Lecture Notes in Computer Science 6586

Commenced Publication in 1973
Founding and Former Series Editors:
Gerhard Goos, Juris Hartmanis, and Jan van Leeuwen

Editorial Board

David Hutchison
Lancaster University, UK
Takeo Kanade
Carnegie Mellon University, Pittsburgh, PA, USA
Josef Kittler
University of Surrey, Guildford, UK
Jon M. Kleinberg
Cornell University, Ithaca, NY, USA
Alfred Kobsa
University of California, Irvine, CA, USA
Friedemann Mattern
ETH Zurich, Switzerland
John C. Mitchell
Stanford University, CA, USA
Moni Naor
Weizmann Institute of Science, Rehovot, Israel
Oscar Nierstrasz
University of Bern, Switzerland
C. Pandu Rangan
Indian Institute of Technology, Madras, India
Bernhard Steffen
TU Dortmund University, Germany
Madhu Sudan
Microsoft Research, Cambridge, MA, USA
Demetri Terzopoulos
University of California, Los Angeles, CA, USA
Doug Tygar
University of California, Berkeley, CA, USA
Gerhard Weikum
Max Planck Institute for Informatics, Saarbruecken, Germany

Mario R. Guarracino Frédéric Vivien Jesper Larsson Träff
Mario Cannataro Marco Danelutto Anders Hast
Francesca Perla Andreas Knüpfer Beniamino Di Martino
Michael Alexander (Eds.)

Euro-Par 2010 Parallel Processing Workshops

HeteroPar, HPPC, HiBB, CoreGrid, UCHPC, HPCF, PROPER, CCPI, VHPC
Ischia, Italy, August 31 – September 3, 2010
Revised Selected Papers

Volume Editors

Mario R. Guarracino
CNR, ICAR, 80131 Napoli, Italy, E-mail: mario.guarracino@cnr.it

Frédéric Vivien
INRIA, ENS Lyon, 69364 Lyon, France, E-mail: frederic.vivien@inria.fr

Jesper Larsson Träff
University of Vienna, 1090 Vienna, Austria, E-mail: traff@par.univie.ac.at

Mario Cannataro
University of Catanzaro, 88100 Catanzaro, Italy
E-mail: cannataro@unicz.it

Marco Danelutto
University of Pisa, 56122 Pisa, Italy, E-mail: marcod@di.unipi.it

Anders Hast
Creative Media Lab, 80632 Gävle, Sweden, E-mail: aht@hig.se

Francesca Perla
University of Naples Parthenope, 80133 Napoli, Italy
E-mail: francesca.perla@uniparthenope.it

Andreas Knüpfer
TU Dresden, 01062 Dresden, Germany, E-mail: andreas.knuepfer@tu-dresden.de

Beniamino Di Martino
Seconda Università di Napoli, 81031 Aversa, Italy, E-mail: beniamino.dimartino@unina.it

Michael Alexander
scaledinfra technologies GmbH, 1010 Vienna, Austria, E-mail: malexand@scaledinfra.com

ISSN 0302-9743
e-ISSN 1611-3349
ISBN 978-3-642-21877-4
e-ISBN 978-3-642-21878-1
DOI 10.1007/978-3-642-21878-1
Springer Heidelberg Dordrecht London New York

Library of Congress Control Number: 2011929849

CR Subject Classification (1998): C.4, D.2, C.2, D.4, C.2.4, C.3

LNCS Sublibrary: SL 1 – Theoretical Computer Science and General Issues

© Springer-Verlag Berlin Heidelberg 2011

This work is subject to copyright. All rights are reserved, whether the whole or part of the material is concerned, specifically the rights of translation, reprinting, re-use of illustrations, recitation, broadcasting, reproduction on microfilms or in any other way, and storage in data banks. Duplication of this publication or parts thereof is permitted only under the provisions of the German Copyright Law of September 9, 1965, in its current version, and permission for use must always be obtained from Springer. Violations are liable to prosecution under the German Copyright Law.
The use of general descriptive names, registered names, trademarks, etc. in this publication does not imply, even in the absence of a specific statement, that such names are exempt from the relevant protective laws and regulations and therefore free for general use.

Typesetting: Camera-ready by author, data conversion by Scientific Publishing Services, Chennai, India

Printed on acid-free paper

Springer is part of Springer Science+Business Media (www.springer.com)

Preface

Euro-Par is an annual series of international conferences dedicated to the promotion and advancement of all aspects of parallel and distributed computing. Euro-Par 2010 was the 16th edition in this conference series. The conference took place at the congress Center of Hotel Continental Terme, on the beautiful island of Ischia, Italy. The success of the conference series has provided a convenient venue for many workshops to meet and discuss. The focus of these workshops is on specialized topics in parallel and distributed computing, with the aim of bringing together a community on research themes in early stages of development.

The 2009 experience was quite successful, and it was extended to a larger size in 2010, where 11 events were co-located with the main Euro-Par Conference. With respect to the 2009 edition, seven out of nine workshops confirmed their presence at Euro-Par 2010 from the previous edition, while four new workshops were organized on emerging aspects. HiBB (High-Performance Bioinformatics and Biomedicine), UCHPC (UnConventional High-Performance Computing), HPCF (High-Performance Computing applied to Finance) and CCPI (Cloud Computing Projects and Initiatives) are newcomers, while ROIA (Real-Time Online Interactive Applications) and UNICORE were discontinued. Here follows a brief description of the workshops:

HeteroPar 2010 is a workshop on Algorithms, Models and Tools for Parallel Computing on Heterogeneous Platforms. HeteroPar 2010 was the eighth edition of this workshop, and the second edition co-located with the Euro-Par conference. The workshop intends to be a forum for people working with heterogeneous platforms and trying to find efficient problem solutions on heterogeneous systems. The 2010 edition started with an invited talk by Marco Danelutto, who discussed *structured programming models targeting heterogeneous architectures.*

HPPC—Highly Parallel Processing on a Chip workshop—is a forum for presentation and discussion of new research into parallel single-chip/node (multi/many-core) architectures, programming models, languages, libraries, algorithms, and software tools, including the efficient use of highly parallel special-purpose architectures for efficient general-purpose parallel processing. The workshop aims to attract new and tentative work that seriously addresses the problems of managing significant amounts of on-chip parallelism at the levels mentioned. To be able to relate to the parallel processing community at large, the workshop is organized in conjunction with Euro-Par, the main European (but international) conference on all aspects of parallel processing. The format of the workshop is to sandwich a selection of contributed, thoroughly reviewed papers between two prominent invited talks providing a broader outlook.

HiBB 2010 was the First Workshop on High-Performance Bioinformatics and Biomedicine (HiBB). This workshop aimed to bring together scientists in the fields of high-performance computing, computational biology and medicine to discuss the parallel implementation of bioinformatics algorithms, the application of high-performance computing in biomedical applications, as well as the organization of large-scale databases in biology and medicine. Furthermore, the use of novel parallel architectures and dedicated hardware to implement bioinformatics and biomedical algorithms was discussed.
CoreGRID/ERCIM provided a forum for discussing the latest developments in the field of large-scale grid, cloud and peer-to-peer computing. The original goal of CoreGRID was strengthening and advancing technological excellence in the areas of grid and peer-to-peer technologies. However, the interests of the network have evolved and now additionally embrace the emerging service-based cloud computational model. The 2010 CoreGRID meeting followed on from previous meetings held in Pisa (2005), Krakow (2006), Heraklion (2007), Gran Canaria (2008) and Delft (2009).
UCHPC 2010 was the Third Workshop on UnConventional High-Performance Computing 2010. As the word "UnConventional" in the title suggests, the workshop focuses on hardware or platforms used for HPC, that were not intended for HPC in the first place. Reasons could be raw computing power or especially low cost. Thus, UCHPC tries to capture solutions for HPC which are unconventional today but perhaps conventional tomorrow. For example, the computing power of platforms for games recently grew rapidly. This motivated the use of GPUs for computing (GPGPU), or building computational grids from game consoles. Other examples for "unconventional" hardware would be embedded, low-power processors, FPGAs or DSPs. Only imagination sets the limit for their usage for HPC. The goal of the workshop is to present the latest research in how hardware and software (yet) unconventional for HPC is or can be used to reach goals such as best performance per watt. UCHPC also covers programming models, compiler techniques, and tools.
HPCF 2010 was the first workshop on the computational issues in the evaluation of financial instruments on advanced architectures. The workshop aims to bring together scientists from finance, statistics, numerical analysis and computer science, decision-makers and strategists from the financial industries in order to discuss recent challenges and results in using high-performance technologies for the evaluation of financial instruments. The workshop was enriched by two invited lectures; the first lecture by Gilberto Castellani and Luca Passalacqua on "Applications of Distributed and Parallel Computing in the Solvency II Framework: The DISAR System", and the second one by Andreas Grothey on "Massively Parallel Asset and Liability Management".
The PROPER workshop series on productivity and performance serves as a forum to present novel work on scalable methods and tools for high-performance computing. This covers parallel program development and analysis, debugging, correctness checking, and performance measurement and

evaluation. Furthermore, it is the right place to present experiences and success stories reporting optimization or improvements of parallel scalability achieved using tools. Besides the computing performance, the programmer and user productivity is also addressed. This focuses on the entire process of application development, parallelization, performance optimization, and scalability enhancement. The PROPER workshop is supported by the Virtual Institute—High Productivity Supercomputing (VI-HPS), an initiative to promote the development and integration of HPC programming tools.

CCPI, Cloud Computing Projects and Initiatives workshop, a satellite workshop organized by the Europen ICT-FP7 Project mOSAIC (http://www.mosaic-cloud.eu), gathered together scientists, engineers and industrial users from collaborative international and national projects and initiatives on cloud computing. A number of key projects funded by the European Commission and by National Government and Research Agencies, addressing several issues and challenges of cloud computing were presented at the workshop, and are in these proceedings.

VHPC 2010, the 5th Workshop on Virtualization in High-Performance Cloud Computing, brought together researchers and practitioners presenting their recent results. With the cloud paradigm and its enabling technology of virtualization moving into the mainstream of scientific and commercial large-scale computing, aspects of operational significance were emphasized. In addition, this year's guest speaker, Chris Kemp, IT CIO of NASA, provided an overview of the NASA Nebula cloud platform which is in-use at HPC sites worldwide.

XtreemOS: Large-scale distributed systems like grids and clouds provide means for executing complex scientific and business applications. But they often involve installing and interacting with several layers of middleware, a difficult task for inexperienced users. Tools developed for grid use are demanding and complex, especially because they are based on operating systems that are not designed to manage distributed and versatile resources. The aims of this summit are: to familiarize participants with the usage of the main XtreemOS services (virtual organization management and grid security mechanisms, application execution management, XtreemFS - distributed data storage etc.); to present the XtreemOS Grid system from the user's point of view; to demonstrate some XtreemOS main functionalities; to provide a unique opportunity for people interested in the XtreemOS technology to meet developers, users and researchers who initiated the technology, share experiences and discuss research work.

Gecon 2010: The commercial exploitation of technologies of distributed computing is slowly starting to become popular under the term "cloud computing". These solutions allow selling and buying of resources (i.e., computing resources, network resources, software resources, and data resources) on demand. Existing solutions in this area are diverse, ranging from intrastructure-as-a-service (IaaS) models via platform-as-a-service (PaaS) to software-as-a-service (SaaS) models. Although the economics of these services is not understood yet and the interoperability of the services is still

VIII lacking, a common market for simple computing services is slowly developing. It allows buyers and sellers of computing services to trade easily. However, it is still not possible that any market participant can act as a resource provider or resource seller, depending on the current demand level. Another example of a developing open market is the Web2.0 service system, which enables consumers to create new services. The purpose of this workshop is to gather original work and build a strong community in this increasingly important area of the future economy.

The present volume includes the proceedings of the first nine workshops; the remaining two have separate proceedings. Each workshop had a Program Committee managing the peer-review process. We would like to thank the authors who submitted their papers to the various workshops. Without the contribution of the members of the Program Committees and many reviewers, the organization of the workshops would not have been possible.

Last but not least, we would like to thank all Euro-Par Steering Committee members, and in particular Luc Bougé for the valuable advice and for following all phases of the workshop organization. We also thank Euro-Par 2009 workshop organizer Hai-Xiang Lin for sharing his experience with us. Many other people, institutions and companies supported the organization of the Euro-Par 2010 conference and workshops. Their names and logos can be found on the conference website at `http://www.europar2010.it`.

It was a pleasure and honor to organize and host the Euro-Par 2010 workshops in Ischia. We also thank the Yes Meet people involved in the conference secretariat for the kind and collaborative support they provided during the preparation and actual course of the workshops.

March 2011

Mario R. Guarracino
Frédéric Vivien
Jesper Larsson Träff
Mario Cannataro
Marco Danelutto
Anders Hast
Francesca Perla
Andreas Knüpfer
Beniamino Di Martino
Michael Alexander

Organization

Euro-Par Steering Committee

Chair

Christian Lengauer	University of Passau, Germany

Vice-Chair

Luc Bougé	ENS Cachan, France

European Representatives

José Cunha	New University of Lisbon, Portugal
Marco Danelutto	University of Pisa, Italy
Rainer Feldmann	University of Paderborn, Germany
Christos Kaklamanis	Computer Technology Institute, Greece
Paul Kelly	Imperial College, UK
Harald Kosch	University of Passau, Germany
Thomas Ludwig	University of Heidelberg, Germany
Emilio Luque	Universitat Autònoma de Barcelona, Spain
Tomàs Margaalef	Universitat Autònoma de Barcelona, Spain
Wolfgang E. Nagel	Technische Universität Dresden, Germany
Rizos Sakellariou	University of Manchester, UK
Henk Sips	Delft University of Technology, The Netherlands

Honorary Members

Ron Perrott	Queen's University Belfast, UK
Karl Dieter	Reinartz University of Erlangen-Nuremberg, Germany

Observers

Domenico Talia	University of Calabria, Italy
Emmanuel Jeannot	LaBRI-INRIA, Bordeaux, France

Euro-Par 2010 Local Organization

Euro-Par 2010 was organized by the High-Performance Computing and Networking Institute of National Research Council of Italy (ICAR-CNR).

Conference Chairs

Domenico Talia	University of Calabria and ICAR-CNR
Pasqua D'Ambra	ICAR-CNR
Mario R. Guarracino	ICAR-CNR

Local Organizing Committee

Laura Antonelli	ICAR-CNR
Eugenio Cesario	ICAR-CNR
Agostino Forestiero	ICAR-CNR
Francesco Gregoretti	ICAR-CNR
Ivana Marra	ICAR-CNR
Carlo Mastroianni	ICAR-CNR

Web and Technical Support

Francesco Gregoretti ICAR-CNR

Publicity

Ivana Marra ICAR-CNR

Workshop Proceedings

Giuseppe Trerotola ICAR-CNR

Secretariat

Francesco Schisano Yes Meet

Euro-Par 2010 Workshop Program Committees

8th International Workshop on Algorithms, Models and Tools for Parallel Computing on Heterogeneous Platforms (HeteroPar 2010)

Steering Committee

Domingo Giménez	University of Murcia, Spain
Alexey Kalinov	Cadence Design Systems, Russia
Alexey Lastovetsky	University College Dublin, Ireland
Yves Robert	Ecole Normale Supérieure de Lyon, France
Leonel Sousa	INESC-ID/IST, Technical University of Lisbon, Portugal
Denis Trystram	LIG, Grenoble, France

Program Chair

Frédéric Vivien	LIP, École normale supérieure de Lyon, and INRIA, France

Program Committee

Jacques Mohcine Bahi	University of Franche-Comté, France
Mark Baker	University of Reading, UK
Jorge Barbosa	Faculdade de Engenharia do Porto, Portugal
Olivier Beaumont	INRIA Bordeaux Sud Ouest, LABRI, France
Andrea Clematis	IMATI-CNR, Italy
Michel Daydé	IRIT-Université de Toulouse / INPT-ENSEEIHT, France
Frédéric Desprez	INRIA, ENS Lyon, France
Pierre-François Dutot	LIG, Grenoble, France
Alfredo Goldman	University of São Paulo, Brazil
Abdou Guermouche	University of Bordeaux, France
Shuichi Ichikawa	Toyohashi University of Technology, Japan
Emmanuel Jeannot	INRIA, France
Heleni Karatza	Aristotle University of Thessaloniki, Greece
Tahar Kechadi	University College Dublin, Ireland
Zhiling Lan	Illinois Institute of Technology, USA
Pierre Manneback	University of Mons, Belgium
Loris Marchal	CNRS, ENS Lyon, France
Kiminori Matsuzaki	Kochi University of Technology, Japan
Wahid Nasri	Ecole Sup. des Sciences et Techniques de Tunis, Tunisia
Dana Petcu	University of Timisoara, Romania
Serge Petiton	CNRS/LIFL and INRIA, France
Antonio J. Plaza	University of Extremadura, Spain
Casiano Rodríguez	University of La Laguna, Spain

Mitsuhisa Sato	University of Tsukuba, Japan
Franciszek Seredynski	PJIIT and Polish Academy of Sciences, Poland
H. J. Siegel	Colorado State University, USA
Leonel Sousa	INESC-ID/IST, Technical University of Lisbon, Portugal
Antonio M. Vidal	Universidad Politécnica de Valencia, Spain
Ramin Yahyapour	University of Dortmund, Germany

Highly Parallel Processing on a Chip (HPPC)

Steering Committee

Martti Forsell	VTT, Finland
Jesper Larsson Träff	Faculty of Computer Science, University of Vienna, Austria

HPPC 2010 Proceedings Editor

Jesper Larsson Träff	Faculty of Computer Science, University of Vienna, Austria

Program Chairs

Martti Forsell	VTT, Finland
Jesper Larsson Träff	University of Vienna, Austria

Program Committee

Martti Forsell	VTT, Finland
Jim Held	Intel, USA
Peter Hofstee	IBM, USA
Chris Jesshope	University of Amsterdam, The Netherlands
Ben Juurlink	Technical University of Berlin, Germany
Jörg Keller	University of Hagen, Germany
Christoph Kessler	University of Linköping, Sweden
Dominique Lavenier	IRISA - CNRS, France
Ville Leppänen	University of Turku, Finland
Lasse Natvig	NTNU, Norway
Sabri Pllan	University of Vienna, Austria
Jürgen Teich	University of Erlagen-Nuremberg, Germany
Jesper Larsson Träff	University of Vienna, Austria
Theo Ungerer	University of Augsburg, Germany
Uzi Vishkin	University of Maryland, USA

Workshop on High-Performance Bioinformatics and Biomedicine (HiBB)

Program Chair

Mario Cannataro	University Magna Græcia of Catanzaro, Italy

Program Committee

Pratul K. Agarwal	Oak Ridge National Laboratory, USA
David A. Bader	Georgia University of Technology, USA
Ignacio Blanquer	Universidad Politécnica de Valencia, Spain
Daniela Calvetti	Case Western Reserve University, USA
Werner Dubitzky	University of Ulster, UK
Ananth Y. Grama	Purdue University, USA
Concettina Guerra	University of Padova, Italy
Vicente Hernández	Universidad Politécnica de Valencia, Spain
Salvatore Orlando	University of Venice, Italy
Omer F. Rana	Cardiff University, UK
Richard Sinnott	University of Glasgow, UK
Fabrizio Silvestri	ISTI-CNR, Italy
Erkki Somersalo	Case Western Reserve University, USA
Paolo Trunfio	University of Calabria, Italy
Albert Zomaya	University of Sydney, Australia

Additional Reviewers

Giuseppe Agapito
Gianluigi Folino
Gionata Fragomeni
Pietro H. Guzzi
Marcelo Lobosco
Maria Mirto
Giuseppe Tradigo
Pierangelo Veltri

CoreGRID/ERCIM Workshop on Grids, Clouds and P2P Computing

Program Chairs

M. Danelutto	University of Pisa, Italy
F. Desprez	LIP, ENS Lyon, France
P. Fragopoulou	FORTH-ICS, Greece
A. Stewart	Queen's University of Belfast, UK

Program Committee

Artur Andrzejak	I2R, Singapore
Marco Aldinucci	University of Pisa, Italy
Alvaro Arenas	STFC Rutherford Appleton Laboratory, UK
Rosa M. Badia	Technical University of Catalonia, Spain
Alessandro Bassi	HITACHI, France
Augusto Ciuffoletti	University of Pisa, Italy
Marios Dikaiakos	University of Cyprus, Cyprus
Dick H.J. Epema	Delft University of Technology, The Netherlands
Thomas Fahringer	University of Innsbruck, Austria
Gilles Fedak	INRIA, France
J. Gabarro	Technical University of Catalonia, Spain
Vladimir Getov	University of Westminster, UK
Sergei Gorlatch	University Münster, Germany
T. Harmer	Belfast e-Science Center, UK
Ruben S. Montero	Complutense University of Madrid, Spain
Peter Kacsuk	MTA SZTAKI, Poland
Thilo Kielmann	Vrije Universiteit, The Netherlands
Derrick Kondo	INRIA, France
Philippe Massonet	CETIC, Belgium
Carlo Mastroianni	ICAR-CNR, Italy
Norbert Meyer	Poznan, Poland
Ignacio M. Llorente	Complutense University of Madrid, Spain
Christian PÃľrez	INRIA/IRISA, France
Ron Perrott	Queen's University of Belfast, UK
Thierry Priol	INRIA, France
Omer Rana	Cardiff University, UK
Rizos Sakellariou	University of Manchester, UK
Junichi Suzuki	University of Massachusetts, Boston, USA
Domenico Talia	University of Calabria, Italy
Ian Taylor	Cardiff University, UK
Jordi Torres	Technical University of Catalonia, Spain
Paolo Trunfio	University of Calabria, Italy
Ramin Yahyapour	University of Dortmouth, Germany
D. Zeinalipour-Yazti	University of Cyprus, Cyprus
Wolfgang Ziegler	Fraunhofer SCAI, Germany

Third Workshop on UnConventional High-Performance Computing 2010 (UCHPC 2010)

Organizers and Program Chairs

Anders Hast	University of Gävle, Sweden
Lars Bengtsson	Chalmers University, Sweden
Josef Weidendorfer	Technische Universität München, Germany
Ren Wu	HP Labs, Palo Alto, USA

International Program Committee

Michael Bader	Universität Stuttgart, Germany
Lars Bengtsson	Chalmers, Sweden
Duncan A. Buell	University of South Carolina, USA
Karl Fürlinger	UC Berkeley, USA
Dominik Göddeke	TU Dortmund, Germany
Anders Hast	University of Gävle, Sweden
Rainer Keller	ORNL, USA
Gaurav Khanna	University of Massachusetts Dartmouth, USA
Dominique Lavenier	INRIA, France
Malcolm Low Yoke Hean	Nanyang Technological University, Singapore
Ingela Nyström	UPPMAX, Sweden
Douglas Leslie Maskell	Nanyang Technological University, Singapore
Ioannis Papaefstathiou	Technical University of Crete, Greece
Art Sedighi	Softmodule
Bertil Schmidt	Nanyang Technological University, Singapore
Carsten Trinitis	Technische Universität München, Germany
Josef Weidendorfer	Technische Universität München, Germany
Jan-Phillipp Weiss	KIT, Germany
Ren Wu	HP Labs, Palo Alto, USA

Additional Reviewers

Markus Geveler	TU Dortmund, Germany
Hans Hacker	Technische Universität München, Germany
Tilman Küstner	Technische Universität München, Germany
Thomas Müller	Technische Universität München, Germany
Alin Murarasu	Technische Universität München, Germany

Workshop on High-Performance Computing applied to Finance (HPCF 2010)

Program Chair

Francesca Perla	Università di Napoli “Parthenope” and ICAR-CNR, Italy

Steering Committee

Stefania Corsaro	Università di Napoli “Parthenope” and ICAR-CNR, Italy
Zelda Marino	Università di Napoli “Parthenope”, Italy
Paolo Zanetti	Università di Napoli “Parthenope”, Italy

Program Committee

Gilberto Castellani	Sapienza, Università di Roma, Italy
Pasquale L. De Angelis	Università di Napoli “Parthenope”, Italy
John Miller	Trinity College, Dublin, Ireland

Michael Mascagni	Florida State University, USA
Panos M. Pardalos	University of Florida, USA
Giovanni Sacchi	IMATI-CNR, Italy
Marián Vajterŝic	University of Salzburg, Austria

PROPER Organization

Organizers

- Andreas Knüpfer, TU Dresden, Germany (Chair)
- Jens Doleschal, TU Dresden, Germany
- Matthias Müller, TU Dresden, Germany
- Felix Wolf, German Research School for Simulation Sciences, Aachen, Germany

Program Committee

- Dieter an Mey, RWTH Aachen, Germany
- Taisuke Boku, Tsukuba University, Japan
- Jens Doleschal, TU Dresden, Germany
- Karl Fürlinger, University of California at Berkeley, USA
- Michael Gerndt, TU München, Germany
- Andreas Knüpfer, TU Dresden, Germany
- Allen Malony, University of Oregon, Eugene, USA
- Federico Massaioli, CASPUR, Rome, Italy
- Kathryn Mohror, Lawrence Livermore National Lab, CA, USA
- Shirley Moore, University of Tennessee, USA
- Matthias Müller, TU Dresden, Germany
- Martin Schulz, Lawrence Livermore National Lab, CA, USA
- Josef Weidendorfer, TU München, Germany
- Felix Wolf, German Research School for Simulation Sciences, Aachen, Germany

Workshop on Cloud Computing Projects and Initiatives (CCPI)

Program Chairs

Beniamino Di Martino	Second University of Naples, Italy
Dana Petcu	West University of Timisoara, Romania
Antonio Puliafito	University of Messina, Italy

Program Committee

Pasquale Cantiello	Second University of Naples, Italy
Maria Fazio	University of Messina, Italy
Florin Fortis	West University of Timisoara, Romania
Francesco Moscato	Second University of Naples, Italy
Viorel Negru	West University of Timisoara, Romania
Massimo Villari	University of Messina, Italy

5th Workshop on Virtualization in High-Performance Cloud Computing (VHPC 2010)

Program Chairs

Michael Alexander	scaledinfra technologies GmbH, Austria
Gianluigi Zanetti	CRS4, Italy

Program Committee

Padmashree Apparao	Intel Corp., USA
Volker Buege	University of Karlsruhe, Germany
Roberto Canonico	University of Naples Federico II, Italy
Tommaso Cucinotta	Scuola Superiore Sant'Anna, Italy
Werner Fischer	Thomas Krenn AG, Germany
William Gardner	University of Guelph, Canada
Wolfgang Gentzsch	Max Planck Gesellschaft, Germany
Derek Groen	UVA, The Netherlands
Marcus Hardt	Forschungszentrum Karlsruhe, Germany
Sverre Jarp	CERN, Switzerland
Shantenu Jha	Louisiana State University, USA
Xuxian Jiang	NC State, USA
Kenji Kaneda	Google, Japan
Yves Kemp	DESY Hamburg, Germany
Ignacio Llorente	Universidad Complutense de Madrid, Spain
Naoya Maruyama	Tokyo Institute of Technology, Japan
Jean-Marc Menaud	Ecole des Mines de Nantes, France
Anastassios Nano	National Technical University of Athens, Greece
Oliver Oberst	Karlsruhe Institute of Technology, Germany
Jose Renato Santos	HP Labs, USA
Borja Sotomayor	University of Chicago, USA
Deepak Singh	Amazon Webservices, USA
Yoshio Turner	HP Labs, USA
Kurt Tuschku	University of Vienna, Austria
Lizhe Wang	Indiana University, USA

Table of Contents

Eighth International Workshop on Algorithms, Models and Tools for Parallel Computing on Heterogeneous Platforms (HeteroPar'2010)

Forth Workshop on Highly Parallel Processing on a Chip (HPPC 2010)

Workshop on High Performance Bioinformatics and Biomedicine (HiBB 2010)

2010 CoreGRID/ERCIM Workshop on Grids, Clouds and P2P Computing

Third Workshop on UnConventional High Performance Computing (UCHPC 2010)

Workshop on High-Performance Computing Applied to Finance (HPCF 2010)

Third Workshop on Productivity and Performance - Tools for HPC Application Development (PROPER 2010)

Workshop on Cloud Computing Projects and Initiatives (CCPI 2010)

Fifth Workshop on Virtualization in High-Performance Cloud Computing (VHPC 2010)

Eighth International Workshop on Algorithms, Models and Tools for Parallel Computing on Heterogeneous Platforms (HeteroPar'2010)

HeteroPar'2010: Eighth International Workshop on Algorithms, Models and Tools for Parallel Computing on Heterogeneous Platforms

Frédéric Vivien

LIP, École normale supérieure de Lyon, and INRIA, France

Foreword

Networks of computers are now the most common and available parallel architecture. Unlike dedicated parallel computer systems, networks are inherently heterogeneous. They consist of diverse computers of different performance interconnected via heterogeneous network equipment providing communication links with different latencies and bandwidths. Traditional parallel algorithms and tools are aimed at homogeneous multiprocessors and cannot be efficiently used for parallel computing on heterogeneous networks. New ideas, dedicated algorithms and tools are needed to efficiently use this new type of parallel architecture.

The HeteroPar workshop series is intended to be a forum for people working on algorithms, programming languages, tools, and theoretical models aimed at efficient problem solutions on heterogeneous networks. The covered topics target heterogeneous systems and platforms, and include parallel programming languages and libraries, fault tolerance, tools for grid, cloud and green computing, and the usage of these complex platforms for solving different types of problems and applications.

HeteroPar'2010 was the eighth edition of this workshop, and the second one co-located with the Euro-Par conference. Out of 12 manuscripts submitted this year, 7 were accepted for presentation at the Workshop in Ischia on August 30. Each submission received 4 reviews. Apart from the presentation of the 7 accepted papers, the workshop had one invited speaker of international reputation, Marco Danelutto, who talked about *Structured programming models targeting heterogeneous architectures.*

As program chair, I wish to acknowledge all those who contributed to the success of HeteroPar'2010, in particular to the authors of the submitted papers, to the Program Committee members for their invaluable time and expertise, and to the organizers of EuroPar 2010.

M.R. Guarracino et al. (Eds.): Euro-Par 2010 Workshops, LNCS 6586, p. 3, 2011.
© Springer-Verlag Berlin Heidelberg 2011

Accurate Emulation of CPU Performance

Tomasz Buchert[1], Lucas Nussbaum[2], and Jens Gustedt[1]

[1] INRIA Nancy – Grand Est
[2] LORIA / Nancy-Université

Abstract. This paper addresses the question of CPU performance emulation, which allows experimenters to evaluate applications under a wide range of reproducible experimental conditions. Specifically, we propose Fracas, a CPU emulator that leverages the Linux Completely Fair Scheduler to achieve performance emulation of homogeneous or heterogeneous multi-core systems. Several benchmarks reproducing different types of workload (CPU-bound, IO-bound) are then used to thoroughly compare Fracas with another CPU emulator and hardware frequency scaling. We show that the design of Fracas results in a more accurate and a less intrusive CPU emulation solution.

1 Introduction

The evaluation of algorithms and applications for large-scale heterogeneous platforms is a very challenging task. Different approaches are in widespread use [3]: *simulation* of course, but also *in-situ* experiments (where a real application is tested on a real environment), and *emulation* (where a real application is tested on a simulated environment).

It is often difficult to perform experiments in a real environment that suits the experimenter's needs: the available infrastructure might not be large enough or have the required characteristics. Moreover, controlling experimental conditions in heterogeneous and distributed systems, like grids or the Internet, makes the experimental validation error-prone. Therefore, *in-situ* experiments are often not feasible, and the use of an emulated or simulated environment is often preferred. Many distributed system emulators (e.g. MicroGrid, Modelnet, Emulab, Wrekavoc [1]) have been developed over the years, but most of them focus on network emulation.

Surprisingly, the question of the emulation of CPU speed and performance is rarely addressed by them. However, it is crucial to evaluate applications under a set of different experimental conditions: to know how application's performance is related to the performance of the CPU (as opposed to the communication network), or how an application would perform when executed on clusters of heterogeneous machines, with different CPUs.

This paper explores the emulation of CPU performance characteristics, and proposes a new implementation of a CPU emulator: Fracas. After exposing the related works in Section 2, the problem is clarified and formalized in Section 3. Fracas is then described in Section 4, and evaluated extensively in Section 5.

M.R. Guarracino et al. (Eds.): Euro-Par 2010 Workshops, LNCS 6586, pp. 5–12, 2011.
© Springer-Verlag Berlin Heidelberg 2011

2 Related Work

Due to unforeseen changes in the number of pages for the proceedings version, it was not possible to include that section in the final paper. It can be found in the corresponding Research Report: `http://hal.inria.fr/inria-00490108/en/`.

3 Problem Statement

In this section *core* is the smallest processing unit that can execute the code of the program independently on a processor. It is equivalent to a core of a physical processor. Consequently, *processor* is a set of cores and is equivalent to a physical processor. Additionally, a distinction is made between *real* processor/core (the one existing as a hardware implementation) and *emulated* processor/core (the one being emulated).

Let's assume that a computer system consists of N cores with speeds $\alpha_1 \leq \alpha_2 \leq \alpha_3 \leq \ldots \leq \alpha_N$. The goal is to emulate M processors, using this physical processor. The m-th emulated processor, denoted C_m occupies a subset of real cores: $C_m \subset \{1, 2, \ldots, N\}$. None of the physical cores will be occupied by more than two emulated ones so $C_i \cap C_j = \emptyset$ for $1 \leq i < j \leq M$.

Finally, for each emulated processor C_m $(1 \leq m \leq M)$, a core $k \in C_m$ has the emulated speed β_k. If $k \notin C_m$ for every $1 \leq m \leq M$ then by definition $\beta_k = 0$.

It is also reasonable to assume that $\alpha_i \geq \beta_i$ for $i \in \{1, \ldots, N\}$, so that each emulated core can be mapped to a physical one. Also, in most real-life scenarios it is true that $\alpha_1 = \alpha_2 = \alpha_3 = \ldots = \alpha_N$. If not stated differently, this is always assumed in the following sections.

An example of the problem instance is presented in Figure 1.

The following special cases of this problem are of particular interest and are considered in this paper:

(A) $M = 1$ and C_1 has one element – a single core processor is emulated.
(B) $M = 1$ and C_1 has exactly N elements – the only emulated processor spans all physical cores.

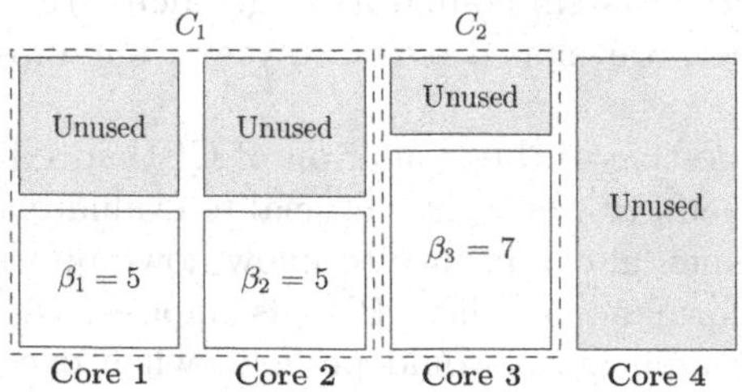

Fig. 1. An example of a CPU emulation problem. Here: $N = 4$, $\alpha_1 = \alpha_2 = \alpha_3 = \alpha_4 = 10$, $M = 2$, $C_1 = \{1, 2\}$, $C_2 = \{3\}$, $\beta_1 = \beta_2 = 5$, $\beta_3 = 7$, $\beta_4 = 0$.

This is a hardly a complete formalization of the general problem. In a more general setting one may relax some previous assumptions or take other properties of the computer systems into account: speed of the random access memory, the CPU cache size and properties, Simultaneous Multi Threading (SMT) (e.g. Intel Hyper-Threading technology) or Non-Uniform Memory Architectures (NUMA).

4 Proposed Solution

Fracas is using an approach similar to KRASH. On every processor core a CPU-intensive process is created. It burns a required amount of CPU cycles on its core. All other tasks in the system are moved to another group which spans all cores. CPU time is distributed to groups proportionally to their weights so, by adjusting them properly, the latter group will acquire the desired amount of the CPU time. Figure 2 presents the idea graphically.

This method uses Completely Fair Scheduler (CFS) by Ingo Molnar which is a default scheduler in the current Linux release (2.6.34). It was merged into kernel mainline in version 2.6.23. Cpusets, which also play an important role, were introduced in version 2.6.12 of the Linux kernel. The O(1) scheduler (also by Ingo Molnar) used back then does not possess the features as required by Fracas [6].

The following CFS parameters [5] have been experimentally verified to have impact on the work of Fracas: `latency` (default kernel value: 5ms) – targeted preemption latency for CPU-bound tasks, and `min_granularity` (default kernel value: 1ms) – minimal preemption granularity for CPU-bound tasks. The first one defines the time which is a maximum period of a task being in a preempted state and the latter is a smallest quantum of CPU time given to the task by the scheduler.

Ignoring rounding, the kernel formula for computing the period in which every running task should be ran once is (n_r - a number of running tasks) $\max(n_r \cdot \texttt{min\_granularity}, \texttt{latency})$. Therefore, setting `latency` and `min_granularity` to the lowest possible values (which is 0.1ms for both of them) will force the scheduler to compute the smallest possible preemption periods and,

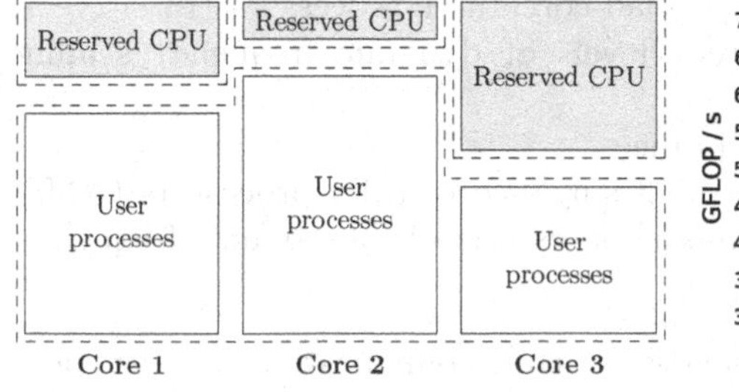

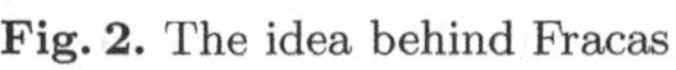

Fig. 2. The idea behind Fracas

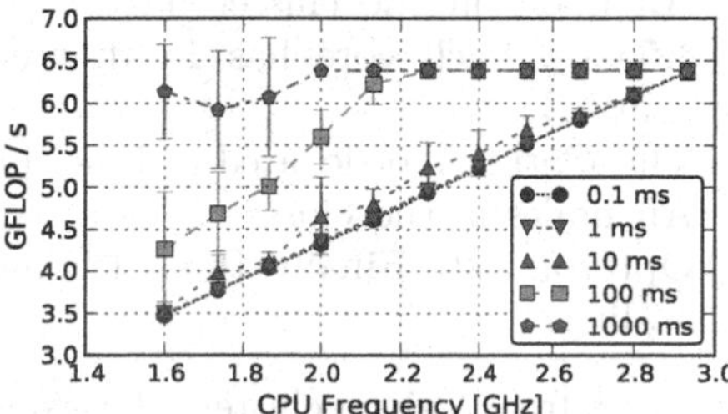

Fig. 3. Latency of the scheduler & Fracas

as a result, the highest possible activity of the scheduler. This substantially improves the accuracy of Fracas (see Figure 3). In this figure each plot presents the result for `Linpack` benchmark (see Section 5.2) under different scheduler latency. As can be seen, the lower the latency, the more the results converge to the perfect behavior.

5 Evaluation

In the following sections three different methods are evaluated which can be used to emulate the CPU speed: dynamic frequency scaling (abbreviated to *CPU-Freq*), CPU-Lim and Fracas.

There are many pitfalls related to the experiments involving processors. Contemporary processors have a very complex architecture – due to cache, branch prediction, simultaneous multithreading technology, code alignment in the memory and other factors, the behavior of programs may vary significantly in similar conditions. Another problem is posed by external factors that may change the execution conditions on the fly. For instance, dynamic frequency scaling is used to conserve power or to generate less heat than during a normal operation. Preferably this feature should be turned off during all the experiments. Nevertheless, even if turned off, most CPUs may also throttle their frequency down in the case of dangerous overheat, leading to an unexpected performance loss. To make things even worse, the newest Intel processors in the Nehalem family (used in our experiments) may introduce an "unexpected" performance gain: *Turbo Mode* technology allows a processor core to overclock itself when the other cores are idle. In the following experiments this technology was knowingly turned off as well as Intel Hyper-Threading.

The experimental scientist must be aware of these problems to perform the experiments reliably.

5.1 Experimental Setup

All experiments were performed on the Grid'5000 experimental testbed [2]. Specifically, the following clusters were used:

- The *Parapide* cluster located in Rennes, France.
  All nodes in the cluster have two quad-core Intel processors (Intel Xeon X5570). Each core has 11 different levels of dynamic frequency scaling available.
- The *Chti* cluster located in Lille, France.
  All nodes in the cluster have a pair of single-core AMD processors (AMD Opteron 252). Finally, this CPU model offers 6 levels of dynamic frequency scaling.

All nodes from a given cluster offer exactly the same configuration so it was possible to perform experiments in parallel. To achieve this, a client-server application was created to distribute the tests automatically. The order in which tests are distributed is randomized. Nodes involved in the experiments were deployed with the same instance of Linux operating system (kernel version: 2.6.33.2).

The experimental framework as well as instructions to reproduce the results are available at `http://www.loria.fr/~lnussbau/files/fracas.html`.

5.2 Benchmarks

The following benchmarks, testing important aspects of the CPU emulation, were used:

- `Linpack` (GFLOP/s) – a well known benchmark used to measure floating point computing power. The version used is a slightly modified version included in the HPCC Benchmark suite (version 1.4.0, released 2010-03-26) [4].
- `Sleep` (Loops/s) – a test performing CPU-intensive work, sleeping for the amount of time that was required to perform the work, and finally running the same computation once again. The result is the number of the computation cycles performed divided by the the time of the whole computation.
- `UDP` (Sends/s) – a program that measures the time required to send many UDP packets to the network. The result is a number of `sendto()` invocations divided by the time required to perform them.
- `Threads` (Loops/s) – a benchmark that creates a few threads (5 threads for the Parapide cluster and 2 threads for the Chti cluster). After a simple integer computation all threads are joined (using `pthread_join`) and the result is the number of computation cycles performed by each thread divided by the time required to join all of them.
- `Processes` (Loops/s) – a modification of `Threads` benchmark. Instead of the threads, processes are created. They are joined using `waitpid` syscall.
- `STREAM` (GB/s) – a synthetic benchmark that measures sustainable memory bandwidth. It is available at [7].

Each benchmark performs a small calibration loop at the beginning to assure that the computation time is big enough as to yield meaningful results (i.e. it's not affected by the granularity of system clock). Please also note that the results from different benchmarks, even though sometimes measured in the same units, are not comparable in any sensible way.

5.3 Results and Discussion

All tests were performed ten times each and the final plot value is the average of all results. The whiskers describe the 95% confidence intervals of this value. The results from the Chti cluster are attached only if they significantly differ from the results obtained on the Parapide cluster. The majority of the results is identical and differences can be easily explained. This further convinces us that the results are independent and general. Most of the time the results obtained by CPU-Freq method are used as a reference, as a model we want to emulate using other methods.

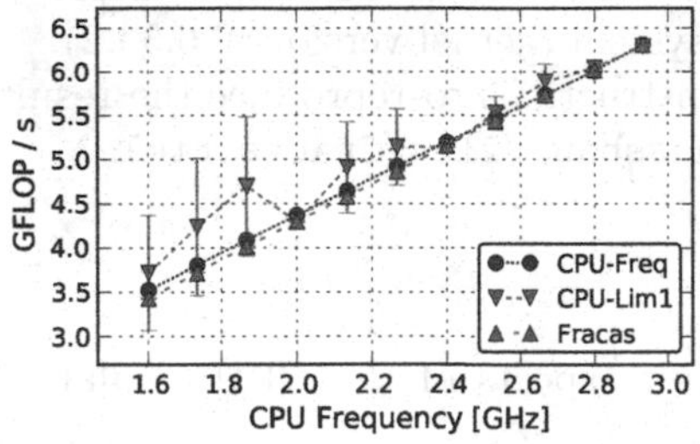

Fig. 4. `Linpack` benchmark

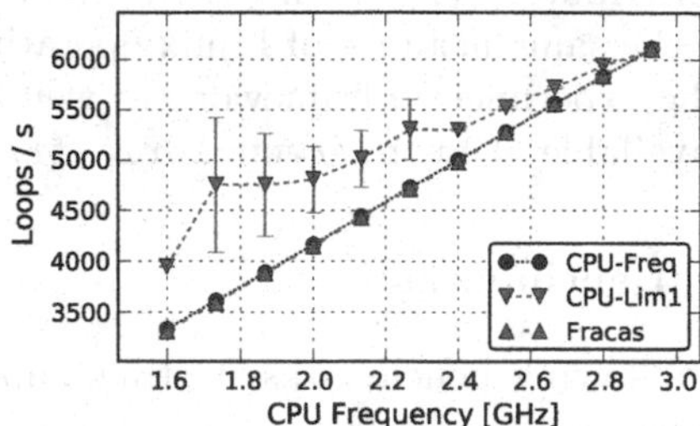

Fig. 5. `Sleep` benchmark

For every emulated frequency f, let's define $\mu = \frac{f}{f_{max}}$ as a *scaling ratio* (where f_{max} is the maximum processor speed).

For a CPU intensive work the execution speed should be proportional to the ratio μ. In Figure 4 one can see that all three methods behave similarly for a CPU intensive work. Nevertheless CPU-Lim gives less predictable results and the slope of a plot with Fracas results is different than the one obtained from CPU-Freq. The observed difference between Fracas and CPU-Freq while emulating processor at 1.6 GHz speed is around 2.5%. This shows that dynamic frequency scaling on Intel processors affects the performance by a different factor than just the ratio μ.

The time when processes sleep, either voluntarily or waiting for IO operation to finish, should not influence the behavior after the process is woken up. However, from Figure 5 it is evident that CPU-Lim has problems with controlling processes which perform this type of work. Both Fracas and CPU-Freq behave as expected.

Generally, IO operations should not be affected by the CPU scaling because they depend on the hardware traits (like network card speed). Results from the Parapide cluster show that the time required to perform intensive access to the hardware does not scale with emulated CPU speed on the tested Intel processor. However, the results from the Chti cluster show (see Figure 9) that it scales by a factor of 16% when emulating the lowest possible frequency using CPU-Freq. It is because the AMD Opteron 252 processor has a wider range of available frequencies than Intel Xeon X5570 (but a smaller set of possible values). If scaled to 1.0 GHz, the time required to prepare UDP packet is becoming a significant factor. This is a proper behavior of all methods.

The CPU time is a resource shared by all the tasks running in the system. All the methods should scale down the total CPU usage and not only the one perceived by every process. Multiple tasks doing the same work simultaneously on different cores should finish at the same time and the total time should be roughly the same as the CPU time consumed by one task. In Figure 6 and Figure 7 the results for this kind of work are presented. A strange behavior of Fracas was observed – the time required to finish the work is much longer than the expected time. This odd behavior is of course a wrong one. CPU-Lim

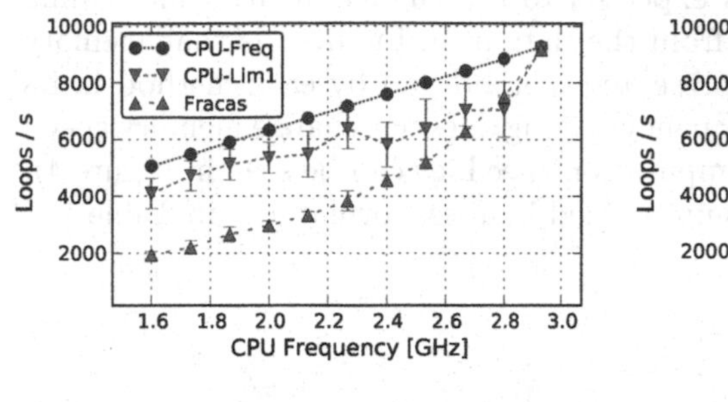

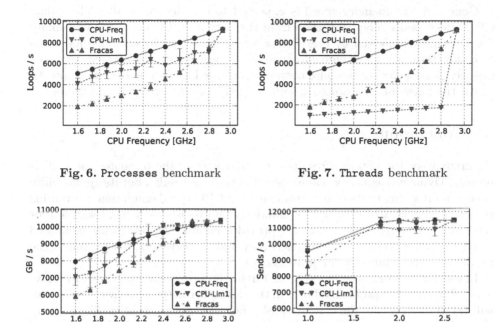

Fig. 6. Processes benchmark

Fig. 7. Threads benchmark

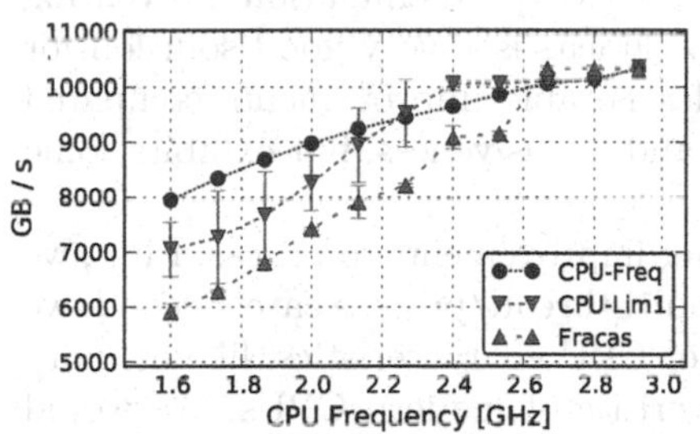

Fig. 8. STREAM benchmark

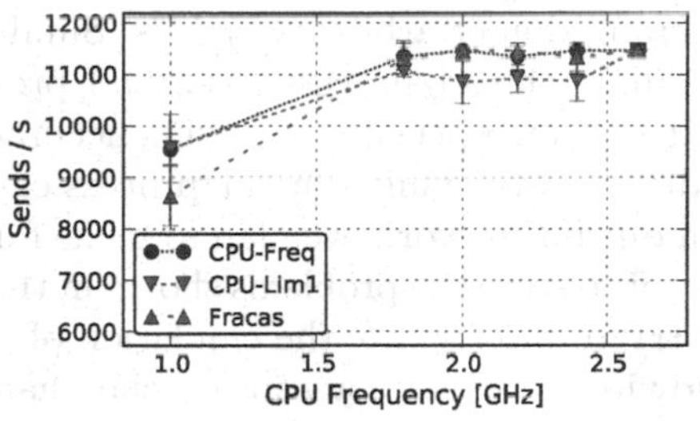

Fig. 9. UDP benchmark (on Chti cluster)

performs much better but its results are very unstable. Additionally, a significant overhead of CPU-Lim method can be observed when used to control even just 5 processes – the results of CPU-Lim method oscillate in the range 77% ÷ 89% of the respective CPU-Freq result (excluding the case of emulating the highest possible frequency when CPU-Lim processes are not started at all).

The only significant difference between Figure 7 and Figure 6 is the behavior of CPU-Lim. The observed phenomenon was described in Section 2 as *Incorrect measurement of CPU usage* – the whole process (consisting of 5 threads) is controlled and the CPU usage is an accumulated value from all the threads. Therefore, CPU-Lim stops the process too often. As predicted, each result of CPU-Lim equals almost exactly 20% percent of CPU-Freq's one.

Table 1. Summary of the presented emulation methods

	CPU-Freq	CPU-Lim	Fracas
Granularity of emulation	Coarse	Very good	Very good
Accuracy of results	Excellent	Mediocre	Depends on work
Stability of emulation	Excellent	Mediocre	Very good
Scalability (with no. of tasks)	Unlimited	Very bad	Very good
Intrusiveness	None	Very high	Almost none

Generally, the memory speed is expected to not change at all while scaling CPU speed down. The conclusion from the data from Figure 8 is that memory speed is indeed affected by every presented method and by each method in its own way. Interestingly dynamic frequency scaling does not change memory speed linearly (as opposed to the pure computation speed, as can be seen in Figure 4).

All the above observations are summarized in a less formal way in Table 1.

6 Conclusions

Unfortunately, the obtained results show that none of the presented methods is perfect. Dynamic frequency scaling provides the best results, but its applicability is very limited due to its coarse granularity of CPU speed emulation, preventing the emulation of arbitrary speeds. Similarly, Fracas is a very good solution for the single thread/process case, and provides notable improvements compared to CPU-Lim, especially regarding accuracy and intrusiveness, but exhibits some problems in the multi-thread/process case.

In our future work, we plan to make further improvements to Fracas. First, we will try to solve the problems shown in the multi-thread/process case. Second, we will try to incorporate the emulation of other CPU characteristics, like memory bandwidth, as it becomes a crucial characteristic of modern CPUs. We would also like to emulate common features such as simultaneous multi-threading. The ultimate goal is to create a reliable, fine-grained solution to cover all important aspects of CPU emulation.

In order to provide an easy way to run experiments with Fracas, we will integrate it into the Wrekavoc emulator, enabling experimenters to combine CPU emulation with Fracas, and network emulation on large clusters.

References

1. Canon, L.C., Dubuisson, O., Gustedt, J., Jeannot, E.: Defining and Controlling the Heterogeneity of a Cluster: the Wrekavoc Tool. Journal of Systems and Software 83, 786–802 (2010)
2. The Grid'5000 experimental testbed, `https://www.grid5000.fr`
3. Gustedt, J., Jeannot, E., Quinson, M.: Experimental Validation in Large-Scale Systems: a Survey of Methodologies. Parallel Processing Letters 19, 399–418 (2009)
4. HPC Challenge Benchmark, `http://icl.cs.utk.edu/hpcc/`
5. Jones, M.T.: Inside the Linux 2.6 Completely Fair Scheduler: Providing fair access to CPUs since 2.6.23, `http://www.ibm.com/developerworks/linux/library/l-completely-fair-scheduler/`
6. Perarnau, S., Huard, G.: Krash: reproducible CPU load generation on many cores machines. In: IPDPS 2010: Proceedings of the 2010 IEEE International Symposium on Parallel&Distributed Processing (2010)
7. STREAM: Sustainable Memory Bandwidth in High Performance Computers, `http://www.cs.virginia.edu/stream/`

Case Studies in Automatic GPGPU Code Generation with `llc`*

Ruymán Reyes and Francisco de Sande

Dept. de E. I. O. y Computación
Universidad de La Laguna, 38271–La Laguna, Spain
{rreyes,fsande}@ull.es

Abstract. The evolution of high performance computers is progressing toward increasingly heterogeneous systems. These new architectures pose new challenges, particularly in the field of programming languages. New tools and languages are needed if we want to make a full use of the advantages offered by these new architectures. `llc` is a language with a C-like syntax where parallelism is expressed using compiler directives. In this work we focus our attention on the new backend of our prototype compiler for `llc` which generates CUDA code. We evaluate the performance of the target code using three different applications. The preliminary results that we present make us believe that our approach is worth to be explored more deeply.

Keywords: GPGPU, CUDA, OpenMP, compiler, code performance, automatic parallelization, `llc`.

1 Introduction

At the present time, HPC technology is living a time of fast changes. The range of computer architectures capable to achieve high performance [3] has broadened. With a reasonable cost, it is easy at this moment to build a HPC system interconnecting computing nodes where each node consists of several many-core processors plus computational accelerators. These deep changes in the hardware are immediately followed by the corresponding movements in the software layer.

Before the end of the Gigahertz race, the situation at the time to exploit parallelism was not satisfactory in terms of programmability. From our point of view, MPI or OpenMP, the prevailing tools to program parallel systems, are not acceptable if we take into account that those users who have the need for HPC are not experts in this field. The inclusion in this cocktail of hardware accelerators such as graphic processors (GPUs) [5] or field-programmable gate arrays (FPGAs) [6] does nothing but complicate the landscape. The new architectures pose new challenges, particularly in the field of programming languages. New

* This work has been partially supported by the EU (FEDER), the Spanish MEC (Plan Nacional de I+D+I, contract TIN2008-06570-C04-03) and the Canary Islands Government (ACIISI, contract SolSubC200801000285).

M.R. Guarracino et al. (Eds.): Euro-Par 2010 Workshops, LNCS 6586, pp. 13–22, 2011.
© Springer-Verlag Berlin Heidelberg 2011

tools and languages are clearly needed if we want to take advantage of the new hardware capabilities.

The OpenCL [8] standard represents an effort to create a common programming interface for heterogeneous devices, which many manufacturers have joined. However, it is still immature, and its programming model is not simple.

CUDA [9] is a more mature and extended approach, although currently only supports NVIDIA devices. It offers a programming interface (mostly C with a small set of extensions). This framework allows HPC users to re-implement their codes using GPU devices. Despite of being partially simple to build a code using this framework, it is hard to achieve a good performance rate, requiring a huge coding and optimization effort to obtain the maximum performance of the architecture.

`llc` is a high level parallel language [4] where parallelism is expressed through the use of compiler directives that follow the OpenMP syntax. The performance of the MPI and hybrid MPI+OpenMP code generated by the `llc` compiler has been studied in previous works [10]. The aim of this work is to use our language and the new CUDA backend of its compiler to study different cases in the parallelization of loops. The computational environment where we develop our experiments is equiped with a multicore system and an attached GPU.

The remainder of the paper is organized as follows. We begin with an introduction of the `llc` language and its compiler in Section 2. Different situations considered when extracting parallelism from a code annotated with `llc` directives are studied in Section 3. We guide our explanations through the use of three applications implemented in `llc` for which we present computational results. We summarize a few concluding remarks and future work in Section 4.

2 The `llc` Language and Its Compiler

We believe that simplicity and programmability are key aspects in the success of any parallel language. With this consideration in mind, in the last years we have been working on a project that tries to combine simplicity from the user side with reasonable performance and portability. We expose to the HPC programmer a simple and well known language that hides the hardware complexity. On the other side, we present templates, representing the most common parallel patterns, where we can introduce optimized versions without too much effort. The bridge is a software architecture, conformed by a powerful transformation tool.

`llc` is a high level parallel language with a C based syntax where parallelism is expressed using compiler directives. The syntax of these directives is compatible with OpenMP where it is possible. `llCoMP` is a source to source compiler that translates C code annotated with `llc` directives into high-level parallel code. `llCoMP` uses the information present in the directives to produce the parallel code. Although `llc` supports the most usual parallel patterns: *forall*, *sections*, *pipelines* and *task queues* [4], the new CUDA `llCoMP` backend only supports parallel loops (*forall*), although in the future we plan to introduce support for additional patterns.

As all OpenMP directives and clauses are recognized by `llCoMP`, from a single source code we can obtain different binaries (sequential or parallel) depending on the compiler selected to translate the target code produced by `llCoMP`. The OpenMP directives not relevant to the actual CUDA backend are simply ignored by `llCoMP`.

The new version of the `llc` compiler can be considered an automatic translator from OpenMP to CUDA, but we prefer to consider it as a prototyping tool. It represents an intermediate software layer between `llc` and different backends. It has been designed in such a way that targeting different architectures will not require a huge effort. `llCoMP` has been implemented using Python and following an object oriented approach. Reusing the code from the pycparser project [2], we have been able to build a C frontend supporting OpenMP in a short time, and our software architecture design allowed us to write a translation system compound by a set of classes and methods, which encapsulate most of the work.

To make its work, `llCoMP` starts translating the abstract syntax tree (AST) corresponding to the input source code to an internal representation (IR) based on a class hierarchy. Those parts of the IR corresponding to sequential code in the source are written in the target code without transformation. The compiler searches in the AST for specific patterns using what we call a *Filter*. These patterns corresponds to different high-level parallel constructs. The compiler has a filter class hierarchy that deals with this search task. Once a pattern is located in the AST, we can apply different mutators to achieve the desired translation. *Mutators* produce local modifications in the AST where they insert the high-level (CUDA) code corresponding to the desired translation. After all *Mutators* have been applied, the new AST is processed by the *CudaWriter* module to produce the target code.

The code generation in `llCoMP` uses the *code pattern* concept. A *code pattern* is an abstraction that represents a specific task in the context of the translation. `llCoMP` uses two kind of code patterns: static and dynamic. The simplest code patterns are implemented using code templates, while the most complex cases require the implementation of a *Mutator*.

A code template is a code fragment in the target language that will be modified accordingly to some input parameters. This code is interpreted and translated to the IR and afterwards it is grafted in the AST. The design of the backend using code templates will ease the implementation of new future backends.

Every time we need to use a device, we can identify several common tasks: initialization, local data allocation, device invocation, data retrieval and memory deallocation, among others. Each of these tasks identifies a pattern which is implemented through a code template. To manipulate these code templates and insert them in the IR `llCoMP` defines a set of operations that are collected in a library and exhibit a common facade.

In our first approach to automatic code generation for CUDA, we have prevailed on simplicity, rather than focusing on code performance. However, we have detected some situations where improvements in the target code will enhance the performance. We are currently working on the implementation of these improvements and some other complex optimizations that will be included in future releases of `llCoMP`.

3 Case Studies

In order to study different relevant situations during the translation from `llc` to CUDA we have used three applications: the Mandelbrot set computation, the solution of a finite difference equation using the Jacobi iterative method and a Molecular Dynamic (MD) simulation. With each code we will focus our attention on different aspects that offer opportunities to optimize the code produced by `llCoMP`. The source code for all the applications is available at the `llc` project home page.

For the OpenMP and sequential versions of the codes we have used GCC while the target codes generated by `llCoMP` have been compiled using the CUDA C NVIDIA compiler. The speedups are computed using exactly the same source code, for the `llCoMP` and OpenMP versions. The sequential code was obtained deactivating the OpenMP flags.

The computational experience we present here has been carried out in a system build from two AMD Opteron QuadCore processors (8 cores) with 4 GB of RAM. This system has attached through a PCI-express 16x bus a Tesla C1060 card with 4 GB and 1 GPU with 240 cores.

Some of our computational results compare the performance of OpenMP code executed with 8 threads against the execution in the GPU. Our purpose is to exhibit the improvement obtained just by adding a GPU card to a small multicomputer. In addition, the peak power consumption of such a system is much lower than the corresponding to an equivalent homogeneous system.

3.1 The Mandelbrot Set Computation

The Mandelbrot set is the convergence domain of the complex series defined by $Z_n = {Z_{n-1}}^2 + C$. The area of the set is an open question in Mathematics. Using a Monte-Carlo method, the algorithm in Listing 1 computes an estimation of the set area. In line 1, with a syntax taken from [1], we specify the target device for the parallel loop in line 5. When `llCoMP` translates to CUDA, it looks for parallel regions preceded by an `omp target` directive (line 1) whose device is CUDA. Once this situation is detected, the compiler inserts in the target code the memory transfer pattern and encapsulates the body of any parallel loop into a CUDA kernel. Finally, the patterns for data gathering and resources deallocation are also inserted.

The CUDA backend of our compiler uses a specialized kernel to perform reduction operations. The kernel implemented in the compiler [7] uses interleaved addressing and makes the first add during data fetching from global memory. This improvement benefits from using the device to perform the reduction and minimizes the size of the transfer between host and device.

Our approach when translating from `llc` to CUDA takes advantage of specialized CUDA kernels in additional situations. If the programmer is aware that

```
#pragma omp target device(cuda) copy_in(c)
#pragma omp parallel for reduction(+:numoutside) private(i,j,ztemp,z) shared(nt,c)
{
  numoutside = 0;
  for(i = 0; i < npoints; i++) {
    z.creal = c[i].creal;
    z.cimag = c[i].cimag;
    for (j = 0; j < MAXITER; j++) {
      ztemp = (z.creal * z.creal) - (z.cimag * z.cimag) + c[i].creal;
      z.cimag = z.creal * z.cimag * 2 + c[i].cimag;
      z.creal = ztemp;
      if (z.creal * z.creal + z.cimag * z.cimag > THRESOLD) {
        numoutside++;
        break;
      }
    } /* for j */
  } /* for i */
}
```

Listing 1. The Mandelbrot set computation in llc

certain operation has an efficient implementation in the target language, she can provide such information through the use of the `implements` clause also proposed in [1].

Another issue that has a large impact on the performance of the CUDA code is the number of threads per block, particularly in the presence of irregular computations. Figure 1 shows the execution time for three increasing problem sizes (number of points computed) in the Mandelbrot set area computation varying the number of threads involved in the computation.

Although it seems counterintuitive, the best performance for a problem size is achieved with the lesser number of threads per block. This effect is due to the multiprocessors occupancy. With a lesser number of threads, a larger number of

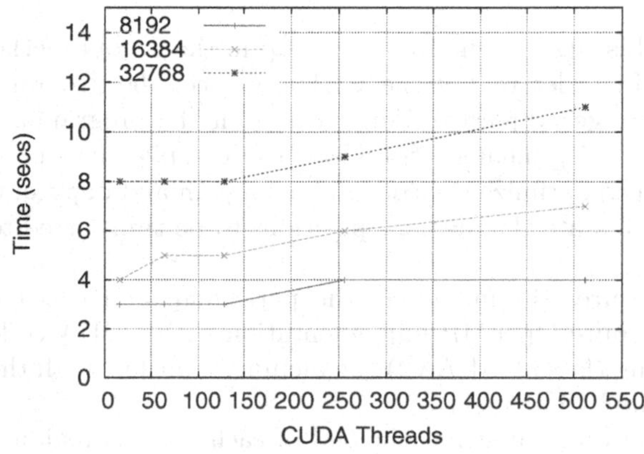

Fig. 1. Execution time for the Mandelbrot code for different number of threads

blocks can be allocated to the same multiprocessor, and therefore more blocks are executing concurrently.

This is only one of the tradeoffs involved in the execution of CUDA programs. Information has to be provided by the user in order to increase the performance. High level transformations of the parallel loops directly turns into an improvement of the multiprocessor occupancy and therefore in a performance gain.

3.2 The Jacobi Method

A key issue to enhance the performance in the CUDA architecture is the reduction of data transfer between host and device. In our PCI express × 16 bus this data transfer rate is 1.7 GB/s between CPU and GPU, and it constitutes a critical bottleneck.

```
1  while ((k < maxit) && (error > tol)) {
2    error = 0.0;
3    #pragma omp target device (cuda) copy_in(uold, f, u) copy_out(u)
4    #pragma omp parallel shared(uold, u, ...) private(i, j, resid)
5    {
6      #pragma omp for
7      for (i = 0; i < m; i++)
8        for (j = 0; j < n; j++)
9          uold[i][j] = u[i][j];
10     #pragma omp for reduction(+:error )
11     for (i = 0; i < (m - 2); i++) {
12       for (j = 0; j < (n - 2); j++) {
13         resid = ...
14         ...
15         error += resid * resid;
16       }
17     }
18   }
19   k++;
20   error = sqrt(error) / (double) (n * m);
21 }
```

Listing 2. Iterative loop in the Jacobi method implementation in `llc`/OpenMP

The code in Listing 2 is the iterative loop in the Jacobi method both in `llc` and OpenMP. In order to use the CUDA device, the programmer just need to specify the `target` directive. Furthermore, if the programmer uses the `llc` capabilities to specify memory transfers, the compiler can take advantage of this information to optimize the code. The `copy_in` and `copy_out` clauses in the directive at line 3 state the memory positions to be transferred to and from the device.

Figure 2 measures the impact in the performance of this language feature by comparing a pure OpenMP implementation with CUDA code generated by `llCoMP` specifying (label CUDA v2) the memory transfers with these clauses and not doing so (label CUDA v1).

In our translation strategy, at the end of each parallel region we synchronize host and device memories. Inside a parallel region we assume that memory locations allocated in the host remain unchanged. The programmer has to use the

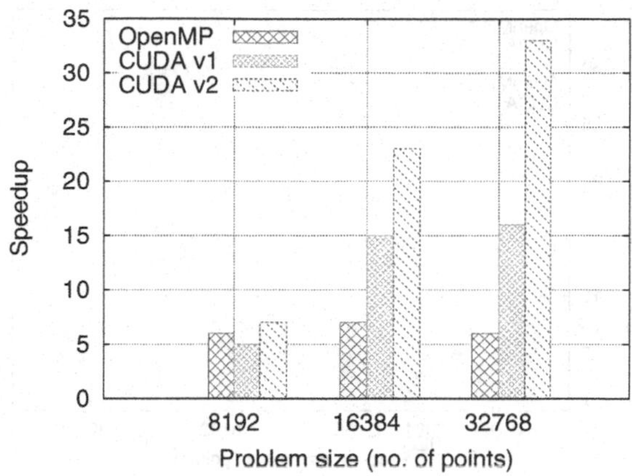

Fig. 2. Speedup of the Jacobi code for different problem sizes

OpenMP `flush` construct in order to synchronize host and device in the case that access to variables computed in the device in a previous parallel loop is needed inside the parallel region. The insertion of the `flush` construct is not required in the case of function calls because they are automatically translated into device code.

With the Jacobi code we also want to measure differently the impact of memory transfers in the CUDA parallelization. The code in Listing 2 has been coded in two different ways:

`1-REG`: with a single parallel region containing the parallel loops (as it is shown in Listing 2).

`2-REG`: using two different parallel regions, one for each parallel loop. In this case, at the end of the first parallel region the GPU memory is released and data have to be transferred again, while in the former case we take advantage of the persistence of the GPU memory between kernel calls.

The performance of these alternative parallelizations are presented in Figure 3. The size of the problem correspond to the dimension of the square matrices used in the computation. The OpenMP versions of the code slightly benefits when enclosing both parallel loops in a single parallel region, but the benefit is exceeded by CUDA versions of the code, and this benefit is larger when the problem size grows.

3.3 Molecular Dynamic Simulation

Given positions, masses and velocities of `np` particles, the routine shown in listing 3 computes the energy of the system and the forces on each particle. The code is an implementation in `llc` of a simple Molecular Dynamics (MD) simulation. It employs an iterative numerical procedure to obtain an approximate solution whose accuracy is determined by the time step of the simulation.

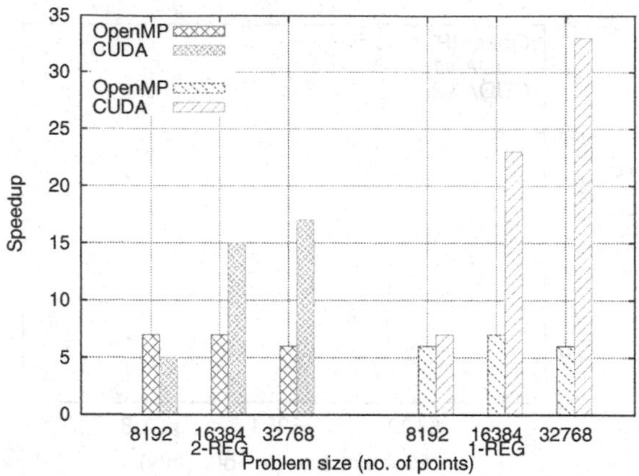

Fig. 3. Speedup of the Jacobi code depending on the number of parallel regions

```
void compute(int np, int nd, double *box, vnd_t *pos, ...) {
  double x, d, pot, kin;
  int i, j, k;
  vnd_t rij;

  pot = kin = 0.0;
 #pragma omp target device(cuda) copy_in(f,vel,pos,box) copy_out(f)
 #pragma omp parallel for default(shared)
                 private(i, j, k, rij, d) reduction(+ : pot, kin)
    for (i = 0; i < np; i++) {      /* Pot. energy and forces */
      for (j = 0; j < nd; j++)
        f[i][j] = 0.0;
      for (j = 0; j < np; j++) {
        if (i != j) {
          d = dist(nd, box, pos[i], pos[j], rij);
          pot = pot + 0.5 * v(d);
          for (k = 0; k < nd; k++) {
            f[i][k] = f[i][k] - rij[k] * dv(d) /d;
          }
        }
      }
      kin = kin + dotr8(nd, vel[i], vel[i]); /* kin. energy */
    }
    kin = kin * 0.5 * mass;
    *pot_p = pot;
    *kin_p = kin;
  }
```

Listing 3. Molecular Dynamic code simulation in `llc`

On each simulation step, the algorithm perform two basic operations: *compute* (shown in Listing 3) and *update*. The *update* operation is simply a for loop that runs over the particles, updating their positions, velocities and accelerations. From a computational point of view, *compute* is more intensive than *update*.

With this application we want to study the best combination of GPU/CPU to target the parallel code. If we state **C** for CPU and **G** for GPU we have measured four different versions of the code: **CC**: both routines in the CPU (pure OpenMP

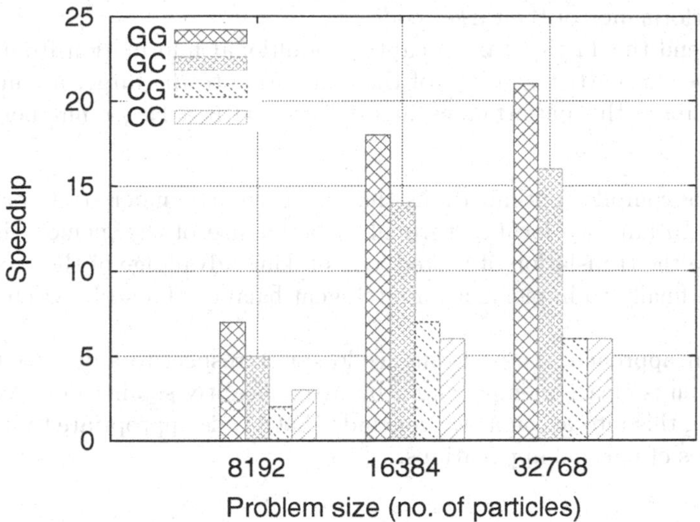

Fig. 4. Speedup of the MD simulation code for different parallelization strategies

code) **GG**: both routines in the GPU (pure CUDA code) **GC**: *compute* in the GPU and *update* in the CPU **CG**: *compute* in the CPU and *update* in the GPU Figure 4 shows the speedup obtained for three different problem sizes (number of particles). The best case is to place both routines in the GPU. For the hybrid OpenMP/CUDA codes, the best choice is to allocate the coarser grain routine in the GPU. The pure OpenMP version of the code do not scale up when increasing the problem size, probably due to memory constrains.

4 Conclusions and Future Work

This work represents a preliminary evaluation of the results obtained with the new backend of the `llc` compiler. We have got a new version of a source to source compiler, written in a modern, flexible and portable language that represents a starting point for future works. The architectural design of our proposal make our compiler a powerful prototyping tool to research in code transformation and optimization.

With the experience achieved in the development of the CUDA backend, we believe that the incorporation of new target languages (we plan to target OpenCL) should not require an unaffordable effort. From now on, our goal is to evolve the language to increase its capabilities balancing simplicity and performance.

Work in progress within the framework of this project includes the following:

- To increase the number of applications parallelized using our compiler, with particular attention to commercial applications.

- To study and implement additional compiler optimizations that will enhance the performance of the target code.
- To extend the `llc` syntax to capture additional information from the programmer for better adaption of the translation to the target architecture.
- To compare the performance in platforms with a larger number of CPU cores.

Some of the compiler optimizations that are currently under study or development are: To improve locality through a better use of the memory hierarchy, To enhance the translation of nested loops taking advantage of the architecture design and finally to implement an intelligent balance of load between host and device.

With our approach, the performance loss with respect to a direct CUDA implementation is clearly compensated by a significantly smaller development effort. Taking this into account, we conclude that `llc` is appropriate to implement some classes of parallel applications.

References

1. Ayguadé, E., Badia, R.M., Cabrera, D., et al.: A proposal to extend the openMP tasking model for heterogeneous architectures. In: Müller, M.S., de Supinski, B.R., Chapman, B.M. (eds.) IWOMP 2009. LNCS, vol. 5568, pp. 154–167. Springer, Heidelberg (2009)
2. Bendersky, E.: Pycparse (2010), `http://code.google.com/p/pycparser/`, `http://code.google.com/p/pycparser/`
3. Brodtkorb, A.R., Dyken, C., Hagen, T.R., Hjelmervik, J.M., Storaasli, O.O.: State-of-the-art in heterogeneous computing. Scientific Programming 18, 1–33 (2010)
4. Dorta, A.J., López, P., de Sande, F.: Basic skeletons in `llc`. Parallel Computing 32(7-8), 491–506 (2006)
5. Fatahalian, K., Houston, M.: A closer look at GPUs. Commun. ACM 51(10), 50–57 (2008)
6. Ghosh, S.: An asynchronous approach to efficient execution of programs on adaptive architectures utilizing FPGAs. J. Netw. Comput. Appl. 20(3), 223–252 (1997)
7. Harris, M.: Optimizing parallel reduction in CUDA (2007), `http://tiny.cc/t2phi`
8. Khronos Group: OpenCL the open standard for parallel programming of heterogeneous systems, `http://www.khronos.org/opencl/`
9. Nickolls, J., Buck, I., Garland, M., Skadron, K.: Scalable parallel programming with CUDA. Queue 6(2), 40–53 (2008)
10. Reyes, R., Dorta, A.J., Almeida, F., de Sande, F.: Automatic hybrid mPI+OpenMP code generation with `llc`. In: Ropo, M., Westerholm, J., Dongarra, J. (eds.) PVM/MPI. LNCS, vol. 5759, pp. 185–195. Springer, Heidelberg (2009)

On the Evaluation of JavaSymphony for Heterogeneous Multi-core Clusters*

Muhammad Aleem, Radu Prodan, and Thomas Fahringer

Institute of Computer Science, University of Innsbruck,
Technikerstraße 21a, A-6020 Innsbruck, Austria
{aleem,radu,tf}@dps.uibk.ac.at

Abstract. Programming hybrid heterogeneous multi-core cluster architectures is today an important topic in scientific and mainstream communities. To address this challenge, we developed JavaSymphony providing high-level programming abstraction and a middle-ware that facilitates the development and high-performance execution of Java applications on modern shared and distributed memory architectures. In this paper we present results of programming and executing a three-dimensional ray tracing application on a heterogeneous many-core cluster architecture.

1 Introduction

Multi-core processors have emerged today as a viable source of processing power. The emergence of multi-core trend was the result of heat dissipation and power consumption problems related to high clocked single-core processors. A multi-core processor consists of several homogeneous or heterogeneous cores packaged in a single chip. Already, there are many-core processors with hundreds of cores and the majority of top 500 supercomputers is being based on multi-core cluster architectures.

To exploit the underlying many-cores, applications need to be re-engineered and parallelised with user controlled load balancing and locality, heterogeneity of machines, and complex memory hierarchies. The Java programming constructs related to threads, synchronisation, remote method invocations, and networking are well-suited to exploit medium to coarse grained parallelism. Today, there are many research efforts [2,5,6,9,10] which focus on parallel Java applications for multi-core shared memory systems and clusters. Most of these efforts, however, do not provide user-controlled locality of task and data to exploit the complex memory hierarchies on many-core clusters. The locality of task and data have significant impact on an application's performance as demonstrated in [3,8].

In previous work [1,4], we developed JavaSymphony (JS) as a Java-based programming paradigm for programming conventional parallel and distributed infrastructures such as heterogeneous clusters, computational Grids, and shared memory multi-cores. JS provides a unified API to program both shared, as well as

* This research is partially funded by the "Tiroler Zukunftsstiftung", Project name: "Parallel Computing with Java for Manycore Computers".

M.R. Guarracino et al. (Eds.): Euro-Par 2010 Workshops, LNCS 6586, pp. 23–30, 2011.
© Springer-Verlag Berlin Heidelberg 2011

distributed memory applications. JS's design is based on the concept of dynamic virtual architecture, which allows programmer to define a hierarchical structure of heterogeneous computing resources (e.g. cores, processors, machines, clusters) and to control load balancing, locality, and code placements. On top of the virtual architecture, objects can be explicitly distributed, migrated, and invoked, enabling high-level user control of parallelism, locality, and load balancing. Previously [1], we described JS run-time system and locality control mechanism for shared and distributed memory applications. In this paper, we present new experiments based on a 3D ray tracing application using a heterogeneous multi-core cluster architecture.

The paper is organised as follows. Next section discusses the related work. Section 3 presents the JS overview, including JS run-time system, dynamic virtual architectures, and locality control mechanisms. Section 4 presents experimental results and section 5 concludes the paper.

2 Related Work

Proactive [2] is a Java-based library and parallel programming environment for parallel and distributed applications. Proactive provides high-level programming abstractions based on the concept of remote *active objects* [2]. In contrast to Proactive's single-threaded *active objects*, JS provides multi-threaded remote objects. Alongside programming, Proactive also provides deployment-level abstractions. Proactive has no functionality to map an *active object* and thread to specific processors or cores of a multi-core cluster.

Jcluster [9] is a Java-based message passing library for programing parallel applications. Jcluster provides a dynamic load balancing scheduler that is based on the Transitive Random Stealing algorithm. The dynamic scheduler enables any node in a cluster to get a task from other used nodes to balance the load. Jcluster scheduler has no support for multi-core processors and no functionality to map a task or object to specific processor and core in a multi-core cluster environment.

Parallel Java [5] is a Java-based API for shared and distributed memory parallel applications. It provides programming constructs similar to MPI and OpenMP. A hybrid programming model can also be used to combine both shared and distributed memory features in a parallel program. Although Parallel Java provides a multi-threaded approach for shared memory multi-cores, it has no capability to map threads to specific processors and cores in a cluster.

VCluster [10] implements a new programming model which allows migration of virtual threads (instead of complete processes) to other JVMs on the same or on different multi-core nodes in a cluster. Thread migration can be used for dynamic load balancing in a parallel multi-threaded application. VCluster does not provide any functionality to map a thread to a specific processor or core of a multi-core cluster.

MPJ Express [6] is a Java-based message passing framework that provides a portable and efficient communication layer. Although MPJ Express uses shared memory communication inside a multi-core computing node, it has no capability to control the locality of threads at processor or core level.

Most of the related work either prevents the application developer from controlling the locality of data and tasks, or engage the developer in time consuming and error-prone low-level parallelization details of the Java language. High-level user-controlled locality of the application, object, and task distinguishes JavaSymphony from other Java-based frameworks for multi-core cluster programming.

3 JavaSymphony

JavaSymphony (JS) is a Java-based programming paradigm for developing parallel and distributed applications. JS provides high-level programming constructs which abstract low-level infrastructure details and simplify the tasks of controlling parallelism, locality, and load balancing. Furthermore, it offers a unified solution for user-controlled locality-aware mapping of applications, objects and tasks on shared and distributed memory infrastructures. In this section, we provide an overview of some of the JS features, while complete description and implementation details can be found in [1,4].

3.1 Dynamic Virtual Architectures

The Dynamic Virtual Architecture (VA) [4] concept introduced by JS allows the programmer to define structure of heterogeneous computing resources and to control mapping, load balancing, migration of objects, and code placements. Most existing work assumes flat hierarchy of computing resources. In contrast to that, JS allows programmer to fully specify the multi-core architectures [1].

VA has a tree like structure, where each VA element has a certain level representing a specific resource granularity. Figure 1 depicts a four-level VA representing a heterogeneous cluster architecture consisting of a set of shared memory (NUMA or UMA) nodes on level 2, multi-core processors on level 1, and individual cores on the leaf nodes (level 0).

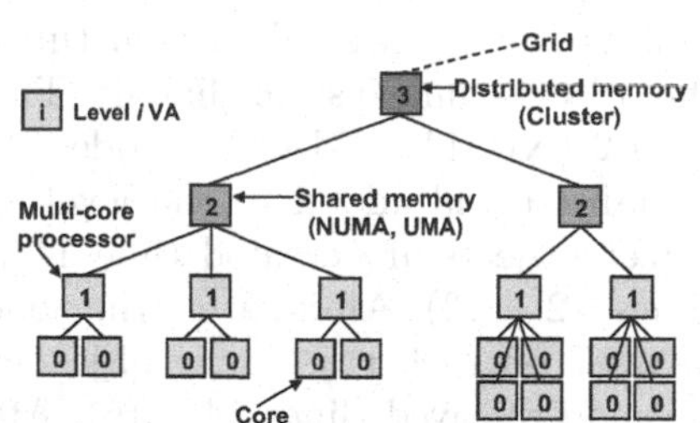

Fig. 1. Four-level locality-aware VA

3.2 JavaSymphony Objects

Writing a parallel JavaSymphony application requires encapsulating Java objects into so called *JS objects*, which are then distributed and mapped onto the hierarchical VA nodes (levels 0 to n). A JS object can be either a single or a multi-threaded object supporting three types of method invocations: asynchronous, synchronous, and one-sided.

3.3 Object Agent System

The Object Agent (OA) System [1], a part of JS run-time (JSR), processes remote as well as shared memory jobs. An OA is responsible for creating jobs, mapping objects to VAs, migrating, and releasing objects. An OA has a multi-threaded job queue which is associated with n job processing threads called *Job Handlers*. The results returned by the jobs are accessed using `ResultHandle` objects.

3.4 Locality Control

The Locality Control Module [1] applies and manages locality on the executing JS application by mapping the JS objects and tasks onto the VA nodes. In JS, we can specify locality constraints at three levels of abstraction: application, object, and task-level. Mapping an application, object, or task to a specific core will constrain the execution to that core. Mapping them on a higher-level VA node (e.g. multi-core processor, SMP, NUMA, cluster) will constrain the execution on the corresponding resource and delegate the scheduling to the inferior VA nodes.

4 Experiments

We developed a JS-based version of a multi-threaded 3D ray tracing application (JSRT) that is part of the Java Grande Forum (JGF) benchmark suite [7]. JSRT is a large-scale application that creates several ray tracer objects, initialises them with scene (64 spheres) and interval data, and renders at $N \times N$ resolution. The JSRT application is parallelised by distributing the outermost loop (over rows of pixels) to n JS objects which are mapped to the cores of the parallel machine. We experimented on a heterogeneous cluster (HC), which consists of two types of nodes outlined in Table 1:

Listing 1 shows the core of the JSRT application. First, it creates and initialises the required data structures (lines 1 – 3) and then registers itself to the JS run-time system (line 4). Then, it creates a level-3 (cluster) and several level-2 (NUMA, UMA) VA nodes (lines 5 – 6). The level-2 VA nodes are then initialised and added to the level-3 VA node (lines 7 – 9). Then, several ray tracer objects are created (line 11), initialised, and mapped to the VA nodes (lines 12 – 13). Afterwards, the rendering method (`render`) is asynchronously invoked on each `rayTracer` object and the handle objects (`ResultHandle`) returned are saved (lines 14 – 16). After collecting the results (checksum values)

Table 1. The heterogeneous cluster architecture

Node architecture	*No. of nodes*	*Processor*	*Processors per node*	*Network*	*Shared caches*
NUMA	2	Quad-core Opteron 8356	8	Gigabit ethernet	L3/Processor
UMA	13	Dual-core Opteron 885	4	Gigabit ethernet	Nil

from all invoked JS objects, they are validated (line 18) to check the correctness of the algorithm. Then, the rendered images are collected (lines 19 – 21) from all `rayTracers` and merged into one file. Finally, the JSRT application un-registers from the JS run-time system (line 23).

```
1 boolean bSingleThreaded = false; int npPerMachine = 8; int np = 64;
2 long checksum=0; int nMachines = np/npPerMachine; int k=0; int i, j;
3 ResultHandle[] rhSet = new ResultHandle[np];
4 JSRegistry reg = new JSRegistry("JSRTApp"); //register JSRTApp to JSR
5 VA cluster = new VA(3,nMachines); //level-3 VA node
6 VA[] computeNodes = new VA[nMachines];
7 for(i=0; i<nMachines; i++) {
8  computeNodes[i] = new VA(2); //level-2 VA nodes
9  cluster.addVA(computeNodes[i]); } //add level-2 VA nodes to level-3
10 ... //Initialization of data structures
11 JSObject[] rayTracers = new JSObject[nMachines]; //distributed
     objects
12 for(i=0; i<nMachines; i++) //create raytracers at level-2 VA nodes
13  rayTracers[i] = new JSObject(bSingleThreaded,"jsRayTracer.Worker",
      new Object[]{width,height,np},computeNodes[i]);
14 for(i=0; i<nMachines; i++)
15  for(j=0; j<npPerMachine; j++, k++) //invoke render tasks
16   rhSet[k] = rayTracers[i].ainvoke("render",new Object[]{k});
17 ... //get and sum the checksum values
18 jsRayTracerValidate(checksum); //check for correctness
19 for(i=0; i<nMachines; i++) { //get and save rendered images
20  rhSet[i] = rayTracers[i].sinvoke("getImage",new Object[]{});
21  renderdImage[i] = (int[]) rhSet[i].getResult(); }
22 ... //merge and save Image data to file
23 reg.unregister(); //un-register from JSR
```

Listing 1. The core JS code of the JSRT application

4.1 Heterogeneous Cluster

On the heterogeneous cluster, we experimented using up to 128 cores and five different versions of the JSRT application. The default version labelled `JSRT` is based on a *machine-fill* scheduling strategy, in which we first entirely filled the NUMA-based nodes by invoking up to 64 parallel tasks before moving to the UMA-based nodes (8 tasks per node). We select NUMA nodes first, since they have four times as many cores as the UMA nodes. This scheme requires less number of nodes, thus results in low VA and communication overheads.

Figure 2(a) shows that, although the default version (`JSRT`) achieved decent speedup, the machine-fill scheduling negatively affected the application performance on the NUMA nodes. In particular, we observed that 22% of the threads were slower, as illustrated by the load imbalance metric in Figure 2(b), calculated as follows:

$$LI = \frac{T_{\max} - T_{avg}}{T_{\max}} \cdot 100,$$

where $T_{\max}$ and T_{avg} represent the maximum and the average times of the parallel threads. To eliminate the load imbalance, we applied first two optimisations labelled `JSRT+OPT1` and `JSRT+OPT2` that shifts 10%, respectively 20% of the threads from the NUMA nodes to other free nodes of the cluster. These versions achieved better speedup results (see Figure 2(a)) and reduced the load imbalance to about 9% – 11%, respectively 2.81% – 4.83%, as displayed in Figure 2(b).

In the next step, we applied locality constraints on the optimised versions (labelled `JSRT+OPT1+LOC` and `JSRT+OPT2+LOC`) and achieved up to 50.14% more speedup over the default version (see Figure 2(a)).

Figure 2(c) shows the efficiency of these experiments calculated as the ratio between the speedup S and the weighted processor count due to the slight difference in processor speed of the two clusters:

$$E = \frac{S}{\sum_{\forall C \in HC} \frac{T_{\min}}{T_C}},$$

where T_C is the sequential execution time of the JSRT application on core C and $T_{\min}$ is the sequential execution time on the fastest core: $T_{\min} = \min_{\forall C \in HC} \{T_C\}$. The efficiency achieved by the different `JSRT` versions is quite good (95% – 52%), although it dropped down to 45% and 39% for the 112 and 128 machine sizes. To understand this reduced efficiency, we measured the overheads T_O encountered in each execution and calculated their *severity* as the ratio to the total parallel execution time T: $S = \frac{T_O}{T}$ (see Figure 2(d)). For the large machines size (112 – 128 cores), we observed increasing overhead severities related to the JSR and VA creation (7.53% – 9.53%), instantiation of JS objects on remote nodes (6.67% – 7.82%), communication (4.10% – 4.55%), and I/O (10.86% – 14.26%) limited the application performance and caused the efficiency to decrease below 50%.

The efficiency can be improved by choosing larger problem sizes. For example, Figure 2(e) illustrates that the larger 6000 × 6000 problem size labelled `JSRT+OPT2 (6k)` achieves up to 38.82% increase in efficiency compared to the 4000 × 4000 problem size labelled `JSRT+OPT2 (4k)`.

To investigate the effects of the locality constraints, we measured the number of instructions per cycle that are up to 13.46% higher for the locality-aware implementation compared to the non-locality aware version (see Figure 2(f)). The locality constraints keep the threads close to the node and processor where the data has been allocated, which results in a high number of local DRAM memory accesses that significantly improve overall performance (see Figure 2(h)). We also observed less number of data cache (L1) misses for the locality-aware `JSRT` version compared to the non-locality-aware version (see Figure 2(g)). Figure 2(i) illustrates that the number of L3 cache misses has increased for the locality-aware version because of contention on the L3 cache shared by multiple threads on the NUMA nodes.

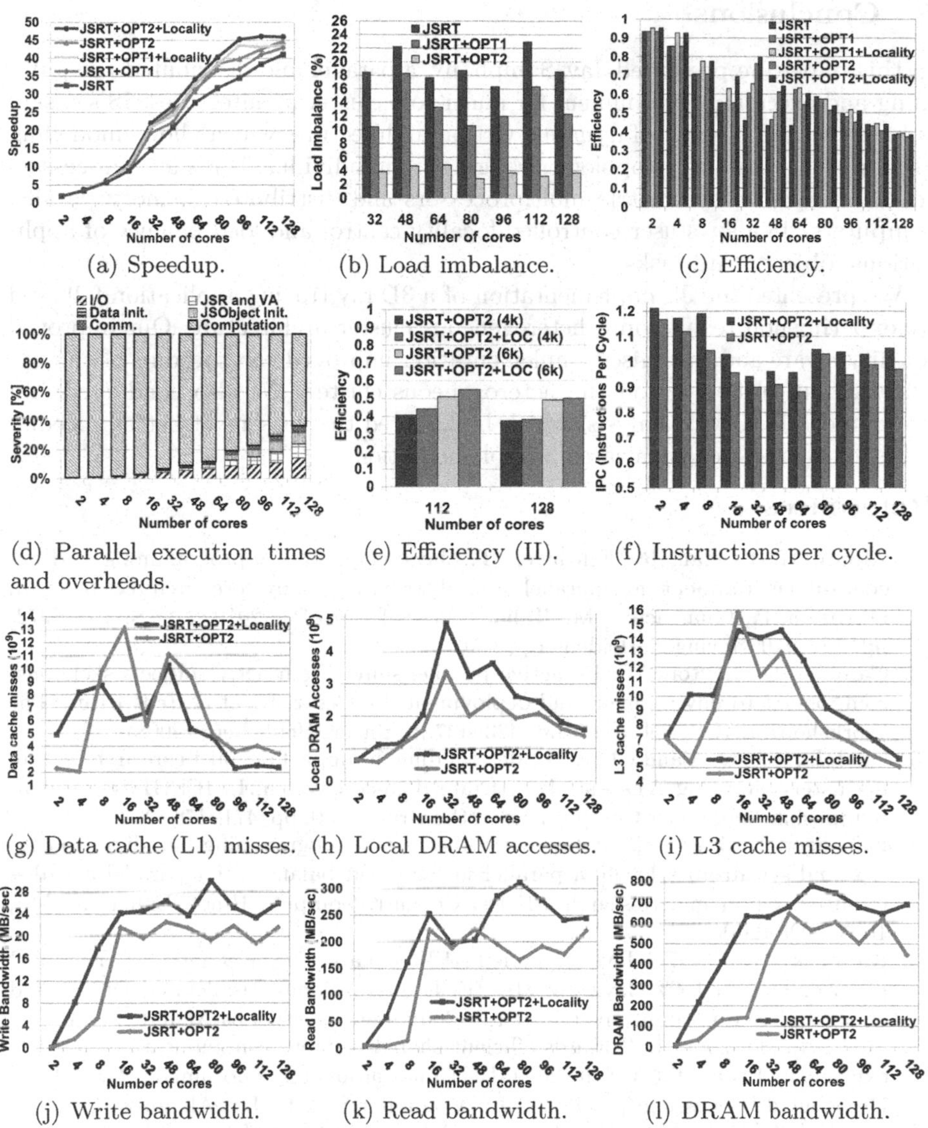

(a) Speedup. (b) Load imbalance. (c) Efficiency.

(d) Parallel execution times and overheads. (e) Efficiency (II). (f) Instructions per cycle.

(g) Data cache (L1) misses. (h) Local DRAM accesses. (i) L3 cache misses.

(j) Write bandwidth. (k) Read bandwidth. (l) DRAM bandwidth.

Fig. 2. Heterogeneous cluster experimental results

We further investigated the performance results by measuring system read, write, and DRAM bandwidth utilisation in the locality-aware and non-locality-aware versions. Figure 2(j) shows that the locality-aware version has a higher write bandwidth of up to 10.51% to 55.05% for large machine sizes (32 – 128 cores). The locality-aware version also shows 4.27% to 87.47% higher system read bandwidth for large machine sizes between 32 – 128 cores (see Figure 2(k)) and the DRAM bandwidth utilisation shown in Figure 2(l) is similarly between 3.93 – 54.78% higher.

5 Conclusions

In this paper, we presented JavaSymphony, a parallel and distributed programming and execution environment for multi-core cluster architectures. JS's design is based on the concept of dynamic virtual architecture, which allows modelling of hierarchical resource topologies ranging from individual cores and processors to more complex symmetric multiprocessors and distributed memory parallel computers. JS allows user controlled locality control and load balance of applications, objects, and tasks.

We presented the JS implementation of a 3D ray tracing application followed by experimental results on a heterogeneous cluster architecture. Our improved locality-aware and optimised implementation improved the speedup of the application up to 50.14% on the heterogeneous cluster. We also conducted and presented a low-level analysis, which highlighted the reasons of better speedup achieved by the locality-aware JS implementation.

References

1. Aleem, M., Prodan, R., Fahringer, T.: JavaSymphony: A programming and execution environment for parallel and distributed many-core architectures. In: D'Ambra, P., Guarracino, M., Talia, D. (eds.) Euro-Par 2010. LNCS, vol. 6272, pp. 139–150. Springer, Heidelberg (2010)
2. Caromel, D., Leyton, M.: Proactive parallel suite: From active objects-skeletons-components to environment and deployment. In: César, E., et al. (eds.) Euro-Par Workshops. LNCS, vol. 5415, pp. 423–437. Springer, Heidelberg (2008)
3. Chai, L., Gao, Q., Panda, D.K.: Understanding the impact of multi-core architecture in cluster computing: A case study with intel dual-core system. In: IEEE International Symposium on Cluster Computing and the Grid, vol. 0, pp. 471–478 (2007)
4. Fahringer, T., Jugravu, A.: Javasymphony: a new programming paradigm to control and synchronize locality, parallelism and load balancing for parallel and distributed computing: Research articles. Concurr. Comput.: Pract. Exper. 17(7-8), 1005–1025 (2005)
5. Kaminsky, A.: Parallel Java: A unified API for shared memory and cluster parallel programming in 100% Java. In: 21st IEEE International Parallel and Distributed Processing Symposium, pp. 1–8. IEEE Computer Society, Los Alamitos (2007)
6. Shafi, A., Manzoor, J.: Towards efficient shared memory communications in MPJ express. In: Proceedings of the 2009 IEEE International Symposium on Parallel and Distributed Processing, pp. 1–7. IEEE Computer Society, Los Alamitos (2009)
7. Smith, L.A., Bull, J.M.: A multithreaded Java grande benchmark suite. In: Third Workshop on Java for High Performance Computing. pp. 97–105 (2001)
8. Yang, R., Antony, J., Rendell, A.P.: A simple performance model for multithreaded applications executing on non-uniform memory access computers. In: Proceedings of the 2009 11th IEEE International Conference on High Performance Computing and Communications, pp. 79–86. IEEE Computer Society, Los Alamitos (2009)
9. Zhang, B.Y., Yang, G.W., Zheng, W.M.: Jcluster: an efficient Java parallel environment on a large-scale heterogeneous cluster: Research articles. Concurr. Comput.: Pract. Exper. 18(12), 1541–1557 (2006)
10. Zhang, H., Lee, J., Guha, R.K.: VCluster: a thread-based Java middleware for smp and heterogeneous clusters with thread migration support. Softw., Pract. Exper. 38(10), 1049–1071 (2008)

MAHEVE: An Efficient Reliable Mapping of Asynchronous Iterative Applications on Volatile and Heterogeneous Environments

Raphaël Couturier, David Laiymani, and Sébastien Miquée

University of Franche-Comté, LIFC laboratory, France
{raphael.couturier,david.laiymani,sebastien.miquee}@univ-fcomte.fr

Abstract. The asynchronous iteration model, called AIAC, has been proven to be an efficient solution for heterogeneous and distributed architectures. An efficient mapping of application tasks is essential to reduce their execution time. In this paper we present a new mapping algorithm, called MAHEVE (Mapping Algorithm for HEterogeneous and Volatile Environments) which is efficient on such architectures and integrates a fault tolerance mechanism to resist computing node failures. Our experiments show gains on a typical AIAC application execution time up to 65%, executed on distributed clusters architectures containing more than 400 computing cores with the JaccP2P-V2 environment.

1 Introduction

In the parallel computing area, in order to execute very large applications on heterogeneous architectures, iterative methods are well adapted [2]. These methods repeat the same instructions block until a convergence state and a desired approximation of the solution are reached. They constitute the only known approach to solving some kinds of problems and are relatively easy to parallelize. The Jacobi or the Conjugate Gradient methods are examples of such methods. To parallelize them, one of the most used methods is the message passing paradigm which provides efficient mechanisms to exchange data between tasks. As such a method, we focus here on the asynchronous parallel iterative model, called AIAC (*Asynchronous Iterations Asynchronous Communications*).

In this model, as can be seen on Figure 1, after each iteration, a task sends its results to its neighbors and immediately starts the next iteration with the last received data. The receiving and sending mechanisms are asynchronous and tasks do not have to wait for the reception of dependency messages from their neighbors. Consequently, there is no idle time between two iterations. Furthermore, this model is tolerant to message loss and even if a task is stopped the remaining tasks continue the computation, with the last available data. Several experiments [2] show the relevance of the AIAC algorithms in the context of distributed clusters with high latency between clusters. These works underline the good adaptability of AIAC algorithms to network and processor heterogeneity.

In a previous study [6] we proposed the implementation of two static task mapping algorithms dedicated to the AIAC model on heterogeneous distributed

M.R. Guarracino et al. (Eds.): Euro-Par 2010 Workshops, LNCS 6586, pp. 31–39, 2011.
© Springer-Verlag Berlin Heidelberg 2011

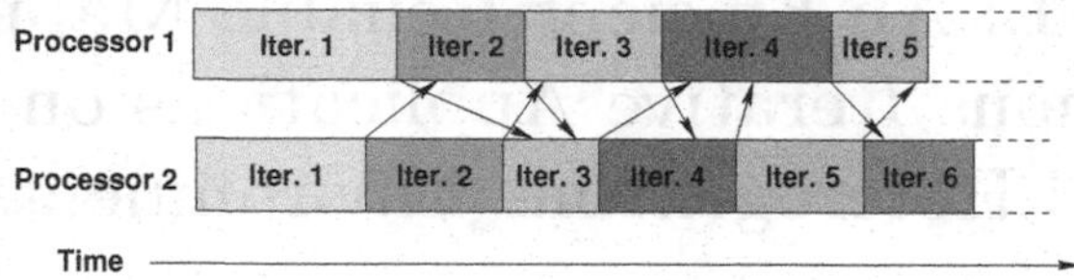

Fig. 1. Two processors computing in the AIAC model

clusters. Both these two algorithms, AIAC-QM (for *AIAC Quick-quality Map*) and F-EC (for *Farhat Edges-Cuts*) showed an important performance improvement by significantly reducing the application execution time. These experiments were performed by using the fully fault tolerant JaceP2P-V2 environment, described in the next section. In these experiments no computing node failures were introduced during the computation. As architecture heterogeneity continually evolves according to node volatility, we have to take care more precisely about the heterogeneity of the target platform. Thus in this paper we propose a new mapping algorithm called MAHEVE (*Mapping Algorithm for HEterogeneous and Volatile Environments*). This algorithm explicitly tackles the heterogeneity issue and introduces a level of dynamism in order to adapt itself to the fault tolerance mechanisms and to the evolution of the executing platform. Our experiments show gains up to 65% on application execution time, with faults during executions, which is about 10 points better than AIAC-QM and about 25 points better than F-EC, and MAHEVE also outperforms them in experiments with no fault during executions.

The rest of this paper is organized as follows. Section 2 presents the JaceP2P-V2 middleware by describing its architecture and briefly presenting its fault tolerance mechanisms. Section 3 formalizes our mapping and fault tolerance problems and quotes existing issues to address them. Section 4 describes the new mapping strategy we propose, MAHEVE. In Section 5 we present the experiments we conducted on the Grid'5000 testbed with more than 400 computing cores. Finally, we give some concluding remarks and plan our future work in Section 6.

2 JaceP2P-V2

JaceP2P-V2 [5] is a distributed platform implemented in Java, dedicated to developing and executing parallel iterative asynchronous applications. It is fully fault tolerant allowing it to execute parallel applications over volatile environments. To our knowledge this is the only such existing platform.

The JaceP2P-V2 platform part, which is based on the daemons and supervisors paradigm, is composed of three main entities: the "super-nodes", which are in charge of supervising free computing nodes connected to the platform; the "spawner", which is launched by a user wanting to execute a parallel application. It is in charge of a group of computing nodes and monitors them. If one fails, it requires a replacing one to a super-node; the "daemon", first connects to a super-node and waits for a task to execute. Each daemon can communicate directly with its computing neighbors.

To be able to execute AIAC applications, JaceP2P-V2 has an asynchronous messaging mechanism, and to resist daemon failures, it implements a checkpoint/restart mechanism by using a distributed backup mechanism called the *uncoordinated distributed checkpointing* [7]. This decentralized procedure allows the platform to be very scalable, with no weak point and does not require a secure nor a stable station for backups. When a daemon dies, it is replaced by another one, as we suppose that there are enough available free nodes. For more details on the JaceP2P-V2 platform, interested readers can refer to [5].

3 Mapping and Fault Tolerance Problems

Application modeling. The TIG [11] (*Task Interaction Graph*) model is the most appropriate to our problem, as it only models relationships between tasks. They are considered simultaneously executable and communications can take place at any time during the computation, with no precedence nor synchronization.

In this model, a parallel application is represented by a graph $GT(V,E)$, where $V = \{V_1, V_2, \dots V_v\}$ is the set of $|V|$ vertices and $E \subset V \times V$ is the set of undirectional edges. Vertices represent tasks and edges represent the mutual communication among tasks. A function $EC : V \longrightarrow \mathbb{R}^+$ gives the computation cost of tasks and $CC : E \longrightarrow \mathbb{R}^+$ gives the communication cost for message passing on edges. We define $|V| = v$, $EC(V_i) = e_i$ and $CC(V_i, V_j) = c_{ij}$. Another function $D : V \longrightarrow \mathbb{N}^+$ gives the amount of dependencies of a task, noted $D(V_i) = d_i$.

Architecture modeling. A distributed clusters architecture can be modeled by a three-level-graph. The levels are *architecture* (a) (here the Grid'5000 grid), *cluster* (c), and *computing node* (n) levels. Let $GG(N,L)$ be a graph representing a distributed clusters architecture, where $N = \{N_1, N_2, \dots N_n\}$ is the set of $|N|$ vertices and L is the set of $|L|$ undirectional edges. The vertices represent the computing nodes and the edges represent the links between them. An edge $L_i \in L$ is an unordered pair $(N_x, N_y) \in N$, representing a communication link between nodes N_x and N_y. A function $WN : N \longrightarrow \mathbb{R}^+$ gives the computational power of nodes and another function $WL : L \longrightarrow \mathbb{R}^+$ gives the communication latency of links. We define $WN(N_i) = wn_i$ and $WL(L_i, L_j) = wl_{ij}$. Let be $|C|$ the number of clusters contained in the architecture. A function $CN : C \longrightarrow \mathbb{N}^+$ gives the amount of computing nodes contained in a cluster, and another function $CF : C \longrightarrow \mathbb{N}^+$ gives the amount of available computing nodes (not involved in computation) of a cluster. We define $CN(C_i) = C_{Ni}$ and $CF(C_i) = C_{Fi}$. We also define $C_{\overline{P}fi}$ as the average power of available resources of cluster C_i.

We evaluate the *heterogeneity degree* of the architecture, noted hd, by using the *relative standard deviation* method, with $hd = \frac{\sigma_{PN}}{avg_{PN}}$ where avg_{PN} is the average computing power of nodes and σ_{PN} represents the standard deviation of computing node power. This measure provides us the coefficient of variation of the platform in percentage – we only consider $0 \leq hd \leq 1$ as considering values of $hd > 1$ is not relevant, as $hd = 1$ denotes a fully heterogeneous platform.

Mapping functions. When a parallel application *App*, represented by a graph GT, is mapped on a distributed clusters architecture, represented by a graph GG, the execution time of the application, $ET(App)$, can be defined as the execution time of the slowest task. Indeed, an application ends when all the tasks have detected convergence and reached the desired approximation of the solution. We define $ET(App) = \max_{i=1...v}(ET(V_i))$, where the execution time of each task i $(i = 1 \ldots v)$, $ET(V_i)$, is given by $ET(V_i) = \frac{e_i}{wn_i} + \sum_{j \in J} c_{ij} \times wl_{ij}$ where e_i is the computational cost of V_i, wn_i is the computational power of the node N_i on which V_i is mapped, J represents the neighbors set of V_i, c_{ij} is the amount of communications between V_i and V_j, and wl_{ij} is the link latency between the computing nodes on which V_i and V_j are mapped. As described in this formula, the execution time of a task depends on the task weight and on the communications which may occur between this task and its neighbors. We underline here that in the AIAC model, it is impossible to predict the number of iterations of a task. So it is difficult to evaluate a priori its cost e_i.

An important point to take into consideration is that the execution of multiple tasks on the same node is not allowed, as this provides a fall of performance in such a context. This task mapping problem is similar to the classical graph partitioning and task assignment problem, and is thus NP-complete.

Fault tolerance. In volatile environments, computing nodes can disconnect at any time during the computation, and have thus to be efficiently replaced. The replacing nodes should be the best ones at the fault time, by finding them in available nodes. As executing environments can regularly evolve, due to computing node volatility, a mapping algorithm has to keep a correct overview of the architecture, in real time. Thus, criteria to assign tasks to nodes should dynamically evolve too.

Another problem appears after multiple crashes: some tasks may have migrated over multiple computing nodes and clusters, and the initial mapping may be totally changed. So, after having suffered some node failures the task mapping could not always satisfy the mapping criteria (not on the most powerful available machine, too far away from its neighbors...). A good fault tolerance policy has to evolve dynamically with the executing environment.

3.1 Related Work

In the literature of the TIG mapping many algorithms exist, which can be broadly classified into two categories. The first one is the *Edge-cuts optimization* class, which minimizes the use of the penalizing links between clusters. As tasks are depending on neighbors, which are called dependencies, the goal is to choose nodes where distance, in term of network, is small to improve communications between tasks. Here we can cite Metis [9] and Chaco [8] which are libraries containing such kind of algorithms. The second category is the *Execution time optimization* class, which aims at minimizing the whole application execution time. These algorithms look for nodes which can provide the smallest execution time of tasks using their computational power. We can cite QM [12] and MiniMax [10] as such kind of algorithms. Both classes of algorithms may fit with our goals as in our model we have both the computational power of nodes and communication costs which may influence the applications performance.

All mentioned algorithms do not tackle the computing node failures issue, or only basically by applying the same policy. As explained in Section 3, a more efficient and dedicated replacement function is needed. Nevertheless, to the best of our knowledge, no task mapping algorithm, addressing explicitly both the executing platform heterogeneity and the computing node failures issues, exists.

4 MAHEVE

Here we present our new task mapping strategy, called MAHEVE (for *Mapping Algorithm for HEterogeneous and Volatile Environments*). This algorithm aims at taking the best part of each category mentioned in Section 3.1, the edge-cuts minimization and the application execution time optimization algorithms.

This new algorithm can be divided into two parts. The first part aims at performing the initial mapping, and the second part is devoted to search replacing nodes when computing node failures occur.

4.1 Initial Mapping

In this section we will study the main mechanisms of the *static mapping* done by MAHEVE, which is composed of three phases: sort of clusters, sort of tasks, and the effective mapping, which maps tasks (in their sort order) on nodes of clusters (also in their sort order) with a reservation of some nodes in each cluster.

Sorting clusters. The first step of the initial mapping is to sort clusters according to the executing platform heterogeneity degree hd. The main principles are that a cluster obtains a better mark M_i when $hd < 0.5$ and it contains more computing nodes than other clusters (C_{Fi}, the number of available free nodes, is privileged), and when $hd \geq 0.5$ and it contains more powerful computing nodes ($C_{\overline{P}fi}$, the average free computation power, is privileged). These choices come from several experiments with the AIAC model, which show that in such environments it is more efficient to privilege the computation power or the number of nodes. As the number of nodes, C_{Fi}, and the average free computing power, $C_{\overline{P}fi}$, are not in the same order of magnitude, we normalize them with two functions, $normN$ and $normP$. We note $normN\,(C_{Fi}) = NC_{Fi}$ and $normP(C_{\overline{P}fi}) = NC_{\overline{P}fi}$. The formula used to give a mark, M_i, to a cluster is $M_i = NC_{\overline{P}fi}^{hd} + NC_{Fi}^{1-hd}$ (1).

This compromise function allows us to privilege clusters following our criteria, as explained previously, according to the heterogeneity degree. If we study its limits for the hd extremities, $hd = 0$ and $hd = 1$, we obtain $\lim_{hd \to 0} M_i = NC_{Fi} + 1$ and $\lim_{hd \to 1} M_i = NC_{\overline{P}fi} + 1$, which fit with our objectives.

Clusters are so sorted and placed in a list containing them, starting from the cluster which receives the better mark to the one which receives the lower mark.

Sorting tasks. Like clusters, tasks are also sorted according to the heterogeneity degree of the executing platform, *hd*. This sort is done in the same way as previously, as when $hd < 0.5$ tasks with higher dependencies will be privileged, and when $hd \geq 0.5$ tasks with higher computing cost are privileged. The main function used to classified tasks is $Q_i = {e_i}^{hd} \times {d_i}^{1-hd}$ (2)

where Q_i is the evaluation of the task i according to the heterogeneity degree hd and d_i, the amount of dependencies of task i.

Then tasks are taken in the order of the first sort, determined with equation (2), and each task is placed in a new list (the final one) and some of its dependencies are added. We note $Nb_i = {d_i}^{1-hd}$ this amount of dependencies as the lower the heterogeneity degree is the higher this number will be. This final operation allows to control the necessary locality of tasks according to *hd*.

Mapping method. The third step of the initial mapping is to allocate tasks to nodes. As clusters and tasks have been sorted accordingly to the executing platform heterogeneity degree, ordered from the highest mark to the lowest, this function maps tasks on almost all available computing nodes of clusters, in their respective order in lists (for example a task classified first in the task list is mapped on an available node of the cluster classified first in the cluster list). The idea here is not to fulfill each cluster, but to preserve some computing nodes in each cluster. These conserved nodes will be used to replace failed nodes.

4.2 Replacing Function

During the initial mapping some nodes in each cluster have been preserved. When a node fails this function replaces it by a free node of the same cluster. If none is available this function sorts again clusters, to take into consideration platform modifications, and replaces the failed node by one available in the new sorted cluster list. This mechanism allows to retain task locality and a real time overview of the executing platform.

5 Experimentation

5.1 A Typical AIAC Application and the Execution Platform

We used a variation of the "Kernel CG" application of the NAS Parallel Benchmarks (NPB) [4] to evaluate the performance of our new mapping algorithm. The Conjugate Gradient method is replaced by the multisplitting method, which supports the asynchronous iterative model. More details about this method can be found in [3]. We used used a matrix of size $5,000,000$ with a bandwidth fixed to $35,000$, which generates between 8 and 20 neighbors per task. This application was executed on 64 nodes selected among more than 100.

The platform used to realize our tests, called Grid'5000 [1], is a French nationwide experimental set of clusters which provides us with distributed clusters architectures (28 heterogeneous clusters spread over 9 sites). We used three distributed clusters architectures, each having a different heterogeneity degree.

Table 1. Application execution time in seconds and corresponding gains on various platforms using different mapping algorithms, with fault free (FF) executions and with 2 node failures each 20 seconds (WF) executions

hd	Default		FT-AIAC-QM		FT-FEC		MAHEVE	
	FF	WF	FF	WF	FF	WF	FF	WF
0.08	80	229	63 (21%)	178 (22%)	61 (23%)	154 (33%)	60 (25%)	113 (50%)
0.50	67	242	61 (9%)	118 (51%)	63 (6%)	133 (45%)	54 (20%)	85 (65%)
0.72	67	192	59 (12%)	99 (45%)	65 (3%)	121 (33%)	52 (22%)	86 (53%)

The first one was composed of four clusters spread over four sites, with a total of 106 computing nodes representing 424 computing cores with $hd = 0.08$; the second one was composed of four clusters spread over three sites, with a total of 110 computing nodes representing 440 computing cores with $hd = 0.50$; and finally the third one was composed of five clusters spread over four sites with 115 computing nodes representing 620 computing cores with $hd = 0.72$.

All nodes can communicate with each other through an efficient network, but as it is shared with many other users, high latencies appear during executions.

5.2 Experiments

We compared MAHEVE with FT-AIAC-QM (for *Fault Tolerant AIAC-QM*) and FT-FEC (for *Fault Tolerant F-EC*) which are respectively the fault tolerant versions of the AIAC-QM and F-EC mapping algorithms presented in [6]. During some executions, we introduced two failures in computing nodes involved in the computation every 20 seconds to simulate a volatile environment. Table 1 shows the execution times of each mapping algorithm compared to the default mapping strategy of the JaceP2P-V2 platform, with the corresponding gains on application execution time, given in brackets. It presents both the executions with faults (WF) and the fault free (FF) ones.

First of all, we can note that all mapping algorithms provide an enhancement of the application performance by considerably reducing its execution time, especially for executions with node failures, with an average gain of about 45% in general in comparison to the default policy. If we focus on executions with node failures (WF), FT-FEC is efficient on architectures with a low heterogeneity degree ($hd = 0.08$) by providing gains of about 33%, and gains are roughly the same on heterogeneous architectures ($hd = 0.72$). FT-AIAC-QM is efficient on architectures with a high heterogeneity degree ($hd = 0.72$) by providing gains of about 45%, whereas it is not so efficient on homogeneous architectures ($hd = 0.08$) by providing gains of about 22%. We can note here that on an architecture with a heterogeneity degree of 0.50 FT-AIAC-QM is more efficient than FT-FEC by providing gains up to 50%. Here we point out that in fault free executions (FF), both algorithms also provide gains on their respective favorite architectures, though gains are lower than in executions with faults (WF).

Now if we focus on the performance of our new solution MAHEVE, we can see that it is all the time better than other algorithms. As can be seen in Table 1, in executions with faults (WF), it reduces the application execution time by about 50% on homogeneous architectures (here of 0.08 heterogeneity degree) which is more than 25 points better than FT-FEC and near 30 points better than FT-AIAC-QM. On heterogeneous architectures (here of 0.72 heterogeneity degree) it also outperforms other mapping algorithms by reducing the application execution time by about 53% which is almost 10 points better than FT-AIAC-QM and 20 points better than FT-FEC. On middle heterogeneity degree architectures (here of 0.50), MAHEVE is once again better than its two comparative mapping algorithms by reducing the application execution time by about 65%. These good performance come from the fact that it is designed to be efficient on both architectures, homogeneous and heterogeneous. Moreover, as it integrates a fault tolerance *security* in the initial mapping, it is more efficient when computing nodes fail. Here we can point out that this algorithm allows in general gains on application execution time of about 55%. In fault free executions (FF), it outperforms once again the two other algorithms.

6 Conclusion and Future Work

In this paper we have presented a new mapping algorithm, called MAHEVE, to address the AIAC mapping issue on heterogeneous and volatile environments. It aims at doing an efficient mapping of tasks on distributed clusters architectures by taking the best part of the two known approaches, application execution time optimization and edge-cuts minimization. We have shown that it is all the time better than the two other comparative mapping algorithms, FT-AIAC-QM and FT-FEC. This can be explained by the fact that it not only takes care about computing nodes and clusters, but also about the task properties (computing cost and dependencies), what refines the mapping solution.

In our future work we plan to enhance the MAHEVE algorithm performance by modifying the notation of clusters, since their locality has not yet been taken into consideration, and enhanced fault tolerance functions should be tried. We also have to validate the algorithm performance with other AIAC applications.

References

1. Grid 5000, `http://www.grid5000.fr`
2. Bahi, J., Contassot-Vivier, S., Couturier, R.: Performance comparison of parallel programming environments for implementing AIAC algorithms. Journal of Supercomputing 35(3), 227–244 (2006)
3. Bahi, J., Contassot-Vivier, S., Couturier, R.: Asynchronous Iterations. In: Parallel Iterative Algorithms: from Sequential to Grid Computing. Numerical Analysis & Scientific Computating, vol. 1. Chapman & Hall/CRC, Boca Raton (2007)
4. Bailey, D., et al: The NAS Parallel Benchmarks. Tech. Rep. RNR-94-007, NASA Advanced Supercomputing (NAS) Division (March 1994)
5. Charr, J.C., Couturier, R., Laiymani, D.: JACEP2P-V2: A fully decentralized and fault tolerant environment for executing parallel iterative asynchronous applications on volatile distributed architectures. In: Abdennadher, N., Petcu, D. (eds.) GPC 2009. LNCS, vol. 5529, pp. 446–458. Springer, Heidelberg (2009)

6. Couturier, R., Laiymani, D., Miquée, S.: Mapping asynchronous iterative applications on heterogeneous distributed architectures. In: PDSEC 2010 (2010)
7. Elnozahy, E.N., Alvisi, L., Wang, Y., Johnson, D.: A survey of rollback-recovery protocols in message-passing systems. ACM Comput. Surv. 34(3), 375–408 (2002)
8. Hendrickson, B., Leland, R.W.: The Chaco User's Guide (1995)
9. Karypis, G., Kumar, V.: A fast and high quality multilevel scheme for partioning irregular graphs. SIAM Journal on Scientific Computing 20(1), 359–392 (1998)
10. Kumar, S., Das, S.K., Biswas, R.: Graph partitioning for parallel applications in heterogeneous grid environments. In: IPDPS (2002)
11. Long, D.L., Clarke, L.A.: Task interaction graphs for concurrency analysis. In: ICSE, pp. 44–52 (1989)
12. Phinjaroenphan, P.: An Efficient, Pratical, Portable Mapping Technique on Computational Grids. Ph.D. thesis, RMIT University (2006)

Dynamic Load Balancing of Parallel Computational Iterative Routines on Platforms with Memory Heterogeneity

David Clarke, Alexey Lastovetsky, and Vladimir Rychkov

School of Computer Science and Informatics, University College Dublin, Belfield, Dublin 4, Ireland
David.Clarke.1@ucdconnect.ie,
{Alexey.Lastovetsky,vladimir.rychkov}@ucd.ie

Abstract. Traditional load balancing algorithms for data-intensive iterative routines can successfully load balance relatively small problems. We demonstrate that they may fail for large problem sizes on computational clusters with memory heterogeneity. Traditional algorithms use too simplistic models of processors performance which cannot reflect many aspects of heterogeneity. This paper presents a new dynamic load balancing algorithm based on the advanced functional performance model. The model consists of speed functions of problem size, which are built adaptively from a history of load measurements. Experimental results demonstrate that our algorithm can successfully balance data-intensive iterative routines on parallel platforms with memory heterogeneity.

Keywords: iterative algorithms, dedicated heterogeneous platforms, dynamic load balancing, data partitioning, functional performance models of heterogeneous processors.

1 Introduction

In this paper we study load balancing of data-intensive parallel iterative routines on heterogeneous platforms. These routines are characterised by a high data-to-computation ratio in a single iteration. The computation load of a single iteration can be broken into any number of equal independent computational units [2]. Each iteration is dependent on the previous one. The generalised scheme of these routines can be summarised as follows: (i) data is partitioned over the processors, (ii) at each iteration some independent calculations are carried out in parallel, and (iii) some data synchronisation takes place. Typically computational workload is directly proportional to the size of data. Examples of scientific computational routines include Jacobi method, mesh-based solvers and routines used in signal processing and image processing.

Our target architecture is a dedicated cluster with heterogeneous processors and heterogeneous distributed memory. High performance of iterative routines on this platform can be achieved when all processors complete their work within the same time. This is achieved by partitioning the computational workload

M.R. Guarracino et al. (Eds.): Euro-Par 2010 Workshops, LNCS 6586, pp. 41–50, 2011.
© Springer-Verlag Berlin Heidelberg 2011

and, hence, data unevenly across all processors. Workload should be distributed with respect to the processor speed, memory hierarchy and communication network [4]. Load balancing of parallel applications on heterogeneous platforms has been widely studied for different types of applications and in various aspects of heterogeneity. Many load balancing algorithms are not appropriate to either the applications or platforms considered in this paper. Applicable algorithms use models of processors performance which are too simplistic. These traditional algorithms are suitable for problem sizes, which are small relative to the platform, but can fail for larger problems.

This paper presents a new dynamic load balancing algorithm for data-intensive iterative routines on computational clusters with memory heterogeneity. In contrast to the traditional algorithms, our algorithm is adaptive and takes into account heterogeneity of processors and memory. Load balancing decisions are based on functional performance models which are constantly improved with each iteration [10]. Use of the functional performance models remove restrictions on the problem size which can be computed. This allows a computational scientist to utilise the maximum available resources on a given cluster. We demonstrate that our algorithm succeeds in balancing the load even in situations when traditional algorithms fail.

This paper is structured as follows. In Section 2, related work is discussed. In Section 3, we describe the target class of iterative routines and the traditional load balancing algorithm. Then we analyse the shortcomings of the traditional algorithm and present experimental results. In Section 4, we describe our algorithm and demonstrate that it can successfully balance data-intensive iterative routines with large problem sizes.

2 Related Work

In this section, we classify load balancing algorithms and discuss their applicability to data-intensive iterative routines and dedicated computational clusters with memory heterogeneity.

Load balancing algorithms can be either static or dynamic. **Static** algorithms [8,11,13] use *a priori* information about the parallel application and platform. This information can be gathered either at compile-time or run-time. These strategies are restricted to applications with pre-determined workload and cannot be applied to such iterative routines as adaptive mesh refinement [12], for which the amount of computation data grows unpredictably. **Dynamic** algorithms [1,3,5,6,7] do not require *a priori* information and can be used with a wider class of parallel applications. In addition, dynamic algorithms can be deployed on non-dedicated platforms. The algorithm we present in this paper is dynamic.

Another classification is based on how load balancing decisions are made: in a centralised or non-centralised manner. In **non-centralised** algorithms [1,5], load is migrated locally between neighbouring processors, while in **centralised** ones [3,6,7,8,11,13], load is distributed based on global load information. Non-centralized algorithms are slower to converge. At the same time, centralized algorithms typically have higher overhead. Our algorithm belongs to the class of centralised algorithms.

Centralised algorithms can be subdivided into two groups: task queue and predicting the future [4]. **Task queue** algorithms [3,7] distribute tasks. They target parallel routines consisting of independent tasks and schedule them on shared-memory platforms. **Predicting-the-future** algorithms [6,8,11,13] can distribute both tasks and data by predicting future performance based on past information. They are suitable for data-intensive iterative routines and any parallel computational platform.

A traditional approach taken for load balancing of data-intensive iterative routines belongs to static/dynamic centralised predicting-the-future algorithms. In these traditional algorithms, computation load is evaluated either in the first few iterations [13] or at each iteration [6] and globally redistributed among the processors. Current load measurements are used for prediction of future performance. Neither memory structure nor memory constraints are taken into account. As it will be demonstrated in Section 3, when applied to large scientific problems and parallel platforms with memory heterogeneity, this strategy may never balance the load, because it uses simplistic models of processors' performance.

It has been shown in [9] that it is more accurate to represent performance as a function of problem size, which reflects contributions from both processor and memory. In this paper, we propose a new dynamic load balancing algorithm based on partial functional performance models of processors [10]. Unlike traditional algorithms, our algorithm imposes no restriction on problem sizes.

We would also like to mention some advanced load balancing strategies which are not directly applicable to data-intensive iterative routines on heterogeneous clusters. It has been shown that the task queue model implemented in [3] can outperform the model [7] because decisions are based on adaptive speed measurements rather then single speed measurements. The algorithm presented in this paper also applies an adaptive performance model, but in such a way that it is applicable to scientific computational iterative routines.

In this paper, we focus on dynamic load balancing with respect to processor performance and memory hierarchy, and to this end we do not take into account communication heterogeneity. Future work could be the development of a hybrid approach, similar to [11], in which our algorithm is combined with one of the many existing communication models.

3 Traditional Load Balancing Algorithm of Iterative Routines

Iterative routines have the following structure: $x^{k+1} = f(x^k)$, $k = 0, 1, ...$ with x^0 given, where each x^k is an n-dimensional vector, and f is some function from $\mathbb{R}^n$ into itself [1]. The iterative routine can be parallelized on a cluster of p processors by letting x^k and f be partitioned into p block-components. In an iteration, each processor calculates its assigned elements of x^{k+1}. Therefore, each iteration is dependent on the previous one.

The objective of load balancing algorithms for iterative routines is to distribute computations across a cluster of heterogeneous processors in such a way that all processors will finish their computation within the same time and thereby minimising the overall computation time: $t_i \approx t_j, 1 \leq i, j \leq p$. The computation is spread across a cluster of p processors P_1, ...,P_p such that $p \ll n$. Processor P_i contains d_i elements of x^k and f, such that $n = \sum_{i=1}^{p} d_i$.

Traditional load balancing algorithms work by measuring the computation time of one iteration, calculating the new distribution and redistributing the workload, if necessary, for the next iteration. The algorithm is as follows:

Initially. The computation workload is distributed evenly between all processors, $d_i^0 = n/p$. All processors execute n/p computational units in parallel.

At each iteration

1. The computation execution times $t_1(d_1^k)$, ..., $t_p(d_p^k)$ for this iteration is measured on each processor and gathered to the root processor.
2. If $\max_{1 \leq i,j \leq p} \left| \frac{t_i(d_i^k) - t_j(d_j^k)}{t_i(d_i^k)} \right| \leq \epsilon$ then the current distribution is considered balanced and redistribution is not needed.
3. Otherwise, the root processor calculates the new distribution of computations d_1^{k+1}, ..., d_p^{k+1} as $d_i^{k+1} = n \times \frac{s_i^k}{\sum_{j=1}^{p} s_j^k}$ where s_i^k is the speed of the i'th processor given by $s_i^k = \frac{d_i^k}{t_i(d_i^k)}$.
4. The new distribution d_1^{k+1}, ..., d_p^{k+1} is broadcast to all processors and where necessary data is redistributed accordingly.

3.1 Analysis of Traditional Load Balancing

The traditional load balancing algorithm is based on the assumption that the absolute speed of a processor depends on problem size but the speed is represented by a constant at each iteration. This is true for small problem sizes as depicted in Fig. 1(a). The problem is initially divided evenly between two processors for the first iteration and then redistributed to the optimal distribution in the second iteration.

Consider the situation in which the problem can still fit within the total main memory of the cluster but the problem size is such that the memory requirement of n/p is close to the available memory of one of the processors. In this case paging can occur. If paging does occur, the traditional load balancing algorithm is no longer adequate. This is illustrated for two processors in Fig. 1(b, c). Let the real performance of processors P_1 and P_2 be represented by the speed functions $s_1(x)$ and $s_2(x)$ respectively. Processor P_1 is a faster processor but with less main memory than P_2. The speed function drops rapidly at the point where main memory is full and paging is required. First, n independent units of computations are evenly distributed, $d_1^0 = d_2^0 = n/2$, between the two processors and the speeds of the processors, s_1^0, s_2^0, are measured. Then at the second iteration the computational units are divided according to $\frac{d_1^1}{d_2^1} = \frac{s_1^0}{s_2^0}$, where $d_1^1 + d_2^1 = n$.

Therefore in the second iteration, P_1 will execute less computational units than P_2. However P_1 will perform much faster and P_2 will perform much slower than the model predicts, Fig. 1(b). Moreover the speed of P_2 at the second iteration is slower than P_1 at the first iteration.

Based on the speeds of the processors demonstrated at the second iteration, their constant performance models are changed accordingly, Fig. 1(c), and the computational units are redistributed again for the third iteration as: $\frac{d_1^2}{d_2^2} = \frac{s_1^1}{s_2^1}$, where $d_1^2 + d_2^2 = n$. Now the situation is reversed, P_2 performs much faster than P_1. This situation will continue in subsequent iterations with the majority of the computational units oscillating between processors.

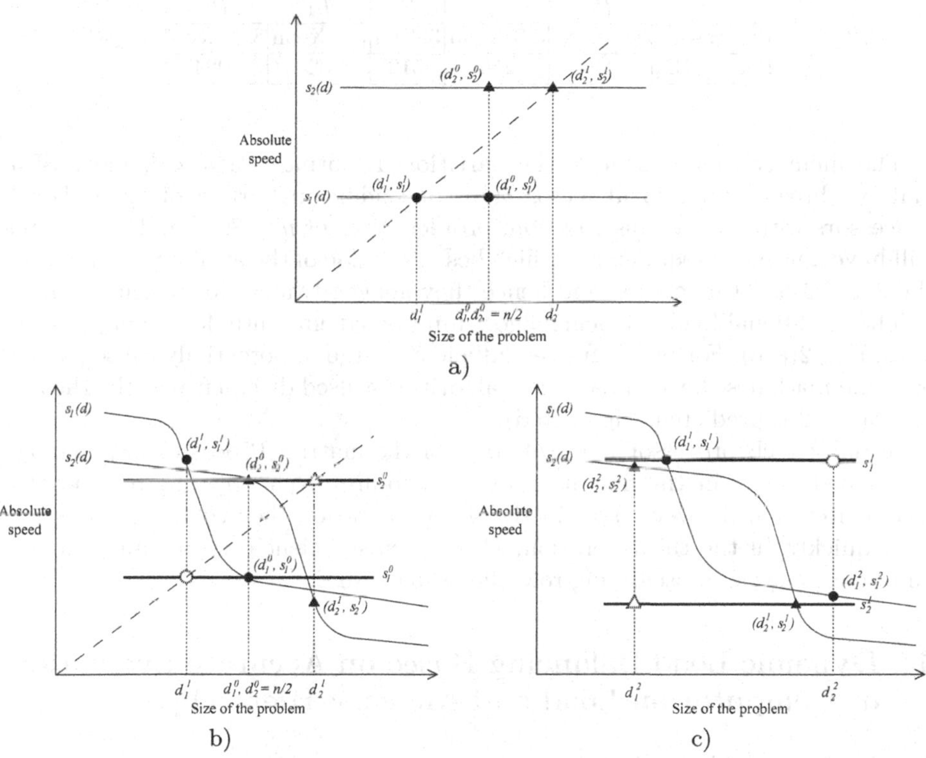

Fig. 1. Predicted results from dynamic load balancing on two processors using constant performance models. In (a) the problem size is small relative to available main memory and balance is achieved. In (b, c) the problem size is large and may require paging, the balancing algorithm causes further unbalance. (b) shows first and second iterations, (c) shows second and third iterations. Outlined points represent performance predicted by constant performance model.

3.2 Experimental Results of the Traditional Load Balancing Algorithm

The traditional load balancing algorithm was applied to the Jacobi method, which is representative of the class of iterative routines we study. The program was tested successfully on a cluster of 16 processors. For clarity the results presented here are from two configurations of 4 processors, Table 1. The essential difference is that cluster 1 has one processor with 256MB RAM and cluster 2 has two processors with 256MB RAM.

Table 1. Specifications of test nodes. Cluster 1 consists of nodes: P_1, P_3, P_4, P_5. Cluster 2 consists of nodes: P_1, P_2, P_3, P_4.

	P_1	P_2	P_3	P_4	P_5
Processor	3.6 Xeon	3.0 Xeon	3.4 P4	3.4 Xeon	3.4 Xeon
Ram (MB)	256	256	512	1024	1024

The memory requirement of the partitioned routine is a $n \times d_i$ block of a matrix, three n dimensional vectors and some additional arrays of size p. For 4 processors with an even distribution, problem sizes of $n = 8000$ and $n = 11000$ will have a memory requirement which lies either side of the available memory on the 256MB RAM machines, and hence they are good values for benchmarking.

The traditional load balancing algorithm worked efficiently for small problem sizes, Fig. 2(a, c). For problem sizes sufficiently large to potentially cause paging on some machines the load balancing algorithm caused divergence as the theory, in section 2.1, predicted, Fig. 2 (b,d).

Initially each processor has $n/4$ rows of the matrix. Processors P_1 and P_2 performed slowly in the first iteration and so are given very few rows in the second iteration. However now in the second iteration they compute these few rows quickly. In the third iteration, P_1 is given sufficient rows to cause paging and hence a cycle of oscillating row allocation ensues.

4 Dynamic Load Balancing Based on Accurate Evaluation of Computation Load and Memory Hierarchy

Our dynamic load balancing algorithm is based on functional performance models [9], which are application centric and hardware specific. Functional performance models reflect both processor and memory heterogeneity. In this section, we describe how the load can be balanced with help of these models.

The functional performance models of the processors are represented by their speed functions $s_1(d)$, ..., $s_p(d)$, with $s_i(d) = \frac{d}{t_i(d)}$, where $t_i(d)$ is the execution time for processing of d elements on the processor P_i. As in traditional algorithms, load balancing is achieved when $t_i \approx t_j$, $1 \leq i, j \leq p$. This can be expressed as $\frac{d_1}{s_1(d_1)} \approx \frac{d_2}{s_2(d_2)} \approx ... \approx \frac{d_p}{s_p(d_p)}$, where $d_1 + d_2 + ... + d_p = n$. These

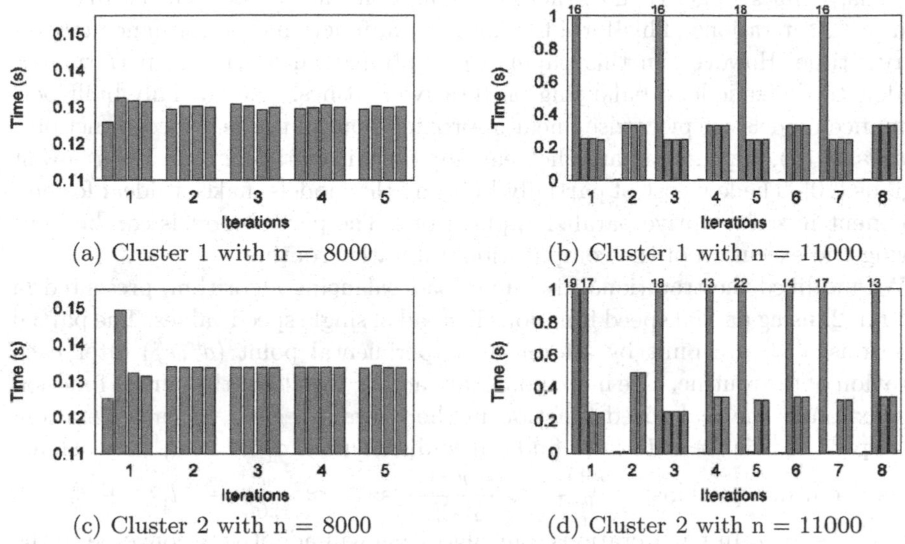

Fig. 2. Time taken for each of the 4 processors to complete their assigned computational units for each iteration 1,2,3, ... In (a) and (c) the problem fits in main memory the load converges to a balanced solution. In (b) and (d) paging occurs on some machines and the load remains unbalanced.

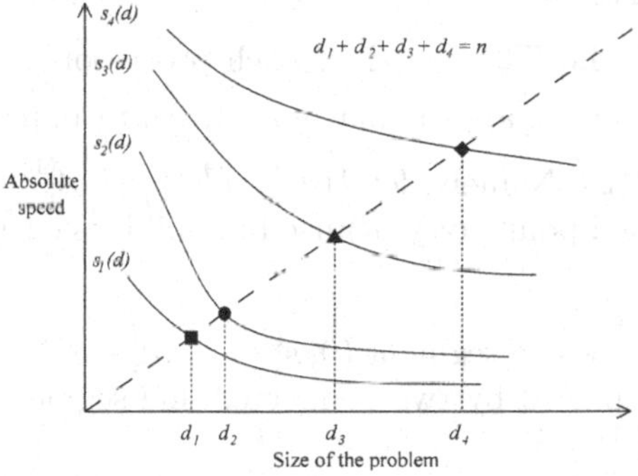

Fig. 3. Optimal distribution of computational units showing the geometric proportionality of the number of chunks to the speed of the processor

equations can be solved geometrically by noting that the points $(d_i, s_i(d_i))$: $\frac{d_1}{s_i(d_i)}$, where c is a constant, lie on the intersection of the speed functions with a line passing through the origin of the coordinate system (Fig. 3). This approach can be used for static load balancing.

Functional performance models are built experimentally. Their accuracy depends on the number of experimental points. Unfortunately, generating these speed functions is computationally expensive, especially in the presence of paging. To create just 20 points of a function in Fig. 5(b) took approximately 1473 seconds, 4 times longer then the actual calculation with a homogeneous distribution for 20 iterations. This forbids building full functional performance models at run time. However, in this paper, we apply partial functional performance models to dynamic load balancing of iterative routines. The partially built performance models are piecewise linear approximations of the real speed functions, $s'_i(d) \approx s_i(d)$, which estimate the real functions in detail only in the relevant regions [10]. The low cost of partially building the models makes it ideal for employment in self-adaptive parallel applications. The partial models can be built during the execution of the computational iterative routine.

We modified the traditional dynamic load balancing algorithm, presented in Section 2, using partial speed functions instead of single speed values. The partial functions $s'_i(d)$ are built by adding an experimental point (d_i^k, s_i^k) after each iteration of the routine. The more points are added, the closer the partial function approximates the real speed function in the relevant region. At each iteration, we apply the balance criteria to find a new distribution $d_1^{k+1}, ..., d_p^{k+1}$ by solving the system of equations: $\frac{d_1^{k+1}}{s'_1(d_1^{k+1})} \approx \frac{d_2^{k+1}}{s'_2(d_2^{k+1})} \approx ... \approx \frac{d_p^{k+1}}{s'_p(d_p^{k+1})}$, $d_1^{k+1} + d_2^{k+1} + ... + d_p^{k+1} + = n$. In few iterations, our algorithm will adaptively converge to the optimal data distribution, since $s'_i(d) \to s_i(d)$. Let us outline how the partial functions $s'_i(d)$ are constructed.

The first iteration. The speed of each processor is calculated as $s_i^0 = \frac{n/p}{t_i(n/p)}$. The first approximation of the partial speed function, $s'_i(d)$, is created as a constant $s'_i(d) = s_i^0$, Fig. 4(a).

Subsequent iterations. The speed of each processor is calculated as $s_i^k = \frac{d_i^k}{t_i(d_i^k)}$. The piecewise linear approximations $s'_i(d)$ are improved by adding the points (d_i^k, s_i^k), Fig. 4(b). Namely, let $\{(d_i^{(j)}, s_i^{(j)})\}_{j=1}^m$, $d_i^{(1)} < ... < d_i^{(m)}$, be the experimentally obtained points of $s'_i(d)$ used to build its current piecewise linear approximation, then

- If $d_i^k < d_i^{(1)}$, then the line segment $(0, s_i^{(1)}) \to (d_i^{(1)}, s_i^{(1)})$ of the $s'_i(d)$ approximation will be replaced by two connected line segments $(0, s_i^k) \to (d_i^k, s_i^k)$ and $(d_i^k, s_i^k) \to (d_i^{(1)}, s_i^{(1)})$;
- If $d_i^k > d_i^{(m)}$, then the line $(d_i^{(m)}, s_i^{(m)}) \to (\infty, s_i^{(m)})$ of this approximation will be replaced by the line segment $(d_i^{(m)}, s_i^{(m)}) \to (d_i^k, s_i^k)$ and the line $(d_i^k, s_i^k) \to (\infty, s_i^k)$;
- If $d_i^{(j)} < d_i^k < d_i^{(j+1)}$, the line segment $(d_i^{(j)}, s_i^{(j)}) \to (d_i^{(j+1)}, s_i^{(j+1)})$ of $s'_i(d)$ will be replaced by two connected line segments $(d_i^{(j)}, s_i^{(j)}) \to (d_i^k, s_i^k)$ and $(d_i^k, s_i^k) \to (d_i^{(j+1)}, s_i^{(j+1)})$.

4.1 Experimental Results

For small problem sizes ($n = 8000$, $p = 4$), our algorithm performed in much the same way as the traditional algorithm. For larger problem sizes ($n = 11000$),

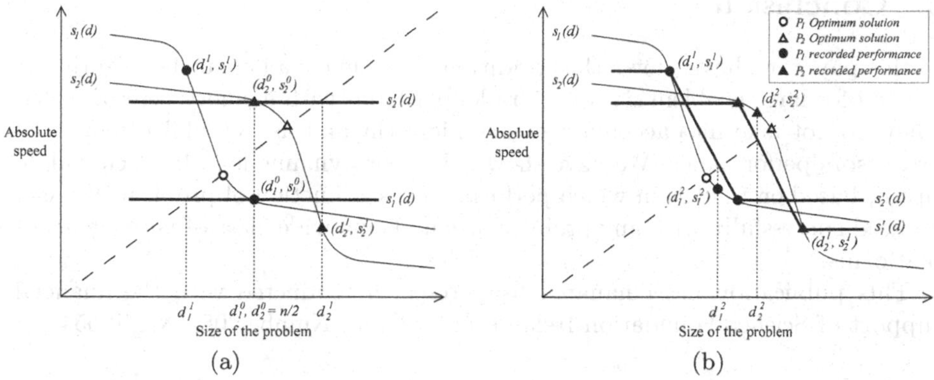

Fig. 4. Dynamic load balancing using partial estimation of the functional performance model

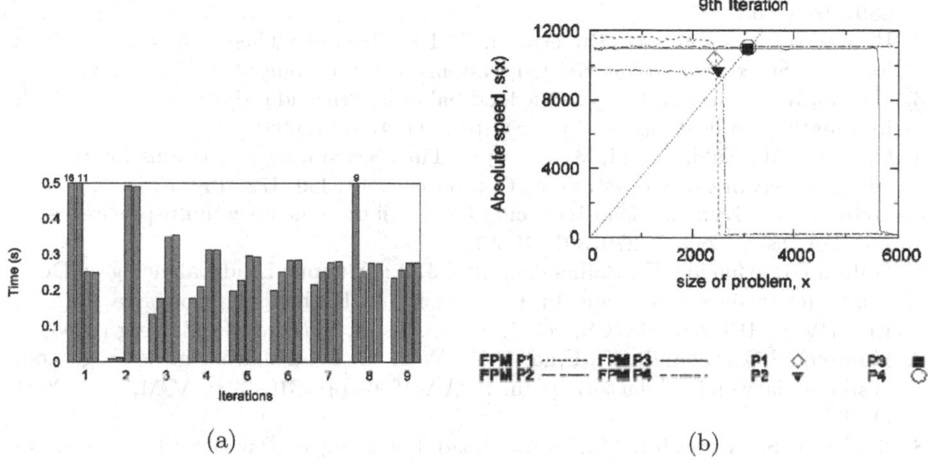

Fig. 5. Results of load balancing in the first 9 iterations using partial estimation of the functional performance model for problem size $n = 11000$. (a) Time taken for each of the 4 processors to complete an iteration. (b) Showing full functional performance models and the near optimum distribution at the 9th iteration. The line intersecting the origin represents the optimum solution and points converge towards this line.

our algorithm was able to successfully balance the computational load within a few iterations (Fig. 5). As in the traditional algorithm, paging also occurred but our algorithm experimentally fit the problem to the available RAM. Paging at the 8th iteration on P_1 demonstrates how the algorithm experimentally finds the memory limit of P_1. The 9th iteration represents a near optimum distribution for the computation on this hardware. A plot of speed vs. problem size, Fig. 5(b), shows how the computational distribution approaches an optimum distribution within 9 iterations.

5 Conclusion

In this paper, we have shown that traditional dynamic load balancing algorithms can fail for large problem sizes on parallel platforms with memory heterogeneity. They do not take into account memory hierarchy and use simplified models of processors performance. We have shown that our dynamic load balancing algorithm, based on models in which performance is a function of problem size, can be used successfully with any problem size and on a wide class of heterogeneous platforms.

This publication has emanated from research conducted with the financial support of Science Foundation Ireland under Grant Number 08/IN.1/I2054.

References

1. Bahi, J., Contassot-Vivier, S., Couturier, R.: Dynamic Load Balancing and Efficient Load Estimators for Asynchronous Iterative Algorithms. IEEE T. Parall. Distr. 16, 289–299 (2005)
2. Bharadwaj, V., Ghose, D., Robertazzi, T.: Divisible Load Theory: A New Paradigm for Load Scheduling in Distributed Systems. Cluster Comput. 6, 7–17 (2003)
3. Cariño, R., Banicescu, I.: Dynamic load balancing with adaptive factoring methods in scientific applications. J. Supercomput. 44, 41–63 (2008)
4. Cierniak, M., Zaki, M., Li, W.: Compile-Time Scheduling Algorithms for Heterogeneous Network of Workstations. Computer J. 40, 356–372 (1997)
5. Cybenko, G.: Dynamic load balancing for distributed memory multi-processors. J. Parallel Distr. Com. 7, 279–301 (1989)
6. Galindo, I., Almeida, F., Badía-Contelles, J.M.: Dynamic Load Balancing on Dedicated Heterogeneous Systems. In: Lastovetsky, A., Kechadi, T., Dongarra, J. (eds.) EuroPVM/MPI 2008. LNCS, vol. 5205, pp. 64–74. Springer, Heidelberg (2008)
7. Hummel, S.F., Schmidt, J., Uma, R.N., Wein, J.: Load-sharing in heterogeneous systems via weighted factoring. In: SPAA 1996, pp. 318–328. ACM, New York (1996)
8. Ichikawa, S., Yamashita, S.: Static Load Balancing of Parallel PDE Solver for Distributed Computing Environment. In: PDCS 2000, pp. 399–405. ISCA (2000)
9. Lastovetsky, A., Reddy, R.: Data Partitioning with a Functional Performance Model of Heterogeneous Processors. Int. J. High Perform. Comput. Appl. 21, 76–90 (2007)
10. Lastovetsky, A., Reddy, R.: Distributed Data Partitioning for Heterogeneous Processors Based on Partial Estimation of Their Functional Performance Models. In: Lin, H.-X., Alexander, M., Forsell, M., Knüpfer, A., Prodan, R., Sousa, L., Streit, A. (eds.) Euro-Par 2009. LNCS, vol. 6043, pp. 91–101. Springer, Heidelberg (2010)
11. Legrand, A., Renard, H., Robert, Y., Vivien, F.: Mapping and load-balancing iterative computations. IEEE T. Parall. Distr. 15, 546–558 (2004)
12. Li, X.Y., Teng, S.-H.: Dynamic Load Balancing for Parallel Adaptive Mesh Refinement. In: Ferreira, A., Rolim, J.D.P., Teng, S.-H. (eds.) IRREGULAR 1998. LNCS, vol. 1457, pp. 144–155. Springer, Heidelberg (1998)
13. Martínez, J., Garzón, E., Plaza, A., García, I.: Automatic tuning of iterative computation on heterogeneous multiprocessors with ADITHE. J. Supercomput. (2010) (to appear)

Dealing with Heterogeneity for Mapping MMOFPS in Distributed Systems*

Ignasi Barri, Josep Rius, Concepció Roig, and Francesc Giné

Computer Science Department, University of Lleida, Spain
{ignasibarri,jrius,roig,sisco}@diei.udl.cat

Abstract. In this paper, we present a distributed heterogeneous system called *OnDeGaS* (On Demand Game Service), that fits the scalability and latency requirements of MMOFPS networked games. To exploit platform capabilities efficiently, the *OnDeGaS* system performs a mapping mechanism that assigns the game sessions of a MMOFPS, taking advantage of the specific available computational resources of individual nodes. We show through simulation that this mapping mechanism is able to deal with different heterogeneity conditions in the distributed area. It allows the system to grow at any moment according to the existing demand, while latency values are maintained under the acceptable threshold permitted in MMOFPS games.

1 Introduction

Massively Multiplayer Online Games (MMOG) are the most popular genre in the computer game world. They can be divided into three categories: *MMORPG* Role Games, *MMORTS* based on Real Time Strategy and *MMOFPS* known as First Person Shooter. The execution requirements vary with the way of playing in each of them [11]. On the one hand, MMORPG and MMORTS can have thousands of players in a single party, so bandwidth is an important feature for supporting them [5]. On the other hand, in MMOFPS, players are divided into many isolated game sessions, each with a handful of players, who are continuously interacting. Thus, response latency is the key factor in this case. In this paper, we focus on the optimization of MMOFPS games.

Traditionally, client-server systems have been the platforms to provide service to massively networked games. However, when the number of players increases this approach reaches its limits due to problems of scalability. The research community has proposed some alternatives to overcome client-server limits with decentralized structures where each machine contributes to, and benefits from, a large service oriented network. The way to distribute the entire game into the machines varies according to the category it belongs to. For MMORPG, some authors present solutions [6,7,8] where the exploitation of the distributed area is based on mapping the pieces of the splitted game world, or groups of players, into

* This work was supported by the MEyC-Spain under contract TIN2008-05913 and the CUR of DIUE of GENCAT and the European Social Fund.

M.R. Guarracino et al. (Eds.): Euro-Par 2010 Workshops, LNCS 6586, pp. 51–61, 2011.
© Springer-Verlag Berlin Heidelberg 2011

the distributed nodes. Other proposals of game distribution are focused on the execution requirements of MMRPOG and MMORTS, such as solving cheating problems [8]. In the case of MMOFPS, cheating is not a key issue to face because it will potentially affect a single game service, having a negative impact for a small set of players, and a duration of the order of minutes. Then, for MMOFPS the research community focuses other challenges. Nharambe et al [3] proposes a solution to assign game sessions to a pure P2P system. The increase in latency time, inherent to this kind of architecture, is solved by proposing new rules in many features of current MMOFPS games, such as the size of the AOI (Area of Interest) of players in order to decrease the number of messages transferred among players. These improvements need to be included in the internal code of the game, which implies important implementation efforts.

In this paper, we propose a new system named *OnDeGaS* (On Demand Game Service), devoted to execute the game sessions of a MMOFPS without affecting the game's internal code. *OnDeGaS* is a hybrid system that combines the functionalities of a centralized server infrastructure with a distributed area composed of players' machines. A preliminary version of *OnDeGaS* was reported in [1]. This proposal was designed taking into account a study of the execution of MMOFPS's servers, where real traces of player's activity were monitored in order to tune and analyze the proper values for the configuration parameters, that determine the way to add and to remove game services in the distributed area. In the present paper, we propose the mapping mechanism for *OnDeGaS*, to assign game sessions to nodes, taking heterogeneity features into account such as latency and available cores. To the best of our knowledge, only the work presented by Iosup et al. [9], is also based in the dynamic assignment of resources in MMOFPS's. However they propose a prediction based mechanism that does not take into account the existing demand. The effectiveness of our approach, based on the resource assignment taking into account current demand, has been evaluated by means of simulation. Our results show that the *OnDeGaS* mapping mechanism is able to deal with different heterogeneity conditions, by properly exploiting the computational resources making up the distributed area of the system. We also show that latency values of the entire game are maintained under an acceptable threshold for MMOFPS in all cases.

The remainder of this paper is organized as follows. Section 2 describes the *OnDeGaS* system and the proposed mapping mechanism. Section 3 evaluates the *OnDeGaS* mapping performance taking system heterogeneity into account. Finally, Section 4 outlines the main conclusions and future work.

2 OnDeGaS System Description

In this section, the *OnDeGaS* system is described globally, discussing the components, their operation and implementation details.

2.1 System Model

Figure 1 shows the *OnDeGaS* system model that is made up of two main areas: one central area performing central services and a distributed area with several zones composed of a set of heterogeneous nodes.

The central area is devoted to performing the global control of the system and also to supplying players with services. Its components are the following:

- *Master Server (MS)* is the system's main server and acts as the bootstrap point.
- *Waiting Queue (WQ)* is a logical space in MS used to insert those players who cannot be served due to overload situations. It is a transitory state for players, who will be distributed in a short term.
- *Zones Queue (ZQ)* is a logical space in MS used to keep the information about the created zones updated. This information is used for distributing players to the already created zones.

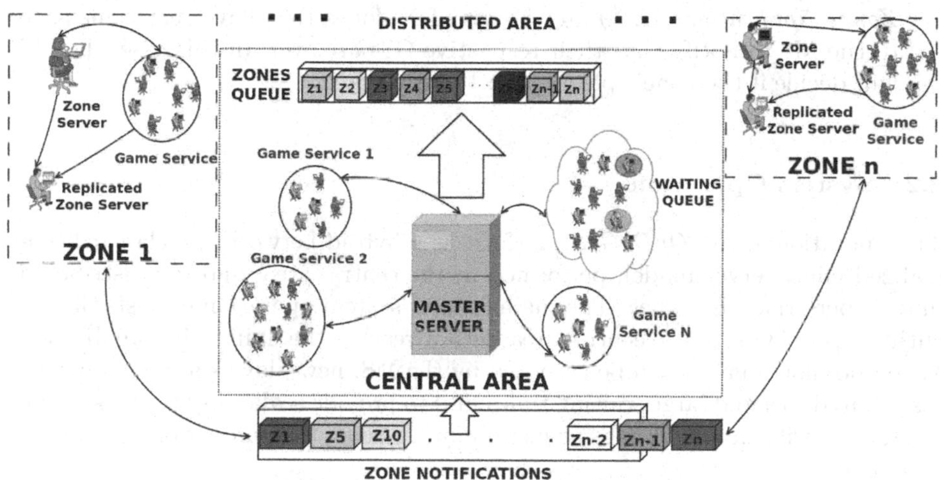

Fig. 1. OnDeGaS system model

The distributed area is composed of players' machines that are logically grouped in zones. A Zone number i, Z_i, has the following components:

- *Zone Server (ZS)* is the current server of the Zone.
- *Replicated Zone Server (RZS)* is the current replicated server of the Zone. It has the role of implementing fault tolerance policies. The role of RZS is to replace the ZS in case of failure. For this reason, players in the distributed area play against the ZS and its RZS, and the ZS sends the game state to both, players and the RZS. Players also update to RZS, to avoid losses of the state of the game, when the RZS replaces ZS.

Due to the inherent heterogeneity of nodes conforming the distributed area, each player in the system is characterized by two determinant computational attributes: latency in relation to the MS and the number of cores conforming its CPU. Both attributes are taken into account to find the best ZS and RZS for each Zone among the players waiting in the WQ. It is worth remarking that memory is not taking into account due to the low requirements of the MMOFPS games (order of tens MB per game service).

Regarding games, the following elements are distinguished:

- *Player (P_i)* is a client who connects to the system in order to play a MMOFPS.
- *Game Service (GS)* is an instance of a game, where a set of players is connected to play. Each GS will be hosted in the MS or in a single core of a ZS. At any moment, each GS can be in two different states: *active* when players are interacting in the GS, or *over*, when the GS has ended due to player disconnections or caused by the rules of the GSs. Normally, in MMOFPS, the *number of players* per GS is in the order of tens, while the *duration of the GS* is in the order of a few minutes.
- *Zones Notifications (Z^N)* are the set of N Zones that have sent a message to the MS to notify that their respective GSs are over. In this case, the MS will decide if the zone's players can be reaccepted.

2.2 System Operation

The operation of the *OnDeGaS* platform is a hybrid between the classical centralized client-server model, performed in the central area, and the distributed model, performed in Zones. The main idea of system operation consists of executing a set of GSs in the central area until it reaches the limit of its capabilities. When no more players can be accepted by the MS, new players are dynamically distributed to avoid large waiting times and to provide scalability to the system. Each Zone will execute N GSs as maximum, N being the number of cores of the chosen ZS.

The system operation is controlled by the continuous execution of Alg. 1, which has two input flows: new player connections (P_i) and zones (Z_i) that have ended their GS and want to enter the MS. At each iteration the MS checks its state (*MS.state*). According to this, the two following cases are considered:

1. **MS.State() == OVERLOAD**, If the MS is overloaded, each new player (P_i), will be added to the WQ queue. Next, the MS checks if the number of players in the WQ is greater than or equal to a predefined value α, or whether the uptime of the WQ is greater than or equal to a predefined value β, too. If either of these two conditions is true, the algorithm tries to distribute all players located in the WQ, with function *MS.Distribute_Players* (see Alg. 2), to one already created zone in ZQ. If the previous function fails, then the MS will create a new Zone with function *MS.Create_Zone* (see Alg. 3).

```
Input: ∀P_i connecting to MS
Input: Z^N = {Z_i, Z_{i+1}, ..., Z_{n-i}, Z_n} notifying to MS
while True do
    switch MS.State() do
        case MS.State() == OVERLOAD
            if ∃ P_i then MS.Enqueue(P_i,WQ);
            if (WQ.size() ≥ α or WQ.uptime() ≥ β) then
                if (MS.Distribute_Players(WQ,ZQ) == FALSE) then
                    Z_i=MS.Create_Zone(WQ);
                    ZQ=ZQ+{Z_i};


        endsw
        case MS.State() == NOT OVERLOAD
            if WQ.uptime() ≥ β then
                forall the P_i in WQ do
                    MS.Accept(P_i);
                end
            if Z^N ≠ ∅ then MS.Reaccept(P_i);
            if ∃ P_i then MS.Accept(P_i);
        endsw
    endsw
end
```

Algorithm 1. OnDeGaS main Algorithm

The *MS.Distribute_Players* function (see Alg. 2) looks for those zones of ZQ whose ZS has at least one free core (*ZS.freeCores()*). If there are available zones, the function will select the one which has the lowest latency between the respective ZS and the MS (*MS.lowestLatency()*). Then the ZS and RZS of the selected Zone will accept all players located in the WQ and finally, a boolean is returned.

The *Create_Zone* functionality (see Alg. 3) executes the *lowestLatency* function to find the best ZS and RZS, in latency and computational resource terms. Moreover, the function ensures that RZS is able to serve at least the same number of GSs as the ZS to avoid problems when the fault tolerance mechanisms acts (*if* statement with function *swap*). Then, all players in the WQ are linked to the new ZS/RZS (*ZS/RZS.accept()*) with the aim of RZS keeping the same information as the updated ZS. Thus, a fault tolerance mechanism is maintained by the system. Then, a Zone Z_i comprises the ZS, the RZS and the set of players previously located in the WQ.

2. **MS.state() == NOT OVERLOAD**. When the MS is not overloaded, Alg. 1 evaluates the three following conditional statements:
   - The first condition evaluates if the uptime of the WQ is greater than or equal to β; if it is, players located in the WQ will be accepted to play in the MS (*MS.accept()*). This acceptance flow acts like a *FIFO*, the first

```
Input: ZQ,WQ
Output: Boolean
MS.Distribute_Players(ZQ,WQ):
begin
    Available Zones = AZ = ∅;
    forall the ((ZS and RZS) ∈ Z_i) ∈ ZQ do
        if (ZS.freeCores() and RZS.freeCores()) then AZ =AZ +{Z_i};
    end
    if (AZ!= ∅) then
        Z_i=MS.lowestLatency(AZ);
        Z_i.Accept(WQ);
        return TRUE;
    else
        return FALSE;
    end
end
```

Algorithm 2. OnDeGaS *Distribute_Players* function

```
Input: WQ
Output: Z_i
MS.Create_Zone(WQ):
begin
    ZS=MS.lowestLatency(WQ);
    RZS=MS.lowestLatency(WQ-{ZS});
    if (ZS.freeCores() > RZS.freeCores()) then swap(ZS,RZS);
    ZS/RZS.accept(WQ);
    Z_i = {ZS ∪ RZS};
    return Z_i;
end
```

Algorithm 3. OnDeGaS Create_Zone function

player in the WQ queue is the first to be connected to the MS if it has enough space.

- The second conditional statement gives priority of entry into the MS to players of those zones that sent an *over* message to notify that they had finished the GS, and wanted to start another GS in the MS. This happens whenever a round of the game has finished and players are waiting for the next round. In this case, if the set of notifying zones, Z^N, is not empty, the MS executes the *Reaccept* function. Note that distributed players are playing continuously in the MS or the zones, and the time transitions from WQ to the zones, and from the zones to the MS are of the order of seconds, which is an acceptable delay for the players.
- The last conditional statement allows to connect new players to the MS.

2.3 Implementation Issues

The following needs to be considered for the proper performance of the system:

Lowest Latency Functionality. *lowestLatency* function is based on a loop that checks the latency of all players located in the WQ (case Alg. 3) or all the ZS located in the ZQ with respect to the MS (case Alg. 2). Then, it selects the closest ZS or Zone to the MS to assign the players located in the WQ respectively.

System Overload State. To determine the system overload state, real traces of player's activity of a MMOFPS have been monitored and analyzed during two months, which allowed us to verify that the state of system overload is determined by the number of concurrent players playing in the MS. Many authors also corroborate this [2,5,11], as it has been proved experimentally that the number of concurrent players is directly related to the CPU and network usage.

Free Cores Functionality. In Alg. 2 and 3, the *freeCores* function is used. This function returns the number of free cores of the ZS or RZS (depending on which node executes the function). The studies carried out by Ye and Cheng in [11] show that with an idle processor, is possible to provide a MMOFPS with QoS easily. Thus, if the number of GSs per core was increased the QoS would decrease. Likewise, our system assumes that the player's computational resources are totally dedicated to the MMOFPS and therefore, it is feasible to take advantage of all these computational resources of a player. Thus, the maximum number of GSs that a Zone is able to execute is equal to the number of cores of the ZS, given that, a ZS reserves a core to run its own GS when the ZS is involved in a player role, apart from the ZS role.

3 Experimental Results

In this section, experimentation is conducted to demonstrate the feasibility and good performance of the proposed mapping mechanism for *OnDeGaS* system. The experimentation was performed through simulation using SimPy [10]. SimPy is a discrete-event simulation language based on standard Python. SimPy tools have been used to implement nodes of the platform, which can fulfill four distinct roles: player, ZS, RZS and MS. The SimPy procedures allow random behavior of the simulation to be created to represent the real behavior of a player.

Each simulation consists of 100,000 player connections to the MS. The connections are sequential with constant inter-arrival time (≈ 1 second) to submit the MS to a constant stress situation or constant peak load, in order to verify that the distributed area is dynamically adapted to the on-demand queries of players. When the MS reaches its limit, 2,000 concurrent players, (since the computational resources of a typical single machine server can support 2,000 to 6,000 concurrent clients [7]), no more players will be accepted, and new ones will be distributed to zones. Another important issue is the calculus of the players' latency against MS. This is determined by a triangulated heuristic, delimiting the 2-Dimensional Euclidean Space to ($x = [-110, +110], y = [-110, 110]$). This methodology is based on the relative coordinates explained in [4]. Furthermore, each player has a lifetime determined by a Weibull distribution scaled from 0 seconds up to 24 hours. For the parameters α and β used in Alg. 1, we considered the values of 32 players and 120 seconds respectively, it having been demonstrated in [1], that they are appropriate values to ensure a good performance of the whole system taking the characteristics of real MMOFPS into account. The length of a GS is 900 seconds [3] on average, following an exponential distribution.

To configure a heterogeneous system, we considered that a player can have 2, 4 or 8 cores, where ω_2, ω_4 and ω_8 are the percentages of players with this number of cores in the system. Let $\omega_{max} = max(\omega_2, \omega_4, \omega_8)$ and ω_i and ω_j the remaining two percentages excluding this ω_{max}. We define the heterogeneity degree of the system (*het_degree*) with equation (1).

$$het\_degree = 1 - \frac{\frac{(\omega_{max} - \omega i)}{\omega_{max}} + \frac{(\omega_{max} - \omega j)}{\omega_{max}}}{2} \quad (1)$$

The values of *het_degree* range from 0 to 1, where 0 means that is a homogeneous system, while 1 corresponds to a system with the same percentages of each type of players ($\omega_2 = \omega_4 = \omega_8$), it means totally heterogeneous.

According to the previous assumptions and functionalities, in the next Subsection, the performance provided by the mapping mechanism of *OnDeGaS* according to the *het_degree* is shown. The cases of the study are: ability to scale the distributed area and the QoS of the system, measured by the zone's average latency and the waiting time for players located in the WQ.

3.1 Performance Evaluation

The scalability of the *OnDeGaS* system indicates its ability to manage more zones on demand, while the QoS of the whole system is maintained.

Table 1 shows the average (AVG) and standard deviation (SD) for the number of created zones and QoS parameters under two conditions of heterogeneity: (a) *h_d=0* (*het_degree=0*), where all players have two cores ($\omega_2 = 100\%, \omega_4 = \omega_8 = 0\%$) and, (b) *h_d=1* (*het_degree=1*) with $\omega_2 = \omega_4 = \omega_8$. In each case we evaluated 100 different simulations. As can be observed in Zones column of Table 1, the distribution performed by *OnDeGaS* is able to exploit the additional cores of the heterogeneous system, as it creates a lower number of zones with more GSs. In practice, this will suppose a significant decrease in the overhead for the management of the set of ZS and RZS in the distributed area.

Regarding QoS, Table 1 shows similar average in the latency values in both cases, but the standard deviation vary between the homogeneous and heterogeneous case. This is due to the fact that in the heterogeneous, fewer zones are created and this behavior means that the set of potential ZS to distribute players located in the WQ was smaller than the homogeneous case. However, it is worth remarking that in all the cases, both systems, latency values are below the maximum acceptable threshold for MMOFPS (180 ms).

Table 1. System performance analysis

	Zones (No.)		Latency (ms)		WQ Time (sec.)		FT Gain (sec.)	
	$h\_d = 0$	$h\_d = 1$	$h\_d = 0$	$h\_d = 1$	$h\_d = 0$	$h\_d = 1$	$h\_d = 0$	$h\_d = 1$
AVG	888.38	395.84	87.43	87.79	30.16	24.40	1007.865	1007.865
SD	193.37	76.92	0.293	0.955	4.70	6.30	166.65	166.65

For the waiting time of players located in the WQ, the experiment reveals a significant impact on the average, depending on the number of cores. Whenever a new Zone is created, a new ZS and RZS must be searched for. This process takes 30 seconds on average. This situation happens frequently in the homogeneous case (considering 2 cores) as indicated by the average of 30.16 sec. Nevertheless, this happens less often in the heterogeneous case as more players are mapped to zones already created, 24.40 sec. in this case.

It is also shown in Table 1 the benefits of the fault tolerance policy (FT Gain) that is implemented by the use of the RZS. On average, implementing zones with a single RZS represents an extra lifetime of $\approx$ 16 minutes for zones, which means an average increase of 22% of the zones' lifetime. The standard deviation points out a small deviation of $\approx$ 3 minutes, caused by the player's lifetime determined by a Weibull distribution. Thus, the heterogeneity of the system has not any influence in the effectiveness of the fault tolerance mechanisms.

To expand the study of the influence carried out by heterogeneity of the distributed area, we evaluated its effects in the number of created zones, as a representative case. Figure 2 points out its trend according to different values of *het_degree*, where the total number of cores in the whole system and the percentage values for ω_2, ω_4 and ω_8 vary. Figure 2a corresponds to a system where the majority of the players have 2 cores ($\omega_{max} = \omega_2$) and the weights have the relation: $\omega_2 \geq \omega_4 \geq \omega_8$. In the same way, Figure 2b, shows the results for a system with a relation of $\omega_2 \leq \omega_4 \leq \omega_8$, where $\omega_{max} = \omega_8$. As can be

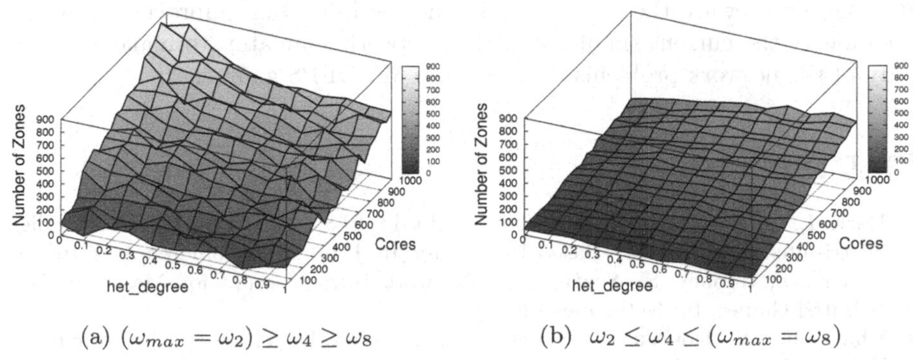

(a) $(\omega_{max} = \omega_2) \geq \omega_4 \geq \omega_8$ (b) $\omega_2 \leq \omega_4 \leq (\omega_{max} = \omega_8)$

Fig. 2. Number of zones created in function of *het_degree*

observed, the number of cores and their distribution among players drastically determines the number of zones created in both plots. When $\omega_{max} = \omega_2$, the number of created zones is, in most of the series, larger than when $\omega_{max} = \omega_8$. Thus, the system creates new zones only when the cores of the existing zones are busy. It can also be seen that the number of created Zones increases in all cases when the total number of cores is also increasing. Regarding the *het_degree*, there is a different trend in the plots of the figure. When $\omega_{max} = \omega_2$, the number of zones increases when het_degree decreases as most players have only 2 cores. However, the trend is the opposite when $\omega_{max} = \omega_8$, as most players have 8 cores. Thus, we can conclude that the *OnDeGaS* mapping system is able to deal with different heterogeneity conditions by properly exploiting the system's computational resources.

4 Conclusion and Future Work

In this paper, we presented a distributed heterogeneous system called *OnDeGaS* (On Demand Game Service), that fits the scalability and latency requirements of MMOFPS networked games. The proposed new system is made up of a Master Server (MS) carrying out centralized functionalities, and several zones that make up a distributed area. Whenever the MS is overload, the system scales by creating zones to execute game sessions. Zones are created taking latency with respect to the MS and the available number of cores composing their CPUs into account.

By means of simulation, experimental results show that the system is able to scale according to the demand. Moreover, it has been demonstrated that the number of created zones depends directly on the heterogeneity degree (*het_degree*) value. For higher *het_degree* values, fewer zones are created, thus avoiding excessive fragmentation of the system. Likewise, it has also been shown that this scalability does not damage the average latency, which is always below the maximum threshold allowed in MMOFPSs. Furthermore, the waiting time for players located in the WQ is reduced as the *het_degree* of the system is increased.

In future work, we are interested in improving the fault tolerance taking the *het_degree* characteristics of the system into account and also implementing market policies to reward the ZS and RZS. Another important improvement would be to merge the current simulator with a network simulator, to make a deeper study of the network problems derived from MMOFPS gaming.

References

1. Barri, I., Giné, F., Roig, C.: A Scalable Hybrid P2P System for MMOFPS. Parallel, Distributed, and Network-Based Processing. In: Euromicro Conference (2010)
2. Bauer, D., Rooney, S., Scotton, P.: Network Infrastructure for Massively Distributed Games. In: NetGames (2002)
3. Bharambe, A., Douceur, J., Lorch, J.R., Moscibroda, T., Pang, J., Seshan, S., Zhuang, X.: Donnybrook: Enabling Large-Scale, High-Speed, Peer-to-Peer Games. In: SIGCOMM (2008)

4. Eugene, T.S., Zhang, H.: Predicting Internet Network Distance with Coordinates-Based Approaches. In: INFOCOM (2001)
5. Huang, G., Ye, M., Cheng, L.: Modeling System Performance in MMORPG. In: Global Telecommunications Conference Workshops (2004)
6. Keller, J., Simon, G.: Solipsis: A Massively Multi-Participant Virtual World. In: PDPTA (2003)
7. Knutsson, B., Lu, H., Xu, W., Hopkins, B.: Peer-to-Peer Support for Massively Multiplayer Games. In: INFOCOM (2004)
8. Liu, H.I., Lo, Y.T.: Dacap-A Distributed Anti-Cheating P2P Architecture for Massive Multiplayer On-line Role Playing Game. In: CCGRID (2008)
9. Nae, V., Iosup, A., Prodan, R.: Dynamic Resource Provisioning in Massively Multiplayer Online Games. IEEE Transactions on Parallel and Distributed Systems (2010)
10. IBM Developers Works: Charming Python: SimPy Simplifies Complex Models (Simulate Discrete Simultaneous Events for Fun and Profit) (2002)
11. Ye, M., Cheng, L.: System-Performance Modeling for Massively Multiplayer Online Role-Playing Games. IBM Syst. J. (2006)

Max-Plus Algebra and Discrete Event Simulation on Parallel Hierarchical Heterogeneous Platforms

Brett A. Becker and Alexey Lastovetsky

School of Computer Science and Informatics, University College Dublin, Belfield, Dublin 4, Ireland
{brett.becker,alexey.lastovetsky}@ucd.ie

Abstract. In this paper we explore computing max-plus algebra operations and discrete event simulations on parallel hierarchal heterogeneous platforms. When performing such tasks on heterogeneous platforms parameters such as the total volume of communication and the top-level data partitioning strategy must be carefully taken into account. Choice of the partitioning strategy is shown to greatly affect the overall performance of these applications due to different volumes of inter-partition communication that various strategies impart on these operations. One partitioning strategy in particular is shown to reduce the execution times of these operations more than other, more traditional strategies. The main goal of this paper is to present benefits waiting to be exploited by the use of max-plus algebra operations on these platforms and thus speeding up more complex and quite common computational topic areas such as discrete event simulation.

Keywords: Data Partitioning, Heterogeneous Computing, Parallel Computing, Tropical Algebra, Max-Plus algebra, Discrete Event Simulation, Hierarchal Algorithms, Square-Corner Partitioning.

1 Introduction

Max-plus algebra is a relatively new field of mathematics which grew from the advent of tropical geometry in the early 1980s and has since been shown to have many diverse application areas. MPA is (along with min-plus algebra) a sub-category of tropical algebra. MPA obeys most laws of basic algebra with the operations of addition $(a+b)$ and multiplication $(c\times d)$ replaced by the operations $\max(a,b)$ and addition $(c+d)$ respectively. Min-plus algebra is similar, but with the maximum operation replaced with a minimum function.

Discrete event simulation is an extremely expansive area of continuing and intense research which may broadly be characterised as a collection of techniques and methods which when applied to the study of discrete-event dynamical systems generate sequences which characterize system behaviour. This includes modelling concepts for abstracting essential features of a system into a set of precedence and mathematical relationships, which can be used to describe the

M.R. Guarracino et al. (Eds.): Euro-Par 2010 Workshops, LNCS 6586, pp. 63–70, 2011.
© Springer-Verlag Berlin Heidelberg 2011

system and more importantly for system design, to predict behaviour, performance, and drawbacks/bottlenecks. DES is used to design and model a vast number of systems including travel timetables, operating systems, communication networks, autonomous guided vehicles, operating systems, CPUs and other complex systems. There are many approaches to designing DES including Petri nets, alphabet based approaches, perturbation methods, control theoretic techniques and expert systems design. Recently MPA and other techniques involving both logical and algebraic components have shown to be capable of simplifying simulations while maintaining the desired outputs [11]. One such method is explored later in this paper.

The square-corner partitioning (SCP) is a top-level partitioning method for parallel hierarchal heterogeneous computing which when applied to problems such as matrix-matrix multiplication (MMM) and all linear algebra kernels reducible to MMM, optimally reduces the total volume of communication (TVC) between computing entities (processors, clusters, etc.) when the power ratios between entities meet certain, yet numerous and very common ratios. This partitioning also has other benefits including simpler communication schedules and the possibility of overlapping communication and computation [2,3]. As this paper demonstrates the SCP can extend these benefits to many application areas.

The rest of this paper is outlined as follows: In Section 2 we review and formally define the MPA, and introduce a specific approach for solving DES problems. We then outline the SCP and its application to these operations on heterogeneous parallel platforms. Section 3 presents results of MPI experiments applying the SCP to MPA operations and a DES example which uses a mixed algebraic/logical approach. Section 4 presents our conclusions and future work.

2 Background and Related Work

2.1 Max-Plus Algebra

Max-plus algebra is a relatively new field in mathematics, dating back approximately 30 years. It has since been shown to have several application areas such as discrete event simulation, dynamic programming, finite dimensional linear algebra, modelling communication networks, operating systems, combinatorial optimization, solving systems of linear equations, biological sequence comparisons and even problems such as crop rotation [4,8,9,11,13]. In many scientific and computational applications the structure of MPA matrix multiplication is an important aspect. Additionally, higher powers of MPA matrices are of significant interest and necessary in many application areas [5,11].

MPA is based on replacing the "normal" algebraic addition operation with a binary max function, and the "normal" multiplication operation with addition. Formally, if we define $\epsilon \stackrel{\text{def}}{=} -\infty$ and $e \stackrel{\text{def}}{=} 0$ then denote $\mathbb{R}_{\max}$ to be the set $\mathbb{R} \cup \{\epsilon\}$ then for elements $a, b \in \mathbb{R}_{\max}$, the operations $\oplus$ and $\otimes$ are defined respectively by the following.

$$a \oplus b \stackrel{\text{def}}{=} \max(a, b) \text{ and } a \otimes b \stackrel{\text{def}}{=} a + b \quad (1)$$

Therefore, $a \oplus \epsilon = \max(\epsilon, a) = a$ and $a \otimes \epsilon = \epsilon + a = \epsilon$. We can now formally define max-plus algebra as $\mathfrak{R}_{\max} = (\mathbb{R}_{\max}, \oplus, \otimes, \epsilon, e)$. Finally, the $\otimes$ operation has priority over the $\oplus$ operation.

MPA matrices are denoted $\mathbb{R}^{n \times m}_{\max}$, where n and m are the matrix dimensions. For the MPA matrices $A \in \mathbb{R}^{n \times m}_{\max}$ and, $B \in \mathbb{R}^{m \times q}_{\max}$ the matrix product $A \otimes B$ is the same as in normal linear algebra, but following the operation substitutions in (1). From this, matrix powers are straight-forward, and represented $A^{\otimes k}$ for the kth power of A. As max-plus matrix multiplication and max-plus matrix powers are integral parts of many applications of MPA we further discuss this in Section 3.1.

2.2 Discrete Event Simulation

Discrete event simulation is a very broad and well-studied field and therefore the purpose of this Section is to acquaint the reader with the specific technique utilized in this paper. Briefly, DES is a collection of techniques and methods which when applied to the study of a discrete-event dynamical system generates sequences which characterize the system behaviour. This includes modelling concepts for abstracting essential features of the system into a set of precedence and mathematical relationships, which can be used to describe the system and more importantly for design, and to predict its behaviour, performance, and drawbacks/bottlenecks. For more see any good DES text such as [7].

As most DES algorithms are computationally intensive, efforts to parallelize them are numerous. The complexity of most practical DES algorithms however poses numerous obstacles in effective and efficient parallelization. Amongst these are synchronization and timing inconsistencies, synchronous vs. asynchronous simulation, deadlock avoidance and detection, conservative vs. optimistic simulation, recovery strategies, and memory management to name a few [6].

In Section 3.2 we present results of the parallelization of a DES modelling technique which although as presented in [13] is sequential, lends itself to parallelization due to a computationally intensive algorithmic core which can be efficiently ported to hierarchal heterogeneous parallel platforms. This core is very similar to a max-plus matrix operation but using logical and/or operations instead of max-plus operations. We employ this technique — called the Matrix Discrete Event Model (MDEM) — using MPI and utilizing the SCP [2,3], for the core routine.

The Matrix Discrete Event Model. The authors of [13] note that the design, simulation, and analysis of large-scale, complex systems using existing DES techniques such as Petri nets, alphabet-based approaches, perturbation methods, control theoretic techniques, and expert systems design are often difficult to implement and are very labour and time intensive. The MDEM is a hybrid system with logical and algebraic components that seeks to make these processes more efficient. Although the examples in [13] focus on manufacturing systems, the formulation is also applicable to many DES situations such as travel timetables, communication networks, autonomous guided vehicles, operating systems, and many others. Clearly the number of degrees of freedom, state possibilities, and general complexity of such systems often result in simulations with several thousands (or more) event components.

The MDEM approach is a rule-based model described by four equations: the model state equation, start equation, resource release equation, and the product output equation. Each of these equations are *logical*, only using *or, and,* and *negation* operations. Additionally, all vectors and matrices in these equations are binary — only composed of 0's and 1's. For instance, the vector which is the output of the start equation contains a '1' for each job which is to be started at the given state of the simulation, and a '0' otherwise.

The simulation itself is carried out by first calculating initial conditions from the description of the system. The core of the simulation is carried out by the successive calculation of 'firing vectors' which carry the simulation to the next state. This amounts to the repeated calculation of an equation which has the form of a matrix-matrix multiplication except that since the approach of the MDEM technique is hybrid — having both algebraic and logical components — the algebraic multiplication and addition operations are replaced with logical 'or' and 'and' operations respectively. It is this step that constitutes the bulk of the calculation time for the MDEM technique as all other calculations only need to be carried out once.

2.3 The Square-Corner Partitioning

The square-corner partitioning is a partitioning method for parallel hierarchal heterogeneous computing which when applied to problems such as matrix-matrix multiplication and all linear algebra kernels reducible to MMM reduces the total volume of communication (TVC) between clusters optimally when the power ratios between clusters is greater than 3:1[1]. This partitioning also has other benefits such as simplified communication schedules and the possibility of overlapping communication and computation. A defining feature of the SCP is that it removes the restriction that all partitions be rectangular, which at first may seem unintuitive [12].

An existing state-of-the-art heterogeneous partitioning scheme (referred to here as the straight line partitioning or SLP) which does carry such a restriction is introduced in [1] which presents a column based partitioning based on that of [10]. The SLP balances the workload between processors of different speeds in an attempt to minimize the TVC between processors. First the matrix is partitioned into rectangles proportional in area to the speed of each processor. These rectangles are then arranged into columns in a defined manner. The TVC is proportional to the sum of the half-perimeters s of each rectangle, given by (2), where p is the number of processors and h_i and w_i are the height and width of the rectangle assigned to processor i, respectively.

[1] In this Section the words processor and cluster are used more or less interchangeably as some papers simulate individual clusters with processors for simplicity of modelling/verification purposes.

$$s = \sum_{i=1}^{p} (h_i + w_i) \tag{2}$$

Since the perimeter of any rectangle enclosing a given area is minimized when that rectangle is a square, there is a natural lower bound l of (2), shown by (3), where a_i is the area of the partition belonging to processor i.

$$l = 2 \times \sum_{i=1}^{p} \sqrt{a_i} \tag{3}$$

In considering the case of two clusters, we can inspect the case with relative speeds such that cluster 1 receives a rectangle of area $a_1 = 1 - \epsilon$, and cluster 2

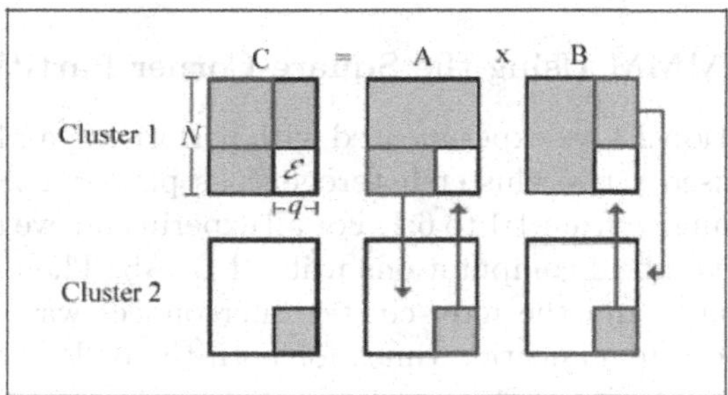

Fig. 1. The square-corner partitioning (for two partitions) and the necessary communication steps. Shaded areas belong to the respective clusters. Clearly if $\epsilon = 0$, no communication is necessary at all.

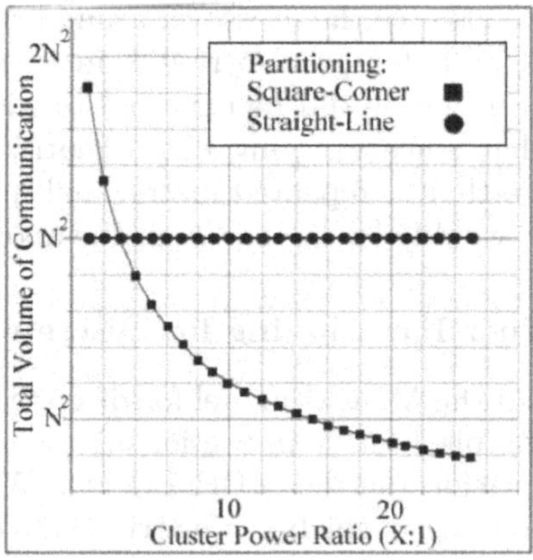

Fig. 2. Comparison of the total volume of communication between two clusters for the square-corner and straight-line partitionings

receives a rectangle of area $a_2 = \epsilon$, where $\epsilon > 0$ is an arbitrarily small number. In order to partition the unit matrix into two rectangles using the straight line partitioning, a line of length 1 must divide the matrix. Using (2) this results in a sum of half-perimeters equal to 3, regardless of the value of ϵ, but (3) shows that the lower bound can get arbitrarily close to 2, (as $\epsilon \to 0$).

A glance at Figure 1 illustrates that for the SCP (unlike the SLP), as $\epsilon \to 0$, the sum of half-perimeters — and therefore the TVC — approaches 2, showing that the SCP is optimal. A more detailed discussion and proof are given in [2].

Figure 2 shows the TVC of the SCP compared to that of the SLP. It is clear that when the power ratio between clusters is 3:1, the TVC values are equal, and for ratios above 3:1 the SCP TVC is less. By the time the ratio reaches 15:1, the SCP TVC is exactly half that of the SLP.

3 MPI Experiments

3.1 Max-Plus MMM Using the Square-Corner Partitioning

As outlined in Section 2.1 we experimented with performing a MPA MMM using C and MPI. We used a two cluster heterogeneous platform with power ratios between clusters ranging from 1:1 to 6:1. For all experiments we use double precision and N = 7,000. Local computations utilized BLAS. The local interconnect was 2Gb/s Infiniband and the inter-cluster interconnect was 1Gb/s Ethernet. Figure 3 shows the communication times for both the SCP and SLP partitionings. Firstly, it can be seen that as expected the SCP does not show improvement in communication time until the power ratio is 3:1, as this is when the SCP results in a lower TVC as shown in [2]. After this (as the system becomes more heterogeneous), the gap between the two communication times widens, and would be expected to widen further.

Figure 3 shows the resulting difference in execution times between the SCP and SLP. As expected we also see the crossover around ratio 3:1, and note that the lower TVC that the SCP brings also results in lower execution times for ratios above 3:1. Again this gap would be expected to widen.

It is worth noting that since carrying out a matrix power operation A^n amounts to nothing more than n repeated matrix multiplications, carrying out matrix power operations would also benefit from the above.

3.2 The Square-Corner Partitioning for Discrete Event Simulation

In Section 2.2 we outlined the MDEM model for discrete event simulations. We use the same experimental platform as in Section 3.1 to demonstrate results on a parallel, heterogeneous platform of the MDEM model. We utilize both the SLP and the SCP for the core routine which is a matrix "and/or" multiplication. We generate the initial conditions so that the core routine involves a large system (N = 5000). All initial calculations and cleanup are carried out on a single processor as these calculations are carried out only once and make up a very small percentage of the overall execution time.

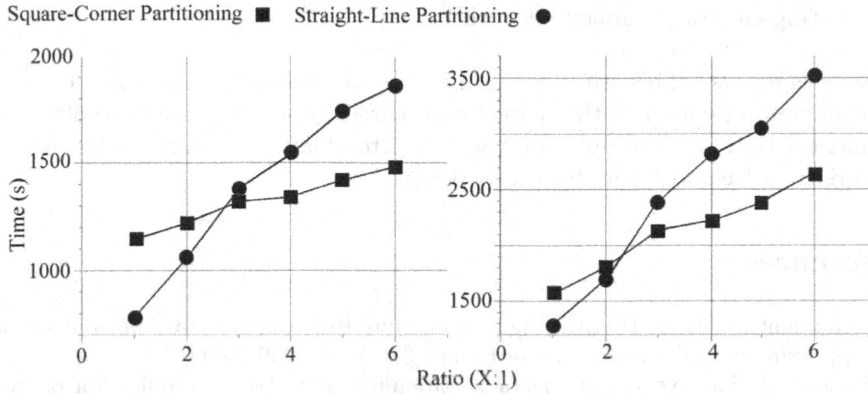

Fig. 3. Communication times (left) and execution times (right), Max-Plus MMM, $N = 7000$

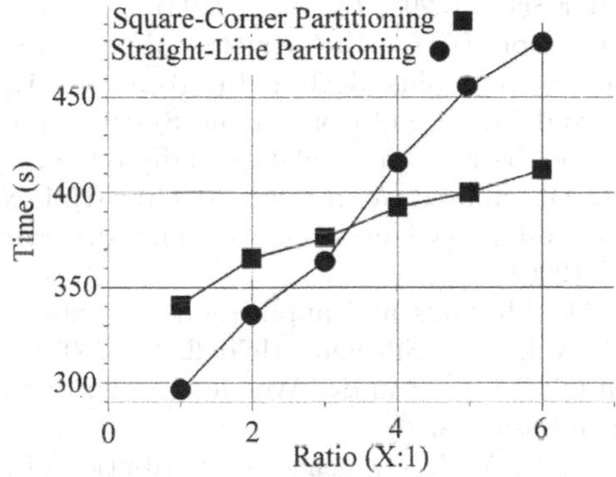

Fig. 4. Total execution times, MDEM DES model, $N = 5000$

Figure 4 shows the execution times for the MDEM DES using both partitioning techniques. All times are averaged over five runs. It is seen that the use of the SCP for the core kernel of the MDEM DES algorithm significantly reduces the execution time for ratios above 3:1. Again the expected crossover occurs near the ratio of 3:1. The overall shapes of the curves are similar to those of Section 3.1 as the "and/or" MMM in the MDEM involves a similar computational cost as the max-plus MMM.

4 Conclusion and Future Work

We found that the initial top-level data partitioning significantly affects overall execution time due to the total volume of inter-cluster communication involved. Notably the square-corner partitioning outperformed the straight-line partitioning in all cases. Future work involves applying similar strategies to speed up more complex routines on parallel hierarchal heterogeneous platforms and experimenting on more complex networks.

Acknowledgments. This work was supported by Science Foundation Ireland. Experiments presented in this paper were carried out using the Grid'5000 experimental testbed. The authors would like to thank Dr. Mark Dukes of the University of Iceland for useful suggestions.

References

1. Beaumont, O., et al.: Partitioning a Square into Rectangles: NP-Completeness and Approximation Algorithms. Algorithmica 34(3), 217–239 (2002)
2. Becker, B., Lastovetsky, A.: Data partitioning for matrix multiplication on two interconnected processors. In: Cluster 2006. IEEE, Los Alamitos (2006)
3. Becker, B.A., Lastovetsky, A.: Towards data partitioning for parallel computing on three interconnected clusters. In: ISPDC 2007 (2007)
4. Comet, J.: Application of max-plus algebra to biological sequence comparisons. Theoretical Computer Science 293, 189–217 (2003)
5. De Schutter, B., De Moor, B.: On the sequence of consecutive matrix powers of boolean matrices in the max-plus algebra. In: Tornamb, A., Conte, G., Perdon, A.M. (eds.) Theory and Practice of Control and Systems, pp. 672–677 (1999)
6. Fersha, A.: Parallel and distributed simulation of discrete event systems. In: Handbook of Parallel and Distributed Computing. McGraw-Hill, New York (1995)
7. Fishman, G.S.: Discrete-Event Simulation: Modeling, Programming, and Analysis. Springer, New York (2001)
8. Gaubert, S., Plus, M.: Methods and applications of (max,+) linear algebra. In: STACS 2007. LNCS, vol. 3088. Springer, Heidelberg (2007)
9. Heidergott, B., Jan Olsder, G., van der Woude, J.: Max Plus at Work. Princeton University Press, Princeton (2006)
10. Kalinov, A., Lastovetsky, A.: Heterogeneous Distribution of Computations While Solving linear algebra Problems on Networks of Heterogeneous Computers. In: Sloot, P.M.A., Hoekstra, A.G., Bubak, M., Hertzberger, B. (eds.) HPCN-Europe 1999. LNCS, vol. 1593. Springer, Heidelberg (1999)
11. Kirov, M.V.: The transfer-matrix and max-plus algebra method for global combinatorial optimization: Application to cyclic and polyhedral water clusters. Physica A 388, 1432–1445 (2009)
12. Lastovetsky, L., Dongarra, J.: High Performance Heterogeneous Computing. Wiley-Blackwell, Hoboken (2009)
13. Tacconi, D., Lewis, F.: A new matrix model for discrete event systems. application to simulation. IEEE Control Systems 97, 6–71 (1997)

Forth Workshop on Highly Parallel Processing on a Chip (HPPC 2010)

HPPC 2010: Forth Workshop on Highly Parallel Processing on a Chip

Martti Forsell[1] and Jesper Larsson Träff[2]

[1] VTT – Technical Research Centre of Finland
Oulu, Finland
Martti.Forsell@vtt.fi

[2] Faculty of Computer Science, Department of Scientific Computing
University of Vienna, Vienna, Austria
traff@par.univie.ac.at

Foreword

In response to the stagnant growth in conventional, single-processor performance increased on-chip parallelism is seen as a solution to the demands for high performance and power efficiency for general purpose, mainstream computing. While many general-purpose architectures with a moderate number of processing cores are already on the market, architectures with much more significant on-chip parallelism are generally expected, as is already seen for many special purpose processors. How the processing power of such many-core systems can be leveraged for general purpose computing is a most critical and completely open issue, as witnessed by the lack of convergence towards standard architecture and programming models. A major challenge for the coming years therefore is the design of highly parallel single-chip architectures that can support manageable programming abstractions to allow the mainstream programmer to take advantage of the processing power furthered by the technological developments.

The workshop on *Highly Parallel Processing on a Chip* (HPPC), now in its 4th incarnation, is dedicated to the interface between single-chip/node multi/many-core architectures and programming paradigms, models, and languages towards supporting parallel algorithms and applications development in an efficient and manageable way. HPPC is a forum for **bold**, *new* ideas on architectural organization (general- and special-purpose processors, heterogeneous designs, memory organization, on-chip communication networks, etc.), parallel programming models, languages, and libraries, many-core parallel algorithms, and application studies on both existing and envisaged architectures.

In response to the call-for-papers that was issued early in 2010, HPPC 2010 received 18 submissions that were all of relevance to the general workshop themes. Based on relevance and quality of the submissions as judged by the program committee (which did most of the reviewing with few external reviewers) this year a slightly higher number of papers than in previous years were selected for presentation by the program chairs. This made for an acceptance rate of 44%, which is not a measure of anything, anyway, in case this bothers anyone.

M.R. Guarracino et al. (Eds.): Euro-Par 2010 Workshops, LNCS 6586, pp. 73–75, 2011.
© Springer-Verlag Berlin Heidelberg 2011

The workshop organizers and program chairs thank sincerely all contributing authors, and hope that they will also find it worthwhile to submit contributions next year. Most contributions received *four* reviews (which is what HPPC strives for), a few having only three (which we regret), and were thus given an all in all fair consideration. The members of the program committee are likewise all thanked for the time and expertise they put into the reviewing work, and for getting it done within the rather strict time limit.

The Euro-Par 2010 workshop day featured a number of workshops, and was very lively, well-attended and generally well-organized. The HPPC workshop was conducted in an informal atmosphere and gave, hopefully, enough room for interaction and discussion between presenters and audience. HPPC 2010 had a high, cumulative attendance of more than 70. In addition to the 8 contributed talks, the workshop featured two longer, invited talks by Rolf Hoffmann (on "The massively parallel computing model CGA") and Jim Held (on "Single-chip Cloud Computer, an IA tera-scale research processor"). The workshop organizers thank all attendees, who contributed much to the workshop with questions, comments and discussion, and hope they found something of interest in the workshop, too. We also thank the Euro-Par organization for creating the opportunity to arrange the HPPC workshop in conjunction with the Euro-Par conference, and of course all Euro-Par 2010 organizers for their help and support both before and during the workshop. HPPC sponsors VTT, University of Vienna, and Euro-Par 2010 are warmly thanked for the financial support that made it possible to invite Rolf Hoffmann and Jim Held, both of whom we sincerely thank for accepting our invitation to speak and for their excellent talks.

These post-workshop proceedings include the final versions of the presented HPPC 2010 papers (accepted papers not presented at the workshop will not be included in the proceedings, but HPPC 2010 had all authors present and presenting), taking the feedback from reviewers and workshop audience into account. In addition to the reviews by the program committee prior to selection, an extra, post-workshop (blind) "*reading*" of each presented paper by one of the other presenters has been introduced with the aim of getting fresh, uninhibited high-level feedback for the authors to use at their discretion in preparing their final version (no papers would have been rejected at this stage – bar major flaws). This idea was introduced with HPPC 2008, and will be continued also for HPPC 2011.

The contributed papers are printed in the order they were presented at the workshop. A full version of the invited talk by Rolf Hoffmann and an abstract of Jim Held's talk have also been included in the proceedings. Thematically, the contributed papers cover aspects of memory organization ("Evaluation of low-overhead organizations for the directory in future many-core CMPs" by Ros and Acacio), programmability ("A work stealing scheduler for parallel loops on shared cache multicores" by Tchiboukdjian, Danjean, Gautier, Le Mentec and Raffin, "Resource-agnostic programming for many-core microgrids" by Bernard, Grelck, Hicks, Jesshope and Poss, "Programming heterogeneous multicore systems using Threading Building Blocks" by Russell, Keir, Donaldson, Dolinsky, Richards and Riley), applications and optimization for accellerators and special processors ("Fine-grain parallelization of a Vlasov-Poissoin application on GPU" by Latu, "Highly parallel implementation of Harris corner detector on CSX SIMD architecture" by Hosseini, Fijany and Fontaine, "Static speculation as post-link optimization for the Grid Alu Processor" by Jahr, Shehan, Uhrig and Ungerer), and on-chip networks and routers ("A multi-level routing scheme and router architecture to support hierarchical routing in large network on chip platforms" by Holsmark, Kumar and Palesi).

The HPPC workshop is planned to be organized again in conjunction with Euro-Par 2011.

Sponsors

VTT, Finland	`http://www.vtt.fi`
University of Vienna	`http://www.univie.ac.at`
Euro-Par	`http://www.euro-par.org`

The Massively Parallel Computing Model GCA

Rolf Hoffmann

Technische Universität Darmstadt, FB Informatik, FG Rechnerarchitektur,
Hochschulstraße 10, D-64289 Darmstadt, Germany
{hoffmann}@ra.informatik.tu-darmstadt.de

Abstract. The Global Cellular Automata Model (GCA) is an extension of the Cellular Automata Model (CA). Whereas in the CA model each cell is connected via fixed links to its local neighbors, in the GCA model each cell is connected via data dependent dynamic links to any (global) cell of the whole array. The GCA cell state does not only contain data information but also link information. The cell state is synchronously updated according to a local rule, modifying the data and the link information. Similar to the CA model, only the own cell state is modified. Thereby write conflicts cannot occur. The GCA model is related to the CROW (concurrent read owners write) model and it can be used to describe a large range of applications. GCA algorithms can be described in the language GCA-L which can be compiled into different target platforms: a generated data parallel multi-pipeline architecture, and a NIOS II multi-softcore architecture.

Keywords: Global Cellular Automata, Parallel Programming Model.

1 Introduction

Since the beginning of parallel processing a lot of theoretical and practical work has been done in order to find a parallel programming model (PPM) which fulfills at least the following properties

- *User-friendly:* easy to model and to program
- *System-designer-friendly:* parallel processing target architectures supporting the model are easy to design and to implement, and programs can easily be translated into these architectures
- *Efficient:* The applications can efficiently be executed on the target architecture
- *Platform independent:* The PPM can also be mapped (interpreted, simulated) without much effort onto other standard platforms and can there be executed with a satisfying performance.

In the following sections such a model (Global Cellular Automata) will be described, and how it can be implemented and used. This model was introduced in [1], then further investigated, implemented, and applied to different problems. This paper is based on the results of former publications, mainly [1] [2] [3] [4] [5] [6] [7] [8] [9] [10].

M.R. Guarracino et al. (Eds.): Euro-Par 2010 Workshops, LNCS 6586, pp. 77–84, 2011.
© Springer-Verlag Berlin Heidelberg 2011

2 The GCA Model (Global Cellular Automata)

The definition of the GCA model was inspired by the CA (Cellular Automata) model. The CA model consists of an array of cells arranged in an n-dimensional grid. Each cell (also called the "Center Cell" is connected to its local neighbors belonging to the neighborhood, e.g. to **N**orth, **E**ast, **S**outh, **W**est. The next state of the center cell is defined by a local rule f residing in each cell: $C \leftarrow f(C, N, E, S, W)$. All cells are applying the same rule synchronously and thereby a new generation of cell states is defined. As a cell changes only its own state, no write conflicts can occur which makes the model simple and elegant. Many applications with a local neighborhood can nicely be described as a CA, and CAs can easily be simulated or implemented in hardware.

The idea for the GCA model was (1) to retain the property that a cell can only modify its own state, and (2) to introduce more flexibility. Flexibility was obtained by using (2a) computed dynamic links to the neighbors and (2b) by allowing any cell in the array to be a neighbor (global neighbors). Thus a GCA can informally be described as follows:

A GCA consists of an indexed set of cells (e.g. an n-dimensional array). The cells' states are updated synchronously according to a local rule. Each cell has k global neighbors which can dynamically be changed by the local rule (Fig. 1). Write conflicts cannot occur, therefore the model can easily be supported by hardware for a large number of cells. A GCA is initialized by an initial state for each cell (initial configuration *CFG(t=0)*). The result of the computation is the state of the finial configuration (all cell states) at time-step t_{final}. We can also speak of a "GCA algorithm", meaning the transformation of the initial generation to the final generation.

Three model variants are distinguished, the *basic model*, the *general model* and the *condensed model*. They are closely related to each other and can be transformed into each other. It depends on the application or the implementation which one will be preferred.

Basic model. The cell state is a composition $(data, pointer) = (d, p)$ (Fig. 2a). The pointer p is used to access the global neighbor $p = k^*$. The remote state (d^*, p^*) is read from the global cell via the dynamic link. Then the new state components are computed: $d' = e(d, p, d^*, p^*)$ and $p' = g(d, p, d^*, p^*)$. Then

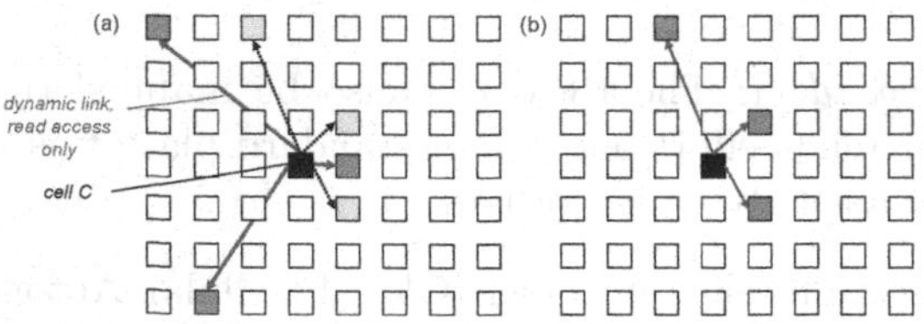

Fig. 1. (a) In generation t each cell is connected to k neighbors (e.g. $k = 3$), and it selects k new neighbors. (b) In generation $t + 1$ each cell is connected to its new neighbors.

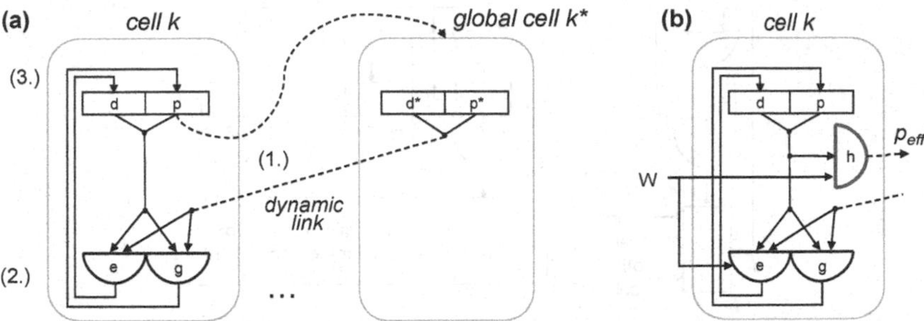

Fig. 2. (a) Basic model. The cell state is a composition of one or more data fields d and one or more pointer (link) fields p. A global cell k^* is accessed via p and a data link is dynamically established from the global cell k^* to the cell k (1.). Then the function e computes the next data and the function g computes the next pointer (2.). Then all cells are updated synchronously (3.). – (b) General model. An additional function $h(d,p)$ is used which computes an effective address p_{eff} to select the global neighbor. Central control parameters W from the simulation environment can be taken into account.

all cells are updated synchronously: $d \leftarrow d', p \leftarrow p'$. In general several data and pointer fields can be used $(d_1, d_2, ..., p_1, p_2, ...)$ and several neighbors can be accessed.

General model. In addition to the basic model the general model (Fig. 2b) uses an addressing function $h(d,p)$ which computes the effective address $p_{eff} = h(d,p)$ of the global neighbor. For many applications this addressing technique is more convenient than the direct addressing with p of the basic model. In addition, central parameters W, supplied by the simulation environment (e.g. generation counter t, cell index k, etc.) are useful to be available in the functions: $h(d,p,d^*,p^*,W), e(d,p,d^*,p^*,W)$, and $g(d,p,d^*,p^*,W)$.

Condensed model. In the condensed model the cell state is not separated into a data part and pointer part. Instead only a data part q is used. The meaning of q is a matter of interpretation, it can be interpreted as a data or a pointer field. Either parts of q are interpreted as data or pointer, or q is interpreted alternatively as data or pointer depending on a data type subfield of q (like an operation code of an instruction) or on additional information like the generation counter t.

Relation to the CROW model. The GCA model is related to the CROW (concurrent read owner write) model [11], a variant of the PRAM (parallel random access machine) models. The CROW model consists of a common global memory and P processors, and each memory location may only be written by its assigned owner processor. In contrast, the GCA model consists of P cells, each with its local state (data and pointer fields) and its local rule (together acting as a small processing unit updating the data and pointer field). Thus the GCA model is (1) "cell" based, meaning that the state and processing unit are

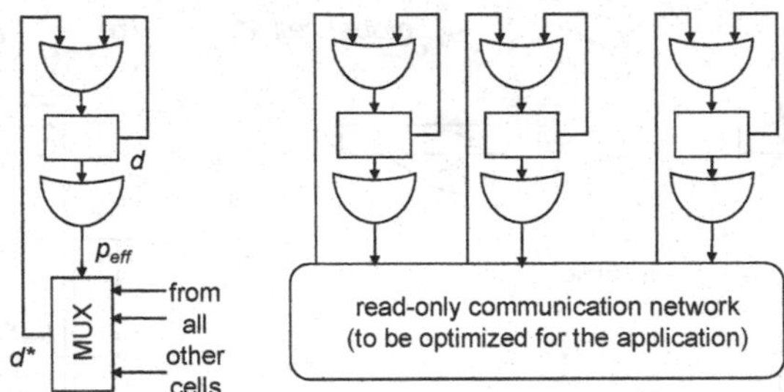

Fig. 3. Fully parallel implementation. Communication implemented by a multiplexer in each cell (a). Communication implemented by a common network (b).

encapsulated, similar as objects in the object oriented languages, and (2) the cells are structured according to the application. The processing units of the GCA can be seen as virtual processors, having just the processing features which are needed for the application. On the other hand the CROW model uses "universal" processors independent of the application. Furthermore the GCA updates in each generation the data and pointer fields simultaneously, whereas in the PRAM model only one memory location per processor is updated simultaneously.

3 GCA Architectures

A variety of architectures can be designed or used to support the GCA model. In the following three architectures are proposed. The *fully parallel architecture* can be very powerful for small dedicated applications. The *data parallel architecture* can be used for medium size dedicated applications to be configured on an FPGA. The *multisoftcore* system is programmable and can be applied to medium or large applications. Other interesting architectures could be designed, e.g. cells with programmable rules, or pipelines with programmable rules, but these are out of the scope of this paper. Furthermore standard platforms like standard multicores or GPUs can be used to execute the GCA model.

In a student's work Benjamin Milde and Niklas Büscher showed an acceleration of 13 for bitonic merging and 150 for a diffusion algorithm on an NVIDIA GFX 470 compared to an Intel Q9550@3GHz with 4 threads. Although these results cannot be generalized, GPUs seem to be a promising platform to execute the GCA model.

Fully Parallel Architecture. "Fully parallel" means that the whole GCA for a specific application is completely implemented in hardware (Fig. 3). The question is how many hardware resources are needed. The number of cells is n. Therefore the logic (computing the effective address and the next state) and the number of registers holding the cells' states are proportional to n. The local interconnections (wiring) are proportional to n, too. As the GCA generally allows to access from each cell any other global cell, the wiring effort is $(n-1) \times n$ *global* wires. The length of a global wire is not a constant, it depends on the

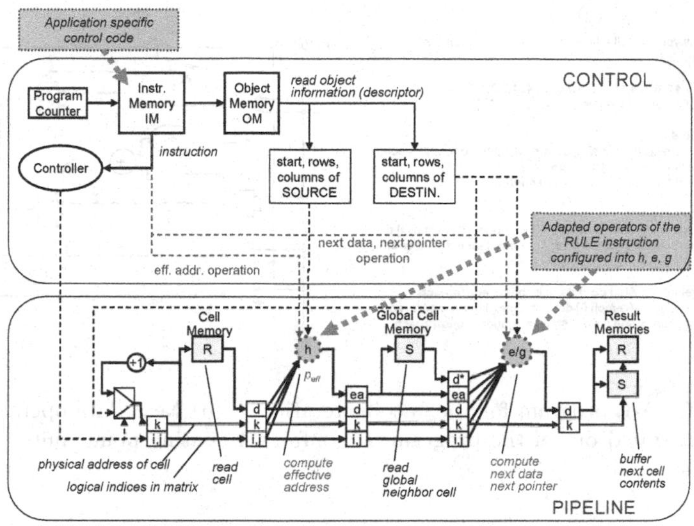

Fig. 4. Data parallel architecture (DPA) with one pipeline

physical distance. If the cells are arranged in a *2d* square grid the shortest distance is one and the longest (Manhattan) distance is $2\sqrt{n}$. Thus the total wiring (with respect to the mean distance) is of the order $O(n^2)$. Note that the longest distance also determines the maximal clock rate. Many applications / GCA algorithms do not require a total interconnection fabric because only a subset of all communications (read accesses) are required for a specific application. Therefore the amount of wires and switches can be reduced significantly for one or a limited set of applications. In addition for each global wire a switch is required. The switches can be implemented by a multiplexer in each cell, or by a common switching network (e.g. crossbar). Note that the number of switches of the network can also be reduced to the number of communication links used by the specific application. Another aspect is the multiple read (concurrent read) feature. In the worst case one cell is accessed from all the other cells which may cause a fanout problem in the hardware implementation.

Data Parallel Architecture. The data parallel architecture (DPA) uses p pipelines in order to process p cell rules in parallel [6][8]. The whole address space is partitioned into (sub) arrays, also called "cell objects". In our implementation a cell object represents either a cell vector or a cell matrix. A cell object is identified by its start address, and the cells within it are addressed relatively to the start address. The *destination object* D stores the cells to be updated, and the *source object* S stores the global cells to be read. Although for most applications D and S are disjunct, the may overlap or be the same.

The DPA consists of a control unit and p pipelines, in Fig. 4 only one pipeline is shown. In the case of one pipeline only, the cells of S are processed sequentially using a counter k. In the first pipeline stage the cell *D[k]* is read from memory

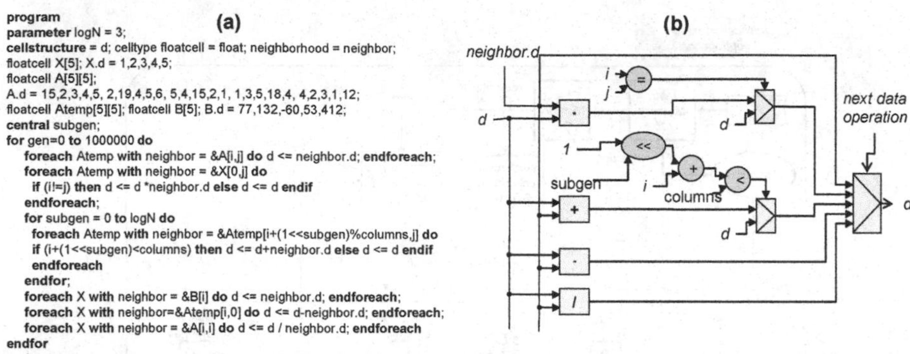

(a)
program
parameter logN = 3;
cellstructure = d; celltype floatcell = float; neighborhood = neighbor;
floatcell X[5]; X.d = 1,2,3,4,5;
floatcell A[5][5];
A.d = 15,2,3,4,5, 2,19,4,5,6, 5,4,15,2,1, 1,3,5,18,4, 4,2,3,1,12;
floatcell Atemp[5][5]; floatcell B[5]; B.d = 77,132,-60,53,412;
central subgen;
for gen=0 to 1000000 do
foreach Atemp with neighbor = &A[i,j] do d <= neighbor.d; endforeach;
foreach Atemp with neighbor = &X[0,j] do
if (i!=j) then d <= d *neighbor.d else d <= d endif
endforeach;
for subgen = 0 to logN do
foreach Atemp with neighbor = &Atemp[i+(1<<subgen)%columns,j] do
if (i+(1<<subgen)<columns) then d <= d+neighbor.d else d <= d endif
endforeach
endfor;
foreach X with neighbor = &B[i] do d <= neighbor.d; endforeach;
foreach X with neighbor=&Atemp[i,0] do d <= d-neighbor.d; endforeach;
foreach X with neighbor = &A[i,i] do d <= d / neighbor.d; endforeach
endfor
endprogram
(b)
neighbor.d
i
j
=
d
next data operation
d
1
<<
+
subgen
i
<
columns
d
+
d
-
/

Fig. 5. (a) GCA-L program for the Jacobi iteration. – (b) Next data operator e automatically generated out of the program. It contains 4 floating point units and several integer units.

R. In the second stage the effective address ea is computed by h. In the third stage the global cell $S[ea]$ is read. In the fourth stage the next cell state d is computed. Then the next cell state is stored in the buffer memories R' and S' at location k. When all cells of the destination object are processed, the memories (R, S) and (R', S') are interchanged.

An application specific DPA with p pipelines can automatically be generated out of a high level description in the experimental language GCA-L [6]. The program (Fig. 5a) describes the Jacobi iteration [7] solving a set of linear equations.

The most important feature of GCA-L is the *foreach D with neighbor* $= \&S[..]$ *do .. endforeach* construct. It describes the (parallel) iteration over all cells $D[i, j]$ using the global neighbors *&S[h(i,j)]*. Our tool generates Verilog code for the functions h, e, g to be embedded in the pipeline(s). These functions are also pipelined. In addition control code for the control unit is generated. The most important control codes are the *rule* instructions. A rule instruction triggers the processing of all cells in a destination object and applies the so called *adapted operators* h, e, g coded in the rule. All necessary application specific rule instructions are extracted from the source program [7]. Fig. 5b shows a generated next data operation used by a rule instruction. It contains 4 floating point units and several integer units. The floating point operations are internally also pipelined (- :14, * :11, + :14, / :33 stages). Our tool generates Verilog code which further is used for synthesis with Quartus II for Altera FPGAs. For $p = 8$ pipelines, normalized to the amount needed for one pipeline, the relative increments for the FPGA Altera Stratix II EP2S180 were: 8.3 for the ALUTs (logic elements), 7.5 for the registers, 4.5 for the memory bits (note that the required memory bits are theoretically proportional to $(p+1)/2$ for the pipeline architecture). The speedup was 6.8 for 8 pipelines compared to one. Thus the scaling behavior was very good and almost linear for up to 8 pipelines.

Multisoftcore. The basic idea is to use many standard softcores together with specific GCA support. Each core is responsible to handle a subset of all cells

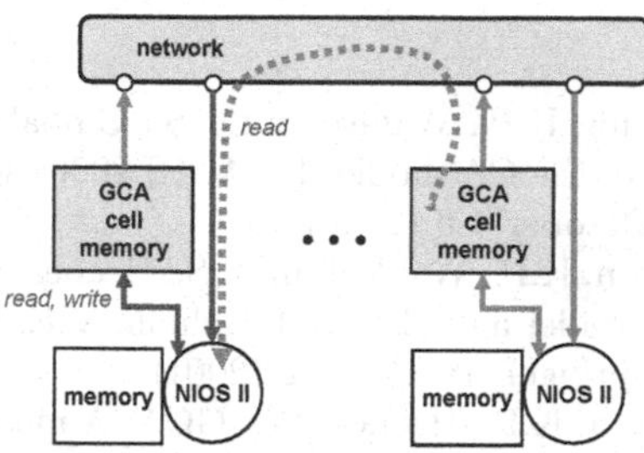

Fig. 6. Multisoftcore system implemented on an FPGA. A local GCA cell memory is attached to each NIOS II softcore. Each core can read and write its own GCA cell memory and read from any other GCA cell memory via the network.

being processed in one generation. In our implementation, p NIOS II softcores were used [9][10]. To each processor a GCA cell memory is attached (Fig. 6). A processor can read via the network the state of a global cell residing in another cell memory. Only the cells residing in the own cell memory need to be updated according to the GCA model. No write access via the network is needed, thereby the network can be simplified. In case that only a specific application has to be implemented, the network can be minimized according to the communication links used by the application. The machine instruction set of the NIOS processors was extended (custom instructions), e.g. read a cell via the network, read/write local cell memory, floating point operations, synchronize and copy new cell states into the current cell states.

A tool was developed that can automatically generate C code (extended by custom instructions) out of a GCA-L program for such a multisoftcore system. Then this C code is compiled and loaded into the cores of the system configured on an FPGA.

4 Conclusion

In the GCA parallel programming model, applications are modeled as a set of cells which are dynamically connected to other cells. Applications can be described in the experimental language GCA-L. Different GCA target architectures can easily be designed and implemented, e.g. a fully parallel architecture, a data parallel architecture, and a multisoftcore architecture. Tools allow to translate GCA-L programs into such architectures or generate them for FPGAs. These architectures can be optimized for specific applications and adjusted to the performance requirements. First investigations have shown that the GCA model can also be efficiently executed on standard multicores and especially on GPUs.

Acknowledgment. I would like to thank Benjamin Milde and Niklas Büscher who implemented the model on Quadcores and GPUs.

References

1. Hoffmann, R., Völkmann, K.P., Waldschmidt, S.: Global cellular automata GCA: an universal extension of the CA model. In: ACRI 2000 "work in progress" session, Karlsruhe, Germany, October 4-6 (2000)
2. Hoffmann, R., Völkmann, K.P., Waldschmidt, S., Heenes, W.: GCA: Global cellular automata. A flexible parallel model. In: Malyshkin, V.E. (ed.) PaCT 2001. LNCS, vol. 2127, pp. 66–73. Springer, Heidelberg (2001)
3. Hoffmann, R., Völkmann, K.P., Heenes, W.: GCA: A massively parallel model. In: IPDPS 2003, Nice, France, April 22-26 (2003)
4. Heenes, W., Hoffmann, R., Jendrsczok, J.: A multiprocessor architecture for the massively parallel model GCA. In: IEEE Proceedings of 20th International Parallel & Distributed Processing Symposium, IPDPS/SMTPS 2006, Rhodes Island, Greece, April 25-29. IEEE, Los Alamitos (2006)
5. Jendrsczok, J., Ediger, P., Hoffmann, R.: The Global Cellular Automata Experimental Language GCA-L1. Technical Report RA-1-2007, Technische Universität Darmstadt (2007)
6. Jendrsczok, J., Ediger, P., Hoffmann, R.: A Scalable Configurable Architecture for the Massively Parallel GCA Model. International Journal of Parallel, Emergent and Distributed Systems (IJPEDS) 24(4), 275–291 (2009)
7. Jendrsczok, J., Hoffmann, R., Ediger, P.: A Generated Data Parallel GCA Machine for the Jacobi Method. In: 3rd HiPEAC Workshop on Reconfigurable Computing, Paphos, Cyprus, January 25, pp. 73–82 (2009)
8. Jendrsczok, J., Hoffmann, R., Lenck, T.: Generated Horizontal and Vertical Data Parallel GCA Machines for the N-Body Force Calculation. In: Berekovic, M., Müller-Schloer, C., Hochberger, C., Wong, S. (eds.) ARCS 2009. LNCS, vol. 5455, pp. 96–107. Springer, Heidelberg (2009)
9. Schäck, C., Heenes, W., Hoffmann, R.: A Multiprocessor Architecture with an Omega Network for the Massively Parallel Model GCA. In: Bertels, K., Dimopoulos, N., Silvano, C., Wong, S. (eds.) SAMOS 2009. LNCS, vol. 5657, pp. 98–107. Springer, Heidelberg (2009)
10. Schäck, C., Heenes, W., Hoffmann, R.: Network Optimization of a Multiprocessor Architecture for the Massively Parallel Model GCA. In: Mitteilungen - Gesellschaft für Informatik e. V., Parallel-Algorithmen und Rechnerstrukturen, Wolfgang Karl and Rolf Hoffmann and Wolfgang Heenes, vol. 26, pp. 48–57 (Dezember 2009)
11. Dymond, P., Ruzzo, W.: Parallel RAMs with owned global memory and deterministic context-free language recoginition. In: Kott, L. (ed.) ICALP 1986. LNCS, vol. 226, pp. 95–104. Springer, Heidelberg (1986)

“Single-chip Cloud Computer”, an IA Tera-scale Research Processor

Jim Held

Intel Fellow & Director Tera-scale Computing Research
Intel Labs, USA
jim.p.held@intel.com

Abstract

As part of our Tera-scale Computing Research Program, Intel Labs has created a second generation experimental “Single-chip Cloud Computer” (SCC). It contains the most Intel Architecture cores ever integrated on a silicon CPU chip: 48 cores. It incorporates technologies intended to scale multi-core processors to 100 cores and beyond, such as an on-chip network, advanced power management technologies and support for *message-passing*.

Architecturally, SCC is a microcosm of a cloud data-center. Each core can run a separate OS and software stack and act like an individual compute node that communicates with other compute nodes over the on-die packet-based network fabric, thus supporting the "scale-out" message passing programming models that have been proven to scale to 1000s of processors in cloud data-centers.

The SCC serves as an experimental platform for a wide range of software research and is currently being used by a worldwide community of academic and industry co-travelers. This talk will describe the architecture of the SCC platform and discuss its role in the broader context of our Tera-scale research. For more information, see www.intel.com/info/scc

Short Biography

Jim Held is an Intel Fellow who leads a virtual team of architects conducting Tera-Scale Computing Research in Intel Labs. Since joining Intel in 1990, he has led research and development in a variety of Intel's labs concerned with media and interconnect technology, systems software, multi-core processor architecture and virtualization. He earned a Ph.D. (1988) in Computer and Information Science at the University of Minnesota.

M.R. Guarracino et al. (Eds.): Euro-Par 2010 Workshops, LNCS 6586, p. 85, 2011.
© Springer-Verlag Berlin Heidelberg 2011

Evaluation of Low-Overhead Organizations for the Directory in Future Many-Core CMPs*

Alberto Ros[1] and Manuel E. Acacio[2]

[1] Dpto. de Informática de Sistemas y Computadores
Universidad Politécnica de Valencia, 46022 Valencia, Spain
[2] Dpto. de Ingeniería y Tecnología de Computadores
Universidad de Murcia, 30100 Murcia, Spain
aros@gap.upv.es, meacacio@ditec.um.es

Abstract. If current trends continue, today's small-scale general-purpose CMPs will soon be replaced by multi-core architectures integrating tens or even hundreds of cores on-chip. Most likely, some of these many-core CMPs will implement the hardware-managed, implicitly-addressed, coherent caches memory model. Cache coherence in these designs will be probably maintained through a directory-based cache coherence protocol implemented in hardware. The organization of the directory structure will be a key design point due to the requirements in area that it will pose. In this work, we study the effects on performance, network traffic and area that the use of compressed sharing codes for the directory will have in many-core CMPs. In particular, we select two compressed sharing codes previously proposed in the context of large-scale shared-memory multiprocessors that have very small area requirements. Simulation results of 32-core CMPs show that degradations of up to 32% in performance and 350% in network traffic are experienced. Additionally, since some proposals for efficient multicast support in on-chip networks have recently appeared, we also consider the case of using this support in combination with the compressed sharing codes. Unfortunately, we found that multicast support is not enough to remove all the performance degradation introduced by the compressed sharing codes and barely can reduce network traffic.

1 Introduction

In the last years we have witnessed the substitution of single-core processors by multi-core ones. Following the Moore's Law that establishes that the number of transistors doubles every 18 months, it is expected that current small-scale general-purpose chip-multiprocessors (CMPs) will soon be followed by multi-core architectures integrating tens or even hundreds of cores on-chip [1]. Architectures of this type are usually known as many-core CMPs.

* We would like to thank anonymous reviewers for their suggestions. This research was supported by the Spanish MEC and MICINN, as well as European Commission FEDER funds, under Grants CSD2006-00046 and TIN2009-14475-C04, and PROMETEO from Generalitat Valenciana (GVA) under Grant PROMETEO/2008/060.

M.R. Guarracino et al. (Eds.): Euro-Par 2010 Workshops, LNCS 6586, pp. 87–97, 2011.
© Springer-Verlag Berlin Heidelberg 2011

Many-core CMPs will be probably designed as arrays of identical or close-to-identical building blocks (tiles) connected over a switched direct network [2,3]. Tiled architectures provide a scalable solution for supporting families of products with varying computational power, managing the design complexity, and effectively using the resources available in advanced VLSI technologies. As an example, Intel has recently announced the 48-core Single-chip Cloud Computer [4], an experimental research microprocessor that has been developed in the context of the Tera-scale Computing Research Program. The Single-chip Cloud Computer consists of 24 tiles with two IA cores per tile, which are interconnected by means of a 24-router mesh network providing 256 GB/s bisection bandwidth.

On the other hand, if current trends continue, future many-core CMP architectures will implement the hardware-managed, implicitly-addressed, coherent caches memory model [5]. With this memory model, all on-chip storage is used for private and shared caches that are kept coherent in hardware by using a cache coherence protocol. In this way, each tile contains at least one level of cache memory that is private to the local core (the L1 in this work), and the first level of shared cache (commonly, the L2 cache) is physically distributed between the tiles of the system.

The cache coherence protocol will be a key design issue in these architectures since it will add requirements of area and energy consumption to the final design, and therefore, could restrict severely its scalability. When the number of cores is large, as is the case of many-core CMPs, the best way today of keeping cache coherence is by implementing a directory-based protocol, which reduces energy consumption compared to broadcast-based protocols by keeping track of the caches that hold copies of each block in a directory structure. In tiled CMPs, the directory structure is distributed between the L2 cache banks, usually included into the L2 tags' portion [3]. In this way, each tile keeps the sharing information of the blocks mapped to the L2 cache bank that it contains. This sharing information comprises two main components: the *state bits* used to codify one of the three possible states the directory can assign to the line (*Uncached*, *Shared* and *Private*), and the *sharing code*, that holds the list of current sharers. Most of the bits of each directory entry are devoted to codifying the sharing code.

In a traditional directory organization, each directory entry keeps track of the sharers of the corresponding memory block through a simple bit-vector (one bit per private cache). In Figure 1, we plot the area (in mm^2) that one 1MB 4-way L2 module would take as the number of cores grows from 2 to 256 (area estimations are based on CACTI. Refer to Section 4 for more details). As it can be seen, while the number of cores keeps below 16 the bit-vector sharing code barely impacts area requirements. However, from 16 cores and onwards, the use of bit-vectors would entail too much area overhead and more area efficient sharing codes would be required.

One approach for reducing directory area requirements in the context of traditional shared-memory multiprocessors is the use of compressed sharing codes. Compressed sharing codes store the directory information in a compressed way

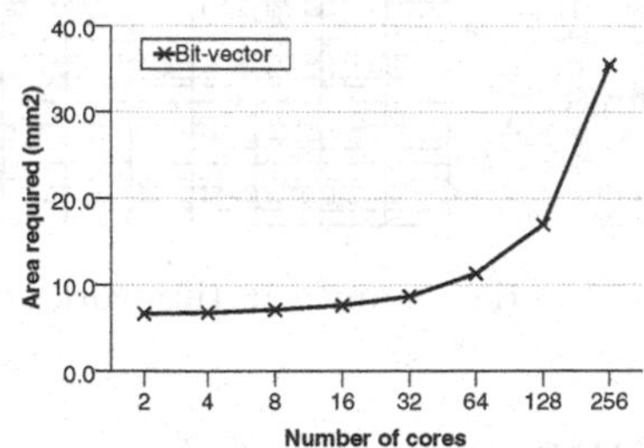

Fig. 1. Area (mm^2) required for a 1MB cache module when the bit-vector sharing code is used

to use fewer number of bits, introducing a loss of precision compared to *exact* ones (e.g., bit-vector). This means that when this information is reconstructed, some of the cores codified in the sharing code are real sharers and must receive the coherence messages, whereas some other cores are not sharers actually and *unnecessary* coherence messages will be sent to them. Unnecessary coherence messages lead to increased miss latencies, since more messages are required to resolve caches misses. These messages also entail extra traffic in the interconnection network and useless cache accesses, which will increase energy consumption. Conversely, a bit-vector directory does not generate unnecessary coherence messages and thus shows the best results in terms of both performance and energy consumption.

In this work we study the effects on performance, network traffic and area required by the directory structure that the use of compressed sharing codes will have in many-core CMPs. In particular, we select two area-efficient compressed sharing codes previously proposed by us in the context of large-scale shared-memory multiprocessors, namely Binary Tree (BT) and Binary Tree with Symmetric Nodes (BT-SN) [6]. Simulation results of 32-core CMPs show that degradations of up to 32% in performance and 350% in network traffic are experienced. Additionally, since some proposals for efficient multicast support in on-chip networks have recently appeared [7], we also consider the case of using this kind of support in combination with the compressed sharing codes. Unfortunately, multicast support is not enough to completely remove the performance degradation that the compressed sharing codes introduce (performance degradations of 10% on average are still observed when BT is used) and barely can reduce network traffic.

The rest of the paper is organized as follows. First of all, we will give more details regarding the target CMP architecture in Section 2. Subsequently, in Section 3 we will present a couple of compressed sharing codes based on the concept of multilayer clustering. Next, in Section 4, we will describe the evaluation environment that we are assuming, and the results of the evaluation will be shown in Section 5. Finally, Section 6 closes the work.

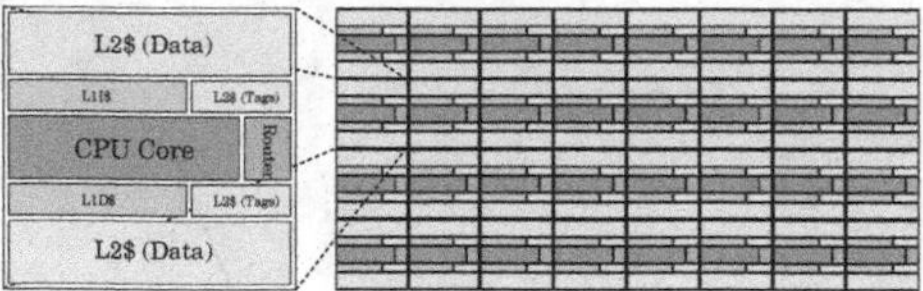

Fig. 2. Organization of the tile assumed in this work and a 4×8 tiled CMP

2 Base Architecture

A tiled CMP architecture consists of a number of replicated *tiles* connected over a switched direct network. Each tile contains a processing core with primary caches (both instruction and data caches), a slice of the L2 cache, and a connection to the on-chip network. Cache coherence is maintained at the L1 caches. In particular, a directory-based cache coherence protocol with directory information stored in the tags' part of the L2 cache modules is employed. The L2 cache is shared among the different processing cores, but it is physically distributed between them. Therefore, some accesses to the L2 cache will be sent to the local slice while the rest will be serviced by remote slices (L2 NUCA architecture [8]). Moreover, for simplicity the L1 and L2 caches are inclusive, that is to say, all the blocks included in any L1 cache keep an entry in the L2 cache. Figure 2 shows the organization of a tile (left) and a 16-tile CMP (right). From now on, we will use the terms tile and node interchangeably.

3 BT and BT-SN Compressed Sharing Codes

The two compressed sharing codes considered in this work (BT and BT-SN) were derived from the multi-layer clustering concept introduced in [6]. Multi-layer clustering assumes that nodes are recursively grouped into clusters of equal size until all nodes are grouped into a single cluster. Compression is achieved by specifying the smallest cluster containing all the sharers (instead of indicating *all* the sharers). Compression can be increased even more by indicating only the level of the cluster in the hierarchy. In this case, it is assumed that the cluster is the one containing the home node for the memory block. Although clusters can be formed by grouping any integer number of clusters in the immediately lower layer of the hierarchy, we analyze the case of using a value equal to two. That is to say, each cluster contains two clusters from the immediately lower level. By doing so, we simplify binary representation and obtain better granularity to specify the set of sharers. This recursive grouping into layer clusters leads to a logical binary tree with the nodes located at the leaves.

Since nodes are located at the leaves of a tree, the set of nodes (sharers) holding a copy of a particular memory block can be expressed as the minimal subtree that includes the home node and all the sharers. This minimal subtree is codified using the level of its root (which can be expressed using just $\lceil \log_2 (\log_2 N + 1) \rceil$ bits). Intuitively, the set of sharers is obtained from the home node identifier by

Table 1. System parameters

32-core CMP			
GEMS Parameters		**SICOSYS Parameters**	
Processor frequency	4 GHz	Network frequency	2 GHz
Cache hierarchy	Inclusive	Topology	8x4 Mesh
Cache block size	64 bytes	Switching technique	Wormhole, Multicast
Split L1 I & D caches	128KB, 4 ways, 4 hit cycles	Routing technique	Deterministic X-Y
		Message size	4 flits data, 1 flit control
Shared unified L2 cache	1MB/tile, 4 ways, 7 hit cycles	Routing time	2 cycles
		Link latency (one hop)	2 cycles
Memory access time	300 cycles	Link bandwidth	1 flit/cycle

changing the value of some of its least significant bits to *don't care*. The number of modified bits is equal to the level of the above mentioned subtree. It constitutes a very compact sharing code (observe that, for a 128-node system, only 3 bits per directory entry are needed). This sharing code is known as *binary tree* or BT.

We also considered the concept of symmetric nodes of a particular home node. Assuming that 3 additional symmetric nodes are assigned to each home node, they are codified by different combinations of the two most-significant bits of the home node identifier (note that one of these combinations represents the home node itself). In other words, symmetric nodes only differ from the corresponding home node in the two most significant bits. Now, the process of choosing the minimal subtree that includes all the sharers is repeated for the symmetric nodes. Then, the minimum of these subtrees is chosen to represent the sharers. The intuitive idea is the same as before but, in this case, the two most significant bits of the home identifier are changed to the symmetric node used. Therefore, the size of the sharing code of a directory entry is the same as before plus the number of bits needed to codify the symmetric nodes (for 3 sym-nodes, 2 bits). This sharing code is known as *binary tree with symmetric nodes* or BT-SN.

4 Evaluation Environment

We perform the evaluation using the full-system simulator Virtutech Simics [9] extended with Multifacet GEMS 1.3 [10], that provides a detailed memory system timing model. Since the network modeled by GEMS 1.3 is not very precise, we have extended it with SICOSYS [11], a detailed interconnection network simulator. We simulate a 32-tile CMP architecture as the one described in Section 2. The values of the main parameters used for the evaluation are shown in Table 1. Cache latencies have been calculated using the CACTI 5.3 tool [12] for 45nm technology. We also have used CACTI to measure the area of a 1MB 4-way L2 cache bank that includes the different sharing codes assumed in this work. In this study, we assume that the length of the physical address is 44 bits, like in the SUN UltraSPARC-III architecture [13].

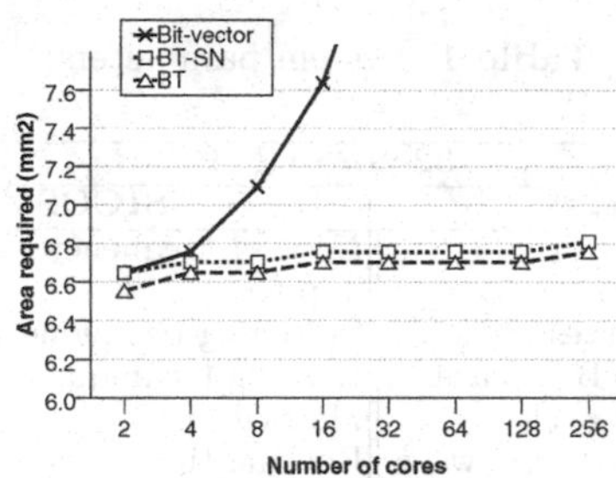

Fig. 3. Area (mm^2) required for a 1MB cache module when bit-vector, BT or BT-SN are used

The ten applications used in our simulations cover a variety of computation and communication patterns. *Barnes* (8192 bodies, 4 time steps), *FFT* (256K points), *Ocean* (258x258 ocean), *Radix* (1M keys, 1024 radix), *Raytrace* (teapot), *Volrend* (head) and *Water-Sp* (512 molecules, 4 time steps) are scientific applications from the SPLASH-2 benchmark suite [14]. *Unstructured* (Mesh.2K, 5 time steps) is a computational fluid dynamics application. *MPGdec* (525_tens_040.m2v) and *MPGenc* (output of *MPGdec*), are multimedia applications from the APLBench suite [15]. We account for the variability in multithreaded workloads by doing multiple simulation runs for each benchmark in each configuration and injecting random perturbations in the memory systems timing for each run.

5 Evaluation Results

We start this section by comparing the area overhead introduced by the different organizations for the sharing code considered in this work. Next, we study the impact that the compressed sharing codes have on network traffic, considering both a network with and without multicast support. Finally, we compare the execution times for the three directory organizations.

5.1 Impact on Area Overhead

Figure 3 plots the total area (in mm^2) that would be required by a 1MB 4-way cache module when bit-vector, BT and BT-SN sharing codes are used. Due to the limited number of cores used in our simulations (32), we evaluate BT-SN assuming only one symmetric node. In this way, the size of BT-SN is equal to the size of BT plus 1 bit to codify whether the home node or the symmetric node is being used in the codification.

As shown in Figure 3 (and discussed in the introduction of this work), the area overhead that the bit-vector sharing code entails does not scale with the number of cores. Obviously, the size of the bit-vector (in bits) increases linearly with the

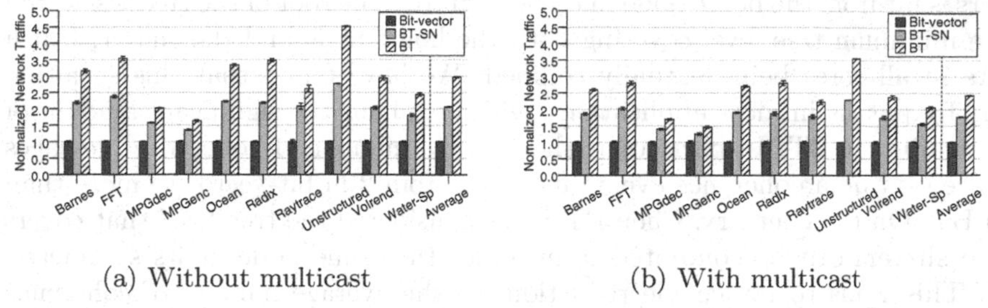

(a) Without multicast (b) With multicast

Fig. 4. Normalized network traffic for bit-vector, BT and BT-SN

number of cores. For this reason, the bit-vector could be a good option for a small number of cores. However, for 16 or more cores the increase in area that the bit-vector conveys makes it infeasible (the area overhead becomes almost 100% for the 64-core configuration). On the other hand, the size of BT and BT-SN barely increases with the number of cores. Moreover, the total number of bits needed by BT and BT-SN is very small in all cases ($\lceil \log_2 (\log_2 N + 1) \rceil$ bits and $\lceil \log_2 (\log_2 N + 1) \rceil + 1$ bits, respectively). In this way, the area overhead of BT and BT-SN is very low (less than 5% for the 256-core configuration) and keeps almost constant with the number of cores. This makes BT and BT-SN promising alternatives to bit-vector for future may-core CMPs, since besides introducing very small overheads in terms of area, they would allow to support families of CMPs with varying number of cores using the same tile structure (without requiring any modifications in the directory).

5.2 Impact on Network Traffic

Although compressed sharing codes can drastically reduce the size of the directory, their drawback is that they could increase the number of coherence messages as a consequence of the in-excess codification of the sharers that they perform. Increasing the number of coherence messages leads to more traffic being injected in the interconnection network of the CMP. Since previous works have identified the interconnection network as one of the most important elements of the CMP from the point of view of energy consumption (consuming almost 40% of the total energy budget in the Raw processor [16]), more traffic at the end means more energy.

Figure 4 shows the amount of network traffic that would be generated for bit-vector, BT and BT-SN for the 32-core CMP configuration assumed in this work. In particular, each bar plots the number of bytes transmitted through the interconnection network (the total number of bytes transmitted by all the switches) normalized with respect to the bit-vector case. We present results considering both a network with unicast support (a) and with multicast support (b).

As shown in Figure 4(a), the use of BT has severe impact on the amount of network traffic and degradations ranging from approximately 50% for *MPGenc* to 350% for *Unstructured* are found. The problem with BT is that when one of the sharers is far from the home node in the logical tree, the root of the tree is selected as the minimum tree level covering both the home node and the sharer, which results in all cores being actually codified. We have found that this situation occurs frequently in most applications, which explains the significant amount of extra traffic for BT. In particular, the average number of coherence messages that are sent on a coherence event[1] increases from 2 in bit-vector to more than 20 in BT. On the contrary, when BT-SN is considered the tree level that covers all the sharers can be computed from either the home node or its symmetric node. This leads to noticeable reductions in the average number of coherence messages (12 in BT-SN), which leads to important savings in network traffic when compared with BT. Unfortunately, BT-SN does not mitigate completely the extra traffic introduced by BT and degradations of approximately 100% on average are still observed. Again, when two or more cores, distant in the logical tree, share a memory block, the root of the tree would be codified by BT-SN.

Obviously, the provision of multicast support at the interconnection network level can alleviate the levels of extra traffic. More specifically, in Figure 4(b) we show the results obtained when we take advantage of multicast support for sending coherence messages (invalidations and cache-to-cache transfer commands). Efficient implementations of such kind of multicast support in on-chip networks have recently been proposed [7]. Unfortunately, using multicast support for also the response messages is not a trivial issue. So, in this work we assume that responses to coherence commands are unicast messages. As it can be seen, the use of multicast support is a step forward in achieving the network traffic levels obtained by bit-vector, and it is especially useful when BT is considered (average traffic overhead is reduced from 200% without multicast support to 150%). Anyway, the fact that multicast support is available just for the coherence commands and not for their associated responses limits its benefits.

5.3 Impact on Execution Time

The degradations previously reported in terms of network traffic finally translate into increases in terms of execution time. In Figure 5 we show how the use of BT and BT-SN impacts applications' execution times, considering an interconnection network with and without multicast support, (a) and (b) respectively. Again, all results have been normalized with respect to the bit-vector case.

As observed in Figure 5(a), the use of BT without multicast support has important consequences on performance. In particular, the execution time grows from less than 10% for *Barnes* and *Water-Sp* to more than 30% for Raytrace (19% on average). In general, the greater number of messages that are needed with BT to resolve every coherence event leads to longer cache miss latencies, and therefore, execution times. Obviously, the extent of the degradation in execution time will depend on the particular characteristics of each application (L1

[1] By coherence event we refer to a situation where the home node must use the sharing code to send coherence messages (invalidations or cache-to-cache transfer commands).

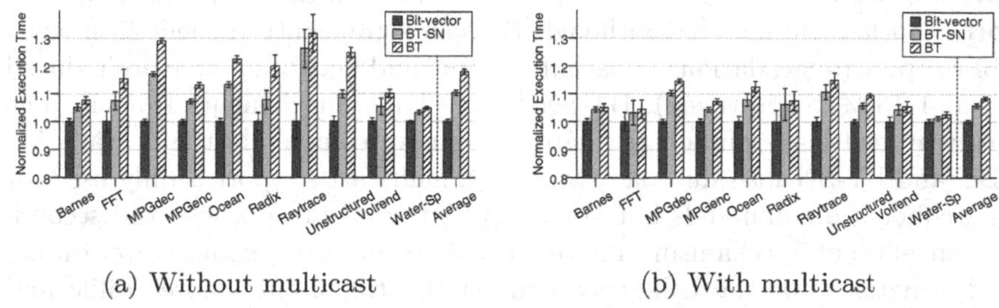

(a) Without multicast (b) With multicast

Fig. 5. Execution time for 32 cores

cache miss rate, average number of coherence messages per cache miss, kind of synchronization used, etc.). This is why there is no direct correlation between the amount of extra traffic reported in Figure 4(a) and the degradation in execution time shown in Figure 5(a). On the other hand, when BT-SN is used instead of BT, the average overhead in terms of execution time is reduced to a half (10%). In this case, significant reductions in execution time are observed for most applications. The exceptions are *Barnes* and *Water-Sp*, that hardly see their execution times reduced when BT-SN is used, even when significant savings in terms of network traffic were reported.

The effects of using multicast support with BT and BT-SN are analyzed in Figure 5(b). As before, multicast support has significant impact on execution time when BT is assumed. In this case, average degradation falls from 19% to less than 10%. Although all applications benefit from multicast support, *FFT*, *MPGdec*, *Radix*, *Raytrace* and *Unstructured* are the most affected (in all these cases performance degradation entailed by BT is reduced to more than a half). Finally, and as it was reported for network traffic, multicast support does not help much in reducing performance overhead when BT-SN is considered. In this case, what dominates cache miss latencies is the time taken to collect all responses to a coherence event, which is not optimized with the assumed multicast support.

6 Conclusions

The organization of the directory needed to maintain cache coherence will be a key design point in future many-core CMPs. In this work, we have analyzed the effects that the BT and BT-SN compressed sharing codes have on area, network traffic (as representative of the energy consumed in the interconnection network), and performance in the context of many-core chip-multiprocessors. In particular, we have found that although very area-efficient directories could be derived based on these two sharing codes (with area overheads of less than 5%), the degradations in terms of network traffic (200% for BT and 100% for BT-SN) as well as execution time (20% for BT and 10% for BT-SN) that they entail could preclude them from being employed in future many-core CMPs. Moreover, we have studied the case of having an interconnection network with multicast support, and have found that although BT can significantly benefit from such kind of support (degradations in execution time and network traffic are reduced to 8% and 150% respectively), BT-SN barely finds any benefits from it. The reasons why multicast support is unable to remove completely the degradation that BT and BT-SN introduce are two. First, multicast support is only used for sending coherence commands but not for collecting the responses. And second, even if an efficient mechanism able to provide combined responses were used, more destinations for the coherence commands still implies more traffic and longer cache miss latencies.

References

1. Borkar, S.: Thousand core chips: A technology perspective. In: 44th Annual Design Automation Conference, pp. 746–749 (2007)
2. Taylor, M.B., Kim, J., Miller, J., et al.: The raw microprocessor: A computational fabric for software circuits and general purpose programs. IEEE Micro 22, 25–35 (2002)
3. Zhang, M., Asanović, K.: Victim replication: Maximizing capacity while hiding wire delay in tiled chip multiprocessors. In: 32nd Int'l Symp. on Computer Architecture (ISCA), pp. 336–345 (2005)
4. Intel Res.: Single-chip Cloud Computer (2010), http://techresearch.intel.com/articles/Tera-Scale/1826.htm
5. Leverich, J., Arakida, H., Solomatnikov, A., Firoozshahian, A., Horowitz, M., Kozyrakis, C.: Comparing memory systems for chip multiprocessors. In: 34th Int'l Symp. on Computer Architecture (ISCA), pp. 358–368 (2007)
6. Acacio, M.E., González, J., García, J.M., Duato, J.: A new scalable directory architecture for large-scale multiprocessors. In: 7th Int'l Symp. on High-Performance Computer Architecture (HPCA), pp. 97–106 (2001)
7. Rodrigo, S., Flich, J., Duato, J., Hummel, M.: Efficient unicast and multicast support for CMPs. In: 41st IEEE/ACM Int'l Symp. on Microarchitecture (MICRO), pp. 364–375 (2008)
8. Kim, C., Burger, D., Keckler, S.W.: An adaptive, non-uniform cache structure for wire-delay dominated on-chip caches. In: 10th Int. Conf. on Architectural Support for Programming Language and Operating Systems (ASPLOS), pp. 211–222 (2002)
9. Magnusson, P.S., Christensson, M., Eskilson, J., et al.: Simics: A full system simulation platform. IEEE Computer 35, 50–58 (2002)
10. Martin, M.M., Sorin, D.J., Beckmann, B.M., et al.: Multifacet's general execution-driven multiprocessor simulator (GEMS) toolset. Computer Architecture News 33, 92–99 (2005)
11. Puente, V., Gregorio, J.A., Beivide, R.: SICOSYS: An integrated framework for studying interconnection network in multiprocessor systems. In: 10th Euromicro Workshop on Parallel, Distributed and Network-based Processing, pp. 15–22 (2002)
12. Thoziyoor, S., Muralimanohar, N., Ahn, J.H., Jouppi, N.P.: CACTI 5.1. Technical Report HPL-2008-20, HP Labs (2008)
13. Horel, T., Lauterbach, G.: UltraSPARC-III: Designing third-generation 64-bit performance. IEEE Micro 19, 73–85 (1999)

14. Woo, S.C., Ohara, M., Torrie, E., Singh, J.P., Gupta, A.: The SPLASH-2 programs: Characterization and methodological considerations. In: 22nd Int'l Symp. on Computer Architecture (ISCA), pp. 24–36 (1995)
15. Li, M.L., Sasanka, R., Adve, S.V., Chen, Y.K., Debes, E.: The ALPBench benchmark suite for complex multimedia applications. In: Int'l Symp. on Workload Characterization, pp. 34–45 (2005)
16. Wang, H., Peh, L.S., Malik, S.: Power-driven design of router microarchitectures in on-chip networks. In: 36th IEEE/ACM Int'l Symp. on Microarchitecture (MICRO), pp. 105–111 (2003)

A Work Stealing Scheduler for Parallel Loops on Shared Cache Multicores

Marc Tchiboukdjian, Vincent Danjean, Thierry Gautier*, Fabien Le Mentec, and Bruno Raffin

MOAIS Project, INRIA- LIG
{marc.tchiboukdjian,vincent.danjean,fabien.lementec,bruno.raffin}@imag.fr, thierry.gautier@inrialpes.fr

Abstract. Reordering instructions and data layout can bring significant performance improvement for memory bounded applications. Parallelizing such applications requires a careful design of the algorithm in order to keep the locality of the sequential execution. In this paper, we aim at finding a good parallelization of memory bounded applications on multicore that preserves the advantage of a shared cache. We focus on sequential applications with iteration through a sequence of memory references. Our solution relies on a work stealing scheduler combined with a dynamic sliding window that constrains cores sharing the same cache to process data close in memory. This parallel algorithm induces the same number of cache misses as the sequential algorithm at the expense of an increased number of synchronizations. Experiments with a memory bounded application confirm that core collaboration for shared cache access can bring significant performance improvements despite the incurred synchronization costs.

1 Introduction

Many applications in scientific computing are memory bounded. Favoring the locality of access patterns through data and computation reordering can bring significant performance benefits. When designing parallel algorithms, one must be extra careful not to lose the locality of the sequential application, which is the key for good performance. In most last generation multicores, the last level of cache is shared among all cores of the chip. For instance the Intel Nehalem, the AMD Phenom and Opteron (only for the quadcores and hexacores) and the IBM Power7 all have a shared L_3 cache.

In this paper, we focus on one specific aspect of the parallelization of memory bounded applications: how to adapt the scheduling to take advantage of the shared caches of multicore processors. The goal is to propose a scheduling algorithm that improves performance by reducing cache misses, compared to parallel algorithms that do not take into account the shared cache amongst several cores.

* Part of this work was done while the third author was visiting the ArTeCS group of the University Complutense, Madrid, Spain.

M.R. Guarracino et al. (Eds.): Euro-Par 2010 Workshops, LNCS 6586, pp. 99–107, 2011.
© Springer-Verlag Berlin Heidelberg 2011

We propose to have cores working on independent but close (regarding the memory layout) data sets that can all fit in the shared cache. If a core needs a data that is not in its data set, there is a good chance it will find it in the data set loaded in the cache by one of its neighbors, thus saving cache misses. The algorithm behaves as if each core would benefit from a full-size private cache, at the price of a few extra synchronizations required to ensure a proper collaboration between cores.

This paper focuses on algorithms that take an input sequence to produce an output sequence of results. Such algorithms encompass many of the C++ Standard Template Library (STL) functions like `for_each` or `transform`. Moreover, many parallel libraries such as Intel TBB or the GNU STL parallel mode provide parallel implementations of the STL. Thus providing shared cache aware parallelizations of these algorithms can improve performance of many applications.

We provide a cache constraint that parallel algorithms should respect to induce no more cache misses than the sequential algorithms. We present two new algorithms respecting this cache constraint and two implementations, one based on PThread and the other one based on work-stealing allowing efficient dynamic load balancing. We also implement those new algorithms with the parallel library TBB and the GNU parallel STL and compare them with our implementations.

2 Scheduling for Efficient Shared Cache Usage

2.1 Window Algorithms for Sequence Processing

We consider algorithms that take an input sequence $i_1, i_2, \ldots, i_n$ (different input elements can share some data) and a function *op* to be applied on all elements of the input producing an output sequence $o_1, o_2, \ldots, o_{n'}$. Notice that treating one element may produce a different number of elements in the output sequence. Most STL algorithms are variations over this model. The sequential algorithm processes the sequence in order from i_1 to i_n. We assume that the sequential algorithm already performs well with respect to temporal locality of data accesses. Data processed closely in the sequential execution are also close in memory. We focus on the case where all elements of the sequence can be processed in parallel.

We introduce two parallel algorithms to process such a sequence in parallel. These two algorithms are parameterized by m, the maximum distance between the threads. In the first one, denoted *static-window*, the sequence is first divided into n/m chunks of m contiguous elements. Then, each chunk is processed in parallel by the p processors sharing the same cache. Several strategies can be used to parallelize the processing of each chunk. The m elements could be statically partitioned into p groups of m/p elements, one per processor, or a work-stealing scheme can be used to dynamically balance the load. The second parallel algorithm, denoted *sliding-window*, is a relaxed version of the *static-window* algorithm. At the beginning of the algorithm, the first m elements of the sequence are ready and can be processed in any order. Each time the first element i_k not yet processed in the sequence is treated by a processor, it enables the element i_{k+m} at the end of a window of size m. These two algorithms will be compared with an algorithm denoted *no-window* that do not respect the cache constraint. All the elements of the sequence can be processed in any order. This algorithm induces more cache misses than the sequential algorithm and the window algorithms, but it requires fewer synchronizations.

2.2 Cache Performance of Window Algorithms

The re-use distance captures the temporal locality of a program [1]. Let consider a series of memory references $(x_k)_{k \geq 0}$. When a reference x_k access an element for the first time, the re-use distance of x_k is infinite. If the element has been previously accessed, $x_{k'} = x_k$ with $k' > k$, the re-use distance of $x_{k'}$ is equal to the number of distinct elements accessed between these two references x_k and $x_{k'}$. Let h_d denote the number of memory references with a re-use distance d. The number of cache misses of a fully associative LRU cache of size C is equal to $M_{\text{seq}} = \sum_{d=C+1}^{\infty} h_d$. We can extend this definition to sequence processing algorithms: if processing i_k and $i_{k'}$ uses similar data, the re-use distance is $k' - k$.

We consider now p processors sharing the same cache that process the sequence in parallel in distant places like the *no-window* algorithm. As we assumed the sequence has good temporal locality, elements far-away in the sequence use distinct data. In this case, the re-use distance is multiplied by p as to each access of one processor corresponds $p - 1$ accesses of the others to distinct elements. Thus, the number of cache misses is $M_{\text{no-win}} = \sum_{d=C+1}^{\infty} h_{d/p} \approx \sum_{d=C/p+1}^{\infty} h_d$. The *no-window* algorithm induces as many cache misses as the sequential algorithm with a cache p times smaller. We now restrain the processors to work on elements at distance less than m like in the window algorithms. Let $r(m)$ be the maximum number of distinct memory references when processing $m - 1$ consecutive elements of the input sequence. In the worst case, when processing element i_k, all elements $i_{k+1}, \ldots, i_{k+m-1}$ have already been processed accessing at most $r(m)$ additional distinct elements compared to the sequential order. Thus the re-use distance is increased by at most $r(m)$. The number of cache misses is $M_{\text{window}} \leq \sum_{d=C+1}^{\infty} h_{d-r(m)} = M_{\text{seq}} + \sum_{d=C+1-r(m)}^{C} h_d$. As we assumed the sequence has good temporal locality, $r(m)$ is small compared to m and h_d is small for large d. Therefore $\sum_{d=C+1-r(m)}^{C} h_d$ is small and the window algorithms induce approximately the same number of cache misses as the sequential algorithm.

2.3 PThread Parallelization of Window Algorithms

We present here the implementation of the *no-window* and *static-window* algorithms using PThreads. The PThread implementation allows a fine grain control on synchronizations with very little overhead.

For the *no-window* algorithm, the sequence is statically divided into p groups. Each group is assigned to one thread bound to one processor and all threads synchronize at the end of the computation. For the *static-window* algorithm, the sequence is first divided into chunks of size m. Then each chunk is statically divided into p groups and all threads synchronize at the end of each chunk before

```
typedef struct {
  InputIterator        ibeg;
  InputIterator        iend;
  OutputIterator       obeg;
  size_t               osize;
} Work_t ;

void dowork(...) {
  complete_work:
    while (iend != ibeg) {
      kaapi_stealpoint(..., &splitter);
      for(i=0; i<grain; ++i, ++ibeg)
        op(ibeg, obeg, &osize);
      kaapi_preemptpoint(..., &reducer);
    }
    if ( kaapi_preempt_next_thief(...) )
      goto complete_work ;
} // no more work -> become a thief

void reducer(Work_t *victim, Work_t *thief) {
  memmove( victim->obeg, thief->obeg,
           thief->osize );
  victim->osize += thief->osize;
  victim->ibeg   = thief->ibeg;
  victim->iend   = thief->iend;
} // victim -> dowork / thief -> try to steal
```

```
void splitter( Work_t *victim, int count,
               kaapi_request_t* request ) {
  int i = 0;
  size_t size = victim->iend - victim->ibeg;
  size_t bloc = size / (1+count);
  InputIterator local_end = victim->iend;
  Work_t *thief;

  if (size < gain)
    return;
  while (count >0) {
    if (kaapi_request_ok(&request[i])) {
      thief->iend  = local_end;
      thief->ibeg  = local_end - bloc;
      thief->obeg  = intermediate_buffer;
      thief->osize = 0;
      local_end   -= bloc;
      kaapi_request_reply_ok(thief,
                             &request[i]);
      --count;
    }
    ++i;
  }
  victim->iend  = local_end;
} // victim and thieves -> dowork
```

Fig. 1. C implementation of the adaptive *no-window* algorithm using the KAAPI API

starting to compute the next one. Each synchronization is implemented with a `pthread_barrier`. Threads wait at the barrier and are released when all of them have reached the barrier. Although we expect the threads in the *static-window* algorithm to spend more time waiting for other threads to finish their work, the reduction of cache misses should compensate this extra synchronization cost. The *sliding-window* algorithm has not been implemented in PThread because it would require a very complex code. We present in the next section a work-stealing framework allowing to easily implement all these algorithms.

3 Work-Stealing Window Algorithms with Kaapi

In this section, we present the low level API of KAAPI [2] and detail the implementation of the windows algorithms.

3.1 Kaapi Overview

KAAPI is a programming framework for parallel computing using work-stealing. At the initialization of a KAAPI program, the middleware creates and binds one thread on each processor of the machine. All non-idle threads process work by executing a sequential algorithm (`dowork` in fig. 1). All idle threads, the thieves, send work requests to randomly selected victims. To allow other threads to steal part of its work, a non-idle thread must regularly check if it received work requests using the function `kaapi_stealpoint`. At the reception of `count` work requests, a `splitter` is called and divides the work into `count+1` well-balanced pieces, one for each of the thieves and one for the victim.

When a previously stolen thread runs out of work, it can decide to preempt its thieves with the `kaapi_preempt_next_thief` call. For each thief, the victim merges part of the work processed by the thief using the `reducer` function and takes back the remaining work. The preemption can reduce the overhead of storing elements of the output sequence in an intermediate buffer when the final place of an output element is not known in advance. To allow preemption, each thread regularly checks for preemption requests using the function `kaapi_preemptpoint`.

To amortize the calls to the KAAPI library, each thread should process several units of work between these calls. This number is called the *grain* of the algorithm. In particular, a victim thread do not answer positively to a work request when it has less than *grain* units of work.

Compared to classical WS implementations, tasks (`Work_t`) are only created when a steal occurs which reduces the overhead of the parallel algorithm compared to the sequential one [3]. Moreover, the steal requests are treated by the victim and not by the thieves themselves. Although the victim has to stop working to process these requests, synchronization costs are reduced. Indeed, instead of using high-level synchronization functions (mutexes, etc.) or even costly atomic assembly instructions (compare and swap, etc.), the thieves and the victim can communicate by using standard memory writes followed by memory barriers, so no memory bus locking is required. Additionally, the `splitter` function knows the number `count` of thieves that are trying to steal work to the same victim. Therefore, it permits a better balance of the workload. This feature is unique to KAAPI when compared to other tools having a work-stealing scheduler.

3.2 Work-Stealing Algorithm for Standard (*no-window*) Processing

It is straightforward to implement the *no-window* algorithm using KAAPI. The work owned by a thread is described in a structure by four variables: `ibeg` and `iend` represents the range of elements to process in the input sequence, `obeg` is an iterator on the output sequence and `osize` is the number of elements written on the output. At the beginning of the computation, a unique thread possesses the whole work: `ibeg=0` and `iend=n`. Each thread processes its assigned elements in a loop. Code of Fig. 1 shows the main points of the actual implementation.

3.3 Work-Stealing Window Algorithms

The *static-window* algorithm is very similar to the *no-window* algorithm of the previous section. The first thread owning the total work has a specific status, it is the *master* of the window. Only the master thread has knowledge of the remaining work outside the m-size window. When all elements of a window have been processed, the master enables the processing of the new window by updating its input iterators `ibeg = iend` and `iend += m`. This way, when idle threads request work to the master thread, the stolen work is close in the input sequence. Moreover, all threads always work on elements at distance at most m.

The *sliding-window* algorithm is a little bit more complex. In addition to the previous iterators, the master also maintains `ilast` an iterator on the first

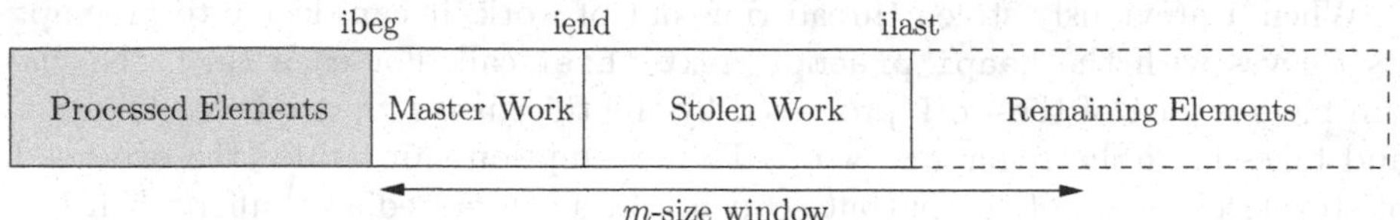

Fig. 2. Decomposition of the input sequence in the *sliding-window* algorithm

element after the stolen work in the input sequence (see Fig. 2). When the master does not receive any work request, then `iend == ilast == ibeg+m`. When the master receives work requests, it can choose to give work on both sides of the stolen work. Distributing work in the interval `[ibeg,iend]` corresponds to the previous algorithm. The master thread can also choose to distribute work close to the end of the window, in the interval `[ilast,ibeg+m]`.

4 Experiments

We base our experiments on a common scientific visualization filter: extracting an isosurface in an unstructured mesh using the marching tetrahedra (MT) algorithm [4].

We first calibrate the grain for the work-stealing implementation and the window size m for the window algorithms. Then, we compare the KAAPI framework with other parallel libraries on a central part of the MT algorithm which can be written as a `for_each`. Finally we compare the *no-window*, *static-window* and *sliding-window* algorithms implementing the whole MT.

All the measures reported are averaged over 20 runs and are very stable. The numbers of cache misses are obtained with PAPI [5]. Only last level cache misses are reported as the lower level cache misses are the same for all algorithms. Two different multicores are used, a quadcore Intel Xeon Nehalem E5540 at 2.4Ghz with a shared 8MB L_3 cache and a dualcore AMD Opteron 875 at 2.2Ghz with two 1MB L_2 private caches. If the window algorithms reduce the number of cache misses on the Nehalem but not on the Opteron, one can conclude that this is due to the shared cache.

4.1 Calibrating the Window Algorithms

Fig. 3(left) shows the number of L_3 cache misses for the *static-window* algorithm compared to the sequential algorithm and the *no-window* algorithm. The *static-window* algorithm is very close to the sequential algorithm for window sizes less than 2^{20}. It does not exactly match the sequential performance due to additional `reduce` operations for managing the output sequence in parallel. With bigger windows, L_3 misses increase and tend to the *no-window* algorithm. For the remaining experiments, we set $m = 2^{19}$.

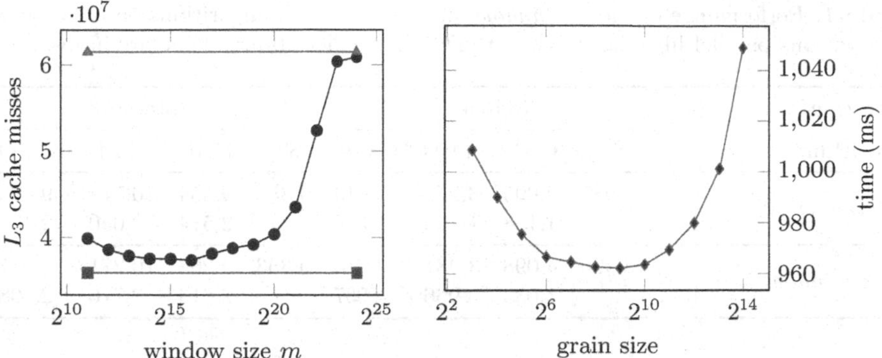

Fig. 3. (Left) Number of L_3 cache misses for the PThread implementation of the *static-window* algorithm —●— for various window sizes compared to the sequential algorithm —■— and the *no-window* —▲— algorithm. (Right) Parallel time for the KAAPI implementation of the *static-window* algorithm —◆— with various grain sizes. (Both) All parallel algorithms use the 4 cores of the Nehalem processor.

Fig. 3(right) shows the parallel time of the *static-window* algorithm with the KAAPI implementation for various grain sizes. Performance does not vary much, less than 10% on the tested grains. For small grains, the overhead of the KAAPI library becomes significant. For bigger grains, the load balancing is less efficient. For the remaining experiments, we choose a grain size of 128. We can notice that the KAAPI library allows very fine grain parallelism: processing 128 elements takes approximately 3μs on the Nehalem processor.

4.2 Comparison of Parallel Libraries on `for_each`

Table 1 compares KAAPI with the GNU parallel library (from gcc 4.3) (denoted GNU) and Intel TBB (v2.1) on a `for_each` used to implement a central sub-part of the MT algorithm. The GNU parallel library uses the best scheduler (parallel balanced). TBB uses the auto partitioner with a grain size of 128. TBB is faster than GNU on Nehalem and it is the other way around on Opteron. KAAPI shows the best performance on both processors. This can be explained by the cost of the synchronization primitives used: POSIX locks for GNU, compare and swap for TBB and atomic writes followed by memory barriers for KAAPI.

4.3 Performance of the Window Algorithms

We now compare the performance of the window algorithms. Table 1 shows that the *static-window* algorithm improves over the *no-window* algorithm for all libraries on the Nehalem processor. However, on the Opteron with only private caches, performances are in favor of the *no-window* algorithm. This was expected as the Opteron has only private caches and the *no-window* algorithm has less synchronizations. We can conclude that the difference observed on Nehalem is indeed due to the shared cache.

Table 1. Performance of the *no-window* and *static-window* algorithms on a `for_each` with various parallel libraries. GNU is the GNU parallel library. Time are in ms.

Time (ms)		Nehalem				Opteron			
Algorithms	#Cores	STL	GNU	TBB	KAAPI	STL	GNU	TBB	KAAPI
no-window	1	3,987	4,095	3,975	4,013	9,352	9,154	10,514	9,400
	4		1,158	1,106	1,069		2,514	2,680	2,431
static-window	1	3,990	4,098	3,981	4,016	9,353	9,208	10,271	9,411
	4		1,033	966	937		2,613	2,776	2,598

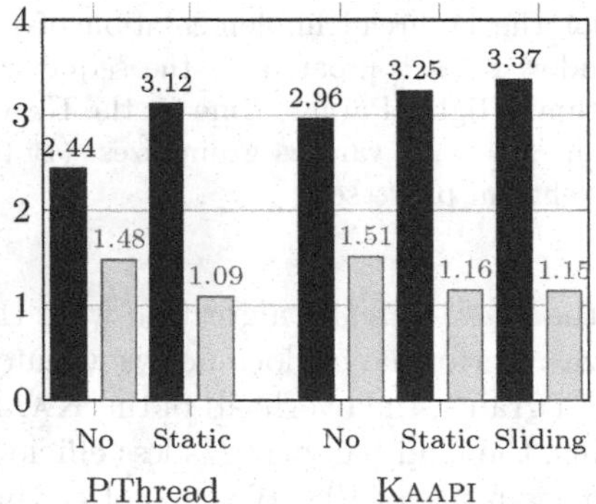

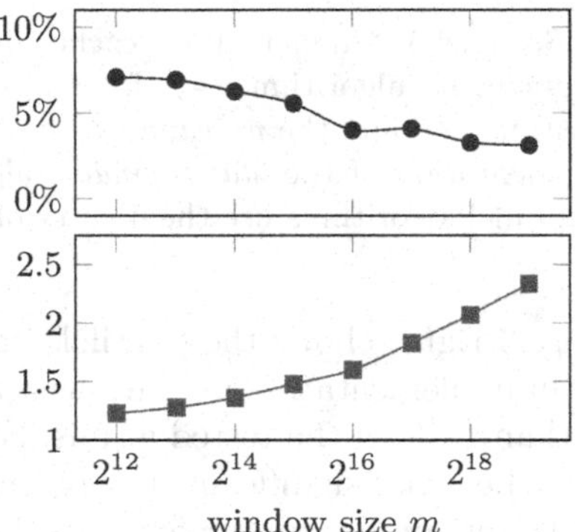

Fig. 4. (Left) Speedup ▬ and ratio of increased cache misses ▭ over the sequential algorithm for the *no-window*, *static-window* and *sliding-window* algorithms with PThread and KAAPI implementations. (Right) Speedup —●— and ratio of saved steal operations —■— for the *sliding-window* algorithm over the *static-window* algorithm with the KAAPI implementation. (Both) All algorithms run on the 4 cores of the Nehalem.

Fig. 4(left) presents speedup of all algorithms and ratio of cache misses compared to the sequential algorithm. The *no-window* versions induces 50% more cache misses whereas the window versions only 13% more. The window versions are all faster compared to the *no-window* versions. Work stealing implementations with KAAPI improves over the static partitioning of the PThread implementations. The *sliding-window* shows the best performance. Fig. 4(right) focus on the comparison of the *sliding-window* and *static-window* algorithms. Due to additional parallelism, the number of steal operations are greatly reduced in the *sliding-window* algorithm (up to 2.5 time less) leading to a 5% additional gain.

5 Conclusions

Previous experimental approaches have shown the interest of efficient cache sharing usage, on a recent benchmark [6] and on data mining applications [7].

Many parallel schemes have been proposed to achieve good load balancing for isosurface extraction [8]. However, none of these techniques take into account the shared cache of multicore processors. Optimization of sequential locality for mesh applications has been studied through mesh layout optimization [9].

The algorithms for parallel sequence processing proposed in this paper focus on exploiting the shared cache of last generation multicores. Experiments confirm that these techniques increase performances by 10% to 30%.

References

1. Cascaval, C., Padua, D.A.: Estimating cache misses and locality using stack distances. In: Proc. of ICS (2003)
2. Gautier, T., Besseron, X., Pigeon, L.: KAAPI: A thread scheduling runtime system for data flow computations on cluster of multi-processors. In: PASCO (2007)
3. Traoré, D., Roch, J.L., Maillard, N., Gautier, T., Bernard, J.: Deque-free work-optimal parallel STL algorithms. In: Luque, E., Margalef, T., Benítez, D. (eds.) Euro-Par 2008. LNCS, vol. 5168, pp. 887–897. Springer, Heidelberg (2008)
4. Schroeder, W., Martin, K., Lorensen, B.: The Visualization Toolkit, An Object-Oriented Approach To 3D Graphics, 3rd edn. Kitware Inc. (2004)
5. Browne, S., Dongarra, J., Garner, N., Ho, G., Mucci, P.: A portable programming interface for performance evaluation on modern processors. In: The International Journal of High Performance Computing Applications, vol. 14 (2000)
6. Zhang, E.Z., Jiang, Y., Shen, X.: Does cache sharing on modern CMP matter to the performance of contemporary multithreaded programs? In: PPoPP (2010)
7. Jaleel, A., Mattina, M., Jacob, B.: Last level cache (LLC) performance of data mining workloads on a CMP. In: HPCA (2006)
8. Zhang, H., Newman, T.S., Zhang, X.: Case study of multithreaded in-core isosurface extraction algorithms. In: EGPGV (2004)
9. Tchiboukdjian, M., Danjean, V., Raffin, B.: Binary mesh partitioning for cache-efficient visualization. TVCG 16(5), 815–828 (2010)

Resource-Agnostic Programming for Many-Core Microgrids*

Thomas A.M. Bernard, Clemens Grelck, Michael A. Hicks, Chris R. Jesshope, and Raphael Poss

University of Amsterdam, Informatics Institute, Netherlands
{t.bernard,c.grelck,m.a.hicks,c.r.jesshope,r.c.poss}@uva.nl

Abstract. Many-core architectures are a commercial reality, but programming them efficiently is still a challenge, especially if the mix is heterogeneous. Here granularity must be addressed, i.e. when to make use of concurrency resources and when not to. We have designed a data-driven, fine-grained concurrent execution model (SVP) that captures concurrency in a resource-agnostic way. Our approach separates the concern of describing a concurrent computation from its mapping and scheduling. We have implemented this model as a novel many-core architecture programmed with a language called μTC. In this paper we demonstrate how we achieve our goal of resource-agnostic programming on this target, where heterogeneity is exposed as arbitrarily sized clusters of cores.

Keywords: Concurrent execution model, many core architecture, resource-agnostic parallel programming.

1 Introduction

Although a mainstream task today, programming many-core architectures is still difficult [6]. Concurrency must be exposed, and often it is also explicitly managed [9]. For example, low-level constructs must be carefully assembled to map computations to hardware threads and achieve synchronisation without introducing deadlocks, livelocks, race conditions, etc. From a performance perspective, any overhead associated with concurrency creation and synchronisation must be amortised with a computation of a sufficient granularity. The difficulty of the latter is under-estimated and in this paper we argue that this mapping task is too ill-defined statically and too complex to remain the programmer's responsibility. With widely varying resource characteristics, generality is normally discarded in favour of performance on a given target, requiring a full development cycle each time the concurrency granularity evolves.

We have addressed these issues in our work on *SVP* (for Self-adaptive Virtual Processor [2]), which combines fine-grained threads with both barrier and

* This work is supported by the European Union through the Apple-CORE project, grant no. FP7-ICT-215216.

M.R. Guarracino et al. (Eds.): Euro-Par 2010 Workshops, LNCS 6586, pp. 109–116, 2011.
© Springer-Verlag Berlin Heidelberg 2011

dataflow synchronisation. Concurrency is created hierarchically and dependencies are captured explicitly. Hierarchical composition aims to capture concurrency at all granularities, without the need to explicitly *manage* it. Threads are not mapped to processing resources until run-time and the concurrency exploited depends only on the resources made available dynamically. Dependencies are captured using dataflow synchronisers, and threads are only scheduled for execution when they have data to proceed. In this way, we automate thread scheduling and support asynchrony in operations.

SVP's ability to define concurrency hierarchically and its data-driven scheduling brings it close to Cilk [4] and the DDM architecture [10]. SVP differs from DDM mainly in that synchronisation is implemented in registers instead of cache, and that yet unsatisfied dependencies cause threads to suspend.

In the context of this paper, where SVP is implemented in a processor's ISA [5], we have very efficient concurrency creation and synchronisation. Setting up a new family of threads only costs a few processor cycles, regardless of the number of threads. The latency of actually creating a large number of threads can be tolerated through asynchronous completion of instruction. The same holds for other long-latency instructions such as loads from a distributed shared memory. The mapping of threads to a cluster of cores in our *Microgrid* hybrid dataflow chip architecture is fully automatic. Compiled code can express more concurrency than is available in a cluster. Granularity mismatches are resolved by automatically switching to sequential execution when hardware thread slots are exhausted. Hence, the minimal requirement for any SVP program is a single thread slot, which implies pure sequential execution, even though the code is expressed concurrently. It is through this technique and the latency tolerance that we achieve resource-agnostic code with predictable performance.

The main contribution of this paper is that we show simply implemented, resource agnostic SVP programs that adapt automatically to the concurrency effectively available in hardware and can achieve extremely high execution efficiency. We also show that we can predict the performance of these programs based on simple throughput calculations even in the presence of non-deterministic instruction execution times. This demonstrates the effectiveness of the self-scheduling supported by SVP. In other words, we promote our research goal:

"Implement once, compile once, run anywhere."

2 The SVP Concurrency Model and Its Implementation

In SVP programs *create* multiple threads at once as statically homogeneous, but dynamically heterogeneous *families*. The parent thread can then perform a barrier wait on termination of a named family using a *sync* action. This fork-join pattern captures concurrency hierarchically, from software component composition down to inner loops. A family is characterised by its index sequence, a thread function and the definition of unidirectional dataflow channels from, to and within the family. Channels are I-structures [1], *i.e.* blocking reads and single non-blocking writes.

We have built an implementation of SVP into ISA extensions of a novel chip architecture called the *Microgrid*, described in more details in [5]. In this hybrid dataflow architecture, SVP channels are mapped onto the cores' registers. Dependencies between threads mapped to the same core share the same physical registers to allow fast communication. With threads spread over different cores, communication is induced automatically upon register access. The latter is still a low-latency operation since constraints on dependency patterns ensure that communicating cores are adjacent on chip. Implementing I-structures on the registers also enforces scheduling dependencies between consumers and producers. Hence, long-latency operations may be allowed to complete asynchronously giving out-of-order completion on instructions with non-deterministic delay. Examples include memory operations, floating point operations (with FPU sharing between cores) and barrier synchronisation on termination of a family.

Also, the number of active threads per core is constrained by a block size specified for each family or by exhaustion of thread contexts. Additional expressed concurrency is then scheduled by reusing thread contexts non-preemptively. Deadlock freedom is guaranteed by restricting communication to forward-only dependency chains. The dataflow scheduling, in combination with a large number of hardware threads per core, provide latency tolerance and high pipeline utilisation. Another key characteristic of SVP is the separation of concerns between the program and its scheduling onto computing nodes. Space scheduling is achieved by binding a bundle of processors, called a *place*, to a family upon its creation. This can happen at any concurrency nesting level in the program by dynamic arbitration. On the Microgrid, places are clusters of cores implementing an SVP run-time system in hardware.

The Microgrid is targeted by a system language μTC [8] and a compiler that maps this code to the Microgrid [3]. μTC is not intended as an end-user language; work is ongoing to target μTC from a data-parallel functional language [7] and a parallelising C compiler [11].

3 Performance Model and Results

Our aim in this paper is to show how we can obtain deterministic performance figures, even though the code is compiled from naive μTC code, with no knowledge of the target. In order to analyse the performance, we need to understand the constraints on performance. For this we define two measures of arithmetic intensity (AI). The first AI_1 is the ratio of floating point operations to instructions issued. For a given kernel that is not I/O bound, this limits the FP performance. For P cores at 1 GHz, the peak performance we can expect therefore is $P \times AI_1$, the ideal case of full pipeline utilisation (one apparent cycle per operation). In some circumstances, we know that execution is constrained by dependencies between floating point operations, so we modify AI_1 to take this into account giving an effective intensity AI_1'. The second measure of arithmetic intensity is the ratio of FP operations to I/O operations, AI_2 FLOPs/byte. I/O bandwidth IO is usually measured at the chip boundary (25.6GB/s), unless we can identify

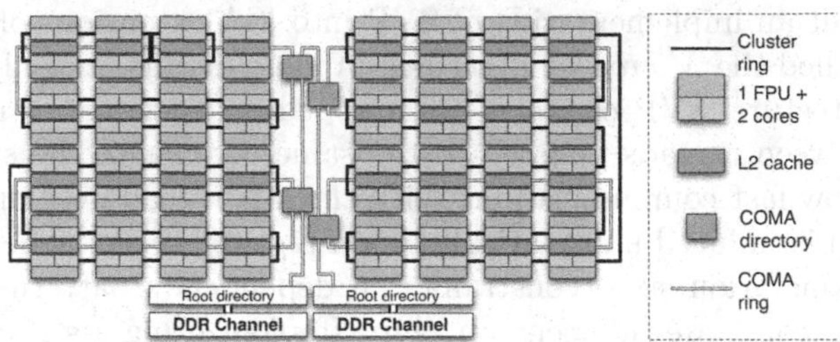

Fig. 1. Functional diagram of a 128 core Microgrid. Each pair of two cores shares 1 FPU with separate *add*, *mul*, *div* and *sqrt* pipelines. Each core supports up to 256 threads in 16 families using up to 1024 integer and 512 floating-point registers. On-chip memory consists of 32 L2 caches of 32KB each, one L2 cache per four cores. There are 4 rings of 8 L2 caches; the 4 directories are connected in a top-level ring subordinated to a master directory. Two DDR3-1600 channels connect the master directory to external storage. The on-chip memory network implements a Cache-Only Memory Architecture (COMA) protocol [12]: a cache line has no home location and migrates to the point of most recent use. Each DDR channel provides 1600 million 64-bit transfers/s, *i.e.* a peak bandwidth of 25.6GB/s overall. Each COMA ring provides a total bandwidth of 64GB/s, shared among its participants. The bus between cores and L2 caches provides 64GB/s of bandwidth; the SVP cores are clocked at 1GHz.

bottlenecks on the COMA rings (64GB/s). These I/O bandwidths are independent of the number of cores used, so it also provides a hard performance limit. We can then combine these two intensities to obtain a *maximum performance envelope* for a given code and problem size. A program is either constrained by AI_1 if $P \times AI_1 \leq AI_2 \times IO$ or AI_2 when $P \times AI_1 \geq AI_2 \times IO$.

The results presented in this paper are produced using cycle-accurate emulation of a Microgrid chip (Figure 1) that implements SVP in the ISA. It assumes custom silicon with current technology [5]. It defines all states that would exist in a silicon implementation and captures cycle-by-cycle interactions in all pipeline stages. We have used realistic multi-ported memory structures, with queueing and arbitration where we have more channels than ports. We also simulate the timing of standard DDR3 channels.

3.1 Example: Parallel Reduction

The first example is the IP kernel from the Livermore suite, which computes the Euclidean norm of a vector. The μTC code is given in Figure 2. In a first experiment we only use the inner function 'ik3' to compute the Euclidean norm of an entire vector. 'ik3' compiles to 7 instructions including 2 FP operations. So $AI_1 = 2 \div 7 \approx 0.29$. However, every thread must wait for its predecessor to produce its result before reducing. The cost of communicating the result from thread to thread requires between 6 and 11 cycles per add depending on the scheduling of threads, with the difference representing the cost of waking up a waiting thread and getting it to the read stage of the pipeline, which may

```
typedef double flt;
/* Livermore loop 3: Inner product
   Q ← Σ_i Z_i × X_i */
thread LMK3_IP(shared flt Q, int N,
               flt Z[N], flt X[N])
{
   int P = get_ncores();
   create(DEFAULT; 0; P)
      redk3(Qr = 0, Z, X, N/P);
   sync();
   Q = Qr;
}
```

```
thread redk3(shared flt Q, flt*Z, flt *X, int sp)
{
   index ri;
   create(LOCAL; ri * span; (ri+1) * sp)
      ik3(Qr = 0, Z, X);
   sync();
   Q += Qr;
}
thread ik3(shared flt Q, flt*Z, flt *X) {
   index i;
   Q += Z[i]*X[i];
}
```

Fig. 2. Inner product in μTC using a parallel reduction. Entry point LMK3_IP creates a family at the *default* place, *i.e.* the entire cluster. The family contains P threads where P is the number of cores. Each thread runs 'redk3', identified by 'ri'. Each 'redk3' thread further creates one family of N/P threads running 'ik3'. The keyword 'LOCAL' hints that the concurrency be kept local relative to 'redk3', *i.e.* on the same core if 'redk3' is spread over multiple cores. The reduced sums trickle from the inner family to the entry point through dataflow channel Q.

be overlapped by other independent instructions in the pipeline. This implies $2 \div (7+11) \approx 0.11 \leq AI'_1 \leq 0.16 \approx 2 \div (7+6)$, *i.e.* an expected single core performance of 0.11 to 0.16 GFLOP/s. As shown in Figure 3 with P=1 we observe 0.12 to 0.15 GFLOP/s, in accordance with the envelope.

In a second experiment we exploit the associativity of addition for a two-level implementation (full code of Figure 2). The (dynamic) number of cores in the 'current place' is exposed to programs as a language primitive. The reduction is split in two stages: LMK3_IP creates a family of one thread per core, which performs a local reduction and then completes the reduction between cores. When the number of threads per core is significantly larger than the number of cores, the cost of the final reduction is small and the performance should scale linearly with the number of cores. Given the single core performance of ≈ 0.15 GFLOP/s we would expect a maximum performance of $0.15 \times 64 = 9.6$ GFLOP/s. However, for this code $AI_2 = 0.125$ FLOPs/byte and so performance would be memory limited to 3.2 GFLOP/s.

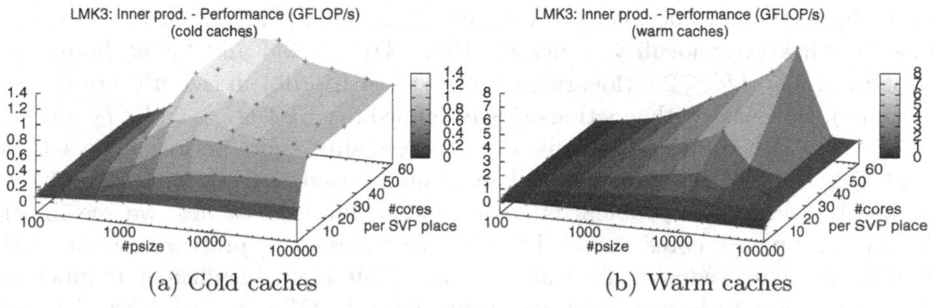

(a) Cold caches

(b) Warm caches

Fig. 3. IP performance, using N/P reduction. Working set: 16×#psize bytes.

We achieve only 1.4 GFLOP/s, dropping to 0.88 GFLOP/s, for cold caches with the largest problem size. This deviation occurs when the working set does not fit in the L2 caches, because then loads to memory must be interleaved with line evictions. Even though evictions do not require I/O bandwidth, they do consume COMA ring bandwidth. In the worst case a single load may evict a cache line where the loaded line is used only by one thread before being evicted again. A single 8 byte load could require as much as two 64-byte line transfers, *i.e.* a perceived bandwidth for loads of 4 GB/s rising to 32GB/s if all 8 words are used. This translates into a peak performance of between 0.5 and 4 GFLOP/s with $AI_2 = 0.125$ FLOPs/byte, when the caches become full. Note also, at a problem size of 20K on 64 cores, between 17 and 22% of the cycles required are for the sequential reduction, a large overhead and at a problem size of 100K, when this overhead is significantly smaller, only 1/6th of the problem fits in cache for up to 32 cores (1/3 for 64 cores).

With warm caches, this transition to on-chip bandwidth limited performance is delayed and more abrupt. For $P = 32$ the maximum in-cache problem size is N=16K and for $P = 64$, N=32K (ignoring code etc.). As would be expected for ring-limited performance, we see peak performance at N=10K and 20K resp. for these two cases. Any increase in problem size beyond this increases ring bandwidth to the same level as with cold caches.

3.2 Data-Parallel Code

We show here the behaviour of three data-parallel algorithms which exhibit different, yet typical communication patterns. Again, our μTC code is a straightforward parallelisation of the obvious sequential implementation and does not attempt any explicit mapping to hardware resources. The equation of state fragment (ESF, Livermore kernel 7) is a data parallel kernel with a high arithmetic intensity, $AI_1 = 0.48$. It has 7 local accesses to the same array data by different threads. If this locality can be exploited, then $AI_2 = 0.5$ FLOPs/byte from off-chip memory. Matrix-matrix product (MM, Livermore kernel 21) has significant non-local access to data, in that every result is a combination of all input data. MM is based on multiple inner products and hence $AI_1 = 0.29$. However, for cache bound problems and best case for problems that exceed the cache size, $AI_2 = 3$ FLOPs/byte from off-chip memory. Finally, FFT lies somewhere between these two extremes: it has a logarithmic number of stages that can exploit reuse but has poor locality of access. Here $AI_1 = 0.33$ and for cache-bound problems $1.6 \leq AI_2 \leq 2.9$ (logarithmic growth with problem size if there are no evictions). However, with evictions this is defined per FFT stage and $AI_2 = 0.21$.

For ESF, with sufficient threads, the observed single core performance is 0.43 GFLOP/s, *i.e.* 90% of the expected maximum based on AI_1 for this problem (4a). Also, while the problem is cache bound, for cold caches, we see linear speedup on up to 8 cores, 3.8 GFLOP/s. For 8 cores this problem size has 128 threads per core, reducing to 8 at 64 cores. This is an insufficient number of threads to tolerate latency and we obtain 6.6 GFLOP/s for 64 cores, 54% of the maximum limited by AI_2 (12.3 GFLOP/s). As the problem size is increased,

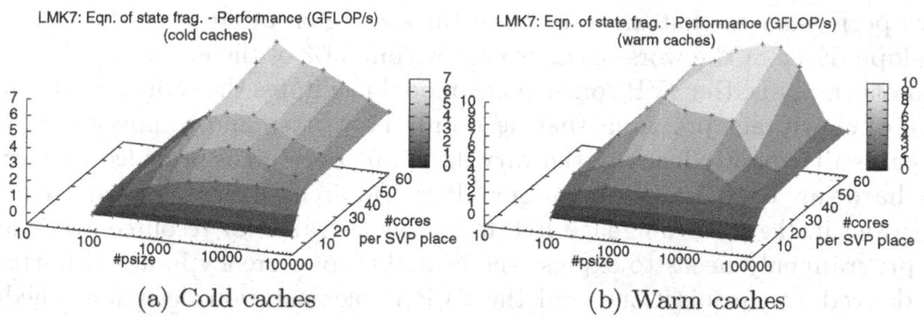

(a) Cold caches (b) Warm caches

Fig. 4. Performance of the ESF. Working set: 32×#psize bytes.

cache evictions limit effective I/O bandwidth to 12.3GB/s at the largest problem sizes, *i.e.* an AI_2 constraint of around 6 GFLOP/s. We see saturation at 67% of this limit for both warm and cold caches. With warm caches and smaller problem sizes, greater speedups can be achieved (4b) and we achieve 9.87 GFLOP/s or 80% of the AI_2 constrained limit for a cache bound problem.

MM naively multiplies 25×25 matrices by 25×N matrices using a local IP algorithm. As $AI_2 = 3.1$ FLOPs/byte, the I/O limit of 75 GFLOP/s exceeds the theoretical peak performance, namely 9.8 GFLOP/s. Our experiments show an actual peak of 8.7 GFLOP/s, or 88% of the maximum.

For FFT, the observed performance on one core is 0.23 GFLOP/s, or 69% of the AI_1 limit. When the number of cores and the problem size increase, the program becomes AI_2 constrained, as now every stage will require loads and evictions, giving an effective bandwidth of 12.3GB/s and as $AI_2 = 0.21$, an I/O constrained limit of 2.6 GFLOP/s. We observe 2.24 GFLOP/s, or 86% of this.

Extra benchmark results are illustrated in Figure 5.

Program	AI_1	AI_2	Bounded by	Max. envelope	Observed	Eff.
DNRM2 (BLAS)	0.14-0.22	0.375	AI_1	0.15-0.22	0.12-0.22	> 80%
MM	0.11-0.16	3.1	AI_1	P×0.16	P×0.13	> 85%
ESF	0.48	0.5	AI_1	P×0.48	P×0.43	> 85%
ESF (cache bound)	0.48	0.5	AI_2	2-6.15 (IO=4-12.3G/s)	2.7	> 40%
FFT1D	0.33	0.21	AI_1	P×0.33	P×0.23	> 65%
FFT1D (cache bound)	0.33	0.21	AI_2	0.84-2.6 (IO=4-12.3G/s)	2.24	> 85%

Fig. 5. Observed performance *vs.* performance envelope for various kernels

4 Conclusion

The results presented in this paper show high pipeline utilisation of single SVP places by naive implementations of computation kernels. Moreover, we are able to predict performance using a simple performance envelope defined by purely architectural bandwidth constraints. Provided we have sufficient threads we observe performances that are very close (in the region of 80%) to the expected envelope. Even in the worst cases we are within 50% of the envelope.

In other words, the SVP concurrency model facilitates the writing and generation of concurrent programs that need only be written and compiled once but yet can still exploit efficiently the varying parallel resources provided by particular hardware configurations. On our Microgrid architectures programs can be expressed in the μTC language free from the restraints of resource awareness; the program only needs to express the available concurrency in algorithms and the desired synchronisations, and the SVP implementation derives a schedule that achieves high resource utilisation automatically.

References

1. Arvind, Nikhil, R.S., Pingali, K.K.: I-Structures: Data Structures for Parallel Computing. ACM Trans. Program. Lang. Syst. 11(4), 598–632 (1989)
2. Bernard, T., Bousias, K., Guang, L., Jesshope, C.R., Lankamp, M., van Tol, M.W., Zhang, L.: A General Model of Concurrency and its Implementation as Many-core Dynamic RISC Processors. In: Proc. Intl. Conf. on Embedded Computer Systems: Architecture, Modeling and Simulation, SAMOS 2008, pp. 1–9 (2008)
3. Bernard, T., Grelck, C., Jesshope, C.: On the Compilation of a Language for General Concurrent Target Architectures. Parallel Processing Letters 20(1) (2010)
4. Blumofe, R.D., Joerg, C.F., Kuszmaul, B.C., Leiserson, C.E., et al.: Cilk: an efficient multithreaded runtime system. SIGPLAN Not. 30(8), 207–216 (1995)
5. Bousias, K., Guang, L., Jesshope, C., Lankamp, M.: Implementation and Evaluation of a Microthread Architecture. J. Systems Architecture 55(3), 149–161 (2009)
6. Chapman, B.M.: The Multicore Programming Challenge. In: Xu, M., Zhan, Y.-W., Cao, J., Liu, Y. (eds.) APPT 2007. LNCS, vol. 4847, pp. 3–3. Springer, Heidelberg (2007)
7. Grelck, C., Herhut, S., Jesshope, C., Joslin, C., Lankamp, M., Scholz, S.B., Shafarenko, A.: Compiling the Functional Data-Parallel Language SaC for Microgrids of Self-Adaptive Virtual Processors. In: 14th Workshop on Compilers for Parallel Computers (CPC 2009), Zürich, Switzerland (2009)
8. Jesshope, C.R.: muTC - An Intermediate Language for Programming Chip Multiprocessors. In: Asia-Pacific Computer Systems Architecture Conference (2006)
9. Kasim, H., March, V., Zhang, R., See, S.: Survey on Parallel Programming Model. In: Cao, J., Li, M., Wu, M.-Y., Chen, J. (eds.) NPC 2008. LNCS, vol. 5245, pp. 266–275. Springer, Heidelberg (2008)
10. Kyriacou, C., Evripidou, P., Trancoso, P.: Data-driven multithreading using conventional microprocessors. IEEE Trans. Parallel Distrib. Syst. 17(10) (2006)
11. Saougkos, D., Evgenidou, D., Manis, G.: Specifying loop transformations for C2μTC source-to-source compiler. In: 14th Workshop on Compilers for Parallel Computers (January 2009)
12. Zhang, L., Jesshope, C.: On-chip COMA cache-coherence protocol for microgrids of microthreaded cores. In: Bougé, L., Forsell, M., Träff, J.L., Streit, A., Ziegler, W., Alexander, M., Childs, S. (eds.) Euro-Par Workshops 2007. LNCS, vol. 4854, pp. 38–48. Springer, Heidelberg (2008)

Programming Heterogeneous Multicore Systems Using Threading Building Blocks*

George Russell[1], Paul Keir[2], Alastair F. Donaldson[3], Uwe Dolinsky[1], Andrew Richards[1], and Colin Riley[1]

[1] Codeplay Software Ltd., Edinburgh, UK
firstname@codeplay.com
[2] School of Computing Science, University of Glasgow, UK
pkeir@dcs.gla.ac.uk
[3] Computing Laboratory, University of Oxford, UK
alad@comlab.ox.ac.uk

Abstract. Intel's Threading Building Blocks (TBB) provide a high-level abstraction for expressing parallelism in applications without writing explicitly multi-threaded code. However, TBB is only available for shared-memory, homogeneous multicore processors. Codeplay's Offload C++ provides a single-source, POSIX threads-like approach to programming *heterogeneous* multicore devices where cores are equipped with private, local memories—code to move data between memory spaces is generated *automatically*. In this paper, we show that the strengths of TBB and Offload C++ can be combined, by implementing part of the TBB headers in Offload C++. This allows applications parallelised using TBB to run, without source-level modifications, across all the cores of the Cell BE processor. We present experimental results applying our method to a set of TBB programs. To our knowledge, this work marks the first demonstration of programs parallelised using TBB executing on a heterogeneous multicore architecture.

1 Introduction

Concurrent programming of multicore systems is widely acknowledged to be challenging. Our analysis is that a significant proportion of the challenge is due to the following:

Thread management: It is difficult to explicitly manage thread start-up and clear-down, inter-thread synchronization, mutual exclusion, work distribution and load balancing over a suitable number of threads to achieve scalability and performance.

Heterogeneity: Modern multicore systems, such as the Cell [1], or multicore PCs equipped with graphics processing units (GPUs) consist of cores with differing instruction sets, and contain multiple, non-coherent memory spaces. These heterogeneous features can facilitate high-performance, but require writing duplicate code for different types of cores, and orchestration of data-movement between memory spaces.

Threading Building Blocks (TBB) [2] is a multi-platform C++ library for programming homogeneous, shared-memory multicore processors using parallel loop and reduction operations, pipelines, and tasks. These constructs allow the user to specify what

* This work was supported in part by the EU FP7 STREP project PEPPHER, and by EPSRC grant EP/G051100/1.

M.R. Guarracino et al. (Eds.): Euro-Par 2010 Workshops, LNCS 6586, pp. 117–125, 2011.
© Springer-Verlag Berlin Heidelberg 2011

```
void SerialUpdateVelocity() {
  for(int i=1; i<Height-1; ++i)
    for(int j=1; j<Width-1; ++j)
      V[i][j] = D[i][j]*(V[i][j]+L[i][j]*
        (S[i][j]-S[i][j-1]+T[i][j]-T[i-1][j]));
}
```

Fig. 1. A serial simulation loop

can be safely executed in parallel, with parallelisation coordinated behind-the-scenes in the library implementation, thus addressing the above *thread management* issues.

Offload C++ [3] extends C++ to address *heterogeneity*. Essentially, Offload C++ provides single source, thread based programming of heterogeneous architectures consisting of a host plus accelerators. Thread management must be handled explicitly, but code duplication and movement of data between memory spaces is handled automatically. Offload C++ for the Cell processor under Linux is freely available [4].

In this paper, we combine the strengths of TBB and Offload C++ by implementing the crucial TBB *parallel for* construct. This allows applications that use these constructs to run, *without source-level modifications*, across *all* cores of the Cell BE architecture.

We also discuss data-movement optimisations for Offload C++, and describe the design of a portable template-library for bulk data-transfers. We show that this template-library can be integrated with TBB applications, providing optimised performance when Offload C++ is used on Cell. We evaluate our approach experimentally using a range of benchmark applications. In summary, we make the following contributions:

- We describe how an important fragment of TBB implemented using Offload C++ allows a large class of programs to run across all the cores of the Cell architecture
- We show how performance of TBB programs on Cell can be boosted using a *portable* template-library to optimise data-movement
- We demonstrate the effectiveness of our techniques experimentally

2 Background

The TBB `parallel_for` construct. We illustrate the `parallel_for` construct using an example distributed with TBB that simulates seismic effects. Figure 1 shows a serial loop. In Figure 2 the loop body is expressed as a C++ function object whose **`operator`**`()` method can process elements in a given range. The `parallel_for` function template takes a function object and an iteration space parameter. When invoked, the function object is applied to each element in the iteration space, typically in parallel. The programmer specifies neither the number of threads nor tasks.

Offload C++. The central construct of Offload C++ is the *offload block*, a lexical scope prefixed with the **`__offload`** keyword. In the Cell BE implementation of Offload C++, code outside an offload block is executed by the host processor (PPE). When an offload block is reached, the host creates an accelerator (SPE) thread that executes the code inside the block. This thread runs asynchronously, in parallel with the host thread. Multiple SPE threads can be launched concurrently via multiple offload blocks. Each offload block returns a handle, which can be used to wait for completion of the associated SPE thread. For full details, see [3].

```
struct UpdateVelocityBody {
  void operator()( const blocked_range<int>& r ) {
    for(int i=r.begin(); i!=r.end(); ++i)
      for(int j=1; j<Width-1; ++j)
        V[i][j] = D[i][j]*(V[i][j]+L[i][j]*
          (S[i][j]-S[i][j-1]+T[i][j]-T[i-1][j]));
} };
void ParallelUpdateVelocity() {
  parallel_for(blocked_range<int>(1, Height-1), UpdateVelocityBody());
}
```

Fig. 2. Simulation loop body as a C++ function object, executable using `parallel_for`

3 Offloading TBB Parallel Loops on the Cell BE Architecture

The example of Figure 2 demonstrates the ease with which TBB can parallelise regularly structured loops. TBB does not however support heterogeneous architectures such as the Cell BE. We now show that, by implementing the `parallel_for` construct in Offload C++ we can allow the code of Figure 2 to execute across *all* cores of the Cell. The key observation is that TBB tasks are an abstraction over a thread-based model of concurrency; of the kind provided by Offload C++ for heterogeneous architectures.

We implement the parallel loop templates of TBB to distribute loop iterations across both the SPE and PPE cores of the Cell. These template classes are included in a small set of header files compatible with the Offload C++ compiler. Figure 3 shows a simple version of `parallel_for`, while `parallel_reduce` can be implemented similarly.

The implementation in Figure 3 performs static work division. Multiple distinct implementations with different static and dynamic work division strategies across subsets of the available cores can be achieved via additional overloads of the `run` function. Dynamic work division is achieved by partitioning the iteration space dynamically to form a work queue, guarded by a mutex, from which the worker threads obtain work units. This provides dynamic load balancing, as workers with less challenging work units are able to perform more units of work. Overloaded versions of `parallel_for` allow the user to select a specific work partitioner, *e.g.* to select static or dynamic work division.

Work division between the SPE cores *and* the PPE core is performed in the `run` method of the `internal::start_for` template. Offload's automatic call graph duplication makes this straightforward, despite the differences between these cores: in Figure 3, `local_function` is called on both the SPE (inside the offload block) and PPE (outside the offload block) without modification to the client code.

In Figure 3, `NUM_SPES` holds the number of SPEs available to user programs. To use all the cores, we divide work between `NUM_SPES+1` threads. One thread executes on the PPE, the others on distinct SPEs. The body of `run` spawns offload threads parameterised with a sub-range and the function object to apply; it then also applies the function object to a sub-range on the PPE, before finally awaiting the completion of each offload thread.

When passing function objects into class and function templates, the methods to invoke are known statically. Therefore, the Offload C++ compiler is able to automatically compile the function object **`operator`**`()` routine for both SPE and PPE, and generate the data transfer code needed to move data between global and SPE memory [3].

```
template<typename Range, typename Body>
void parallel_for( const Range& range, const Body& body ) {
  internal::start_for<Range,Body>::run(range,body);
}

template<typename Range, typename Body>
struct start_for<Range, Body> {
  static void run( const Range& range, const Body& body ) {
    typedef Range::const_iterator iter;

    unsigned NUM_SPES       = num_available_spes();
    iter start              = range.begin(); // Simple 1D range work division
    iter end                = range.end();
    iter chunksize          = (end - start)/(NUM_SPES+1);
    offloadThread_t handles[NUM_SPES];
    const Body local_body = body;

    for (int i = 0; i < NUM_SPES; ++i) {
      iter local_begin = start + chunksize*i;
      iter local_end   = local_begin + chunksize;
      if (local_end > end) local_end = end;
      Range local_range(local_begin,local_end);
      handles[i] = __offload(local_body, local_range) { // Sub-range offloaded
        local_body(local_range);                        // to SPE for
      };                                                // asynchronous execution
    }
    {  // PPE also executes a sub-range
        iter local_begin = start + chunksize*NUM_SPES;
        Range local_range(local_begin,end);
        local_body(local_range);
    }
    for (int i = 0; i < NUM_SPES; i++)
      offloadThreadJoin(handles[i]); // Await completion of SPE threads
} };
```

Fig. 3. An Offload C++ implementation of `parallel_for` for the PPE and SPE cores

4 Portable Tuning for Performance

Offload C++ enables code written for a homogeneous shared-memory multicore architecture to run on heterogeneous multicore architectures with fast local memories. A consequence of this is that the relative cost of data access operations differs, depending on the memory spaces involved. We discuss both the default data-movement strategy employed by Offload; and the portable, manual optimisations we develop to tackle this.

Default data-movement: software cache. The compiler ensures that access to data declared in host memory results in the generation of appropriate data-movement code. The primary mechanism for data-movement on Cell is DMA. However, issuing a DMA operation each time data is read or written tends to result in many small DMA operations. This can lead to inefficient code, since providing standard semantics for memory accesses requires synchronous DMA transfers, introducing latency into data access.

A software cache is used to avoid this worst-case scenario. When access to host memory is required, the compiler generates a cache access operation. At runtime, a synchronous DMA operation is only issued if the required data is not in the software cache. Otherwise, a fast local store access is issued. When contiguous data is accessed, or the same data is accessed repeatedly, the overhead associated with cache-lookups is ameliorated by eliminating the far greater overhead associated with DMA. Writes to global memory can be buffered in the cache and delayed until the cache is flushed or the cache-entry is evicted to make room for subsequent accesses.

The software cache is small: 512 bytes by default. The cache is a convenience, and can significantly improve performance over naïve use of DMA. However, accessing the cache is significantly more expensive than performing a local memory access, even when a cache hit occurs. For bulk transfers, where each cache-line is evicted without being reused, the cache leads to overhead without benefit.

Local shadowing. A common feature of code offloaded for Cell without modification is repeated access to the same region of host memory by offloaded code. In this case, rather than relying on the software cache, a better strategy can be to declare a local variable or array, copy the host memory into this local data structure *once*, and replace accesses to the host memory with local accesses throughout the offloaded code. If the offloaded code modifies the memory then it is necessary to copy the local region back to host memory before offload execution completes. We call this manual optimisation *local shadowing*, as illustrated below with a fragment of the raytracer discussed in §5.1:

```
Sphere spheres[sphereCount]; // Allocated in host memory
__offload {
  RadiancePathTracing(&spheres[0], sphereCount, ... );
};
```

The scene data in the `spheres` array, allocated in host memory, is passed into the `RadiancePathTracing` function, which repeatedly accesses its elements using the software cache. We can instead apply local shadowing by copying scene data from `spheres` into a locally-allocated array, `local`, declared within the offload block:

```
Sphere spheres[sphereCount]; // Allocated in host memory
__offload {
  Sphere local[sphereCount]; // Allocated in local memory
  for (int i = 0; i < sphereCount; ++i)
    local[i] = spheres[i];
  RadiancePathTracing(&local[0], sphereCount, ... );
};
```

A pointer to `local` is now passed to `RadiancePathTracing`, redirecting accesses to scene data to fast, local memory. This optimisation reduces access to scene data via the software cache to the “copy-in” loop; after this, accesses are purely local.

Local shadowing does not compromise portability: in a system with uniform memory the copy-in and copy-out are unnecessary, but yield equivalent semantics. Assuming that the code using the locally shadowed data is substantial, the performance hit associated with local shadowing when offloading is not applied is likely to be negligible.

Bulk data transfers. Offload C++ provides a header-file library of portable, type-safe template classes and functions to wrap DMA intrinsics and provide support for various data access use cases. Templates are provided for read-only (`ReadArray`), write-only (`Write-Array`) and read/write (`ReadWriteArray`) access to arrays in host memory.

The array templates follow the Resource Acquisition is Initialisation (RAII) pattern [5], where construction and automatic destruction at end of scope can be exploited to perform processing. Transfers into local memory are performed on construction of `ReadArray`/`ReadWriteArray` instances, and transfers to host memory are performed on destruction of `ReadWriteArray`/`WriteArray` instances.

```
struct UpdateVelocityBody {
  void operator()( const blocked_range<int>& range ) const {
    for( int i=range.begin(); i!=range.end(); ++i ) {
      ReadArray      <float, Width> lD(&D[i][0]), lL(&L[i][0]), lpT(&T[i-1][0]),
                                    lS(&S[i][0]), lT(&T[i][0]);
      ReadWriteArray<float, Width> lV(&V[i][0]);
      for( int j=1; j < Width-1; ++j )
        lV[j] = lD[j]*(lV[j]+lL[j]*(lS[j]-lS[j-1]+lT[j]-lpT[j]));
} } };
```

Fig. 4. Using DMA template wrappers for efficient data transfer

Figure 4 illustrates optimising the example of Figure 2 with bulk transfers. The declaration `ReadArray<float, Width> lD(&D[i][0])` declares `lD` a local **`float`** array, of size `Width`, and issues a synchronous DMA to fill `ld` with data from host array `D` (hence `lD` stands for "local `D`"). The `ReadWriteArray` instance `lV` is similar, except that when destroyed (on scope exit), a synchronous DMA restores the contents of `lV` to `V`. Velocity update is now performed with respect to local arrays only.

Bulk transfer templates share similarities with local shadowing. However, they hide details of copy-in and copy-out operations, and bypass the software cache completely, which is often significantly more efficient than an element-by-element copy would be.

At compile time, when targetting the PPE, a zero-copy template instantiation is invoked instead. This implementation is also usable on systems with single memory spaces, maintaining portability of code using the templates. Additional data-movement use cases can be implemented by users using the same template functions abstracting transfer operations used to implement the array templates.

Automation. The Offload C++ compiler provides feedback on memory access patterns which can guide the manual application of local shadowing and bulk data transfers. In principle, the compiler could conservatively perform these optimisations automatically, given good general-purpose heuristics for when such transformations are beneficial.

5 Experimental Evaluation

We demonstrate the effectiveness of our approach using a set of parallel TBB programs. Experiments are performed on a Sony PlayStation 3 (with six SPEs accessible), running Fedora Core 10 Linux and IBM Cell SDK v3.0. Parallel benchmarks are compiled using Offload C++ v1.0.4. Serial versions of the benchmarks are compiled using both GCC v4.1.1, and Offload C++ v1.0.4. The faster of the two serial versions is taken as the baseline for measuring the speedup obtained via parallelisation. Optimisation level `-O3` is used in all cases.

- **Seismic simulation.** Simulation discussed in §2 for a 1120×640 pixel display
- **SmallPT-GPU Raytracer.** Global illumination renderer generating 256×256 pixel images from scenes of 3 to 783 spheres, computing sphere-ray intersections with specular, diffuse, and glass reflectance with soft shadows and anti-aliasing [6]
- **Image processing kernels.** A set of 8 kernels operating on a 512×512 pixel image, performing black-and-white median, colour median and colour mean filtering; embossing; sharpening; greyscale conversion; Sobel and Laplacian edge detection

- **PARSEC Black-Scholes.** Partial differential equations modelling the pricing of financial options, from the PARSEC benchmark suite [7] using the *large* data set
- **PARSEC Swaptions.** Simulates pricing a portfolio of swaptions using the Heath-Jarrow-Morton and Monte Carlo methods; from PARSEC using the *large* data set

5.1 Results

We present results showing the performance increases obtained by parallelising each benchmark across all available cores of the Cell (6 SPEs + PPE), compared with PPE-only execution. In some cases, the speedup using all cores is more than $7\times$. The SPE cores are significantly different to the PPE, so we would not expect them to be directly comparable; a specific program may run faster across the SPEs due to higher floating point performance, or efficient use of scratch-pad memory.

Seismic Simulation: After an initial offload of the original code, we found that the data transfer intensive nature of this code results in non-optimal performance on the SPE as the data being processed is still held in the global memory, and not in fast SPE local store. To address this, we used the `ReadArray` and `ReadWriteArray` templates, as shown in Figure 4, to obtain a $5.9\times$ speedup over the PPE alone.

Image Processing Kernels: Figure 5 shows performance results. We used local shadowing to hold input pixel rows in stack allocated arrays, implementing a sliding window over the input image. Fetching a new pixel row would over-write the local buffer storing the oldest, and here we utilised our bulk data transfer template operations. Writes of individual output pixels were also buffered, and written out via bulk transfer.

SmallPT-GPU Raytracer: Figure 6 shows performance results for three versions of the SmallPT raytracer in raytracing six scenes compared to the serial baseline. The first version uses `parallel_for` to execute on the SPEs and PPE. The second version uses local shadowing of the scene data, as discussed in §4. The last version uses a dynamic scheduling implementation of `parallel_for` where the SPE and PPE threads dequeue work from a shared queue, and thereby load balance amongst themselves.

Kernel	B&W Median	Col. Mean	Col. Median	Emboss	Laplacian	Sharpen	Sobel	Greyscale
Speedup	$7.7\times$	$7.4\times$	$4.5\times$	$3.6\times$	$3.1\times$	$5.3\times$	$5.7\times$	$3\times$

Fig. 5. Speedup for Image Kernels

Scene	caustic	caustic3	complex	cornell large	cornell	simple
Global scene data	$2.5\times$	$2.6\times$	$1.4\times$	$4.5\times$	$4.4\times$	$2.7\times$
Local scene data	$2.8\times$	$3.0\times$	$7.1\times$	$7.2\times$	$7.1\times$	$3.1\times$
Dynamic parallel_for	$4.9\times$	$5.2\times$	$10.1\times$	$8.9\times$	$8.5\times$	$5.1\times$

Fig. 6. Speedup for SmallPT Raytracer using `parallel_for`

PARSEC Black-Scholes: Conversion of the Black-Scholes benchmark was straightforward. A single `parallel_for` template function call represents the kernel of the application. We obtained a speedup of 4.0× relative to the serial version on PPE.

PARSEC Swaptions. The code was refactored in two stages. First, dynamic memory allocations were annotated to distinguish between memory spaces. Secondly, unrestricted pointer usage was replaced with static arrays. Local shadowing optimisations were also applied. After these modifications, a 3.0× speedup was obtained.

6 Conclusions

We have shown how, using Offload C++, the TBB `parallel_for` construct can be readily used to distribute work across the SPE and PPE cores of the Cell processor. Our proof of concept implementation provides both static and dynamic work division and supports a subset of the TBB library; `parallel_for` and `parallel_reduce`; the associated `blocked_range` templates, and the `spin_mutex` class object.

We have also demonstrated that data transfer operations can be portably implemented, exploiting target-specific DMA transfer capabilities when instantiated in the context of code to be compiled for the SPE processors.

While related work is available for Cell, the approach of Offload C++ remains distinct. OpenMP targets *homogeneous* shared-memory architectures; although distributed and heterogeneous implementations do exist [8,9]. In contrast to OpenMP on Cell [9], the Offload compiler can use C++ templates to reflect information obtained statically from the call graph, allowing users to optimise code using "specialised" template strategies selected for a specific target architecture *e.g.* the SPE. OpenCL [10] also permits programming in heterogeneous parallel environments. Unlike Offload, OpenCL introduces "boilerplate" code to transfer data between distinct memory spaces via an API, and requires accelerator code to be written in the OpenCL language.

Extending Offload C++ to massively parallel systems, such as GPUs, is likely to follow. However, GPU-like architectures are not an ideal fit for the current Offload C++ programming model, which anticipates random access to a shared global store. Adapting existing application code and Offload C++ to work with the restricted programming models associated with GPUs will be a significant research challenge.

References

1. Hofstee, H.P.: Power efficient processor architecture and the Cell processor. In: HPCA, pp. 258–262. IEEE Computer Society, Los Alamitos (2005)
2. Intel, Threading Building Blocks 3.0 for Open Source, http://www.opentbb.org
3. Cooper, P., Dolinsky, U., Donaldson, A., Richards, A., Riley, C., Russell, G.: Offload – automating code migration to heterogeneous multicore systems. In: Patt, Y.N., Foglia, P., Duesterwald, E., Faraboschi, P., Martorell, X. (eds.) HiPEAC 2010. LNCS, vol. 5952, pp. 337–352. Springer, Heidelberg (2010)
4. Codeplay Software Ltd, Offload: Community Edition, http://offload.codeplay.com
5. Stroustrup, B.: The Design and Evolution of C++. Addison-Wesley, Reading (1994)

6. Bucciarelli, D.: SmallPT-GPU, `http://davibu.interfree.it/opencl/smallptgpu/smallptGPU.html`
7. Bienia, C., Kumar, S., Singh, J.P., Li, K.: The PARSEC benchmark suite: Characterization and architectural implications. In: PACT 2008, pp. 72–81. ACM, New York (2008)
8. Hoeflinger, J.P.: Extending OpenMP to Clusters (2006), `http://www.intel.com`
9. O'Brien, K., O'Brien, K.M., Sura, Z., Chen, T., Zhang, T.: Supporting OpenMP on Cell. International Journal of Parallel Programming 36(3), 289–311 (2008)
10. Khronos Group, The OpenCL specification, `http://www.khronos.org`

Fine-Grained Parallelization of a Vlasov-Poisson Application on GPU

Guillaume Latu[1,2]

[1] CEA, IRFM, F-13108 Saint−Paul−lez−Durance, France
[2] Strasbourg 1 University & INRIA/Calvi project
guillaume.latu@cea.fr

Abstract. Understanding turbulent transport in magnetised plasmas is a subject of major importance to optimise experiments in tokamak fusion reactors. Also, simulations of fusion plasma consume a great amount of CPU time on today's supercomputers. The Vlasov equation provides a useful framework to model such plasma. In this paper, we focus on the parallelization of a 2D semi-Lagrangian Vlasov solver on GPGPU. The originality of the approach lies in the needed overhaul of both numerical scheme and algorithms, in order to compute accurately and efficiently in the CUDA framework. First, we show how to deal with 32-bit floating point precision, and we look at accuracy issues. Second, we exhibit a very fine grain parallelization that fits well on a many-core architecture. A speed-up of almost 80 has been obtained by using a GPU instead of one CPU core. As far as we know, this work presents the first semi-Lagrangian Vlasov solver ported onto GPU.

1 Introduction

The present paper highlights the porting of a semi-Lagrangian Vlasov-Poisson code on a GPU device. The work, described herein, follows a previous study made on the LOSS code described in other papers [CLS06, CLS09, LCGS07]. A classical approach in the Semi-Lagrangian community involves the use of cubic splines to achieve the many interpolations needed by this scheme. The application we describe here, uses a local spline method designed specifically to perform decoupled numerical interpolations, while preserving classical cubic spline accuracy. In previous papers, this scalable method was described, and was benchmarked in academic and industrial simulators. Only relatively small MPI inter-processor communication costs were induced and these codes scaled well over hundreds of cores (1D and 2D domain decompositions were investigated).

Particle-in-Cell (PIC) codes are often used in plasma physics studies and they use substantial computer time at some of the largest supercomputer centers in the world. Particle-in-Cell, yet less accurate, is a most commonly used numerical method than the semi-Lagrangian one. Several papers has been published on PIC codes that harness the computational power of BlueGene and GPGPU hardwares [SDG08, BAB$^+$08] and provide good scalability. Looking for new algorithms that are highly scalable in the field of Tokamak simulations is important to mimic plasma devices with more realism.

M.R. Guarracino et al. (Eds.): Euro-Par 2010 Workshops, LNCS 6586, pp. 127–135, 2011.
© Springer-Verlag Berlin Heidelberg 2011

We will describe how to enrich the Semi-Lagrangian scheme in order to obtain scalable algorithms that fits well in the CUDA framework. In the sequel, the numerical scheme and the accuracy issues are briefly introduced and the parallelization of the main algorithm with CUDA is described. The speedup and accuracy of the simulations are reported and discussed.

2 Mathematical Model

In the present work, we consider a reduced model for two physical dimensions (instead of six in the general case), corresponding to x and v_x such as $(x, v_x) \in \mathbb{R}^2$. The 1D variable x represents the configuration space and the 1D variable v_x stands for the velocity along x direction. Moreover, the self consistent magnetic field is neglected because v_x is considered to be small in the physical configurations we are looking at. The Vlasov-Poisson system then reads:

$$\frac{\partial f}{\partial t} + v_x\,.\nabla_x f + (E + v_x \times B)\,.\nabla_{v_x} f = 0, \tag{1}$$

$$-\varepsilon_0 \nabla^2 \phi = \rho(x,t) = q \int f(x, v_x, t) d\,v_x, \qquad E(x,t) = -\nabla\phi. \tag{2}$$

where $f(x, v_x, t)$ is the particle density function, ρ is the charge density, q is the charge of a particle (only one species is considered) and ε_0 is the vacuum permittivity, B is the applied magnetic field.

Eq. (1) and (2) are solved successively at each time step. The density ρ is evaluated in integrating f over v_x and Eq. (2) gives the self-consistent electrostatic field $E(x,t)$ generated by particles. Our work focuses on the resolution of Eq. (1) using a backward semi-Lagrangian method [SRBG99]. The physical domain is defined as $\mathcal{D}_p^2 = \{(x, v_x) \in [x_{\min}, x_{\text{Max}}] \times [v_{x_{\min}}, v_{x_{\text{Max}}}]\}$. For the sake of simplicity, we will consider that the size of the grid mapped on this physical domain is a square indexed on $\mathcal{D}_i^2 = [0, 2^j - 1]^2$ (it is easy to break this assumption to get a rectangle). Concerning the type of boundary conditions, a choice should be made depending on the test cases under investigation. At the time being, only periodic extension is implemented.

3 Algorithmic Analysis

3.1 Global Numerical Scheme

The Vlasov Equation (1) can be decomposed by splitting. It is possible to solve it, through the following elementary advection equations:

$$\partial_t f + v_x \partial_x f = 0, \quad (\hat{x} \text{ operator}) \qquad \partial_t f + \dot{v_x} \partial_{v_x} f = 0. \quad (\hat{v}_x \text{ operator})$$

Each advection consists in applying a shift operator. A splitting of Strang [CK76] is employed to keep a scheme of second order accuracy in time. We took the sequence $(\hat{x}/2, \hat{v}_x, \hat{x}/2)$, where the factor 1/2 means a shift over a reduced time step $\Delta t/2$. Algorithm 2 shows how the Vlasov solver of Eq. (1) is interleaved with the field solver of Eq. (2).

3.2 Local Spline Method

Each 1D advection (along x or v_x) consists in two substeps (Algorithm 1). First, the density function f is processed in order to derive the cubic spline coefficients. The specificity of the local spline method is that a set of spline coefficients covering one subdomain can be computed concurrently with other ones. Thus, it improves the standard approach that unfortunately needs a coupling between all coefficients along one direction. Second, spline coefficients are used to interpolate the function f at specific points. This substep is intrinsically parallel wether with the standard spline method or with the local spline method: one interpolation involves only a linear combination of four neighbouring spline coefficients.

In Algorithm 1, x^o is called the origin of the characteristic. With the local spline method, we gain concurrent computations during the spline coefficient derivation (line 2 of the algorithm). Our goal is to port Algorithm 1 onto GPU.

Algorithm 1. Advection in x dir., dt time step

```
  Input : f
  Output: f
1 forall v_x do
2     a(.) ← spline coeff. of sampled function f(., v_x)
3     forall x do
4         x^0 ← x − v_x.dt
5         f(x, v_x) ← interpolate f(x^0, v_x) with a(.)
```

Algorithm 2. One time step

```
Input : f_t
Output: f_{t+Δt}
// Vlasov solver, part 1
1D Advection, operator x̂/2 on f(., ., t)
// Field solver
Integrate f(., ., t+Δt/2) over v_x
        to get density ρ(., t+Δt/2)
Compute Φ_{t+Δt/2} with Poisson solver
        using ρ(., t+Δt/2)
// Vlasov solver, part 2
1D Advection, operator v̂_x (use Φ_{t+Δt/2})
1D Advection, operator x̂/2
```

3.3 Floating Point Precision

Usually, semi-Lagrangian codes make extensive use of double precision floating point operations. The double precision is required because pertubations of small amplitude often play a central role during plasma simulation. For the sake of simplicity, we focus here on the very classical linear Landau damping test case (with $k=0.5, \alpha=0.01$) which highlights the accuracy problem one can expect in Vlasov-Poisson simulation. The initial distribution function is given by $f(x, v_x, 0) = \frac{e^{-\frac{{v_x}^2}{2}}}{\sqrt{2\,\pi}}(1 + \alpha\ \cos(k\,x))$. Other test cases are available in our implementation, such as strong Landau damping, or two stream instability. They are picked to test the numerical algorithm and for benchmarking.

The problem arising with single precision computations is shown on Fig. 1. The reference LOSS code (CPU version) is used here. The L^2 norm of electric potential is shown on the picture (electric energy) with logarithmic scale along the Y-axis. The double precision curve represents the reference simulation. The difference between the two curves indicates that single precision is insufficient; especially for long-time simulation. With an accurate look at the figure, one can notice that the double precision simulation is accurate until reaching a plateau value near 10^{-20}. To go beyond this limit, a more accurate interpolation is needed.

3.4 Improvement of Numerical Precision

For the time being, one has to consider mostly single precision (SP) computations to get maximum performance out of a GPU. The double precision (DP) is much slower than single precision (SP) on today's devices. In addition, the use of double precision may increase pressure on memory bandwidth.

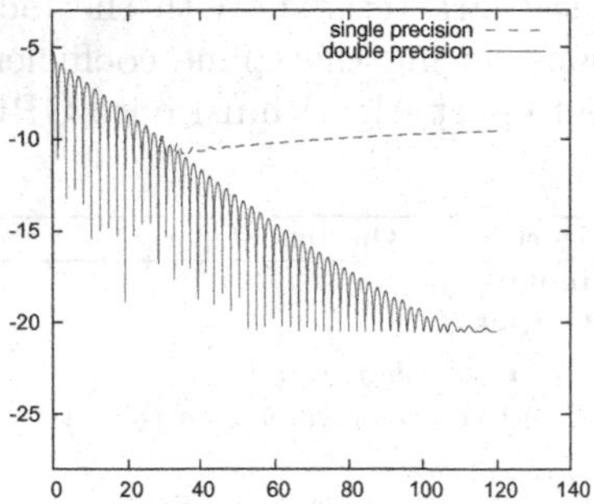

Fig. 1. Electric energy for Landau test case 1024^2, single versus double precision (depending on time measured as a number of plasma period $\omega_c{}^{-1}$)

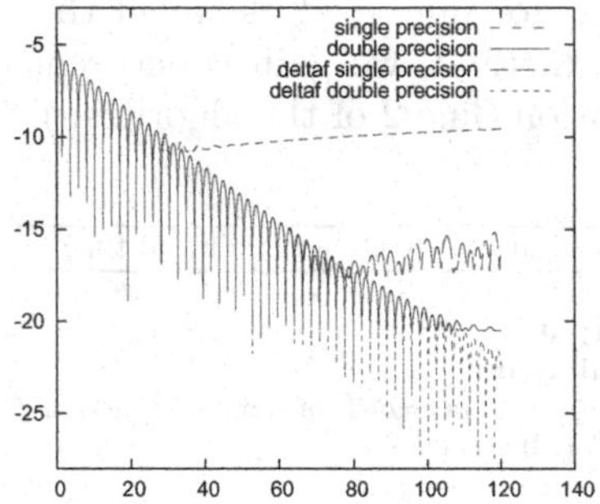

Fig. 2. Electric energy for Landau test case 1024^2, using δf representation or standard representation

The previous paragraph shows that SP leads to unacceptable numerical results. It turns out that our numerical scheme could be modified to reduce numerical errors even with only SP operations during the advection steps. To do so, a new function $\delta f(x, v_x, t) = f(x, v_x, t) - f_{\text{ref}}(x, v_x)$ is introduced. Working on the δf function could improve accuracy if the values that we are working on are sufficiently close to zero. Then, the reference function f_{ref} should be chosen such that the δf function remains relatively small (in L_∞ norm). convenient to assume that f_{ref} is a constant along the x dimension. For the Landau test case, we choose $f_{\text{ref}}(v_x) = \frac{1}{\sqrt{2\pi}} e^{-\frac{v_x{}^2}{2}}$. As the function f_{ref} is constant along x, the x-advection applied on f_{ref} leaves f_{ref} unchanged. Then, it is equivalent to apply $\hat{x}$ operator either on function δf or on function f. Working on δf is very worthwile ($\hat{x}$ operator): for the same number of floating point operations, we increase accuracy in working on small differences instead of large values. Concerning the $\hat{v_x}$ operator however, both f_{ref} and f are modified. For each advected grid point (x, v_x) of the $f^\star$ function, we have (v_x^o is the foot of the characteristic):

$$f^\star(x, v_x) = f(x, v_x^o) = \delta f(x, v_x^o) + f_{\text{ref}}(v_x^o), \qquad \delta f^\star(x, v_x) = f^\star(x, v_x) - f_{\text{ref}}(v_x),$$

$$\delta f^\star(x, v_x) = \delta f(x, v_x^o) - (f_{\text{ref}}(v_x) - f_{\text{ref}}(v_x^o)).$$

Working on δf instead of f changes the operator $\hat{v_x}$. We now have to interpolate both $\delta f(x, v_x^o)$ and $(f_{\text{ref}}(v_x) - f_{\text{ref}}(v_x^o))$. In doing so, we increase the number of computations; because in the original scheme we had only one interpolation per grid point (x, v_x), whereas we have two in the new scheme. In spite of this cost increase, we enhance the numerical accuracy using δf representation (see Fig. 2). A sketch of the δf scheme is shown in Algorithm 3.

4 CUDA Algorithms

4.1 CUDA Framework

Designed for NVIDIA GPUs (Graphics Processing Units), CUDA is a C-based general-purpose parallel computing programming model. Using CUDA, GPUs can be regarded as coprocessors to the central processing unit (CPU). They communicate with the CPU through fast PCI-Express ports. An overview of the CUDA language and architecture could be found in [NVI09]. Over the past few years, some success in porting scientific codes to GPU have been reported in the literature. Our reference implementation of LOSS, used for comparisons, uses Fortran 90 and MPI library. Both sequential and parallel versions of LOSS have been optimized over several years. The CUDA version of LOSS presented here mixes Fortran 90 code and external C calls (to launch CUDA kernels).

Algorithm 3. One time step, δf scheme

Input : δf_t
Output: $\delta f_{t+\Delta t}$

1D advection on δf, operator $\frac{\hat{x}}{2}$
Integrate $\delta f(.,.,t+\Delta t/2) + f_{\text{ref}}(.)$
  to get $\rho(.,t+\Delta t/2)$
Compute $\Phi_{t+\Delta t/2}$,
  with Poisson solver on $\rho(.,t+\Delta t/2)$
1D advection on δf, operator $\hat{v_x}$
  $\rightarrow$ stored into δf
Interpolate $f_{\text{ref}}(v_x) - f_{\text{ref}}(v_x^o)$
  $\rightarrow$ results added into δf
1D advection on δf, operator $\frac{\hat{x}}{2}$

Algorithm 4. Skeleton of an advection kernel

Input : f_t in global memory of GPU
Output: f_{t+dt} in global memory of GPU

`// A) Load from global mem. to shared mem.`
Each thread loads 4 floats from global mem.
Floats loaded are stored in *shared memory*
Boundary conditions are set (extra floats are read)
Synchro.: 1 thread block owns n *vectors* of 32 floats
`// B) LU Solver`
1 thread over 8 solves a LU system (7 are idle)
Synchro.: 1 block has n vectors of spline coeff.
`// C) Interpolations`
Each thread computes 4 interpolations
`// D) Writing to GPU global memory`
Each thread writes 4 floats to global mem.

4.2 Data Placement

We perform the computation on data δf of size $(2^j)^2$. Typical domain size varies from 128×128 (64 KB) up to 1024×1024 (4 MB). The whole domain fits easily in global memory of current GPUs. In order to reduce unnecessary overheads, we decided to avoid transferring 2D data δf between the CPU and the GPU as far as we can. So we kept data function δf onto GPU global memory. CUDA computation kernels update it in-place. For diagnostics purposes only, the δf function is transfered to the RAM of the CPU at a given frequency.

4.3 Spline Coefficients Computation

Spline coefficients (of 1D discretized functions) are computed on patches of 32 values of δf. As explained elsewhere [CLS06], a smaller patch would introduce significant overhead because of the cost of first derivative computations on the patch borders. A bigger patch would increase the computational grain which is a bad thing for GPU computing that favors scheduling large number of threads.

The 2D domain is decomposed into small 1D vectors (named "patches") of 32 δf values. To derive the spline coefficients, tiny LU systems are solved. The assembly of right hand side vector used in this solving step can be summarized as follows: keep the 32 initial values, add 1 more value of δf at the end of the patch, and then add two derivatives of δf located at the borders of the patch. Once the right hand side vector is available (35 values), two precomputed matrices L and U are inverted to derive spline coefficients (using classical forward/backward substitution). We decided not to parallelize this small LU solver: a single CUDA thread is in charge of computing spline coefficients on one patch That point could be improved in the future in order to use several threads instead of one.

4.4 Parallel Interpolations

On one patch, 32 interpolations need to be done (except at domain boundaries). These interpolations are decoupled. To maximize parallelism, one can even try to dedicate one thread per interpolation. Nevertheless, as auxiliary computations could be factorized (for example the shift $v_x.dt$ at line 4 of Algo. 1), it is relevant to do several interpolations per thread to reduce global computation cost. The number of such interpolations per thread is a parameter that impacts performance. This blocking factor is denoted K.

4.5 Data Load

The computational intensity of the advection step is not that high. During the LU phase (*spline coefficients computation*), each input data is read and written twice and generates two multiplications and two additions in average. During the *interpolation step*, there are four reads and one write per input data and also four multiplications and four additions. The low computational intensity implies that we could expect shortening the execution time in reducing loads and writes from/to GPU global memory. So, there is a benefit to group the spline computation and the interpolations in a single kernel. Several benchmarks have confirmed that with two distinct kernels (one for building splines and one for interpolations) instead of one, the price of load/store in the GPU memory increases. Thus, we now describe the solution with only one kernel.

4.6 Domain Decomposition and Fine Grain Algorithm

We have designed three main kernels. Let us give short descriptions: `KernVA` operator $\hat{v_x}$ on $\delta f(x, v_x)$, `KernVB` adding $f_{\mathrm{ref}}(v_x) - f_{\mathrm{ref}}(v_x^o)$ to $\delta f(x, v_x)$, `KernX` operator $\hat{x}$ on $\delta f(x, v_x)$. The main steps of `KernVA` or `KernX` are given in Algorithm 4. The computations of $8\,n$ threads acting on $32\,n$ real number values are described (it means $K = 4$ hardcoded here).

First `A)` substep reads floats from GPU global memory and puts them into fast GPU shared memory. When entering the `B)` substep, all input data have been copied into shared memory. Concurrently in the block of threads, small *LU* system are solved (but 87% of the threads stays idle). Spline coefficients are then stored in shared memory. In substep `C)`, each thread computes $K = 4$ interpolations using spline coefficients. This last task is the most computation intensive part of the simulator. Finally, results are written into global memory.

5 Performance

5.1 Machines

In order to develop the code and perform small benchmarks, a cheap personal computer has been used. The CPU is a dual-core E2200 Intel (2.2Ghz), 2 GB of RAM, 4 GB/s peak bandwidth, 4 GFLOPS peak, 1 MB L2 cache. The GPU is a GTX260 Nvidia card: 1.24 Ghz clock speed, 0.9 GB global memory, 95 GB/s peak bandwidth, 750 GFLOPS peak, 216 cores. Another computer (at CINES, FRANCE) has been used for benchmarking. The CPU is a bi quad-core E5472 Harpertown Intel (3 Ghz), 1 GB RAM, 5 GB/s peak bandwidth, 12 GFLOPS peak, L2 cache 2×6 MB. The machine is connected to a Tesla S1070, 1.44Ghz, 4 GB global memory, 100 GB/s peak bandwidth, 1000 GFLOPS peak, 240 cores.

5.2 Small Test Case

Let us first have a look on performance of the δf scheme. We consider the small testbed (E2200-GTX260), and a reduced test case (256^2 domain). The simulation ran on a single CPU core, then on the 216 cores of the GTX260. Timing results and speedups (reference is the CPU single core) are given in Table 1. The speedup is near 30 for the two significant computation steps, but is smaller for the field computation. The field computation part includes two substeps: first the integral computations over the 2D data distribution function, second a 1D poisson solver. The timings for the integrals are bounded up by the loading time of 2D data

Table 1. Computation times inside a time step and speedup (in parentheses) averaged over 5000 calls - 256^2 Landau test case, E2200/GTX260

Substeps in one time step	CPU (deltaf 4B)	GPU (deltaf 4B)
X Advection	5123 μs (*1.0*)	172 μs (*29.7*)
V Advection	4850 μs (*1.0*)	144 μs (*33.7*)
Field computation	133 μs (*1.0*)	93 μs (*1.4*)
Complete Iteration	10147 μs (*1.0*)	546 μs (*18.6*)

from global memory of the GPU (only one addition to do per loaded float). The second substep that solves Poisson equation is a small sequential 1D problem. Furthermore, we loose time in lauching kernels on the GPU (25 μs per kernel launch included in timings shown).

5.3 Large Test Case

In Tables 2-3, we look at a larger test case with data size equal to 1024^2. Compared to a single CPU core, the advection kernels have speedups from 75 to 90 for a GPU card (using260 000 threads.). Here, the field computation represents a small computation compared to the advections and the low speedup for the field solver is not a real penalty. A complete iteration reaches a speedup of 76.

Table 2. Computation time and speedups (in parentheses) averaged over 5000 calls - 1024^2 Landau test case - E2200/GTX260

Substeps in one time step	CPU (deltaf 4B)	GPU (deltaf 4B)
X Advections	79600 μs (*1.0*)	890 μs (*90*)
V Advections	89000 μs (*1.0*)	1000 μs (*89*)
Field computation	1900 μs (*1.0*)	180 μs (*11*)
Complete Iteration	171700 μs (*1.0*)	2250 μs (*76*)

Table 3. Computation time and speedups (in parentheses) averaged over 5000 calls - 1024^2 Landau test case - Xeon/Tesla1070

Substeps in one time step	CPU (deltaf 4B)	GPU (deltaf 4B)
X Advections	67000 μs (*1.0*)	780 μs (*86*)
V Advections	42000 μs (*1.0*)	960 μs (*43*)
Field computation	1500 μs (*1.0*)	200 μs (*7*)
Complete Iteration	110000 μs (*1.0*)	2200 μs (*50*)

6 Conclusion

It turns out that δf method is a valid approach to perform a Semi-Lagrangian Vlasov-Poisson simulation using only 32-bit floating-point precision instead of classical 64-bit precision. So, we have described the implementation on GPU of the advection operator used in Semi-Lagrangian simulation with δf scheme and single precision. A very fine grain parallelization of the advection step is presented that scales well on thousands of threads. We have discussed the kernel structure and the trade-offs made to accommodate the GPU hardware.

The application is bounded up by memory bandwidth because computational intensity is small. It is well known that algorithms of high computational intensity are able to be efficiently implemented on GPU. We have demonstrated that an algorithm of low computational intensity can also benefit from GPU hardware. Our GPU solution reaches a significant speedup of overall 76 compared to a single core CPU execution. In the near future, we expect to have a solution for 4D semi-Lagrangian codes (2D space, 2D velocity) that runs on a GPU cluster.

References

[BAB+08] Bowers, K.J., Albright, B.J., Bergen, B., Yin, L., Barker, K.J., Kerbyson, D.J.: 0.374 pflop/s trillion-particle kinetic modeling of laser plasma interaction on roadrunner. In: Proc. of Supercomputing. IEEE Press, Los Alamitos (2008)

[CK76] Cheng, C.Z., Knorr, G.: The integration of the Vlasov equation in configuration space. J. Comput Phys. 22, 330 (1976)

[CLS06] Crouseilles, N., Latu, G., Sonnendrücker, E.: Hermite spline interpolation on patches for a parallel solving of the Vlasov-Poisson equation. Technical Report 5926, INRIA (2006), http://hal.inria.fr/inria-00078455/en/

[CLS09] Crouseilles, N., Latu, G., Sonnendrücker, E.: A parallel Vlasov solver based on local cubic spline interpolation on patches. J. Comput. Phys. 228(5), 1429–1446 (2009)

[LCGS07] Latu, G., Crouseilles, N., Grandgirard, V., Sonnendrücker, E.: Gyrokinetic semi-lagrangian parallel simulation using a hybrid openMP/MPI programming. In: Cappello, F., Herault, T., Dongarra, J. (eds.) PVM/MPI 2007. LNCS, vol. 4757, pp. 356–364. Springer, Heidelberg (2007)

[NVI09] NVIDIA. CUDA Programming Guide, 2.3 (2009)

[SDG08] Stantchev, G., Dorland, W., Gumerov, N.: Fast parallel particle-to-grid interpolation for plasma PIC simulations on the GPU. J. Parallel Distrib. Comput. 68(10), 1339–1349 (2008)

[SRBG99] Sonnendrücker, E., Roche, J., Bertrand, P., Ghizzo, A.: The semi-lagrangian method for the numerical resolution of the Vlasov equations. J. Comput. Phys. 149, 201–220 (1999)

Highly Parallel Implementation of Harris Corner Detector on CSX SIMD Architecture

Fouzhan Hosseini, Amir Fijany, and Jean-Guy Fontaine

Italian Institute of Technology, Genova, Italy
{fouzhan.hosseini,amir.fijany,jean-guy.fontaine}@iit.it

Abstract. We present a much faster than real-time implementation of Harris Corner Detector (HCD) on a low-power, highly parallel, SIMD architecture, the ClearSpeed CSX700, with application for mobile robots and humanoids. HCD is a popular feature detector due to its invariance to rotation, scale, illumination variation and image noises. We have developed strategies for efficient parallel implementation of HCD on CSX700, and achieved a performance of 465 frames per second (fps) for images of 640x480 resolution and 142 fps for 1280x720 resolution. For a typical real-time application with 30 fps, our fast implementation represents a very small fraction (less than %10) of available time for each frame and thus allowing enough time for performing other computations. Our results indicate that the CSX architecture is indeed a good candidate for achieving low-power supercomputing capability, as well as flexibility.

1 Introduction

Mobile robots and humanoids represent an interesting and challenging example of embedded computing applications. On one hand, in order to achieve a large degree of autonomy and intelligent behavior, these systems require a very significant computational capability to perform various tasks. On the other hand, they are severely limited in terms of size, weight, and particularly power consumption of their embedded computing system since they should carry their own power supply. The limitation of conventional computing architectures for these types of applications is twofold: first, their low computing power, second, their high power consumption. Emerging highly parallel and low-power SIMD and MIMD architectures provide a unique opportunity to overcome these limitations of conventional computing architectures. Exploiting these novel parallel architectures, our current objective is to develop a flexible, low-power, lightweight supercomputing architecture for mobile robots and humanoid systems for performing various tasks and, indeed, for enabling new capabilities.

Computer vision and image processing techniques are very common in robotic, e.g. tracking, 3D reconstruction and object recognition. Feature detection is a low-level image processing task which is usually performed as the first step in many computer vision applications such as object tracking [1] and object recognition [2]. Harris Corner Detector (HCD) [3] is a popular feature detector due to its invariance to rotation, scale, illumination variation and image noises.

M.R. Guarracino et al. (Eds.): Euro-Par 2010 Workshops, LNCS 6586, pp. 137–144, 2011.
© Springer-Verlag Berlin Heidelberg 2011

Fast implementations of HCD on various architectures have been considered in the literature including Application Specific Integrated Circuit (ASIC) [4], Field Programmable Gate Array (FPGA) [5], Graphics Processing Units (GPU) [6], and Cell processor [7]. A performance comparison of these implementations is given in Section 5. ASICs and FPGAs could be used to design custom hardware for low-power high performance applications. GPU and Cell processor are more flexible, but the main limitation is the rather prohibitive power consumption. None of the above mentioned solutions satisfies our requirements for mobile system vision processing including low power consumption, flexibility, and real time processing capability simultaneously.

In this paper, we present a fast implementation of HCD on a highly parallel SIMD architecture, the ClearSpeed CSX700. The CSX700 has a peak computing power of 96 GFLOPS, while consuming less than 9 Watts. In fact, it seems that CSX provides one of the best (if not the best) performance in terms of GFLOPS/Watt among available computing architectures. Considering the CSX architecture, we have developed strategies for efficient parallel implementation of HCD. We have achieved a performance of 465 fps for images of 640x480 resolution and 142 fps for 1280x720 resolution. These results indeed represent a much faster than real-time implementation and better than those previously reported in the literature. Our experimental results, presented in this paper, clearly indicate that the SIMD architectures such as CSX can indeed be a good candidate for achieving low-power supercomputing capability, as well as flexibility, for embedded applications.

This paper is organized as follows. In Section 2, we briefly discuss the HCD algorithm. In Section 3, we briefly review the CSX architecture. In Section 4, our approach for parallel implementation of HCD on CSX architecture is described and experimental results are discussed in Section 5. Finally, some concluding remarks are presented in Section 6.

2 The Harris Corner Detector Algorithm

To detect corners in a given image, the HCD algorithm [3] proceeds as follows. Let $I(x, y)$ denotes the intensity of a pixel at row x and column y of the image.

1. For each pixel (x, y) in the input image compute the elements of the Harris matrix $G = \begin{bmatrix} g_{xx} & g_{xy} \\ g_{xy} & g_{yy} \end{bmatrix}$ as follows:

$$g_{xx} = \left(\frac{\partial I}{\partial x}\right)^2 \otimes w \quad g_{xy} = \left(\frac{\partial I}{\partial x}\frac{\partial I}{\partial y}\right) \otimes w \quad g_{yy} = \left(\frac{\partial I}{\partial y}\right)^2 \otimes w, \tag{1}$$

   where $\otimes$ denotes convolution operator and w is the Gaussian filter.
2. For all pixel (x, y), compute Harris' criterion:

$$c(x, y) = \det(G) - k(trace(G))^2 \tag{2}$$

   where $\det(G) = g_{xx} \cdot g_{yy} - g_{xy}^2$, k is a constant which should be determined empirically, and $trace(G) = g_{xx} + g_{yy}$.

3. Choose a threshold τ empirically, and set all $c(x, y)$ which are below τ to 0.
4. Non-maximum suppression, i.e. extract points (x, y), which have the maximum $c(x, y)$ in a window neighborhood. These points represents the corners.

3 The CSX700 Architecture

In this section, we briefly review the ClearSpeed CSX700 architecture with emphasis on some of its salient features that have been exploited in our implementation (see, for example, [8] for more detailed discussion). As illustrated in Fig. 1(a), CSX700 has two similar cores, each core has a DDR2 memory interface and a 128KB SRAM, called external memory. Each core also has a standard, RISC-like, control unit, also called *mono execution unit*, which is coupled to a highly parallel SIMD architecture called *poly execution unit*.

Poly execution unit consists of 96 processing elements (PEs) and performs parallel computation (see Fig. 1(b)). Each PE has a 128 bytes register file, 6KB of SRAM, an ALU, an integer multiply-accumulate (MAC) unit, and an IEEE 754 compliant floating point unit (FPU) with dual issue pipelined add and multiply. The CSX700 has clock frequency of 250 MHz [9]. Considering one add and one multiply floating point units working in parallel and generating one result per clock cycle, the peak performance of each PE is then 500 MFLOPS, leading to a peak performance of 96 GFLOPS for two cores (one chip). However, sequential (i.e., scalar) operations, wherein single add or multiply is performed, take 4 clock cycles to be performed [9]. This results to a sequential peak performance of 12 GFLOPS for two cores. This indeed represents a drastic reduction in the peak, and hence, achievable performance. However, vector instructions which operate on sets of 4 data are executed much faster, e.g, vector add or multiply instructions take 4 cycles to be completed [9]. Therefore, vector instructions allow greater throughput for operations. However, the code generated by compiler may not be optimized. Therefore, in order to achieve the best performance, we have also written part of our codes in assembly language of the CSX.

Poly execution unit includes a Programmable I/O (PIO) unit (Fig. 1(b)) which is responsible for data transfer between external memory and PEs' memories, called poly memory. The architecture of poly execution unit enables the computational units and the PIO unit to work in parallel, i.e. it allows overlapping of communication with computation. This feature is fully exploited in our implementation to reduce I/O overhead

Moreover, as shown in Fig. 1(b), a dedicated bus called *swazzle path* connects the register files of neighboring PEs. Consequently, on each cycle, PEs are able to perform a register-to-register data transfer to either their left or right neighbor, while simultaneously receiving data from the other neighbor.

4 Proposed Parallel Implementation

Considering the SIMD architecture of CSX, we have employed data parallel model of computation. Here, we first discuss our data decomposition strategy. Then, we discuss more details of our parallel implementation.

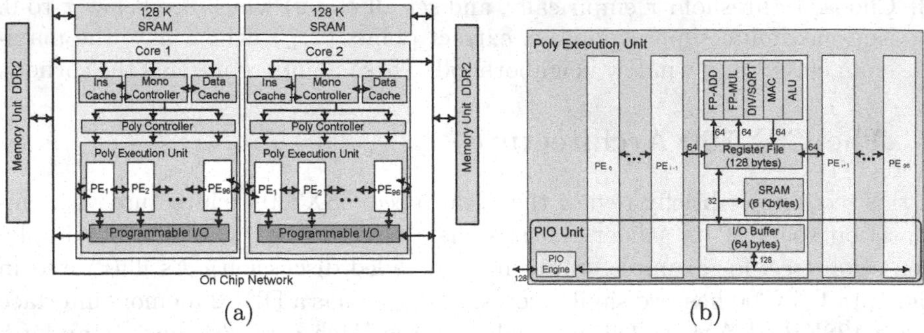

(a) (b)

Fig. 1. (a)Simplified CSX Chip Architecture (b) Poly Execution Unit Architecture [8]

4.1 Data Decomposition

Having an image and an array of PEs, various data distributions schemes could be considered. The most obvious schemes are row (column)-stripe distribution, block distribution, and row (column)-cyclic distribution. Here, we discuss the effectiveness of each of these data distribution schemes for parallel implementation of HCD algorithms on the CSX architecture. An important consideration for the CSX architecture is the size of PE's memory which is rather limited. For the CSX architecture, various data distributions should be compared in terms of the following parameters: (a) required memory space for each PE; (b) redundant external memory communication; and (c) inter-PE communication time.

In the following, c and r denote the number of columns and rows in image matrix, respectively. According to the algorithm description in Section 2, HCD performs a set of operations in windows around each pixels. In fact, HCD uses windows which may have different sizes in 3 stages: calculating partial derivatives, Gaussian smoothing, and non-maximal suppression. Let ω be the sum of these window sizes. Also, let p indicate the number of PEs. Finally, in each memory communication, each PE reads or writes m bytes of data (pixel) from/into the external memory. Π is the memory space needed to calculate the elements of Harris matrix for m pixels.

Block distributions. In this scheme, as illustrated in Figure 2(a), the image is divided into $p = d * s$ blocks, with each block having c/d columns and r/s rows. The first block is assigned to the first PE, the second one to the second PE, and so on. Each block can be identified by an ordered pair (i, j) where $1 \leq i \leq s$ and $1 \leq j \leq d$. In the following, $P(i, j)$ denotes the PE which is responsible for processing the block (i, j) and refers to PE $((i - 1)s + j)$.

Figure. 2(b) depicts the boundary data needed for computation by $P(i, j)$ and its four immediate neighbors. To handle boundary data, needed by two neighboring PEs, there are two possible alternatives: transferring boundary data from external memory to both PEs, hence performing redundant data communication, or transferring to one PE and then using swazzling path to transfer it to the other PE. The former takes more time, and the latter requires more PE memory

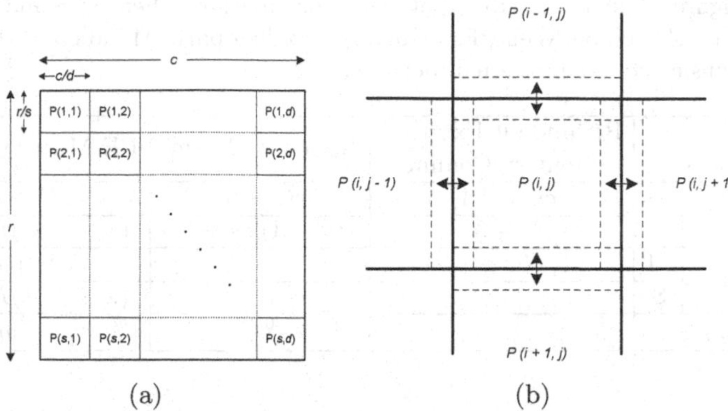

Fig. 2. (a)Block distribution. P(i, j) refers to $PE(i-1)s+j$ (b) Boundary data for each PE in block distribution.

space to store boundary data as discussed in the following. To process first rows (columns), $P(i,j)$ requires the last rows (columns) of $P(i-1,j)$ $(P(i,j-1))$, but these PEs have not yet received the data which $P(i,j)$ requires. Therefore, if the swazzling path is used then $P(i,j)$ should skip processing these boundary data, until $P(i-1,j)$ $(P(i,j-1))$ provides the required data. Also, for processing the last rows (columns) of data, $P(i,j)$ requires data which has already been sent to $P(i+1,j)$ $(P(i,j+1))$. For these PEs to provide the boundary data to $P(i,j)$, they need to store this part of data in their memory which is a limited resource. It should be noted that on the CSX architecture, the distance between $P(i,j)$ and $P(i+1,j)$ which process two neighboring blocks is d.

Row-strip distribution. The first r/p rows are assigned to the first PE, the second r/p rows are assigned to the second PE, and so on. To handle boundary data, $PE(i)$ requires last rows of $PE(i-1)$ and first rows of $PE(i+1)$. In fact, like block distribution, boundary data could be transfered from external memory to both PEs or from one PE to another via swazzling path. As discussed above, the former takes more time, and the latter requires more PE memory space.

Row-cyclic distribution. In this scheme, the first row is assigned to the first PE, the second row to the second PE, and so on. Since one row is assigned to each PE, each PE needs to communicate with the PEs which are at most at the distance of $(w-1)/2$. Here, each PE needs data just after its neighbor has finished processing that same data. So, swazzle path can be utilized without using extra poly memory space.

Table 1 summarizes the parameters calculated for each data distribution strategy. As can be seen, block and row-strip distribution schemes require either more PE memory space or more redundant external memory communications. In fact, for these schemes, the required poly memory space increases linearly with ω. Note that, the size of windows in HCD are determined empirically for each application. For larger ω, e.g. 7 or 11, using these data distributions, the required PE memory will be larger than poly memory space. Row-cyclic distribution needs less poly

Table 1. Figure of merit for different data distribution schemes. S indicates that boundary data is shared between PEs by using swazzling path. M indicates that boundary data is transferred from external memory.

Data Dist.		Redundant External Memory Comm.	Inter-PE Comm.	PE Memory Space
Block Dist.	M	$cs(\omega-1)$	$r(\omega-1)$	$\omega\Pi+m$
	S	-	$(\omega-1)[cs+r]$	$(\omega+\frac{\omega-1}{2})\Pi+m$
Row-strip Dist.	M	$pc(\omega-1)$	-	$\omega\Pi+m$
	S	-	$c(\omega-1)$	$(\omega+\frac{\omega-1}{2})\Pi+m$
Row-cyclic Dist.		-	$c\frac{\omega(\omega-1)}{2}$	$\Pi+m$

memory space and no redundant external memory communication. Although row-cyclic distribution uses inter-PE communication more than row-strip distribution by a factor of $\omega/2$, this overhead will be negligible since communication via swazzle path is very fast (see Section 3). Therefore, row-cyclic distribution scheme is the most efficient for implementing HCD on the CSX architecture.

4.2 Parallel Implementation of Harris Corner Detector Algorithm

In this section, we discuss parallel implementation of HCD on the CSX architecture, based on row-cyclic distribution scheme. Since, each CSX core includes 96 PEs, the input image is divided into groups of 96 rows. The computation of each group represents a sweep and sweeps are performed iteratively. Also, to utilize both cores of CSX700 processor, the input image is divided into two nearly equal parts. The first $\lceil r/2 \rceil + (\omega-1)/2$ rows are assigned to the first core and the last $\lfloor r/2 \rfloor + (\omega-1)/2$ rows are assigned to the second core. Sending boundary lines to both cores enables each core to perform all computation locally. In the following, implementation of HCD on one core is explained (for one sweep).

Memory Communication Pattern. In our parallel implementation, communication and computation overlapping is greatly exploited, and PEs are never idle to receive data (except the initial phase) from external memory. In fact, each image row is divided into segments of almost equal size (32 or 64 pixels, depending on the image size). After receiving the first segment of data, while each PE is processing the segment of data which is already in its memory, in the background, PIO transfers new sets of data from external memory to memories of PEs and the last sets of results to external memory.

Computation Steps. In this section, we present the computation of one segment of data which consists of 5 steps: calculating partial derivative of I in x and y directions, Gaussian smoothing, computing Harris criterion, non-maximum suppression, followed by thresholding.

To calculate partial derivative of I, we have used Prewitt operator. Prewitt operator uses two 3x3 kernels which are convolved with the original image. In our implementation, we take advantages of the fact that these convolution kernels are separable, i.e. they can be expressed as the outer product of two vectors.

So, the x and y derivative can be calculated by first convolving in one direction (using local data), then swazzling data and convolving in the other direction.

In the next step, Gaussian smoothing, elements of Harris matrix, g_{xx}, g_{xy}, and g_{yy} are calculated using (1). Since Gaussian kernel is also separable, the 2-D convolution can be performed by first convolving with a 1-D Gaussian in the x direction, and then swazzling the calculated values and convolving with another 1-D Gaussian in the y direction. Then, Harris' criterion is computed using (2).

In the next step, non-maximum suppression, the maximum value of Harris criterion in each 3x3 neighborhood is determined. First, each PE obtains the maximum value in 1x3 neighborhood. Then, each PE swazzles the maximum values to both its neighbors. Receiving the maximal values of two neighboring rows, the maximum value in 3x3 neighborhood can then be obtained.

5 Results and Performance of Parallel Implementation

To evaluate the performance, we have implemented the following HCDs on the CSX700 architecture: $HCD_{3\times3}$ and $HCD_{5\times5}$ which uses a 3×3 and 5×5 Gaussian kernel, respectively. Since our proposed parallel approach provides flexibility, it can be easily applied to images with different sizes, and various sizes of Gaussian filter or non-maximum suppression window. The performance of implemented algorithms in terms of latency, fps, and sustained GFLOPS for different image resolutions are summarized in Table 2. As Table 2 shows, for all tested image resolutions, even for resolution of 1280x720, our implementation is much faster than real-time.

The arithmetic intensity, i.e., number of operation per pixel, of $HCD_{3\times3}$ and $HCD_{5\times5}$ is 40 and 64 respectively. As Table 2 shows, the sustained GFLOPS depends also on the image size. One reason is that in processing the last sweep of data, some PEs may be idle, and the number of idle PEs depends on image size.

Table 2. Performance of HCD on CSX700 architecture using 3×3 and 5×5 Gaussian filter

Image	Latency (ms)		fps		Sustained GFLOPS	
Resolution	$HCD_{3\times3}$	$HCD_{5\times5}$	$HCD_{3\times3}$	$HCD_{5\times5}$	$HCD_{3\times3}$	$HCD_{5\times5}$
128x128	.165	.224	6060	4464	3.97	4.68
352x288	.8	1.22	1250	819	5.06	5.31
512x512	1.74	2.63	574	380	6.02	6.37
640x480	2.15	3.28	465	304	5.71	5.99
1280x720	7.04	10.89	142	91	5.23	5.41

Table 3. Comparison with other implementations in the literature

Image Resolution	fps reported in [ref]	fps achieved by our approach
128x128	1367 [4]	4464
352x288	60 [5]	819
640x480	99 [6]	304

Table 3 compares our implementation results with those reported in the literature. As can be seen, our approach provides much better performance in terms of latency or frame per second while providing a high degree of flexibility in terms of problem size and parameters.

6 Conclusion and Future Work

We presented a much faster than real-time implementation of Harris Corner Detector (HCD) on a low-power, highly parallel, SIMD architecture, the ClearSpeed CSX700. Considering the features of the CSX architecture, we presented strategies for efficient parallel implementation of HCD. We have achieved a performance of 465 fps for images of 640x480 resolution and 142 fps for 1280x720 resolution. These results indeed represent a much faster than real-time implementation. Our experimental results, presented in this paper, and our previous work [10] clearly indicate that the CSX architecture is indeed a good candidate for achieving low-power supercomputing capability, as well as flexibility, for embedded computer vision applications.

References

1. Yilmaz, A., Javed, O., Shah, M.: Object tracking: A survey. ACM Computing Surveys 38(4), 13 (2006)
2. Roth, P.M., Winter, M.: Survey of appearance-based methods for object recognition. Technical Report ICG-TR-01/08, Inst. for Computer Graphics and Vision, Graz University of Technology (2008)
3. Harris, C., Stephens, M.: A combined corner and edge detector. In: 4th Alvey Vision Conference, pp. 147–151 (1988)
4. Cheng, C.C., Lin, C.H., Li, C.T., Chang, S.C., Chen, L.G.: iVisual: an intelligent visual sensor SoC with 2790fps CMOS image sensor and 205GOPS/W vision processor. In: 45th Annual Design Automation Conference (DAC 2008), pp. 90–95 (2008)
5. Dietrich, B.: Design and implementation of an FPGA-based stereo vision system for the EyeBot M6. University of Western Australia (2009)
6. Teixeira, L., Celes, W., Gattass, M.: Accelerated corner-detector algorithms. In: 19th British Machine Vision Conference(BMVC 2008), pp. 625–634 (2008)
7. Saidani, T., Lacassagne, L., Bouaziz, S., Khan, T.M.: Parallelization strategies for the points of interests algorithm on the cell processor. In: Stojmenovic, I., Thulasiram, R.K., Yang, L.T., Jia, W., Guo, M., de Mello, R.F. (eds.) ISPA 2007. LNCS, vol. 4742, pp. 104–112. Springer, Heidelberg (2007)
8. ClearSpeed. Clearspeed Whitepaper: CSX Processor Architecture (2007), `http://www.clearspeed.com`
9. ClearSpeed: CSX600/CSX700 Instruction Set Reference Manual, 06-RM-1137 Revision: 4.A (August 2008), `http://www.clearspeed.com`
10. Hosseini, F., Fijany, A., Safari, S., Chellali, R., Fontaine, J.G.: Real-time parallel implementation of SSD stereo vision algorithm on CSX SIMD architecture. In: Bebis, G., Boyle, R., Parvin, B., Koracin, D., Kuno, Y., Wang, J., Wang, J.-X., Wang, J., Pajarola, R., Lindstrom, P., Hinkenjann, A., Encarnação, M.L., Silva, C.T., Coming, D. (eds.) ISVC 2009. LNCS, vol. 5875, pp. 808–818. Springer, Heidelberg (2009)

Static Speculation as Post-link Optimization for the Grid Alu Processor

Ralf Jahr, Basher Shehan, Sascha Uhrig, and Theo Ungerer

Institute of Computer Science
University of Augsburg
86135 Augsburg
Germany
{jahr,shehan,uhrig,ungerer}@informatik.uni-augsburg.de

Abstract. In this paper we propose and evaluate a post-link-optimization to increase instruction level parallelism by moving instructions from one basic block to the preceding blocks. The Grid Alu Processor used for the evaluations comprises plenty of functional units that are not completely allocated by the original instruction stream. The proposed technique speculatively performs operations in advance by using unallocated functional units.

The algorithm moves instructions to multiple predecessors of a source block. If necessary, it adds compensation code to allow the shifted instructions to work on unused registers, whose values will be copied into the original target registers at the time the speculation is resolved.

Evaluations of the algorithm show a maximum speedup of factor 2.08 achieved on the Grid Alu Processor compared to the unoptimized version of the same program due to a better exploitation of the ILP and an optimized mapping of loops.

1 Introduction

The Grid Alu Processor (GAP, see Section 3) was proposed to speed up the execution of single threaded sequential instruction streams. Compared to other designs, GAP multiplies the number of Functional Units (FUs) instead of entire cores. To configure it, a superscalar-like processor frontend loads a standard sequential instruction stream that is dynamically mapped onto an array of FUs by a special configuration unit. Execution speed is gained very much from the high level of parallelism supplied by the FUs. The main influences on the mapping process are control and data flow dependencies as well as resource conflicts caused by limited resources, which restrict the level of instruction level parallelism (ILP) that can be exploited.

The algorithm presented in this paper tackles this by moving parts of a basic block (source block) to one or more preceding blocks (target blocks). By this, results that might be required in the near future, e. g. after upcoming branches, are calculated speculatively on otherwise unused resources. At the time the reason for the speculation is resolved, these results are made visible by compensation instructions (if required).

As the GAP shall be able to replace a superscalar RISC or CISC processor and, hence, be able to execute the same binaries, no recompilation would be needed to make

M.R. Guarracino et al. (Eds.): Euro-Par 2010 Workshops, LNCS 6586, pp. 145–152, 2011.
© Springer-Verlag Berlin Heidelberg 2011

use of it. To preserve this advantage, we suggest using a post-link optimizer to apply platform-dependent code optimizations because the source code of the program to optimize is not needed in this case. Therefore, static speculation has been designed for use in a post-link-optimizer, hence after instruction selection, register assignment, and scheduling[1].

Static speculation is able to handle all types of control flow independent from domination- or post-domination-relations or the number of the source block's predecessors. The only exceptions are basic blocks that are targets of indirect jumps. A binary analysis together with profiling of the application delivers information about the execution frequency of basic blocks that can be selected as candidates for the modification.

In the remainder of the paper we give an overview of related approaches in Section 2 followed by a brief introduction of the GAP as target processor in Section 3. The algorithm is described in Section 4 followed by an evaluation of its effects on the execution of selected benchmarks in Section 5. The paper is concluded in Section 6.

2 Related Work

The GAP is a unique approach and no other code optimizations are yet suggested for it. However, similar challenges arise in compilation for superscalar or VLIW architectures as well as in hardware design. This section gives an overview.

For VLIW architectures, trace scheduling [5] is used to expose parallelism beyond basic block boundaries; it is implemented e. g. in the Multiflow Trace Scheduling Compiler [9]. This compiler also moves instructions above splits in the control flow graph but does this only if compensation instructions are not necessary. Other scheduling techniques for speculation working on the level of superblocks have been introduced and evaluated by e. g. Bergmann [2] and Mahlke [10]. These techniques require sophisticated knowledge of the program to optimize and, therefore, cannot be applied as post-link optimizations.

Without giving details, Bernstein et al. [1] suggest for scalar and superscalar architectures moving single instructions speculatively. Similar work is done by Tirumalai et al. [14]. The main difference to the work presented here is that we try to move as many instructions of a basic block as possible or reasonable at one time which decreases the overhead caused by repeatedly executing analyses. Beyond this, we also cope with the duplication of instructions to execute them speculatively.

Similarities also exist with *tail duplication* (see e. g. [6]).We also try to expose parallelism by duplicating instructions but handle only the important parts of basic blocks. Hence, the program is not as heavily rewritten but the modification effort is even smaller.

As shown in Section 4 our algorithm also has parallels with software pipelining (e. g., Llosa [8]) because it can split a loop formed by a single block into two parts and rearrange them (i. e., a prologue is formed). Nevertheless, it does not reach the complexity of most algorithms for software pipelining because we assume that instructions

[1] Nevertheless, additional implementation effort arises from this and it can happen that the optimization performs not as well as if implemented directly in the compiler. Somehow this is the price to pay for not having access to the source code.

in blocks have already been scheduled. Accordingly, we do not try to divide the source block into equal blocks in terms of approximated execution time and support only one stage.

Regarding processor design techniques, out-of-order execution as implemented by scoreboarding [12,13] or Tomasulo's scheme [15] – both in combination with branch prediction – execute instructions speculatively, too. The hardware-effort needed to allow out-of-order execution is very high and adds new limitations e. g. for the issue unit of a processor as shown by Cotofana et al. [4].

Hence, the outstanding features of the algorithm presented here are its large number of instructions which can be handled in one iteration, its ability to handle different constellations of blocks independent of the number of the source block's predecessors or the domination and/or post-domination relation between a source block and its predecessors. Beyond this, it is a post-link optimization that uses only information available from the analysis of the binary file and profiling. This causes also the struggle to modify only small parts of the program with the aim of achieving maximal effects.

3 Target Platform: Grid Alu Processor

The Grid Alu Processor (GAP) has been developed to speed up the execution of conventional single-threaded instruction streams. To achieve this goal, it combines the advantages of superscalar processor architectures, those of coarse grained reconfigurable systems, and asynchronous execution.

A superscalar-like processor front-end with a novel configuration unit is used to load instructions and map them dynamically onto an array of functional units (FUs) accompanied by a branch control unit and several load/store units to handle memory accesses.

The array of FUs is organized in columns and rows. Each column is dynamically and per configuration assigned to one architectural register. Configuration and execution in the array is always from the top to the bottom, data can flow only in this direction. The rows of the array are used to model dependencies between instructions. If an instruction B is dependent of an instruction A than it must be mapped to a row below the row of A.

To be able to save configurations for repeated execution all elements of the array are equipped with some memory cells which form configuration layers. The array is quasi three-dimensional and its size can be written as `columns x rows x layers`. So, before clearing the array it is first checked if the next instruction to execute is equal to any first instruction in one of the layers. Then, in all cases, the new values of registers calculated in columns are copied to the register file at the top of the columns. If a match is found, the corresponding layer is set to active and execution continues there. If no match is found, the least recently used configuration is cleared and used to map new instructions. With this technique, the execution of loops can be accelerated very much because instructions do not have to be re-issued.

For a detailed description of the GAP please refer to Uhrig et al. [16] and Shehan et al. [11].

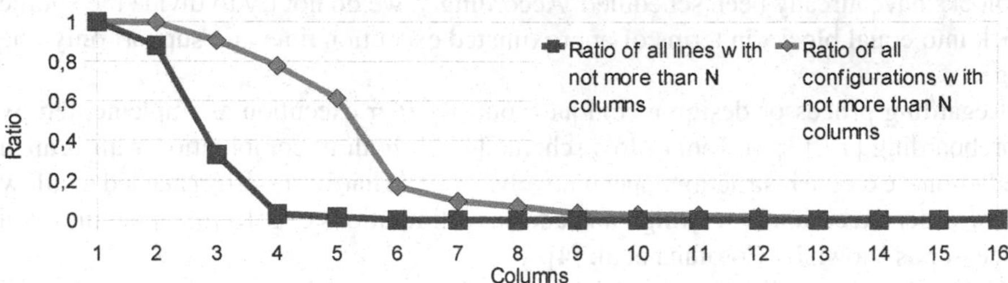

Fig. 1. Ratio of the configurations/rows which use the number of columns shown on the axis to the right for the benchmark `jpeg_encode` executed on GAP with 16x16x16 array

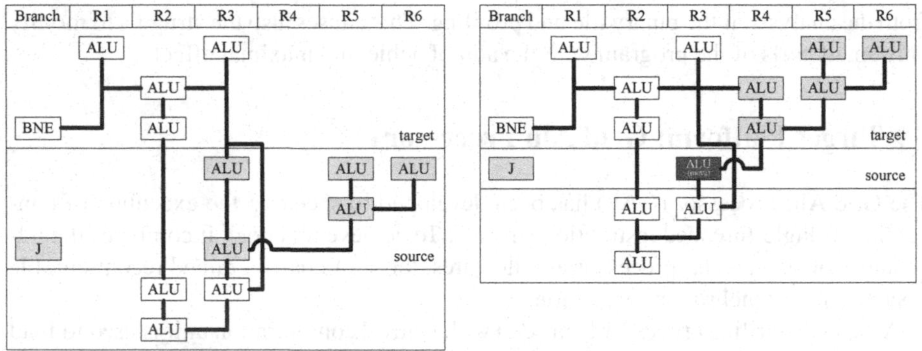

Fig. 2. Layout of three basic blocks in the GAP array without (left) and with (right) speculation

4 Static Speculation

In this section, we describe the algorithm to move instructions to preceding basic blocks together with the aim of the proposed program transformation.

When running code generated by the default compiler (GCC 2.7.2 with `-O3`, the latest version available for SimpleScalar/PISA), in most rows of the array only a small number of FUs is configured with instructions (see Figure 1). So there are enough FUs that could be used to calculate additional results, even if they might not be needed, because they would consume only little or no additional time. To use these spare resources we try to speculatively execute instructions from following blocks.

An example is shown in Figure 2. It shows three basic blocks which could stand for an *if-then*-structure and have been placed into the array of the GAP. The influence of data dependencies on the instruction placement can be observed. Also, after each control flow instruction synchronization, which is a special pecularity of GAP and shown by a horizontal line in Figure 2, is required. In this example, all instructions of the second block can be moved to the first block and executed speculatively.

If the second block shall not be executed, i. e., the branch from the first block to the third block is taken, its effects must not be visible. In the example, `R3` is the only register which would have been modified by the speculatively executed instructions and overwrite a value which is used by subsequent instructions. Therefore, the moved instructions work on `R4`, which was initially unused, instead of the original `R3`. The overhead for executing the speculative instructions is zero in this example, because they are executed in parallel to the first block.

If the second block shall be executed, the content of `R4` must be copied to `R3`, the original target register. In the figure, this additional compensation instruction is marked by a dark box. Even if multiple compensation instructions would be required, they can be placed in the same row of the array and can be executed in parallel because they do not have any interdependencies. In our example, the overhead for the compensation instruction is zero because it is executed in parallel with the branch instruction. In the worst case, all compensation instructions can be executed in parallel because they do not have any dependencies on each other and, hence, consume the same time as a single additional *move* instruction.

Depending on the critical path and the resource utilization of the source and the target block, the number of rows of the array that are required to map the combined blocks should be lower. If a lower number of rows is needed for the modified blocks the average number of instructions per row increases. Hence, the number of instructions that can be executed in parallel increases resulting in a higher instructions per cycle (IPC) value.

To avoid executing too many unnecessary instructions, we move instructions only if the probability of the usage of the calculated results is above a fixed value, e. g. 30%. This value has been found to be a good tradeoff between performance and additionally executed instructions. Also we want to modify blocks only if they contribute significantly to the total program performance. Hence a block must be executed more often than a fixed boundary, e. g. more than 10 times.

Nevertheless, we cannot be sure that the total configuration length will be shorter after the modification of the blocks. This is because of the eventually required additional row for the compensation instructions, the potential inconvenient layout of the critical paths of the blocks, and resource restrictions. For example, if memory operations are moved into a block which already uses many memory access units, then additional rows will be needed to map the moved memory operations. Hence, resource restrictions can also restrict the degree of parallelism of instructions. This problem is solved by introducing an objective function to estimate the height of the modified configuration. The additional height could also be limited by a parameter, but currently it is set to zero.

This objective function is mainly taken into account when selecting the number of instructions to move. It is maximized in respect to the objective function and the availability of enough registers to use them as temporary registers.

A special case is to move instructions across a loop branch. As example, imagine a block with a conditional branch to its first instruction, so it forms a very simple loop. If we shift a part of the source block to all the preceding blocks, we shift instructions from its beginning to one or more blocks with edges to the loop and also to the end of the loop. these re-ordered parts of the loop can be executed with a higher degree of parallelism. Loop carried dependencies are also handled because the speculatively

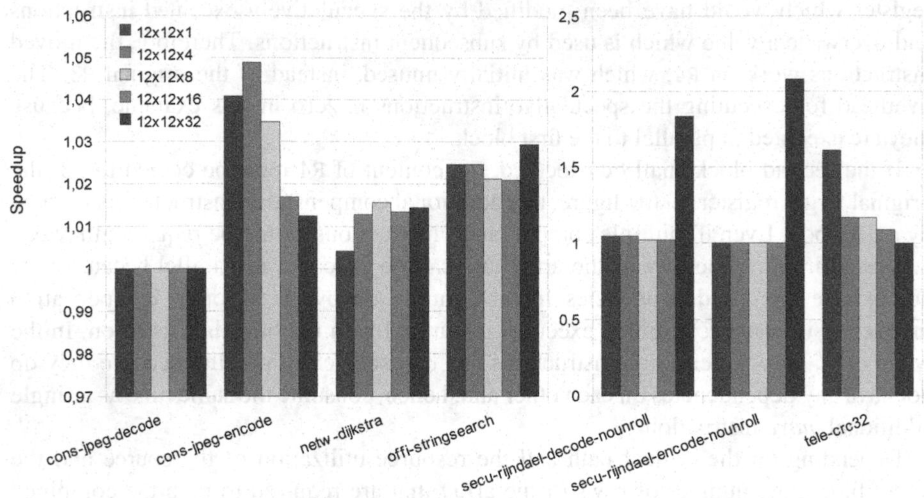

Fig. 3. Maximum speedup for selected benchmarks on GAP array of 12x12xN FUs

calculated results are not copied to the target registers until it is clear that the loop will be executed at least one more time.

To sum up, we expect better performance in terms of execution time. In an optimal case a better use of the FUs of the array is achieved because more columns and less rows are used. This leads to less reconfigurations of the array and a higher degree of parallelism inside the array.

5 Evaluation

We evaluated the static speculation algorithm using seven selected benchmarks of the MiBench Benchmark Suite [7]. We first compiled them using a standard compiler (GCC with optimizations turned on, $-O3$). Second, we performed on these binaries a static analysis and applied the proposed post-link-optimization with our tool GAPtimize.

The GAP is simulated by a cycle accurate simulator which can execute the same binary files as the SimpleScalar simulator [3] using the PISA instruction set architecture. For all benchmarks, we used a *bimod* branch predictor and an identical cache configuration.

Figure 3 shows the speedup that can be gained for the seven selected benchmarks and several configurations of the GAP by the optimization technique over unmodified code. They have been distributed on the two charts according to the main reason for the speedup. The maximum speedup of 2.08 is achieved for benchmark `secu-rijndael-encode` (AES) with an array of 12 rows, 12 columns and 32 layers (i. e. 12x12x32). The speedup is calculated as the number of total clock cycles for the unmodified program divided by the number of clock cycles needed for the modified program executed on GAP with identical configuration.

The speedup for the benchmarks secu-rijndael-decode-nounroll, secu-rijndael-encode-nounroll, and tele-crc32 is caused by effects beyond those described in Section 4. The main reason for the speedup is here GAP's ability to accelerate the execution of loops if the loop body fits completely into the array. This is more often the case if the program has been modified with reduction of the length of configurations as objective. As example, GAP with the 12x12x1 configuration executing tele-crc32 accelerates 108310 loop iterations after applying the algorithm instead of 428 without modifications. This is because the configuration of the loop is short enough after applying the static speculation optimization to map it onto the single available configuration layer. In other words, the static speculation and the hardware architecture are working hand in hand.

The more configuration layers are available the less is the impact of the optimization for tele-crc32 and cons-jpeg-encode. This is because larger loops can be mapped to multiple layers anyway and, hence, the advantage of the static speculation is not as high as with a small number of layers. The acceleration of the two secu-rijndael-*-nounroll benchmarks is caused by the same effects. Hereby, a very long loop is mapped to multiple layers and by static speculation the number of layers required for the loop is reduced. Consequently, more layers are available to configure other code fragments.

Nevertheless, speed up can also be gained for benchmarks without dominant loops like cons-jpeg-encode. This is due to a higher level of ILP (more FUs er line of the array are used) and less instruction cache misses. Again, these effects are reduced if the number of configuration layers is increased.

6 Conclusion

In this paper, we present an algorithm for a post-link-optimizer to increase the degree of ILP in some parts of a program. Therefore, instructions are moved from one basic block to the preceding blocks. This modification allows in-order architectures with high fetch and execute bandwidth to execute these instructions speculatively. The speculative instructions are statically modified to use registers not required by the original program flow at that time. If the following branch is resolved the results are copied into the original target registers, if necessary. Otherwise, they are discarded. Additional hardware for speculative execution is not required. Our evaluations show a maximum speedup factor of 2.08 for a standard benchmark using GAP.

A side effect of the static speculation algorithm is that moving instructions over a loop back branch is similar to software pipelining. In the future we will focus more on this aspect. As example, it would be possible to add an additional step to reschedule the instructions of the source block before modification to increase the number of instructions that can be moved to the target blocks.

Another topic that we will examine is the real-time capability of the proposed approach. Speculative execution is also applied within out-of-order processors but, in contrast to our approach, its timing behavior is nearly unpredictable because of its dynamic nature.

References

1. D. Bernstein and M. Rodeh. Global instruction scheduling for superscalar machines. *SIGPLAN Not.*, 26(6):241–255, 1991.
2. R. A. Bringmann. *Enhancing instruction level parallelism through compiler-controlled speculation.* PhD thesis, University of Illinois, Champaign, IL, USA, 1995.
3. D. Burger and T. Austin. The SimpleScalar tool set, version 2.0. *ACM SIGARCH Computer Architecture News*, 25(3):13–25, June 1997.
4. S. Cotofana and S. Vassiliadis. On the design complexity of the issue logic of superscalar machines. In *EUROMICRO '98: Proceedings of the 24th Conference on EUROMICRO*, page 10277, Washington, DC, USA, 1998. IEEE Computer Society.
5. J. Fisher. Trace scheduling: A technique for global microcode compaction. *IEEE Transactions on Computers*, 30:478–490, 1981.
6. D. Gregg. Comparing tail duplication with compensation code in single path global instruction scheduling. In *CC '01: Proceedings of the 10th International Conference on Compiler Construction*, pages 200–212, London, UK, 2001. Springer-Verlag.
7. M. Guthaus, J. Ringenberg, D. Ernst, T. Austin, T. Mudge, and R. Brown. Mibench: A free, commercially representative embedded benchmark suite. pages 3 – 14, dec. 2001.
8. J. Llosa. Swing modulo scheduling: A lifetime-sensitive approach. In *PACT '96: Proceedings of the 1996 Conference on Parallel Architectures and Compilation Techniques*, page 80, Washington, DC, USA, 1996. IEEE Computer Society.
9. P. G. Lowney, S. M. Freudenberger, T. J. Karzes, W. D. Lichtenstein, R. P. Nix, J. S. O'Donnell, and J. Ruttenberg. The multiflow trace scheduling compiler. *The Journal of Supercomputing*, 7(1-2):51–142, 1993.
10. S. A. Mahlke, W. Y. Chen, R. A. Bringmann, R. E. Hank, W. mei W. Hwu, B. Ramakrishna, R. Michael, and S. Schlansker. Sentinel scheduling: a model for compiler-controlled speculative execution. *ACM Transactions on Computer Systems*, 11:376–408, 1993.
11. B. Shehan, R. Jahr, S. Uhrig, and T. Ungerer. Reconfigurable grid alu processor: Optimization and design space exploration. In *Proceedings of the 13th Euromicro Conference on Digital System Design (DSD) 2010, Lille, France*, 2010.
12. J. E. Thornton. Parallel operation in the Control Data 6600. In *AFIPS '64 (Fall, part II): Proceedings of the October 27-29, 1964, fall joint computer conference, part II: very high speed computer systems*, pages 33–40, New York, NY, USA, 1965. ACM.
13. J. E. Thornton. *Design of a Computer—The Control Data 6600.* Scott Foresman & Co, 1970.
14. P. Tirumalai and M. Lee. A heuristic for global code motion. In *ICYCS'93: Proceedings of the third International Conference on Young Computer Scientists*, pages 109–115, Beijing, China, China, 1993. Tsinghua University Press.
15. R. M. Tomasulo. An efficient algorithm for exploiting multiple arithmetic units. *IBM J Res Dev*, 11(1):25–33, 1967.
16. S. Uhrig, B. Shehan, R. Jahr, and T. Ungerer. The two-dimensional superscalar GAP processor architecture. *International Journal on Advances in Systems and Measurements*, 3:71–81, 2010.

A Multi-level Routing Scheme and Router Architecture to Support Hierarchical Routing in Large Network on Chip Platforms

Rickard Holsmark[1], Shashi Kumar[1], and Maurizio Palesi[2]

[1] School of Engineering, Jönköping University, Sweden
{rickard.holsmark,shashi.kumar}@jth.hj.se
[2] DIIT, University of Catania, Italy
mpalesi@diit.unict.it

Abstract. The concept of hierarchical networks is useful for designing a large heterogeneous NoC by reusing predesigned small NoCs as subnets. In this paper we show that multi-level addressing is a cost-effective implementation option for hierarchical deadlock-free routing. We propose a 2-level routing scheme, which is not only efficient, but also enables co-existence of algorithmic and table-based implementation in one router. Synthesis results show that a 2-level hierarchical router design for an 8*x*8 NoC, can reduce area and power requirements by up to ~20%, as compared to a router for the flat network. This work also proposes a new possibility for increasing the number of nodes available for subnet-to-subnet interfaces. Communication performance is evaluated for various subnet interface set-ups and traffic situations.

Keywords: Networks on Chip, Hierarchical Networks, Router Architecture.

1 Introduction

NoC will be the ideal communication infrastructure for next generation SoCs with hundreds of cores as predicted by ITRS. The concept of hierarchy will be helpful in designing and using such NoC platforms with growing number of cores. Whether hierarchical or not, the formation of packet deadlocks may be fatal to any network communication. To avoid this, several deadlock-free routing schemes have been proposed in literature, e.g. Turn model [1], Odd-Even [2] and Up*/Down* [3]. Deadlock freedom may be compromised when combining different networks, each with its own deadlock-free routing algorithm. Therefore, an important new issue in hierarchical NoCs is the design of deadlock-free routing algorithms.

Holsmark et al. [4] proposed hierarchical deadlock-free routing and showed that if subnets are interconnected by "safe boundary" nodes, it is possible to design a deadlock-free global routing algorithm without altering any internal subnet routing algorithm. But Holsmark et al. [4] assumed a flat implementation with a common address space for all network nodes. In this work we propose that a hierarchical routing function is implemented in two levels. The higher level routing function will determine if the destination for a packet is inside or outside the local subnet. If the destination is outside the current subnet, the address of the entry node of the

M.R. Guarracino et al. (Eds.): Euro-Par 2010 Workshops, LNCS 6586, pp. 153–161, 2011.
© Springer-Verlag Berlin Heidelberg 2011

destination subnet is used for routing the message. Upon reaching the destination subnet, the lower level routing function determines the route using the local address of the destination node. Hence, multi-level routers need only to store addresses to subnet entry-nodes for destinations in other subnets, rather than addresses to all nodes. This reduces router table-sizes and we show that the 2-level router architecture indeed enables significant reduction in area and power consumption.

One important parameter which affects performance is the number of safe boundary nodes of a subnet [4]. Since some routing algorithms provide very few safe nodes, we propose the concept of "safe channels" to attain higher connectivity, and hence higher performance of a network. We have compared the performance of 2-level routing with common deadlock-free routing algorithms and explored the effect of varying the number of boundary nodes.

Recently the topic of hierarchical NoCs has caught the attention of researchers. Several aspects have been studied, for example Bourduas et al. [5] have proposed a hybrid ring/mesh interconnect topology to remove limitations of lengthy diameter of large mesh topology networks. Deadlock-free routing in irregular networks often implies a strongly limited set of routing paths. To increase the available paths, Lysne et al. [6] developed a routing scheme, which avoids deadlock by assigning traffic into different layers of virtual channels.

2 Safe Channels for Increased Connectivity in Hierarchical Routing Algorithms

The methodology for hierarchical routing algorithms [4] used the concept of safe boundary nodes to ensure deadlock freedom. Whether a node is "safe" or not depends on each subnet routing algorithm and is checked by analysis of internal CDG (Channel Dependency Graph [7]) paths. If there are no internal paths from any output to any input of a node, it is *safe* (see Fig. 1). If such a path exists, the node is *unsafe* and may enable formation of CDG cycles with paths in other subnets. The requirement that all boundary nodes should be safe often reduces the number of possible boundary nodes in a network.

For deterministic routing algorithms, like XY, all boundary nodes are safe. Partially adaptive algorithms provide only a few safe boundary nodes, e.g. an *NxN* network with Odd-Even [2], or West-First [1] provides only *N*, whereas Negative-First [1] provides *N*+ (*N*-1) nodes. To remedy this situation we propose the concept of

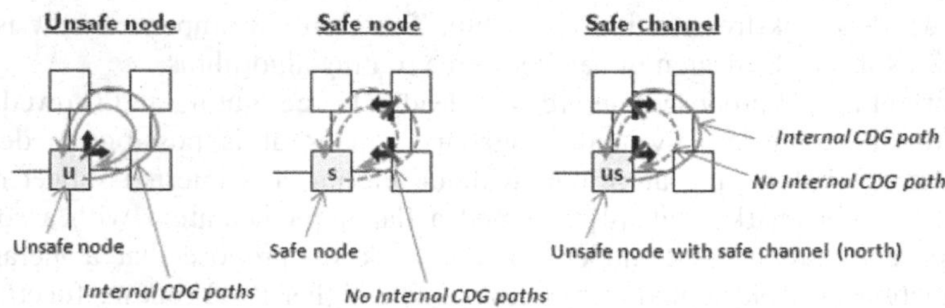

Fig. 1. Examples of unsafe boundary nodes, safe boundary nodes and safe channels

safe *channels*. Given a node *n*, and an internal output channel *c* of node *n*, *c* is a safe channel if there does not exist an internal CDG path from channel *c* to any input channel of *n*.

Fig. 1 illustrates the differences between unsafe nodes, safe nodes and safe channels. The node ***u*** is *unsafe* because the routing restriction allows CDG paths between its internal ports. The restrictions in the *safe* node example prevent such CDG paths and ***s*** is therefore safe. In the safe *channel* example, it is straightforward to see that only one of the internal output channels of node ***us*** (unsafe with safe channel) is on a CDG path to an input channel of ***us*** itself. Using this safe channel and restricting the use of the other channel would, from a deadlock freedom perspective, be equivalent to using a safe node. Note that safe channels cannot relax the requirement of at least one safe boundary node in each subnet. The effect of adding unsafe nodes with safe channels is explored in the evaluation section.

3 Two-Level Routing Scheme

3.1 Addressing and Routing Protocol

Availability of multiple boundary nodes requires that information of the destination subnet boundary node is added (see example in section 3.3). Therefore a source node tags the header destination address with three fields [*subnet id, boundary node, node id*]. The routing protocol is identical for all nodes. Each node first checks to which subnet a packet is destined. If it is in the current subnet, an internal routing function determines the route. Otherwise, it is forwarded by an external routing function.

If subnets are heterogeneous, the encoding of node address in the source subnet may differ from the encoding in the destination subnet, both with respect to size and topology. In general, the header field for node address must be adjusted according to the subnet requiring largest number of bits for node address. The size of the field for subnet addressing depends on the number of subnets.

3.2 Two-Level Routing Function

The 2-level routing function is partitioned into an external routing function R_G and a subnet internal routing function R_i. The internal routing function is identical to the routing function as if the subnet is a stand-alone network. One feature which is enabled by 2-level routing is the possibility to mix implementation techniques of the internal routing functions in different subnets. This implies that routers in some subnets may be table-based while other routers may implement algorithmic routing.

Fig. 2 gives pseudo-code of the main hierarchical routing function R_H and the proposed router architecture. The routing function takes *dst* which contains the destination subnet *dst.sn*, destination boundary node *dst.bn* and node address *dst.addr*. If both destination subnet and node addresses match with current subnet and node addresses, the function returns the local resource channel. If the destination resides in the same subnet as the current node, the local routing function R_i is called with the destination node address *dst.addr*. The returned output channel *c_out* will in this case always be internal. Should the subnets not match, the external routing function is invoked with destination subnet *dst.sn* and boundary node *dst.bn*. The external routing function can return both external and internal channels if current node is a boundary node. If current node is not a boundary node it will only return internal channels. The 2-level router tables are built similarly to the flat router tables, using breadth-first search for computing paths. The main difference is that only paths to destination subnets and boundary nodes are stored in the external table. This means that during the search, for each source-destination pair, the node where the last transition between different subnets was made is stored as boundary node for the destination. This information is used for addressing by the source node. Simultaneously, the output channel from which the boundary node can be reached is stored in the router table.

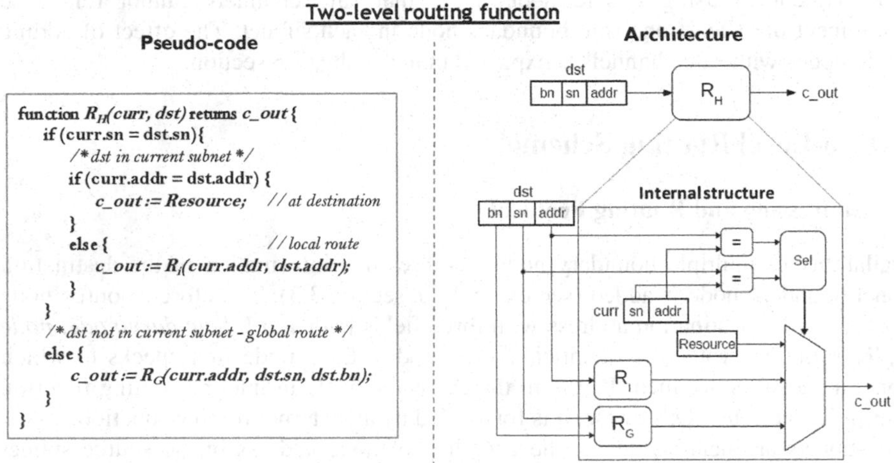

Fig. 2. Pseudo-code and architecture of two-level routing function

Since all paths are obtained using the hierarchical deadlock-free routing methodology [4], it can be shown that the 2-level scheme is deadlock free and connected as well. If the destination is in another subnet, such paths must traverse a boundary node in the source subnet and a boundary node in the destination subnet.

3.3 A Small Example of Routing in Two-Level Router Networks

This small example illustrates routing in 2-level networks as well as the requirement of boundary node id for external destinations. Study Fig. 3 where each subnet S_1, S_2 and S_3 is a 2*x*2 mesh with routing algorithms XY, YX and XY respectively. The external algorithm in this case is assumed to be YX. Boundary nodes are indicated by double border.

Consider routing a message from source node $n_{1,1}$ in subnet S_1 to the destination node $n_{2,2}$ in subnet S_2. The source node is identified with subnet and node address, *src* = (S_1, $n_{1,1}$). Destination address contains subnet, boundary node and node address, *dst* = (S2, b2, n2,2). When the routing function is called in src, the subnet fields do not match and the external function will be used. The external function returns the *East* channel, i.e. $R_G((n_{1,1}), S_2, b_2)$ = *East*. Note that this is the only allowed route according to the internal XY algorithm. At node *curr* = (S_1, $n_{1,2}$), the external algorithm returns *South*. Using *East* would neither violate the internal algorithm restriction. However, this shows the necessity for boundary node specification in the packet header. If the external address is specified using subnet id alone, it would not be possible to distinguish between destinations in row 1 and row 2 in subnet S_2.

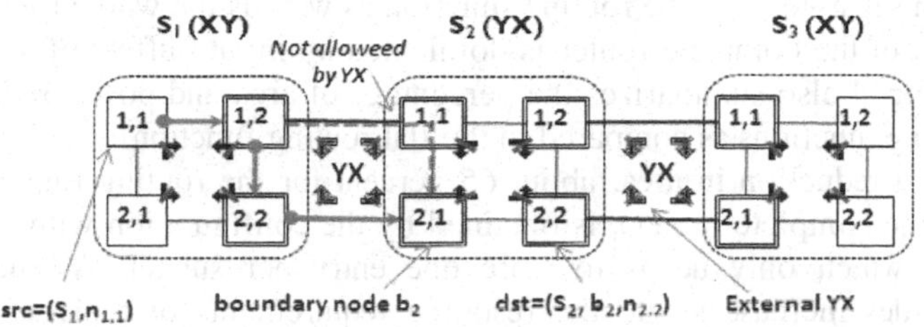

Fig. 3. Example of two-level addressing

In this case, for reaching node *dst* the *only* allowed route is *South*, as the packet cannot make this turn at row 1 in subnet S_2 since both the internal algorithm and external algorithm is YX. After turning south, eventually the packet arrives at node $n_{2,1}$ in subnet S_2. Since the current subnet is now the same as the destination subnet, the node address and local algorithm is used for routing to the destination, i.e. R_i = ($n_{2,1}$, $n_{2,2}$) = *East*.

4 Synthesis Results

We evaluate area and power requirements for the network structures given in Fig. 5(right). Straightforwardly compared, flat addressing in this case requires 64 (8x8) entries per router whereas, e.g., 2-level addressing with one boundary node requires one table of 4 entries for subnet addresses and one table with 16 (4x4) entries for local addresses.

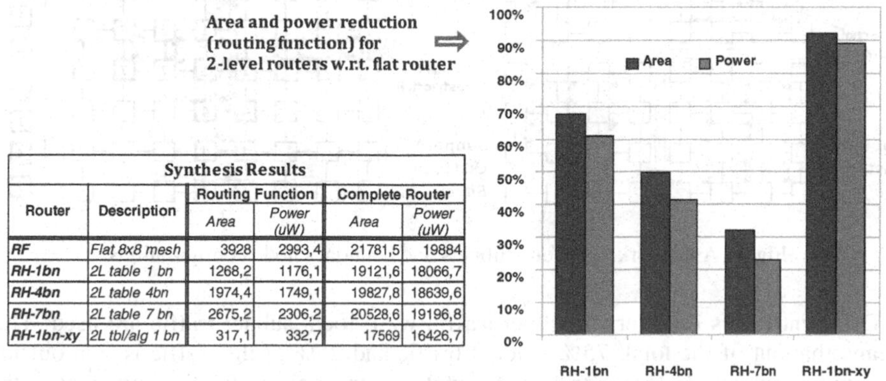

Synthesis Results

Router	Description	Routing Function		Complete Router	
		Area	*Power (uW)*	*Area*	*Power (uW)*
RF	*Flat 8x8 mesh*	3928	2993,4	21781,5	19884
RH-1bn	*2L table 1 bn*	1268,2	1176,1	19121,6	18066,7
RH-4bn	*2L table 4bn*	1974,4	1749,1	19827,8	18639,6
RH-7bn	*2L table 7 bn*	2675,2	2306,2	20528,6	19196,8
RH-1bn-xy	*2L tbl/alg 1 bn*	317,1	332,7	17569	16426,7

Fig. 4. Area and power for different two-level router versions (RH-*x*bn) and a flat router (RF)

Fig. 4 presents synthesis results from UMC 65nm technology library, assuming 1 GHz clock frequency. The results for implementation of a flat routing function are indicated by the label *RF*. The 2-level variants are indicated according to the number of boundary nodes (*RH-1bn*, *RH-4bn* and *RH-7bn*). The table also provides data for 2-level routing with one boundary node and algorithmic XY routing (*RH-1bn-xy*). Results are given for one routing function per router. The table gives area and power consumption separately for the routing function as well as the whole router. The main share of cost of the complete router is dominated by input buffers of 4 flits for each input port. Fig. 4 also summarizes the percentage of area and power reduction of the 2-level routing functions as compared to the flat routing function.

The largest reduction in area, about 65 percent for the routing function (and ~12 percent for the complete router), is obtained by the configuration with one boundary node (*bn1)*, which only needs to store one entry per subnet. As the number of boundary nodes increase so do the resource requirements of the routing function. Power reduction is slightly less than area reduction for all configurations. Considering the algorithmic implementation with XY as local routing function, it is shown that area and power for the routing function can be reduced by about 90 percent.

5 Simulation Based Performance Evaluation

The evaluations are performed with a simulator designed in SDL using Telelogic SDL and TTCN Suite 6.2. Wormhole switching is employed, with packet size fixed at 10 flits. Routers are modeled with input buffers of size 4 and flit latency of 3 cycles per router. Packet injection rate *pir* is given in average number of packets generated per cycle. Thus at *pir*=0.02, each node generates on average 2 packets per 100 cycles.

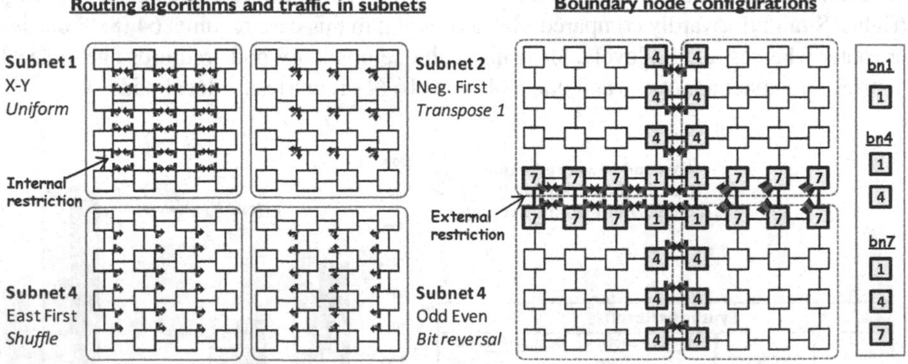

Fig. 5. A network with four subnets and boundary node configurations

Different levels of external subnet traffic w.r.t. local subnet traffic are used. This means that out of the total, 75% is local traffic and 25% of the traffic is sent outside the source subnet. External traffic destinations are uniformly distributed over the whole network. The used subnet configurations are given in Fig. 5(left). Each subnet exhibits a specific traffic type, which in the case of hierarchical routing is matched with a suitable routing algorithm, (e.g. Subnet 2: Negative First, Transpose1). Fig. 5(right) shows the three configurations of boundary nodes and external routing restrictions in the evaluations. Nodes labeled 1, represent the one boundary node per subnet case (bn1).The four boundary node set-up (bn4) additionally uses the nodes labeled 4, while the seven boundary node instance (bn7) includes all numbered nodes.

The bn1 and bn4 set-ups utilize only safe nodes, where bn4 represents the maximum attainable connectivity with safe nodes. The bn7 case allows safe channels of unsafe nodes in subnets 3 and 4 and achieves the maximum connectivity of the topology. Flat algorithms are global, e.g. in the case of XY this means that XY is used for routing all messages. Note that XY is only applicable to the bn7 configuration. The Up*/Down* algorithm is applicable to all different configurations and is annotated similarly to the hierarchical cases, i.e. ud_bn*x*.

5.1 Simulation Results

Fig. 6(left) compares average latency (duration from when a packet was generated at the source to when its tail flit was received at the destination) of the hierarchical *hr_bn7* configuration with XY and Up*/Down* for 100, 95 and 75 percent of message subnet locality. Performance is adversely affected for all algorithms when reducing the internal traffic. The highest performance is obtained by *hr_bn7* with 100% local traffic (hr_bn7_100). Notable is that *hr_bn7* also for 95 % local traffic performs considerably better than both XY and Up*/Down* for 100% local traffic.

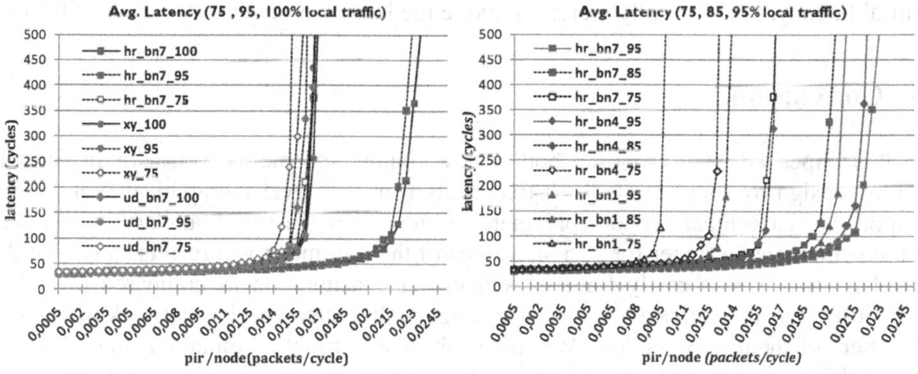

Fig. 6. Average latency: hr vs. other algorithms (left), different hr configurations (right)

For 75% of local traffic the differences are reduced, especially compared to XY. This is quite expected, since XY is known to be a very good algorithm for uniformly distributed traffic (which is the distribution of the external traffic). Studying the results for four- and one- boundary node hierarchical (hr_bn4_95 and hr_bn1_95 respectively) in Fig. 6(right), we see that both outperform XY for 95% local traffic (Fig. 6(left)), even though their average distances increase due to longer routes. As the local traffic is reduced, fewer boundary nodes result in significantly higher average latency than XY. The very few external links in *hr_bn1* are effective bottlenecks and the congestion rapidly propagates into the internal subnet traffic.

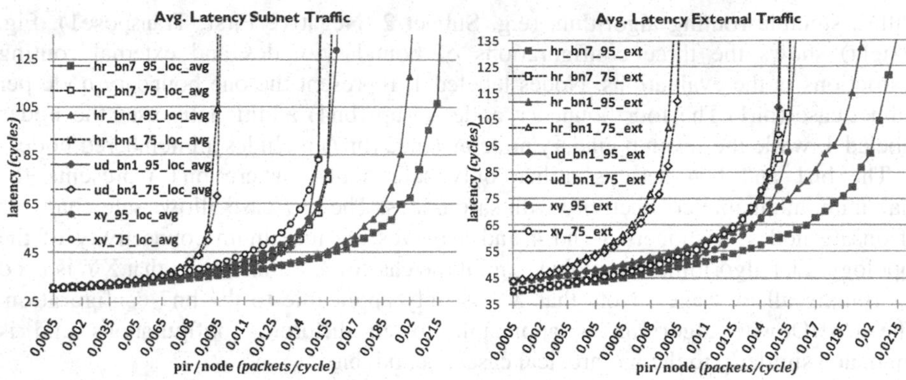

Fig. 7. Average latency for internal subnet traffic (left), external traffic (right)

Fig. 7.(left) compares average latency for different algorithms and internal subnet traffic. Both *hr_bn7* and *hr_bn1* show considerably lower latency values for high load in the 95% local traffic scenario. Note that XY is on a higher curve than Up*/Down* (ud_bn1_95) at low *pir* but improves as *pir* is increased. This indicates that Up*/Down* may have advantage of adaptive routes at lower *pir* compared to XY routing algorithm. Fig. 7(right) complement the subnet latency by showing the latency of the external traffic. The higher base latency for *ud_bn1*and *hr_bn1*, due to fewer external links, is visible at both 75% and 95% of local traffic. But, in spite of lower initial latency, *xy_95* rapidly increases above the latency of *hr_bn1_95* at *pir* of 0.015.

6 Conclusions

In this paper we have proposed both a new routing scheme as well as a structured router design to support deadlock-free routing in a 2-level hierarchical NoC. One important hierarchical network parameter is the number of safe boundary nodes. We have synthesized a router for various values of this parameter and results show that 2-level routing is less costly for area and power consumption as compared to a flat solution. The importance of this advantage will increase with network size and number of boundary nodes. We also observe through simulation that 2-level hierarchical routing with maximum number of boundary nodes, in general, provides higher performance compared to flat routing algorithms. Although it seems that the proposed 2-level scheme will recursively extend itself to *n*-levels, implementation of such schemes will open new challenges.

References

1. Glass, C., Ni, L.: The Turn Model for Adaptive Routing. In: Proceedings of the 19th Annual International Symposium on Computer Architecture, 1992, pp. 278–287 (1992)
2. Chiu, G.-M.: The odd-even turn model for adaptive routing. IEEE Transactions on Parallel and Distributed Systems 11, 729–738 (2000)

3. Schroeder, M., Birrell, A., Burrows, M., Murray, H., Needham, R., Rodeheffer, T., Satterthwaite, E., Thacker, C.: Autonet: a high-speed, self-configuring local area network using point-to-point links. IEEE Journal on Selected Areas in Communications 9, 1318–1335 (1991)
4. Holsmark, R., Kumar, S., Palesi, M., Mejia, A.: HiRA: A methodology for deadlock free routing in hierarchical networks on chip. In: 3rd ACM/IEEE International Symposium on Networks-on-Chip, NoCS 2009, pp. 2–11. IEEE Computer Society, Los Alamitos (2009)
5. Bourduas, S., Zilic, Z.: A Hybrid Ring/Mesh Interconnect for Network-on-Chip Using Hierarchical Rings for Global Routing. In: Proc. of the ACM/IEEE Int. Symp. on Networks-on-Chip (NOCS) (2007)
6. Lysne, O., Skeie, T., Reinemo, S., Theiss, I.: Layered Routing in Irregular Networks. IEEE Trans. Parallel Distrib. Syst. 17, 51–65 (2006)
7. Duato, J.: A new theory of deadlock-free adaptive routing in wormhole networks. IEEE Transactions on Parallel and Distributed Systems 4, 1320–1331 (1993)

Workshop on
High Performance Bioinformatics
and Biomedicine
(HiBB 2010)

HiBB 2010: Workshop on High Performance Bioinformatics and Biomedicine

Mario Cannataro

Department of Experimental Medicine and Clinic,
University Magna Græcia of Catanzaro,
88100 Catanzaro, Italy,
cannataro@unicz.it

Foreword

High-throughput technologies such as microarray and mass spectrometry and clinical diagnostic tools such as medical imaging, are producing an increasing amount of experimental and clinical data. In such a scenario, large scale databases and bioinformatics tools are key tools for organizing and exploring biological and biomedical data with the aim to discover new knowledge in biology and medicine.

High-performance computing may play an important role in many phases of life sciences research, from raw data management and processing, to data integration and analysis, till data exploration and visualization. In particular, at the raw data layer, Grid infrastructures may offer the huge data storage needed to store experimental and biomedical data, while parallel computing can be used for basic pre-processing (e.g. parallel BLAST) and for more advanced analysis (e.g. parallel data mining). In such a scenario, novel parallel architectures (e.g. CELL processors, GPU, FPGA, hybrid CPU/FPGA) coupled with emerging programming models may overcome the limits posed by conventional computers to the mining and exploration of large amounts of data.

At an higher layer, emerging biomedical applications need to use bioinformatics tools, biological data banks and patient's clinical data, that require seamless integration, privacy preservation and controlled sharing. Service Oriented Architectures and semantic technologies, such as ontologies, may allow the building and deployment of the so called "collaboratories", where experimental research may be conducted by remote scientists in a collaborative way.

The *1st Workshop on High Performance Bioinformatics and Biomedicine* (HiBB) aimed to bring together scientists in the fields of high performance computing, computational biology and medicine to discuss the parallel implementation of bioinformatics algorithms, the application of high performance computing in biomedical applications, as well as the organization of large scale databases in biology and medicine. Furthermore, the use of novel parallel architectures and dedicated hardware to implement bioinformatics and biomedical algorithms has been discussed.

M.R. Guarracino et al. (Eds.): Euro-Par 2010 Workshops, LNCS 6586, pp. 165–166, 2011.
© Springer-Verlag Berlin Heidelberg 2011

To be able to reach the parallel processing community, the workshop has been organized in conjunction with Euro-Par, the main European (but international) conference on all aspects of parallel processing. The Call for Papers for the HiBB workshop was launched early in the year 2010, and at the passing of the submission deadline we had received 16 submissions, which were of good quality and generally relevant to the theme of the workshop. The papers were swiftly and expertly reviewed by the program committee, each of them receiving at least three qualified reviews.

The program chair thanks the whole of the program committee and the additional reviewers for the time and expertise they put into the reviewing work, and for getting it all done within the rather strict time limit. Final decision on acceptance was made by the program chair based on the recommendations from the program committee. Being an half-day event, there was room for accepting only 8 of the contributions, resulting in an acceptance ratio of about 50%. All the accepted contributions were presented at the workshop yielding an interesting discussion on the role that parallel processing may play in bioinformatics and biomedicine.

Presentations were organized in two sessions: in the former (High Performance Bioinformatics) four papers discussing the parallel implementation of bioinformatics and systems biology algorithms were presented, while in the latter (High Performance Biomedicine) four papers describing the application of high performance computing in clinical laboratories and hospitals were presented. This post-workshop proceedings includes the final versions of the presented HiBB papers, taking the feedback from reviewers and workshop audience into account.

The program chair sincerely thanks the Euro-Par organization for providing the opportunity to arrange the HiBB workshop in conjunction with the Euro-Par 2010 conference. The program chair also warmly thanks the Faculty of Medicine of the University of Catanzaro and Euro-Par for financial support which made it possible to organize the workshop. Finally, the program chair thanks all attendees at the workshop, who contributed to a lively day. Based on the mostly positive feedback the program chair and organizers plan to continue the HiBB workshop in conjunction with Euro-Par 2011.

October 2010

Mario Cannataro

StochKit-FF: Efficient Systems Biology on Multicore Architectures

Marco Aldinucci[1,⋆], Andrea Bracciali[2,⋆], Pietro Liò[3,⋆], Anil Sorathiya[3], and Massimo Torquati[4]

[1] Computer Science Department, University of Torino, Italy
aldinuc@di.unito.it
[2] ISTI - CNR, Italy
braccia@di.unipi.it
[3] Computer Laboratory, Cambridge University, UK
{pl219,as883}@cam.ac.uk
[4] Computer Science Department, University of Pisa, Italy
torquati@di.unipi.it

Abstract. The stochastic modelling of biological systems is informative and often very adequate, but it may easily be more expensive than other modelling approaches, such as differential equations. We present StochKit-FF, a parallel version of StochKit, a reference toolkit for stochastic simulations. StochKit-FF is based on the FastFlow programming toolkit for multicores and on the novel concept of selective memory. We experiment StochKit-FF on a model of HIV infection dynamics, with the aim of extracting information from efficiently run experiments, here in terms of average and variance and, on a longer term, of more structured data.

Keywords: Stochastic biological models, simulation, multicore.

1 Introduction

The immune system is an example of a complex system formed out of its intercellular and intracellular components, which organise in space and time the immune response to pathogens through a system of positive and negative regulatory nested feedbacks. The modelling of part of the immune response to HIV infection is a paradigmatic scenario illustrating the challenges that computer-based modelling and analysis present for this class of problems. The immune system can be both modelled by deterministic differential equations (ODEs) and by stochastic modelling approaches. ODEs are effective in characterizing the system dynamics when the molecular copy number of each species is sufficiently large. A stochastic model is much more accurate when the number of molecules considered is small. The numerical solvability of stochastic models is limited to pretty

⋆ MA and AB have been partially supported by the HPC-Europa 2 *Transnational Access* programme, MA by the Regione Piemonte *BioBITs* Project AB by the CNR project RSTL-XXL, and PL by the EC's IST SOCIALNETS project (217141) and the U.S. Army Research Lab. and U.K. Ministry of Defence (W911NF-06-3-0001).

M.R. Guarracino et al. (Eds.): Euro-Par 2010 Workshops, LNCS 6586, pp. 167–175, 2011.
© Springer-Verlag Berlin Heidelberg 2011

small dimensions (e.g. number of species) due to their exponential complexity. The behaviour of larger systems can be described by stochastic simulations, e.g. those based on the *Gillespie's algorithm*, which simulates the system dynamics step by step. These methods, although often more accurate than the deterministic ones, can be highly demanding in terms of computational power, e.g. when considering many simulations for increasing the precision of the model. Stochastic methods represent a challenging methodological areas of system biology and play a growing role in modelling immune responses to pathogens.

We here illustrate the use of parallelism for supporting efficient and informative stochastic analysis of one such model. Multiple simulations exhibit a natural independence that would allow them to be treated in an *embarrassingly parallel* fashion. However, this is not possible whenever the results need to be concurrently combined or compared. Often, recombination is done in a post-processing phase as a sequential process whose cost in time and space depends on the number and the size of the simulation results and can be comparable to the cost of the simulation phase. Besides, independent simulations exhibit good parallel scalability only if executed onto truly independent platforms (e.g., multicomputers, clusters or grids), but they might exhibit serious performance degradation if run on multicores due to the concurrent usage of underlying resources. This effect is particularly significative for I/O-bound applications since typically I/O and memory buses are shared among cores.

We introduce StochKit-FF, a parallel version of the popular StochKit [1], aiming at supporting the execution of multiple simulations and at combining their results on cache-coherent, shared memory multicores. These architectures are currently being developed by the whole computer industry and equip many computing platforms. StochKit-FF has been designed and developed as a low-effort, efficient porting of StochKit by means of the FastFlow C/C++ programming framework, which supports efficient applications on multicore and makes it possible to run multiple parallel stochastic simulations and combine their results. This relies on *selective memory*, a novel data structure we designed to perform the online *alignment* and *reduction* of multiple streams of simulation results: different data streams are aligned according to simulation time and combined together according to a user-defined function, e.g. the average or others. By discussing the HIV case-study, we intend to show that this framework represents an efficient way for running multiple simulations and for the development of effective modelling techniques. We focus here on producing averaged values, and on more structured and informative data on a longer term project.

2 A Stochastic Model of the Immune Response to HIV

ODEs based models have long been used for immune system and viral infection modeling [2,3]. They focus on the average behavior of large populations of identical objects and need often to be solved numerically. When considering a small number of molecules, which is highly probable if we consider immune cell interactions in a small volume, or when considering randomness and irregularities

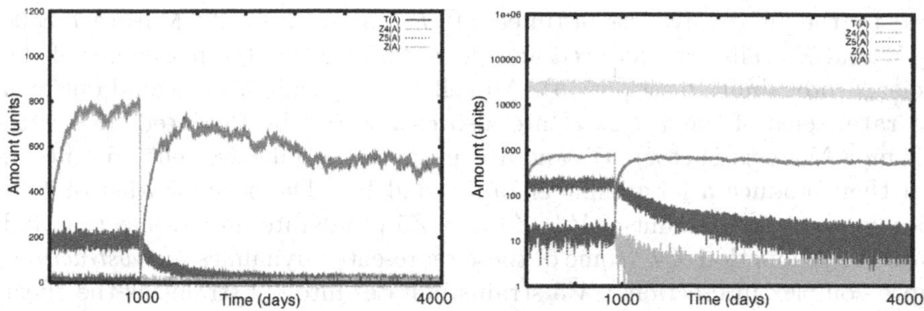

Fig. 1. a) The "noisy" immune cell dynamics over 4000 days: mutation around day 1000 and then T (mid-curve) degrades. b) A log-scale view: the high peak perturbation of $V4+V5$ during mutation and the dynamics for the small amounts of degrading cells.

found at all levels of life, then a stochastic model is much more accurate on a mesoscale. Stochastic methods are based on the *Gillespie's algorithm*, which simulates the reactions step by step [4]. Such stochastic methods are more effective than the deterministic ones to describe the above mentioned irregularities and crucial chemical reactions. They observe emerging properties of the behaviour of a system composed of a large number of simple agents (viruses and cells), following local rules [5].

Briefly, agent behaviour consists of actions, e.g. cellular interactions, that cause a state transition of the modelled system, e.g. a variation in the amount of agents. Actions are stochastic, as their occurrence in time has an associated probability distribution, which is generally memoryless, typically negative exponential distributions with the rate as parameter. Hence the overall system behaviour can be interpreted as a Continuous Time Markov Chain (CTMC). Systemic emergent properties can be sensitive to the local presence of minimal (integer) quantities of agents/molecules/cells [6]. The combined behavior of these agents is observed in a discrete-time stochastic simulation, from given initial conditions: a single transition amongst the possible ones in the current state is selected, and the state updated accordingly. The Gillespie's algorithm [4] determines the next transition and the time at which it occurs, exactly according to the given probability distributions. Each such possible evolution of the system is called a *trajectory*. Large computing resources may be required to correctly determine fluctuations and averages from the system simulated trajectories.

HIV and the immune response. We recapitulate here our model here, see [2,7] for details. During the HIV infection multiple strains of the virus arise, we consider two phenotype classes, $V5$ and $V4$, which invade cells through different membrane receptors. The mutation from $V5$, initially prevailing, to the more aggressive $V4$ has been correlated to the progression to the AIDS phase. The immune response is based on the action of several cells (T, $Z5$ and $Z4$), some of which strain specific, which can also be infected by the viruses. The Tumor

Necrosis Factor F induces bystander death of several cells. Infection is characterised by the progressive loss of (infected) T, $Z5$ and $Z4$ cells. Mature T cells and $Z4$ and $Z5$ cells are produced at a constant rate (i.e. the parameter of the associated probability distribution). All cells are typically also cleared out at a given rate, some of them, e.g. T, are also cleared out by the interaction with F (Tumor Necrosis Factor). $V5$ and $V4$ produce the infected cells $I5$ and $I4$, which then produce a large number of $V5$ and $V4$. The accumulation of F is proportional to the amount of $V4$. $Z4$ and $Z5$ proliferate due to infection and sustain the production of T (some of these represented dynamics are *abstractions* of more complex interactions). $V5$ strains mutates into $V4$ strains as the effect of a stochastic triggering event expected to occur around a desired time. The parameters used have been referred from literature, e.g. [2,3] and sometimes tuned against the known behaviour of the system. Simulations start from given initial conditions, e.g. $T = 1000, Z5 = 250$ and $V5 = 100$. See Fig. 1 for a trajectory of the modelled infection dynamics.

3 Parallel Stochastic Simulations

In stochastic simulations, many trajectories might be needed to get a representative picture of how the system behaves on the whole. Processing and combining many trajectories may lead to very high compulsory cache miss-rate and thus become a memory-bound (and I/O-bound) problem. This in turn may require a huge amount of storage space (linear in the number of simulations and the observation size of the average trajectory) and an expensive post-processing phase, since data should be retrieved from permanent storage and processed. Eventually, the computational problem hardly benefits from the latest commodity multi-core architectures. These architectures are able to exhibit an almost perfect speedup with independent CPU-bound computations, but hardly replicate such a performance for memory-bound and I/O-bound computations, since the memory is still the real bottleneck of this kind of architectures. Tackling these issues at the low-level is often unfeasible because of the complexity of the code and of the need to keep the application code distinct from platform-specific performance tricks. Typically, low-level approaches only provide the programmers with primitives for flow-of-control management, synchronisation and data sharing.

Designing suitable high-level abstractions for parallel programming is a long standing problem [8]. Recently, high-level parallel programming methodologies are receiving a renewed interest, especially in the form of pattern-based programming [9,10]. FastFlow belongs to this class of programming environments.

The FastFlow Parallel Programming Environment. FastFlow is a parallel programming framework aiming at *simplifying* the development of *efficient* applications for multicore platforms, being these applications either brand new or ports of existing legacy codes. The key vision underneath FastFlow is that effortless development and efficiency can both be achieved by raising the level of abstraction in application design, thus providing designers with a suitable set of parallel programming patterns that can be compiled onto efficient networks of parallel activities on the target platforms. The FastFlow run-time support is completely based on lock-free and memory fence-free synchronizations. This approach significantly reduces cache reconciliation overhead, which is the primary source of inefficiency in cache-coherent multicore platforms. We refer to [12,11] for any further details. FastFlow is open source available at [11] under LGPL3.

3.1 Parallel StochKit: StochKit-FF

StochKit [1] is an extensible stochastic simulation framework developed in the C++ language. It implements the popular Gillespie algorithm, explicit and implicit tau-leaping, and trapezoidal tau-leaping methods.

StochKit-FF extends StochKit (version 1) with two main features: The support for the parallel run of multiple simulations on multicores, and the support for the online (parallel) *reduction* of simulation results, which can be performed according to one or more user-defined associative and commutative functions. StochKit v1 is coded as a sequential C++ application exhibiting several non-reentrant functions, including the random number generation. Consequently, StochKit-FF represents a significative test bed for the FastFlow ability to support parallelisation of existing complex codes. The parallelisation is supported by means of high-level parallel patterns, which could also be exploited as *parametric code factories* to parallelise existing, possibly complex C/C++ codes [11].

In particular, StochKit-FF exploits the FastFlow *farm* pattern, which implements the functional replication paradigm: a stream of independent data items are dispatched by an *Emitter* thread to a set of independent *Worker* threads. Each worker produces a stream of results that is gathered by a *Collector* thread into a single output stream [12].

In StochKit, a simulation is invoked by way of the `StochRxn()`, which realises the main simulation loop; the propensity function and initial conditions are among its parameters. StochKit-FF provides programmers with `StochRxn_ff()` function, which has a similar list of parameters, but invokes a parametric simulation modelling either a number of copies of the same simulation or a set of parameter-sweeped simulations. `StochRxn_ff()` embodies a *farm*: the emitter unrolls the parametric simulation into a stream of standard simulations (represented as C++ objects) that are dispatched to workers. Each worker receives a set of simulations, which are sequentially run by way of the `StochRxn()`, which is basically unchanged with respect to the original StochKit. Each simulation produces a stream of results, which are locally *reduced* within each worker into a single stream [13]. The collector gathers all worker streams and *reduces* them again into a single output stream. Overall, the parallel *reduction* happens in a systolic (tree) fashion via the so-called *selective memory* data structure.

Selective Memory. Together with StochKit-FF, we introduce the *selective memory* concept, i.e. a data structure supporting the on-line *reduction* of time-aligned trajectory data by way of user-defined associative functions. Selective memory distinguishes from standard *reduce* operation [13] because it works on

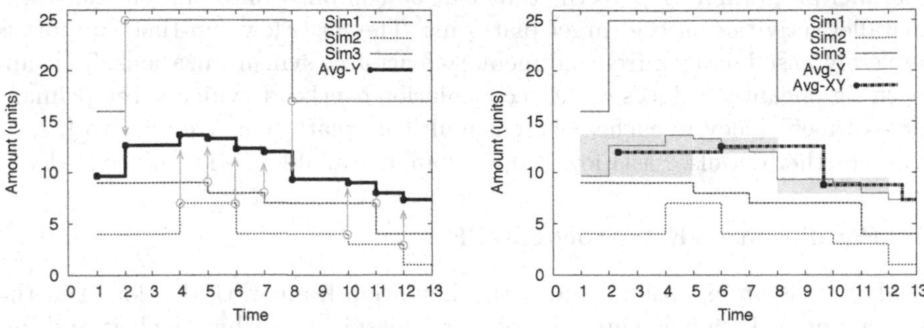

Fig. 2. Selective Memory with average. Left: a) Curve Avg-Y is derived via oversampling and time-aligned reduction (average along Y axis) of k independent simulations (arrows highlight oversampling). Right: b) Avg-XY is derived by the reduction (average along X axis) of k successive points of Avg-Y (grey boxes highlight averaging zone).

unbound streams, and aligns simulation points (i.e. stream items) according to simulation time before reducing them: since each simulation proceed at a variable time step, simulation points coming from different simulations cannot simply be reduced as soon as they are produced. Selective memory behaves as a sliding window in a buffer that follows the wavefront of generated simulation points. It keeps the bare minium amount of data from different simulations to produce a slice of simulation points that are aligned to simulation time.

The behaviour of selective memory is shown in Fig. 2 using average as combining function. Simulation points from different simulations are first averaged at aligned simulation time points: such computed average results oversampled with respect to single simulations (Fig. 2 a). This oversampling is possibly reduced by applying the same technique along time axis (Fig. 2 b). Overall, selective memory produces a combined simulation that has been adaptively sampled: time intervals exhibiting a higher variability across different simulations exhibit an higher sampling rate. Selective memory effectively mitigates the memory pressure of result logging when many simulations are run on a multicore, as it substantially reduces the output size, and thus capacity misses and the memory bus pressure.

4 Experiments and Discussion

Figure 3 a) is a focus on the immune response averaged over 16 simulations, performed on the `ness.epcc.ed.ac.uk` platform (Sun X4600 SMP - 8 x Dual-Core AMD Opteron 1218, 32 Gb memory) hosted at EPCC, University of Edinburgh. The averaged amounts and the variance of $Z4$, $Z5$, their sum Z, and T are reported. The variance of $Z4$ and $Z5$ is large till 2500 days, showing tight coupling i.e. interdependence. Then, the variance of T decreases continuously, while the one of $Z5$ decreases with the amount of $Z5$: it is not much involved in dynamics after the mutation to $V4$. Figures 3 b)-d) describe a sensitivity analysis for δ_t, which has resulted in being very influential by a large analysis of the model: it

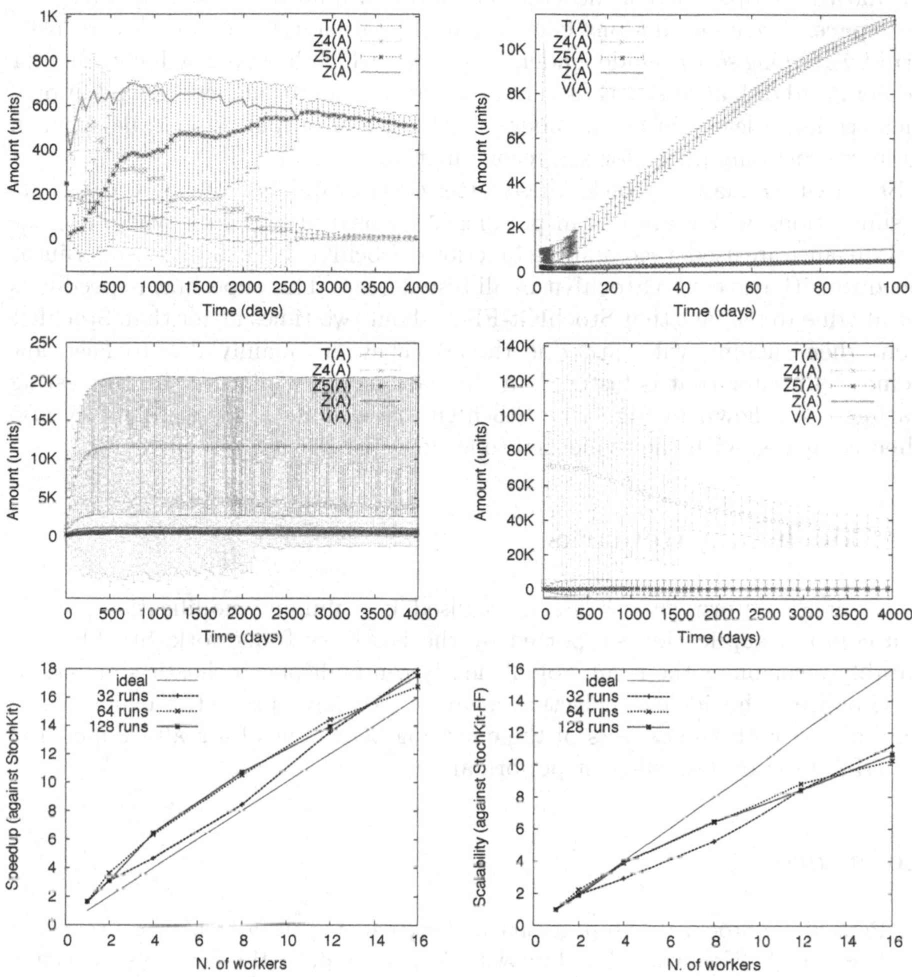

Fig. 3. Experimental results. Left to right: a) A focus on the immune response, and b) c) d) Sensitivity analysis for $\delta_t = 5.0, 3.0$ and 0.5 (average and variance for multiple trajectories (16x)). e) Speedup of StochKit-FF against StochKit. f) Scalability of StochKit-FF(n) against StochKit-FF(1), where with n is the number of worker threads.

strongly impacts on the diffusion of $V_{5,4}$. In b) V is immediately (in the interval [0,100]) cleared out, T rapidly increases, and the system is very stable, with a low variance. In c) the immune response still prevails, but the system appears much perturbed. In d), well below the standard value of δ_t, the virus clearly prevails. Variance is initially high, then it stabilises towards a steady state.

The performances of StochKit-FF have been evaluated on multiple runs of the HIV case-study. A single run of the simulation with StochKit produces $\sim$ 150M simulation points for 4000 days of simulated time (sampled from $\sim$ 6 GBytes of raw data); multiple runs of the same simulation will need a linearly greater time and space. These simulations can be naively parallelised on a multicore platform by running several independent instances, which however, will compete for memory and disk accesses, thus lead to suboptimal performances. An additional linear time (at least) in the number and the size of outputs should be spent in the postprocessing phase for the recombination of results.

StochKit-FF mainly attacks these latter costs by online reducing the outputs of simulations, which are run in parallel. As shown in Fig. 3 e), where average and variance are used as combining functions, StochKit-FF exhibits a superlinear speedup with respect to StochKit in all tested cases. This superlinear speedup is mainly due to the fact that StochKit-FF is about two times faster than StochKit even when running with just one thread. They are mainly due to FastFlow memory allocator that is faster than standard memory allocator on the testing platform. As shown in Fig. 3 f), StochKit-FF exhibits a good scalability also when compared with the sequential (one-thread) version of StochKit-FF.

5 Concluding Remarks

StochKit-FF we presented has been realised as a minimal-modification porting of a complex application supported by the FastFlow framework. StochKit-FF suitably recombines the results of efficiently run multiple stochastic simulations by exploiting the idea of selective memory. We have presented experiments, highlighting both the aspects of the emerging behaviour of a realistic model of the HIV infection and efficient performances.

References

1. Petzold, L.: StochKit web page, `http://engineering.ucsb.edu/~cse/StochKit`
2. Perelson, A., Neumann, A., Markowitz, M., Leonard, J., Ho, D.: HIV-1 dynamics in vivo: Virion clearance rate, infected cell life-span, and viral generation time. Science 271, 1582–1586 (1996)
3. Sguanci, L., Bagnoli, F., Liò, P.: Modeling HIV quasispecies evolutionary dynamics. BMC Evolutionary Biology 7(2), S5 (2007)
4. Gillespie, D.: Exact stochastic simulation of Coupled Chemical Reactions. The Journal of Physical Chemistry 81(25), 2340–2361 (1977)
5. Chao, L., Davenport, M., Forrest, S., Perelson, A.: A stochastic model of cytotoxic t cell responses. Journal Theoretical Biology 228, 227–240 (2004)
6. Wilkinson, D.: A stochastic model of cytotoxic T cell responses. CRC press, Boca Raton (2006)
7. Sorathiya, A., Liò, P., Bracciali, A.: Formal reasoning on qualitative models of coinfection of HIV and Tuberculosis and HAART therapy. BMC Bioinformatics 11(1) (2010); Asia Pacific Bioinformatics Conference
8. Cole, M.: Algorithmic Skeletons: Structured Management of Parallel Computations. Research Monographs in Parallel and Distributed Computing. Pitman (1989)
9. Intel Threading Building Blocks, `http://software.intel.com/en-us/intel-tbb`

10. Asanovic, K., Bodik, R., Demmel, J., Keaveny, T., Keutzer, K., Kubiatowicz, J., Morgan, N., Patterson, D., Sen, K., Wawrzynek, J., Wessel, D., Yelick, K.: A view of the parallel computing landscape. CACM 52(10), 56–67 (2009)
11. Fastflow project (2009), `http://mc-fastflow.sourceforge.net`
12. Aldinucci, M., Meneghin, M., Torquati, M.: Efficient smith-waterman on multi-core with FastFlow. In: Proc. of Intl. Euromicro PDP 2010: Parallel Distributed and Network-Based Processing, Pisa, Italy, pp. 195–199. IEEE, Los Alamitos (February 2010)
13. Aldinucci, M., Gorlatch, S., Lengauer, C., Pelagatti, S.: Towards parallel programming by transformation: The FAN skeleton framework. Parallel Algorithms and Applications 16(2-3), 87–121 (2001)

ProtTest-HPC: Fast Selection of Best-Fit Models of Protein Evolution

Diego Darriba[1,2], Guillermo L. Taboada,[2], Ramón Doallo[2], and David Posada[1]

[1] Bioinformatics and Molecular Evolution Group, University of Vigo, 36310 Vigo, Spain
[2] Computer Architecture Group, University of A Coruña, 15071 A Coruña, Spain
{ddarriba,taboada,doallo}@udc.es, dposada@uvigo.es
http://darwin.uvigo.es/software/prottesthpc

Abstract. The use of probabilistic models of amino acid replacement is essential for the study of protein evolution, and programs like ProtTest implement different strategies to identify the best-fit model for the data at hand. For large protein alignments, this task can demand vast computational resources, preventing the justification of the model used in the analysis.

We have implemented a High Performance Computing (HPC) version of ProtTest. ProtTest-HPC can be executed in parallel in HPC environments as: (1) a GUI-based desktop version that uses multi-core processors and (2) a cluster-based version that distributes the computational load among nodes. The use of ProtTest-HPC resulted in significant performance gains, with speedups of up to 50 on a high performance cluster.

1 Introduction

The evolution of protein sequences can be studied using statistical models that describe the probabilities of particular amino acid replacements along specific lineages. Because the number of parameters in these models can be large, in most cases the 20×20 replacement matrices are not estimated *de novo* for each data set. Instead, replacement rates previously estimated from large empirical databases are adopted. Among these, some of the more popular are the Dayhoff [4], JTT [7], mtREV [3], WAG [18], mtArt [1] or LG [10] matrices. Importantly, many phylogenetic calculations like the estimation of tree topologies, branch lengths, nodal support, divergence times or replacement rates benefit from the use of explicit models of evolution. Because, the use of different models can change the outcome of the analysis [15], different model selection tools for protein alignments have been implemented in the past, like ProtTest [2] or ModelGenerator [9]. In addition, some model selection capabilities have been added to more general phylogenetic programs like HYPHY [12], Treefinder [6] or TOPALi [11].

M.R. Guarracino et al. (Eds.): Euro-Par 2010 Workshops, LNCS 6586, pp. 177–184, 2011.
© Springer-Verlag Berlin Heidelberg 2011

2 ProtTest

The program ProtTest is one of the most popular tools for selecting models of protein evolution, with almost 4,000 registered users. ProtTest is written in Java and uses the program PhyML [5] for the maximum likelihood (ML) estimation of phylogenetic trees and model parameters. The current version of ProtTest (2.4) includes 14 different rate matrices that result in 112 different models when we consider rate variation among sites (+I: invariable sites; +G: gamma-distributed rates) and the observed amino acid frequencies (+F). ProtTest uses the Akaike Information Criterion (AIC) and other information criteria to find which of the candidate models best fits the data at hand. In addition, it can perform multi-model inference and estimate parameter importances [13]. The time required to complete the likelihood calculations, that take most of the runtime of the program, can be variable depending on the size and complexity of the alignments. For large alignments, this task cannot be completed in a reasonable time using a single core. While ModelGenerator/MultiPhyl [8] and TOPALi implement grid computing to speed-up the analyses, they consider fewer models and do not implement model averaging.

3 Java for High Performance Computing

There are several programming options in Java for HPC [16]:

Java Shared Memory Programming. As Java has built-in multithreading support, the use of threads is quite extended due to its portability and high performance, although it is a rather low-level option. Nevertheless, Java now provides concurrency utilities, such as thread pools, tasks, blocking queues, and low-level high-performance primitives (e.g., *CyclicBarrier*), for a higher level programming. However, this option is limited to shared memory machines, which provide less computational power than distributed memory architectures.

Java Distributed Memory Programming. Message-passing is the preferred programming model for distributed memory architectures (e.g., clusters) due to its portability, scalability and usually good performance, although it generally requires significant development efforts. Among currently available Java Message-Passing Java (MPJ) libraries, F-MPJ [17] and MPJ Express [14] deserve to be mentioned for their nested parallelism (MPJ+threads) support for exploiting performance on clusters of multi-core processors.

4 ProtTest-HPC

ProtTest-HPC is a high performance computing application for protein model selection, based on ProtTest, but completely redesigned in order to grant model extensibility, traceability and encapsulation. ProtTest-HPC includes four main hierarchies:

- **Substitution Models** contain the amino-acid model data, although they can be extended to also support nucleotide models.
- **Likelihood Estimators** optimize model parameters as a previous step to model selection. This optimization relies on third-party applications.
- **Execution Strategies** determine how the optimization of the candidate set of models is scheduled (i.e., how the workload is distributed among the available computational resources).
- **Information Criteria** drive the model selection task according to the previous optimization and provide the basis for model-averaging calculations.

4.1 Shared Memory Implementation

ProtTest-HPC uses a thread pool to handle the execution of tasks on shared memory architectures. This implementation is totally portable using thread pools from the Java Concurrence API, which is included in the Java SDK. The task queue contains the whole set of tasks (i.e., candidate models to optimize) which will be processed by the thread pool in a particular order (reverse complexity estimate) (Figure 1).

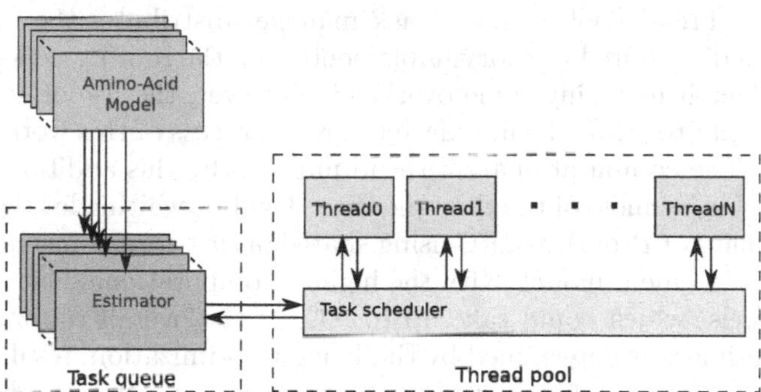

Fig. 1. ProtTest-HPC shared memory strategy

4.2 Distributed Memory Implementation

In order to handle the computation of tasks on distributed memory architectures (e.g., clusters), ProtTest-HPC manages processes, which rely on message-passing communication. ProtTest-HPC uses a distributor process to allocate the workload (Fig. 2) according to three different strategies, one static and two dynamic.

The static approach performs the whole distribution of the tasks before their actual optimization. This distribution is based on the workload estimate for each task, which is key to provide balanced workload assignments. Therefore, message-passing among processes is avoided during computation. As long as the computational load is very hard to estimate, this strategy will usually result in significant runtime differences among processes. The performance of this strategy is highly dependent on the workload estimate and the number of processes

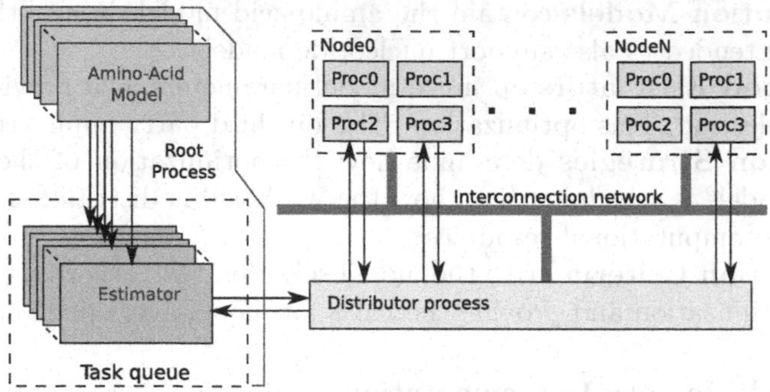

Fig. 2. ProtTest-HPC distributed memory strategy

used (i.e., an inaccurate estimate when scheduling a small number of tasks per process will show poor performance), so it is usually less scalable than dynamic approaches. However, shorter running times will be obtained for small datasets, where the time spent in message-passing becomes more significant.

On the other hand, the behavior of the dynamic approaches is more similar to that of the thread pool, where a task manager distributes the tasks among processes. In a distributed memory implementation, the root process can assume this role, although incurring some overhead. However, the use of an additional dedicated distributor thread can relieve the root process of this work, increasing performance. The computational overhead imposed by this additional thread is almost negligible, as most of the time the thread will be waiting for the processes.

The scalability of ProtTest-HPC using shared or distributed memory was limited by the replacement models with the highest computational load, usually the "+I+G" models, which could take up to 90% of the overall runtime. In these cases, the runtime was determined by the longest optimization, resulting in poor speedups. Moreover, the higher the number of cores, the higher the workload imbalance due to runtime differences. In fact, it is expected that ProtTest-HPC could take advantage of up to 50 cores, approximately. This important limitation suggests that the combination of the distributed memory version with a parallel maximum-likelihood computation can increase significantly the scalability of ProtTest-HPC. Therefore, this two-level parallelism approach can result in a much more efficient exploitation of the available computational resources.

5 Performance Evaluation

We evaluated the performance of ProtTest-HPC on a representative multi-core cluster under two different scenarios:

- shared memory, using the available cores in a machine.
- distributed memory, running the message-passing version on the whole cluster.

Table 1. Test data sets used for performance evaluation. The base tree used for parameter estimation can be a BIONJ tree fixed across models or the particular ML tree for each model. Execution times are given in minutes.

Data set/ Analysis	Protein	Number Sequences	Length	Base tree	Execution Time
RIB	Ribosomal protein	21	113	Fixed BIONJ	5
RIBML	"	"	"	ML tree	30
COX	Cytochrome C oxidase II	28	113	Fixed BIONJ	10
COXML	"	"	"	ML tree	58
HIV	HIV polymerase	36	1,034	Fixed BIONJ	45
HIVML	"	"	"	ML tree	185
10K	Simulated alignment	50	10,000	Fixed BIONJ	552
20K	"	"	20,000	"	1,470
100K	"	"	100,000	"	4,785

To evaluate the performance of ProtTest-HPC we used 6 real and simulated alignments (Table 1). In all cases the set of candidate models included all 112 models available in ProtTest.

5.1 Shared Memory Benchmarking

Figure 3 and Table 2 show the performance of ProtTest-HPC in an 8-core Harpertown cluster node using shared memory. Here ProtTest-HPC was limited to the use of up to 8 threads (one thread per core). In this scenario, where the number of available threads is significantly lower than the number of models to be optimized, the computational workload was usually well-balanced, and the scalability almost reached the ideal case (i.e., obtaining speedups close to n with n threads). Nevertheless, for the simplest analyses (e.g., COX and RIB) the performance results when using 8 threads were poorer than for more computationally intensive tasks (e.g., COXML and RIBML) as the overhead of threads operation (e.g., synchronizations) and the workload imbalance had a higher impact on the overall performance.

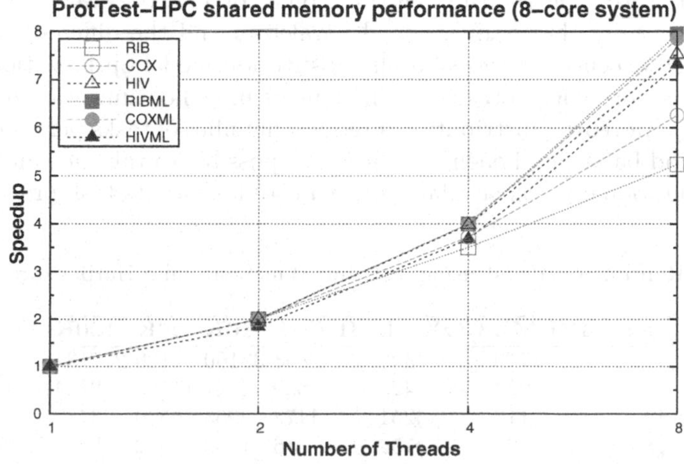

Fig. 3. Scalability of ProtTest-HPC in an 8-core node using shared memory

Table 2. Runtime (seconds) using shared memory on an 8-core Harpertown node

Threads	RIB	COX	HIV	RIBML	COXML	HIVML
1	330	563	2544	1710	3300	9498
2	165	282	1269	851	1647	5149
4	94	151	639	427	825	2581
8	63	90	338	215	415	1300

5.2 Distributed Memory Benchmarking

We explored three different distribution strategies for message-passing. Here we only evaluated the dynamic option because it provided the most balanced workloads without incurring significant penalties (the core devoted to the dedicated distributor thread represents a small percentage of the total number of available cores, 256).

Starting from 16 cores, we ran on the cluster the message-passing parallel implementation of ProtTest-HPC using multiples of 14 cores. The reason for this is that the computational load for a given model depends on the rate heterogeneity and frequency parameters because the replacement matrix is given. Thus, for a specific parameter combination like "+I+G" there are 14 models with similar workload. This suggested the use of a number of cores multiple of 14, so the workload would be more balanced. In this case the number of tasks processed per core is likely to be the same. Additionally, it is expected that models with similar workloads would be optimized by different processes. Finally, ProtTest-HPC currently includes 112 models, and as each model is optimized sequentially by a single core, the maximum number of cores that can be used is 112. Performance in this case was almost linear for the simple analyses up to 28 cores, while in other cases (HIVML) the biggest speedups were obtained with 56 cores (Figure 4 and Table 3). ProtTest-HPC could only take advantage of around 56 cores on a 256-core cluster, as the running times on 56 or 112 cores were similar. This happens because of the coarse-grained paralelism and the differences between the sequential execution times of each substitution model optimization, so this is the main performance bottleneck (the longest model optimization determines the runtime). Moreover, distributing a reduced number of tasks per core severely limits the load balancing benefits, as it is not possible to take advantage of the spare computational power available once a core finishes its task processing.

Table 3. Runtime (seconds) using distributed memory on a Harpertown testbed

Cores	RIBML	COXML	HIVML	10K	20K	100K
1	1710	3300	9498	33160	88129	287134
8	224	429	1880	4421	11750	38284
16	113	251	1172	2963	6590	23417
28	71	152	516	1960	4972	15275
56	64	93	207	1032	3148	7988
112	49	78	206	1028	2593	7178

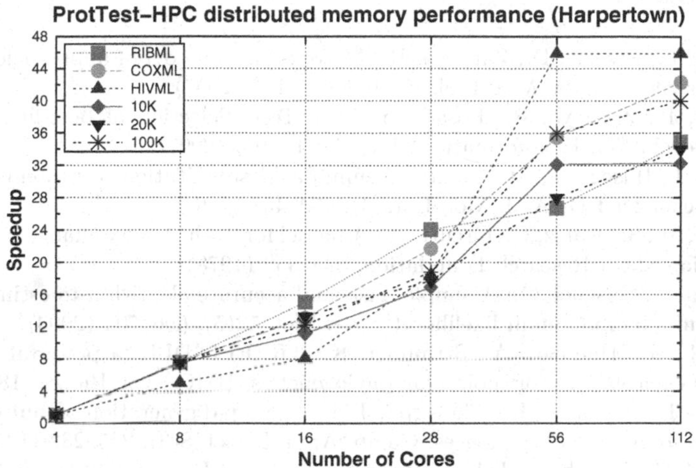

Fig. 4. Scalability of ProtTest-HPC using distributed memory

6 Conclusions

We have developed a high performance computing version of ProtTest for the fast selection of best-fit models of protein evolution. In order to allow for the parallel execution of ProtTest in high performance computing environments, our implementation can work either (i) as a GUI-based desktop version that supports the execution using the available multi-core processors, or (ii) as a cluster-based version that distributes the computational load among the available compute nodes. We show that ProtTest-HPC achieves a significant performance gain over ProtTest, with speedups of up to 50 on an HPC cluster, although the combination of the cluster-based version with a parallel maximum-likelihood computation can increase significantly ProtTest-HPC scalability. For very large alignments, this can be equivalent to a reduction of the running time from more than one day to around half an hour. In this way, statistical model selection for large protein alignments becomes feasible, not only for cluster users, but also for the owners of standard multi-core desktop computers. Moreover, the flexible design of ProtTest-HPC will allow developers to extend future functionalities, whereas third-party projects will be able to easily adapt its capabilities to their requirements.

Acknowledgments. Special thanks to Stephane Guindon for his continuous help with PhyML. This work was financially supported by the European Research Council [ERC-2007-Stg 203161-PHYGENOM to D.P.] the Spanish Ministry of Science and Education [BFU2009-08611 to D.P. and TIN2010-16735 to R.D.] and by the Xunta de Galicia [Bioinformatics (to D.P.) and HPC (to R.D.) Galician Thematic Networks].

References

1. Abascal, F., Posada, D., Zardoya, R.: MtArt: a new model of amino acid replacement for Arthropoda. Mol. Biol. Evol. 24(9), 1–5 (2007)
2. Abascal, F., Zardoya, R., Posada, D.: ProtTest: Selection of best-fit models of protein evolution. Bioinformatics 24(1), 1104–1105 (2007)
3. Adachi, J., Hasegawa, M.: Model of amino acid substitution in proteins encoded by mitochondrial DNA. J. Mol. E 42(4), 459–468 (1996)
4. Dayhoff, M., Schwartz, R., Orcutt, B.: A model for evolutionary change in proteins. Nat'l Biomedical Research Foundation, 345–352 (1978)
5. Guindon, S., Gascuel, O.: A simple, fast, and accurate algorithm to estimate large phylogenies by maximum likelihood. Syst. Biol. 52(5), 696–704 (2003)
6. Jobb, G., von Haeseler, A., Strimmer, K.: TREEFINDER: a powerful graphical analysis environment for molecular phylogenetics. BMC Evol. Biol. 4, 18 (2004)
7. Jones, D.T., Taylor, W.R., Thornton, J.M.: The rapid generation of mutation data matrices from protein sequences. Comp. Appl. Biosci. 8(3), 275–282 (1992)
8. Keane, T.M., Naughton, T.J., McInerney, J.O.: MultiPhyl: a high-throughput phylogenomics webserver using distributed computing. Nucleic Acids Res. 35(Web Server issue), W33–W37 (2007)
9. Keane, T., Creevey, C., Pentony, M., Naughton, T., Mclnerney, J.: Assessment of methods for amino acid matrix selection and their use on empirical data shows that ad hoc assumptions for choice of matrix are not justified. BMC Evol. Biol. 6(1), 29 (2006)
10. Le, S.Q., Gascuel, O.: An improved general amino acid replacement matrix. Mol. Biol. Evol. 25(7), 1307–1320 (2008)
11. Milne, I., Lindner, D., Bayer, M., Husmeier, D., McGuire, G., Marshall, D.F., Wright, F.: TOPALi v2: a rich graphical interface for evolutionary analyses of multiple alignments on HPC clusters and multi-core desktops. Bioinformatics 25(1), 126–127 (2009)
12. Pond, S.L.K., Frost, S.D., Muse, S.V.: HyPhy: hypothesis testing using phylogenies. Bioinformatics 21, 676–679 (2005)
13. Posada, D., Buckley, T.R.: Model selection and model averaging in phylogenetics: advantages of akaike information criterion and bayesian approaches over likelihood ratio tests. Syst. Biol. 53(5), 793–808 (2004)
14. Shafi, A., Carpenter, B., Baker, M.: Nested parallelism for multi-core HPC systems using Java. J. Parallel Distr. Com. 69(6), 532–545 (2009)
15. Sullivan, J., Joyce, P.: Model selection in phylogenetics. Annu Rev. Ecol. Evol. S 36, 445–466 (2005)
16. Taboada, G.L., Tourino, J., Doallo, R.: Java for high performance computing: assessment of current research and practice. In: Proc. 7th Intl. Conf. on Principles and Practice of Programming in Java, Calgary, Canada, pp. 30–39 (2009)
17. Taboada, G.L., Tourino, J., Doallo, R.: F-MPJ: scalable Java message-passing communications on parallel systems. J. Supercomput. (2010) (in press)
18. Whelan, S., Goldman, N.: A general empirical model of protein evolution derived from multiple protein families using a maximum-likelihood approach. Mol. Biol. Evol. 18(5), 691–699 (2001)

Gridifying the TINKER Conformer Generator Application for gLite Grid

Attila Kertész[1], Ferenc Ötvös[2], and Péter Kacsuk[1]

[1] MTA SZTAKI Computer and Automation Research Institute
H-1518 Budapest, P.O. Box 63, Hungary
{attila.kertesz,kacsuk}@sztaki.hu
[2] Biological Research Center
H-6701 Szeged, P.O. Box 521, Hungary
otvos@brc.hu

Abstract. Grid Computing provides an efficient way for parallelizing and gridifying computationally and data intensive applications of various research fields. One of these application areas is molecular dynamics. In this paper we examine a biochemical application that generates conformers by unconstrained molecular dynamics at high temperature to overcome conformational bias then finishes each conformer by simulated annealing and energy minimization to obtain reliable structures. We provide a general way for turning biochemical applications into Grid workflows that can be executed by Grid portals exploiting the computational power of available production Grids. First we describe the gridification process, then provide experimental results that show the achieved speed-up of the ported application.

Keywords: Grid Computing, Grid portal, molecule conformer generation, TINKER application.

1 Introduction

E-Science infrastructures play an important role in enabling large-scale scientific research. In order to establish such e-infrastructures, various Grid systems have been created and run in production as a service for the scientific community. While several years ago users and companies having computation and data intensive applications looked sceptical at the forerunners of Grid solutions, Grid Computing [3] has become a separate research field: currently Grids are targeted by many world-wide projects. Research groups were forming around specific middleware components and different research branches have arisen. Many user groups from various research fields put their trust in Grids, and usage statistics and research results show that they were undoubtedly right. Nowadays research directions are focusing on user needs, therefore more efficient utilization and interoperability play the key roles. The current wave of Grid research targets user support [4]. Though several production Grid solutions are available today (eg. [1], [9], [8]), the application of these systems is still not widespread.

M.R. Guarracino et al. (Eds.): Euro-Par 2010 Workshops, LNCS 6586, pp. 185–192, 2011.
© Springer-Verlag Berlin Heidelberg 2011

Nevertheless we already have good examples that show how beneficial these systems can be [11], especially for biology, chemistry and physics.

In this paper we examine a biochemical application that generates conformers of flexible molecules, here a tetrapeptide (Tyr-Pro-Phe-Phe-NH2), by unconstrained molecular dynamics at high temperature to overcome conformational bias then finishes each conformer by different statistical modeling (SM) methods to obtain reliable structures. These structures were successfully used to obtain the active conformation of the peptide for its receptor (mu opioid receptor) by QSAR modeling assisted with an efficient variable selection algorithm. We provide a way for turning biochemical applications into Grid workflows that can be managed and executed through high level graphical interfaces offered by Grid portals exploiting the computational power of available production Grids. Regarding related works, Valverde in [13] has already shown, how to execute TINKER binaries [12] in EGEE Grids [1], but this solution used only low-level, command line interface. On the contrary, we propose a general, high-level solution using Grid portals, which provide graphical user interface for non-Grid expert users. The general gridification process we introduce in this paper can be applied to any parallelizable application, but the final Grid workflow is highly dependent on the structure (the number and order of algorithms used) of the appropriate application.

The rest of the paper is organized as follows. In Section 2 we introduce the biochemical application and discuss its requirements. In Section 3 we introduce our approach for gridification, and in Section 4 we present the evaluation result of our proposed solution. Finally, we conclude our paper in Section 5.

2 The TINKER Conformer Generator Application

The application (shown in Figure 1) generates conformers by unconstrained molecular dynamics at high temperature to overcome conformational bias (T) then finishes each conformer by simulated annealing and/or energy minimization to obtain reliable structures. The parameter files contain reference for the molecular force field (here Amber99), vacuum/implicit water (here GBSA) environment, target temperatures, etc. The aim is to obtain conformation ensembles to be evaluated by multivariate statistical modeling. It uses the TINKER library [12] for molecular modeling for further QSAR studies and drug development. The target end users are biologists or chemists, who need to examine molecule conformers with the TINKER package. The conformer generation algorithm in its present form comprises five different conformer finishing methods:

(i) minimizing the initial conformational states generated at high temperature (TM),
(ii) performing a short low temperature (e.g. 300 K) dynamics with the high temperature conformations to simulate a low temperature thermodynamical ensemble (TD),
(iii) minimizing the above low temperature states (TDM),

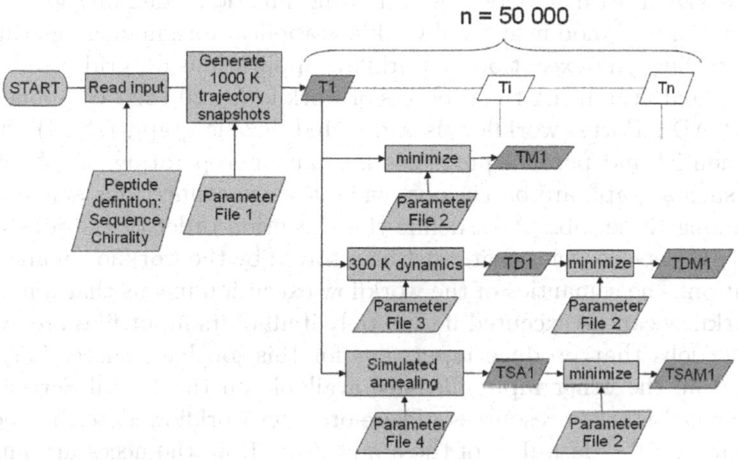

Fig. 1. TINKER Conformer Generator application

(iv) cooling the high temperature states by simulated annealing, e.g. to 50 K, or completely to 0 K (TSA),

(v) minimizing the annealed states (TSAM).

The reason why to generate the conformational states or conformers (which are conformational states at some local energy minima) is to investigate which of them suits better for the subsequent multivariate statistical modeling (namely quantitative structure-activity relationships studies, QSAR), then the algorithm may be simplified. Our most recent successful QSAR modeling makes use of the TSAM structures which is the most computationally costly method, but may serve as a reference method to obtain the most reliable thermodynamical ensembles. Regarding execution times, these are the average run times (in hours) of the various methods in the vacuum environment used in the application on a single 2GHz CPU machine: T – 13, TM – 28, TD – 3, TDM – 28, TSA – 26 and TSAM – 28 (the abbreviations discussed in this paragraph correspond to the ones shown in Figure 1). If we use the implicit water (GBSA) environment, the execution of the different steps takes 1,5 times longer. This means that the execution of the whole application takes around 5-8 days.

3 Gridifying the Application

The P-GRADE Grid Portal [6] is a workflow-oriented grid portal with the main goal to support all stages of grid workflow development and execution processes. It enables the graphical design of workflows created from various types of executable components (sequential and parallel jobs), executing these workflows in Globus-based computational Grids relying on user credentials, and finally, analyzing the monitored trace-data by the built-in visualization facilities.

The P-GRADE Portal provides the following functions: defining grid environments, creation and modification of workflow applications, managing grid certificates, controlling the execution of workflow applications on grid resources and monitoring and visualizing the progress of workflows and their component jobs.

A P-GRADE Portal workflow is a directed acyclic graph (DAG) that connects sequential and parallel programs into an interoperating set of jobs. The nodes of such a graph are batch jobs, while the arc connections define data relations among these jobs. Arcs define the execution order of the jobs and the input/output dependencies that must be resolved by the workflow manager during execution. The semantics of the workflow execution means that a node (job) of the workflow can be executed if, and only if all of its input files are available, i.e., all the jobs that produce input files for this job have successfully terminated, and all the other input files are available on the Portal Server and at the pre-defined storage resources. Therefore, the workflow describes both the control-flow and the data-flow of the application. If all the necessary input files are available for a job, then the workflow manager transfers these files – together with the binary executable – to the computational resource where the job is allocated for execution. Managing the transfer of files and recognition of the availability of the necessary files is the task of the workflow manager component of the Portal Server.

The WS-PGRADE Portal [7] is the latest member of the P-GRADE portal family. It is a web-based frontend of the gUSE infrastructure [5], which is a lose collection of web services supporting high-level distributed deployment and scalability. It supports development and submission of distributed applications executed on the computational resources of production Grids. The workflow semantics of gUSE builds on the successful concept of the original P-GRADE Portal, but it also provides several new features: Job-wise parametrization gives a flexible and computing efficient way of parameter study (or sweep) (PS) applications, permitting the submissions of different jobs in different numbers within the same workflow. During workflow execution, so-called workflow instances are created. In this way different submissions can be managed and tracked of the same concrete workflow. Web service calls and different sub-workflows can also be embedded into the jobs/nodes of the workflow.

The original application has been gridified by creating P-GRADE and WS-PGRADE workflows shown in Figure 2. Though these two versions of the application workflow are similar, we present both versions in order to exemplify gridification in both portals. The open-source P-GRADE portal can be attractive for many scientists, while the WS-PGRADE portal has some new enhancements and provide further development support. The grid workflow application consists of three phases (denoted by dashed areas in the figures):

1. The first phase is a generator job responsible for the generation of input data for parameter studies in the next phase.
2. The second phase consist of a PS sub-workflow, in which three PS jobs are defined for executing three different algorithms (discussed in Section 2), and an additional PS job that collects the outputs of the three threads and copies

them in a compressed file to a pre-defined remote storage. (In the P-GRADE workflow we can see an additional job as the first job of the sub-workflow that is responsible for copying the PS input files one-by-one from a remote storage (created by the generator job in the first phase) to the other three PS jobs. There is no need for such a job in the WS-PGRADE portal, because this feature is supported by its workflow interpreter.)

3. Finally in the third phase, a collector job gathers the output files of the PS sub-workflows and uploads them in a single compressed file to the remote storage, which can be easily downloaded by the user.

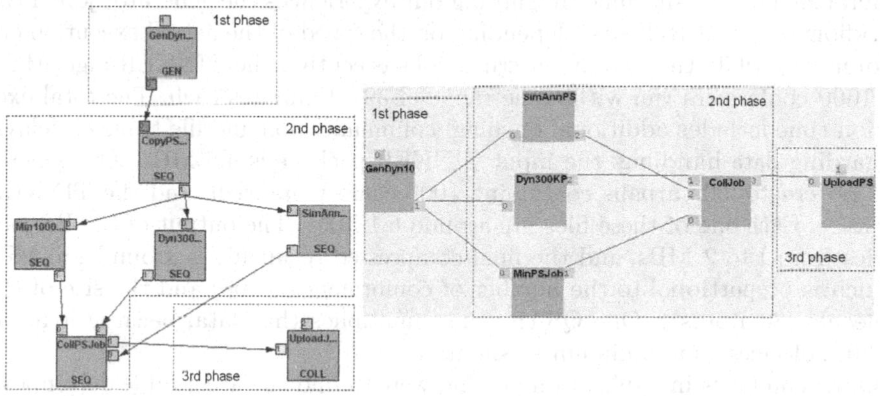

Fig. 2. TINKER Conformer Generator workflow in the P-GRADE and WS-PGRADE portals

In the original sequential application, the TINKER algorithms are executed by Bash Unix scripts, which are also applicable in EGEE infrastructures [1]. The sequential generation of 50 000 conformers cannot be parallelized, this is done by the first generator job. This job has an input file containing the required binaries of the TINKER library and a user script that perform the execution of the TINKER algorithms (which comes from the original user application). During execution it reads the arguments (that can be used for parameterizing the workflow) and generates the conformers, then sorts them to 50 output files containing 1000 conformers, the TINKER library and the pre-defined parameters. Finally these files are uploaded to a pre-defined remote storage. These files represent the input files of the parameter study sub-workflow instances.

The second phase of the workflow application is parallelized by the parameter study construct. Instead of executing the three TINKER algorithms (minimization, dynamics and simulated annealing) sequentially on 50 000 conformers, we decided to divide the computation into several parts. Since performing an algorithm on one conformer takes less then a second and thousands of jobs may flood the Grid resources, we decided to pack 1000 conformers to feed sequentially to the algorithms, and gathered the algorithms into three threads. Each thread processes 1000 conformers 50 times, therefore this decomposition resulted in 3 times 50 parameter study jobs. After the execution of the TINKER algorithms, the output of these threads are gathered, compressed and copied to a storage by the last job of this phase. Since these PS jobs are executed 50 times parallelly (for each input file), this phase means 200 job submissions. (In the P-GRADE portal version we have an additional copy PS job, which makes 250 total job submissions in this phase.) Finally in the third phase the last collector job of the workflow compresses all the output files into a single result file, and uploads it to a storage. Altogether the gridified workflow application consists of 202 jobs in the WS-PGRADE and 252 jobs in the P-GRADE portals.

Regarding execution times, the original application runs for about a week on a general single CPU machine. Regarding our experiences the generator job of the workflow run for 9-18 hours (depending on the speed of the actual execution environment), while the parameter study jobs executing the TINKER algorithms on 1000 conformers run within the range of 30-60 minutes each. The total execution time includes additional queuing, communication and file transfer delays. Regarding data handling: the input TINKER package is 4.5 MBs. The generator job creates 50 tarballs containing 1000 conformers each, and the TINKER package. Each one of these files are around 6.1 MBs. The output of the PS jobs varies from 1 to 2 MBs, and the final compressed result file is around 280 MBs (which is proportional to the number of conformers (50000) and the size of the molecule (80 atoms)). One QSAR study multiplies this data, because it needs 15-20 molecules as a minimum to simulate.

Our main tasks in application porting were to find the acceptable decomposition, to modify the original application scripts to work separately with a selected algorithm on the decomposed input sets, and to create additional wrapper scripts that set up the working environment on the selected grid resources right before executing the algorithms, and clear up the working directory after execution. After the scripts have been created, we designed the workflow structure and set its properties according to the available Grid environments (further described in the next Section). In the preliminary tests we experienced that some Grid resources failed to execute the TINKER binaries correctly. Later we found out that the invoked Fortran programs could not manage files with long path names (eg. /var/scratch/jobs/540873.ce.ui.savba.sk/ https_3a_2f_2flb2.egee.ces-net.cz_3a90-00_2f1wvjmGCIwWLIDrsdmH8yg), which is typical in the utilized VOs. First we used the default HOME of the resources (which are usually different from the pre-defined working directories), but in some cases we still experienced failures, because sometimes more jobs were sent to different cores of the same host and tried to use the same working directories. The final solution was to create unique temporary working directories (for which we used the *mktemp* Unix command).

The application is the first part of a drug design toolbox, whose first step is to generate high number of conformers of extremely flexible molecules (in our case it is a tetrapeptide). The description of highly flexible molecules can only be considered adequate when they are treated as thermodynamical ensembles and the rules of statistical thermodynamics are applied. Therefore a successful QSAR study on this kind of molecules can only be performed when they are treated as statistical ensembles and this kind of molecular description serves as an input for the multivariate statistical analysis step. As a result, we will use the gridified application to perform several QSAR studies (including 15-20 molecule explorations each).

4 Performance Evaluation

In order to execute applications (and use any service of production Grids) scientists have to acquire Grid certificates from a certificate authority (eg. [2]) and register themselves to the selected Grids or Virtual Organizations (VO). We have applied for membership into two multidisciplinary and one biomedical application specific VOs of EGEE for evaluation and further utilization: VOCE [14], SEEGRID [10] and BIOMED [15]. We have executed the workflow several times in all three VOs. The total execution time (the makespan) varied between one and three days. The actual execution time is highly dependent on the actual load of the resources in the utilized VO. The summary of the average execution times can be seen in Figure 3 on the left.

By the time we carried out these experiments, we could reach 21 resources in VOCE, 41 in SEEGRID and 183 in BIOMED. During the evaluation we experienced a little load on VOCE, medium on SEEGRID and high on BIOMED. Regarding reliability, no execution errors happened in VOCE, but we encountered several resubmissions in SEEGRID and some in BIOMED. These environmental conditions affected the measured values. As a result we can state that the gridified application can be executed 4 to 7 times faster on real production Grids compared to general single CPU machines. Finally we can see the detailed execution times of different workflow application phases for selected evaluation runs in Figure 3 on the right.

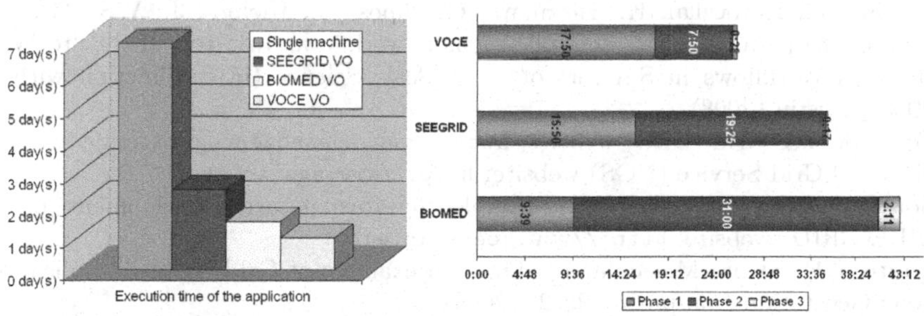

Fig. 3. Evaluation of the application on different Grid infrastructures

5 Conclusions

In this paper we have shown how to port a legacy biochemical application to a parameterizable Grid workflow that can be executed by non-Grid expert users from Grid portals providing a graphical user interface for production Grids. We have successfully parallelized the application and evaluated it on three Virtual Organizations of the EGEE Grid. The presented results show that we have achieved a significant speed-up with at most 7 times faster execution compared to general single CPU machines. Though the presented worklows have been designed for EGEE VOs, using the gUSE infrastructure it is possible to execute the workflow in different Grids (eg. GT4, BOINC). Our future work aims at creating a graphical portlet for workflow submissions in the P-GRADE and WS-PGRADE portals, which will further simplify user interactions with production Grids.

Acknowledgement

The research leading to these results has received funding from EGI-InSPIRE project (contract number RI-261323) and the Enabling Grids for E-sciencE project (contract number INFSO-RI-031688).

References

1. Enabling Grids for E-sciencE (EGEE) project website, http://public.eu-egee.org/
2. e-Science grid authentication in Europe, http://www.eugridpma.org/
3. Foster, I., Kesselman, C.: The Grid 2: Blueprint for a New Computing Infrastructure. Morgan Kaufmann Publishers Inc., San Francisco (2003)
4. Grid Application Support Centre website, http://www.lpds.sztaki.hu/gasuc/
5. Grid User Support Environment (gUSE) website, http://www.guse.hu/
6. Kacsuk, P., Sipos, G.: Multi-Grid, Multi-User Workflows in the P-GRADE Grid Portal. Journal of Grid Computing, 1–18 (February 2006)
7. Kacsuk, P., Karóczkai, K., Hermann, G., Sipos, G., Kovács, J.: WS-PGRADE: Supporting parameter sweep applications in workflows. In: Proc. of the 3rd Workshop on Workflows in Support of Large-Scale Science (in conjunction with SC 2008), Austin (2008)
8. Open Science Grid (OSG) website, http://www.opensciencegrid.org/
9. National Grid Service (NGS) website, http://www.ngs.ac.uk/
10. South Eastern European Grid-Enabled eInfrastructure Development project (SEE-GRID) website, http://www.see-grid.eu/
11. Tantoso, E., et al.: Molecular Docking, an example of Grid enabled applications. New Generation Computing 22(2) (2004)
12. TINKER molecular modeling software website, http://dasher.wustl.edu/tinker/
13. Valverde, J.R.: Simplifying job management on the Grid. EMBnet.news 14(2), 25–32 (2008)
14. Virtual Organisation for Central Europe (VOCE) website, http://egee.cesnet.cz/en/voce/
15. Virtual Organisation for biomedical applications (BIOMED) website, https://twiki.cern.ch/twiki/bin/view/EGEE/LifeSciences

On the Scalability of Multi-Criteria Protein Structure Comparison in the Grid

Gianluigi Folino[1], Azhar Ali Shah[2], and Natalio Krasnogor[2,*]

[1] Institute of High Performance Computing and Networking, Italian National Research Council, Cosenza 87036, Italy
folino@icar.cnr.it
[2] School of Computer Science, University of Nottingham, NG81BB, UK
{azhar.shah,natalio.krasnogor}@nottingham.ac.uk

Abstract. Multi-Criteria Protein Structure Comparison (MC-PSC) is one of the Grand Challenge Applications (GCAs) in the field of structural proteomics. The solution of the MC-PSC grand challenge requires the use of distributed algorithms, architectures and environments. This paper is aimed at the analysis of the scalability of our newly developed distributed algorithm for MC-PSC in the grid environment. The scalability in the grid environment indicates the capacity of the distributed algorithm to effectively utilize an increasing number of processors across multiple sites. The results of the experiments conducted on the UK's National Grid Service (NGS) infrastructure are reported in terms of speedup, efficiency and cross-site communication overhead.

Keywords: Protein Structure Comparison, Grid, Scalability, Bioinformatics.

1 Introduction

The theoretical analysis of the scalability of the *'computation-centric'* parallel applications on the grid appears in [4] with a prompt to the Grid community for the demonstration of this idea in terms of real Grid computing environments. This theoretical analysis is based on the idea of *'Homogeneous Computational Grid' (HCG)* and fits well with the real Grid computing infrastructure provided by the UK National Grid Service (NGS) [8] (please see section 3 for the details of the NGS infrastructure). The HCG model is based on the concept of *'Hierarchical Resource Manager'* [3] and assumes that the Grid consists of C number of identical Computing Elements ($CE's$) and each CE (being a HPC system) has p number of identical processors connected using the same type of network. The workload decomposition on such a system consists of two-level hierarchy: at first the un-decomposed work (W expressed e.g. in Mflops) is equally distributed in C CE's (i.e W/C decomposition) and then within each CE the portion of the work is assigned to each of the p processors (i.e $(W/C)/p$ decomposition). Consequently, this two-level hierarchy gives rise to two sources of communication

* Corresponding author.

M.R. Guarracino et al. (Eds.): Euro-Par 2010 Workshops, LNCS 6586, pp. 193–200, 2011.
© Springer-Verlag Berlin Heidelberg 2011

overhead, i.e. the communication overhead among C CE's $Q_1(W, C)$ and the communication overhead among p processors of each CE $Q_2(W/C, p)$. With this formalism, the execution time on HCG could be defined as:

$$T_{C,p}(W) = \frac{W_p}{pC\Delta} + Q_2(W/C, p) + Q_1(W, C) \quad (1)$$

Where Δ indicates the computing capacity of a processor e.g Mflops/s. Please note that if $C = 1$ and if $Q_1(W, 1) = 0$ then the overhead of equation 1 returns to the standard parallel case i.e $Q_2(W, p) = Q(W, p)$.

Equation 1 makes it clear that running the parallel application on more than one CE's introduces an additional communication overhead in terms of $Q_1(W, C)$ which increases the execution time. However, this increase in the execution time could be masked by the value of C, which decreases the execution time by increasing the number of processors and also by reducing the communication overhead in terms of $Q_2(W/C, p)$ as compared to $Q(W, p)$ on one CE.

In order to analyze the added value of parallelism we normally compare the parallel execution time on P processors with the sequential execution time on 1 processor. However, as suggested by [4], in a Grid environment, we need to compare the parallel execution time on C CE's with the parallel execution time on 1 CE. This comparison is named as *Grid Speedup* and is mathematically defined as:

$$\Gamma_p^C = \frac{T_1, p(W)}{T_C, p(W)} \quad (2)$$

where, Γ_p^C is the 'Grid Speedup' (with p processors and C CE's), T_1 is the execution time on a single CE and T_C is the execution time on C CE's.

The Grid Speedup (equation 2) is one of the scalability metrics for the parallel applications on the Grid. Its value indicates how better a parallel application performs when decomposed on C CE's as compared to its performance on a single CE in terms of execution time. From equation 2 we could also derive the expression for the Grid efficiency as:

$$\gamma_p^C = \frac{T_1, p(W)}{CT_C, p(W)} \quad (3)$$

where, γ_p^C is the 'Grid efficiency' and p, C, T_1 and T_C represent the same parameters as described in eq. 2.

The description of the 'Grid Efficiency' in eq. 3 follows Amdahl's popular statement that "for a given instance of a particular problem, the system efficiency decreases when the number of available processors is increased " [1]. In the case of the Grid efficiency, in addition to the number of processors, it is the value of the C (number of CE's) that affects the system efficiency.

Based on these concepts of scalability, this paper performs empirical analysis of our parallel algorithm for MC-PSC as described in the following sections.

The remainder of this paper is organized as follows: section 2 describes the background related to the MC-PSC Grand Challenge, section 3 describes the experimental setup; section 4 presents the results and discussions and finally section 5 concludes the paper.

2 The MC-PSC Grand Challenge

The problem of large scale MC-PSC could be represented as a 3D cube. The x and y axis of the cube representing the different proteins being compared, while the z axis representing different comparison methods being used such as such as the *Universal Similarity Metric* (USM), *Maximum Contact Map Overlap* (MaxCMO), *Distance Alignment Matrix* (DaliLite), *Combinatorial Extension* (CE), *Fast Alignment And Search Tool* (FAST) and TM-Align etc. While processed, each cell of this 3D cube holds the output of each comparison method in terms of different measures and metrics. That is, each cell of the 3D cube represents both the processing as well as the storage perspective of the problem space while cell boundaries specify the communication overhead. Given the ever growing number of protein structure comparison methods as well as the number of protein structures being deposited in the PDB; the dimensions of this cube go on increasing and making its computation, in our opinion, to be one of the Grand Challenge Applications (GCAs) in the field of structural biology. GCAs are defined as "fundamental problems in science and engineering with great economic and scientific impact, whose solution is intractable without the use of state-of-the-art parallel/distributed systems" [11]. Many examples of the use of parallel/distributed systems for the solution of GCAs in the field of life sciences in general and structural proteomics in particular are available in the literature [10]. It is believed that most of the GCAs may have several parallel solutions; therefore, a methodological approach based on an exploratory nature will help in finding the best available solution [2]. An example of such approach that is widely used for the design of parallel and distributed algorithms is the PCAM (*Partitioning, Communication, Agglomeration, and Mapping*) approach. Introduced by Ian Foster in [2], the beauty of this approach is that it enables the designer to consider the machine-independent issues (e.g. concurrency, scalability and communication) first and machine-specific issues (e.g granularity and load-balancing) later in the design process. Based on the philosophy of the PCAM approach, a high-throughput distributed framework for the solution of the grand challenge of MC-PSC using *Message Passing Interface* (MPI) model of parallel programming has been introduced [9]. The performance of this framework along with different load balancing strategies was evaluated on a 64-node cluster as reported in [9]. However, it was observed that for datasets having relatively large number of proteins (e.g. 1000+), even the 64-node cluster becomes a bottleneck and it takes about 11 days for the computation to complete. Hence, we tried to deploy our algorithm on the UK National Grid Service (NGS) to take advantage of greater number of cores available across multiple sites. The deployment on the NGS is reported in the next section.

3 Deployment on the NGS Infrastructure

The *National Grid Service* (NGS), provides the *eScience* infrastructure to all the UK-based scientists free of cost [8]. For our case we used the Globus-based MPIg [7] (grid-based implementation of MPI) to spawn the jobs across two NGS sites; one at Leeds and the other at Manchester. Like its predecessors (e.g MPICH-G and MPICH-G2), the MPIg library extends the Argonne MPICH implementation of MPI to use services provided by the Globus Toolkit for cross-site job execution using IP-based communication for inter-cluster messaging. However, being the latest implementation, the MPIg includes several performance enhancements such as in the case of inter-cluster communication it uses multiple threads as compared to the single thread communication of the previous implementations. Furthermore, besides being backward compatible with the pre-web service Globus, the MPIg also makes use of the new web services provided by Globus version 4x. By making use of the new web services, the MPIg provides much more enhanced functionality, usability and performance. The use of the MPIg for cross-site runs requires advanced resource reservation so that jobs (processes) can run simultaneously across all the sites. To facilitate this, NGS provides the *High-Available Resource Co-allocation* (HARC) [6] as a command line utility to perform automatic reservation. Each of the two NGS sites (Leeds and Manchester) consists of 256 cores (AMD Opteron with 2.6GHz and 8GB of main memory) interconnected with Myrinet M3F-PCIXD-2. However, the NGS policies allow the advance reservation of maximum of 128 cores at each site for the maximum duration of 48 hours. Once the reservation is done, then the Globus-based job submission could be achieved with the *Resource Specification Language* (RSL) scripts and other Globus services could be used for job monitoring and control. For the MPI based jobs to run on different sites, the source code of the application needs to be compiled with MPIg libraries at each site and the executable placed in the appropriate working directory under the respective local file system. The compilation of the MPI based application with MPIg does not require any change in the source code and hence from the user's perspective the deployment is as straight forward as running the parallel application on a single site/cluster with the exception that the RSL scripts specifies the resources of the additional site to be used. Figure 1, shows the overall architecture and setup of deploying the MC-PSC application on the Grid.

3.1 Dataset

The dataset used in these experiments is the one introduced by Kinjo et al [5] consisting of 1012 non-redundant protein chains having a total of $252,569$ residues. The 1012 chains result in as many as $1,024,144$ pairwise comparisons for each method/algorithm. While using all the six methods (i.e., USM, MaxCMO, CE, DaliLite, FAST and TM-Align), the total number of pairwise comparisons becomes $1,024,144 \times 6 = 6,144,864$. Given that the average time for the comparison of 1 pair using all the six methods on a single processor machine is about 8 secs, this computation requires about 569 days to complete on a single

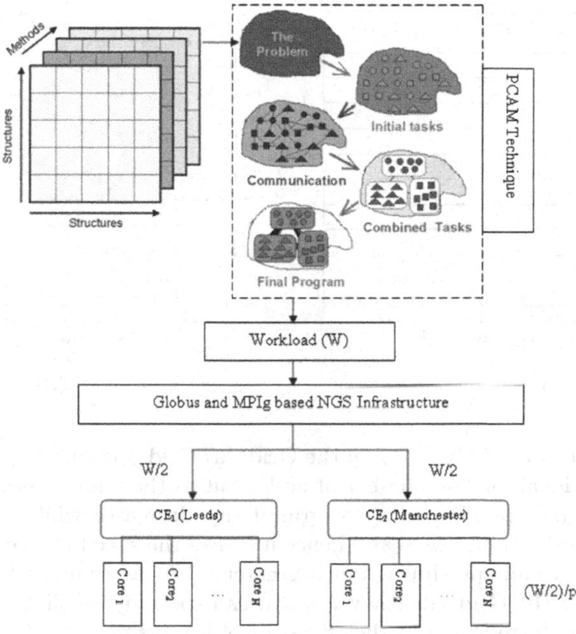

Fig. 1. Deployment of the MC-PSC application on the Grid: the application takes protein 3-D structures as input and prepares the balanced workload W to be distributed on the Grid. Half of the total workload (W/2) is assigned to each site (CE). Each site further distributes the W/2 into p number of cores.

processor and it took about 10.7 days to complete on a 64-node cluster [9]. The results on the Grid infrastructure are presented in the next section.

4 Results and Discussions

Both the single-site and cross-site experiments for MC-PSC were conducted with varying number of processors using the Kinjo et al [5] dataset. The Grid speedup and efficiency (eq. 2 and eq. 3 respectively) were calculated based on the results of these experiments and are shown in figure 2. Figure 2(a) shows that initially (for less number of processors), running the MC-PSC experiments across two sites almost doubles the performance to that of the single-site. However, as the number of processors increases (thereby decreasing the level of granularity and increasing the communication overhead), the speedup decreases slightly and finally reaches to about 1.65. There is also same trend in the Grid efficiency as shown in figure figure 2(b).

Figure 3 provides the comparison of the algorithmic speedup on a single-site (S_1, having 128 processors) and the speedup obtained while running the experiments on the two sites (S_2, having a total of 256 processors). The speedup in this case is taken as the ratio of the execution time on single-machine

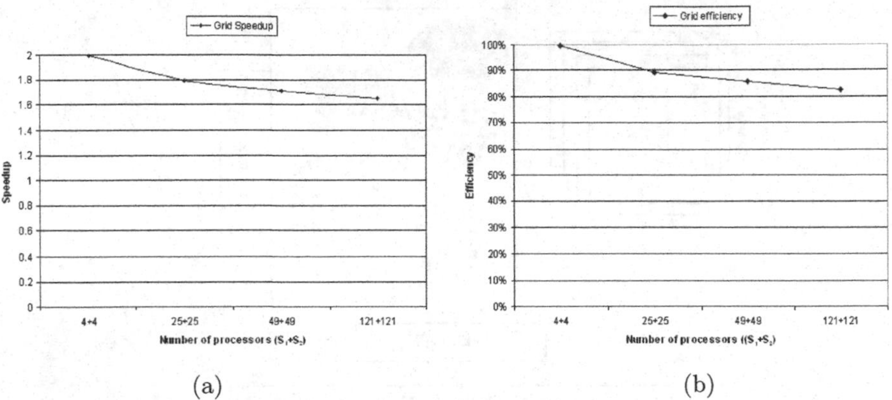

Fig. 2. Performance of the MC-PSC on the Grid: (a) Grid Speedup (eq 2); initially the speedup is almost ideal for less number of nodes but as the number of nodes increases on each site the corresponding level of granularity decreases while the the level of communication overhead increases and hence it causes the speedup to degrade slightly. Nevertheless, the overall speedup is much greater (1.6) as compared to speedup on the single site (¡1). (b) Grid efficiency (eq. 3); as expected the slight degradation of speedup causes the degradation in the efficiency of the system.

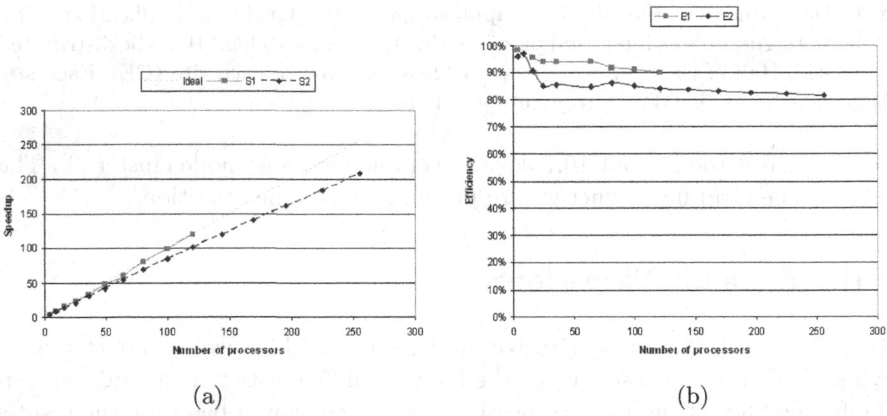

Fig. 3. Single-Site and Cross-Site: (a) Speedup; the graph shows that though initially, the cross-site speedup ($S2$) is slightly low as compared to the single-site speedup ($S1$); however, given the large number of processors available on the later, the overall speedup ($S2$) increases by almost a factor of 2. (b) Efficiency; as expected the cross-site efficiency ($E2$ is slightly less as compared to the single-site efficiency ($E1$ due to extra communication overhead.

(single processor) (T_1) to the execution time on p processors (T_p) (i.e $S_1 = S_2 = \frac{T_1}{T_p}$). As indicated by Figure 3(a), though initially, the cross-site speedup is slightly low as compared to the single-site speedup; however, given the large number of processors available on the later, the overall speedup increases by almost a factor of 2. The total time for the computation of the given dataset on 256 cores (2.4GHz each) was reduced to 38.6 hours. Comparing this with the 569 days on the single-machine and 10.7 days required on a 64-node (though having less processor power i.e 1.4GHz each) cluster we observe a good scalability and performance of our algorithm on the Grid. The boast in the speedup and performance is two folds i.e the large number of processors (*physical speedup*) coupled with high speed of each individual processor (*power scalability*). Figure 3(b), shows the corresponding efficiency of the algorithm on single-site and cross-site architecture. The efficiency, in this case measures the effective use of the hardware and is equal to the ratio of the speedup on p processors to p (i.e $E = \frac{S_p}{p}$). Figure 4 shows the cross-site communication overhead in terms of running the MC-PSC application in the Grid. It shows that, when a few processors are used, the load of the processors and the amount of data to be exchanged is high and consequently there is a considerable communication overhead. However, when we use a larger number of processors, the overhead is negligible in comparison with the computation time.

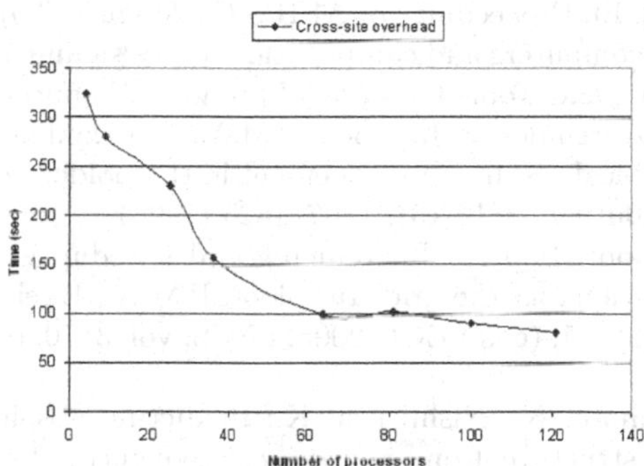

Fig. 4. Cross-site communication overhead. The graph shows that when a few processors are used the load of the processors and consequently the amount of data to be exchanged is high and consequently there is considerable communication overhead. However, when we use a larger number of processors, the overhead is negligible in comparison with the computation time.

4.1 Concluding Remarks and Future Directions

The quality of our parallel algorithm for MC-PSC has been measured in terms of Grid speedup and efficiency. The results of the single-site and cross-site experiments indicate that by making use of the Grid resources, the algorithm scales well and that the cross-site communication overhead does not cause performance degradation. The current cross-site experiments were conducted on two sites based on the HCG model of the National Grid Service (NGS), UK. As the NGS is still in the process of adding more sites, in future we would like to extend this study by increasing the number of sites as well as incorporating the heterogeneous architecture of the Grid. Because, at present the maximum time allocated for continuous execution of a job/process at NGS is limited to 48 hours, it does not allow evaluating the performance of the application with larger datasets; hence the software developed so far could be upgraded by adding fault tolerance mechanisms in the form of checkpoint/restart. The checkpoint/restart mechanism could be added without changing the code of the application by using some libraries such as the *Berkeley Lab Checkpoint/Restart* (BLCR). With these improvements, it would be possible for the MC-PSC to perform real time computation with even large datasets and to develop a database of pre-computed results.

Acknowledgments. All the authors would like to acknowledge the use of the UK National Grid Service in carrying out this work; Azhar A. Shah acknowledges The University of Sindh for the scholarship SU/PLAN/F.SCH/794.

References

1. Amdahl, G.: Validity of the single processor approach to achieving large-scale computing capabilities. In: Proceedings of AFIPS Conference, (30), pp. 483–485 (1967)
2. Foster, I.: Parallel computers and computation. In: Designing and Building Parallel Programs: Concepts and Tools for Parallel Software Engineering (1995)
3. Halderen, A.W., Overeinder, B.J., Sloot, P.M.A., van Dantzig, R., Epema, D.H.J., Livny, M.: Hierarchical resource management in the polder metacomputing initiative. Parallel Computing 24(12-13), 1807–1825 (1998)
4. Hoekstra, A.G., Sloot, P.M.A.: Introducing grid speedup g: A scalability metric for parallel applications on the grid. In: Sloot, P.M.A., Hoekstra, A.G., Priol, T., Reinefeld, A., Bubak, M. (eds.) EGC 2005. LNCS, vol. 3470, pp. 245–254. Springer, Heidelberg (2005)
5. Kinjo, A.R., Horimoto, K., Nishikawa, K.: Predicting absolute contact numbers of native protein structure from amino acid sequence. Proteins Struct. Funct. Bioinf. 58, 158–165 (2005)
6. MacLaren, J., Keown, M.M., Pickles, S.: Co-allocation fault tolerance and grid computing. In: UK e-Science AHM (2006)
7. Manos, S., Mazzeo, M., Kenway, O., Coveney, P.V., Karonis, N.T., Toonen, B.: Distributed mpi cross-site run performance using mpig. In: HPDC 2008: Proceedings of the 17th International Symposium on High Performance Distributed Computing, pp. 229–230. ACM, New York (2008)
8. Richards, A., Sinclair, G.M.: UK National Grid Service. CRC Press, Boca Raton (2009)
9. Shah, A.A., Folino, G., Krasnogor, N.: Towards high-throughput, multi-criteria protein structure comparison and analysis. IEEE Transactions on NanoBioscience 9, 1–12 (2010)
10. Shah, A., Barthel, D., Lukasiak, P., Blacewicz, J., Krasnogor, N.: Web and grid technologies in bioinformatics, computational biology and systems biology: A review. Current Bioinformatics 3(1), 10–31 (2008)
11. Silva, L., Buyya, R.: Parallel programming models and paradigms, pp. 27–42. Prentice Hall PTR, NJ (1999)

Real-Time Electron Tomography Based on GPU Computing

José A. Martínez[1], Francisco Vázquez[1],
Ester M. Garzón[1], and José J. Fernández[2,*]

[1] Dpt Computer Architecture, Almería University, 04120 Almería, Spain
[2] National Center for Biotechnology (CSIC) Cantoblanco, 28049 Madrid, Spain

Abstract. Electron tomography (ET) has emerged as the leading technique for the structural analysis of unique complex biological specimens. Recently, real-time ET systems have appeared on the scene and they combine the computer-assisted image collection with the 3D reconstruction, and provide the users a preliminary structure of the specimen. This rough structure allows the users to easily evaluate the quality of the specimen and decide whether a more time-consuming processing and thorough analysis of the dataset is worthwhile. The aim of this work is to develop software for real-time ET systems. The principle of ET is based upon 3D reconstruction from projections. By means of tomographic reconstruction algorithms, the projection images in the tilt series can then be combined to yield the 3D structure of the specimen.The 3D structure has poor signal to noise ratio, so it is necessary an additional non linear filtering process in order to achieve enough resolution. Then, Matrix Weighted Back Projections (Matrix WBP) and Beltrami methods have been selected as reconstruction and filter procedures, respectively. First the Matrix WBP is applied to the input sinograms to obtain the three-dimensional structure and, next, Beltrami filter de-noises the image. Both methods are highly accelerated by GPU platforms. The power of GPU computing is then exploited to further improve the performance and yield reconstructions of biological datasets in seconds, it allows to integrate both methods on real time electron tomography systems.

Keywords: Electron tomography, Real time, Matrix Weighted Back-Projection, GPU, Beltrami filter.

1 Introduction

Electron tomography (ET) has made it possible to directly visualize the molecular architecture of organelles, cells and complex viruses and, in particular, it has been crucial for recent breakthroughs in life sciences [6,10,3,11,1]. It allows to automate specimen tilting, area tracking, focusing and recording of images

* Work supported by grants CSIC-PIE-200920I075, MCI-TIN2008-01117, JA-P08-TIC-3518.

M.R. Guarracino et al. (Eds.): Euro-Par 2010 Workshops, LNCS 6586, pp. 201–208, 2011.
© Springer-Verlag Berlin Heidelberg 2011

under low electron-dose conditions in order to preserve the specimen from radiation damage. But, as a consequence, the images exhibit poor signal-to-noise ratio (SNR).

Recently, real-time ET systems have appeared on the scene [15,17]. These systems provide rough structure which allows the users to easily evaluate the quality of the specimen and decide whether a more time-consuming processing and also guide the users to select further target areas to be imaged [15,17,5]. Therefore, for fully exploitation of these real-time ET systems, reconstruction and noise reduction methods are necessary. These methods should fulfill a number of requisites to be suitable for integration in real-time ET systems:(1) reconstruction method should supply the enough accurate 3D structure and the nonlinear denoising methods should be used so that the noise is reduced while structural features are preserved and not blurred; (2) the methods should not have complicated parameters to be tuned, as these systems are not intended to run under interactive mode and (3) the methods should be fast to approach solutions in real-time.

Weighted backprojection (WBP) is the standard reconstruction method in the field [6,10]. In this work, three-dimensional reconstruction with WBP is addressed from a matrix perspective by formulating the problem as a set of sparse matrix-vector products [16]. Moreover, the Beltrami flow filter has been chosen as an efficient noise reduction method based on a geometric diffusion flow approach [9], because it reduces the noise preserving the structural features at no huge computation time. Then, the combination of both methods is an appropriated approach to develop real-time electron tomography because it verifies the three requisites before mentioned.

In the last few years, new emerging platforms are shaking up the HPC scene. Graphics processing units (GPUs) offer massive parallelism and provide outstanding performance-to-cost ratio for scientific computing. The use of GPUs for general purpose applications has exceptionally increased in the last few years thanks to the availability of Application Programming Interfaces (APIs), such as Compute Unified Device Architecture (CUDA) [12], that greatly facilitate the development of applications targeted at GPUs. This work proposes the combination of Matrix WBP and Beltrami methods based on GPU computing in order to get reconstructed 3D structures with enough resolution. These methods fulfill the requisites to be integrable in current real-time ET systems. The GPU platforms are selected to accelerate both methods, achieving a significant reduction of the computing time.

The rest of the paper is organized as follows: Sections 2 and 3 describe the main foundations of Matrix WBP and Beltrami methods as reconstruction and denoising approaches respectively. Section 4 analyzes the keys of the parallel implementations of these methods on multiGPU architectures. Section 5 evaluates the GPU implementations experimentally. This paper ends with some conclusions and future work.

2 Tomographic Reconstruction Based on Matrix WBP

Assuming single tilt axis geometry, the 3D problem can be decomposed into a set of independent two-dimensional (2D) reconstruction subproblems corresponding to the slices perpendicular to the tilt axis [5]. The 3D volume is obtained by stacking the 2D slices reconstructed from the corresponding sinogram (i.e. the set of 1D projections). Now we will thus focus on the 2D reconstruction problem. The projection process can be modeled as follows. The sinogram $\mathbf{p}$ is related to the slice $\mathbf{g}^\star$ by the discrete Radon Transform or projection operation:

$$p_i = \sum_{j=1}^{m} A_{i,j} g_j^\star \quad with \quad 1 \leq i \leq n, \tag{1}$$

where $n = n_{tilts} n_{bins}$ is the dimension of $\mathbf{p}$, n_{tilts} being the number of projection angles and n_{bins} the number of projection values obtained for every projection angle; $m = m_x m_y$ is the dimension of $\mathbf{g}^\star$, i.e. the total number of voxels in every slice, with m_x and m_y being the number of voxels in the x and y dimensions, respectively; and $A_{i,j}$ is a weighting factor representing the contribution of the voxel j to the projection value i, and its value only depends on the geometry of the projections. The set of weighting factors defines the $n \times m$ matrix $\mathbf{A}$. This matrix is sparse, therefore, the projection operation can be defined as a sparse matrix-vector product, $\mathbf{p} = \mathbf{A}\mathbf{g}^\star$, where $\mathbf{A}$ is usually called the forward projection operator. Then, the system $\mathbf{p} = \mathbf{A}\mathbf{g}^\star$ must be solved to compute the unknown slice $\mathbf{g}^\star$. In practice, the system is ill-conditioned and a least square problem must thus be solved to compute an approximation of $\mathbf{g}^\star$. WBP is the standard method to solve this problem [14], which reconstructs the specimen by uniformly distributing the specimen density present in the projection images over computed backprojection rays. Formally, the backprojection operator can be defined by means of the matrix $\mathbf{B}$ as:

$$g_j = \sum_{i=1}^{n} B_{j,i} p_i \qquad 1 \leq j \leq m \tag{2}$$

where $\mathbf{B}$ is the transpose of matrix $\mathbf{A}$, and when the number of tilt angles is large enough, the vector $\mathbf{g}$ is a good estimation of the slice $\mathbf{g}^\star$. In WBP a high-pass filter is applied to the projections before backprojection [14], whose burden is usually negligible. In the following, we assume that the projections are already weighted. Our Matrix WBP approach then reconstructs a 3D object as a set of independent SpMV products: $\mathbf{g^s} = \mathbf{B}\ \mathbf{p^s}$ with $1 \leq s \leq N_{slices}$ where N_{slices} is the total number of slices in the volume. Note that the matrix $\mathbf{B}$: (1) is involved in all the products, since the projections have the same geometry for all slices; and (2) is sparse and the location of nonzero coefficients (referred to as nonzeroes) exhibits some regular pattern related to its definition (i.e. $B_{j,i} = A_{i,j}$).

Nowadays, the memory requirements to store the sparse matrix are fulfilled in current computers and GPUs. Specific data structures have proven suited for the particular SpMV operation of WBP with GPU [16], since the regularity and the symmetry relationships between the nonzeroes of **B** can be exploited to reduce the memory access and thus accelerate the SpMV operations on GPUs. These symmetries led reduce the storage space of the data structure in nearly 75%, as it is explained in depth in [16].

3 Reduction Noise by Beltrami Method

The Beltrami flow is an efficient noise reduction method based on a geometric diffusion flow approach [9]. As such, it considers images as maps that are embedded into a higher dimension, that is, a 2D image is considered as a 2-manifold embedded in 3D, i.e. the image $I(x, y)$ is regarded as a surface $S = (x, y, I(x, y))$ in a 3D space [7]. In this work, this idea has been extended to 3D, that is, a 3D volume $I(x, y, z)$ is considered as a 3-manifold embedded in a 4D space $S = (x, y, z, I(x, y, z))$. Embedding the multidimensional image into a higher dimension allows the use of powerful differential geometry operators [9]. In that sense, the Beltrami flow is a geometric flow approach that aims at minimizing the area of the image manifold, driving the flow towards a minimal surface solution while preserving edges [9]. The Beltrami flow is formulated as follows [8]:

$$I_t = \frac{1}{\sqrt{g}} \mathrm{div} \left(\frac{\nabla \mathbf{I}}{\sqrt{g}} \right) \tag{3}$$

where $I_t = \partial I/\partial t$ denotes the derivative of the image density I with respect to the time t; $\nabla \mathbf{I}$ is the gradient vector, that is $\nabla \mathbf{I} = (I_x, I_y, I_z)$, being $I_x = \partial I/\partial x$ the derivative of I with respect to x (similar applies for y and z); g denotes the determinant of the first fundamental form of the surface, which is $g = 1 + |\nabla \mathbf{I}|^2$; Finally, div is the *divergence* operator. The term $\frac{1}{\sqrt{g}}$ in Eq. (3) acts as an edge indicator since it is proven to be the projection of the normal-to-the-surface to the vector representing the 4th dimension [9].

Therefore, the Beltrami flow is a selective noise filtering method that preserves structural features as minimizes diffusion at and across edges whereas it applies extensive diffusion elsewhere [8]. The implementation of the partial differential equation derived from Eq. (3) is based upon an explicit finite difference discretization [13], using an Euler forward difference approximation for I_t and central differences to approximate the spatial derivatives. The reader is referred to that previous work [4,7] for an in-depth analysis of the denoising method.

The noise reduction method based on the Beltrami flow has no complicated parameters to be tuned, as the detection of the edges and estimation of their strength is performed based on g, which is directly computed from the gradient. Nevertheless, the method is solved in an iterative way, and hence a number of iterations have to be specified. In a previous work it was shown that a number of iterations around 100 yielded, in general, good denoising results in ET [4].

Fig. 1 is intended to illustrate the performance of this method in terms of noise reduction and feature preservation over a representative ET dataset that was taken from the Electron Microscopy Data Bank (http://emdatabank.org).

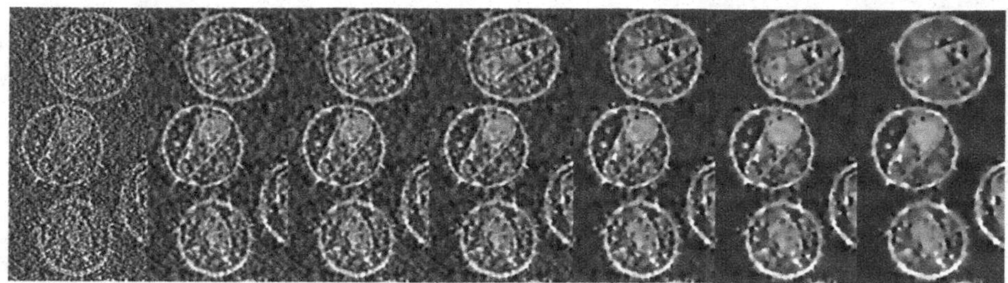

Fig. 1. From left to right, the original HIV-1 reconstruction and the results with the noise reduced at 10, 25, 50, 100, 150 and 200 iterations are shown. Only a representative slice of the 3D reconstruction is presented.

The dataset, whose accession code was emd-1155, is a 3D reconstruction of human immunodeficiency virions (strain HIV-1) [2]. It is clearly observed how the noise is progressively reduced with the iterations. These results show that a number of iterations of 100 are appropriate in terms of noise reduction and preservation of features.

4 Matrix WBP-Beltrami on MultiGPU

The GPU architecture is an accelerator of CPU computation and the input/output data involved in every kernel executed on GPU are communicated between the main memory of CPU and the device memory of GPU. From the programmer's point of view, every GPU card is considered as a set of SIMT (Single Instruction, Multiple Threads) multiprocessors. Each kernel (parallel code) is executed as a batch of threads organized as a grid of thread blocks. In order to optimize the exploitation of the NVIDIA GPU architecture the programmer has to attend to maximize: (1) the *multiprocessor occupancy*, that is the ratio between the number of active warps per multiprocessor and the maximum number of possible active warps; and (2) the *bandwidth memory*, the memory management can be optimized if the access pattern of the different threads belonging to every half-warp (16 threads) verifies the coalescence and alignment conditions.

Both methods previously described have been implemented taking account the keys about the exploitation of the multi-GPU architecture. Two levels of parallelism have been applied in the multi-GPU implementations of WBP-Beltrami method: (1) at high level the volume is distributed among P GPU cards, then every GPU computes WBP-Beltrami method on the corresponding sub-volume stored on its local device memory, consequently, communications processes between GPUs are necessary to solve data dependencies, these communications are set by means of the CPU memory; and (2) at more low level every sub-volume is computed exploiting massive parallelism of every GPU card, thus, hundreds of threads collaborate to compute WBP-Beltrami method on the sub-volume stored in the local device memory.

Matrix WBP has been formulated as a set of specific sparse matrix-vector products without data dependence among them. The sinograms are distributed

Table 1. Run-times (s) of sequential code on a core of CPU based on 2 Quad Core Intel Xeon 2,26Ghz and GPU code on one and two Tesla C1060 cards

Vol	128		192		256		384		512		640		768	
Sequential														
Standard WBP	6,7		21,6		51,3		169,7		404,7		782,7		1347,7	
Beltrami	8,2		28,2		98,7		335,5		800,5		1552,1		2729,3	
Total	14,9		49,8		150,0		505,2		1205,2		2334,8		4077,0	
1 GPU (left) and 2 GPUs (right)														
Matrix WBP	0,6	0,4	1,0	0,5	1,4	0,8	2,7	1,5	5,4	3,0	7,9	4,3	11,4	6,1
Beltrami	0,5	0,4	1,0	0,7	2,1	1,4	5,7	3,2	14,6	8,1	22,9	12,7	38,7	21,6
Total	1,1	0,8	2,0	1,2	3,5	2,2	8,4	4,7	20,0	11,1	30,7	16,9	50,1	27,7

among the P GPU cards. The matrix B is computed by every card, aligned in the device memory and so the coalesced memory access is achieved to read the nonzeroes of B. Every reconstructed slice is related to one product accelerated by one GPU, so P cards can simultaneously accelerate the reconstruction of P slices, and the reconstructed volume is distributed among the P cards. Next, every GPU sends its volume to CPU main memory and the float data format is changed to integer format and it is also distributed among the GPU cards with an additional slice in the boundaries between two sub-volumes (called halo) in order to solve the data dependence of Beltrami method to denoise the corresponding sub-volume. Then, every Beltrami iteration is accelerated by P cards, when it finishes the halo slices are communicated among GPUs by means CPU.

5 Experimental Evaluation

The Matrix WBP-Beltrami approach was implemented with CUDA and evaluated on one core of CPU based on 2 Quad Core Intel Xeon E5520 2,26Ghz with 24GB SDRAM DDR3 1333Mhz ECC, under Linux, and an architecture of two GPUs Tesla C1060 with 4GB GDDR3 and 30 multiprocessors of 8 cores (i.e. 240 cores) at 1.2 GHz. Synthetic datasets were created to carry out an extensive performance evaluation. They comprised a number of aligned projection images to yield cubic 3D reconstructions. The datasets had different image sizes (128, 192, 256, 512, 640 and 768) and number of tilt angles 180. In the general implementation, the memory demands rapidly increase with the problem size, up to 2GB in the largest test case. This amount does not turn out to be a problem in modern GPUs.

The datasets were subjected to tomographic reconstruction with the standard WBP, based on recomputation of the coefficients following by the Beltrami filter on the CPU (Standard WBP-Beltrami). The computation times of every phase of Standard WBP-Beltrami are summarized in Table 1 and are taken as reference to evaluate the speed-up achieved by the GPUs. Moreover, Table 1 includes the run times of the Matrix WBP code on one and two GPUs Tesla C1060. The run-times values shown on Table 1 highlight that: (1) The computational load of the tomographic reconstructions based on WBP-Beltrami method strongly increases when the dimensions of volume increases because the sequential times

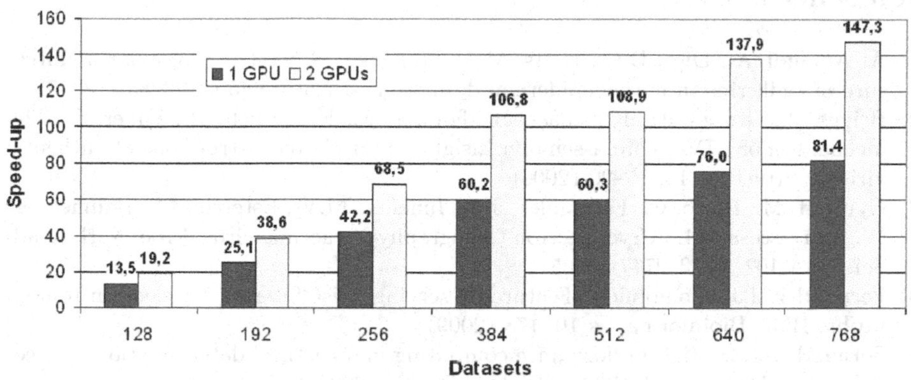

Fig. 2. (a) Speed-up factors of Matrix WBP-Beltrami implementation on one and two GPUs vs. Standard WBP-Beltrami on the test CPU

of larger test volumes are very long; (2) the GPU architecture relevantly reduces the run-times since the run times on one GPU card is reduced by two magnitude orders and (3) the GPU implementation scales on two cards due to the reduction of run-times by even half when the volume is distributed between the two cards. Fig. 2 shows that the acceleration factor thanks to exploitation of the GPU architecture is in the range [13.5x, 81.4x] on one GPU card and in the range [19.2x, 147.3x] on two cards, regardless of the problem size.

These results demonstrate that Matrix WBP-Beltrami based on GPU computing relevantly reduces the computing time required for tomographic. This acceleration factors lead to the capability of computing reconstructions and filter of 0.5 – 1.5 GB in size in around 11–27 s, as Table 1 shows. Therefore the tomography based on Matrix WBP-Beltrami on GPUs can be joined to a real-time ET system which helps the users to select the samples with relevant information.

6 Conclusions and Future Work

This work has accelerated the tomographic reconstruction problem by means of GPU computing. Two methods have been selected to solve the reconstruction and denoising problems: Matrix WBP and Beltrami filter. Both methods have the appropriated characteristics to join to real-time tomographic systems, that is, the images supplied have enough resolution, they do not include complicated parameters to be tuned and their computational requirements are available on the current GPU platforms. The evaluation results have shown that both methods exploit the multi-GPU architectures achieving high acceleration factor over the run-times on CPU. Therefore these methods could be easily integrated in current real-time electron tomography systems. Consequently, the approach described in this work is expected to be of invaluable help for scientists to assess the quality of their datasets acquired during their ET sessions, and also to use this information as a guide for subsequent data collection.

References

1. Al-Amoudi, A., Diez, D.C., Betts, M.J., Frangakis, A.S.: The molecular architecture of cadherins in native epidermal desmosomes. Nature 450, 832–837 (2007)
2. Briggs, J., Grunewald, K., Glass, B., Forster, F., Krausslich, H., Fuller, S.: The mechanism of HIV-1 core assembly: Insights from 3D reconstructions of authentic virions. Structure 14, 15–20 (2006)
3. Cyrklaff, M., Risco, C., Fernández, J.J., Jimenez, M.V., Esteban, M., Baumeister, W., Carrascosa, J.L.: Cryo-electron tomography of vaccinia virus. Proc. Natl. Acad. Sci. USA 102, 2772–2777 (2005)
4. Fernandez, J.J.: Tomobflow: Feature-preserving noise filtering for electron tomography. BMC Bioinformatics 10, 178 (2009)
5. Fernández, J.J.: High performance computing in structural determination by electron cryomicroscopy. J. Struct. Biol. 164, 1–6 (2008)
6. Fernández, J.J., Sorzano, C.O.S., Marabini, R., Carazo, J.M.: Image processing and 3D reconstruction in electron microscopy. IEEE Signal Process. Mag. 23(3), 84–94 (2006)
7. Fernández, J., Martínez, J.: Three-dimensional feature-preserving noise reduction for real-time electron tomography. Digital Signal Processing 20(4), 1162–1172 (2010)
8. Kimmel, R., Malladi, R., Sochen, N.A.: Images as embedded maps and minimal surfaces: Movies, color, texture, and volumetric medical images. Int. J. Comput. Vis. 39, 111–129 (2000)
9. Kimmel, R., Sochen, N.A., Malladi, R.: From high energy physics to low level vision. In: ter Haar Romeny, B.M., Florack, L.M.J., Viergever, M.A. (eds.) Scale-Space 1997. LNCS, vol. 1252, pp. 236–247. Springer, Heidelberg (1997)
10. Leis, A.P., Beck, M., Gruska, M., Best, C., Hegerl, R., Baumeister, W., Leis, J.W.: Cryo-electron tomography of biological specimens. IEEE Signal Process. Mag. 23(3), 95–103 (2006)
11. Nicastro, D., Schwartz, C., Pierson, J., Gaudette, R., Porter, M.E., McIntosh, J.R.: The molecular architecture of axonemes revealed by cryoelectron tomography. Science 313, 944–948 (2006)
12. NVIDIA: CUDA Programming guide. Version 2.3 (August 2009)
13. Press, W.H., Flannery, B.P., Teukolsky, S.A., Vetterling, W.T.: Numerical Recipes: The Art of Scientific Computing. Cambridge University Press, Cambridge (1992)
14. Radermacher, M.: Weighted back-projection methods. In: Frank, J. (ed.) Electron Tomography: Methods for Three-Dimensional Visualization of Structures in the Cell, 2nd edn., pp. 245–273. Springer, Heidelberg (2006)
15. Schoenmakers, R.H.M., Perquin, R.A., Fliervoet, T.F., Voorhout, W., Schirmacher, H.: New software for high resolution, high throughput electron tomography. Micros. Anal. 19(4), 5–6 (2005)
16. Vazquez, F., Garzon, E.M., Fernandez, J.J.: A matrix approach to tomographic reconstruction and its implementation on gpus. J. Struct. Biol. 170(1), 146–151 (2010)
17. Zheng, S.Q., Keszthelyi, B., Branlund, E., Lyle, J.M., Braunfeld, M.B., Sedat, J.W., Agard, D.A.: UCSF tomography: An integrated software suite for real-time electron microscopic tomographic data collection, alignment, and reconstruction. J. Struct. Biol. 157, 138–147 (2007)

Hybrid Parallel Simulations of Fluid Flows in Complex Geometries: Application to the Human Lungs

Mathias J. Krause*, Thomas Gengenbach, and Vincent Heuveline

Karlsruhe Institute of Technology (KIT)
Engineering Mathematics and Computing Lab (EMCL)
Institute for Applied and Numerical Mathematics 4
Fritz-Erler-Str. 23, Bldg. 01.86
76133 Karlsruhe, Germany
{mathias.krause,thomas.gengenbach,vincent.heuveline}@kit.edu
http://www.united-airways.eu, http://openlb.org
http://numhpc.math.kit.edu, http://emcl.kit.edu

Abstract. In this paper a hybrid parallel strategy dedicated to the simulations of fluid flows in complex geometries by means of Lattice Boltzmann methods (LBM) is introduced. The approach allows coping with platforms sharing both the properties of shared and distributed architectures and relies on spatial domain decomposition where each subdomain represents a basic block entity which is solved on a symmetric multi-processing (SMP) system. Main emphasis is placed on testing its realization and studying its efficiency on a realistic fluid flow problem with a highly complex geometry. Therefore, as a suitable problem the simulation of the expiration in the human lung, whose functionality is described by a dedicated two-scale model, is considered.

Keywords: Numerical Simulation, Lattice Boltzmann, High Performance Computing, Computational Fluid Dynamics, Human Lungs, Modeling, Respiratory System.

1 Introduction

The numerical simulation of the full human respiratory system corresponds to one of the *Grand Challenges* in scientific computing nowadays. The main difficulties are not only related to the highly complex multiphysics phenomenology involving multi-scale features but also to the complex geometry. Many other problems especially in the field of biotechnology and medical sciences are also characterized by underlying highly complex computational domains. Furthermore, related applications like the analysis of possible implications due to surgeries in advance or cognition-guided surgeries require to consider patient-individual geometries. A widely automated preprocessing as well as efficient

* Corresponding author.

M.R. Guarracino et al. (Eds.): Euro-Par 2010 Workshops, LNCS 6586, pp. 209–216, 2011.
© Springer-Verlag Berlin Heidelberg 2011

parallelization strategies are both necessary conditions aiming to enable real-time simulations. In this context, it is of great importance to take advantage of nowadays available hardware architectures like IBM Cell processors, Graphic Processing Units (GPUs), multi-core processors and especially hybrid high performance technologies that blur the line of separation between architectures with shared and distributed memory.

The goal of this work is to present a highly efficient parallelization strategy dedicated to the numerical simulation of fluid flows in complex geometries which takes great advantage of today's typical hybrid high performance computers. The approach is based on LBM which have evolved to a mature tool in computational fluid dynamics (CFD) and related topics in the landscape of both commercial and academic software in the last decade (cf. literature e.g. [1,2]). The simplicity of the core algorithms as well as the locality properties resulting from the underlying kinetic approach lead to methods which are very attractive in the context of parallel and high performance computing (HPC). The LBM, which are employed here, are discretization strategies for families of BGK-Boltzmann equations [3] which are related to the Navier-Stokes equations as shown by Saint-Raymond in [4]. Junk and Klar [5] interpret particular LB schemes of the presented type directly as Chorin-type projection methods for incompressible Navier-Stokes equations.

In [6,7], Krause et al. propose a hybrid parallelization strategy for LB simulations. In the following, this idea is picked up and extended for simulations with underlying complex computational domains. Its realization is tested for the simulation of an expiration in a human lung. The underlying two-scale model [8] is based on the coupling of a bronchiole model with a model describing the incompressible Newtonian fluid flow in the upper part of the human lungs which can be resolved using standard medical imaging like computer tomography (CT) or Magnetic Resonance Imaging (MRI).

The paper is organized as follows: In Section 2, the hybrid parallelization strategy is explained. A test case is formulated in Section 3 which relies on a patient-specific lung geometry. Details concerning the discretization method are stated. Finally, the measured performance results on the *Jülich Research on Peta-flop Architectures (JUROPA)*[1] supercomputer are presented and analyzed.

2 Hybrid Parallelization Strategy for LBM

The most time demanding steps in LB simulations are usually the collision and the streaming operations. Since the collision step is purely local and the streaming step only requires data of the neighboring nodes, parallelization by domain partitioning leads to low communication costs and is therefore very efficient [9,10,11].

The hybrid parallelization strategy proposes to partition the data of a considered discrete position space Ω_h, which is a uniform mesh with spacing $h > 0$,

[1] http://www.fz-juelich.de/jsc/juropa

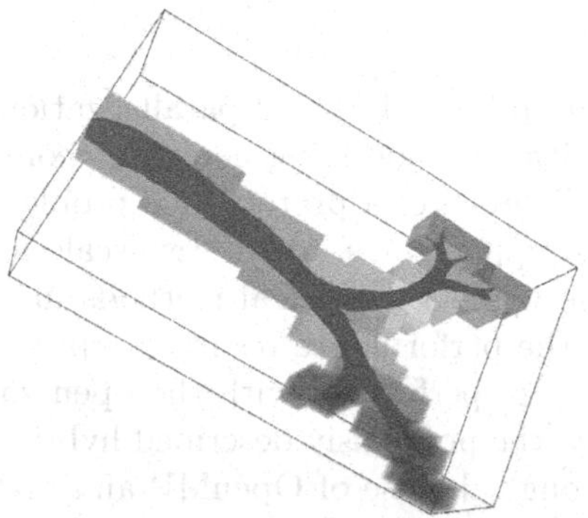

(a) The geometry of a human lung split into $n = 139$ cuboids which are assigned to processing units. Different colors represent different processing units. Each cuboid comprise about 50^3 computing grid points which are shared by cores within the same shared memory area.

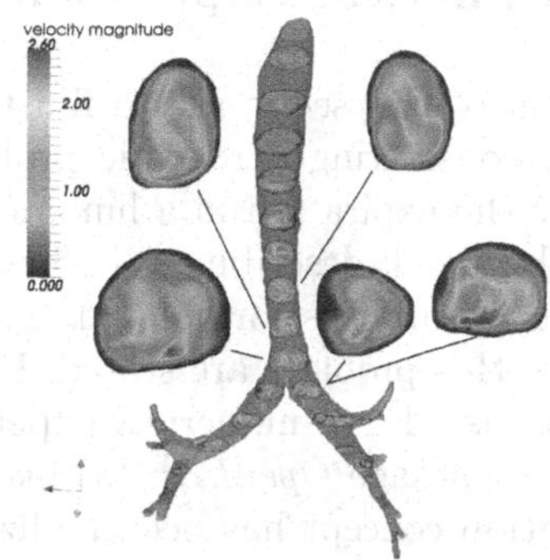

(b) The simulated flow field for an expiration in the human lungs in various planes. The intersections are colored according to the computed velocity magnitude in m/s. Cf. [8]

Fig. 1. Partition of the geometry data (a) and resulting flow field (b)

according to their geometrical origin into $n \in \mathbb{N}$ disjoint, preferably cube-shaped sub-lattices Ω_h^k $(k = 0, 1, ..., n-1)$ of almost similar sizes.

This becomes feasible by extending Ω_h to a cuboid-shaped lattice $\widetilde{\Omega}_h$ through the introduction of ghost cells. Then, $\widetilde{\Omega}_h$ is split into $m \in \mathbb{N}$ disjoint, cuboid-shaped extended sub-lattices $\widetilde{\Omega}_h^l$ $(l = 0, 1, ..., m-1)$ of approximately similar size and as cube-shaped as possible. Afterwards, all those extended sub-lattices $\widetilde{\Omega}_h^l$ which consist solely of ghost cells are neglected. The number of the remaining extended sub-lattices $\widetilde{\Omega}_h^l$ $(l_0, l_1, ..., l_{n-1})$ defines n. Finally, one gets for each $k \in \{0, 1, ..., n-1\}$ the wanted Ω_h^k as a subspace of $\widetilde{\Omega}_h^{l_k}$ by neglecting the existing ghost cells.

For $p \in \mathbb{N}$ the number of available processing units (PUs) of a considered hybrid high performance computer which communicates by means of a network, an even load balance for complex geometries in particular will be assured if the domain Ω_h is partitioned in a sufficiently large number $n \in \mathbb{N}$ of sub-lattices. Then, several of the sub-lattices Ω_h^k $(k = 0, 1, ..., n-1)$ can be assigned to each of the available PUs. In order to find an optimal distribution where the communication costs between the PUs are kept low, a sophisticated graph-based partitioning algorithm can be applied. Then, each PU in turn, distributes its load for any of its sub-lattices Ω_h^k among the available threads sharing the local memory of the PU. The sub-lattice Ω_h^k is always a uniform mesh. Hence, a dedicated parallelization paradigm for the shared memory part of the platform can be applied in a way that takes advantage of the regular structure by means of efficiency.

3 Numerical Experiments

The aim of this section is to illustrate the proposed hybrid parallelization approach considering a realistic problem with an underlying complex geometry, namely the expiration in a human lung. Thereunto, a prototypical problem for the sub-model, describing the flow in the upper lungs, of the two-scale model introduced in [8] is formulated. Then, the applied numerical methods in order to solve this problem are stated. Finally, the performance results are presented and discussed. All numerical experiments are performed with the open source software package *OpenLB*[2]. In this library, the previously described hybrid parallelization concept has been realized through the use of OpenMP and MPI. A detailed description of both the implementation and performance tests for a simple underlying geometry are provided in detail in [6,7]. The obtained numerical results, see Figure 1b, for this simulation set-up are presented in detail in [8].

3.1 Case Study Description and Discretization Issues

An expiration for a realistic everyday situation is to be simulated. Thereby, the flow rate is fixed to be $Q = 150$ ml/s which is typically observed for adult males in situations of resting or sitting awake [12]. The air is considered at normal conditions, i.e. $1,013$ hPa and $20\,°$C. Thus, its kinematic viscosity is $\nu = 1.4 \cdot 10^{-5}$ m^2/s.

In order to set up flow simulations, it is necessary to determine a couple of parameters, hence the velocity profiles can be set at the considered bronchi $i \in I$ in accordance with Poiseuille's law. The area of the boundary at the trachea is found to be approximately $A \approx 0.9065$ cm^2. To reach the desired flow rate of $Q = 150$ ml/s a mean speed of $U_{mean}(Q) \approx 1.65$ m/s is needed. This mean speed is considered to be the characteristic macroscopic velocity. The characteristic macroscopic length $L = 0.015$ m is fixed to be the diameter of A. With it, one obtains the Reynolds number $Re \approx 1768$. As a suitable test geometry, the lung of a middle-aged male human is considered. The computational domain Ω is extracted from CT data with a resolution of 0.4 mm. To solve the fluid flow problem in the upper part of the human lungs Ω a standard $D3Q19$ LB model with BGK collision operator [1,2] is applied. This discretization approach requires the computational domain to be a uniform, hence, a voxel mesh Ω_h. The patient specific mesh is created in a preprocessing step [13] which leads to $h = 0.23$ mm$/N$ for three different refinement levels $N = 1, 2, 3$. For $N = 3$ one obtains approximately 57.7 million fluid voxels, which results in about 1.1 billion unknowns for the $D3Q19$ LB scheme.

3.2 Performance Results

According to the concept presented in Section 2, the considered lattices Ω_h with $h = 0.23$ mm$/N$ and $N = 1, 2, 3$ need to be partitioned. Thereto, at first

[2] http://www.openlb.org

all Ω_h are extended to cuboid-shaped lattices $\widetilde{\Omega}_h$ through the introduction of ghost cells. An overview concerning the dimensions of the different considered extended lattices $\widetilde{\Omega}_h$ as well as its corresponding numbers of fluid, non-boundary and boundary cells is given in Table 1. In Figure 1a the obtained remaining extended sub-lattices obtained for $m = 1,000$ but also for the geometry of the upper human lungs are visualized.

Table 1. The considered extended discrete lattices $\widetilde{\Omega}_h$ representing the geometry of human lungs for different discretization parameters $h = 0.23$ mm/N whereby $N = 1, 2, 3$ is the corresponding refinement level

refinement level N	dimension of $\widetilde{\Omega}_h$	fluid cells	non-boundary / fluid cells	boundary/ fluid cells
1	$452 \times 234 \times 859$	$2,327,357$	87.8%	12.2%
2	$900 \times 464 \times 1714$	$17,465,152$	93.6%	6.4%
3	$1350 \times 696 \times 2571$	$57,675,848$	95.7%	4.3%

Then, the three considered extended lattices $\widetilde{\Omega}_h$ ($h = 0.23$ mm/N with $N = 1, 2, 3$) are split into $m = 1,200,\ 12,000,\ 24,000,\ 48,000$ disjoint extended sub-lattices $\widetilde{\Omega}_h^l$ ($l = 0, 1, ..., m-1$). Afterwards, all sub-lattices which just consist of ghost cells are neglected, leaving a certain number $n \leq m$ of extended sub-lattices $\widetilde{\Omega}_h^{l_k}$ ($k = 0, 1, ..., n-1$). This leads to twelve different test cases which are listed in Table 2. There, for each of the test cases ($h = 0.23$ mm/N with $N = 1, 2, 3$) the obtained number n of remaining lattices $\widetilde{\Omega}_h^{l_k}$ ($k = 0, 1, ..., n-1$) as well as the minimal and maximal number of cells in the respective remaining lattices $\widetilde{\Omega}_h^{l_k}$ are specified. According to the presented strategy, all remaining extended sub-lattices $\widetilde{\Omega}_h^{l_k}$ ($k = 0, 1, ..., n-1$) are distributed among the available PUs. In the presented case, they are spread by building blocks with respect to the numbering.

The twelve test cases are executed on the supercomputer *JUROPA*. Thereby, in every case a different number of cores p, but always with just one core per node, is employed. The C++ source code is compiled with the Intel compiler using optimization level 3. In order to keep the total execution times low, the number of the time steps to be performed is always set to 100. The time in seconds measured for these 100 steps obtained employing p processes, respectively nodes, is captured by the variable t_p. In order to compare performances of LB implementations obtained on different computers or obtained for different implementation techniques, the measuring unit *million fluid-lattice-site updates per second* MLUP/s is frequently introduced, e.g. in [14]. In the following, this terminus is extended to also enable comparisons of LB code executed in parallel by introducing the measuring unit MLUP/ps, which stands for *million fluid-lattice-site updates per process and second.* The performance results obtained for the test cases are measured in this unit and captured by the variable P_{LB} which is defined according to $P_{LB} := N_c/(10^4 t_p p)$ whereby N_c denotes the number of fluid cells.

Table 2. The table shows all considered test cases and provides for each of the cases ($h = 0.23$ mm$/N$ with $N = 1, 2, 3$) the initial number m of sub-lattices $\tilde{\Omega}_h^l$ ($l = 0, 1, ..., m-1$), the remaining number n of sub-lattices $\tilde{\Omega}_h^{l_k}$ ($k = 0, 1, ..., n-1$) as well as the minimal and maximal number of cells in the respective remaining lattices $\tilde{\Omega}_h^{l_k}$

case name	refinement level N	initial cuboids m	remaining cuboids n	max. cell cuboid	min. cell cuboid
N1m1200	1	1, 200	152	73,710	77,142
N1m12000	1	12, 000	744	6,859	8,000
N1m24000	1	24, 000	1, 347	3,375	4,096
N1m48000	1	48, 000	2, 258	1,728	2,028
N2m1200	2	1, 200	161	581,256	602,454
N2m12000	2	12, 000	741	57,798	62,400
N2m24000	2	24, 000	1, 310	28,830	30,752
N2m48000	2	48, 000	2, 254	14,440	15,625
N3m1200	3	1, 200	158	2,000,349	2,026,056
N3m12000	3	12, 000	734	198,476	205,320
N3m24000	3	24, 000	1, 296	97,336	103,776
N3m48000	3	48, 000	2, 210	47,952	52,022

In Figure 2 the measured performances P_{LB} are plotted as a function of the employed number of MPI-processes $p = 2^0, 2^1, ..., 2^8$. Considering the obtained graphs of all test cases, a general observation made is a slight decline of P_{LB} for increasing p. This is in accordance with the obtained performance results for the problem with an underlying simple geometry presented in [6,7].

For all considered test cases ($m = 1,200,\ 12,000,\ 24,000,\ 48,000$ and $p = 2^0, 2^1, ..., 2^8$) it is observed that the greater the refinement level N is chosen the better are the obtained performances P_{LB}. The best value $P_{LB} \approx 2.14$ MLUP/ps is measured for $m = 12,000$ and $N = 3$ on $p = 8$ nodes. This characteristics can be explained by the fact that the computational costs for a boundary cell are usually higher than for a non-boundary cell and that the ratio of boundary cells to fluid cells increases for smaller problem sizes as stated in Table 1.

Further, it is observed that for the cases where the number of initial cuboids m is the smallest, i.e. $m = 1,200$, in general the obtained performances P_{LB} are the smallest. In these cases, the number of obtained sub-lattices ranges from $n = 152$ to $n = 161$, while for the other cases it is much greater ($n \geq 734$). This leads to a relative bad load balance especially where $p \geq 64$. However, for a fixed problem size, which is characterized by N, the overhead due to communication costs will be greater if m and n increases. Thus, increasing m, it is expected that the positive effect of a better load balance is compensated by additional costs due to increasing effort for the three steps *blocking*, *communicating* and *writing to ghost cells* needed for the MPI-based implementation [7]. This is indeed observed in the test results. By trend, in the case where $N = 1$ the best result is obtained for $m = 12,000$ and for the cases $N = 2, 3$ for $m = 24,000$. Yet, it is to be noted

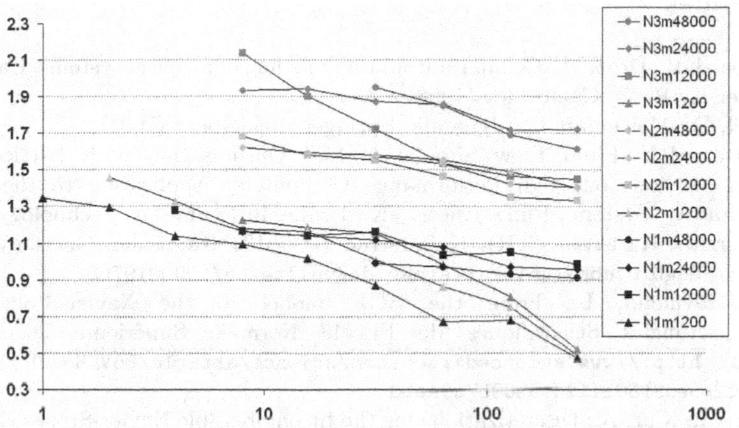

Fig. 2. The graph shows the obtained values for P_{LB} in MLSUP/ps (million fluid-lattice-site updates per process and second) as a function of the number of employed MPI-processes p for 100 times steps of an *D3Q19* LB algorithm obtained on the *JUROPA*. The underlying computational domain is obtained by CT scans of the upper human lungs.

that the measured performances P_{LB} are relatively close to each other in the majority of the considered cases with $m \geq 12,000$. In particular, comparing the results obtained for $m = 24,000$ to those for $m = 48,000$, no significant drop of the performances P_{LB} is observed.

4 Conclusions

A hybrid parallelization strategy dedicated for LB simulations of fluid flow problems with underlying complex geometries is introduced. The approach is based on a partition of a domain into blocks which are distributed across the nodes of a cluster. Its realization takes advantage of the paradigms MPI and OpenMP and is part of the open source software *OpenLB*. It is tested for a realistic problem with an underlying highly complex computational domain, namely the upper part of a human lung extracted from CT data.

The obtained parallel performance results confirm the efficiency of the underlying approach in terms of the computing time that can almost be halved if the number of employed nodes is doubled. Thereunto, it is important to ensure a good load balance, which is accomplished by splitting the computational domain in a sufficient large number of sub-domains. The associated overhead is observed to be rather small. It is expected that applying a sophisticated graph-based partitioning algorithm would lead to a reduction of this overhead since relative expensive network communication could be replaced by memory operations. With the obtained progress in terms of efficiency of the hybrid parallelization, the simulation of a complete breathing cycle in the complete human lungs becomes technically feasible.

References

1. Chopard, B., Droz, M.: Cellular automata modeling of physical systems. Cambridge University Press, Cambridge (1998)
2. Hänel, D.: Molekulare Gasdynamik. Springer, Heidelberg (2004)
3. Krause, M.J.: Fluid Flow Simulation and Optimisation with Lattice Boltzmann Methods on High Performance Computers: Application to the Human Respiratory System. Ph.D. thesis, Karlsruhe Institute for Technology (KIT), Universität Karlsruhe (TH), Kaiserstrae 12, 76131 Karlsruhe, Germany (2010), http://digbib.ubka.uni-karlsruhe.de/volltexte/1000019768
4. Saint-Raymond, L.: From the BGK model to the Navier-Stokes equations. Annales Scientifiques de l'École Normale Supérieure 36, 271–317 (2003), http://www.sciencedirect.com/science/article/B6VKH-48HS9DK-5/2/4b7102c9ed9f501112dc9b08b7c9ae3d
5. Junk, M., Klar, A.: Discretizations for the Incompressible Navier-Stokes Equations Based on the Lattice Boltzmann Method. SIAM J. Sci. Comput. 22, 1–19 (2000)
6. Heuveline, V., Krause, M.J., Latt, J.: Towards a hybrid parallelization of lattice Boltzmann methods. Computers & Mathematics with Applications 58, 1071 (2009)
7. Heuveline, V., Krause, M.J.: OpenLB: Towards an Efficient Parallel Open Source Library for Lattice Boltzmann Fluid Flow Simulations. In: International Workshop on State-of-the-Art in Scientific and Parallel Computing. PARA, vol. 9 (2010) (accepted)
8. Gengenbach, T., Heuveline, V., Krause, M.: Numerical Simulation of the Human Lung: A Two-scale Approach. In: BMT 2010 - Reguläre Beiträge (BMT 2010 Reguläre Beiträge), Rostock-Warnemünde, Germany (2010)
9. Massaioli, F., Amati, G. Achieving high performance in a LBM code using OpenMP. In EWOMP 2002, The Fourth European Workshop on OpenMP (2002)
10. Pohl, T., et al.: Performance Evaluation of Parallel Large-Scale Lattice Boltzmann Applications on Three Supercomputing Architectures, p. 21 (2004)
11. Zeiser, T., Götz, J., Stürmer, M.: On performance and accuracy of lattice Boltzmann approaches for single phase flow in porous media: A toy became an accepted tool - how to maintain its features despite more and mor complex (physical) models and changing trends in high performance computing! In: Resch, M., Shokin, Y., Shokina, N., et al. (eds.) Proceedings of 3rd Russian-German Workshop on High Performance Computing, Novosibirsk, July 2007. Springer, Heidelberg (2008)
12. Valentin, J.: Basic Anatomical and Physiological Data for Use in Radiological Protection: Reference Values - ICRP Publication 89. Annals of the ICRP 32, 1–277 (2002), http://www.ingentaconnect.com/content/els/01466453/2002/00000032/00000003/art00002
13. Gengenbach, T.: Modellierung und numerische Simulation der menschlichen Atemwege auf Hochleistungsrechnern. Master's thesis, Universitaet Karlsruhe (TH) (2009)
14. Wellein, G., Zeiser, T., Hager, G., Donath, S.: On the single processor performance of simple lattice Boltzmann kernels. Computers & Fluids 35, 910 (2006)

Parallel Implementation of a Computational Model of the Human Immune System

Alexandre Bittencourt Pigozzo, Marcelo Lobosco, and Rodrigo Weber dos Santos

Mestrado em Modelagem Computacional, Universidade Federal de Juiz de Fora, 36036-330, Juiz de Fora, MG, Brazil
{alexandre.bittencourt,marcelo.lobosco}@ice.ufjf.br, rwdsantos@yahoo.com

Abstract. Our work aims to develop and implement a mathematical and computational model for the primary immune system response in a microscopic section of a tissue. A large amount of computation is required to solve the set of equations related to the mathematical model, for this reason in this work we present an initial attempt to improve the performance of the implementation via the use of parallel computing.

1 Introduction

The development of computational systems that simulates an entire living system was proposed by the UK Computing Research Committee as one of the grand challenges in computing research for 2010 and beyond [5]. This class of system is known as iViS (in Vivo-in Silico). The potential benefits of iViS are enormous, so are the challenges along this long way. Currently, the development of such iViS systems is in its early stages. In this scenario, our work aims to develop and implement a mathematical and computational model of the Human Immune System (HIS). The complete modeling of the HIS demands a large amount of work to be performed by a large multidisciplinary team. In this work we focus on one specific task: the simulation of the immune response to pathogenic agents in a microscopic section of a tissue, reproducing, for this purpose, the initiation, maintenance and resolution of immune response. Our model describes a set of Partial Differential Equations (PDEs) used to reproduce important HIS phenomena. The simulation of these phenomena is computationally very expensive. Depending on how accurate is the simulation, it can take hours or even some days to compute the simulation results for a small section of tissue. Therefore, the use parallel computing is very important in order to reduce the execution times. In this work, we present and analyze the performance of a OpenMP (*Open Specifications for Multi Processing*) [3] version of the simulator.

The remainder of this work is organized as follows. Section 2 includes the biological background necessary for understanding this work. Section 3 describes the mathematical model implemented in this work. Section 4 describes our sequential implementation. Sections 5 and 6 describes our parallel version and

M.R. Guarracino et al. (Eds.): Euro-Par 2010 Workshops, LNCS 6586, pp. 217–224, 2011.
© Springer-Verlag Berlin Heidelberg 2011

presents the results, respectively. Our conclusions and plans of future works are presented in Section 7.

2 Biological Background

The HIS is composed of two distinct parts, the innate immune system and the adaptive immune system. Our work focuses on the modeling of the innate immune system. The innate immune system is responsible for powerful nonspecific defenses that prevent or limit infections by most pathogenic microorganisms [9]. This first line of defense against pathogenic microorganisms consists of physical barriers, such as the skin and mucous membranes, and the second line consists of cells that recognize specific parts of pathogenic microorganisms, herein called antigens. After the antigens are recognized, the immune system cells, like the macrophage, attack them. The induction of an inflammatory response as a result of the activation of the innate immune system recruits other cells to the point of attack, such as the neutrophils. Dendritic cells (DC) uptakes antigens, transporting them to the linfatic nodes where the adaptive immune response starts. Activated DC produces chemokines, that are responsible for the regulation of the immune response. A third line of defense, the adaptive immune system, is activated by the innate response. Its role is to adapt the immune system response during an infection to improve its recognition of the pathogenic microorganism [9]. The cells that participate in the adaptive immune response are very specialized, called lymphocytes. B-Cells and T-Cells are the major types of lymphocytes. Chemokines plays an important role in regulating the migration of lymphocytes and other cells types in the immune and inflammatory responses.

3 Mathematical Model

Our HIS simulator is based on a set of PDEs originally proposed by [11]. The main differences between our model and the original one are: a) we use a simplified model; and b) we adopt distinct boundary conditions: Neumann boundary conditions are used in our work, while the original one uses Dirichlet boundary conditions for neutriphils and chemokines. Our main contribution is to show that even a simple model can reproduce qualitatively the behaviour of neutrophils during an immune response to an antigen (PAMPs). The main characteristics of the mathematical model are: a) neutrophils interacts with chemokines and antigens to control the infection; b) in the local of infection neutrophils diffuses and moves in the direction of chemokine gradient; and c) the chemokine attracts neutrophils to the local where the antigen concentration is higher. Our set of equations is given below, where A, N and CH represent the population of Antigens, Neutrophils and chemokines, respectively.

$$\begin{cases} \frac{\partial A}{\partial t} = -\mu_A A - \lambda_{A|N} AN + D_A \Delta A + g(x,t) \\ A(x,0) = 0, \, \frac{\partial A(.,t)}{\partial n}|_{\partial\Omega} = 0 \end{cases} \tag{1}$$

In Equation 1, μ_A is the decay rate for the antigen, $\lambda_{A|N}$ is the phagocytosis rate, D_A is the diffusion coefficient and the function g is the source term of infection.

$$\begin{cases} \frac{\partial N}{\partial t} = -\mu_N N - \lambda_{N|A} AN - \nabla.(\chi_N N \nabla CH) - \delta_{N|CH} CHN + D_N \Delta N \\ N(x,0) = N_0, \frac{\partial N(.,t)}{\partial n}|_{\partial\Omega} = 0 \end{cases} \quad (2)$$

In Equation 2, μ_N is neutrophil decay rate, $\lambda_{N|A}$ is the uptake rate by antigens, χ_N is the chemotaxis coefficient, $\delta_{N|CH}$ is the regulation coefficient and D_N is the diffusion coefficient.

$$\begin{cases} \frac{\partial CH}{\partial t} = \beta_{CH|N} NA - \mu_{CH} CH + D_{CH} \Delta CH \\ CH(x,0) = 0, \frac{\partial CH(.,t)}{\partial n}|_{\partial\Omega} = 0 \end{cases} \quad (3)$$

In Equation 3 $\beta_{CH|N}$ is the production rate of the chemokine (IL-8), μ_{CH} is the decay rate and D_{CH} is the diffusion coefficient.

This set of equations tries to model the role of chemotaxis and chemokinesis on the migration of immune cells to sites of inflammation and infection. Both cells are of fundamental importance in this process. We believe that our computational model can enhance the comprehension of inflammatory and immune processes. A better understanding of these processes is essential since they trigger a cascade of events that activate and coordinate the global response of the immune system [1]. The understanding of the neutrophils role is also important because of its specific regulatory effectors of immunity: they orchestrate immature DC, recruit T cells, and the chemokines released by them display chemotactic activity for macrophages, dendritic cells, NK cells, and T cells [2].

4 Sequential Implementation

The mathematical model can be discretized in many distinct ways using, for example, explicit, implicit or Crank-Nicholson schemes in time. Different numerical approaches have been proposed [8,4] to solve this kind of equations. Our implementation is based on the finite volume technique for the spatial discretization and an explicit method for the time evolution with an upwind scheme for the advection term of the equation, i.e. the chemotaxis term. The sequential code was implemented in C.

A numerical library, such as NAG[10], could be used to solve the PDEs. However, we decided to implement the numerical method to solve PDEs because a) we have the possibility to parallelize the code; b) most of the numerical libraries offer few functions that are suitable to our problem; and c) functions offered by such numerical libraries are hard to use because arguments supplied to functions must be in a specific format.

In this simulation we considered an unidimensional domain with dimension $4mm$ and the number of time steps equal to (10^6), which represents an interval of approximately 2.4 hours. The simulations we are interested in are made on much larger length and time scales, which takes about two days to execute. Due to this huge execution time, we simulate in this paper a smaller instance of the problem. Table 1 presents the initial conditions, the time discretization (δT), the space discretization (δX) and all the parameters used in our simulations.

Table 1. Simulation parameters

Parameter	Value	Units
N_0	$25, 0 < x < 4000$	cell
CH_0	$0, 0 < x < 4000$	cell
A_0	$300, 2500 < x < 4000$	cell
δT	10^{-7}	s
δX	1	μm
μ_A	0.005	1/day
$\lambda_{A\|N}$	0.5	1/cell.day
D_A	7x10^6	μm^2/day
$g(x,t)$	300	cell
μ_N	0.33	1/day
$\lambda_{N\|A}$	0.55	1/cell.day
$\delta_{N\|CH}$	0.3	1/cell.day
X_N	1.44x10^5	μm^2/day
D_N	1.44x10^6	μm^2/day
$\beta_{CH\|N}$	0.1	1/day
μ_{CH}	0.03	1/day
D_{CH}	9.216x10^4	μm^2/day

The numerical results of some simulations are presented in Figures 1, 2 and 3. As can be observed, the results show that initially the neutrophil population is equally distributed over the entire domain. As the time goes by, the concentration of the chemokine increases. As a result, the antigen population starts to decrease due to the higher concentration of neutrophil in the area.

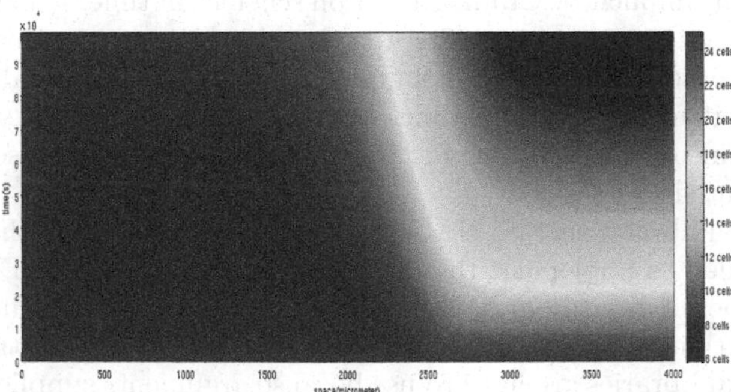

Fig. 1. Temporal evolution of neutrophil concentration. The x-axis represents the space (in μm), the y-axis represents the time steps. The colormap represents the number of neutrophil (in cells).

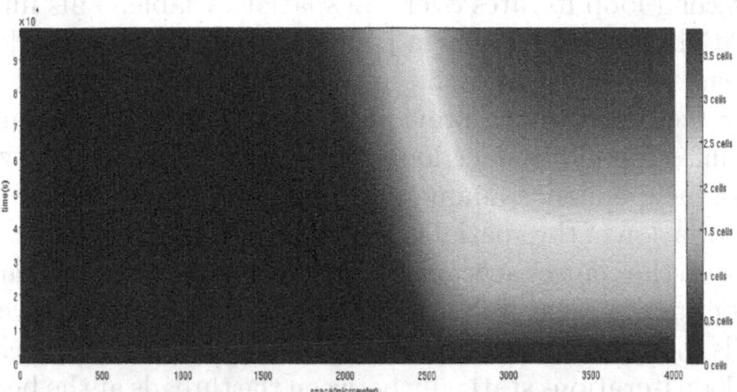

Fig. 2. Temporal evolution of chemokine concentration. The x axis represents the space (in μm), the y-axis represents the time steps. The colormap represents the number of chemokine (in cells).

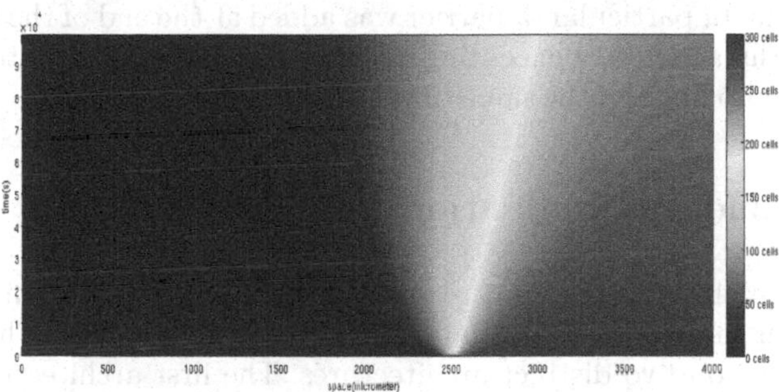

Fig. 3. Temporal evolution of antigen concentration. The x-axis represents the space (in μm), the y-axis represents the time steps. The colormap represents the number of antigen (in cells).

5 Parallel Implementation

The parallel version of the HIS simulator was implemented using OpenMP (*Open Specifications for Multi Processing*) [3], which offers a programming interface for shared memory parallel machines. The programmer uses compilation directives to identify the portions of the source code that should be executed in parallel and may also specify how the code should be executed.

This parallelization requires us to identify sections of the code that demands the large amounts of CPU time and that could be executed in parallel. The instrumentation of the sequential version of the HIS simulator has shown that the code associated with the temporal resolution of the PDEs consumes almost 99% of the total execution time. The step that followed the identification of hotspot was its parallelization. The code is composed by two distinct loops. The first one implements the temporal evolution of the system. For each time iteration, a second loop iterates over the spatial variable. This inner loop solves the discretization of the PDEs for a position in the simulation domain. Due to the data dependency between each temporal time step, we could not parallelize the first loop: the result of the previous temporal step is necessary to calculate the current time step. The inner loop was chosen to be parallelized due to the complete data independence among all iteration steps.

The parallelization of the spatial loop was implemented with the *#pragma omp for* directive with the clauses *schedule(static)* and *nowait*. The *nowait* clause allows a thread to continue the execution after leave the loop without have to wait for all others threads to finish the loop execution. The *schedule(static)* clause was used to divide the loop iterations statically between the threads at the beginning of loop execution. This is due to its lower overhead in comparison with the dynamic division of iterations among threads. We tried to avoid overheads associated with thread creation and synchronization. So in our implementation threads are created only once, at the beginning of the temporal loop. The synchronization of the threads was necessary only in one point of the code, and was used to guarantees the correctness of the program. In particular, a barrier was added at the end of the temporal loop to prevent a thread to start executing a new temporal iteration without all others threads have also finished the same time step.

6 Experimental Evaluation

In this section the experimental results obtained by executing five times both versions of our simulator, sequential and parallel, are presented. The experiments were performed on two distinct architectures. The first architecture is a 2 GHz Intel Core 2 Quad processor (Q8200), with 4 GB RAM and 2 MB L2 cache, running Linux kernel 2.6.18. The second architecture is a 1.2 GHz Intel Core i7-860 processor, with 8 GB RAM, 8 MB L2 cache, running Linux kernel 2.6.31. In both architectures, the *gcc* version 4.4.2 was used to compile all versions of our program. Although both processors have four physical cores, the i7 processors come with Hyper-Threading (HT) technology, so it effectively scales 8 threads.

To evaluate the parallel implementation of the HIS simulator, we vary the number of threads from 2 to 4 in the Quad processor and from 2 to 8 in the i7 processor, due to its HT capabilities. Both sequential and parallel versions of our simulator were executed five times. The standard deviation was less than 1.5%. The speedup figures were obtained by dividing the average sequential execution time by the parallel one. Table 2 present the results.

As can be observed in Figure 4, the speedup achieved when running on the Quad ranges from 1.4 up to 2.8 on 4 cores. The speedup achieved when running on the i7 processor ranges from 1.4 up to 3.1 on 4 HT cores. We believe that both processors do not achieve a linear speedup because we scaled down the problem size. The speedup results presented in Figure 4 are quite surprising from an intuitive point of view: one could expected that the i7 would achieve a better speedup than the Quad processor, specially because some works [12,6] describe a memory contention issue in the Quad processor. The reason why the HIS simulator code do not suffer from

Table 2. Serial and parallel execution time, in seconds, for both architectures

		Number of Threads							
		serial	2	3	4	5	6	7	8
Core 2 Quad	execution time	197.4	137.6	92.6	70.1	-	-	-	-
	% std deviation	<0.1	<0.1	<0.1	<0.1	-	-	-	-
i7	execution time	119.3	85.7	65.3	50.7	56.8	49.1	43.6	38.9
	% std deviation	1.3	0.3	0.4	0.7	1.2	0.3	1.5	0.1

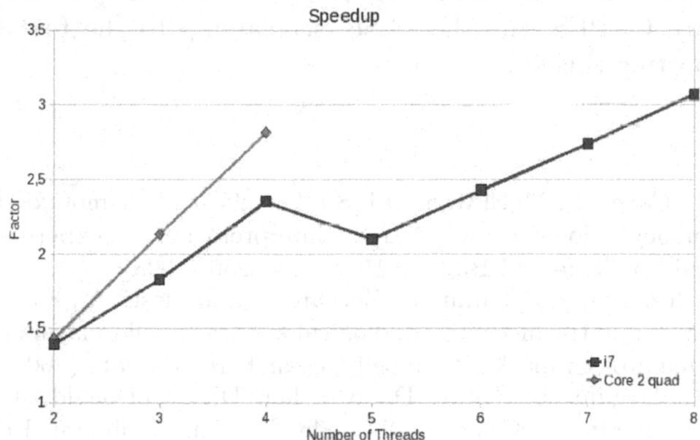

Fig. 4. HIS simulator speedup curve

the memory contention in the Quad processor is simple: the amount of memory it uses completely fits in the processor cache. Also, i7 performed worse than the Quad processor because it is faster than the Quad. The sequential code executes almost 1.65 times faster in the i7 processor than in the Quad. So, the parallel overheads in the code, such as the time spent doing thread creation and destruction, synchronization and so on, become more prominent: we reduced the computation time, but not the parallel overheads in the code.

7 Conclusions and Future Works

In this work we presented a mathematical and computational model that simulates the immune response to pathogenic agents in a microscopic section of a tissue. To achieve this objective, the model reproduces the initiation, maintenance and resolution of immune response. A set of PDEs are used to model the main agents involved in this processes, like the antigen, chemokines and neutrophils. However, the resolution of the PDEs is computationally a very expensive task. So this work also presented an initial attempt to improve the performance of the computational implementation through the use of parallel programming techniques. The numerical experiments developed herein show that the parallelization was effective in improving the program performance, providing gains up to 2.8, when using a Core 2 Quad processor, or 3.1, when using a i7 processor.

As future works, we plan to implement a more complete mathematical model including, for example, the description of DC, T cells and macrophages. This more complex model will require even more computation power. To cope with this problem we are currently developing another parallel version of our code using the new high-performance platform based on GPGPUs (*General-Purpose computation on Graphics Processing Units*)[7].

Acknowledgment

The authors would like to thank FAPEMIG (CEX APQ 01326/08), CNPq (481535/2008-0), CAPES (for the M.Sc. scholarship to the first author) and UFJF for supporting this study.

References

1. Byrne, H.M., Cave, G., McElwain, D.L.S.: The effect of chemotaxis and chemokinesis on leukocyte locomotion: A new interpretation of experimental results. Mathematical Medicine and Biology 15(3), 235–256 (1998)
2. di Carlo, E., Iezzi, M., Pannellini, T., Zaccardi, F., Modesti, A., Forni, G., Musian, P.: Neutrophils in anti-cancer immunological strategies: Old players in new games. Journal of Hematotherapy & Stem Cell Research 10, 739–748 (2001)
3. Chandra, R., Dagum, L., Kohr, D., Maydan, D., MacDonald, J., Menon, R.: Parallel Programming in OpenMP, 1st edn. Morgan Kaufmann Publishers, San Francisco (2001)
4. Filbet, F.: A finite volume scheme for the patlak–keller–segel chemotaxis model. Numerische Mathematik 104, 457–488 (2006)
5. Hoare, T., Miller, R.: Grand Challenges in Computing Research. British Computer Society (2004)
6. Jin, H., Hood, R., Chang, J., Jespersen, J.D.D., Taylor, K., Biswas, R., Mehrotra, P.: Characterizing application performance sensitivity to resource contention in multicore architectures. Tech. Rep. NAS-09-002, NAS Division, NASA Ames Research Center (November 2009)
7. Kirk, D., Hwu, W.: Massively Parallel Processors: A Hands-on Approach. Morgan Kaufmann, San Francisco (2010)
8. Marrocco, A.: Numerical simulation of chemotactic bacteria aggregation via mixed finite elements. Math. Mod. Num. Analysis 37, 617–630 (2003)
9. Paul, W.E. (ed.): Fundamental immunology, 6th edn. Lippincott Williams & Wilkins, Philadelphia (2008)
10. Pennington, S.V., Berzins, M.: New nag library software for first-order partial differential equations. ACM Trans. Math. Softw. 20(1), 63–99 (1994)
11. Su, B., Zhou, W., Dorman, K.S., Jones, D.E.: Mathematical modelling of immune response in tissues. Computational and Mathematical Methods in Medicine: An Interdisciplinary Journal of Mathematical, Theoretical and Clinical Aspects of Medicine 10, 1748–6718 (2009)
12. Xavier, C.R., dos Santos Amorim, E.P., Amorim, R.M., Lobosco, M., Goldfeld, P., Dickstein, F., dos Santos, R.W.: Performance evaluation of a reservoir simulator on a multi-core cluster. In: Taniar, D., Gervasi, O., Murgante, B., Pardede, E., Apduhan, B.O. (eds.) ICCSA 2010, Part IV. LNCS, vol. 6019, pp. 395–408. Springer, Heidelberg (2010)

Parallel Pre-processing of Affymetrix Microarray Data

Pietro Hiram Guzzi and Mario Cannataro

Department of Experimental Medicine and Clinic,
University Magna Græcia, 88100 Catanzaro, Italy
{hguzzi,cannataro}@unicz.it

Abstract. The study of genes is currently carried out by systematic analysis that relies on data produced by the microarray technology. The recent development of such technology and the increasing number of analysed samples result in an increased volume of raw data for each experiment. The time for preprocessing represents an important amount of the analysis, so the need to introduce tools for the efficient preprocessing arises. This paper presents a system able to manage and preprocess microarray data in a parallel way. First experimental results on Affymetrix data showing appreciable improvements in term of execution times are discussed.

1 Introduction

Biological processes within cells are carried out by genes that can be studied using microarray technology. For processing and studying DNA microarrays many different technologies as well as algorithms and tools have been introduced [2,3,7]. A typical workflow for analysing microarray data is structured on four main phases: *(i)* preprocessing, that comprises summarisation and normalization, *(ii)* annotation; *(iii)* statistical and data mining analysis, and *(iv)* biological interpretation.

Raw data generated from microarray platforms, e.g. Affymetrix Cel Files or Illumina Tagged Images, need to be preprocessed. The first step in preprocessing, known as summarisation, aims to recognise the position of different genes in raw images, associating different regions of pixels to the unique gene that generated them. Normalisation aims to correct the variation of gene expression in the same array due to experimental bias. Filtering reduces the number of investigated genes on the basis of biological considerations, e.g. genes of known functions, or considering statistical criteria (e.g. associated p-value). Finally, the annotation process associates each gene to a set of functional information, such as biological processes that are related to gene, and a set of cross reference database identifiers. Statistical and data mining analysis phases aim to identify biological meaningful genes, e.g. by finding differentially expressed genes among two groups of patients on the basis of their expression values.

The typical dimension of microarray datasets is growing for two main reasons: the dimension of files encoding a single chip and the number of the arrays involved in a single experiment are increasing. Let us consider, for instance, two

M.R. Guarracino et al. (Eds.): Euro-Par 2010 Workshops, LNCS 6586, pp. 225–232, 2011.
© Springer-Verlag Berlin Heidelberg 2011

common Affymetrix microarray files (named CEL files): the older Human 133 Chip CEL file that has a dimension of 5 MB and contains 20000 different genes while the newer Human Gene 1.0 st that has a typical dimension of 10 MB and contains 33000 genes. A single array of the Exon family (e.g. Human Exon or Mouse Exon) can have up to 100 MB of size. Moreover the recent trend in genomics is to perform microarray experiment considering a large number of patients.

From this scenario, the need for the introduction of tools and technologies to process such huge volume of data in an efficient way arises. A possible way to develop the efficient preprocessing of microarray data is represented by the parallelization of existing algorithms on parallel computing, e.g. clusters. In the scenario we envision the whole computation is distributed onto different processors, that perform computations on smaller sets of data and results are finally integrated. Such scenario requires the design of new algorithms for summarisation and normalisation that take advantage of the underlying parallel architectures. Nevertheless, a first step in this direction can be represented on the replication on different nodes of existing preprocessing software that runs on smaller datasets.

This paper presents a software system based on a master-worker architecture for the parallel preprocessing of Affymetrix data. The core of the system is in fact based on a master node that distributes data on different nodes. Each node performs preprocessing on a subset of the dataset employing the Affymetrix Power Tools (APT)[1]. Finally, results are moved to the master node and are integrated.

Despite its relevance, the parallel processing of microarray data is a relatively new field. An important work is represented by affyPara [8] that is a Bioconductor package for parallel preprocessing of Affymetrix microarray data. It is freely available from the Bioconductor project. Compared to affyPara, our approach presents three main advantages: (i) the possibility to realize more summarisation scheme such as Plier, (ii) the easily extension to newer SNP arrays, (iii) it does not require the installation of Bioconductor platform.

The rest of the paper is structured as follows. Section 2 discusses the sequential preprocessing of Affymetrix data, Section 3 presents a parallel preprocessing algorithm and Section 4 presents a case study discussing the preprocessing of Affymetrix data. Finally Section 5 concludes the paper and outlines future work.

2 Preprocessing of Affymetrix Microarray Data

The preprocessing of microarray data can be structured as a pipeline of sequential steps, as data feeds along next steps, it becomes more and more refined. Each step can be performed by using different algorithms that are designed for each chip of different platforms. Usually, software tools are designed ad hoc for a vendor and are tailored to the properties of data; they do not allow the preprocessing in an general way.

[1] www.affymetrix.com

From a technical point of view CEL files store the results of the intensity calculations obtained from the pixel values of the raw image files (also referred as DAT files). The structure of the current version of CEL files (see Figure 1) is represented by a binary file where values are stored in little-endian format.

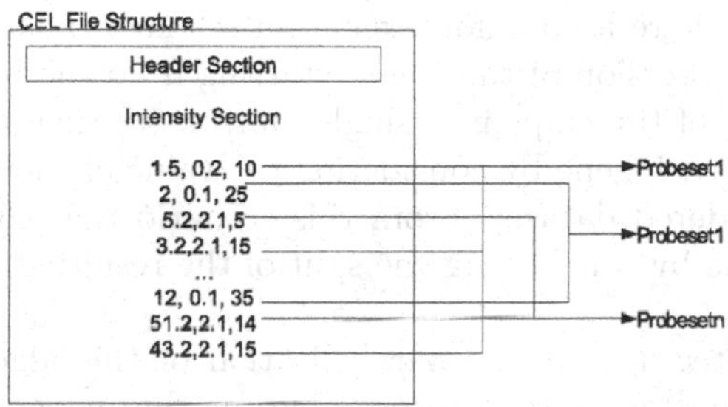

Fig. 1. The internal structure of a CEL file

Preprocessing of Affymetrix arrays start from multiple CEL files and produces as output a matrix whose element (i, j) represents the intensity of the i-th gene in the j-th sample. Preprocessing can be structured as: (i) background correction and quality control, (ii) normalisation, (iii) summarisation, and (iv) annotation.

Background correction aims to identify the background noise and to remove it [7]. Normalisation consists of reducing the bias among chips and within different regions of the same chip [2], aiming at removing non-biological variability within a dataset. Both biological and technical variations introduce artifacts and variability into the system. Summarisation combines multiple preprocessed probe intensities to a single expression value. All arrays employ more than one probe for each genes as introduced before. Summarisation takes into account all of the probes for the same gene and averages them by enhancing the signal-to-noise ratio.

All of these algorithms are based on several assumptions on the data distribution and they require a set of specific libraries in order to correctly access binary data. For Affymetrix arrays, there exist two main summarisation algorithms: Robust Multi-array Average (*RMA*) algorithm [6], and Probe Logarithmic Intensity Error (*PLIER*) algorithm [1].

Finally, a process known as *annotation*, associates to each probe its known annotations such as Gene Symbol or Gene Ontology [4] by matching probes to public databases or knowledge bases. Often annotation files are provided by the chip manufacturer and contain different levels of annotation, e.g. database identifier, description of molecular function, associated protein domains.

Affymetrix Power Tools are a set of command line programs provided by Affymetrix that implements different algorithms for preprocessing Affymetrix arrays. In particular apt-probeset-summarize implements summarization and normalization methods (e.g. RMA- RMA-SKETCH and PLIER) for expression arrays. APT-Tools are able to read a set of *CEL* files and produce a data matrix.

3 A Parallel System for Preprocessing Affymetrix Microarray Data

The preprocessing of Affymetrix files can be easily executed in a parallel way by considering the structure of RMA, RMA-SKETCH and PLIER algorithms. All the algorithms share a common execution scheme: (a) they initially find a raw value for the expression of the gene i starting from the binary file, (b) they merge all the genes of the chips in a single matrix, (c) then they normalize the expression value of each gene by considering the value of the gene i in the other arrays of the considered dataset. From this scenario the parallelization of the step (c) can be done by considering the split of the resulting matrix in different arrays.

A suitable architecture for the parallelisation of this algorithm is depicted in Figure 2. The master node is responsible for the invocation of the worker nodes, each worker node receives as input a copy of the whole dataset and a list of probeset to be preprocessed, then it performs their summarisation and normalization. Finally, it sends to the master node the subset of summarised probesets. Master node merges together results and builds the resulting matrix.

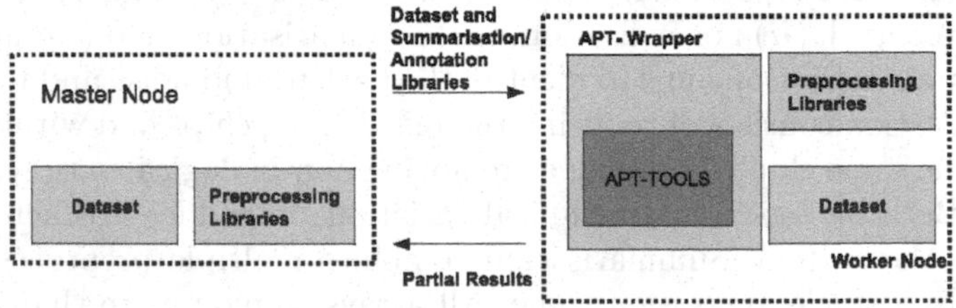

Fig. 2. Architecture of the system

Considering the APT-Tools, the parallelization can be performed by invoking APT on a subset of probesets specified in an input file (e.g. subset.txt), as explained in the following. The rest of the Section explains the execution of these steps on a cluster architecture as depicted in Figure 3:

- **Invocation of Master Node.** The Master node computes the number of needed nodes and the list of probeset for each node. We consider a simple load distribution strategy that assigns to each node the same load. Let N_{pbs} the number of probesets of a chip, and Nwk the number of desired workers, each worker will process $\frac{N_{pbs}}{Nwk}$ probes.
- **Data Distribution.** The Master Node replicates the whole dataset on each worker node and sends the list of probesets to be considered to each node.
- **Parallel execution of APT.** Each Worker node executes the APT-Tool on a subset of probesets and sends the resulting output to the Master node.
- **Integration of results.** The Master node, after the completion of each job collects the results and builds the final data matrix.

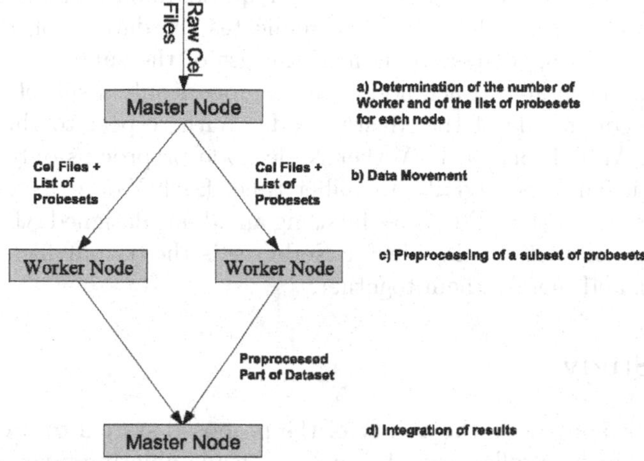

Fig. 3. Flow of data for the execution of parallel preprocessing

The following fragments of pseudo code show the main steps executed, respectively, by the master node and the worker nodes.

---

procedure: Master Node
Input: Dataset // Microarray Dataset (CEL Files), each file contains N_{pbs} probesets,
Input: N_{wk} **// Number of Workers**
Input: L_a, L_s: **Annotation and Summarisation Libraries**
begin
Computation of jobs and generation of the list of probesets for each node,
Each node will receive, $\frac{N_{pbs}}{N_{wk}}$ probesets; $Probeset[j], j = 1...N_{wk}$:Array;
Replication of Data and Libraries for each node
Delivery to each node the corresponding list of probes $Probeset[j]$ and the preprocessing parameters
FOR EACH $Workerj : send(Probeset[j], Parameters[j])$ $j = 1...N_{wk}$
Collection of partial results
Fusion of partial results
end

---

procedure: Worker Node
Input: (D,L_a,L_s,Preprocessed[j],Parameters[j])
// Preprocessing of dataset
$Results[j] = RunAPT(D, L_a, L_s, Probeset[j], Parameters[j])$
// Partial Results are moved to the Master Node
send($Results[j], MasterNode$)

The Master Node receives the preprocessing requests (a dataset and the number of desired workers) from the user, then replicates the dataset on the available worker nodes and sends to each of them the list of the subset of probesets to summarize and normalize. Each node will preprocess only a subset of probesets following the commands of the Master Node. With respect to the traditional invocation of APT-Tools, each Worker Node node preprocess only a subset of probesets so it employs trivially a smaller time. Each Worker Node is able to invoke an instance of the APT-Tools by using an ad hoc designed APT-Wrapper. After the jobs completion, the Master Node reads the output files sent by the worker nodes, and merges them together.

4 Case Study

This section demonstrates the ability of the proposed system to preprocess microarray data in a parallel way showing a considerable improvement in term of consumed time. We considered a publicly available dataset of 21 Affymetrix HumanGene 1.0 st arrays and we split this dataset onto three subsets respectively of 7 (Dataset1 hereafter), 14 (Dataset2 hereafter), and 21 arrays (Dataset3 hereafter). The dimension of three datasets are respectively: 75Mb, 150Mb, and 220Mb.

For each dataset we measured the sequential execution time for preprocessing considering three possible preprocessing schemas: RMA, RMA-SKETCH and PLIER. Then we considered the execution time for the parallel preprocessing. The execution time of each preprocessing has to consider the overhead of data-movement among nodes as well as the execution time of the successive merging of the jobs of the nodes. The measured transfer time is considerably lower than the execution time, so we do not include it in this discussion. We measured the execution times of such preprocessing respectively considering an increasing number of worker nodes. Table 1, shows the comparison among the sequential, (T_{seq}) and parallel execution of preprocessing, (T_{10}, T_{15}, and T_{20}), for each dataset considering the RMA, RMA-SKETCH and PLIER algorithms.

Table 1. Execution Times for Datasets

Algorithm - Times	Dataset1				Dataset2				Dataset3			
	T_{seq}	T_{10}	T_{15}	T_{20}	T_{seq}	T_{10}	T_{15}	T_{20}	T_{seq}	T_{10}	T_{15}	T_{20}
RMA	310	31	20	19	150	10	8	8	480	50	30	29
RMA-SKETCH	205	20	15	14	100	10	7	7	295	29	20	18
PLIER	460	50	35	26	230	23	15	12	710	80	46	46

We measured also the speed-up for each dataset measuring the ratio $Speed-Up = \frac{T_{seq}}{T_{par}}$, where T_{par} is the time for the parallel processing considering the different number of workers. Figures 4(a), 4(b), and 4(c) depict the speed-up respectively for Dataset 1, 2, and 3.

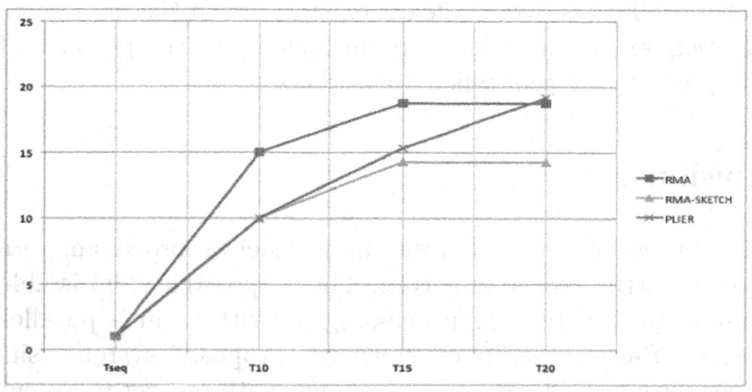

(a) Dataset 1

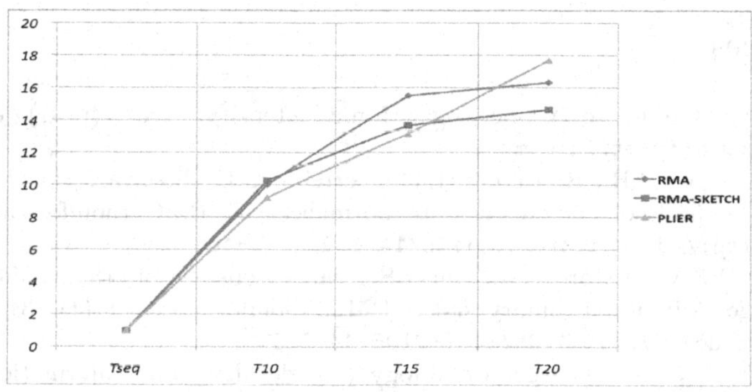

(b) Dataset 2

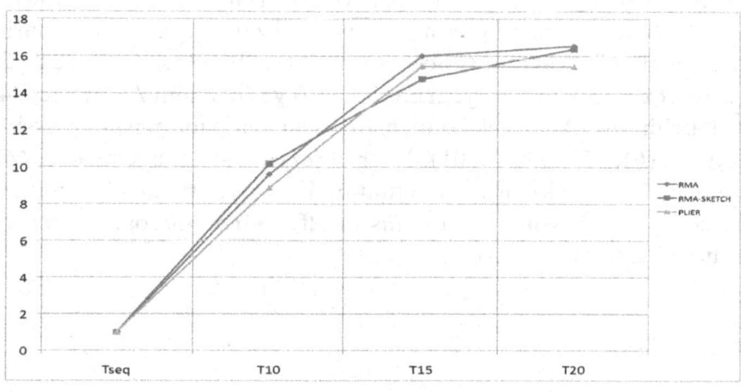

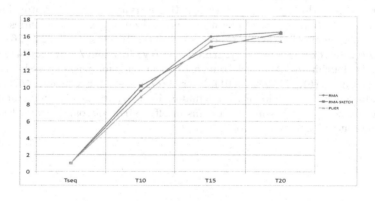

(c) Dataset 3

Fig. 4. Speed-Up for Dataset 1,2, and 3

As evidenced in all the figures the parallel execution initially presents a superlinear [5] speed-up. This is due to the decrease of size of the number of probesets and to the consequently allocation in main memory of the problem. The superlinear speed-up is only present when 10 workers are used.

5 Conclusion

In this work we presented a system for the parallel preprocessing of microarray data based on a distributed architecture. The proposed system is able to collect data from user, run different preprocessing algorithms in a parallel way, and integrate results. Early experiments with the proposed system using publicly available Affymetrix data showed improvements with respect to execution times. This gain will be more evident considering the constant increase of the volume of data. Future work will focus on the complete realization of the system.

References

1. Affymetrix: Guide to probe logarithmic intensity error (plier) estimation, http://www.affymetrix.com
2. Fujita, A., Sato, J.R., Rodrigues, L.O., Ferreira, C.E., Sogayar, M.C.: Evaluating different methods of microarray data normalization. BMC Bioinformatics 7, 469 (2006), http://dx.doi.org/10.1186/1471-2105-7-469
3. Guzzi, P.H., Cannataro, M.: mu-CS: An extension of the TM4 platform to manage Affymetrix binary data. BMC Bioinformatics 11(1), 315+ (2010), http://dx.doi.org/10.1186/1471-2105-11-315
4. Harris, M.A., et al.: The gene ontology (go) database and informatics resource. Nucleic Acids Res. 32(Database issue), 258–261 (2004)
5. Helmbold, D.P., McDowell, C.E.: Modeling speedup (n) greater than n. IEEE Trans. Parallel Distrib. Syst. 1(2), 250–256 (1990)
6. Irizarry, R.A., Hobbs, B., Collin, F., Beazer-Barclay, Y.D., Antonellis, K.J., Scherf, U., Speed, T.P.: Exploration, normalization, and summaries of high density oligonucleotide array probe level data. Biostat. 4(2), 249–264 (2003), http://biostatistics.oxfordjournals.org/cgi/content/abstract/4/2/249
7. Rocke, D., Durbin, B.: A model for measurement error for gene expression arrays. J. Comput. Biol. 8(6), 557–569 (2001), http://citeseer.ist.psu.edu/447387.html
8. Schmidberger, M., Vicedo, E., Mansmann, U.: affypara. a bioconductor package for parallelized preprocessing algorithms of affymetrix microarray data. Bioinform. Biol. Insights 30(22), 83–87 (2009)

2010 CoreGRID/ERCIM Workshop on Grids, Clouds and P2P Computing

2010 CoreGRID/ERCIM Workshop on Grids, Clouds and P2P Computing

Marco Danelutto[1], Frédéric Desprez[2], Paraskevi Fragopoulou[3], and Alan Stewart[4]

[1] Dept. Computer Science, Univ. of Pisa, Italy
[2] LIP, ENS Lyon, France
[3] FORTH-ICS, Heraklion, Greece
[4] EEECS, The Queen's University of Belfast, UK

Foreword

CoreGRID is a European research Network of Excellence (NoE) that was initiated in 2004 as part of the EU FP6 research framework. The NoE developed theoretical foundations and software infrastructures to support the development of large-scale Grid and P2P applications. A CoreGRID Working Group, sponsored by ERCIM, was established in 2008 to ensure the continuity of the CoreGrid programme after the official end of NoE. The Working Group has the goals of:

- sustaining the operation of the CoreGRID Network; and
- establishing a forum to encourage collaboration between the Grid and P2P Computing research communities.

The original interests of CoreGrid have broadened to include the emerging field of service-based Cloud computing which is crucially important to the development of the European software industry. The CoreGRID community is using the experience gained from constructing inter-operable Grid middle-ware to contribute to the development of a service-oriented paradigm. CoreGrid members are playing an active part in developing service-based models such as Infrastructure as a Service (IaaS), Platform as a Service (PaaS) and Software as a Service (SaaS).

The CoreGRID organisation has organised a series of workshops to discuss state of the art developments in Grid, P2P and Cloud computing. The workshops have been attended by CoreGRID members and also by international experts in the area of distributed computing. Previous workshops took place in Pisa (2005), Krakow (2006), Heraklion (2007), Gran Canaria (2008) and Delft (2009). CoreGRID 2010 was held in Ischia-Naplesis. Topics open for discussion included Service Level Agreements, Data & Knowledge Management, Scheduling, Virtual environments, Network monitoring, Volunteer Computing Systems, Trust & Security, Self-* and adaptive mechanisms, Advanced programming models including IaaS, PaaS and SaaS, Tools and Environments for Application Development and Execution.

The workshop received 18 submissions, of which 8 were accepted. The accepted papers where in the following areas:

M.R. Guarracino et al. (Eds.): Euro-Par 2010 Workshops, LNCS 6586, pp. 235–236, 2011.
© Springer-Verlag Berlin Heidelberg 2011

- adaptive software management:
  A framework for autonomic management of multiple non- functional concerns by M. Aldinucci, M. Danelutto, P. Kilpatrick, V. Xhagjika; and *Adaptive instantiation of service workflows using a chemical approach* by C. Di Napoli, M. Giordano, Z.Németh, N. Tonellotto,
- interoperation and SLA negotiation in services:
  Multi-level Brokering Solution for Interoperating Service and Desktop Grids by A. Kertesz, Z. Farkas and P. Kacsuk; and
  Dynamic Service Configurations for SLA Negotiation
  by I. ul Haq, K. Koer, E. Schikuta,
- programming models and tools for grids and clouds:
  First Class Futures: Specification and implementation of Update Strategies by L. Henrio, M. Uzair Khan, N. Ranaldo, and E. Zimeo;
  Actor-driven Workflow Execution in Distributed Environments
  by S. Skorupa, F. Berretz, V. Sander, A. Belloum and M. Bubak; and
  GroudSim: An Event-based Simulation Framework for Computational Grids and Clouds
  by S. Ostermann, K. Plankensteiner, R. Prodan, and T. Fahringer,
- license management in distributed environments:
  Software Licenses as Mobile Objects in Distributed Computing Environments by C. Cacciari, D. Mallmann, C. Zsigri, F. D'Andria, B. Hagemeier, D. GarcIa Peréz, A. Rumpl, W. Ziegler, M. Gozalo, and J. Martrat.

In addition to regular papers, three invited lectures were organized to discuss topics of current interest. The lectures were given by S. Newhouse, R. Yahyapour and V. Getov and an interesting discussion on the future of CoreGRID community activities followed.

The Workshop took place on 31 August 2010, with the various sessions being attended by between 50 and 70 participants.

We wish to thank all those that contributed to the success of the workshop: authors submitting papers, invited speakers, colleagues participating in the refereeing process / discussion session and Euro-Par 2010 organizers whose invaluable support greatly helped in the organisation of the Workshop.

October 2010

M. Danelutto
F. Desprez
P. Fragopoulou
A. Stewart

LIBERO: A Framework for Autonomic Management of Multiple Non-functional Concerns*

Marco Aldinucci[1], Marco Danelutto[2], Peter Kilpatrick[3], and Vamis Xhagjika[2]

[1] University of Torino
[2] University of Pisa
[3] Queen's University Belfast

Abstract. We describe a lightweight prototype framework (LIBERO) designed for experimentation with *behavioural skeletons*—components implementing a well-known parallelism exploitation pattern *and* a rule-based autonomic manager taking care of some non-functional feature related to pattern computation. LIBERO supports multiple autonomic managers within the same behavioural skeleton, each taking care of a different non-functional concern. We introduce LIBERO–built on plain Java and JBoss–and discuss how multiple managers may be coordinated to achieve a common goal using a two-phase coordination protocol developed in earlier work. We present experimental results that demonstrate how the prototype may be used to investigate autonomic management of multiple, independent concerns.

Keywords: structured parallel/distributed programming, behavioural skeletons, non-functional concerns, performance, security, autonomic management.

1 Introduction

A behavioural skeleton (BS) is the result of the co-design of a well-known, efficient parallelism exploitation pattern *and* of a rule-based control loop implementing an autonomic manager of (one or more) non-functional properties related to the pattern [1,2]. The concept was introduced to tackle the problem of efficient, autonomic management of non-functional features of parallel/distributed computations, such as performance, security, fault tolerance, power management, etc. The BS parallel pattern makes use of well-understood techniques to implement that particular pattern on target architectures. The BS autonomic manager executes a classical Monitor, Analyse, Plan, Execute (MAPE) control loop to monitor and adjust the system to modify some non-functional characteristics.

Behavioural skeletons were originally designed in the framework of GCM, the Grid Component Model [8] developed within CoreGRID [7] and subsequently

* This work has been partially supported by ERCIM/CoreGRID.

M.R. Guarracino et al. (Eds.): Euro-Par 2010 Workshops, LNCS 6586, pp. 237–245, 2011.
© Springer-Verlag Berlin Heidelberg 2011

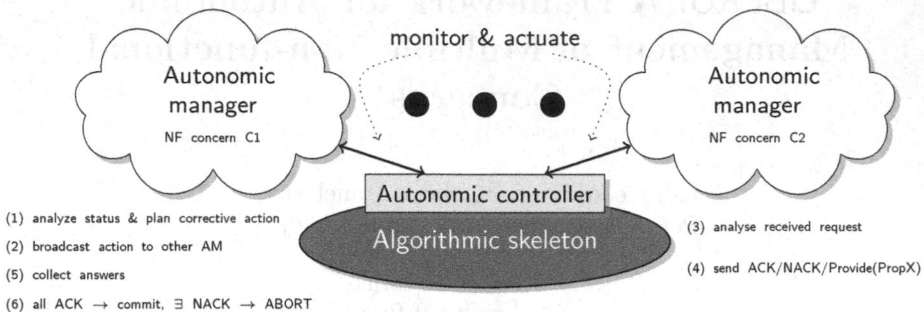

Fig. 1. Coordinating activities of distinct autonomic managers in a BS

implemented in the GCM reference implementation built on top of ProActive [14] in GridCOMP [11]. GridCOMP produced a GCM BS prototype supporting common stream parallel patterns–pipelines and farms–with managers taking care of performance issues. Those BS were demonstrated to be effective in managing (best-effort) user-supplied *performance contracts*. In [2] it was shown how contracts requiring a given throughput can be guaranteed when a single BS models the entire application. In [3] we introduced techniques that support the coordination of the different managers in a BS hierarchy.

In the general case, however, *multiple* non-functional concerns have to be addressed within the same computation. The BS concept can be easily extended in such a way that multiple managers are associated with the same parallel pattern, each taking care of a different concern. In [4] we identified the need for such managers to interact to achieve consensus before effecting changes to the managed system. We also identified protocols for achieving such consensus. However, no actual implementation was presented. In this paper we introduce LIBERO (LIightweight BEhaviouRal skeletOn framework), which is a lightweight prototype implementing several BS–including pipes and farms–and supporting multiple autonomic managers within a single BS.

2 Autonomic Manager Coordination

Problems may arise when *independent* autonomic managers are run within the same behavioural skeleton. In a scenario such as that depicted in Fig. 1, multiple managers are associated with the same algorithmic skeleton in a single BS. The algorithmic skeleton implements a well-know parallelism exploitation pattern. Through its *autonomic controller* (AC) it provides i) methods to access its internal state (to support monitoring) and ii) methods to operate on its internal state (to modify its behavior). Each associated autonomic manager takes care of a distinct non-functional concern.

When different AMs associated with the same BS independently decide to take some action those actions must be coordinated as they may produce effects that are mutually incompatible. In [4] we introduced a two-phase approach to coordinate different manager activities. In this approach each action planned by an AM is validated by the other AMs in the BS before being executed. The manager taking care of non-functional concern X (e.g. performance), analyzes system behaviour and decides to take some action (① in Fig. 1). It informs the other managers of the decision ②. These managers evaluate ③ the decision with respect to any consequences for their non-functional concern. Eventually they return ④ one of three answers: `ACK`, meaning the decision can be safely taken by the first manager, `NACK`, meaning the decision is in conflict with the managed non-functional concern and therefore should be aborted, or `provide(property)`, meaning the decision may be actuated provided `property` is ensured (e.g. securing of connections). The manager initiating the process gets answers from the other managers ⑤ and either actuates its decision (the original plan or a modified one to accomplish `property`) or aborts it ⑥.

This two-phase protocol has not previously been experimented with, due mainly to the difficulty of embedding a complex management structure in the reference implementation of BS in ProActive/GCM. We implemented LIBERO to allow assessment of the feasibility of this protocol as well as to experiment with other protocols regulating autonomic management.

3 LIBERO

LIBERO is a prototype supporting BS with multiple autonomic managers implemented using lightweight components. Each component implementing a parallel computation has a managing entity–the AM–that deals with the *non-functional* aspects of the parallel computation in a local and autonomic way. The AM management functions operate through the operations provided by the component Autonomic Controller [8]–the AC–which exports its internal computation state and provides a set of operations to modify component state and functioning.

LIBERO implements the BS previously investigated in GridCOMP, namely those modelling the usual stream parallel patterns, such as *task farms* and *pipelines* [6], and equipped with a single autonomic manager taking care of a single non-functional concern. In addition, LIBERO supports *Multiple Concern Management*, implementing the coordination algorithm outlined in Sec. 2. All LIBERO components are native *Java* objects. This simplifies investigation of multi-concern management as compared with the ProActive/GCM BS prototype. The ProActive/GCM prototype requires a more complex runtime and does not support multiple AMs in a single BS. LIBERO, like the ProActive/GCM BS implementation, uses the DROOLS [10] library middleware to implement autonomic managers' control cycles.

3.1 LIBERO Base Mechanisms

LIBERO implements component deployment on remote nodes using a small Java RMI-based runtime.This runtime allows deployment of LIBERO components and management of their life cycle. Management activities access the runtime to check

BS name	Features
Sequential	models sequential code, no actuator supported in AC, provides service time and executed task number through monitoring AC interface
Farm	models embarrassingly parallel stream parallel computations, constructor parameter used to pass the worker component class, AC supports increase/decrease parallelism degree actuators, provides service time, total task number and number of workers through the AC monitoring interface
Pipeline	models computations organized in stages, constructor parameters used to pass stage component classes, no actuator supported in AC, provides service time and total task number through monitoring AC interface

Fig. 2. LIBERO Behavioural Skeletons

machine dependent parameters peculiar to the node where the runtime is running, and may also access parameters associated with other nodes of the system, if needed.

The functional interfaces of LIBERO components are implemented using permanent Java TCP socket connections (either normal or SSL connections, depending on security requirements), with the use of serialisation for input/output object delivery between BS components. These permanent TCP connections imply the use of a discovery mechanism to locate the distributed components. Implementation of this mechanism assumes a global naming scheme for the components. A centralized multicast discovery component is used as a *Nameserver*.This component allows registration, removal and lookup requests using the specified component IDs. *Non-functional* interfaces (those related to BS managers) need stronger expressiveness and ease of use, and thus are implemented using RMI.

3.2 LIBERO BS

The LIBERO BS framework is provided as a set of classes [15]. A `Behavioural-Skeleton` class provides the common mechanisms (such as those needed for registration/removal of sub-components) and interfaces of BS and can be extended to implement new BS. Table 2 summarizes the main features provided by LIBERO.

Multiple managers, specialized by their contracts, can be declared using the appropriate LIBERO classes and associated with the same LIBERO BS. The actions of these cooperating AM are coordinated by means of the two-phase protocol proposed in [4]. The AM behaviour (that is, its contract) is expressed in terms of JBoss rules. The DROOLS rule pre-conditions are evaluated using the parameters monitored through the BS AC interface. Actions of the rules eventually fired by the DROOLS rule engine are executed using the BS AC interface.

The consensus protocol is implemented using JBoss rules and allows use of runtime values as contract parameters. As a consequence, the protocol is not embedded in the manager code but rather in the rule language. Fig. 3 (right) shows a sample JBoss rule. This is the rule fired when a new worker is added to a farm due to a breach of contract (fewer than 8 workers in the farm). The action part of the rule consists in setting up and broadcasting the consensus request.

Autonomic controllers provide mechanisms to monitor BS behaviour and to actuate manager decisions on the embedded skeleton. In particular, each AC implements the `executeOperation` and `getMeasure` methodsto change/export

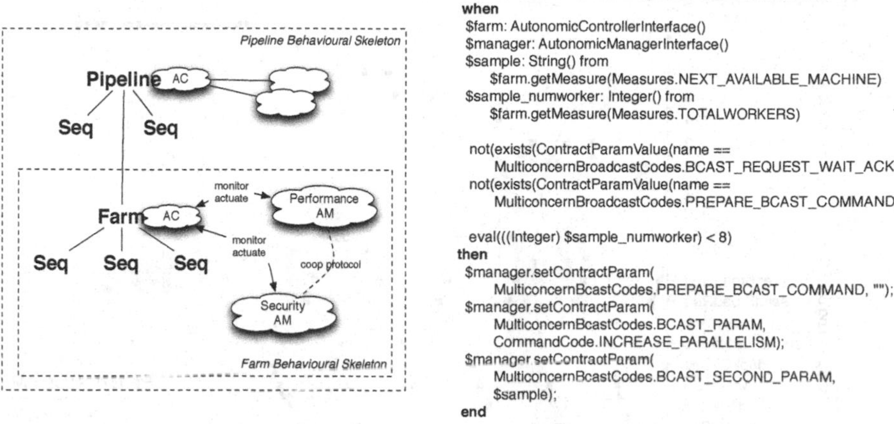

Pipeline Behavioural Skeleton
Pipeline
AC
Seq
Seq
Farm
AC
Seq
Seq
Seq
monitor
actuate
Performance
AM
monitor
actuate
coop protocol
Security
AM
Farm Behavioural Skeleton
rule "FarmPerformanceManagerRuleToAskForConsensus"
when
$farm: AutonomicControllerInterface()
$manager: AutonomicManagerInterface()
$sample: String() from
$farm.getMeasure(Measures.NEXT_AVAILABLE_MACHINE)
$sample_numworker: Integer() from
$farm.getMeasure(Measures.TOTALWORKERS)
not(exists(ContractParamValue(name ==
MulticoncernBroadcastCodes.BCAST_REQUEST_WAIT_ACK)))
not(exists(ContractParamValue(name ==
MulticoncernBroadcastCodes.PREPARE_BCAST_COMMAND)))
eval(((Integer) $sample_numworker) < 8)
then
$manager.setContractParam(
MulticoncernBcastCodes.PREPARE_BCAST_COMMAND, "");
$manager.setContractParam(
MulticoncernBcastCodes.BCAST_PARAM,
CommandCode.INCREASE_PARALLELISM);
$manager.setContractParam(
MulticoncernBcastCodes.BCAST_SECOND_PARAM,
$sample);
end

Fig. 3. Sample use case application (left) and Sample JBoss rule (right)

the internal execution state. The AC also implements methods for accessing machine dependent parameters, fetched from the runtime support of the node.

Machine dependent properties are made accessible through the runtime support; these properties are described in an XML file parsed at startup by the runtime. The configuration file may host metadata relative to properties of the machines used for program execution.

4 Experimental Results

A set of experiments to assess LIBERO functionality and efficiency has been performed on an Intel/Linux cluster, with Java (version 1.5 or higher) and JBoss DROOLS (version 5.0). The nodes in the cluster were interconnected by FastEthernet and NFS was used. Here we report on one experiment illustrating multiple non-functional concern management in LIBERO.

This experiment uses a synthetic application structured as a three stage `Pipeline` component, as depicted in Fig. 3 (left): the first and the third stages are `Sequential` components, while the second stage is a `Farm` component. Each component is placed on a different node in the cluster and 3 machines, each running the LIBERO runtime are assigned as resources for the `Farm` workers.

The scenario under test is the following. *Both a performance contract and a security contract have been supplied by the user.* The performance contract requires that a given number of workers (8) be employed and that that level be maintained. It can be ensured by recruiting increasing numbers of resources to the point where the required number is operating. New resources may also be dynamically recruited for the computation in the event that existing ones become less effective due to temporary overloads or faults. The security contract demands that, where nodes are recruited from external, possibly unreliable domains, such nodes must be suitably secured by, for example, encrypting data

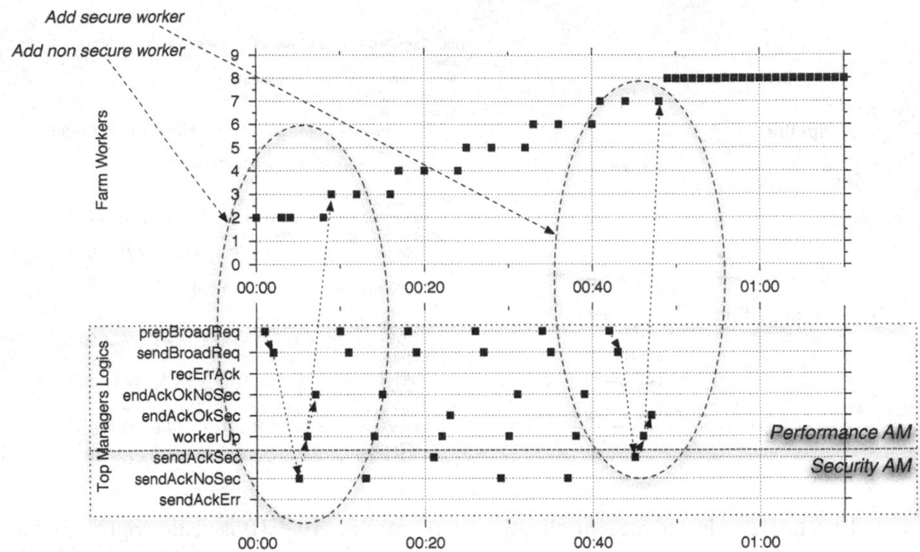

Fig. 4. Event distribution over time (secs from system startup). *W.r.t. Fig. 1:* prepBroadReq *corresponds to* ①, SendBroadReq *to* ②, SendAckSec/SendAckNoSec *to* ③/④, workerUp *to* ⑤/⑥ *and* endAckOkNoSec/endAckOkSec *to end of* ⑥.

and code communications; nodes internal to the user domain may be considered secure. Thus, if the performance manager identifies failure of the performance contract it will prompt the recruitment of further resources. If some of these are in an external domain the security manager may in turn demand the securing of communications with such potentially unsafe resources.

To implement this scenario, two autonomic managers are associated to the Farm component, one handling security and the other performance. The run time nodes host metadata classifying each node that may be recruited as secure or insecure.We used both secure and insecure nodes in the experiment to check both types of answers from the consensus phase: simple ACK (i.e. accept recruitment of a new node to host a `Farm` worker implemented using plain TCP sockets) and conditional ACK (i.e. accept recruitment of the node provided SSL sockets are used for communications).

The life cycle of the managers (the period used to run the DROOLS engine) is set to 500ms so that the plot of the runtime is sufficiently discrete to allow observation of the events, but smaller life cycles are possible down to 100ms.

In the use case we start the Farm component with two workers. The performance manager immediately detects a contract violation and asks the other managers for permission to add another worker. If other violations are encountered then the same set of operations is applied repeatedly, until no further violation is encountered.

The plot in Fig. 4 is automatically generated (but for arrows and ovals, added for clarification) from the application log files and shows evolution of the Farm component and the distribution of manager events over the same period of time.

As can be seen, consensus is sought and achieved according to the two phase protocol. In some cases workers are added using plain TCP connections (workers that happen to be placed on "secure" nodes – see on the right of Fig. 4). In other cases, the security manager detects that resources identified to host new workers are not secure and so it requests `property(Security)` in the ACK message. At this point the performance manager changes the plan used to add the worker from that employing plain TCP to one incorporating secure SSL connection, and eventually recruits the new worker using this modified action plan.

Overall, the consensus protocol takes an overhead of at most 4 manager life-cycles plus the execution time of the rules, which depends only on the communication overhead between managers. This gives a total overhead time of $T_{overhead} = 4 * (T_{LyfeCycle} + T_{Com})$, where T_{Com} is the average number of RMI calls * average RMI latency. In this simple case the entire reconfiguration of the system takes 45s, and reconfiguration time for worker allocation on average (including decision making and synchronization) is about 5 secs (including about 2 secs of idle time spent waiting 4 times for the next iteration of the control loop). These times are of the same order of magnitude as the times spent in the ProActive/GCM BS prototype to achieve an unmediated reconfiguration (i.e. a reconfiguration decided autonomically by a single, uncoordinated manager), which underlines the "lightweight" nature of LIBERO.

5 Related Work

The IBM blueprint paper on autonomic computing has already established, in a slightly different context, the need to orchestrate independent autonomic managers [12]. In [9] strategies to handle performance and power management issues by autonomic managers are discussed. However the approach is much more oriented to the generic combination of target functions relating to the two non-functional concerns considered, rather than to the constructive coordination of the actions planned by the two managers.

A framework that can be used to reason on multiple concerns was introduced in [13]. Based on the concepts of state and action (i.e. state transition) adopted from the field of artificial intelligence, this framework maps three types of agenthood concepts (action, goal, utility-function) into autonomic computing policies. Action policies may produce and consume resources, which are used by a *resource arbiter* (i.e. a super manager) to harmonize conflicting concerns. The framework does not, however, provide specific support for policy design and distributed management overlay.

A similar approach was followed in [5], which also exploits the same policies (action, goal, utility-function) defined on the *state* and *configuration* space of the system. These policies are extended with *resource-definition* policies, which specify how the autonomic manager exposes the system to its environment; this makes it possible to dynamically extend manager knowledge with other resources/parameters, possibly coming from other managers, thus supporting management overlay.

6 Conclusion

LIBERO supports the implementation of behavioural skeletons with multiple autonomic managers, each managing a different non-functional concern, and runs on any distributed architecture supporting Java. The prototype allows investigation of coordination aspects of autonomic management of non-functional concerns. The lightweight implementation of LIBERO, and in particular of the monitoring and actuator mechanisms implemented in the autonomic controllers, allows us to experiment with various consensus building strategies without being burdened by the complexities of fully-fledged distributed/parallel implementations, such as that provided by the ProActive/GCM BS implementation.

References

1. Aldinucci, M., Campa, S., Danelutto, M., Dazzi, P., Kilpatrick, P., Laforenza, D., Tonellotto, N.: Behavioural skeletons for component autonomic management on grids. In: CoreGRID Workshop on Grid Prog. Model, Grid and P2P Systems Architecture, Grid Systems, Tools and Environments, Heraklion, Greece (June 2007)
2. Aldinucci, M., Campa, S., Danelutto, M., Vanneschi, M., Dazzi, P., Laforenza, D., Tonellotto, N., Kilpatrick, P.: Behavioural skeletons in GCM: autonomic management of grid components. In: Baz, D.E., Bourgeois, J., Spies, F. (eds.) Proc. of Intl. Euromicro PDP 2008: Parallel Distributed and Network-Based Processing, Toulouse, France, pp. 54–63. IEEE, Los Alamitos (February 2008)
3. Aldinucci, M., Danelutto, M., Kilpatrick, P.: Autonomic management of non-functional concerns in distributed and parallel application programming. In: Proc. of Intl. Parallel & Distributed Processing Symposium (IPDPS), Rome, Italy (2009)
4. Aldinucci, M., Danelutto, M., Kilpatrick, P.: Autonomic Management of Multiple Non-Functional Concerns in Behavioural Skeletons. In: Desprez, F., Getov, V., Priol, T., Yahyapour, R. (eds.) Proc. of the CoreGRID Symposium 2009, Delft, The Netherlands. CoreGRID, pp. 89–103. Springer, Heidelberg (August 2009), http://www.di.unipi.it/~aldinuc/papers/2009_CGSymph_Autonomic_BeSke.pdf, ISBN: 978-1-4419-6793-0, doi:10.1007/978-1-4419-6794-7_8
5. Calinescu, R.: Resource-definition policies for autonomic computing. In: Proc. of the 5th Intl. Conference on Autonomic and Autonomous Systems (ICAS), pp. 111–116. IEEE, Los Alamitos (April 2009)
6. Cole, M.: Bringing skeletons out of the closet: A pragmatic manifesto for skeletal parallel programming. Parallel Computing 30(3), 389–406 (2004)
7. The CoreGRID home page (2007), http://www.coregrid.net
8. CoreGRID NoE deliverable series, Institute on Programming Model. Deliverable D.PM.04 – Basic Features of the Grid Component Model (February 2007) (assessed)
9. Das, R., Kephart, J.O., Lefurgy, C., Tesauro, G., Levine, D.W., Chan, H.: Autonomic multi-agent management of power and performance in data centers. In: Proc. of the 7th Intl. Conf. on Autonomous Agents and Multiagent Systems (2008)
10. Drools 5 - The Business Logic integration Platform (2010)
11. GridCOMP Project. Grid Programming with Components, An Advanced Component Platform for an Effective Invisible Grid (2008), http://gridcomp.ercim.org

12. IBM Corp. An Architectural Blueprint for Autonomic Computing (2005), `http://www-01.ibm.com/software/tivoli/autonomic/`
13. Kephart, J.O., Walsh, W.E.: An artificial intelligence perspective on autonomic computing policies. In: Proc. of the 5th Intl. Workshop on Policies for Distributed Systems and Networks (POLICY 2004). IEEE, Los Alamitos (2004)
14. ProActive home page (2009), `http://www-sop.inria.fr/oasis/proactive/`
15. Xhagjika, V.: Implementation of a prototype for experimenting with autonomic hierarchical managers in java (thesis, in italian). Dept. of Computer Science, Univ. of Pisa, Italy (December 2009)

Adaptive Instantiation of Service Workflows Using a Chemical Approach*

Claudia Di Napoli[1], Maurizio Giordano[1],
Zsolt Németh[2], and Nicola Tonellotto[3]

[1] Istituto di Cibernetica "E. Caianiello" - C.N.R.
Via Campi Flegrei 34, 80078 Pozzuoli, Naples - Italy
{c.dinapoli,m.giordano}@cib.na.cnr.it
[2] MTA SZTAKI Computer and Automation Research Institute,
P.O. Box 63, H-1518 - Hungary
zsnemeth@sztaki.hu
[3] Istituto di Scienze e Tecnologie dell'Informazione - C.N.R.
Via G. Moruzzi 1, 56124 Pisa - Italy
nicola.tonellotto@isti.cnr.it

Abstract. Service oriented technologies allow Service Based Applications (SBAs) to be easily built by composing independent services available in a network and provided by many actors under conditions that may change in time. Therefore services need to be dynamically selected and composed when an SBA is required along with parameters representing the service delivery conditions. In this paper we propose to use a chemical computational approach to model the process of selecting the required service functionalities with the required conditions as an evolving and always running middleware mechanism. The chemical evolving behaviour of the middleware allows to take into account environmental changes coming from both the providers and users side.

1 Introduction

Service Oriented Architecture (SOA) technologies are becoming very popular in the context of Future Internet [1] where enterprises and diverse organizations take up the role of *service providers*, while users exploit such services in combined ways to fulfill their needs. In this context, it becomes necessary to organize Service Based Applications (SBAs) on demand in response to dynamic requirements and circumstances. In fact, service providers can provide the same functionality with different conditions, or even the same provider can provide one functionality with different conditions, usually related to non-functional characteristics of a service (like price, time to deliver, and so on). Conditions may change in time depending on both provider policies and consumer's needs. For example, the cost associated to a service may vary according to market conditions (driven by demand-supply mechanisms), or the time to deliver may vary according to

* This research is funded by EC FP7/2007-2013 under grant N. 215483 (S-Cube).

M.R. Guarracino et al. (Eds.): Euro-Par 2010 Workshops, LNCS 6586, pp. 247–255, 2011.
© Springer-Verlag Berlin Heidelberg 2011

the workload of the provider. Given the dynamic nature of these characteristics, they have to be managed at the time a service is required.

In the present work this problem is addressed by decoupling the process of selecting services composing an SBA requested by a user from their actual enactment. We propose to use the chemical computational model [2] to represent the problem of selecting service instances that match an SBA requested by a user specifying functionality of service components, their dependence constraints and some preferred non-functional characteristics of the whole composition.

Applying this metaphor to the problem of selecting service instances allows to reduce the search space considerably, and more important, to model the service selection process as an "evolving" and always running mechanism that can adapt to environmental changes as they occur, so providing adaptability to non-functional characteristics changes. Furthermore, decoupling service instantiation from their execution makes it possible to interleave the two processes, so that services can be instantiated or replaced during workflow execution.

2 The Chemical Computational Model

The γ-calculus is a formal definition of the chemical paradigm aimed at relaxing the artificial sequentializing of algorithms. The fundamental data structure of the γ-calculus is the *multiset*, i.e., a set that may contain multiple occurrences of the same element. Multisets are modified by *reactions* taking place independently and potentially simultaneously, according to local and actual conditions. There is no centralized control, ordering, serialization, but rather the computation is carried out in an indeterministic, inherently parallel, self-evolving way. γ-terms (molecules) are: variables x, γ-abstractions $\gamma\langle x\rangle.M$, multisets (M_1, M_2) and solutions $\langle M\rangle$ [2]. Juxtaposition of γ-terms is commutative and associative. These properties realize the basic principle of 'Brownian-motion', i.e., the free distribution and unspecified reaction order among molecules [3]. γ-abstractions are the reactive molecules that can take other molecules and replace them by reduction. Molecules, and solutions participating in the reaction are extracted by pattern matching. The semantics of a γ-reduction is $(\gamma\langle x\rangle.M), \langle N\rangle \rightarrow_\gamma M[x := N]$ i.e., the two reacting terms on the left hand side are replaced by the body of the γ-abstraction where free occurrences of x are replaced by parameter N [3].

Reactions may depend on conditions expressed by C in $\gamma\langle x\rangle\lfloor C\rfloor.M$ that can be reduced only if C evaluates to true before the reaction. Reactions can capture multiple molecules in a single atomic step and are governed by: (i) locality law, i.e. a reaction occurs irrespectively of the environment; and (ii) membrane law, i.e. reactions can occur in nested solutions separated by a membrane. The γ-calculus is a *higher order* model where abstractions, just like any other molecules, can be passed as parameters or yielded as a result of a reduction.

The Higher Order Chemical Language (HOCL) [4], based on the γ-calculus extended with expressions, types, pairs, empty solutions and names, is adopted in this work. HOCL uses the self-explanatory **replace... by... if...** construct to express active molecules. **replace** P **by** M **if** C formally corresponds to

$\gamma(P)\lfloor C \rfloor.M$ with the difference that γ-abstractions are destroyed by the reactions, while HOCL rules remain in the solution.

3 Chemical Representation of the Problem

It is assumed that users requiring SBAs submit their requests by specifying both the functionality of each component of the application, and the dependence constraints occurring among the components, i.e. the order of execution in which the components should be delivered. They also provide values for parameters representing some non-functional characteristics they would "prefer" the application to be delivered with. They will drive the selection of the suitable service components.

The required SBA functionalities together with their dependence constraints are expressed in the form of an *abstract workflow* (AW), a Directed Acyclic Graph (DAG) $AW = (S, E)$ where $S = \{s_i, \ldots, s_n\}$ is a set of nodes in the graph, and $E \subseteq S \times S$ is a set of directed edges in the graph. Each node represents a service interface whose implementation can be provided by one or more service instances with different non-functional characteristics. Each directed edge represents a data, or a control (or both) dependence between two nodes it connects. An AW has four types of nodes: (1) a *start* node with an in-degree equal to 0; (2) a *stop* node with an out-degree equal to 0; (3) a *split* node with an out-degree equal to 2; (4) a *merge* node with an in-degree equal to 2.

An AW specifies only topological relations between nodes, i.e. edges between two nodes and in- and out-degree of each node, while the interpretation of these relations is relevant to the workflow instantiation and enactment phases. An AW *node* is represented by the solution of Eq.1, where the attribute *id* is a unique integer identifying the node, *in* is the number of the node incoming edges (in-degree), and *out* is the number of the node outgoing edges (out-degree).

$$Node_i = \langle id : s_i, in : n_i, out : m_i, ... \rangle \tag{1}$$

$$Edge_{ij} = \langle from : s_i, to : s_j, ... \rangle \tag{2}$$

$$Offer_i = \langle e^i : s_i, qos : c^i \rangle \tag{3}$$

Nodes are ordered by their identifiers, i.e. there is a path in the AW from node s_i to node s_j if $i \leq j$. This is a baseline model for a workflow of services where the control constructs taken into consideration are sequence, if-then, and/or, and parallel fork/join. The type of construct can be specified by using an optional attribute *type:<value>* in the solution of Eq.1.

An *edge* of the abstract workflow is represented by the solution of Eq.2, where *id* is an integer identifying the edge, $from$ is the identifier of the source node and *to* is the identifier of the sink node.

Service providers make their services available as "offers". An offer is composed of the identifier of the service instance it refers to, and the value of the QoS parameter representing the non-functional characteristics they can provide the service with. So, for each service interface s_i of the AW a set of actual service implementations may be available, $e_1^i, \ldots, e_{m_i}^i$. An offer is represented by the solution of Eq.3, where the e^i is a generic endpoint of service s_i offered with a QoS c^i. If a provider offers the same service instance s_i with different *qos* values, more offers for the same service will be available in the chemical system.

It is assumed that the user specifies a value at the time when the request is issued representing the Quality of Service (QoS) he/she requires for the entire composition. It is also assumed that this value is related to the QoS value of each service offer. Of course, it is not always possible to relate a global preference on a composition of services to the QoS value of each service offer, but for the time being we refer to cases in which this exemplification is acceptable, i.e. where a cumulative property holds for the QoS.

4 Workflow Instantiation as Chemical Reactions

Once service offers are available in the system, the ones matching the user's requirements have to be selected to obtain the actual workflow to be enacted, called an *instantiated workflow* (IW). The process that leads from an abstract workflow to an instantiated workflow is the *workflow instantiation process.*

This process is expressed in terms of chemical reactions [5] that occur when some conditions are satisfied, i.e. as long as there are molecules that match the rule conditions. When no more chemical reactions can take place an inert state is reached. IWs are created when service endpoints are assigned to all the corresponding nodes of the requested AW.

To model the instantiation process in terms of chemical reactions, in addition to the molecules representing the AW and the offered services, also partially instantiated workflows built by chemical reactions are represented with the same formalism. A *partially instantiated workflow* (pIW) is composed of either a single node (elementary pIW), or a set of nodes (IW subgraph) with the following conditions: 1) each node different from the first and last node of the set (where first and last refer to the node ordering) must all have edges with sink and source nodes belonging to the subgraph; 2) the first node must have all outgoing edges with sink nodes belonging to the subgraph; 3) the last node must have all incoming edges with source nodes belonging to the subgraph. The chemical molecule representing a pIW is the following:

$$\langle first : \langle e^i : s_i \rangle, last : \langle e^j : s_j \rangle, \ldots, qos : c \rangle \tag{4}$$

where s_i is the first node of the pIW associated to the service endpoint e^i, s_j is the last node associated to the service endpoint e^j, dots represent some intermediate nodes if any, and *qos* is the value of the considered non-functional parameter associated to the pIW obtained by combining the *qos* values of its component nodes. For an elementary pIW $s_i = s_j$, $e^i = e^j$.

Elementary pIWs are the starting building blocks of the workflow instantiation process. So, before the instantiation process takes place, all service offers are converted into elementary pIWs using a chemical rule called *prerule* reported in

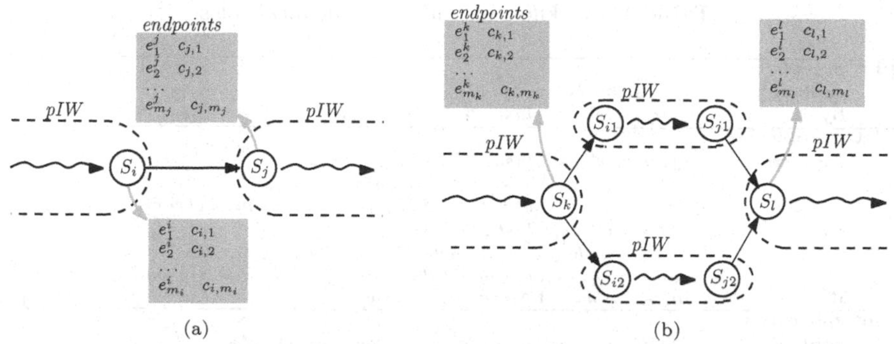

Fig. 1. (a) Concatenating pIWs; (b) Dealing with split/merge nodes

Table 1(1). The *prerule* matches all service offers and thus it applies to all of them, i.e. no condition (**if** part) is specified to trigger the reaction.

Two pIWs can be concatenated to form new pIWs containing a sequence of consecutive nodes if the first one ends with a node that is not a *split* node, and the second one starts with a node that is not a *merge* node, and they are connected by an edge. The sequences can be further concatenated producing longer sequences. The rule that concatenates pIWs is named *chainrule* reported in Table 1(2). The **replace** part of the rule contains the pIWs to be chained (line 2 and 3 of the rule), while the other solutions (line 4 of the rule) represent the AW information used by the **if** part to check whether the pIWs are in the right topological relation to be chained. These solutions are catalysts since they remain intact after the reaction. The **if** part also checks that the *qos* values of the two pIWs satisfy a boolean condition expressed by the function ψ. The **by** part of the rule produces a new pIW that is the concatenation of the two input pIWs, and its *qos* value is obtained combining the *qos* values of the two input pIWs. ω symbols are wildcards to match anything inside the input molecules that is not relevant to the reaction to take place: in this rule all information matching the wildcards is reinserted in the new produced molecule.

To concatenate two pIWs where the first one ends with a *split* node and the second one starts with a *merge* node, the *splitrule* reported in Table 1(3) is introduced. As depicted in Fig.1(b), the rule links together four pIWs: one ending with a *split* node (line 2 of the rule), one starting with the corresponding *merge* node (line 3), and two pIWs representing the subgraphs of the right and left branch of the split (line 4 and 5). The other solutions (line 6 and 7) represent the AW edges connecting the pIWs that are matched by the rule to check their topological relation. These solutions are catalysts available in the system for further reactions. The **if** part of the rule checks if the input *qos* values of the pIWs (once combined) satisfy a boolean condition to meet the QoS requirement specified in the user request. The **by** part of the rule produces a new pIW representing the combination around the split and merge nodes (lines 8-11).

Table 1. Workflow instantiation chemical rules

(1) **let** *prerule* =	
replace	$\langle e^i : s_i, qos, c_{e^i} \rangle,$
by	$\langle first : \langle e^i : s_i \rangle, last : \langle e^i : s_i \rangle, qos : c_{e^i} \rangle$
(2) **let** *chainrule* =	
replace	$\langle first : \langle e^l : s_l \rangle, last : \langle e^i : s_i \rangle, qos : c_1, \omega_1 \rangle,$
	$\langle first : \langle e^j : s_j \rangle, last : \langle e^k : s_k \rangle, qos : c_2, \omega_2 \rangle,$
	$\langle id : s_i, in : n_i, out : m_i \rangle, \langle id : s_j, in : n_j, out : m_j \rangle, \langle from : s_i, to : s_j \rangle,$
by	$\langle first : \langle e^l : s_l \rangle, last : \langle e^k : s_k \rangle,$
	$node : \langle e^i : s_i \rangle, node : \langle e^j : s_j \rangle, qos : c_{1,2}, \omega_1, \omega_2 \rangle$
	$\langle id : s_i, in : n_i, out : m_i \rangle, \langle id : s_j, in : n_j, out : m_j \rangle, \langle from : s_i, to : s_j \rangle,$
if	$m_i = 1 \wedge n_j = 1 \wedge \psi(c_1, c_2) = \mathbf{true}$
(3) **let** *splitrule* =	
replace	$\langle first : \langle e^i : s_i \rangle, last : \langle e^k : s_k \rangle, qos : c_1, \omega_1 \rangle,$
	$\langle first : \langle e^l : s_l \rangle, last : \langle e^j : s_j \rangle, qos : c_2, \omega_2 \rangle,$
	$\langle first : \langle e^{i1} : s_{i_1} \rangle, last : \langle e^{j1} : s_{j_1} \rangle, qos : c_3, \omega_3 \rangle,$
	$\langle first : \langle e^{i2} : s_{i_2} \rangle, last : \langle e^{j2} : s_{j_2} \rangle, qos : c_4, \omega_4 \rangle,$
	$\langle from : s_k, to : s_{i_1} \rangle, \langle from : s_k, to : s_{i_2} \rangle,$
	$\langle from : s_{j_2}, to : s_l \rangle, \langle from : s_{j_2}, to : s_l \rangle,$
by	$\langle first : \langle e^i : s_i \rangle, last : \langle e^j : s_j \rangle, split : \langle e^k : s_k \rangle, merge : \langle e^l : s_l \rangle,$
	$\langle first : \langle e^{i1} : s_{i_1} \rangle, last : \langle e^{j1} : s_{j_1} \rangle, \omega_3 \rangle,$
	$\langle first : \langle e^{i2} : s_{i_2} \rangle, last : \langle e^{j2} : s_{j_2} \rangle, \omega_4 \rangle,$
	$qos : c_{1,2,3,4}, \omega_1, \omega_2 \rangle,$
	$\langle from : s_k, to : s_{i_1} \rangle, \langle from : s_k, to : s_{i_2} \rangle,$
	$\langle from : s_{j_2}, to : s_l \rangle, \langle from : s_{j_2}, to : s_l \rangle$
if	$\phi(c_1, c_2, c_3, c_4) = \mathbf{true}$
(4) **let** *lazysplitrule* =	
replace	$\langle first : \langle e^i : s_i \rangle, last : \langle e^k : s_k \rangle, qos : c_1, \omega_1 \rangle,$
	$\langle first : \langle e^l : s_l \rangle, last : \langle e^j : s_j \rangle, qos : c_2, \omega_2 \rangle,$
	$\langle first : \langle e^{i1} : s_{i_1} \rangle, last : \langle e^{j1} : s_{j_1} \rangle, qos : c_3, \omega_3 \rangle,$
	$\langle from : s_k, to : s_{i_1} \rangle, \langle from : s_k, to : s_{i_2} \rangle,$
	$\langle from : s_{j_2}, to : s_l \rangle, \langle from : s_{j_2}, to : s_l \rangle,$
	$\langle id : s_k, type : ifthen, \omega_4 \rangle,$
by	$\langle first : \langle e^i : s_i \rangle, last : \langle e^j : s_j \rangle, split : \langle e^k : s_k \rangle, merge : \langle e^l : s_l \rangle,$
	$\langle first : \langle e^{i1} : s_{i_1} \rangle, last : \langle e^{j1} : s_{j_1} \rangle, \omega_3 \rangle,$
	$\langle first : \langle future : s_{i_2} \rangle, last : \langle future : s_{j_2} \rangle \rangle,$
	$qos : c_{1,2,3}, \omega_1, \omega_2 \rangle,$
	...
if	$\phi(c_1, c_2, c_3) = \mathbf{true}$

5 Lazy Instantiation of Workflows

In this section we introduce the possibility to exploit the additional attributes necessary for the execution phase also in the AW instantiation process by specifically managing *split* nodes with an if-then attribute. In order to do so, a special pIW, called *lazy pIW*, is introduced and it is represented by the molecule of Eq.5. The *future* attributes represent placeholders for nodes not yet instantiated that will be replaced by actual service instances when necessary; *qos* values are not present since they are related to service instances.

$$\langle first : \langle future : s_i \rangle, last : \langle future : s_j \rangle, \ldots \rangle \tag{5}$$

In the instantiation process all paths of the AW have to be instantiated to obtain an IW even though some of them will not be executed because of the if-then nodes. The introduction of lazy pIWs relaxes this constraint, so allowing for the "lazy" enactment of an IW containing lazy pIWs. The *lazysplitrule* has been introduced to build lazy pIWs when if-then nodes are present in the AW.

The proposed extension is compliant with the pIW definition, so it guarantees that lazy pIWs produced by the *lazysplitrule* can be reused as input for further reactions.

At the end of the workflow instantiation process the resulting IWs can be passed to the enactment stage, although some paths are not yet instantiated. If during the IW execution an if-then node fires the execution of a non-instantiated path, the enactment system will suspend the IW execution to request the chemical middleware to instantiate the missing branch on the demand.

6 Related Work

(Self-)adaptive service composition is coined due to the changing behavior of services (mobility, quality, faults, etc.), extreme dynamicity, unreliability, large scale [6], and high complexity, already beyond the human capability to deal with [7]. Also, it has been argued and generally accepted, that such self-adaptable, evolvable and context-aware systems require innovative approaches that take inspiration from nature, e.g. [6].

Viroli et al. [8] proposed a concept where above a common biochemical substrate (defining the basic "laws of nature"), different individuals interact, compete, and combine with each other to serve their own individual needs as well as the sustainability of the overall system. Ding et al. [7], Sun et al. [9] take the neuroendocrine-immune (NEI) system as a metaphor and create a decentralized, evolutionary, scalable, and adaptive system for Web service composition and management. Bio-entities represent services able to obtain the desirable characteristics in a self-organizing way and emerge the requested services.

Banâtre et al. [10] use HOCL to model and express various issues related to service invocations. Their approach is very similar to ours; they are aimed at a general conceptual model whereas we are focused on specific aspects of service composition. Canfora et al. apply genetic algorithms to assist QoS aware service composition [11]. The composition takes into consideration non-functional features, cost and time constraints and it is traced back to an optimisation problem. Multimedia service composition based on ant colony optimisation is presented in [12]. Ensuring quality criteria is challenging due to the continuous flow, synchronisation issues and dynamic characteristics.

7 Conclusions

The present work proposes to decouple the workflow instantiation from its execution, so that the first one can be modeled as an independent, autonomous, and always running mechanism. In such a way it is possible to take into account environmental changes, i.e. new provider availability, or changes in the provided QoS, as they occur without discharging IWs already produced. The chemical approach allows to change at runtime the state of the system (i.e. the number and/or the QoS offers), so allowing new compositions to be found because new chemical reactions may take place in a way that simulate an *adaptation* of the system to different configurations not planned in advance. Furthermore, the proposed approach allows also to dynamically change the selection criteria coming from user requirements because they are represented as chemical reactions that are manipulated in the same way as molecules; reactive molecules can be removed from the system, and new ones can be inserted in it, so changing the system behaviour. In such a way the chemical mechanism provides adaptability from both the provider side, by giving the possibility to insert new offers and so to re-activate chemical reactions, and from the user side, by giving the possibility to change his/her preferences during the instantiation phase.

Another advantage is the possibility to generate an IW also when there are missing service offers for some AW nodes. In fact, once the IW enactment takes place, and a path with missing service instances has to be executed, the execution may be suspended to query the chemical system for the missing parts if available by instantiating the placeholders in the IW. This is because the chemical middleware may run concurrently with the enactment engine. New offers activate reactions as soon as they appear in the system, so it is possible to exploit them, yielding partially instantiated workflows that were not possible before the enactment started. Finally, the instantiation process can be completely distributed since all reactions take place concurrently, independently and in a not deterministic way.

References

1. DG Information Society and Media: Future internet 2020: Visions of an industry expert group (May 2009)
2. Banâtre, J.P., Fradet, P., Radenac, Y.: Principles of chemical programming. In: Fifth International Workshop on Rule-Based Programming, RULE 2004. Electronic Notes in Theoretical Computer Science (2004)
3. Banâtre, J.P., Radenac, Y., Fradet, P.: Chemical specification of autonomic systems. In: Proc. of the 13th Int. Conf. on Intelligent and Adaptive Systems and Software Engineering (IASSE 2004) (2004)
4. Banâtre, J.P., Fradet, P., Radenac, Y.: Generalised multisets for chemical programming. Math. Struct. in Comp. Science 16, 557–580 (2006)
5. Di Napoli, C., et al.: Using chemical reactions to model service composition. In: Proc. Second Int. Workshop on Self-Organizing Architectures, pp. 43–50. ACM, New York (2010)
6. Babaoglu, O., et al.: Design patterns from biology for distributed computing. ACM Transactions on Autonomous and Adaptive Systems 1(1), 26–66 (2006)
7. Ding, Y., Sun, H., Hao, K.: A bio-inspired emergent system for intelligent web service composition and management. Knowledge-Based Sys. 20, 457–465 (2007)
8. Viroli, M., Zambonelli, F.: A biochemical approach to adaptive service ecosystems. Inform. Sci. (2009)
9. Sun, H., Ding, Y.: A scalable method of e-service workflow emergence based on the bio-network. In: Fourth International Conference on Natural Computation

10. Banâtre, J.P., Priol, T.: Chemical programming of future service-oriented architectures. JSW 4(7), 738–746 (2009)
11. Canfora, G., Di Penta, M., Esposito, R., Villani, M.L.: An approach for qos-aware service composition based on genetic algorithms. In: GECCO 2005: Proceedings of the 2005 Conference on Genetic and Evolutionary Computation, pp. 1069–1075. ACM, New York (2005)
12. Hossain, M.S., Alamri, A., El-Saddik, A.: A biologically inspired framework for multimedia service management in a ubiquitous environment. Concurrency and Computation: Practice and Experience 21(11), 1450–1466 (2009)

CoreGRID and Clouds - Future Perspectives

Ramin Yahyapour

Technische Universität Dortmund,
IT and Media Center,
44227 Dortmund, Germany

Abstract. Since 2004 the research interests of the CoreGRID community has evolved from distributed large scale computing to service-based computing and Clouds. The adoption of the SOA paradigm and virtualization has resulted in an unprecedented flexibility in creating distributed applications. Old and new research challenges need to be mastered to exploit fully the potential of cloud infrastructures. In this article we present outstanding cloud-related research questions that need to be addressed. It is proposed that a pan-European research community is needed to bridge existing knowledge gaps.

Keywords: Cloud Computing, HPC, Grid Computing.

1 Introduction

One key requirement for the CoreGRID network is dynamic adaption to changes in the scientific landscape. New research challenges have arisen which need to be addressed. Lately, the advent of clouds has caused disruptive changes in the IT infrastructure world. However, there is a significant overlap between the scientific questions related to Grid and Cloud research. Naturally, part of the Grid community is also active in Cloud research. Current and future cloud research challenges are considered by means of selected examples. It is argued that these outstanding challenges need to be addressed at a European scale.

Grids and clouds have many similarities as they both address questions concerning access to resources in a large-scale distributed environment. Thus, there is significant overlap between the two areas in the ways that infrastructures may evolve. The CoreGRID programme of work has focused mostly on Grids with particular questions in application engineering and middleware management for Grids. The underlying use-case was typically resource sharing between different administrative domains for collaborated problem solving in virtual organizations. Due to the size of the research network, CoreGRID has provided a wide variety of results e.g. component models, schedulers, SLA management, or workflow management. With the advent of Cloud Computing, it is reasonable to reconsider the future research questions and to compare them between the different application fields.

M.R. Guarracino et al. (Eds.): Euro-Par 2010 Workshops, LNCS 6586, pp. 257–262, 2011.
© Springer-Verlag Berlin Heidelberg 2011

2 Research Challenges in Cloud Computing and Grids

Cloud computing is very successful in creating a layered architecture that separates the infrastructure access from applications. Infrastructure as a Service can be utilized to run arbitrary applications. Similarly, applications can be broken down to several software services which run on such virtual infrastructures. Grids target a similar space by combining resources from different providers in a networked infrastructure. Grids also require substantial middleware efforts to form the basis of core services. Thus, there is a significant overlap between Grid and Cloud research challenges. The following is - a quite subjective - selection of main research themes that we are currently facing.

2.1 Scalability

The HPC world has significant experience in exploiting large-scale systems. The use of 1.000s of processors is challenging but well understood for many application scenarios. However, we are still in the early days of many-core infrastructures; we will see a dramatic increase in processing cores in the next years. We are already at the verge of deploying Exa-scale systems with millions of processor cores. Similarly we will also see federations of such systems in large-scale distributed infrastructures. Currently, there is doubt as to whether science has the right scalability answers. Existing approaches are not sufficient to cope with this challenge. We will need new models for supporting future Cloud infrastructures. This is not only limited to application design and parallelization, but also to aspects of infrastructure management. A multi-layered architecture will need suitable solutions to cope with the size of such infrastructures.

2.2 Improve Efficiency

High-performance computing is heavily focused on optimization. Considerable research effort has been expended to decrease response-time for relevant problems or to increase the throughput of infrastructures. This included optimization for efficient utilization of machines. As such, efficiency was and remains a crucial aspect for managing Grids and Clouds for the future. However, efficiency may well extend to more areas that considered in the past. We already live in a time in which energy consumption and Green IT became major aspects in running IT infrastructures. Most Cloud computing models are based on a clear business model and so costs in general will become a crucial aspect in optimizing service executions. As such, our assumption is that Grid and Cloud management will require novel solutions supporting multi-criteria optimization.

2.3 Reliability

Due to the size of future infrastructures and the dynamic composition of applications from many different services, we will increasingly face reliability questions. This will require better understanding of software design and novel programming paradigms for such infrastructures. Moreover, managing quality-of-service will play a major role to handle these large-scale software and infrastructure landscapes. The multiple layers in large-scale distributed infrastructures will require a suitable abstraction of service quality. Models on creating redundancy, fault-tolerance, and automatic adaption will be crucial. For instance, service-level agreements are already an industry standard in ITIL-compliant IT management. However, there is not yet sufficient support for automatically managing large infrastructures by SLAs. This will have to be taken into account in future systems.

2.4 Reducing Complexity

Most aspects mentioned above relate to the overall challenge of mastering system complexity. These systems are large-scale, very dynamic, and span multiple administrative domains. Such systems will require a high degree of automatic and autonomous management. Current approaches try to tackle this. however, it seems necessary to completely revise the way that infrastructures are managed with the transition from thousands to millions of cores or software components. Our systems are still too complicated. As a consequence, many potential user groups cannot fully exploit the technology. There is a clear need to lower the entry barrier and to also target non-experts as users. This can only be achieved by hiding the complexity and by providing easy-to-use tools, portals, or programming environments. Suitable user support systems will be essential for the broad proliferation of Clouds.

2.5 Data Management

The handling of data in distributed environments was one of the main questions in Grid systems. Data Grids have been one of the first usage scenarios. After several years of research in data management, the challenge seems larger than ever. Managing huge amounts of data seems more of an issue than managing processing power. As of now, we still have no clear understanding on how to handle data on a global scale. Map-Reduce and Hadoop became common infrastructures for many usage scenarios. But this does not yet bridge from globally distributed data repositories to individual data stores. There remains a significant gap in efficient and automatic data management. Again, it seems necessary to revisit this data challenge and to come up with fresh ideas for the future of Clouds and Grids.

2.6 Trust and Security

Grid environments already have quite sophisticated security management, e.g. through virtual organizations, certificate management, or support for secure communication channels. But it is also obvious that many of these approaches do not scale well for main stream adoption and future infrastructures. Clouds currently have even less well established security methods than Grids. It is obvious that trust and security will remain high up on the scientific agenda. It needs to be easy-to-use, non-intrusive, but at the same time reach an even higher security levels than before. Industrial adoption of cloud-based services may require support for ISO/IEC 27001, SAS 70, or SOX compliance which is typically not found in Grid infrastructures.

3 HPC and Cloud Computing

A significant part of the CoreGRID research was linked to HPC-related Grid computing. Today Grids offer common production facilities in e-Science [4]. Many scientific communities rely on Grids for resource sharing and collaboration in virtual organizations. It is not foreseeable that this will change in the near future. On the contrary, we see that more scientific communities are likely to require Grid infrastructures [2].

There is still a vivid discussion on the relation between Grid computing and Cloud computing [7]. Our understanding is that Grids and Clouds and Clouds are different. Both approaches address similar research areas but with different use-cases in mind (HPC/e-Science vs. Commercial operations) and with different technologies (common access to different infrastructure resources vs. virtualization abstraction). Both environments successfully co-exist and will have their share in their respective application realm.

However, there is no strong trend for Grids to be adopted as main stream technology for the service economy beyond e-Science and HPC. Instead, Cloud computing is taking this role. It changes the way applications are executed and infrastructure are managed. Almost all large data centers have adopted virtualization as a core technology to increase flexibility and resource utilization. Similarly, we see more applications being run as cloud-based services. There is a trend to adopt private public or hybrid clouds as an operational model for many organizations.

HPC remains an important application area, but we see more differences in the user communities requesting access to such resources. On one hand, we have the top end of HPC resources in the renowned global super-computing centers. Users of such resources are typically experts who are able to adapt to the available HPC resources. A very good understanding of the underlying hardware is required (e.g. on the specific cache structure, the interconnection network, processor capabilities). This user group is able to extract very high performance from such systems. On the other hand, we see many users who also need access to HPC resources but who are unable or unwilling to adapt to the specific hardware infrastructures. For those users it would be inefficient to access the top end HPC super computers. Instead they need easy and fast access to resources which are similar to the infrastructures which they know.

For HPC experts, the adoption of virtualization and cloud computing would be counter-productive. Application performance would suffer, while top end super computers would not be well utilized. However, for the second group clouds may be a viable alternative. This group might not require the fine grain optimization of their application to gain the final percent in performance. Instead, a fast and easy transition from existing computers to a larger resource set would suffice. Here, a Cloud infrastructure might provide on demand the required compute resources on which an arbitrary number of virtual machines with the necessary applications can run. Thus, we might see that Cloud computing will also become an operational model in the HPC eco-system in the low- and mid-range market. These are typically local or regional data centers with HPC resources for their user community. Similarly, we already see HPC services provided by commercial providers such as Amazon [3].

Obviously, this will not apply to all applications: Software that is tightly coupled with high communication demand will not be well suited for a Cloud. Today cloud computing is usually agnostic of the underlying hardware and network infrastructure. For HPC applications, we will need specific support to realize acceptable network performance. This combination of Cloud with HPC is an interesting scientific research subject.

4 Outlook

While CoreGRID gained significant international visibility in the Grid realm, there is no similar impact on the Cloud community. However, many (not all) of its members are very active in service-based computing and Clouds. This is quite natural as the research challenges mentioned above are shared in Grids and Clouds. Unfortunately, we see again a large fragmentation in the European research landscape.

Several good attempts have been made to provide a joint research agenda, e.g. by the NESSI European technology platform [1] or the S-Cube network of excellence [5]. However, none of these serves as a pan-European Cloud research center focusing on basic scientific research questions. These research challenges mentioned above are major and need to be addressed. Due to the size of these challenges, it is unlikely that single research groups or companies can solve those. It will require again a joint effort by many scientists to overcome these obstacles.

CoreGRID can play an important role to support such efforts. However, this will require a significant evolution in its research structure and membership. Despite the overlap in research questions, the scientific community for cloud research is not identical. It will require a gathering of experts from different disciplines to achieve a similar successful network as CoreGRID constitutes for Grids.

References

1. Nessi strategic research agenda, vol. 3 (May 2009)
2. Bird, I., Jones, B., Kee, K.F.: The organization and management of grid infrastructures. Computer 42, 36–46 (2009)
3. Evangelinos, C., Hill, C.N.: Cloud computing for parallel scientific hpc applications: Feasibility of running coupled atmosphere-ocean climate models on amazon's ec2. Cloud Computing and Its Applications (October 2008)

4. Jones, B.: The use of grids for fusion applications in europe and future directions. In: GMAC 2009: Proceedings of the 6th International Conference Industry Session on Grids Meets Autonomic Computing, pp. 39–40. ACM, New York (2009)
5. Metzger, A., Pohl, K.: Towards the next generation of service-based systems: The S-cube research framework. In: van Eck, P., Gordijn, J., Wieringa, R. (eds.) CAiSE 2009. LNCS, vol. 5565, pp. 11–16. Springer, Heidelberg (2009)
6. Meyer, N., Talia, D., Yahyapour, R.: Grid and Services Evolution. Springer Publishing Company, Heidelberg (2008) (incorporated)
7. Schwiegelshohn, U., Badia, R.M., Bubak, M., Danelutto, M., Dustdar, S., Gagliardi, F., Geiger, A., Hluchy, L., Kranzlmüller, D., Laure, E., Priol, T., Reinefeld, A., Resch, M., Reuter, A., Rienhoff, O., Rüter, T., Sloot, P., Talia, D., Ullmann, K., Yahyapour, R., von Voigt, G.: Perspectives on grid computing. Future Gener. Comput. Syst. 26(8), 1104–1115 (2010)

From Invisible Grids to Smart Cloud Computing

Vladimir Getov[1] and Savitha Srinivasan[2]

[1] School of Electronics and Computer Science, University of Westminster, 115 New Cavendish St., London W1W 6UW, UK
V.S.Getov@westminster.ac.uk

[2] IBM Venture Capital Group, IBM Almaden Research Center, 650 Harry Rd., San Jose, CA 95120, USA
savitha@almaden.ibm.com

Abstract. In recent years the concepts and implementations of modern distributed computing infrastructures have been developing rapidly. The cloud computing paradigm emerged shortly after the introduction of the "invisible" grid concepts. In both cases however providing support for a variety of autonomic properties is of primary importance for constructing those large-scale complex systems of high quality. This paper gives an overview of our reference smart cloud computing architecture which is proposed as a solution to these problems. Some of the available directions for future work are also discussed.

Keywords: Cloud computing, invisible grids, smarter planet.

1 Introduction

The main challenges for our planet are becoming grimly clear – the first decade of the twenty-first century has been a series of wake-up calls [5], with a single subject of focus, the reality of global integration:

- Climate change and global warming in particular;
- Population growth;
- Frozen credit markets and limited access to capital;
- Energy crisis including energy shortfalls and erratic commodity prices;
- Healthcare management and delivery around the world;
- Increasingly complex supply chains and empowered consumers.

Just being connected is not sufficient to address our challenges. There is a need to make these global systems better. Energy systems – 170 billion kilowatt-hours wasted each year by consumers due to insufficient power usage information. Healthcare systems – that don't link from diagnosis, to drug discovery, to healthcare deliverers, to insurers, to employers while facing pandemic challenges such as the outbreak of swine flu. Traffic systems – congested roadways cost us billions of lost hours, billions litres of wasted petrol as well as a huge impact on the air quality.

In order to start tackling the above challenges we need qualitatively new large-scale computing infrastructures with smart properties. The emerging cloud

M.R. Guarracino et al. (Eds.): Euro-Par 2010 Workshops, LNCS 6586, pp. 263–270, 2011.
© Springer-Verlag Berlin Heidelberg 2011

computing paradigm looks quite suitable for this purpose but it needs significant improvements towards providing full autonomy. This is the topic area of our current research.

The rest of this paper is organised as follows. Section 2 gives a brief overview of recent and related work including projects that introduced the "invisible" grid concepts. Section 3 summarized the smarter planet vision. Section 4 introduces our reference smart cloud architecture while Section 5 gives conluding remarks and identifies directions for future work.

2 The Invisible Grid Concepts

We have been investigating the services design methodology in dynamically reconfigurable distributed platforms supporting flexible and fault-tolerant composition and execution of workflows. Our approach, objectives, methodology, and existing tools and environments contribute directly to the long-term objectives for developing ICT infrastructures in Europe [2,7]. Also, the increased interest and motivation in the partnership related to services and service oriented architectures, will address several problems and objectives recently stated in EU research guidelines such as the NESSI Technology Platform.

The proposed research activity builds on results of, completes and complements current research frameworks, and in particular those related to:

- advanced Grid programming models and workflow management systems, including initiatives from the US and other non-EU countries, those related to the SCA initiative by IBM and all the results achieved within CoreGRID and the "Invisible Grid" concepts in particular as well as the other recent EU-funded projects in FP6 and FP7, including XtreemOS, GridCOMP, EDGeS, Reservoir and S-Cube.
- autonomic management of non-functional features in distributed and parallel programming, such as those from the GrADs project, or by IBM's autonomic computing initiative.
- complex (web) service orchestration and choreography, such as those related to WSO with BLEP4WS or WSCI.
- cloud computing framework design, including the Google App engine.
- algorithmic skeletons, design patterns, and more in general distributed programming abstractions, with communities active in Europe and in US.
- utility computing achievements, as well as theoretical and practical results from the global computing community.

3 The Smarter Planet Vision

Based on the launch of IBM's campaign in Nov 2008 the smarter planet vision [8] has three elements:

First, our world is becoming *instrumented*. Sensors are being embedded across entire ecosystems, supply-chains, healthcare networks, cities and even natural systems like rivers.

Second, our world is becoming *interconnected*. Systems and objects can now "speak" to one another. Soon there will be a trillion connected and intelligent things – cars, appliances, cameras, roadways, pipelines, pharmaceuticals, and even livestock. The amount of information produced by the interaction of all those things will be unprecedented.

Third, all things are becoming *intelligent*. Advanced analytics can turn the mountains of data from these systems and objects into decisions and actions that make the world smarter.

Today's demands on a broad range of city resources, from road availability to electrical power, effluent emission and water usage are being subjected to increasing pressure as approximately 50% of the world's population moves to within 200 kilometres of a coastline. Through the more efficient use of these resources, it is possible to reduce these pressures. This efficiency is obtained through accurate measurement of the lifecycle of these resources through data which can be captured from today's wide range of sensors as presented in the recent review of key market revenue trends, technology snapshots, and growth perspectives [4]. By connecting this data to increasingly sophisticated mathematical models it becomes possible to accurately monitor and manage the lifecycle of a resource. The Instrumented Planet [3] is a notion which uses the idea of connecting data from sensors to models to business processes ultimately enabling transparency in the use and control of resources according to a specific objective.

Current capabilities of data acquisition, modelling and optimization are not yet capable of managing the entire resource lifecycle without considerable customized coding. Our experience shows that as cities look to manage a specific resource, such as carbon emission or traffic or water, the need to simultaneously manage these resources becomes increasingly more acute. The interdependence of these resource systems becomes even clearer as the demand on the resource becomes more acute since every aspect of managing the resource lifecycle becomes critical. It is thus important in situations where a particular resource is being optimized, to provide a framework, enabling rapid service and mode integration while identifying resource lifecycle dependencies.

Early engagements also show the importance of including humans in the resource management process, as models, particularly interacting models of this type cannot be relied upon to make sensible decision under all conditions. These issues notwithstanding, the use of an instrumented planet approach where data are transformed into models which in turn allow cities to make decisions about which roads to make available under specific conditions, or where to pump water or to generate renewable energy is a rapidly evolving domain, which requires the integration of ICT, mathematics and business processes.

The agenda for a Smarter Planet is a transformational agenda to create and manage a new future for these instrumented, interconnected, and intelligent systems that come together and to bring solutions that chart the course for real time collaborative ecosystem management.

4 A Reference Smart Cloud Architecture

The smart cloud will be the key enabler for the implementation of our smarter planet vision contributing significant innovation in smart cloud services for sustainable cities. We envision two types of sustainable services:

The first will address socio-environmental challenges like water management, thermal energy management and traffic prediction, and create sustainable cities with an integrated view of the disparate city services. The second will drive economic sustainability for cities with the ability to develop and pilot industry services for Telco, Retail and Media using in-market pilots to create greater value.

4.1 Smart Cloud Infrastructure

We plan to introduce and implement the design methodology of a generic component based smart cloud platform with a single software services infrastructure. One of the main goals of his proposal is to focus on the research challenges for rapid development and highly efficient execution of extreme-scale future Internet applications suitable for deployment on cloud infrastructures.

The cloud infrastructural innovations necessary for achieving our objectives will be driven by the requirements of the sustainable cities based on in-market use cases. Following our application-driven approach, we propose to address a range of technical challenges that span the spectrum of a smart cloud infrastructure, a smart cloud data bus and a set of smart cloud services. We plan to give special attention to the design of mobile cloud infrastructures. More specifically our reference smart platform architecture includes the following major layers as shown in Figure 1:

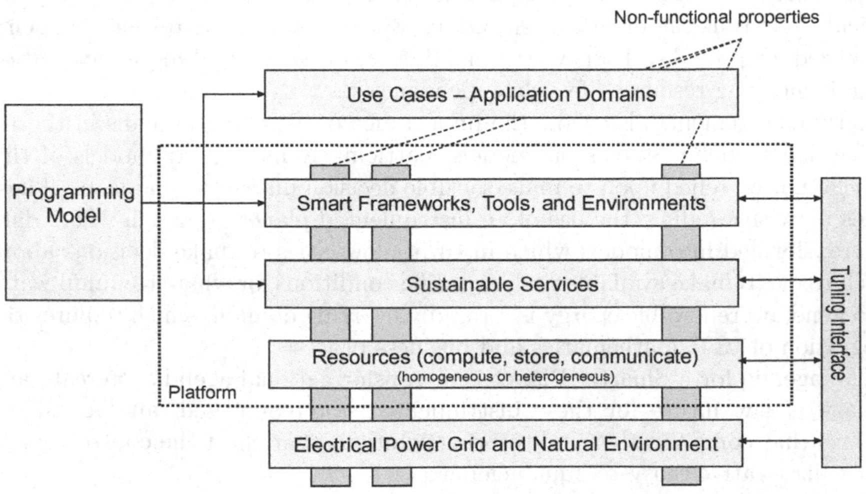

Fig. 1. Smart Cloud Infrastructure Architecture

– Natural environment (sensors);
– Electrical power grid and other industrial establishments (sensors);
– Smart computer communication networks;
– Information resources, infrastructures, and repositories;
– Sustainable services;
– Smart programming models, tools, and environments;
– Use cases in strategic application domains.

Three of the layers – Information resources, infrastructures, and repositories; Sustainable services; and Smart programming models, tools, and environments – constitute the Smart Cloud Platform. They are considered further below.

4.2 Information Resources, Infrastructures, and Repositories

Most of the data volume for sensors will not come from *in situ* devices, but rather from remote sensors (e.g., active sensors like radar, etc. or passive sensors like multi-spectral images, video systems, etc.). Of course, there will be far more *in situ* devices, but they will have relatively small and simple data streams. The challenge will be in handling of the diversity of data (modalities, sampling strategies, data rates), properly registering them geospatially and temporally, and how to fuse, analyze, visualize and disseminate them, etc.

We propose to address the challenge of data intensive smart cloud services with the design and architecture of a smart cloud data bus that serves as a logical single point of entry of the real time data streams generated and transmitted by various sensors including mobile phones. The volume of data transmitted can be of the order of million updates a day, given the smart services use cases where the mobile phone is an example of a ubiquitous sensor. The cloud data bus will receive the transmitted data and ensure intelligent routing and updates of the stream with the persistent store associated with the corresponding service.

4.3 Sustainable Services

The smart cloud infrastructure will incorporate service and infrastructure management technologies that enable the delivery and management of IT services in an automated fashion in a virtualized environment. This will build upon currently available technologies that provide a level of automated cloud management and request-driven-provisioning, but will require further research innovation and development in key areas to support the vision of the smart cloud for sustainable cities.

Base Cloud Services. Currently available technology offerings provide core services in the cloud related to provisioning and basic management of virtualized infrastructure. Users are able to configure virtual servers and the accompanying storage and connectivity, and deploy virtual images containing preconfigured software stacks.

Advanced Cloud Services. The core services above are available in current cloud service offerings that offer a basic infrastructure service model. Realizing the vision of a cloud platform to support Smart City services requires a number of additional capabilities. Some of the key additional areas of required innovation include support for workload elasticity, workload migration, data integration, policy-based data sharing, and template-based service creation in the cloud.

Live Migration of Virtualized Services: many virtualization technologies support live migration of single virtual machines to balance load within a data center. In the Smart Cloud Infrastructure, services may need to be moved for a number of additional reasons including, for example, relocating services closer to specific data sources or populations, or to overcome restrictions on data availability. Moreover, smart services are solutions that consist of multiple interconnected modules which must be moved in concert and reconnected to data sources or other services in the target location. Hence, there is a need for automation to collect dependency information to ensure that all relevant services are relocated (or accessible), plan the migration, and perform post-migration reconfiguration. This migration must work within a data center and also across the wide area where additional challenges arise in terms of network latency and network reconfiguration.

Elastic Services: as data volumes or usage of services grows, there will be a need to dynamically extend compute capacity based on workload utilization for a resource pool. The trigger for the change may not be as simple as CPU utilization thresholds – the challenges are to provide a way to use service-level metrics to invoke changes, and also to determine the right way to extend the capacity. For example, there may be scenarios when migration to alternate physical resources, or replication of the service, are necessary.

Template-based Service Creation and Provisioning: Creation of cloud services for Smart Cities will require collaboration between domain experts (e.g., water management engineers, transportation planners) and IT experts who understand the artefacts needed implement the service in the cloud. Without standard models and specifications which can be leveraged for a wide variety of services, the creation process is ad-hoc, time-consuming, and expensive. The notion of service templates or "service appliances" should be developed to provide a framework in which services can be defined, including their interfaces to ancillary services and management components. These templates also enable rapid provisioning by standardizing, for example, the specification of software images, configuration automation scripts, and security parameters.

Service Catalogue Management: Smart service components are expected to be developed for a variety of scenarios and by a number of different service creators or providers. The Smart Service Catalogue brings these services together with a unified way to present services to various user roles, and provides capability to automatically update and manage the content as new services are added.

4.4 Smart Programming Models, Tools and Environments

Recent advances in software service technology increasingly provide interoperable frameworks and tools suitable for development of new applications/services from existing ones, but using intelligent and automatic decision-making based on a set of smart properties. Unfortunately, however, the level of abstraction presented to the service developer is currently relatively low. New paradigms are necessary to raise the level of abstraction presented to service users, particularly in the following areas:

a) Advanced Programming Models for Services. The effort needed to combine existing services to develop a new service/application, should be made less onerous and less costly by providing new paradigms which offer the service user/developer new and effective means to operate on/with services, means that should be far from the low level, machine-oriented service mechanisms currently used.

b) Smart Autonomic Management of Service Applications. Support for the development of autonomic service managers to manage smart (non-functional) properties should be provided through abstractions that may be instantiated, generalized or specialized by service users to implement autonomic service management.

Both these areas require substantial investigation, and, where appropriate, reuse of existing results in other research areas, together with the development of new, service-oriented mechanisms, tools, programming models and frameworks. This area includes a number of related research challenges and opportunities for future development.

5 Conclusions

The results obtained within this research activity can be exploited directly in the Smart Cloud Infrastructures scenario. In particular, when designing tools to support Cloud programming, autonomic aspects must be given primary consideration, due to the need to decouple programmer activities from actual knowledge of the target architecture.

Within our generic smart cloud infrastructures model, future research activities include development of composition support interoperable with other service-oriented platforms including platforms conforming to the net-centric operating systems approach. Further research work also focuses on the integration with and the adoption of emerging standards [1]. This involves the development of meta-data-based decision-taking support via high flexibility and dynamic properties integrated within the future SOA-oriented distributed systems. The ultimate goal is the design methodology of fully integrated framework based on both service-oriented and peer-to-peer-oriented approaches for rapid development and execution of extreme-scale distributed applications.

Because of the early development stages of the cloud computing field, little consensus about it has been reached so far. A particularly interesting activity is to expand and develop further support for both software development and deployment in systems based on the cloud computing concepts [6]. Important related opportunities stem from further developing and implementing the cloud computing concepts of Infrastructure as a Service (IaaS) and Software as a Service (SaaS).

Regarding IaaS, open questions are how compute and storage clouds can be used as resources for grid applications. One such question is the introduction of virtual machine configuration management to application deployment mechanisms. Regarding SaaS, it is interesting and important to investigate if and how hosted services can be used to execute code of grid use cases, possibly by a means of dynamically composing applications from existing services with user-defined ones, while also introducing meta-data support for service composition.

As a generalization of the research questions above, it remains to be investigated which use cases (with which properties) lend themselves for execution on cloud computing infrastructures, or in other words: What is the suitability for services computing of certain classes of applications? Therefore, the research work on this topic will address directly the rapid development and execution support of future Internet applications based on their suitability properties.

References

1. Baskey, M., Black, A., Drescher, M., Lipton, P., Matsumoto, Y., Perazolo, M., Salahshour, A., Snelling, D., Vaught, J.: Symptoms Framework White Paper, Version 1.0, OASIS (2010)
2. Campolargo, M.: e-Infrastructures: Catalysts of a New Scientific Renaissance. Computer 42(1), 43 (2009)
3. Chen-Ritzo, C.-H., Harrison, C., Paraszczak, J., Parr, F.: Instrumenting the planet. IBM J. Res. and Dev. 53(3), paper 1 (2009), `http://www.research.ibm.com/journal/rd53-3.html`
4. Global Sensor Outlook – 2009. Frost and Sullivan (March 2009)
5. Friedman, T.L.: Hot, Flat, and Crowded. Farrar, Straus and Giroux, New York (2008)
6. The Future of Cloud Computing. Expert Group Report, Information Society and Media, European Commission, Brussels (2010)
7. ICT Infrastructures for e-Science. Communication from the European Commission, Brussels (2009)
8. Palmisano, S.: A Smarter Planet: The Next Leadership Agenda. IBM (2008), `http://www.ibm.com/ibm/ideasfromibm/us/smartplanet/20081106/sjp_speech.shtml`

Multi-level Brokering Solution for Interoperating Service and Desktop Grids*

Attila Kertész, Zoltán Farkas, and Péter Kacsuk

MTA SZTAKI Computer and Automation Research Institute,
H-1518 Budapest, P.O. Box 63, Hungary
{attila.kertesz,zfarkas,kacsuk}@sztaki.hu

Abstract. User communities have gathered around various Grid systems forming separate islands that represent borders they cannot cross. As these communities are growing and demanding more and more computational power, uniting these islands draws more attention in Grid research and development. This problem is called the Grid Interoperability problem. This issue may be tackled at different levels in the Grid middleware, this paper targets the level of Grid resource management also called as Grid brokering. This paper introduces a meta-brokering approach that means a higher level resource management by enabling automatic and simultaneous utilization of various Grid brokers managing resources of different Grid systems. Desktop Grids are using not only different interfaces, but also different technologies. Here we also introduce a novel solution to access Desktop Grids through specific brokers that can be managed by our Meta-Broker. In this way with our multi-level brokering solution we can unify several Service and Desktop Grids without modifying their implementation, policies or interfaces, providing the greatest computational power possible for all Grid user communities.

Keywords: Grid Interoperability, Grid Interoperation, Grid Resource Management, Grid Meta-brokering.

1 Introduction

E-Science infrastructures play an important role in enabling large-scale scientific research. In order to establish such e-infrastructures, various Grid systems have been created and run as a service for the scientific community. Originally, the aim of Grid systems was that anyone (called donors) could offer resources for the Grid, and anyone (called users) could claim resources dynamically, according to their actual needs, in order to solve a computational or data intensive task. This twofold aim has however not fully been achieved, and today we can observe two different trends in the development of Grid systems: Service Grids and Desktop Grids. In Service Grids, computational resources are offered as Grid services

* The research leading to these results has received funding from the European Community's Seventh Framework Programme FP7/2007-2013 under grant agreement 215483 (S-Cube) and from EDGI (RI-261556).

M.R. Guarracino et al. (Eds.): Euro-Par 2010 Workshops, LNCS 6586, pp. 271–278, 2011.
© Springer-Verlag Berlin Heidelberg 2011

that can be accessed by a large number of users. A resource can become part of the Grid by installing a predefined software set, or middleware. The middleware is, however, so complex that it often requires extensive effort to maintain. On the other hand, Desktop Grids are commonly known as volunteer computing systems, because they often rely upon the general public to donate compute resources, or spare cycles. Unlike Service Grids, which are based on complex architectures, volunteer computing has a simple architecture and has demonstrated the ability to integrate dispersed, heterogeneous computing resources with ease, successfully scavenging cycles from tens of thousands of idle desktop computers. The Grid research community considers Desktop Grids only as particular and limited forms of e-infrastructures, because they cannot work as services nor be used by anyone who has not already setup their projects to function in this environment. Additionally, unlike most Service Grids, which have reciprocal agreements for resource utilization among partners, participants in Desktop Grid systems, cannot use the system for their own goals. Until now, these two kinds of Grid systems have been completely separated, hence there has not been a mechanism to exploit their advantageous, individual features in a unified environment. However, with the objective to support new scientific communities who need extremely large numbers of resources, the solution could be to interconnect these two kinds of Grid systems into an integrated Service Grid – Desktop Grid infrastructure. User communities have gathered around various Grid systems (including Service and Desktop Grids) forming separate islands that represent borders they cannot cross. As these communities are growing and demanding more and more computational power, uniting these islands draws more attention in Grid research and development, which is called the Grid Interoperability problem [8]. Grid Resource Management tools evolved from manual discovery and task submission to sophisticated brokering solutions. To ease the simultaneous utilization of different Service Grids, researchers have started to revise current brokering solutions by extending existing resource brokers with multiple middleware support. In this paper we introduce a meta-brokering approach, which acts as a higher level brokering service by enabling automatic and simultaneous utilization of various Grid brokers managing resources of different Grid systems. Since Desktop Grids are using different technologies and lacking such brokers Service Grids have, here we introduce a novel solution to access Desktop Grids through specific gateways that act as service brokers and can be managed by our meta-brokering solution. In this way we can unify several Service and Desktop Grids without modifying their implementation, policies or interfaces, providing the greatest computational power possible for all user communities.

The rest of the paper is organized as follows. In Section 2 we present the related work for interoperation research with high-level brokering directions. In Section 3, we present a meta-brokering solution for service Grids, and in Section 4, we show how the Desktop Grids can be interfaced to meta-brokering with a novel service called 3G Bridge. In Section 5 we describe the multi-level brokering solution for Grid interoperation.

2 Related Work

The problem of Grid interoperability and interoperation is a crucial issue to solve [8]. Meta-brokering approaches seek for interoperable solutions at the level of Grid resource management by enabling a higher level brokering solution that schedules user jobs among various Grid brokers/domains. Some of these meta-brokering solutions, such as the meta-scheduling project in LA Grid [9], the delegated matchmaking with Koala [4] and decentralized scheduling with Gridway [3], aim at enabling communication among existing resource brokers in a sense that different domains are being examined as a whole, but they rather delegate resource information among domains, broker instances or gateways through their own, implementation-dependent interfaces. Usually the local domain has preference, and when a job is forwarded, the result should be transferred back to the initial instance. On the other hand, the advantage of our proposed meta-brokering concept is that it does not require any modification of the existing Grid resource managers, since it utilizes and delegates broker information by reaching them through their current interfaces.

Regarding Grid interoperability solutions achieved so far, they are based on short-term solutions. The paper in [8] focuses on different Grid components (like job management, data management, information systems), and urges the usage of standards-based solutions. The interoperability solution for UNICORE and Globus described in [7] uses a translation mechanism to allow the execution of jobs submitted to UNICORE on Globus. In paper [2], authors show two solutions for using Condor resources in an OGSA-based infrastructure. The first option hides the details of the Condor system: job submission, job execution management and resource information providers are offered for the OGSA Grid to hide Condor details. On the other hand, the second option embeds OGSA within the Condor framework in order to provide controlled access to the Condor resources. These solutions target low-level interoperability of service Grids. Interoperability of service and Desktop Grids has been solved within the EDGeS [1] project with the help of the Generic Grid-Grid (3G) Bridge technology [10]. The architecture of 3G Bridge has been proven to be generic enough to easily solve interoperability of a number of service (gLite, ARC, Unicore) and Desktop (BOINC, XtremWeb, OurGrid) Grid systems. In this paper we introduce an extension of the 3G Bridge that allows us using it as part of our meta-brokering approach, that helps to solve Grid interoperability at higher levels.

3 Meta-Brokering for Service Grids

In order to access resources of different Grids simultaneously, we use a meta-brokering approach. The *Grid Meta-Broker Service* (GMBS) [6] is a higher level tool that matches resource brokers to user requests. The system is implemented as a web-service (WS), which is independent from middleware-specific components. In the following we describe the role of the components (depicted in Figure 1) and their interaction. The *Translator* components of GMBS are responsible for translating the resource specification defined by the user to the language of the appropriate resource broker that the meta-broker selects to invoke for a given job. We also use an extendable *Broker Property Description Language* (BPDL) [6] to express metadata about brokers. The *Information Collector* (IC) component of the GMBS stores the data of the reachable brokers and historical data of the previous submissions. During broker utilization the successful submissions and failures are tracked, and regarding these events a rank is modified for each special attribute in the BPDL of the appropriate broker. In this way, the BPDL documents represent and store the dynamic states of the brokers. When a large number of jobs with similar requirements are sent to GMBS, the so-called best effort matchmaking (choosing the less loaded one) may flood a broker and its utilized resources. To cope with this problem, there is an *IS Agent* (IS stands for Information System) service reporting to IC, which regularly checks and stores the load of the Grids of each connected broker.

The *Invoker* components are used to contact the brokers. Therefore the Invokers are broker-specific components: they communicate with the interconnected brokers, calling them with job requests and collecting the results. The user has to upload the job, Grid certificate proxies and input files along with the job description (JSDL) to the GMBS, and the Matchmaker component tries to find a proper broker for the request. If it could not find a broker that would be able to fulfil the user requirements, the request is discarded, otherwise the JSDL is translated to the language of the selected broker. In the JSDL extension the middleware constraint fields can be used to specify certificate proxy names for Grids/VOs. This information is used by the Invokers to select the valid certificate proxy from the uploaded files for the actual job submission. Then the responsible Invoker takes care of transferring the necessary files to the selected Grid environment. After job submission, it stages back the output files and upgrades the historical data stored in the Information Collector with the log of the utilized broker. The *Core* component of the service is responsible for managing the communication (information and data exchange) among the other components. Generally the following operations can be done through this interface: adding a new broker with BPDL, querying the available brokers and the name of the tracked Grids/VOs, adding new Information Systems to be tracked, submitting jobs and signaling submitted job results.

4 3G Bridge: A Service Broker for Desktop Grids

The Generic Grid-Grid Bridge (3G Bridge) has been created within the scope of the EDGeS project to solve Grid interoperability. The aim of 3G Bridge is to offer a generic implementation for a gateway service that allows the execution of jobs within different Grid middleware using Grid plugins. On the other hand, it offers a very simple web service interface for submitting jobs into its internal job database. An overview of the 3G Bridge architecture can be seen in Figure 1. The central component of the 3G Bridge is the *3G Bridge Job Database*. This database is responsible for storing data of jobs and plugins. The design is

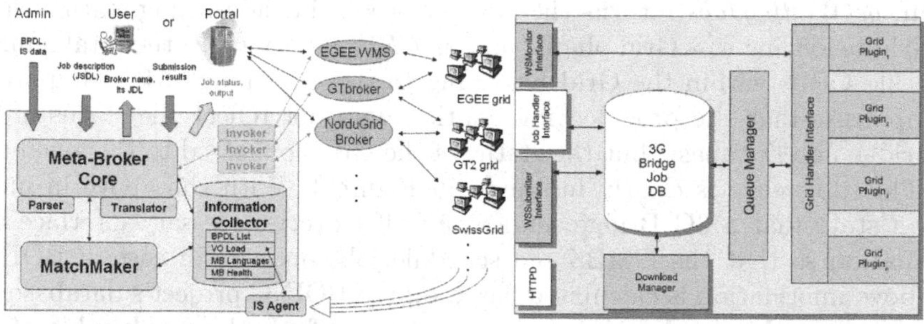

Fig. 1. The Grid Meta-Broker Service for Service Grids (on the left) and 3G Bridge for Desktop Grids (on the right)

very simple, for every job the following minimal set of attributes is kept track of: the internal identifier of the job, the name of the destination plugin, the name of the executable, the status of the job, the Grid identifier of the job, the command-line arguments of the job, the timestamp when the job has been added to the database, the list of input files and their locations and finally the list of output files (and their locations given that they have been produced). Based on this information, the *Queue Manager* interacts with the *Grid Plugins* through the generic *Grid Handler Interface*. The Grid Plugins have to implement some functions of the interface in order to create a working plugin: submit a set of jobs, update the status of all jobs belonging to the plugin, and poll the status of one job. These functions are responsible for managing jobs assigned to the given Grid plugin. Using this design we managed to create Grid plugins for gLite, BOINC, XtremWeb, OurGrid and BES-compatible resources. Clients of the 3G Bridge have two possibilities to submit new jobs to a new plugin: the *WSSubmitter Interface* and the *Job Handler Interface*. The WSSubmitter interface is a web service-based interface, offering very simple operations: *submit* – to send a set of jobs to 3G Bridge, the response of the submission operation is the list of 3G Bridge job identifiers assigned to the jobs; *getStatus* – to query the status of jobs from the 3G Bridge, the response is the sequence of job statuses; *delete* – to cancel jobs; *getOutput* – to get the list of names and URLs of output files produced by jobs; *getFinished* – to get the list of job identifiers assigned to a Grid plugin that have finished; and finally *getVersion* – to get the version of the 3G Bridge service.

The *Download Manager* and *HTTPD* components have responsible for managing input and output files of jobs. The Download Manager is responsible for fetching input files of submitted jobs onto the 3G Bridge server machine. The HTTP component is a simple web server that makes 3G Bridge clients able to fetch output files produced by 3G Bridge jobs. All this information makes 3G Bridge usable as a Grid gateway, but the information needed for brokering is not propagated yet. In order to make 3G Bridge usable for our meta-brokering solution, the *WSMonitor Interface* has been created. This is a web service interface offering basic information about Grid plugins: *getRunningJobs* returns the number of jobs in the running status within the Grid belonging to a Grid plugin, *getWaitingJobs* returns the number of jobs in the waiting status within the Grid belonging to a Grid plugin, and *getCPUCount* returns the total number of usable CPUs within the Grid belonging to the Grid plugin. It is important to emphasise that the provided information does not reflect the status of the 3G Bridge Job Database, but the status of the Grid connected to the given plugin. This difference is clearly indicated in Figure 1. With the above in mind, we can state that a 3G Bridge service can offer every necessary interface and information so that the GMBS can schedule jobs onto it. In case of BOINC, the above information is calculated based on the BOINC project's database the following way: the number of running jobs comes from the *result* table of the BOINC database. The number of waiting jobs is determined in the same way, the difference is the value the query looks for. The CPU count is collected from the *host* table of the BOINC database. The query summarizes the number of CPUs of the hosts, whose last connection was within the last 24 hours, thus the host is assumed to be active.

5 Meta-brokering among Service and Desktop Grids

In order to bring Desktop Grid resources to our meta-brokering environment presented in Section 3, we use the 3G Bridge described in Section 4. The GMBS sees 3G Bridges as service brokers, therefore we have created a new Invoker that uses the WSSubmitter web-service interface of the 3G Bridge (described by a WSDL). The IS Agent of GMBS is also interfaced to the WSMonitor web-service interface of the 3G Bridge. Through this interface the GMBS can be informed about the number of running and waiting jobs, and also about the number of available CPUs in the actual Desktop Grid. Exactly these attributes are used by the IS Agent to store the actual load information in the BPDL descriptions of the utilized brokers by GMBS. The Translator component has also been extended to convert the JDSL description of the job provided by the user to the XML description needed by the 3G Bridge (which contains the name of the executable, arguments, possible input/output files and the name of the target Desktop Grid).

Regarding security issues, in Section 3 we have stated that the Invokers use the attached proxies named in the JSDL extension of the submitted job for authentication by the selected service broker and other related Grid services. Additionally, the GMBS makes use of the EDGeS Application Repository [1]: this service contains application descriptions. For each application, the hash of the executable and supporting Desktop Grid resources are stored within the repository. Eg. in BOINC, for a given application we can collect the set of BOINC projects that support the application based on its hash. With the EDGeS Application Repository the Meta-Broker service can have an overview of which application is supported by which BOINC project, and selects a 3G Bridge service during scheduling if and only if the given application is supported by the given BOINC project. To enable this validation, the IS Agent has been extended to periodically fetch the contents of the Application Repository as there could be updates, and stores the MD5 hashes of the available applications in the BPDL of the appropriate 3G Bridge. The validation is done during matchmaking: the MD5 hash of the application to be scheduled is compared to the ones found in the repository and stored in the BPDLs. If the validation fails for a given 3G Bridge (which means that the job is not supported by the Desktop Grid reachable by the 3G Bridge), the 3G Bridge is filtered out from the candidate brokers.

In general, the matchmaking process of GMBS remains the same: the list of available brokers are filtered according to the special requirements of the submitted job, then the actual load and performance data stored in the BPDLs of the brokers (including 3G Bridges) are used to select the best candidate. In this way at the meta-level the GMBS schedules user jobs among brokers of different Grids, then the invoked broker schedules the job among resources in its Grid environment. The extended meta-brokering solution is depicted in Figure 2, which serves as an interoperable brokering service among both Service and Desktop Grids.

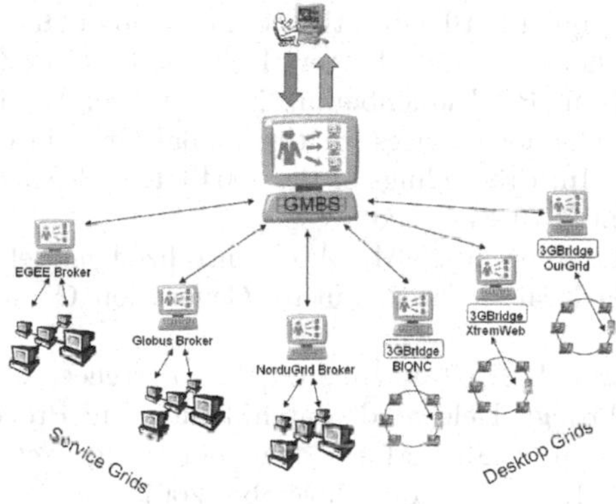

Fig. 2. Interoperation between Service and Desktop Grids with meta-brokering

6 Conclusions

Grid interoperability and interoperation among different Grid systems gets more and more attention due to the increasing number of users and Grid applications. Though some low level solutions for interconnecting different middleware systems have already appeared, a higher level brokering solution was still missing. In this paper we have shown how the Grid Meta-Broker Service can serve as an interoperable service to interconnect several Service and Desktop Grids. The design and the architecture of the GMBS enable a multi-level interoperable brokering by utilizing existing resource brokers of different Grid systems. It gathers and utilizes meta-data about existing widely used brokers from various Service Grid systems, and communicates with 3G Bridge instances to reach resources of Desktop Grid systems in a brokered way. The novel advantage of our extended meta-brokering concept is that it does not require any modification of the existing Grid systems, since it gathers and delegates broker-related information and utilizes them through their current interfaces. In this way the presented multi-level brokering solution can unify several Service and Desktop Grids without modifying their implementation, policies or interfaces, providing the greatest computational power possible for all Grid user communities. Several ideas of the described meta-brokering and the 3G Bridge solution have built into the P-GRADE and WS-PGRADE portal that provide workflow level interoperability among various gLite, GT2, GT4 and BOINC Grids [5]. Our future work aims at investigating different scheduling policies for the coordinated use of these heterogeneous resources, and extending our meta-brokering solution to Cloud infrastructures.

References

1. Balaton, Z., Farkas, Z., Gombás, G., Kacsuk, P., Lovas, R., Marosi, A., Emmen, A., Terstyánszky, G., Kiss, T., Kelley, I., Taylor, I., Lodygensky, O., Cardenas-Montes, M., Fedak, G., Araujo, F.: EDGeS: the common boundary between service and desktop grids. Parallel Processing Letters 18(3), 433–445 (2008)
2. Chapman, C., Wilson, P., Tannenbaum, T., Farrellee, M., Livny, M., Brodholt, J., Emmerich, W.: Condor services for the Global Grid: interoperability between Condor and OGSA. In: Proceedings of the 2004 UK E-Science All Hands Meeting, Nottingham, UK, pp. 870–877 (2004)
3. Leal, K., Huedo, E., Llorente, I.M.: A decentralized model for scheduling independent tasks in Federated Grids. Future Generation Computer Systems 25(8), 840–852 (2009)
4. Iosup, A., Epema, D.H.J., Tannenbaum, T., Farrellee, M., Livny, M.: Inter-Operating Grids through Delegated MatchMaking. In: Proceedings of the International Conference for High Performance Computing, Networking, Storage and Analysis (SC 2007), Reno, Nevada (November 2007)
5. Kacsuk, P., Karóczkai, K., Hermann, G., Sipos, G., Kovács, J.: WS-PGRADE: Supporting parameter sweep applications in workflows. Proc. of the 3rd Workshop on Workflows in Support of Large-Scale Science, Austin (2008)
6. Kertész, A., Kacsuk, P.: GMBS: A New Middleware Service for Making Grids Interoperable. Future Generation Computer Systems 26, 542–553 (2010)
7. Rambadt, M., Weider, P.: UNICORE – Globus: Interoperability of Grid Infrastructures. In: Proceedings of Cray User Group Summit, Manchester (2002)
8. Riedel, M., et al.: Interoperation of World-Wide Production e-Science Infrastructures. Concurrency and Computation: Practice and Experience (2008)
9. Rodero, I., Guim, F., Corbalan, J., Fong, L.L., Liu, Y.G., Sadjadi, S.M.: Looking for an Evolution of Grid Scheduling: Meta-brokering. In: Coregrid Workshop in Grid Middleware 2007, Dresden, Germany (June 2007)
10. Urbah, E., Kacsuk, P., Farkas, Z., Fedak, G., Kecskeméti, G., Lodygensky, O., Marosi, A., Balaton, Z., Caillat, G., Gombás, G., Kornafeld, Á., Kovács, J., He, H., Lovas, R.: EDGeS: Bridging EGEE to BOINC and XtremWeb. Journal of Grid Computing, Special Issue: Grid Interoperability 7(3), 335–354 (2009)

Software Licenses as Mobile Objects in Distributed Computing Environments

Claudio Cacciari[1], Daniel Mallmann[2], Csilla Zsigri[3], Francesco D'Andria[4], Björn Hagemeier[2], David García Peréz[6], Angela Rumpl[5], Wolfgang Ziegler[5], Miriam Gozalo[7], and Josep Martrat[4]

[1] CINECA, 40033 Casalecchio di Reno, Italy
c.cacciari@cineca.it
[2] Forschungszentrum Jülich GmbH, 52428 Jülich, Germany
{d.mallmann,b.hagemeier}@fz-juelich.de
[3] The 451 Group, London, WC1E6HH, United Kingdom
csilla.zsigri@the451group.com
[4] Atos Origin - Research and Innovation, Barcelona, 08011, Spain
{francesco.dandria,josep.martrat}@atosorigin.com
[5] Fraunhofer Institute SCAI, 53754 Sankt Augustin, Germany
{wolfgang.ziegler,angela.rumpl}@scai.fraunhofer.de
[6] Foundation CESGA, Santiago de Compostela, 15705, Spain
dgarcia@cesga.es
[7] Gridcore AB, Göteborg, 411 33, Sweden
miriam.gozalo@gridcore.se

Abstract. Current praxis of software licensing has been identified as major obstacle for Grid computing a couple of years ago already. Recent surveys of Clouds indicate that the same holds true for Cloud computing. As a consequence, using commercial applications that require access to a license server for authorisation at run-time has been quite limited until recently in distributed computing environments. Due to the mandatory centralised control of license usage during application run-time traditional software licensing practices are not suitable. In this paper we present a novel approach for managing software licenses as web service resources in distributed service oriented environments. Licenses become mobile objects, which may move to the environment where required to authorise the execution of a license protected application. The SmartLM solution, which has been recently implemented as a prototype decouples authorisation for license usage from authorisation for application execution.

1 Introduction

So far, commercial software is rarely used in Grids due to the limitations both with respect to the license management technology and the missing business models of the independent software vendors (ISV) for using their software in the Grid. Only recently MathWorks has provided a technical solution (and a business model) allowing to use their MATLAB suite in the EGEE Grid environment [5].

M.R. Guarracino et al. (Eds.): Euro-Par 2010 Workshops, LNCS 6586, pp. 279–286, 2011.
© Springer-Verlag Berlin Heidelberg 2011

However, this is a bilateral agreement only and has so far no implications for using MathWorks software in other Grids. The license management technology for software licenses is still based on the model of local computing centres providing both resources for computation and the software used for simulations together with the required licenses locally. Thus, these licenses are provided on the basis of named users, IP-addresses, or as a site license for the administrative domain of an organisation. Executing software in a distributed service oriented infrastructure is impossible using resources that are spread across different administrative domains, that do not host the application's license server. The licenses usually are bound to hardware within the domain of the user and do not allow access from outside, e.g. due to firewalls.

The increasing role Grid environments and virtualized infrastructures play in resource provisioning requires a solution. Traditional licensing practices are under pressure from a variety of alternative options (Software as a Service, open source, low-cost development environments, and the increasing software piracy [6] etc.) and are tightening vendors profit margins, pushing down licensing costs and giving more negotiating power to users. On the one hand, software manufacturers need to change the way licensing works and use flexible and non-hardware based licensing solutions that better fit into a virtual environment (one of the top ten obstacles for Cloud Computing mentioned in [1]). End users want fairness and flexibility and software vendors do not vote for a reduction in revenue. Hence, the achievement of a win-win situation between software vendors and software users is the main requirement for a mutually advantageous change. The major part of the licensing technology presented in this paper has been designed, implemented and evaluated with three industrial applications (ANSYS CFX, INTES PERMAS and LMS OPTIMUS) in the SmartLM project [9].

The remainder of the paper is organised as follows. Section 2 presents related work. Section 3 addresses the new business models (based on new license models) and the technology. Section 4 presents the SmartLM approaches for security. Validation and enforcement of virtualised licenses are described in Section 5. The paper concludes with a summary and plans for future research.

2 Related Work

To our best knowledge little research has been focusing on licensing technology since the new IT infrastructure paradigms Grids, Clouds and SOA became serious enhancements of traditional IT infrastructures. Only recently when these new paradigms gained ground in productive environments where e.g. more commercial simulation codes are used than in the e-Science domain license technology came to the fore. In [4] the authors give an overview on current licensing technology and models and describe two approaches developed in European projects to overcome the limitations. One of the presented approaches breaks with the current technology and is currently implemented in the SmartLM project while the second approach circumvents some of the limitations imposed by the defacto standard. The authors of [2] describe another approach, which is similar to SmartLM but lacks the integrated accounting and billing service and still requires network connectivity with the ISV when a user requests a license from the local license management server. As we will explain in the following sections SmartLM has taken a holistic approach for all services around license management while effectively making dispensable the requirement for permanent network connectivity between the license management service, the execution site of the application during runtime or to the ISV when requesting a license. In the European project BEinGRID another approach was developed which allows the use of existing licenses in Grid environments through tunneling of the communication of the license server to the application [7]. While technically feasible this approach raises a number of legal issues since many license contracts limit the use of a software license outside a company or outside a certain radius from the company.

3 Mobile Licenses

3.1 New Business Models

Through close collaboration with stakeholders - software vendors, application providers, end users - we identified some real licensing gaps and have developed new models that would help fill them in.

'Featuring the ASP' - In this model we find the Application Service Provider (ASP) offering various solutions to various problems. We highlight the following cases:

1. Customer license hosting: the customer owns a license for a specific application and deploys the license in the ASP's environment. This case also allows for aggregation of licenses.
2. Embedded license: a dependant software vendor commercialises its templates through the ASP. This case implies a license dependency to be solved, accounted and billed by the ASP.
3. License redirection: a third party (external consultant) owns a license and deploys the full license or part of it (sub-license) to carry out a specific project for the customer. Proper accounting is needed.
4. License reselling: the ASP resells the ISV's licenses for third-party use. ISVs may prefer to minimise the number of contacts they sell directly to and eventually minimise the risk for non-payments. Also for small software vendors, the ASP makes the access to market easier.

License extension - The license extension model allows end users to extend their licenses in both their Local Area Network (LAN) and distributed environments on-demand, e.g. for workload peaks. The license server manages the process of the extension of licenses, e.g. in terms of accounting and license administration. **License aggregation** - Most contracts between ISVs and end users restrict the license usage to LAN. The license aggregation model allows the use of licenses that belong to different sites and brings them together to form a single license token. These licenses can come from either the ISV or the ASP.

3.2 Architecture

The SmartLM License Service follows a layered architecture comprising 6 layers: Coallocation, Authentication, Administration, Management, Business, and Persistency. Figure 1 depicts the layered architecture of SmartLM highlighting the major communication paths between the components. The following paragraphs describe the different layers, the components inside a layer, and their interaction with other components. Finally, since security affects all layers, the fundamentals of the orthogonal SmartLM security are described.

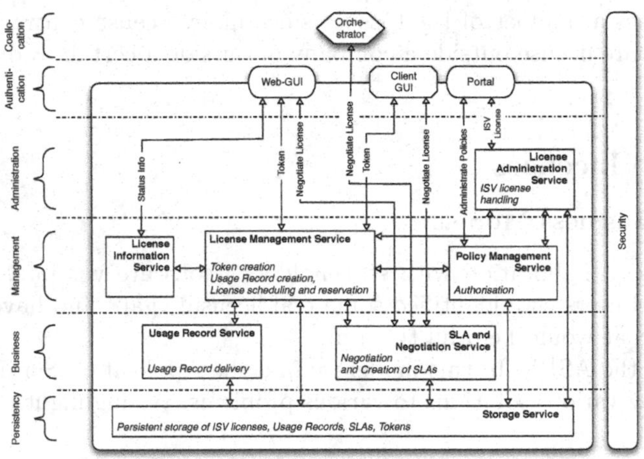

Fig. 1. Architecture of the license service

3.3 License Service

The license service is capable to manage all licenses that support the new licensing mechanism owned by a company. It provides a single point for license management and an easy and comfortable access to the entire license information either through a graphical user interface or the command-line. For redundancy multiple synchronised instances of the service may be hosted on different servers. When a company buys a license from a software vendor, the license is added to the license service using the License Administration Service (LAS). This is the main contact point for the ISV and the license service administrators in general. It acts as a proxy to forward the requests to the various internal components of the license service not accessible for external actors like ISVs or users and to report back the responses. In particular it interacts with the License Management Service, the License Information Service (LIS) and the Policy Management Service. The actions performed through the LAS interface are related to license, authorisation and policy management. The License Management Service may then fork software license tokens from this license once the user's request for a license has been accepted. Policies of the ISV and local policies are used by the policy management service to authorise the user's request.

The License Information Service allows both users and administrators to retrieve information on installed ISV licenses, licenses available or in use. When a user requests a license for an application or a feature of an application from the license service, the terms of license usage are negotiated between the user and the service through the SLA and negotiation service and then embedded in a Service Level Agreement document following the WS-Agreement [3] specification. The negotiation is based on templates specific to the application. The cost resulting from license request is calculated beforehand and becomes part of the SLA. This allows to easily check the license cost against budget constraints for users or user groups implemented in UVOS [10]. After creating the token the information relevant for accounting and billing is passed to the Accounting and Billing Service (ABS) through the usage record service in form of a usage record.

3.4 SLAs and Negotiation

The SLA and Negotiation service provides license mechanisms based on WS-Agreement/WS-Agreement Negotiation [8]. The Service is responsible of creating Service Level Agreements as a result of a user request for a license addressed to the license server. The created SLA describes all specific conditions of the application usage the user is entitled to, e.g. application id, duration, number of processors and guarantees like the maximum cost, etc. In order to implement WS-Agreement and WS-Agreement Negotiation, the SmartLM component SLA and Negotiation Service uses the WS-Agreement Framework for Java (WSAG4J) [11]. WSAG4J implements the WS-Agreement protocol and also the negotiation extension.

4 Security

One of the strict requirements of the SmartLM project was to enable licensing without constant connection to the network and thus without constant connection to the license server hosted by the user's home organisation. This was achieved by introducing signed documents conveying the information in an unalterable manner, such that their contents can be verified at the appropriate locations, i. e. in the application. The documents we introduced were *licenses*, *authorisations*, and *license tokens*. Figure 2 shows the flow of documents when using the SmartLM license mechanism. After a license has been requested from the ISV for a particular license server, a license is sent to the license server and it is ensured that a valid authorisation is available. Authorisations express the trust of the ISV in the license server. Tokens are needed by an application to run and verify its execution according to license restrictions. They contain information about features of the application which may be used, or the number of threads that can be run in accordance with the license.

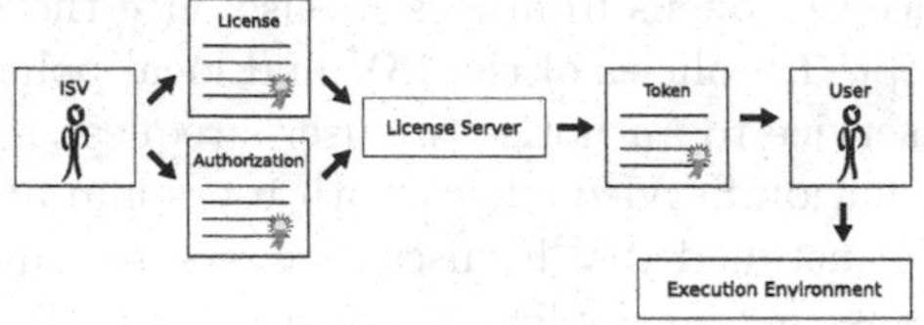

Fig. 2. License workflow

4.1 Licenses

Licenses are issued by ISVs to be used by a certain license server. The association with a particular server is ensured by enclosing the server's certificate in the signed part of the license. The server software will only accept licenses that have been specifically issued to the license server it is running in. If the license has been issued to a different license server, it will refuse to use the license. Licenses contain features, which are reserved by the license server when a token that uses these features is created.

4.2 Authorisation

An authorisation is a signed document expressing the trust of the ISV in a particular license server. Ingredients to this document are the ISV, who expresses the trust, the certificate of the license server, and a duration for which this authorisation is valid. We have decoupled authorisations from licenses for several reasons. **First** of all, one means for the application to validate the authorised issuance of tokens for the application would be to see the entire license document, as it was signed by the ISV. However, the license may contain information about the owner that may not be intended for the general public. E.g., if a large ASP buys licenses by the hundreds or thousands and receives these in one license document, then a user may gain insight into the capabilities and cost model of the provider. **Secondly**, the lifetime of a license can be much longer than the ISV can trust in the license server or its owner. Thus, authorisations are short lived compared to licenses. **Lastly**, tokens can have multiple parent licenses, which would all have to be included if the verification would be done using the server. It is thus easier to include a single authorisation, if the parent licenses are located in the same license server.

4.3 License Tokens

License tokens are issued by license servers and can be seen as children of the licenses available in the server. It is the license tokens that are necessary for a protected application to run. Multiple licenses can be parents of one token. The license server thus aggregates the features available from all licenses of the same type, which are available to it. Features need to be scheduled in order to ensure that the total of checked out features in all child tokens never exceeds the total of available features in all parent licenses. A license token is bound to a job's input by including digests of the input files in the token. As these digest values are signed by the license server, the token can only be used for a specific set of input files. Thus, a user gains no additional value from using the token multiple times. The digest values are contained in the InputHashes element of the license token and identified by file name. Some vendors used their own license enforcement mechanisms up to now. In order to foster the uptake of the SmartLM mechanism and to gain vendors' trust in the solution, a special `VendorKey` can be embedded into the token. It is computed given the token constraints and would in most cases just be a different encoding of these, e. g. using the vendor's legacy encoding. The license server supports vendor or even application specific plugins responsible for creating these VendorKeys. Thus, it is up to the vendor to provide such plugins for the license servers that use their tokens.

5 License Enforcement

The enforcement of the license constraints during the runtime of the application is the crucial point. This is the point where the above mentioned documents are validated and their contents evaluated. Remember, the application only receives the license token and the authorisation. For ease of use and most of all transmission of the token, the authorisation is embedded in the license token. The validation process of the two documents can be separated into three steps.

The **first step** is the validation of the documents' integrity. This is done by validating their respective digital signatures. If any of the documents fails to validate against its signature, then the application will not be executed. Also, the issuer of the authorisation must be the correct ISV, i. e. the vendor of the application. And lastly, the subject of the authorisation must be the license server which issued the token. If these conditions are met, then the license token can be considered trustworthy by the application and it can proceed with the evaluation of the token's contents. In the **second step**, some general restrictions of the token are checked. This mainly concerns the period in time, during which the token is valid. **Finally,** once all these generic constraints have been checked, through its SmartLM API the application can query the token for the features which need to be available for the application to execute. Also, whenever an input file is accessed for reading by the application, the digest value of the file needs to be compared with the one mentioned in the token. If the digest value does not match, then the token is invalid.

6 Conclusions and Future Work

We discussed a new approach for software licensing in distributed computing infrastructures based on Service Level Agreements presenting the basics of the SmartLM technology, new business models considering the interest of the software vendors, the users and the application service providers. Managing software licenses as Web service resources allows to achieve the flexibility required by distributed environments such as Grid or Clouds. The project is currently focussing on three crucial aspects of the licensing process: the re-negotiation of the Service Level Agreements [8], the accounting based on the actual usage of the resources and additional security and trustability of the license tokens. Moreover, additional enhancements like (i) the introduction of trusted clocks limiting the possibilities of cheating by manipulating time and date of the execution environment and (ii) the realisation of a trusted entity are under investigation and will become part of the system in near future.

Acknowledgements

Work reported in this paper has been co-funded by the European Commissions ICT programme in the FP7 project SmartLM under grant #216759 and by the German Federal Ministry of Education and Research in the D-Grid project under grant #01AK800A.

References

1. Armbrust, M., Fox, A., Griffith, R., Joseph, A.D., Katz, R., Konwinski, A., Lee, G., Patterson, D., Rabkin, A., Stoica, I., Zaharia, M.: Above the Clouds: A Berkeley View of Cloud Computing. Technical Report UCB/EECS-2009-28, University of California, Berkeley (2009)
2. Dalheimer, M., Pfreundt, F.-J.: GenLM: License Management for Grid and Cloud Computing Environments. In: Proceedings of the CCGrid Conference 2009 (2009)
3. Andrieux, A., et al.: Web Services Agreement Specification (WS-Agreement). Grid Forum Document GFD.107, Open Grid Forum, GFD.107 proposed recommendation (2007), `http://www.ogf.org/documents/GFD.107.pdf`
4. Li, J., Wldrich, O., Ziegler, W.: Towards sla-based software licenses, pp. 139–152 (2008)
5. EGEE now running Matlab parallel computing products (May 25, 2010), `http://www.scientific-computing.com/news`
6. Seventh Annual BSA/IDC Global software - 09 piracy study (May 25, 2010), `http://portal.bsa.org/globalpiracy2009/index.html`
7. Raekow, Y., Simmendinger, C., Krmer-Fuhrmann, O.: License management in grid and high performance computing. Computer Science, Research + Development 23(3-4), 275–281 (2009)
8. Rumpl, A., Wäldrich, O., Ziegler, W.: Extending WS-AGREEMENT with multi-round negotiation capability. In: Proceedings of Grid 2009 Workshop on SLA Usage in Grids. Springer, Heidelberg (2010)
9. SmartLM - Grid-friendly software licensing for location independent application execution (June 8, 2010), `http://www.smartlm.eu/`
10. UVOS - Unicore Virtual Organisation System (February 8, 2010), `http://uvos.chemomentum.org/`
11. WSAG4J - Web Services Agreement for Java (June 8, 2010), `http://packcs-e0.scai.fraunhofer.de/mss-project/wsag4j/index.html`

Actor-Driven Workflow Execution in Distributed Environments

Frank Berretz[1], Sascha Skorupa[1], Volker Sander[1], Adam Belloum[2], and Marian Bubak[2,3]

[1] FH Aachen University of Applied Sciences, Juelich, Germany
[2] University of Amsterdam, Amsterdam, Netherlands
[3] AGH University of Science and Technology, Krakow, Poland

Abstract. Currently, most workflow management systems (WfMS) in Grid environments provide push-oriented task distribution strategies, where tasks are directly bound to suitable resources. In those scenarios the dedicated resources execute the submitted tasks according to the request of a WfMS or sometimes by support of a Meta-Scheduling service. This approach has specific problems, especially because of various conditions and constrains that have to be taken into account like local policies or the sites' autonomy. To deal with such issues, this paper takes a closer look to the task distribution strategies. The established Grid WfMSs essentially support control-flow and data perspectives. However, they neglect the resource perspective. This paper exposes the advantages to deal with this perspective and demonstrates its feasability by a prototype implementation that integrates the missing resource patterns into UNICORE.

Keywords: Grid WfMS, Resource Pattern, UNICORE, jBPM, Human Tasks.

1 Introduction

Current e-Science infrastructures provide support for complex scientific processes that consist of orchestrated resources such as pure computational devices, data repositories, scientific instruments or applications. Grid environments are the common technical approach used to build these e-Science infrastructures on a middleware platform by a proper service layer. In order to support the orchestration of scientific tasks, many Grid middleware platforms offer a WfMS either as an integrative part or as an enactment service build on top of the middleware. So far, all popular Grid WfMSs use an approach that follows push patterns [4]. Here, a software agent, e.g. the workflow engine, actively exercises control about the progress of a workflow by pushing the individual tasks to selected resources according to the dependencies, provided by the workflow description. Consequently, in either case it is the WfMS that takes the initiative and causes the distribution process of newly created workflow tasks to occur. The alternative solution would be a pull-based actor-driven approach, where the commitment to undertake a specific task

M.R. Guarracino et al. (Eds.): Euro-Par 2010 Workshops, LNCS 6586, pp. 287–294, 2011.
© Springer-Verlag Berlin Heidelberg 2011

is initiated by the resource itself rather than the system. But the implementation of the associated pull patterns are not considered in today's Grid WfMSs that all prefer a system-initiated resource allocation [4]. In fact, all Grid WfMSs and their corresponding description languages focus on control-flow and data issues when mapping scientific processes onto workflows. In such data-centric systems resources are just regarded as dedicated machines that execute software as instructed. Within this paper the term "actor" is used to describe the entity that is actually responsible for the execution of a task. This means, e.g. an actor can be a computing Grid resource that executes a job according to a specific task. The proposal of this paper is to take a closer look on the resource perspective and especially the work distribution strategies. The participating resources who actually are the actors of a workflow should not be treated as passive automata with little influence to the assigned tasks and the way work is distributed. The modeling of the acting resources should be considered in a proper way and the connection between the resources and WfMSs is not just unidirectional. In the following paragraphs the focus is on the pros and cons of push- and pull-based work distribution approaches. Furthermore, this paper presents a possible prototype implementation of the pull-based approach on the example of the well known jBPM WfMS [11] and the UNICORE Grid middleware [7].

2 Related Works

This paper presents a novel concept for WfMSs in Grid environments. All known Grid WfMS approaches follow the push pattern. Desktop Grids, such as BOINC, EDGeS or pilot jobs in the DIRAC Pilot framework [10][9] can be viewed as intermediate approaches that emulate a pull concept. The presented task repository can be realized by using mechanism such as UNICORE XML-spaces [6], where computational resources request for jobs from a shared job queue implemented as tuple space. However, the space is targeted towards high-throughput computing and that's why it is a thin application without any logical layer that is required for our application domain. Clearly, the work among the emerging WS-HumanTask [12] standard is related to the presented concept. There, a model is described that enables the integration of human beings in service-oriented applications like BPEL processes. In the proposed architecture the WfMS is separated from a task processor, which is a standalone component, exposed as a service to manage tasks' lifecycles. But in contrast to the task processor of WS-HumanTask the task repository should manage tasks for any kind of actors.

3 Task Distribution to Resources

As indicated in the introduction the currently used Grid WfMSs primarily focus on the control-flow and data perspectives, while neglecting the resource perspective of the well-known workflow patterns. From a resource's perspective the manner in which tasks are advertised and ultimately bound for execution is of particular importance. In Figure 1 a part of the state transition diagram for

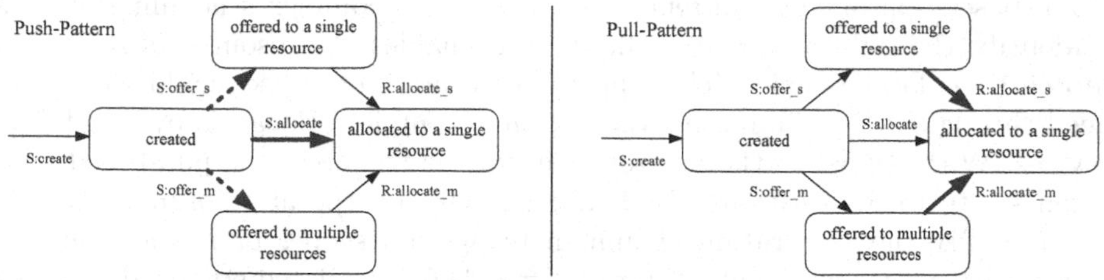

Fig. 1. Patterns of the resource perspective to bind resources to tasks [1]. Possible task states are denoted by boxes and transitions by edges. Blue edges indicate the applicable transitions supported by the particular pattern. Dash doted edges indicate that this state transitions only make sense if there is a transition of a pull pattern.

tasks is illustrated according to Aalst et al. [1]. In this paper, we focus on the allocation process, which is performed after a task is created and before it is executed by a suitable resource.

After a workflow task comes into existence, it is set into the `created` state, indicating that it is capable of being executed. Here, the task has not been bound to a specific resource for execution. Obviously, there are multiple possible paths through these states for an individual task. The edges within this diagram are prefixed with either an `S` or an `R` indicating that the transition is initiated by the WfMS or resource respectively. Essentially, there is a distinction between push- and pull-patterns, identified by the initiator of the various transitions. The state transitions that belong to the push-patterns are typically initiated by the WfMS for `created` tasks. So, these push-patterns concentrate on the subject of making resources aware of available tasks to execute. This can be realized in three different ways leading to distinct subsequent states. In today's Grid WfMSs, a task is usually allocated to a suitable resource explicitly denoted by the `s:allocate` operation. Hence, the resources are always allocated by the system. Indeed, most Grid WfMSs use schedulers and information systems to identify the most appropriate resource for the task allocation. Nevertheless, the real binding of a task to a resource is initiated by the system. Consequently, the alternative courses of action indicated by the states `offered to a single resource` and `offered to multiple resources` are not considered in common Grid WfMSs. This means in turn that the resource-initiated operations of the pull-patterns like `R:allocate_s` and `R:allocate_m` are not implemented in current Grid WfMSs. This is exactly the gap that the concepts presented in this paper aimed to bridge. The feasibility of our concepts is discussed in section 3.

The integration of such pull-pattern might solve various existing problems with regard to the interactions between the WfMSs and the resources. For instance, pushing each job from the WfMS to the resources requires efficient working Meta-Schedulers [3] that have to be to be able to coordinate and allocate resources across multiple administrative domains. These Meta-Schedulers have to consider various conditions and constraints, like local policies and the autonomy of each site, security issues like authentication and authorization as well as the heterogeneity of the different sites and their local scheduling systems.

A pull-based approach could remove the need for a complex scheduling process to identify the right resource explicitly and enables the resource providers to enforce their local policies. This approach to distribute tasks could effectively speed throughput by eliminating the notion of complex allocation by scheduling services. With regard to the heterogeneity of the resources the pull-based allocation strategies for tasks are also benificial. The incorporation of more specific resources like the integration of human beings, telescopes or medical devices is, however, a rather difficult task that often lacks of related standards such as JSDL for job submission to computational resources. Standards like the emerging WS-HumanTask [12] that might address this issue are neither sufficiently supported by Grids nor cover all kinds of specific resources. We believe the main reasons for the troublesome incorporation of specific resources are the commonly used push-based allocation mechanism, which postulates that a WfMS or any other job distributer require a set of well-known interfaces to interact with the resources. While OGSA provides a general framework for this, more details such as provided by JSDL are needed for specific resources. Because this assumption cannot be fulfilled with reasonable expenditure and in absence of related standards, it is currently hard to join the push-oriented model to the ambition of integrating special resources. The proposed pull-based task distribution strategy makes this goal relatively easy to realize because it opens the way to integrate resources that do not have a well-defined interface. Therefore, it is necessary to offer tasks to execute to resources, e.g. by informing multiple suitable resources of the existence of a specific task. In this case the WfMS does not attempt, which resource should undertake the task. So the resources, to which the task is offered, are free to choose whether they are interested in undertaking the task or not. Generally, this procedure results in the task being placed on a specific task list of the individual resources for later execution. In the proposed pull concept actors are the driving force of the execution of a workflow. Indeed, this approach makes a centralized resource control e.g. by scheduling systems impractical. But, at the same time it opens new perspectives with respect to community approaches, where members delegate their resources to execute tasks as actors for the benefit of a community.

4 UNICORE Middleware Integration

The above discussed concept of using pull patterns to bind resources to tasks has been ported to existing Grid technologies in the scope of the ongoing project HiX4AGWS [8]. In particular, the UNICORE Grid middleware has been extended by establishing a corresponding task repository to allow an actor-driven execution of tasks. The resulting UNICORE architecture is illustrated in figure 2. A starting point for integrating the pull-based approach has been the jBPM WfMS [11]. The jBPM engine that is a suitable candidate for the realization of the pull-based approach especially because of its expandability supports the usual workflow control-flow and data patterns [1].

In the first step the jBPM engine has been integrated to UNICORE framework similarly to the actually used Chemomentum engine [7]. The fundamental

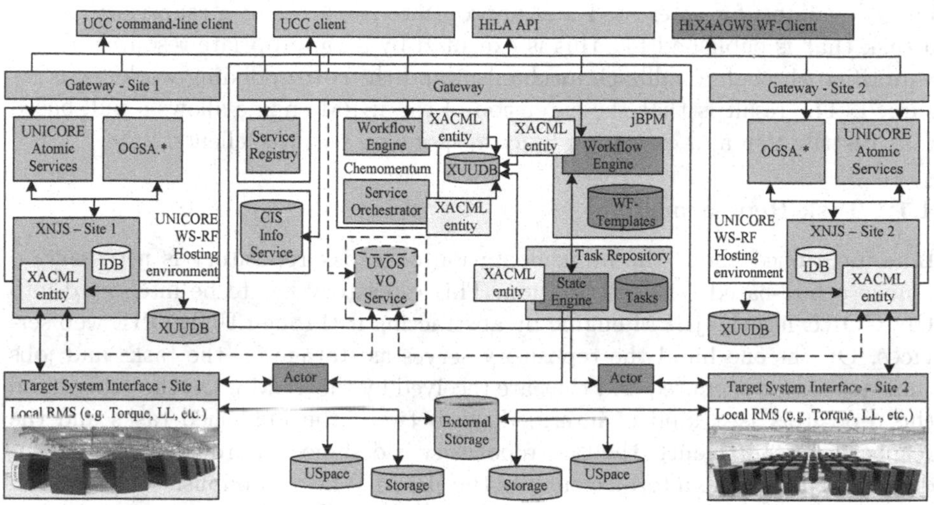

Fig. 2. Architecture of the prototype and its integration into UNICORE. The grey boxes represent the UNICORE components that have not been changed. Green highlighted boxes indicate the components implemented within the HiX4AGWS project.

difference between these two WfMSs is the concept of abstract and concrete workflows. Thereby an abstract workflow can be regarded as a generalization of a business case whose instances are referred to as concrete workflows. In jBPM an abstract workflow has to be deployed before it can be instantiated as often as desired to finally execute several concrete workflows. The Chemomentum system lacks of this concept to distinct between abstract and concrete workflows. Here, a workflow modeled by a user is executed just once immediately after the submission. Therefore, the jBPM engine offers some advantages, particularly with respect to the reusability of workflows and hence to a collaborative working.

For the purpose of the UNICORE integration of jBPM, the essential interfaces of the WfMS, e.g. to deploy or delete abstract workflows, has been abstracted through web services. Endpoint references (EPRs) are used to explicitly identify workflows. For instance, once a abstract workflow is deployed, in form of a jPDL schema conform XML document [11], the associated web service operation returns the relevant EPR to the invoking entity. Afterwards, this EPR can then be used to create concrete workflows or to delete the deployment and all associated instances. If, e.g., a wrong EPR is used to instantiate a workflow or any other internal or external failures occur, all web service operations are able to notify the invoking entity with the help of a corresponding exception handling. After successfully integrating jBPM into UNICORE by the explained web services, the next step is to focus on the actually intended goals: Autonomous resources should be able to apply for jobs in a pull-based way. Therefore, a new kind of task has been introduced to jBPM. During the processing of this new task, jBPM contacts an external repository, where the associated task description is published. That means the task is not executed by the WfMS on the local UNICORE site, but is available for interested and appropriate resources in a repository. After, a task that is published like this is executed by an appropriate resource, jBPM is notified through a callback mechanism and the corresponding workflow is resumed. The result is that the extension of the jBPM engine allows a pull-based task distribution and execution by corresponding resource clients.

4.1 Task Repository

Like mentioned above the implementation of a task repository is necessary to realize a pull-based task distribution. This repository has to be integrated into UNICORE like the jBPM engine by abstracting it through UNICORE web services. On the one hand the repository serves as storage for the tasks and jobs that need to be executed and that are received by the WfMS. On the other hand the repository is a kind of intermediary between the published tasks and the respective actors. Hence, the task repository is designed to provide two independent interfaces. One interface enables the jBPM WfMS to publish jobs that can be executed by appropriate actors. The second interface allows resources to deal with tasks, e.g. to query for tasks, waiting for them and to work on these tasks.

Once the WfMS publishes a task, a wrapper object is created and stored in the repository. This object consists of the task description, which can be a JSDL job and resource description. The resource description is used to define which role a resource must possess to claim and execute the task. This process corresponds to a role-based access control, which also allows working across various VOs. If a resource provider wants to apply for specific kinds of tasks, he just has to get the associated role. Besides this information, which is particularly necessary for the communication to the actors, the wrapper object also consists of callback information. This information allows notifying the WfMS and respectively the corresponding workflow instance about a successful execution of a task to trigger the workflow's progress. The current status of a task is additional an essential information stored in the wrapper object. For this purpose a state engine has been implemented to manage the different states of a published task and the transitions between them. The associated state diagram for the tasks is shown in figure 3. The presented actions and their resulting state transitions are abstracted by web service operations that can be invoked by the actors. Hence, the actors are able to communicate with the task repository by web service operations like claim(), start(), finish() or cancel(). The unique identification of a task is again directed through EPRs. An integrated exception framework notifies the actors about invalid state transitions or faulty accesses to EPRs.

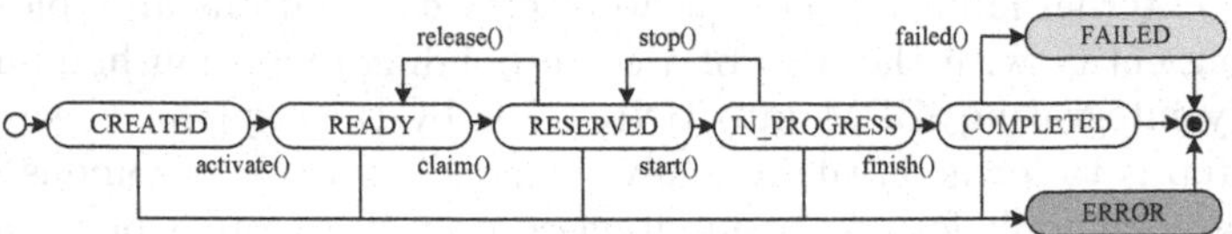

Fig. 3. The task repository's state engine including all states represented by oval boxes, transitions and its triggering actions represented by the arrows and its labels

4.2 Evaluation - Human Tasks in Unicore

UNICORE uses the Chemomentum engine to execute workflows. In this WfMS the resource allocation is done by the service orchestrator, who submits JSDL jobs to appropriate resources, supervises their execution and informs the workflow enginge of job completion. So, the service orchestrator can be identified as the resource broker or scheduler working according to the push pattern, because he determines which resource is used for a specific job. The process of job submission only works, if the service orchestrator knows the interfaces of the resources, which makes the integration of more specific resources like humans hard to realize. Because sometimes a resource may even be a person, one goal of our project was to integrate human tasks into UNICORE workflows. This is a useful feature, if workflows require a human step, such as verification by a scientist that the workflow is proceeding correctly. To integrate human resources into a workflow execution, our jBPM integration prefer a hybrid usage of pull and push patterns for task distribution. This approach also serves as an evaluation for the implemented pull patterns. In the hybrid approach, a task to be executed by a human can explicitly be denoted as "pull"-task in the workflow description. The jBPM engine sends such a task to the task repository where a human can pick up it for execution according to the pull pattern. Each task that is not denoted as pull-task is treated like a common Grid job that can be sent to the service orchestrator by using its web service interface. This solution enables the integration of human resources into UNICORE workflows, whereby a first project goal can be complied. Furthermore, the pull-based approach can be evaluated by executing a workflow that contains a human step on our system. At this time, it is not possible to make performance analysis because the task repository and the corresponding pull concept lacks a comprehensive security concept. For this reason, it is inequitable to compare workflow execution of the jBPM and the Chemomentum engine. Such analysis are planned for the future.

5 Conclusions and Future Works

This paper has shown that current Grid WfMSs neglect the resource perspective of the workflow patterns resulting in several problems that are mentioned in the previous sections. Developments as mentioned in section 4 try to integrate the resources' point of view into Grids. But these approaches continue to place importance on well known standards. The proposed actor-driven approach binds resources to tasks through an intermediate task repository presented in this paper. The prototype prepares a way to cleanly integrate pull patterns into UNICORE. Important components are the task repository and the actors. Therefore, the Grid resources as well as human resources are connected to the task repository. Thus, e.g. human beings are able to claim and execute tasks like the qualitative evaluation of interim results resulting in a clean integration in scientific workflows. The next steps consist of the integration of additional resources by proper actors into the Grid. Particularly, the expansion of the actor-based pull concept by using Cloud computing technologies e.g. to incorporate resources from community clouds may increase the elasticity of the system with respect to the amount of users as well as the amount of available resources.

Acknowledgements. This research is conducted in the context of the History tracing XML for an Actor-driven Grid-enabled Workflow System project, supported by the Federal Ministry of Education and Research and the Federation of Industrial Research Associations in Germany.

References

1. Van der Aalst, W.M.P., et al.: Workflow Resource Patterns. BETA Working Paper Series, WP 127, Eindhoven University of Technology, Eindhoven (2004)
2. Van der Aalst, W.M.P., et al.: Workflow Patterns. Distributed Parallel Databases 14(1), 5–51 (2003)
3. Wldrich, O., Wieder, P., Ziegler, W.: A Meta-Scheduling Service for Co-allocating Arbitrary Types of Resources. CoreGRID Technical Report, Nr TR-0010 (2005)
4. Buyya, R., Yu, J.: A taxonomy of scientific workflow systems for grid computing. Journal of Grid Computing 3(3-4), 171–200 (2005)
5. Foster, I., Kesselman, C., Tuecke, S.: The Anatomy of the Grid: Enabling Scalable Virtual Organization. International Journal of Supercomputer Applications 15(3), 200–222 (2001)
6. Schuller, B., Schumacher, M.: Space-Based Approach to High-Throughput Computations in UNICORE 6 Grids. In: Euro-Par 2008 Workshops, pp. 75–83 (2009)
7. Schuller, B., et al.: Chemomentum - UNICORE 6 based infrastructure for complex applications in science and technology. In: Bougé, L., Forsell, M., Träff, J.L., Streit, A., Ziegler, W., Alexander, M., Childs, S. (eds.) Euro-Par Workshops 2007. LNCS, vol. 4854, pp. 82–93. Springer, Heidelberg (2008)
8. Berretz, F., Skorupa, S., Sander, V., Belloum, A.: Towards an Actor-Driven WfMS for Grids. In: Proceedings of CTS 2010, Chicago, pp. 611–617 (2010)
9. Casajus, A., et al.: DIRAC Pilot Framework and the DIRAC Workload Management System. Journal of Physics: Conference Series 219(6) (2010)
10. Urbah, E., et al.: EDGeS: Bridging EGEE to BOINC and XtremWeb. Journal of Grid Computing 7(3), 335–354 (2009)
11. jBPM Developers Guide (January 2010), `http://docs.jboss.com/jbpm/v4/devguide`
12. WS-HumanTask V1.0. (June 2007), `http://xml.coverpages.org/WS-HumanTask-V1-0706.pdf`

First Class Futures: Specification and Implementation of Update Strategies

Ludovic Henrio[1], Muhammad Uzair Khan[1],
Nadia Ranaldo[2], and Eugenio Zimeo[2]

[1] INRIA – CNRS – I3S – Université de Nice Sophia-Antipolis
{mkhan,lhenrio}@sophia.inria.fr
[2] University of Sannio
{ranaldo,zimeo}@unisannio.it

1 Introduction

Futures are language constructs that improve concurrency in a natural and transparent way. A *future* is a place holder for a result of a concurrent computation [5]. Once the computation is complete and a result (called *future value*) is available, the placeholder is *replaced* by the result. Access to an unresolved future results in the caller being blocked, until the result becomes available. Results are only awaited when they are really needed which helps in improving the parallelization. Futures may be created transparently or explicitly. For explicit creation, specific language constructs are necessary to create the futures and to fetch the result. *Transparent* futures, on the other hand, are managed by the underlying middleware and the program syntax remains unchanged; futures have the same type as the actual result. Some frameworks allow futures to be passed to other processes. Such futures are called *First class futures* [2]. Replacing a future reference by the corresponding calculated value is called "future update". In this case additional mechanisms to update futures are required not only at the creator, but also on all processes that receive a future. First class futures offer greater flexibility in application design and can significantly improve concurrency both in object-oriented and procedural paradigms like workflows [12].

Our work focuses on various future update strategies; it can be considered as an extension of [2] and [10] through a language-independent approach that makes it applicable to various existing frameworks that support first class futures. The experiments are performed with ProActive [1], which is a middleware providing first-class futures. Formal semantics for our strategies are presented in [6]. The main contributions of this paper are: a semi-formal event-like notation to model the future update strategies, and a description of three different update strategies using this notation (Section 2); results from experiments carried out to study the efficiency of strategies (Section 3).

1.1 Related Works

Futures, first introduced in Multilisp [5] and ABCL/1 [11] are used as constructs for concurrency and data flow synchronization. Frameworks that make

M.R. Guarracino et al. (Eds.): Euro-Par 2010 Workshops, LNCS 6586, pp. 295–303, 2011.
© Springer-Verlag Berlin Heidelberg 2011

use of explicit constructs for creating futures include Multilisp [5], λ-calculus [9], SafeFuture API [13] and ABCL/f [11]. In contrast, futures are created implicitly in frameworks like ASP [2], AmbientTalk [4] and ProActive [1]. This implicit creation corresponds to asynchronous invocation. A key benefit of the implicit creation is that no distinction is made between local and remote operations in the program. Additionally, the futures can be accessed explicitly or implicitly. In case of explicit access, operations like *claim* and *touch*, etc., are used to access the future [7, 11]. For implicit access, the synchronization on the future is triggered automatically by the operations manipulating the actual result value. Accessing a future that has not been updated, results in the caller being blocked.

Creol [3] allows for explicit control over data-flow synchronizations. Creol has been extended to support first class futures. In contrast to our work, future creation and manipulation in Creol is explicit. ASP [2] and ProActive [1], have transparent first-class futures and the synchronization is transparent and data-flow oriented. In AmbientTalk, futures are also first-class and transparently manipulated; but the future access is a non-blocking operation thus avoiding the possibility of a dead lock as there is no synchronization. Processes interested in the future value are registered as observers, and results are sent to registered observers when they are computed. The future update strategy in AmbientTalk is close to the eager-message based strategy presented here. [13] provides a *safe* extension to Java futures, but with explicit creation and access.

2 Modeling Different Future Update Strategies

This section gives a semi-formal definition for the three main future update strategies. Those strategies explain how future references can be updated when they are spread into different processes.

2.1 General Notation

This section presents a brief overview of the various notation and entities that we use to model the future update strategies. We denote by $\mathcal{A}$ the set of processes (also called *activities*); α, β, ... $\in \mathcal{A}$ range over processes. $\mathcal{F}$ denotes the set of future identifiers, each future identifier is of the form $f^{\alpha\rightarrow\beta}$, which represents the future f created by the activity α, and being calculated by β. As each object needs to keep track of the futures it has received, we make use of some local lists for this purpose. There is one *future list* for each activity α. It represents the location where the futures are stored in local memory.

$$\mathcal{FL}_\alpha \colon \mathcal{F} \mapsto \mathcal{P}(Loc)$$

Locations, called *loc* in the following and of type *Loc*, refer to the in-memory position of the future. To keep track of activities to which a future is to be sent, a *future recipient* list is stored in each process.

$$\mathcal{FR}_\delta \colon \mathcal{F} \mapsto \mathcal{P}(\mathcal{A})$$

$\gamma \in \mathcal{FR}_\delta\,(f^{\alpha\to\beta})$ if the future value for $f^{\alpha\to\beta}$ has to be sent from δ to γ. It should be noted that each $f^{\alpha\to\beta}$ can be mapped to several locations in $\mathcal{FL}$ or several activities in $\mathcal{FR}$. $\mathcal{FR}$ and $\mathcal{FL}$ are initialized to empty mapping on all processes. We use an event-like notation to define the different strategies. Operations triggered by the strategies, and events triggered by the rest of the middleware are described respectively in bellow. Events are indexed by the activity on which they occur, or $\alpha \to \beta$ for a communication from α to β.

Operations

Register Future - Reg: $\mathcal{F} \times \mathcal{B} \times \mathcal{F} \mapsto \mathcal{P}(\mathcal{B})$

We define an operation *Reg* that is given a future, a process and a mapping $\mathcal{F} \mapsto \mathcal{P}(\mathcal{B})$ (either $\mathcal{FL}$ when $\mathcal{B} = Loc$, or $\mathcal{FR}$ when $\mathcal{B} = \mathcal{A}$). $Reg_\gamma(f^{\alpha\to\beta}, b, L)$ replaces the list L by the list L' defined as follows:

$$L'(f_2^{\alpha'\to\beta'}) = \begin{cases} L(f^{\alpha\to\beta}) \cup \{b\} & \text{if } f_2^{\alpha'\to\beta'} = f^{\alpha\to\beta} \\ L(f_2^{\alpha'\to\beta'}) & \text{else} \end{cases}$$

The *Reg* operation replaces the old mapping L with a new one containing the additional mapping. An example of its usage could be $Reg_\gamma(f^{\alpha\to\beta}, loc, \mathcal{FL}_\gamma)$ which adds to the $\mathcal{FL}_\gamma$ list, a new location *loc* associated to future $f^{\alpha\to\beta}$.

Locally Update future with value - Update: $Loc \times Value$

Once the value for a given future is received, this operation is triggered to update all corresponding local futures with this value. The operation $Update_\gamma(f^{\alpha\to\beta}, v)$ replaces, in the activity γ, each reference to the future $f^{\alpha\to\beta}$ by the value v. Remember the set of locations of these references is $\mathcal{FL}_\gamma(f^{\alpha\to\beta})$.

Clear future from list - Clear: $\mathcal{F} \times \mathcal{F} \mapsto \mathcal{P}(\mathcal{B})$

The clear operation $Clear(f^{\alpha\to\beta}, L)$ removes the entry for future $f^{\alpha\to\beta}$ from the list L. It will be used after a future update to clear entries for the updated future. It replaces the list L by the list L' defined by:

$$L'(f_2^{\alpha'\to\beta'}) = \begin{cases} L(f_2^{\alpha'\to\beta'}) & \text{if } f_2^{\alpha'\to\beta'} \neq f^{\alpha\to\beta} \\ \emptyset & \text{else} \end{cases}$$

Send future value: SendValue: $\mathcal{F} \times Loc \times Value$

Send is used when a process needs to send the value of a computed future to another process in order to update the future there. $SendValue_{\delta\to\gamma}(f^{\alpha\to\beta}, loc, v)$ sends the value v for the future $f^{\alpha\to\beta}$ from δ to γ. Sending a future value can trigger send future reference events, *SendRef*, for all the future references contained in the value v. This operation is detailed in Sections 2.2, 2.3, and 2.4

Events. Future update strategies react to events, triggered by the application or the middleware, presented below.

Create future: Create: $\mathcal{F} \times Loc$

$Create_\alpha(f^{\alpha\to\beta}, loc)$ is triggered when α creates a future that will be calculated by the process β. The semantics of this event is similar for all strategies: it registers the future in the future list $\mathcal{FL}$ of the creating process.

$$Create_\alpha(f^{\alpha\to\beta}, loc) \triangleq Reg_\alpha(f^{\alpha\to\beta}, loc, \mathcal{FL}_\alpha)$$

Send future reference: SendRef: $\mathcal{F} \times Loc$
$SendRef_{\delta \rightarrow \gamma}(f^{\alpha \rightarrow \beta}, loc)$ occurs when the process δ sends the future reference $f^{\alpha \rightarrow \beta}$ to γ and the future is stored at the location *loc* on the receiver side. The details of this operation will be described in Sections 2.2, 2.3, and 2.4.

Future computed: FutureComputed: $\mathcal{F} \times Value$
$FutureComputed_{\beta}(f^{\alpha \rightarrow \beta}, val)$ occurs when the value *val* of future $f^{\alpha \rightarrow \beta}$ has been computed by β.

Wait-by-necessity: Wait: $\mathcal{A}$
This event is triggered when a process accesses an unresolved future. This corresponds to *get* or *touch* operation in [8, 7, 11]. For the two eager strategies it simply causes the process to be blocked until the value is received. For the lazy strategy, this event retrieves the future value, see Section 2.4.

2.2 Eager Forward-Based Strategy

In this strategy, each process remembers the processes to which it has forwarded the future. When the value is available, it is sent to all such processes. The list of processes to which a process β should send the future value for $f^{\alpha \rightarrow \beta}$ is $\mathcal{FR}_{\beta}(f^{\alpha \rightarrow \beta})$. It is the list of processes to which β has sent the future reference.

Figure 1 shows an example of this strategy. Process A makes an asynchronous call on process H and receives the future $f^{A \rightarrow H}$. A then passes this future to B, which in turn passes the future to C, D and E. Finally C passes the future to F. Each time a future is forwarded, i.e., upon a *SendRef* message, the forwarding process δ adds the destination to its $\mathcal{FR}_{\delta}(f^{A \rightarrow H})$. When the result for $f^{A \rightarrow H}$ is available, it is communicated to A using *SendValue* message. A then forwards the update on B ($\mathcal{FR}_A(f^{A \rightarrow H}) = \{B\}$). B can make concurrent updates on C, E and D ($\mathcal{FR}_B(f^{A \rightarrow H}) = \{C, E, D\}$). Finally, the occurrence in F is updated by C ($\mathcal{FR}_F(f^{A \rightarrow H}) = \{C\}$).

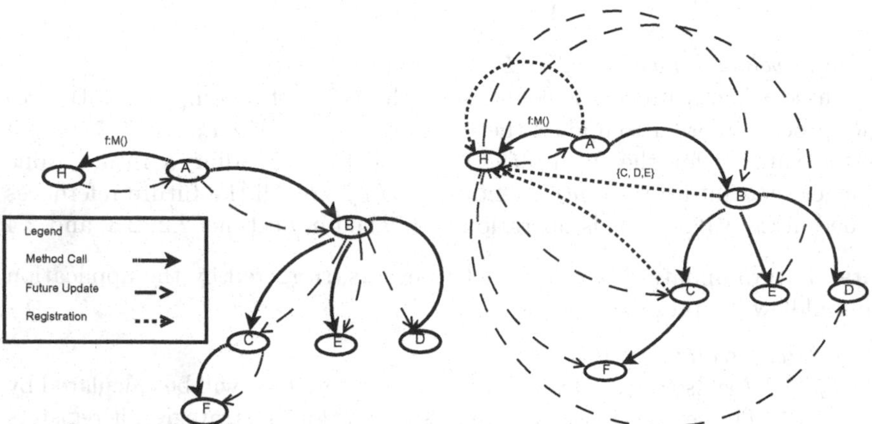

Fig. 1. Eager Forward Based

Fig. 2. Eager Message Based

Send Future Reference. When a process δ sends a future $f^{\alpha\to\beta}$ to a process γ, the sender registers the destination process in $\mathcal{FR}_\delta$, and the destination process registers the location of the future in $\mathcal{FL}_\gamma$.

$$SendRef_{\delta\to\gamma}(f^{\alpha\to\beta}, loc) \triangleq Reg_\delta(f^{\alpha\to\beta}, \gamma, FR_\delta);\quad Reg_\gamma(f^{\alpha\to\beta}, loc, \mathcal{FL}_\gamma)$$

Future Computed. Once the value (val) of a future $f^{\alpha\to\beta}$ has been computed at process β, it is immediately sent to all the processes that belong to $\mathcal{FR}_\beta(f^{\alpha\to\beta})$. This will trigger chains of *SendValue* operations. Once the future value have been sent, the future recipient list is no longer useful:

$$\begin{aligned} FutureComputed_\beta(f^{\alpha\to\beta}, val) \triangleq\ & \forall\, \delta \in \mathcal{FR}_\beta(f^{\alpha\to\beta}),\ SendValue_{\beta\to\delta}(f^{\alpha\to\beta}, val) \\ & Clear_\beta(f^{\alpha\to\beta}, \mathcal{FR}_\beta)) \end{aligned}$$

Send Future Value. When a future value is received, the receiver first updates all the local references, and then sends the future value to all the processes to which it had forwarded the future (the processes in its $\mathcal{FR}$ list). The operation is recursive, because the destination process of *SendValue* may also need to update further futures. This operation can potentially trigger the *SendRef* operation in case of nested futures. The future locations and future recipient lists for this future are not needed anymore after those steps:

$$\begin{aligned} SendValue_{\delta\to\epsilon}(f^{\alpha\to\beta}, value) \triangleq\ & \forall\, loc \in \mathcal{FL}_\epsilon(f^{\alpha\to\beta}),\ Update_\epsilon(loc, value), \\ & Clear_\epsilon(f^{\alpha\to\beta}, \mathcal{FL}_\epsilon) \\ & \forall\, \gamma \in \mathcal{FR}_\epsilon(f^{\alpha\to\beta}),\ SendValue_{\epsilon\to\gamma}(f^{\alpha\to\beta}, value), \\ & Clear_\epsilon(f^{\alpha\to\beta}, \mathcal{FR}_\epsilon) \end{aligned}$$

2.3 Eager Message-Based Strategy

In eager message-based strategy, the process β, computing the future value, is responsible for updating all processes which receive a future. Opposed to forward-based strategy where futures updates are performed in a distributed manner, here all updates are performed by same process β (home) in a centralized manner. Whenever, a process δ forwards a future to another process γ, it sends a message *SendRegReq* to the home process β, and updates the list of future recipients $\mathcal{FR}_\beta$. $\mathcal{FR}_\beta(f^{\alpha\to\beta})$ contains the set of processes to which $f^{\alpha\to\beta}$ has been forwarded.

Figure 2 shows an example of this strategy. When A forwards the future to process B a registration message *SendRegReq* is sent from A to H, registering B in $\mathcal{FR}_H$. Similarly we have a registration message sent to H from B adding C, E, and D to $\mathcal{FR}_H$; finally we have $\mathcal{FR}_H(f^{A\to H}) = \{A, B, C, D, E, F\}$.

Once the future result is available, H uses the *SendValue* message to communicate the value to all processes in $\mathcal{FR}_H(f^{A\to H})$.

Send Future Reference. In the message-based strategy when a future $f^{\alpha\to\beta}$ is forwarded by a process δ to a process γ, a registration message is sent to the process that will compute the future, β.

$$SendRef_{\delta\to\gamma}(f^{\alpha\to\beta}, \gamma, loc) \triangleq Reg_\beta(f^{\alpha\to\beta}, \gamma, \mathcal{FR}_\beta);\quad Reg_\gamma(f^{\alpha\to\beta}, loc, \mathcal{FL}_\gamma)$$

The registration $Reg_\beta(f^{\alpha\to\beta}, \gamma, \mathcal{FR}_\beta)$ is performed using a communication addressed to the home process β, and is called *SendRegReq* in Figure 2.

Future Computed. Once the execution is completed and the value is available in β, the process β sends the value to all the processes in $\mathcal{FR}_\beta(f^{\alpha\to\beta})$.

$$\begin{aligned}FutureComputed_\beta(f^{\alpha\to\beta}, val) \triangleq \forall\, \delta \in \mathcal{FR}_\beta(f^{\alpha\to\beta})\ SendValue_{\beta\to\delta}(f^{\alpha\to\beta}, val);\\ Clear_\beta(f^{\alpha\to\beta}, \mathcal{FR}_\beta)\end{aligned}$$

Send Future Value. Contrarily to forward-based strategy, there is no need to forward the future value when received, only local references are updated, and then the $\mathcal{FL}$ list can be cleared.

$$\begin{aligned}SendValue_{\beta\to\gamma}(f^{\alpha\to\beta}, val) \triangleq \forall\, loc \in \mathcal{FL}_\gamma(f^{\alpha\to\beta})\ Update_\gamma(loc, val);\\ Clear_\gamma(f^{\alpha\to\beta}, \mathcal{FL}_\gamma)\end{aligned}$$

The received future value may contain other futures as well. In this case, it can potentially trigger the send future reference operation.

2.4 Lazy Message-Based Strategy

The lazy strategy differs from the eager strategies in the sense that future values are only transmitted when absolutely required. When a process accesses a unresolved future, the access triggers the update. This strategy is somewhat similar to message-based strategy except the futures are updated only when and if necessary. In addition, each process now needs to store all the future values that it has computed. For this, we introduce another list, $\mathcal{FV}$ that stores these values: $\mathcal{FV}$: $\mathcal{F} \mapsto \mathcal{P}(Value)$. $\mathcal{FV}_\beta(f^{\alpha\to\beta})$, if defined, contains a singleton, which is the future value of $f^{\alpha\to\beta}$.

Compared to Figure 2, in the lazy strategy only the processes that require the future value register in $\mathcal{FR}_H$, $\mathcal{FR}_H(f^{A\to H}) = \{C, D\}$ if only C and D access the future. When the result is available, H communicates it to processes in $\mathcal{FR}_H(f^{A\to H})$. In addition, the value is stored in $\mathcal{FV}_H(f^{A\to H})$. If the future value is required later, it will be retrieved from $\mathcal{FV}_H(f^{A\to H})$.

Send future reference. This strategy does not require registration with home process when forwarding a future. Incoming futures are registered in FL_γ on the receiver. Once the value is received, all local references can be updated.

$$SendRef_{\delta\to\gamma}(f^{\alpha\to\beta}, \gamma, loc) \triangleq Reg_\gamma(f^{\alpha\to\beta}, loc, \mathcal{FL}_\gamma)$$

Wait-by necessity. Wait-by-necessity is triggered when the process tries to access the value of the future. We register the waiting process at β:

$$\textit{Wait-by-necessity}_\gamma(f^{\alpha\to\beta}) \triangleq SendRegReq_{\gamma\to\beta}(f^{\alpha\to\beta}, \gamma)$$

If the future has already been computed by β, the value is transmitted immediately. Otherwise, the request is added to the Future receivers list of β.

$$SendRegReq_{\gamma\to\beta}(f^{\alpha\to\beta}, \gamma) \triangleq \begin{cases} SendValue_{\beta\to\gamma}(f^{\alpha\to\beta}, val) & \text{if } \mathcal{FV}_\beta(f^{\alpha\to\beta}) = \{val\} \\ Reg_\beta(f^{\alpha\to\beta}, \gamma, \mathcal{FR}_\beta) & \text{if } f^{\alpha\to\beta} \notin dom(\mathcal{FV}_\beta)\end{cases}$$

Future Computed. When a result is computed, the value is stored in the future value list. Moreover, if there are pending requests for the value, then the value is sent to all the awaiting processes.

$$FutureComputed_{\beta}(f^{\alpha\rightarrow\beta}, val) \triangleq \forall\,\delta \in \mathcal{FR}_{\beta}(f^{\alpha\rightarrow\beta}) SendValue_{\beta\rightarrow\delta}(f^{\alpha\rightarrow\beta}, val)$$
$$Clear_{\beta}(f^{\alpha\rightarrow\beta}, \mathcal{FR}_{\beta});\quad Reg_{\beta}(f^{\alpha\rightarrow\beta}, val, \mathcal{FV}_{\beta})$$

Send Future Value. The *SendValue* operation is the same as for the eager message-based strategy:

$$SendValue_{\beta\rightarrow\gamma}(f^{\alpha\rightarrow\beta}, val) \triangleq \forall\, loc \in \mathcal{FL}_{\gamma}(f^{\alpha\rightarrow\beta})\ Update_{\gamma}(loc, val);$$
$$Clear_{\gamma}(f^{\alpha\rightarrow\beta}, \mathcal{FL}_{\gamma})$$

3 Experimental Evaluation

We conducted an experimentation with a real system in order to test the efficiency of the various strategies. We implemented our strategies using ProActive programming library(4.1). ProActive is based on the notion of active objects, abstracting processes with a unique thread and message queue. We deployed an application featuring a tree topology where each node is an active object. For the scope of the analysis, we kept the number of nodes accessing future value constant. The graph in Figure 3 compares the time needed to update futures for the evaluated strategies. Experiments are realized over trees of varying heights. Lazy strategy takes less time to update the futures since much less updates have to be made. Update time required for lazy and eager message-based strategies is roughly independent of the height of the tree. Eager-forward based strategy can take advantage of concurrent updates. On the other hand, it also gets more time to reach the bottom of high trees as shown by the shape of the graph. As the height of the tree increases, overheads increases due to time spent at intermediate nodes. As a result, at height 7, the time needed for updates is higher.

Figure 4 shows the time necessary to update a future along a simple chain of processes. Time taken by the lazy strategy is constant because only one update is made. Both the forward-based and message-based strategies scale in a linear

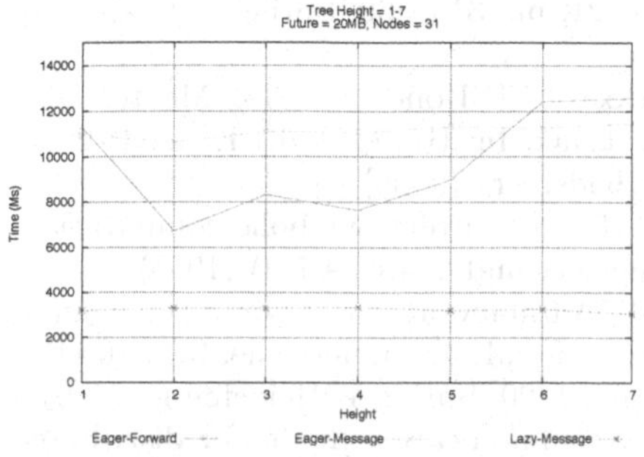

Fig. 3. Tree Configuration

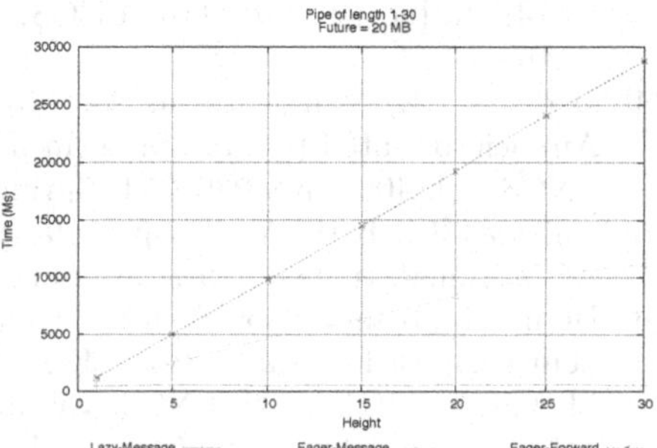

Fig. 4. Pipe configuration

manner. Future updates in eager forward-based strategy go through a number of intermediate steps before arriving at the final node, introducing additional delay. In message-based strategies, all updates are performed by same node in single step, resulting in a relatively constant update time.

4 Conclusion

This paper presented a semi-formal description of three strategies for updating first class futures. Our main contributions are: *A semi-formal event-like notation*: A language independent notation for modeling future update strategies; other frameworks using futures may benefit from our work. *Experimental results*: Implementation of different strategies in the ProActive to study the efficiency.

We hope this article will help answering the non-trivial question: "Which is the best future update strategy"? There is no single *best* strategy, rather the strategy should be adopted based on the application requirements, to summarize:

*E*ager forward-based strategy is more suitable when the number of intermediate processes and the future value are relatively small. *E*ager message-based strategy is more adapted for process chains since it ensures that all updates are made in relatively constant time. Due to its centralized nature, it may require more bandwidth and resources at the process that computes the future. *L*azy strategy is better suited for scenarios where not all processes with a given future require its result value. Considerable savings in network load can be achieved but this has to be balanced against the additional delay inherent in the design of lazy approach. Also results have to be stored for longer time.

References

[1] Caromel, D., Delbé, C., di Costanzo, A., Leyton, M.: ProActive: an integrated platform for programming and running applications on grids and P2P systems. Computational Methods in Science and Technology 12(1), 69–77 (2006)

[2] Caromel, D., Henrio, L.: A Theory of Distributed Object. Springer, Heidelberg (2005)

[3] de Boer, F.S., Clarke, D., Johnsen, E.B.: A complete guide to the future. In: De Nicola, R. (ed.) ESOP 2007. LNCS, vol. 4421, pp. 316–330. Springer, Heidelberg (2007)

[4] Dedecker, J., Van Cutsem, T., Mostinckx, S., D'Hondt, T., De Meuter, W.: Ambient-oriented programming in ambientTalk. In: Hu, Q. (ed.) ECOOP 2006. LNCS, vol. 4067, pp. 230–254. Springer, Heidelberg (2006)

[5] Halstead Jr., R.H.: Multilisp: A language for concurrent symbolic computation. ACM Transactions on Programming Languages and Systems 7(4) (1985)

[6] Henrio, L., Kammüller, F., Uzair Khan, M.: A framework for reasoning on component composition. In: de Boer, F.S., Bonsangue, M.M., Hallerstede, S., Leuschel, M. (eds.) FMCO 2009. LNCS, vol. 6286, pp. 1–20. Springer, Heidelberg (2010)

[7] Johnsen, E.B., Owe, O.: An asynchronous communication model for distributed concurrent objects. In: SEFM 2004 (2004)

[8] Johnsen, E.B., Owe, O., Chieh Yu, I.: Creol: a type-safe object-oriented model for distributed concurrent systems. Theor. Comput. Sci. 365 (2006)
[9] Niehren, J., Schwinghammer, J., Smolka, G.: A concurrent lambda calculus with futures. Theoretical Computer Science 364 (November 2006)
[10] Ranaldo, N., Zimeo, E.: Analysis of Different Future Objects Update Strategies in ProActive. In: IEEE International on IPDPS 2007, pp. 23–66 (2007)
[11] Taura, K., Matsuoka, S., Yonezawa, A.: ABCL/f: A Future-Based Polymorphic Typed Concurrent Object-Oriented Language - Its Design and Implementation. In: DIMACS 1994, vol. 18 (1994)
[12] Tretola, G., Zimeo, E.: Activity pre-scheduling for run-time optimisation of grid workflows. Journal of Systems Architecture 54(9) (2008)
[13] Welc, A., Jagannathan, S., Hosking, A.: Safe futures for java. SIGPLAN Not. 40(10), 439–453 (2005)

GroudSim: An Event-Based Simulation Framework for Computational Grids and Clouds

Simon Ostermann, Kassian Plankensteiner, Radu Prodan, and Thomas Fahringer*

Institute of Computer Science, University of Innsbruck, Technikerstr. 21a, 6020 Innsbruck, Austria
{simon,kassian.plankensteiner,radu,tf}@dps.uibk.ac.at

Abstract. We present GroudSim, a Grid and Cloud simulation toolkit for scientific applications based on a scalable simulation-independent discrete-event core. GroudSim provides a comprehensive set of features for complex simulation scenarios from simple job executions on leased computing resources to calculation of costs, and background load on resources. Simulations can be parameterised and are easily extendable by probability distribution packages for failures which normally occur in complex environments. Experimental results demonstrate the improved scalability of GroudSim compared to a related process-based approach.

1 Introduction

Scientific applications have a continuous demand for fast and scalable execution environments such as computational Grids to deliver results for ever increasing problem sizes or concurrent requests in a required timeframe. Today, a new trend named *Cloud computing* is to rent modern computational capabilities from specialised hosting companies, which frees research institutions from the burden of buying, operating, and maintaining expensive and rapidly deprecating hardware. This new class of Cloud resources raises new research questions in the field of resource management, scheduling, fault tolerance, or Quality of Service, requiring hundreds to thousands of simulation experiments for finding valid solutions. To enable and support such research, a scalable simulation framework is typically required for early testing and validation of results before the real deployment is performed. In Clouds, the role of a simulator becomes even more important, since cost models are an integrated part of any Cloud environment, in contrast to computational Grids where resources are often freely shared.

In previous research [11], we have demonstrated how Clouds have the potential of complementing Grids for large applications that do not benefit from fast enough resources required by their computational demands. Nevertheless, there is a lack of support in the community for scalable and easy to use simulation frameworks able to aid combined Grid and Cloud scientific research.

* This work is partially funded by the European Union under grant agreement number 261585/SHIWA Project.

M.R. Guarracino et al. (Eds.): Euro-Par 2010 Workshops, LNCS 6586, pp. 305–313, 2011.
© Springer-Verlag Berlin Heidelberg 2011

Existing simulators such as GridSim [12] and CloudSim [3] follow a *process-based* approach that runs a separate thread for each entity in the system resulting in poor scalability when the number of entities in the system becomes large. To address this issue, we describe in this paper GroudSim, a new *event-based* simulator for scientific applications on Grid and Cloud environments that requires one simulation thread only (instead of one thread per entity). We present experimental results that demonstrate the scalability of our approach with respect to sequential and parallel job submissions and file transfers, as well as the superiority over the process-based approach for simulating the execution of two real-world workflows.

The paper is organised as follows. Section 2 summaries the related work, followed by an introduction to the discrete-event simulation technology in Section 3. Section 4 presents the GroudSim simulator in detail, while Section 5 shows the results of the evaluation. Section 6 concludes the paper.

2 Related Work

GridSim [12] is a simulation toolkit for resource modelling and application scheduling for Grid computing. GridSim uses SimJava [10] as the underlying simulation framework, which is a process-based discrete event simulation package that runs a separate thread for each entity in the system resulting in poor performance. Evaluation results show that this toolkit suffers when simulating more than 2000 Grid sites concurrently, because of large memory consumption. CloudSim [3] extends GridSim by modelling and simulating Cloud computing infrastructures and services showing the same scalability problems.

SimGrid [4] is a simulation framework for evaluating cluster, Grid, and peer-to-peer algorithms and heuristics. The approach is comparable to the one used in GroudSim, but uses C instead of Java as the main development language, which makes its integration with existing Java tools and services more difficult. SimGrid does not address simulation of Cloud infrastructures.

3 Discrete-Event Simulation

A discrete system [8] is one in which the state variables change only at discrete points in time called *events*, whose chronological sequence describe the behaviour of the system. The following terms are important when working with a discrete-event simulation system: (1) *event* being an instant occurrence that changes the state of a system; (2) *future event list* (FEL) being a list of future events that is ordered by their occurrence in time; (3) *clock* being a variable representing the time at which the simulation currently stands; (4) *entity* being any object or component in the system that requires explicit representation in the model; and (5) *system state* being a collection of variables that contain all the information necessary to describe the system at any time. In our case, the system variables are the Grid and Cloud resources and their assigned jobs.

Further, a discrete-event simulation system also needs a so called *time advance algorithm*, which is used to advance the simulation clock when there are no more external requests. An *event scheduling algorithm* is another very important part of a discrete-event simulator, responsible for the correct processing order of events. An event can influence other events that are stored in the FEL that might need to be removed or altered, leading to a critical dependency in the order of event processing.

4 GroudSim

In this section, we describe the technical details of GroudSim by referencing to the most important Java API classes available at [2] where also the sources are available under GPL. Following the API it is easy to write test scenarios that can be controlled using XML configuration files.

Entities. `SimEngine` is the main GroudSim class which implements the time advance algorithm, the clock, and the FEL, and keeps track of the so called *registered entities* used for tracing during a simulation. There are three options when starting a simulation: (1) simulate as long as there are events in FEL; (2) simulate for a specified simulation time; and (3) simulate until an arbitrary point in time and shutdown the `SimEngine` afterwards. The Grid and Cloud resources classes share most of the common functionality implemented in the `groud` package, and override the specialised behaviour in the `groud.grid` and `groud.cloud` packages. To allow manipulation of the state of entities (e.g. `CloudSite`, `GridSite`), a level of indirection for forwarding events directly to the destination entity is added. `GroudEntity` is an abstract class which provides all method stubs for manipulating the state of entities.

Jobs. A `GroudJob` has an identifier, a problem size (in million of instructions (MI)), a source (needed for cancelling it), and can be executed on a Grid or a Cloud site. A `GroudJob` also has a state which is changed during the execution of the specific `JobEventTypes`: `unsubmitted`, `submitted`, `queued`, `activated`, `finished`, `failed`, and `cancelled`. Grid and Cloud jobs that specialise a `GroudJob` differ in their execution policy. Grids follow a job queuing policy by putting the jobs into a waiting queue until a CPU becomes available. For using a Cloud, resources, also called *instances*, need first to be acquired, after which a resource policy sharing upon job arrival is applied (no queuing mechanism employed). For each state in the job state transition diagram, there exists a corresponding event type in the `groud.event.job` package implementing a callback method on the source of the event, on its destination, or on both. The only classes that the end-user directly needs to use in his simulation are `JobSubmitEventType` for submitting `JobCancelEventType` for cancelling jobs. Figure 1 shows the interaction of three possible entities: a user, a `SimEngine`, and one `GridSite`. The first step has to be initiated by the user, while the rest are done automatically by GroudSim:

1. The user adds a `JobSubmitEventType` to the `SimEngine`;
2. The `submit` event occurs and the `submitJob` method of the target Grid site is called. The job is in state `submitted`;
3. The Grid site creates a `JobQueuedEventType` and adds it to the `SimEngine`;
4. The `queued` event occurs and the `handleJobQueued` method of both the user and the Grid site is called. The job is in state `queued`;
5. The user needs to implement the `handleJobQueued` method. The Grid site adds `JobActivatedEventType` and `JobFinishedEventType` events to the `SimEngine`, as it already knows how much time the job will need to finish;
6. The `activated` event occurs and the `handleJobActivated` method of both the user and the Grid site is called. The job is in state `activated`. The Grid site resets the consumed MI of the job, indicating that it is starting to run;
7. The `finished` event occurs and the `handleJobFinished` method of both the user and the Grid site is called. The job is in state `finished`. The Grid site releases the CPU occupied by the job and calculates its costs. The user can now analyse the costs, the runtime, or submit new jobs.

Several Cloud instances of the same `InstanceType` can be acquired using a `ResourceReservation`. Each Cloud instance is an object of type `CloudSite` registered properly with the simulation engine. If there are jobs still running on a `CloudSite` once it is released, they are simply cancelled before the release of the `ResourceReservation` is confirmed.

Cost. We support two cost models in the simulation environment. For Grid resources, the computation time is typically free, but can be charged per time unit of CPU core used. Cloud instances have to be paid for their usage, typically on an hourly basis as charged by most of today's commercial Cloud providers. GroudSim allows keeping track of the costs resulting from a simulation and supports custom billing intervals to study the their influence on the overall cost. The cost introduced by file transfers is calculated per gigabyte of data to allow rich simulation scenarios and detailed analysis on Cloud or mixed resource setups. The end-user can retrieve these costs during runtime to allow steering of scheduling polices or at the end of the simulation for later analysis.

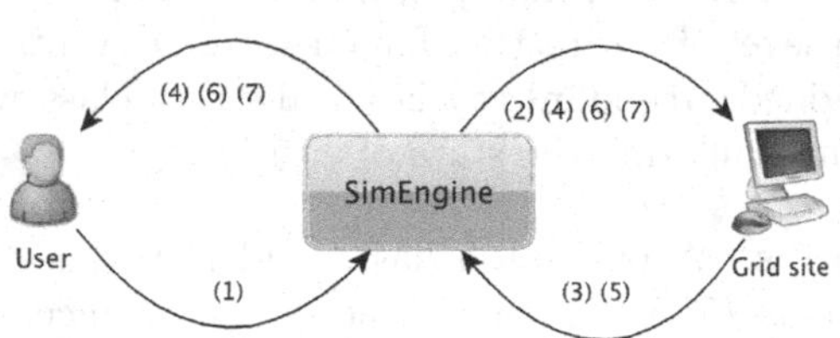

Fig. 1. Job submission workflow

Tracing. Tracing is an essential tool to support the offline evaluation of simulation results. GroudSim provides two different configurable tracing types: (1) *entity state tracing* for analysing the system state of all entities in the current simulation including active entities like `GridSites` and `CloudSites`, and passive entities such as users; and (2) *event-based tracing* is based on the simulated events and hence more powerful than the static entity-based tracing. Nevertheless, there are simulation results which are more intuitive to gather with entity-based tracing such as the the utilisation of the current `Groud` entities. We designed a tracing architecture similar to the one used by `java.util.logging` which includes three important additional classes: (1) `Tracer` defines the link between the simulation engine and the visualisation of the tracing stream; (2) `Handlers` are responsible for the visualisation of the current tracing stream, including the writing of information to a console or a tracing file as, well as the creation of predefined charts; and (3) `Filters` are used to remove unnecessary information from the tracing stream for a specific handler.

Probability Distributions. As GroudSim is based on a time sharing system with a lot of different initial timespans and stochastic decisions, distributions are used at multiple points in a simulation. This affects the runtime and the failure behaviour of Grid sites and Cloud instances, as well as the distribution of the initial jobs simulated. The `groud.dist` package introduces an adapter pattern to use different stochastic distributions from different packages while providing a homogeneous interface. A wide range of different distributions including the widely-used exponential and logarithmic, as well as simpler distributions such as normal or uniform are included. Our implementation uses the standard `ssj.jar` stochastic package [6, 9], which gives the possibility to run deterministic and nondeterministic simulations by using precise or random initial seeding values.

Failures. As real Grids and Clouds are distributed systems prone to failures, the simulator provides the possibility to let some of the registered resources fail for certain time intervals. Furthermore, the problem size and the occurrence probability can be configured for each failure. The simulator provides two different types of failures implemented in the `groud.failure` package: job and file transfer-related. Each `GroudEntity` defines its own failure behaviour. The standard behaviour is configurable via the `GroudSimEntityProp` and follows a stochastic distribution for each failure property. As already mentioned, these properties consist of the size of the failure, the duration of the failure and the mean time to next failure for both jobs and file transfers. For activating the failure behaviour for all registered entities, one has to introduce and register the `GroudFailureGenerator` in the simulation engine. From an abstract point of view, this failure generator is another passive simulation entity registered. The failure generator iterates over all registered entities before the simulation starts and adds one reactivation event to the FEL for each entity. Once the simulation reaches such a reactivation event, the failure generator gets activated and injects a failure with the defined size at the target entity. At the same time, events for recovering the affected entity and for reactivating the failure generator are added to the FEL. Using this "circle" of simulated events, each failure behaviour can be simulated for Grid, Cloud, as well as for network resources.

Background Load. GroudSim offers functionality to introduce background load into the current simulation by building an interface to the file format of the Grid Workload Archive [7]. The `BackgroundLoader` class located in the `groud.bg` package contains the main functionality of background loading able to introduce new `GroudEvents` into the `SimEngine` and to handle the generated callbacks for each `GroudJob` executed. For each GWA entry that is properly parsed, the `BackgroundLoader` introduces a new `GroudJob` into the current simulation.

5 Evaluation

We run the GroudSim evaluation experiments on an Intel Core Duo E6750 (2.67 gigahertz) with 2048 megabytes DDR2-RAM using the Java^{TM}SE Runtime Environment (build 1.6.0_16-b01). Each experimental result presented represents the average of ten separate runs. The simulated workflow runs were compared with real executions on the Austrian Grid and resulted in a runtime in a reasonable range of 10% of real executions.

5.1 GridSim Comparison

We start our evaluation by comparing GroudSim with the GridSim [12] simulator. We implemented a simple workflow execution environment capable of working with both GridSim and GroudSim as back-end and used two real-world workflow applications in our evaluation: WIEN2k and MeteoAG. The size of the simulated workflows can be changed using a parameter x called *parallelization size*, which corresponds to the problem size of the input data. We generated the performance models for these applications from real trace data logged in the Austrian Grid environment over the course of the last few years.

WIEN2k [1] is a material science workflow for performing electronic structure calculations of solids using density functional theory based on the full-potential (linearised) augmented plane-wave ((L)APW) and local orbital (lo) method. The WIEN2k workflow contains two parallel sections of size x, with sequential synchronisation activities in between. The total number of activities in a Wien2k workflow is: $N_{wien2k} = 2 \cdot x + 3$.

MeteoAG [5] is a workflow designed for meteorological simulations based on the RAMS numerical atmospheric model. The simulations produce spatial and temporal fields of heavy precipitation cases over the western part of Austria to resolve most alpine watersheds and thunderstorms. The workflow structure, in which a large set of simulation cases x (parallelization size) is modelled as a parallel loop, where For each simulation, another nested parallel loop is executed with different parameter values. The total number of activities in a MeteoAG workflow is: $N_{meteoag} = 69 \cdot x + 2$.

Figure 2 shows that for growing parallelization sizes, the GridSim simulation time increases significantly faster than the GroudSim for both workflows. The reason for this advantage is in the event-based nature of GroudSim, in which the number of simulated resources (Grid sites, Cloud instances) has very little impact on the runtime performance, as demonstrated by the experiments following.

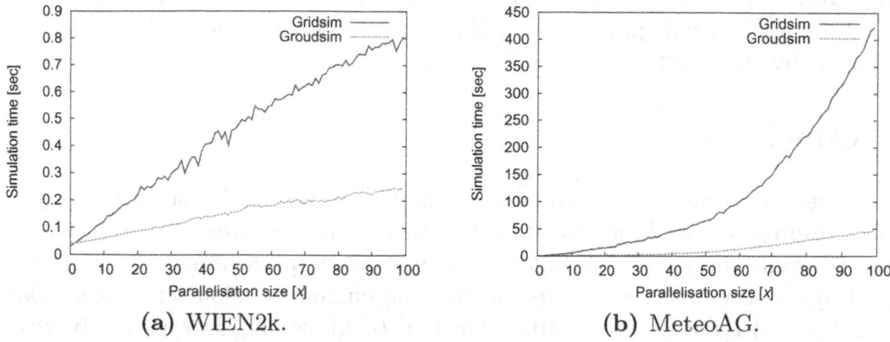

(a) WIEN2k. (b) MeteoAG.

Fig. 2. GroudSim and GridSim comparison

5.2 Job Submission

Figure 3a shows the results of the parallel submission of multiple jobs to Grid sites with 32 CPUs each and a computing power of 1000 MI per second (MIPS) for each CPU. We ran the tests on 8 to 32, 768 Grid sites and submitted between 16, 384 and 1, 048, 576 jobs. Submitting four times as many jobs to a given number of Grid sites requires four times as long simulation time to complete, slightly longer due to the Java Virtual Machine (JVM) garbage collector. The comparison between the clusters shows that the simulation also scales with the number of registered Grid sites, the execution times being almost independent of the number of entities except for cases when when the available memory is low. Different amounts of computing power per CPU did not affect the runtime at all, therefore the results of these experiments are not presented. The different number of CPUs per Grid site means the creation of additional objects, however, the overhead caused by this parameter is negligible.

Figure 3b presents the scenario where the jobs were submitted sequentially to Cloud resources, showing that the simulation scales linearly with the number of jobs. Moreover, the number of acquired Cloud instances does not have a

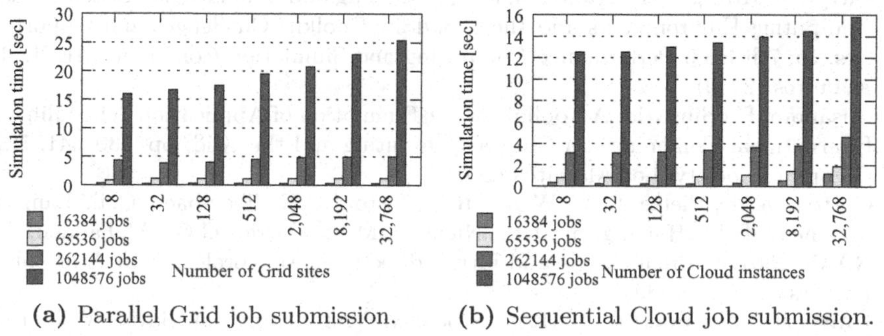

(a) Parallel Grid job submission. (b) Sequential Cloud job submission.

Fig. 3. Job submission experimental results

significant impact on the simulation time, which gets slightly worse the more Cloud instances are acquired due to the huge amount of objects that need to be managed by the JVM.

6 Conclusion

We presented GroudSim, a Java-based simulation toolkit for scientific applications running on combined Grid and Cloud infrastructures. GroudSim uses a discrete-event simulation toolkit that offers better performance then process-based approaches used in related work. The current version offers some basic statistics and analysis views after runtime to allow the user to easily writer more complex analysis. The developed simulation framework supports modelling of Grid and Cloud computational and network resources, job submissions, file transfers, as well as integration of failure, background load, and cost models. A sophisticated textual and visual tracing mechanism and a library-independent distribution factory give extension possibilities to the simulator: a new tracing mechanisms can be easily added by implementing new handlers or filters in the event system, and additional distribution functions can be included by adding a new library and writing an appropriate adapter. We provided experimental results that demonstrate the scalability of the job submission mechanisms, as well as the superiority of our solution over a related process-based approach for simulating the execution of two real-world scientific workflow applications.

The GroudSim framework is integrated as a back-end in the ASKALON Grid computing environment, which enables to perform both real and simulated executions of real-world applications using the same integrated development, monitoring, and analysis interface.

References

1. Blaha, P., Schwarz, K., Luitz, J.: WIEN2k, a full potential linearized augmented plane wave package for calculating crystal properties. TU Wien (2001)
2. Bodner, D., Kraler, G., Joerer, S.: GroudSim Java docu (2009), `http://www.assembla.com/code/groudsim/subversion/node/blob/trunk/doc/index.html`
3. Buyya, R., Ranjan, R., Calheiros, R.N.: Modeling and Simulation of Scalable Cloud Computing Environments and the CloudSim Toolkit: Challenges and Opportunities. In: 7th High Performance Computing and Simulation Conference. IEEE, Los Alamitos (2009)
4. Casanova, H.: SimGrid: A Toolkit for the Simulation of Application Scheduling. In: International Conference on Cluster Computing and the Grid, pp. 430–441. IEEE Computer Society, Los Alamitos (2001)
5. Cotton, W.R., Pielke, R.A., Walko, R.L., Liston, G.E., Tremback, C.J., Jiang, H., McAnelly, R.L., Harrington, J.Y., Nicholls, M.E., Carrio, G.G., McFadden, J.P.: RAMS 2001: Current status and future directions. Meteorology and Atmospheric Physics 82, 5–29 (2003)
6. University of Montreal DIRO. Stochastic Simulation in Java. Web Page, `http://www.iro.umontreal.ca/~simardr/ssj/indexe.html` (accessed in March 2010)

7. Iosup, A.: The Grid Workloads Archive. Future Generation Computer Systems 24(7), 672–686 (2008)
8. Nelson, B., Banks, J., Carson, J., Nicol, D.: Discrete-Event System Simulation. Pearson Prentice Hall, London (2005)
9. L'Ecuyer, P., Meliani, L., Vaucher, J.: SSJ: a framework for stochastic simulation in Java. In: WSC 2002: Proceedings of the 34th Conference on Winter Simulation, pp. 234–242. Winter Simulation Conference (2002)
10. McNab, R., Howell, F.W.: Using java for discrete event simulation. In: Twelfth UK Computer and Telecommunications Performance Engineering Workshop (UKPEW), pp. 219–228. Univ. of Edinburgh, Edinburgh (1996)
11. Ostermann, S., Prodan, R., Fahringer, T.: Extending Grids with Cloud resource management for scientific computing. In: International Conference on Grid Computing, pp. 42–59. IEEE Computer Society, Los Alamitos (October 2009)
12. Sulistio, A., Cibej, U., Venugopal, S., Robic, B., Buyya, R.: A toolkit for modelling and simulating data Grids: an extension to GridSim. Concurrency and Computation: Practice and Experience 20(13), 1591–1609 (2008)

Dynamic Service Configurations for SLA Negotiation

Irfan ul Haq, Kevin Kofler, and Erich Schikuta

Department of Knowledge and Business Engineering
University of Vienna, Austria
kevin.kofler@chello.at, {irfan.ul.haq,erich.schikuta}@univie.ac.at

Abstract. Utility Computing based infrastructures such as Cloud Computing promise on-demand packaging of resources similar to metered public utilities, i.e. electricity, water, gas and telephone. However, computing resources, which are traded as services are very different from the usual commodities due to their dynamically changing behavior and (re)configurable properties. Service Level Agreements(SLA) ensure the necessary guarantees to the highly dependent service consumers. There may be several rounds of negotiation before a formal SLA is established. During automated negotiation sessions, the service provider needs to understand consumer requests and is required to offer the closest possible service configuration fulfilling these requirements, keeping in view the preferences of the consumer on one hand and the business rules and configuration constraints of the service provider on the other. Service providers need to be prepared to expect demands for all possible permutation of service attributes. This requires a mechanism to map given expected values onto a discrete or continuous set of possibilities and then their refinement through multiple negotiation rounds. In this paper, we present a formal approach to compute feasible configurations of services, which fulfill the consumer preferences as well as the service provider's constraints and then introduce an SLA negotiation process based on this formal model.

1 Introduction

With the popularization of utility computing in the form of Cloud Computing infrastructures, there is a high likelihood for an IT-based service economy to cause a major shift from Capital Expenditure (CAPEX) to Operational Expenditure (OPEX) based enterprise setups. This will bring about new business models which will encourage resellers and Composite Service Providers [4] [5], not only affecting Small and Medium Enterprises (SME) but also directly promoting the micro-economical sector. For this, services of varying granularity and customizable configurations will be contracted through SLAs as on-demand consumable resources similar to the metered public utilities such as electricity, gas, water and telephone. However, computing utilities are very different from other commodities due to their highly dynamic nature and flexibly configurable attributes. This requires new trade mechanisms. A supermarket approach [6] i.e.,

M.R. Guarracino et al. (Eds.): Euro-Par 2010 Workshops, LNCS 6586, pp. 315–323, 2011.
© Springer-Verlag Berlin Heidelberg 2011

a take-it-or-leave-it negotiation model, is drastically insufficient to harness the optimal business value of IT-based service markets. In IT-based service market, a single service can be packaged into several different products depending upon its varying configurations. Moreover these configurations cannot be prepackaged due to customized requirements of clients. To cope with this situation, in addition to many other enabling requirements, there is a strong need for dynamic and flexible negotiation mechanisms, which allow service providers to dynamically compute customizable service configurations against consumer specifications following the business policies of the service provider at the same time. We argue that to enable an IT-based service economy, it is essential to promote such flexible SLA-based negotiation models.

For this, an SLA template initiated by either a service provider or a consumer may pass through several rounds of negotiation before becoming a legal contract. The interests of the client may go beyond cheap price and high quality of services and include preferences demanding strict specifications in case of certain properties and relaxation for the others. For instance, a client may be very strict with the output resolution of an image processing service but may not bother about the throughput of the service for a batch job. The service provider on the other hand would make an utmost effort to find some ways to match the client's requirements while protecting its business rules and thus not risking the overall profit margin and deliverable QoS (Quality of Service) levels. For this purpose, the service provider must be able to configure services dynamically, in accordance with the client's preferences and compliant to the business rules. The resultant configurations may not exactly match clients' requirements but would reflect the best that the service provider could offer. This may lead to another round of negotiation if the client slightly modifies its requirements or preferences in order to get a better quotation.

In this paper we present a formal model to facilitate the process of SLA negotiation. The negotiation model is not a symmetric model because the service provider and the consumer have different roles and need to act accordingly within their non-identical scopes. The proposed formal model:

- allows the clients and the service providers to express and offer customized configuration and reconfiguration of services, and
- forms the basis of a multi-round negotiation/renegotiation protocol

In section 2 we explain the concept of dynamic configuration of SLA offers, whereas in section 3 we present our formal model in this regard. Section 4 depicts a motivational scenario to realize various aspects of the model, whereas section 5 explains a negotiation protocol based on the formal model. Section 6 concludes the paper with an overview of the contribution and future work.

2 Dynamic Configuration of SLA Offers

In this section, we explain how the service provider can customize service configurations dynamically in response to the client's requirements and priorities.

We assume that both the service provider and the service consumer are able to express their requirements in their respective SLA templates and any of them can initiate the negotiation process by sending its SLA offer to the other. For the sake of the argument, let's say that the client initiates the process.

Service Consumer's Role. For the service provider to better understand the consumer's exact requirements and to reciprocate with its best offer, the consumer should be able to express its requirements precisely along with their priorities. This will allow the service provider more flexibility to come up with the cheapest and most desirable offer possible for the client. The client can express its requirements expressing the desired values of service attributes and assigning weights to them to highlight its priorities.

Service Provider's Role. The service provider is required to compute a configuration of the service fulfilling the client's requirements in accordance with its business rules, compute the corresponding price and respond to the client with its counteroffer. The counteroffer need not contain the exact configuration that the client required but the closest possible that the service provider can offer. The client, on examining this offer, can redefine certain values or weights of its requirements in order to expect a better offer.

Negotiation and Renegotiation. The negotiation round will go on until both parties agree on certain terms. In the next section, we formulate these concepts in a formal model that will serve as a basis for computing service configurations as part of a dynamic and flexible SLA negotiation protocol. A similar communication pattern can be followed for a renegotiation round. In case of renegotiation the previously established SLA will remain intact even in case of a failure of the process whereas in case of negotiation an SLA does not exist before and in fact is the output of the process.

3 Formal Model for Dynamic Service Configurations

In this section, we will formalize the concept of dynamic service configurations based on the client requirements and preferences. These service configurations will be presented to the clients in the form of SLA offers.

3.1 Definitions

We define a service through its attributes and a service configuration as a set of specific values assigned to the service attributes.

Definition (Service Attribute and Attribute Value). A *service attribute* is a pair $a_i = (D_i, n_i)$ where D_i is a set called the *definition domain* (most commonly, we will have $D_i \subseteq \mathbb{R}$, this also covers booleans if we identify *true* as 1 and *false* as 0) and $n_i : D_i \to [0, 1]$ is a map called the *normalization map* for the attribute. It represents a QoS parameter such as the compression rate. The definition domain specifies the possible values the QoS attribute can take, the normalization map specifies how to map those values to a quality between 0 and 1, where 0 is the worst possible quality and 1 the best one. The map can be increasing or decreasing: it will be increasing for attributes which directly indicate a quality, it will be decreasing for attributes such as latencies where less is better. An *attribute value* is a value $(q_0)_i \in D_i$. It specifies a concrete value the attribute can take.

Definition (Service). A *service* s is a list of attributes $a_1, \ldots, a_m$ (i.e. we define a service by its attributes). It models a specific service offered by a specific provider, e.g. the video compression service of company XYZ. The *normalization map* $n : D = D_1 \times \ldots \times D_m \to [0,1]^m$ for the service is the map mapping each attribute value $(q_0)_i$ to $n_i((q_0)_i)$. In other words, each component of the normalization map for the service is the normalization map for the respective attribute.

Definition (Configuration). A *configuration* of the service s is an *attribute vector* $q_0 \in D$, i.e. a vector of specific attribute values for the attributes of a service. We assume that all the relevant properties of the service are given as such QoS attributes, so those fully define the service. Note that this is a vector of attribute values $(q_0)_i \in D_i$. This attribute vector maps under n to a *quality vector* $q = n(q_0) \in [0,1]^m$.

Definition (Set of Feasible Configurations). For each service, we assume that only a subset F of the set $D = D_1 \times \ldots \times D_m$ of all possible configurations can actually be fulfilled by the service provider. We call F the *set of feasible configurations*. An attribute value q_0 will be called *feasible* if and only if $q_0 \in F$, *infeasible* otherwise. The exact nature of F will in general only be known to the service provider, not to the client.

Definition (Price Function). Each service has a given *price function* $f : D \to \mathbb{R}_+$ which maps each feasible attribute value q_0 to its monetary cost $f(q_0)$. We set $f(q_0) = \infty$ for infeasible q_0. This price function will also usually only be known to the service provider.

Definition (Weights). A vector $w \in \mathbb{R}_+^m$, where m is again the number of attributes of a given service s, will be called a vector of *weights* corresponding to the service s. During the renegotiation process, it allows the client to define which attribute values carry most importance to him, which influences the service provider's idea of the closest feasible point.

Definition (Negotiation Function). If the client requests an infeasible configuration q_0, the service provider computes the closest feasible configuration

$\hat{q}_0 = g(q_0, w)$ using a *negotiation function* defined as follows:

$$g(q_0, w) = \begin{array}{l} \arg\min_{\hat{q}_0} d_w(\hat{q}_0, q_0) \\ \text{s.t. } \hat{q}_0 \in F, \end{array}$$

i.e. the $\hat{q}_0$ in the set F of feasible configurations which minimizes $d_w(\hat{q}_0, q_0)$, where

$$d_w(\hat{q}_0, q_0) = \|n(\hat{q}_0) - n(q_0)\|_w$$

and $\|u\|_w = \sqrt{\sum_{i=1}^{m} w_i^2 u_i^2}$ is the 2-norm weighted by w.

If we write $q = n(q_0)$ and $\hat{q} = n(\hat{q}_0)$, d_w can be written as

$$d_w(\hat{q}_0, q_0) = \sqrt{\sum_{i=1}^{m} w_i^2 (\hat{q}_i - q_i)^2}.$$

Figure 1 shows a geometric interpretation of the weighted 2-norm distance d_w defined above in an example with a 2-dimensional, triangular set of feasible configurations F. In the absence of weights, the 2-norm is the Euclidean norm and the closest point under the 2-norm is given by an orthogonal projection. Setting weights w corresponds to stretching, for all i, the ith coordinate axis by a factor w_i (the ith coordinate of w). This deforms the orthogonal projection, yielding a point which deviates less in the coordinates weighted higher at the expense of those weighted lower. An analogous geometric interpretation is possible in higher dimensions.

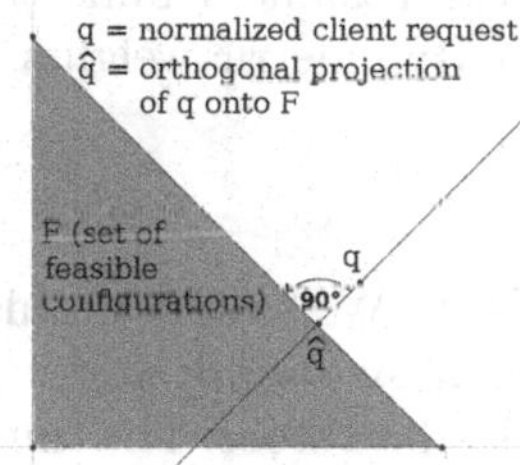

(a) For the trivial weights $w = (1; 1)$, g corresponds to an orthogonal projection.

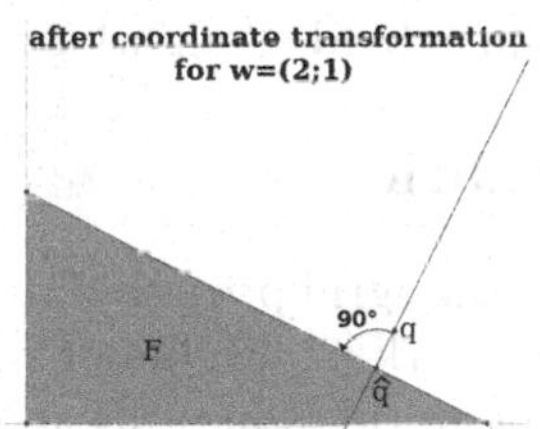

(b) Nontrivial weights w correspond to a coordinate stretch by factors w.

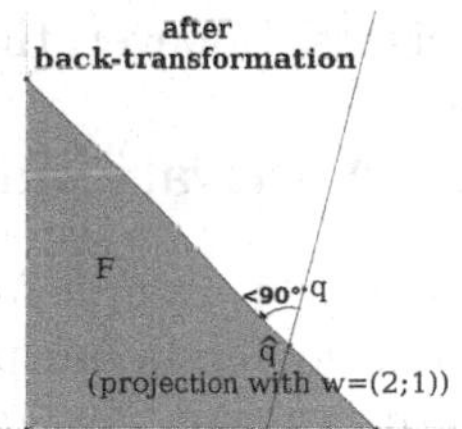

(c) The effects of the coordinate transformation in the original coordinates.

Fig. 1. Geometric interpretation of the negotiation function g and the distance d_w

3.2 Extensions

Here we discuss some possibilities to extend the formal model described above.

Parameter Vector. Both the set F of feasible configurations (and thus the renegotiation function g) and the price function f may depend on additional outside parameters known to the service provider, such as the amount of idle CPU power currently available on the server infrastructure, or such as the number of services from the same provider being purchased by the client, to be considered for mass purchase rebates. This can be modeled by introducing an additional *parameter vector* θ which is added to the definition of F, f and g, turning the set F into a set-valued function $F(\theta)$ and adding an additional parameter to $f(\theta, q_0)$ and $g(\theta, q_0, w)$. (In the definition of g, we only need to replace F by $F(\theta)$, all the other quantities do not depend on θ.)

If the vector θ is assumed constant throughout the negotiation process, we can ignore it during computation and just consider F, f and g for a given fixed value of θ.

Asymmetric Weights. Due to the symmetricity of the distance relation d_w used in the renegotiation function g, the client has no way to specify that for a given attribute, e.g. the resolution of the video, getting a higher quality than requested is not a big problem, but getting a lower one is. Instead, a violation by the same amount in either direction will always be the same.

This limitation can be addressed by introducing *asymmetric weights* $w^+ \in \mathbb{R}_+^m$ and $w^- \in \mathbb{R}_+^m$ and redefining d_w as the *asymmetric distance*

$$d_w(\hat{q}_0, q_0) = \sqrt{\sum_{i=1}^{m} \begin{cases} {w_i^+}^2 (\hat{q}_i - q_i)^2, & \text{if } \hat{q}_i \geq q_i \\ {w_i^-}^2 (\hat{q}_i - q_i)^2, & \text{if } \hat{q}_i < q_i. \end{cases}}$$

It shall be noted that this asymmetric distance is no longer a distance relation in the classical sense, which would require symmetricity, i.e. $d(u, v) = d(v, u)\ \forall u, v$.

For simplicity, throughout the rest of this paper, we will assume symmetric weights. However, the results extend straightforwardly to asymmetric weights.

4 Motivational Scenario

We use an example from the Datagrid project of the CERN [1]. We have used this scenario also in our previous work [2] [3]. In our scenario, physicists are working at distributed locations in the world requesting access to the data store. The time which elapses between sending the request and retrieving / storing the required data locally is defined as the response time of the system. The location of the client application has an important impact on the response time because a LAN normally has a much higher bandwidth than a WAN. This results in a shorter response time which we consider as the major performance measurement for the data store. We have the following requirements for the data storage service.

1. The minimum requirement for the bandwidth to access the data is 10 Mbps.
2. Due to parallel access, the available disk size may change dynamically, but the disk size at the storing location always has to be at least 5 GB.
3. For the application characteristics of the running example in focus, a high compression rate is desired.
4. The data needs to be replicated to at least one extra location.
5. A very high level (e.g. 99.9 percent) of availability of the service is desired.

Data Storage Service (Client's Preferences)		
Service Attribute	Desired Value (qo)	Weight (w)
Availability	99.9 %	1
Bandwidth	10 MB	0.8
Disk Size	5 GB	0.5
Compression	2	0.5
Degree of Replication	2	1

(a)

Data Storage Service (Service Provider's Options)				
Availability	BandWidth	Disk Size	Compression	Degree of Replication
99.9 %	8 MB/s	2 GB	1	1
–	15 MB/s	4 GB	2	2
–	20 MB/s	8 GB	4	3
–	30 MB/s	16 GB	–	4

(b)

Fig. 2. (a) Client's Preferences, (b) Service Provider's Options

Following our formal model, we have formulated the client requirements and preferences mentioned above in Figure 2(a). It must be noted that the service provider is not in a position to fulfill every preference of the client. But that is where it will use the priorities of the client expressed in terms of weights and will compute the most suitable configuration closest to the client's requirements following the negotiation function:

$$g(q_0, w) = \begin{array}{l} \arg\min_{\hat{q}_0} d_w(\hat{q}_0, q_0) \\ \text{s.t. } \hat{q}_0 \in F. \end{array}$$

Note that this simple example has been chosen such that the possible values for each attribute are independent of each other and thus the weights have no effect.

So instead of the bandwidth of 10 Mbps and the desired diskspace of 5 GB, the client is offered a bandwidth of 8 Mbps and diskspace of 4 GB, which are the closest available values to the ones the client requested.

5 Negotiation Process Based on SLA Configurations

Now we explain the step by step detail of the negotiation process based on the dynamic configuration of services as depicted in Figure 3.

1. Initiation of the Negotiation Process: Any party can initiate the negotiation process. However, this is not a symmetric protocol because the real world is not symmetric. Both the service consumer and the service provider need to maximize their interests so their activities within their scopes vary from each other. In Figure 3, we have assumed that the client first gets the SLA template and fills in its preferences.
2. Preparation of SLA quotation by the service consumer: The client provides two types of information to the service provider. It fills in the desired values of service attributes within the SLA template, and it also informs about its priorities regarding those attributes. This information can either be a part of the SLA template or can be sent separately. The idea is to give clues to

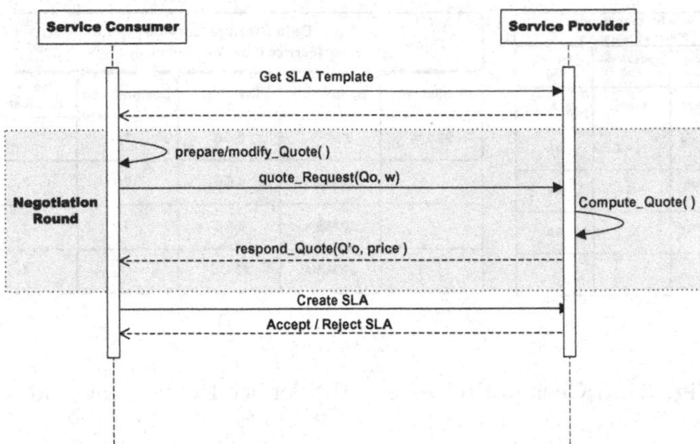

Fig. 3. Negotiation Protocol for SLA configuration

the service provider about where adjustments can be tolerated and which attributes are a must-have requirement. The service consumer will send the values shown in the Figure 2(a).

3. Computation of the best configuration offer by the service provider: The service provider, following the difference function described in the formal model, computes a service configuration, which is closest to the desired service configuration. It also computes the price using the price function described in section 3. As depicted in Figure 2(b), it is quite possible that no configuration exists that matches the service consumer's preferences exactly. In that case, during the configuration selection, a relaxation is assumed on the attributes with the least priority. The exact computational criteria have been described in the formal model. The service provider in our scenario will offer a bandwidth of 8 Mbps and a disk size of 4 GB while fulfilling the rest of the requirements of the client.
4. Analysis of the offer and modification of service preferences by the consumer: After receiving the best possible configuration matching the consumer's request, the service consumer analyzes the offered configuration and can opt to proceed in three different ways, i.e., accept, reject or further negotiate the offer. The client can decide to further negotiate the offer either by changing/modifying certain attribute values or by relaxing certain priorities (changing weights). In case of a modified quote, the negotiation process keeps on going until both parties agree or disagree to continue it further.
5. SLA establishment: If the client agrees with the SLA offer of the service provider, it can opt to commit and send an acceptance call thus binding itself to the agreement. If the service provider also accepts then a contract is formed and an SLA is formally established. Conversely, if either of parties reject the SLA offer then the negotiation round is failed.

6. Renegotiation: The same process can also be utilized for renegotiation. In case of a successful renegotiation process, the newly formed SLA takes the place of the old one, otherwise the previous SLA survives and remains intact.

6 Conclusion

The provision of such flexible configurability of services discusses in this paper is essential to increase the market liquidity where service consumers and service providers can adapt themselves to market situations in accordance with the dynamically changing resources. In the future, we intend to implement and simulate this model in connection with service composition scenarios.

References

1. Stockinger, H., Stockinger, K., Schikuta, E., Willers, I.: Towards a Cost Model for Distributed and Replicated Data Stores. In: Proc. 9th Euromicro Workshop on Parallel and Distributed Processing (PDP 2001). IEEE CS Press, Los Alamitos (2001)
2. Schikuta, E., Wanek, H., Haq, I.U.: Grid Workflow Optimization regarding Dynamically Changing Resources and Conditions. Journal of CCPE (2008)
3. Haq, I.U., Kofler, K., Schikuta, E.: Using Blackboard Systems to Automate and Optimize Workflow Orchestrations. In: Proceedings of 5th IEEE Conference on Emerging Technologies (ICET 2009), Islamabad (2009)
4. Ludwig, A.: COSMA – an approach for managing sLAs in composite services. In: Bouguettaya, A., Krueger, I., Margaria, T. (eds.) ICSOC 2008. LNCS, vol. 5364, pp. 626–632. Springer, Heidelberg (2008)
5. Buyyaa, R., Yeo, C.S., Venugopal, S., Broberg, J., Brandic, I.: Cloud computing and emerging IT platforms: Vision, hype, and reality for delivering computing as the 5th utility. Future Generation Computer Systems 25, 599–616 (2010)
6. McKee, P., Taylor, S., Surridge, M., Lowe, R., Ragusa, C.: Strategies for the Service Market Place. In: Veit, D.J., Altmann, J. (eds.) GECON 2007. LNCS, vol. 4685, pp. 58–70. Springer, Heidelberg (2007)

Third Workshop on UnConventional High Performance Computing (UCHPC 2010)

UCHPC 2010: Third Workshop on UnConventional High Performance Computing

Anders Hast[1], Lars Bengtsson[2], Josef Weidendorfer[3], and Ren Wu[4]

[1] University of Gävle, Sweden
[2] Chalmers University, Sweden
[3] Technische Universität München, Germany
[4] HP Labs, Palo Alto, United States

Foreword

As the word "UnConventional" in the title suggests, the UCHPC workshop focuses on hardware or platforms used for HPC, which were not intended for HPC in the first place. Reasons could be raw computing power or especially low cost. Thus, UCHPC tries to capture solutions for HPC which are unconventional today but perhaps conventional tomorrow. For example, the computing power of platforms for games recently raised rapidly. This motivated the use of GPUs for computing (GPGPU), or building computational grids from game consoles. Other examples for "unconventional" hardware would be embedded, low-power processors, FPGAs or DSPs. Only imagination sets the limit for their usage for HPC. The goal of the workshop is to present latest research in how hardware and software (yet) unconventional for HPC is or can be used to reach goals such as best performance per watt. UCHPC also covers according programming models, compiler techniques, and tools.

It was the 3rd time the UCHPC workshop took part, with previous workshops held in 2008 in conjunction with the *International Conference on Computational Science and Its Applications 2008*, and in 2009 with the *ACM International Conference on Computing Frontiers 2009*. This year, the organizers were very pleased by a large number of high quality submissions. This made it possible to accept nine out of sixteen submitted papers. While there only was a half-day available, it was no problem for the speakers to stay in time, although a very tight schedule had to be met. We were able to group the talks into three topics. These formed the structure of the workshop sessions, and made up for a very exciting program:

- *Accelerator Usage for Applications* with four talks about applications from electromagnetics, medical image processing, molecular dynamics simulation, and object detection,
- *Accelerator Usage Infrastructure* with two talks on GPU/CPU callbacks and static GPU workgroups, and

M.R. Guarracino et al. (Eds.): Euro-Par 2010 Workshops, LNCS 6586, pp. 327–328, 2011.
© Springer-Verlag Berlin Heidelberg 2011

- *Speeding up Algorithms with Accelerators* with three talks on domain-independent irregular kernels, multi-coloring preconditioning, and custom precision arithmetics with FPGAs.

This post-workshop proceedings includes the final versions of the presented UCHPC papers, taking the feedback from reviewers and workshop audience into account.

Finally, the organizers and program chairs of the UCHPC workshop want to thank the authors of the papers. Without them, the workshop would not have been able to come up with the interesting topics for discussion. But also, we sincerely thank the EuroPar organization for providing the opportunity to arrange the workshop in conjunction with the EuroPar 2010 conference. Last but not least, we especially appreciated the hard work of the members of our International Program Committee. They did a perfect job at reviewing the submissions. And we thank all attendees at the workshop, who contributed to a lively day, and we hope they too found something of interest in the workshop. Based on the very positive feedback, the program chairs and organizers plan to continue the UCHPC workshop in conjunction with EuroPar 2011.

October 2010

Anders Hast
Lars Bengtsson
Josef Weidendorfer
Ren Wu

Iterative Solution of Linear Systems in Electromagnetics (And Not Only): Experiences with CUDA

Danilo De Donno, Alessandra Esposito,
Giuseppina Monti, and Luciano Tarricone

Department of Innovation Engineering,
University of Salento,
Via per Monteroni - 73100 - Lecce, Italy
{danilo.dedonno,alessandra.esposito,giuseppina.monti,
luciano.tarricone}@unisalento.it

Abstract. In this paper, we propose the use of graphics processing units as a low-cost and efficient solution of electromagnetic (and other) numerical problems. Based on the software platform CUDA (Compute Unified Device Architecture), a solver for unstructured sparse matrices with double precision complex data has been implemented and tested for several practical cases. Benchmark results confirm the validity of the proposed software in terms of speed-up, speed and GPU execution time.

Keywords: linear system, GPU, CUDA, biconjugate gradient, BiCG.

1 Introduction

Software simulations are continuously requested to become faster, more accurate, and able to handle new, bigger and more complex problems. Recently, thanks to the continuous impulse coming from video game industry, graphics processors (GPUs) are affirming as a valid solution to accelerate time-demanding scientific computations. This is facilitated by the publication of simple-to-use libraries such as CUDA [1] which greatly ease software implementation.

An important research effort is currently devoted to the implementation of GPU-enabled linear solvers, since modern software simulations often depend on the solution of a computationally demanding linear system. A wide range of linear solvers exist, the choice of which depends fundamentally on the properties of the system matrix. For instance, when the matrix is known to be sparse, real symmetric or complex Hermitian, an iterative solver, such as the conjugate gradient (CG) algorithm, is usually preferred [2]. The biconjugate gradient (BiCG) method is a generalization of the CG suited to handle real nonsymmetric and complex non-Hermitian matrices. This feature is a significant advantage in many areas, such as computational electromagnetics (CEM) for the analysis and design of EM structures. In this case, a key role is played by the Method of Moments (MoM) [4] which transforms the integral-differential Maxwell's equations into

M.R. Guarracino et al. (Eds.): Euro-Par 2010 Workshops, LNCS 6586, pp. 329–337, 2011.
© Springer-Verlag Berlin Heidelberg 2011

a linear system of algebraic equations. MoM usually generates unstructured, sparse, symmetric and non-Hermitian matrices with complex coefficients. Moreover, double precision is needed in order to achieve a satisfying accuracy.

Starting from the requirements of such a category of problems, we implemented a new BiCG solver for GPUs. Indeed, available GPU-enabled iterative solvers, such as Iterative CUDA [5], CUSP [6], SpeedIT [7] and *"Concurrent Number Cruncher"* (CNC) [8], deal with real coefficient matrices, most concentrating on the CG algorithm.

Our solver is implemented in CUDA and tackles unstructured complex sparse matrices. It has been tested on matrices coming from concrete scientific problems, some being taken from well recognized matrix collections, others being generated during in-house experimentation in the area of EM circuit design.

2 Design and Implementation

2.1 CUDA Background

A NVIDIA GPU is built around an array of multiprocessors, each of which supporting up to 1024 threads. CUDA is a standard C language extension for thread-based application development on GPU. A CUDA application consists of a sequential *host* code that executes parallel programs (*kernels*) on a parallel *device* (the GPU). Kernels are SIMT (Single Instruction Multiple Thread) computations that are executed by a potentially large number of *threads* organized into a *grid* of thread *blocks*.

Great benefits are obtained when threads access a contiguous part of device memory: in this case the individual memory instructions are replaced by a single memory access (*memory coalescence*).

2.2 The BiCG Algorithm

BiCG is an extension of the CG algorithm. It produces two mutually orthogonal sequences of vectors in place of the orthogonal sequence of residuals generated in the CG algorithm.

We implemented the complex BiCG algorithm with Jacobi preconditioning, in the form presented by Jacobs in [9]. First, we define initial variables: the residual r and bi-residual $\overline{r}$, the direction vector p and the bi-direction vector $\overline{p}$, the preconditioned residual d and bi-residual $\overline{d}$, the residual error ρ. Then, assuming that b is the rigth-hand side (r.h.s) of the linear system $Ax = b$, M the Jacobi preconditioner and x_0 the initial guess of the solution, the following steps are repeated for each iteration (the asterisk denotes the complex conjugate):

1. calculate the step length parameter and form the new solution estimate

$$q_i = Ap_{i-1} \qquad \overline{q}_i = A^H\overline{p}_{i-1} \tag{1}$$

$$\alpha_i = \rho_{i-1}/p^*_{i-1}q_i \tag{2}$$

$$x_i = x_{i-1} + \alpha_i p_{i-1} \tag{3}$$

2. update residual and bi-residual, with and without preconditioning

$$r_i = r_{i-1} + \alpha_i q_i \qquad \overline{r}_i = \overline{r}_{i-1} + \alpha_i^* \overline{q}_i \tag{4}$$

$$d_i = M^{-1} r_i \qquad \overline{d}_i = M^{-1} \overline{r}_i \tag{5}$$

3. calculate the residual error ρ and bi-conjugacy coefficient β

$$\rho_i = d_i^T \overline{r}_i^* \tag{6}$$

$$\beta_i = \rho_i / \rho_{i-1} \tag{7}$$

4. update next direction and bi-direction vectors

$$p_i = d_{i-1} + \beta_i p_{i-1} \qquad \overline{p}_i = \overline{d}_i + \beta_i^* \overline{p}_{i-1} \tag{8}$$

Iteration is continued till a termination condition of the form:

$$\left\| r^i \right\|_2 / \left\| b \right\|_2 \leq \epsilon \tag{9}$$

is satisfied. Values of ϵ used in literature range from $10^{-6}/10^{-7}$ [3].

2.3 Matrix Format

There is a multitude of sparse matrix representations, each with different storage requirements, computational characteristics and methods of accessing and manipulating entries of the matrix. We focused on schemes which efficiently store matrices with arbitrary sparsity patterns. Moreover, we preferred formats suited for the GPU use, where the amount of available memory is strictly limited and memory accesses should be as regular as possible. Based on these considerations, we considered two matrix formats: Compressed Row Storage (CRS) and the hybrid (HYB) Ellpack-Coordinate format [10].

CRS is the most common data structure used to represent general sparse matrices. It makes no assumptions about the matrix sparsity and provides a compact representation. It uses three one-dimensional arrays, from where non-zero elements, column indices and pointers to the first element of each row are retrieved. HYB joins features from the so-called Ellpack (ELL) and Coordinate (COO) formats. ELL is suited for matrices whose maximum number of non-zeros per row does not substantially differ from the average; it stores the non-zero values in a dense bi-dimensional array and the corresponding column indices in a vector. COO, instead, is a very simple format which uses three vectors to store the row indices, column indices, and non-zero values of the matrix. The HYB format, proposed in [10], calculates the *typical* number of non-zeros per row and stores the majority of matrix entries in ELL and the remaining in COO.

2.4 Implementation

In the CUDA implementation of the BiCG algorithm, the main loop controlling the iterations is kept on the CPU, whilst the computations inside are performed

Table 1. Summary of BiCG functions and floating point operations (N is the matrix dimension, nnz is the number of non-zeros)

OPERATION	FORMULAS	DESCRIPTION	FLOPS
SpMV	Eq. 1	sparse matrix-vector product	$8nnz$
dot product	Eq. 2, 6	scalar product of two vectors	$8N$
e. w. product	Eq. 5	element-wise product of two vectors	$6N$
axpy	Eq. 3, 4, 8	$ax + y$ (a scalar, x and y vectors)	$8N$

on the GPU. Four kernels are in charge of the operations carried out in the BiCG main loop (see Table 1). Among them, the sparse matrix-vector product (SpMV) is the heaviest operation, even though each of the listed operations deserves being optimized on the GPU hardware. The implementation of the four kernels is shortly described below.

SpMV - this kernel implements the Bell and Garland algorithm [10], which is, at our knowledge, the best performing code currently available for solving sparse matrix-vector product on GPUs. This algorithm is avaible in the CUSP library [6] only for single and double precision real coefficients. Therefore, we adapted it in order to tackle matrices and vectors having double precision complex values and replicated the sophisticated optimization strategies, such as loop unrolling and shared memory exploitation, described in [10]. Memory accesses were optimized according to the storage format: one warp was assigned to each matrix row in the CRS format, whilst one thread was assigned to each row of the matrix in the HYB format. In addition to the matrix-vector product Ap_{i-1}, BiCG requires computing a Hermitian product $A^H\overline{p}_{i-1}$ (see equation 1). In a distributed-memory context, there will be extra communication costs associated with one of the two matrix-vector products, depending upon the storage scheme for A. To alleviate this problem, in the initialization phase we precalculate A^H at the cost of doubling the storage requirements for the matrix.

Dot product - cuBLAS complex dot function provided with CUDA is available only for single precision coefficients. Therefore, we implemented such function from scratch. Our kernel is an adaptation and generalization of the well known parallel reduction algorithm proposed by Harris et al. in [11]. Such algorithm deals with the sum of vector elements and is appreciated for its efficiency due to the adoption of advanced optimization strategies such as shared memory exploitation, loop unrolling and algorithm cascading (combine parallel and sequential reduction). The result is a function which, given as input two complex double precision arrays, provides as output their dot product, with performances aligned with those obtained by Harris.

Element-wise product and axpy - also in these cases, the cuBLAS functions provided with CUDA don't support double precision complex coefficients. Therefore, we implemented such functions from scratch by taking advantage of the CUDA cuComplex library [1] and by adopting optimization strategies finalized to the maximization of coalesced accesses. Moreover, in order to reduce the overhead due to communication between host and device we aggregated multiple calls in a single kernel wherever possible.

In addition to the optimization strategies briefly mentioned above, we also took advantage from CUDA texture memory, which provided relevant performance gains, as it caches data spatially closed together. Texture memory is normally read from kernels by using device functions called fetches. We implemented our own fetching functions since CUDA provides them only for real single precision data. Moreover, thanks to the exploitation of the so-called CUDA built-in arrays we efficiently minimized the cost of memory accesses.

3 Experiments and Results

The GPU-enabled solver has been tested on the CUDA-compatible nVidia GeForce GTX 260 GPGPU, featuring 24 streaming processors. The code was compiled by using CUDA 2.3 with driver version 190.53. For comparison we used a serial code implemented in C and all calculations were performed by a single core of an Intel Core2 Quad CPU Q9550 @ 2.83 GHz. The CPU code was compiled by GCC 4.3.4 with the "-O3" optimization option enabled on a PC equipped with 4 GB of DDR2 RAM, Ubuntu 9.10 as the 32-bit Linux operating system and ATLAS 3.6 [14] as BLAS library.

We tested our algorithms on sparse matrices, some of which were obtained from the application of the MoM to the design of EM circuits, the remaining were taken from the *"University of Florida Sparse Matrix Collection"* [12]. In both cases, based on GPU characteristics, we maximized multiprocessor occupancy and adopted equation (9) as convergence criterion with ϵ set to 10^{-7}.

3.1 EM Matrices

As to EM matrices derived from MoM, they concern the design of branch-line couplers in microstrip technology, which are four ports devices widely adopted in microwave and millimetre-wave applications like power dividers and combiners [13]. More specifically, the analyzed layout consists of two branch-line couplers connected by means of a 360° microstrip line and operating in the 2.5-3.5 GHz frequency band (see Fig. 1). The desired sparsity pattern was obtained by making a thresholding operation which determines the number of non-zero elements while maintaining a good accuracy of the final solution (error less than 2%).

The left side of Fig. 2 shows the convergence times of the host (CPU) and device (GPU) code for different matrix sizes (N) and formats. The percentage of non-zero elements is kept to 5% of the total number of entries by thresholding. The maximum matrix size was imposed by the memory limit of the available CPU, as before thresholding the entire dense matrix had to be loaded. Table 2 lists the achieved speed-ups. They are higher when matrix dimension allows for an optimum exploitation of hardware resources.

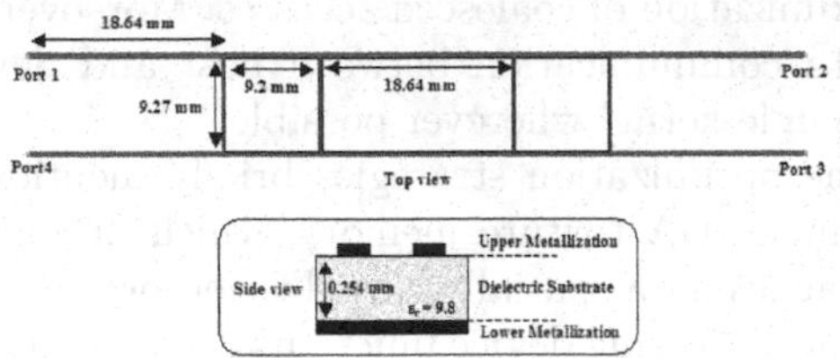

Fig. 1. Layout of the EM circuit used for testing

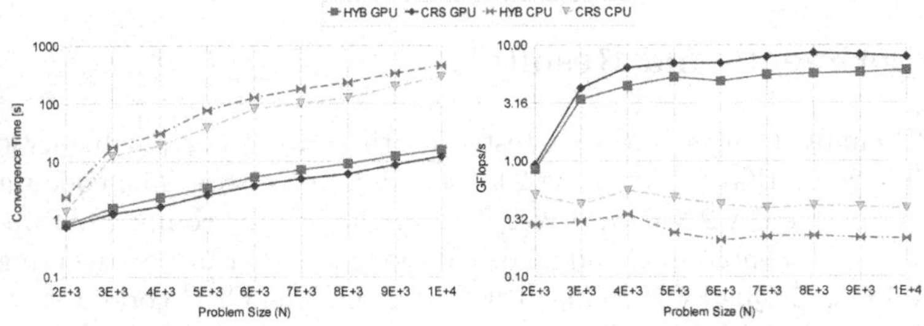

Fig. 2. BiCG convergence time (left) and performance in GFlops/s (right) for EM matrices

The right side of Fig. 2 shows the BiCG performance in terms of number of floating point operations (FLOPs) per second. For clarity, we report the equation used for calculating performance:

$$GFlops/s = \frac{C_{init} + n_{it} \cdot (2C_{spmv} + 2C_{ewp} + 2C_{dot} + 5C_{axpy})}{10^9 \cdot T_e} \qquad (10)$$

where C_{init} is the number of FLOPs in the initialization phase of the algorithm, C_{spmv}, C_{ewp}, C_{dot} and C_{axpy} respectively represent FLOPs required for SpMV, element-wise product, dot product and axpy functions (see last column of Table 1), n_{it} is the number of iterations of BiCG main loop and T_e is the total execution time of the algorithm. The multiplying factors of each C term in the numerator indicates the number of corresponding operations in the BiCG main loop.

In all EM matrices we analyzed, CRS format always produces faster results because of the high variability of the non-zero number per row (see Fig. 3). It is

Table 2. Achieved speed-ups for EM matrices

Problem Size (N)	Speed-Up CRS	Speed-Up HYB
2E+3	3.01	1.84
4E+3	12.8	11.5
6E+3	23.79	21.36
8E+3	25.17	20.74
10E+3	28.57	23.69

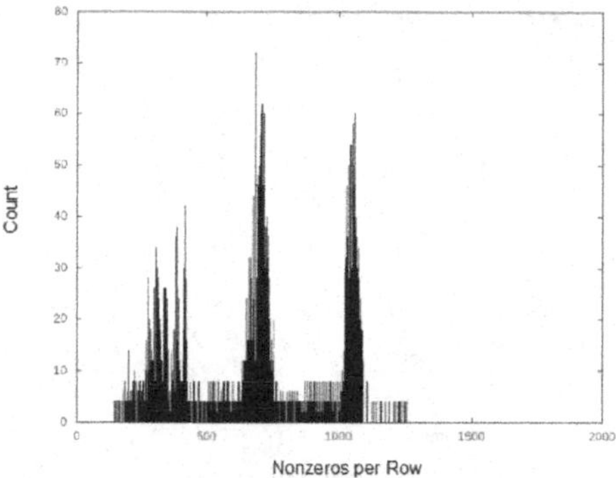

Fig. 3. Distribution of number of non-zeros per row for EM-MoM matrices

well known that convergence behavior of BiCG may be quite irregular, and the method may even break down, but in practical cases of EM circuit analysis we never observed this phenomenon in agreement with what observed in [3].

3.2 Florida Matrices

As to the *"University of Florida Collection"* [11], we identified ten complex sparse matrices (see table 3), belonging to different research areas and exhibiting different size, sparsity pattern and number of non-zeros.

The left side of Fig. 4 shows the performance obtained in the ten cases. Results are shown in terms of number of floating point operations and calculated according to equation (10). As the number of non-zeros per row was substantially constant for all the chosen matrices, the HYB format performed better than the CRS in all cases. Therefore we reported in the table on the right side of Fig. 4 only the speed-up obtained for the HYB format. As shown, the obtained speed-ups are even higher than those reached with EM matrices since we could better exploit GPU hardware resources as much bigger matrices were elaborated.

Table 3. Florida matrices used for performance testing

ID.	GROUP	NAME	SIZE	Non-zeros	Kind of problem
1	Bindel	ted_AB	10605^2	522387	thermal
2	Sinclair	3Dspectralwave2	292008^2	12935272	materials
3	Rost	RFdevice	74104^2	365580	semiconductor device
4	QCD	conf6_0-8x8-80	49152^2	1926928	chemistry
5	Puri	ABACUS_shell_md	23412^2	218484	model reduction
6	Lee	fem_hifreq_circuit	491100^2	20239237	electromagnetic
7	Kim	kim2	456976^2	11330020	2D/3D mesh
8	FreeFieldTech.	mono_500Hz	169410^2	5033796	acoustic
9	Dehghani	light_in_tissue	29282^2	406084	electromagnetic
10	Lee	fem_filter	74062^2	1731206	electromagnetic

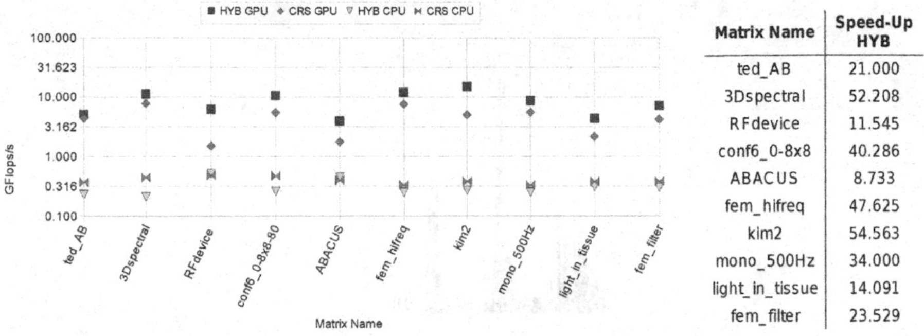

Matrix Name	Speed-Up HYB
ted_AB	21.000
3Dspectral	52.208
RFdevice	11.545
conf6_0-8x8	40.286
ABACUS	8.733
fem_hifreq	47.625
kim2	54.563
mono_500Hz	34.000
light_in_tissue	14.091
fem_filter	23.529

Fig. 4. Performance results (left) and speed-ups (right) for Florida matrices

4 Conclusions

In this paper, the achievement of peak-performance for EM solvers through the use of the inexpensive and powerful GPUs has been investigated. Based on the requirements coming from CEM, a sparse iterative solver for GPUs has been proposed. Taking advantage from CUDA library, we implemented a BiCG algorithm which tackles unstructured sparse matrices with two different storaging schemes. It has been tested on several matrices, both from well recognized matrix collections and from in-house experimentation in the area of EM circuit design. Results in terms of speed-up, execution time and GPU speed have been provided as a validation and assessment of solver efficiency.

References

1. NVIDIA, CUDA Zone, `http://www.nvidia.com/cuda`
2. Saad, Y.: Iterative methods for sparse linear systems, 3rd edn. SIAM, Philadelphia (2000)
3. Smith, C.F., et al.: The biconjugate gradient method for electromagnetic scattering. IEEE Trans. on Antennas and Propagation 38, 938–940 (1990)
4. Harrington, R.F.: Field Computation by Moment Methods. Krieger, Melbourne (1982)
5. Iterative CUDA, `http://mathema.tician.de/software/iterative-cuda`
6. CUSP Library v.0.1, `http://code.google.com/p/cusp-library`
7. SpeedIT Tools, `http://vratis.com/speedITblog`
8. Buatois, L., et al.: Concurrent number cruncher - A GPU implementation of a general sparse linear solver. International Journal of Parallel, Emergent and Distributed Systems 24(3), 205–223 (2009)
9. Jacobs, D.A.H.: A generalization of the conjugate gradient method to solve complex systems. IMA J. Numerical Analysis. 6, 447–452 (1986)
10. Bell, N., Garland, M.: Efficient sparse matrix-vector multiplication on CUDA. NVIDIA Tech. Rep. NVR-2008-004, NVIDIA Corporation (December 2008)

11. Harris, M., Sengupta, S., Owens, J.D.: Parallel prefix sum (scan) with CUDA. In: Nguyen, H. (ed.) GPU Gems, vol. 3. Addison Wesley, Reading (August 2007)
12. Davis, T.A.: The University of Florida Sparse Matrix Collection. Tech. Report of the University of Florida, `http://www.cise.ufl.edu/research/sparse/matrices`
13. Mongia, R.K., et al.: RF and Microwave Coupled-Line Circuits. Artech House, Boston (1999)
14. ATLAS Library, `http://math-atlas.sourceforge.net`

Distributed Computation of Feature-Detectors for Medical Image Processing on GPGPU and Cell Processors

Peter Zinterhof

Salzburg University, Austria
peter.zinterhof3@sbg.ac.at

Abstract. Automated classification of medical (computed tomography) images may ultimately lead to faster and improved diagnosis, benefiting both patients and clinicians. We describe a software system, that can be trained for classification purposes in the area of medical image processing. The underlying algorithm is based on a set of perceptron-like feature detectors, which are combined to short feature vectors. Those are used to form self-organized Kohonen maps, which will be used for the classification of new image data. The exact description of the feature detectors is derived from a large set of sample images by way of an evolutionary strategy. This leads to a computationally demanding process of iterated image decomposition, Kohonen map training and quality assessment. To make our method feasible, we rely on clusters of rather cheap commodity hardware, namely general purposes graphics processing units (GPGPU [5]) and the STI Cell Broadband Engine Architecture (Cell), as it comes with the PS3 gaming console.

1 Introduction

Medical image processing is applied on a wide range of levels, such as database-centered storage/retrieval applications, systems that physicians' strategic planning, automated counting of cells in histology and many more. Our work focuses on the automated detection of kidneys within computed tomography (CT) data. Although seemingly trivial for a human (even one without much medical experience), the task is difficult to accomplish on a computer system, due to the many possible shapes, sizes, levels of contrast, and medical anomalies a human kidney can display. In a training phase some 12000 image samples undergo a perceptron based filtering process that leads to a set of feature vectors. These feature vectors are both used for training of a Kohonen self-organizing feature map and for assessment of the resulting recall quality. The process starts with randomized perceptron weights, which subsequently are being refined by application of an evolutionary strategy (ES). According to ES a population of many individuals, each one describing a distinct set of perceptrons, has to be evolved for many generations to find proper settings. Fortunately, this computationally very demanding process is highly parallel in itself, so we can easily map it onto clusters

M.R. Guarracino et al. (Eds.): Euro-Par 2010 Workshops, LNCS 6586, pp. 339–347, 2011.
© Springer-Verlag Berlin Heidelberg 2011

of Cell Broadband Engine Architecture (Cell) processors and general purpose graphics processing units (GPU). The proposed system is domain specific by training, rather than by architecture. So there happen to be no restrictions to the domain of medical image processing.

2 Related Work

Several approaches for the automated segmentation and registration of organ tissue have been proposed, not necessarily restricted to kidney tissue. These include contour-based [3], graph-based [4], texture-based, and statistical [9] methods. The latter seems especially promising, because of its ability to cope with cysts, that may distort the kidney and make the detection even more difficult. Due to a lack of appropriate data, we could not yet test our system with images of pathologically distorted kidneys. Petkov [6] describes a system of n parallel 1-dimensional Kohonen self-organizing maps for general image classification purposes. Although not based on evolutionary strategies, it displays some similarity with the proposed system, in that it makes use of different 'views' of the data (cortical images) which are subjected to self-organizing maps. In principle, the texton-based approach [8] also bears a rather close resemblance with our approach, but we rely on Kohonen maps for classification instead of support vector machines. Additionally, in our case the filter masks (textons) are not derived from the set of training samples, but their formulation is left to evolution. A more general approach is taken by Pinto et al. [7] who describe a very efficient method of high-throughput screening of good visual representations on Cell and GPU hardware. By evaluating a large population for a single generation, the proposed system effectively mimics the latter approach. Generally, by adding more generations our approach extends high-throughput screening, thus constituting the well-known evolutionary process. Currently, we are not aware of approaches for automated kidney detection on Cell or GPU hardware.

3 Perceptron-Based Image Filtering

Image samples are filtered by a sliding window scheme based on 4x4 pixel wide perceptrons (a good introduction can be found in [1]). Every window location is preprocessed by a thresholding mechanism, that determines which of the 16 gray values fall within a given interval V. Pixels are set to 1 when lying within V and set to 0 otherwise, forming a temporary image P consisting of black and white pixels only. Convolving P and W with $c = \sum_{y=0}^{3} \sum_{x=0}^{3} P_{y,x} W_{y,x}$ leads to a local output of T=0, if $c < \Theta$ and T=1, if $c \geq \Theta$. The final result is given by $F_n = \sum_{0}^{Sy} \sum_{0}^{Sx} T_{y,x}$, with Sx, Sy denoting the dimension of the sample image in pixels reduced by the width of the perceptron (4 pixels) to account for the image boundaries. For each dimension k of the feature vector different weight matrices

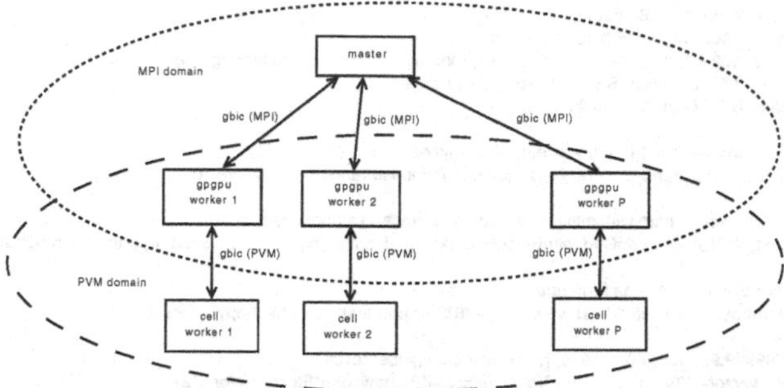

Fig. 1. Overview on distributed computation by means of MPI and PVM

W_k and pixel intervals V_k are used and subjected to evolution. The rationale of this process is to enable the evolutionary algorithm to find such weight matrices and pixel intervals, that 'behave well' during self-organization of the Kohonen map.

4 Kohonen Maps

Kohonen self-organizing maps reduce high-dimensional data to lower (e.g. two-) dimensional 'maps'. We employ an 8-dimensional Kohonen map of 192 x 192 elements. The training phase consists of two steps: A) find vector W within the map that has the minimum Euclidean distance to sample vector S and B) within a given radius R around W, change vectors W_r such, that the difference $S - W_r$ is reduced by a small factor $\gamma \in]0.0, 0.3]$, Radius R and learning-rate γ are constantly reduced during training to allow the map to settle to a stable state. The choice of dimensions of the map has been guided by the tight memory constraints of the Cell processor, which allows to store a map of 8x192x192 elements in the local store (LS) of 6 SPEs.

4.1 Parallel Computation

The genetic algorithm utility library (GAUL) was used for parallel and distributed evaluation of the population's fitness scores. GAUL has been linked against the MPICH2 library and parallelization occurs at several levels, depending on the chosen accelerator hardware. We first employ GAUL's distributed evaluation of individuals by which the genotypes are sent to the remote worker processes for fitness evaluation. When based on GPU acceleration, the worker process employs a local GPU for the main steps of our algorithm, namely the image filtering process and the training of the Kohonen map. Obviously, the GPU code is highly parallel in itself. For the filtering step a number of

```
dim3 dimBlock (8,8);   // 64 threads per block
dim3 dimGrid (24, 24);  // 576 blocks per grid
radius= (float)192 / 2.0;  // start values for neighborhood dimension and learing rate
learnrate = 0.29; reduceradABS   = (radius - 2.0) / cycles;
reducelearnABS = (learnrate - 0.001) / cycles;

for (i=0 ;  i < cycles ;  i++ ) {  // repeat e.g. 25000 times
  random_nr = (int)(drand48()*TrainingsImages);  // choose random sample vector

   // find vector within map with minimal euclidian distance to sample vector
  find_best_vector <<< dimGrid, dimBlock >>> (kmap_d, some_big_d, best_vector_d, (random_nr*Channels) );

   // retrieve 576 local minima from gpu
  cudaMemcpy(best_vector, best_vector_d, 576*2*sizeof(float), cudaMemcpyDeviceToHost);

  min = 999999.99;  for (j=0; j < 576; j++) // compute global result
  if (*(best_vector+j*2)< min) { min = *(best_vector+j*2); position=*(best_vector+j*2+1); }

  // adapt neighbours around winning vector
  change_vector_within_radius <<< dimGrid, dimBlock >>>
    (kmap_d, some_big_d, pos_x, pos_y, radius, learnrate,(random_nr*Channels));
  radius-=reduceradABS:   learnrate-=reducelearnABS: }
```

Fig. 2. Outline of GPU-based Kohonen map training

CUDA-blocks equal to the number of image samples are allocated. Within the MP, we make substantial use of the (SIMD-)vector capabilities. The 192x192 map vectors are distributed in blocks of 8x8 vectors onto the MPs, hence we get 576 data-independent CUDA-blocks. Since synchronization of the MPs proofed rather expensive, we moved the reduction of the 576 local minima to the CPU. In order to use Cell as the application's accelerator, we have to engage a second scheme of inter-process-communications for two reasons. MPICH2 does not support little- and big-endian machines within the same setup and LAM-MPI has been too outdated for proper installation on the PS3. OpenMPI should have been a feasible candidate, but as GAUL assumes all participating MPI ranks (worker processes) to be active 'evaluators', we would have had to introduce major changes to the internal workings of GAUL. We therefore employ the parallel virtual machine (PVM 3.4), which manages all necessary data conversions in a transparent way and does not interfere with GAUL's internal structure. CPU-based (x86) workers enroll both within PVM and MPI (Fig. 1) while PS3 based workers enroll within PVM only and establish 1:1-links to their CPU-based counterparts. Due to the very high demand of vector shifts during the sliding-window filter algorithm, we encountered performance levels that did not justify further development efforts and we restricted the Cell code to the Kohonen map training and recall process. Also, 200 MB of available memory would have hampered scalability in terms of the number of training images.

5 Implementation

In this section we will focus on some implementation details which are critical to performance on the various types of hardware.

5.1 GPU

The filtering stage delivers very high performance on the GPU, but we had to test several approaches to reach this goal. As 8 perceptrons have to be applied onto each sample image (64x64 pixels), we chose a grid size of 60. Within each of the 60 rows a single thread loops from index 0 to index 59, summing up the fire events of the perceptrons. To account for the computation of the 8 different perceptrons a second - outer - loop is used. The resulting performance proofed to be insignificantly higher than the CPU code (i7, 2.6GHz), which called for a rearrangement of the GPU code. By mapping the outer loop onto dimension y of the kernel, we change the partitioning from 60 threads to 60x8 threads. By changing the inner loop index (0..59) from row- to column-based computation, performance could also be improved to a high degree, resulting in a total speedup of 18.3 compared to the standard GPU code.

5.2 Cell

For maximum performance on map training we rely on the local store (LS) of the SPEs only. Every SPE manages 32x192 vectors of the map. Because the dimensions are multiples of 4, with 4 quad words taking up 128 bit (the cache line size), we get perfect data alignment which is key for fast vector operations. In the parallel winner-takes-all scheme of Kohonen map training, the winner has to be found after every iteration. In contrast to the GPU code, in which the CPU computes the global minimum, the Cell version operates without CPU interventions. As a consequence, the full algorithm of map training has been encapsulated in a single function, that can be called from within the main PPC-code. It even incorporates the code necessary for the classification of unknown vectors, which is being executed automatically after training. Cell's rather unique mechanism for conditional assignments of vector values (spu_sel, spu_cmpgt) has been extensively used in step A. See an excerpt of the code:

```
// DEMONSTRATION OF spu_cmpgt and spu_sel for a nearest-neighbor search
// mymap: array of Kohonen-map vectors (1/6 of total map)
// testvector: random vector, whose nearest neighbor is computed
for (i=0; i < RES*DIM; i++) {
  sum=(vector float){0.0,0.0,0.0,0.0};  current_nr=spu_splats (i);

  diff = mymap[i][0] - testvector[0]; sum = spu_madd (diff,diff, sum);
  diff = mymap[i][1] - testvector[1]; sum = spu_madd (diff,diff, sum);
      ...
  diff = mymap[i][7] - testvector[7]; sum = spu_madd (diff,diff, sum);

  mask = spu_cmpgt (localbest, sum);
  // if localbest > sum -> arg 1, else arg 0 is new minimum
  localbest=spu_sel(localbest,sum,mask);
  localbest_nr = spu_sel (localbest_nr,current_nr,mask);
}
```

The Cell toolkit (CTK-0.73, [2]) is offering mutex, semaphore, and barrier functions, but we designed our own improved barrier function (Fig. 3), on base of CTK's mutex code. This new function extends the traditional functionality by a means for distributing arbitrary data between the SPUs. 'Value' holds 16 words

```
inline void Barrier_1 (ctk_mutex_ea_t lock)
{
  ctk_mutex_lock(lock);
  ctk_dma_get_block((void*)&value, arg.value_ea, 64);
  value[1]++;
  ctk_dma_put_block((void*)&value, arg.value_ea, 64);
  ctk_mutex_unlock(lock);

  while (value[1]%NR_SPE_THREADS !=0) // modulo 6
   {
    ctk_dma_get_block((void*)&value, arg.value_ea, 64);
   }
}
```

Fig. 3. Cell barrier function

(64 bytes total size). The first 4 words are reserved for 4 distinct barrier variables, the remaining 12 words are dedicated to the 6 SPUs. Accesses to the array 'value' are protected by a single mutex. The SPUs store the locally computed values of the minimum search, along with the vector position at places $2*spu\_id, 2*spu\_id+1$ of the array 'value'. As the SPUs call the barrier function, they are not only being synchronized but the additional data are communicated within the group of 6 SPUs. The crucial point is the lack of additional data transfers for the SPUs. So each SPU receives the set of 6 local minima, reduces them into the number of the winner and continues with step B. As the SPU has to rely on a PPU-callback for most of the glibc-functions, we face problems in measuring the actual speedup of the new barrier function. Therefore, we take measurements (Tab. 1) from two reasonably large numbers of synchronizations in order to reduce the effects of code startup delays and call overheads. The busy-waiting scheme at the end of the barrier code can - in principle - lead to a race condition. By using two separated barriers, which are being called consecutively, this issue has been solved.

Table 1. Execution times (wall-time) for the standard synchronization and data distribution between 6 SPUs and the improved barrier function, that delivers about 14 % of speedup

number of calls	standard code	improved barrier	speedup
10.000.000	286.10 s	251.08 s	1.13947 x
100.000.000	2858.76 s	2508.87 s	1.13946 x

6 Results

The benchmarks (Tab. 2) show a tremendous advantage in using accelerator hardware during the training phase of the algorithm. We found speedups in the range of 11x (Cell) to 22x (GPU) for the evaluation of single individuals, which makes up the very core of the algorithm and can be directly translated to overall speedups of the application itself. Cell, albeit considerably less powerful than

Table 2. Execution times for the CPU-, Cell- and GPU-based algorithms. The Cell number denotes the sum of both training and recall execution times. CPU timings based on i7, 2.66 GHz, GPU timings based on single NVIDIA GTX 295. Total timings are measured at the level of the CPU-based worker and include all communication (MPI,PVM), as well as memory transfers to and from the GPU.

arch	convolution	Kohonen	quality evaluation	total time	speedup
CPU	6.064 s	182.9 s	6.6 s	195.6 s	1.00 x
Cell	n/a	15.8 s	n/a	16.69 s	11.7 x
GPU	0.351 s	4.2 s	3.18 s	8.86 s	22.05 x

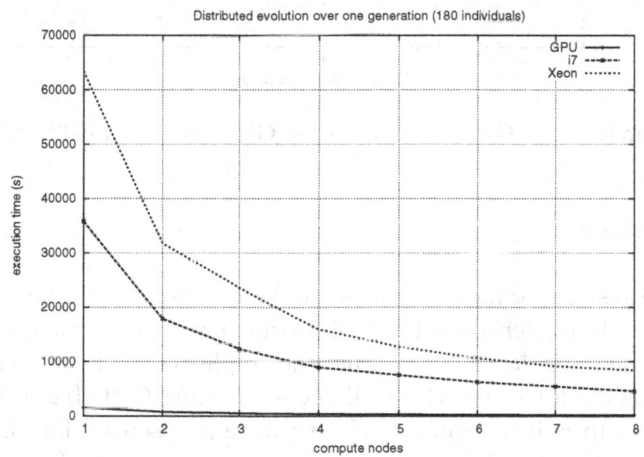

Fig. 4. GPU (up to 4x NVIDIA 295 GTX), i7 (up to 8 cores, 2.66GHz), Xeon (up to 8 cores, 2.3 GHz). Core counts based on 'full' CPUs without HT-support (e.g. numbers for eight i7-cores result from two i7 sockets).

the GPU in terms of the number of processing elements, delivers respectable performance. Fig. 4 displays execution times for up to 8 GPUs (4 dual-node NVIDIA GTX 295) and the corresponding numbers of i7 [1] and Xeon-cores. The GPU-based code clearly outperforms all CPU-based codes. Scalability is nearly linear. Fig. 5 displays execution times for up to 8 GPUs (NVIDIA GTX 295) and Cell processors. Cell timings are split into two setups. In setup 1 each Cell is served by a 'private' GPU, in setup 2 a single global GPU serves all (up to 8) Cell processors. A single GPU easily serves up to 8 Cell processors, therefore a cluster of PS3s does not necessarily have to be accompanied by an equally large GPU cluster.

[1] i7 quad core @2.66 GHz, Xeon 5345 quad core @2.3 GHz, GTX 295 cards consist of 2 GPUs with 240 streaming processors each.

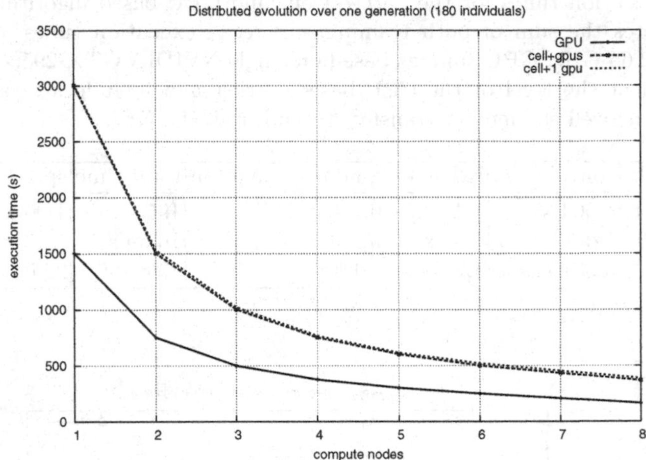

Fig. 5. Comparison of GPU vs. Cell codes, GPU=NVIDIA GTX 295, Cell=PS3

7 Conclusion

The proposed system for medical image classification has been successfully tested on GPU and Cell accelerators. Both platforms leverage performance by at least one order of magnitude, thus making the application of the very demanding algorithms feasible for users who lack access to large CPU-based HPC-systems. The high speedup gained from GPU hardware is essential for the evolution of proper features for the classification process in a reasonable amount of time. Ongoing work will be subject to the next generation of Fermi-based GPUs, which are expected to further improve throughput due to larger shared memory areas and thus shall further increase classification rates.

References

1. Bishop, C.M.: Neural Networks for Pattern Recognition. Oxford University Press, Oxford (1995)
2. Fixstars.com. NCTK: Cell ToolKit Library (2007)
3. Ghosh, P., Mitchell, M.: Segmentation of medical images using a genetic algorithm. In: GECCO, pp. 1171–1178 (2006)
4. Lai, C.-C., Chang, C.-Y.: A hierarchical evolutionary algorithm for automatic medical image segmentation. Expert Syst. Appl. 36(1), 248–259 (2009)
5. NVIDIA. NVIDIA CUDA Compute Unified Device Architecture, Programming Guide. NVIDIA Corporation (2008)
6. Petkov, N.: Biologically motivated computationally intensive approaches to image pattern recognition. Future Generation Computer Systems 11 (4-5), 451–465 (1995)

7. Pinto, N., Doukhan, D., DiCarlo, J.J., Cox, D.D.: A high-throughput screening approach to discovering good forms of biologically inspired visual representation. PLoS Comput. Biol. 5(11), e1000579 (2009)
8. Shotton, J., Johnson, M.: Semantic texton forests. In: Cipolla, R., Battiato, S., Farinella, G.M. (eds.) Computer Vision. Studies in Computational Intelligence, vol. 285, pp. 173–203. Springer, Heidelberg (2010)
9. Touhami, W., Boukerroui, D., Cocquerez, J.-P.: Fully automatic kidneys detection in 2D CT images: A statistical approach. In: Duncan, J.S., Gerig, G. (eds.) MICCAI 2005. LNCS, vol. 3749, pp. 262–269. Springer, Heidelberg (2005)

Preliminary Investigation of Accelerating Molecular Dynamics Simulation on Godson-T Many-Core Processor

Liu Peng[1], Guangming Tan[2], Rajiv K. Kalia[1], Aiichiro Nakano[1], Priya Vashishta[1], Dongrui Fan[2], and Ninghui Sun[2]

[1] Collaboratory for Advanced Computing and Simulation,
University of Southern California, Los Angeles, CA, USA
{liupeng,rkalia,anakano,priyav}@usc.edu
[2] Institute of Computing Technology,
Chinese Academy of Sciences, Beijing, China
{tgm,fandr,snh}@ict.ac.cn

Abstract. Molecular dynamics (MD) simulation is widely used in computational science, however, its irregular memory-access pattern imposes great difficulty on performance optimization. This paper presents a joint application/architecture study to accelerate MD on an emerging unconventional computing platform–*Godson-T* many-core architecture. We propose three incremental optimizations: (1) a divide-and-conquer algorithm adaptive to on-chip memory; (2) a novel data-layout to re-organize linked-list cell data structures to improve data locality; (3) an on-chip locality-aware parallel algorithm to enhance data reuse. Experiments on an event-driven, cycle-accurate *Godson-T* simulator achieve excellent speedup of 62 on 64 cores.

1 Introduction

Molecular dynamics (MD) simulation is widely used to study material properties at the atomistic level. But increasingly large computing power is needed to satisfy the spatiotemporal scale of the real world simulations. The advent of many-core paradigm has provided unprecedented computing power, and promises to enable large-scale and long-time simulation only if we can efficiently harvest the computing power. Challenges to achieve efficient parallel MD algorithm mainly on many-core platform arise from two aspects: (1) MD application is characterized by irregular memory access which imposes difficulty on locality optimization; (2) many-core hardware limitation (volume of on-chip memory, bandwidth of on-chip networking, etc.) constrains the size of working-set per core which imposes difficulty on on-chip parallelization. To address these difficulties, this paper presents a joint study from both application and architecture aspects on how to accelerating MD on *Godson-T* emerging many-core architecture, where we map an MD algorithm to architecture for achieving high on-chip parallel efficiency.

The main contribution of this paper are: (1) An adaptive divide-and-conquer (ADC) algorithm is designed to optimize the use of memory hierarchy; (2) A novel data layout is employed to re-organize linked-list cell data structures to maximize data locality;

M.R. Guarracino et al. (Eds.): Euro-Par 2010 Workshops, LNCS 6586, pp. 349–356, 2011.
© Springer-Verlag Berlin Heidelberg 2011

(3) An on-chip locality-aware parallel algorithm is designed to maximize data reuse; (4) Detailed experiments on an *Godson-T* simulator shows the optimized MD achieves a strong-scaling parallel efficiency 0.92 on 64 cores.

The rest of this paper is organized as follows. Section 2 briefly introduces the DC-MD algorithm used in this work, where key performance bottlenecks are summarized. Section 3 highlights the main architectural features of *Godson-T* , and Section 4 describes our optimization strategies. Section 5 presents the experimental results and detailed analysis. Finally, Section 6 concludes the paper.

2 A Divide-and-Conquer MD Algorithm

We have previously proposed a space-time multiresolution MD (MRMD) algorithm to reduce the $O(N^2)$ time complexity of potential evaluation to $O(N)$ [4]. In the MRMD, $E(r^N)$ consists of two-body $E_2\{r_{ij}\}$ and three-body $E_3\{r_{ijk}\}$ terms within a cutoff radius r_c. In the linked-list cell method, the dimension R_c of the cells is usually chosen to be larger than r_c. For a given atom in a cell, the search space for interacting neighbor atoms is limited to the 26 nearest neighbor cells. Conventional summation rule to compute 3-body interaction is written as $E_3(r_{ijk}) = \sum_{i=1}^{N}\sum_{j=1}^{nbr(i)}\sum_{k\neq i}^{nbr(j)} v(r_i, r_j, r_k)$, where r_i is the coordinate of the $i-th$ atom and $nbr(i)$ is the list of neighbor atoms within the three-body cutoff length from atom i, which acts as the center of atomic triplet (j, i, k). To maximally exploit parallelism in a multi-core cluster, our EDC-STEP-HCD scheme has employed a multi-level parallelization strategy [5,6]. Although this scheme has achieved internode parallel efficiency well over 0.95 for 218 billion-atom MD simulation on 212, 992 BlueGene/L processors [5], it suffers inefficient on-chip parallelism with on-chip parallel efficiency only 0.65 for 8 threads on a dual Intel quadcore Xeon SMP platform [6]. We observe several features that prevent the program from achieving high performance on conventional multi-core architectures: (1)*Irregular memory access*. Straightforward or sparse-matrix-like implementation of linked-list data structure leads to irregular memory accesses in three-body interaction calculation;

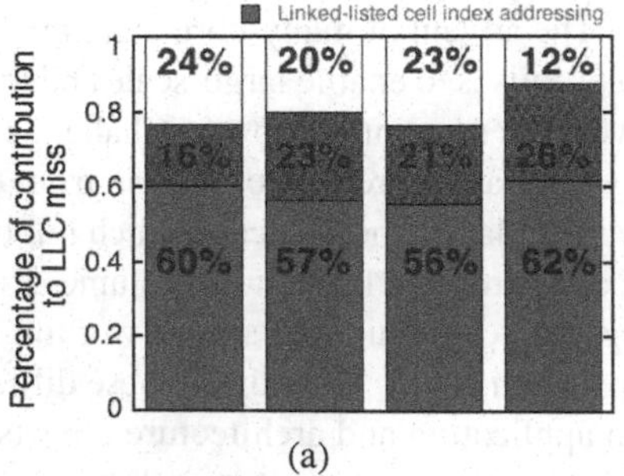

(a)

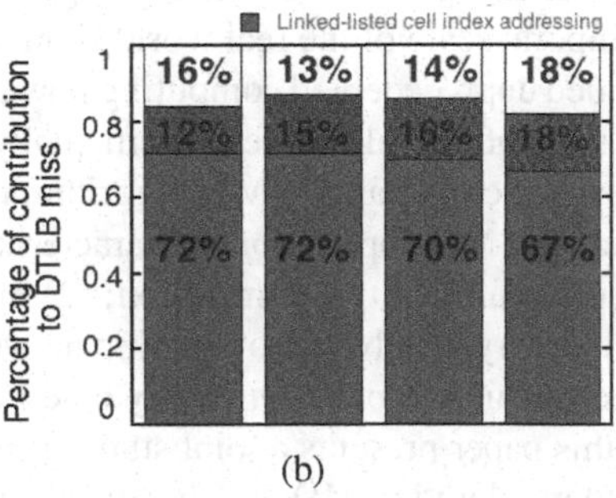

(b)

Fig. 1. (a) and (b) are percentages of events that cause last level cache (LLC) miss and data translation look aside buffer (DTLB) miss for the original DC-MD algorithm on an Intel quadcore core i7 920 platform measured by Intel VTune Performance Analyzer

(2)*High latency to access shared data*. Let N_c denote the number of cells in each Cartesian direction, q the atom density(number of atoms divided by system volume $(N_c R_c)^3$, then the total number of cross-cell pairs in the system is given by $N_c^3 \times qR_c^3 \times 26qR_c^3$. Thereby the size of atomic data for interaction computation easily exceeds that of the last level cache. Combining with the irregular memory access mentioned before, the latency problem becomes even worse, as evidenced by the memory accessing performance in Fig. 1(a) and Fig. 1(b) conducting on Intel quadcore core i7 920 platform measured by the Intel VTune Performance Analyzer. Therefore, it is of great significance to optimize the memory accessing to improve the performance and scalability of our MD application on many-core platforms.

3 *Godson-T* Many-Core Architecture

Godson-T is a low-power many-core architecture developed by Institute of Computing Technology, Chinese Academy of Sciences to serve as a dedicated petaflops computing engine. As shown in Fig. 2, *Godson-T* has 64 homogeneous, dual-issue and in-order processing cores running at 1 GHz, where a floating-point multiply-accumulate operation can be issued to a fully-pipelined function unit in each cycle, resulting in a peak floating-point performance of 128 Gflops. The 8-pipeline processing core supports 32-bit MIPS ISA (64-bit ISA will be supported in latter version) with synchronization instruction extensions. Key architectural features for achieving decent scalability and high performance include the following [1]:

- *Fine-grained parallelism* [8]. Each core works as a lightweight hardware thread unit executing in a non-preemptive manner. A dedicated synchronization manager (SM) is a centralized unit to collect and handle synchronization requests, which provides architectural support for fast mutual exclusion, barrier and signal/wait synchronization. In addition, an extremely efficient thread execution runtime system has been developed to manage thread execution [8,3].
- *Locality-awareness*. Each processing core has a 16KB 2-way set-associative private instruction cache and a 64KB local memory (like data cache). As inspired by

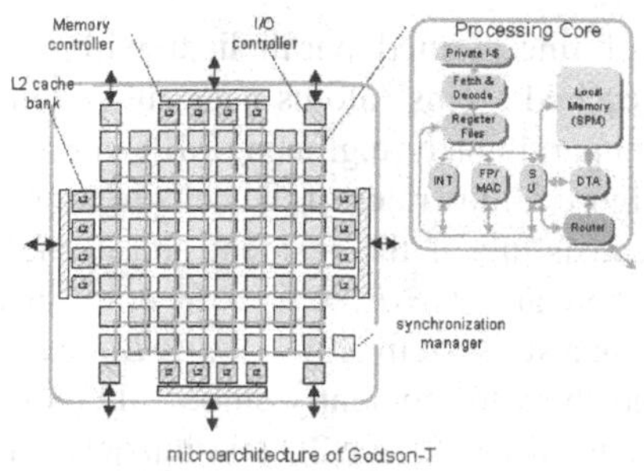

Fig. 2. *Godson-T* architecture: INT is fixed point arithmetic unit, FP/MAC is floating point unit, and CU is communication unit

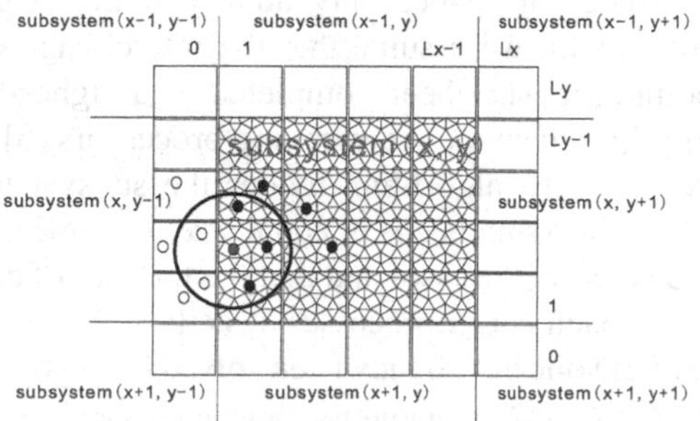

Fig. 3. Cellular decomposition scheme for on-chip parallelization. Cached atoms and resident atoms are shown in white and shaded boxes

IBM CELL and Nvidia GPU, an explicit memory hierarchy is implemented for user to exploit better locality with less complex hardware implementation compared to that of the traditional transparent memory hierarchy. Moreover, in *Godson-T*, each local memory is configured as explicitly-controlled, globally-addressed scratched-pad memory (SPM) to further help programmer maximize locality. An 8×8 packet-switching 2D mesh network connects all on-chip units with a 128bit bandwidth employing deterministic X-Y routing policy, which can provide a total of 2TB/s on-chip bandwidth among 64 processing cores. In addition, there are 16 address-interleaved L2 cache banks (256KB each) distributed along the perimeter of the chip, which are shared by all processing cores and can serve up to 64 cache accessing requests in total. The bandwidth between SPM and L2 cache is 256GB/s, and each four L2 cache banks on the same side of the chip share a memory controller with a 25.6GB/s memory-accessing bandwidth.

- *Latency tolerance* [7]. Since there may exist intensive contention on on-chip network and memory controller, latency to L2 cache will possibly become primary obstacle to achieve decent performance. To address this issue, a DMA (direct memory accessing)-like coprocessor Data Transfer Agent (DTA) is built in each core to do fast data communication, that is, when one core is doing calculations, DTA can be programmed to manage various data communications at backend in parallel.

4 Optimizations on *Godson-T*

In this section, we describe how to design an efficient MD algorithm based on the features provided by *Godson-T* many-core architecture.

4.1 Adaptive Divide-and-Conquer Algorithm

In the original DC-MD algorithm, the physical space is subdivided into spatially localized cells, with local atoms constituting subproblems. The algorithm recursively divides a coarse cell into finer cells until some criterion is satisfied. In our adaptive divide-and-conquer (ADC) algorithm specially designed for many-core architectures, we use the size of the first level memory (i.e. private local memory), C_{pm}, as a critical factor of the criterion.

Since this paper only addresses the issue of fine-grained parallelism within a subsystem, we assume that the interchange of cached atoms (atoms near subsystem boundaries) has been completed by a higher-level parallelism (e.g. using MPI) among multiple many-core computing processors [5]. Figure 3 illustrates of the cells in a subsystem. The algorithm divides the subsystem consisting of the resident and cached atoms into small cells of equal size. Assume that there are $P = P_x \times P_y \times P_z$ cores in a many-core processor and that the number of cells in a subsystem is $L = L_x \times L_y \times L_z$. Then each core i processes $\frac{L}{P}$ cells as Eq. 1 (since how to efficiently embed 3D mesh into 2D one has already been solved by classical algorithms [2], the 2D on-chip network on *Godson-T* is viable for this decomposition): $\{(c_x, c_y, c_z)|c_x \in [\frac{iL_x}{P_x}, \frac{(i+1)L_x}{P_x}), c_y \in [\frac{iL_y}{P_y}, \frac{(i+1)L_y}{P_y}), c_z \in [\frac{iL_z}{P_z}, \frac{(i+1)L_z}{P_z})\}$. Let B denote the memory space for storing one atomic data, N_b denote the number of neighbor atoms per cell. In order for all the resident atomic data to fit in the private local memory, R_c should satisfy

$$qR_c^3 \times (N_b + \frac{L}{P}) \times B \leq C_{pm} \Rightarrow R_c \leq \sqrt[3]{\frac{PC_{pm}}{(PN_b + L)Bq}}. \tag{1}$$

ADC algorithm performs recursive cellular decomposition until Eq. 1 is satisfied. When the atomic data are distributed into each core's local memory, they are reused in both two- and three-body force calculations, as the software controlled SPM provides a mechanism for user to decide what data locate in the private local memory and when. However, a direct implementation based on the linked-list cell data structure is not efficient enough because of MD's irregularity. In the next subsection, we propose a novel data layout optimization to address this problem.

4.2 Data Layout Optimization

At the beginning of MD simulation, each atom is assigned an integer in $[0...N-1]$, which is used as an identifier for the linked-list based algorithm to access atomic data. We refer to this method as *global-ID-centered* addressing. However, during the simulation, the identifiers cannot be kept contiguous due to atom migration between computing nodes/processors. In the ADC algorithm, it is expected that the atomic data is distributed among different cores, where each cell only interacts with 26 neighbor cells. Therefore, if all the atomic data within one cell were grouped together, they would be easily reached through its cell index. Here, we propose a new strategy—*cell-centered* addressing.

Figure 4(a) depicts the data structure designed for the atomic data in SPM, where na denotes the maximum number of atoms in one cell. Since all the atomic data for each cell are grouped, the cell index (cc) can be used to search the neighbor cells, and then the

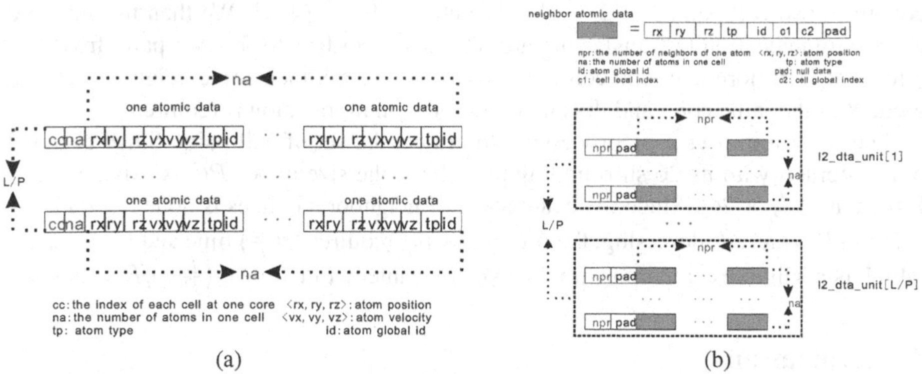

Fig. 4. (a) The atomic data of cells in a core's SPM. (b)The neighbor atomic data of cells in the shared L2 cache or off-chip memory. Pad is used for address alignment. Each L2_data_unit[i] represents a contiguous block of all neighbor atomic data for the $i-th$ cell in L2 cache or off-chip memory ($i = 1, ..., L/P$).

atomic data in each cell can be touched contiguously. Moreover, considering the sequential mapping between cores and cells, the searching of neighbor cells is completed in $O(1)$ time: The scalar value of cc is transformed into a vector (cc_x, cc_y, cc_z), then the neighbor cell index is calculated by the combination of $\{(cc_x + l_x, cc_y, +l_y, cc_z + l_z)|l_x, l_y, l_z \in \{-1, 0, 1\}\}$, where the number of neighbors including itself is 27.

As was shown in section 2, the number of cross-cell atom pairs is $qR_c^3 \times 26qR_c^3$ per cell, and it is impossible to store all the data in each core's private memory. Since the three-body interaction calculation also involves atoms in one cell and its 26 neighbor cells, it can also benefit from the *cell-centered* addressing for contiguous accessing of atomic data in a cell. Similarly, we group the neighbor atoms as well. Figure 4(b) depicts the data layout of neighbor atoms located in L2 cache or off-chip memory, where we group all the neighbor atomic data for the i-th cell together as L2_data_unit[i], which can be transferred to the SPM through a DMA like operation that utilizes high bandwidth provided in *Godson-T*.

4.3 On-Chip Locality Aware Parallel Algorithm

In this subsection, we present our on-chip locality aware parallel algorithm to enhance data reuse and further to alleviate the long latency to access the shared neighbor atomic data in L2 cache or off-chip memory. The two-body force calculation involves core-core communication, and it may cause on-chip network congestion. Moreover, the access to L2 cache also goes through the on-chip network, which may introduce more congestion. Here, we propose a solution to enhance the data reuse and to reduce the remote shared-data memory accessing, thereby alleviating the long latency. Suppose that the atoms in a cell at core i interacts with those in another cell at core j. In order to achieve on-chip locality for core i, we maximize the data reuse of cells from core j, and vice versa for core j. Our solution is first to construct a set of cell pairs $PC[cj] = \{ci0, ci1, .., cik\}$, where cj is the global index of the cell interacting with cells $ci0, ..., cik$ in core i. For example, suppose that core i has cells $\{1, 4, 8\}$, and core j has cells $\{2, 5\}$. Also assume that cell 2 interacts with $\{1, 4\}$ and that cell 5 interacts with $\{4, 8\}$. Then we construct two cell pairs $PC[2] = \{1, 4\}$ and $PC[5] = \{4, 8\}$. We then use the core-core communication to transfer the atomic data according to the cell pairs from core j to core i. If more than one cell are assigned to a core, then some neighbor cells are located in the same core, and thus no core-core communication is required.

The algorithm uses a preprocessing to collect the set of cell pairs. Since each cell only interacts with its 26 surrounding neighbors, the size of set PC is expected to be less than $O(\frac{L}{P} \times 26)$. Since the calculation of neighbor's indices is done in $O(1)$ time using *cell-centered* addressing, the preprocessing requires $O(\frac{L}{P})$ time and $O(\frac{L}{P})$ space, which is negligible compared with the two-body interaction time $O(\frac{L}{P} \times qR_c^3 \times 26qR_c^3)$.

5 Evaluation

In this section, we present the experimental results and detailed analysis of the proposed MD optimization on a *Godson-T* many-core simulator.

Godson-T is an on-going research project for building a petaflops supercomputer, and a real chip is expected to be shipped in late 2010. In order to evaluate its performance at early stage of the architectural development, we here employ an instruction-level simulator. The *Godson-T* simulator is event-driven, cycle-accurate, executing both kernel and application codes, and has modeled all architectural features introduced previously. Since it is an instruction-level simulator, it can produce detailed traces and instruction mix of all executed instructions for any given application after execution. The toolchain on *Godson-T* consists of a gcc-3.3 compiler and a thread execution runtime system, which provides a POSIX thread-like API. Moreover, since our ultimate objective is to build a large-scale parallel computer, where on-chip parallelism is of critical importance, we mainly focus on on-chip parallelization with a fixed problem size, and the speedup on p cores is calculated by $S(p) = \frac{Time_{one\_core}}{Time_{p\_cores}}$, where $Time_{p\_cores}$ represents the executing time on p cores and $Time_{one\_core}$ represents that on one core. And strong-scaling parallel efficiency $E(p)$ is then defined as $E(p) = \frac{S(p)}{p}$ for a fixed problem size. In the following experiments, the MD simulation tested is for a silica system [5]. Within the DC framework, the whole system is divided into subsystems each containing $24,000$ atoms as the fixed problem size for strong scalability analysis.

The experiments compare three incrementally improved versions of MD algorithm:

- *optimization-1*: implementation of ADC algorithm,
- *optimization-2*: implementation of ADC algorithm and data layout optimization,
- *optimization-3*: implementation of ADC algorithm, data layout optimization and on-chip locality-aware algorithm.

We have tested the scalability of the parallel algorithms. Figure 5 shows that *optimization-3* makes MD scale excellently with an on-chip strong-scaling parallel efficiency 0.92 on 64 cores while *optimization-1* begins to deteriorate when the number of cores exceeds 32. It tells that optimizations which take advantage of architectural features to maximize data locality and exploit data reuse benefit scalability most, which is also evidenced by the running time in Fig. 6 as *optimization-3*reduces the execution time by a factor of 2.

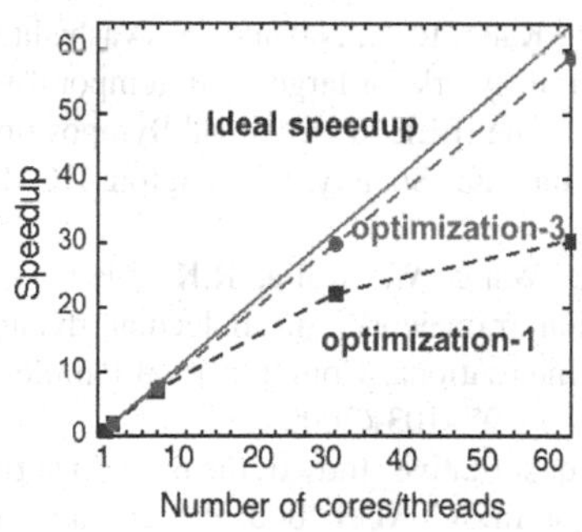

Fig. 5. Speedup as a function of the number of cores for *optimization-1* and *optimization-1*

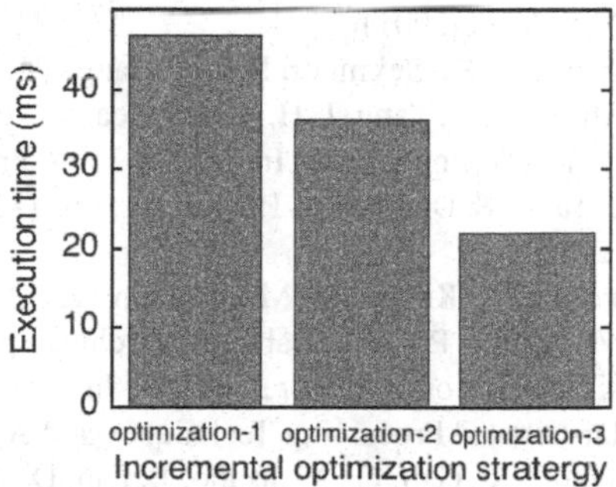

Fig. 6. Execution time in milliseconds on 64-core *Godson-T* . Here, number i represents optimization-i ($i = 1, 2, 3, 4$)

6 Conclusion

The emergence of many-core architecture has provided unprecedented computing power to computational scientists, and it is of great significance to exploit the computational power of such new platforms to improve the performance and scalability of large-scale scientific applications. In this paper, we have described our investigation of accelerating MD simulation on representative many-core architecture *Godson-T* . We have proposed a divide-and-conquer algorithm adaptive to the memory hierarchy to facilitate the on-chip local memory, a novel data layout to improve data locality to alleviate the irregular memory accessing, an on-chip locality-aware parallel algorithm to enhance data reuse to amortize the long latency to access shared data. These techniques have made the parallel MD algorithm scale nearly linearly with the number of cores. Also we have found that the data locality and data reuse schemes taking advantage of explicit memory architecture and high-bandwidth on-chip network are essential to achieve high scalability. The contribution of this work lies not only in giving application scientists advice on how to optimize their applications utilizing architectural mechanisms, but also in guiding future hardware developments.

References

1. Fan, D.R., Yuan, N., Zhang, J.C., Zhou, Y.B., Lin, W., Song, F.L., Ye, X.C., Huang, H., Yu, L., Long, G.P., Zhang, H., Liu, L.: Godson-t: An efficient many-core architecture for parallel program executions. Journal of Computer Science and Technology 24(6), 1061–1073 (2009)
2. Grama, A., Karypis, G., Kumar, V., Gupta, A.: Introdution to Parallel Computing. Benjamin Cummings (2003)
3. Lin, W., Fan, D., Huang, H., Yuan, N., Ye, X.: A low-complexity synchronization based cache coherence solution for many cores. In: CIT 2009: Proceedings of the 2009 Ninth IEEE International Conference on Computer and Information Technology, pp. 69–75. IEEE Computer Society, Washington, DC, USA (2009)
4. Nakano, A., Kalia, R.K., Vashishta, P., Campbell, T.J., Ogata, S., Shimojo, F., Saini, S.: Scalable atomistic simulation algorithms for materials research. In: Supercomputing 2001: Proceedings of the 2001 ACM/IEEE Conference on Supercomputing (CDROM), p. 1. ACM, New York (2001)
5. Nomura, K., Seymour, R., Weiqiang, W., Dursun, H., Kalia, R.K., Nakano, A., Vashishta, P., Shimojo, F., Yang, L.H.: A metascalable computing framework for large spatiotemporal-scale atomistic simulations. In: IPDPS 2009: Proceedings of the IEEE International Symposium on Parallel & Distributed Processing, pp. 1–10. IEEE Computer Society, Washington, DC, USA (2009)
6. Peng, L., Kunaseth, M., Dursun, H., Nomura, K., Wang, W., Kalia, R.K., Nakano, A., Vashishta, P.: A scalable hierarchical parallelization framework for molecular dynamics simulation on multicore clusters. In: Proceeding of International Conference on Parallel and Distributed Processing Techniques and Applications, pp. 97–103 (2009)
7. Wang, X., Gan, G., Manzano, J., Fan, D., Guo, S.: A quantitative study of the on-chip network and memory hierarchy design for many-core processor. In: ICPADS 2008: Proceedings of the 2008 14th IEEE International Conference on Parallel and Distributed Systems, pp. 689–696. IEEE Computer Society, Washington, DC, USA (2008)
8. Yu, L., Liu, Z., Fan, D., Song, F., Zhang, J., Yuan, N.: Study on fine-grained synchronization in many-core architecture. In: SNPD 2009: Proceedings of the 10th ACIS International Conference on Software Engineering, Artificial Intelligences, Networking and Parallel/Distributed Computing, pp. 524–529. IEEE Computer Society, Washington, DC, USA (2009)

Real-Time Stopped Object Detection by Neural Dual Background Modeling

Giorgio Gemignani[1], Lucia Maddalena[2], and Alfredo Petrosino[1]

[1] DSA - University of Naples Parthenope
Centro Direzionale, Isola C/4, 80143 Naples, Italy
[2] ICAR - National Research Council
Via P. Castellino 111, 80131 Naples, Italy

Abstract. Moving object detection is a relevant step for many computer vision applications, and specifically for real-time color video surveillance systems, where processing time is a challenging issue. We adopt a dual background approach for detecting moving objects and discriminating those that have stopped, based on a neural model capable of learning from past experience and efficiently detecting such objects against scene variations. We propose a GPGPU approach allowing real-time results, by using a mapping of neurons on a 2D flat grid on NVIDIA CUDA. Several experiments show parallel perfomance and how our approach outperforms with respect to OpenMP implementation.

Keywords: Video Surveillance, Stopped Object Detection, Neural Model, GPGPU.

1 Introduction

Moving object detection in videos is the first relevant step of information extraction in many computer vision applications. The usual approach is through *background subtraction*, that consists in maintaining an up-to-date model of the scene background and detecting moving objects as those that deviate from such a model. Among the objects detected as extraneous to the background, in visual surveillance, specific attention is given to *stopped objects*, i.e. temporally static image regions indicating objects that do not constitute the original background, but were brought into the scene at a subsequent time. Examples are given by abandoned luggage or illegally parked vehicles [2,3,8]. Approaches proposed in literature are either *tracking-based*, i.e. results are obtained based on the analysis of object trajectories through an application-dependent event detection phase (e.g. most of the papers in [2,3]), or *non tracking-based*, i.e. objects are classified without the aid of tracking modules (e.g. [1,4,7]).

We adopt a non tracking-based approach to stopped object detection in image sequences taken by stationary cameras. Based on the use of a double background strategy [7], we construct separate long- and short-term neural self-organizing backgrounds, based on the approach reported in [5]. The long-term background is the usual background model, holding a model for the scene background, while

M.R. Guarracino et al. (Eds.): Euro-Par 2010 Workshops, LNCS 6586, pp. 357–364, 2011.
© Springer-Verlag Berlin Heidelberg 2011

the short-term model contains temporarily static background elements. Using such models an evidence score is inferred for each pixel as belonging or not to a stationary foreground object. The model, named by us Dual Background SOBS Algorithm, possesses a significant amount of data-level parallelism, suitable for a Single Instruction Multiple Data (SIMD) architecture that allows massively parallel processing. Following the approach of General-Purpose computing on Graphics Processing Units (GPGPU), we decided to exploit the CUDA (Compute Unified Device Architecture) technology on NVIDIA graphical chipsets [6], by organizing both short- and long-term models as neural networks mapped onto 2D flat grids. Section 2 reports the Dual Background SOBS Algorithm, while Sections 3 and 4 respectively report the adopted parallelization technique and performance evaluation.

2 Stopped Object Detection

2.1 Dual Background Approach

In order to automatically detect stopped objects in digital color sequences $I_t, t = 1, \ldots,$. taken by stationary cameras, we adopt a dual background strategy based on the approach proposed in [7]. We construct two separate models (whose specific structure is described in §2.2): a *long-term model* B^L, that models the scene background without moving objects, and a *short-term model* B^S, that contains temporarily static background elements, including moving objects that have been excluded by B^L. By comparing each sequence frame with these models, we obtain two binary masks: the long-term foreground mask F^L, that is true only for objects (both moving and stopped) that are extraneous to the background, and the short-term foreground mask F^S, that is true only for moving objects. An evidence score is inferred at each pixel $\mathbf{x}$ by applying a set of hypotheses on the foreground masks and, to provide temporal consistency, the resulting evidence scores $E_t(\mathbf{x})$ for each pixel $\mathbf{x}$ of sequence frame I_t are aggregated in time as

$$E_t(\mathbf{x}) = \begin{cases} \min(\tau, E_{t-1}(\mathbf{x}) + \Delta t) & \text{if } F^L(\mathbf{x}) \wedge !F^S(\mathbf{x}) \\ \max(0, E_{t-1}(\mathbf{x}) - k) & \text{if } !F^L(\mathbf{x}) \vee F^S(\mathbf{x}) \end{cases} \tag{1}$$

where $\wedge$, $\vee$ and ! indicate logical *and*, *or* and *not* operations, respectively. If $\mathbf{x}$ is not modeled by B^L but it is modeled by B^S, than it must belong to a stopped object, and correspondingly $E_t(\mathbf{x})$ is incremented by the factor Δt. The maximum value τ for $E_t(\mathbf{x})$ corresponds to the *stationarity threshold*, i.e. the minimum number of consecutive frames after that a pixel assuming constant features is classified as stopped; the value for τ is chosen depending on the desired responsiveness of the system. Otherwise, if $\mathbf{x}$ is modeled by B^L or is not modeled by B^S, than it must belong either to the background or to a moving object, and correspondingly $E_t(\mathbf{x})$ is decremented by the factor k, that determines how fast the system should recognize that a stopped pixel has moved again. When thresholded by τ, the aggregated evidence score computed as in (1) provides a binary mask that is true only for pixels belonging to objects extraneous to the background and that stay stopped for at least τ consecutive sequence frames. An example of the stopped object detection procedure is shown in Fig. 1. The sequence frame I_t of Fig. 1-(a) shows a bag that has been left on the floor more than τ frames ago, while a man is moving. The corresponding long-term foreground mask F^L shown in Fig. 1-(b) is true (white colored) only for pixels extraneous to the scene background (i.e. pixels that are not modeled by the long-term background B^L), while the short-term foreground mask F^S (Fig. 1-(c)) is true only for moving pixels, since the short-term background has included pixels belonging to the stopped object. The evidence score E_t, whose normalized version is shown as a gray-level image in Fig. 1-(d), has reached the maximum value τ only for pixels of the stopped object, while gets lower values for pixels that where recently moving. Thresholding the evidence score with respect to τ, the stopped object shown in red in Fig. 1-(e) is obtained.

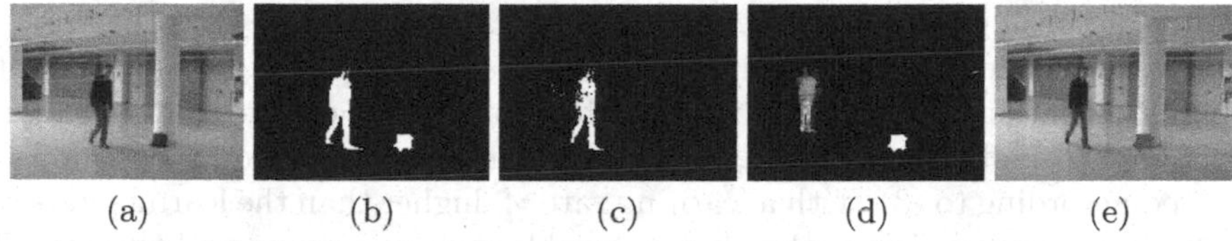

Fig. 1. (a) original sequence frame; (b) F^L; (c) F^S; (d) E; (e) stopped object (in red)

2.2 Neural Self-Organizing Background Model

The background model constructed and maintained in SOBS algorithm [5], here adopted for both the long-term and the short-term backgrounds, is based on a self-organizing neural network arranged as a 2-D flat grid of neurons. Each neuron computes a function of the weighted linear combination of incoming inputs, with weights resembling the neural network learning, and can be therefore represented by a weight vector obtained collecting the weights related to incoming links. An incoming pattern is mapped to the neuron whose set of weight vectors is most similar to the pattern, and weight vectors in a neighborhood of such node are updated; such learning of the neuronal map allows to adapt the background model to scene modifications. Specifically, for each pixel $\mathbf{x}$ we build a neuronal map consisting of $n \times n$ weight vectors $b_0^i(\mathbf{x}), i = 1, \ldots, n^2$ where each weight vector is a 3D vector initialized to the color components of the corresponding pixel of the first sequence frame I_0. The complete set of weight vectors for all pixels of an image I_0 with N rows and M columns is represented as a neuronal map B_0 with $n \times N$ rows and $n \times M$ columns, where adjacent blocks of $n \times n$ weight vectors correspond to adjacent pixels in image I_0. The value $n = 3$, suggested and justified in [5], is adopted for all experiments reported in §4. For each frame I_t, the color $I_t(\mathbf{x})$, at position $\mathbf{x}$ is compared to the weight vectors $b_{t-1}^1(\mathbf{x}), \ldots, b_{t-1}^{n^2}(\mathbf{x})$ related to it in the model B_{t-1}, to determine the weight vector $b_{t-1}^{BM}(\mathbf{x})$ that best matches it according to a metric $d(\cdot)$:

$$d(b_{t-1}^{BM}(\mathbf{x}), I_t(\mathbf{x})) = \min_{i=1,\ldots,n^2} d(b_{t-1}^i(\mathbf{x}), I_t(\mathbf{x})). \tag{2}$$

The best matching weight vector is used as the pixel's encoding approximation, and therefore $\mathbf{x}$ is detected as foreground if the distance in (2) exceeds a threshold ϵ; otherwise, it is classified as background. The adopted color space, the metric $d(\cdot)$ and the threshold ϵ can be suitably chosen as in [5].

Learning is able to adapt the background model B_{t-1} to scene modifications and is achieved by updating the best matching weight vector $b_{t-1}^{BM}(\mathbf{x})$, supposed at position $\mathbf{z}$ of B_{t-1}, and all other weight vectors in its neighborhood $N_{\mathbf{z}}$ according to:

$$b_t(\mathbf{y}) = (1 - \alpha_t(\mathbf{y}, \mathbf{z}))b_{t-1}(\mathbf{y}) + \alpha_t(\mathbf{y}, \mathbf{z})I_t(\mathbf{x}), \quad \forall \mathbf{y} \in N_{\mathbf{z}} \tag{3}$$

Here $\alpha(\mathbf{y}, \mathbf{z}) = \gamma_t \cdot G(\mathbf{y}\text{-}\mathbf{z})$, where γ_t represents the learning rate, that depends from scene variability, while $G(\cdot) = G(\cdot; 0, \sigma^2)$ are the values of a Gaussian filter with zero mean and σ^2 variance in $N_{\mathbf{z}}$. For the purpose of the double background approach to stopped object detection, the long-term background model B_t^L is updated according to (3) in a *selective* way, i.e. only if $d(\cdot, \cdot) \leq \varepsilon$, otherwise, it remains unchanged. Such selectivity allows to adapt the background model to scene modifications without introducing the contribution of pixels not belonging to the background scene. Instead, the short-term background model B_t^S is always updated according to (3), with a learning rate γ_t^S higher than the learning rate γ_t^L for the long-term model, so that it can quickly include moving and temporarily static background elements that have been excluded by the long-term model.

2.3 The Algorithm

The stopped object detection procedure described in the previous section for each pixel $\mathbf{x}$ can be sketched as the following algorithm:

Dual Background SOBS Algorithm

Input: pixel $\mathbf{x}$ in sequence frame $I_t, t = 0, \ldots,$ LastFrame
Output: aggregated evidence score $E_t(\mathbf{x})$

1. $InitializeModels(B_0^L(\mathbf{x}), B_0^S(\mathbf{x}))$
2. **for** t=1, Kinit
3. $\quad CalibrateModels(B_t^L(\mathbf{x}), B_t^S(\mathbf{x}))$
4. **for** t=Kinit+1, LastFrame
5. $\quad (F^L(\mathbf{x}), F^S(\mathbf{x})) = UpdateModels(B_t^L(\mathbf{x}), B_t^S(\mathbf{x}), I_t(\mathbf{x}))$
6. $\quad E_t(\mathbf{x}) = ForegroundCompare(F^L(\mathbf{x}), F^S(\mathbf{x}))$

Steps 1-3 represent the *calibration phase*, that involves initial learning of the two neural networks modeling the long-term and the short-term backgrounds over Kinit initial frames, while steps 4-6 represent the *online phase*, that involves the updating of both neural network models and the computation of the evidence score based on (1), (2), and (3).

Most of the computation for each pixel can be done concurrently, independently from adjacent pixels. Communication is only needed for the update of the background models in the case that the neighborhood of best matching weight vector, computed according to (2), contains weight vectors of adjacent pixels.

A suitable parallelization strategy is therefore based on data decomposition, where each thread is responsible of data needed to perform the whole Dual Background SOBS Algorithm for a single pixel.

3 Parallelizing Stopped Object Detection

To afford the parallelization approach we should firstly point out some costraints of CUDA architectures. Parallel programs for CUDA are organized into three levels of abstraction: elementary sequences of instructions (*threads*) are clustered into different *blocks*, which are themselves grouped into *grids*. All threads execute the same sequence of instructions on different data. Each block is executed on one multiprocessor (consisting of 8 processors), which can alternate with other blocks in order to hide latencies due to not-cached memory accesses. Once a block is assigned to a multiprocessor, it is divided into 32 thread units (called *warps*), effectively scheduled such that the threads within a warp are executed in a somewhat lock-step way called *single-instruction multiple-thread.* Whenever the number of blocks is higher than the number of available multiprocessors, the remaining blocks are queued.

Given a sequence frame consisting of $M \times N$ pixels and fixed the number $th_x \times th_y$ of threads for each block, we define a grid G consisting of $(\frac{2\times M}{th_x}) \times (\frac{N}{th_y})$ blocks. The grid G is subdivided into two subgrids, G_S and G_L, each consisting of $(\frac{M}{th_x}) \times (\frac{N}{th_y})$ blocks, running simultaneously. The subgrid G_S processes the short-term background model B^S, while the subgrid G_L processes the long-term background model B^L.

The implementation is divided into four different *kernels* (program modules executed independently on different data), corresponding to steps 1, 3, 5, and 6 of the Dual Background SOBS Algorithm (cfr. §2.3): the initialization, the calibration, the model update, and the evidence computation, which are launched sequentially by the CPU. The only exchange of memory between CPU and GPU is the one for loading the input images into the global memory device and for sending back the resulting binary evidence image. Since global memory is not cached, it is particularly important to follow the right access pattern to get the maximum bandwidth. The device is capable of reading 4-byte, 8-byte, 16-byte words from memory into registers in a single instruction; for structures larger than 16 bytes the compiler generates several load instructions. Moreover, global memory bandwidth is most efficiently used when the simultaneous memory access by threads in half-warp can be coalesced into a single memory transaction of 32, 64, or 128 bytes, respectively, and this is achieved if all threads access 1-byte, 2-byte, or 4-byte words lying in the same segment, respectively.

Since usually images are stored into 1D arrays in row-major order, we reorganize the image data before transferring them to the global memory device in order to guarantee coalesced access during the parallel processing. As an example, in Figure 2-(a) we show a simple image consisting of $M \times N = 6 \times 6$ pixels, distributed on a grid of 2×2 blocks (identified by different colors), where each block consists of 3×3 threads which are assigned one pixel each. The usual storing into a 1D array in row-major order (shown in Figure 2-(b)) is reorganized as in Figure 2-(c), so that each block accesses data as sequential chunks of the 1D array. This preprocessing phase is done sequentially and should be taken into account for time measurements, as described in the next section.

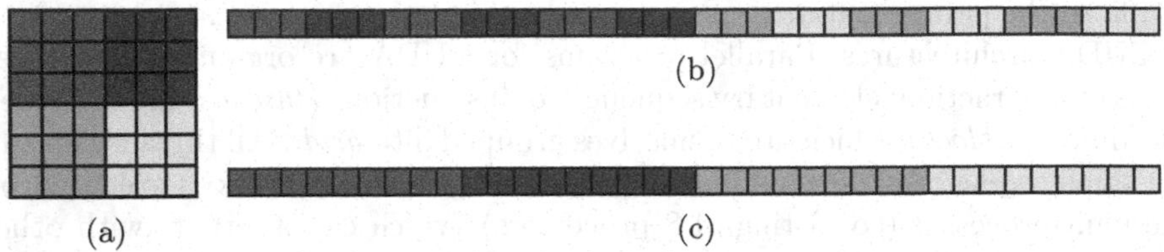

Fig. 2. (a) Image consisting of 6 × 6 pixels distributed on a grid of 2 × 2 blocks (identified by different colors), each consisting of 3 × 3 threads, having one pixel each; (b) usual image memorization pattern; (c) reorganized image memorization pattern

4 Experimental Results

In order to evaluate the performance of the parallel version of the Dual Background SOBS Algorithm we considered several color image sequences resized at a resolution of $M \times N = 720 \times 480$ pixels, belonging to the publicly available i-LIDS 2007 dataset (available at ftp://motinas.elec.qmul.ac.uk/pub/iLids/), that represent typical situations where stopped objects can be of great concern (abandoned luggage in train stations and parked vehicles in no parking zones). Experiments were performed on two Intel Core i7 CPUs at 2.67GHz equipped with two different NVIDIA GPUs, both based on the G80 architecture: a Tesla C1060 (in the following referred to as Tesla), with 30 multiprocessors and 4 GB of global memory, and a GeForce 8400GS (in the following referred to as GeForce), with 2 multiprocessors and 300 MB of global memory. Concerning memory into the NVIDIA G80 chipset, each thread accesses only 32 registers and each block has 16 KB of shared (cached) memory common to all its threads. Furthermore, as memory transfer between CPU and GPU is very time consuming, it is preferable to perform all the calculations on data stored in the global memory. The Tesla card contains 16384 registers, and thus only 512 threads per block should be active at a time; the number of threads per block has to be chosen between 64 and 512 in order to optimize the block distribution and avoid latency. The GeForce card contains 8192 registers, and thus only 256 threads per block should be active at a time; the number of threads per block has to be chosen between 64 and 256 in order to optimize the block distribution and avoid latency.

The serial implementation in such environment has an average execution time $T_{SEQ} = 431.68ms$ per frame; this accounts for only $2.3165fps$, much lower than the $24fps$ required for real-time processing of an image sequence. The parallel processing time T_{PAR} is given by the sum of a sequential time t_s (elapsed time to acquire an image from the video and to re-arrange the image data as described in §3) and a parallel time t_p (elapsed time from the start of storage of the re-arranged image on global memory device to the end of the computation of the binary evidence image). To compare performance on Tesla and GeForce, we fix 8×8 threads per block (optimal configuration supported by GeForce to process the considered 720×480 image sequences) corresponding to a grid of 180×60 blocks, that simultaneously processes B^L and B^S. On GeForce T_{PAR} is $280.13ms$, consisting of $t_s = 3.73ms$ and $t_p = 276.40ms$, while on Tesla T_{PAR} is $20.55ms$, with $t_s = 3.73ms$ and $t_p = 16.82ms$. It turns out that achieved speedups as compared to serial time T_{SEQ} (1.6x for the GeForce and 20x for the Tesla) can be considered satisfactory, although the implementation with GeForce still does not allow for real-time execution. Indeed, the implementation on GeForce achieves $3.57fps$, while that on Tesla $48.64fps$. Other experiments on 720×480 image sequences have been carried out on the most performing Tesla GPU varying the number of block threads, in order to measure the overhead given by block scheduling as shown in Table 1. The number of active blocks per

Table 1. Parallel times T_{PAR} (in ms), Speedups, and fps on Tesla for image size 720×480 and different configurations of Block and Grid sizes

Block size	*Grid size*	T_{PAR}	*Speedup*	*fps*
8×4	180×120	22.63	19.07x	44.18
8×8	180×60	20.84	20.70x	47.97
16×8	90×60	20.55	21.00x	48.64
16×16	90×30	22.19	19.45x	45.05
20×8	72×60	20.86	20.68x	47.91

multiprocessor depends on how many registers per thread and how much shared memory per block are required for a kernel, since the multiprocessor registers and shared memory are split among all the threads of the active blocks. Allocating more threads per block is better for efficient time slicing, but the more threads per block the fewer registers are available per thread, which might prevent the kernel invocation from succeeding.

Further experiments have been done varying the size of the image sequences to assess the extent to which the requirement of real-time processing ($24fps$) is guaranteed. Results on 720×480 , 960×720 and 1200×960 image sequences, with an average execution serial time $T_{SEQ} = 431.68ms$, $T_{SEQ} = 862.94ms$ and $T_{SEQ} = 1430.30ms$ per frame, respectively, are reported in Table 2(a). Finally, we have designed an OpenMP implementation that parallelizes the algorithm on the 8 cores of our CPU through the definition of 8 independent threads working on data stored on shared memory. The parallel processing time (Table 2(b)) reduces 6 times: multicore architecture gets better performance with respect to GeForce 8400GS, even if the real time requirement is not yet satisfied.

Table 2. Parallel times (ms), speedups, and fps on (a) Tesla and (b) OpenMP

(a) Tesla

Image Size	*Block size*	T_{PAR}	*Speedup*	fps
720 × 480	16 × 8	20.55	21x	48.64
960 × 720	8 × 8	40.96	21x	24.9
1200 × 960	16 × 8	65.41	21.8x	15.2

(b) OpenMP implementation

Image Size	T_{PAR}	*Speedup*	fps
720 × 480	76.42	5.64x	13.08
960 × 720	152.08	5.67x	6.57
1200 × 960	254.25	5.62x	3.9

5 Conclusions

We have described a dual background approach to stopped object detection in digital image sequences based on self-organizing neural networks, proposing a data parallel algorithm, which is specifically suitable for SIMD architectures. Parallel performance of our CUDA implementation with two different GPUs has been analyzed, concluding that with the Tesla C1060 GPU significant speedups can be achieved as compared to our serial implementation, allowing for real-time stopped object detection. Further experiments have been carried out in order to check different configurations of the parallel implementation, varying the number of threads, the number of pixels per thread, the number of blocks per multiprocessor and the size of image sequences, also making comparisons with an OpenMP implementation.

References

1. Collins, R.T., et al.: A System for Video Surveillance and Monitoring, The Robotics Institute, Carnegie Mellon University, Tech. Rep. CMU-RI-TR-00-12 (2000)
2. Ferryman, J.M. (ed.): Proceedings of the 9th IEEE International Workshop on PETS, New York, June 18 (2006)
3. Ferryman, J.M. (ed.): Proceedings of the 10th IEEE International Workshop on PETS, Rio de Janeiro, Brazil, October 14 (2007)
4. Herrero-Jaraba, E., et al.: Detected Motion Classification with a Double-background and a Neighborhood-based Difference. Patt. Recogn. Lett. 24, 2079–2092 (2003)
5. Maddalena, L., Petrosino, A.: A Self-Organizing Approach to Background Subtraction for Visual Surveillance Applications. IEEE Transactions on Image Processing 17(7) (July 2008)
6. NVIDIA, CUDA guide, http://www.nvidia.com/object/cuda_home_new.html
7. Porikli, F., Ivanov, Y., Haga, T.: Robust Abandoned Object Detection Using Dual Foregrounds. EURASIP Journal on Advances in Signal Processing (2008)
8. Proc. of Fourth IEEE International Conference on Advanced Video and Signal Based Surveillance (AVSS 2007). IEEE Computer Society, Los Alamitos (2007)

GPU-to-CPU Callbacks

Jeff A. Stuart[1], Michael Cox[2], and John D. Owens[1]

[1] University of California, Davis
[2] NVIDIA Corporation

Abstract. We present GPU-to-CPU callbacks, a new mechanism and abstraction for GPUs that offers them more independence in a heterogeneous computing environment. Specifically, we provide a method for GPUs to issue callback requests to the CPU. These requests serve as a tool for ease-of-use, future proofing of code, and new functionality. We classify the types of these requests into three categories: System calls (e.g. network and file I/O), device/host memory transfers, and CPU compute, and provide motivation as to why all are important. We show how to implement such a mechanism in CUDA using pinned system memory and discuss possible GPU-driver features to alleviate the need for polling, thus making callbacks more efficient with CPU usage and power consumption. We implement several examples demonstrating the use of callbacks for file I/O, network I/O, memory allocation, and debugging.

1 Introduction

Microprocessor architectures are becoming ever more complicated. Even now, the world is moving in the direction of System-on-a-Chip (SoC), wherein the CPU and many specialized cores reside on one common die. With an SoC, systems will inevitably contain more cores than can be concurrently powered. The heat and wattage demands will be such that only a fraction of the cores can run at a time. There is no reason the CPU should not be able to idle or power off while other cores stay functional. Right now, this is impossible because the CPU controls many functions of the machine and is the only core to do so.

There is no insurmountable challenge to having another core, such as the GPU, be capable of managing aspects of a machine. In fact, we contend that the GPU should be able to access hard drives, communicate with network controllers, make other various system calls, and even wake up a sleeping CPU. As of right now, the graphics driver does not allow this, and would require a significant amount of work from driver architects to properly implement.

For now, the concept of a machine controlled by the GPU is attractive, if for no other reason than a CPU often need only sit idle while the GPU is working. In fact, users often split long GPU kernels into multiple smaller kernels simply because CPU intervention is necessary for one reason or another, typically to make a system call or transfer memory from the CPU to the GPU.

In this paper, we detail a new mechanism that allows the GPU to execute system calls and control the CPU, and we provide a library that wraps this

M.R. Guarracino et al. (Eds.): Euro-Par 2010 Workshops, LNCS 6586, pp. 365–372, 2011.
© Springer-Verlag Berlin Heidelberg 2011

functionality via callbacks. By using GPU-to-CPU callbacks, our library exposes a mechanism that allows the GPU to request computation from the CPU, and that allows these tasks to execute concurrently with GPU kernels. This mechanism demonstrates the new model of GPU programming that allows the GPU to execute system calls and control the machine.

In our current implementation, callbacks most often do *not* yield performance improvements, nor are they meant to. We implemented callbacks for two reasons: to make code future-proof (as drivers and systems advance, update the callback library and code runs more efficiently) and to make certain tasks easier, especially those that use either concurrent compute and memory transfers, or concurrent CPU and GPU compute. We predict that performance improvements will come as the GPU driver and system architecture evolve.

2 Existing Methods

Callbacks can used in two ways: the GPU requests some data/computation from the CPU, or the GPU feeds debugging/checkpointing information to the CPU. The GPU currently does not request work from the CPU because there are few mechanisms by which to do so. Instead, most kernels take the data they need, perform their computation, and leave results in GPU memory. Even though there are times when logically it makes more sense for a GPU to request work or data from a CPU, programmers do not write applications this way due to the restrictions of the GPU.

The second general way in which callbacks can be used is debugging. Many GPU-debugging tools have been announced recently, including a fully capable GDB port from NVIDIA called CUDA-GDB [3]. However, CUDA-GDB does not address the problems that arise through dataflow, when a bug in one kernel results in erroneous data used by other kernels, which eventually causes a later kernel to perform incorrectly or even crash. In 2009, Hou et al. used dataflow recording to debug GPU stream programs [2]. This was a solid start to debugging large applications, but it required users to be able to mark their data, fit all debugging information on the GPU along with the data, and interpret a visualization to understand exactly where a problem occurred.

To further address the deficiencies in debugging, NVIDIA ported *printf* functionality to CUDA as *cuPrintf* [4], which lets developers use console output. This eased the burden of debugging for many but had the drawback that results were only printed to *stdout* upon kernel completion. With long-running kernels and kernels that crash the GPU, *cuPrintf* might not function properly.

Stuart and Owens [5] created a mechanism to let the GPU execute system calls using their library DCGN. DCGN relied on concurrent, asynchronous memory copies from the GPU to the CPU, which are not possible on compute-1.0 architectures, are not supported in OpenCL, and are never guaranteed to execute asynchronously. Furthermore, all calls to the CPU in this work are hard-coded, precluding implementions of new system-call requests without heavily modifying the underlying library.

3 Implementation

We implemented callbacks with 0-copy memory and a polling mechanism. Polling goes against our motivation of having idle CPUs, but we expect driver innovations to mitigate this. When issuing a callback, the GPU puts a callback request in 0-copy memory and sets a flag to alert the CPU of said request. The kernel then either continues with its work, busy-waits on the callback, or finishes execution and examines the return value of the callback with a future kernel. On the CPU, our library handles callbacks via polling (modern GPU drivers do not expose any interrupt/signal capabilities). Once a kernel is invoked, the user calls one of two functions. Figure 1 shows a basic overview of how the CPU and GPU interact via callbacks. Calling *callbackSynchronize* ceases all CPU execution except for handling callbacks until both the kernel has finished executing and all callbacks have completed. The other function, *callbackQuery(cudaStream_t)*, polls the status of the kernel and any active/pending callbacks, but does not block. A successful return value from *callbackQuery* implies all callbacks completed and all kernels finished executing. We provide more details below.

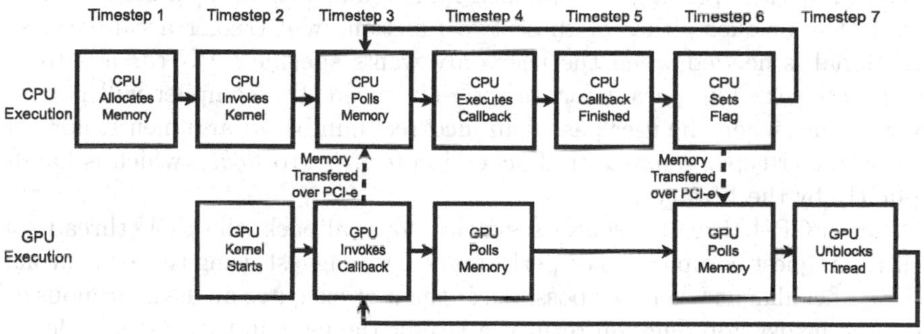

Fig. 1. An overview of callbacks and the CPU-GPU interactions they create. The CPU initializes the callback library and allocates the pool of 0-copy memory. It then invokes a kernel and executes *callbackSynchronize*, and the GPU starts the kernel. Next, the GPU invokes a synchronous callback and the CPU polls 0-copy memory. Then, the GPU halts and the CPU executes the callback. Next, the callback finishes. Now, the CPU sets a 0-copy memory flag to tell the GPU that it handled the callback request. Finally, the GPU unblocks the calling thread and continues its execution.

3.1 CPU Implementation

Our library provides an API to register callbacks and issue them within a kernel, as well as a backend that handles callbacks. The user initializes the library by specifying how many concurrent callback requests the GPU may issue, the maximum number of parameters for any callback, and the number of CPU threads to handle callback requests. The library creates a CPU-thread pool and allocates enough 0-copy memory to hold all concurrent callback requests.

Once the library finishes initialization, it is ready to register callbacks. To do so, a user first creates a data structure that contains information about the callback (parameter type(s), return type, and function address), then registers the callback with the library and receives a unique handle for use on the GPU (which can be passed as a kernel argument). After launching all kernels, the user can either sleep wait or periodically check on the kernels. Both of these must be done using library-supplied functions and not the functions provided by CUDA.

When the CPU detects a callback request, it passes the parameters from 0-copy memory to the user-specified callback function. Once completed, the callback returns a value which the library gives to the GPU, and sets a flag to tell the GPU the callback completed. This method works well, even with many callbacks (on the order of hundreds) in flight.

3.2 GPU Implementation

The user may invoke any number of callbacks in a kernel (though the number of concurrent callbacks is limited). To do so, any GPU thread invokes *callbackExecute* (synchronous callback request) or *callbackExecuteAsync* (asynchronous callback request), passing the callback handle and callback parameters. Every thread that invokes either of these two functions will trigger a callback, so a conditional is needed when the user only wants specific GPU threads to execute a callback. The parameters are loosely typed; the compiler will not issue any warnings when the user passes an incorrect number of arguments, nor when the parameter types require strong coercion (e.g. *int* to *float*), which is handled implicitly by the library.

When a GPU thread executes a synchronous callback, the GPU thread spins until the request completes. For performance, we suggest using the asynchronous version of callbacks whenever possible. If the user executes an asynchronous callback, the invokation function returns a handle the user, in their GPU code, may query or block upon in a manner similar to *cudaStreamQuery* and *cudaStreamSynchronize* (again, these function are host functions, though the functions we provide are device functions). This allows the CPU and GPU to overlap work without stalling the GPU.

When a user invokes a callback, the library coerces the parameters to their correct types and moves them to 0-copy memory. The function identifier is also set in 0-copy memory, and then a *threadfence()* is executed to ensure that the writes to 0-copy memory are flushed. The library returns a handle for querying or waiting. When the user executes a synchronous callback, the function implicitly waits on the handle until the callback is complete. Blocking works by spinning on a region of 0-copy memory until the CPU signals that the specific callback is complete.

To guarantee an upper bound on the number of concurrent callbacks, the library simply uses a queue of freely available "slots." We borrow the notion of slots from DCGN, but instead of explicitly requiring a slot identifier, the library uses an atomicly guarded queue to obtain the next available slot and mark previously unavailable slots as available again. When no slots are available, the library will spin wait. We experimented with a version of callbacks that required explicit slot identifiers (similar to DCGN) but found that slots make sense for communication patterns in DCGN but are often cumbersome and unnecessary for general-purpose callbacks.

4 Tests

We categorize callbacks into three types of combinable requests: system calls, overlapping CPU and GPU compute, and overlapping compute and memory transfers. The most interesting to us is system calls because it shows how programmers will leverage the GPU when it gains such an ability and no longer requires a user-level library to mimic that ability. System calls also allow for command line I/O such as *printf*, a very useful tool during the development and debugging cycle of any application.

A useful callback library must have three characteristics: an ability to scale, an acceptable response time, and be easy to use. Scalability is important because a GPU has many thread processors and the situation may arise that each thread processor has an outstanding asynchronous (or synchronous) callback. As such, it is important for the library to work well when dealing with one callback request or tens-to-hundreds of callback requests. An acceptable response time is important because each millisecond spent on a callback represents numerous FLOPs of wasted compute. And like any library, ease of use is important.

We wrote several applications to demonstrate callbacks, our library, and a proper implementation of each of the above-mentioned requirements, and touch on three of them: a TCP/IP client and server, a CPU-side memory manager for the GPU, and a command-line debugging tool that uses *printf*. All applications use callbacks and are straightforward to write.

For our tests, we used a GTX 280 running in a machine with a 2.5 GHz Intel Core 2 Quad and 4 GB of RAM. The machine is running the 2.6.18 Linux kernel, GCC 4.1.2, the 2.3 CUDA Toolkit, and the NVIDIA 190.53 GPU driver.

4.1 TCP/IP

We wrote a TCP/IP client and server to demonstrate the response time of our library. Both the client and a server operate in the same kernel[1]. The configuration uses two blocks with one thread each. This guarantees each thread is run in a different warp and thus does not deadlock from warp-divergence stalls. The first thread uses callbacks to create a server socket, accept an incoming connection, receive a string, and close both the server socket and the receiving socket. The second thread uses callbacks to create a socket by connecting to the server, send a string, and close the socket. For reference, the device code for the server is shown in Figure 2. This code is representative of most callback code, so for brevity we only show the code for this test and not others.

[1] On our test GPU, this was necessary as the GPU only runs a single kernel at a time. This test also is beneficial as it shows one way to perform interblock communication, though obviously one would avoid network I/O for such a thing in a real application.

```
__device__ void serverKernel(callbackData_t * cdata, callbackFunction_t * funcs)
{
  int serverSocket  = callbackExecute<int>(cdata, funcs[START_SERVER_CALLBACK],
                                            SERVER_PORT);
  int recvSocket    = callbackExecute<int>(cdata, funcs[ACCEPT_CALLBACK]);
  int bytesRead     = callbackExecute<int>(cdata, funcs[RECV_CALLBACK],
                                            recvSocket, 0, 1024, 0);
                      callbackExecute<int>(cdata, funcs[CLOSE_CALLBACK], serverSocket);
                      callbackExecute<int>(cdata, funcs[CLOSE_CALLBACK], recvSocket);
}
```

Fig. 2. The GPU callback code to create a TCP server. *callbackExecute* requires a template parameter for the callback return type, a pointer to a *callbackData_t* structure that contains information about all callbacks registered before kernel invokation, the handle for the callback to be invoked, and the parameters to the callback.

This test is important because it shows callback performance when there is little contention, at most two callbacks run concurrently. The GPU version of this test executes in approximately 2.5 ms, while the CPU version executes in approximately 1 ms. The slowdown can be attributed to several things, but the primary reasons are thread-safety mechanisms in the callback library and the overhead of polling 0-copy memory with active callbacks.

4.2 Memory Manager

We implemented a primitive memory manager and matrix multiplication to showcase the effectiveness of our library at scale. We make a certain number of "pages" available to any number of blocks. Each block uses a callback to request an adequately-sized page to hold three large, square matrices from the CPU. Once the CPU responds, the block generates two random matrices, stores the product of the two, then issues a callback to free the page (the result is essentially ignored). It is possible that every block is stalled waiting for the CPU to return a page, thus providing details on our library's performance with many concurrent callbacks. While this test is trivial and the GPU often would not work on random data, the test is important because it grants a wish for many GPU programmers: dynamic memory allocation from the GPU during runtime[2]. Because a kernel can request new memory while running, and the request goes to the CPU, users are free to implement a heap as complicated as necessary to accomplish their tasks. This is prohibitively difficult without callbacks.

We varied the total number of blocks from 30 to 20000 and the maximum number of concurrently scheduled blocks from 30 to 120 (we did this by using various sizes of shared memory). Our *allocatePage* and *deallocatePage* callbacks each required the use of a lock to either get the next available page or free a page. The locks affected performance in the worst case, but only slightly.

[2] CUDA does not allow any memory management while a kernel or asynchronous memory copy is running. Many writers of GPU renderers have stated that being able to use more complex data structures and dynamic memory on the GPU would be beneficial.

Our average time to service a callback was under 4 ms, the minimum was under 2 ms, and the maximum was approximately 10 ms.

4.3 Debugging

The last test we wrote was one for debugging, something important with either a long-running kernel producing erroneous results, or a kernel that crashes. In either case, the programmer absolutely must find the problem(s) and fix their code. The current methods are 1) allocate GPU memory for debug information that the CPU consumes and displays (Hou et al. did this for stream dataflow debugging), which is very similar to 2) breaking up a kernel into many smaller kernels and inspect certain GPU variables after each kernel completes, which is also similar to 3) removing pieces of a kernel, from last line to first line, until the last executed step is found to be the offending step, 4) use cuda-gdb, which often times does not behave properly when a GPU crashes, or 5) use *cuPrintf*, which only prints to the console upon kernel completion and offers no guarantee of proper functionality if a kernel crashes before completion or if the user executes too many *cuPrintf* statements.

All these options have drawbacks; they are time-consuming to implement, not guaranteed to work, or require significant refactoring of code. Callbacks offer a simple method: the user simply inserts synchronous callbacks so the CPU code will immediately print to the console. The GPU warp halts until the CPU outputs to the console (and if desired, a global barrier can halt the entire GPU), guaranteeing the proper execution of *printf* before the GPU crashes. In fact, even if the GPU crashes, as long as the callback buffers remain uncorrupted, the library will still issue the callback, even after it detects a GPU crash.

We would like to point out some notable tradeoffs in using a *synchronous* callback to execute *printf*, and using *cuPrintf*. *cuPrintf* will execute quickly, because it only writes straight to GPU memory, whereas, on a discrete GPU, the CPU must issue many PCI-e transactions to get the callback's payload. However, we contend that this is fine because of the other tradeoff, *cuPrintf* is delayed until the end of kernel execution, whereas even *synchronous* callbacks execute concurrently with the kernel.

To demonstrate this, we wrote a test wherein each block has a preassigned memory space on the GPU. The block generates two random matrices and multiplies them, then invokes a callback to the print out the determinant of the result. This kernel, when ran with sufficiently many blocks, takes several minutes to complete. During execution, we can see the progress of the GPU as each printed determinant tells us that another block has finished execution.

5 Conclusion

As we have shown, callbacks offers several advantages to users. Perhaps the most important advantage is that code that uses our library is now future-proof (all one must do is use an updated version of the library that takes advantage of new

GPU advancements). As drivers (software) and system architectures (hardware) progress, kernels that are split or use modified algorithms to work around deficiencies in the GPU hardware and driver require modification. Code that takes advantage of callbacks simply requires an update to the callback library to use the new features of the driver and system. This is both in terms of hardware advancements and software advancements.

We see several avenues for advancement. For hardware, the important advancement is that of a more tightly-integrated and powerful (not in of FLOPs but in system control) GPU. AMD is on this path with their Fusion [1] processors; putting a CPU and GPU on the same die. This is great as it lowers memory latency (especially 0-copy) and paves the way for more advancements. It is in these advancements that we hope to see a GPU that can control the machine and put CPU cores to sleep. In terms of software advancement, a mechanism that allows the GPU to send signals or interrupts to the CPU would most benefit callbacks. This is useful as it allows the CPU to be put to sleep and woken up when either the GPU issues a callback or completes a kernel.

Acknowledgements

We would like to say thank you to Dominik Göddeke, the SciDAC Institute for Ultrascale Visualization and the National Science Foundation (Award 0541448), and to NVIDIA for equipment donations.

References

1. Advanced Micro Devices. Coming soon: The AMD fusion family of APUs
2. Hou, Q., Zhou, K., Guo, B.: Debugging GPU stream programs through automatic dataflow recording and visualization. ACM Transactions on Graphics 153(5), 153:1–153:11 (2009)
3. NVIDIA Corporation. CUDA-GDB: The NVIDIA CUDA debugger (2008), http://developer.download.nvidia.com/compute/cuda/2_1/cudagdb/CUDA_GDB_User_Manual.pdf
4. NVIDIA Corporation. NVIDIA CUDA compute unified device architecture programming guide (February 2010), http://developer.nvidia.com/cuda
5. Stuart, J.A., Owens, J.D.: Message passing on data-parallel architectures. In: Proceedings of the 23rd IEEE International Parallel and Distributed Processing Symposium (May 2009)

Static GPU Threads and an Improved Scan Algorithm

Jens Breitbart

Research Group Programming Languages / Methodologies
Universität Kassel
Kassel, Germany
jbreitbart@uni-kassel.de

Abstract. Current GPU programming systems automatically distribute the work on all GPU processors based on a set of fixed assumptions, e. g. that all tasks are independent from each other. We show that automatic distribution limits algorithmic design, and demonstrate that manual work distribution hardly adds any overhead. Our Scan$^+$algorithm is an improved scan relying on manual work distribution. It uses global barriers and task interleaving to provides almost twice the performance of Apple's reference implementation [1].

1 Introduction

Graphics processing units (GPUs) are a compelling platform for High Performance Computing (HPC) as they offer multiple times the processing power and memory bandwidth of modern CPUs. However, GPUs are a rather new HPC platform and their programming systems are still at an early stage of its development. NVIDIAs CUDA and the Open Compute Language (OpenCL) are the most modern systems currently available, yet they limit algorithmic design with a fixed work distribution scheme and the lack of global synchronization.

Current GPUs are tiled many-core systems, consisting of tiles of closely coupled processors. We refer to these tiles as multiprocessing elements (MPEs). In both CUDA and OpenCL, developers must define as many tasks as possible. These tasks are automatically mapped on the MPEs, which allows for transparent scalability, but as the mapping order of the tasks is undefined, one cannot use intertask synchronization. However, intertask synchronization and manual mapping of tasks to MPEs is a requirement for complex algorithm. We introduce the notion of static workgroups, which are similar to CPU threads in the sense that they process not one task but multiple tasks sequentially. Static workgroups are implemented by fully occupying the GPU with workgroups and manually map the tasks to these static workgroups. Using static workgroups in scenarios were they are of no algorithmic benefit decreases performance slightly, since the automatic scheduling is more efficient than our manual scheduling. However, control over task mapping allows for easy sharing of data between tasks mapped to the same workgroup, as data can be kept in fast on-chip memory. For example it

M.R. Guarracino et al. (Eds.): Euro-Par 2010 Workshops, LNCS 6586, pp. 373–380, 2011.
© Springer-Verlag Berlin Heidelberg 2011

allows sharing data between matrix multiplication tiles and thereby prevents reoccurring reads from slow off-chip memory.

Relying on manual work distribution and global synchronization allows for implementing an improved scan (prefix sums) algorithm. We refer to this algorithm as Scan$^+$. The algorithm is based on the algorithm by Blelloch [2], which was e. g. implemented by Harris et al. [5] for GPUs. Scan$^+$removes the need for multiple kernel calls by using global synchronization and interleaves the two phases of the scan algorithm to allow for higher processor utilization. These techniques allow a performance increase of about a factor of two.

We experienced with OpenCL and CUDA and measured the performance of our implementation with a GeForce GTX 280.

The paper is organized as follows. First, Sect. 2 gives a basic introduction in GPU architecture and Sect. 3 explains the CUDA and OpenCL programming model. The next section introduces our concept of static workgroups and shows its performance with a basic matrix multiplication. We show both the overall performance decrease compared to a standard CUDA implementation with automatic work distribution and the speedup to demonstrate that manual work distribution allows for good scalability. Section 5 describes the Scan$^+$algorithm and its benefits compared to the well known algorithm. The paper finishes with related work and a conclusion in Sects. 6 and 7, respectively.

2 GPU Architecture

GPUs are considered to be one of the first many-core architectures with hundreds of slow in-order cores not providing decent single thread performance. The cores are organized in tiles, meaning subsets of the processors are bundled together. These architectures allow for fast communication and synchronization within the tile, but communication between processors of different tiles is rather slow. On current GPUs, communication between tiles must be done using off-chip memory. In NVIDIA hardware these tiles are called streaming multiprocessors. We continue to refer to these tiles as MPEs and call a single processor a processing element (PE). On GPUs, PEs are oversatured with threads and the hardware uses this oversaturation to hide memory latency. The number of threads that can be executed at once depends on a set of factors, e. g. the number of registers required by a thread and the number of registers available in the hardware. Detailed rules can for example be found in [4]. The hardware used for our measurements has 30 MPEs with 8 PE each.

3 OpenCL/CUDA Programming Model

In this section we give a brief introduction to the OpenCL programming model. CUDA's programming model is almost identical to that of OpenCL and mostly differs by names. We use the OpenCL names throughout the following sections, even for programs written in CUDA. In OpenCL the GPU (called *compute device*) is exposed to the CPU (called *host*) as a co-processor with its own memory subsystem. The host launches special functions on the device called *kernels*, which are similar to main functions in CPU programs.

Kernel execution is done in an SPMD fashion with normally up to hundreds of thousands of microtasks (called *workitems* in OpenCL). Microtasks must be bundled together in (data parallel) tasks called *workgroups*. All workitems in one of these groups can be synchronized and share fast on-chip memory called *local memory*. A set of workgroups is scheduled to a MPE, which than executes these groups in parallel. How many workgroups a MPE can execute in parallel depends on the hardware and the kernel, as described before. If there are more groups than the hardware can execute in parallel, an external queue is generated and a group from the queue is executed after another one has completed execution. The order in which the workgroups are scheduled is undefined. User can therefore e. g. not have one workgroup wait for completion of another one, since this can result in a deadlock. Furthermore, a global barrier is not possible, since it is not guaranteed that all workgroups are currently active.

In the following section we enhance the programming model to give users access to the scheduling of the workgroups and also allow for global barrier synchronization.

4 Static GPU Threads

In OpenCL the mapping of tasks (workgroups) to the hardware is intransparent to the user. We now introduce so called static workgroup or MPE threads that compute not only one task but multiple – static workgroups are therefore similar to CPU threads. To implement static workgroups one must identify how many workgroups can be executed at the device at once and than only start this amount of workgroups, so the device is fully utilized and no workgroup is in the external queue. Unfortuatly OpenCL does not allow this to be queried, so the developer must rely on hardware dependent code calculating this number.

One may implement different scheduling schemes to distribute the tasks to the static workgroup, for example a static scheduling can be implemented with a loop, which indexes depend on the (static) workgroup index. However, one may also decide to implement forms of dynamic scheduling using an atomically incremented counter. Without static workgroups, both CUDA and OpenCL do not allow users to specify the work scheduling and expect tasks all of the same size or it may result in poor performance. Furthermore static workgroups allow for synchronization of workitems in different blocks, so it is e. g. possible to have a global barrier for all workitems, since all workitems are active at the same time.

However as the current programming systems do not natively support static workgroups, using them results in more complex programs, as even static scheduling requires an additional loop. More complex kernel may increase the register pressure, which can decrease overall performance. Figure 1 shows matrix multiplication performance implemented in CUDA. The non-optimized version runs the well known blocked matrix multiplication algorithm that is also being used in NVIDIA's CUDA SDK sample. We can see that the implementation using static

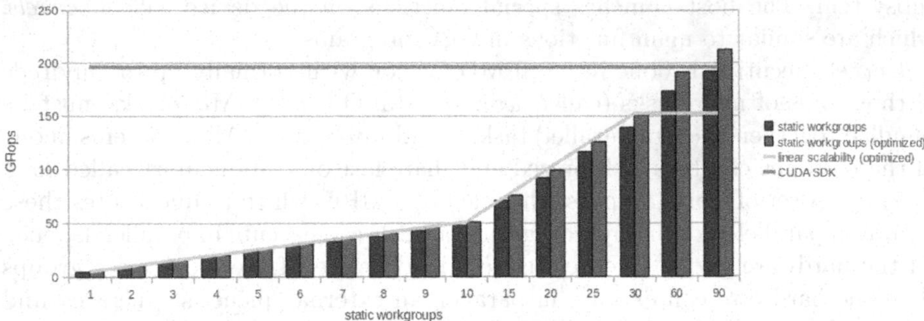

Fig. 1. GTX 280 Matrix multiplication performance (matrix sizes 4800*7200*4800)

threadblocks scales linearly up to the 30 MPEs and oversaturation the MPEs increased performance as well. The overall performance is slightly below that of the SDK implementation. This is the result of the overhead being added by using static threadblocks, however as we can see the overhead is rather small. We have implemented an optimized version that shares data in local memory between tasks. This version calculates not one tile with one static workgroup at a time, but interleaves the computation of two tiles and thereby can utilize the shared memory more efficiently. See figure 2 for an example. The blocks that are in the same row in the result matrix C require the same data from A, so interleaving reduces the amount of data that must be fetched from off-chip memory.

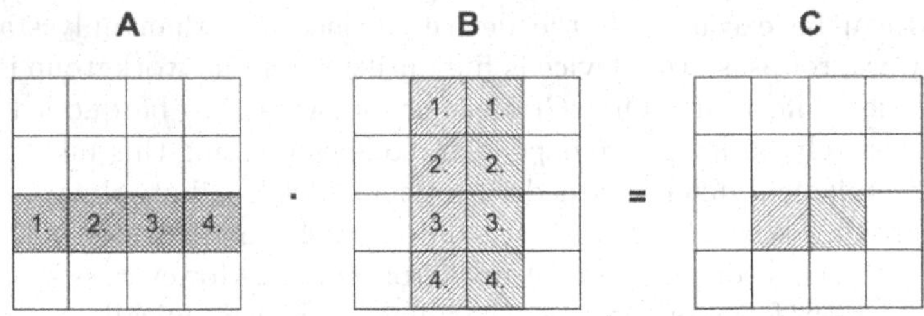

Fig. 2. Optimized blocked matrix multiplication

5 Scan$^+$ Algorithm

In this section we first introduce the CUDA parallel prefix sums implementation suggested by Harris et al. [5] and afterwards outline a way of how this algorithm can be improved using static workgroups. We end this section with a performance comparison to Appel's OpenCL implementation of Harris work.

All prefix sums – also known as scan – is an important parallel building block used in a wide variety of algorithms. Scan takes an input array $[x_0, x_1, ..., x_{n-1}]$

and a binary associative operator $+$ with the identity I as input and returns $[I, x_0, (x_0 + x_1), ..., (x_0 + x_1 + ...x_{n-2})]$. Harris et al. suggested a work-efficient implementation for CUDA, which subdivides the whole array into blocks and uses workgroups to perform a local reduction in every block.

The local reduction is split into two phases: first the up-sweep phase and afterwards the down-sweep phase. The array access pattern in both phases is based on a balanced tree. During the up-sweep phase the tree is traversed from the leaves to the root computing partial sums. In the down-sweep phase the tree is traversed from the root to the leaves using the partial sums to compute the missing elements. Figures 3 and 4 show the algorithm in detail. After the up-sweep, the block sums of every workgroup are written to an auxiliary array (SUM). In a second kernel, SUM is scanned and in a third kernel, the result of the scan are used to update the originally array, so it contains the final result. We identify two major performance problems:

1. This algorithm requires 3 kernel calls in the best case. In case more than 1024 workgroups are used, we must recursively apply the algorithm to scan the SUM array. This complicates implementation by a great deal and every kernel call also imposes overhead to the CPU.

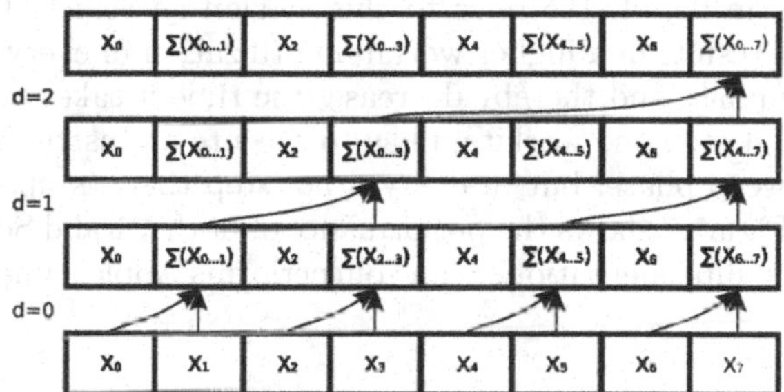

Fig. 3. Up-sweep phase

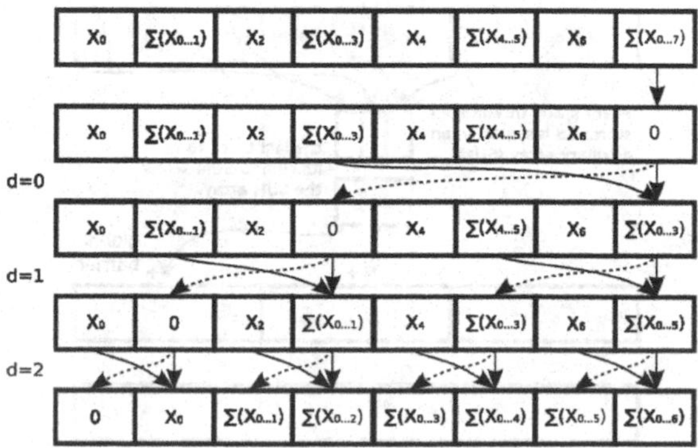

Fig. 4. Down-sweep phase

2. Except $d = 0$ in the up-sweep and $d = maxLevel$ in the down-sweep phase, only a fraction of workitems are active.

We suggest a solution for both problems, by using static workgroups. Figure 5 shows our solution to the first problem. As you can see, the whole computation is done with one kernel call. We subdivide the input array into as many blocks as we use static workgroups and have every static workgroups scan its part. We subdivide every block in smaller blocks and perform the scan identical to the one used by Harris et al. on these sub blocks. After the scan is complete, every static workgroups writes its result out to a SUM array. Note that the number of static workgroups does not depend on the input size of the array, which reduces the size of the SUM array. The SUM array is scanned by the last static workgroup to finish its part of the input array. We identify the last block by atomatically increment a shared counter in global memory. A global barrier is placed, so all other static workgroups wait until the work of the last workgroup is completed. The barrier is implemented following a wait $\rightarrow$ notify all concept. One counter is being used to identify the last block reaching the barrier. The last block notifies all other blocks by setting a flag. After the barrier, the final array is updated. We refer to this version solving problem 1 simply as *V1*.

Our approach to solve problem 2 is to execute both phases in parallel. Figure 6 shows this in detail. We refer to this version as Scan$^+$. Executing both stages in parallel results in a higher workitem utilization in every step of the up- and down-sweep phase and thereby decreases the time it takes to compute both phases. In the first step one workitem has to execute an instruction of both the up- and down-sweep phase, but in every other step there is up to one task for each workitem. Figure 7 shows the performance of both V1 and Scan$^+$in comparison with Apple's implementation. Scan$^+$outperforms Apple's implementation in

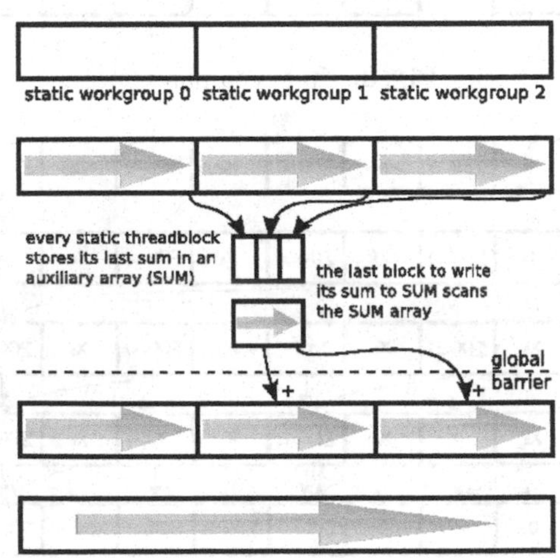

Fig. 5. Global overview of the Scan$^+$algorithm

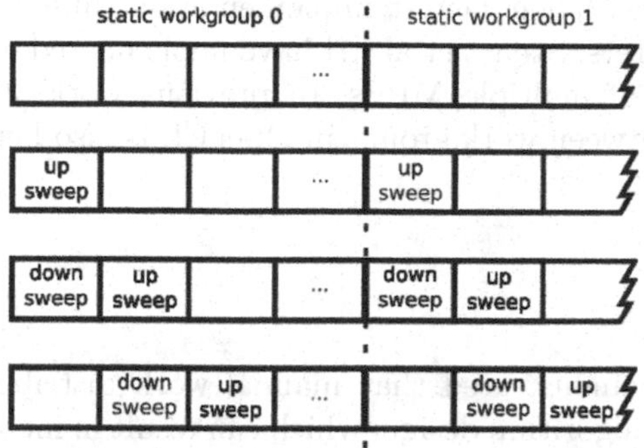

Fig. 6. Overlapping both scan phases

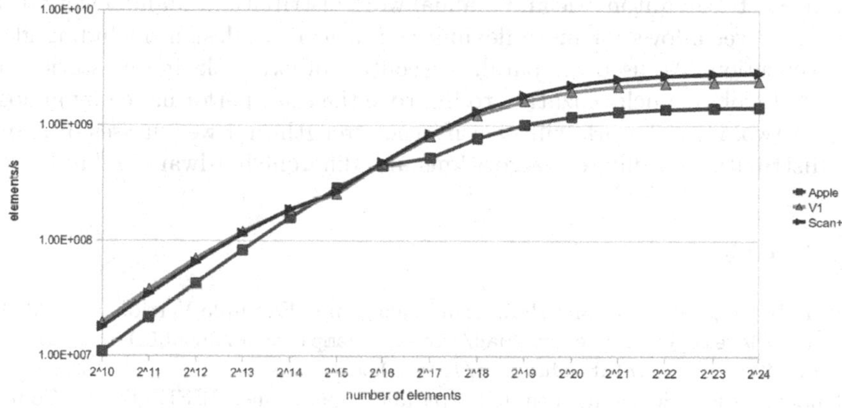

Fig. 7. GTX 280 scan performance

almost all cases. All three version use shared memory padding to prevent shared memory bank conflicts and unrolled loops to increase performance.

Our implementation is mostly limited by register pressure. If hardware would provide us with more registers, we could e. g. implement global memory prefetching as it has been suggested by [4] to increase our performance further. The performance is also limited by the strict synchronization primitives made available by OpenCL. Synchronization within a workgroup is only possible with a classic barrier, meaning every workitem of the workgroup has to reach the same barrier. However, NVIDIA hardware allows for finer grained synchronization [6] with barriers of which only a subset of workitem of a workgroup have to participate.

6 Related Work

Our implementation of the scan algorithm is based on Harris et al.'s work [5] and gains from their optimizations. Xiao et al. [8] studied fast barrier synchronization between threadblocks. Their fastest implementation differs to our solution by using arrays of counters. Stuart et al. [7] have implemented a MPI like interface for cooperate work of multiple MPEs. In previous work [3], we have showed that sharing data between work groups in OpenCL is also beneficial for the Cell Broadband Engine.

7 Conclusion

In this paper, we demonstrated that manual work distribution on GPUs increased flexibility in algorithm design, which can result in increased performance. We introduced the notion of static workgroups to effectively allow manual work distribution and evaluate its overhead compared to the native work distribution based on matrix multiplication. As a result there is hardly any performance difference between automatic and manual work distribution. Manual work distribution however allows for more flexibility in algorithm design, including global synchronization. We used the parallel execution of two tasks in one static workgroup and global synchronization to improve the scan performance by almost a factor of two. Future work will identify the strength and weaknesses of manual work distribution in different algorithms and different hardware architectures.

References

1. Apple Inc. OpenCL Parallel Prefix Sum (aka Scan) Example Version 1.5. (2010), `http://developer.apple.com/mac/library/samplecode/OpenCL_Parallel_Prefix_Sum_Example/Introduction/Intro.html`
2. Blelloch, G.E.: Scans as primitive parallel operations. IEEE Trans. Computers 38(11), 1526–1538 (1989)
3. Breitbart, J., Fohry, C.: OpenCL – an effective programming model for data parallel computations at the Cell Broadband Engine. In: IEEE Int. Parallel and Distributed Processing Symposium (2010) (to appear)
4. Kirk, D., Hwu, W.-m.: Programming Massively Parallel Processors: A Hands-on Approach, 1st edn. Morgan Kaufmann, San Francisco (February 2010)
5. Harris, M., Sengupta, S., Owens, J.D.: Parallel prefix sum (scan) with CUDA. In: Nguyen, H. (ed.) GPU Gems 3, ch. 39, pp. 851–876. Addison Wesley, Reading (August 2007)
6. NVIDIA Corporation. PTX: Parallel Thread Execution ISA Version 2.0 (2010)
7. Stuart, J.A., Owens, J.D.: Message passing on data-parallel architectures. In: Stuart, J.A., Owens, J.D. (eds.) Proceedings of the 23rd IEEE International Parallel and Distributed Processing Symposium (May 2009)
8. Xiao, S., Feng, W.-c.: Inter-Block GPU Communication via Fast Barrier Synchronization. In: Proceedings of the 24th IEEE International Parallel and Distributed Processing Symposium (IPDPS), Atlanta, Georgia, USA (April 2010)

Streaming-Oriented Parallelization of Domain-Independent Irregular Kernels*

Jacobo Lobeiras, Margarita Amor,
Manuel Arenaz, and Basilio B. Fraguela

Computer Architecture Group, University of A Coruña, Spain
{jlobeiras,margamor,manuel.arenaz,basilio.fraguela}@udc.es

Abstract. Current parallelizing and optimizing compilers use techniques for the recognition of computational kernels to improve the quality of the target code. Domain-independent kernels characterize the computations carried out in an application, independently of the implementation details of a given programming language. This paper presents streaming-oriented parallelizing transformations for irregular assignment and irregular reduction kernels. The advantage of these code transformations is that they enable the parallelization of many algorithms with little effort without a depth knowledge of the particular application. The experimental results show the efficiency on current GPUs, although the main goal of the proposed techniques is not performance, but assist the programmer in the parallelization for a better productivity.

Keywords: Stream programming, domain-independent kernels, automatic parallelization, hardware accelerators, GPGPU.

1 Introduction

The development and maintenance of applications that make efficient use of modern hardware architectures is a complex and time consuming task even for experienced programmers. Parallel application lifecycle costs are highly dependent on the hardware advances, especially in domains that change as fast as the GPUs (*Graphics Processing Units*). The use of GPUs for general purpose computation (or *GPGPU*) is becoming more relevant because of the increasing computational power and low cost of last-generation GPUs. However, from a programmability standpoint, CPUs have many advantages over GPUs due to the existence of standard programming languages like *C++* or *Java*, very powerful tools for software development and debugging, and well-known parallel programming *APIs* like *OpenMP*. Nowadays, GPU programming is more complicated as it requires using special languages (like *OpenCL* [9], *NVIDIA's CUDA* [12] or

* This work was supported by the Xunta de Galicia under projects INCITE08PXIB105161PR and 08TIC001206PR, and the Ministry of Science and Innovation, cofunded by the FEDER funds of the European Union, under the grant TIN2007-67536-C03-02. The authors are members of the HiPEAC network.

M.R. Guarracino et al. (Eds.): Euro-Par 2010 Workshops, LNCS 6586, pp. 381–388, 2011.
© Springer-Verlag Berlin Heidelberg 2011

ATI's Brook+ [1]) which often expose hardware features or limitations that restrict the flexibility of GPU programs.

Recently, tools for the parallelization of sequential codes for modern GPUs are beginning to emerge. An *OpenMP*-like semiautomatic approach targeting regular codes as well as read-only irregular computations has been proposed [11]. A step forward towards automatic parallelization for these platforms is a *C*-to-*CUDA* parallel code generator for sequential affine (regular) programs based on the polyhedral model [6]. Despite these advances, the automatic parallelization of irregular applications for GPUs remains a great challenge.

Parallelizing compilers for multiprocessors address irregular applications by recognizing domain-independent computational kernels [5] (e.g. inductions, scalar reductions, irregular reductions and array recurrences) and by applying appropriate parallelizing transformations [8,3]. The main contribution of this paper is the proposal of streaming-oriented parallelizing transformations for the well-known domain-independent kernels called irregular assignment and irregular reduction. Our strategies combine inspector-executor techniques, loop versioning and loop unrolling. A performance analysis using the *Brook+* language for GPU programming is also presented. *Brook+* is well suited for the streaming model that we are going to use in this work.

This paper is structured as follows. Section 2 describes the domain-independent irregular kernels and Section 3 presents the parallelizing transformations for a stream programming model. Section 4 describes our tests and shows the experimental results on a GPU. Finally, section 5 summarizes the main conclusions and future work.

2 Domain-Independent Irregular Kernels

Multiple definitions of computational kernel have been proposed in the literature in the context of automatic program analysis. In this work we use the *domain-independent concept-level computational kernels* recognized by the *XARK* compiler framework [5], which proved to be a useful tool for automatic parallelization of procedural and object-oriented programming languages [4], as well as for data locality optimization [2].

Domain-independent kernels (or simply *kernels* from now on) characterize the computations carried out in a program with independence of the programming language. These kernels do not take into account domain-specific problem solvers. Well-known examples are irregular assignment and irregular reduction, which will be described next.

2.1 Irregular Assignment

An *assignment kernel* consists in storing a value in a memory address. Within a program, this address can be accessed by a scalar variable, a memory pointer or an indexed variable, typically an array. Thus, an *irregular assignment* (see Algorithm 1) may be represented by a loop that computes a sentence $A(f(i)) = e(i)$,

Algorithm 1: Irregular assignment

```
A(...) = ...
for i = 1 to Asize do
    A(f(i)) = e(i)
end for
```

Algorithm 2: Scalar reduction

```
v = ...
for i = 1 to n do
    v = v ⊕ e(i)
end for
```

Algorithm 3: Irregular reduction

```
A(...) = ...
for i = 1 to Asize do
    A(f(i)) = A(f(i)) ⊕ e(i)
end for
```

where A is the output array, f is an indirection array that introduces an unpredictable access pattern at compile-time, and e is an expression. Neither the right-hand side expression $e(i)$ nor any function call within it contain occurrences of A. As a result, unless f is a permutation, output data dependencies will appear at run-time. This kernel can be found in application fields such as computer graphics, finite element applications or sparse matrix computations.

2.2 Irregular Reduction

The distinguishing characteristic of the *reduction kernel* is that the value stored in a memory address is computed using its previous value. The most popular one is the *scalar reduction* (see Algorithm 2), $v = v \oplus e(i)$, where the reduction variable v is a scalar, $\oplus$ is the reduction operator and $e(i)$ is a loop-variant expression whose value is not dependent on v. Scalar reductions appear in financial applications or statistical methods to obtain information of a sample, like the mean value. They are so common that programming languages usually provide some built-in support. An *irregular reduction*, $A(f(i)) = A(f(i)) \oplus e(i)$, is characterized by the use of an indirection array f that selects the locations of an array A to be updated (see Algorithm 3). Note that in this kernel loop-carried output and true data dependencies may appear at run-time. Irregular reductions are very common in many complex scientific applications and adaptive algorithms.

3 Parallelizing Transformations for the Streaming Model

In this section we describe streaming-oriented parallelizing transformations for irregular assignments and irregular reductions targeting current GPUs.

3.1 Irregular Assignment

In the literature, parallel irregular assignments for multiprocessors follow two main approaches. First, loop-partitioning oriented techniques [10] split the iteration space among processors and privatize the output array A. However, this technique is not of practical use on GPUs because memory requirements will grow proportionally to the number of threads (one copy of A for each thread), which limits its scalability and performance. Second, data-partitioning oriented techniques [3] split the iteration space and the output array A, reordering the loop iterations in order to balance the workload among the processors. Hereafter, we propose a data-partitioning oriented parallelizing transformation based on the inspector-executor model tuned for a streaming model.

Algorithm 4: Irr. Assignment Inspector

```
ins_table(1.. Asize) = 0
for i = 1 to Asize do
    ins_table(f(i)) = i
end for
```

Algorithm 5: Irr. Assignment Executor

```
for i = 1 to Asize do
    if ins_table(i) > 0 then
        A(i) = e(ins_table(i))
    end if
end for
```

Algorithm 6: Irr. Reduction Inspector

```
1:  contention(1..Asize) = 0
2:  max_cont = 0
3:  for i = 1 to Asize do
4:      contention(f(i))++
5:      if contention(f(i)) > max_cont then
6:          max_cont = max_cont + 1
7:      end if
8:  end for
9:  ins_table(1..Asize, 1..max_cont) = 0
10: for i = 1 to Asize do
11:     dest = f(i)
12:     j = 1
13:     while ins_table(dest, j) > 0 do
14:         j = j + 1
15:     end while
16:     ins_table(dest, j) = i
17: end for
```

Algorithm 7: Irr. Reduction Executor

```
if max_cont > 4 then
    for i = 1 to Asize do
        j = 0
        while ins_table(i, j) > 0 do
            A(i) = A(i) ⊕ e(ins_table(i, j))
            j = j + 1
        end while
    end for
else
    for i = 1 to Asize do
        if ins_table(i, 0) > 0 then
            A(i) = A(i) ⊕ e(ins_table(i, 1))
        end if
        ...
        if ins_table(i, 3) > 0 then
            A(i) = A(i) ⊕ e(ins_table(i, 3))
        end if
    end for
end if
```

The inspector-executor technique analyzes the contents of the indirection array f at runtime to determine which set of loop iterations must be assigned to each processor to avoid write conflicts. As shown in Algorithm 4, the inspector generates a table *ins_table* to store the last loop iteration that writes to each element of A. Algorithm 5 shows the executor, which uses *ins_table* to determine whether each element of the output array A remains unchanged ($ins\_table(i) = 0$) or will be updated ($ins\_table(i) > 0$) in iteration $ins\_table(i)$.

Finally, some performance issues are briefly discussed. First, a given access pattern is often reused during the execution of an adaptive irregular application (this is called *reusability*). In this case, the extra cost of the inspector is amortized over several calls of the executor. Second, our inspector minimizes the cost of the executor by performing run-time dead code elimination, which removes any loop iterations that compute values of A overwritten in higher iterations.

3.2 Irregular Reduction

Techniques based on loop-partitioning and data-partitioning have also been proposed for irregular reduction parallelization in multiprocessors. In the scope of GPUs, we propose an inspector-executor technique that uses loop versioning and loop unrolling to efficiently exploit the available resources. The inspector code is shown in Algorithm 6. The goal is to create a table *ins_table* that stores all the iterations writing to a given element of A. First, the indirection array f is analyzed (lines 1-8) to compute the degree of contention, that is, the maximum number of writes to the same element of the output array A. Then, the degree of contention *max_cont* is used to statically allocate memory for *ins_table* in the GPU. Note that, in contrast to irregular assignments, all the iterations that contribute to an element need to be stored. Next, the executor presented in Algorithm 7 is called to compute the parallel reduction. A set of conflict-free iterations can be assigned to each processor using *ins_table*. In the CPU each thread will compute a portion of the iterations, while on the GPU each thread will be assigned the reduction of a single location of A. This adaptation is only beneficial for streaming architectures because they heavily depend on multithreading techniques to hide memory access latencies. The GPU can also benefit from the use of both loop versioning and loop unrolling (see lines 11-24), storing the information on one or more *SIMD* short vectors (like *float4* or *int4*) which can be fetched in a single memory access.

4 Performance Evaluation on a GPU Using Brook+

Our test platform is composed by a *Phenom II X4 940* processor running at 3.0 *GHz*, 4 *GB DDR2 800 CL5* memory, a *790X* chipset based motherboard and a *Radeon 4850* GPU. The software setup is *WinXP x64* operating system, using *MS Visual C++ 2005* compiler (x64, release profile) and *Catalyst 9.12* driver.

As the programming language we use *Brook+ 1.4* [1], a *C* extension for *AMD* GPUs that exposes a stream programming model [7], designed to encourage and exploit a high degree of parallelism without significant compiler effort. In this paradigm the same function is applied to a set of inputs in parallel, producing another set of outputs, but there should be no overlapping between the input and the output data to prevent race conditions. The data inputs and outputs of a *streaming kernel* are called *streams* and each thread can only write to a certain location of the output stream, otherwise the performance is greatly reduced.

4.1 Benchmark Suite

We designed several benchmarks to analyze the performance of the GPU using our streaming-oriented parallelization strategies. In the irregular assignment test *Asig_Irr*, the data of a matrix is updated using an indirection array whose values were generated using a uniform random distribution. As the number of indirections is equal to the size of the input, it is very likely that several iterations will try to update the same output address. To simulate a moderate computational load, the right-hand side of the assignment adds 100 integer numbers.

In the irregular reduction test *Red_Irr*, a matrix is updated by adding a value to those matrix locations specified by an indirection array generated using an uniform random distribution, thus again it is highly probable that more than one reduction will be performed on many of the matrix locations. The number of reductions for a given location can be easily estimated by a binomial distribution $B(N, 1/N)$. As in the previous case, in order to simulate some computational load, the reduction function will add 100 integers. Figure 1 shows an implementation using *Brook+* of the executor method for the irregular reduction kernel. It presents a general version for any degree of contention (*gpu_executor*), as well as a specialized version for degrees of contention less or equal to (*gpu_executor_f*4) that uses *float4* data type.

```
// Function to execute, Brook+ GPU version
kernel float
gpu_fun (int pos<>, float val<>, float red<>)
{
    return red + (float)pos * val;
}

// Executor code, Brook+ GPU general version
kernel void
gpu_executor(float src[][], int ins[][],
        float dst_R<>, out float dst_W<>,
        int max_cnt, int dimX)
{
    // 2D texture coordinates to 1D position
    int2 ins2D, pos2D = instance().xy;
    int i, pos = ADR_2Dto1D(ins, dimX);
    // Writes the previous value in the output array
    dst_W = dst_R;
    // Reads the inspector table
    for(i = 0; i < max_cnt; i++) {
        int p = ins[pos2D.y][max_cnt * pos2D.x + i];
        // Calls the reduction function when needed
        if(p < 0) break;
        ins2D = ADR_1Dto2D(p, DIMX);
        dst_W = gpu_fun(p,
                    src[ins2D.y][ins2D.x], dst_W);
    }
}
```

```
// Executor code, Brook+ GPU float4 version
kernel void
gpu_executor_f4(float src[][],
            int4 ins<>, float dst_R<>,
            out float dst_W<>,
            int dimX)
{
    // Obtains the locations to read from ins
    int2 ins2Da = ADR_I1(ins.x, dimX);
    int2 ins2Db = ADR_I1(ins.y, dimX);
    int2 ins2Dc = ADR_I1(ins.z, dimX);
    int2 ins2Dd = ADR_I1(ins.w, dimX);
    // Writes the previous value in the output array
    dst_W = dst_R;
    // Calls the reduction function when needed
    if(ins.x >= 0) dst_W =
        gpu_fun(ins.x, src[ins2Da.y] [ins2Da.x],
                dst_W);
    if(ins.y >= 0) dst_W =
        gpu_fun(ins.y, src[ins2Db.y] [ins2Db.x],
                dst_W);
    if(ins.z >= 0) dst_W =
        gpu_fun(ins.z, src[ins2Dc.y] [ins2Dc.x],
                dst_W);
    if(ins.w>= 0) dst_W =
        gpu_fun(ins.w, src[ins2Dd.y] [ins2Dd.x],
                dst_W);
}
```

Fig. 1. Brook+ versions of the executor for the irregular reduction kernel

Table 1. Execution time (in sec.) and speedup for the 2048 × 2048 problem size

Benchmark		CPU 1P (Original)		CPU 2P (OMP)		CPU 4P (OMP)		GPU (Brook+)	
Asig_Irr	R0	71.44	–	37.20	(1.9x)	22.94	(3.1x)	10.59	(6.7x)
	R100	71.38	–	25.83	(2.8x)	12.70	(5.6x)	0.91	(78.4x)
Red_Irr	R0	75.09	–	65.69	(1.1x)	44.81	(1.7x)	29.98	(2.5x)
	R100	75.12	–	41.09	(1.8x)	19.97	(3.8x)	1.28	(58.7x)

4.2 Performance Analysis

Here we analyze the performance of the proposed parallelization techniques on a GPU and on a multi-core CPU using *OpenMP*. The tests were run in single precision for matrices of sizes 512 × 512, 1024 × 1024 and 2048 × 2048, repeating each test 100 times to obtain meaningful times for the smaller problems. The computational cost of the tests tends to be deliberately low to study a worst case GPU scenario. Table 1 summarizes the execution times obtained in the tests using a 2048 × 2048 problem size as well as the respective speedups enclosed in parentheses. The time measured for the GPU includes the inspector and the data transfer of the analysis table between the CPU and the GPU. The execution of each inspector requires about 0.10 sec. for the *Asig_Irr* test, while the *Red_Irr* test requires about 0.25 sec. due to the additional memory and complexity.

Figure 2 shows the speedup of the two kernels for several problem sizes and for several reusability degrees ($R0$ if the inspector is not reused, $R10$ if it is reused 10

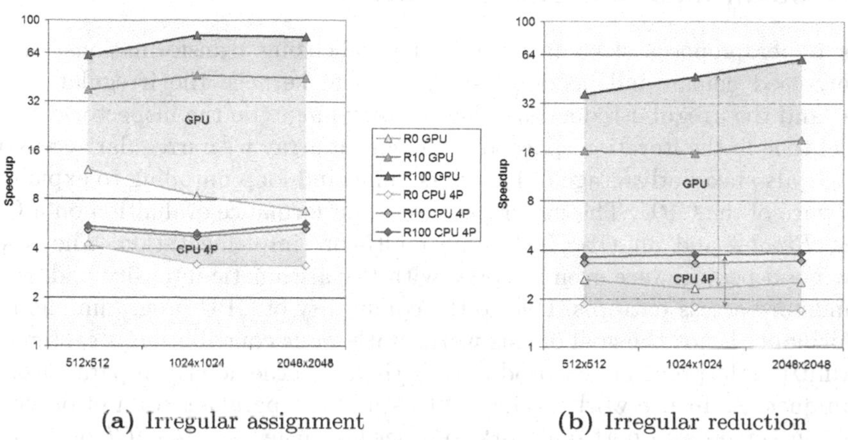

(a) Irregular assignment (b) Irregular reduction

Fig. 2. Performance analysis of domain-independent irregular kernels

times, and $R100$ if it is reused 100 times). Under the same conditions of problem size and reusability, GPU performance is always better than the CPU, but for a good performance there should be some reusability in both cases. Otherwise, the execution time of the additional analysis required by the inspector stage is proportionately high. In the GPU, even a small reusability degree is able to compensate for the memory transfer times.

In the irregular assignment (Figure 2(a)) the optimal GPU performance is obtained for a 1024×1024 input. If there is no reusability, both architectures lose speedup as the problem size increases. The *OpenMP* implementation has superlinearity for the irregular assignment kernel because with the increase in the number of cores, the problem fits better in their caches. Also note that our inspector implementation is performing runtime dead code elimination, so the parallel execution can avoid computing some of the iterations.

Figure 2(b) shows the speedups for the irregular reductions. Although the speedups are not as remarkable as in the case of the irregular assignment, the parallelization is still beneficial. The reason behind this lower *speedup* is the additional bandwidth required by the inspector table in the GPU. Observe that in this case, the bigger the problem size, the more speedup the GPU is able to achieve over the CPU. In the GPU, every thread within a wavefront must execute the same code, so a certain degree of computing power will be wasted if the degree of contention is uneven. In problems where the contention has a large variance, the lookup table could be stored in a sparse matrix format like CRS (compressed row storage), however, accessing the data in the executor would require an additional indirection level, which according to our experiments lowers the efficiency on the GPU.

5 Conclusions and Future Work

This paper proposes streaming-oriented parallelizing transformations for two widely-used domain-independent computational kernels: the irregular assignment and the irregular reduction. The strategy hinges on the inspector-executor model to split the iteration space and the output array with irregular access pattern. It also takes advantage of loop versioning and loop unrolling to exploit the hardware of the GPU. The paper proposes a performance evaluation on a GPU using *Brook+* and an *OpenMP*-based multi-core implementation. The results show good performance even in codes with low arithmetic intensity and irregular memory access patterns. Due to the complexity of GPU programming, peak performance is not the goal of this work. Rather our contribution is centered on maximizing the programmer productivity thanks to the described parallelization techniques. As future work we intend to study the parallelization of other less common kernels and port our work to other languages like *OpenCL* or *CUDA*.

References

1. AMD. AMD Stream Computing User Guide, v1.4.0a (2009)
2. Andrade, D., Arenaz, M., Fraguela, B.B., Touriño, J., Doallo, R.: Automated and Accurate Cache Behavior Analysis for Codes with Irregular Access Patterns. Concurrency and Computation: Practice and Experience 19(18), 2407–2423 (2007)
3. Arenaz, M., Touriño, J., Doallo, R.: An Inspector-Executor Algorithm for Irregular Assignment Parallelization. In: Cao, J., Yang, L.T., Guo, M., Lau, F. (eds.) ISPA 2004. LNCS, vol. 3358, pp. 4–15. Springer, Heidelberg (2004)
4. Arenaz, M., Touriño, J., Doallo, R.: Compiler Support for Parallel Code Generation through Kernel Recognition. In: Proc. of the 18th IEEE International Parallel and Distributed Processing Symposium, Santa Fe, New Mexico, page 79b (2004)
5. Arenaz, M., Touriño, J., Doallo, R.: XARK: An eXtensible Framework for Automatic Recognition of computational Kernels. ACM Transactions on Programming Languages and Systems 30(6), 1–56 (2008)
6. Baskaran, M.M., Ramanujam, J., Sadayappan, P.: Automatic C-to-CUDA Code Generation for Affine Programs. In: Gupta, R. (ed.) CC 2010. LNCS, vol. 6011, pp. 244–263. Springer, Heidelberg (2010)
7. Gummaraju, J., Rosenblum, M.: Stream Programming on General-Purpose Processors. In: Proc. of the 38th Annual IEEE/ACM International Symposium on Microarchitecture (MICRO), Barcelona, Spain, pp. 343–354 (2005)
8. Gutiérrez, E., Plata, O.G., Zapata, E.L.: Data partitioning-based Parallel Irregular Reductions. Concurrency and Computation: Practice and Experience 16(2-3), 155–172 (2004)
9. Khronos OpenCL Working Group. The OpenCL Specification, v1.0.48 (2009)
10. Knobe, K., Sarkar, V.: Array SSA Form and Its Use in Parallelization. In: Proc. of the 25th ACM SIGPLAN-SIGACT Symposium on Principles of Programming Languages (POPL), pp. 107–120 (1998)
11. Lee, S., Min, S., Eigenmann, R.: OpenMP to GPGPU: a Compiler Framework for Automatic Translation and Optimizations. In: Proceedings of the 14th ACM SIGPLAN Symposium on Principles and Practice of Parallel Programming (PPoPP), Raleigh, NC, USA, pp. 101–110 (2009)
12. NVIDIA. NVIDIA CUDA Compute Unified Device Architecture, v2.3.1 (2009)

Scalable Multi-coloring Preconditioning for Multi-core CPUs and GPUs

Vincent Heuveline[1], Dimitar Lukarski[1,2], and Jan-Philipp Weiss[1,2]

[1] Engineering Mathematics and Computing Lab (EMCL)
[2] SRG New Frontiers in High Performance Computing,
Karlsruhe Institute of Technology, Germany
{vincent.heuveline,dimitar.lukarski,jan-philipp.weiss}@kit.edu

Abstract. Krylov space methods like conjugate gradient and GMRES are efficient and parallelizable approaches for solving huge and sparse linear systems of equations. But as condition numbers are increasing polynomially with problem size sophisticated preconditioning techniques are essential building blocks. However, many preconditioning approaches like Gauss-Seidel/SSOR and ILU are based on sequential algorithms. Introducing parallelism for preconditioners is mostly hampering mathematical efficiency. In the era of multi-core and many-core processors like GPUs there is a strong need for scalable and fine-grained parallel preconditioning approaches. In the framework of the multi-platform capable finite element package HiFlow^3 we are investigating multi-coloring techniques for block Gauss-Seidel type preconditioners. Our approach proves efficiency and scalability across hybrid multi-core and GPU platforms.

Keywords: Parallel preconditioners, multi-coloring, Gauss-Seidel, multi-core CPU, GPU, performance analysis.

1 Introduction

Solution methods for linear systems of equations fall into direct methods like LU decomposition or FFT, and iterative methods like splitting methods (Jacobi, Gauss-Seidel, SSOR), Krylov space methods (CG, GMRES) or multigrid solvers. For iterative methods the number of iterations for reaching a prescribed error tolerance depends on the structure of the iteration matrix, in particular on its eigenvalues and condition number. Preconditioning techniques are used to influence the structure and the spectrum of the matrix. On the one hand, the number of necessary iterations shall be reduced, on the other hand extra work for solving additional linear systems shall not outweigh associated benefits.

In the era of multi-core and many-core computing particular emphasis has to be put on fine-grained parallelism within preconditioning approaches. In this work we consider node-level preconditioning techniques on hybrid multi-core CPU and GPU platforms. The impressive power of GPUs originates from processing thousands of lightweighted threads on huge arrays performing uniform operations and coalesced memory transfers via highly capable on-device data paths. For many applications the limitations of the PCIe connection to the host

M.R. Guarracino et al. (Eds.): Euro-Par 2010 Workshops, LNCS 6586, pp. 389–397, 2011.
© Springer-Verlag Berlin Heidelberg 2011

machine are considerable bottlenecks. Moreover, programmability is a major challenge for hybrid and heterogeneous computing platforms since extensions by accelerators introduce different processing models and programming interfaces.

The parallel HiFlow^3 finite element package [8] is built on a two-level library with an inter-node level communication layer based on MPI and an intra-node communication and computation model: the local multi-platform linear algebra toolbox (lmpLAtoolbox) [7]. By unified interfaces with backends to different platforms and accelerators it allows seamless integration of various numerical libraries and devices. The user is freed from any particular hardware knowledge – the final decision on platform and chosen implementation is taken at run time.

This paper investigates parallel symmetric block Gauss-Seidel type preconditioning based on multi-coloring techniques for GPU and CPU platforms. It evaluates performance and scalability characteristics and shows performance benefits for three matrix systems on diverse hybrid multi-core CPU and GPU platforms. Our test scenarios and environments unveil particular behavior with respect to core and memory configuration. Our approach provides an out-of-the box type node-level preconditioning approach for general purpose utilization as well as for use within the complex finite element package HiFlow^3 [8].

To our knowledge there is not much work about parallel preconditioning techniques on GPUs in the literature – although it is a highly important topic. In [5] fined-grained parallel preconditioners and multigrid smoothers are considered for GPUs. But, the approach is limited to banded matrices based on linewise numbering of generalized tensor product meshes. Chebyshev type preconditioners [1] have the appealing of fine-grained parallelism within basic linear algebra routines. However, detailed knowledge of the spectrum of the matrix is required and hence, it is not applicable as a general purpose parallel technique.

2 Parallel Preconditioning Techniques

Due to their work complexity splitting methods are a non-optimal choice for the solution of huge linear system. However, they play an important role as preconditioners for Krylov space methods and smoothers for multigrid solvers. For the Poisson model problem on regular grids Jacobi and Gauss-Seidel methods have an asymptotic complexity of $O(N^{1+2/d})$ where N is the number of unknowns and $d = 1, 2, 3$ is the problem dimension. For Krylov space methods like the conjugate gradient (CG) method work complexity for solving the model problem is only $O(N^{1+1/d})$. By choosing the optimal relaxation parameter SSOR preconditioning for CG reduces work complexity to $O(N^{1+1/(2d)})$ [2]. This is still not the optimal order $O(N)$ like for multigrid methods but this approach circumvents complex treatment of mesh hierarchies, grid transfer operators, and limited parallel scalability due to communication imbalance on coarse grids. An alternative approach is given by algebraic multigrid methods that do not rely on representations of PDEs or any geometric information. Only matrix structures and size of matrix elements are analyzed for constructing a hierarchy of operators. While parallelization of the solution phase is straightforward, this is not true for the setup phase [6]. Hence, we concentrate on Gauss-Seidel type preconditioning. For our investigation we consider the CG-method for symmetric positive definite matrices. Similar to the ILU-preconditioning approach the relaxed symmetric Gauss-Seidel (SSOR) method is purely sequential. By using the splitting $A = D + L + R$ for the system matrix A with diagonal matrix D, strict lower part L, and strict upper part R the SSOR preconditioning within each CG-step requires solution of the linear system

$$Mz = r \text{ with } M = \frac{1}{\omega(2-\omega)}(D+\omega L)D^{-1}(D+\omega R).$$

Since $D+\omega L$ and $D+\omega R$ are triangular systems, the solution procedure is typically sequential. For structured grids and stencil operations parallelism can be introduced by red-black or wavefront ordering of nodes which are not applicable to general matrices and for the latter case has varying degree of parallelism. The restriction to simple Jacobi preconditioners with $M = D$ is highly parallel but without positive effect for many linear systems.

An increased level of parallelism can be introduced by block decomposition of the matrix A as shown in Figure 1 (right). The block diagonal matrix D now consists of B blocks $D_1, \ldots, D_B$. Each block row i, $i = 1, \ldots, B$, has $i-1$ left blocks $L_{i,j}$, $j = 1, ..., i-1$ and $B-i$ right blocks $R_{i,j}$, $j = 1, \ldots, B-i$. The block type solution of $Mz = r$ now reads

$$x_i := D_i^{-1}(r_i - \sum_{j=1}^{i-1} L_{i,j}x_j) \text{ for } i = 1, \ldots, B, \tag{1}$$

$$y_i := D_i^{-1}x_i \text{ for } i = 1, \ldots, B, \tag{2}$$

$$z_i := D_i^{-1}(y_i - \sum_{j=1}^{B-i} R_{i,j}z_{i+j}) \text{ for } i = B, \ldots, 1. \tag{3}$$

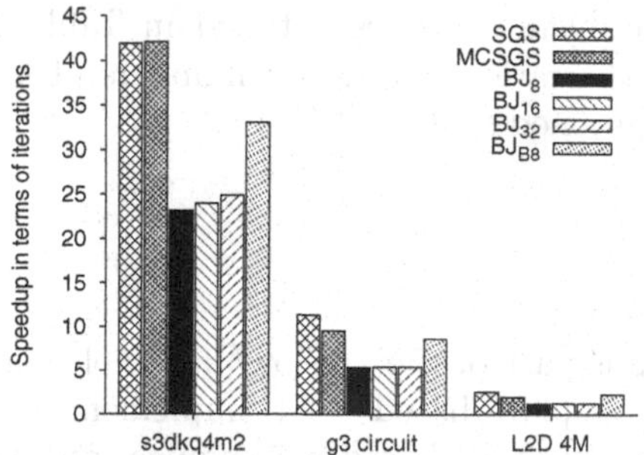

D_1	R_{11}	R_{12}	R_{13}
L_{21}	D_2	R_{21}	R_{22}
L_{31}	L_{32}	D_3	R_{31}
L_{41}	L_{41}	L_{41}	D_4

Fig. 1. Speedup in terms of the ratio of necessary number of iterations of the unpreconditioned system to the necessary number of iterations of the preconditioned system (left); Example of 4-by-4 block-decomposed matrix (right) for $B = 4$; Problem definitions are given in Table 2

The diagonal blocks D_i, $i = 1, \ldots, B$, are square with size $b_i \times b_i$ but b_i may be different for all i. The vectors x_k, y_k and z_k, $k = 1, \ldots, B$, are block vectors of length b_k. The bracket expressions in the right hand sides of (1) and (3) now consist of $i-1$ and $B-i$ matrix-vector products with vector length b_j and b_{i+j}. In total $B^2 - B$ sparse matrix-vector products and $3B$ sparse matrix-inversions are necessary to compute (1)-(3). For equal block size the degree of parallelism is $b_k = N/B$. The major difficulty in computing (1)-(3) arises from solving for the diagonal blocks D_i which are non-diagonal itself in general.

The basic idea of the multi-coloring approach is to resolve neighbor dependencies by introducing neighborship classes (colors) such that for non-vanishing matrix elements $a_{i,j}$ with $A = (a_{i,j})_{i,j}$ i and j are not members of the same class (color). A straightforward algorithm for determining the colored index sets is

```
for i=1,...,N Set Color(i)=0;
for i=1,...,N Set Color(i)=min(k>0:k!=Color(j) for j ∈ Adj(i));
```

where $\mathrm{Adj}(i) = \{j \neq i | a_{i,j} \neq 0\}$ are the adjacents to node i [10]. By renumbering the mesh nodes by colors diagonal blocks D_i become diagonal itself, B is the number of colors, and b_k is the number of elements for color k. Inversion of D_i then is only a component-wise scaling of the source vector. Due to the data parallelism of the associated routines on vectors there is no load imbalance even for varying block sizes (if the number of elements per block is reasonably large).

In the following we consider three different types of preconditioners: sequential symmetric Gauss-Seidel preconditioner (SGS), parallel block-Jacobi preconditioner with prescribed uniform block size and block-level symmetric Gauss-Seidel preconditioning for approximate inversion of diagonal blocks (BJ), and the parallel multi-coloring symmetric Gauss-Seidel preconditioner (MCSGS). Increasing the number of blocks in the BJ approach increases parallelism, decreases the level of coupling, but also decreases efficiency of the preconditioner. The drawback of the BJ preconditioner is that parallelism is only given by the number of blocks introduced (degree of parallelism is B). Hence, this approach is not scalable with respect to the number of cores.

The importance of preconditioning within the CG-method is presented in Figure 1 (left) by means of three test problem matrices detailed in Table 2. It shows the speedup factor in terms of the ratio of iteration numbers of the non-preconditioned system to the preconditioned system.

3 Implementation Aspects

Our collection of preconditioning routines is part of the HiFlow^3 finite element package [8], a generic, modularized and template-based C++ implementation of fluid dynamic solvers. Under the roof of a MPI-based communication and computation layer the lmpLAtoolbox provides backends to heterogeneous nodes built of various processor types like multi-core CPUs (OpenMP-parallel, Intel MKL, Atlas) and NVIDIA GPUs (CUBLAS and own CUDA SPMV kernels). Currently, an extension by means of an OpenCL interface and vendor-specific approaches is under construction. The whole module will be released within the framework of the HiFlow^3 project [8]. More information on the structure of the module and its cross-platform portability can be found in [7].

We have tested our three described preconditioning approaches on platforms detailed in Table 1 and for different matrices taken from [9,11] – see Table 2. The CG method is either implemented on the CPU or on the GPU. We use start vector zero, right hand side constant to one, and stop the solver with relative residual less than 10^{-6}. Preconditioning is performed on the same device with exception of SGS which is solely executed on the CPU due to its sequential nature. All computations are performed in double precision. Matrices and all sub-blocks are stored in compressed sparse row format (CSR). This format is our favorite choice for general matrix structures, whereas DIA and ELL format show benefits for particular matrix structures. See [4,3] for SpMV-kernels in different formats for GPUs. Due to the small number of non-zero elements in FEM matrices we use scalar code (one row per thread) versions on the GPU (see [4]) with and without texture caching. Kernel and thread launch times have a considerable impact on overall performance for small sized matrix problems.

MCSGS relies on a preprocessing step in which the matrix graph is analyzed, the matrix and vectors are permuted, and decomposed into blocks. The number of colors depends on the choice of finite elements (Q1, Q2, or others) and mesh properties. For higher degree elements graph connectivity and number of colors increases. 3D problems typically exhibit more graph-connectivity than 2D problems. In the MCSGS approach the amount of data and work per iteration step is independent of the data decomposition into blocks. As no detailed information is available on matrix properties we use the relaxation parameter $\omega = 1$.

Table 1. CPU and GPU system configuration: Pa/Pi = Pageable/Pinned memory, H2D = host-to-device, D2H = device-to-host, 1c/2c/4c/8c = 1/2/4/8 core(s)

Host			Device			
CPU	BW [GB/s]	H2D [GB/s]	GPU	MEM [GB]	BW [GB/s] BT/daxpy/ddot	D2H [GB/s]
2x Intel Xeon 4c (E5450), 8 cores	8c: 6.14 1c: 2.62	Pa: 1.92 Pi: 5.44	Tesla T10 S1070	4x4	71.8/83.1/83.3	Pa: 1.55 Pi: 3.77
1x Intel Core2 2c (6600), 2 cores	2c: 3.28 1c: 3.08	Pa: 1.76 Pi: 2.57	GTX 480	1.5	108.6/135.0/146.7	Pa: 1.38 Pi: 1.82
1x Intel Core i7 4c (920), 4 cores	4c: 12.07 1c: 5.11	Pa: 5.08 Pi: 5.64	GTX 280	1.0	111.5/124.3/94.8	Pa: 2.75 Pi: 5.31

4 Performance Analysis

Our performance analysis is performed on three different GPU-based platforms detailed in Table 1 giving particular information on the system bandwidth. These configurations and associated results clearly show that not only the internal bandwidth of the GPU but also the PCIe bus speed and the utilization of the bandwidth per core on the CPU need to be considered. Bandwidth values on the GPU are determined by means of the bandwidth test provided by the CUDA SDK (denoted by BT), for the vector update (daxpy), and for the scalar product (ddot). For maximal bandwidth all cores of the CPU need to be active. All our CPU tests are performed on the dual-socket quadcore Xeon system. Although the Tesla S1070 provides four GPUs we only utilize a single GPU in all our tests. Test matrices are listed in Table 2. For the g3 circuit matrix the decomposition into colors is imbalanced (689390, 789436, 106502, 150 entries per color) while for both other examples the block distributions have balanced sizes. In general, smaller matrices (like 3dkq4m2) are better suited for the cache-oriented CPUs.

The MCSGS algorithm shows good scaling properties and load balancing on the test platforms as it is based on fine-grained parallelism of the BLAS 1 vector operations and sparse matrix-vector operations in (1)-(3). For a larger number of unknowns parallelism can be better exploited. As the #colors or #blocks B stays constant the #cores may be increased with N asymptotically. Since the algorithm is bandwidth-bound on most platforms it scales with the bandwidth of the system and hence with core configurations and memory organization.

Table 2. Description and properties of test matrices

Name	Description of the problem	#rows	#non-zeros	#colors	#block-SpMV
s3dkq4m2	FEM - Cylindrical shells	90449	4820891	24	552
g3 circuit	Circuit simulation	1585478	7660826	4	12
L2D 4M	FEM - Q1 Laplace 2D	4000000	19992000	2	2

First, we compare the performance of the non-preconditioned CG solver on our test platforms in Figure 2 - 4. For large matrices we observe that the speedup of the GPU version over the OpenMP-parallel CPU version is basically due to the bandwidth difference. The only exception for the GPU is given for the 3dkq4m2 matrix which is so small that the full internal bandwidth of the GPU device cannot be utilized due to the large number of kernel calls over the PCIe. In all cases we find that texture caching on the GPU slightly improves performance.

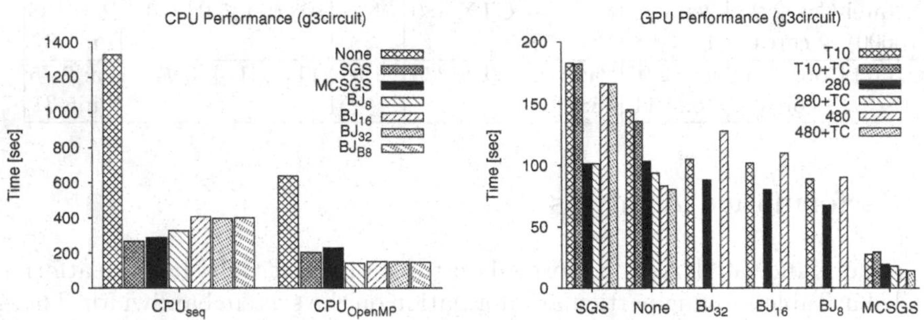

Fig. 2. Performance of preconditioned CG-solver on CPU (OpenMP: 2x4 cores) and GPU (TC: with texture caching) for g3 circuit test matrix

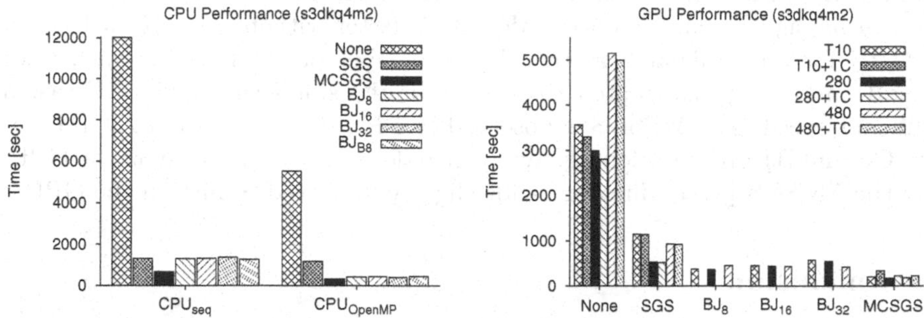

Fig. 3. Performance of preconditioned CG-solver on CPU (OpenMP: 2x4 cores) and GPU (TC: with texture caching) for s3dkq4m2 test matrix

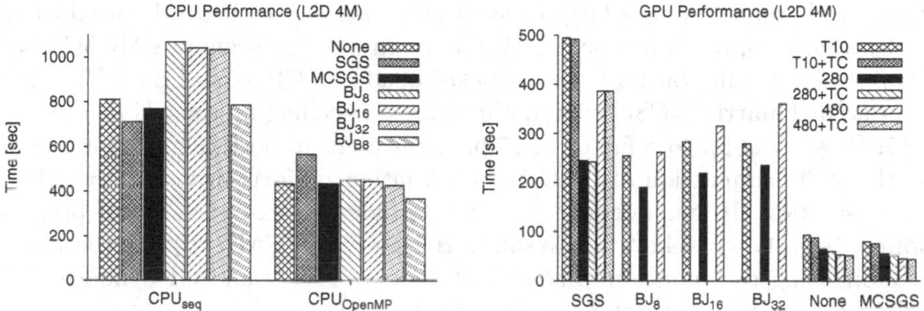

Fig. 4. Performance of preconditioned CG-solver on CPU (OpenMP: 2x4 cores) and GPU (TC: with texture caching) for L2D 4M test matrix

Computation of the SGS preconditioning step sequentially on the CPU – while the CG solver is either performed on the GPU or OpenMP-parallel – emphasizes the limitations due to Amdahl's law.

The BJ preconditioning is improving the number of iterations (see Figure 1) but not in all cases the total time is reduced. The CPU plots in Figures 2-4 show the BJ results in terms of total CG-solver time for block sizes 32, 16, and 8 and for a fixed number of eight blocks (B8). For the L2D 4M matrix on the CPU the best performance is obtained by using BJ preconditioning (see Figure 4) since the CPU cores are optimized for executing large sequential parts.

On the GPU the multi-coloring MCSGS preconditioning yields the best results for all test matrices and CPU-GPU configurations due to its inherent scalable parallelism. Efficiency of the preconditioner is paired with parallel execution within the forward and the backward step. In MCSGS the number of sparse matrix-vector operations in the block decomposition increases quadratically with the number of colors. Therefore, we observe a significant latency for launching GPU kernels and forking CPU threads as the number of colors increases. But even in the scenario with 552 SpMV operations per preconditioning step (s3dq4m2) the speedup over the CPU version is more than a factor of two. For small matrices with large number of colors the latency is further increased when texture caching is used. Therefore, MCSGS is faster without texture caching on the GPU for the s3dkq4m2 matrix. If the number of unknowns in each color is small and evenly distributed then even for the single-threaded CPU-case a significant speedup of MCSGS is observed (see Figure 3). For the L2D 4M matrix SGS and BJ preconditioning give a breakdown in performance on the GPU. Only the MCSGS preconditioner yields slightly improved results on the GPU.

5 Conclusion

We have tested preconditioning techniques for various matrix problems on hybrid multi-core CPU and GPU systems. Our investigated multi-coloring technique for symmetric Gauss-Seidel preconditioning (MCSGS) provides a scalable and fine-grained parallel approach on the level of basic linear routines. It is a robust solution and applicable to a large class of problems. Hence it can be used as an out-of-the-box approach for any FEM matrix. In our test scenarios MCSGS has delivered best results on both the 2-socket quadcore CPUs and on GPUs. For the s3dkq4m2 matrix MCSGS preconditioning is speeding up the CG method on our GPU systems up to a factor of 17.6. Assessment of performance has shown that the PCIe connection of GPUs is not limiting performance and scalability for this solution. In our ongoing work we consider an extended set of preconditioners (e.g. Chebyschev, non-sysmmetric cases with GMRES). Furthermore, preconditioning techniques in a cluster of multicore-CPU and GPU nodes with parallelisation across several devices is investigated.

Acknowledgements

The Shared Research Group 16-1 received financial support by the Concept for the Future of Karlsruhe Institute of Technology in the framework of the German Excellence Initiative and its collaboration partner Hewlett-Packard.

References

1. Asgasri, A., Tate, J.E.: Implementing the Chebyshev Polynomial Preconditioner for the Iterative Solution of Linear Systems on Massively Parallel Graphics Processors. In: CIGRE Canada Conference on Power Systems, Toronto (2009)
2. Axelsson, O., Barker, V.: Finite element solution of boundary value problems: theory and computation. SIAM, Philadelphia (2001)
3. Baskaran, M.M., Bordawekar, R.: Optimizing Sparse Matrix-Vector Multiplication on GPUs. Technical report, IBM (2009)
4. Bell, N., Garland, M.: Implementing sparse matrix-vector multiplication on throughput-oriented processors. In: SC 2009: Proc. of the Conf. on High Perf. Computing Networking, Storage and Analysis, pp. 1–11. ACM, New York (2009)
5. Göddeke, D.: Fast and Accurate Finite-Element Multigrid Solvers for PDE Simulations on GPU Cluster. PhD thesis, Technische Universität Dortmund (2010)

6. Van Henson, E., Yang, U.M.: BoomerAMG: a parallel algebraic multigrid solver and preconditioner. Appl. Numer. Math. 41(1), 155–177 (2002)
7. Heuveline, V., Subramanian, C., Lukarski, D., Weiss, J.P.: A multi-platform linear algebra toolbox for finite element solvers on heterogeneous clusters. In: PPAAC 2010, IEEE Cluster 2010 Workshops (2010)
8. HiFlow^3, `http://www.hiflow3.org`
9. Information Technology Laboratory of the National Institute of Standards and Technology, `http://math.nist.gov/MatrixMarket/`
10. Saad, Y.: Iterative Methods for Sparse Linear Systems. Society for Industrial and Applied Mathematics, Philadelphia (2003)
11. University of Florida Sparse Matrix Collection, `http://www.cise.ufl.edu/research/sparse/matrices/`

Peak Performance Model for a Custom Precision Floating-Point Dot Product on FPGAs*

Manfred Mücke, Bernd Lesser, and Wilfried N. Gansterer

University of Vienna,
Research Lab Computational Technologies and Applications
{bernd.lesser,manfred.muecke,wilfried.gansterer}@univie.ac.at

Abstract. FPGAs have the native feature that reduced resource usage of single operators can be directly translated in additional parallelism. For floating-point (FP) operators, such reduced resource usage can be achieved by reducing the mantissa bit width. The work presented here pursues two objectives: First, the maximum number of operands of a parallel dot product architecture is explored experimentally on an FPGA for different custom precision FP number formats. Given the resources of this FPGA, it is shown that based on non-pipelined basic FP operators, a dot product for input vector size 21, 57 and 123 can be implemented for double-, single- and half-precision, respectively. This corresponds to a respective peak performance of 1, 3.2 and 9.9 GFlop/s. Second, it is shown that the maximum dot product peak performance as a function of used precision can be modeled by a function of the form $P(p) = c_1 + c_2 \cdot p^{c_3}$, given a certain type of FPGA, library and synthesis settings. Fitting experimental data to this model reveals similarities as well as differences among generations of devices.

1 Introduction

It is a basic property of FPGAs that free hardware resources can be used to implement additional functional units and thus to increase chip-level parallelism. Given a specific FPGA, reducing the precision (mantissa bit width) of the FP number format translates directly into more functional units and, in case this additional parallelism can be exploited, to improved performance. There is, however, a trade-off between the effort to be invested in analysis and algorithmic modifications for minimizing the precision and the resulting performance gain. Consequently, key to productive algorithm and application development for FPGAs are reliable performance estimation schemes. The hardware resource usage of FP operators on FPGAs depends on many factors, including the architecture's total size, the chosen library and pipeline depth, the FPGA architecture and feature mix, the synthesis tool and its configuration. It is therefore impossible to

* This work was supported by the Austrian Research Promotion Agency (FFG) under contract 819469 (MixSVM) and by the Austrian Science Fund (FWF) under contract S10608-N13 (NFN SISE).

M.R. Guarracino et al. (Eds.): Euro-Par 2010 Workshops, LNCS 6586, pp. 399–406, 2011.
© Springer-Verlag Berlin Heidelberg 2011

extrapolate the performance data reported in this paper to all FPGAs or all possible constellations. The efforts summarized in this paper should be considered an initial design space exploration with the precision level as a variable while most other influence factors are kept constant. While reported hardware resource usage on FPGAs typically scales linearly with the number of identical functional units, the same is not true for routing resources (affecting the achievable clock frequency). When investigating peak performance, it is therefore important to actually implement designs of a specific size rather than extrapolating from the basic building blocks.

The main contributions of our work are (*i*) extensive measurements of peak performance based on fully synthesized designs up to 100% resource usage on different FPGAs over a wide range of precisions up to double precision (64 bit) in single-bit resolution and (*ii*) a model describing the dot product architecture's peak performance as a function of precision. To the best of our knowledge, this is the most complete investigation to date of a dot product architecture's peak performance on FPGAs.

FPGA designs (and libraries) implementing FP arithmetic often favor deeply pipelined basic operators to maximize clock frequency. This choice boosts peak performance, but lowers the worst-case performance thereby making sustained performance less predictable. We have opted to implement our architecture with unpipelined (combinatorial) basic FP operators. Consequently, the reported peak performance figures are lower than the ones reported by authors using more pipelined architectures while our worst-case performance is better.

Paper Outline. Chapter 2 summarizes related work. Chapter 3 describes the dot product architecture. Based on extensive measurements reported in Chapter 4, we derive a model for the peak performance as a function of precision in Section 4.1. We close with a summary and outlook in Chapter 5.

2 Related Work

Table 1 gives a compact overview over related literature and the respective number formats[1] investigated. The table reveals that most publications deal exclusively with either double- or single precision number formats. Only [1] also gives detailed synthesis results for a limited set of custom-precision number formats.

de Dinechin et. al [1] propose an FPGA-based accumulation- and sum-of-products module for FP numbers. By using the Flopoco code generation tool [5] and by targeting high-end FPGA platforms, they achieve a fast (up to 416 MHz for double-precision) and deeply pipelined architecture. Synthesis results are reported for single modules and for four different FP number formats only. Peak performance achievable on some FPGA is not documented. The data provided makes estimation of the total hardware-resources required to implement a large dot product unreliable.

[1] $s12e10m$ stands short for a FP number representation using a 12 bit wide exponent and a 10 bit wide mantissa, totaling $1 + 12 + 10 = 23$ bit.

Table 1. Floating-point number formats investigated in related literature.

Publication	DP	SP	HP	Custom Precision	Comments
[1]	√	√	–	s10e37m, s7e6m	internal fixed-point register
[3]	–	√	–	–	internal fixed-point register: 2-52 bits
[6]	√	–	–	–	
[2]	√	–	–	–	dot product based, blocked DGEMM
[4]	√	–	–	–	dot product based GAXPY
This work	√	√	√	s11e<4..52>m	

Lopes and Constantinides [3] propose a fused hybrid (floating- and fixed-point) dot product architecture for FPGAs. Hardware resource usage and achieved maximum frequency of their architecture, depending on the bit width of the internal register are reported for three different dot product vector lengths only. The single-precision peak performance for a vector length of m=50 is about 15 GFlop/s (the frequency is not explicitly given) and has a total latency of 80 clock cycles. The worst-case performance for this architecture is 15 [GFlop/s] / 80 [cycles] = 187.5 MFlop/s.

Zhuo et. al [6] investigate different architectures for linear algebra operations on FPGA. Among the considered operations is also a double-precision dot product architecture based on a binary adder tree, which is identical to ours. Different to this work, the authors limit the size of their architecture by an estimate of I/O bandwidth to six input operand pairs. Their dot product module for six operand pairs has a latency of 9 clock cycles and runs at about 170 MHz. This results in a peak performance of 1.87 GFlop/s and a worst-case performance of 207 MFlop/s.

Langhammer and VanCourt [2] report performance results of a highly parallel double-precision DGEMM implementation, using an experimental FP core builder. The resulting implementation is based on a dot product core very similar to our architecture. The implementation achieves a double-precision peak performance of 47.46 GFlop/s for vectors of length 128 and a latency of 55 cycles, resulting in a worst-case performance of 863 MFlop/s. The authors do not investigate different number formats nor do they investigate performance on different FPGAs.

Kestur et. al [4] discuss and evaluate different FPGA architectures to implement BLAS kernels based on a tree-based dot product core, and compare final performance figures with CPU- and GPU-based implementations. The authors use Xilinx's CoreGen tool to generate fully pipelined FP multipliers and adders, making their BLAS-core run at a frequency of 100 MHz. The authors report a peak performance of 3.11 GFlop/s, with a maximum variance of 32% over a variety of problem sizes. They do not mention explicitly the total latency for their overall architectures. Different number formats or FPGAs are not compared.

3 Dot Product Architecture

The canonical dot product of two real-valued input-vectors $\boldsymbol{a} = [a_1, \ldots, a_n]$ and $\boldsymbol{b} = [b_1, \ldots, b_n]$ is defined as: $< \boldsymbol{a}, \boldsymbol{b} >= \boldsymbol{a}^T \boldsymbol{b} = \sum_{i=1}^{n} a_i \cdot b_i$. As n can be arbitrary large, the above formulation requires a dot product operation accepting arbitrary large input vectors. In case a custom dot product operator accepting input vectors of length m exists, the dot product can be rewritten as follows:

$$< \boldsymbol{a}, \boldsymbol{b} >= \sum_{i=1}^{n} a_i \cdot b_i = \sum_{j=0}^{\lfloor \frac{n}{m} \rfloor - 1} \sum_{i=1}^{m} a_{i+j \cdot m} \cdot b_{i+j \cdot m} + \sum_{i=\lfloor \frac{n}{m} \rfloor \cdot m+1}^{n} a_i \cdot b_i$$

Our objective is to document and to model the maximum input vector length m implementable on FPGAs for different FP number formats. We have chosen to implement m parallel multipliers followed by a pipelined binary tree structure of adders to sum the products. Our dot product architecture implements a dot product function accepting 2 vectors of maximum length m input operands each clock cycle, using FP modules from the *FPLibrary*[2]. While the individual FP modules are purely combinatorial (see Section 1 for the motivation), registers are placed between basic operators to achieve a pipelined dot product architecture. The total latency is the depth of the binary adder tree ($\lceil \log_2 m \rceil$) plus one cycle for multiplication and two for pre- and post-conversion of number formats, respectively. This leads to a total latency of $\lceil \log_2 m \rceil + 3$ clock cycles for the computation of a single dot product of two vectors with m entries.

In detail, the architecture performs the following steps: (i) The input-values are being converted from the IEEE custom-precision FP number format to the *FPLibrary* internal number format. (ii) All m products are calculated in parallel by m multipliers. (iii) The m products are summed up by a binary adder tree of depth $\lceil \log_2 m \rceil$ containing a total of $m - 1$ adders. (iv) The final dot product is converted back to the used IEEE custom-precision FP number format.

Assuming a fully filled pipeline, the architecture accepts two new input vectors and outputs one result every clock-cycle. As computing the dot product requires $2m-1$ FP operations, this corresponds to a peak performance of $(2m-1) \cdot f_{\max}$ FP operations per second (Flop/s), where $f_{\max}$ is the maximum clock frequency achievable for the respective architecture.

$$P = (2m - 1) \cdot f_{\max} \tag{1}$$

4 Experiments

In the following, we describe the tools used and steps performed to achieve real-world measurements on the maximum dot product size implementable on a set of FPGAs. We report measurements on three different types of FPGAs. Our initial measurements use the largest available Altera Cyclone II device, the EP2C70[3].

[2] http://www.ens-lyon.fr/LIP/Arenaire/Ware/FPLibrary/ (July 30th, 2010)

[3] http://www.altera.com/products/devices (July 30th, 2010)

To verify the results obtained, we repeat our measurement using two more recent devices: the Cyclone III EP3C80[3] and the Stratix III EP3SL70[3] . Table 2 gives details on the available resources for each FPGA. Finally, we develop a model approximating best the original measurements and verify the model with the measurements obtained from the two more recent devices.

Table 2. Hardware resources of used FPGAs

FPGA Device	FPGA Family	Logic elements	Feature size	DSP blocks [9x9bit blocks]	Emb. Memory [kbits]
EP2C70	Cyclone II	68,416	90nm	300	1,125
EP3C80	Cyclone III	81,264	65nm	488	2,745
EP3SL70	Stratix III	67,500	65nm	576	2,214

We implemented a generic dot product architecture, as described in Section 3, in VHDL, using VHDL `generic` statements to achieve a flexible code accepting the number of input-operands and the mantissa bit width as parameters. We implemented a measurement framework using the TCL scripting language to generate a large set of possible implementations by setting the parameters of the VHDL code accordingly. The TCL script initiates synthesis of multiple implementations of varying size for each chosen FP mantissa bit width and records reported performance figures. The synthesis tool used is the freely available *QuartusII WebEdition v9.1*[4] from Altera. For the optimization goal of the synthesis, the option "speed" was chosen. For the rest of the many available synthesis options, the default options have been used.

Resource Usage vs. Dot Product Size. The first series of measurements targets the hardware-resource usage of the dot product architecture as a function of the number of input operands. The chosen architecture requires one additional adder and one additional multiplier for each new pair of input operands. For multipliers, the hardware-resource usage is expected to increase linearly until all available DSP-blocks are consumed. After this point, the synthesis software assembles further multipliers from LUTs, only. This results in more logic elements per operator and therefore in a steeper increase of total hardware resource usage, until all hardware resources of the FPGA are consumed and no more operators can fit. Figure 1 shows the logic elements and DSP blocks used as well as the maximum achievable clock frequency, when implementing the dot product architecture on an Altera EP2C70 FPGA, for double-, single-, and half-precision, respectively. For each number format, the number of input operand pairs is increased until all available hardware resources are consumed. The logic elements increase linearly over the whole resource range for single- and half-precision while there is a visible change in slope for double-precision when all available DSP blocks are consumed. Table 3 shows the maximum clock frequency and

[4] `http://www.altera.com/products/software/sfw-index.jsp`(July 30th, 2010)

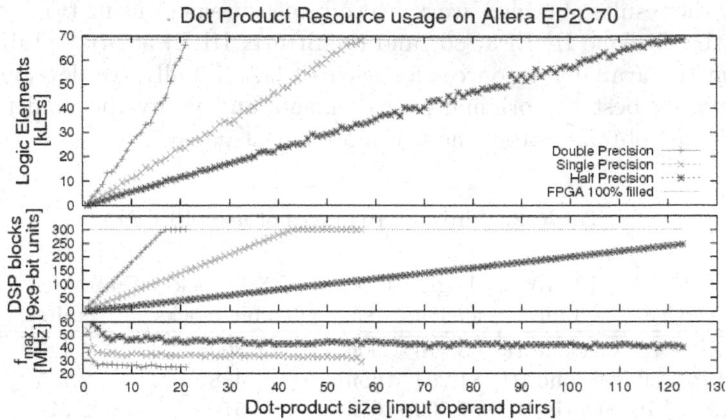

Fig. 1. Dot product hardware resource usage on Altera EP2C70 over dot product size

maximum number of input operand pairs for double-, single-, and half-precision implementable on the EP2C70 using our dot product architecture. The resulting peak performance can be calculated according to equation 1.

FPGA Peak Performance vs. Number Format. In this series of measurements, we identify the maximum dot product size fitting the FPGA for each number format (i.e. adding another pair of input operands would require more resources than are available on the respective FPGA). Figure 2 shows the maximum size and the maximum clock frequency of the dot product architecture over the range of considered number formats on all three FPGAs (EP2C70, EP3C80, EP3SL70). According to Equation (1) we can calculate the corresponding peak performance of our architecture for each mantissa bit width. Figure 3 shows the resulting peak performance for EP2C70, EP3C80 and EP3SL70, respectively. The peak performance for all three FPGAs increases with decreasing mantissa bit width. The peak performance achieved on the EP3C80 is consistently higher than the one achieved on the EP2C70, thanks to additional hardware resources and higher clock frequencies. The performance achieved on th EP3SL70 is consistently higher than the one on EP3C80 due to higher clock frequencies.

Table 3. Dot product peak performance on Altera EP2C70 for selected formats

Floating-point number format	max. input operand pairs m	$f_{\max}$ [MHz]	peak-performance [GFlop/s]
double precision (s11e52m)	21	24.82	1
single precision (s8e23m)	57	28.98	3.2
half-precision (s5e10m)	123	40.42	9.9

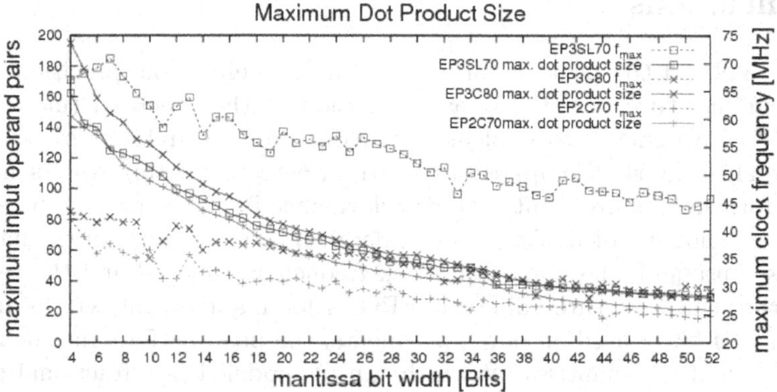

Fig. 2. Maximum dot product input vector length over mantissa bit width

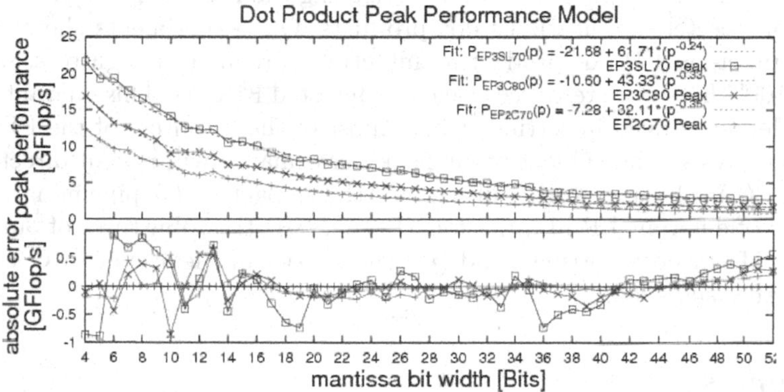

Fig. 3. Dot product peak performance measurements and model

4.1 Dot Product Performance Model

We fit the observed data to fractional polynomials of the form $P(p) = c_1 + c_2 \cdot p^{c_3}$ where p is the precision. Figure 3 shows the peak performance derived from measured data together with the fits for all three FPGAs. The exponents c_3 are -0.35, -0.33 and -0.24 and the weighted sum of squared residuals χ^2 is $1.89, 2.76$ and 9.15 for the EP2C70, EP3C80 and EP3SL70, respectively. The maximum absolute error is about 1 GFlop/s. It is interesting to observe that the exponent c_3 is almost identical for the EP2C70 and the EP3C80 (-0.35 vs. -0.33) while it differs significantly for the EP3SL70 (-0.24). We conclude that for Cyclone devices (even spanning different generations), the peak performance of our dot product architecture scales with the power of about -0.35 of the precision. For the Stratix III device, we see a higher general performance level, but somewhat lower scaling ($c_3 = -0.24$).

5 Conclusions

We have explored the peak performance of a parallel custom precision FP dot product architecture on FPGAs as a function of the precision (mantissa bit width). We have chosen to implement our dot product architecture with minimum pipeline depth. Compared to other architectures, this results in lower peak performance figures, but better performance in the worst case when deep pipelines can not be filled. We provided detailed measurements of the hardware resources consumed, the maximum clock frequency achieved and the resulting peak performance on three different FPGAs for mantissa bit widths from 52 bit down to 4 bit. Based on our experiments, the peak performance achievable as a function of the mantissa bit width can be modeled as a fractional polynomial of order one. The exponent is between -0.35 and -0.24, depending on the FPGA chosen. With this result, the performance benefit of reduced precision can be reliably quantified for the devices considered and comparable settings. We hope that this stipulates work investigating the minimally required FP precision for selected application's dot products. Our experiments show that the custom-precision FP dot product architecture is regular enough to scale up to almost 100% hardware resource usage on all tested FPGAs. This guarantees that our model holds even in settings where most of the resources of the FPGA are used and gives strong evidence that peak performance will benefit directly from larger FPGAs. Future work will explore the impact of (*i*) pipelining, (*ii*) the behavior of different FP libraries for FPGAs, (*iii*) the robustness of our results in terms of synthesis settings, and (*iv*) the impact of the size of FPGAs on the performance achieved.

References

1. de Dinechin, F., Pasca, B., Cret, O., Tudoran, R.: An FPGA-specific approach to floating-point accumulation and sum-of-products. In: International Conference on ICECE Technology, FPT 2008, pp. 33–40 (December 2008)
2. Langhammer, M., VanCourt, T.: Altera Cooperation. Accelerating floating-point DGEMM on FPGAs. HPEC 2008 Poster (2008), `http://www.ll.mit.edu/HPEC/agendas/proc08/Day2/35-Day2-PosterDemoB-VanCourt-abstract.pdf` (last accessed: July 30, 2010)
3. Roldao Lopes, A., Constantinides, G.: A fused hybrid floating-point and fixed-point dot-product for fPGAs. In: Sirisuk, P., Morgan, F., El-Ghazawi, T., Amano, H. (eds.) ARC 2010. LNCS, vol. 5992, pp. 157–168. Springer, Heidelberg (2010)
4. Kestur, S., Davis, J.D., Williams, O.: BLAS Comparison on FPGA, CPU and GPU. Article, Microsoft Research (2007), `http://research.microsoft.com/apps/pubs/default.aspx?id=130834`
5. FloPoCo - Project, `http://www.ens-lyon.fr/LIP/Arenaire/Ware/FloPoCo/` (last accessed: July 30, 2010)
6. Zhuo, L., Prasanna, V.K.: High-performance designs for linear algebra operations on reconfigurable hardware. IEEE Transactions on Computers 57(8), 1057–1071 (2008)

Workshop on High-Performance Computing applied to Finance (HPCF 2010)

HPCF 2010: Workshop on High-Performance Computing Applied to Finance

Francesca Perla

Università degli Studi di Napoli "Parthenope", and ICAR-CNR, Italy

Foreword

The *Workshop on High-Performance Computing applied to Finance* (HPCF) focuses on the computational issues in the solution by advanced architectures of financial problems, particularly concerning the evaluation of financial instruments, asset and liability portfolio management, measuring and monitoring of risks and assessment of solvency requirements.

Kontoghiorghes, Nagurney and Rustem – in the year 2000 – in the guest editorial of a special number of Parallel Computing (in economics, finance and decision-making)[1] stated that "[parallel] computing has evolved into an essential tool in the solution of complex, large scale problems arising in [...] finance, in particular. Nevertheless, [...] its potential to solve problems in [...] finance has neither been fully addressed nor explored."

This statement is at the moment partially still true for high-performance computing.

The critical issue is yet the lack of complex valuation systems, for advanced computing architectures, able to provide "market-consistent evaluation" of values and risks and to perform timely measurements, as required by markets and regulations, in order to carry out continuous verification. The development of such a system requires a strong synergy between high-level theory and high-level technology, that is a synergy between models and techniques of quantitative finance, computational schemes and data management. The appropriateness of data quality and models as well as accuracy and efficiency of computation and the adequacy of the IT infrastructure are more and more preconditions for an efficient governance of financial companies and an effective monitoring of market stability.

The Financial Services Authority (FSA), in a document on Solvency II project[2], stated indeed that to develop, implement and maintain an "internal model" insurance undertakings must make "a cross-functional team: comprising finance, actuarial, risk and IT functions" [p. 29. 5.4], and that "an adequate system of

[1] Kontoghiorghes, J., Nagurney, A., Rustem, B., Parallel computing in economics, finance and decision-making - Guest editorial, Parallel Computing, 26 (2000), 507-509.

[2] Financial Services Authority, Insurance Risk Management: The Path To Solvency II, FSA, September 2008.

M.R. Guarracino et al. (Eds.): Euro-Par 2010 Workshops, LNCS 6586, pp. 409–411, 2011.
© Springer-Verlag Berlin Heidelberg 2011

governance should be carried out by persons with sufficient knowledge of actuarial and financial mathematics and [...] able where appropriate to demonstrate their relevant experience and expertise" [p. 16, 3.19]. Mario Draghi – Governor of Banca d'Italia – in the Concluding Remarks of year 2007[3] claimed as well that "the consolidation of our banking system [...] must be accompanied by a significant acceleration in the integration of networks, organizational structures, IT systems [...] to enable banks to manage the new and complex risks.".

The integration between high-level theory and high-level technology requires a close collaboration between experts in finance, in modelling, in computational mathematics and in computer science. In addition, the new banking regulation (Basilea 2) and insurance and reinsurance regulation (Solvency II) strongly affect the governance of financial companies, thus requiring decision-makers and regulators to make their own contribution to the design, development and validation of valuation systems.

From the hardware point of view, a wider spread of high-performance computing can be achieved by exploring new technology solutions that trade off costs and performance, such as blade systems, cloud computing, gpu computing, many-core processors and so on.

The workshop aims at providing a forum for researchers and practitioners on the challenge of fully addressing the potential of high-performance computing to realize effective systems for the estimation of values and risks that can be used in a business and industry context.

The contributions of the authors certainly concur both to the advance of knowledge in the computational finance field and to the effective solution of financial problems by the application of innovative ideas of other research areas, such as data processing, numerical analysis and high-performance computing, and further stimulate the research on these topics.

The choice of invited lectures has been inspired by the main problem of asset-liability management and in particular by the actual debate on the Solvency II implementing measures.

The first lecture by Gilberto Castellani and Luca Passalacqua addresses computational problems deriving from Solvency II compliance in the context of Italian life insurance. They present DISAR (Dynamic Investment Strategy with Accounting Rules), a relevant example of "internal model" designed for the monitoring of portfolios of "profit sharing" Italian life insurance policies with minimum guarantees, linked to "segregated funds", working on a grid of conventional computers.

The second lecture by Andreas Grothey focuses on asset-liability management of portfolio optimisation by large long-term investors. He shows that realistic simulations lead to problems with many millions of unknowns that now can be really faced-up using stochastic dynamics models on massively parallel architectures. He reviews some of the results and challenges in this framework.

---

[3] Banca d'Italia, The Governor's Concluding Remarks - Ordinary Meeting of Shareholders, 2007 - 114th Financial Year, Rome 31 May 2008.

Both the contributions represent notable examples of synergy between high-level theory and high-level technology and meet the requirement of a strong community of interests between scientific and business and industry context.

Acknowledgments

I wish to thank the Europar organizers for providing the opportunity to carry out the workshop in conjunction with the EuroPar 2010 conference. My gratitude also goes to Gilberto Castellani, Luca Passalacqua and Andreas Grothey for accepting my invitation to give a lecture. For their support in the workshop program's definition, I want to thank the members of the Program committee. Financial support from Università degli Studi di Napoli "Parthenope" and EuroPar, is gratefully acknowledged.

November 2010

Francesca Perla

Applications of Distributed and Parallel Computing in the Solvency II Framework: The DISAR System

Gilberto Castellani and Luca Passalacqua

Sapienza, Università di Roma, Dipartimento di Scienze Statistiche,
Viale Regina Elena, 295, I-00161 Roma, Italy
{gilberto.castellani,luca.passalacqua}@uniroma1.it

Abstract. We address computational problems deriving from Solvency II compliance in the context of Italian life insurance. Solvency II requires insurance undertakings to perform market consistent valuation of technical provisions and continuous monitoring of risks. We examine the case of profit sharing policies with minimum guarantees, which is the most diffused type of life policy in Italy. Market consistent valuation of the complex cash flows generated by these contracts entails modelling of management actions and the use of numerical techniques in a stochastic framework, typically Monte Carlo simulation on a fine grained time grid. Fulfillment of the subsequent highly-demanding computational tasks is possible only by implementing valuation procedures in parallel and distributed architectures. In this work we introduce DISAR, a Solvency II compliant system designed to work on a grid of conventional computers, and discuss its performances.

1 Introduction

The European Directive 2009/138 (Solvency II) [Dir-09] requires insurance undertakings to evaluate technical provisions in a market-consistent way and to measure the Solvency Capital Requirement (SCR) with the Value-at-Risk approach (confidence level = 99.5%, unwinding period = 1 year).

Moreover, insurance undertakings "shall have in place an effective risk-management system comprising strategies, processes and reporting procedures necessary to identify, measure, monitor, manage and report, on a continuous basis the risk, at the individual and at an aggregated level, to which they are or could be exposed, and their interdependencies" [Dir-09, art. 44]. It is possible to identify at least five relevant areas that the risk-management system should cover: 1 – underwriting and reserving; 2 – asset-liability management; 3 – investment; 4 – liquidity and concentration risk management; 5 – risk-mitigation techniques.

The implications and requirements introduced by the Directive become particularly compelling when the undertaking calculates technical provisions and SCR using an "internal model" [Dir-09, art. 112]. The internal model is a system used by the undertaking to assess risks and determine the overall solvency needs,

M.R. Guarracino et al. (Eds.): Euro-Par 2010 Workshops, LNCS 6586, pp. 413–421, 2011.
© Springer-Verlag Berlin Heidelberg 2011

ensuring the quality standards indicated by the Directive and subject to the approval of the national supervisory authority [Dir-09, art. 112-127]. In addition, the new requirements will have strong impact on the IT function responsibilities, which, instead of being restricted to hardware and software solutions, shall be extended to include processes and monitoring of performance and standards.

In such complex scenario, we shall introduce and discuss DISAR (Dynamic Investment Strategy with Accounting Rules), a computational system designed for the monitoring of portfolios of "profit sharing" Italian life insurance policies with minimum guarantees, linked to "segregated funds". Notice that systems like DISAR are required also when the undertaking computes the SCR using the "standard formula", as presently defined by the Committee of European Insurance and Occupational Pensions Supervisors (CEIOPS) in the Quantitative Impact Study 5 (QIS5) [C-10].

2 Life Insurance Policies in Italy

Profit sharing policies with minimum guarantees are one of the most popular contracts in the Italian life insurance market. In this type of policies benefits provided to the insured are periodically adjusted depending on the return of a dedicated fund, the so-called *segregated fund* (in Italian *gestione separata*) [1].

As reference example of the profit sharing mechanism, we consider a single premium pure endowment contract, written at time 0, for a life aged x, with term T years and initial sum insured Y_0. In this case, the benefit Y_T paid by the insurer if the policyholder is alive at time T is determined by incrementing each year the insured sum by a fraction of the interest earned by the insurer in the segregated fund where the premium is invested. Specifically,

$$Y_T = Y_0 \cdot \prod_{k=1}^{T} (1 + \rho_k) \,, \text{ where} \tag{1}$$

$$\rho_k = \frac{\max\{\min\{\beta I_k; I_k - \eta\} - i; \delta^c\}}{1+i} \tag{2}$$

is the so-called *readjustment rate*, $\beta \in (0,1]$ is the participation coefficient, I_k is the annual rate of return of the segregated fund in year $[k-1,k]$, η is the minimum annual rate retained by the insurance company, i is the *technical rate*, and δ^c is the minimum guaranteed annual *cliquet rate.*

The market consistent valuation of the policy must be performed in a stochastic framework where uncertainties are of actuarial and financial type. The valuation principles and the methodological approach are detailed in [DM-05]. The core of market consistent valuation is the fact that value of the benefits at time $t=0$, $V_0(Y_T)$, can be expressed as the expected value of the payoff at time $t = T$,

---

[1] At the end of year 2009 the Italian Supervisory Authority listed 386 segregated funds, belonging to 76 insurance companies, with the overall amount of statutory reserves summing up to about 65% of the total life reserves.

weighted by a suitable state-price deflator. Assuming independence between actuarial and financial uncertainty, the expectation can be factorised. Finally, the expectations can then be rewritten with a change of measure, employing the so-called risk-neutral probability measure Q. Under Q prices measured in units of the value of the money market account are martingales. Accordingly,

$$V_0(Y_T) = \mathbf{E}^Q\left[\frac{Y_T}{e^{\int_0^T r_u du}}\middle|\mathcal{F}_0\right]\, {}_T p_x = \overline{Y}_T\, \mathbf{E}^Q\left[\prod_{k=1}^{T}(1+\rho_k)\; e^{-\int_0^T r_u\, du}\middle|\mathcal{F}_0\right], \tag{3}$$

where r_t is the instantaneous intensity of interest rate determining the value of the money market account, $\mathcal{F}_t$ is the filtration containing the information about financial events, ${}_T p_x$ is the risk-neutral probability that an individual aged x will persist for T more years (lapse included) and $\overline{Y}_T = Y_0\, {}_T p_x$ is the *actuarially expected* benefit. Notice that both ρ_t and r_t are $\mathcal{F}_t$-adapted random variables.

A closer inspection of the payoff of the policy in eq. (1) shows that it includes embedded options, whose underlying is the segregated fund return. The presence of the options can be made explicit by expressing $V_0(Y_T)$ using either a put or a call decomposition [DM-05, p. 91]:

$$V_0(Y_T) = B_0 + P_0 = G_0 + C_0, \tag{4}$$

where B_0 is the value of a risky investment (base component) and P_0 that of a put option; G_0 is the value a guaranteed investment and a C_0 that of a call option, or – in the words of the Directive – the policy guaranteed benefits and its future discretionary benefits.

For this type of policies the fund return is typically defined by "book accounting rules" which offer several strategic handles to control the return of the segregated fund and play a key role in the management strategy of the fund itself. Due to the complexity of the payoff and the management actions involved, the valuation processes are performed numerically using Monte Carlo simulation on a fine grained time grid. Fast evaluations are hindered by at least six different factors: 1 – the maturity of policies (about 100 years); 2 – the control of the investment and accounting strategy; 3 – the computing time required by Monte Carlo simulation; 4 – the large number of policies involved (typically at the million level); 5 – the large number of segregated funds owned by each undertaking; 6 – the large number of securities composing each segregated funds.

3 The DISAR System

DISAR is a system composed by a DataBase Management System and by several calculation engines. The methodological asset-liability management (ALM) framework in which DISAR has been designed is detailed in [CDMP-05] [2].

[2] It is a well established framework embedding all principles of modern finance, rooted in the first works on the market consistent valuation of this type of policies, that date back to 1994 [DM-94] and acknowledging the guidelines suggested in "New Math for Life Actuaries" [B-02] and in [DM-05].

The theoretical framework and the "high technological" infrastructure allow DISAR to meet the requirements needed for the approval of internal models, *i.e.* use test [Dir-09, art. 120], statistical quality standards (art. 121), calibration standards (art. 122), profit and loss attribution (art. 123), validation standards (art. 124), documentation standards (art. 125).

DISAR is able to provide (*inter alia*): the market value of the policies, the net asset value (NAV) of the ALM portfolio and the corresponding components (*base*, *call*, *put* and *guaranteed*); the *Value of Business In Force* (VBIF); the overall SCR and its components (interest rate, equity, mortality, etc.).

3.1 Management Actions

The management of the policy portfolio is modelled defining an asset-liability management *ALM strategy*, *i.e.* a set of rules for the actions to be undertaken by the insurance company until run-off of all policies. The strategy affects:

1. the portfolio of outstanding policies (including expenses);
2. the segregated funds, composed by the assets defining the reference index;
3. an external fund, composed by all remaining assets;
4. a bank account, controlling liquidity positions;
5. the subordinated loan capital.

The set of operations that are performed, either monthly or at the end of each accounting year, include:

1. cash-flow hedging: defines how benefits and expenses are paid;
2. technical provision and solvency margin calculation: it is performed at the end of each accounting year;
3. company capital strategy: defines how capital is allocated from the company to shareholders (and vice versa) and how debt is created/cancelled on the company balance sheet; it is performed at the end of each accounting year;
4. fund allocation: defines how capital is allocated between the segregated fund, the external fund and the bank account.
5. asset portfolio management: defines the asset allocation strategies for the segregated fund and the external fund.

The strategy components are governed by algorithms driven by a set of parameters and embody several constraints. For example, the asset portfolio management is defined by creating a classification scheme (*asset class*) for all possible assets and fixing a range of values for the relative contribution of each class (in terms of value, duration, etc.). Similarly, a target return for the segregated fund can be constrained to be constant or indexed to a financial yield prevailing on the market at that date (*e.g.* the swap rate for a given maturity).

Since the quantities constrained by the strategy assume values that depend on the trajectory of simulated market prices, the constraints should be periodically monitored along the trajectory making proper readjustments when needed. The monitoring frequency of the constraints strongly affects the overall computing time since it is required to repeat the valuation of a large set of contracts with very long maturities.

3.2 Reduction of Computational Complexity

DISAR achieves a reduction of the computation complexity of the valuations by:

1) decomposing the overall valuation into an actuarial valuation and an ALM valuation as done in eq. (3): all actuarially expected cash flows $\overline{Y}$ are computed first and used later as an input for the ALM valuation;
2) performing scenario generation separately from the actuarial and ALM valuation; this decoupling allows to use exogenous reference trajectories; moreover, the simulation of the trajectories can be easily parallelised;
3) performing on the liability side a decomposition of the contracts, followed by an aggregation of *elementary contracts*; these are obtained by decomposing derivatives in baskets of simpler contracts; this operation is fully information-preserving and is different from the traditional model-point technique, where information may be lost;
4) sub-dividing the evaluations to be performed by processing and assembling "atomic units" or *elementary elaboration blocks* (EEB), each corresponding to a given segregated fund, for a given set of parameters.

The above operations allow the implementation of DISAR in a distributed and parallel computing environment.

3.3 Sources of Uncertainty

Two main types of uncertainty are considered: actuarial risks such as mortality/longevity risk, surrender risk (lapses), expense risks and financial risks, such as interest rate risk, equity risk, property risk, credit risk (default and spread risk), currency risk, inflation risk.

Actuarial and financial risks are assumed to be independent. Moreover, actuarial risks are assumed to be independent between each other, while financial risks are possibly correlated. Table 1 reports a list of the main risk drivers with a corresponding model used for the valuation. The list is not exhaustive since in DISAR it is possible to choose between different models: for example credit risk can be modeled either with deterministic credit spreads (as in the "standard formula" QIS5 approach) or with a suitable stochastic model, as in [DS-99]. Ultimately, the financial uncertainty is described by a vector $\mathbf{Z}$ of Brownian motions, *e.g.* $\mathbf{Z} = \{Z_t^p, Z_t^r, Z_t^B, Z_t^{c,j}, Z_t^{e,i}\}$, and a correlation matrix $\mathbf{\Sigma}_Z$.

The number of sources of uncertainties is computationally relevant when computing the capital requirement. For each source of uncertainty s the SCR_s is determined as the impact of a specified scenario on the NAV of the undertaking. Two scenarios are considered: one where the source of uncertainty is stressed up to the reference confidence level, and another where the stress is in the opposite direction. For example, for interest rates, let Δ_t be the NAV central value, $\Delta_t^{u,d}$ the NAV stressed up and down values; then

$$\mathrm{SCR}_{int.rate} = \max\{\Delta_t - \Delta_t^u\, ; \Delta_t - \Delta_t^d\, ; 0\} \tag{5}$$

Table 1. Financial models

risk driver	evolution	model
consumer prices	$dp_t = y_t\, p_t\, dt + \sigma_p\, p_t\, dZ_t^p$	lognormal model
expected inflation	$y_t = y_\infty + (y_0 - y_\infty)\, e^{-\alpha_y\, t}$	deterministic
nominal risk-free int. rates	$dr_t = \alpha\,(\gamma - r_t)\, dt + \rho\,\sqrt{r_t}\, dZ_t^r$	CIR model
nominal risk-free disc. factor	$v(t,s) = A(s-t)\, e^{-B(s-t)\, r_t}$	CIR model
risky nominal disc. factors	$v^j(t,s) = A^j(s-t)\, e^{-B^j(s-t)\, \eta_t^j}$	DS model
credit spreads	$d\eta_t^j = \alpha_j^c(\gamma_j^c - \eta_t^j)dt + \rho_j^c\sqrt{\eta_t^j}\, dZ_t^{c,j}$	DS model
real risk-free rates	$x_t = r_t - (y_t - \sigma_p^2)$	stoch. Fisher eq.
equity benchmark	$dB_t = B_t\, \mu_B\, dt + B_t\, \sigma_B\, dZ_t^B$	Black-Scholes model
equity prices	$dS_t^i = S_t^i\, \mu_S^i\, dt + S_t^i\, (\beta^i\, \sigma_B)\, dZ_t^B$	CAPM
exchange rates	$dC_t^i = C_t^i\, \mu_C^i\, dt + C_t^i\, \sigma_C^i\, dZ_t^{e,i}$	lognormal model

For each segregated fund the number of EEB to be performed is then:

$$N_b = 1(\text{best estimate}) + 2 \times \#\,\text{sources of uncertainty}. \qquad (6)$$

Each elementary block can be processed independently from the other, which allows a trivial parallelisation of the valuation of the different SCR_s. Finally, a dedicated EEB performs the *consolidation* of the SCR_s into the overall SCR.

4 The Computing Environment

DISAR works over a grid of conventional computers. Each node of the grid hosts a service that activates the computing engine upon request. The components of the system are the following.

1. **A Database Server**, hosting a Relational DataBase Management System;
2. **A Master Server**, hosting the *Disar Master Service* (DiMaS), that receives the primary requests from the *Clients*, defines the elementary elaboration blocks, estimates the complexity of the elaborations, establishes the elaboration schedule, distributes the elementary requests to the processing units and monitors the process. If necessary, the Master Service is also able to distribute the data needed for the evaluations and to collect the results and to write them into the Database. In addition, the Master Server hosts also the *Disar Consolidation Service* (DiConS) that performs the aggregation of the individual results at higher levels.
3. **A set of Computing Units:** each unit hosts the *Disar Engine Service* (DiEngS) that manages the *Disar Actuarial Engine* (DiActEng) and the *Disar Alm Engine* (DiAlmEng). The *Disar Engine Service* executes a single run of either one of the two engines. It may write the results directly to the Database or return them to the Master Server.

Table 2. Computing times. No ordering/Ordered refers to the index of complexity.

time	Company A			Company B		
schedule	No ordering	Ordered	Serial	No ordering	Ordered	Serial
monthly	1h 14m	1h 05m	34h 28m	2h 12m	1h 47m	54h 33m
annual	0h 43m	0h 34m	17h 45m	0h 31m	0h 22m	11h 31m

4. **A set of Clients**, each hosting the Disar Interface (DIINT) that allows to set computational parameters and monitors the progress of the elaborations. Moreover, the DIINT allows to start DICONS directly and gives direct access to the outputs.

5 DISAR Performances

DISAR performances were investigated on two (stylised) Italian life insurance companies. Company A (B) has a portfolio of about 5 (1) mln policies referred to 30 (30) segregated funds. The number of policies linked to the same segregated fund ranges from few hundreds to one million (to hundreds of thousands). The number of *representative policies* – that is the policies having equal insurance parameters (same age, sex, etc.) is about 0.35 mln (0.4 mln). In both cases the maximum time horizon of the policies is 109 years.

The computing grid is composed of 7 heterogeneous computing units for a total of 32 cores. The Relational DataBase Management System is Oracle server 10g. Connections between units are provided by a LAN with a 1 Gbit HUB switch. The total number N_{tot} of processed EEB per company was

$$N_{tot} = N_s \left[\underbrace{(1 + 2\,n_a)}_{\text{DIACTENG}} + \underbrace{(1 + 2(n_a + n_f) + 1)}_{\text{DIALMENG}} \right] + \underbrace{1}_{\text{DICONSENG}} ,$$

where N_s is the number of segregated funds, n_a is the number of sources of actuarial uncertainty and n_f is the number of sources financial of uncertainty and we let DIALMENG perform an additional *forward* scenario used to compute the intrinsic and time value of the embedded options (see [CDMP-05], p. 22 for details). In particular, we let $n_a = 2$ (mortality + lapses) and $n_f = 2$ (interest rate + equity), which implied a total of $N_{tot} = 451$ EEB per company, of which 150 are of actuarial type and 300 of ALM type, and 1 the (final) consolidation elaboration. 5000 Monte Carlo simulations were used for each EEB. Stressed up/down scenarios correspond to the 99.5%-quantile.

In general the optimal scheduling is driven mainly by the differences in complexity of the jobs and by the differences in computing power of the CPUs. In this application the ordering in complexity has been made using an heuristic index of complexity, computed on the basis of the time horizon of the evaluation, the number of representative policies times the number of elementary contracts, the

Table 3. Reduction achieved

time schedule	Company A Ordered	Serial	Reduction	Company B Ordered	Serial	Reduction
monthly	1h 05m	34h 28m	31.8	1h 47m	54h 33m	30.6
annual	0h 34m	17h 45m	31.3	0h 22m	11h 31m	31.4

number of assets and asset classes composing the segregated fund and the number of risk drives. The results obtained are not fully optimal since the ordering does not take into account the differences in CPU computing power.

Table 2 reports computing times for the two Companies in 4 different hypotheses: with a monthly/annual time schedule of the ALM strategy and with a casual/ordered submission of the jobs. Computing time is *all inclusive*; input/output Database access time is estimated to be about 6 min. (5 min.) for Company A (B). Finally, Table 3 shows that, when the jobs are submitted in order of increasing complexity, the reduction factors achieved are almost equal to the number of CPUs used, so that the system is almost optimal.

6 Conclusions and Outlook

DISAR has proven to be able to monitor portfolios of profit sharing policies with minimum guarantees as required by the Solvency II Directive. The grid architecture adopted for DISAR is effective, easy to implement and easy to scale. With a small number of non specialised nodes, typical computing times are at most of a couple of hours.

Since the most time consuming jobs are those processed by the ALM engine and involve Monte Carlo calculations, a further improvement of the system is achievable by parallelising the simulations. In fact, it has already been shown that Monte Carlo evaluation in a similar problem scales linearly with the number of CPU's in a "traditional" parallel architecture [CDMP-09]. A promising evolution under study is to use a mixed GPU/CPU architecture where the GPUs are used to speed up the generation of the Monte Carlo sample paths and the conventional CPUs are used whenever a large quantity of data is needed in the calculation.

References

[B-02] Bühlmann, H.: New Math for Life Actuaries. Astin Bulletin 32(2) (2002)

[C-10] CEIOPS: QIS5 Technical Specifications (July 2010)

[CDMP-05] Castellani, G., De Felice, M., Moriconi, F., Pacati, C.: Embedded Value in Life Insurance. Working paper (2005)

[CDMP-09] Corsaro, S., De Angelis, P.L., Marino, Z., Perla, F., Participating life insurance policies: an accurate and efficient parallel software for COTS clusters. Computational Management Science (2009) doi: 10.1007/s10827-009-0100-0, ISSN 1619-697X

[Dir-09] Directive 2009/138/EC of the European Parliament and of the Council of 25 November 2009 on the taking-up and pursuit of the business of Insurance and Reinsurance. Official Journal of the European Union (2009)

[DM-94] De Felice, M., Moriconi, F.: Un modello per la progettazione e la valutazione di polizze indicizzate e rivalutabili. Rapporto per l'INA, Roma (1994)

[DM-05] De Felice, M., Moriconi, F.: Market Based Tools for Managing the Life Insurance Company. Astin Bulletin 35(1), 79 (2005)

[DS-99] Duffie, D., Singleton, K.: Modeling Term Structures of Defaultable Bonds. Review of Financial Studies 12(4), 687 (1999)

Massively Parallel Asset and Liability Management

Andreas Grothey

University of Edinburgh, School of Mathematics, Edinburgh, UK, EH9 3JZ
A.Grothey@ed.ac.uk

Abstract. Multistage Stochastic Programming is a popular method to solve financial planning problems such as Asset and Liability Management (ALM). The desirability to have future scenarios match static and dynamic correlations between assets leads to problems of truly enormous sizes (often reaching tens of millions of unknowns or more). Clearly parallel processing becomes mandatory to deal with such problems.

Solution approaches for these problems include nested Decomposition and Interior Point Methods. The latter class in particular is appealing due to its flexibility with regard to model formulation and its amenability to parallelisation on massively parallel architectures. We review some of the results and challenges in this approach, demonstrate how popular risk measures can be integrated into the framework and address the issue of modelling for High Performance Computing.

1 Introduction

Asset and Liability Management (ALM) is one of the most important applications of portfolio optimization. The basic setup is that a large long-term investor (such as a pension fund or an insurance) has to decide how to invest available capital into a choice of assets (which may be stocks, bonds, real estate, etc) over several time periods. In every time period the investor faces liability payments, but may also receive cash contributions. The problem is to find an optimal investment strategy that maximised net return, while controlling the risk of defaulting on the liability payments. Parameters such as asset returns, liability payments and cash contributions are uncertain, however it is assumed that some information about their (joint) distribution is available.

The simplest model of this kind is the Markowitz Mean-Variance model in which only one period of investment is considered, and all uncertain parameters are assumed to follow a multivariate normal distribution with known expectations and covariances. There has been widespread criticism of this model, most importantly concerning its static nature (which does not take into account effects due to rebalancing or transaction costs), the implicit assumption of normal distributions and the use of variance as a risk measure.

In response a multitude of alternative risk models have been suggested, from simple linear Mean Absolute Deviation through to Stochastic Dominance Constraints. As a result research emphasis as shifted to stochastic dynamic models

M.R. Guarracino et al. (Eds.): Euro-Par 2010 Workshops, LNCS 6586, pp. 423–430, 2011.
© Springer-Verlag Berlin Heidelberg 2011

that (in principle) allow the use of any return distribution and can be adapted to a variety of risk measures.

Realistic models need to account for long planning horizons and adequate capture of the joint distributions of all future events that can influence the return of the portfolio over the planning horizon. These requirements quickly result in astronomical problem sizes. On the other hand progress on solution algorithms (in particular Interior Point Methods) and the use of High Performance Computing techniques have made problems of unprecedented sizes tractable.

The aim of this paper is to present risk-averse ALM models, the challenges inherent in building and solving them and to show how high-performance computing can be leveraged to overcome these challenges. In the following section we discuss the features of stochastic programming models for ALM with various risk measures. Section 3 will give details of solution challenges and HPC approaches to them, while the final Section 4 will summarise some numerical results.

2 The Stochastic Programming Approach to ALM

Let $\mathcal{A}$ be the set of possible investments available over time periods $t = 1, .., T$. With each investment $j \in \mathcal{A}$ and each time period t we associate an (unknown) return $r_{t,j}$. Further there are (again uncertain) cash contributions C_t and liability payments L_t. Denote by $\xi_t = (C_t, L_t, \{r_{t,j}\}_{j\in\mathcal{A}})$ the uncertain data in each time period. The state of the portfolio is denoted by the vector $x^h_t = \{x^h_{t,j}\}_{j\in\mathcal{A}}$, where $x^h_{t,j}$ is the current position in asset j (i.e. the total capital currently invested in this asset). Decisions are x^b_t, x^s_t, the amount to buy and sell of each asset in each time period.

The task is to find optimal investment decisions $x_t = (x^h_t, x^b_t, x^s_t)$ that maximize expected surplus return at the final time stage subject to cash balance and inventory constraint. The discrete-time ALM problem is thus

$$
\begin{array}{lll}
\max \mathbb{E}[X_T], & X_T = (1-\gamma)\sum_{j\in\mathcal{A}} x^h_{T,j} & \\
\text{s.t.} & x^h_{t,j} = (1+r_{t-1,j})x^h_{t-1,j} - x^s_{t,j} + x^b_{t,j} & \text{(inventory)} \\
& L_t + (1+\gamma)\sum_j x^b_{t,j} = C_t + (1-\gamma)\sum_j x^s_{t,j}, \quad t \neq 1 & \text{(cash balance)} \\
& L_1 + (1+\gamma)\sum_j x^b_{1,j} = b_0 &
\end{array}
\tag{1}
$$

where γ are the (assumed proportional) transaction costs and X_T is the value of the portfolio at the final time period when converted into cash.

The model describes a multi-stage decision process in which information ξ_t becomes available at certain discrete points in time, and decisions x_t at time t can be based only on information available at that point in time (non-anticipativity):

$$x_1 \to \xi_2 \to x_2(\xi_2) \to \xi_3 \to x_3(\xi_2, \xi_3) \to \cdots \xi_T \to x_T(\xi_1, \ldots \xi_T).$$

Note that in this setting both the data ξ_t as well as the decisions x_t are described by discrete-time stochastic process, hence problem (1) is a semi-infinite optimization problem and as such very difficult to solve.

The stochastic programming approach to ALM overcomes this problem by replacing the data process ξ_t by a discrete approximation $\tilde{\xi}_t$. That is at every stage there are finitely many different outcomes $\tilde{\xi}_{t,i}$. The resulting process $\tilde{\xi}$ can be visualised by a tree giving the evolution of future data realisation: this is known as the scenario tree. Let $\mathcal{L}_t$ denote the set of all nodes at stage t in the tree, $\mathcal{L} = \bigcup_t \mathcal{L}_t$ the whole tree and for a given node $i \in \mathcal{L}_t$ let $a(i) \in \mathcal{L}_{t-1}$ be the ancestor node. Then the discretised version of (1) reads

$$\max_x \sum_{i\in\mathcal{L}_T} y, \tag{2a}$$

$$\begin{aligned} \text{s.t.}\quad & x^h_{i,j} = (1 + r_{a(i),j})x^h_{a(i),j} - x^s_{i,j} + x^b_{i,j}, \qquad \forall i \in \mathcal{L}\setminus\{0\}, j \in \mathcal{A} \\ & L_i + \sum_{j\in\mathcal{A}} (1+\gamma)x^b_{i,j} = C_t + \sum_{j\in\mathcal{A}} (1-\gamma)x^s_{i,j},\ \forall i \in \mathcal{L}\setminus\{0\} \\ & L_0 + \sum_{j\in\mathcal{A}} (1+\gamma)x^b_{0,j} = b_0 \\ & y = (1-\gamma)\textstyle\sum_{i\in\mathcal{L}_T} \pi_i \sum_{j\in\mathcal{A}} x^h_{T,j,i}. \end{aligned} \tag{2b}$$

which is a standard (if large) linear programming problem. With appropriately chosen matrices W_i, T_i, d_i (see [6]) the Jacobian for the scenario tree given in Figure 1 has the given nested bordered block-diagonal form. In particular note the final constraint in (2b) which stretches over all scenarios and corresponds to the linking row in the constraint matrix. While it would be possible to substitute for y in the objective function, thereby eliminating this row, the presence of y as an explicit variable results in more modelling flexibility and sparser formulations (cf [6] for details).

The question of scenario generation, that is how to construct a discrete approximation $\hat{\xi}_t$ to ξ_t in some optimal sense is an active field of research. An overview can be found for example in [9]. For our purposes it suffices to say that for every node in the scenario tree, the scenarios described by the successor nodes need to capture means, variances and correlations (conditional on the current state) between the $|\mathcal{A}|$ different assets. For a realistic model description the size of the scenario tree quickly reaches astronomical sizes. For a tree with $T = 5$ stages and a branching factor of 30 at each node (barely enough to capture the correlation between say, 60 considered random variables describing the evolution of investments and liabilities), the resulting tree has 24 million scenarios.

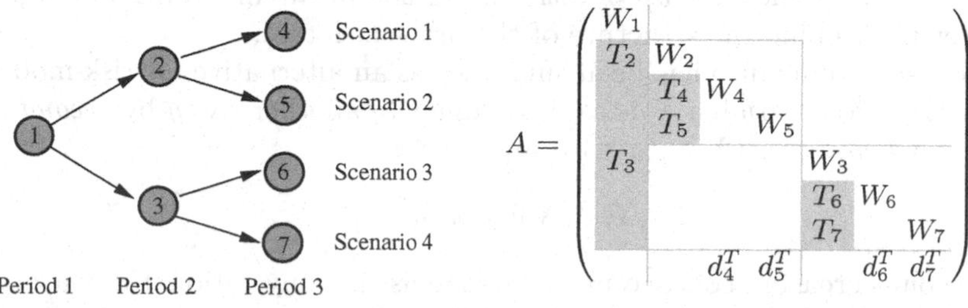

Fig. 1. Scenario tree and resulting structured constraint Jacobian

Assuming 20 different assets, model (2) would have 1.5×10^9 variables and 5.3×10^8 constraints.

2.1 Risk Averse ALM Modelling

The main deficiency of the prototype ALM model in the previous section is that it only aims to maximise expected excess return, without attempting to control risk. The standard approach to handle risk follows the suggestion of Markowitz[12] and uses the variance of the surplus return as a risk measure. In the Markowitz model the twin contradictory objective of maximizing expected return while minimizing risk are combined into a single objective

$$\max_x \mathbb{E}[X_T] - \lambda \mathrm{Var}[X_T], \tag{3}$$

where $\lambda > 0$ is a *risk-aversion parameter.* Using the identity $\mathrm{Var}[X] = \mathbb{E}[X^2] - \mathbb{E}[X]^2$, the variance of the final wealth can be expressed within model the ALM model as

$$\mathrm{Var}[X_T] = (1-\gamma)^2 \sum_{i \in \mathcal{L}_T} \pi_i (\sum_{j \in \mathcal{A}} v_j x_{i,j}^h)^2 - y^2 \tag{4}$$

which can be readily incorporated into the formulation (2) leading to a quadratic programming problem with a block-diagonal Hessian [6].

On the other hand the use of of the variance as a risk measure has been criticised in various places as being to simplistic. Practitioners often recommend the use of a von Neumann-Morgenstern type [15] nonlinear utility formulation

$$\mathbb{E}[U(X_T)] \tag{5}$$

where $U : \mathbb{R} \to \mathbb{R}$ is a *utility function.* Usually U is assumed to be convex and non-decreasing which corresponds to a risk-averse investor. A popular choice for $U(x)$ is $U(x) = -\log x$. Konno et al. [10, 11], suggest the use of skewness (third moment of X_T) in the objective to adequately cover non-symmetrical distribution of return. Pflug [13] suggests the use of lower-semivariance

$$\mathbb{E}[X_T] - \lambda\sqrt{\mathbb{E}[([X_T - \mathbb{E}[X_T]]^-)^2]}$$

for the same reason. As shown in [6] these formulations can be incorporated into the model (2), at the expense of introducing nonlinear constraint and objective terms, while keeping the structure of the problem intact.

Stochastic dominance has been suggested as an alternative for risk modelling by [2]. A random variable X is said to dominate another r.v. y by *second order stochastic dominance* ($X \succeq_{ssd} Y$) if and only if

$$\mathbb{E}[u(X)] \geq \mathbb{E}[u(Y)]$$

for all non-decreasing concave utility functions; i.e. any rational risk-averse investor would prefer portfolio X to portfolio Y. In order to use stochastic dominance within ALM models one can define a *benchmark portfolio* B (whose return is a random variable) and only consider investment decisions whose return outperforms the benchmark by s.s.d.:

$$\max_x \mathbb{E}[X_T(x)] \text{ s.t. } \quad X_T(x) \succeq_{ssd} B \quad \text{(+ inventory \& cash balance constraints)} \tag{6}$$

It has been shown in [2] that $X_T \succeq_{ssd} B$ is equivalent to

$$\mathbb{E}[(\eta - X_T)_+] \leq \mathbb{E}[(\eta - B)_+], \quad \forall \eta, \qquad \text{(here } (x)_+ = \max\{x, 0\}\text{)}. \tag{7}$$

In the case where the benchmark (which is often sampled from historical data) has only discrete outcomes $\{b_j\}_{j=1,..,m}$ and X_T is given by a discrete distribution (as is the case in stochastic programming), constraints (7) can be modelled by the system

$$\sum_{i \in \mathcal{L}_T} \pi_i s_{i,j} \leq v_j, j = 1, ..., m, \qquad s_{i,j} \geq b_j - X_{T,i}, s_{i,j} \geq 0, \quad i \in \mathcal{L}_T, j = 1, ..., m$$

This leads to m constraints that are linking all final stage scenarios (and are thus of the same form as the final constraint in (2b)).

3 Solution Based on Interior Point Methods

Since their emergence in the 1990's Interior Point Methods (IPM) have proven to be among the most efficient methods for solving large stochastic programming problems and multitude of applications to ALM exist [1, 5, 6, 14]. The reasons for the success of IPMs on these problems include their applicability to a wide range of formulations, spanning linear, quadratic and nonlinear models, their comparative non-sensitivity to large problem sizes (IPMs are in practice observed to converge in $\mathcal{O}(\log n)$ iterations, where n is the problem size), and not least the amenability of the linear algebra operations to parallelisation. In the remainder of this section we concentrate on the computational complexity of IPMs for multistage ALM models. A more thorough description of the algorithm can be found in the above references. For the quadratic programming problem

$$\min \; c^T x + \tfrac{1}{2} x^T Q x, \qquad \text{s.t. } Ax = b, x \geq 0 \tag{8}$$

the main computational work consists of solving the Newton system

$$\Phi \begin{bmatrix} \Delta x \\ \Delta y \end{bmatrix} = \begin{bmatrix} \xi_d - X^{-1}\xi_\mu \\ \xi_p \end{bmatrix}, \qquad \Phi = \begin{bmatrix} -Q - \Theta^{-1} & A^T \\ A & 0 \end{bmatrix} \tag{9}$$

where (x_k, s_k, y_k) is the current iterate, $\xi_p = b - Ax_k, \xi_d = c - A^T y_k - s_k + Qx_k, \xi_u = \mu e - X_k S_k e$, $X = \text{diag}(x_1, ..., x_n)$ and $\Theta = XS^{-1}$. For an IPM applied to the nonlinear problem

$$\min_x f(x) \text{ s.t. } g(x) = 0, x \geq 0$$

we need to use $A = \nabla g(x), Q = \nabla^2 f(x) + \sum_{i=1}^m y_i \nabla^2 g_i(x)$ in (9). For the ALM model (2) with the Jacobian as in Figure 1, matrix Φ can be reordered into the nested double-bordered block-diagonal form shown in Figure 2.

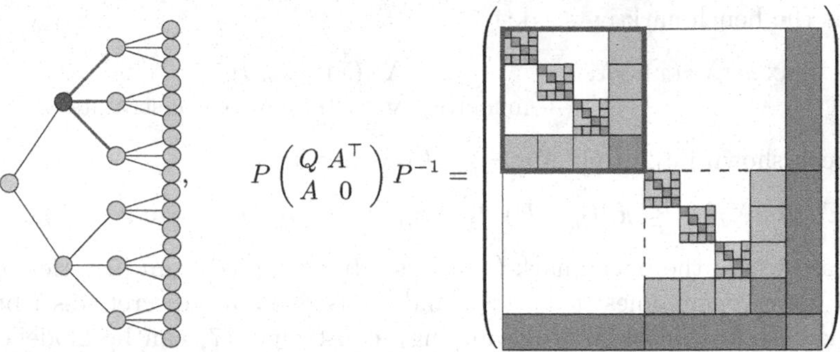

Fig. 2. Scenario tree and resulting nested bordered block-diagonal augmented system matrix Φ: highlighted is a matrix block corresponding to a scenario tree node

3.1 Parallelisation and Modelling

As pointed out earlier, the main computational effort in solving the ALM model (2) by Interior Point Methods consists of the repeated solution of system (9) for an augmented system matrix Φ with the nested structure displayed in Figure 2. Rather than solving this system directly it is more efficient to obtain a Cholesky-like factorisation $\Phi = LDL^T$ and solve system (9) by successive backsolves with L^T, D and L. Naturally parallelisation efforts are primarily targeted at these steps. A appealing property of bordered block-diagonal matrices is that by using Schur complement techniques the factorisation and backsolve operations can be decomposed into corresponding operations on the diagonal sub-blocks. Since these sub-block operations are independent they can be readily parallelised.

To exploit the nested structure in Φ in the parallel IPM solver OOPS the whole matrix is represented by a tree of (simple) bordered block-diagonal matrices, mirroring the scenario tree in Figure 2. Every node of the *matrix tree* is represented by an instance of a *structured matrix* object following object-oriented principles. In this manner linear algebra operations on the root node of the matrix tree (corresponding to the whole matrix) are recursively decomposed into corresponding operations on the leaf node matrices. Parallelism is dealt with in the same manner: to every node in the matrix tree a set of processors $\mathcal{P}_i$ is allocated. Between them the processors in $\mathcal{P}_i$ are responsible for all operations to be performed on this node. This is done by recursively allocating the processors in $\mathcal{P}_i$ to the child nodes of the current node (see Figure 3). The approach has been demonstrated to be scalable up to 1280 processors. Details of the implementation can be found in [7].

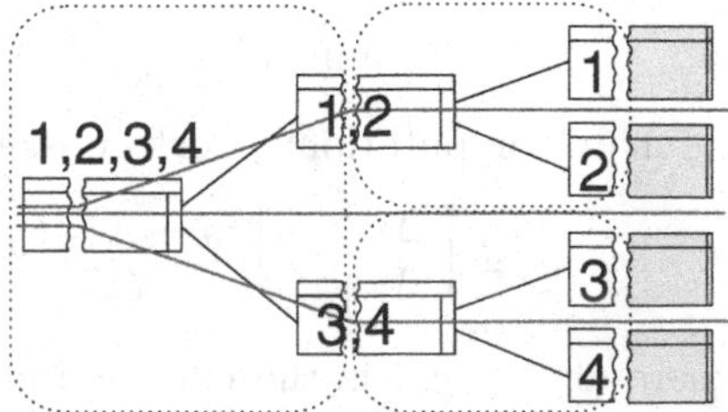

Fig. 3. Allocation of processors to matrix blocks

An important consideration is how to transfer the data needed to describe the problem onto the processors. Two approaches have been used traditionally: Either the model and data is generated in-situ on every processor; while efficient in execution this requires writing carefully handcrafted code for every new model. Alternatively, modelling languages such as AMPL[3] are designed to overcome this problem by providing the user with a descriptive language in which to formulate the model and automating the task of model generation. None of the existing modelling languages, however, support parallelisation of the model generation, creating a major bottleneck. In some of the large ALM problems solved by OOPS, the model description alone requires upwards of 40GB making serial model generation impossible. To overcome this issue OOPS is linked to SPML (Structure-conveying Parallel Modelling Language), a parallel model generator[8]. SPML extends AMPL with keywords to indicate model structure. A preprocessor extracts the model structure, builds processor-sized submodels and distributes them among the available processor, leaving the local model generation to be done on each processor independently.

4 Numerical Results

Numerical results on OOPS and SPML have been reported in various papers[5, 6, 4, 16]. We therefore restrict ourselves to some highlights. OOPS was able to solve an ALM problem with 6 stages, 12.8 million scenarios, and 1.02×10^9 variables on 1280 processors of the 1600-1.7GHz processor machine HPCx in 3020 seconds[4]. OOPS has been applied to various formulations of the ALM problem reported in this paper such as nonlinear utility functions and stochastic dominance constrained problems. In most cases solution times in serial improve (sometimes significantly) on those that can be obtained with the commercial solver CPLEX. On parallel machines a consistent speed-up of 6.22 – 7.64 on 8 processors has been reported[5] as has been a speedup of 27.5 going from 16 to 512 processors[4].

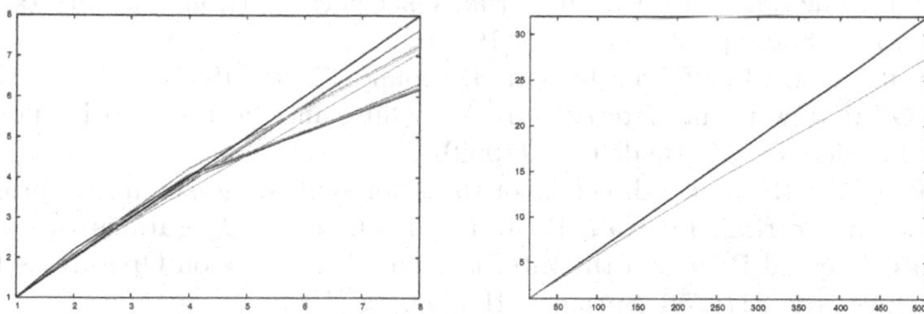

Fig. 4. Speedup for OOPS on 1-8 (a) and 16-512 (b) processors

5 Conclusions

We have presented recent approaches to the parallel solution of multistage portfolio optimization problems using a variety of approaches to model risk. Problems of many millions of variables can now be routinely solved on moderate parallel hardware with almost linear speed-up, while the use of dedicated massively parallel machines makes the solution of problems with 10^9 variables and more feasible.

References

1. Blomvall, J., Lindberg, P.O.: Backtesting the performance of an actively managed option portfolio at the Swedish stock market, 1990–1999. J. Econ. Dyn. Control 27, 1099–1112 (2003)
2. Dentcheva, D., Ruszczyński, A.: Portfolio optimization with stochastic dominance constraints. J. Bank Financ 30, 433–451 (2006)
3. Fourer, R., Gay, D., Kernighan, B.W.: AMPL: A Modeling Language for Mathematical Programming. The Scientific Press, San Francisco (1993)
4. Gondzio, J., Grothey, A.: Direct solution of linear systems of size 10^9 arising in optimization with interior point methods. In: Wyrzykowski, R., Dongarra, J., Meyer, N., Waśniewski, J. (eds.) PPAM 2005. LNCS, vol. 3911, pp. 513–525. Springer, Heidelberg (2006)
5. Gondzio, J., Grothey, A.: Parallel interior point solver for structured quadratic programs: Application to financial planning problems. Ann. Oper. Res. 152, 319–339 (2007)
6. Gondzio, J., Grothey, A.: Solving nonlinear portfolio optimization problems with the primal-dual interior point method. Eur. J. Oper. Res. 181, 1019–1029 (2007)
7. Gondzio, J., Grothey, A.: Exploiting structure in parallel implementation of interior point methods for optimization. Comput. Manage Sci. 6, 135–160 (2009)
8. Grothey, A., Hogg, J., Woodsend, K., Colombo, M., Gondzio, J.: A structure-conveying modelling language for mathematical and stochastic programming. Math. Program. Comput. 1, 223–247 (2009)
9. Høyland, K., Wallace, S.W.: Generating scenario trees for multistage decision problems. Manage Sci. 47, 295–307 (2001)
10. Konno, H., Shirakawa, H., Yamazaki, H.: A mean-absolute deviation-skewness portfolio optimization model. Annals of Operational Research 45, 205–220 (1993)
11. Konno, H., Suzuki, K.-I.: A mean-variance-skewness portfolio optimization model. J. Oper. Res. Soc. Jpn 38, 173–187 (1995)
12. Markowitz, H.M.: Portfolio selection. J. Financ, 77–91 (1952)
13. Pflug, G.C.: How to measure risk. In: Modelling and Decisions in Economics, pp. 39–59. Physica-Verlag, Heidelberg (1999)
14. Steinbach, M.: Recursive direct algorithms for multistage stochastic programs in financial engineering. In: Kall, P., Lüthi, H.-J. (eds.) Operations Research Proceedings, Selected Papers of the International Conference on Operations Research Zürich 1998, pp. 241–250. Springer, Heidelberg (1999)
15. von Neumann, J., Morgenstern, O.: Theory of Games and Economic Behaviour. Princeton University Press, Princeton (1953)
16. Yang, X., Gondzio, J., Grothey, A.: Asset-liability management modelling with risk control by stochastic dominance. J. Ass. Manag. 11, 73–93 (2010)

A Fast and Stable Heston Model Calibration on the GPU

Michael Aichinger[1], Andreas Binder[2],
Johannes Fürst[2], and Christian Kletzmayr[2]

[1] Johann Radon Institute for Computational and Applied Mathematics (RICAM), Austrian Academy of Sciences, Altenberger Strasse 69, A-4040 Linz, Austria
michael.aichinger@ricam.oeaw.ac.at
[2] MathConsult GmbH, Altenberger Strasse 69, A-4040 Linz, Austria

Abstract. For the analysis of many exotic financial derivatives, the Heston model, a stochastic volatility model, is widely used. Its specific parameters have to be identified from sets of options market data with different strike prices and maturities, leading to a minimization problem for the least square error between the model prices and the market prices. It is intrinsic to the Heston model that this error functional typically exhibits a large number of local minima, therefore techniques from global optimization have to be applied or combined with local optimization techniques to deliver a trustworthy optimum. To achieve results in reasonable time, we approach as follows: (1) For the evaluation of the objective function, we use a Fourier cosine method, optimized for parallelization, and (2) the local/global optimization scheme is carried out on parallel architectures. Results are reported for a multi GPU server and a multicore SGI Altix 4700.

Keywords: Heston Model, Calibration, Cosine Method, GPU, Multicore CPU.

1 Model and Methods

1.1 The Heston Model

The Heston stochastic volatility model [1] relaxes the constant volatility assumption in the classical Black Scholes model by incorporating an instantaneous short term variance process (CIR)

$$\begin{aligned} dS_t &= r(t)S_t dt + \sqrt{v_t} S_t dW_t^1 \\ dv_t &= \kappa(\theta - v_t)dt + \lambda\sqrt{v_t} dW_t^2 \qquad v_0 \geq 0 \end{aligned} \tag{1}$$

where r denotes the domestic yield curve, v_t denotes the stock price variance, dW_t^i are standard Brownian motions with correlation ρ, κ is the the mean reversion parameter, Θ is the long term level and λ is the volatility of variance parameter. The variance process is always positive if $2\kappa\theta > \sigma^2$ (Feller condition). The characteristic function of the Heston model is analytically available. (see for example [2]).

M.R. Guarracino et al. (Eds.): Euro-Par 2010 Workshops, LNCS 6586, pp. 431–438, 2011.
© Springer-Verlag Berlin Heidelberg 2011

1.2 The Calibration Problem

Before complex instruments can be priced, the model parameters p_i have to be calibrated to market prices of liquid instruments, e.g. by minimizing the least squares error of model prices compared to market prices [2].

$$\sum_j ||V_j^{Mod}(\{p_i\}) - V_j^{Mar}||^2 \rightarrow \min \tag{2}$$

where the V_j are single calibration instruments, i.e. European call/put options with with different strike prices and different expiries. One of the difficulties in solving the resulting inverse problem is that the market information is insufficient to completely identify a pricing model, which means that several sets of model parameters may reproduce the market prices, leading to ill-conditioned problems and model uncertainty. To overcome the ill-conditioned nature of the problem, regularization methods can be used to guarantee stable parameters [2]. The corresponding optimization problem, formulated as a minimization problem of a least squares functional, is not necessarily convex as a function of the model parameters and is therefore hard to solve. It may happen that several, even a large amount of local minima exist. Another problem that may arise is that the objective function may exhibit an extremely "flat" behaviour such that even if only a unique minimum exists, a parameter set is accepted as optimal although it is far away from the true optimum. Two groups of algorithms can be applied to solve these optimization problems. The first group are locally convergent algorithms which will find a minimum but not necessarily the global one (e.g. Levenberg-Marquardt). The second group of algorithms are globally convergent, which should theoretically (CPU time going to infinity) be able to find the global minimum (simulated annealing, particle swarm methods, evolutionary algorithms, ...) [4]. The disadvantage of the second group is the enormous amount of computation time in comparison to the algorithms of the first group to obtain results. Our key idea to overcome this drawback is to take the best parts of both worlds to improve the quality of the results for the first group and to speed up the computation for algorithms of the second group. We start with quasi-random low-discrepancy sequences to get a good coverage of the parameter space and evaluate the residual function (2) for each of these N_I points. After sorting, a gradient based algorithm (Levenberg-Marquardt) is started from the N_B best points of the initial set. The Levenberg-Marquardt algorithm is an iterative technique that locates the minimum of a function that is expressed as the sum of squares of nonlinear functions. It has become a standard technique for nonlinear least-squares problems and can be thought of as a combination of steepest descent and the Gauss-Newton method [9].

Special attention is turned to the stability of the optimal parameters and of the prices for the exotic instruments obtained under these parameters with respect to time. Crucial for this kind of algorithm is the fast evaluation of the residual value as well as the corresponding gradients with respect to the model parameters.

1.3 Fast Evaluation of European Style Options and Their Derivatives

If the model under consideration does not provide an analytic solution for the European option price efficient numerical methods are required to price European options in order to calibrate the parameters of the model to given market data.

Starting point is the risk neutral valuation formula

$$v(x, t_0) = e^{-r\Delta t}\mathbb{E}Q[v(y, T)|x] = e^{-r\Delta t}\int_{\mathbb{R}} v(y, T)f(y|x)dy \tag{3}$$

where v denotes the option value, Δt is the difference between the maturity T and the valuation date t_0, $f(y|x)$ is the probability density of y given x and r is the risk neutral interest rate. Some of the state of the art numerical integration techniques have in common that they rely on a transformation to the Fourier domain [7]. The main reason for this is that the probability density function appears in the integration in the original pricing domain but is not known analytically for many important pricing processes. Instead, the characteristic functions of these processes, the Fourier transforms of the respective density functions, can often be expressed analytically. The density and its characteristic function form a Fourier pair and the idea of the Fourier-Cosine method [6] is to reconstruct the whole Fourier integral in - not only the integrand - from its Fourier-cosine expansion. In the case of European options one ends up with

$$L[v(x, t_0)] = e^{-r\Delta t}\sum_{k=0}^{\prime N} \mathrm{Re}\left\{L\left[\left[\phi\left(\frac{k\pi}{b-a}, x\right)\right]\exp\left(-i\frac{ka\pi}{b-a}\right)\right\} V_k \tag{4}$$

V_k depends on the payoff of an European option at maturity T. $L[\cdot]$ denotes an operator being id, if the option value or $L = \frac{\partial}{\partial p_i}$ if the gradient of the option value with respect to the ith model parameter should be calculated.

2 Implementation Details

We have implemented the calibration routine on two parallel hardware platforms, a CPU multicore server SGI Altix 4700 with 256 cores in clusters of four with one terabyte memory and a GPU server with two C1060 (240 streaming processor cores) and one GTX 260 (192 CUDA cores) graphic cards from Nvidia, two Intel E5520 CPUs and 24 gigabyte memory. For parallelization Open-MP has been used on the SGI machine and a combination of Open-MP and the Nvidia Cuda framework has been used on the GPU Server.

The key point in programming effective GPU algorithms is the optimal memory management. We used constant memory (which is read-only but cached) for look-up tables and ensured that all memory transactions on global memory are coalesced. Special emphasize has been put on the minimization of memory transfers between host and global memory since this is bottleneck in terms of speed. To achieve the highest performance, it is necessary to get the best combination of the number of registers, the number of threads and the amount of shared memory. All GPU computations has been performed in double precision to ensure the accuracy necessary for calibration purposes. However, at this point in time double precision is much slower than single precision (typically ba a factor of eight). Switching to new hardware with FERMI technology will probably speed up the whole algorithm.

On each of our testing platforms the function evaluations for the N_I starting points are distributed between the processing units - GPUs or Cores. Whereas the parallelization is straight forward in the CPU case, details of the implementation on the GPU can be found in figure (1). The residuals (2) are sorted on

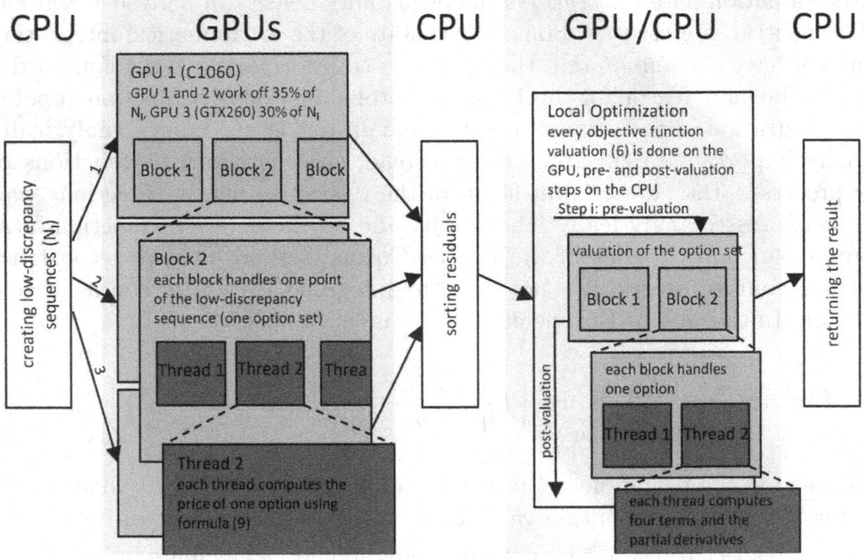

Fig. 1. Implementation details of the calibration algorithm - a combination of quasi-random low-discrepancy sequences and a gradient based Levenberg-Marquardt algorithm

the CPU, and Levenberg-Marquardt algorithms are started from the N_B points with the lowest residuals. Within the Levenberg-Marquardt algorithm, it depends whether the evaluation of the objective function (2) and the derivatives with respect to the model parameters are again performed in a parallel manner. In the case of the Multicore CPU machine each core is used to perform a Levenberg-Marquardt optimization and the residual and the derivatives are computed sequentially. Also in the GPU case, each GPU performs such an optimization but the threads and multiprocessors on each GPU are used to parallelize the summation in (4).

The main difference in the implementation between the GPU and the CPU is the number of summands used in (4). To get the best performance on the GPU, each thread on each Multiprocessor should be equally busy. Therefore it is advantageous to keep the number of summands N fixed. On the other hand, on a CPU or a MultiCore CPU, a processing unit can start with the next parameter set after finishing a valuation task therefore it is advantageous to have a stopping criterion. We use the absolute value of the characteristic function, i.e. the envelope function as stopping criterion and abort the summation if $|\phi(u)| < \epsilon$.

3 Results

Market Data
All results presented in this section are calculated for a set of options on the FTSE-100 index for May 1st 2008. The forward rates (GBP) on that date ranged between 3.4% *p.a.* and 4.52% *p.a.* (continuous compounding).

Evaluation of Points in the Parameter Space
We start with reporting the performance of the first part of our combined algorithm - the evaluation of the residual for a large number of points in the five dimensional parameter space. As mentioned before, the speed of the calculation of one option set (different strikes and maturities) is crucial. Therefore we report the performance using the GPU compared with a single core of the CPU of our GPU Server and using several CPUs on our multicore CPU server in Tab.1. Starting from N_I points we evaluate the objective function for each of these parameter sets. Increasing N_I allows to improve the best residual, as $N_{I_1} \subset N_{I_2}$ if $|N_{I_2}| > |N_{I_1}|$ when using quasi-random low discrepancy sequences (here Sobol points). Unfortunately it is possible that the optimal parameter set violates the Feller condition.

Table 1. This table shows the average computation time (in milliseconds) for one option set (256 options) on the GPU (C1060),on a single core of the CPU server, on three GPUs (2xC1060+1GTX260) and for 8 and 32 cores on the Altix for a fixed number of summands denoted by $N = 512$ as well as for an abort criterion denoted by $\epsilon = 10^{-8}$

N_I	CPU-N	GPU-N	CPU-ϵ	8-CPU-N	32-CPU-N	8-CPU-ϵ	32-CPU-ϵ	3-GPU-N
2^7	217.24	4.05	15.59	9.46	3.52	1.40	1.42	4.19
2^8	217.02	3.29	16.29	9.55	2.75	1.41	0.68	2.34
2^{10}	216.97	2.85	16.92	9.26	2.39	1.14	0.50	1.30
2^{12}	217.03	2.71	17.10	9.27	2.38	1.05	0.47	1.02
2^{14}	217.00	2.68	16.96	9.20	2.34	1.03	0.47	0.97
2^{16}	216.96	2.67	16.94	9.23	2.33	0.93	0.45	0.95

The Gradient Algorithm and the Feller trap
Next we will focus on the gradient part of the calibration algorithm (Levenberg Marquardt). To check whether the analytical derivatives are advantageous to the numerical ones, calculated via finite difference formulas, we have used

our gradient based optimization routine. We have started from the following point in the five dimensional parameter space: $(2.5, 0.5, 0.5, -0.5, 2.5)$ and performed 50 iterations of the Levenberg-Marquardt algorithm (see Tab.2). Again a major drawback for the performance of the Levenberg-Marquardt is the Feller condition. Up to our experience, for some of the starting points the algorithm converges towards parameter sets not satisfying the Feller condition. When hitting the boundary of the area defined by the Feller condition we add/subtract a small number to move the parameter set to the allowed region - slowing down the performance of the whole algorithm. As Tab.3 shows this is especially true for the algorithm using analytic derivatives. Furthermore the values for the optimal parameters can be different for each of the methods used for calculating the derivatives (compare with Tab.2).

Table 2. This table shows the residual and the corresponding calibrated parameter set using the Levenberg Marquardt algorithm starting from $(2.5, 0.5, 0.5, 0.5, -0.5)$ and fixing the number of iterations to 50. The different lines correspond to the different methods for calculating the derivatives with respect to the Heston parameters: analytic means calculation using (4), bd means using a simple backward difference quotient (first order), fd means forward difference quotient (first order), cd means central difference quotient (second order) and cd2 means a higher order central difference quotient (fourth order).

Method	Residual	κ	θ	λ	ρ	v_0
analytic	0.00181063	0.092252	0.486551	0.695210	-0.384361	0.048140
fd	0.00181035	0.090878	0.493407	0.694971	-0.384394	0.048132
bd	0.00181089	0.093595	0.480052	0.695447	-0.384329	0.048147
cd	0.00181063	0.092256	0.486530	0.695211	-0.384361	0.048140
cd2	0.00181063	0.092249	0.486566	0.695210	-0.384361	0.048137

The Overall Calibration Algorithm

Finally we report some results for the whole calibration algorithm - the combination of the quasi-random low discrepancy sequences and the gradient based algorithm, the overall performance on our different computing systems and some comparison with other optimization algorithms. We have used a simulated annealing (SA) algorithm, a direct search simulated annealing (DSSA) algorithm and a differential evolution (DE) algorithm [4],[5] to get values for comparison. All of these algorithms give comparable results for the value of the objective function (2) but the parameter sets are different. The reason for this will be reported elsewhere [10]. In Tab.4 the results for these global optimization algorithms are reported. Furthermore we have added results obtained with our combination algorithm and emphasize the enormous advantage in performance obtained with our method. Table 5 shows the dependence of the residual and the optimal parameters from the starting points N_I and the number of points N_B chosen after sorting to start the gradient based algorithm from.

Table 3. This table shows the influence of the Feller condition on the results when starting from a certain point of the parameter space $(2.5, 0.5, 0.5, 0.5, -0.5)$. The number of iterations for the Levenberg-Marquardt algorithm has been fixed to 20 for these calculations.

Method	Feller y/n	Time[s]	κ	θ	λ	ρ	v_0	R
analytic	y	286	5.16374	0.0535189	0.743359	-0.656857	0.0532264	0.00317053
analytic	n	13	0.490489	0.128122	0.757395	-0.381153	0.0489238	0.00175283
fd	y	142	4.94054	0.0557186	0.741914	-0.634476	0.0474512	0.00300541
fd	n	24	0.599426	0.117699	0.803694	-0.376169	0.0490682	0.0017445
bd	y	40	8.32845	0.0523705	0.926955	-0.409117	0.0488767	0.00341173
bd	n	24	0.609957	0.116568	0.805291	-0.37605	0.049105	0.00174367
cd	y	65	4.45272	0.0525163	0.682833	-0.66807	0.0522633	0.00321284
cd	n	38	0.604866	0.11711	0.804514	-0.376109	0.0490869	0.00174406

Table 4. This table shows results obtained with SA, DSSA, DE and our hybrid method (HM). For the results obtained with the hybrid method we have used $N_I = 16384$, $N_B = 8$ and report the parameters of the best three points.

Method	Time	κ	θ	λ	ρ	v_0	R
SA	$> 1h$	1.37489	0.0659624	0.42583	-0.521524	0.0442002	0.0026999
DSSA	$> 1h$	3.326651	0.056260	0.609410	-0.528481	0.045514	0.002731
DE	$> 1h$	2.19221	0.0606641	0.515656	-0.52504	0.0442017	0.002674
HM	$20s$	2.110270	0.060529	0.503548	-0.532090	0.045330	0.002684
HM	$20s$	2.851548	0.057947	0.574742	-0.512623	0.045789	0.002700
HM	$20s$	4.487206	0.054525	0.699049	-0.509853	0.045819	0.002808

Table 5. This table shows the residual for different combinations of initial points N_I and Levenberg-Marquardt starting points N_B.

$N_I \backslash N_B$	1	2	4	8	16	32	64	128
2^7	0.00441	0.00383	0.00359	0.00353	0.00316	0.00297	0.00293	0.00285
2^8	0.01350	0.01350	0.00343	0.00306	0.00300	0.00287	0.00287	0.00287
2^{10}	0.00394	0.00325	0.00311	0.00311	0.00311	0.00293	0.00288	0.00285
2^{12}	0.00311	0.00311	0.00311	0.00299	0.00290	0.00286	0.00275	0.00275
2^{14}	0.00286	0.00286	0.00286	0.00286	0.00285	0.00285	0.00283	0.00282
2^{16}	0.00286	0.00286	0.00286	0.00286	0.00286	0.00283	0.00283	0.00283

4 Conclusion

We have presented an algorithm for the calibration of the widely used Heston model which is theoretically capable of finding the global minimum. The combination of local and global algorithms together with parallelization on GPUs and CPUs led to a massive speed up compared to global algorithms. Including the

Feller condition has an enormous impact on the results and the performance - these problems will be addressed in further investigations.

Acknowledgement

Part of this work was supported by the Austrian Ministry of Economy, Family and Youth and by the Upper Austrian government within the framework of the "industrial competence centers" program. We thank Michael Schwaiger for useful discussions.

References

1. Heston, S.: A closed-form solution for options with stochastic volatility with applications to bond and currency options. Review of Financial Studies 6, 327–343 (1993)
2. Albrecher, H., Binder, A., Mayer, P.: Einführung in die Finanzmathematik. Birkhäuser, Basel (2009)
3. Albrecher, H., Mayer, P., Schoutens, W., Tistaert, J.: The Little Heston Trap. Wilmott Magazine, 83-92 (January 2007)
4. Brabazon: Biologically Inspired Algorithms for Financial Modelling. Springer, Heidelberg (2006)
5. Hedar, A.-R., Fukushima, M.: Hybrid simulated annealing and direct search method for nonlinear unconstrained global Optimization. Optimization Methods and Software 17, 891–912 (2002)
6. Fang, F., Osterlee, K.: A novel pricing method for European options based on Fourier-Cosine series expansion, MPRA Paper (2008)
7. Carr, P., Madan, D.B.: Option valuation using the fast Fourier transform. J. Comp. Finance 2, 61–73 (1999)
8. O'Sullivan, C.: Path dependent option pricing under Levy processes, EFA 2005 Moscow Meetings Paper, SSRN (February 2005), `http://ssrn.com/abstract=673424`
9. Madsen, K., Nielsen, H.B., Tingleff, O.: Methods for Non-Linear Least Sqares Problems, 2nd edn (2004)
10. Aichinger, M., Binder, A., Fürst, J., Kletzmayr, C.: Advanced Methods for the Calibration of Heston and Bates Models (to be submitted)

High Performance Computing and Economic Scenario Generation: Integrating Expert Forecasts into Plane Price Modeling

El Moufatich Fayssal[1], Willutzky Sebastian[3], and Haitof Houssam[2]

[1] risklab GmbH, Seidlstr. 24a, Munich, Germany
Fayssal.ElMoufatich@risklab.com
[2] TU München, Boltzmannstr. 3, Garching, Germany
haitof@in.tum.de
[3] risklab GmbH, Seidlstr. 24a, Munich, Germany
Sebastian.Willutzky@risklab.com

Abstract. The problem at hand is the integration of expert forecasts for plane prices into a fully calibrated basic economy. The economy is simulated through an Economic Scenario Generator (ESG), which includes macroeconomic processes, interest rate term structures, etc.. By defining the available best-case, worst-case, and mid-case forecasts to correspond to the 95%, the 50% and the 5% quantiles of the plane price distribution, one could describe the problem with the following optimization setting:

$$\min_{(\beta_c, \alpha_{c,i}, \delta_{\mathbf{c}}', \sigma_{c,i})} \{ \| \left(Q\left((\widetilde{I}_{T,S}) \odot \widetilde{P}^{R}_{c,i,T,S}(\beta_c, \alpha_{c,i}, \delta'_{\mathbf{c}}, \gamma'_{\mathbf{c}}, \sigma_{c,i}), \mathbf{q} \right) - \widetilde{FM} \right) \odot W \|_F^2 \}$$

The tilded matrices represent simulation results, i.e. they have the dimension timesteps T and scenarios S. The function $Q(\widetilde{M}_{T,S}, \mathbf{q}) : \mathbb{R}^{T \cdot S} \times [0,1]^q \to \mathbb{R}^{T \cdot q}$ is mapping a matrix $\widetilde{M}_{T,S}$ of simulated scenarios with dimension $(T \times S)$ onto each timestep's quantiles $\mathbf{q}$, resulting in a matrix of dimension $T \times q$. FM is the $(T \times q)$ matrix of expert forecasts, and W is a $(T \times q)$ weighting matrix. $\|\|_F$ denotes the Frobenius norm,[1] and $\odot$ is the element-wise multiplication. The economy simulation is computation-intensive, for which we take benefit of using GPGPU techniques. The optimisation part is also a high-dimensional computation-intensive problem, for which we use a natural computing approach using Differential Evolution.

Keywords: Economic Scenario Generation, Plane Price Modelling, Expert Forecasts, GPU Computation, Differential Evolution.

1 Basis Economy

For the comprehensive modeling of plane prices we use the risklab Economic Scenario Generator (ESG)[2] as the basic theoretical framework. This model builds

[1] Compare e.g. [3].
[2] Compare [11].

M.R. Guarracino et al. (Eds.): Euro-Par 2010 Workshops, LNCS 6586, pp. 439–446, 2011.
© Springer-Verlag Berlin Heidelberg 2011

on fundamental macroeconomic factors to describe the evolution of interest rates and equities. Using a cascade structure, the model captures the long-term economic relationships while allowing for short-term deviations. This structural approach allows for an integrated modeling of financial markets to obtain economically meaningful and consistent scenarios. We assume an arbitrage-free, frictionless financial market in continuous time $t \in [0, T^*]$, where T^* is the end of the given time horizon and the uncertainty in the market is described by the complete filtered probability space $(\Omega, \mathcal{F}, F, \mathbb{P})$. Details on this framework can be found in [10]. The numeraire is represented by a non-defaultable money market account defined by $P(0,t) = \int_0^t e^{r^N(s)} ds$, the process $\{r^N(t)\}_{t\in[0,T^*]}$ represents the nominal short rate. We assume the existence of a probability measure Q equivalent to $\mathbb{P}$, under which all discounted price processes of the financial market under consideration are martingales. Onto this foundation, we impose the cascade structure mentioned before and explained in the following, to incorporate long-term economic dependencies.

The first cascade of the model comprises an inflation process $\{i(t)\}_{t\in[0,T^*]}$ and an economic growth process $\{w(t)\}_{t\in[0,T^*]}$, which are both modeled with Vasicek processes, introduced in [9]. Under the equivalent martingale measure Q they are specified as follows:

$$di(t) = [\theta_i - \hat{a}_i \cdot i(t)]dt + \sigma_i dW_i^Q(t), \tag{1}$$

$$dw(t) = [\theta_w - \hat{a}_w \cdot w(t)]dt + \sigma_w dW_w^Q(t), \tag{2}$$

with the positive real numbers $\theta_i, \theta_w, \hat{a}_i, \hat{a}_w, \sigma_i, \sigma_w$ and the independent standard Brownian motions W_i^Q and W_w^Q. The third risk factor from the first cascade is the real oil price, which is directly relevant for plane price modeling. We assume the real oil price P_o^R to follow a geometric Ornstein-Uhlenbeck process under the real measure $\mathbb{P}$, which is specified as follows:[3]

$$dP_o^R(t) = [\theta_o - a_o \cdot \log P_o^R(t)]P_o^R(t)dt + P_o^R(t)\sigma_o dW_o(t), \tag{3}$$

with θ_o,a_o and σ_o as positive real numbers.

The following second cascade contains the real and nominal interest rate processes. The real short rate process $\{r(t)\}_{t\in[0,T^*]}$ is modeled with a two factor Hull White model. Its dynamics are specified as:

$$dr(t) = [\theta_r(t) + b_{rw} \cdot w(t) - \hat{a}_r \cdot r(t)]dt + \sigma_r dW_r^Q(t), \tag{4}$$

with b_{rw}, $\hat{a}_r$, and σ_r being positive real numbers, θ_r being a time dependent deterministic function and the standard Brownian motion W_r^Q being independent of the Brownian motions mentioned before. The nominal short rate $\{r^N(t)\}_{t\in[0,T^*]}$ comprises real short rate and inflation short rate, and is obtained as the sum of real short rate and inflation, i.e.:

$$r^N(t) = r(t) + i(t). \tag{5}$$

[3] See [2] for more information on the geometric Ornstein-Uhlenbeck process.

The term structure of nominal interest rates can then be derived by the zero-coupon bond prices obtained from this setting. [11] show, that under the presented set of assumptions the price of a zero-coupon bond with maturity $t < T \leq T^*$ is given by:

$$P(t,T) = e^{(A(t,T)-B(t,T)r(t)-C(t,T)i(t)-D(t,T)w(t))}, \tag{6}$$

where

$$\begin{aligned}
B(t,T) &= \tfrac{1}{\hat{a}_r}(1 - e^{(-\hat{a}_r(T-t))}),\\
C(t,T) &= \tfrac{1}{\hat{a}_i}(1 - e^{(-\hat{a}_r(T-t))}),\\
D(t,T) &= \tfrac{b_{rw}}{\hat{a}_r} \cdot \left(\tfrac{1-e^{(-\hat{a}_r(T-t))}}{\hat{a}_w} + \tfrac{e^{(-\hat{a}_w(T-t))} - e^{(-\hat{a}_r(T-t))}}{\hat{a}_w - \hat{a}_r} \right),\\
A(t,T) &= \textstyle\int_t^T (\tfrac{1}{2}(\sigma_r^2 B(l,T)^2 + \sigma_i^2 C(l,T)^2 + \sigma_w^2 D(l,T)^2) - \theta_r(l)B(l,T)\\
&\quad -\theta_i C(l,T) - \theta_w D(l,T))dl.
\end{aligned}$$

The model equations can be derived under the real measure $\mathbb{P}$ instead of the equivalent martingale measure Q using Girsanov's Theorem, by replacing W_i^Q, W_w^Q, W_r^Q with the independent standard Brownian motions W_i, W_w, W_r and using the parameters $a_i = \hat{a}_i - \lambda_i \sigma_i^2$, $a_w = \hat{a}_w - \lambda_w \sigma_w^2$, and $a_r = \hat{a}_r - \lambda_r \sigma_r^2$. The parameters λ_i, λ_w, and λ_r are obtained by the change of measure, as shown e.g in [7]. In addition, we assume the Brownian motion $W_o(t)$ to be correlated with $W_w(t)$ with a constant correlation coefficient $\rho > 0$. As can be seen, the term structure of interest rates is driven by the real short rate process, as well as the underlying macroeconomic factors of economic growth and inflation rates. The third cascade contains equity assets. The equity prices $\{S_t^E\}_{t \in [0,T^*]}$ are driven by the following dynamics:

$$dS^E(t) = [\alpha_E + b_{Er} r(t) - b_{Ei} i(t) + b_{Ew} w(t)]\, S^E(t)dt + \sigma_E S^E(t) dW_E(t), \tag{7}$$

where b_{Er}, b_{Ei}, b_{Ew}, and σ_E are positive real numbers, $\alpha_E \in R$ and $W_E(t)$ is a standard Brownian motion, independent of those mentioned above.

2 Plane Price Model

On the basic economy just described, we will impose our model of the plane price process. As plane prices are dependent on macroeconomic factors, whereas macroeconomic factors do not depend on plane prices, we follow a two-step procedure to simulate plane prices. In a first step, we simulate the basic economy using the risklab ESG, and then impose the plane price process onto the calibrated basic economy. Using the methods of dynamic panel data analysis,[4] one

[4] For a detailed exposition of panel data analysis methods, compare [4]. For log-linear plane price modeling and the inclusion of age dependency compare e.g. [6].

can identify the following model describing the real prices in year t of a plane belonging to class c[5] and built in year i under $\mathbb{P}$:[6]

$$\begin{aligned} P^R_{c,i}(t) = \exp(&\beta_c + \alpha_{c,i} + \rho_c \cdot \log(1 + P^R_{c,i}(t-1)) \\ &+ \delta_{\mathbf{c}}' \cdot \mathbf{A_{c,i}(t)} + \gamma_{\mathbf{c}}' \cdot \mathbf{M(t)} + \sigma_{c,i}\epsilon_{c,i}(t)) - 1, \end{aligned}$$

with the vectors $\mathbf{A_{c,i}(t)}$ and $\mathbf{M(t)}$ defined as:

$$\mathbf{A_{c,i}(t)} := \left(\log(1 + \mathrm{age}_{c,i}(t))),\ (\log(1 + \mathrm{age}_{c,i}(t)))^2,\ (\log(1 + \mathrm{age}_{c,i}(t)))^3\right)',$$

$$\mathbf{M(t)} := \left(w(t),\ \log(1 + P^R_o(t)),\ \frac{1}{P(t, T_M)},\ \log \frac{S^E(t)}{S^E(t-1)}\right)',$$

and the parameter vectors $(\beta_c,\ \alpha_{c,i}) \in \mathbb{R}^2$, $\delta_{\mathbf{c}} \in \mathbb{R}^{\mathbf{3}}$and $\gamma_{\mathbf{c}} \in \mathbb{R}^4$. As introduced before, w_t is GDP-growth, $\mathrm{age}_{c,i}(t)$ is the age of the plane, $P^R_o(t)$ is the real oil price and $P(t, T_M)$ is the price of a zerobond with a notional of 1 currency unit and one year to maturity, and the residual noise $\epsilon_{c,i}(t) \sim N(0, 1)$.

The nominal plane price $P^N_{c,i}(t)$ can then be obtained by multiplying the real price $P^R_{c,i}(t)$ with the inflation index $I(t)$:

$$P^N_{c,i}(t) = P^R_{c,i}(t) \cdot I(t), \tag{8}$$

where $I(t)$ is the value of the inflation index[7] generated by $\{i(t^*)\}_{t^* \in [0,t]}$ at time t. With this model, macroeconomic variables obviously have an impact on plane prices, but not vice versa.

3 Simulation and Calibration

We would like now to integrate plane price model and expert forecasts for plane prices into the calibrated basic economy. As there is only a one-way dependence, i.e. plane prices depend on macroeconomic factors, but not vice versa, the first step of integration is done simply by calculating plane prices given the exogenous factor realizations from the basic economy. However, also the given expert forecasts on plane prices need to be considered. Usually, one is given best-case, worst-case, and mid-case forecasts for plane prices. One approach is then to define these three cases to correspond to specific quantiles of the plane price distribution, e.g. 5% for the worst case, 50% for the mid case and 95% for the worst case. Following this approach, one could describe the problem of integrating the expert forecasts generally by the following optimization setting:[8]

$$\min_{(\beta_c, \alpha_{c,i}, \delta_{\mathbf{c}}', \sigma_{c,i})} \{\| \left(Q\left((\widetilde{I}_{T,S}) \odot \widetilde{P}^R_{c,i,T,S}(\beta_c, \alpha_{c,i}, \delta_{\mathbf{c}}', \gamma_{\mathbf{c}}', \sigma_{c,i}), \mathbf{q}\right) - FM\right) \odot W\|^2_F\}. \tag{9}$$

[5] E.g. widebody, narrowbody, etc.

[6] For the ease of exposition, we present a reduced model. The generalized model considers several economies with their proper economic processes and linking exchange rates.

[7] Starting with $I(0) = 1$.

[8] In this optimisation, we consider only one build-year. Thus, we set $\alpha_{c,i} = 0$.

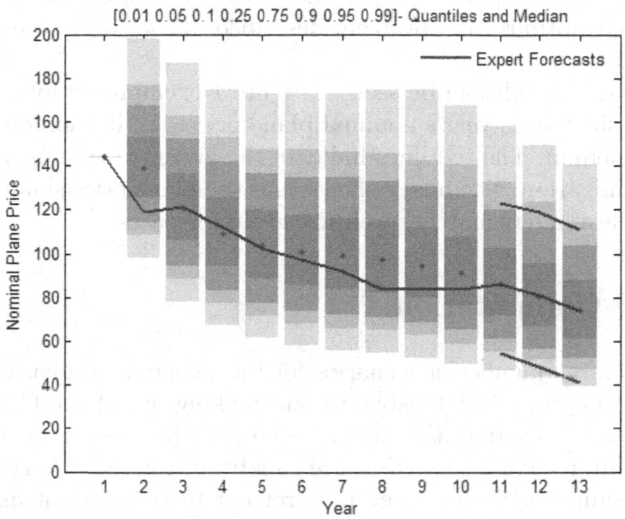

Fig. 1. Simulated Quantiles and Expert Forecats

The tilded matrices represent simulation results, i.e. they have the dimension timesteps T and scenarios S. The matrix $\widetilde{P}^R_{c,i,T,S}$ is for instance composed of the components:

$$P^R_{c,i}(t,s) = \exp(\beta_c + \alpha_{c,i} + \rho_c \cdot \log(1 + P^R_{c,i}(t-1,s)) \\ + \delta_{\mathbf{c}}{}' \cdot \mathbf{A_{c,i}(t)} + \gamma_{\mathbf{c}}{}' \cdot \mathbf{M(t,s)} + \epsilon_{c,i}(t,s)) - 1.$$

The function $Q(\widetilde{M}_{T,S}, \mathbf{q}) : \mathbb{R}^{T \cdot S} \times [0,1]^q \longrightarrow \mathbb{R}^{T \cdot q}$ is mapping a matrix $\widetilde{M}_{T,S}$ of simulated scenarios with dimension $(T \times S)$ onto each timesteps' quantiles $\mathbf{q}$, resulting in a matrix of dimension $T \times q$. FM is the $(T \times q)$ matrix of expert forecasts, and W is a $(T \times q)$ weighting matrix[9]. $\|\|_F$ denotes the Frobenius norm,[10] and $\odot$ is the element-wise multiplication.

In our case, best, worst and mid case forecasts are given. So we set $q = 3$ and $\mathbf{q} = (0.05, 0.5, 0.95)'$. Note that the optimization is only over the parameter vector $(\beta_c, \alpha_{c,i}, \delta_{\mathbf{c}}{}', \sigma_{c,i})$. This is due to the fact that the parameter vector $\gamma_{\mathbf{c}}$ represents economic relationships, i.e. sensitivities of real plane prices to macroeconomic variables and is estimated on empirical data[11]. Thus, this vector should not be altered in the course of the optimization. However, the parameter vector $(\beta_c, \alpha_{c,i}, \delta_{\mathbf{c}}{}')$ controls a deterministic evolution of plane prices over time, and is therefore predestined to incorporate the expert forecasts. The parameter $\sigma_{c,i}$

[9] One has to take into consideration that the components of the weighting matrix will be squared when applying the Frobenius norm. As a result, corresponding transformations should be applied to the weighting matrix when needed.

[10] Compare e.g. [3].

[11] The parameters were in fact estimated on historical data using a generalized method of moments following Arrelano and Bover, which can be found e.g. in [4], p. 53f.

incorporates the experts opinion on quantile spread. Therefore, we face the large-scale unrestricted optimization problem described above, which we solve using differential evolution.

The optimization result can be seen in Figure 1 exemplarily for a one plane-class. The bars show each year's nominal plane price distribution quantiles, the dots show the median. The red lines indicate the given expert forecasts considered in the optimization. The image shows that the plane price simulation using the optimized parameters matches well the given forecasts.

4 GPGPU Computation

As simulating a large number of scenarios for the Economic Scenario Generator could be quite computation-intensive, we are making use of the GPGPU techniques to harness the computation intensivity of the basic economy simulation.

GPUs are computation devices that are capable of running a very large number of threads simultaneously. A key requirement to the efficient use of GPUs for computation is independence of the running threads. This means the running threads are not allowed to interact with each others and will be operating on different data. However, threads are allowed to share data but without I/O flow dependencies. In the context of GPGPU, the main CPU is also known as the **host**, and the GPU devices are known as the **device**. For these two computation devices to coexist without intevening with each other's work, they would need to maintain separate memory spaces, entitled the **host memory** and the **device memory** respectively.

So, for our application, the simulation of the underlying risk factors representing the basic economy as well as the plane price process fit nicely to the target applications of GPGPU techniques. The different processes are data parallel and computation-intensive. For this purpose, we had to separate the different process Stochastic Differential Equations (SDEs) into CUDA functions that are followingly compiled into the instruction set of the GPU device, called **kernels** in CUDA parlance.

The simulated scenarios run independently of each other and have no data dependencies. Since what differentiates the scenarios is the diffusion part of their stochastic differential equation, which stems from the dynamics of the corresponding Brownian motion, generating random numbers is a critical part in our simulation. In addition, the dynamics driving the plane prices and those driving the growth of the economy are positively correlated ($\rho > 0$). We generate the needed random numbers in parallel using a parallel implementation of the **Mersenne Twister** (MT) Pseudo-Random Number Generator (PRNG) that leviates the inherent serial behavior of the Mersenne Twister and allows threads to generate random numbers in parallel, with good statistical properties. The resulting speedups from running the kernels in two hardware sets are illustrated in Figure 2.

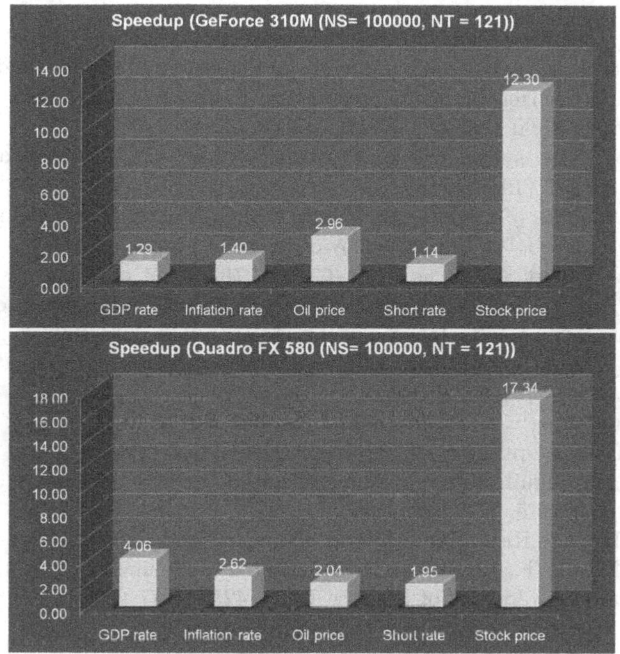

Fig. 2. GPGPU Speedups

5 Differential Evolution

Differential Evolution (DE) is a vector-population-based stochastic optimization method that was introduced to the public in 1995. It has been widely used since then and in various domains of applications. Pointers for further reference in this respect can be found in [5], [8], or [1], among others.

Our parameter vector for the optimisation problem in Setting 9 is composed of 5 parameters[12], namely $(\beta_c, \sigma_{c,i}, \delta_{c,1}, \delta_{c,2}, \delta_{c,3})$ with $\delta'_c = (\delta_{c,1}, \delta_{c,2}, \delta_{c,3})$. At each iteration, DE compares the current population to a competent population. A population is the number of parameter vectors assessed at the given iteration. Hence, at a given iteration k, DE takes the best population from the last iteration and for each individual in the population (target individual), it constructs a competent individual by taking the difference of two randomly chosen individuals and adds it to either the target individual or another randomly selected individual from the population. Then, a single candidate vector is chosen from the two individuals uniformally based on a crossover bound (CR) probabililty. The probabilistic approach for selecting the final vector based on the CR probability is applied per parameter value individually. The selected candidate is then evaluated and used for the next iteration. The algorithm starts by randomly selecting a starting vector from the defined boundaries of the optimization problem.

[12] Remember that $\alpha_{ci} = 0$.

References

1. Chakraborty, U.K.: Advances in Differential Evolution. Springer, Heidelberg (2008)
2. Föllmer, H., Schweizer, M.: A microeconomic approach to diffusion models for stock prices. Mathematical Finance 3, 1–23 (1993)
3. Higham, N.: The symmetric procrustes problem. BIT Numerical Mathematics 28(1), 189–217 (1988)
4. Hsiao, C.: Analysis of Panel Data. Cambridge University Press, Cambridge (2005)
5. Lampinen, J.: Global optimization by differential evolution (2001), `http://www.it.lut.fi/kurssit/01-02/010778000/DE.pdf`
6. Pulvino, T.C.: Do asset fire sales exist? an empirical investigation of commercial aircraft transactions. The Journal of Finance (3), 939–978 (1998)
7. Schmid, B., Zagst, R.: A three-factor defaultable term structure model. Journal of Fixed Income 10(2), 63–679 (2000)
8. Storn, R.M., Price, K.V., Lampinen, J.A.: Differential Evolution: A Practical Approach to Global Optimization. Springer, Heidelberg (2005)
9. Vasicek, O.: An equilibrium characterization of the term structure. Journal of Financial Economics 5, 177–188 (1977)
10. Zagst, R.: Interest Rate Management. Springer, Heidelberg (2002)
11. Zagst, R., Meyer, T., Hagedorn, H.: Integrated modelling of stock and bond markets. International Journal of Finance 19(1), 4252–4277 (2007)

Wavelet Techniques for Option Pricing on Advanced Architectures

Stefania Corsaro[1,2], Daniele Marazzina[3], and Zelda Marino[1]

[1] Dipartimento di Statistica e Matematica per la Ricerca Economica
Università degli Studi di Napoli "Parthenope"
Via Medina 40, I-80133 Napoli, Italy
{stefania.corsaro,zelda.marino}@uniparthenope.it
[2] Istituto di Calcolo e Reti ad Alte Prestazioni (ICAR-CNR)
Via Pietro Castellino 111, I-80131 Napoli, Italy
[3] Dipartimento di Matematica - Politecnico di Milano
Via Bonardi 9, I-20133 Milano, Italy
daniele.marazzina@polimi.it

Abstract. This work focuses on the development of a parallel pricing algorithm for Asian options based on the Discrete Wavelet Transform. Following the approach proposed in [6], the pricing process requires the solution of a set of independent Fredholm integral equations of the second kind. Within this evaluation framework, our aim is to develop a robust parallel pricing algorithm based on wavelet techniques for the pricing problem of discrete monitoring arithmetic Asian options. In particular, the Discrete Wavelet Transform is applied in order to approximate the kernels of the integral equations. We discuss both the accuracy of the method and its scalability properties.

Keywords: Asian options, Discrete Wavelet Transform, Parallel Computing.

1 Introduction

The backward recursion that arises in option pricing can be converted into a set of independent Fredholm integral equations of the second kind by means of the z-transform. This approach is described in [7] for European, Barrier and Lookback options and in [6] for Asian options. Moreover, the development of a grid-enabled pricing algorithm for plain vanilla options is presented in [5].

In this paper we focus on the pricing procedure for Asian options, based on the randomization technique described in [6]; as authors point out, the pricing procedure turns out to be computational demanding. Our purpose in this framework is to develop an accurate and efficient pricing algorithm based on wavelet techniques. In probabilistic terms, most of a wavelet mass is concentrated in a compact subset of $\mathbb{R}$, that is, one of the main features of wavelets is "localization". This property motivates the use of wavelet bases for data compression: wavelet coefficients contain local information, thus, if we neglect the coefficient

M.R. Guarracino et al. (Eds.): Euro-Par 2010 Workshops, LNCS 6586, pp. 447–454, 2011.
© Springer-Verlag Berlin Heidelberg 2011

under a fixed threshold, accuracy can be preserved with a significative gain in efficiency. Even if most applications of wavelets deal with signal analysis, wavelets have been applied in the numerical solution of partial differential and integral equations, and in the approximation and interpolation of data [1]. Much effort has been indeed devoted to the development of routines that perform the computation of the *Discrete Wavelet Transform* (DWT) both on serial and parallel architectures (see, for example, [2] and [4] and references therein).

We project the linear systems which arise from the discretization of the integral equations onto wavelet spaces in order to obtain a sparse representation of the discrete operators, retaining information so to preserve accuracy. We furthermore discuss the parallelization of the pricing wavelet-based procedure.

In Section 2 we briefly describe the pricing method, addressing to existing literature for details. In Section 3 we introduce the DWT operator. In Section 4 we describe the wavelet-based pricing algorithm we developed, which is tested in Section 5. Finally, Section 6 deals with the parallel implementation and the performance analysis.

2 The Randomization Pricing Algorithm

In this section we briefly recall the Asian fixed call randomization pricing algorithm presented in [6]. Authors show that, under the assumption that the underlying asset evolves according to a generic Lévy process, the price of a call option with fixed strike K, N equidistant monitoring dates (Δ being the time interval between them) and maturity T is equal to

$$e^{-rT}\int_{-\infty}^{+\infty}\left(\frac{S_0}{N+1}\left(1+e^x\right)-K\right)^+ f_{B_1}\left(x\right)dx \tag{1}$$

The density f_{B_1} is the key variable: it can be computed exploiting the recursion

$$u\left(x,k\right)=\int_{\mathbb{R}}K\left(x,y\right)u\left(y,k-1\right)dy,\;\; k=1,\ldots,N-1 \tag{2}$$

with initial condition $u\left(x,0\right)=f\left(x\right)$, where $u\left(x,k\right)=f_{B_{N-k}}\left(x\right)$ and $K\left(x,y\right)=f(x-\log\left(e^y+1\right))$, being f the transition probability density function from time t to time $t+\Delta$ of the considered Lévy process.

The randomization technique consists in making the expiry date T to be random according to a geometric distribution of the parameter q and then computing the value of $U\left(x,q\right):=\left(1-q\right)\sum_{k=0}^{+\infty}q^k u\left(x,k\right)$. With some manipulations on (2), we get that the function $U\left(x,q\right)$ satisfies the integral equation:

$$U\left(x,q\right)=q\int_{\mathbb{R}}K\left(x,y\right)U\left(y,q\right)dy+\left(1-q\right)f\left(x\right) \tag{3}$$

Therefore a recursive integral equation for $u\left(x,k\right)$ is transformed into an integral equation for $U\left(x,q\right)$. If we approximate the integral equation (3) with a quadrature rule with nodes x_i, $i=1,\cdots,m$, we obtain the linear system

$$\mathbf{u}-q\mathbf{KDu}=\mathbf{f} \tag{4}$$

with $(\mathbf{u})_i = U(x_i)$, $(\mathbf{K})_{ij} = K(x_i, x_j)$, $(\mathbf{f})_i = (1-q)f(x_i)$ and $\mathbf{D}$ being the diagonal matrix of the quadrature weights. The system (4) is the main computational kernel in the procedure. The unknown function $u(x, N-1)$, i.e., $f_{B_1}(x)$, can be then obtained by de-randomizing the option maturity exploiting the complex inversion integral

$$u(x, N-1) = \frac{1}{2\pi\rho^{N-1}} \int_0^{2\pi} \frac{U\left(x, \rho e^{is}\right)}{1-\rho e^{is}} e^{-i(N-1)s} ds \tag{5}$$

Approximating (5) with a trapezoidal formula, and applying the Euler summation, a convergence-acceleration technique well suited for evaluating alternating series, we obtain

$$f_{B_1}(x) = u(x, N-1) \approx \frac{1}{2^{m_e}\rho^{N-1}} \sum_{j=0}^{m_e} \binom{m_e}{j} b_{n_e+j}(x)$$

where $b_k(x) = \sum_{j=0}^{k}(-1)^j a_j U(x, q_j)$ with $q_j = \rho e^{ij\pi/(N-1)}$, $a_0 = (2(N-1)(1-q_0))^{-1}$, $a_j = ((N-1)(1-q_j))^{-1}$, $j \geq 1$, assuming $N > n_e + m_e$. A sketch of the pricing algorithm is reported in Fig. 1.

Procedure
- `compute` $\mathbf{K}$, $\mathbf{D}$ `and` $\mathbf{f}$
- `for` $j = 0, \cdots, n_e + m_e$, `solve the integral equations` $(\mathbf{I} - q_j\mathbf{KD})\mathbf{u} = \mathbf{f}$
- `reconstruct` $f_{B_1}(x)$ `by means of the solutions of the integral equation`
- `compute the integral` (1)

End Procedure

Fig. 1. Asian fixed call randomization pricing algorithm

3 The Discrete Wavelet Transform

A wavelet $\psi(t)$ is defined as a function belonging to $L^1(\mathbb{R}) \cap L^2(\mathbb{R})$ such that $\int_{\mathbb{R}} \psi(t)dt = 0$. Wavelets have either compact support or the most of information contained in them is concentrated in a compact subset of $\mathbb{R}$ [3]. Each wavelet basis is derived by a *mother wavelet* by means of dilation and translation; in particular, the dilation factor corresponds to a scale within the *Multiresolution Analysis* (MRA). Projecting a function onto a space of a MRA allows one to obtain information about it, depending on the *resolution* of the space. The mapping that leads from the l-th level resolution to the $(l-1)$-th level, retaining the information that is lost in this process, is the Discrete Wavelet Transform. The aforementioned properties justify the use of DWT for data compression [9]: wavelet coefficients contain the detail information, thus, if we neglect the coefficients under a fixed threshold, accuracy can be preserved with a significative gain in efficiency.

Given a MRA, two sequences $(h_k)_{k\in\mathbb{Z}}$ and $(g_k)_{k\in\mathbb{Z}}$, the *low-pass* and the *high-pass filters* of the MRA, respectively, define a change of level within the MRA. More precisely, let $\mathbf{c}^l = (c_n^l)_{n\in\mathbb{Z}}$ be the vector of the coefficients of the projection of a function $f(t)$ onto the l-th resolution subspace of the MRA; the DWT operator W is defined as follows:

$$W : \mathbf{c}^l \in l^2(\mathbb{Z}) \longrightarrow (\mathbf{c}^{l-1}, \mathbf{d}^{l-1}) \in l^2(\mathbb{Z}) \times l^2(\mathbb{Z})$$

where $l_2(\mathbb{Z}) = \{(c_k)_{k\in\mathbb{Z}} : c_k \in \mathbb{C}, \sum_k |c_k|^2 < \infty\}$, $c_n^{l-1} = \sum_{k\in\mathbb{Z}} h_{k-2n} c_k^l$, and $d_n^{l-1} = \sum_{k\in\mathbb{Z}} g_{k-2n} c_k^l$.

In matrix form, if $\mathbf{L} = (\tilde{h}_{i,j} = h_{j-2i})$ is the low-pass operator and $\mathbf{H} = (\tilde{g}_{i,j} = g_{j-2i})$ is the high-pass operator, the above relation can be written in the following way:

$$\begin{pmatrix} \mathbf{c}^{l-1} \\ \mathbf{d}^{l-1} \end{pmatrix} = \begin{pmatrix} \mathbf{L} \\ \mathbf{H} \end{pmatrix} \cdot c^l \Longleftrightarrow \begin{cases} \mathbf{c}^{l-1} = \mathbf{L}\mathbf{c}^l \\ \mathbf{d}^{l-1} = \mathbf{H}\mathbf{c}^l \end{cases}$$

The vector $\mathbf{c}^{l-1}$ retains the information about the low frequencies, while the filters g_k "detect" the high frequencies: so the vector $\mathbf{d}^{l-1}$ contains the *details*, that is, the information that is lost passing from the resolution l to the resolution $l-1$. From a computational point of view, it is worth emphasizing that, if s is the length of the two sequences h_k and g_k, then the number of floating-point operations required for the computation of the DWT of a vector of length m is $O(sm)$.

If $\mathbf{Q} := (\mathbf{L},\ \mathbf{H})^\top$, then the DWT of a matrix $\mathbf{A}$ is defined as $\mathbf{QAQ}^\top$. In practice, the bidimensional DWT is computed in two stages: the product $\mathbf{QA}$ actually requires to transform the columns of the matrix; then, the DWT is applied to the rows of the intermediate matrix $\mathbf{QA}$. Note that if the wavelet basis is orthonormal, then the matrix $\mathbf{Q}$ is orthogonal, thus $\mathbf{QQ}^\top = \mathbf{I}$.

4 The Wavelet-Based Pricing Algorithm

In this work, we consider the Daubechies Wavelets [3], a family of orthonormal compactly supported wavelets. Each family of Daubechies wavelets is characterized by a fixed number of vanishing moments, from which the amplitude of the support depends. Our idea is to increase the sparsity of the coefficient matrices of the linear systems to be solved, so to improve efficiency, by means of a *hard threshold* [9] applied to the projection of the discrete operators onto wavelet spaces, which allows one to better preserve information for the sake of accuracy.

Let us discretize (3) by means of a quadrature rule on a truncated integration domain $[l, u]$. The bounds are chosen in such a way that the tails of the density outside of it are less than 10^{-8} [6]. Moreover, since f is the transition probability density of the log-price of the underlying asset, it is reasonable to expect a decay of the values of f moving towards l or u. For this reason, we expect the most significant elements of the matrix $\mathbf{KD}$ to be localized in a region near its diagonal, and smoothness away from this region. Let us refer to the pricing algorithm reported in Fig. 1: in the solution of the linear systems in step 2, we apply to both sides the DWT operator $\mathbf{Q}$, so for each value of q we obtain the linear system, equivalent to (4), $(\mathbf{I} - q\mathbf{Q}(\mathbf{KD})\mathbf{Q}^\top)\mathbf{Qu} = \mathbf{Qf}$. Therefore, if we denote by $\mathbf{KD}_W, \mathbf{u}_W, \mathbf{f}_W$ the DWT of $\mathbf{KD}, \mathbf{u}, \mathbf{f}$ respectively, we have:

$$(\mathbf{I} - q\mathbf{KD}_W)\mathbf{u}_W = \mathbf{f}_W \tag{6}$$

We then apply a *hard threshold* to the coefficient matrix of (6), thus we actually solve the linear system:

$$(\mathbf{I} - q\mathbf{KD}_W^\epsilon)\mathbf{y} = \mathbf{f}_W \tag{7}$$

where $\mathbf{KD}_W^\epsilon$ is the hard threshold of $\mathbf{KD}$ with threshold ϵ. Finally, the inverse DWT is applied to the solution $\mathbf{y}$ of (7), thus an approximation of $\mathbf{u}$, $\mathbf{Q}^\top\mathbf{y}$, is obtained.

5 Numerical Results

In this section we price an Asian fixed option with 100 monitoring dates, maturity $T = 1$ and strike $K = 100$. The Market data are $S_0 = 100$, $r = 3.67\%$ and the underlying asset is assumed to follow a Jump Diffusion Merton Lévy process with parameters $\sigma = 0.126349$, $\alpha = -0.390078$, $\lambda = 0.174814$ and $\delta = 0.338796$. We consider a Gauss-Legendre quadrature rule with $m = 2048$ nodes and three methods to solve the integral equations: the "standard" quadrature method with Gauss-Legendre nodes, the wavelet transform method, and the Reichel algorithm [11], which is a fast solution method for integral equations based on a low-rank representation of the kernel of the equation. The quadrature rule considered for the wavelet transform method is the Gauss-Legendre one. We fix $n_e = 12$ and $m_e = 10$.

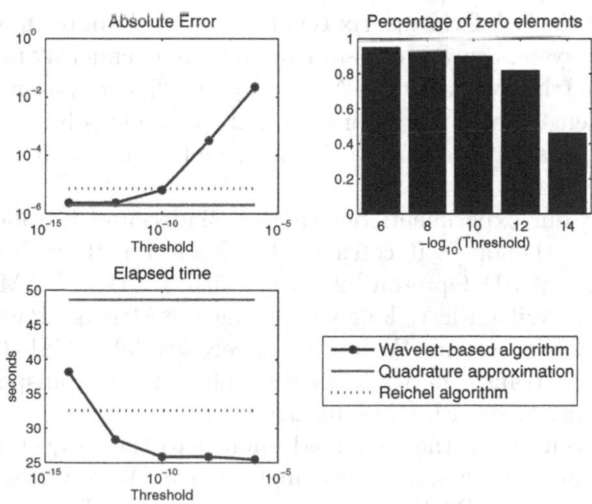

Fig. 2. Top-left: approximation error; top-right: percentage of neglected elements in the hard threshold following the DWT; bottom-left: execution time

In Fig. 2 we report the results concerning a simulation in which two steps of DWT, based on Daubechies wavelets with four vanishing moments, have been performed, for different threshold values ranging between 10^{-14} and 10^{-6}. In the top-left picture the absolute error is represented for different threshold levels, considering the results in [6] as exact solution, the corresponding execution time being represented in the bottom-left graphic. We see that the DWT-based approach is almost always the most efficient and the approximation error has the same order of magnitude up to 10^{-10} threshold level. On the other hand, when the threshold is in the range 10^{-10} – 10^{-6} more than the 80% of the elements are set to zero, as it can be seen in the top-right graphic, where the percentage of elements which are neglected in the threshold procedure are reported, for different threshold values. The same behavior has been observed when the number of DWT steps increases.

6 Parallel Implementation

The performances of our method can be improved using High Performance Computing methodologies. Parallelism has been introduced both in the linear systems solution process and in the DWT computation. In this section we describe the parallel algorithm and we present numerical results from the implementation of the developed software.

As already pointed out, the computation of the bidimensional DWT is performed in two stages; we distribute the matrix **KD** in a row-block fashion. In the first stage, processors concurrently compute the DWT of rows; then, communication is required for globally transposing the matrix, so, processors can concurrently transform the columns of the intermediate matrix. Finally, the matrix is globally transposed again.

While to apply the DWT the matrix **KD** has to be distribute among processor, to solve the linear system each processor can build independently from the others the coefficients matrix. We have then $N_{sys} = n_e + m_e$ linear systems to be solved. We distribute them among processors, so that each one solves $\lfloor N_{sys}/nprocs \rfloor$ systems; in this phase, processors work concurrently. In Fig. 3 a sketch of the algorithm is reported.

We carried out our experiments on an IBM Bladecenter installed at University of Naples "Parthenope". It consists of 6 Blade LS 21, each one of which is equipped with 2 AMD Opteron 2210 and with 4 GB of RAM. The implemented software is written in *C* language, using the Message Passing Interface (MPI) communication system. We use the freely available GSL Library [8] to perform the wavelet transform, while for the global matrix transposition we use the routine `pdtrans` of the PUMMA library [10].

The matrix arising from the threshold applied to the projection of the discrete operators onto wavelet spaces is strongly sparse. We solve the sparse linear systems by means of the GMRES solver, with Incomplete Factorization ILU(0) preconditioner, implemented in the SPARSKIT library [12].

```
Procedure
• apply the DWT operator to KD and to f in parallel
  - distribute the matrix KD in row-block fashion
  - each processor computes the DWT of a row block
  - global transposition
  - each processor computes the DWT of a column block
  - global transposition
• collect the matrix so that each processor stores the whole matrix
• neglect the elements of KD_W below the fixed threshold ε;
• for j = 0, N_sys, solve in parallel (I − q_j KD^ε_W)y = f_W
  - distribute the values of q among processors;
  - each processor solves the linear systems distributed to it;
  - each processor applies the inverse transform to y.
• processor 0 collects local solutions
End Procedure
```

Fig. 3. Sketch of the parallel pricing algorithm for Asian options based on the DWT

To evaluate the parallel performance of the algorithm, in Fig. 4 we report the speed-up for $m = 2^{10}$, $m = 2^{11}$ and $m = 2^{12}$, considering the same pricing problem presented in Section 5. We use the Daubechies wavelets of length 4 and with 4 level of resolution. The graph reveals a decrease in terms of performance with four processors. This is due to the communication overhead of the global transposition. Better results could be obtained if the transposed matrices were built, so to avoid one transposition, as we plan to do in the next future.

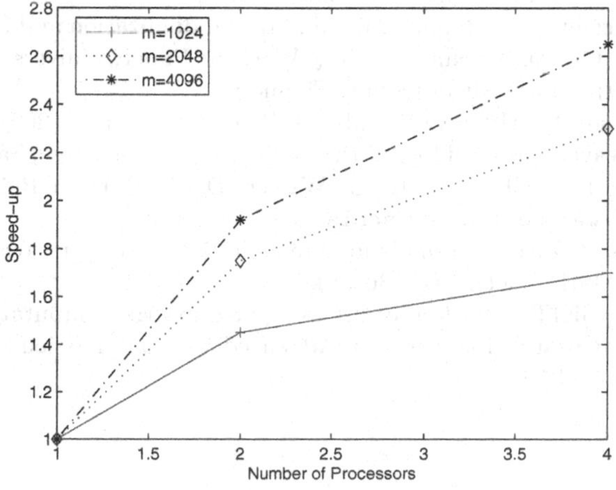

Fig. 4. Speed-up

7 Conclusion

In this paper we focus on the use of wavelet techniques in a pricing procedure for Asian options based on randomization. Preliminary experiments reveal that wavelet bases allow one to improve efficiency without loss in accuracy. Moreover, we discuss the parallelization of the proposed algorithm; parallelism is introduced at two levels, both in the wavelet transform and in the solution of the linear systems arising from the discretization of the involved integral operators. Parallel performance results reveal that the parallel algorithm needs some revisions which we are planning to implement in the next future.

References

1. Cohen, A.: Numerical analysis of wavelet methods. Elsevier, Amsterdam (2003)
2. Corsaro, S., D'Amore, L., Murli, A.: On the Parallel Implementation of the Fast Wavelet Packet Transform on MIMD Distributed Memory Environments. In: Zinterhof, P., Vajtersic, M., Uhl, A. (eds.) ACPC 1999 and ParNum 1999. LNCS, vol. 1557, pp. 357–366. Springer, Heidelberg (1999)
3. Daubechies, I.: Ten lectures on wavelets. Society for Industrial and Applied Mathematics, Philadelphia (1992)
4. Franco, J., Bernabé, G., Fernández, J., Acacio, M.E.: A Parallel Implementation of the 2D Wavelet Transform Using CUDA. In: PDP 2009: Proceedings of the 2009 17th Euromicro International Conference on Parallel, Distributed and Network-based Processing, pp. 111–118. IEEE Computer Society, Washington (2009)
5. Fusai, G., Marazzina, D., Marena, M.: Option Pricing, Maturity Randomization and Distributed Computing. Parallel Comput. 36(7), 403–414 (2010)
6. Fusai, G., Marazzina, D., Marena, M.: Pricing Discretely Monitored Asian Options by Maturity Randomization, SEMeQ Working Paper, University of Piemonte Orientale(2009) (to appear in SIAM J. Finan. Math.)
7. Fusai, G., Marazzina, D., Marena, M., Ng, M.: Randomization and Preconditioning Techniques for Option Pricing, SEMeQ Working Paper, University of Piemonte Orientale (2009) (to appear in Quant. Financ.)
8. Galassi, M., et al.: GNU Scientific Library Reference Manual (2009)
9. Mallat, S.: A Wavelet Tour of Signal Processing. Academic Press, San Diego (2008)
10. Choi, J., Dongarra, J.J., Petitet, A., Walker, D.W.: Pumma Reference Manual (1993), `http://www.netlib.org/scalapack`
11. Reichel, L.: Fast Solution Methods for Fredholm Integral Equations of the Second Kind. Numer. Math. 57(1), 719–736 (1989)
12. Saad, Y.: SPARSKIT: a basic tool kit for sparse matrix computations. Technical Report 90-20, Research Institute for Advanced Computer Science, NASA Ames Research Center, (1990)

A Stock Market Decision Support System with a Hybrid Evolutionary Algorithm for Many-Core Graphics Processors

Piotr Lipinski

Institute of Computer Science,
University of Wroclaw, Wroclaw, Poland
lipinski@ii.uni.wroc.pl

Abstract. This paper proposes a computational intelligence approach to stock market decision support systems based on a hybrid evolutionary algorithm with local search for many-core graphics processors. Trading decisions come from trading experts built on the basis of a set of specific trading rules analysing financial time series of recent stock price quotations. Constructing such trading experts is an optimization problem with a large and irregular search space that is solved by an evolutionary algorithm, based on Population-Based Incremental Learning, with additional local search. Using many-core graphics processors enables not only a reduction in the computing time, but also a combination of the optimization process with local search, which significantly improves solution qualities, without increasing the computing time. Experiments carried out on real data from the Paris Stock Exchange confirmed that the approach proposed outperforms the classic approach, in terms of the financial relevance of the investment strategies discovered as well as in terms of the computing time.

1 Introduction

In recent years, many computational approaches to financial modelling appeared [2]. Neural networks and evolutionary algorithms were applied to stock market data analysis [4], [5], [7]. Genetic programming was used to building decision trees for supporting financial decision making [12]. Evolutionary approaches were constructed for portfolio optimization [8]. Computational intelligence was also applied to money management [10] or option pricing [3].

Although the recent development in computational algorithms leads to an increasing number of applications in stock market data analysis, the data size and the computing time still remain to be the bottleneck for computational methods. Therefore, the increasing computational power of many-core graphics processors enables new horizons for computational approaches and offers a challenge for researchers.

This paper proposes a computational intelligence approach to stock market decision support systems based on a hybrid evolutionary algorithm with local search for many-core graphics processors. Trading decisions come from trading experts built on the basis of a set of specific trading rules analysing financial time series of recent stock price quotations. Constructing such trading experts is an optimization problem with a

M.R. Guarracino et al. (Eds.): Euro-Par 2010 Workshops, LNCS 6586, pp. 455–462, 2011.
© Springer-Verlag Berlin Heidelberg 2011

large and irregular search space that is solved by an evolutionary algorithm, based on Population-Based Incremental Learning [1] - a fast and simple Estimation of Distribution Algorithm [6], with additional local search. Using many-core graphics processors enables not only a reduction in the computing time, but also a combination of the optimization process with local search, which significantly improves solution qualities, without increasing the computing time.

Experiments carried out on real data from the Paris Stock Exchange confirmed that the approach proposed outperforms the classic approach, in terms of the financial relevance of the investment strategies discovered as well as in terms of the computing time.

This paper is structured in the following manner: Section 2 defines the optimization problem of building efficient trading experts. Section 3 describes the hybrid evolutionary algorithm and Section 4 proposes its parallelization. Section 5 reports some experiments performed on real data from the Paris Stock Exchange. Finally, Section 6 concludes the paper.

2 Problem Definition

A stock market trading rule is a function $f : \mathcal{K} \mapsto s \in \mathbb{R}$ that maps a factual financial knowledge $\mathcal{K}$ (e.g. financial time series of recent stock price quotations) to a real number s encoding a trading signal (low values denote a sell signal, high values denote a buy signal). Examples of such trading rules may be found in Technical Analysis [9].

A stock market trading expert is a subset E of the entire set $\mathcal{R}$ of some specific trading rules $f_1, f_2, \ldots, f_d$, available in the decision support system, encoded in a binary vector $\mathbf{e} = (e_1, e_2, \ldots, e_d) \in \{0, 1\}^d$. A trading signal of the trading expert, for a given factual financial knowledge, is the arithmetic average of trading signals of trading rules included in the trading expert.

For a given training period, the trading expert is evaluated in a type of simulation. It starts with an initial capital: an initial amount of cash and an initial number of stocks. In successive days of the training period, the trading expert produces a trading signal. If it is a buy signal, a part of available cash is invested in stocks. If it is a sell signal, a part of available stocks is sold. Each transaction is charged with a transaction fee. Finally, the efficiency of the trading expert is defined by the Sharpe ratio [11] of daily return rates.

Table 1. Simulation settings used in experiments

threshold for a buy signal	+0.05
threshold for a sell signal	-0.05
buy limit	50% of cash
sell limit	50% of stocks
initial cash	10000
initial stocks	100
transaction fee	0.39%

Table 1 presents the simulation settings applied in experiments. Trading rules always produce -1 (sell), 0 (do nothing) or 1 (buy) signals. Thresholds for buy and sell signals concern interpreting the arithmetic average of trading rule signals as trading expert signals. The Sharpe ratio of daily return rates was calculated with the daily risk-free return rate of 0.01%.

Therefore, constructing efficient trading experts is an optimization problem of finding the binary vector $\mathbf{e}$, corresponding to the trading expert, maximizing the efficiency measure ϱ being the Sharpe ratio over a given training period.

However, due to the large number of trading rules in the decision support system (in experiments, $d = 500$), the dimension of the search space is excessively large (in experiments, $|\{0,1\}^d| = 2^{500}$), which constitutes the main bottleneck for many optimization algorithms.

3 Hybrid Evolutionary Algorithm

In order to solve the optimization problem, an hybrid evolutionary algorithm, based on Population-Based Incremental Learning (PBIL) [1], with additional local search, HPBIL-LS, is proposed.

Algorithm 1. Hybrid Population-Based Incremental Learning with Local Search (HPBIL-LS)

```
p = (0.5, 0.5, ..., 0.5);
t = 0;
while not Termination-Condition() do
   P = Random-Population(p);
   Population-Evaluation(P);

   PartialLocalSearch(P);

   e* = Find-Best-Solution(P);

   {updating the probability model};
   p = (1 − α) · p + α · e*;

   {mutating the probability model};
   if random(0, 1) < β then
      u = random-binary-vector();
      p = (1 − γ) · p + γ · u;
   end if

   t = t + 1;
end while
```

Algorithm 1 presents the overview of the HPBIL-LS algorithm. It starts with initializing the probability model $\mathbf{p} = (p_1, p_2, \ldots, p_d) \in [0,1]^d$ with $(0.5, 0.5, \ldots, 0.5)$.

Afterwards, the evolution starts with creating a random population with the probability model $\mathbf{p}$. It generates a population $\mathcal{P}$ of N random trading experts $\mathbf{e} = (e_1, e_2, \ldots, e_d) \in \{0,1\}^d$ in such a way that, for $i = 1, 2, \ldots, d$, $e_i = 1$ with probability p_i and $e_i = 0$ with probability $(1 - p_i)$. Next, the population is evaluated and additionally optimized with local search. Local search selects $0.20 \cdot N$ trading experts from the population at random and tries to improve them by negating one gene (for each trading expert considered, local search checks d possible improvements). Finally, the best trading expert $\mathbf{e}^*$ is taken, the probability model $\mathbf{p}$ is updated with a learning rate $\alpha \in [0,1]$ and mutated with a mutation probability $\beta \in [0,1]$ and a mutation rate $\gamma \in [0,1]$, and the evolution process repeats until a termination condition is held (after a certain number of iterations).

In the sequential approach, local search makes the algorithm very time consuming and impractical in the case of a large population size N and a large number of trading rules d. In the parallel approach, population evaluation as well as local search may be run in parallel, which significantly reduces the computing time.

4 Parallel Hybrid Evolutionary Algorithm

HPBIL-LS was modified for many-core graphics processors and Compute Unified Device Architecture (CUDA), version 2.3, which is a parallel computing architecture for NVidia graphics processors, with a specific parallel programming model and an instruction set architecture, for many-core graphics processors.

Experiments were performed on NVidia GeForce GTX 280 with a many-core graphics processor with 240 cores, but the approach should be compatible with other graphics cards of the NVidia GeForce 200 series supporting CUDA 2.3. Details of the hardware platform specification are presented in Table 2.

Population evaluation was run in parallel – each trading expert from the population was processed in a separate thread. According to CUDA, threads was organized in blocks. Blocks were processed in parallel by multiprocessors, in such a way that a warp of 32 threads were processed at the same time, while the remaining warps of the same block were waiting active in the queue. The number of threads per block depended on the problem size, because only 16 kB of shared memory was accessible for the entire

Table 2. Hardware platform specification (NVidia GeForce GTX 280)

number of multiprocessors	30
number of registers per multiprocessor	16384
maximum number of threads per block	512
number of threads per warp	32
shared memory per multiprocessor	16 kB
constant memory	64 kB
local memory per thread	16 kB
maximum number of active blocks per multiprocessor	8
maximum number of active warps per multiprocessor	32
maximum number of active threads per multiprocessor	1024

block (thus, the number of threads per block was approximately equal to 16 kB divided by the size of the trading expert).

A number of technical issues had to been addressed, as a result of some limitations of CUDA. Due to memory constraints, financial time series of stock quotations were represented in short integer numbers (2 bytes) of euro cents. Simulations of trading expert performances were calculated in either integer numbers (4 bytes) or short integer numbers (2 bytes). Return rates and Sharpe ratios were calculated in float numbers (4 bytes, single precision arithmetic), but stored in integer numbers of 0.0001%, which in certain situations caused some numerical problems (insignificant in the final assessment).

Permanent data structures, such as financial time series and trading rule signals, evaluated before the evolution had started, were stored in texture memory, because of the lack of faster shared memory. Trading experts and objective values were stored in shared memory. Global memory was not used in computations, because of the low bandwidth.

Local search was also run in parallel – each trading expert was optimized in a separate thread. It required a similar architecture than in the case of population evaluation, but smaller numbers of threads were run.

5 Experiments

Experiments were performed on 10 benchmark datasets. Each dataset concerned one stock chosen from the CAC IT 20 index of the Paris Stock Exchange, a training period from January, 2, 2009 to November, 30, 2009 (234 trading days) and a testing period from December, 1, 2009 to December, 31, 2009 (22 trading days).

In each experiment, the same set of 500 trading rules, based on technical analysis indicators [9], was used. Signals of trading rules were evaluated before the evolution had started and were buffered in memory. The learning rate α was 0.15, the mutation probability β was 0.05, the mutation rate γ was 0.05. The population size N was 3600.

The first part of experiments focused on comparing the computing time necessary to construct a trading expert in the sequential approach and the parallel approach with many-core graphics processors. In the sequential approach, the Intel Pentium Core2Duo 3GHz processor was used. In the parallel approach, the NVidia GeForce GTX 280 graphics card was used.

Table 3 presents a summary of the comparison of the computing time. The first two rows correspond to the algorithm with local search turned off. The next two rows correspond to the algorithm with reduced local search, where only $0.04 \cdot d$ randomly chosen genes were examined. The last two rows correspond to the algorithm with full local search (experiments with the sequential algorithm were stopped after 6 hours).

Not surprisingly, the parallel approach outperformed the sequential one in terms of the computing time and enabled to process the cases that were impractical for the sequential approach.

The second part of experiments focused on evaluating the financial relevance of the investment strategies discovered. It focused on the parallel approach, because the financial relevance of both approaches are similar, the difference lies in the computing time.

Figure 1 (a) presents the evolution of the probability model for one chosen experiment with the dataset concerning Neopost (other experiments gave similar results).

Table 3. Comparison of the computing time necessary to construct a trading expert in the sequential and parallel approach (average times for 8 runs)

	parallel	sequential
1000 iterations, without local search	50 s	5 min
5000 iterations, without local search	240 s	25 min
1000 iterations, with reduced local search	2.5 min	11 min
5000 iterations, with reduced local search	12 min	55 min
1000 iterations, with full local search	28 min	> 6 h
5000 iterations, with full local search	2 h	> 6 h

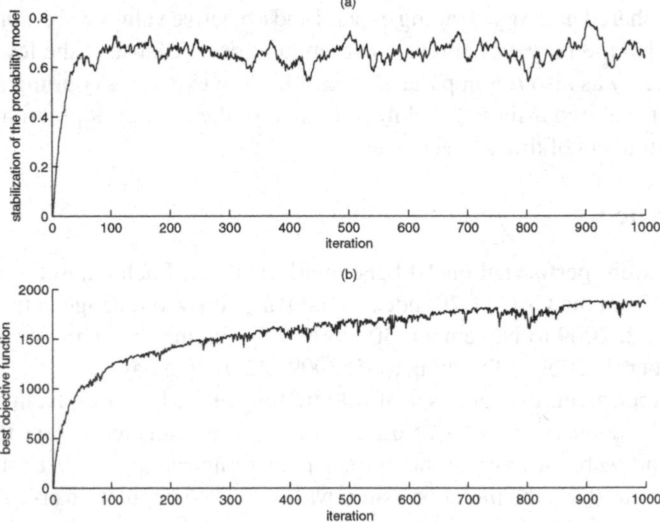

Fig. 1. Evolution of the probability model and the objective function values in successive iterations for an experiment with the dataset concerning Neopost

For each iteration, a stabilization factor ξ was evaluated on the probability model $\mathbf{p} = (p_1, p_2, \ldots, p_d)$ in such a way that

$$\xi = \frac{4}{d} \cdot \sum_{i=1}^{d} (p_i - 0.5)^2, \qquad (1)$$

so that $\xi \approx 0$ denotes that most of p_i are close to 0.5 (i.e. probabilities of including and excluding the i-th trading rule are similar – the model not stabilized) and $\xi \approx 1$ denotes that most of p_i are either close to 0 or to 1 (i.e. the i-th trading rule either should be, or should not be, included in the efficient trading expert – the model stabilized). Figure 1 (b) presents the evolution of the maximum objective function value in successive populations for the same experiment. It is easy to see that the evolutionary algorithm is capable of optimizing the objective function in successive iterations. In addition to this, the model varies and is not stabilized even after a large number of iterations, which

Table 4. Financial relevance of the investment strategies discovered (average values for 8 runs)

Stock	ISIN	Training Time	Training Sharpe Ratio	Training Return Rate	Test Return Rate	Test B&H
Alcatel-Lucent	FR0000130007	52 s	28.19	264.77	1.33	5.84
Alstom	FR0010220475	180 s	20.05	107.89	0.72	4.92
Cap Gemini	FR0000125338	104 s	21.02	75.86	3.20	3.48
France Telecom	FR0000133308	98 s	10.97	18.28	0.08	0.24
Legrand	FR0010307819	69 s	22.96	64.57	1.79	6.09
Neopost	FR0000120560	74 s	19.43	40.25	0.62	-1.15
Schneider Electric	FR0000121972	113 s	25.87	88.43	6.68	11.91
STMicroelectronics	NL0000226223	139 s	20.07	92.76	5.97	19.73
TF1	FR0000054900	83 s	25.72	202.95	1.40	8.29
Vivendi	FR0000127771	127 s	16.19	41.08	2.61	8.03

enables further optimization of the objective function. It may also mean that the search space is irregular and contains many local optima.

Finally, Table 4 presents the financial relevance of the investment strategies discovered. The first two columns define the dataset, the third column presents the computing time to find the best trading expert (for the parallel approach with reduced local search). The next two columns concern the training period and present the Sharpe ratio and the average return rate. The last two columns concern the testing period and present the return rate and the Buy-and-Hold benchmark, which consists of investing the entire cash in stocks at the beginning and keeping it until the end of the testing period. In all the experiments, the investment strategy discovered had a positive return rate. In one case, the dataset concerning Neopost, the investment strategy discovered outperformed the Buy-and-Hold benchmark.

6 Conclusions

This paper proposed a hybrid evolutionary algorithm with local search for many-core graphics processors for building efficient trading experts. Parallelization of the sequential approach concerned population evaluation and local search. Despite some constraints of many-core graphics processors, mainly related to memory management, the parallel approach not surprisingly outperformed the sequential approach and enabled to process the cases that were impractical for the sequential approach.

However, further research on parallelization of the approach may lead to additional improvements. First, recent developments in many-core graphics processors in CUDA 3.0 led to a new mechanism of memory management with up to 64kB of shared memory for a block of threads and the 2nd level cache, which allows to load permanent data, such as financial time series and trading rule signals, to the shared memory in order to speed up computation. Second, other models of the thread organization should be studied in order to optimally balance computation on multiprocessors. Third, parallelization may also be applied to other parts of the evolutionary algorithms, such as finding the best trading expert (searching through the population), updating and mutating the probability model.

Finally, further studies on parallelization of other evolutionary algorithms, such as SGA, ECGA or BOA, which may solve the optimization problem more efficiently, may reduce the computing time of more advanced approaches.

References

1. Baluja, S.: Population-Based Incremental Learning: A Method for Integrating Genetic Search Based Function Optimization and Competitive Learning, Research Report CMU-CS-94-163, Carnegie Mellon University (1994)
2. Brabazon, A., O'Neill, M.: Biologically Inspired Algorithms for Financial Modelling. Springer, Heidelberg (2006)
3. Dang, J., Brabazon, A., O'Neill, M., Edelman, D.: Estimation of an EGARCH Volatility Option Pricing Model using a Bacteria Foraging Optimisation Algorithm. In: Natural Computing in Computational Finance. Studies in Computational Intelligence, vol. 100, pp. 109–127. Springer, Heidelberg (2008)
4. Dempsey, I., O'Neill, M., Brabazon, A.: Adaptive Trading with Grammatical Evolution. In: Proceedings of the 2006 Congress on Evolutionary Computation, CEC 2006, pp. 2587–2592. IEEE, Los Alamitos (2006)
5. Korczak, J., Lipinski, P.: Evolutionary Building of Stock Trading Experts in a Real-Time System. In: Proceedings of the 2004 Congress on Evolutionary Computation, CEC 2004, pp. 940–947. IEEE, Los Alamitos (2004)
6. Larranaga, P., Lozano, J.: Estimation of Distribution Algorithms, A New Tool for Evolutionary Computation. Kluwer Academic Publishers, Dordrecht (2002)
7. Lipinski, P.: Evolutionary Decision Support System for Stock Market Trading. In: Dochev, D., Pistore, M., Traverso, P. (eds.) AIMSA 2008. LNCS (LNAI), vol. 5253, pp. 405–409. Springer, Heidelberg (2008)
8. Lipinski, P.: Evolutionary Strategies for Building Risk-Optimal Portfolios. In: Natural Computing in Computational Finance. Studies in Computational Intelligence, vol. 100, pp. 53–65. Springer, Heidelberg (2008)
9. Murphy, J.: Technical Analysis of the Financial Markets, NUIF (1998)
10. Saks, P., Maringer, D.: Evolutionary Money Management. In: Giacobini, M., Brabazon, A., Cagnoni, S., Di Caro, G.A., Ekárt, A., Esparcia-Alcázar, A.I., Farooq, M., Fink, A., Machado, P. (eds.) EvoWorkshops 2009. LNCS, vol. 5484, pp. 162–171. Springer, Heidelberg (2009)
11. Sharpe, W.: Capital Asset Prices: A Theory of Market Equilibrium under Conditions of Risk. Journal of Finance 19, 425–442 (1964)
12. Tsang, E., Li, J., Markose, S., Er, H., Salhi, A., Iori, G.: EDDIE In Financial Decision Making. Journal of Management and Economics 4(4) (2000)

Numerical Methods for the Lévy LIBOR Model

Antonis Papapantoleon[1,2] and David Skovmand[3]

[1] Institute of Mathematics, TU Berlin, Straße des 17. Juni 136, 10623 Berlin, Germany
[2] Quantitative Products Laboratory, Deutsche Bank AG, Alexanderstr. 5, 10178 Berlin, Germany
papapan@math.tu-berlin.de
[3] Aarhus School of Business, Aarhus University, Fuglesangs Allé 4, 8210 Aarhus V, Denmark
davids@asb.dk

Abstract. The aim of this work is to provide fast and accurate approximation schemes for the Monte Carlo pricing of derivatives in the Lévy LIBOR model of Eberlein and Özkan [4]. Standard methods can be applied to solve the stochastic differential equations of the successive LIBOR rates but the methods are generally slow. We propose an alternative approximation scheme based on Picard approximations. Our approach is similar in accuracy to the full numerical solution, but with the feature that each rate is evolved independently of the other rates in the term structure. This enables simultaneous calculation of derivative prices of different maturities using parallel computing. We include numerical illustrations of the accuracy and speed of our method pricing caplets.

Keywords: LIBOR models, Lévy processes, Lévy LIBOR model, Picard approximation, parallel computing.

1 Introduction

The LIBOR market model has become a standard model for the pricing of interest rate derivatives in recent years. The main advantage of the LIBOR model in comparison to other approaches, is that the evolution of discretely compounded, market-observable forward rates is modeled directly and not deduced from the evolution of unobservable factors. Moreover, the log-normal LIBOR model is consistent with the market practice of pricing caps according to Black's formula (cf. [2]). However, despite its apparent popularity, the LIBOR market model has certain well-known pitfalls.

On the one hand, the log-normal LIBOR model is driven by a Brownian motion, hence it cannot be calibrated adequately to the observed market data. An interest rate model is typically calibrated to the implied volatility surface from the cap market and the correlation structure of at-the-money swaptions. Several extensions of the LIBOR model have been proposed in the literature using jump-diffusions, Lévy processes or general semimartingales as the driving

M.R. Guarracino et al. (Eds.): Euro-Par 2010 Workshops, LNCS 6586, pp. 463–470, 2011.
© Springer-Verlag Berlin Heidelberg 2011

motion (cf. e.g. Glasserman and Kou [5], Eberlein and Özkan [4], Jamshidian [7]), or incorporating stochastic volatility effects (cf. e.g. Andersen and Brotherton-Ratcliffe [1]).

On the other hand, the dynamics of LIBOR rates are not tractable under every forward measure due to the random terms that enter the dynamics of LIBOR rates during the construction of the model. In particular, when the driving process has continuous paths the dynamics of LIBOR rates are tractable under their corresponding forward measure, but they are not tractable under any other forward measure. When the driving process is a general semimartingale, then the dynamics of LIBOR rates are not even tractable under their very own forward measure. Consequently: if the driving process is a *continuous* semimartingale caplets can be priced in closed form, but *not* swaptions or other multi-LIBOR derivatives. However, if the driving process is a *general* semimartingale, then even caplets *cannot* be priced in closed form. The standard remedy to this problem is the so-called "frozen drift" approximation, where one replaces the random terms in the dynamics of LIBOR rates by their deterministic initial values; it was first proposed by Brace et al. [3] for the pricing of swaptions and has been used by several authors ever since.

Although the frozen drift approximation is the simplest and most popular solution, it is well-known that it does not yield acceptable results, especially for exotic derivatives and longer horizons. Therefore, several other approximations have been developed in the literature. We refer the reader to Joshi and Stacey [8] for a detailed overview of that literature, and for some new approximation schemes and numerical experiments.

In this article we develop a general method for the approximation of the random terms in the drift of LIBOR models. In particular, by applying Picard iterations we develop a generic approximation where the individual rates can be evolved independently in a Monte Carlo simulation. This enables the use of parallel computing in the maturity dimension. Our method is universal and can be applied to any LIBOR model driven by a general semimartingale. We illustrate the accuracy and speed of our method in a case where LIBOR rates are driven by a normal inverse Gaussian process.

2 The Lévy LIBOR Model

The Lévy LIBOR model was developed by Eberlein and Özkan [4], following the seminal articles of Sandmann et al. [11], Miltersen et al. [9] and Brace et al. [3] on LIBOR market models driven by Brownian motion; see also Glasserman and Kou [5] and Jamshidian [7] for LIBOR models driven by jump processes and general semimartingales respectively. The Lévy LIBOR model is a *market model* where the forward LIBOR rate is modeled directly, and is driven by a time-inhomogeneous Lévy process.

Let $0 = T_0 < T_1 < \cdots < T_N < T_{N+1} = T_*$ denote a discrete tenor structure where $\delta_i = T_{i+1} - T_i$, $i \in \{0, 1, \ldots, N\}$. Consider a complete stochastic basis $(\Omega, \mathcal{F}, \mathbf{F}, \mathbb{P}_{T_*})$ and a time-inhomogeneous Lévy process $H = (H_t)_{0 \leq t \leq T_*}$

satisfying standard assumptions such as the existence of exponential moments and absolutely continuous characteristics. The law of H_t is described by the Lévy–Khintchine formula:

$$\mathbb{E}_{\mathbb{P}_{T_*}}\left[e^{iuH_t}\right] = \exp\left(\int_0^t \kappa_s(iu)ds\right). \tag{1}$$

Here κ_s is the *cumulant generating function* associated to the infinitely divisible distribution with Lévy triplet $(0, c, F^{T_*})$, i.e. for $u \in \mathbb{R}$ and $s \in [0, T_*]$

$$\kappa_s(iu) = -\frac{c_s}{2}u^2 + \int_{\mathbb{R}} (e^{iux} - 1 - iux)F_s^{T_*}(dx). \tag{2}$$

The canonical decomposition of H is:

$$H = \int_0^\cdot \sqrt{c_s} dW_s^{T_*} + \int_0^\cdot \int_{\mathbb{R}} x(\mu^H - \nu^{T_*})(ds, dx), \tag{3}$$

where W^{T_*} is a $\mathbb{P}_{T_*}$-standard Brownian motion, μ^H is the random measure associated with the jumps of H and ν^{T_*} is the $\mathbb{P}_{T_*}$-compensator of μ^H. We further assume that the following conditions are in force.

(LR1). For any maturity T_i there exists a bounded, continuous, deterministic function $\lambda(\cdot, T_i) : [0, T_i] \to \mathbb{R}$, which represents the volatility of the forward LIBOR rate process $L(\cdot, T_i)$. Moreover, we assume that (i) for all $s \in [0, T_*]$, there exist $M, \epsilon > 0$ such that $\int_0^{T_*} \int_{\{|x|>1\}} e^{ux} F_t(dx)dt < \infty$, for $u \in [-(1 + \varepsilon)M, (1 + \varepsilon)M]$, and (ii) for all $s < T_i$

$$\sum_{i-1}^{N} \left|\lambda(s, T_i)\right| \leq M.$$

(LR2). The initial term structure $B(0, T_i)$, $1 \leq i \leq N + 1$, is strictly positive and strictly decreasing. Consequently, the initial term structure of forward LIBOR rates is given, for $1 \leq i \leq N$, by

$$L(0, T_i) = \frac{1}{\delta_i}\left(\frac{B(0, T_i)}{B(0, T_i + \delta_i)} - 1\right) > 0. \tag{4}$$

The construction of the model starts by postulating that the dynamics of the forward LIBOR rate with the longest maturity $L(\cdot, T_N)$ is driven by the time-inhomogeneous Lévy process H and evolve as a martingale under the terminal forward measure $\mathbb{P}_{T_*}$. Then, the dynamics of the LIBOR rates for the preceding maturities are constructed by backward induction; they are driven by the same process H and evolve as martingales under their associated forward measures. For the full mathematical construction we refer to [4].

We will now proceed to introduce the stochastic differential equation that the dynamics of log-LIBOR rates satisfy under the terminal measure $\mathbb{P}_{T_*}$. This will be the starting point for the approximation method that will be developed in the next section.

In the Lévy LIBOR model the dynamics of the LIBOR rate $L(\cdot, T_i)$ under the terminal forward measure $\mathbb{P}_{T_*}$ are given by

$$L(t,T_i) = L(0,T_i)\exp\left(\int_0^t b(s,T_i)\mathrm{d}s + \int_0^t \lambda(s,T_i)\mathrm{d}H_s\right), \tag{5}$$

where $H = (H_t)_{0\le t\le T_*}$ is the $\mathbb{P}_{T_*}$-time-inhomogeneous Lévy process. The drift term $b(\cdot, T_i)$ is determined by no-arbitrage conditions and has the form

$$\begin{aligned} b(s,T_i) = &-\frac{1}{2}\lambda^2(s,T_i)c_s - c_s\lambda(s,T_i)\sum_{l=i+1}^{N}\frac{\delta_l L(s-,T_l)}{1+\delta_l L(s-,T_l)}\lambda(s,T_l)\\ &-\int_{\mathbb{R}}\left(\left(\mathrm{e}^{\lambda(s,T_i)x}-1\right)\prod_{l=i+1}^{N}\beta(s,x,T_l)-\lambda(s,T_i)x\right)F_s^{T_*}(\mathrm{d}x), \end{aligned} \tag{6}$$

where

$$\beta(t,x,T_l,) = \frac{\delta_l L(t-,T_l)}{1+\delta_l L(t-,T_l)}\left(\mathrm{e}^{\lambda(t,T_l)x}-1\right)+1. \tag{7}$$

Note that the drift term in (5) is random, therefore we are dealing with a general semimartingale, and not with a Lévy process. Of course, $L(\cdot, T_i)$ is not a $\mathbb{P}_{T_*}$-martingale, unless $i = N$ (we use the conventions $\sum_{l=1}^{0} = 0$ and $\prod_{l=1}^{0} = 1$).

Let us denote by Z the log-LIBOR rates, that is

$$\begin{aligned} Z(t,T_i) &:= \log L(t,T_i)\\ &= Z(0,T_i) + \int_0^t b(s,T_i)\mathrm{d}s + \int_0^t \lambda(s,T_i)\mathrm{d}H_s, \end{aligned} \tag{8}$$

where $Z(0,T_i) = \log L(0,T_i)$ for all $i \in \{1,\dots,N\}$.

Remark 1. Note that the martingale part of $Z(\cdot, T_i)$, i.e. the stochastic integral $\int_0^{\cdot} \lambda(s,T_i)\mathrm{d}H_s$, is a time-inhomogeneous Lévy process. However, the random drift term destroys the Lévy property of $Z(\cdot, T_i)$, as the increments are no longer independent.

3 Picard Approximation for LIBOR Models

The log-LIBOR can be alternatively described as a solution to the following linear SDE

$$\mathrm{d}Z(t,T_i) = b(t,T_i)\mathrm{d}t + \lambda(t,T_i)\mathrm{d}H_t, \tag{9}$$

with initial condition $Z(0,T_i) = \log L(0,T_i)$. Let us look further into the above SDE for the log-LIBOR rates. We introduce the term $Z(\cdot)$ in the drift term

$b(\cdot, T_i; Z(\cdot))$ to make explicit that the log-LIBOR rates depend on all subsequent rates on the tenor.

The idea behind the Picard approximation scheme is to approximate the drift term in the dynamics of the LIBOR rates; this approximation is achieved by the Picard iterations for (9). The first Picard iteration for (9) is simply the initial value, i.e.

$$Z^{(0)}(t, T_i) = Z(0, T_i), \tag{10}$$

while the second Picard iteration is

$$\begin{aligned} Z^{(1)}(t, T_i) &= Z(0, T_i) + \int_0^t b(s, T_i; Z^{(0)}(s))\mathrm{d}s + \int_0^t \lambda(s, T_i)\mathrm{d}H_s \\ &= Z(0, T_i) + \int_0^t b(s, T_i; Z(0))\mathrm{d}s + \int_0^t \lambda(s, T_i)\mathrm{d}H_s. \end{aligned} \tag{11}$$

Since the drift term $b(\cdot, T_i; Z(0))$ is deterministic, as the random terms have been replaced with their initial values, we can easily deduce that the second Picard iterate $Z^{(1)}(\cdot, T_i)$ is a Lévy process and equivalent to the well known frozen drift approximation. Finally a third Picard iteration can be performed to get a more refined approximation:

$$Z^{(2)}(t, T_i) = Z(0, T_i) + \int_0^t b(s, T_i; Z^{(1)}(s))\mathrm{d}s + \int_0^t \lambda(s, T_i)\mathrm{d}H_s, \tag{12}$$

This process is clearly no longer a Lévy process due to dependence on $Z^{(1)}(s)$ in the drift. However, the main advantage is that the resulting SDE for $Z^{(2)}(\cdot, T_i)$ can be simulated more easily than the equation for $Z(\cdot, T_i)$. Indeed, looking at (9) and (6) again, we can observe that each log-LIBOR rate $Z(\cdot, T_i)$ depends on all subsequent log-rates $Z(\cdot, T_l)$, $i+1 \le l \le N$. Hence, in order to simulate $Z(\cdot, T_i)$, we should start by simulating the furthest rate in the tenor and proceed iteratively from the end. On the contrary, the dynamics of $Z^{(2)}(\cdot, T_i)$ depend only on the Lévy processes $Z^{(1)}(\cdot, T_l)$, $i+1 \le l \le N$, which are independent of each other. Hence, we can use *parallel computing* to simulate all approximate LIBOR rates simultaneously. This significantly increases the speed of the Monte Carlo simulations as will be demonstrated in the numerical example.

3.1 Caplets

The price of a caplet with strike K maturing at time T_i, using the relationship between the terminal and the forward measures can be expressed as

$$\mathbb{C}_0(K, T_i) = \delta_i B(0, T_*)\, \mathrm{E}_{\mathbf{P}_{T_*}}\Big[\prod_{l=i+1}^{N} \big(1 + \delta_l L(T_i, T_l)\big)(L(T_i, T_i) - K)^+ \Big]. \tag{13}$$

This equation will provide the actual prices of caplets corresponding to simulating the full SDE for the LIBOR rates. In order to calculate the Picard approximation prices for a caplet we have to replace $L(\cdot, T_\cdot)$ in (13) with $L^{(2)}(\cdot, T_\cdot)$. Similarly, for the frozen drift approximation prices we must use $L^{(1)}(\cdot, T_\cdot)$ instead of $L(\cdot, T_\cdot)$.

4 Numerical Illustration

The aim of this section is to demonstrate the accuracy and efficiency of the Picard approximation scheme for the valuation of options in the Lévy LIBOR model. We will consider the pricing of caplets, although many other interest rate derivatives can be considered in this framework.

We will examine a simple example with a flat volatility structure of $\lambda(\cdot, T_i) = 18\%$ and zero coupon rates generated from a flat term structure of interest rates: $B(0, T_i) = \exp(-0.04 \cdot T_i)$. The tenor structure has 6 month increments (i.e. $\delta_i = \frac{1}{2}$).

The driving Lévy process H is a normal inverse Gaussian (NIG) process with parameters $\alpha = \bar{\delta} = 12$ and $\mu = \beta = 0$, resulting in a process with mean zero and variance 1. We denote by μ^H the random measure of jumps of H and by $\nu(\mathrm{d}t, \mathrm{d}x) = F(\mathrm{d}x)\mathrm{d}t$ the $\mathbb{P}_{T_*}$-compensator of μ^H, where F is the Lévy measure of the NIG process. The necessary conditions are then satisfied for term structures up to 30 years of length because $M = \alpha$, hence $\sum_{i=1}^{60} |\lambda(\cdot, T_i)| = 10.8 < \alpha$. The NIG Lévy process is a pure-jump process with canonical decomposition

$$H = \int_0^\cdot \int_{\mathbb{R}} x(\mu^H - \nu)(\mathrm{d}s, \mathrm{d}x). \tag{14}$$

The cumulant generating function of the NIG distribution, for all $u \in \mathbb{C}$ with $|\Re u| \leq \alpha$, is

$$\kappa(u) = \bar{\delta}\alpha - \bar{\delta}\sqrt{\alpha^2 - u^2}. \tag{15}$$

4.1 Accuracy of the Method

The Picard approximation should be considered primarily as a parallelizable alternative to the standard Euler discretization of the model. The Euler scheme will therefore be the benchmark to which we compare. In order to avoid Monte Carlo error we use the same discretization grid (5 steps per tenor increment) and the same pseudo random numbers (50000 paths) for each method. The pseudo random numbers are generated from the NIG distribution using the standard methodology described in Glasserman [6].

Figure 1 shows the difference between the Euler discretization and the frozen drift (9) and Picard approximation (12) respectively. The difference in price is expressed in basis point of implied volatility. As can been seen the errors from the Picard approximation are a full order of magnitude smaller than the errors from the frozen drift. Implied volatility is normally quoted in units of 1 basis point while bid-ask spreads are usually around at least 5 bp of implied volatility. The errors from the Picard approximation are therefore at acceptable levels. Note also that in experiments not shown we found that the levels and patterns of the errors are insensitive to the number of discretization points as well the number of paths.

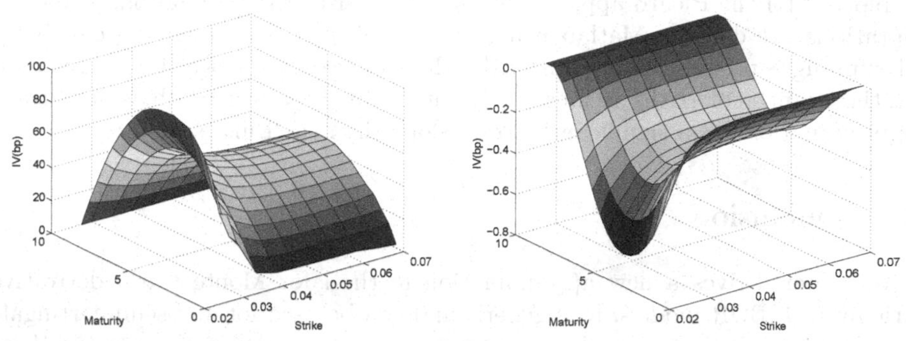

Fig. 1. Difference in implied caplet volatility (in basis points) between the Euler discretization and the frozen drift prices (left), and the Euler discretization and the Picard approximation (right)

The errors display a non-monotonic behavior as a function of maturity with peaks around mid-maturity. The non-monotonicity can be explained by the fact that volatility dominates the price of options in the short end, making the drift, and any error in it, less relevant. As maturity increases the importance of the drift grows relative to volatility but the state dependence becomes less critical as the number of "live" rates decreases. These two opposing effects result in the mid-maturity peak that we observe. This pattern is also noted in the study by Joshi and Stacey [8].

4.2 Speed of the Method

The gains from parallelization using the Picard approximation can be seen in Figure 2. There, indicative CPU times as a function of the number of paths

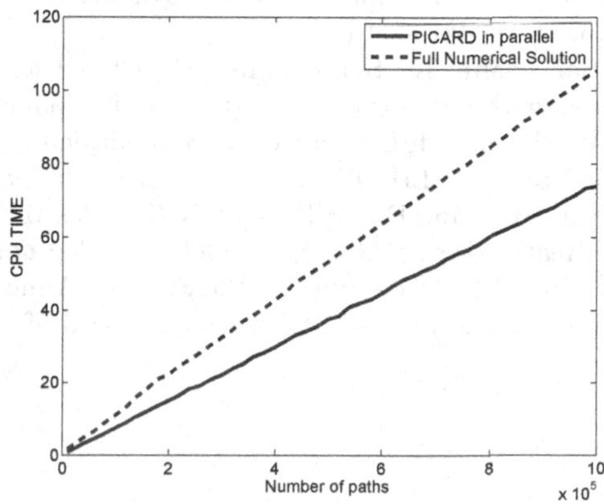

Fig. 2. CPU time vs. number of paths

is plotted for the Picard approximation and the Euler discretization. The computations are done in Matlab using an Intel i7 processor with the capability of running 8 processes simultaneously. Here we see the typical linear behavior as the number of paths is increased, but it can be observed that the Picard approximation has a significantly lower slope than the Euler scheme.

5 Conclusion

This paper derives a new approximation method for Monte Carlo derivative pricing in LIBOR models. It is generic and can be used for any semimartingale driven model. It decouples the interdependence of the rates when moving them forward in time in a simulation, meaning that the computations can be parallelized in the maturity dimension. We have demonstrated both the accuracy and speed of the method in a numerical example. The interested reader is referred to Papapantoleon and Skovmand [10] for a more detailed analysis.

References

1. Andersen, L., Brotherton-Ratcliffe, R.: Extended LIBOR market models with stochastic volatility. J. Comput. Finance 9, 1–40 (2005)
2. Black, F.: The pricing of commodity contracts. J. Financ. Econ. 3, 167–179 (1976)
3. Brace, A., Gątarek, D., Musiela, M.: The market model of interest rate dynamics. Math. Finance 7, 127–155 (1997)
4. Eberlein, E., Özkan, F.: The Lévy LIBOR model. Finance Stoch. 9, 327–348 (2005)
5. Glasserman, P., Kou, S.G.: The term structure of simple forward rates with jump risk. Math. Finance 13, 383–410 (2003)
6. Glasserman, P.: Monte Carlo Methods in Financial Engineering. Springer, Heidelberg (2003)
7. Jamshidian, F.: LIBOR market model with semimartingales. Working Paper, NetAnalytic Ltd (1999)
8. Joshi, M., Stacey, A.: New and robust drift approximations for the LIBOR market model. Quant. Finance 8, 427–434 (2008)
9. Miltersen, K.R., Sandmann, K., Sondermann, D.: Closed form solutions for term structure derivatives with log-normal interest rates. J. Finance 52, 409–430 (1997)
10. Papapantoleon, A., Skovmand, D.: Picard approximation of stochastic differential equations and application to LIBOR models. Preprint, arXiv/1007:3362 (2010)
11. Sandmann, K., Sondermann, D., Miltersen, K.R.: Closed form term structure derivatives in a Heath–Jarrow–Morton model with log-normal annually compounded interest rates. In: Proceedings of the Seventh Annual European Futures Research Symposium Bonn, pp. 145–165. Chicago Board of Trade (1995)

Measuring Default Risk in a Parallel ALM Software for Life Insurance Portfolios

Stefania Corsaro[1,2], Zelda Marino[1], Francesca Perla[1,2], and Paolo Zanetti[1]

[1] Dipartimento di Statistica e Matematica per la Ricerca Economica
Università degli Studi di Napoli "Parthenope"
Via Medina 40, I-80133 Napoli, Italy
{corsaro,marino,perla,zanetti}@uniparthenope.it

[2] Istituto di Calcolo e Reti ad Alte Prestazioni (ICAR-CNR)
Via Pietro Castellino 111, I-80131 Napoli, Italy

Abstract. In this paper we investigate the computational issues in the use of a stochastic model – the *doubly stochastic intensity default* model – to measure *default risk* in the development of "internal models", according to the new rules of the Solvency II project. We refer to the valuation framework used in DISAR, an asset-liability management system for the monitoring of portfolios of "Italian style" profit sharing life insurance policies with minimum guarantees. The computational complexity of the overall valuation process requires both efficient numerical algorithms and high performance computing methodologies and resources. Then, to improve the performance, we apply to DISAR a parallelisation strategy based on the distribution of Monte Carlo simulations among the processors of a last generation blade server.

Keywords: high performance computing, credit risk, life insurance policies, asset-liability management, reduced-form models.

1 Introduction

The aim of the work is to investigate the computational issues in the use of stochastic models to measure *default risk* in the development of "internal models", according to the rules of the European Directive 2009/138 (Solvency II) [7].

The analysis is carried out on "Italian style" *profit sharing* (PS) *life insurance policies* with minimum guarantees, briefly introduced in Sect. 2. In these contracts, the benefits which are credited to the policyholder are indexed to the annual return of a specified investment portfolio (*segregated fund*); the return is transferred to the policyholders by retrocession. Then, a part of the counterparty default risk falls on the insurance company, because of the minimum guarantees, and a part is transferred to the policyholders, by the retrocession mechanism.

We consider a *reduced-form* approach, illustrated in Sect. 3, for valuing defaultable bonds in the segregated fund, by modeling the default probability by means of a suitable stochastic *intensity process* [6,8,9].

M.R. Guarracino et al. (Eds.): Euro-Par 2010 Workshops, LNCS 6586, pp. 471–478, 2011.
© Springer-Verlag Berlin Heidelberg 2011

We use the DISAR (Dynamic Investment Strategy with Accounting Rules) system [2] – an Asset Liability Management (ALM) system – as valuation framework.

From the computational point of view, the implementation of stochastic models for default risk in ALM procedures implies a rise of computational complexity. In [2] a computing grid approach is adopted to monitor portfolios of profit sharing policies. Here, as shown in Sect. 5, we improve the performance by parallelising Monte Carlo simulations [3], the most time consuming tasks involved in the valuation process.

2 Valuation Framework: The DISAR System

We use the valuation framework of DISAR [2], a risk-management system designed to monitor portfolios of Italian style PS policies with minimum guarantees. A profit sharing policy is a "complex" structured contract, with underlying the segregated fund return; the models for values and risks evaluation of the policy must provide "market-consistent valuation", thus requiring the use of a stochastic framework and of Monte Carlo simulation techniques. For an exhaustive analysis of the basic principles and the methodological approach for a valuation system of profit sharing policies with minimum guarantees we address to [4,5].

The core of the problem is the computation, at the evaluation time ($t = 0$), of the *stochastic reserve* $V_0(Y_T)$ (see [2], eq. (3) and [5], eq. (15)), that plays a crucial role for the insurance company. The annual minimum guarantees in PS policies imply that a series of financial options written on the segregated fund return are embedded in the policies. The stochastic reserve $V_0(Y_T)$ can be expressed using either a put or a call decomposition (see [2], eq. (4) and [5], p. 91)

$$V_0(Y_T) = B_0 + P_0 = G_0 + C_0, \tag{1}$$

where B_0 is the "base value" of the policy and P_0 is the value of a put option; G_0 is the cost of the non-participating policy and C_0 is the participating cost.

About the financial risks evaluation models, for the interest rate risk we refer to the well-known one-factor Cox, Ingersoll and Ross (CIR) model. In this work, we just consider the risk-neutral dynamics of the spot rate, $r(u)$, since the risk adjusted parameters, usually denoted in literature with $r(0)$, $\tilde{\alpha}$, $\tilde{\gamma}$, and ρ (see [4], p. 38), are the parameters required when the CIR model has to be used for pricing purpose. We do not consider the computation of the risk-capital (the Solvency Capital Requirement, SCR, in Solvency II jargon).

In a risk-neutral setting, it is well known that the closed form of the price at time $t = 0$ of the unitary default-free zero-coupon bond (zcb) with maturity T, that is the value of the risk-free discount factor, $B(0,T)$ is available [4].

3 Stochastic Default Risk Simulation

In the last decade, *reduced-form* default risk models have become popular. According to these models, default is treated as an unexpected event with likelihood governed by a *default intensity process* [6,8,9,10].

In this work we refer to the reduced-form approach. The time of default τ is modeled as the first arrival time of a Poisson process with random arrival rate λ. We therefore consider a *doubly stochastic process*, in that we have two layers of uncertainty, both the time and the intensity of default [6]. In a risk-neutral setting, the survival probability in $[0, T]$ is given by

$$P(0,T) = E^Q\left[e^{-\int_0^T \lambda(u)du}\right],$$

where Q denotes, as usual, the risk-neutral measure. A very useful result, proven by Lando [9], provides the following expression for the price at time 0 of a defaultable unitary zcb with maturity T, that is the value of the risky discount factor, denoted by $\bar{B}(0,T)$, in terms of short rate and default intensity

$$\bar{B}(0,T) = E^Q\left[e^{-\int_0^T r(u)+\lambda(u)\, du}\right]. \tag{2}$$

We moreover assume r and λ to be stochastically independent; in this case, the expected value in (2) can be factorised in the following way [9,10]

$$\bar{B}(0,T) = B(0,T)P(0,T).$$

Defaultable coupon bonds may be valued as a linear combination of defaultable zero-coupon bonds [6].

We choose to model the default intensity λ following the CIR process; in a risk-neutral setting, the stochastic equation governing the process is

$$d\lambda(t) = \tilde{k}[\tilde{\theta} - \lambda(t)]\, dt + \sigma\sqrt{\lambda(t)}\, d\tilde{Z}_\lambda(t). \tag{3}$$

A closed form for survival probability in $[0, T]$ can be obtained, which depends on the parameters of the intensity process in (3) and on the value of λ at $t = 0$

$$P(0,T) = A_\lambda(0,T)e^{-\lambda(0)\beta_\lambda(0,T)}, \tag{4}$$

$$\text{where } A_\lambda(0,T) = \left[\frac{d_\lambda e^{\phi_\lambda T}}{\phi_\lambda(e^{d_\lambda T}-1)+d_\lambda}\right]^{\nu_\lambda}, \beta_\lambda(0,T) = \frac{e^{d_\lambda T}-1}{\phi_\lambda(e^{d_\lambda T}-1)+d_\lambda}$$

$$d_\lambda = \sqrt{\tilde{k}^2 + 2\sigma^2}, \quad \nu_\lambda = \frac{2\tilde{k}\tilde{\theta}}{\sigma^2}, \quad \phi_\lambda = \frac{\tilde{k}+d_\lambda}{2}, \tag{5}$$

following the Brown-Dybvig parametrisation [1].

3.1 The Data and Calibration Method

Our aim is to model the evolution of a collection of term structures of defaultable bonds credit spreads for different credit classes (ratings).

Let $\bar{B}_j(0,T)$ be the price, at time 0, of a zero-recovery zcb in the j-th credit class of corporate bonds with maturity T, we have

$$\bar{B}_j(0,T) = E^Q\left[e^{-\int_0^T r(u)+\lambda_j(u)\, du}\right]. \tag{6}$$

Hence, $\lambda_j(u)$ is the intensity of a Poisson process used to model the event of default of the j-th credit class.

The data. We refer to data on investment-grade bonds from Finance sector with Moody's rating Aa3 e Baa1. We consider current market data of a set of coupon bonds at the evaluation date April 30th 2010; we refer to the closing prices. We have initially examined 75 Aa3 and 62 Baa1 Finance corporate coupon bonds with residual maturities ranging from three months up to twenty years for Aa3 bonds and up to ten years for Baa1 ones.

Even within a fairly homogeneous credit quality sample, the credit spreads of some bonds can noticeably vary [10]. A problem which arises is then the removal of outliers. We use a two-stage procedure to remove outliers. In the first stage a bond is removed if its yield deviates more than twice the standard deviation from the average yield in the same maturity bracket. Afterwards, the same procedure is repeated[1].

The calibration method. Defaultable bond yields have two components: the risk-free interest rate and the default spread. We choose the risk-free term structure implied by the single-factor CIR model. Risk neutral parameters for CIR model have been calibrated on market data using the methodology described in [4] ($r(0) = 0.00560384$, $\tilde{\alpha} = 0.30368297$, $\tilde{\gamma} = 0.04367279$, $\rho = 0.13681307$).

We estimate the vector of default risk parameters, $(d_\lambda, \nu_\lambda, \phi_\lambda, \lambda(0))$, by performing a non-linear fit procedure on the two different sets of corporate bonds. The estimation is then done by means of a non linear least-square method that minimizes the sum of the quadratic differences between the market prices and the model prices.

In the calibration phase, the second stage of the outliers removal procedure, as described in [10], has been performed by removing those defaultable bonds whose pricing errors exceed two times the average root-mean square relative pricing errors; and afterwards by repeating the calibration procedure. For the implementation of the above calibration and selection procedure, we use the Matlab software environment (*trust-region reflective Newton* method).

At the end of the removal procedure, we obtain a set of 40 Aa3 and a set of 49 Baa1 Finance bonds.

In Table 1 we report the resulting estimates of the default risk parameters in (4) and (5), using the two different sets of selected corporate bonds, and the sample standard deviation of residuals.

In Fig. 1, for both the two credit classes, we plot on the left the term structures of credit spreads (in basis points), over a range of thirty years of maturities, obtained using the calibrated default risk parameters; in the same figure, on the right, we plot the related risk-neutral default intensity $\lambda(u)$. Credit spreads range from about 33 to 176 basis points for Aa3-rated zero-coupon bonds and from 101 to 219 basis points for Baa1-rated ones.

---

[1] We refer to a criteria applied by ECB when selecting bonds for the estimation of yield curves (www.ecb.int/stats/money/yc/html/index.en.html).

Table 1. Default risk parameters

$t = 04/30/2010$	Aa3-Finance	Baa1-Finance
$\lambda(t)$	0.00079011351155	0.00762255771740
d_λ	0.32209372929069	0.36215265757040
ϕ_λ	0.30328555876149	0.36208344131790
ν_λ	1.00000000000468	321.544667798335
sqmr	0.37561488234354	0.29840697224378

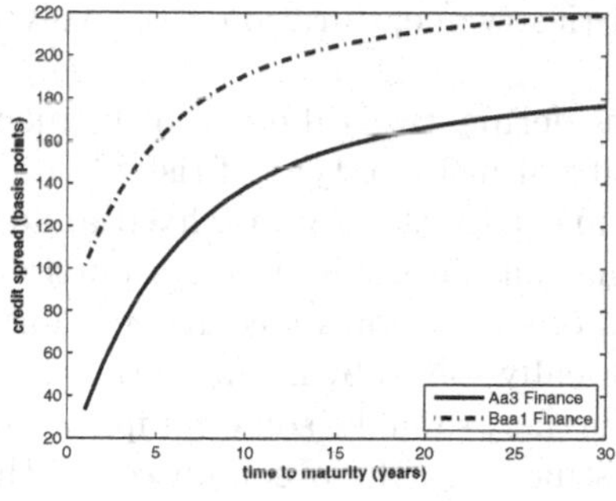

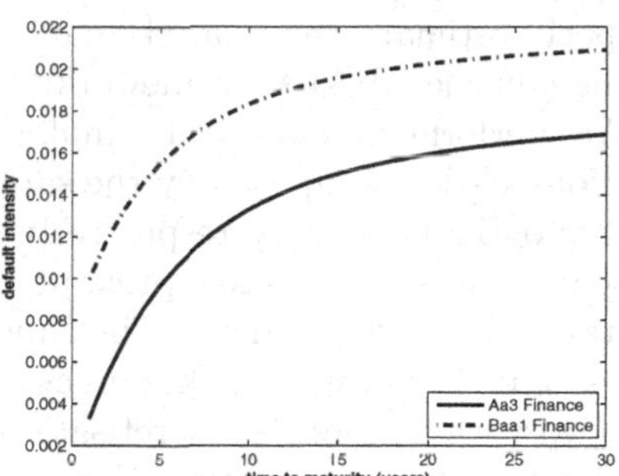

Fig. 1. Credit spreads term structure and default intensity for Aa3 and Baa1 Finance zcb

4 Computational Issues

Stochastic default risk simulation in DISAR increases the computational complexity of the system in terms of both amount of data to be managed and of computing time.

Specifically, the system has to be able to manage a set of default-risk adjusted term structures, each of them related to a combination of rating and economic sector – the choice of the combinations and the number of the term structures to consider depending on the company investment strategy –; the default intensity parameters computation requires a pre-processing phase implementing the procedure described in Sect. 3.1; this phase has an impact on the amount of data, needed to properly calibrate the parameters, to be included in the DataBase system; it has also an impact on the execution time required to perform the calibration procedure on each set of data.

After the pre-processing phase, the DataBase must be enriched with all the default risk parameters calibrated for each default intensity process; the DataBase Management System has to be able to identify and then to manage credit risky bonds on the basis of the appropriate rating and sector.

The default risk simulation in DIALMENG – the ALM computing unit of DISAR [2] – requires, for each set of calibrated default intensity parameters:

1 – simulation of stochastic default intensity processes,
2 – simulation of stochastic default probabilities,
3 – computation, at the evaluation date, of the default-risk adjusted term structures.

The simulations at points 1 and 2 require the use of numerical methods for solving stochastic differential equations (SDEs) and Monte Carlo methods. The computation at point 3 requires the evaluation of (6), for each considered class.

Each risky bond in the fund has to be managed in order to be "linked" to the pertaining default-risk adjusted term structure and default probabilities, to properly estimate the related financial quantities (value, duration, ...) involved in the considered ALM framework.

We performed numerical simulations considering two different investment portfolios, each composed by the same quantity of just one type of risky bond – Aa3 and Baa1 Finance, respectively –, with maturity three years, fixed annual coupons and same market price at the evaluation date. The policies portfolio contains about 200 policies. The time horizon of simulation we consider is forty years. The SDEs for the risk sources are numerically solved by means of the Euler method with a monthly discretisation step. Further, to make some comparisons, we carried out a simulation also on an investment portfolio composed by the same quantity of a risk-free coupon bond, with same maturity and market price.

The experiments have been carried out on an IBM Bladecenter installed at *Università di Napoli "Parthenope"*. It consists of 6 Blade LS 21, each one of which is equipped with 2 AMD Opteron 2210 and with 4 GB of RAM.

In Table 2 we report the values, in euro, of the stochastic reserve $V_0(Y_T)$ (and the related standard error) and of the components of the put and call decompositions in (1), for the three different segregated funds, obtained performing N=5000 Monte Carlo simulations.

Table 2. $V_0(Y_T)$, put and call components for three different segregated funds

N=5000	risk-free bond	Aa3-Finance bond	Baa1-Finance bond
$V_0(Y_T)$	711.793.017	716.334.673	722.241.384
std. err.	523.798	535.177	543.725
B_0	690.066.024	697.948.820	705.637.021
P_0	21.726.993	18.385.853	16.604.364
G_0	704.994.119	705.134.076	705.134.076
C_0	6.798.898	11.200.598	17.107.309

Table 3. Execution times (in seconds) for two different segregated funds

N	risk-free bond	Aa3-Finance bond	time increment
6000	135.812	163.423	20.3 %
12000	269	326.333	21.3 %

To quantify the increment of computing time overhead due to the stochastic default risk simulation, we report in Table 2 the execution times of the overall ALM procedure on the investment portfolio composed by risk-free coupon bonds and on that composed by Aa3-Finance risky bonds (the execution times being the same for the investment portfolio composed by the Baa1-Finance), respectively, for N=6000 and N=12000 MC simulations on one processor. We observe that the default risk valuation implies an increment of about 20% of the computing time, for both the considered values of N, including just one credit risk class in the investment portfolio.

5 Parallel Implementation and Performance Results

The most time consuming processes are those involved in MC simulation, thus an improvement of performance is achievable by parallelising the simulations, as we showed in [3]. Here we implement the same parallelisation strategy in DIALMENG.

We use the Mersenne-Twister generator included in the *Intel Math Kernel Library* for the generation of pseudo-random sequences. We use the MPI communication system to handle the message passing among the processors.

To analyse the performance of the parallel procedure, we report, on the left hand of Fig. 2, the execution times, expressed in seconds, for two values of global number of simulated trajectories, $N = 6000$ and $N = 12000$, versus the number of processors involved in the computation. To evaluate the parallel efficiency, we show, on the right hand of Fig. 2, the related speed-up. The graph reveals the good scalability properties of the algorithm. Indeed, speed-up is almost linear. The same behavior was observed in all our experiments.

procs	N = 6000	N = 12000
1	163.423	326.333
2	85.687	169.048
4	43.234	85.651
6	29.673	59.249
8	22.285	44.494
10	17.899	35.729
12	15.105	30.120

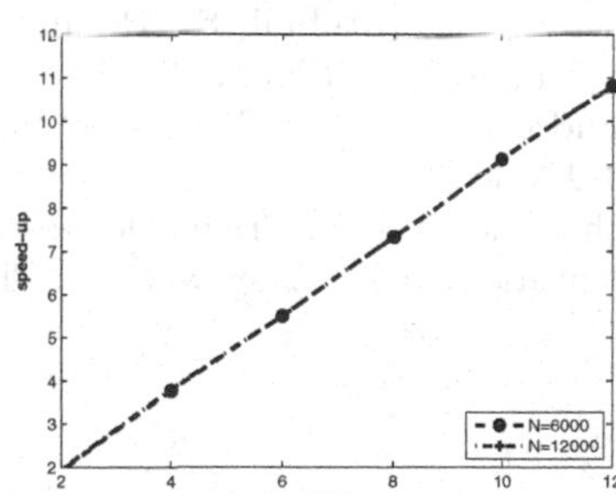

Fig. 2. On the left hand the execution time (in seconds); on the right hand the speed-up versus number of processors

6 Conclusions and Prospects

A market-consistent valuation of default risk is a very relevant task in the development of internal models. Nevertheless, stochastic default risk simulation increases the computational complexity of the valuation process, thus motivating the use of high performance computing. A parallelisation strategy, based on the distribution of Monte Carlo simulations among the processors of blade systems, allows to pull down the execution time, thus allowing to efficiently deal with this complex task. The combined use of the showed parallelisation strategy with a grid approach [2] could allow further reductions of the computing time, so the experimentation of new technology solutions, as, for example, gpu computing.

References

1. Brown, S.J., Dybvig, P.H.: The empirical implications of the Cox, Ingersoll, Ross theory of the term structure of interest rates. J. Financ. 41, 617–630 (1986)
2. Castellani, G., Passalacqua, L.: Applications of distributed and parallel computing in the Solvency II framework – the DISAR system. In: Guarracino, M.R., et al. (eds.) Euro-Par 2010 Workshops. LNCS, vol. 6586, pp. 413–422. Springer, Heidelberg (2011)
3. Corsaro, S., De Angelis, P.L., Marino, Z., Perla, F.: Participating life insurance policies: an accurate and efficient parallel software for COTS clusters. Comput. Manag. Science (2009) doi: 10.1007/s10827-009-0100-0
4. Castellani, G., De Felice, M., Moriconi, F., Pacati, C.: Embedded Value in Life Insurance, Working paper, 7.3 (2005)
5. De Felice, M., Moriconi, F.: Market Based Tools for Managing the Life Insurance Company. Astin Bulletin 35(1), 79–111 (2005)
6. Duffie, D., Singleton, K.J.: Modeling Term Structures of Defaultable Bonds. Rev. Financ. Stud. 12, 686–720 (1999)
7. Directive 2009/138/EC of the European Parliament and of the Council of 25 November 2009 on the taking-up and pursuit of the business of Insurance and Reinsurance. Official Journal of the European Union (2009)
8. Jarrow, R., Turnbull, S.: Pricing Derivatives on Financial Securities Subject to Default Risk. J. Financ. 50, 53–85 (1995)
9. Lando, D.: On Cox Processes and Credit Risky Securities. Rev. Deriv. Res. 2, 99–120 (1998)
10. Schonbucher, P.J.: Credit Derivatives Pricing Models - Models, Pricing and Implementation. John Wiley & Sons, Chichester (2005)

Third Workshop on Productivity and Performance

–

Tools for HPC Application Development (PROPER 2010)

PROPER 2010: Third Workshop on Productivity and Performance – Tools for HPC Application Development

Andreas Knüpfer[1], Jens Doleschal[1], Matthias Müller[1], and Felix Wolf[2]

[1] ZIH, TU Dresden, Germany
[2] GRS-SIM, Aachen, Germany

Foreword

The PROPER workshop addresses the need for productivity and performance in high performance computing. Productivity is an important objective during the development phase of HPC applications and their later production phase. Paying attention to the performance is important to achieve efficient usage of HPC machines. At the same time it is needed for scalability, which is crucial in two ways: Firstly, to use higher degrees of parallelism to reduce the wall clock time. And secondly, to cope with the next bigger problem, which requires more CPUs, memory, etc. to be able to compute it at all.

Tool support for the user is essential for productivity and performance. Therefore, the workshop covers tools and approaches for parallel program development and analysis, debugging and correctness checking, and for performance measurement and evaluation. Furthermore, it provides an opportunity to report successful optimization strategies with respect to scalability and performance.

This years contributions reflect this spectrum nicely. The invited paper by Torsten Höfler proposes to combine the so far disjoint approaches from performance modeling and tool based performance analysis. The paper by Chee Wai Lee et.al. presents an online extension to the TAU tools. Robert Schöne et.al. introduce a plug-in mechanism for adding new performance counter sources to the VampirTrace run-time measurement system. Judit Giménez et.al. propose a combined profiling and event tracing solution which is demonstrated with the Paraver tools. Christian Iwainsky et.al. present an in-depth analysis of memory access behavior on Intel Nehalem-EX CPUs. Stas Negara et.al. present the challenges of automatic transformation of MPI codes to adaptive MPI. Stefano Masini et.al. discuss the use of Python for HPC.

The PROPER workshop was initiated and is supported by the Virtual Institute - High Productivity Supercomputing (VI-HPS), an initiative to promote the development and integration of HPC programming tools.

October 2010

Andreas Knüpfer
Jens Doleschal
Matthias Müller
Felix Wolf

M.R. Guarracino et al. (Eds.): Euro-Par 2010 Workshops, LNCS 6586, p. 481, 2011.
© Springer-Verlag Berlin Heidelberg 2011

Bridging Performance Analysis Tools and Analytic Performance Modeling for HPC

Torsten Hoefler

University of Illinois at Urbana-Champaign, IL, USA
htor@illinois.edu

Abstract. Application performance is critical in high-performance computing (HPC), however, it is not considered in a systematic way in the HPC software development process. Integrated performance models could improve this situation. Advanced analytic performance modeling and performance analysis tools exist in isolation but have similar goals and could benefit mutually. We find that existing analysis tools could be extended to support analytic performance modeling and performance models could be used to improve the understanding of real application performance artifacts. We show a simple example of how a tool could support developers of analytic performance models. Finally, we propose to implement a strategy for integrated tool-supported performance modeling during the whole software development process.

1 Motivation

High performance computing (HPC) software development differs from traditional software development in several aspects. In addition to the forus on reliability, correctness and productivity, HPC software development strives to achieve maximum performance. This is reflected throughout the whole development process and tool-chain. HPC libraries and APIs such as BLAS, LAPACK, and the Message Passing Interface (MPI) focus mostly on the highest performance and performance portability. HPC applications are mostly scientific codes that are usually dominated by floating-point and memory operations and are often regular. Languages such as Fortran and High Performance Fortran thus pick their default semantics (e.g., dense arrays) to support such regular scientific codes.

In addition to the traditional software development tools such as debuggers and profilers, advanced (parallel) *performance analysis tools* are often necessary to understand the complex performance characteristics of HPC applications. Large scientific codes are often significant investments at a national level, but a clear software engineering methodology that integrates performance into all layers of the development process has not been established yet. The field of *performance engineering* [15] made some advances in this direction and first strategies exist to incorporate performance models into standard software development using UML [10,14].

M.R. Guarracino et al. (Eds.): Euro-Par 2010 Workshops, LNCS 6586, pp. 483–491, 2011.
© Springer-Verlag Berlin Heidelberg 2011

2 State of the Art

We advocate the idea that performance should play a central role in software development and maintenance. This means that expected performance of codes or parts of codes are expressed as *analytic performance models*. The development and maintenance of such models should be supported by *tools* that become an essential part of HPC software development and maintenance.

In this position paper, we point out that both, performance tools and performance models, exist separately and could be combined to improve HPC software development. We begin with an (due to space limitations incomplete) overview of the state of the art techniques for performance modeling, which is followed by a similar discussion for performance analysis tools.

2.1 Overview of Analytic Performance Modeling

Performance modeling is important for many aspects of HPC. It has been used to compare system performance, validate large system installations (acceptance testing), for routine tests during the lifetime of a computer system to detect anomalies and degradation, to guide hardware-software co-design, to guide re-engineering of large applications, to optimize schedulers and batch systems, and to predict costs to solve a particular scientific problem. Performance models are generally less accurate than actual benchmark studies but allow *predicting* performance on different systems.

Alam and Vetter propose code annotations, called "Modeling Assertions" [2] that combine empirical and analytical modeling techniques and help the developer to derive performance models for his code. Kerbyson et al. propose a performance modeling approach [11] that is based on manually developed human expert knowledge about the application. Those modeling techniques rely on empirical execution of serial parts on the target architecture and are usually applied to stable codes which limits their usefulness during software development. Snavely et al. uses an application's memory access pattern and processing requirements to predicts its performance on a target architecture [16]. This approach relies on memory profiles of the application and automated, simulation-based prediction. Hoefler et al. define strategies to trade the accuracy and complexity for modeling the performance of Message Passing Interface implementations [7].

Several other research works, such as [9], use analytic performance modeling to understand the performance characteristics of different codes or to guide optimizations.

Analytic performance modeling of scientific codes is usually performed in three phases: (1) identify the performance-critical input parameters, (2) formulate and test a hypothesis about the performance as function of the performance-critical input parameters, and (3) parametrize the function. Empirical modeling strategies that benchmark parts of the code (kernels) on the target architecture are often employed to maintain human-manageable performance models. Steps (2) and (3) of developing analytic performance models are often performed with the help of performance tools even though performance tools do not offer explicit support for the modeling workflow. **Analytic performance models strive to capture the applications' performance characteristics in a *human-understandable* form.**

2.2 Overview of Performance Analysis Tools

Performance tools are an integral part of the HPC ecosystem. They allow deep insights into the behavior of machines and their performance by displaying the performance characteristics of executed applications. Tools allow us to find bottlenecks and tune applications. They can also guide re-engineering of applications and they are often used to collect the data to design application models.

HPCToolkit [1] provides a framework for measurement and analysis of program performance, collects call path profiles, and can display hierarchical space-time diagrams. Periscope [5] monitors performance online and uses a distributed search to detect performance bottlenecks automatically. This approach omits time-and space-intensive offline trace analysis and allows the specification of "performance properties" to check during runtime. The TAU project [13] offers multiple tracing, profiling, and analysis tools to collect and analyze performance data of large-scale parallel applications. Vampir [12] uses the Open Trace Format and supports the visualization of performance traces and profiles. Scalasca [4] is targeted at large-scale architectures and offers scalable performance views and analyses.

In general, performance tools strive to guide performance analysis by displaying performance behavior. This enables users to understand the performance characteristics. Advanced analysis tools try to support users by pinpointing possible performance bottlenecks, hotspots, or other potential problems. Fully-automated tools are often imperfect and allow some guidance (such as Periscope's "performance properties") to be specified by the user. **Performance tools strive to extract *performance properties* of applications that enable users to understand application performance.**

We now discuss how performance tools and performance-models could be combined to benefit the software development process.

3 Combining Performance Tools and Analytic Modeling

We showed in the previous section that there already exists some overlap between performance analysis tools and analytic performance modeling. Analytic performance modeling can be seen as *top-down* approach where the user formulates an expectation based on an algorithm or implementation and tries to validate and parametrize it to predict performance. Performance analysis tools can be seen as a *bottom-up* approach that records performance artifacts and strive to trace the artifacts back to the original implementation or algorithm.

It is now obvious that performance analysis and analytic performance modeling can benefit from each other. Performance tools could use analytic performance models to filter the displayed information or even to pinpoint possible problems automatically and during runtime. Creating analytic performance models could

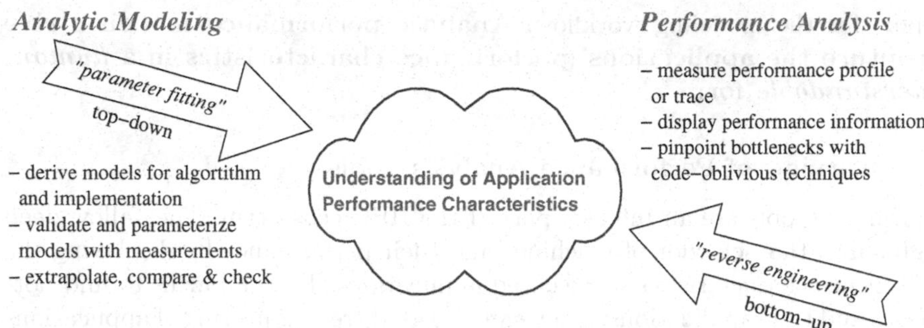
Analytic Modeling
"parameter fitting"
top–down
- derive models for algortithm and implementation
- validate and parameterize models with measurements
- extrapolate, compare & check
Understanding of Application Performance Characteristics
Performance Analysis
- measure performance profile or trace
- display performance information
- pinpoint bottlenecks with code–oblivious techniques
"reverse engineering"
bottom–up

Fig. 1. Comparison of Performance Modeling and Performance Analysis Approaches

benefit largely from effective tool support that could automatize the benchmark and fitting cycle. Both scenarios require human input of an initial model and model inputs (performance-critical input parameters). However, such models are often easy to derive and already used in algorithm design.

We now describe the first option, i.e., how a performance analysis tool could assist users in deriving performance models. For this, we propose a possible work-flow based on tools and human input.

The first step would be to identify performance-critical input parameters. This has to be done by an application expert. Performance-critical input parameters (called *critical parameters* in the following) are for example the dimensions of the simulated system or parameters that influence convergence. Other parameters, such as initial starting values (e.g., heats or masses) might not change the runtime of the algorithm and are thus not critical in performance models. More complex parameters such as the shape of the input systems need to be approximated into a single value by the application expert.

The set of critical parameters could now be used by a static analysis framework to identify the propagation though the code. This could help to guide the user through the second step, the identification of *critical blocks* which exhibit similar performance characteristics. This often means identifying parts of the call-tree for which the runtime can be modeled by a single analytic expression.

The third step requires the user to define abstract parametric models for the performance of each code block. For example, the user can specify that the expected runtime of a matrix-matrix multiplication is $T_{MM} = a+b\cdot(c\cdot N)^3$ where N is the size of the matrix (a critical input parameter), and a,b,c are parameters that depend on the performance characteristics of the implementation and the target machine. Such performance expectations are often low-order polynomials or simple logarithmic functions and a tool could support the user with pre-defined functions. Additionally, a tool could support modeling of caches by pre-defining segmented functions, such as $T_{MMc} = a + min\{C_N, N\} \cdot b_1 \cdot (c_1 \cdot N)^3 + max\{N-C_N, 0\}\cdot b_2\cdot(c_2\cdot N)^3$ where C_N specifies the number of elements $x\cdot N$ that can be stored in fast cache-memory. The variables b_1 and c_1 model the in-cache execution and b_2 and c_2 out-of-cache execution. Such simple transformations can easily be extended to deeper memory hierarchies and supported by tools.

The performance tool could then assist in conducting a series of benchmarks with different values of N and perform user-guided statistical fits to the target function in order to parametrize the model.

Communication analysis could similarly be guided by tools. A communication model usually includes the number of messages and the communicated sizes for each critical block. Those counts are then used to parametrize network models such as the LogGPS model. Tools and techniques to parametrize the LogGPS machine model exist elsewhere [8].

The model validation phase could similarly be automated with an appropriate tool which then benchmarks different parameter configurations in order to certify the model's prediction. Several well-known methods from statistics exist to perform such checks. This would imply that tools need to be extended to run multiple experiments instead of analyzing only a single experiment.

The two main impediments to wide adoption of analytic performance modeling are (1) that the software developer needs to be familiar with the details of the modeling strategy and (2) the necessary manual work and missing standardization and guidance for notation (cf. UML). The proposed tool-support would address both in that it offers an integrated interface to performance analysis and performance modeling. Tools would also be able to adopt UML-like syntax and add performance assertions (cf. [10,14]). This would enhance the software development cycle in HPC and help the developers to focus on end-to-end performance and thus improve productivity.

4 A Motivating Modeling Example: MILC

We now present a brief overview about manual analytic performance modeling for the MIMD Lattic Computation (MILC) code [3]. This code is highly regular and the code- and data-flow is mostly deterministic and very structured. The balanced computation is performed on a regular four-dimensional grid.

The critical parameters of the MILC code are the size of each dimension `nx`, `ny`, `nz`, `nt`, the number of warmups (`warms`) and trajectories (`trajecs`), steps per trajectory (`steps`) and trajectories between measurements (`meas`). The number of CG iterations is determined by different input parameters (masses and convergence factors) but a single step usually requires around 2,100 iterations.

Identifying the critical blocks can often be done by analyzing the call-graph and identifying subtrees with common performance characteristics. The MILC developers already identified five significant blocks: (1) LL (`load_longlinks`), (2) FL (`load_fatlinks`), (3) CG (`ks_congrad`), (4) GF (`imp_gauge_force`), and (5) FF (`eo_fermion_force_twoterms`).

The expected runtime of each of the serial blocks scales linearly with the number of grid points per process V. Thus, a simple linear function, for example $T_{GF}(V) = t_{1,GF} \cdot V$ can be used to model the performance. In order to model the cache hierarchy, we split the linear model into two pieces $T_{GF}(V) = t_{1,GF} \cdot \min\{s_{GF}, V\} + t_{2,GF} \cdot max\{0, V - s_{GF}\}$ with $t_{1,GF}$ being the in-cache time per grid point and $t_{2,GF}$ being the out-of-cache time.

Parametrizing $t_{1,GF}$ and $t_{2,GF}$ and finding the exact switching point s is usually done via curve-fitting. Figure 2(a) shows the benchmarked and parametrized model ($t_{1,GF} = 88\mu s$, $t_{2,GF} = 157\mu s$, and $s_{GF} = 1900$). The model was parametrized by least-squares curve-fitting which could be easily supported by tools. This time-consuming step needs to be repeated for each target architecture and can easily be automatized.

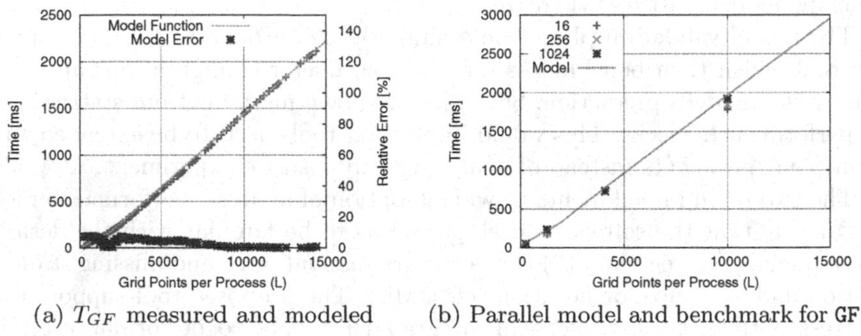

(a) T_{GF} measured and modeled (b) Parallel model and benchmark for GF

Fig. 2. Performance Modeling on POWER5+

A complete serial application model can now be constructed from either a detailed understanding of the code execution or by analyzing multiple different program runs and observing the number of invocations of each critical block. The complete serial model for MILC is a simple linear model:

$$T_{serial}(V) = (\texttt{trajecs} + \texttt{warms}) \cdot \texttt{steps} \cdot [T_{FF}(V) + T_{GF}(V) + 3(T_{LL}(V) + T_{FL}(V))] + \left\lfloor \frac{\texttt{trajecs}}{\texttt{meas}} \right\rfloor [T_{LL}(V) + T_{FL}(V)] + \texttt{niters} \cdot T_{CG}(V)$$

Parallel execution models can often be derived from serial performance models. For MILC, it is sufficient to add the communication overheads to the serial time. The communication overhead depends on the number and sizes of messages sent via point-to-point and collective communication calls. Those parameters can either be derived from the source-code or measured with performance tools. Using the latter approach, we were able to construct a simple linear model for detailed message counts and sizes for nearest-neighbor (along the four-dimensional grid) and collective (CG convergence checks) communication. We omit the detailed linear equations for brevity. Tool support for automatic counting and data correlation could improve productivity significantly.

Figure 2(b) shows the parallel performance model for GF on 16, 256, and 1024 CPUs. The used LogGPS model ignores congestion and shows thus some little deviation from the benchmark for large V.

4.1 Application of the Model

After successfully deriving and parametrizing the model for POWER5+, we are able to make a first prediction for the performance of a large-scale system like Blue Waters. At this point, there is only a single POWER7 MR system available for testing but the network parameters are known to us. First, we construct a serial performance model as described before. Figure 3(a) shows the serial model in comparison to POWER5+. Figure 3(b) shows the parallel model prediction for 1,024 CPUs.

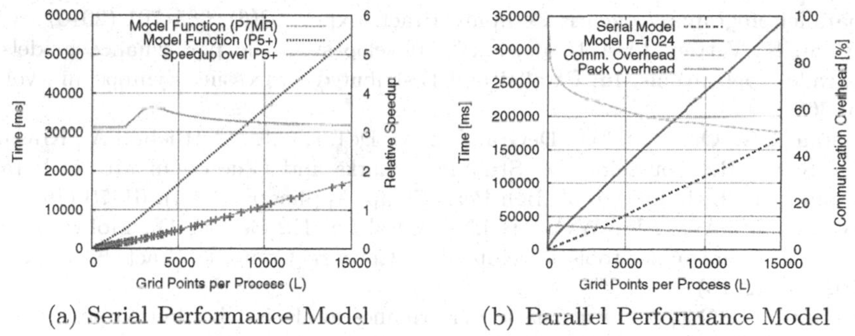

(a) Serial Performance Model (b) Parallel Performance Model

Fig. 3. Performance Models of POWER7 MR

The parallel model allows us to predict the performance and identify potential improvements. For example, a possible optimization which could save up to 15% for small V is the replacement of the pack routine with MPI Datatypes. The benefits of this approach were demonstrated in practice [6].

5 Summary and Conclusion

We support the idea of making analytic performance modeling part of the HPC software development cycle in order to improve programmer productivity and code maintainability.

We show that a huge body of knowledge, techniques and tools exist in the analytic performance modeling and the performance analysis tools communities. We show how performance tools and performance modeling could mutually benefit from each other and we propose an easy roadmap to extend existing tools with the capability to support simple performance models.

We also show a simplified exemplary model for the MILC application which could be used as a starting point to explore tool support for analytic performance modeling. More complex (less regular) applications most likely require more advanced techniques. However, techniques like clustering are already employed in current performance analysis tools such as Vampir and TAU.

We propose to both communities to analyze the mutual benefits and develop a roadmap to synchronize the efforts in analytic modeling and performance analysis.

Acknowledgments. The author thanks William Gropp, Bill Kramer, and Marc Snir for many helpful discussions and ideas regarding concepts of analytic modeling. Thanks to Steven Gottlieb for discussions about MILC and Shirley Moore, Fredrik Kjolstad and all anonymous reviewers for comments on early drafts of this work.

References

1. Adhianto, L., et al.: HPCTOOLKIT: tools for performance analysis of optimized parallel programs. Concurr. Comput.: Pract. Exper. 22(6), 685–701 (2010)
2. Alam, S., Vetter, J.: A framework to develop symbolic performance models of parallel applications. In: Parallel and Distributed Processing Symposium, vol. 0, p. 368 (2006)
3. Bernard, C., Ogilvie, M.C., DeGrand, T.A., DeTar, C.E., Gottlieb, S.A., Krasnitz, A., Sugar, R., Toussaint, D.: Studying Quarks and Gluons On MIMD Parallel Computers. Intl. Journal of High Perf. Comp. Applications 5(4), 61–70 (1991)
4. Geimer, M., Wolf, F., Wylie, B.J.N., Ábrahám, E., Becker, D., Mohr, B.: The Scalasca performance toolset architecture. Concurr. Comput.: Pract. Exper. 22(6), 702–719 (2010)
5. Gerndt, M., Ott, M.: Automatic performance analysis with Periscope. Concurr. Comput.: Pract. Exper. 22(6), 736–748 (2010)
6. Hoefler, T., Gottlieb, S.: Parallel Zero-Copy Algorithms for Fast Fourier Transform and Conjugate Gradient using MPI Datatypes. In: Keller, R., Gabriel, E., Resch, M., Dongarra, J. (eds.) EuroMPI 2010. LNCS, vol. 6305, pp. 132–141. Springer, Heidelberg (2010)
7. Hoefler, T., Gropp, W., Thakur, R., Träff, J.L.: Toward Performance Models of MPI Implementations for Understanding Application Scaling Issues. In: Keller, R., Gabriel, E., Resch, M., Dongarra, J. (eds.) EuroMPI 2010. LNCS, vol. 6305, pp. 21–30. Springer, Heidelberg (2010)
8. Hoefler, T., Lichei, A., Rehm, W.: Low-Overhead LogGP Parameter Assessment for Modern Interconnection Networks. In: Proceedings of the 21st IEEE International Parallel & Distributed Processing Symposium (March 2007)
9. Shan, H., Strohmaier, E., Qiang, J., Bailey, D.H., Yelick, K.: Performance Modeling and Optimization of a High Energy Colliding Beam Simulation Code. In: Supercomputing, SC 2006 p. 48 (2006)
10. Hopkins, R.P., Smith, M.J., King, P.J.B.: Two approaches to integrating UML and performance models. In: WOSP 2002: Proceedings of the 3rd International Workshop on Software and Performance, pp. 91–92. ACM, New York (2002)
11. Kerbyson, D.J., et al.: Predictive performance and scalability modeling of a large-scale application. In: Proceedings of the 2001 ACM/IEEE Conference on Supercomputing (CDROM), pp. 37–37. ACM, New York (2001)
12. Knüpfer, A., Brunst, H., Doleschal, J., Jurenz, M., Lieber, M., Mickler, H., Müller, M.S., Nagel, W.E.: The Vampir Performance Analysis Tool-Set. In: Tools for High Performance Computing, pp. 139–155. Springer, Heidelberg (2008)
13. Lee, C.W., Malony, A.D., Morris, A.: TAUmon: Scalable Online Performance Data Analysis in TAU. In: 3rd Workshop on Productivity and Performance (August 2010)

14. Pllana, S., Fahringer, T.: UML based modeling of performance oriented parallel and distributed applications. In: Winter Simulation Conference, vol. 1, pp. 497–505 (2002)
15. Pooley, R.: Software engineering and performance: a roadmap. In: ICSE 2000: Proceedings of the Conference on The Future of Software Engineering, pp. 189–199. ACM, New York (2000)
16. Snavely, A., Carrington, L., Wolter, N., Labarta, J., Badia, R., Purkayastha, A.: A framework for performance modeling and prediction. In: Supercomputing, SC 2002, Los Alamitos, CA, USA, pp. 1–17 (2002)

TAUmon: Scalable Online Performance Data Analysis in TAU

Chee Wai Lee, Allen D. Malony, and Alan Morris

Department Computer and Information Science,
University Oregon, Eugene, Oregon, 97403

Abstract. In this paper, we present an update on the scalable online support for performance data analysis and monitoring in TAU. Extending on our prior work with TAUoverSupermon and TAUoverMRNet, we show how online analysis operations can also be supported directly and scalably using the parallel infrastructure provided by an MPI application instrumented with TAU. We also report on efforts to streamline and update TAUoverMRNet. Together, these approaches form the basis for the investigation of online analysis capabilities in a TAU monitoring framework TAUmon. We discuss various analysis operations and capabilities enabled by online monitoring and how operations like event unification enable merged profiles to be produced with greatly reduced data volume prior to application shutdown. Scaling results with PFLOTRAN on the Cray XT5 and BG/P are presented along with a look at some initial performance information generated from FLASH through our TAUmon prototype frameworks.

1 Introduction

As the level of parallelism increases in large-scale systems, performance measurement of parallel applications will be affected by the size of the performance data being maintained per process/thread, the effects of measurement overhead, and the cost of output, both during and at the end of execution. The traditional approach of post-mortem (offline) analysis of performance experiments will come under increasing pressure as the sheer volume and dimensionality of performance information drives up I/O and analysis complexity. Enhancing performance measurement systems with online monitoring support is a necessary step to address both challenges. In our prior research, we have explored extensions to the TAU performance system [9] that allow access to the parallel performance data measurement for an application at runtime. The TAUoverSupermon [13] (ToS) and TAUoverMRNet [12] (ToM) prototypes leveraged the online transport infrastructures, Supermon [15] and MRNet [1], respectively. While ToS and ToM demonstrate monitoring functionality, it is becoming increasingly clear that we need to push forward on the scalable algorithms for performance analysis and evaluate their efficiency in real application scenarios.

In this paper, we reconsider the approaches and capabilities of online performance monitoring from a perspective of the online operations necessary to support scalable performance measurement and runtime analysis requirements. In

M.R. Guarracino et al. (Eds.): Euro-Par 2010 Workshops, LNCS 6586, pp. 493–499, 2011.
© Springer-Verlag Berlin Heidelberg 2011

addition to updating ToM to support new machines, we investigate the approach of directly using the parallel infrastructure provided by MPI as an alternative, complementary monitoring framework. Together these different approaches for operations via different transports form the foundation of a framework for TAU performance monitoring we call *TAUmon*. We will structure the rest of the paper as follows. Related work is discussed in section 2. In section 3, we describe the statistical analysis operations enabled by TAUmon. Section 4 briefly covers the changes to ToM and the use of the MPI transport. Section 5 presents scaling results for analysis operations implemented using MPI and ToM for the PFLOTRAN [11] application and FLASH [4]. These experiments were conducted on Jaguar, Oak Ridge National Lab's Cray XT5 and Intrepid, Argonne National Lab's IBM BlueGene/P.

2 Related Work

Prior literature that guided our work can be classified roughly into 2 categories: work that seek to provide general monitoring interfaces and those that seek scalable transport support. The Online Monitoring Interface Specification (OMIS) [8] project provided a general interface between tools and a monitoring system. An event-action paradigm mapped events to requests and responses to actions as part of that interface. J-OMIS [2] was built on top of this interface to provide extensible monitoring facilities for the support of tools for Java applications. Specific target tools were performance characterization and debugging tools. Lee [7] explored the effectiveness of asynchronously collecting profile data transformed from performance traces generated within a running Charm++ application. The work demonstrated how an adaptive runtime system like Charm++ was able to serve as an effective transport medium for such purposes. Periscope [5] made use of hierarchical monitor agents working with applications and an external client in order to address scalability issues with transport. The Distributed Performance Consultant [10] in Paradyn made use of MRNet to support introspective online performance diagnosis. In addition, a number of computation steering frameworks [6,14,16,3] exist where performance information is collected, analyzed and fed through parameter-modifying interfaces in order to change an application's behavior. What distinguishes TAUmon is the attempt to design an integrated abstraction to TAU's interface for swapping independent transport mechanisms in order to provide maximum flexibility for efficiently delivering and processing performance data.

3 Online Performance Monitoring

Our efforts to build monitoring support have grown out of more general concerns of reducing the size, time, and number of files needed to offload parallel profile data at the end of the application execution. For several years, we have been extending the TAU measurement infrastructure with scalable capabilities to access performance data online via different transports, what we call *performance monitoring.* There are several benefits to performance monitoring including offloading of performance data, on-the-fly analysis, and performance feedback. With performance data offload, it becomes possible to capture a running time-series snapshots of event statistics, histograms and cluster-averages. Presentation of these snapshots as they appear permits on-the-fly analysis, possibly on a remote client while the application is still executing. We now describe the monitoring operations currently supported as a part of the TAUmon framework.

Profile Merging: By default, TAU creates a file for every thread of execution in the parallel program. In this case, the number of files required to save the full parallel profile grows as an application scales. We have added to the monitoring framework an operation that merges profile streams in order to reduce the number of files required. The operation is a concatenation operation used only at the end of the run. The root processor requests for the profiles of the other processors one at a time. On receipt of these profiles, the data is immediately concatenated to a single file by the root processor to avoid running out of memory. When profile merging is coupled with and preceded by event unification, the gains in overall data volume when compared with the traditional approach of profile output are significant with low overhead costs. For example, 27 GB of PFLOTRAN profile output for 131k cores was reduced to 600 MB, taking 12.96 seconds on the Cray XT5.

Event Unification: In TAU, because events are instantiated locally, each thread assigns a unique event identifier. This results in full event maps that need to be stored for each thread. Event unification begins by sorting each processor's events by name. The information is propagated up the transport's reduction tree, where at each stage, the output to the next level of the tree is the unified and sorted by the list of events from the set of inputs. At the same time, each intermediate node in the tree maintains the reverse event maps. When the fully-unified event information arrives at the root, it is broadcast back through the tree during which the full event map for each processor can be constructed using the local maps maintained at each intermediate node. Note that event unification is the pre-requisite to all other monitoring operations that do not involve simple concatenation and thus require global event identification consistency.

Statistics Operations: Basic reductions in the transport support the computation of sum, sum of squares, minimum and maximum values of events across processors. From these, we can derive mean profiles and compute histograms with fixed-sized bins. The mean profile is useful as a summary from which additional statistical information can be sought via other operations. As time-series data, it is capable of highlighting the relative significance of events and their relative rate of growth. Histograms are useful for highlighting work distribution across processors for events which cannot be captured by mean profiles.

4 Transport Infrastructure Updates

Our original ToM instantiation scheme was designed to allow additional MRNet resources to be initialized flexibly and semi-transparently to both the application and job scheduling system. This was achieved to a reasonable degree through the splitting of MPI communicators as described in [12]. This instantiation scheme, however, did not foresee other flexibility problems in the way MRNet trees may have to be set up. For example, because of the way MRNet trees are currently implemented, intermediate tree nodes may only be allocated on the service nodes of BG/P. As a result, we have had to update ToM to make use of new versions of MRNet with the latter's support for much larger machines like the Cray XT5 and BG/P platforms and specialized batch environments.

In addition, we have adopted MPI as an online monitoring transport. This was derived from our work to reduce the overheads associated with end-of-execution profile output and analysis. We found it necessary to deal with a large number of profiles using more efficient profile representations. We had separately implemented parallel event unification, profile merging, and profile data analysis (average, min, max and histogramming) using MPI for use at the end of the execution, and considered how these solutions could be applied to other monitoring operations. The monitoring operations were then implemented in parallel using a binomial reduction tree based on the algorithms used in MPI reduction. Enabling them for online monitoring was a then simple matter.

5 Experiments and Results

Our experiments with TAUmon had two goals. First, we aimed to observe transport performance against different online monitoring operations. Second, we wanted to observe expected performance structures over time not normally captured by a final application profile. We targeted two applications: PFLOTRAN [11], a 3-D reservoir simulator that models subsurface reactive flows, and FLASH [4], a multi-physics multi-scale simulation code that has been used to simulate type Ia supernovae explosions. The input data set used for PFLOTRAN modeled a large 2 billion degree-of-freedom river simulation. This data set was used for both our preliminary experiments as well as our strong scaling experiments above 4,096 processor cores on the Cray XT5 and BG/P machines. For FLASH, we employed the Sod 2d input dataset with varying maximum refinement levels.

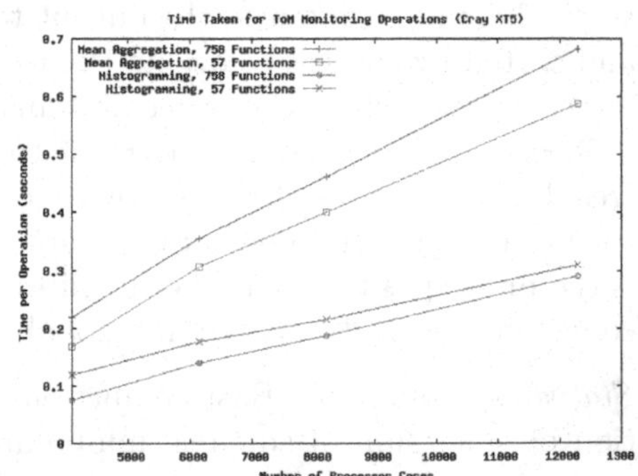

Fig. 1. Time taken for PFLOTRAN monitoring operations on the XT5 using ToM as the transport layer

At each major iteration, event unification followed by monitoring operations to compute per-event means and histograms over 20 bins. In the case of ToM, this is measured by the front-end process which marks the beginning and end of each operation's communication protocol. For MPI transport, the root process of our reduction tree takes responsibility for measuring when the collective operation was begun and when the performance data was finally gathered at the root. To get a perspective on the effects of data volume on online monitoring overhead, we made comparisons of PFLOTRAN when executed with full instrumentation against selective instrumentation of significant events. The full event set numbered around 756, while selective instrumentation yielded about 57 events.

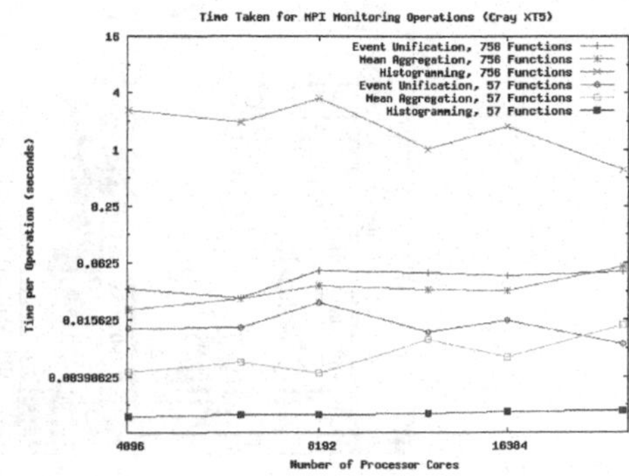

Fig. 2. Time taken for PFLOTRAN monitoring operations on the XT5 using MPI as the transport layer

Figure 1 shows the scaling results for the Cray XT5 using ToM from 4K to 12K cores. Since event unification has not yet been implemented with MRNet, we used MPI event unification results for the other analyses. All times are less than 0.7 seconds, with histogramming taking longer than averaging. Times increase with larger cores counts. Both of these results were expected. We are investigating performance in more detail to determine if optimizations are possible.

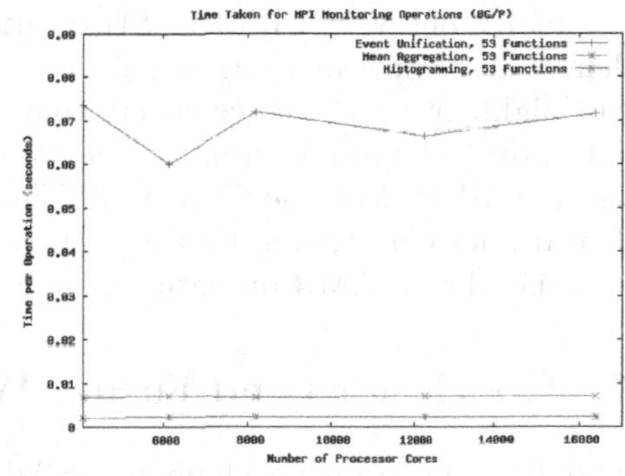

Fig. 3. Time taken for PFLOTRAN monitoring operations on the BG/P using MPI as the transport layer

In contrast, Figure 2 shows the scaling results for the Cray XT5 using the MPI transport for 4K to 24K cores. Except for histogramming on 758 events, MPI analysis operations are all less than 0.06 seconds. Compared to ToM, this is significantly faster. Furthermore, there is little effect of scaling on these times. Clearly, the anomaly is the histogramming results for 758 events. More investigation is needed to uncover the poor performance here. Our suspicions are that there is an interaction between the histogramming algorithm and the core locality boundaries that disrupt performance. In addition to being high, the execution times have the weird behavior of declining at larger scale.

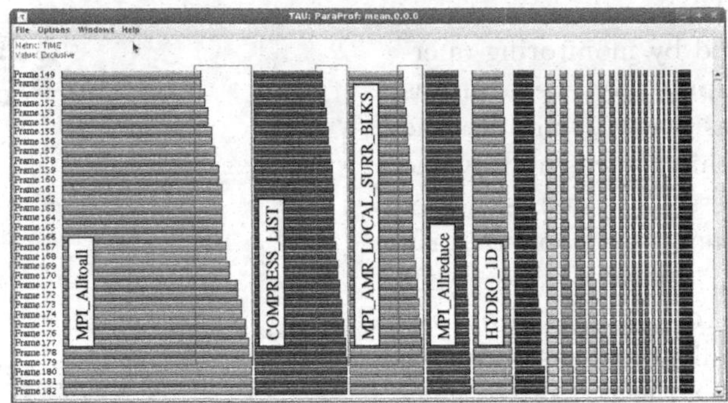

Fig. 4. Online profile snapshots of FLASH execution on 1,536 Cray XT5 processes

Moving to the IBM BG/P, Figure 3 shows the scaling results using MPI transport for 4K to 16K cores and 57 events. Again, the execution times are all less than 0.06 seconds. The interesting effect is the larger event unification time relative to mean and histogram analysis. This is also represented in the XT5 results for 57 events, keeping in mind that Figure 2 is a log-log plot. As before, monitoring analyses with MPI transport appears to be minimally affected by scaling.

Finally, our work with FLASH returned to online monitoring experiments to demonstrate how analysis of parallel profile snapshots taken during execution can highlight performance effects that would otherwise be missed in an aggregate profile. Figure 4 highlights 34 frames of mean profiles from 1,536 processes running FLASH on the Cray XT5. The most significant five events are labeled. The frames were chosen because they show the step-like behavior in the events associated with AMR operations.

6 Conclusions and Future Work

The TAU project is developing a scalable parallel monitoring framework called TAUmon, based on past research prototypes, but with an eye toward leveraging current scalable infrastructure like MRNet and high-performance MPI libraries. The results from initial experiments reported here give confidence that end-of-execution and online monitoring capabilities will provide opportunities for large-scale performance analysis. The parallel performance of the TAU event, merging, and reduction (mean, histogram) operations are good for both MRNet and MPI transport designs. We are currently developing other analysis operations, such as clustering and wavelet analysis, as well as tuning the monitoring analysis for higher efficiency. Long term, we hope to provide a monitoring interface for parallel applications to interrogate performance online from TAUmon, for purposes of adaptive performance optimization.

Acknowledgments. The research was by a grant from the U.S. Department of Energy, Office of Science, under contract DE-SC0001777.

References

1. Arnold, D.C., Pack, G.D., Miller, B.P.: Tree-based Overlay Networks for Scalable Applications. In: 11th International Workshop on High-Level Parallel Programming Models and Supportive Environments (HIPS 2006) (April 2006)
2. Bubak, M., Funika, W., Smętek, M., Kiliański, Z., Wismüller, R.: Architecture of monitoring system for distributed java applications. In: Dongarra, J., Laforenza, D., Orlando, S. (eds.) EuroPVM/MPI 2003. LNCS, vol. 2840, pp. 447–454. Springer, Heidelberg (2003)
3. Eisenhauer, G., Schwan, K.: An object-based infrastructure for program monitoring and steering. In: SPDT 1998: Proceedings of the SIGMETRICS Symposium on Parallel and Distributed Tools, pp. 10–20. ACM, New York (1998)
4. Fryxell, B., Olson, K., Ricker, P., Timmes, F.X., Zingale, M., Lamb, D.Q., MacNeice, P., Rosner, R., Truran, J.W., Tufo, H.: FLASH: An Adaptive Mesh Hydrodynamics Code for Modeling Astrophysical Thermonuclear Flashes. The Astrophysical Journal Supplement Series 131(1), 273–334
5. Gerndt, M., Furlinger, K., Kereku, E.: Periscope: Advanced Techniques for Performance Analysis. Parallel Computing: Current and Future Issues of High-End Computing, 15–26 (September 2005)
6. Gu, W., Eisenhauer, G., Schwan, K., Vetter, J.: Falcon: On-line monitoring for steering parallel programs. In: Ninth International Conference on Parallel and Distributed Computing and Systems, pp. 699–736 (1998)
7. Lee, C.W.: Techniques in Scalable and Effective Parallel Performance Analysis. PhD thesis, Department of Computer Science, University of Illinois, Urbana-Champaign (December 2009)
8. Ludwig, T., Wismuller, R., Sunderam, V., Bode, A.: OMIS - on-line monitoring interface specification (version 2.0). LRR-TUM Research Report Series, 9 (1998)
9. Malony, A.D., Shende, S., Bell, R., Li, K., Li, L., Trebon, N.: Advances in the TAU Performance System, pp. 129–144 (2004)
10. Miller, B.P., Callaghan, M.D., Cargille, J.M., Hollingsworth, J.K., Irvin, R.B., Karavanic, K.L., Kunchithapadam, K., Newhall, T.: The paradyn parallel performance measurement tools. Computer 28(11), 37–46 (1995)
11. Mills, R.T., Lu, C., Lichtner, P.C., Hammond, G.E.: Simulating Subsurface Flow and Transport on Ultrascale Computers using PFLOTRAN. Journal of Physics: Conference Series 78, 012051 (2007)
12. Nataraj, A., Malony, A.D., Morris, A., Arnold, D.C., Miller, B.P.: A Framework for Scalable, Parallel Performance Monitoring using TAU and MRNet. International Workshop on Scalable Tools for High-End Computing (STHEC 2008) (June 2008)
13. Nataraj, A., Sottile, M., Morris, A., Malony, A.D., Shende, S.: TAUoverSupermon: Low-Overhead Online Parallel Performance Monitoring. In: Kermarrec, A.-M., Bougé, L., Priol, T. (eds.) Euro-Par 2007. LNCS, vol. 4641, pp. 85–96. Springer, Heidelberg (2007)
14. Ribler, R.L., Simitci, H., Reed, D.A.: The autopilot performance-directed adaptive control system. Future Gener. Comput. Syst. 18(1), 175–187 (2001)
15. Sottile, M.J., Minnich, R.G.: Supermon: a high-speed cluster monitoring system. In: Proceedings of IEEE International Conference on Cluster Computing, 2002, pp. 39–46 (2002)
16. Tapus, C., I-Hsin Chung, Hollingsworth, J.K.: Active harmony: Towards automated performance tuning. In: ACM/IEEE 2002 Conference on Supercomputing, November 16-22, pp. 44–44 (2002)

References

The VampirTrace Plugin Counter Interface: Introduction and Examples

Robert Schöne, Ronny Tschüter, Thomas Ilsche, and Daniel Hackenberg

Center for Information Services and High Performance Computing (ZIH)
Technische Universität Dresden – 01062 Dresden, Germany
{robert.schoene,ronny.tschueter,thomas.ilsche, daniel.hackenberg}@tu-dresden.de

Abstract. The growing complexity of microprocessors is not only driven by the current trend towards multi-core architectures, but also by new features like instruction set extensions, additional function units or specialized processing cores. The demand for more performance and scalability also results in an increasing complexity of the software stack: operating systems, libraries, and applications all need to exploit more parallelism and new functionalities in order to meet this demand. Both aspects – hardware and software – put pressure on performance monitoring infrastructures that face two conflictive requirements. On the one hand, performance tools need to be somewhat stable without entailing significant software changes with every additional functionality. On the other hand they need to be able to monitor the influence of new hardware and software features. We therefore present a plugin interface for our performance monitoring software VampirTrace that allows users to write libraries that feed VampirTrace with data from new (platform dependent) performance counters as well as hardware features that may not be accessed by Open Source software. This paper describes the interface in detail, analyzes its strength and weaknesses, depicts examples, and provides a comparison to other plugin-like performance analysis tools.

1 Introduction

Profiling and event tracing are the two major analysis techniques to evaluate performance and pinpoint bottlenecks within parallel programs on high performance computing (HPC) systems. A well-established event tracing infrastructure is VampirTrace. Its main focus is to instrument and trace parallel programs written in Fortran or C that are parallelized with the Message Passing Interface MPI [1]. However, VampirTrace also supports OpenMP parallelized programs and hybrid MPI & OpenMP programs, Pthreads, UNIX processes and parallel Java programs [2,3]. The tool is jointly developed by the Forschungszentrum Jülich and the Technische Universität Dresden. It is shipped with OpenMPI [4] and therefore available as a software package for all major Linux distributions.

VampirTrace supports numerous performance counters to track metrics such as PAPI or I/O events. These performance counters are typically standardized

M.R. Guarracino et al. (Eds.): Euro-Par 2010 Workshops, LNCS 6586, pp. 501–511, 2011.
© Springer-Verlag Berlin Heidelberg 2011

and portable. New processor or operating system features are often system specific and not compatible with previous or upcoming systems. However, they influence the overall system performance and need to be tracked by performance monitoring tools. To branch a monitoring infrastructure for each different platform would enlarge the code base significantly – this is inefficient and slows down the development progress. The inclusion of all the new features within the main branch is also not feasible since it would increase both the code size and the error-proneness of the software. We therefore extend our performance monitoring software VampirTrace with the presented VampirTrace plugin counter infrastructure that effectively resolves the described issues. The new interface allows developers to write libraries that feed VampirTrace with data from new (platform dependent) performance counters as well as hardware features that may not be accessed by Open Source software. This effort is an important step towards a VampirTrace infrastructure that enables arbitrary, platform specific performance counters while remaining stable and consistent.

The paper is structured as follows: Section 2 topics design and implementation details of the VampirTrace plugin counter infrastructure. Three different plugin counter libraries that extend the functionality of VampirTrace are presented in Section 3. We discuss design limitations in Section 4 and address related work with respect to plugins for performance analysis tools in Section 5. Finally, Section 6 presents conclusions and outlines future work.

2 The Plugin Counter Interface

2.1 Design

Currently, there are four possible types of plugin counters that differ with respect to their type of synchronicity:

Synchronous plugin counters are very similar to other performance events in VampirTrace. Whenever a VampirTrace event occurs (e.g., the call of an instrumented function or a call into the MPI library), the current value of such a plugin counter is gathered and merged into the event trace.

Asynchronous Callback plugin counters usually start background threads that report data by calling a function of the VampirTrace counter interface. The event data can be gathered from a buffered local or even remote location. Such plugin counter libraries have to provide timestamps along with the counter values since they can not be matched directly to a VampirTrace event. Functions to generate timestamps in a supported format are passed on to the plugin counter library during the initialization phase of VampirTrace.

Asynchronous Post-mortem plugin counters collect tracing information during the full runtime of a program. The event data is collected by VampirTrace after the program has finished. Function calls that implicate overhead occur either prior to or after the program runtime, thus minimizing the program perturbation. If the plugin library itself gathers its data from an external source over a network, the measurement process is not influenced at all.

Asynchronous On-event plugin counters are a hybrid approach. While performance events are collected asynchronously, VampirTrace retrieves the data only when a classic event (e.g., function or MPI call) occurs. The advantage of this plugin counter type is that the event buffer size can be decreased compared to post-mortem plugin counters while still allowing a similar asynchronous collection method.

Another distinction for plugin counter libraries is the scope of their counters. For example, PAPI counters can be related to a thread while CPU-related counters are not thread specific. Thread-independent counters can be associated to a host (e.g., network interface counters) or to the whole system (e.g., usage of an NAS). The current implementation of the plugin counter interface allows measuring counters per thread, per process, on the first thread of the first process of each host ("once per host"), or only on the first thread of the first process ("once").

Plugin libraries can also define counter datatypes such as unsigned and signed integer or floating point values. The relation of values to time can be defined as "relates to the current timestamp" (e.g., temperature of components), "relates to the time frame from the last event to the current" (e.g., average power consumption for the last time frame), "relates to the time frame from the current event to the next one" (e.g., the current processor, a thread is scheduled on), "relates to the time frame from the first time stamp to the current" (e.g., PAPI reads).

2.2 Implementation

The VampirTrace plugin counter interface is developed using C. It depends only on POSIX functions and definitions declared in `dlfcn.h` and `stdint.h`. Functions from `dlfcn.h` enable dynamic loading of plugins at runtime. The interface defines functions for initialization, adding counters, enabling and disabling counters, providing results, and finalization. A subset of at least five functions has to be implemented, others are optional. A minimal useful plugin can be written in less then 50 lines of code.

Specific plugin counters can be added by the user who can define the environment variable `VT_PLUGIN_CNTR_METRICS`. This variable consists of the library name followed by the counter name. For example, setting it to `Power_watts` would define the library `libPower.so` and the counter name `watts`. Multiple plugin counters can be passed by separating them with colons. VampirTrace evaluates the specified metrics and checks for the existence of implicitly defined libraries. This is done for every process that is monitored by VampirTrace (e.g., for every MPI rank). Afterwards, the plugin counter libraries are loaded using `dlopen`. Each plugin counter library has to implement the function `get_info`, which provides VampirTrace with pointers to all needed functions. For instance, the `get_event_info` function assigns meaningful names and units to the counters. Furthermore, plugin developers can use this function to extend the passed counter name to multiple counters. The functionality of wildcards can be a possible use case. If the user sets `VT_PLUGIN_CNTR_METRICS` to `Power_*`, `get_info`

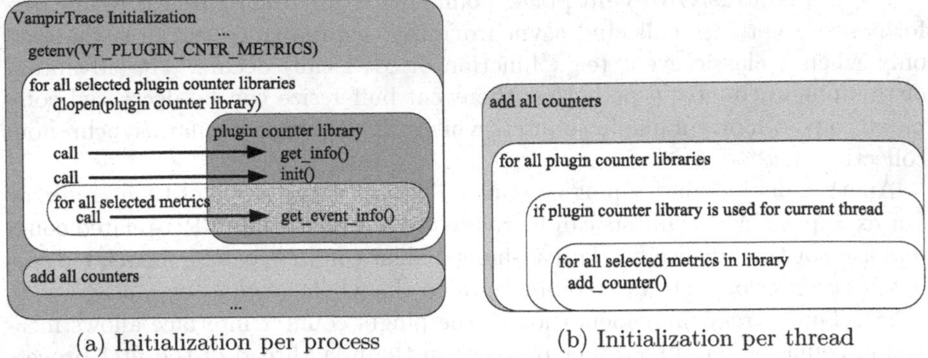

(a) Initialization per process (b) Initialization per thread

Fig. 1. Initialization procedures for plugin counters

might add one counter per available node and provide a comprehensible name (e.g., "power for node 1") and unit ("watts") for each. Finally, VampirTrace activates all defined metrics for the corresponding library. The entire process is depicted in detail in Figure 1a. Additionally, for every new thread of the program the required metrics are determined and added as pointed out in Figure 1b.

The trace buffer for the measured thread is shared by VampirTrace and all used plugins. Writing a trace entry is not an atomic operation and a plugin thread can therefore not write to this buffer directly. Mutexes could assure mutual exclusion when writing events but this would add an unacceptable overhead. Therefore, each callback plugin needs to create separate event buffers. The buffer sizes need to be chosen carefully by the plugin library developer to avoid both event loss and excessive memory usage.

2.3 Overhead Analysis

Monitoring tools typically influence the runtime behavior of the monitored application. In our case, both VampirTrace itself as well as the plugins create a certain overhead. The latter is fully in control of the plugin developer and we therefore focus on the overhead that is induced by VampirTrace and the plugin interface itself. We use a synthetic, OpenMP-parallel program that runs 4 threads on the test system. The system consists of 4 Intel Xeon 7560 processors and 128 GiB registered DDR3-1066 memory. Each processor runs at a core frequency of 2.27 GHz. The TurboBoost overclocking feature allows processor cores to increase their frequency up to 2.67 GHz. All measurements are performed with Linux kernel version 2.6.32.12. This configuration is also used for the examples presented in Section 3. The benchmark repeatedly calls an empty function (immediate return), a worst-case scenario in terms of trace overhead. We compare a minimal synchronous and a minimal asynchronous post-mortem plugin counter to the runtime with no counters. The runtime is measured at the beginning and the end of the program, ignoring the initialization and finalization phase of VampirTrace.

When no counter is added, each function call lasts about 1.65 μs. Every synchronous counter increases this time by about 600 ns, most of which is required to write the counter value to the trace buffer. Asynchronous post-mortem counters do not influence the runtime of the program. Therefore, plugin libraries that record events on an external system and gather the data in the finalization phase have no impact on the program execution at all.

2.4 Additional Software Infrastructure

For the examples presented in Section 3, we use two additional tools. The DBUS-based *perf event server* provides enhanced access to kernel tracing events. The *Dataheap* is a distributed counter collection system.

The Linux kernel tracing infrastructure [5] enables event counting on a user level, but certain restrictions apply in a non-privileged context. Users can only read counters that are attached to their processes (*per-task-counters*). This affects some of our use cases in Section 3, for example in case of a plugin that monitors the operating system scheduler events. When the time slice of the observed process ends, the operating system scheduler selects a new task and starts its execution on the CPU. These actions are executed from the context of the observed (previous) process. Scheduling events that are created whenever the own process is stripped *from* a CPU will be reported correctly. Scheduling the observed process *to* a CPU is performed from the context of a different task and will not be reported by a *per-task-counter*. It is therefore necessary to trace scheduling events for all processes. This implies the usage of *per-CPU-counters* that trace all events of a specific type on one CPU. These counters gather information of foreign processes and therefore require privileged rights. Our DBUS-based *perf event server* allows applications to send tracing requests that include their PID, the event that shall be traced, and the desired memory to buffer the data. The server checks for appropriate user rights and available memory and starts the monitoring if both requirements are satisfied. The plugin collects the gathered data from the server after the task finishes and merges it into the trace file (see Figure 2).

The distributed counter collection system *Dataheap* uses a central management daemon that runs on a dedicated server and collects performance data from information sources. The *Dataheap* manager then distributes this data to arbitrary clients, for example monitoring tools. The default usage scenario of the *Dataheap* framework implies a distributed set-up, where sources and clients run on different nodes. We use this infrastructure for several different purposes, for example monitoring I/O activity by reading information from network attached storage servers, or for measuring the power consumption of compute nodes.

3 Examples

In this Section we demonstrate the potential of the VampirTrace plugin counter interface. Two plugin counters exploit the Linux kernel tracing infrastructure,

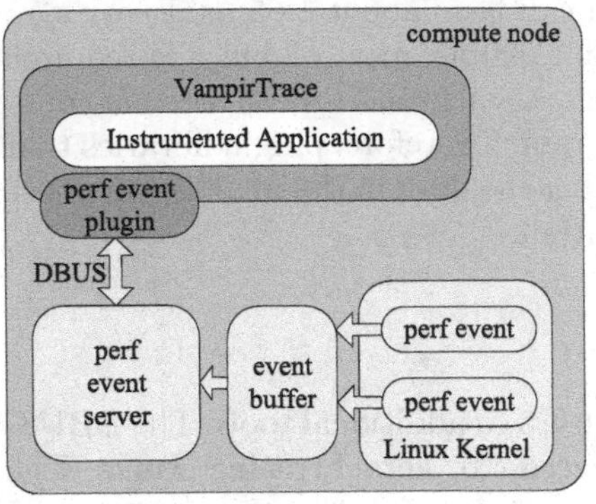

(a) Perf event server and plugin

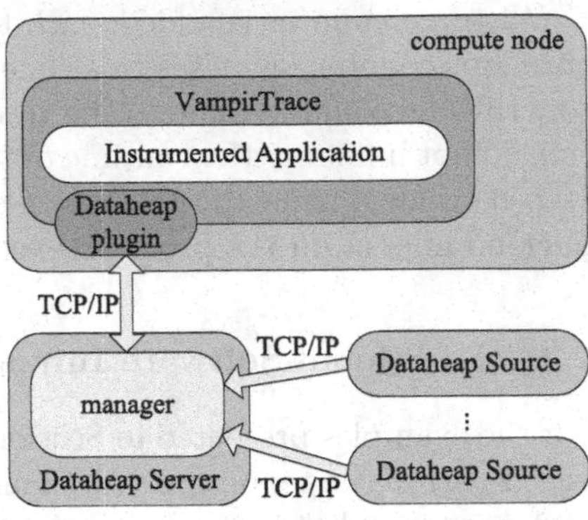

(b) Dataheap infrastructure and plugin

Fig. 2. Comparison of perf event and Dataheap Plugin infrastructure

which was introduced with kernel version 2.6.31. The third one utilizes the *Dataheap* infrastructure. For our tests we use a small MPI program that executes the following commands:

```
0: all ranks: sleep 1 second
1: rank 0: sleep 1 second
2: all ranks: sleep 1 second
3: rank 0: sleep 1 second
4: all ranks: sleep 1 second
5: all ranks: busy waiting for 1 second
6: all ranks: sleep 1 second
7: all ranks: busy waiting for 1 second
8: all ranks: sleep 1 second
```

Each of these commands is followed by an `MPI_Barrier` to synchronize all ranks. The resulting traces are presented in Figure 3, 4, and 5.

3.1 Power State Tracing

We use three different kernel events to determine the C-state and clock frequency of a CPU: *power:power_frequency*, *power:power_start*, and *power:power_end*. A *power:power_frequency* event is created every time a CPU changes its frequency. *power:power_start* and *power:power_end* correlate with a CPU entering or leaving a sleep state. The plugin is implemented as post-mortem type to reduce the overhead within VampirTrace. This means that the event buffers for the kernel events have to be large enough to hold all events.

The possibility of dynamically overclocking a processor (e.g., via Turbo Boost) is not considered, as both the current availability of overclocking and its real frequency are not passed from the operating system to userspace. This could be fixed by adding information about the registers `aperf` and `mperf` to the reported event. Moreover, switching to another C-state has to be done in kernel

(a) Test application - frequency and C-state for every CPU

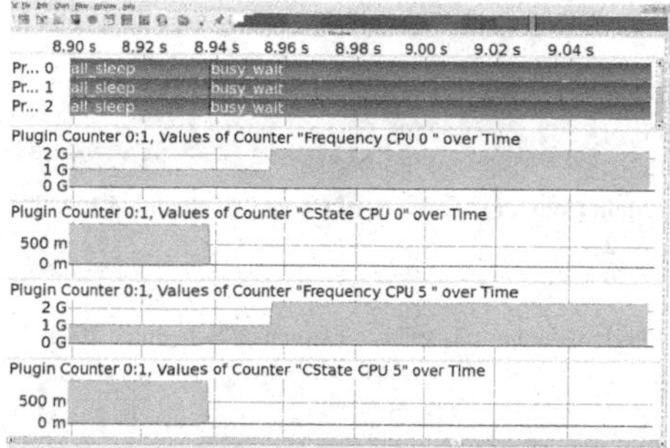

(b) Frequency of a CPU is increased with a short delay after it leaves a C-state

Fig. 3. Power state tracing, frequency and C-state for every CPU

mode since all routines initiating a C-state (e.g., `mwait` or `hlt`) require privileged rights. Therefore we use the *perf event server* introduced in Section 2.4. Switching to another frequency is mostly done by a governor that adapts the processors frequencies automatically based on the recent load (ondemand/conservative governor). The counters displayed in Figure 3a show that whenever a process starts sleeping, its processor immediately switches to a higher C-state. As shown in Figure 3b, the adaption of the frequency is not quite as fast, as the CPU governor bases its frequency scaling decisions on the recent load.

3.2 Scheduler Tracing

Processes or threads that migrate to other cores have to rebuild their register content and their cache entries. The induced overhead can be performance relevant and of interest for an optimization task. Our next plugin therefore monitors *sched:sched_switch* events that are created whenever a process is scheduled onto a CPU or stripped from it. Figure 4a depicts the trace visualization of our test application including scheduler events. Figure 4b shows that there is periodical scheduler activity during the busy waiting phase in a blocking `MPI_Barrier` routine (see process 1 with PID 20049). The counter values correspond to the CPU number that a selected process is scheduled to. For example, when process 0 (with PID 20048) is active, it is scheduled onto CPU 3. Whenever process 0 is put into a sleep state, it is unscheduled (-1).

Since a *sched:sched_switch* event is created every time the operating system scheduler is invoked, tracing this event makes excessive use of the result buffer. With the support for *sched:sched_migrate_task* events, our plugin provides an alternative to trace scheduling behavior. Such a *sched:sched_migrate_task* event is created when a process is scheduled onto a different CPU. This occurs less frequently and reduces the required buffer size significantly. The reduced buffer size comes along with the drawback that the *sched:sched_migrate_task* event can not detect phases, where the observed process is not scheduled onto a CPU.

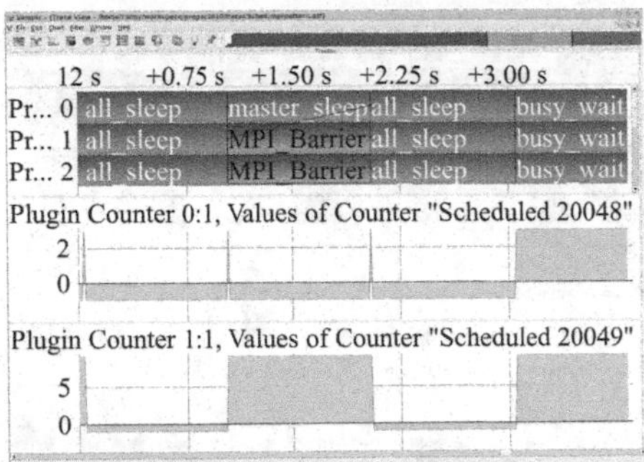

(a) Overview of scheduler behavior for the test application. Processes are unscheduled (-1) when they enter a sleep state

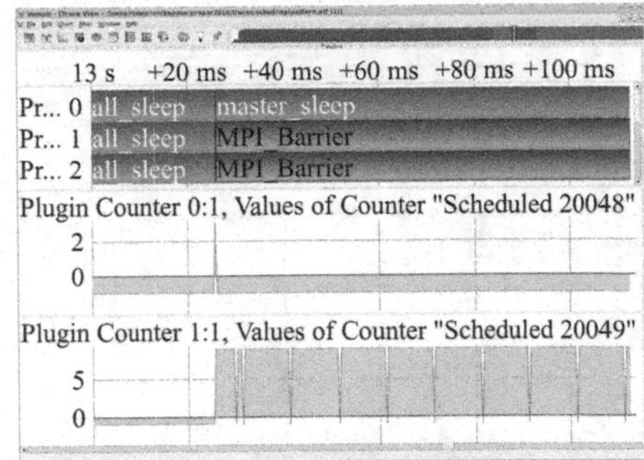

(b) Counter 1:1 shows periodical operating system interrupts every 10 ms during busy waiting in a blocking MPI routine

Fig. 4. Scheduler event tracing, CPU id for every rank

3.3 Power Consumption Tracing

There are currently three distinct *Dataheap* counter plugins, each with its own advantages and disadvantages. We use the asynchronous post-mortem plugin, which only registers at the management daemon and collects the written data after the application has finished. This solution is clearly preferable in terms of trace overhead. The trace depicted in Figure 5 uses the *Dataheap* framework to provide information about the power consumption of our test system (see Section 2.3).

We use a ZES LMG 450 power meter with a 10 Hz sampling frequency that reports its measurement data to the *Dataheap* manager. The trace shows how the power state changes of the CPUs reduce the power consumption of the whole system. We can see that the OpenMPI implementation of `MPI_Barrier` uses a busy waiting algorithm that consumes considerably more power than our busy waiting loop.

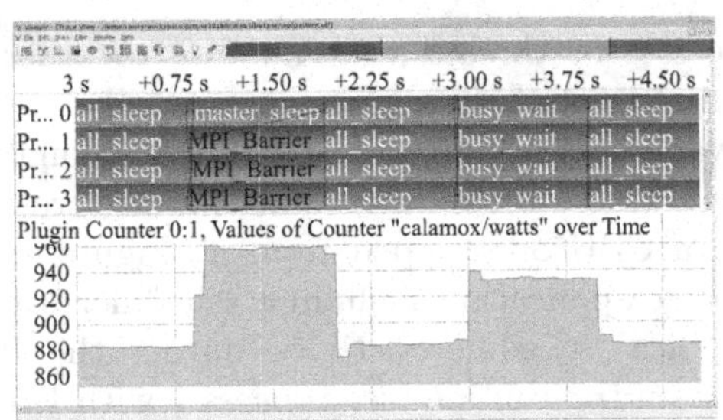

Fig. 5. Power consumption in Watts, collected from an external counter database

4 Limitations

Recording events from performance counters always increases the overall tracing overhead. The proposed VampirTrace extension allows using a post-mortem interface that moves the overhead for the actual event generation within VampirTrace from within the program runtime to after the program has finished. Therefore, the program perturbation is small (kernel tracing) or zero (tracing of external events, see Section 3.3). However, the post-mortem runtime overhead as well as the memory overhead for the event buffers can be significant. These overheads are not introduced by the plugin counter interface, but by the plugins themselves.

Another limitation is that only one counter is internally measured at a time. This can be a drawback when using numerous synchronous events. In contrast, PAPI and the Linux kernel tracing infrastructure allow reading multiple events with only one function call, thereby avoiding some overhead.

5 Related Work

While there is a wide range of performance analysis tools and libraries, only some of them provide a plugin interface. The *Collector Plugins* of Open|SpeedShop [6] are comparable to our approach. However, while Open|SpeedShop focuses on profiling with only limited tracing support, the focus of VampirTrace clearly is event tracing.

The PAPI project specifies an application programming interface for accessing hardware performance counters. Monitoring these counters can for example give hints how software can be optimized for a specific platform. PAPI version 4 provides the possibility to implement own counters called *Components*, which can be read using PAPI. For design reasons, PAPI has to be recompiled for every new component. Moreover, its design prohibits asynchronous events. However, for synchronous events that are counted for every thread, it is a more flexible and well accepted interface.

The Vampir framework is a well established performance analysis tool chain with a strong focus on scalable high performance computing applications [2,3,7]. Recent work hast demonstrated the applicability of both the event monitor VampirTrace and the performance visualizer Vampir on state of the art systems including hardware accelerators [8,9]. While we used the kernel tracing infrastructure to trace scheduling events, Kluge et al. [10] follow a different approach. They use an additional thread, which monitors all other threads with a specific polling interval. A high polling frequency strongly influences the test system even if no rescheduling events occur. A too low frequency increases the possibility of missed events and reduces the time accuracy of scheduling events.

6 Conclusion and Future Work

This paper presents the design and implementation of the VampirTrace plugin counter interface along with some typical usage scenarios. The main goal of this work is to address the issue of the constantly increasing number of performance events sources that are typically highly platform specific. The plugin counter interface allows these events to be recorded with VampirTrace while at the same time strongly reducing the need to modify the core source code of the tool. Its tight integration into VampirTrace and the availability of asynchronous events further increase the benefit of this extension. Our exemplary implementation of three different plugins demonstrates the potential of the newly defined plugin infrastructure. All three plugins are used in current research efforts to analyze programs and libraries with respect to performance and energy efficiency. Future work will focus on making the plugin counter interface generally available within the VampirTrace trunk. Moreover, other plugins are currently under development, e.g., a libsensors plugin to read hardware information asynchronously.

Acknowledgment

The authors would like to thank Matthias Jurenz for his continuous and valuable contributions to the VampirTrace project as well as Michael Kluge for his support and his work on the Dataheap project. The authors also thank Intel Germany for providing us with the Intel Nehalem EX evaluation platform. This work has been funded by the Bundesministerium für Bildung und Forschung via the Spitzencluster CoolSilicon (BMBF 13N10186).

References

1. The MPI Forum: MPI: A Message Passing Interface (2010), `http://www.mpi-forum.org/`
2. Knüpfer, A., Brunst, H., Doleschal, J., Jurenz, M., Lieber, M., Mickler, H., Müller, M.S., Nagel, W.E.: The Vampir Performance Analysis Tool-Set. In: Proceedings of the 2nd International Workshop on Parallel Tools for High Performance Computing, pp. 139–155. Springer, Heidelberg (2008)
3. Müller, M.S., Knüpfer, A., Jurenz, M., Lieber, M., Brunst, H., Mix, H., Nagel, W.E.: Developing Scalable Applications with Vampir, VampirServer and VampirTrace. In: Bischof, C.H., Bücker, H.M., Gibbon, P., Joubert, G.R., Lippert, T., Mohr, B., Peters, F.J. (eds.) PARCO. Advances in Parallel Computing, vol. 15, pp. 637–644. IOS Press, Amsterdam (2007)
4. Gabriel, E., Fagg, G.E., Bosilca, G., Angskun, T., Dongarra, J.J., Squyres, J.M., Sahay, V., Kambadur, P., Barrett, B., Lumsdaine, A., Castain, R.H., Daniel, D.J., Graham, R.L., Woodall, T.S.: Open MPI: Goals, concept, and design of a next generation MPI implementation. In: Kranzlmüller, D., Kacsuk, P., Dongarra, J. (eds.) EuroPVM/MPI 2004. LNCS, vol. 3241, pp. 97–104. Springer, Heidelberg (2004)
5. Eranian, S.: Linux new monitoring interface: Performance Counter for Linux. In: CSCADS Workshop 2009 (2009) `http://cscads.rice.edu/workshops/summer09/slides/performance-tools/cscads09-eranian.pdf`
6. Schulz, M., Galarowicz, J., Maghrak, D., Hachfeld, W., Montoya, D., Cranford, S.: Open|SpeedShop: An open source infrastructure for parallel performance analysis. Sci. Program. 16, 105–121 (2008)
7. Brunst, H., Hackenberg, D., Juckeland, G., Rohling, H.: Comprehensive Performance Tracking with Vampir 7. In: Müller, M.S., Resch, M.M., Schulz, A., Nagel, W.E. (eds.) Tools for High Performance Computing 2009, pp. 17–29. Springer, Heidelberg (2010)

8. Hackenberg, D., Brunst, H., Nagel, W.: Event Tracing and Visualization for Cell Broadband Engine Systems. In: Luque, E., Margalef, T., Benítez, D. (eds.) Euro-Par 2008. LNCS, vol. 5168, pp. 172–181. Springer, Heidelberg (2008)
9. Hackenberg, D., Juckeland, G., Brunst, H.: High resolution program flow visualization of hardware accelerated hybrid multi-core applications. IEEE International Symposium on Cluster Computing and the Grid, vol. 0, pp. 786–791 (2010)
10. Kluge, M., Nagel, W.: Analysis of Linux Scheduling with VAMPIR. In: Shi, Y., van Albada, G., Dongarra, J., Sloot, P. (eds.) ICCS 2007. LNCS, vol. 4488, pp. 823–830. Springer, Heidelberg (2007), doi:10.1007/978-3-540-72586-2_116

Guided Performance Analysis Combining Profile and Trace Tools

Judit Giménez[1], Jesús Labarta[1], F. Xavier Pegenaute[1], Hui-Fang Wen[2], David Klepacki[2], I-Hsin Chung[2], Guojing Cong[2], Felix Voigtländer[3], and Bernd Mohr[4]

[1] BSC-UPC
{judit.gimenez,jesus.labarta,xavier.pegenaute}@bsc.es
[2] IBM T.J. Watson
{hfwen,klepacki,ihchung,gcong}@us.ibm.com
[3] RWTH Aachen University
felix.voigtlaender@gmail.com
[4] Jülich Supercomputing Centre
B.Mohr@fz-juelich.de

Abstract. Performance analysis is very important to understand the applications' behavior and to identify bottlenecks. Performance analysis tools should facilitate the exploration of the data collected and help to identify where the analyst has to look. While this functionality can promote the tools usage on small and medium size environments, it becomes mandatory for large-scale and many-core systems where the amount of data is dramatically increased. This paper proposes a new methodology based on the integration of profilers and timeline tools to improve and facilitate the performance analysis process.

1 Introduction

The performance of an application is influenced by multiple and complex factors. Performance measurement and analysis tools allow to understand the application performance behavior and give hints on how they can be optimized. There are two main approaches on such performance analysis tools:

Profile-based tools accumulate statistics over the time dimension, keeping the metrics per function and/or process. Despite the time aggregation, the volume of data can still become huge if a large number of processes is measured or a very large number of metrics is precomputed. But usually the accumulation over time drastically reduces the data volume. The profiled data is presented structured in tables or trees. These two facts (size and type of display) facilitate the correlation between metrics. Many of the profiler tools can link the metric values with the source code showing the location and in some cases the code can be edited from the profiler GUI.

Timeline visualization tools work with performance data in the 2D space defined by processes and time. This approach yields a lot of data, and the justification is that the variance over time is very important. The advocates for traces defend that the aggregation could mask the metrics, preventing the analyst from

M.R. Guarracino et al. (Eds.): Euro-Par 2010 Workshops, LNCS 6586, pp. 513–521, 2011.
© Springer-Verlag Berlin Heidelberg 2011

looking at the metrics details and variance. Keeping the time dimension allows the user to dynamically compute separate values for different time regions while doing the analysis. In addition, some of these tools are capable of computing new metrics defined on the fly increasing the search tree size. Many timeline tools allow the user to accumulate the metrics in tables to obtain profile-like views or histograms for a given metric.

There are clear strengths in both approaches that make them complementary, but usually these tools are disconnected. A first reason is that profilers and timeline tools work with different types of data, but even if there is a translator, the integration does not go further than being able of working with performance data from the other tool. To make things more difficult, each tool has its own format despite initiatives to promote a common format like OTF [1] for traces and PERI-XML [2] for profiles. The contribution of this work is to demonstrate how profilers and timeline tools can interoperate defining a new methodology that uses at each step the tool that easily answers the analyst question.

The methodology defined herein benefits from both approaches. The analysis is initiated using the profiler to identify regions or metrics of interest for a deep analysis. For these regions/metrics, the timeline tool is used to display the details, e.g., to investigate the context or history of a source of unusual metric values. The integration should provide the feeling of a unified environment capable of collecting all the information required in a single run and the tools should be responsible for keeping the analysis context as transparent as possible. In our work we have interfaced KOJAK and PeekPerf profilers with the Paraver analysis tool. The focus of the methodology is not on the data adquisition but on the analysis phase because we consider it more complex.

Due to the limit of the proceedings number of pages, this paper has been drastically reduced eliminating sections like tools description, related work and conclusions and future plans. The full version of the paper can be found as technical report UPC-DAC-RR-CAP-2010-28.

2 Performance Analysis Workflows

Post-mortem performance analysis is usually defined in two steps for both profile and timeline tools. The first step collects data from the execution and the second one displays the data to the analyst. If a user wants to use a profiler and a timeline for the analysis, usually this would require to do two different executions of the application, unless there is a translator and the data required by one tool can be extracted from the data collected by the other. Some tools like KOJAK divide the second step in two parts: the automatic analyzer (EXPERT) extracts metrics from the trace that are presented to the user with CUBE.

The proposed approach (Figure 1) extends this structure to explore new paths between the collected data and its visualization. The initial path connects the profile and the tracefile views combining them to carry out the analysis. Other interesting paths would be to generate new profile views from the visualization modules (usually trace visualization, but even from a profile view). This approach refines the metrics based on the results of a previous analysis step.

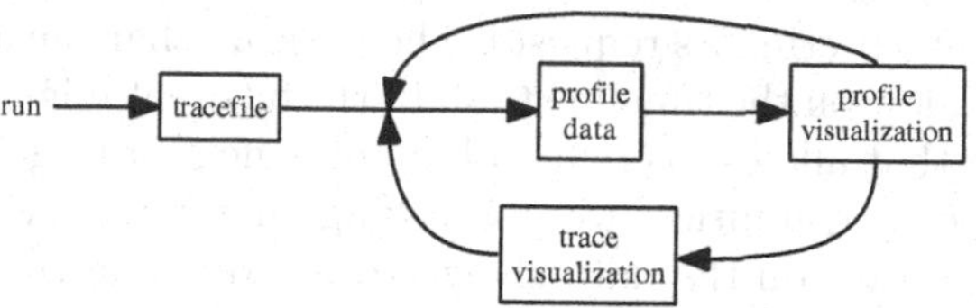

Fig. 1. Proposed workflow

In the current implementation, the selection is controlled by the user, who decides what to do next. This includes a manual refinement to extract new metrics based on the previous step. But this process can be done automatically by an expert system. The methodology would be defined on a search tree and the intermediate results would decide the branch for the next step. The system would present the relevant data to the analyst who can decide where and how to refine the analysis. An example of semi-automatic approach is the IBM's High Productivity Computing System toolkit (HPCST) [3] which actively searches for known performance patterns instead of recording information. The toolkit integrates performance tools, compiler and expert knowledge.

3 Coupling Profile and Timeline Analyzers

As depicted in the previous section, one of our objectives is to obtain all the information from a single run. It is not only a matter of conserving resources, but also to avoid correlating different runs measurements. When data is collected with instrumentation (as opposite to sampling) the overhead of gathering the information is similar for both timeline and profiling except on the regions where the tracing buffer is flushed to disk. The proposed approach is to collect the timeline information and to extract from it the profiled data.

The module that processes trace data to obtain the profiler input corresponds to the EXPERT module in the KOJAK environment. It is a kind of filter that extracts and aggregates the data relevant to the selected metrics. The user is able to select the metrics to be explored, but it is important to provide a good default set. Examples of performance metrics to be analyzed by the profiling environment are: time, instructions per cycle, load balance, L2 misses, L1/L2 miss ratio and message size. The filter program may use the functionality provided by the trace tool to generate a profile. In order to be able to later connect the profile visualization with the timeline visualization, in this phase some additional references have to be included on the profile data. The references should define which views can be generated and how to compute them (for instance being on a given user function or being on a region with a late sender).

The profile visualizer is used to analyze the generated metrics. The tool has to offer a new functionality for the coupling with the timeline visualizer: it needs to accept as part of its input new hidden metrics used to send a request to an external presenter and to offer to the user the possibility to call the timeline.

Finally, the timeline visualizer provides a mechanism to be driven by the profile analysis, interpreting its requests. The basic mechanism allows the profiler to raise a new window on the timeline tool. In the future it might be interesting to use a mechanism that allows to create a kind of dialog, or to get feedback. There is a wide range of possibilities: from checking that the view was successfully presented to get details on the data shown to be added on the profiler display.

4 The Tools

The tools used to validate this methodology are PeekPerf [5] and KOJAK [6] as profile tools and Paraver [8,9] as timeline analyzer. The modifications required to support this approach were very simple: PeekPerf and Kojak were extended with a new menu option to invoque a external tool and Paraver was extended with a signal command functionality to enable external applications to trigger loading new views on a selected time range or zooming on a previous view.

5 Examples of Analysis with the Proposed Framework

This section shows how the combination of profile and timeline tools improves the ease-of-use and accuracy of the analysis using the profiler to focus and the timeline tool to look for details/distribution. While the first example uses the trace visualization to complement the facts identified on the profiler, the second example covers the approach of refining the data depending on previous results.

5.1 KOJAK and Paraver

The example is based on a measurement of WRF-NMMii [11], a public-domain numerical weather forecast code developed by the U.S. National Oceanic and Atmospheric Administration (NOAA) National Centers for Environmental Prediction (NCEP), consisting of the Nonhydrostatic Mesoscale Model (NMM) within the Weather Research and Forecasting (WRF) system. It consists of some 530+ source files with over 300 thousand lines of code (75% Fortran, 25% C). Simulations were analyzed using the Eur-12km dataset with a default configuration, apart from varying the duration of the forecast and disabling intermediate checkpoints. The data shown here are from an experiment with 64 processors on the MareNostrum machine at Barcelona Supercomputing Center.

After instrumenting the application with KOJAK tools, executing it on the parallel system, and analyzing the traces with EXPERT, it is possible to investigate the generated pattern profile with CUBE (see Figure 2). In the "Metric tree" pane on the left side, one can quickly see that KOJAK found two main problems: First, more than half of the point-to-point traffic is *Late Senders* (3.69 seconds compared to 3.41 seconds spent in regular MPI point-to-point functions). More than half of the *late Senders* can be attributed to *Messages in Wrong Order* (1.99 vs. 1.70 seconds). The second detected problem is *WaitAt-NxN* with a severity of 0.68 seconds. Selecting the collective operation pattern

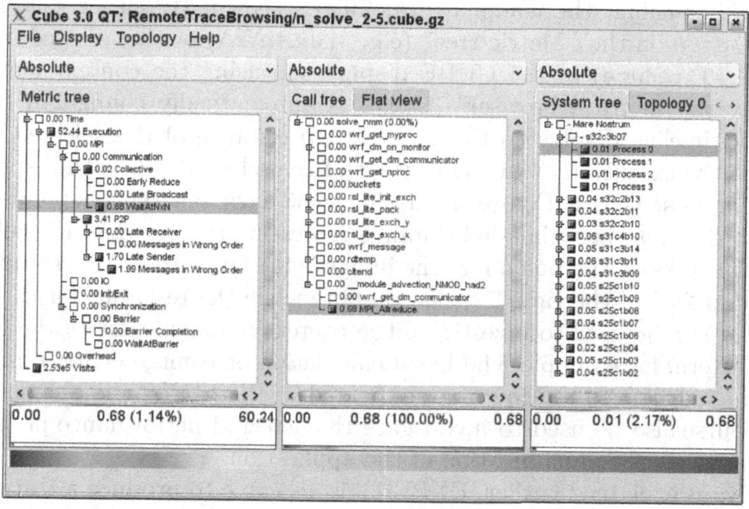

Fig. 2. KOJAK's analysis results for WRF shown in the CUBE browser

(as shown in Figure 2), displays in the middle "Call tree" pane where this pattern occurred in the program. In the example, it is a single call of `MPI_Allreduce` from the module function `advection::had2` called from `solvenmm`. By selecting `MPI_Allreduce` in the call tree pane, the distribution of the imbalance over the nodes and processes can be investigated in the "System tree" pane on the right.

It is important to note that waiting time in front of a collective is more of a symptom than a cause of a performance problem. When the problem cannot be resolved by looking at the corresponding portion of the source code, the context of this pattern can be investigated with timeline tools like Paraver. To do this easily, one can use the "Connect to trace browser" item of the "File" menu. This automatically starts a new instance of Paraver, loading the corresponding trace file via remote control. By default, it brings up the "State as is" display of Paraver which shows the change of MPI states over time. The dialog window also allows the user to select other Paraver configuration files if desired.

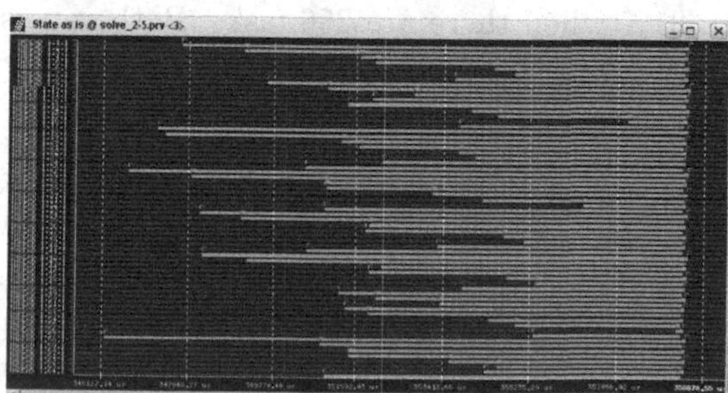

Fig. 3. Zoomed-in Paraver timeline display of a WRF trace showing just the instance of the WaitAtNxN pattern with maximum severity

In the beginning, the complete timelime is shown. By either selecting the desired pattern in the "Metric tree" (e.g. *WaitAtNxN*) or the affected call path (e.g. `MPI_Allreduce`) in the CUBE display and using the context menu item "Max severity in trace browser", CUBE is automatically configured to zoom Paraver's timeline display to the most severe instance of the selected pattern overall in the execution or in the context of the selected call path respectively. The result is shown in Figure 3. In this view dark blue corressponds to the unbalanced computing while light orange represents time in the MPI collective. One of the tasks on the bottom of the image is the latest to end its computation and around 25% of the time 3 tasks compute while the rest wait for them.

Paraver can be used to investigate the context or the history of the instance of the pattern, for example whether a calculation or communication imbalance causes the imbalanced waiting times indicated by *WaitAtNxN*. The same method can of course also be used to investigate the detected performance problems of the point-to-point communication of the application.

Finally, as explained earlier, EXPERT is also able to produce a trace of patterns in addition to the pattern profile report. So in this example, we could have done the same analysis steps also with the pattern trace, or even with both traces. In this case, when a zoom to the most severe instance of a pattern is requested, CUBE zooms both timeline displays via remote control of Paraver.

5.2 PeekPerf and Paraver

The environment was used to analyze the scalability of GROMACS [12], a versatile package to perform molecular dynamics, with "nucleosome" testcase. As the scalability decreases over 256 tasks, the analysis compares the run of 256 tasks with the 64 tasks case that achieves better performance. We obtained traces for these configurations and extracted a first set of global metrics to measure the efficiency at the whole execution level such as parallel efficiency and load balance as described in [13]. The values range from 0 to 1 (except IPC) with high values reporting a good performance and low values identifying a problem.

The analysis starts from PeekPerf (Figure 4 captures the metrics for both runs). As PeekPerf displays all global metrics on a line, it is very simple and quick to analyze and compare their values. The parallel efficiency is 55% with 64 tasks decreasing to 31% when there are 256 tasks. Both values indicate a poor performance, but with 256 tasks more than 2/3 of the resources are wasted.

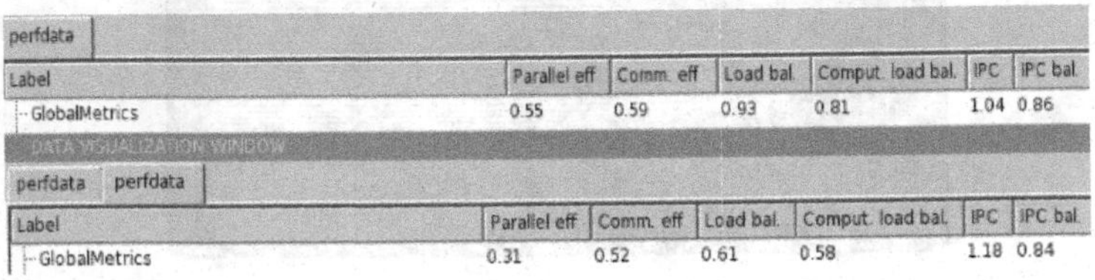

perfdata

Label	Parallel eff	Comm. eff	Load bal.	Comput. load bal.	IPC	IPC bal.
GlobalMetrics	0.55	0.59	0.93	0.81	1.04	0.86

DATA VISUALIZATION WINDOW

perfdata perfdata

Label	Parallel eff	Comm. eff	Load bal.	Comput. load bal.	IPC	IPC bal.
GlobalMetrics	0.31	0.52	0.61	0.58	1.18	0.84

Fig. 4. Global metrics displayed on PeekPerf (top: 64 tasks case; botton: 256)

We can observe that the poor scalability is mainly due to load imbalance (duration) and computation imbalance (instructions) as those are the factors with a higher decrease. But, the communication efficiency is also very poor in both runs. These observations drive the next analysis step to focus on two targets: (1) analyze time and computation balance to understand the poor scalability and (2) analyze the communication performance with 64 tasks.

With respect to the first issue, as we are interested in the time and processes distribution, the timeline analysis tool is foreseen as the best alternative. The PeekPerf contextual menu offers the choice "Call Back to the Integrated Tool" that allows to easily raise a set of predefined Paraver windows. Selecting the duration of the computation bursts we detect that GROMACS is composed by two kinds of tasks: a subset performs FFTs that are characterized by a sequence of medium size computations (around 8ms with 64 tasks) while the rest execute particle computations significantly larger (around 20ms for the same case). For simplicity, the details on the load balance are provided only for the FFTs tasks– Figure 5 compares their execution. The x-axis represents time and the y-axis the MPI tasks. Despite the image of the FFTs for the 256 case is compresed and with this window size we cannot isolate the behavior of a given task, it provides enough details on the global behavior (structure, imbalance, duration, etc.).

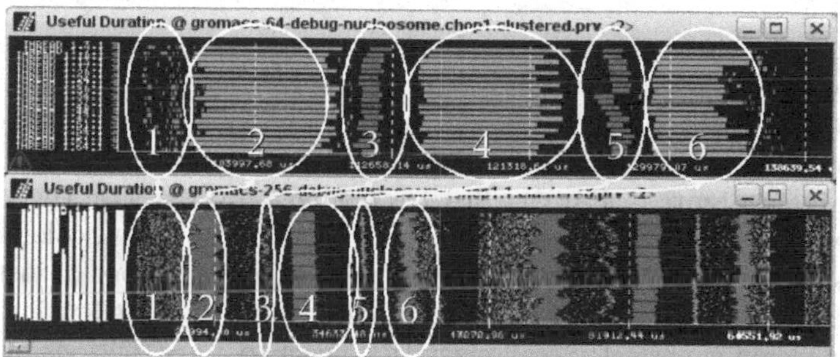

Fig. 5. Analysis of the FFTs duration scalability (top: 64 tasks case; botton: 256). Black corresponds to MPI. 6 ellipsis denote 6 code regions. Note the poor speed-up achieved by the fourth marked region due to imbalance.

On a perfect speed-up, the duration of a region with 256 tasks should be 1/4 of the execution with 64 tasks. Both windows have the same time scale, showing that on the interval where the 64 tasks run executes one iteration with 256 tasks executes a little bit more than two iterations. Observe that the main computation regions (zones 2, 4 and 6) obtain good time reductions. Zone 4 has a problem of imbalance: while with 64 tasks it has a small impact, in the 256 tasks case it becomes the bottleneck as this imbalance does not scale. Zone 1 is dominated by communications and as would be expected, it achieves a poor speed-up. Within Paraver the callstack can be used to identify where any of those regions are in the source code. Notice that this part of the analysis was easily done opening the Paraver views while would be very complex using a profiler.

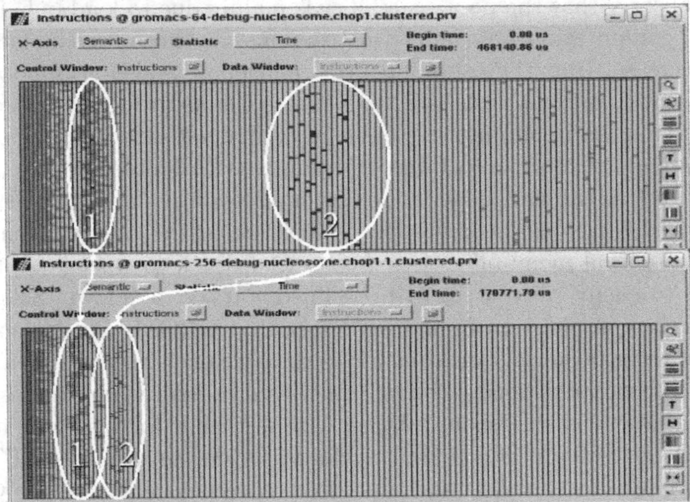

Fig. 6. Analysis of the computation (#instructions) imbalance (top: 64 tasks case; botton: 256). Note that region 1 #instructions is not reduced and imbalance increases.

Restating the hints given by the PeekPerf analysis, the metrics reported a computation balance problem. To analyze this issue, from PeekPerf we opened the instructions histogram. Again, this analysis is done with the timeline tool because we are interested on the distribution. With both histograms at the same scale, we obtain Figure 6. Paraver histograms have processes on the y-axis and the selected metric on the x-axis. In the instructions histogram, colored cells on the right side of the image represent areas with a large number of instructions, colored cells on the left side correspond to regions that execute few instructions.

If a code region is perfectly scalable with respect to #instructions, when tasks are multiplied by 4, the #instructions/task is reduced to 1/4, so both versions execute the same number of instructions (no code replication). This reduction is reflected on the histogram as a proportional shift to the left. With a perfect speed-up the displacement would be 3/4 on the x-axis. While zone 2 (with a high number of instructions) obtains a good reduction (the displacement is close to a perfect scenario), zone 1 obtains a poor reduction and increases the imbalance.

Finally, to analyze the poor communication performance with 64 tasks, we extracted new metrics applied at the level of the MPI call lines. These metrics include time, number of calls, average duration and message size. Computing these metrics at the level of the call line allows to separate, for instance, different broadcasts depending on the calling context. Due to space limitations it is not possible to discuss the details but we would like to remark that the profiling view is the most appropriate tool for this analysis. Notice that with the proposed methodology based on refinements, this new profiling would be generated only because a previous step identified it as a relevant peformance data.

Acknowledgments. This paper has been partially supported by the Spanish Ministry of Science and Innovation (contract number TIN2007-60625) and the MareIncognito project under the IBM-BSC collaboration agreement.

References

1. Knüpfer, A., Brendel, R., Brunst, H., Mix, H., Nagel, W.E.: Introducing the Open Trace Format (OTF). In: ICCS (2006)
2. `http://www.peri-scidac.org/wiki/index.php/PERI_XML`
3. Cong, G., Chung, I.-H., Wen, H., Klepacki, D., Murata, H., Negishi, Y., Moriyama, T.: A holistic approach towards automated performance analysis and tuning. In: Sips, H., Epema, D., Lin, H.-X. (eds.) Euro-Par 2009. LNCS, vol. 5704, pp. 33–44. Springer, Heidelberg (2009)
4. Wolf, F., Mohr, B.: Automatic performance analysis of hybrid MPI/OpenMP appl. Journal of Systems Arch. 49(10-11), 421–439 (2003)
5. Chung, I.-H., et al.: Productivity Centered Framework for Application Performance Tuning. In: Proceedings of the 2nd International Conference on Performance Evaluation Methodologies and Tools
6. Geimer, M., et al.: The Scalasca performance toolset architecture. Concurrency and Computation: Practice and Experience 22(6), 702–719 (2010)
7. Geimer, M., et al.: Scalable Collation and Pres. of Call-Path Profile Data with CUBE. In: Proc. of the Parallel Computing Conf (ParCo). NIC series, vol. 38, pp. 645–652 (2007)
8. Pillet, V., et al.: PARAVER: A Tool to Visualize and Analyze Parallel Code. In: 18th World OCCAM and Transputer User Group Technical Meeting (April 1995), `http://www.bsc.es/paraver`
9. Labarta, J., Gimenez, J.: Performance Analysis: Till When an Art. In: Herroux, M.A., et al. (eds.) Parallel Processing for Scientific Computing. SIAM, Philadelphia (2006)
10. Jost, G., Labarta, J., Gimenez, J.: Paramedir: A Tool for Programmable Performance Analysis. In: Int. Conf. on Computational Science (ICCS 2004) (June 2004)
11. Weather Research Forecast code, `http://www.wrf-model.org/`
12. GROningen MAchine for Chemical Simulations, `http://www.gromacs.org`
13. Casas-Guix, M., Badia, R.M., Labarta, J.: Automatic analysis of speedup of MPI appl. In: Int. Conf. on Supercomputing (ICS 2008) (June 2008)
14. Jost, G., Chun, R., Jin, H., Labarta, J., Gimenez, J.: An Expert Asssistant for Computer Aided Parallelization. In: Dongarra, J., Madsen, K., Waśniewski, J. (eds.) PARA 2004. LNCS, vol. 3732, pp. 665–674. Springer, Heidelberg (2006)

An Approach to Visualize Remote Socket Traffic on the Intel Nehalem-EX

Christian Iwainsky[1], Thomas Reichstein[1], Christopher Dahnken[2], Dieter an Mey[1], Christian Terboven[1], Andrey Semin[2], and Christian Bischof[1]

[1] Center for Computing and Communication
RWTH Aachen University
{iwainsky,reichstein,anmey,terboven,bischof}@rz.rwth-aachen.de

[2] Intel GmbH
Dornacher Str. 1
85622 Feldkirchen bei München

Abstract. The integration of the memory controller on the processor die enables ever larger core counts in commodity hardware shared memory systems with Non-Uniform Memory Architecture properties. Shared memory parallelization with OpenMP is an elegant and widely used approach to leverage the power of such systems. The binding of the OpenMP threads to compute cores and the corresponding memory association are becoming even more critical in order to obtain optimal performance. In this work we provide a method to measure the amount of remote socket memory accesses a thread generates. We use available performance monitoring CPU counters in combination with thread binding on a quad socket Nehalem EX system. For visualization of the collected data we use Vampir.

1 Introduction

With the ever increasing demand for compute power to satisfy the demand of scientists and engineers, hardware vendors assemble larger and larger systems. Considering the Top 500 list [1], current clusters are ranging in the tens of thousands of compute nodes, typically in a dual socket Non Uniform Memory Architecture (NUMA) configuration focused on distributed memory computation. At the same time "fat" commodity nodes with up to eight sockets and up to 128 logical threads become available. They satisfy the need of heavily communicating workloads, shared memory constrained applications and memory requirements up to 2TB [2].

Developing efficient algorithms for such platforms poses a serious problem for developers, particularly if one takes into account that the sockets of these systems might not even be fully connected, i.e. one requires a number of hops between sockets to deliver a piece of data from one processor core to the other[1]. Based

[1] Notice that the terms cores, CPUs, sockets and nodes are often used in a confusing fashion, mostly due for historical reasons. Here we refer to a core as compute core (which a OS will denote as a CPU). A CPU we refer to as a single package compute device mounted in a socket.

M.R. Guarracino et al. (Eds.): Euro-Par 2010 Workshops, LNCS 6586, pp. 523–530, 2011.
© Springer-Verlag Berlin Heidelberg 2011

on todays most widely supported programming models, OpenMP and MPI (or a hybrid version of both), one has to develop highly parallelizable algorithms taking into account the memory location across as well as within the NUMA nodes in order to minimize communication and synchronization times. A variety of software tools are available that help developers to detect various inefficiencies of their software by addressing important issues like hotspots or thread correctness checking (examples: [3,4,5]). None of these tools, however, specifically helps developers to optimize for the now ubiquitous NUMA platforms.

In this work we address this shortcoming by presenting a technique to directly measure and visualize the used bandwidth between sockets on a four socket NUMA platform based on the Intel Xeon 7500 Series processor. The remainder of this work is structured as follows: First we describe the features and the layout of our test system. We then detail on our methodology and implementation approach. After a brief evaluation of a test code we apply our method to a Jacobi solver kernel to evaluate our approach.

2 Test System Description

We conduct our research on a Xeon X7560 4-socket system, with the CPUs being clocked at 2.26 GHz nominal frequency. The Xeon 7560 CPU features 8 cores capable of symmetric multi-threading (SMT) resulting in 16 possible hardware threads per CPU. The core details are not of particular interest here since we are mostly concerned with the memory subsystem. As for the cache hierarchy, there are three levels on each die as follows: 32kB 1st and 256kB 2nd level cache, both 8 way set associative and individual to each core, and a 24MB 24-way set associative 3rd level cache that is shared between the cores.

An important design principle of this CPU is a fundamental differentiation between the processing cores and the remaining environment, like memory controllers, caches, etc., called *uncore*. Memory accesses that cannot be satisfied by the LLC are either routed to the local or remote memory via the uncore routing facility (R-Box), depending on the physical memory location. In this setup, given a homogeneous memory layout with an equal number of DIMMs per memory channel, the cores have only direct access at native speed to a fraction of the total memory of the system via four separate memory channels. The remaining memory then has to be accessed through the QPI links on a 64-byte cache line basis.

Due to the rather complex memory architecture there are several latencies for a single piece of data, depending where that data resides and if the neighboring caches, i.e. caches on one of the CPUs of another socket, have to be queried or not. Our initial research on a quad socket Nehalem EX system shows up to 6 different access times that could occur for a single memory access:

- LLC hit that does not need snooping (non-shared line): order of 40 cycles
- LLC hit requiring snooping (shared line), clean response: order of 65 cycles
- LLC hit requiring snooping (shared line), dirty response: order of 75 cycles
- LLC miss, answer from local DRAM: order of 180 cycles

– LLC miss, answer from remote LLC: order of 200 cycles
– LLC miss, answer from remote DRAM: order of 300 cycles

Evidently, there are large differences between local and remote memory responses, which strongly underlines the need to optimize multi-threaded applications for memory affinity [6].

As each of the CPUs of each socket has four QPI links, a quad socket system can be build fully interconnecting each of the packages to each other. Therefore three of the QPI links are used to connect a single package to all its neighbors. This leaves one link free for I/O or other purposes.

3 Measurement of Cross Socket Traffic

3.1 Performance Monitoring

Performance monitoring is an ubiquitous feature of modern CPUs of all flavors, not only providing the CPU designers with means to debug hardware units, but also benefiting the user with feedback on the quality of the execution[7]. Generally the configuration of a performance monitoring unit (PMU) is quite simple, although low level. In order to obtain the number of occurrences of a given event in a given time one has to touch three types of model specific registers (MSR)[2] on the CPU: a control register which globally enables the tracking of events, a configuration register telling the CPU to which event to accumulate and a counter register which gets incremented each time the event occurs.

The Nehalem EX provides a manifold of hardware events to track a wide variety of observables on a per core basis, such as executed floating point operations, cache misses, branch-mispredictions, etc[8]. Seven core events can be measured at the same time, three of which are fixed events and four can be programmed for general purpose[9].

In contrast to earlier CPUs, however, the Nehalem CPUs also include special counter registers not associated with specific cores, but with the uncore itself. It is important to notice that, unlike the conventional core PMU, not all events on the uncore-PMU can be programmed in every register reflecting the internal layout. For this work the events and counters of the routing facility (R-Box) are of interest, as there the requests for cache-lines are routed to either the local memory or dispatched to the adjunct sockets for fulfillment.

3.2 Programming the Uncore MSRs

Even though there is no direct counter to measure the request for remote-cache lines it is possible to count the responses with the *NEW_PACKETS_RECV* event. This event can be configured to track many different incoming message types, like snoop message replies (compare [10, p2-92]), but also to count all incoming data responses being received through a specific QPI-link. The number

[2] MSRs can generally change with every new generation of a CPU, although some of them are *architectural*, being guaranteed to be found on every new generation.

Table 1. Uncore counter initialization sequence

1: U_MSR_PMON_GLOBAL_CTL[29]=1	Reset global uncore counters
2: R_MSR_PMON_GLOBAL_CTL_7_0[7-0]=1	Enable R-Box counters for ports 0-3 (counters 0-7)
3: R_MSR_PORT0_IPERF_CFG0[3,6,7]=1	Configure event "Data Response Any" for port 0
4: R_MSR_PMON_CTL0=0x01	Set the control of counter 0 to monitor the event set in R_MSR_PORT0_IPERF_CFG0
5: U_MSR_PMON_GLOBAL_CTL[0,28]=1	Globally enable performance monitoring

of incoming packets along with the payload of each packet can then be used to compute a close estimate of the actually used uni-directional bandwidth of that link. As the router of the CPU (R-Box) has eight separate counter registers, it is possible to track the traffic of each QPI-link separately, facilitating the measurement of all QPI-links within a multi-socket system for performance analysis.

We detail on the programming of the uncore registers. The configuration sequence in (Tab. 1) sets exactly one counter to monitor the packages received at a particular QPI port on one socket. The counter register *R_MSR_PMON_CTR0*, which is controlled by *R_MSR_PMON_CTL0*, will now start incrementing each time a package is received that represents a data response[3].

Ideally one would like to directly measure whether a given LLC-miss was serviced from local or remote memory on a per-instruction level to get the most accurate information on that instructions impact to the whole application performance. Although this would be feasible in a statistical sampling approach, the implementation of a sampling driver is certainly beyond the scope of this work. Here we therefore measured the counters on an OpenMP-construct level, similar to ompP[5]. This results in a more coarse measurement interval, but helps to reduce the overhead. This also helps to associate the data with the parallelism described by the OpenMP constructs.

Unfortunately one is only able to measure on a per socket basis. Therefore a method to map the remote access to the thread with the LLC miss has to be found. This again splits up into two distinct issues.

On the one hand the operating system is altering the scheduling on the system, potentially moving processes and threads from one socket to another. As there are no hooks to intercept such occurrences it is not possible to measure the traffic up to that point and associate this with the new core the thread is running on. To circumvent this issue one can use process/thread-binding to pin the threads of the program to specific cores. Therefore a given thread will always execute on a specified core and no special runtime handling is necessary.

[3] Notice that we haven't configured any interrupt firing upon overflow of this register, so that we currently have to make sure that an overflow does not occur.

On the other hand there is no further mechanism available to us, to directly identify which core caused the cache miss on a given socket. For this work, our approach therefore schedules only one thread per socket, in order to directly associate its misses with the QPI-traffic. For two or more threads per socket this would not be possible and is not handled.

3.3 Implementation and Visualization

In order to obtain the counter data from an execution of an OpenMP program we used the OPARI tool[11]. It is a source-to-source instrumenter and can be used to insert measurement hooks for all OpenMP constructs. These hooks then provide the means to attach a measurement library to the program. With this we are able to instrument any given OpenMP program without any manual modification of the code.

Within the backend-library we gathered the 12 (one for each link on each of the four CPUs) *NEW_PACKETS_RECV* counter values at the beginning and end of each OpenMP construct directly from the R-Box of each Nehalem CPU. As currently no generic API, like PAPI[12], exists that supports the uncore counters of the Nehalem EX, we used the MSR interface of current Linux Kernels to directly interface with the CPU. This interface provides special files (/dev/cpu/x/msrm, where 'x' denotes the OS CPU number) by the msr kernel module which allow direct access to the model specific registers.

After obtaining the traffic through each of the 12 QPI links responsible for inter socket communication the open trace format (OTF)[13] is used to time-stamp and store the data to a trace-file on the hard-drive for post-mortem analysis. We selected the OTF due to its scalability, ease of use, wide acceptance and availability of a library implementation.

Because the QPI-links and messages through these links bear some resemblance to message passing we visualized the traces with Vampir[14], a renowned MPI-performance analysis tool. Vampir uses time-line visualization, i.e. it displays the message passing behavior as horizontal bars displaying function calls, one for each process, and vertical lines representing messages (Fig. 1A). This approach can be adapted to the view of our Nehalem EX system. To achieve this, we mapped in a post-mortem processing step the sockets to (MPI-)processes and the transfer of data within a region through a QPI link to a (MPI) message from the source socket to the target socket with the same time frame.

However as we always observed some traffic through any given QPI-link this would lead to the creation of a message for every QPI-link at every possible location. This would result in message-lines at all possible locations resulting in an overwhelming magnitude of messages to analyze. To account for this, we utilized Vampir's capability to filter its display with regard to the communicator of a message. We sorted the measured QPI bandwidths into different groups of ascending bandwidth-ranges (<100MiB/s, <200MiB/s, <1GiB/s, ...) and assigned to each bandwidth-group a different communicator. With this approach the user is later able to use Vampir's communicator filtering mechanism to select which group of "messages" he would like to investigate, with the ability to "on the fly" suppress any noise or message ranges of low and uninteresting bandwidths. This will in the end enable the user to focus on regions where the cache traffic exhibits interesting behavior.

4 Results

4.1 Basic Functionality Test

For the initial test we used an for this purpose designed OpenMP test code. This code executes with one thread per socket and allocates and initializes one continuous block of 1GiB memory with the first OpenMP-thread. As the whole block is initialized by the first thread of the process, the memory location for that block will be on the memory of the socket that the thread was running on according to the first touch policy of Linux. Afterwards we read this block of memory once per thread, whilst using an OpenMP-single construct to limit the access to that memory to one single thread at a time. We also ensured that each time a different OpenMP thread entered the single construct. This code was then executed on our four socket system exclusively. We used four OpenMP threads, where each of the underlying system-threads was bound to the first core on each of the different sockets using the "taskset" command of Linux. With our approach we were able to measure and identify which socket each thread was running on and which QPI link was used to access the remote memory. As the QPI can transmit 64 bytes per transfer, we confirmed at least 16 million hits for 1 GiB (the QPI communicates always a whole cache line) of remote memory accesses.

4.2 Jacobi Kernel

Besides our test code, we also tested our approach on a simple implementation of a Jacobi-solver kernel. To evaluate our analysis method we started with a simple NUMA unaware implementation.

We applied our analysis technique to this code with the aforementioned setup (4 threads, binding, etc.) and a $28k \times 28k$ matrix size. The resulting program execution took $7.6s$ in total runtime, which corresponds to $0.08s$ for the compute- and $0.18s$ for the copy-back loop per iteration. As predicted the initial display of our measurement-data showed traffic-lines (messages) between all packages at all times. Using the described communicator filtering approach, we filtered any traffic below 100MiB/s out, which we concluded to be "background noise". The resulting display (Fig. 1A) showed the bulk of the inter-socket communication. From the regularly structured message-lines we concluded that a significant portion of the used memory was not evenly distributed to all sockets resulting in increased QPI-traffic (and memory latency). We confirmed this with Vampirs "communication matrix"-view for the whole program as well as for a single Jacobi-iteration (see fig. 1B). The numbers showed that 4 multiples of 1/4th of the matrix was transfered from package 1 to each other socket and 1 multiple

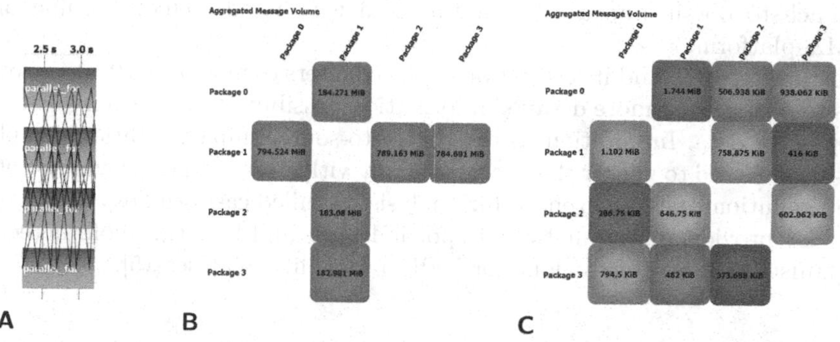

Fig. 1. A) Excerpt of the Vampir-timeline; Visualization of the QPI-message-volume of a typical iteration for **B**) the non optimized and **C**) NUMA optimized Jacobi

was collected back to the initial thread socket. This indicated that all the Jacobi matrix data was residing only on socket one. For this case the highest total transferred data observable was 11.2 GiB.

To alleviate this potential "performance issue" we included the initialization of the matrix into the parallel region and used an OpenMP-for construct in combination with the first-touch policy to distribute the memory to the sockets where it would later be used in the iterations. Re-evaluation of the program showed a 45% improvement in runtime. The improvement for the compute loop was $0.67s$ and for the copy-back loop $0.15s$ (22% and 19% improvement respectively). The change in behavior was easily observed in the graphical presentation of the performance data. In contrast to the NUMA unaware implementation the highest observable bandwidth was well below 200 MiB/s. After again filtering out the background noise, the timeline showed only one occurrence of barely increased traffic. As this did not reoccur with any of the other Jacobi iterations we concluded this to be an artefact. Investigating the "communication matrix" we observed a significant lower and more distributed amount of transferred data, peaking at 69.9 MiB. Matching the improvements of the total message volume, the highest traffic for a single Jacobi iteration was typically in the range of 0.4 to 1.74 MiB (Fig. 1C).

5 Conclusion

Analyzing an OpenMP code to adapt it to modern NUMA hardware architectures is currently a difficult task. Obtaining and interpreting information about the codes memory behavior on current NUMA-platforms is a key part when striving for good performance. In this work we introduced a novel approach to visualize the remote socket cache traffic of an shared-memory parallelized application on the Intel Nehalem EX platform. Granted the current prototypical approach with its restrictions in the setup is in its current form of limited use as it cannot map the gathered data to each core within a socket, it is a viable approach to obtain and analyze initial data for shared memory tuning on a NUMA platform.

Further research and investigation of the counters of modern CPUs may overt ways to obtain even more detailed information possibly enabling even a per core mapping of data. In addition to the source-to-source implementation sampling may also be used to gather the necessary data within a region to provide a better time resolution enabling even better analysis. Detailed case studies and research may also provide an automatic hot-spot indicator and best-threshold detection mechanism as it is already done for MPI in tools like Scalasca[15].

References

1. Top500.org: Top 500 List June 2010 (July 2010), `http://www.top500.org/`
2. HP: HP ProLiant DL980 G7 Server Data Sheet
3. Intel(R): Intel(r) thread checker, `http://software.intel.com/en-us/intel-thread-checker/`
4. Sun Microsystems: Thread analyzer user's guide, `http://dlc.sun.com/pdf/820-0619/820-0619.pdf`
5. Fürlinger, K., Gerndt, M.: A profiling tool for OpenMP. In: OpenMP Shared Memory Parallel Programming, Dresden, Germany. Springer, Heidelberg (2008)
6. Terboven, C., an Mey, D., Schmidl, D., Jing, H., Wagner, M.: Data and thread affinity in OpenMP programs. In: Memory Access on future Processors: A solved problem? In: ACM International Conference on Computing Frontiers, Ischia, Italy (May 2008)
7. Jarp, S., Jurga, R., Nowak, A.: Perfmon2: A leap forward in performance monitoring. In: International Conference on Computing in High Energy and Nuclear Physics. Journal of Physics: Conference Series, vol. 119, p. 042017 (2008)
8. Intel: Intel 64 and IA-32 Architectures Optimization Reference Manual (2009)
9. Intel: Intel 64 and IA-32 Architectures Software Developer's Manuals Volume 3B (2010)
10. Intel(R): Intel(R) Xeon(R) processor 7500 series uncore programming guide (2010), `http://www.intel.com/Assets/pt_BR/PDF/designguide/323535.pdf`
11. Mohr, B., Malony, A.D., Shende, S., Wolf, F.: Design and prototype of a performance tool interface for OpenMP. J. Supercomput. 23(1), 105–128 (2002)
12. Terpstra, D., Jagode, H., You, H., Dongarra, J.: Collecting performance data with papi-c. In: Proceedings of the 3rd Parallel Tools Workshop (2010) (to appear)
13. Knüpfer, A., Brendel, R., Brunst, H., Mix, H., Nagel, W.E.: Introducing the open trace format (OTF). In: Alexandrov, V.N., van Albada, G.D., Sloot, P.M.A., Dongarra, J. (eds.) ICCS 2006. LNCS, vol. 3992, pp. 526–533. Springer, Heidelberg (2006)
14. Knüpfer, A., Brunst, H., Doleschal, J., Jurenz, M., Lieber, M., Mickler, H., Müller, M.S., Nagel, W.E.: The vampir performance analysis tool-set. In: Proceedings of the 2nd HLRS Parallel Tools Workshop, Stuttgart, Germany (July 2008)
15. Wolf, F., Wylie, B.J.N., Ábrahám, E., Becker, D., Frings, W., Fürlinger, K., Geimer, M., Hermanns, M.-A., Mohr, B., Moore, S., Pfeifer, M., Szebenyi, Z.: Usage of the scalasca toolset for scalable performance analysis of large-scale parallel applications. In: Proceedings of the 2nd HLRS Parallel Tools Workshop, Stuttgart, Germany (July 2008)

Automatic MPI to AMPI Program Transformation Using Photran

Stas Negara[1], Gengbin Zheng[1], Kuo-Chuan Pan[2], Natasha Negara[3], Ralph E. Johnson[1], Laxmikant V. Kalé[1], and Paul M. Ricker[2]

[1] Department of Computer Science
University of Illinois at Urbana-Champaign
Urbana, IL 61801, USA
{snegara2,gzheng,rjohnson,kale}@illinois.edu
[2] Department of Astronomy
University of Illinois at Urbana-Champaign
Urbana, IL 61801, USA
{kpan2,pmricker}@illinois.edu
[3] Department of Computing Science
University of Alberta
Edmonton, Alberta T6G 2E8, Canada
negara@ualberta.ca

Abstract. Adaptive MPI, or AMPI, is an implementation of the Message Passing Interface (MPI) standard. AMPI benefits MPI applications with features such as dynamic load balancing, virtualization, and checkpointing. Because AMPI uses multiple user-level threads per physical core, global variables become an obstacle. It is thus necessary to convert MPI programs to AMPI by eliminating global variables. Manually removing the global variables in the program is tedious and error-prone. In this paper, we present a Photran-based tool that automates this task with a source-to-source transformation that supports Fortran. We evaluate our tool on the multi-zone NAS Benchmarks with AMPI. We also demonstrate the tool on a real-world large-scale FLASH code and present preliminary results of running FLASH on AMPI. Both results show significant performance improvement using AMPI. This demonstrates that the tool makes using AMPI easier and more productive.

1 Introduction

The Message Passing Interface (MPI) is a standardized library API for a set of message passing functions. It has become the *de facto* standard for parallel programming on a wide range of platforms. The conventional implementations of the MPI standard tend to associate one MPI process per processor, which limits their support of the dynamic nature of these applications, for example, load balancing is challenging, and must be handled by the application programmer. As a result, application performance and programmer productivity suffer.

One approach to decouple an MPI process from its OS process is to adopt a finer grained decomposition using light-weight threads. In this execution model, each MPI "process" is running in the context of a thread, and there are multiple

M.R. Guarracino et al. (Eds.): Euro-Par 2010 Workshops, LNCS 6586, pp. 531–539, 2011.
© Springer-Verlag Berlin Heidelberg 2011

threads running on a processor. One advantage of this approach is to allow automatic adaptive overlap of communication and computation, i.e., when one MPI "process" (or thread) is blocked to receive, another MPI thread on the same processor can be scheduled for running. Another advantage is that it allows different mapping of MPI threads to processors to take advantage of the multicore architectures. With sophisticated thread migration techniques [12], dynamic load balancing via migratable user-level threads can be supported at the run-time. Adaptive MPI (AMPI) [3] exemplifies this approach. It is an adaptive implementation and extension of MPI with migratable threads, implemented on top of CHARM++ [5]. More recent work in FG-MPI [6] also follows this direction; however, it does not support thread migration and dynamic load balancing yet.

One major obstacle for switching a legacy MPI application to this multithreaded MPI execution model is global (and static) variables. These variables in the MPI code cause no problem with traditional MPI implementations, since each process image contains a separate copy. However, they are not safe in the multi-threading paradigm. Therefore, the global variables in the MPI code need to be privatized to ensure thread safety. One approach is to manually remove global variables at source code level. However, this process is mechanical and sometimes cumbersome. Other more sophisticated approaches described in [12] enable run-time to automatically privatize global variables by analyzing GOT (Global Offset Table) in ELF (Executable and Linkable Format) executables. These approaches however do not handle static variables, and are limited to the platforms that support ELF executables.

In this paper, we present a compiler-based tool that automatically transforms a user program to run with MPI implementations that support the multithreaded execution model. Since a significant number of legacy MPI applications are written in Fortran, we will mainly target Fortran language in this paper. Our tool employs Photran's [7] source-to-source compiler infrastructure for Fortran that we discuss in more details in Sect. 2. We will focus only on AMPI as the target MPI implementation for code transformation from now on. However, the transformed code is a legitimate Fortran MPI program with only a couple of AMPI specific extensions to support thread migration and load balancing. The transformed program is portable and can run on any other MPI implementation as long as the AMPI thread migration feature is disabled.

2 MPI to AMPI Code Transformation

The design goal of our tool is to automatically transform Fortran 90 MPI programs to run on AMPI, and take full advantage of AMPI's load balancing capability. The major task is to privatize global variables.

Fortran Global Variables Privatization. Global variables are those variables that can be accessed by more than one subprogram (including several calls of the same subprogram) and are not passed as arguments of these subprograms. In Fortran 90, global variables are module variables, variables that

```
PROGRAM MyProg
  include 'mpif.h'
  INTEGER :: i, ierr
  COMMON /CB/ i
  CALL MPI_Init(ierr)
  i = 3
  CALL PrintVal
  CALL MPI_Finalize(ierr)
END PROGRAM

SUBROUTINE PrintVal
  INTEGER :: v
  COMMON /CB/ v
  print *, ''val='', v
END SUBROUTINE
```

```
MODULE GeneratedModule
  TYPE GeneratedType
    INTEGER :: f
  END TYPE GeneratedType
END MODULE GeneratedModule

SUBROUTINE MPI_Main
  USE GeneratedModule
  include 'mpif.h'
  INTEGER :: ierr
  TYPE(GeneratedType) :: p
  CALL MPI_Init(ierr)
  p%f = 3
  CALL PrintVal(p)
  CALL MPI_Finalize(ierr)
END SUBROUTINE MPI_Main

SUBROUTINE PrintVal(p)
  USE GeneratedModule
  TYPE(GeneratedType) :: p
  print *, ''val='', p%f
END SUBROUTINE
```

Fig. 1. Example of the code transformation that privatizes a common block variable. The original code of an MPI program is on the left; the transformed code, which can be executed on AMPI, is shown on the right.

appear in common blocks, and local variables that are `saved` (i.e. local variables that keep their values between subprogram calls like `static` variables in C).

Privatizing global variables means giving every MPI "process" its own copy of these global variables. This happens automatically in most MPI implementations, where each MPI process is a separate operating system process, while multithreaded AMPI requires that it be ensured by the programmer. One way to do this is, essentially, to put all of the global variables into a large object (a derived type in Fortran, or `struct` in C), and then to pass this object around between subprograms. Each AMPI thread can be given a different copy of this object. Figure 1 presents an example of privatizing a common block variable. Although this variable has two different names (`i` in `MyProg` and `v` in `PrintVal`), it is a single global variable in the original program.

We implemented global variables privatization for Fortran 90 using the refactoring infrastructure in Photran, an Eclipse-based [1] Integrated Development Environment (IDE) for Fortran [7]. Photran IDE exposes an Application Programming Interface (API) that provides functionality to parse a Fortran program and construct its Abstract Syntax Tree (AST) representation. The produced *rewritable* AST is augmented with information about *binding* of program's entities. Our tool analyzes the underlying Fortran program using information from its AST and transforms the program by manipulating its AST.

2.1 Code Analysis and Transformation

The overall code transformation performed by our tool proceeds in four steps:

1. Stubs are generated for the derived type and the module that contains this type. Our tool ensures that their names do not conflict or shadow names of other entities in the program.

2. Subprograms are processed. An extra parameter is added to each subprogram and each call site within its body. Components for `saved` variables are inserted into the derived type, accesses to these variables are replaced with accesses to the corresponding derived type components, and finally, the `saved` variables are deleted from the subprogram.
3. Common blocks are eliminated in a manner similar to `saved` local variables.
4. Module variables are eliminated similarly.

As a result of the code transformation, every global variable is replaced in the program's code with the corresponding field of the generated derived type. The type and specifications of the replacing field should be consistent with those of the replaced global variable. According to the Fortran standard, specifications of a variable may be defined by multiple specification statements. Our tool uses variable binding information provided by Photran infrastructure to collect the type and all specifications of a particular global variable, which are combined in a single declaration statement of the replacing field.

Declarations with Constants. Declarations of global variables may contain constants, e.g. a variable may be initialized with a constant, or dimensions of an array may be specified using constants. To make the declaration of the replacing field in the generated derived type consistent with the declaration of such global variable, our tool moves declarations of all constants contained in the variable's declaration to the generated module (i.e. the declarations of constants are deleted from the original code and placed in the generated module, and all accesses to the deleted constants in the original code are replaced with accesses to the corresponding constants from the generated module). These moved declarations of constants may contain some other constants, whose declarations also need to be moved to the generated module, and so on.

Figure 2 illustrates a code sample (on the left), where declarations of two global variables, `boundary` and `ar`, contain constants `y` and `total` respectively. Declarations of constants `y` and `total` contain other constants. Moreover, the declaration of constant `total` contains constant `y`. To generate the correct code, we need to detect all constants that are immediately or transitively contained in the declarations of global variables `boundary` and `ar` and also, we need to establish an order of appearance of these declarations in the generated module such that if a declaration of some constant `C1` contains constant `C2`, then the declaration of constant `C2` comes before the declaration of constant `C1` in the generated module.

To achieve this goal, our tool constructs a graph, where nodes represent constants and edges represent "is contained in" relationship, i.e., there is an edge going from a node that represents constant `C1` to a node that represents constant `C2` if and only if constant `C1` is contained in the declaration of constant `C2`. The graph construction starts with the initial set of nodes for constants that are immediately contained in the declarations of global variables and proceeds recursively by adding nodes and edges for constants that are contained in the declarations of constants that are already present in the graph. The order of

```
SUBROUTINE MySub
  INTEGER, PARAMETER :: offset = 5
  INTEGER, PARAMETER :: x = offset + 10
  INTEGER, PARAMETER :: y = offset + 20
  INTEGER, PARAMETER :: total = x * y
  INTEGER :: boundary = y
  REAL, SAVE :: ar(total)
  ...
END SUBROUTINE
```

```
MODULE GeneratedModule
  INTEGER, PARAMETER :: CN_offset = 5
  INTEGER, PARAMETER :: CN_y = CN_offset + 20
  INTEGER, PARAMETER :: CN_x = CN_offset + 10
  INTEGER, PARAMETER :: CN_total = CN_x * CN_y
  TYPE GeneratedType
    INTEGER :: MySub_boundary = CN_y
    REAL :: MySub_ar(CN_total)
  END TYPE GeneratedType
END MODULE GeneratedModule
```

Fig. 2. Example of two global variable declarations that contain constants (on the left), and the corresponding generated module (on the right)

appearance of the declarations of these constants in the generated module is the topological order of the graph. Figure 2 (on the right) presents the resulting generated module.

Global Fixed Size Arrays. In real-world scientific computation programs (like the one we use for our case study) there are many large fixed size arrays declared in different modules. If all these global arrays are placed in the generated derived type, its size would exceed the maximum allowed size of a derived type, which may vary for different Fortran compilers, and is usually around several megabytes. To avoid this problem, our tool transforms global fixed size arrays into pointer arrays and generates an initialization subroutine that allocates these arrays according to their sizes in the original program. This initialization subroutine is called right after `MPI_Init`, ensuring that every MPI process gets its own allocated and initialized copy of the transformed arrays.

3 Evaluation

This section offers comparative evaluations between the original MPI code and the transformed version with AMPI using NAS Benchmarks and a real-world application FLASH.

3.1 Multi-zone NAS Benchmark

NAS Parallel Benchmark (NPB) is a well known parallel benchmark suite. Benchmarks in its Multi-Zone version [4], LU-MZ, SP-MZ and BT-MZ, which are written in Fortran, solve discretized versions of the unsteady, compressible Navier-Stokes equations in three spatial dimensions. Among these benchmarks, LU and SP are well-balanced, while BT is imbalanced application. In BT, the partitioning of the mesh is done such that the sizes of the zones span a significant range, therefore creating imbalance in workload across processors, which provides a good case study for AMPI and its load balancing capability.

We transformed the above mentioned three benchmarks, and evaluated the transformed code on the Queen Bee cluster at LSU. The native MPI we used for comparison is MVAPICH, which takes advantage of the Infiniband interconnect. Figure 3(a) illustrates the execution time of the original benchmarks

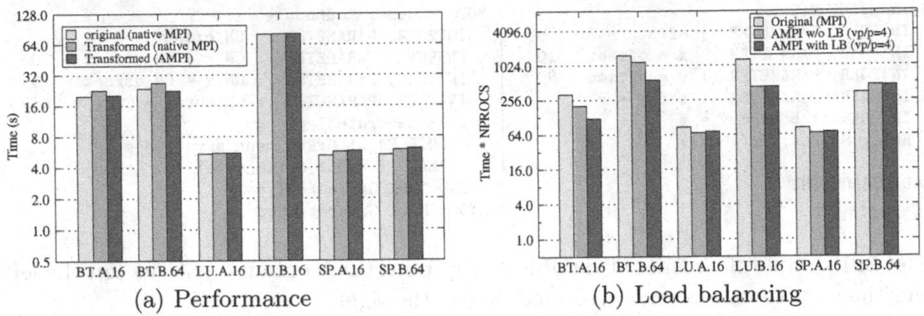

(a) Performance (b) Load balancing

Fig. 3. Comparing NAS benchmarks time on a logarithmic scale (Queen Bee cluster)

on the native MPI, and the transformed benchmarks on the native MPI and AMPI. The X axis displays the name of a benchmark, the problem class, and the number of processors it was run on. The transformed code introduces some overhead that ranges from a fraction of one percent for LU.B.16 up to 14% for BT.A.16. Although the transformation overhead is the highest for both BT-MZ benchmarks, running on AMPI almost completely eliminates it. Note that in this comparison, we associate one MPI thread per physical processor, and thus, do not employ any specific benefits of AMPI. The observed speed up is solely due to the efficient implementation of the AMPI's communication layer.

Figure 3(b) compares the total resource consumption (execution time multiplied by the number of physical processors used) between the native MPI and AMPI. In AMPI runs, we map four MPI threads to a single physical processor, thus reducing the number of physical processors used by a factor of four. The second bar in Fig. 3(b) shows the AMPI resource consumption without load balancing. The decrease in the total processor time demonstrates one of the benefits of using AMPI, i.e., adaptive overlapping of the computation/communication. The third bar shows the AMPI resource consumption with dynamic load balancing. We employed a greedy-based load balancer that is called once after the third simulation step. We see that BT-MZ benchmarks take advantage of both computation/communication overlap and load balancing, while LU.A.16, LU.B.16, and SP.A.16 benefit only from computation/communication overlap (since there is no load balance problem in both LU and SP). SP.B.64 is the only case that does not benefit from any advantages offered by AMPI.

3.2 Case Study – FLASH

We evaluated our tool on a large-scale project: FLASH, version 3 [2]. FLASH is a parallel, multi-dimensional code used to study astrophysical fluids. It is written mainly in Fortran 90 and parallelized using MPI. It is essentially a collection of code pieces, which are combined in different ways to produce different simulation problems, e.g., FLASH supports both uniform grid and a block-structured adaptive mesh refinement (AMR) grid based on the PARAMESH library.

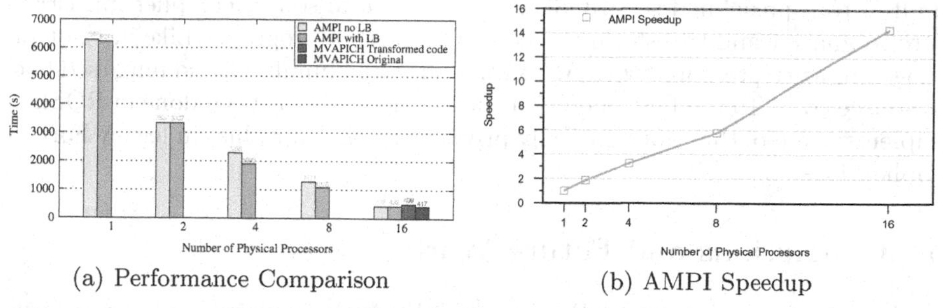

(a) Performance Comparison (b) AMPI Speedup

Fig. 4. Sedov simulation performance (Abe cluster, NCSA)

We transformed and evaluated Sedov-Taylor explosion simulation problem [9], which is a common test problem for strong shocks and non-planar symmetry. The problem is set up using a delta function initial pressure perturbation in an uniform medium. We use 9 AMR levels and two-dimensional fluids for our tests. The experiments are run on the Abe cluster at NCSA.

Figure 4(a) compares the execution time of the transformed Sedov simulation on AMPI with and without load balancing. For load balancing we employ a refinement-based load balancer that is called every 100 simulation steps. We vary the number of physical processors (X axis) from 1 to 16, while the number of virtual processors is 16 for all AMPI runs. The maximum benefit from load balancing is achieved for the execution on 4 physical processors (vp/p ratio 4) which is 16.8%. The two additional bars of the last group reflect the execution time of the original and the transformed Sedov simulation on the native MPI (MVAPICH). The code transformation incurs about 20% overhead compared to the original code when both running on MVAPICH. However, we see that the overhead is almost completely eliminated while running on AMPI. The corresponding speedup of the simulation with AMPI is illustrated in Fig. 4(b).

Although our evaluation of Sedov simulation shows that code transformation incurs considerable overhead for this application, the results prove the usefulness of AMPI features. After we fix the overhead problem in the next version of our tool, we believe that AMPI execution would demonstrate considerably better performance than the original MPI execution.

4 Related Work

TMPI [11] uses multithreading for performance enhancement of multi-threaded MPI programs on shared memory machines. More recent work in FG-MPI [6] shares the same idea with AMPI by exploiting fine grained decomposition using threads. However, FG-MPI does not support thread migration and dynamic load balancing. The source-to-source transformation implemented in our tool will benefit these MPI implementations as well.

SPAG [10] is a tool for analyzing and transforming Fortran programs. It provides both static and dynamic analysis, but its transformation capabilities are limited to a predefined set. ROSE [8] is a source-to-source compiler infrastructure to analyze and transform C, C++, and Fortran programs. Like in Photran, programs are represented with ASTs that can be manipulated and unparsed back to source code. To the best of our knowledge, no work has been done in ROSE to implement a tool that automatically privatizes global variables in legacy Fortran applications.

5 Conclusions and Future Work

In this paper, we presented a Photran-based tool that automatically transforms legacy Fortran MPI applications to run on any MPI implementation that supports multi-threaded execution model. Specifically, we presented techniques to remove global variables in Fortran applications. We demonstrated the utility of the tool on AMPI, an MPI implementation that supports processor virtualization using user-level threads and dynamic load balancing with thread migration. We demonstrated the effectiveness of our tool on both NAS benchmarks and a real-world large scale FLASH application.

We plan to continue our performance evaluation. In particular, we would like to consider more complex and larger problems, which are expected to be inherently more load imbalanced, and, consequently, could benefit more from dynamic load balancing offered by AMPI.

Acknowledgments. This work was partially supported by the Institute for Advanced Computing Applications and Technologies (IACAT) at the University of Illinois at Urbana-Champaign. FLASH was developed by the DOE-supported ASC / Alliance Center for Astrophysical Thermonuclear Flashes at the University of Chicago. We used running time on Queen Bee cluster (LSU) and Abe cluster (NCSA), which is under TeraGrid allocation grant ASC050040N supported by NSF.

References

1. Eclipse - an open development platform, `http://www.eclipse.org/`
2. Fryxell, B., et al.: Flash: An adaptive mesh hydrodynamics code for modeling astrophysical thermonuclear flashes. ApJS 131, 273 (2000)
3. Huang, C., Lawlor, O., Kalé, L.V.: Adaptive MPI. In: Rauchwerger, L. (ed.) LCPC 2003. LNCS, vol. 2958, pp. 306–322. Springer, Heidelberg (2004)
4. Jin, H., der Wijngaart, R.F.V.: Performance characteristics of the multi-zone nas parallel benchmarks. In: Proceedings of the International Parallel and Distributed Processing Symposium (IPDPS) (2004)
5. Kale, L.V., Zheng, G.: Charm++ and AMPI: Adaptive Runtime Strategies via Migratable Objects. In: Parashar, M. (ed.) Advanced Computational Infrastructures for Parallel and Distributed Applications, pp. 265–282. Wiley Interscience, Hoboken (2009)
6. Kamal, H., Wagner, A.: Fg-mpi: Fine-grain mpi for multicore and clusters. In: The 11th IEEE International Workshop on Parallel and Distributed Scientific and Engineering Computing (PDESC). IEEE, Los Alamitos (April 2010)

7. Photran - An IDE for Fortran, `http://www.eclipse.org/photran/`
8. ROSE, `http://www.rosecompiler.org/`
9. Sedov, L.I.: Similarity and Dimensional Methods in Mechanics (1959)
10. SPAG, `http://www.polyhedron.co.uk/spag0html`
11. Tang, H., Shen, K., Yang, T.: Program transformation and runtime support for threaded MPI execution on shared-memory machines. ACM Transactions on Programming Languages and Systems 22(4), 673–700 (2000)
12. Zheng, G., Lawlor, O.S., Kalé, L.V.: Multiple flows of control in migratable parallel programs. In: 2006 International Conference on Parallel Processing Workshops (ICPPW 2006), Columbus, Ohio, pp. 435–444 (August 2006)

High-Performance Parallel Computations Using Python as High-Level Language

Stefano Masini and Paolo Bientinesi

RWTH Aachen, AICES, Aachen, Germany
stefano@stefanomasini.com, pauldj@aices.rwth-aachen.de

Abstract. High-performance and parallel computations have always represented a challenge in terms of code optimization and memory usage, and have typically been tackled with languages that allow a low-level management of resources, like Fortran, C and C++. Nowadays, most of the implementation effort goes into constructing the bookkeeping logic that binds together functionalities taken from standard libraries. Because of the increasing complexity of this kind of codes, it becomes more and more necessary to keep it well organized through proper software engineering practices. Indeed, in the presence of chaotic implementations, reasoning about correctness is difficult, even when limited to specific aspects like concurrency; moreover, due to the lack in flexibility of the code, making substantial changes for experimentation becomes a grand challenge.

Since the bookkeeping logic only accounts for a tiny fraction of the total execution time, we believe that for such a task it can be afforded to introduce an overhead due to a high-level language. We consider Python as a preliminary candidate with the intent of improving code readability, flexibility and, in turn, the level of confidence with respect to correctness. In this study, the bookkeeping logic of SMP-MRRR, a C & Fortran highly optimized multi-core eigensolver, is ported to Python. We report here on the porting process and on the pros and cons of using a high-level language in a high-performance parallel library.

Keywords: Productivity, Code Development, High-Performance Computations, Python, High-Level Languages.

1 Introduction

The scientific computing community spends a great deal of effort in developing numerical routines and libraries. The codes are often both large and difficult to manage. As an example, representative codes for 3D Finite Element solvers normally include hundreds of files, thousands of routines, surpass the 100K lines of code, and are entirely written in one or more of the classic languages: C, C++ and Fortran. Even though the situation is considered to be sub-optimal, it is often tacitly accepted in the name of high-performance.

Typically, complex numerical solvers and simulations are organized into layers: the key logic is expressed at high level in terms of simpler algorithms that perform

M.R. Guarracino et al. (Eds.): Euro-Par 2010 Workshops, LNCS 6586, pp. 541–548, 2011.
© Springer-Verlag Berlin Heidelberg 2011

most of the number crunching. A large number of separate routines, taken from consolidated libraries and often used as black boxes, needs to be orchestrated through proper data structures, function calls and thread synchronization. The libraries themselves are organized in the same fashion. As an example, LAPACK, the de facto standard linear algebra library, is layered on top of the routines of levels 3, 2 and 1 of the BLAS library. Such a modular approach helps separating the computation—confined to well-defined functions—from the data and thread management.

A considerable challenge arises when concurrency is required: in that situation it is generally hard to be highly confident with respect to correctness and absence of deadlock. The typical approach is to try to keep the logic as simple as possible so that the intricate implementation remains confined to limited sections. Unfortunately, always in the name of high-performance, Fortran and C are often misused to obtain low-level optimizations over instructions, registers and the memory hierarchy. Applying these practices when not strictly necessary makes it unlikely that code rich in semantics is also simple and compact. Furthermore, if achieving correctness is already time consuming, it becomes even more expensive to experiment with algorithmic variants, despite this activity is precisely what scientific research is all about.

The main concerns for numerical code and libraries are correctness and performance. We believe that nowadays other concerns should be considered as equally important: code modularity, flexibility, and development time. In this paper we focus on the development of the logic for the management of data, functions and threads (bookkeeping) in high-performance parallel libraries. For this specific task, high-level languages might be better suited than C or Fortran: we chose Python in our first attempt to investigate the pros and cons of replacing C as the main programming language.

The paper is organized as follows. In Section 2 we describe our experimental setup and compare with related approaches. In Section 3 we report on the concrete advantages that we experienced in porting to Python. Section 4 explains the impact of the Global Interpreter Lock in order to understand the performance numbers presented in Section 5, together with future directions. In Section 6 we draw conclusions.

2 Setup

Python is a very appealing language for the scientific computing community at large [6]. Its applicability, even to large projects, has been proven fruitful for a long time already [13]. Most of the investigations and studies targeting parallel computations have only considered the model of distributed memory and message passing [4,7,8,9,10,11,12]. In that scenario Python has been used to steer the computation by organizing and synchronizing processes containing number-crunching operations performed by libraries normally written in C, C++ or Fortran. By targeting shared memory parallelism, our investigation departs sharply from previous efforts.

We aim at using Python *within* a high-performance numerical library, i.e., a piece of code that is highly optimized for speed. Our computing model is SMP (Symmetric MultiProcessing), in which parallelism is obtained through multithreading, and synchronization is based on primitives like semaphores. When compared to approaches based on MPI or BSP, multithreading leads to a different type of parallelism: thanks to fast shared memories and the absence of costly message passing operations, algorithms are parallelized at a much finer granularity.

There is a diffuse perception that Python is not mature enough to be used in this context because of its slow interpreted nature and well known limitations like the Global Interpreter Lock. While some of these criticisms are well founded, we are nonetheless interested in exploring the boundaries of applicability of Python to scenarios in which we feel developers would highly benefit from an expressive language. The goal of this study is to shed some light on Python's current actual limits. We envision two favorable consequences: on the one hand scientific developers might come to the realization that some of the drawbacks of the language are not as severe as expected; on the other hand, Python's developers could pinpoint specific weaknesses that is worth improving on.

In the attempt of stressing the limits of the language, we set out for a rather challenging goal: using Python within a highly-optimized parallel numerical library. We selected SMP-MRRR, a multi-core version of the MRRR symmetric eigensolver [2,3]. Eigensolvers are at the core of innumerable scientific computations and are included in all the standard numerical libraries. SMP-MRRR is currently the fastest eigensolver available for multi-core architectures. It is written in C and Fortran, and makes use of routines from LAPACK and BLAS. It is designed for systems comprising up to 60-80 cores. SMP-MRRR constitutes an especially disadvantageous choice for our goal: not only is it a high-performance library, it also has the lowest algorithmic complexity among all the existing eigensolvers, $O(n^2)$[1]. As a consequence, any overhead introduced by Python will impact the overall execution time much more noticeably than it would had the algorithm had $O(n^3)$ complexity, like most of the dense linear algebra algorithms have. With such a complexity, the overhead would be easily hidden under a much higher amount of computations, quickly becoming negligible.

The execution of SMP-MRRR unfolds by computing an initial approximation of the eigenvalues first, and the eigenvectors together with more accurate eigenvalues later. Depending on the number of available cores, the initial eigenvalue computation is either performed sequentially by the fast *dqds* algorithm, or in parallel by *bisection*. The eigenvectors, together with more accurate eigenvalues, are then computed in parallel by organizing the computation according to a tree of tasks, and utilizing a task queue based approach.

[1] Given an input matrix of size n, SMP-MRRR computes all the eigenvalues and eigenvectors of the matrix in $O(n^2)$ floating point operations. While such a complexity is an upper bound, the actual completion time depends on the input matrix.

The way that tasks are created, their execution order and the portion of data they manipulate represent the core contribution to the algorithm implementation, and accounts for most of the development time. We will refer to this portion of code as the *bookkeeping logic*, implemented in roughly 5000 lines of C code. The remaining code, mostly written in Fortran, is what we consider actual computation, or informally, *number crunching.*

Porting the bookkeeping logic to Python introduces overhead, so it is useful to start from a clear understanding of this portion of the code in relation to the actual number crunching. In our experiments we considered two different types of matrices: Wilkinson and Hermite[2] The number of calls to Fortran routines ranges approximately from 10 to 50 thousands accounting for 0.83% to 4.18% of the total running time [1]. This indicates that the sections of number crunching are highly fragmented and interspersed with bookkeeping logic; the exact figures depend on the nature of the matrices. With Hermite matrices, the amount of time spent inside the bookkeeping logic decreases with larger matrices, as expected, due to the quadratic complexity of the algorithm. The trend for Wilkinson matrices is not as apparent, because of the numerical properties of these matrices.

All the experiments were run on a Mac Pro with two 2.4Ghz Quad-Core Intel Xeon processors, for a total of 8 available cores. We limited the runs to only 6 cores in order to avoid interference with others applications and collect more stable results.

3 The Advantages of Python and Refactoring

We chose Python as target high-level language because of its clean syntax, powerful semantics and rich standard library. When compared against more traditional languages, Python presents a much lighter cognitive load, so developers become more productive and are less likely to introduce subtle bugs.

The Python code makes use of the NumPy and Cython packages in order to manipulate multi-dimensional arrays and call the Fortran routines. Please refer to the techical report [1] for details on the porting process.

The porting was performed by one of the authors, without specific knowledge of the mathematics involved in the eigensolver. Nonetheless he became intimately familiar with the algorithm and was able to refactor the code and introduce a more Object Oriented design. In the process, thanks to the improved readability, he was able to uncover a subtle bug that in some corner cases could lead to deadlock.

In the context of parallel computing, such defects are especially dangerous as they both add unnecessary complications to the logic—which is already difficult to keep in sync with the mathematical model—and might lead to idling processors. An effective practice is then to keep the code in the best possible shape

[2] In order to avoid the possible overhead due to the contention of shared data structures we performed the measurements in single threaded executions.

in order to maintain a high level of confidence in the correct behaviour of the system.

The competencies required to develop high quality software are largely independent of domain specific knowledge so, in general, sane software engineering practices can and should be applied in order to keep the complexity under control, regardless of the programming language used.

Code refactoring is a necessary activity but it requires knowledge and discipline. Learning and applying it though seems to be easier on modern dynamic languages like Python because of their simplicity and flexibility. We believe that by using such languages developers have a better chance of becoming more conscious about software engineering issues thus writing better code and becoming more productive. Some references to available literature can be found in [1].

4 Simulating the Global Interpreter Lock

Python supports multithreading but the internal implementation of its most commonly used interpreter (CPython, written in C) limits the effectiveness of this model in the case of multi-core CPUs. A Global Interpreter Lock (GIL) needs to be acquired by a thread before its execution can continue. Fortunately the GIL can be released during execution of C or Fortran code, therefore in our case all the available core were effectived used.

The presence of locks is standard in the SMP model because they are required to protect shared data structures, e.g., the task queue. This kind of locks though is very fine grained, therefore we were interested in measuring the impact on the overall performance when a coarse grained lock like the GIL is introduced. This will be of primary importance to understanding the overhead introduced by Python, as described in Section 5.

In order to reproduce the contention caused by the GIL in Python, we created a modified C version of SMP-MRRR in which we artificially introduced a global lock. Since the modified and the original versions have no other differences, the resulting measured overhead is a direct indication of the amount of extra contention introduced. Our implementation is much simpler than that of the Python GIL, therefore our measurements represent a lower bound on the amount of overhead introduced by the real interpreter.

We report on the execution of the modified version of SMP-MRRR for two types of input matrices, Wilkinson and Hermite. The eigenspectrum of Wilkinson matrices is such that the computation of eigenvalues and eigenvectors is especially involved, which translates to number-crunching sections that take longer to complete. The Hermite matrices are instead quite favorable, meaning that the outputs can be computed with shorter number-crunching sections. The impact of the bookkeeping logic will therefore be significantly more evident in the latter case. In the case of Hermite matrices, a larger problem size makes the bookkeeping become less noticeable, as more and more time is spent within number-crunching sections. For Wilkinson such a trend is more subtle, because the complexity of the eigenspectrum increases together with the problem size.

Table 1. Execution time penalty due to the use of a global lock

Wilkinson				Hermite			
Size	2 cores	4 cores	6 cores	Size	2 cores	4 cores	6 cores
3001	0.60%	1.07%	2.62%	3001	0.85%	1.42%	4.76%
5001	0.66%	1.82%	3.28%	5001	0.65%	1.16%	5.81%
10001	0.60%	2.17%	3.53%	10001	0.20%	0.43%	0.56%

Finally a note about multithreading: as the number of threads increases, there is a higher chance of threads competing for the lock to start a bookkeeping section, thus increasing the overhead.

Table 1 shows the impact on the overall running time. The two C versions of the algorithm were tested 30 times for every combination of matrix type, size and number of cores. The percentage represents the amount of overhead computed using the average values across the runs. The standard deviation for the original algorithm always remains below 10% of the minimum value, indicating that the behaviour of the system is quite stable and predictable. In the case of the global lock instead we measured an increase also of the standard deviation, of up to 2 to 3 times in some cases, indicating that the contention not only decreased the overall performance, but also made it somewhat less predictable.

For space reasons we have not included measurements about the lock usage. More details can be found in [1].

5 Performance Hit and Future Work

In Table 2 we compare the execution time of the original SMP-MRRR and the Python version. The overhead should be considered in light of the observations made in Section 4 about the Global Interpreter Lock. There is no clear way to identify precisely the amount of overhead due to the GIL, but it certainly has an impact and explains why the overhead increases with the number of cores.

Table 2. Overall performance overhead: Python over C

Wilkinson matrix				Hermite matrix			
Size	2 cores	4 cores	6 cores	Size	2 cores	4 cores	6 cores
3001	11.80%	28.20%	57.80%	3001	95.40%	231.30%	386.90%
5001	15.00%	22.20%	40.10%	5001	85.20%	121.20%	197.80%
10001	13.20%	15.00%	19.20%	10001	43.50%	54.60%	53.00%

The interpreted nature of Python is the other obvious source of overhead. Previous studies [5]have shown that for some simple calculations there can be a difference of up to 2 orders of magnitude between the speed of a Python implementation and the equivalent C. The bookkeeping logic cannot be considered proper algorithmic code because it does not include loops and numerical calculations but, still, we expect it to be much slower than C.

There are well known approaches to circumvent the speed limit of the Python interpreter. Ultimately they are all based on the generation of efficient machine code, or C source code that can in turn be compiled.

We experimented with Psyco, a Just In Time (JIT) that has been shown to increase the performance even by 70-80% in the case of simple numerical computations with nested loops [5]. Unfortunately, in our case we have observed a consistent performance loss of up to 15%. The reason lies in the very nature of the bookkeeping code that, by definition, does not include computation intensive loops that can outweight the startup cost of the compilation step.

Other tools include PyPy, RPython, Cython and ShedSkin. Some of them allow for a low level approach that could help circumvent the GIL limitation and could be the subject of further study. Please see [1] for a more complete description.

We foresee two possible directions for future development of our experiments. On the one hand we could optimize the current Python implementation by adopting one or more of the tools described above. It would be interesting to see how close we can get to the original C performance by still maintaining a high-level Python development environment. On the other hand, we could look at different languages that perform better than Python when used in our context. We could see how they relate to Python and if they can be considered as equally attractive and productive from the point of view of the developer.

6 Conclusions

Porting the bookkeeping logic from C to Python proved to be an incredibly valuable exercise: it yielded a code readable and easy to reason about. Thanks to this, we were able to thoroughly investigate the correctness of the implementation. As a result, we spotted possible deadlocks and hidden constraints that could affect performance. The new code also lends itself for experimentation and testing of new design and algorithm strategies. We believe that proper software engineering practices should discipline the development process even for scientific codes. High-level languages like Python can greatly enhance this opportunity and so they deserve full attention by the scientific computing community.

On the downside, Python added overheads, as expected, and is still far from being a concrete alternative to traditional languages like C or C++ in performance critical environments. Nonetheless, considering the extremely disadvantageous situation represented by an $O(n^2)$ SMP-parallel algorithm, we observed an interesting performance in spite of the Global Interpreter Lock and the slow interpreted nature of Python. We believe that in many cases these limitations are outweighed by the enhanced flexibility of the language.

The high-level dynamic languages scene is rapidly evolving, so it will be interesting to see how these performance issues will be addressed in the coming years.

References

1. Masini, S., Bientinesi, P.: High-Performance Parallel Computations using Python as High-Level Language.Technical Report AICES-2010/08-01, Aachen Institute for Computational Engineering Sciences, RWTH Aachen (August 2010), `http://www.aices.rwth-aachen.de:8080/aices/preprint/documents/AICES-2010-08-01.pdf`
2. Dhillon, I.: A new $O(n^2)$ Algorithm for the Symmetric Tridiagonal Eigenvalue/Eigenvector Problem. Ph.D. thesis, University of California, Berkeley (1997)
3. Petschow, M., Bientinesi, P.: The Algorithm of Multiple Relatively Robust Representations for Multi-Core Processors. In: PARA 2010: State of the Art in Scientific and Parallel Computing, Python in HPC (submitted)
4. Nilsen, J.K., Cai, X., Høyland, B., Langtangen, H.P.: Simplifying parallelization of scientific codes by a function-centric approach in Python. Submitted to Computational Science & Discovery for publication (2010)
5. Wilbers, I., Langtangen, H.P., Ødegard, Å.: Using Cython to Speed up Numerical Python Programs. In: Skallerud, B., Andersson, H.I. (eds.) Proceedings of MekIT 2009, pp. 495–512. NTNU, Tapir (2009)
6. Langtangen, H.P.: Python Scripting for Computational Science, 3rd edn. Springer Publishing Company, Heidelberg (2009) (incorporated)
7. Langtangen, H.P., Cai, X.: On the Efficiency of Python for High-Performance Computing: A Case Study Involving Stencil Updates for Partial Differential Equations. Proceedings of the Third International Conference on High Performance Scientific Computing, Hanoi, Vietnam, pp. 337-357 (2008)
8. Hinsen, K.: Parallel Scripting with Python. Computing in Science and Engineering 9(6), 82–89 (2007)
9. Hinsen, K., Langtangen, H.P., Skavhaug, O., Ødegard, Å.: Using BSP and Python to simplify parallel programming. Future Generation Computer Systems 22(1-2), 123–157 (2006)
10. Cai, X., Langtangen, H.P.: Parallelizing PDE solvers using the Python programming language. In: Bruaset, A.M., Tveito, A. (eds.) Numerical Solution of Partial Differential Equations on Parallel Computers. Springer Lecture Notes in Computational Science and Engineering, vol. 51, pp. 295–325. Springer, Heidelberg (2006)
11. Cai, X., Langtangen, H.P., Moe, H.: On the performance of the Python programming language for serial and parallel scientific computations. Scientific Programming 13(1), 31–56 (2005)
12. Hinsen, K., Sadron, R.C.: High-Level Parallel Software Development with Python and BSP. Parallel Processing Letters 13 (2003)
13. Hinsen, K.: The Molecular Modeling Toolkit: a case study of a large scientific application in Python. In: Proceedings of the 6th International Python Conference, San Jose, California (1997)

Workshop on
Cloud Computing
Projects and Initiatives
(CCPI 2010)

CCPI 2010: Workshop on Cloud Computing Projects and Initiatives

Beniamino Di Martino[1], Dana Petcu[2], and Antonio Puliafito[3]

[1] Second University of Naples, Italy
[2] Western University of Timisoara, Romania
[3] University of Messina, Italy

Foreword

Cloud computing is a recent computing paradigm for enabling convenient, on-demand network access to a shared pool of configurable computing resources (e.g., networks, servers, storage, applications, and services) that can be rapidly provisioned and released with minimal management effort or service provider interaction1. Clouds are currently used mainly in commercial settings and focus on on-demand provision of IT infrastructure. Cloud computing can play a significant role in a variety of areas including innovations, virtual worlds, ebusiness, social networks, or search engines. But currently, it is still in its early stages, with consistent experimentation to come.

The *Workshop on Cloud Computing Projects and Initiatives* (CCPI) gathered together scientists, engineers, computer users both from industry and academia to exchange and share experiences, new ideas, and research results from collaborative international and national projects and initiatives on Cloud Computing. A number of key projects funded by the European Commission and by National Government and Research Agencies, addressing several aspects of the Cloud Computing arena were presented at the workshop, and now in the following post-workshop proceeding papers.

The paper The "Cloud@Home Project: Towards a New Enhanced Computing Paradigm" describes the Cloud@Home Italian Research Ministry funded project aiming at creating a new Cloud paradigm, Cloud@Home, in which both the commercial/business and the volunteer/scientific viewpoints coexist. The Cloud@Home infrastructure has to be able to provide adequate resources to satisfy user requests also taking into account QoS requirements. The goal of the project is to design, to implement and to test on real case studies a complete middleware able to demonstrate the feasibility of the Cloud@Home vision.

The paper "Cloud-based mediation and access of healthcare data in the @neurIST project" by Martin Koehler, Siegfried Benkner, Gerhard Engelbrecht, and Steven Wood describes the utilization of Cloud technologies for the management of unruptered aneurysms and associated research into risk factors in the @neurIST EC funded project. Diagnosis and treatment of aneurysms relies on the interpretation and integration of information, coming from the patients themselves, from the experience of clinicians, and from derived information from medical literature and other biomedical information sources. Within the @neurIST

M.R. Guarracino et al. (Eds.): Euro-Par 2010 Workshops, LNCS 6586, pp. 551–553, 2011.
© Springer-Verlag Berlin Heidelberg 2011

project a data service infrastructure has been built on top of state-of-the art Grid and Cloud technologies that supports the provisioning of virtual data sources. Virtual data sources enable transparent access to and integration of distributed heterogeneous biomedical and clinical data sources. Virtual data and mediation nodes ensure an easy distribution, hosting and deployment of virtual data sources by utilizing Cloud computing technologies.

The paper "Building a Mosaic of Clouds" describes the concept behind an open-source API and platform under construction as part of the EC funded mOSAIC project that intends to use multiple Cloud offers to satisfy the deployment requirements of component-based long-running applications. It emphasizes the need of such a platform by use cases mainly related to data-intensive applications.

The paper "Cloud@Home: Performance Management Components" from R. Aversa, D. Bruneo, A. Cuomo, B. Di Martino, S. Distefano, A. Puliafito, M. Rak, S. Venticinque and U. Villano deals with the design of performance components and their integration into a coherent subsystem for the management of the SLA/QoS of Cloud@Home, a cloud environment based on voluntarily-offered resources currently under development in the context of Cloud@Home project.

The paper "A Cloud Agency for SLA Negotiation and Management" presents the architectural design of an agent based software conceived within the mOSAIC project in order to provide facilties for brokering an negotiation of Cloud resources from different providers that fulfills at the best the requirements of user's applications. The user is able to delegate to this Agency the necessary checks of the agreement fulfilment, the monitoring of resource utilization and eventually necessary re-negotiations.

The paper "Running business applications in the Cloud: a use case perspective" presents a methodology based on the EC funded RESERVOIR project's cloud infrastructure, which automates most of the work needed to migrate an application to the cloud and eases the use of the Cloud itself. As the Cloud computing paradigm is gaining wide consensus among academic and industries, the need to have infrastructures and well know procedures to ease the migration of industrial applications to such paradigm rises. Current solutions such as EC2 might need low level expertise resulting in complex and tedious procedures, which tend to delay the decision of users to use the Cloud. We present here a real use case of a complex SAP ERP 6.0 application which has been ported on the RESERVOIR Cloud infrastructure.

The paper "Minimizing technical complexities in emerging cloud computing platforms" from Andreas Menychtas, Georgios Kousiouris, Dimosthenis Kyriazis and Theodora Varvarigou, analyses the complexities of cloud platforms, which disallow their wide adoption as business and technological solutions for applications and services. It identifies and analyses the key challenges for the emerging cloud platforms in order to minimize these technical complexities and presents various innovative approaches from European research activities.

This post-workshop proceedings includes the final versions of the presented CCPI papers, taking the feedback from reviewers and workshop audience into account.

The program chairs sincerely thank the EuroPar Program Chairs and Organization for providing the opportunity to arrange the CCPI workshop in conjunction with the EuroPar 2010 Conference, the reviewers of the submitted papers and of their final proceeding versions, and all the participants (speakers and attendees) to the Workshop.

October 2010

Beniamino Di Martino
Dana Petcu
Antonio Puliafito

The Cloud@Home Project: Towards a New Enhanced Computing Paradigm*

Rocco Aversa[5], Marco Avvenuti[2], Antonio Cuomo[4], Beniamino Di Martino[5], Giuseppe Di Modica[3], Salvatore Distefano[1], Antonio Puliafito[1], Massimiliano Rak[5], Orazio Tomarchio[3], Alessio Vecchio[2], Salvatore Venticinque[5], and Umberto Villano[4]

[1] Dipartimento di Matematica, Università of Messina
{sdistefano,apuliafito}@unime.it
[2] Dipartimento di Ingegneria dell'Informazione, Università di Pisa
a.vecchio@ing.unipi.it, m.avvenuti@iet.unipi.it
[3] Dipartimento di Ingegneria Informatica e delle Telecomunicazioni, Università di Catania
dimodica@unict.it, orazio.tomarchio@diit.unict.it
[4] Dipartimento di Ingegneria, RCOST, Università del Sannio
{villano,antonio.cuomo}@unisannio.it
[5] Dipartimento di Ingegneria dell'Informazione, Seconda Università di Napoli
{salvatore.venticinque,massimiliano.rak,rocco.aversa,
beniamino.dimartino}@unina2.it

Abstract. Cloud Computing is emerging as a promising paradigm capable of providing a flexible, dynamic, resilient and cost effective infrastructure for both academic and business environments. The aim of this project is to create a new Cloud paradigm, "Cloud@Home", in which both the commercial/business and the volunteer/scientific viewpoints coexist. The Cloud@Home infrastructure has to be able to provide adequate resources to satisfy user requests also taking into account QoS requirements. The goal of the project is to design, to implement and to test on real case studies a complete middleware able to demonstrate the feasibility of the Cloud@Home vision. In this paper we try to summarize the the Cloud@Home project, identifying the tasks in order to implement the Cloud@Home middleware.

1 Introduction and Motivations

Cloud computing is a *service-centric*, distributed computing paradigm in which all capabilities and resources (usually geographically distributed) are provided to users *as a service*, to be accessed through the Internet without any specific knowledge of, expertise with, or control over the underlying technology infrastructure that supports them. It offers a user-centric interface that acts as a unique, user friendly, point of access for users' needs and requirements. Moreover, Cloud computing provides *on-demand service provision*, *QoS guaranteed offer*, and *autonomous system* for managing hardware, software and data transparently to users [9].

* The work described in this paper has been partly supported by MIUR-PRIN 2008 project "Cloud@Home: a New Enhanced Computing Paradigm".

M.R. Guarracino et al. (Eds.): Euro-Par 2010 Workshops, LNCS 6586, pp. 555–562, 2011.
© Springer-Verlag Berlin Heidelberg 2011

In order to achieve such goals it is necessary to implement a level of abstraction of physical resources, uniforming their interfaces and providing means for their management, adaptively to user requirements. This is done through *virtualizations*, *service mashups* (Web 2.0) and *service oriented architectures* (SOA). The development and the success of Cloud computing is due to the maturity reached by such technologies.

A great interest on Cloud computing has been manifested from both academic and private research centers, and numerous projects from industry and academia have been proposed. In commercial contexts, among the others we highlight: Amazon Elastic Compute Cloud, IBMs Blue Cloud, Sun Microsystems Network.com, Microsoft Azure Services Platform, Dell Cloud computing solutions. There are also several scientific activities, among the others: Reservoir [7], Nimbus-Stratus-Wispy-Kupa [8], OpenNEbula [2], Eucalyptus [4], OCCI [5], Open Cyrrus [3] and Open QRM [6]. All of them support and provide an on-demand computing paradigm, in the sense that a user submits his/her requests to the Cloud that remotely, in a distributed fashion, processes them and gives back the results. This client-server model well fits aims and scopes of commercial Clouds: the business. But, on the other hand, it represents a restriction for scientific Clouds, that have a view closer to *Volunteer computing*. Volunteer computing (also called *Peer-to-Peer computing*, *Global computing* or *Public computing*) uses computers volunteered by their owners, as a source of computing power and storage to provide distributed scientific computing [1].

We believe the Cloud computing paradigm is applicable also at lower scales, from the single contributing user, that shares his/her desktop, to research groups, public administrations, social communities, small and medium enterprises, which make available their distributed computing resources to the Cloud. Both free sharing and pay-per-use models can be adopted in such scenarios. We therefore propose a more "democratic" form of Cloud computing, in which the computing resources of single users accessing the Cloud can be shared with the others, in order to contribute to the elaboration of complex problems. Since this paradigm is very similar to the Volunteer computing one, it has been named *Cloud@Home*. Both hardware and software compatibility limitations and restrictions of Volunteer computing can be solved in Cloud computing environments, allowing to share both hardware and software resources or *services*. The Cloud@Home paradigm could be also applied to commercial Clouds, establishing an *open computing-utility market* where users can both buy and sell their services.

2 Aims and Goals

The Cloud@Home paradigm is inspired to the Volunteer computing one. In this new paradigm, user's hosts are not passive interfaces to Cloud services anymore, but they can interact (for free or by charge) with other Clouds. Fig. 1 depicts the Cloud@Home reference scenario, identifying the different stakeholders characterized by their role: consuming and/or contributing. Arrows outgoing from the Cloud represent consuming resources, from which a Cloud@Home client submits its requests; otherwise, arrows incoming to the Cloud represent contributing resources providing their services to Cloud@Home clients. Therefore, infrastructure providers, datacenters, Grids, clusters, servers, till desktops and mobile devices can both contribute and consume.

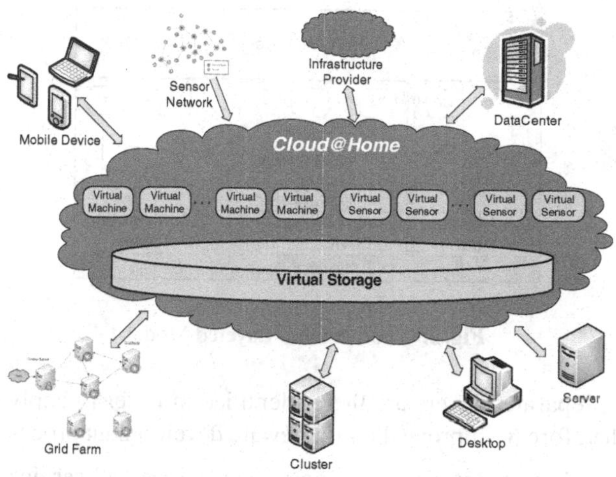

Fig. 1. Cloud@home Reference Scenario

In fact, we believe that the Cloud@Home paradigm is widely applicable, from research groups, public administrations, social communities, SMEs, which make available their distributed computing resources to the Cloud, till, potentially, the single contributing user, that autonomously decides to share his/her resources.

According to the Cloud@Home vision, all the users can be, at the same time or in different moments, both clients and active parts of the computing and storage infrastructure. A straightforward application of this concept to the world of mobile devices is not so much useful, because of the limited computing power and storage capacity that are available on such nodes. Still, an active participation of the mobile nodes to the cloud services can be opportune if we start considering as resources, not only computing and storage, but also the peculiar and commonly available peripherals/sensors available on mobile phones (e.g., camera, GPS, microphone, accelerometer, etc) or other devices such as the nodes of a sensor network. In other words Cloud@Home, besides virtualizing the computing and storage resources, aims at virtualizing also the sensing infrastructure. Such infrastructure, consistently with the other functionalities, has to be accessed as a service (*sensor as a service*, SEAAS). According to this perspective, in Fig. 1 mobile devices are considered as both contributing and consuming resources, since they can provide their sensors to Cloud@Home and/or they can access the Cloud for submitting their requests as common clients, respectively.

The project framework will be based on a Cloud@Home software system which provides readily available functionality in the areas of directory/information services, security and management of resources. In order to implement such a form of computing the following issues should be taken into consideration: resources management, user interface, security, accounting, identity management, virtualization; interoperability among heterogeneous Clouds; business models, billing, QoS and SLA management. A possible rationalization of the tasks and the functionalities the Cloud@Home middleware has to implement can be performed by considering the layered view shown

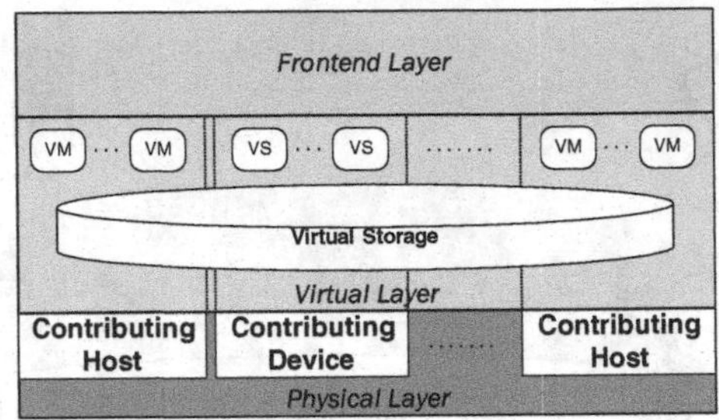

Fig. 2. Cloud@home Layered Model

in Fig. 2. Three separated layers are there identified in order to apply a separation of concerns and therefore to improve the middleware development process:

- The Frontend Layer that globally manages resources and services (coordination, discovery, enrolment) implements the user interface for accessing the Cloud (ensuring security reliability and interoperability), and provides QoS and business models and policies management facilities.
- The Virtual Layer that implements a homogeneous view of the distributed Cloud system offered to the higher frontend layer (and therefore to users) in form of two main basic services: the execution service that allows to set up a virtual machine, and the storage service that implements a distributed storage Cloud to store data and files as a remote disk, locally mounted or accessed via Web. Virtual Sensors (VSs) provide the access points to the sensing infrastructure.
- The bottom Physical Layer that provides both the physical resources for elaborating the requests and the software for locally managing such resources. It is composed of a "cloud" of generic nodes and/or devices geographically distributed across the Internet.

3 Insights

Fig. 3 identifies and groups all the tasks of the Cloud@Home project into six blocks: frontend, SLA, QoS, service composition, security management and virtualization. In the following we provide some details on them.

3.1 Frontend

The user frontend provides tools for Cloud@Home-user interactions. It collects and manages the users' requests issued by the Cloud@Home clients. All such requests are transferred to the underlying layer for processing. The frontend is made up of three subtasks: *mobile access*, *Web access* and *Web service access*. The mobile access provides user interfaces specifically customized for being accessed by devices with small screens and limited input capabilities. The Web access provides all mechanisms and tools for implementing the Web access to the Cloud@Home infrastructure. The Web service access instead focuses on the interface to Web services of the Cloud@Home infrastructure.

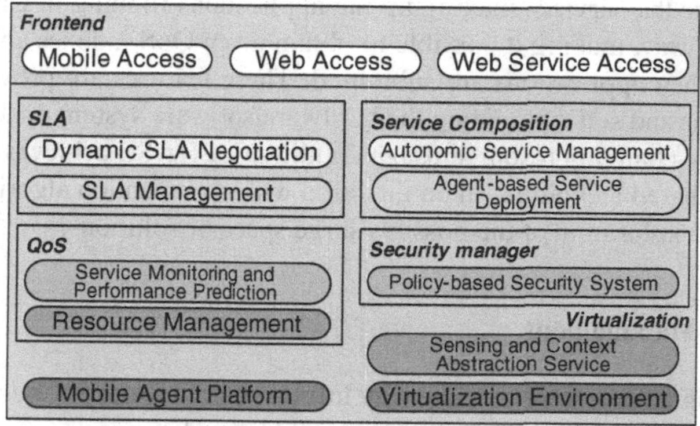

Fig. 3. Cloud@Home infrastructure middleware development tasks allocation

3.2 SLA and QoS

The SLA block will take into account the high dynamicity of the Cloud@Home volunteer context, so it is split into: *dynamic SLA negotiation* and *SLA management*. The dynamic SLA negotiation module provides a framework for the negotiation of non-functional parameters in complex environments of resource and service sharing, composition and virtualization. The SLA management system is responsible for the service lifecycle. This includes service definition, deployment, management, monitoring, compliance and termination. Users require services which are incorporated within contracts containing business terms with no reference to raw resources. The system manages the service by automatically configuring and deploying it. In order to meet the contract terms, the system will monitor SLAs and take any opportune action, such as reconfiguration, re-location or resource re-allocation.

One of the Cloud@Home project aims is to deal with QoS in both open and commercial environments. In this context several issues concerning the QoS and SLA management have to be adequately considered, faced, and solved, as mentioned above. Resource optimization within the Cloud becomes a key requirement.

The Cloud@Home project QoS activity is organized in two sub-activities: *service monitoring and performance prediction* and *resource management*. The service monitoring and performance prediction will be carried out at three different levels:

- **Application Level:** the mobile agent platform will offer a set of a monitoring agents, able to move between the virtual resources collecting performance indexes;
- **Platform Level:** both SLA Engine and CHASE will collect information from the monitored resources using their proprietary solutions;
- **Resource Level:** (some of) partecipating resources will be enriched with monitoring tools that can be remotely interrogated.

3.3 Service Composition

Cloud@Home will exploit CHASE (Cloud@Home Autonomic Service Engine) in order to manage resources: the main goal of CHASE is to schedule, allocate, and possibly migrate the services making up the applications running in Cloud@Home in an "intelligent" way, making it possible to obtain given QoS indexes and to fulfil SLA agreed upon when applications are submitted. These features are provided automatically, self-tuning and self-optimizing the hardware/software system under dynamic and possibly rapidly-changing resource usage conditions. CHASE achieves this results using simulation based techniques in conjunction with optimization algorithms, avoiding the brute-force exploration of the possibly large space of solutions.

3.4 Security Management

In order to design a prototype of a security infrastructure to support the use cases of the Cloud@Home project, the following issues will be faced:

- *Protection level agreement*. The agreement between a service provider and a client normally contains guarantees over non functional requirements, reflecting the client business objectives. These objectives determine the Quality of Service (QoS) that the provider should guarantee during service provisioning.
- *Policy specification languages*. Our objective in this area is to analyse several languages for the specification of security policy and to identify the most suitable for the specification of cloud security policies, by possibly extending existing proposals, that do not provide some critical features.
- *Security-aware resource/service discovery and selection*. The discovery and selection of services/resources in Cloud@Home will take into consideration security among the main requirements. Thanks to the specific security policy adopted by a provider, a potential client will be able to explicitly describe and to impose constraints on security aspects, which will be accounted for in the process of discovery and resource selection.

3.5 Virtualization

The virtualization of the Cloud@Home infrastructure is one of the most important task to implement. All the Cloud@Home computing, storage and sensors resources have to be virtualized in order to be provided as a service. Thus, the activity is organized into three main sub-activities: *sensing and context abstraction service*, *virtualization environment* and *mobile agent platform*.

The sensing and context abstraction service (SCAS) implements the virtual sensor concept, and provides sensing and context information to applications executed within the Cloud.

In the considered scenarios, the context could also include the nature of the device, the quality and availability of wireless connection, the residual power, the physical location of the user. To protect the users from unwanted accesses to their data, the system will include mechanisms useful to specify and enforce access policies.

The virtualization environment provides solution to the problem of heterogeneous hardware and software (OS, libraries, compilers, etc.) by means of virtualization techniques, based on Virtual Machine Monitors such as VMware, VirtualBox, Xen, Qemu and so on. They create virtual execution environments that satisfy individual requirements in terms of memory, disk space, operating system, adapting the runtime environment to the application instead of adapting the application to the runtime environment.

Similar problems must be tackled in organizing and managing storage resources. In fact it is necessary to provide an adequate architecture able to split data in chunks and to store such chunks into the distributed disks. Problems of data security such as confidentiality and integrity, have to be adequately considered and solved in the implementation of the virtual storage environment system.

In order to face the flexibility of virtualized resources, the Cloud@Home platform is enriched with a mobile agent platform which offers a flexible programming paradigm and adaptable services. The mobile agent platform will be adopted to easily deploy new application on the virtual resources, to perform application level monitoring, to develop brokering services and to build up customized interfaces between users and the platform.

4 Case Studies

The Cloud@Home middleware will be tested by using some real reference scenarios, involving organizations external to the project, such as Oracle, Insirio, IBM, and Inquadro, in order to highlight the needs that could decisively encourage its adoption. The first one refers to the utilization of complex enterprise software systems requiring specific hardware resources. Since one of the main source of costs and complexity for companies is related to expand, to tune and to optimize the hardware resources in order to effectively satisfy high demanding, domain-specific technical software and to ensure adequate productivity levels, we consider the utilization of complex enterprise software systems requiring specific hardware resources as the first use case of Cloud@Home. The use of the Cloud@Home technology allows to adequately exploit the company computing resources, which are sometimes distributed over several sites, to meet the demands of the mentioned software, building a private Cloud. Cloud@Home also enables to create, customize and use resources and services running in remote interoperable Clouds. In this scenario powerless terminals can be used to implement remote-desktop connections with both computing and storage delegated to the Cloud. Optimized management of hw/sw platforms and services, simpler monitoring and maintenance, QoS and security provision are some of the further benefits inherent in such approach.

A volunteer computing scenario is instead identified in the second case study, which intends to set up a federated Cloud@Home environment, composed of "local" Clouds located in each research group. This case study intends to highlight the free-sharing and volunteer contributing vocation of Cloud@Home. Each research group involved in the project will build its own local Cloud, starting from the available resources and services in its organization. The Clouds thus created will be federated, implementing a unique Cloud@Home environment, also open to individual contributors. In this way we will set up a significant testbed for experimenting the Cloud@Home middleware and all its capabilities (interoperability, QoS, security, resource management, etc) and scenarios (heterogeneous nodes, wireless devices, ubiquitous and pervasive computing, location based services, etc).

The third use case is mainly focused on mobile environments, in which we imagine the following scenario: a cloud computing system hosts an application dedicated to the management of traffic lights and parking lots of an urban area. Users equipped with mobile phones could voluntarily share their positioning information with the management application. Information gathered in this way could be used to dynamically compute more efficient vehicle routing strategies. The presence of supporting and shared mechanisms for the abstraction of sensing information within the cloud infrastructure foster the reuse of available data in different applications.

5 Conclusions

In this paper we proposed an innovative computing paradigm that merges volunteer contributing and Cloud approaches into Cloud@Home. This proposal represents a solution for building Clouds starting from heterogeneous and independent nodes, not specifically conceived for such a purpose.

In this way Cloud@Home opens the Cloud computing world to scientific and academic research centers, as well as to communities or single users: anyone can voluntarily support projects by sharing his/her resources. On the other hand, it opens the utility computing market to the single user that wants to sell his/her computing resources. To realize this broader vision, several issues must be adequately taken into account: reliability, security, portability of resources and services, interoperability among Clouds, QoS/SLA and business models and policies.

References

1. Anderson, D.P., Fedak, G.: The computational and storage potential of volunteer computing. In: CCGRID 2006, pp. 73–80 (2006)
2. Distributed Systems Architecture Research Group. OpenNEbula Project. Universidad Complutense de Madrid (2009), http://www.opennebula.org/
3. HP, Intel, Yahoo! Open Cirrus^{TM} the HP/Intel/Yahoo! Open Cloud Computing Research Testbed. OGF (June 2010), Open Cirrus^{TM} website, https://www.opencirrus.org/
4. Nurmi, D., Wolski, R., Grzegorczyk, C., Obertelli, G., Soman, S., Youseff, L., Zagorodnov, D.: The eucalyptus open-source cloud-computing system. In: Proceedings of Cloud Computing and Its Applications (October 2008)
5. OGF Open Cloud Computing Interface Working Group. Open Cloud Computing Interface. OGF (June 2010), OCCI website http://www.occi-wg.org/
6. openQRM Development Community. openQRM: open-source Data-center management platform (June 2010), openQRM website http://www.openqrm.com/
7. Reservoir Consortium. Reservoir Project (2009), http://www-03.ibm.com/press/us/en/pressrelease/23448.wss/
8. University of Chicago-University of Florida-Purdue University-Masaryk University. Nimbus-Stratus-Wispy-Kupa Projects (January 2009), http://workspace.globus.org/clouds/nimbus.html/, http://www.acis.ufl.edu/vws/, http://www.rcac.purdue.edu/teragrid/resources/#wispy, http://meta.cesnet.cz/cms/opencms/en/docs/clouds
9. Wang, L., Tao, J., Kunze, M., Castellanos, A.C., Kramer, D., Karl, W.: Scientific Cloud Computing: Early Definition and Experience. In: HPCC 2008, pp. 825–830 (2008)

Cloud-Based Mediation and Access of Healthcare Data in the @neurIST Project

Martin Koehler[1], Siegfried Benkner[1],
Gerhard Engelbrecht[2], and Steven Wood[3]

[1] University of Vienna, Faculty of Computer Science,
Department of Scientific Computing, Vienna, Austria
[2] Center for Computational Imaging & Simulation Technologies in Biomedicine
Universitat Pompeu Fabra, Barcelona, Spain
[3] Department of Medical Physics,
Sheffield Teaching Hospitals Trust, Sheffield, UK

Abstract. Managing and sharing data and information related to the understanding of human disease processes represents a huge challenge for medical researchers and clinicians. The European @neurIST project addressed this challenge by developing an advanced service-oriented IT infrastructure for the management of all processes linked to research, diagnosis and treatment development for complex and multi-factorial diseases. The @neurIST infrastructure relies on a service-oriented architecture comprising data services and compute services encompassing data repositories, computational analysis services and information systems handling multi-scale, multi-modal information at distributed sites. The @neurIST data services infrastructure offers tools based on Grid and Cloud technologies for constructing virtual data sources that enable transparent access to and integration of distributed heterogeneous biomedical and clinical data sources. Pre-configured virtual data nodes and a virtual mediation node ensure an easy distribution, hosting and deployment of data services by utilizing latest Cloud computing technologies.

1 Introduction

The @neurIST Information Society Technologies (IST) Integrated Project funded within the European Commission's (EC) Sixth Framework Programme focused on supporting the research and treatment of cerebral aneurysms. @neurIST is part of a wider vision, which aims at addressing the problem of inequalities in healthcare and outcomes across the European Union. At the heart of the project is a clinical problem, managing unruptered cerebral aneurysms and associated research into risk factors. Diagnosis and treatment of aneurysms relies on the interpretation and integration of numerous pieces of information, coming from the patients themselves in the form of radiographic images, family history and physiological measurements, from the experience of clinicians, and from derived information from medical literature and many other biomedical information sources.

M.R. Guarracino et al. (Eds.): Euro-Par 2010 Workshops, LNCS 6586, pp. 563–570, 2011.
© Springer-Verlag Berlin Heidelberg 2011

The @neurIST consortium, comprised of more than 30 partners including hospitals, universities, research institutes and the industry across Europe, addressed this challenge by developing an advanced service-oriented IT infrastructure for the management of all processes linked to research, diagnosis and treatment development for complex and multi-factorial diseases. The @neurIST infrastructure has been built on top of state-of-the art Grid and Cloud technologies encompassing data repositories, computational analysis and simulation services and information systems handling multi-scale, multi-modal information at distributed sites. The infrastructure supports personalized patient management including data capture, referral, decision support, and treatment planning, as well as clinical research in cerebral aneurysms.

The @neurIST infrastructure relies on a flexible, generic service framework with support for advanced security mechanisms that ensure the stringent privacy and security requirements of patient-specific data. At the heart of the @neurIST infrastructure are generic services to support complex analysis and simulation tasks, and to provide transparent access to and integration of heterogeneous data from diverse, distributed sources comprising text, images, and other structures. A new ontology, formalizing the conceptual space of @neurIST, has been developed and supports semantic service discovery and data integration. Several advanced end-user applications for risk assessment, for linking genetic information to the disease, for multi-modal image processing, and for virtual endovascular treatment planning have been developed on top of these services.

2 @neurIST Architecture

Providing end users with seamless access to distributed medical data and computational resources is a major goal of the @neurIST system. The @neurIST system provides two main modes of operation to end users. The first mode of operation targets clinical practitioners by providing an integrative decision support system. The second mode of operation targets in silico research, linking genetic and phenotypic evidence so that new knowledge can be extracted, structured and transposed for its later exploitation in the decision support operation cycle. Due to privacy and security requirements, the research system has only access to anonymized data sets while the decision support system also deals with specific patient-related data. A versatile middleware layer comprising data and compute services is utilized by the application suites for transparent access to diverse data and information resources as well as to computational resources for performing compute-intensive analysis and simulation tasks. The middleware layer takes care of data transport, security, data access and integration, and management of computational tasks.

The @neurIST system and infrastructure has been developed using multiple technologies and is deployed across a wide geographic distribution. @neurIST adopts a service-oriented architecture to integrate the diverse components of the system, and uses open standards and technologies from the Internet, Grid, Cloud and medical domains. A layered view of the @neurIST reference architecture is shown in Fig. 1 including the constituent components. The system can be logically divided into three layers application, middleware and resource layer.

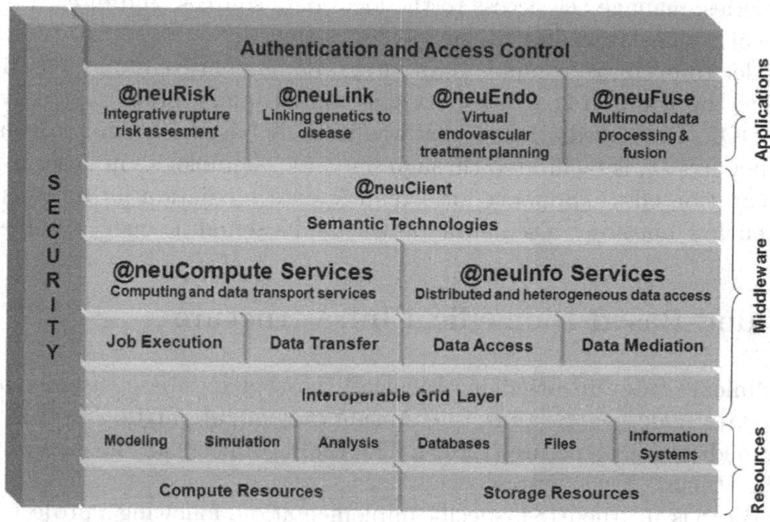

Fig. 1. @neurIST System Architecture

3 @neuInfo - Data Services

A generic data management and integration framework that supports the provisioning and deployment of data services is provided by the @neuInfo middleware. @neuInfo enables the virtualization of heterogeneous scientific databases and information sources as Web services which allows transparent access to and integration of relational databases, XML databases and flat files. The development of data services has been based on the Vienna Grid Environment (VGE) [3] and utilize advanced data mediation and distributed query processing techniques based on GDMS, OGSA-DAI [2], and OGSA-DQP [1].

Data services hide the details of distributed data sources, resolving heterogeneities with respect to access language, data model and schema. Data integration is based on a mediator approach where local data sources are integrated bottom-up by mapping local data base schemes into a virtual global schema. This is done to preserve the autonomy of data sources and to ensure up-to-date data, which are key requirements of the project. Internally, data services utilize the defacto standard for Grid-based data access and integration (OGSA-DAI). Client applications usually access data services by submitting SQL queries and downloading query results in the form of OGSA-DAI-compliant XML documents.

Data services can be deployed with different configurations, all providing the same interface to clients. Data access services (DAS) provide access to a single data source, anonymized image services (AIS) support the transfer of large image data of different modalities, and data mediation services (DMS) offer transparent access to multiple data sources via a global virtual schema. The virtual schema of a DMS provides an integrated, global view of the underlying local data sources. Data mediation services translate queries with respect to the global schema into local queries, manage the access to the local data sources, and integrate results from local queries according to the global schema.

In order to optimize complex data integration scenarios, data mediation services may be configured to support distributed query processing, relying on OGSA-DQP. Data mediation, which was initially based on hand-written mapping schemas [10], is facilitated through semantic technologies in order to reduce the integration effort. Support for semantic data mediation [9] relies on using the @neurIST ontology, a semantic broker, and a semantic query resolver.

4 Cloud-Based Biomedical Infrastructure

Each clinical center involved in @neurIST hosts a database, usually inside a virtual data node (see Section 4.1), storing patient information from a part of the Biomedical Infostructure (BioIS). The BioIS connects all the clinical centers with the @neurIST framework.

The BioIS is an @neurIST-specific implementation, following a project-defined data schema called CRIM (Clinical Reference Information Model) which is driven by the need to gather clinical data from multiple clinical centers for research purposes. The CRIM data schema lists and defines all data items needed by the @neurIST project. The BioIS supports various different patient identification and de-identification mechanisms to ensure that private information cannot be used outside of the hospital, while ensuring that new patient data generated by @neurIST services can be associated with the patient and reviewed by the clinician.

The BioIS system utilizes @neuInfo services (distributed queries and updates) for providing information to the application suites. The BioIS supports requests for clinical data, as well as patient-specific data obtained from other @neurIST services. Clinical information does always remain at its source within the clinical information systems (CIS) of participating centers. The BioIS sub-system does interface with the CIS databases for accessing actual data. Two BioIS models have been implemented. Following the anonymised (ANO) model, data from the original patient record is anonymised and copied to a separate database (called anoDB) in the de-militarized zone of a hospital and then accessed by means of an @neuInfo data service. In the on-the-fly (OTF) model, a corresponding @neuInfo data service directly accesses patient records within the CIS.

Stakeholders are able to transparently access all BioIS instances via the virtual mediation node hosting an @neuInfo data mediation service. Access to the underlying clinical centers is done behind the scenes utilizing distributed query mechanisms.

4.1 Virtual Data Node

The virtual data node, shown in Fig. 2, is based on a virtual appliance and encapsulates the BioIS ANO Model installation of @neuInfo providing access to the anoDB following the CRIM schema. A fully configured system installation

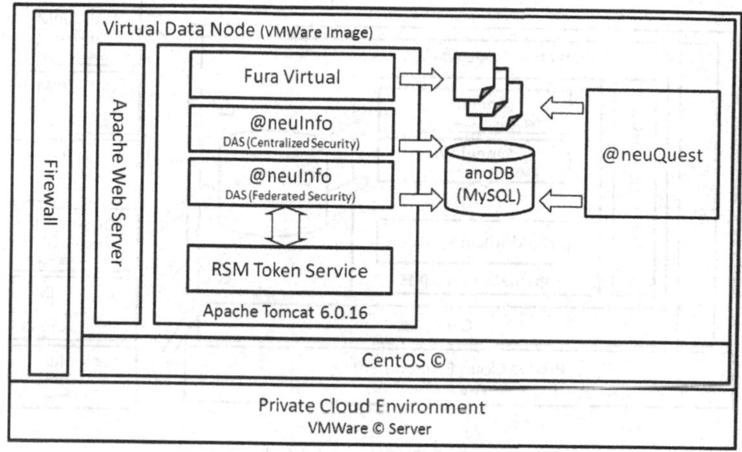

Fig. 2. @neurIST Virtual Data Node

is provided as a virtual machine, including preconfigured system components such as Apache, Tomcat and SSL configuration. This allows simple deployment for test and production use at new clinical partners and supports future Cloud computing infrastructures. The @neurIST software needed for the ANO model is preinstalled, including an @neuInfo data service, an anoDB installation that follows the CRIM schema, the @neuQuest tool for capturing data of new patients, and a Fura Virtual File[1] system providing access to medical images. The Virtual data node has been implemented on top of VMWare and CentOS.

4.2 Virtual Mediation Node

The virtual mediation node encapsulates the installation of @neuInfo data mediation services providing transparent access to all the virtual data nodes at different clinical sites. Queries against the mediation service within the virtual mediation node are automatically resolved and the underlying data access services are accessed in a distributed fashion. A fully configured system installation is provided as a virtual machine, deployable on an VMWare server. New data mediation nodes may be set up to provide specialised views onto the distributed set of clinical data for new usage scenarios or different stakeholders. Providing the service with a preconfigured virtual machine allows replicating and scaling service instances on demand by utilizing the capabilities of Cloud computing infrastructures. The @neurIST software required for the virtual mediation node is preinstalled, including an @neuInfo data mediation service, and a CRIM-compliant data mediation schema that integrates all participating clinical centers. The mediation service is hosted using a Tomcat server and the VMWare server is secured by using a firewall. The configuration of the virtual mediation node is depicted in Fig. 3.

[1] Fura: http://fura.sourceforge.net/

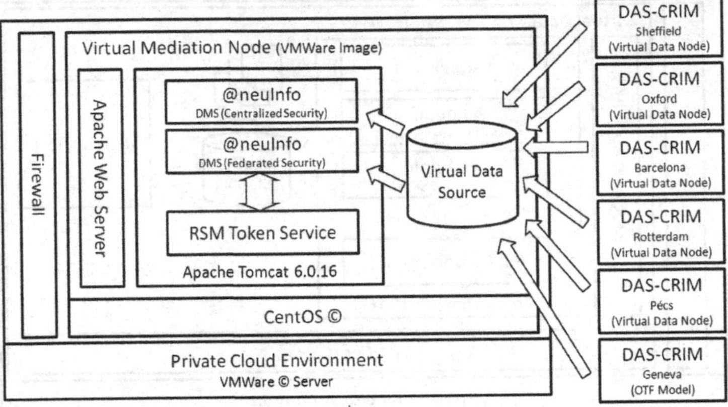

Fig. 3. @neurIST Virtual Mediation Node

The virtual data and mediation nodes utilize the centralized security model with SSL and HTTP authentication. Moreover, a federated security model is also supported, but has not been adopted by all users, which typically prefer the centralized security model. The federated security model comprises a Relationship Manager (RSM) as well as the RSM token service [5].

4.3 Cloud-Based @neurIST System

The @neurIST BioIS data mediation system has been set up in a test bed comprising a variety of services at different sites in Europe. At the clinical partner sites in Barcelona, Geneva, Oxford, Rotterdam and Sheffield, patient data (CRIM) and images are made available via a corresponding virtual data node comprising an @neuInfo data access service (DAS-CRIM) and an anonymized image service (AIS). In order to provide an integrated view of all patient data, a data mediation service (DMS-CRIM) is hosted at the University of Vienna. The DAS-CRIM and the DMS-CRIM services are hosted in private Cloud environments at the Grid sites based on VMWare. Due to the architectural conception of virtual nodes, services can be scaled and replicated on-demand. The @neurist system includes additional compute and data services utilized by the application suites.

5 Related Work

A Grid-based healthcare platform providing a seamless integration of traditional and emerging sources of biomedical information was developed by the Health-e-Child project [4]. The US caBIG initiative [8] developed a Grid-based collaborative information network for sharing of data and knowledge that aims at accelerating the discovery of new approaches for the detection, diagnosis, treatment, and prevention of cancer. They introduced a Cancer Knowledge Cloud that enables remote access to data, analytical tools, and computing power. Additionally there are several research projects on Cloud computing which can enable the development of biomedical Cloud infrastructures. The European RESERVOIR project [7] couples virtualization, grid computing, and business service management techniques to develop system and service technologies that serve as the infrastructure for Cloud computing.

The Virtual Physiological Human [6] Initiative (VPH-I) aims to provide a systematic framework for understanding physiological processes in the human body in terms of anatomical structure and biophysical mechanisms at multiple length and time scales. Research projects under this initiative aim to develop patient-specific computational modeling and simulations of such mechanisms. The European commission has identified that to achieve this objective a combined data/compute infrastructure will need to be developed and have called for proposals in the area of Cloud computing to address these needs (ICT Call 6 FP7-ICT-2009-6).

6 Conclusion

The @neurIST project developed an advanced service-oriented IT infrastructure that supports seamless access to computational resources and distributed medical data in an easy to use and secure way. The @neurIST system fosters multiple high-level application suites facilitating the analysis and treatment of aneurysms.

The @neuInfo data access and mediation services are utilized for seamlessly integrating the biomedical infostructures from multiple hospitals. A virtual data node was developed for the BioIS that enables easy distribution and deployment of @neuInfo services based on Cloud computing technologies. The virtual mediation node supports the deployment of different tailor-made views on distributed and heterogeneous data by creating a virtual database. The virtual mediation host is deployed in a Cloud environment and can be easily adopted and duplicated for different usage scenarios.

The @neurIST infrastructure is generic and applicable to other diseases. It can be utilized for future analysis and decision support systems not only in the clinical context. In particular, the utilization of Cloud technologies, which have been integrated during the final phase of the project, represents a significant step beyond the limits of Grid technologies by completely decoupling the physical execution environment from the infrastructure, ensuring easy migration to future IT infrastructures.

Furthermore, to cope with the complexity and diversity of the data underlying multi-factoral diseases, a semantic environment supporting data access and integration including a domain specific ontology has been developed including semantic annotation technologies, a semantic query resolver, and a semantic broker. Fully leveraging these semantic technologies for increasing the level of automation in data mediation remains, however, a topic of future research activities.

References

1. Alpdemir, M.N., Mukherjee, A., Gounaris, A., Paton, N.W., Watson, P., Fernandes, A.A.A., Fitzgerald, D.J.: OGSA-DQP: A service for distributed querying on the grid. In: Hwang, J., Christodoulakis, S., Plexousakis, D., Christophides, V., Koubarakis, M., Böhm, K. (eds.) EDBT 2004. LNCS, vol. 2992, pp. 858–861. Springer, Heidelberg (2004)
2. Antonioletti, M., Atkinson, M., Baxter, R., Borley, A., Hong, C., Neil, P., Collins, B., Hardman, N., Hume, A.C., Knox, A., Jackson, M., Krause, A., Laws, S., Magowan, J., Paton, N.W., Pearson, D., Sugden, T., Watson, P., Westhead, M.: The design and implementation of grid database services in ogsa-dai: Research articles. Concurrency and Computation: Practice and Experience 17(2-4), 357–376 (2005)
3. Benkner, S., Engelbrecht, G., Koehler, M., Woehrer, A.: Virtualizing scientific applications and data sources as grid services. In: Cao, J. (ed.) Cyberinfrastructure Technologies and Applications. Nova Science Publishers, New York (2009)
4. Freund, J., Comaniciu, D., Ioannis, Y., Liu, P., McClatchey, R., Morley-Fletcher, E., Pennec, X., Pongiglione, G., Zhou, X.: Health-e-child: An integrated biomedical platform for grid-based paediatrics. In: Challenges and Opportunities of HealthGrids: Proceedings of Healthgrid 2006, pp. 259–270. IOS Press, Amsterdam (2006)
5. Gruschka, N., Lo Iacono, L., Rajasekaran, H.: Security architecture for federated medical information systems. Phil. Trans. A Journal (2008)
6. Hunter, P., Coveney, P.V., de Bono, B., Diaz, V., Fenner, J., Frangi, A.F., Harris, P., Hose, R., Kohl, P., Lawford, P., McCormack, K., Mendes, M., Omholt, S., Quarteroni, A., Skar, J., Tegner, J., Thomas, R., Tollis, I., Tsamardinos, I., van Beek, J.H.G.M., Viceconti, M.: A vision and strategy for the virtual physiological human in 2010 and beyond. Philosophical Transactions of the Royal Society (2010)
7. Rochwerger, B., Breitgand, D., Levy, E., Galis, A., Nagin, K., Llorente, I.M., Montero, R., Wolfsthal, Y., Elmroth, E., Caceres, J., Ben-Yehuda, M., Emmerich, W., Galan, F.: The reservoir model and architecture for open federated cloud computing. IBM Journal of Research and Development 53(4), 4:1–4:11 (2009)
8. Tsiknakis, M., Brochhausen, M., Nabrzyski, J., Pucacki, J., Sfakianakis, S.G., Potamias, G., Desmedt, C., Kafetzopoulos, D.: A semantic grid infrastructure enabling integrated access and analysis of multilevel biomedical data in support of postgenomic clinical trials on cancer. IEEE Transactions on Information Technology in Biomedicine 12 (March 2008)
9. Wöhrer, A., Benkner, S., Brezany, P.: Towards a reference model for the runtime-phase of semantic data mediation. In: Essaaidi, M., Malgeri, M., Badica, C. (eds.) Intelligent Distributed Computing IV. Studies in Computational Intelligence, vol. 315, pp. 89–95. Springer, Heidelberg (2010)
10. Wöhrer, A., Brezany, P., Min Tjoa, A.: Novel mediator architectures for grid information systems. Future Generation Computer Systems 21(1), 107–114 (2005)

Building a Mosaic of Clouds

Beniamino Di Martino[1], Dana Petcu[2], Roberto Cossu[3], Pedro Goncalves[4], Tamás Máhr[5], and Miguel Loichate[6]

[1] Second University of Naples, Italy
[2] Institute e-Austria Timişoara, Romania
[3] European Space Agency, France
[4] Terradue SRL, Italy
[5] AITIA International Inc., Hungary
[6] Fatronik Tecnalia, Spain

Abstract. The current diversity of Cloud computing services, benefic for the fast development of a new IT market, hinders the easy development, portability and inter-operability of Cloud oriented applications. Developing an application oriented view of Cloud services instead the current provider ones can lead to a step forward in the adoption of Cloud computing on a larger scale than the actual one. In this context, we present a position paper exposing the concepts behind a recent proposal for an open-source application programming interface and platform for dealing with multiple Cloud computing offers.

Keywords: Cloud programming model, Federation of Clouds, Cloud-based applications.

1 Introduction

Cloud computing, currently used mainly in commercial settings and focusing on on-demand provision of services, has a clear potential to play a significant role in a variety of areas including innovations or e-business, virtual worlds or social networks. Cloud computing offers until date have been developed without addressing a common programming model, open standard interfaces, adequate service level agreements or portability of applications. Neglecting these issues current Cloud computing offers force people to be stranded into locked, proprietary systems. Developers making an effort in Cloud-ifying their applications cannot port them elsewhere. Moreover, users put in the hands of commercial providers applications and data without negotiable quality of service agreements. From these points of view, Cloud computing is still in its early stages with consistent experimentation to come.

In order to respond to the above described community needs, the mOSAIC project has been initiated in the frame of FP7-ICT programme. It intends to create and promote an open-source Cloud application programming interface and a platform targeted for developing multi-Cloud oriented applications. This early position paper about mOSAIC offer describes its concepts and expectations. It is organized as follows. Section 2 is dedicated to mOSAIC's manifest.

M.R. Guarracino et al. (Eds.): Euro-Par 2010 Workshops, LNCS 6586, pp. 571–578, 2011.
© Springer-Verlag Berlin Heidelberg 2011

The user requirements motivating the concepts implementation are described through several scenarios in Section 3. Section 4 identifies the main challenges and components of the proposed software developments. Finally, Section 5 comments the implementation status and the benefits of mOSAIC offer usage.

2 Manifesto

The mOSAIC proposal is motivated by existing weaknesses of the current research and practice in Cloud computing: (a) lack of common programming model for Cloud-oriented applications; (b) lack of tools for easy deployment of scalable applications and (multi)-Cloud-based service compositions; (c) lack of standard interfaces for resource virtualisation; (d) lack of adequate service level agreements and their dynamic negotiation; (e) platform dependability and non-portability due to different APIs for different types of resources. To these weaknesses mOSAIC intends to respond by providing the followings:

1. Design a language- and platform-agnostic application programming interface for using multi-Cloud resources and Cloud usage patterns.
2. Build an open-source and portable platform for using Cloud services based on the proposed API and Cloud usage patterns.
3. Design a generic agent skeleton for representing various stakeholders, e.g. vendors and their resources, users of various types, and collection of modules that can be used to adapt agent skeleton to support needed functionalities.
4. Design user-centric service level agreements, a Cloud ontology and mechanisms for dynamic negotiation of resources based on multi-agent technologies and semantic data processing.
5. Build proof-of-concept applications with emphasis on data intensive applications.

The open-source platform will be a proof-of-the-concept prototype ready to be tested, exploited or extended by its users. It will include instances of the APIs for at least two programming languages and applications tools. Its semantic engine that, based on the Cloud ontology, will express the application's needs for Cloud resources in terms of SLAs and QoS requirements that are the inputs of a negotiation module. This module initiates a bid to the agents representing different Cloud resources providers. Cloud resources can vary from software services (including virtual appliances) or data services to hardware services.

In the current context of the Cloud market, mOSAIC is expected to offer the freedom of choice at programming level as well as at the resource level.

3 Usage Scenarios and Proof-of-the-Concept Applications

3.1 An Entreprise Usage Scenario

In order to describe an example of use of the mOSAIC API and the related framework and platform, we refer to a common Enterprise-to-Cloud use case reported in [1] which involves an enterprise using Cloud services for its internal processes. Suppose that the context is the one of a project with limited duration and that will be a need which will stress the internal resource, reducing the SLA for all the other tasks of the enterprise. The enterprise has a fixed project fund for computational use and will acquire external computational resources from Cloud. Actual Clouds offer a large set of solutions able to solve this kind of problems: as an example the enterprise may acquire computational resources from EC2, customize the machines, deploy its data on the Amazon S3 storage system, setup their software on the target resources, define a set of procedures for accessing the Cloud resources from internal ones and viceversa, and only after that they will proceed to the target project. Even if the procedure remain the same for every kind of Cloud resources (e.g. EC2 or GoGRID), they should be completely re-executed from scratch, changing Cloud provider: different machine images, needing a new customization, new setup of software, probably different procedure to access the external resource from internal ones, and so on. Moreover, as side effect, once the project started using a given Cloud provider, even if a cheaper one arises, e.g. after more detailed evaluation, another Cloud proves to be cheaper than the chosen one, the change will probably be too expensive. Furthermore, if two different Cloud providers offer different features at different prices, and the best solution (in term of quality/cost ratio) is to use both for the different tasks, the cost of setting up the procedure on both will be very high. The overall cost may be not acceptable for a project with limited time and budget.

We expect that in this context the enterprise will use mOSAIC solutions to describe the kind of resources, to request them, and setup internal-external communication. Thanks to the mOSAIC the enterprise will have access to all the (supported) Cloud providers independently. No cost in changing the provider or difficulties in accessing different providers are foreseen. Moreover the solution developed may be easily reused for different applications and projects (the overall development cost and time are reduced). Furthermore is possible to use the mOSAIC framework in order to enrich the needed resource description with an expected quality/cost ratio or the expected cost, so that the framework, in an autonomous way setup a different set of resources or stop using them when the costs grows too high.

3.2 Application Scenarios

A special attention will be given to the validation of the API and platform through data-intensive applications and simulations. The motivation for data-intensive applications is the emergency of the fourth paradigm of scientific and technological discovery, the data-intensive science: the availability of diverse data is shifting scientific approaches from hypothesis-driven scientific method to science based on exploration. The following Gray' laws were recently postulated in the book [2]: scientific computing is becoming increasingly data intensive; the solution is in a "scale-out" architecture; bring computations to the data, rather than data to the computations. In this context Cloud computing offers consists in: allowing groups to host, process, and analyze large volumes of data;

consolidating computing and storage in very large data centers as an economical efficient solution; offering hosting facilitates for long-term data preservation.

On another hand the current scientific and business simulations can scale to a point where they are either computationally too expensive, or require too much memory to be able to run on simple computers, servers, or supercomputers. Simulations are therefore obvious candidates as Cloud applications, their extra needs being satisfied by customized resource allocations.

The mOSAIC's proof-of-the concept applications described in what follows have different requirements and intend to validate not only the usage of Cloud services and the proposed APIs but also the semantic engine for the selection of Cloud resources vendors.

Earth Observation Scenarios. Due to its intensive data processing and highly distributed organization, the multidisciplinary Earth Science (ES) applications community is uniquely positioned for the validation and exploitation of Cloud computing infrastructures. Petabytes of already acquired data are presently under-exploited (under 10%), because for getting the results in a reasonable time not enough computing resources are available. However, even if they were to be made available, an efficient infrastructure to handle and treat very large data sets is still missing. In particular mOSAIC will focused on Earth Observation (EO), a specific discipline of ES that well represents their needs and challenges.

Storage and data distribution. With the growth of network bandwidths and local storage capacities, the media for the distribution of EO data has a new approach. Users are able to discover, select and download data eventually combined with processing services. While the access to near-real time isi currently addressed, the EO systems are not able to respond to peaks of demand. Moreover, providing on-line access to huge amounts of data is challenging and different data policies and controlled access are issues that need to be addressed. Cloud computing for EO on-line data access can split the archiving/preservation from the on-line data access while providing a number of clearly identified benefits: (a) controlled access: access to data can be made private or public and specific rights can be granted to specific users; (b) several data access protocols: http/https and Bittorrent are common among Cloud computing providers; (c) high uptime rates, protected by SLAs; (d) controlled and simple cost model.

EO mission reprocessing. The EO mission re-processing targets improvements of the EO data quality. These improvements can be achieved with the development of new and enhanced algorithms, tuning of auxiliary parameters, processor re-design, instrument calibration or threshold and scaling factor corrections. Huge volumes of data of an EO mission need to be processed. The input data can then be pushed into Cloud storage for the duration of the processing and the reprocessed data can be published on Cloud storage with the extra benefit of possibly being used for on-line data access and distribution.

Routine production. EO routine production includes the generation, archiving and eventually the distribution of high-level products following data- or date-driven scheduled services. These products have different goals and purposes, but a common point is that it is the same data being processed over and over again during specific moments of the production cycle and then no longer used. With this in mind, Cloud storage could host the amount of input data required for the generation of these products using Cloud computing processing power.

Fast data access for crisis situations. EO data has proven to be an excellent source of information for damage assessment for both natural and man-made disasters. There are several services fully dedicated in providing EO-based crisis mapping. The applications behind it rely on an on-line archive continuously feed with new data acquired taken from rolling-archives and on a number of computing resources to do the processing. The common issues for these applications are the fast access to post-crisis data in near-real time and to archived historical data, and the fact that the computing resources have to be "on-call", i.e. continuously available for processing in case of a crisis event. Moreover, the interest for related data is concentrated in a short time span; this situation may put strain on the on-line data distribution and eventually lead to its unavailability. Since the Cloud provides scalable storage capacity, the EO historical archive and near-real time data could be hosted on such infrastructure. Furthermore, the processing resources needed to provide the higher-level products and maps could also be provided by Cloud computing thus removing the need for maintaining "on-call" computing resources. Furthermore, Cloud storage provides high transfer rates even when numerous users access the same data at the same time.

Distributed Intelligent Maintenance. Another scenario involves the development of a distributed intelligence maintenance tool based on advanced data processing techniques, more precisely based on data mining and artificial intelligence paradigms. A generic platform is intended to be build to target industrial systems and processes in the fields of energy and transport where data-intensive tasks must be performed for analysis, diagnosis, anomaly detection and resource optimization. The data load is usually non-uniform and it presents peaks and stagger increments during intensive workloads or when the park of monitored units increases; for these data-intensive telemetry scenarios, on-demand and distributed storage allocation and computing is needed. Fast deployment on Clouds using mOSAIC's platform will be possible without a considerable investment in application re-writing.

Agent-Based Simulations: from Cluster to Cloud. Agent-based models usually depend on several input parameters, which in turn have several possible values. When the parameter space is explored, the number of simulations required runs easily out of hands. A simulation running tool named MEME [3] is extended in the frame of mOSAIC to allow users to run their parameter sweep distributed using Cloud services. Currently the prototype can utilize a local or remote cluster of machines to distribute the parameter sweep operation on the machines. Similar speed-up can be achieved by accessing Cloud services with the extra advantage of more flexible resource provisioning. Typical business cases for running simulations can be explored, such as asap/money does not matter, minimize cost/ no deadline, anything in between.

An important function of the mOSAIC platform will be that it will be able to compose virtual services by matching applications' requirements to service descriptions provided by Cloud vendors. In iterative experiment designs, in particular, the simulations periodically need several parallel VMs to run experiments, followed by en evaluation phase using a single VM, which determines further computations to carry out. The resource need of such experiments therefore fluctuate between a single VM and several parallel VMs. A semantic description of an actual simulation service requested can describe the varying resource needs of this type of simulations, and will help the platform to find a best possible composition of cloud service providers.

The sweeping through the parameter space of distributed simulations that use several machines themselves requires a special service profile where VMs that cooperate in running one simulation should have a fast Internet connection, while other instances of the same simulation can be run anywhere. That is, parameter sweeping of distributed simulations require several clusters of computer, where there is fast network connection within a cluster, but can be slower connections between the clusters. Semantic description of such simulations will be provided by the users who write the simulations to enable the mOSAIC platform to compose appropriate service considering the different processor, storage, and communication needs of different parameter settings.

4 Main Challenges for the Technical Solutions

From the five main challenges identified in [4] for Cloud, mOSAIC will address application and data portability and interoperability. The use of standard interfaces could allow the flexibility to create new solutions enabled by applications and data that interoperate with each other regardless of a specific Cloud type; in this context vendor-independent application interfaces (as mOSAIC's one) are emerging. Moreover currently the term of virtualisation is understood differently in the context of different technologies such as storage, processing, networking, and a unified resource representation is needed to be considered. Furthermore, mOSAIC investigates the Cloud usage patterns in order to expose them through the proposed API.

The selection of Cloud providers for a particular application is an intricate issue due to the complex business model associated with such computing systems. RESERVOIR project [5] is the first initiative intending to provide open source technology to enable deployment and management of complex services across different administrative domains. mOSAIC proposes a complementary solution, based on software agents and semantic data processing, for Cloud resource negotiations and service level agreements.

In what concerns the data services, data lock-in (lack of standardized APIs) is one of the important issues to deal with. The solution proposed by mOSAIC is to use semantics to identify the application requirements in terms of Cloud data services. We further consider that service requirements of applications can change over time and thus may require amendments of original service requests.

mOSAIC proposes Cloud specific SLAs and QoS requirements that allow negotiation and re-negotiation solutions during run-time.

The starting point in order to build a comprehensive API is to consider the emerging standards and to build the missing pieces. The current emerging standards to be considered are OCCI, UCI, OVF and CDMI. For building the Cloud ontology the starting point is the design of a Cloud taxonomy - the recent proposals for taxonomies (e.g. [8]) are taken into consideration. One of the most challenging goals of the semantic engine is to design and develop semantic-based Cloud services discovery; a prototypical tool will be built based on syntactic and structural schema matching.

The mOSAIC platform has two parts: Resource Broker and Application Executor. The Resource Broker, responsible with resource negotiation and booking, has also two sub-systems: Client interface and Cloud agency. The first one uses an application specification document for describing application resources needs and supplementary resource specification document for requesting supplementary resources by the Application Executor. The second one includes a monitor, a negotiator, a mediator, a service registry and a client semantic engine, provider semantic engines represented by agents, and uses a Cloud ontology and QoS parameters. Moreover, it validates the application specifications and generates a SLA document for resource negotiation and booking, as well as a resource contract used by the Application Executor to access the physical resources for application execution. The Application Executor, in charge with application execution using the resources booked and stated in Resource contract document, has also several sub-systems like: API Execution Engine that is the user's API for accessing the physical resources; Virtual Cluster including the booked resources; Providers wrappers as special connectors ensuring a uniform interface to the Clouds resources available in resource contract; Resource manager ensuring resource availability and management, including Resource scheduler and Resource monitor, and handling supplementary resources request.

Agents will represent different Cloud resources providers and users; e.g. each agent representing a vendor that offers resources understands the requirements specified in the unified representation of resources and translates them in vendor specific requirements. A core set of agents will implement the basic services provided by the Cloud agency. Some agents will be in charge of interacting with users and providers in order to negotiate and to broker the needing resources. The agents of the selected resources during the negotiation will further represent the Cloud resources during the execution of an application, as they will understand the application requests and translate them into vendor specific requests (acts as wrappers). Starting from the MAGDA toolset [6], mOSAIC platform component related to the agent layer will provide facilities to design, develop and deploy agents-based services.

A special platform component is the Virtual cluster (named so by folowing the proposal from [7]), an agent-based resource management facility. The Resource contract will refer this cluster build for an application. The platform will build up a Vc on the basis of a given SLA established within a certain application.

5 Conclusions

The main benefit of using the mOSAIC solutions will be a transparent and simple access to heterogeneous Cloud computing resources and the avoidance of lock-in proprietary solutions. The open-source platform will enables applications to negotiate Cloud services as requested by their users. Using a specific Cloud ontology, applications will be able to specify their service requirements and communicate them to the platform via the innovative API. The platform will implement a multi-agent brokering mechanism that will search for services matching the applications' request, and possibly compose the requested service if no direct hit is found. Cloud-application developers and maintainers will be able to postpone their decision on the procurement of Cloud services until run-time, while end-user applications will be able to find best-fitting Cloud services to their actual needs and efficiently outsource computations. The platform will also facilitate competition between Cloud providers, who, in return, will be able to reach customers they could not reach before.

The developments scheduled in the mOSAIC project have recently started and there is a long way until its promises will become a reality. The first open-source stable version of the API will be publicly available in autumn 2011 and the full platform and proof-of-the concept applications in two years. Until this early date of the project, the Cloud computing offers, emerging standards, usage patterns and semantic solutions were tested or analyzed to identify the inputs for the developments that are scheduled in the near future.

Acknowledgements. This research is partially supported by the grant FP7-ICT-2009-5-256910 (mOSAIC).

References

1. Cloud Computing Use Case Discussion Group, Cloud Computing Use Cases, White Paper v0.1 (August 2009)
2. Hey, T., Tansley, S., Tolle, K. (eds.): The fourth paradigm: data-intensive scientific discovery, Microsoft Research (October 2009)
3. Gulyás, L., Szemes, G., Kampis, G., de Back, W.: A Modeler-friendly API for ABM Partitioning. In: Procs. ASME (2009)
4. Open Cloud Manifesto (Spring 2009), `www.opencloudmanifesto.org`
5. Rochwerger, B., et al.: The RESERVOIR Model and Architecture for Open Federated Cloud Computing. IBM J. Research & Development 53 (4) (2009)
6. Aversa, R., Di Martino, B., Mazzocca, N., Venticinque, S.: MAGDA: A Mobile Agent based Grid Architecture. J. Grid Computing 4(4), 395–412 (2006)
7. Keahey, K., Tsugawa, M., Matsunaga, A., Fortes, J.A.B.: Sky Computing. IEEE Internet Computing 13(5), 43–51 (2009)
8. Lenk, A., Klems, M., Nimis, J., Tai, S.: What's Inside the Cloud? An Architectural Map of the Cloud Landscape. In: Procs. ICSE, pp. 23–31. IEEE Computer Press, Los Alamitos (2009)

Cloud@Home: Performance Management Components*

Rocco Aversa[1], Dario Bruneo[3], Antonio Cuomo[2], Beniamino Di Martino[1], Salvatore Distefano[3], Antonio Puliafito[3], Massimiliano Rak[1], Salvatore Venticinque[1], and Umberto Villano[2]

[1] Dipartimento di Ingegneria dell'Informazione,
Seconda Università di Napoli
{rocco.aversa,beniamino.dimartino,massimiliano.rak, salvatore.venticinque}@unina2.it

[2] Dipartimento di Ingegneria,
Università del Sannio
{villano,antonio.cuomo}@unisannio.it

[3] Dipartimento di Matematica,
Università di Messina
{apuliafito,dbruneo,sdistefano}@unime.it

Abstract. This paper shows the design and the mode of operation of the SLA/QoS subsystem devised for Cloud@Home, a cloud environment based on voluntarily-offered resources currently under development in the context of a PRIN-MIUR funded project.

Keywords: Cloud Computing, Volunteer Computing, Performance, SLA.

1 Introduction

Cloud computing is a new emerging paradigm that merges a large set of different technologies and solutions. The main idea driving the cloud computing approach is that all resources, hosted by providers in large datacenters, should be accessed through the network with a service-oriented model. Even if the basic principle is relatively simple, it is very hard to give a precise and clear definition of cloud computing [12]. Volunteer computing is a type of distributed computing in which computer owners donate their computing resources (essentially, processing power and storage space) to one or more "projects". The goal is to build up a single infrastructure from small resources, distributed and administrated independently.

The Cloud@Home project (shortly, C@H) is a proposal for a new enhanced paradigm which integrates both cloud and volunteer computing approaches. It is supported by a grant from the Italian Government in the context of MIUR-PRIN 2008, and has received letters of interests from relevant companies active

* The work described in this paper has been partly supported by MIUR-PRIN 2008 project "Cloud@Home: a New Enhanced Computing Paradigm" and by II Univ. of Naples PRIST 2009, "Fruizione assistita e context aware di siti ...".

M.R. Guarracino et al. (Eds.): Euro-Par 2010 Workshops, LNCS 6586, pp. 579–586, 2011.
© Springer-Verlag Berlin Heidelberg 2011

in the cloud computing field. The main idea behind the Cloud@Home project is to build up a cloud by collecting many different kinds of voluntarily-offered resources. This cloud can provide computing, storage and sensor resources both to the contributing "volunteers" and to commercial users, for free or for charge, guaranteeing service levels, negotiated and agreed upon at service request time.

The Cloud@Home project is thoroughly described in a companion paper [13]. In this paper, we focus on the architectural solution proposed to tackle the performance problems, which are particularly complex in a system made up of distributed and independently-administered resources. The remainder of this paper is structured as follows. The next section opens with a brief overview of the Cloud@Home architecture, followed by a detailed description of the components devised for performance management. Section 3 describes how these components, which perform tasks as performance evaluation, prediction and management, have been integrated in the Cloud@Home performance subsystem. In the last section we draw the conclusions and outline the future work.

2 Cloud@Home Architecture

Figure 1 shows the layered architecture of Cloud@Home. The **Hardware Layer** collects all the physical resources available. These range from clusters, datacenter and computing grids to PCs, notebooks or even smartphones (the last are mainly used to exploits their *sensors*).

The **Virtual Engine Layer** offers a *virtualized* version of the physical resources available. The virtual engines have a key role in cloud computing, because

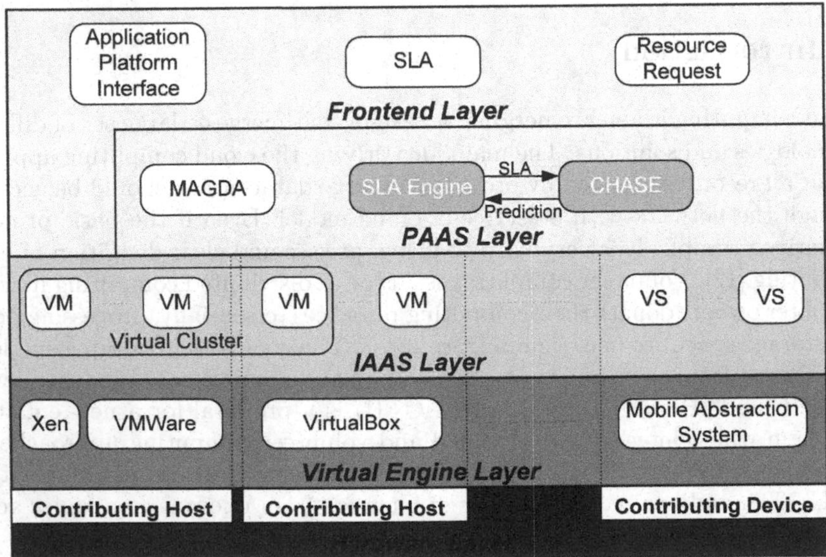

Fig. 1. The *Cloud@Home* architecture

they guarantee the full independence of the resources as they are perceived by the users from the physically available ones.

The **C@H IaaS Layer** offers the typical cloud *Infrastructure as a Service* services. It is composed of a set of different cloud middlewares, previously developed by research units involved in the project (*PerfCloud*[7] and *Clever*[14]). A *discovery* layer, which may be implemented in a centralized or distributed way, grants uniform access to the available resources. The discovery layer might be extended in order to support open-source cloud middleware (such as Eucalyptus[11], Nimbus[2] or Open Nebula[1]) or commercial cloud providers (e.g., Amazon EC2). In fact, this extension is not planned within the Cloud@Home project, even if it will be possibly made in the context of future research.

The **C@H PaaS Layer** integrates a set of components that offer a high-level view of the cloud infrastructure and aim at providing the functionalities (services) needed to face the performance problems mentioned previously. Its main components are the SLA Engine, the CHASE autonomic engine, the mobile agents platform and the mobile device middleware.

The **C@H Frontend Layer** is a *vertical* layer (in that it cooperates with all the others) that operates as an interface between final users and the Cloud@Home components. It provides services for user request of resources, for request enriched with a SLA, or for starting up mobile agent-based applications.

The focus in this paper is on the subsystem for SLA/QoS management, in green in Figure 1. This subsystem has to provide suitable mechanisms to negotiate SLAs and to guarantee QoS on the top of the virtual environments making up the platform. The proposed architecture involves two components for performance management: SLAEngine and CHASE (developed by two different units in the project organization). The first component is involved with resource utilization monitoring and SLA management, whereas the latter (CHASE) enables the application to integrate autonomic self-optimization features. In the following we will briefly describe the two tools, showing successively how they are integrated in the Cloud@Home platform.

2.1 SLA Engine

Two specific components of the Cloud@Home middleware have been identified in the SLA Engine system. These are the SLA and the QoS subsystems, which ensure the seamless execution of applications (Figure 2a).

SLA Negotiator. The SLA Negotiator is responsible for the service lifecycle. This includes service definition, deployment, management, monitoring, compliance and termination. Users call for services that incorporate contracts made up of business terms, with no reference to raw resources. Service invocations are enriched with SLAs, adopting languages such as SLAng[3]. The system manages the service by configuring and deploying it automatically. In order to meet the contract terms, the system is monitored and the SLAEngine takes any required action, such as the re-configuration or re-allocation of resources. Finally, when the service fruition finishes, the system frees the resources. It should be noted

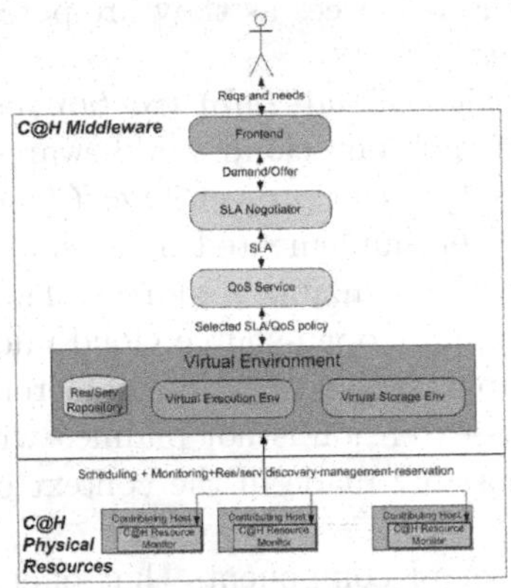

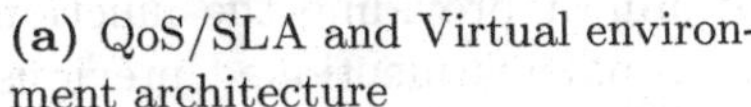
(a) QoS/SLA and Virtual environment architecture

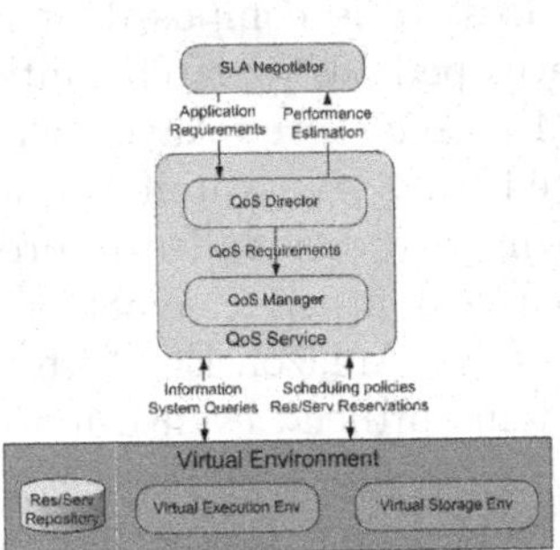

(b) interactions with the C@H infrastructure

Fig. 2. Cloud@Home SLA and QoS subsystems

that the ultimate goal for the infrastructure is the maximization of the number of services executed. The SLA Negotiator needs to monitor service performance levels, in order to detect dynamically contract violations.

QoS service. The QoS service is responsible for the management of the cloud resources and the services needed to achieve the application requirements established by the SLA negotiator. It translates the application requirements (expressed in terms of high-level parameters such as time execution, throughput, transaction rate) into low-level criteria related to computing, storage and network distributed resources. The QoS service also has an important role during the negotiation phase, carried out by the SLA Negotiator. In fact, it acts as an estimator able to predict the computational load generated by applications and the corresponding performance obtained.

Fig. 2b shows the communication between the SLA Negotiator and the QoS service. It is possible to identify two different sub-modules in the QoS service: the *QoS director* and the *QoS manager*. The former accepts requests from the SLA Negotiator and invokes the QoS manager to submit applications with appropriate QoS criteria, in terms of computing and network services. In other terms, the QoS director translates the high-level QoS specifications of the SLA Negotiator into the low level requirements (in terms of raw resource requests) for the QoS manager. Moreover, the QoS director has to inform the SLA Negotiator about the estimated processing time of a particular application.

In order to perform the right choices and to provide correct information to the SLA Negotiator, the QoS director has to estimate the computational, storage and network resources needed for the execution of the applications. This goal can be accomplished querying the cloud information system to check the availability of the requested resources.

2.2 The CHASE Component

CHASE (Cloud@Home Autonomic Service Engine) is based on the MAWeS framework, which was developed to support the predictive autonomicity in web service-based architectures [6]. MAWeS itself leverages on the MetaPL language [9] and the HeSSE simulation environment [10]. The first is used to describe the software system and the interactions inside it; the latter, to describe the system behaviors and to predict performances using simulation. Following a bottom-up approach, we will briefly describe the features of these tools and then show at the end of the section how CHASE operates on top of them.

HeSSE. HeSSE is a simulation tool that allows to simulate the performance behavior of a wide range of distributed systems for a given application, under different computing and network load conditions. It makes it possible to describe distributed heterogeneous systems by interconnecting simple components, which reproduce the performance behavior of a section of the complete system.

MetaPL. MetaPL is an XML-based meta-language for parallel program description and prototyping [9,4]. It provides a core language that can be extended through *Extensions* (XML DTDs) to support different programming paradigms and to enrich the semantics of the description. A MetaPL program can be processed by *filters* (XSLT transformations) to produce different program *views*: one of these set of filters can produce traces to be simulated in HeSSE, thus providing reliable performance predictions even at the early phases of software development [8].

MAWeS. The MAWeS framework relies on MetaPL to run HeSSE simulations and to obtain performance data. The user can specify through the autonomic MetaPL language extension [5,6], the set of parameters that can be modified by the optimization engine. MAWeS will automatically perform a set of simulations varying the values of these parameters to find the set of values that optimizes the software execution according to one or more criteria (e.g., shortest execution time).

MAWeS is structured in three layers (Figure 3). The *MAWeS frontend* includes a standard client application interface, `MAWeSclient`, providing the general services that can be used and extended to develop new applications. The *MAWeS Core* exploits environment services (i.e., the services offered by the environment to monitor and to manage itself) and the *MetaPL/HeSSE WS interface*, using the application information contained in the MetaPL description to find out optimal execution conditions.

CHASE. It is now easy to illustrate how the Cloud@Home Autonomic Service Engine operates. CHASE acts as a special client of MAWeS. It hands in to MAWeS the configuration of the cloud system (in a format suitable for HeSSE) and of the service/application (in MetaPL format) and receives in response the optimal configuration parameters. In order to perform these tasks, the MAWeS framework must also be extended to predict the behavior of virtualized applications, which is an ongoing work within the Cloud@Home project.

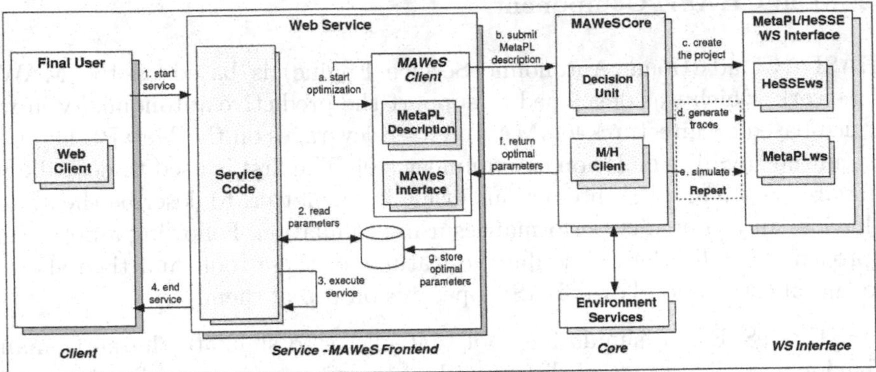

Fig. 3. The three layers of the MAWeS Framework. The client functionalities in the Frontend can be integrated in applicative software.

3 C@H Component Integration

SLAEngine and CHASE have similar aims, but follow different approaches:

- **SLAEngine** accepts a task submission enriched by a SLA description, which describes the application requirements. The SLA Engine accepts, refuses or negotiates it, deploys the needed resources and monitors the application execution, in order to grant that SLA requirements are respected.
- **CHASE** accepts a task submission enriched by a MetaPL description, which describes the application behavior together with application optimization parameters, predicts the application execution performance in different configurations, and returns the optimal application configuration.

In fact, the two components focus on different characteristics of the application execution. The SLA Engine takes into account the resource usage optimization and so aims at granting resources quality and availability (i.e., reserving a network with granted bandwidth to an application). On the other hand, CHASE focuses on application execution optimization, choosing the suitable resources that can lead to the optimization of user-oriented application performance indexes (e.g., response time), even when the application behavior changes (i.e., there is a variation of the number of processes making up the task or of the way in which data are partitioned). The two approaches are orthogonal: SLAEngine can change the resources available to the application, but cannot change the application behavior. CHASE does not directly manage resources (just asks for them), but it, through MetaPL, knows which parameters affect the application behavior and it is able to change them optimally. In Cloud@Home the two functionalities are integrated in order to get the advantages of both approaches.

In order to clarify how the invocation of a service behaves, Figure 4a illustrates the SLA-based service invocation process. Just after the invocation, an evaluation step takes place (the Service Evaluation activity), in order to predict the best configuration in terms of both resource usage and application behavior. If the result respects the SLA requirements, the Service Execution activity will follow; otherwise, a negotiation step driven by the SLA Engine will take place. In the current state of the project, the negotiation phase is absent, and so the service invocation is possibly rejected (Service Refusal). During service execution, a warning may occur if a SLA requirement is nearly to be violated (i.e., a resource crashes, an unpredicted load is detected, ...). In this case, the service is re-evaluated, taking into account the actual resource state, and possibly suspended and re-executed with a new resource utilization scenario.

The CHASE-SLAEngine integration implements the above described behavior, as shown in Figure 4b. The user invokes the service through the C@H Frontend. This starts up the request collecting both the SLA request and the application behavior description (for simplicity's sake, the diagram does not show the user/Frontend interaction). The service invocation is redirected to the SLA Negotiator and to the QoS Director. This latter is integrated in CHASE, and asks it for an optimal application behavior. CHASE makes its prediction by evaluating a set of different resource configurations and finding the optimal one, than returns the result to the QoS director which evaluates the SLA requirements and checks if they are respected. If so, the result is returned to the SLA Negotiator and to the FE, which finally starts up the service.

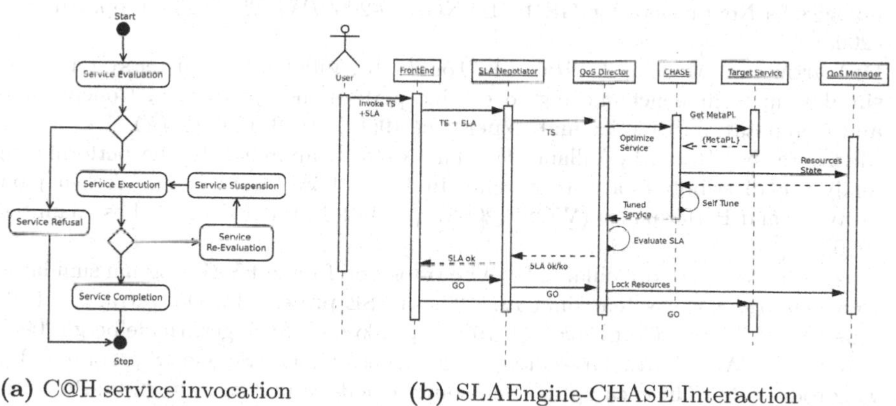

(a) C@H service invocation (b) SLAEngine-CHASE Interaction

Fig. 4. Cloud@home SLAEngine-CHASE Interaction

4 Conclusions and Future Work

The adoption of the volunteer computing paradigm poses problems related to unreliability and low performance. In the Cloud@Home project, whose objective is to build a cloud environment based on volunteer resources, we propose two components that jointly aim at supporting SLA/QoS requirements. One of them focuses on resource utilization, the other on application behavior. In this paper we have shown how both components work, and how it is possible to integrate them in order to obtain a very flexible system for SLA/QoS management. We will apply the proposed approach and evaluate it in the project case studies.

References

1. Fontán, J., Vázquez, T., Gonzalez, L.: RS Montero, and IM Llorente. OpenNebula: The open source virtual machine manager for cluster computing. In: Open Source Grid and Cluster Software Conference (2008)
2. Hoffa, C., Mehta, G., Freeman, T., Deelman, E., Keahey, K., Berriman, B., Good, J.: On the use of cloud computing for scientific workflows. In: IEEE Fourth International Conference on eScience, 2008, pp. 640–645. IEEE, Los Alamitos (2009)
3. Lamanna, D.D., Skene, J., Emmerich, W.: Slang: A language for defining service level agreements. In: Proc. of the 9th IEEE Workshop on Future Trends in Distributed Computing Systems-FTDCS, pp. 100–106 (2003)
4. Mancini, E., Mazzocca, N., Rak, M., Villano, U.: Integrated tools for performance-oriented distributed software development. In: Proc. SERP 2003 Conf., USA, vol. 1, pp. 88–94 (June 2003)
5. Mancini, E., Rak, M., Torella, R., Villano, U.: A simulation-based framework for autonomic web services. In: Proc. of the Eleventh International Conference on Parallel and Distributed Systems, Fukuoka, Japan, pp. 433–437 (July 2005)
6. Mancini, E., Rak, M., Torella, R., Villano, U.: Predictive autonomicity of web services in the MAWeS framework. Journal of Computer Science 2(6), 513–520 (2006)
7. Mancini, E.P., Rak, M., Villano, U.: Perfcloud: Grid services for performance-oriented development of cloud computing applications. In: Proc. of Emerging Technologies for Next generation GRID (ETNGRID-2009/WETICE-2009), pp. 201–206 (2009)
8. Di Martino, B., Mancini, E., Rak, M., Torella, R., Villano, U.: Cluster systems and simulation: from benchmarking to off-line performance prediction. Concurrency and Computation: Practice and Experience 19(11), 1549–1562 (2007)
9. Mazzocca, N., Rak, M., Villano, U.: The MetaPL approach to the performance analysis of distributed software systems. In: Proc. of 3rd International Workshop on Software and Performance (WOSP 2002), pp. 142–149. IEEE Press, Los Alamitos (2002)
10. Mazzocca, N., Rak, M., Villano, U.: The transition from a PVM program simulator to a heterogeneous system simulator: The heSSE project. In: Dongarra, J., et al. (eds.) PVM/MPI 2000. LNCS, vol. 1908, pp. 266–273. Springer, Heidelberg (2000)
11. Nurmi, D., Wolski, R., Grzegorczyk, C., Obertelli, G., Soman, S., Youseff, L., Zagorodnov, D.: The eucalyptus open-source cloud-computing system. In: Proceedings of the 2009 9th IEEE/ACM International Symposium on Cluster Computing and the Grid, pp. 124–131. IEEE Computer Society, Los Alamitos (2009)
12. Mell, P., Grance, T.: The nist definition of cloud computing (2009)
13. Puliafito, A., et al.: The Cloud@Home Project: Towards a New Enhanced Computing Paradigm. In: Guarracino, M.R., et al. (eds.) Euro-Par 2010 Workshops. LNCS, vol. 6586, pp. 513–520. Springer, Heidelberg (2011)
14. Tusa, F., Paone, M., Villari, M., Puliafito, A.: CLEVER: A cloud-enabled virtual environment. In: 2010 IEEE Symposium on Computers and Communications (ISCC), pp. 477–482. IEEE, Los Alamitos (2010)

A Cloud Agency for SLA Negotiation and Management

Salvatore Venticinque[1], Rocco Aversa[1], Beniamino Di Martino[1], Massimilano Rak[1], and Dana Petcu[2]

[1] Second University of Naples, Italy,
[2] Institute e-Austria Timişoara, Romania

Abstract. Resources management facilities, based on service level agreements, are needed in the Cloud in order to negotiate a collection of inter-connected and virtualized computers between resource providers and consumers. In this paper we present the architectural design of a system named `Cloud Agency` which aims to respond to this need and to offer added value to the existing Cloud services. This system is in charge to broker the collection of Cloud resources from different providers that fulfills at the best the requirements of user's applications. The user is able to delegate to the Agency the necessary checks of the agreement fulfilment, the monitoring of resource utilization and eventually necessary re-negotiations.

1 Introduction

Cloud computing is an emerging paradigm that, due to an intensive use of the virtualization approach, offers to users resources on which they have full administrative control. Cloud computing is expected to be the paradigm that will deliver a basic level of computing service that is considered essential to meet the everyday needs of the general community [1]. Such a computing utility is targeted to a market of consumers who require specific QoS to be maintained by their providers in order to meet their objectives and sustain their operations. In this context the need of SLA-oriented resource management represents the solution to negotiate a collection of inter-connected and virtualized computers between resource providers and consumers (or between resource providers and a third-party broker) [2]. The selection of Cloud providers that fulfills the requirements of a particular application is a complex issue due to the different business models associated with such computing systems. Cloud providers usually employ a system-centric resource management architecture. According to [1] a market-oriented resource management is needed in order to regulate the supply and demand of Cloud resources, providing feedback in terms of economic incentives for both Cloud consumers and providers, and promoting QoS-based resource allocation mechanisms that differentiate service requests based on their utility. The current Cloud computing technologies offer a limited support for dynamic negotiation of SLAs between participants. There are no mechanisms for automatic allocation of resources to multiple competing requests. Furthermore,

M.R. Guarracino et al. (Eds.): Euro-Par 2010 Workshops, LNCS 6586, pp. 587–594, 2011.
© Springer-Verlag Berlin Heidelberg 2011

current Cloud computing technologies are not able to support customer-driven service management based on customer profiles and requested service requirements. Also it is impossible according to [1] to derive appropriate market-based resource management strategies that encompass both customer-driven service management and computational risk management to sustain SLA-oriented resource allocation. New SLA-oriented resource management strategies must be designed for Clouds in order to provide personalized attention to customers. Service requirements of users can change over time, due to continuing changes in business operations and operating environment, and thus may require amendments of original service requests. We proposed recently in the frame of the EC-FP7-ICT project proposal, named mOSAIC, a solution, based on software agents and semantic data processing, for Cloud resource negotiations and service level agreements. The mOSAIC project (www.mosaic-cloud.eu) intends to improve the state-of-the-art in Cloud computing by creating, promoting and exploiting an open-source Cloud application programming interface and a platform targeted for developing multi-Cloud oriented applications. The main benefit of using the mOSAIC software package will be a transparent and simple access to heterogeneous Cloud computing resources and the avoidance of lock-in proprietary solutions. A special attention will be given to the applications that are data-intensive: the Earth Observation community is strongly involved in the platform testing. In this paper we present an important component of mOSAIC framework, we named `Cloud Agency`, which aims at offering value added Cloud services. It will be in charge to broker a collection of Cloud resources from different providers that fulfills at the best the requirements of user's applications. According to the available offers it will generate a SLA document that represents the result of resource negotiation and booking with supported Cloud providers. The user will be able to delegate to the Agency the necessary checks of SLA fulfilment, the monitoring of resource utilization and eventually necessary renegotiations. The paper is organized as follows. The second section discusses the motivation of our research and the state of art of Cloud dealing with the resource brokering. The third section introduces the requirements for Cloud Agency design. In the fourth section the Cloud Agency design is described. Finally, in the last section, some conclusion are provided.

2 Requirements for SLA Negotiation and Management

The mOSAIC team plans to investigate Cloud-specific SLAs and QoS requirements in order to support resources management. The proposed approach is to start from Cloud usage patterns. Such patterns were recently identified in [3], reflecting a business view.

Definition of QoS parameters. One of the preliminary requirements, which are relevant to support negotiation activities into the Cloud, is the definition of QoS parameters for existing service. Of course this can be done after an exhaustive study of available Cloud platforms and services. There are critical QoS parameters to consider in a service request for Cloud computing, such as for instance:

time, cost, computer power, storage size, reliability, trust, security, or even location of resources due to business constraints. An attempt to define several QoS metrics is presented in [4]. Authors define response time, availability, reliability, cost and reputation. A reference of SLA model is provided in [5], where SLA objectives (SLOs) are used to compose a SLA. The existence of a number of service levels and performance metrics for each resource results in multiple SLOs for every service.

Role of users, brokers and providers. As actors of the Cloud market needs to be defined. Users submit service requests from anywhere in the world to the Cloud. Cloud providers offer resources, allocate the one acquired and bill their consumption. They need to control that there is no overloading of resources whereby many service requests cannot be successfully fulfilled. This leads the decision on whether to accept or reject the request. On the other hand users need to be aware about the resources they are really exploiting and the service level they are provided with at any time. The monitoring of QoS level is relevant to detect SLA violation which can be regulated by penalties that providers must pay. Applications and new services have to be designed in order to let user delegate to applications the automatic negotiation and management of SLA, resources and services on behalf of users and providers.

SLA negotiation and renegotiation. SLA negotiation with multiple Cloud providers is a first example of complex application that could be delegated to a third party, represented by a broker in a market based context. A broker intermediates between users and providers in order to negotiate the best SLA for both consumer and vendors. On user behalf it can:

- search for available Cloud services, compliant with user needs;
- check of trustness of providers;
- decide with whom to negotiate, according to user requirements and past experiences;
- negotiate the best price for the same offer by different providers;
- negotiate multiple SLAs, with different providers, to overcome the lackness of one compliant offer by a single provider.

Since consumers' requirements can potentially vary over time it needs to support dynamic re-negotiation of SLA. Some mechanisms to reconfigure virtual resources are already available, but it needs policies and protocols for changing the SLA parameters, to include new amendments and withdraw previous ones. Re-negotiation is another service that can be provided to solve some inconsistencies between the SLA and the real user's requirements which can change dynamically. Dynamic SLA re-negotiation has actually limited support. Issues to be investigated are:

- withdraw of a SLA and negotiation of a second one;
- deletion/addittion of a SLA objective;
- redefinition of a QOS parameter;
- negotiation of boundaries within which the SLA can be re-negotiated at the same price or with a pre-defined price adjustment.

Monitoring. The utilization of Cloud resources is another service that can be delegated. Providers monitor utilization of their resources for billing, to change bid prices in order to optimize profit, to not exceed in resource allocation beyond the capability of fulfill the agreements. On the other hand, the user, who has conflicting interests with providers, needs to trust a third party that can be delegated to monitor the satisfaction of the agreed service levels. Monitoring process should provide information about:

- under-utilization of cloud resources, in order to negotiate cheaper agreements;
- saturation of resources, to not let the users's applications work under the QoS level granted to users' clients;
- unbalanced utilization of Cloud resources, in order to check the correctness of negotiated parameters, or to tune the execution of applications in the Cloud;
- violation of SLA by providers.

3 A Cloud Agency in mOSAIC

Applications for SLA negotiation and management should act on behalf of their users and should be able to compose available Cloud services. They will be proactive applications that, beyond the stateless SOA model, are aware about the status of their user's resources and services and interact with brokers, providers and eventually with other Cloud actors in order to pursue user's objectives. Because of these considerations, we modeled the services as agents who implement a *Cloud Agency* [6] in a framework that aims at deliver and manage Cloud resources and services provided by different Cloud platforms.

3.1 Architecture and Agents' Role

The Cloud Agency architecture is showed in Figure 1. The main service provided by the Agency is the negotiation of Cloud resources. The core agents are enumerated in Table 1. A *Client Agent* acts as an access point for the user who is exploiting proactive services. It maintains the user profile and cooperates with the Negotiator in order to provide to the user the services with the requested quality levels. A *Mediator Agent* retrieves a list of available Provider Agents from the *Registry Agent*. It contacts each Provider Agent and requests a bid for the needed resources. Once it obtains responses from Provider Agents, it assesses the following: the QoS provided; the quality of the provider itself (requesting historical data from an Archiver Agent); after assessing the bid responses, it should put together a contract with the winning providers on behalf of the client; it replies to the Client Agent with the attached contract. The Negotiation Agent could try to optimize the contract by applying different trade-offs between performance or availability and costs, but within the bounds specified by the client. A *Provider Agent* accepts bid requests from the Mediator Agent, and tries to propose a contract for the resources it could provide. A *Registry Agent* will allow

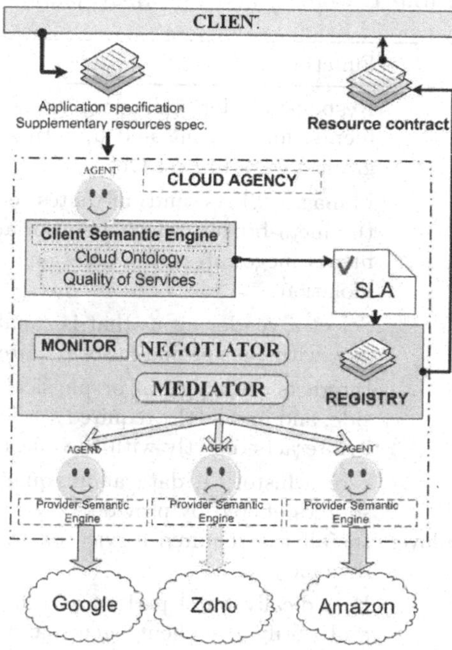

Fig. 1. The Cloud Agency Architecture

the publication of services which are available and accessible by the mOSAIC framework and their discovery. An important project activity includes an exhaustive study of the most important Cloud platforms, in order to recognize what services they can provide and how to use them. Agents exploit a *Semantic Engine* that will allow also semantic validation and translation of messages that use different ontologies and will refine the application specification document into a correct and complete SLA on behalf of the user. The monitoring of Cloud resources utilization is necessary to evaluate the satisfaction of SLA and the effective utilization of resources by the user's applications. A *Monitor Agent* will be in charge to collect all the available information from Cloud providers and from the user's application themselves to figure out the effective values of QoS parameters and the application performance. Even when the resource utilization is accessible for evaluation from outside the virtual environment, it could be relevant to measure the system performance inside the virtual resource in order to evaluate the perceived quality of service by the application without trusting the provider. Specific exceptions can be generated when particular events occur. For example a SLA violation, or saturation of resources by user's application can be notified to the user or directly to the *Client Agent* that will be responsible to ask for a re-negotiation of the SLA.

Table 1. Core agents of mOSAIC platform

Agent type	Function
Client agent	Responsible for collecting users' application requirements, for creating and updating the SLAs in order to grant always to best QoS
Negotiator	Manages SLAs and mediates between the user and the meta-broker, selects appropriate protocols for agreements, negotiates SLA creation, handles fulfilment and violation
Mediator	Select a vendor agent that is capable of deploying a service with the specified user requirements
Vendor agent	Interacts with virtual or physical resources at provider side, and in case the required service needs to be deployed it interacts directly with the automatic service deployer
Archiver	Stores historical data about quality of services and resources offered by providers
Automatic service deployer	Install the required service on the selected resource on demand
Benchmarker	Periodically build performance figures of used resources and notify the client agents about values of measured parameters

3.2 MAGDA as Agents Technology

The MAGDA toolset [7] will be the base for developments of the Cloud Agency in mOSAIC. Its architecture is showed in Figure 2. MAGDA provides a set of agents based services for distributed computing. Users can exploit existing

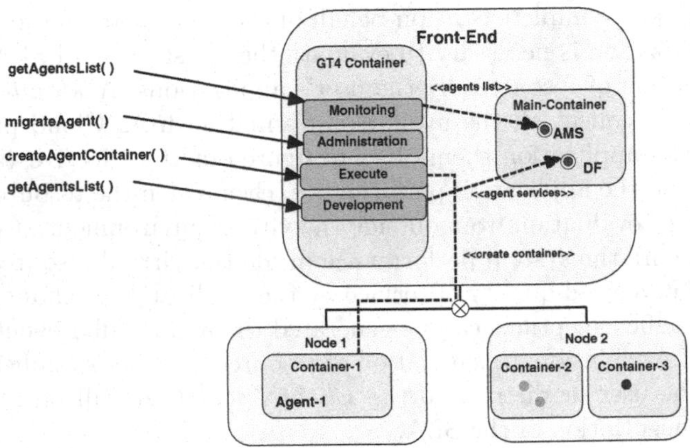

Fig. 2. MAGDA Architecture

services by different protocols, eventually being unaware about the agent technology, accessing a front-end and controlling the agent execution on available resources. On the other hand they can develop new agent based services. Advanced facilities such as strong authentication, agent migration across multiple domains, workload balancing, or dynamic resource allocations are provided [8]. MAGDA provides facilities to design, develop and deploy agents-based services. Services will be stored in the repository and will be able to execute on Cloud resources. Agents will communicate one with th other via standard ACL (Agent Communication Language) messages over http, or over other transport protocols if it will be necessary. Services provided by agents are exposing a Web Services interface that works as a Message Gateway: SOAP to ACL and ACL to SOAP.

3.3 Ontology and Semantic Engine

In order to support interoperability among users and different providers, an uniform *Cloud Ontology* will be defined. It represents a common vocabulary to be used for different purposes. First of all, requests and responses (SLA's, bid requests, and contracts) should be described according to that specific ontology that governs the Cloud domain. Because each user or proder could natively use a different ontology, agents could also implement a semantic mapping between the native ontology and the uniform one. The ontology will be used to implement a semantic discovery facility to find all relevant services and resources published in the Clouds. The ontology will describe Cloud resources and services, Cloud actors, Quality of Service Parameters, the negotiation protocol and the SLA. OWL is prposed as th onntology language. The benefit of using an ontology language is that it acts as a general method for the conceptual description or modeling of information that is implemented by actual resources. This approach will allow to easily take a Cloud resource model and adapt it within other ontology languages making it both platform and vendor agnostic. In this respect, mOSAIC aims to develop ontologies that would offers the main building block to describe the services at the three delivery models. In order to enable algorithms for matching different types of resources, functionalities and capabilities must be captured in these ontologies: a clear description and categorization of existing functionalities, capabilities and specificities of different resources (possibly existing in the Cloud) will ease rapid development of successful applications of the Cloud/over the Cloud. Matching algorithms will equally apply at the different layers of the Cloud architecture selecting the best available Cloud application from a large base of available applications, based on matching customers needs with application specificities. One of the most challenging goals of the semantic engine is to design and develop semantic-based Cloud services discovery. A prototypical tool will be built based on syntactic and structural schema matching. The input will be an ontology describing a service request and services descriptions. This can be achieved on the syntactic level through a service description language (like WSDL), or on the semantic level, through service ontologies (like in OWL-S and WSDL-S). Semantic matching is possible since service request and services descriptions are semantically annotated based on concepts from ontologies adopted for modelling the specific domain of application. The result of a semantic discovery is a new set of exploitable Cloud services and providers.

4 Conclusion

A step forward in the Cloud computing evolution is the development of tools that allows the negotiation and composition of services offered by different Cloud providers. The complexity of the business model related to a multi-Cloud environment imposes the automatization of the offer selections. In this context, mOSAIC proposes to use agent technologies incorporated in a Cloud Agency and a Virtual Cluster to enable the easy development and deployment of multi-Cloud based applications. The on-going development of mOSAIC's proof-of-the-concept prototypes and ready-to-use platform are based on the reasons, concepts, architectures and technologies that were exposed in this paper.

Acknowledgements. This research is partially supported by the grant FP7-ICT-2009-5-256910 (mOSAIC).

References

1. Buyya, R., Yeo, C.S., et al.: Cloud computing and emerging IT platforms: Vision, hype, and reality for delivering computing as the 5th utility. Future Generation Computer Systems 25(6), 599–616 (2009)
2. Sim, K.M.: Towards Complex Negotiation for Cloud Economy. In: Bellavista, P., Chang, R.-S., Chao, H.-C., Lin, S.-F., Sloot, P.M.A. (eds.) GPC 2010. LNCS, vol. 6104, pp. 395–406. Springer, Heidelberg (2010)
3. Cloud Computing Use Case Discussion Group, Cloud Computing Use Cases, White Paper v0.1 (August 2009)
4. Cao, B.-Q., Li, B., Xia, Q.-M.: A Service-Oriented Qos-Assured and Multi-Agent Cloud Computing Architecture. In: Jaatun, M.G., Zhao, G., Rong, C. (eds.) CloudCom 2009. LNCS, vol. 5931, pp. 644–649. Springer, Heidelberg (2009)
5. Kaminski, H., Perry, M.: SLA Negotiation System Design Based on Business Rules. In: Procs. 2008 IEEE International Conference on Services Computing, vol. 2, pp. 609–612 (2008)
6. Aversa, R., Di Martino, B., Rak, M., Venticinque, S.: Cloud Agency: A Mobile Agent Based Cloud System. In: Procs. 2010 International Conference on Complex, Intelligent and Software Intensive Systems, pp. 132–137 (2010)
7. Aversa, R., Di Martino, B., Mazzocca, N., Venticinque, S.: MAGDA: A Mobile Agent based Grid Architecture. Journal of Grid Computing. Journal of Grid Computing 4, 395–412 (2006)
8. Aversa, R., Di Martino, B., Venticinque, S.: Integration of Mobile Agents Technology and Globus for Assisted Design and Automated Development of Grid Services. In: Procs. 12th IEEE International Conference on Computational Science and Engineering, vol. 1, pp. 118–125. IEEE Computer Society, Los Alamitos (2009)

Running Business Applications in the Cloud: A Use Case Perspective

Carmelo Ragusa and Antonio Puliafito

Faculty of Engineering, University of Messina,
Contrada di Dio, Messina, Italy
{cragusa,apuliafito}@unime.it

Abstract. Cloud computing leverages the use of abstracted resources. However, migrating an industrial application to well-known Cloud solutions such as EC2 might be complex and low level expertise is indeed needed. In this use case we present a methodology, based on practical experience matured on the ground, that allows service providers to enable complex applications to the RESERVOIR cloud infrastructure. We also show an example of how a complex business application, such as the SAP ERP 6.0, can be automatically fully deployed and scaled up and down as resource needs change, easing the use of a cloud system for service providers that might experience difficulties or have mental barriers to carry out such task.

Keywords: Cloud computing, Industrial applications, Use case, RESERVOIR, cloud enabling methodology.

1 Introduction

Today a growing number of companies, such as start-up and SMEs, is using Cloud computing to carry out their business, due to the easy requirements to be satisfied and to the fast high competitiveness gained at lower investment costs. However, Cloud computing is far from being definitive, since the always changing requirements are constantly modifying this paradigm. Enterprises are analysing the use of Cloud to carry out some of their processes, which add even more requirements. For example, many enterprise processes are time-critical, with secure and privacy requirements. Also the scale of enterprise applications is in the order of thousands of concurrent services, which is in contrast with SMEs that have a number of services orders of magnitude lower than enterprises. Another aspect in favour of SMEs for the Cloud adoption is that their system have a low number of functions, making no difference between data and logic, and therefore less complex to be "cloudified". This is not feasible for enterprises that have much more complex functions to be taken into account. The result is that Cloud solutions face difficulties to cope with both opposite class of customers and so the use of Cloud within enterprises is still low. However, the benefits in using Cloud are many and Cloud providers, pushed by the hype of the IT environment, are progressing fast to meet the new demands. Although there are

M.R. Guarracino et al. (Eds.): Euro-Par 2010 Workshops, LNCS 6586, pp. 595–602, 2011.
© Springer-Verlag Berlin Heidelberg 2011

efforts [1] to design new enterprise applications to be cloud oriented, they are far from being a reality. Thereby, adopting the Cloud for legacy applications can give enterprises advantages as well as speed up the usage of this paradigm.

The RESERVOIR solution provides an infrastructure able to run not only applications for SMEs, but also for large complex enterprises. The system offers capabilities such as rapid provisioning, elasticity, applications coexistence, federation and security. In this paper we focused on the first two features through a SAP ERP use case, showing how such complex application can be fully automatically deployed and scaled according to specific user requirements, without requiring any modification of the application. This will be an advantage not only for large enterprises using this application, but also for SMEs that are normally afraid of installing and configuring SAP systems due to their complexity. Finally, SAP itself can benefit because it can reach discouraged clients.

The reminder of the paper is organized as follows: section 2 discusses the related work. In section 3 we present the RESERVOIR solution along its main components. Next is discussed the use case, we give details about the application, the testbed and the scenarios performed. After, we describe the lesson learnt. Finally we draw the conclusions and discuss the future work.

2 Related Work

Different Cloud solutions (e.g. RightScale, Scalr, Flexiscale and Elastra) are available, offering high level functionalities on top of Cloud infrastructures such as Amazon EC2, Google App Engine and GoGrid. Such Cloud solutions try to fill the gap between Cloud infrastructures' offers and the Service Providers (SPs) that use them, by providing automation services to control the virtual resources assigned. However, their service definition is not comprehensive. In fact each Virtual Machine (VM) needs to be installed, configured and managed singularly, which restricts the service deployment. Moreover, the automation controls, such as auto-scaling, are too rigid due to the use of predefined monitored variables within the server templates offered, thereby not allowing the SPs to define their own service indicators. As result, SPs have to constantly monitor the VMs running state in order to instantiate or remove VMs to scale the service up or down.

In [2], the authors point out how elasticity is an important feature which allows SPs to save on costs of over-provisioning and risks of under-provisioning. Motahari et al [3] also highlights from a business perspective how such ability has a positive impact on the enterprise business processes management. In [4], the authors discuss the issues commented above and identify four goals, service abstraction level, automatic scalability, smart scaling and avoidance of Cloud vendor lock-in, thus reinforcing the importance to address those issues. On the other hand, migrating enterprises' IT systems to the Cloud, needs to be carefully studied. In [5] the authors investigated the implication to migrate an IT system to the Cloud. Few other works studied the impact of such migration from an enterprise perspective [6], showing also a real use case [7]. In the latter, the authors show how migrating an IT infrastructure to a Cloud system can significantly reduce costs opposite to create and maintain an in-house solution.

The RESERVOIR project addresses the limits of current solutions, by providing a Cloud infrastructure where SPs can easily define their services that run in a fully automated fashion.

3 The RESERVOIR Solution

The RESERVOIR cloud solution [8][9][10] is shown in figure 1. SPs are external entities requiring resources for their applications based on high level business requirements.

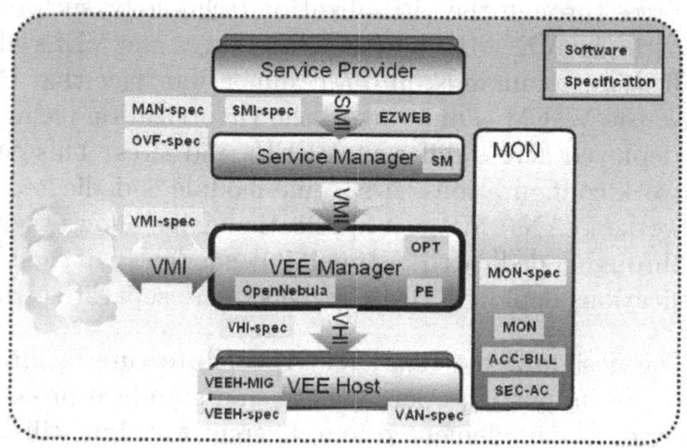

Fig. 1. RESERVOIR Cloud Architecture

A service in RESERVOIR is a set of Virtual Execution Environments (VEEs). Each VEE essentially wraps part of a SP's application. The SP specifies the terms of the service requested through a Service Manifest based on an extended version of the OVF [11].

Service Manager (SM). The SM is the module that interacting with the service providers, deals with the service deployment, checks elasticity rules and SLA compliance, and handles the service billing. The aim of this component is to automate a manual, complex and lengthy service delivery process. The SM processes the service requirements embedded within the manifest and determines the VEEs needed by the service, along their placement constrains based on cost, licensing, affinity, etc. SLAs are checked over the service life cycle and capacity is adjusted according to elasticity rules within the service manifest. This is accomplished by evaluating the application specific KPIs and deploying or removing the relative VEE instances. Finally, an accounting system within the SM processes the resources utilization of the service and creates bills according to post-paid or pre-paid billing models.

Virtual Execution Environment Manager (VEEM). The VEEM interacts with the SM and VEE Hosts (VEEHs) within the same site, and with remote VEEMs. The VEEM, based on the SM instructions, creates VEEs and places them in the VEEHs. Placement is done first to satisfy the SM constrains derived from the manifest, and second to optimize the site utilization according to the current local optimization policy such us of load balancing or power saving. Site policies can be easily plugged within the VEEM, so that each site can have its own optimization strategy. Cloud federation is also performed by this component. This feature allows to extend the cloud capacity over the physical limit of a single site. The VEEM can, within the manifest constraints, place VEEs across remote sites with which agreements have been created.

Virtual Execution Environment Host (VEEH). The VEEH interacts with the lower resources through the virtualization technology, such as XEN, KVM, etc, and also with the VEEM. The VEEH manages the VEEs abstracting the specific virtualization commands, into a common interface that the VEEM can use. In this way, the VEEM is unaware of the virtualization technology in place. VEEs can be deployed across different VEEHs and sites. This component also deals with network configurations. A specific module is dedicated to create Virtual Area Networks (VANs) for each application. This allows the application to communicate through a dedicated channel, independently of each VEE location. Therefore applications deployed in the same site are separated from each other.

Interfaces. The design of the RESERVOIR architecture facilitates the layers interoperability, by supporting open, generic and standard protocols and interfaces. Each layer can be implemented in a different way, but still able to intercat with each other. This approach will encourage new cloud enabling solutions. The Service Management Interface (SMI) allows service providers to access the RESERVOIR solution through the use of the OVF manifest. This means that different RESERVOIR providers use a common business requirements language. The VEE Management Interface (VMI) facilitates the use of different VEEMs within the RESERVOIR stack allowing to experiment with different management strategies. This interface allows also the cross-site communication needed to support the federation feature. Finally, the VEE Host Interface (VHI) supports the use of new virtualizaion technologies.

Monitoring Framework. The monitoring framework stretches across all layers. Its task is to pass information from lower to higher layers, in order for each component to take due action at runtime [12]. Applications running locally as well as across sites need to be monitored. Data can come from physical and virtual resources. For example, the SM needs to continuously check that elasticity rules and SLAs are satisfied. Therefore, probes have been developed and embedded within each VEE, to collect high level specific service data in the form of KPIs. Also, other probes interacting with the hypervisor and collecting CPU, memory and network usage were developed.

4 Use Case

The SAP Business Application. The use case presented in this paper is based on the SAP ERP 6.0, which is part of the SAP Business Suite. The ERP facilitates the flow of information among all business functions within a company. The suite runs over SAP NetWeaver Application Server (NWAS), a three tier architecture shown in figure 2. The application layer is made of two elements:

- **Central Instance (CI):** only one CI is present in a system and implements many services such as dialog, update, batch, spool, gateway, message server and enqueue server. Also, it provides higher level locking mechanism on the message server. It has high availability requirements and cannot be scaled out.
- **Dialog Instance (DI):** it processes user requests or Remote Function Call (RFC) from remote systems. Requests are handled in the form of work processes which can be dynamically parallelized. It can be scaled out.

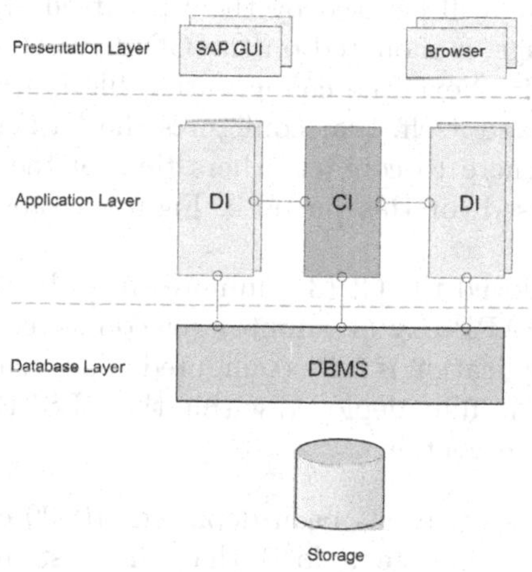

Fig. 2. SAP NETWeaver 3 tier architecture

The SAP NWAS can be configured either as 2-tier or 3-tier system. In a 2-tier system Database and Application layers form a single layer. A system deals with growing load by dynamically scaling up the DI instances. In our case, the NWAS was configured in a 2-tier fashion, where the CI and database were installed within the same VEE while the DI in a different VEE. As Presentation layer a proxy was installed within a VEE. The CI VEE requested 4 CPUs and 7GB of RAM, and its image was 120GB growing to 150GB with the swap area. The DI VEE requested 2 CPUs and 3GB of RAM, with an image of 1.5GB growing to 10GB with the swap area. The proxy requested 2 CPUs and 2GB of RAM. These VEEs requirements were coded within the service manifest.

Testbed Configuration. The RESERVOIR testbed is made of 4 sites, geographically distributed at UniMe (University of Messina, Italy), Umea (Umea University, Sweden), Thales (France) and IBM (Israel). For the presented scenario, the Umea site was used since the SAP application fitted in it. The Umea site is composed of 2 VEEHs and a management node running the SM and VEEM components. Each physical machine is equipped with Quad Xeon X3330 (2.66GHz), 8G RAM, and 160GB of Disk. A storage node stores the images.

4.1 Scenarios

Rapid Provisioning. The goal of this scenario is to demonstrate an automated full deployment of the SAP ERP 6.0 system. The system starts from an OVF descriptor, containing the details of the SP service, such as location of the images, minimum number of instances, VEE description (hypervisor, number of CPUs, memory, network) and elasticity rules to scale up and down the system. The SM contains an OVF parser [11] which extracts all necessary information to create, for each VEE, a descriptor file needed by the VEEM for the deployment, and a configuration file that will be used by the VEE itself. The configuration file, created as an ISO image, is mounted on the CD drive of the VEE that is then mounted by the VEEH. Next, the configuration file is used by the Activation Engine, within the image itself, that configures the VEE after the boot phase. Tiers need to know where to contact others tiers of the application, and the activation engine is used for this purpose. Figure 3 shows the process so far described.

As result, once deployed the CI (3-5 minutes from boot to running), the DI (3 minutes) and the SAPProxy (1 minute) get connected through a dedicated VAN, and the SAP application is fully configured. The result is a complex multi-tier business application, fully deployed within the RESERVOIR infrastructure, without any human intervention.

Elasticity. After the system has been deployed, 10000 concurrent users were simulated in order to generate a load that the system could not manage.

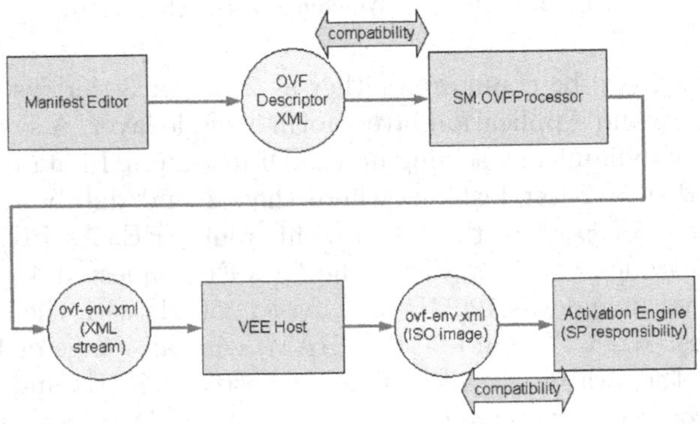

Fig. 3. SAP manifest processing

This was done through a load generator within the SAPProxy. The number of users represents the KPI for the SAP application, which was reported up to the SM, through the probe within the SAPProxy image that sends this data to the monitoring system. Since the Manifest contained elasticity rules to scale the system in such situations, a further DI was created and added to the SAP system, so that all users could be served. After a while the number of concurrent users was reduced by the load generator, which led the extra allocated DI to be removed by the SM.

5 Lesson Learnt

The SAP use case represents a complex class of applications, an enterprise multi-tier system, which allowed us to develop a methodology, based on our practical experience, to enable applications within the RESERVOIR cloud:

- **Virtualization of the application:**
  - embed the application in one or more VMs;
  - verify in-house that the application works;
- **Development of the OVF manifest:**
  - map the virtualized application into the manifest;
  - identify the valuable KPIs for the application;
  - create the appropriate elasticity rules;
- **Development of the activation engine:** configure each VM of the application appropriately;
- **Development of application's probes:** create the appropriate probes to push out the right KPIs from the VEEs;
- **Testing:** tests on deployment and elasticity in a real RESERVOIR environment.

6 Conclusions

This paper presented a complex business use case, the SAP ERP 6.0, running over the RESERVOIR cloud infrastructure. Two different scenarios were presented, the rapid provisioning and the elasticity. The former showed how the SAP ERP could be automatically deployed, starting from an OVF-based Manifest. The role of the Activation Engine to internally configure the VM, was also described. The latter scenario showed how the SAP application could be automatically scaled up and down, accordingly to the KPI. The process to bring this use case on the RESERVOIR cloud system allowed us to develop a methodology, which we formalized in a set of practical steps, that each SP can follow to enable its application to use the RESERVOIR solution.

Next we are going to demonstrate more features of the RESERVOIR system: *applications coexistence*: deploying more applications within the same site, in a transparent and secure fashion; *federation*: extending the infrastructure by setting agreements with other sites; and *cross sites live-migration* of VMs.

Acknowledgments. The research leading to the results presented in this paper has received funding from the European Unions seventh framework programme (FP7 2007-2013) Project RESERVOIR under grant agreement number 215605.

References

1. Chappell, D.: A short introduction to cloud platforms, an enterprise-oriented view. White paper, Chappell & Associates, 13 pages (August 2008)
2. Armbrust, M., Fox, A., Griffith, R., Joseph, A.D., Katz, R.H., Konwinski, A., Lee, G., Patterson, D.A., Rabkin, A., Stoica, I., Zaharia, M.: Above the clouds: A berkeley view of cloud computing. Tech. Rep. UCB/EECS-2009-28, EECS Department, University of California, Berkeley (February 2009)
3. Motahari-Nezhad, H.R., Stephenson, B., Singhal, S.: Outsourcing business to cloud computing services: Opportunities and challenges. Tech. Rep. HPL-2009-23, HP Laboratories (February 2009)
4. Rodero-Merino, L., Vaquero, L.M., Gil, V., Galn, F., Fontn, J., Montero, R.S., Llorente, I.M.: From infrastructure delivery to service management in clouds. Future Generation Computer Systems, Corrected Proof (2010) (in press)
5. Sriram, I., Khajeh-Hosseini, A.: Research agenda in cloud technologies. CoRR, abs/1001.3259 (2010)
6. Khajeh-Hosseini, A., Sommerville, I., Sriram, I.: Research challenges for enterprise cloud computing. CoRR, abs/1001.3257 (2010)
7. Khajeh-Hosseini, A., Greenwood, D., Sommerville, I.: Cloud migration: A case study of migrating an enterprise it system to iaas. CoRR, abs/1002.3492 (2010)
8. Rochwerger, B., Breitgand, D., Levy, E., Galis, A., Nagin, K., Llorente, I.M., Montero, R., Wolfsthal, Y., Elmroth, E., Caceres, J., Ben-Yehuda, M., Emmerich, W., Galan, F.: The reservoir model and architecture for open federated cloud computing. IBM Journal of Research and Development 53 (2009)
9. Rochwerger, B., Galis, A., Levy, E., Cáceres, J.A., Breitgand, D., Wolfsthal, Y., Llorente, I.M., Wusthoff, M., Montero, R.S., Elmroth, E.: Reservoir: management technologies and requirements for next generation service oriented infrastructures. In: IM 2009: Symposium on Integrated Network Management, Piscataway, NJ, USA, pp. 307–310. IEEE Press, Los Alamitos (2009)
10. Rochwerger, B., Galis, A., Breitgand, D., Levy, E., Cáceres, J.A., Llorente, I.M., Wolfsthal, Y., Wusthoff, M., Clayman, S., Chapman, C., Emmerich, W., Elmroth, E., Montero, R.S.: Design for future internet service infrastructures. In: Towards the Future Internet - A European Research Perspective, pp. 227–237. IOS, Amsterdam (2009)
11. Galán, F., Sampaio, A., Rodero-Merino, L., Loy, I., Gil, V., Vaquero, L.M.: Service specification in cloud environments based on extensions to open standards. In: COMSWARE 2009: Communication System Software and Middleware, pp. 1–12. ACM, New York (2009)
12. Clayman, S., Galis, A., Toffetti, G., Rodero-Merino, L., Vaquero, L.M., Nagin, K., Rochwerger, B.: Monitoring service clouds in the future internet. In: Towards the Future Internet - Emerging Trends from European Research, pp. 1–12. IOS, Amsterdam (2010)

Minimizing Technical Complexities in Emerging Cloud Computing Platforms

Andreas Menychtas, George Kousiouris, Dimosthenis Kyriazis, and Theodora Varvarigou

National Technical University of Athens,
Zografou Campus, 9 Iroon Polytechniou Str. 15773, Athens, Greece
{ameny,gkousiou,dimos}@mail.ntua.gr, dora@telecom.ntua.gr

Abstract. Cloud Computing is considered nowadays as the future of ICT systems leveraging new methodologies for developing, providing and consuming services. Even though many people believe that "Cloud" is just another buzzword for utility computing, this new computing paradigm is not only changing the design of modern computing platforms in technical level, but it also impels, from the market perspective, the creation of new value chains and business models. However, many technical complexities still remain, which disallow the wide adoption of Clouds to eventually address the new business trends and requirements of end-users. In this paper we identified and analyzed the key challenges for the emerging cloud platforms in order to minimize these technical complexities while the innovative approaches emerging from European research activities are presented.

1 Introduction

Although cloud computing [1] as another distributed computing paradigm is not something new, nowadays seems that the number of people and organizations exploiting the cloud computing capabilities is increasing and the research interest in cloud technologies is expanding. The main IT players such as Google and Microsoft have already developed platforms [2,3] to offer cloud services hosted in their datacenters and at the same time hundreds of new companies worldwide are involved in the service delivery value chain either by using their owned infrastructures or by providing added value services utilizing the infrastructures of the main players.

The new cloud ecosystems are changing the way the computing, storage and networking resources are purchased and consumed creating new business models and value chains. In contrast with the proprietary software where the license schemas are rather simple, the cloud based services -exploiting the advantages of the cloud features for scalability, multi-tenancy and reliability- are strongly related with the business aspects of the application and platform influencing all process of the service lifecycle. Currently, this is getting even more complex since the IT services are not independent each other but are often federation

M.R. Guarracino et al. (Eds.): Euro-Par 2010 Workshops, LNCS 6586, pp. 603–610, 2011.
© Springer-Verlag Berlin Heidelberg 2011

of other services, aggregating data and information from various sources. However, a number of technical complexities in the new computing environments deter the placement of composite applications and services. As cloud computing passed the "Peak of Inflated Expectations" and is moving towards the "Plateau of Productivity" according to the Hype Cycle of Gartner Research [4], issues like interoperability, data lock-in and QoS degradation are considered of major importance for the wide adoption of such systems. Therefore minimizing the technical complexities allows the involvement of more players in the elastic services market offering cost efficient services with high QoS and security guarantees without large investments on infrastructures.

The technical challenges for the emerging cloud systems span all layers of the established cloud model (SaaS, PaaS and IaaS) [5] with most of them affecting the functionality and the performance of system components (both in the same and cross layer). In the following figure we summarize the most important of them, which are also expected to draw the main research interest for the next few years. In addition, as the tight coupling of system components is of high importance for the future cloud platforms in order to provide efficient management and operation capabilities, we also present and analyze the main architectural design and cross-layer challenges.

Fig. 1. The challenges for the future cloud computing platforms

The rest of the paper is structured as follows. In Chapter 2 we identify the main technical challenges which will be addressed the next years and illustrate approaches on how to minimize their complexities. Cloud architectural issues are presented in Chapter 3, along a series of critical cross-layer issues that need to be addressed in the forthcoming period. Chapter 4 contains the conclusions of this work.

2 Technical Challenges of Future Cloud Platforms

In order to enable the wide adoption of Clouds and the involvement of SMEs, independent users and developers, the future cloud infrastructures have to be attractive as technical and business solutions. This implies providing advanced capabilities for all infrastructure layers and mechanisms to support the individual business and market requirements of each application. In next sections we have identified and analyzed the technical challenges from this perspective.

2.1 Performance Analysis

One of the most critical issues in modern cloud platforms is the performance analysis of the application running on a distributed infrastructure. This problem has been thoroughly investigated the previous years in the context of grid technologies (like in the works of [6,7,8]. However, in the current cloud business model, the different roles of SaaS, PaaS and IaaS limit the flow of information from one layer to the other (like source code or hardware capabilities knowledge). In this context, the task of analyzing performance characteristics of an unknown application running on unknown resources becomes almost impossible. In order to minimize the complexity inserted, the IRMOS project [9] follows a multilevel approach that meets most of the PaaS responsibilities.

First of all, the application and its components are described in an XML format through the Papyrus tool. This way, the platform has a complete description of the application, its structure and a number of behavioral and functional characteristics of each individual component. Afterwards, each component is benchmarked through a process analysed in [10]. This aids in modeling the application behavior with regard to changing resources assigned and the effect on the QoS output. From the IaaS part, further analysis is conducted on whether co-scheduling of VMs in the same host influences the performance of each individual VM, thus reducing the effective resource allocation performed by the cloud provider.

2.2 Interoperability

One of the main challenges of future cloud platforms is the interoperability issue. To this direction, the emerging REST protocol [11] is expected to have increased uptake. This is due to the fact that through the standardized interfaces that are required from the former interoperability at least in terms of interfaces is achieved.

This alleviates from the need to have advanced mechanisms for service composition. However the need for semantic bridging between the different providers still remains. Having the same interface is only the first step. The choice of what type of service to use and what type of resources is needed is critical. Research up to now, like in the FUSION [12] project, has progressed to some extent in this area, through the usage of an intermediate, bridging semantic description to which each provider adapts. However, if we are to meet the full expectations of a global and diversified IT market, this process must be performed on the fly and automatically, without the need for intermediate adjusting mechanisms that usually include manual intervention at some level.

2.3 Cloud Federation

Like in the previous case regarding interoperability, the realization of cloud federation in projects like RESERVOIR [13] is based on a predefined schema that is followed by both providers that wish to federate. However this implies human intervention and it limits the amount of dynamicity. In order to have a full scale autonomous platform that is able to federate on the fly with other IaaS providers, automated semantic bridging between e.g. the ontologies used by both is compelling.

A number of issues arise, from the usage of distributed IT infrastructures, which are not technical from a first glance. This mainly has to do with legal issues (e.g. data location) regarding the operational aspects of cloud platforms. The new project OPTIMIS [Optimis] aims to investigate, among others, the aforementioned critical parameters. Having as a starting point a legal analysis of requirements posed by a number of involved parties like legislation dictations or specific user constraints, OPTIMIS data services will be called to implement inter-Cloud data transfer mechanisms that will cover both the functional and the performance-driven point of view. Furthermore policies enforcement mechanisms for data that are transported to federated Clouds and for selecting the optimal data for federation with regard to their nature and characteristics will be investigated.

In order to meet these goals, aspects such as QoS requirements, functional requirements (e.g. how data are accessed from an external network across multiple domains), energy efficiency, performance constraints, data locality and integrity must be taken under consideration. For this purpose, modeling of the data mechanisms will be pursued in order to aid in the management of data sets during operational deployment of the latter in federated (or not) cloud platforms. What is more, a decision needs to be made regarding which parts of existing or newly deployed data will be federated in order to save resources. This decision must weigh critical factors such as what is the nature or usage of the data sets contained at the moment in the infrastructure. For this purpose, profiling mechanisms must be in place in order to assist in this process.

2.4 Data Management

Given that a major limitation of existing distributed and vitalized environments is the insufficient support for data-intensive services, the data management features of the cloud platforms are determinant for delivering cost effective applications and services to the ICT players and end-users. Therefore a great challenge for the success of the future cloud platforms is the integration, both in technical and business levels, of the computational, storage and network resources in an efficient manner to facilitate the delivery of data intensive services with QoS and security guarantees. This is one of the challenges that will be addressed by the VISION project.

VISION Cloud will include several innovative technical and technological approaches in data management. First of all it will raise the abstraction level of storage, encapsulating the data into objects with user-define and system defined attributes. Metadata will be used for effective access, management and manipulation of the storage enabling scalability and simplification of all storage and data functions. In addition, the problem of data interoperability and data lock-in will be addressed with the implementation of advanced data management functionality for migration and federation of data across geographically distributed administrative domains. Certainly data resources are not independent from the computational ones. To this direction, solutions providing secure execution of computational tasks near their data will be architected. The access to storage will be also highly simplified and efficient with mechanisms to define domain-specific optimizations which will make the content visible to users instead of its underlying storage container. The aforementioned advancements in data management are expected to achieve significant and quantifiable improvements in service delivery productivity, quality, availability, reliability and cost.

2.5 Application and Service Marketplaces

The notions of low-entry cost, scalability and dynamic total ownership cost for using the cloud technologies are fundamental for the Cloud adoption and its economic success. However, in the existing cloud paradigms this comes with limitations regarding the involvement of players with competitive applications in the cloud ecosystem because of the various, often complex, business and technical requirements. In addition, third parties are difficult to deploy their applications in the cloud infrastructures, create new business models and establish synergies since these cannot be fulfilled from a single provider.

In the mobile phones paradigm there are several approaches addressing this problem with the most known and successful the iPhone App Store. The developers and providers join these marketplaces selling their applications and services using various business and revenue models. These solutions leaded many developers and providers to be involved extending their businesses in the mobile market while end users are able to discover hundreds of services and applications to satisfy their needs. In cloud computing paradigm, the marketplace concept is still immature and with many technical complexities.

4CaaSt project [14] targets to minimize these technical complexities designing a cloud marketplace that supports all phases of the service lifecycle (knowledge, intentions, contract and settlement). The marketplace will offer to the providers the ability to publish services and applications in a managed environment, which controls the business terms and conditions (price, revenue sharing, promotion, etc) and also includes integrated rating and billing capabilities, unlike most existing marketplace environments. The 4CaaSt infrastructure will be designed to allow a hosting of compositions allowing the definition of combined models and end-to-end SLAs. While existing marketplaces focus on the trading with standalone services, 4CaaSt service compositions can be published in the marketplace supporting various business terms and conditions. It allows defining business policies taking into account the price models of a service, handling revenue sharing among multiple partners, and executing composed SLAs.

2.6 APIs

The interoperability, federation and marketplace capabilities of future cloud environments need to be supported by advanced, but also efficient and dynamic, APIs. Developing programming interfaces for deploying applications on the Cloud as well as blueprints for describing these applications is a complicated process because of the need to support tailored applications which may be in addition compositions of existing or new applications. Besides, the variety of business characteristics of the applications should be reflected on the design of the APIs. The above introduce additional complexity and overhead in the process of developing and adapting applications for clouds. To eliminate these complexities for all the involved entities -users, developers, providers- the APIs should allow automated or guided human-interactive facilitation of applications and compositions without reducing though the cloud capabilities for interoperability, scalability and QoS provisioning. IRMOS project [9] follows an approach to this direction for applications with real-time requirements. Modeling tools not only enable the deployment of applications on the Cloud but also allow the description of their rich set of high level operational and business requirements in a language that can be interpreted by the platform to a set of low level performance parameters. Furthermore application wrappers can be configured for providing high level monitoring data to the platform for evaluation and comparison with data from the infrastructure to guarantee, through automated corrective decisions during runtime such as resource renegotiation and migration, the smooth operation of the application.

3 Cloud Architectures

Clouds of the future will not be able only to manage and virtualize several types of resources (network, storage, computational) but also to communicate with legacy systems and internet enabled "things" such as wifi locators. The challenge for the system architects is to design a system tha includes services that interact dynamically and continuously, spanning between different domains, and ranging from the application level and down to the level of network resources management and the execution environment. This inlcude a careful synchronization of this rich set of services so as to efficiently operate, manage and reconfigure all the resources under real-time conditions, providing to the end-users the required Quality of Service, agreed in the SLAs. IRMOS project followed an architectural approach that included services to support application developers in engineering their applications, while other services support, in real-time, the application execution.

A major challenge for SaaS providers wanting to exploit the benefits of cloud computing is to manage QoS commitments to customers throughout the lifecycle of a service. The PaaS offers SaaS providers services and tools for estimating resource needs in advance of execution, negotiating QoS with service providers, provisioning virtualized resources. Furthermore, assessment tools for the technical and economic outcomes of provisioning policies and management actions are provided in case either the application or resources do not perform as expected or need to be adjusted. The IRMOS approach considers analysis and decision support to determine which actions are triggered. In addition, the performance of the monitoring and control between cloud layers is as essential factor in ensuring that QoS guarantees are maintained.

An essential element of cloud computing is the ability to deliver on-demand services with minimal manual configuration. All subsystems need to be self-managed and reconfigured in order to achieve management efficiencies, to react to QoS failures (such as an SLA violation or network link failure) in a timely way and avoid the escalation of such problems. Cloud utilization involves several processes that span in different cloud layers and stakeholders. Therefore, the cloud platforms of the future must not only provide a set of services but also cross layer workflows that consider the control channels and information exchanges which are required to support management of applications and application compositions throughout the full lifecycle.

3.1 Cross Layer Issues

The current business model that dominates the service oriented computing paradigm dictates the 3-tier approach. While very adaptive and flexible from a business point of view, this separation of roles between software, platform and infrastructure providers creates another series of challenges.

First of all, the issue of hardware description exists. Up to now, there is no accurate and widely accepted hardware metric in order to describe a computational resource. The unit that is widely used refers to the processor clock speed. However this is far from sufficient. The PaaS provider is not aware of the scheduling policies of the IaaS provider. Therefore, when a virtual machine (VM) is requested based only on processor speed, the effect of co-scheduling other VMs on the same host is not taken into account, despite the fact that the latter influences significantly in some cases the performance of the application. Furthermore, hardware failures may affect the application execution. The identification of the responsible in this case is critical given that this layer should be held accountable for breaching the SLA contract. Third party presence may be necessary in order to ensure that the allocation of resources in IaaS layer are the requested. However, the existence of third party software internally to the cloud provider is not expected to be something the latter would easily permit. If these points are addressed, then the responsibility for not meeting QoS levels falls on the estimation from the PaaS layer.

Another issue, this time between the SaaS and PaaS roles is the confidentiality regarding the source code of the various application components. While the most promising performance estimation techniques require some knowledge of the source code for accurately depicting the dependencies from various performance characteristics, this is not available in the context of current distributed computing infrastructures due to the lack of willingness to disclose application internal characteristics. This feature leaves the PaaS provider with the only option of 'black box' approaches for the prediction of the application behavior.

4 Conclusions

While cloud infrastructures have up to now fulfilled part of their promises and have emerged as sound technological solutions for end users and providers, a number of issues still exist that hinder the harvest of the potential benefits of this paradigm. These issues, coming both form the technical and business constraints of the current cloud implementations are close related each other and span all the layers of cloud model, obstructing the wide adoption of Clouds and the involvement of SMEs and individuals. Clouds have the power to extend the technological barriers for providing distributed services in global scale and to create new value chains and networks for applications. However, many challenges still remain and to this direction, a number of European research projects are significantly contributing so as to minimize the technical complexities and leverage the cloud platforms to the higher levels of innovation and automation.

References

1. Buyya, R., Yeo, C.S., Venugopal, S., Broberg, J., Br, I.: Cloud computing and emerging it platforms: Vision, hype, and reality for delivering computing as the 5th utility
2. Google app engine - google code, `http://code.google.com/appengine`
3. Windows azure platform, `http://www.microsoft.com/windowsazure`
4. Hype cycle definition i& overview, gartner research, `http://www.gartner.com/technology/research/methodologies/hype-cycle.jsp`
5. Lenk, A., Klems, M., Nimis, J., Tai, S., Sandholm, T.: What's inside the cloud? an architectural map of the cloud landscape. In: CLOUD 2009: Proceedings of the 2009 ICSE Workshop on Software Engineering Challenges of Cloud Computing, pp. 23–31. IEEE Computer Society, Washington, DC, USA (2009)
6. Chen, Y., Iyer, S., Liu, X., Milojicic, D., Sahai, A.: Sla decomposition: Translating service level objectives to system level thresholds, p. 3 (June 2007)
7. Lee, J.W., Asanovic, K.: Meterg: Measurement-based end-to-end performance estimation technique in qos-capable multiprocessors. In: Proc. of the 12th IEEE Real-Time and Embedded Technology and Applications Symp., pp. 135–147 (2006)
8. Stube, A.O., Rexachs, D., Luque, E.: Software probes: Towards a quick method for machine characterization and application performance prediction. In: International Symposium on Parallel and Distributed Computing, vol. 0, pp. 23–30 (2008)
9. Irmos project, `http://www.irmosproject.eu`
10. Kousiouris, G., Checconi, F., Mazzetti, A., Zlatev, Z., Papay, J., Voith, T., Kyriazis, D.: Distributed interactive real-time multimedia applications: A sampling and analysis framework. In: Proceedings of the 1st International Workshop on Analysis Tools and Methodologies for Embedded and Real-time Systems (WATERS) (2010)
11. Fielding, R.T.: Architectural styles and the design of network-based software architectures. PhD thesis (2000); Chair-Taylor, Richard N.
12. Alexakis, S., Bauer, M., Pace, A., Schumacher, A., Friesen, A., Bouras, A., Kourtesis, D.: Application of the fusion approach for assisted composition of web services. In: Establishing The Foundation of Collaborative Networks. IFIP International Federation for Information Processing, pp. 531–538. Springer, Boston (2007)
13. Reservoir project, `http://www.reservoir-fp7.eu`
14. 4caast project, `http://4caast.morfeo-project.org`

Fifth Workshop on Virtualization in High-Performance Cloud Computing (VHPC 2010)

VHPC 2010: Fifth Workshop on Virtualization in High-Performance Cloud Computing

Michael Alexander[1] and Gianluigi Zanetti[2]

[1] scaledinfra technologies GmbH, Vienna, Austria
[2] CRS4, Italy

Foreword

Virtualization has become a common abstraction layer in modern data centers, enabling resource owners to manage complex infrastructure independently of their applications. Conjointly virtualization is becoming a driving technology for a manifold of industry grade IT services. Piloted by the Amazon Elastic Computing Cloud services, the cloud concept includes the notion of a separation between resource owners and users, adding services such as hosted application frameworks and queuing. Utilizing the same infrastructure, clouds carry significant potential for use in high-performance scientific computing. The ability of clouds to provide for requests and releases of vast computing resource dynamically and close to the marginal cost of providing the services is unprecedented in the history of scientific and commercial computing.

Distributed computing concepts that leverage federated resource access are popular within the grid community, but have not seen previously desired deployed levels so far. Also, many of the scientific datacenters have not adopted virtualization or cloud concepts yet. This workshop aims to bring together industrial providers with the scientific community in order to foster discussion, collaboration and mutual exchange of knowledge and experience.

This year's workshop featured 10 papers on diverse topics relating to HPC virtualization. Papers of note include Han et al. examining adverse effects of non-uniform memory latency in NUMA architectures along with a proposed soft real-time scheduler by Cucinotta et al. The guest speaker Chris Kemp, IT CIO of NASA, provided an overview of the NASA Nebula cloud environment.

The chairs would like to thank the Euro-Par organizers and the members of the program committee, Mr. Chris Kemp along with the paper presenters and attendees, whose interaction contributed to a stimulating environment. VHPC is planning to continue the successful co-location with Euro-Par in 2011.

M.R. Guarracino et al. (Eds.): Euro-Par 2010 Workshops, LNCS 6586, p. 613, 2011.
© Springer-Verlag Berlin Heidelberg 2011

The Effect of Multi-core on HPC Applications in Virtualized Systems

Jaeung Han[1], Jeongseob Ahn[1], Changdae Kim[1],
Youngjin Kwon[1], Young-ri Choi[2], and Jaehyuk Huh[1]

[1] Computer Science, KAIST, Daejeon, Korea
[2] Korea Institute of Science and Technology Information (KISTI), Daejeon, Korea

Abstract. In this paper, we evaluate the overheads of virtualization in commercial multicore architectures with shared memory and MPI-based applications. We find that the non-uniformity of memory latencies affects the performance of virtualized systems significantly. Due to the lack of support for non-uniform memory access (NUMA) in the Xen hypervisor, shared memory applications suffer from a significant performance degradation by virtualization. MPI-based applications show more resilience on sub-optimal NUMA memory allocation and virtual machine (VM) scheduling. However, using multiple VMs on a physical system for the same instance of MPI applications may adversely affect the overall performance, by increasing I/O operations through the domain 0 VM. As the number of cores increases on a chip, the cache hierarchy and external memory will become more asymmetric. As such non-uniformity in memory systems increases, NUMA and cache awareness in VM scheduling will be critical for shared memory applications.

1 Introduction

Virtualization has become popular to improve system utilization by consolidating multiple servers into a physical system. In addition to the improved utilization, other benefits of virtualization, such as flexible resource management, fault isolation, and support for different operating systems, have led to the increase of interest in the virtualization of computing clusters for high performance computing (HPC). Public cloud computing services, such as Amazon EC2 [1], also accelerated the adoption of virtualization for HPC applications. However, the characteristics of compute-intensive HPC applications are quite different from those of I/O-intensive server applications. To adopt virtualization for HPC applications, thorough analysis of their performance characteristics in virtualized systems is necessary. Furthermore, the fast increase of core counts in multicore architectures, combined with virtualization techniques, affects the performance of HPC applications significantly.

In multicore architectures, the effects of complicated memory hierarchies, such as non-uniform memory access (NUMA), have become significant for HPC applications. Virtualization hides the underlying non-uniformity in memory access, and thus a guest operating system may not be able to make optimal scheduling decisions.

M.R. Guarracino et al. (Eds.): Euro-Par 2010 Workshops, LNCS 6586, pp. 615–623, 2011.
© Springer-Verlag Berlin Heidelberg 2011

In this paper, we investigate the overheads of virtualization on HPC applications running on multicore systems with uniform and non-uniform memory access latencies. Using the Xen hypervisor, we evaluate both a shared-memory multi-threaded benchmark, PARSEC [4], and a MPI-based benchmark, NAS Parallel Benchmark (NPB) [3] in various configurations.

The experimental results show that for shared memory applications, the performance overheads by virtualization are minor with uniform memory latency. However, in non-uniform memory access architecture, the current Xen hypervisor [6] adds a significant overhead for shared-memory applications and small overhead for MPI applications. However, for MPI applications, the granularity of VMs, the number of virtual CPUs (vCPUs) per VM, is important.

2 Methodology

2.1 Target Multicore Architectures

We use two different types of commercial multicore systems to evaluate HPC applications with virtualization. The first system is a single-socket system with a 12-core AMD Opteron 6168 processor (`single-socket`), which is a multi-chip module with two dies packaged together. Each die has six cores. Each core has separate 64KB instruction and data caches, and 512KB L2 cache. Six cores in a die share a 6MB L3 cache. The twelve cores in the system have almost uniform memory latencies to any memory modules.

The second system (`dual-socket`) uses two Intel Nehalem E5530 processors, which have four cores in each processor. Each core has separate 32KB instruction and data caches, and a 256KB private L2 cache. Four cores in a processor share an 8MB L3 cache. In the dual-socket system, two quad-core processors are connected by QPI interconnections. With the QPI interconnections, each processor has its own DRAM memory banks. An important characteristic of the system is non-uniform memory access (NUMA).

2.2 Methodology

To evaluate the effects of virtualization, we use the Xen hypervisor (version 3.4.2) [6]. We compare the performance of two selected benchmarks on virtualized configurations to that on non-virtualized (native) configurations. The guest operating system in the virtualized configurations is a Linux (kernel version 2.6.31.13) modified to support the para-virtualization mode of the Xen hypervisor. For the operating system in the native configurations, the same version of the Linux kernel is used.

We use two benchmarks representing different uses of HPC clusters: PARSEC [4] is a shared-memory multi-threaded benchmark with a single physical machine. We use the native input set for PARSEC. As a MPI-based benchmark, we evaluate the NAS parallel benchmark (NPB) [3]. To evaluate the overheads of MPI communications, we connected two systems by a 1gigabit Ethernet switch, and used the MPICH 1.2 library [2]. For NPB, we use the class C input set.

2.3 Virtual Machine Scheduling

In the Xen hypervisor, the unit of scheduling is a virtual CPU (vCPU). Each VM may have multiple vCPUs, emulating a multiprocessor system. The Xen hypervisor assigns credits to each vCPU periodically to guarantee fairness among vCPUs. Since vCPUs are scheduled independently, there is no guarantee that the vCPUs from a single VM are scheduled together. The Xen hypervisor maintains queues for each physical core, but vCPUs may migrate to all the physical cores freely unless they are pinned to specific cores. In the default setting, the scheduler will try to maximize the overall throughput by not wasting any CPU cycles. Whenever a core becomes idle, it will attempt to steal active vCPUs waiting in the queues of other cores.

In the target dual-socket system, relocating a thread across the processor boundary may cause two effects: shared L3 cache and NUMA effects. When a thread migrates from a processor to the other processor, it can no longer access the cached data in the L3 cache in the old processor directly. The other effect is non-uniform memory access latencies. Depending on which memory modules a thread mostly accesses, the processor where the thread is running may have a significant effect on the overall performance due to non-uniform memory access latencies.

3 Shared Memory Applications: PARSEC

3.1 Performance

Single Socket Results: To isolate the effect of NUMA, we first evaluate the effect of virtualization by using a system with one processor (single-socket). Among 12 cores, we use only 8 cores to be consistent with dual-socket results. Figure 1 presents the execution times of the PARSEC benchmark normalized to those of the native system with the same number threads. In this experiment, the vCPUs are not pinned to physical cores, and thus the Xen scheduler can migrate vCPUs without any restriction to minimize unused CPU cycles. For each application, three bars are shown: one, four, and eight vCPUs. The number of threads in each application is set to the number of vCPUs.

In general, for the single-socket system, the performance overheads by virtualization are insignificant, regardless of the number of vCPUs. The Xen hypervisor

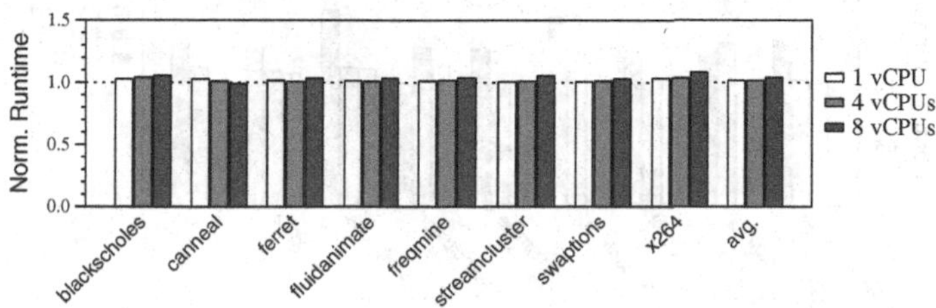

Fig. 1. Single socket (*unpinned* vCPUs): execution times with 1, 4, and 8 vCPUs

supports efficient virtualization for compute-intensive shared-memory applications for the single-socket system with uniform memory access. To further investigate the effect of scheduling, we fix vCPUs to physical cores. Figure 2 presents the execution times normalized to those of the native system, when vCPUs are pinned to physical cores. The results are similar to those with the unpinned configuration. With uniform memory access latencies, mapping between vCPUs and physical cores does not have a significant impact on the performance of the PARSEC applications. Furthermore, the cost of vCPU migration across shared L3 caches is minor, as shown by the almost same performance by the pinned and unpinned configurations.

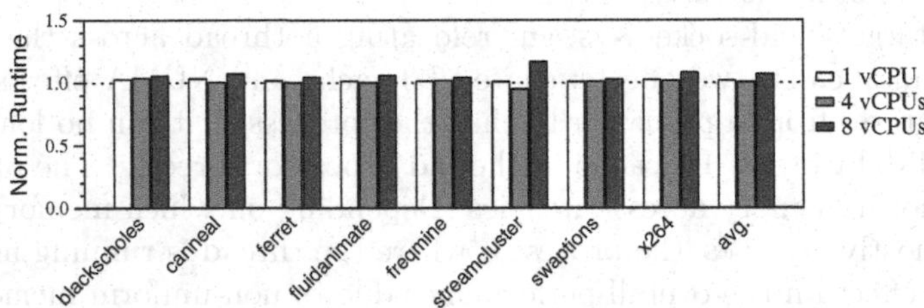

Fig. 2. Single socket (*pinned* vCPUs): execution times with 1, 4, and 8 vCPUs

Dual Socket Results. To include the NUMA effect, we use a dual-socket system in which each socket has four cores. Figure 3 presents the execution times with the dual-socket system normalized to those of the native system. In this experiment, the vCPUs are not pinned to physical cores. Unlike the previous single socket results, the performance degrades significantly. The performance degradation is 12% for 1 vCPU, 16% for 4 vCPUs, and 37% for 8 vCPUs on average, respectively.

To eliminate the effect of vCPU migration, we fix each vCPU to a physical core. Figure 4 presents the normalized execution times (to those of the native system) with the pinned configuration. For the one and four vCPU configurations, the performance degradations reduce to 8% and 9% respectively. However, for the eight vCPU configuration, the performance degradation increases slightly to 40%.

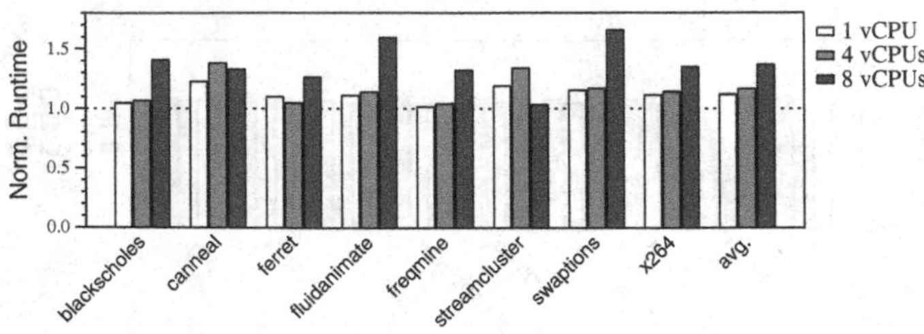

Fig. 3. Dual socket (*unpinned* vCPUs): execution times with 1, 4, and 8 vCPUs

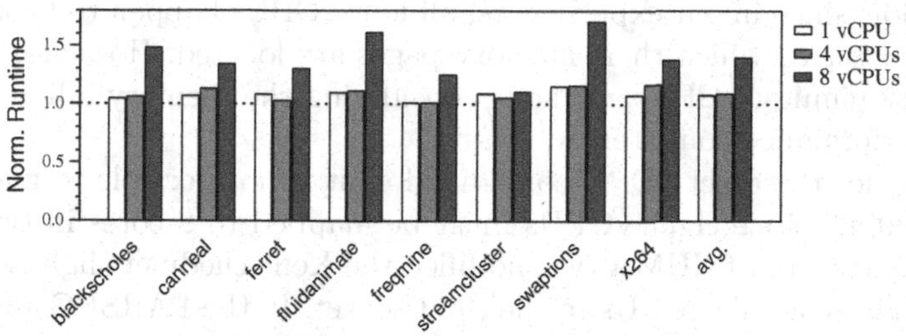

Fig. 4. Dual socket (*pinned* vCPUs): execution times with 1, 4, and 8 vCPUs

When the number of vCPUs is in the range from 1 to 4, pinning vCPUs makes the system use only one socket for the vCPUs, reducing the effect of NUMA and eliminating the cost of vCPU migration across the shared L3 cache boundary. However, for 8 vCPUs, pinning may eliminate the cost of vCPU migration across the shared L3 cache boundary, but it does not mitigate the effect of NUMA. Eight vCPUs must use all the cores in both sockets, but the memory pages of the VM are mostly located in one of the socket.

3.2 Mitigating the NUMA Effect

In this section, we isolate the effect of NUMA to further investigate its performance impact on HPC applications. To explain the benefit of pinning in the dual-socket system (as shown in Figure 4), we evaluate the "worst" and "best" case scheduling for the four vCPU configuration. Considering the NUMA effect, the worst case scheduling is to map all four vCPUs on a socket to which memory pages are not allocated. The best case scheduling is to map all four vCPUs on the same socket to which all the memory pages are located. Figure 5 presents the execution times normalized to those of the native system with the worst and best case scheduling for four vCPUs, as well as the unpinned and pinned configurations.

As shown in Figure 5, the performance with the unpinned configuration is slightly better than that with the worst case range-pinned configuration. The performance with the pinned configuration is similar to that with the best case range-pinned configuration. Pinning vCPUs has a similar effect to the best case

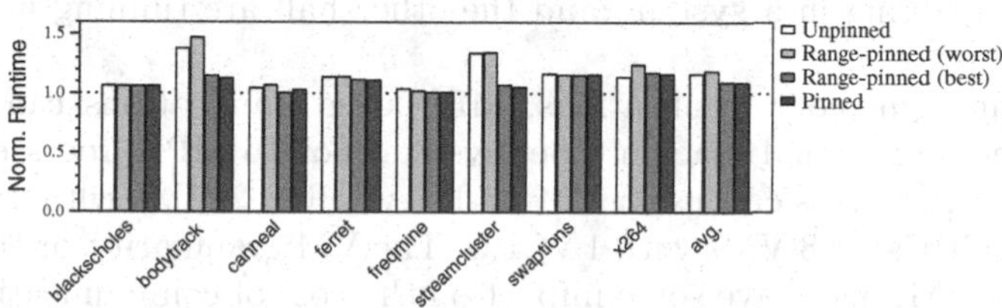

Fig. 5. The worst and best range pinning schemes for 4 vCPUs (dual-socket)

configuration, since in our experiments, all four vCPUs happen to be mapped to the same socket to which their memory pages are located. However, we expect that blindly pinning vCPUs, without considering the memory affinity, will not improve performance consistently.

However, for the eight vCPU configuration, it is not possible to find the best case scheduling, since eight vCPUs must be mapped to 8 cores in two sockets. To reduce the effect of NUMA, we modified the Xen scheduler slightly such that it attempts to schedule vCPUs to the right socket. In the PARSEC applications, all the eight vCPUs are not always used, since available parallelism dynamically changes. If less than eight vCPUs are used, active vCPUs are scheduled as much as possible to the socket in which their memory pages reside. However, we do not make any physical core idle, if there are active vCPUs not scheduled to any core. Thus, if no core in the right socket is available, a vCPU will be scheduled to the other socket. This rudimentary optimization, called `NUMA-first`, provides a significant improvement in performance. Figure 6 presents the normalized execution times with the unpinned, pinned, and NUMA-first configurations. With the NUMA-first scheduling, the average performance degradation is reduced to 18% from 37% of the unpinned configuration. The NUMA-aware scheduling requires further investigation to make it adaptable to more complex cases than our configurations.

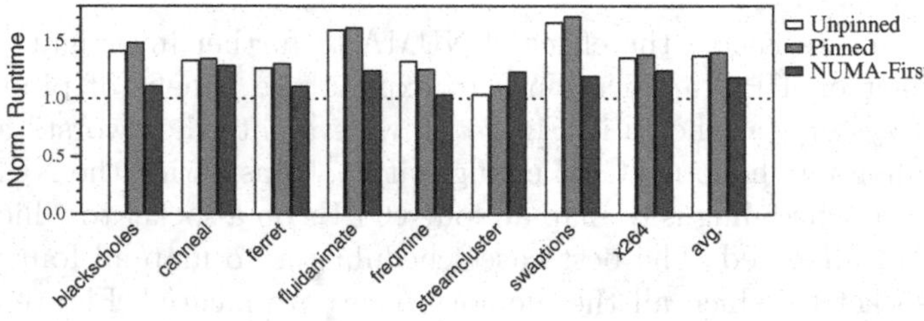

Fig. 6. *NUMA-first* optimization for 8 vCPUs (dual-socket)

4 MPI-Based Applications: NPB

In this section, we evaluate the performance overheads of virtualization with the MPI-based NPB. For the experiments in this section, the half of the total MPI processes are running in a system, and the other half are running in the other system.

Unlike shared memory applications, MPI-based applications can run with various numbers of virtual machines per system. For 16 MPI processes, in each system, 8 MPI processes can use a VM with 8 vCPUs, 2 VMs with 4 vCPUs, 4 VMs with 2 vCPUs, or 8 VMs with 1 vCPU. The VM granularity, or the number of vCPUs per VM, may have some impact on the cost of communication among MPI processes. MPI communications among processes in a VM are done only within the guest operating system. MPI communications among the VMs in a system do not access the network hardware, but the communications must pass through the hypervisor and the domain0 VM. MPI communications among the VMs in different systems must access the network hardware, hypervisor, and the domain0 VM.

Figure 7 presents the execution times with different numbers of VMs for 16 MPI processes without pinning. Firstly, for all applications, using the largest VM (8 vCPUs per VM) is better than using multiple VMs in a system. It is because MPI communications within a VM have lower overheads than those across VMs. Secondly, for each application, if the best VM granularity (8 vCPUs per VM) is used, the performance overheads on MPI-applications by virtualization are much lower than those on shared memory applications. Even though all the 8 cores are used for each system, the average execution time is only 11% higher than that of the native system. Due to the I/O activities, NUMA effect does not dominate the overall performance.

Figure 8 presents the execution times with vCPUs pinned to physical cores. Pinning vCPUs does not improve the NPB performance for the best VM granularity, with a similar 11% average increase of execution times. However, pinning improves performance for any VM granularity other than 8 vCPU per VM.

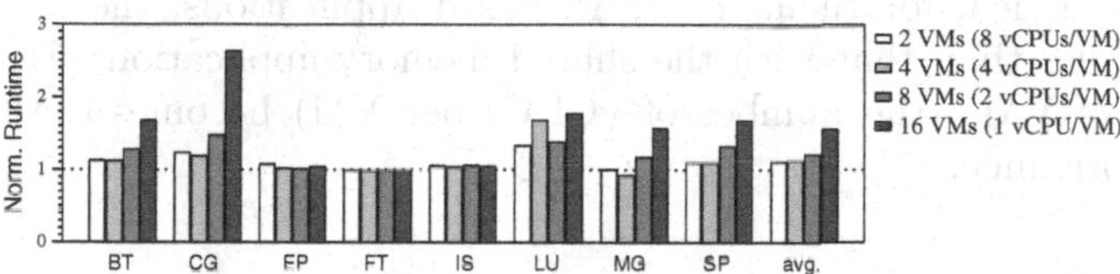

Fig. 7. NPB execution times (*unpinned* vCPUs): varying vCPUs per VM

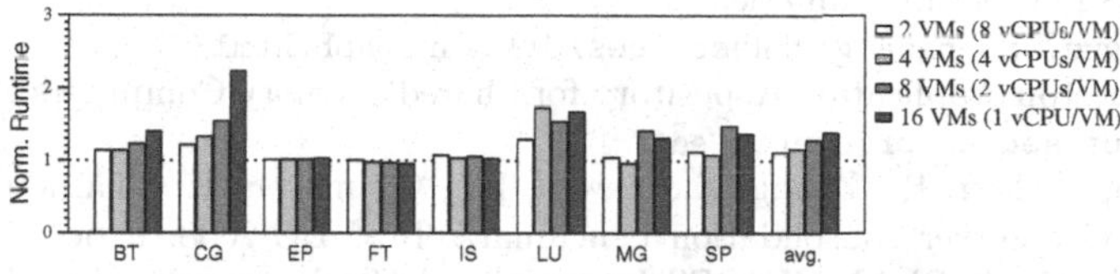

Fig. 8. NPB execution times (*pinned vCPUs*): varying vCPUs per VM

5 Related Work

The effects of virtualization on the performance of applications have been studied in previous work. Due to space limitation, we review some of such work in this section. Huang et al showed that I/O virtualization overhead is the major issue for virtualization, and proposed VMM-bypass I/O to reduce I/O virtualization overhead [9]. In [12], the effects of resource sharing (specially, sharing an Infiniband interconnect) on the performance of HPC applications were studied in a virtualized multicore cluster. In [13], the performance of the compute-bound benchmark applications was analyzed, and in [11], the performance overheads for network I/O device virtualization were measured. A simulation-driven approach was presented in [7], which analyzes the virtualization overheads of I/O intensive workloads. The performance impact of a consolidated workload, composed of server applications, was evaluated in [5]. In our paper, we focus on how the complex memory hierarchy affects the performance of HPC applications in virtualized systems.

A VM-aware MPI library was developed to reduce the communication overhead for HPC application in [8]. To improve I/O performance, Liao et al presented cache-aware scheduling which co-schedules Dom0 and I/O intensive DomUs to communicate more efficiently via a last level cache, and credit-stealing which steals credits for I/O intensive vCPUs [10].

6 Conclusion

In this paper, we evaluate single and dual socket multicore systems with the Xen hypervisor. For shared memory applications, NUMA awareness is critical for performance in dual-socket systems. As the complexity and non-uniformity in memory systems increase, NUMA and cache awareness in VM scheduling will become critical for them. For MPI-based applications, the NUMA effect is much smaller than that with the shared memory applications. However, the granularity of VMs (the number of vCPUs per VM) becomes critical for the overall performance.

References

1. Amazon EC2, `http://aws.amazon.com/ec2/`
2. MPICH, `http://www.mcs.anl.gov/research/projects/mpich2/`
3. The NAS Parallel Benchmarks, `http://www.nas.nasa.gov/Resources/Software/npb.html/`
4. The Princeton Application Repository for Shared-Memory Computers (PARSEC), `http://parsec.cs.princeton.edu/`
5. Apparao, P., Iyer, R., Zhang, X., Newell, D., Adelmeyer, T.: Characterization & analysis of a server consolidation benchmark. In: VEE 2008: Proceedings of the Fourth ACM SIGPLAN/SIGOPS International Conference on Virtual Execution Environments, pp. 21–30. ACM, New York (2008)
6. Barham, P., Dragovic, B., Fraser, K., Hand, S., Harris, T., Ho, A., Neugebauer, R., Pratt, I., Warfield, A.: Xen and the art of virtualization. In: SOSP 2003: Proceedings of the Nineteenth ACM Symposium on Operating Systems Principles, pp. 164–177. ACM, New York (2003)
7. Chadha, V., Illiikkal, R., Iyer, R., Moses, J., Newell, D., Figueiredo, R.J.: I/o processing in a virtualized platform: a simulation-driven approach. In: VEE 2007: Proceedings of the 3rd International Conference on Virtual Execution Environments, pp. 116–125. ACM, New York (2007)
8. Huang, W., Koop, M.J., Gao, Q., Panda, D.K.: Virtual machine aware communication libraries for high performance computing. In: SC 2007: Proceedings of the 2007 ACM/IEEE Conference on Supercomputing, pp. 1–12. ACM, New York (2007)

9. Huang, W., Liu, J., Abali, B., Panda, D.K.: A case for high performance computing with virtual machines. In: ICS 2006: Proceedings of the 20th Annual International Conference on Supercomputing, pp. 125–134. ACM, New York (2006)
10. Liao, G., Guo, D., Bhuyan, L., King, S.R.: Software techniques to improve virtualized i/o performance on multi-core systems. In: ANCS 2008: Proceedings of the 4th ACM/IEEE Symposium on Architectures for Networking and Communications Systems, pp. 161–170. ACM, New York (2008)
11. Menon, A., Santos, J.R., Turner, Y., Janakiraman, G.J., Zwaenepoel, W.: Diagnosing performance overheads in the xen virtual machine environment. In: VEE 2005: Proceedings of the 1st ACM/USENIX International Conference on Virtual Execution Environments, pp. 13–23. ACM, New York (2005)
12. Ranadive, A., Kesavan, M., Gavrilovska, A., Schwan, K.: Performance implications of virtualizing multicore cluster machines. In: HPCVirt 2008: Proceedings of the 2nd Workshop on System-Level Virtualization for High Performance Computing, pp. 1–8. ACM, New York (2008)
13. Tikotekar, A., Vallée, G., Naughton, T., Ong, H., Engelmann, C., Scott, S.L.: An analysis of hpc benchmarks in virtual machine environments, pp. 63–71 (2009)

Proposal of Virtual Network Configuration Acquisition Function for Data Center Operations and Management System

Hideki Okita, Masahiro Yoshizawa, Keitaro Uehara, Kazuhiko Mizuno, Toshiaki Tarui, and Ken Naono

Central Research Laboratory, Hitachi, Ltd.
{hideki.okita.pf,masahiro.yoshizawa.bt,keitaro.uehara.tb, kazuhiko.mizuno.pq,toshiaki.tarui.my,ken.naono.aw}@hitachi.com

Abstract. Virtualization technologies have been widely deployed in data centers to improve the system utilization. However, they cause increased workload for operators to clarify the structure of virtual networks in data centers. To reduce the operation time, this paper provides the virtual-network management system which automates the integration of the configurations of the virtual networks. The proposed system collects the configurations from server virtualization platforms and VLAN-supported switches, and integrates these configurations according to the newly developed XML-based management information model for virtual-network configurations. The preliminary evaluations show that the proposed system helps to reduce the time to collect and update the configurations by about 40 percent. This result implies that the proposed system is effective for improving the configuration management process for virtual networks in data centers.

1 Introduction

In 2013, the scale of the data-center service market in Japan, which was 88 billion dollars in 2009, is expected to reach 140 billion dollars [9]. Reducing management costs is the main motivation for the server consolidation in data centers [11]. To achieve this server consolidation, servers are being increasingly virtualized. In addition, High-Performance Computing (HPC) platforms are also being virtualized [7].

To operate efficiently data centers in which server-virtualization technology is used, data-center operators have to manage virtual networks as well as virtual machines (VMs). For such virtual-network management, prior works provide several methods for clarifying the structure of virtual networks in accordance with the configurations of virtual LAN (VLAN) [3] switches and network-connection information [8,10].

However, to reduce the implementation costs of management functions, the servers with server-virtualization functions (virtualized servers) have configurations with their own forms that differ from those of VLAN switches. As a

M.R. Guarracino et al. (Eds.): Euro-Par 2010 Workshops, LNCS 6586, pp. 625–632, 2011.
© Springer-Verlag Berlin Heidelberg 2011

result, to manage the virtual-network structure in data centers in which server-virtualization technology is used, operators need to collect data on multiple forms of configurations. Configuration management time thereby increases.

To improve interoperability of management information, DMTF (Distributed Management Task Force) is developing a standard management model [4]. However, this model covers only virtual VLAN switches created on virtualized servers and does not cover physical VLAN switches. Therefore, the configurations of virtualized servers still differ from those of physical network devices.

In the present study, to reduce the time taken to collect the configuration data about virtual networks in a data center, a "virtual-network-configuration acquisition function" has been developed.

2 Issues in Virtual-Network Configuration Management

2.1 Prior Virtual-Network Configuration Management

In a network without VLAN, which is standardized as IEEE802.1Q, all servers can communicate with each other. On the other hand, in a VLAN-enabled network, multiple and isolated virtual networks can exist on a physical network.

The logical structure of the VLAN-enabled networks varies according to VLAN configurations. Therefore, to clarify the structure of the networks, operators have to manage the VLAN configurations.

Management Information Base (MIB), a part of the Internet Standard Management Framework [5], is a standard approach for defining management information. Fig.1 shows the management procedure for the previously described VLAN configurations through a MIB.

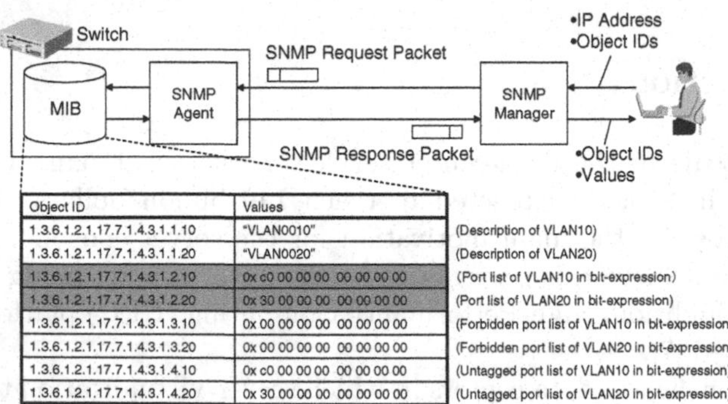

Fig. 1. Collecting VLAN configuration with MIB

The two key issues regarding configuration management of virtual networks with MIBs are described as follows.

The first issue concerns the reusability of configuration information. Although the data of MIBs include sets of object IDs and values, MIBs lack information about data structure. Therefore, when other management tools reuse VLAN configurations collected through MIBs, they require additional information about the data structure. As a result, the complexity of configuration information causes a decrease in manageability.

The second issue concerns the integrity of configuration information. A MIB contains information only about the switch that the configuration is acquired from. Therefore, as the scale of the managed network expands, the number of VLAN configurations that the operators have to manage increases. In turn, the increased workload to manage the configurations becomes another serious issue.

2.2 Virtual-Network Configuration Management in Server Virtualization Environments

Virtualized servers, as shown in Fig.2, run virtual switches to connect VMs on the same server in data centers in which server virtualization is used. Since most of these virtual switches support VLAN technology, the structure of a virtual network varies according to their VLAN configurations.

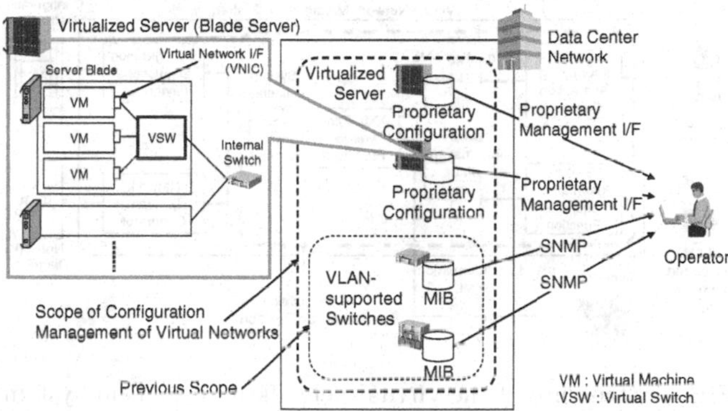

Fig. 2. Virtual network management in the server-virtualized environment

To clarify the structure of virtual networks, the data-center operators therefore have to manage the configurations of the virtualized servers in addition to those of the virtual switches. However, the configurations of the virtualized servers are vendor-specific, unlike those of the Internet-standard MIBs. This makes significant differences in data structure between them. Operators therefore have to manage multiple forms of configurations and thus face increased workload. Additionally, the management interface (I/F) of the virtualized servers is also a vendor-specific I/F and thus leads to increased workload.

2.3 Challenges Facing Virtual-Network Configuration Management

To resolve the three above-described issues, the following three challenges must be faced. First, we should improve the reusability of configuration data so that operators can easily recognize its data structure. Second, we should improve the integrity of configurations so that operators can manage multiple devices as a whole. Third, we should improve the extensibility of configurations so that operators can manage virtualized servers that have their own forms of configurations.

3 Virtual-Network Configuration Acquisition Function

3.1 Architecture

A virtual-network management system that manages the configurations of the whole data-center network (including virtualized servers and switches) was developed. These configurations are called the "system configuration."

Fig.3 shows the architecture of the proposed system. The proposed system consists of a server-information acquisition function, a switch-information acquisition function, and an XML merge function. These functions collect configurations from virtualized servers and switches and aggregate them into a system configuration. Operators then add link information if needed.

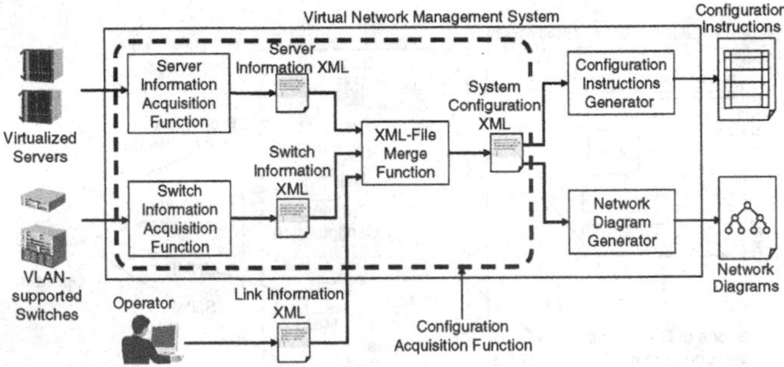

Fig. 3. Structure of the virtual network management system

The proposed system configuration has three characteristics. First, the system configuration is defined as an XML document. Since XML documents have a textual and structured data format, they are easily processed by programs. The XML-based system configuration can therefore improve reusability of configurations from the viewpoint of other management systems.

Second, the system configuration includes XML elements used to represent the overall network. These elements aggregate multiple elements, which are equivalent to managed network devices. The system configuration can therefore describe the overall structure of the managed network in an integrated manner.

Third, the system configuration includes the XML elements that represent the configuration of a managed node. These elements can keep the configurations specific to device type. The system configuration can therefore describe multiple types of configurations.

3.2 System Configuration XML

Fig.4 and Fig.5 show the XML trees of the system-configuration. The XML tree shown in the Fig.4 has *configurations* elements to represent device configurations.

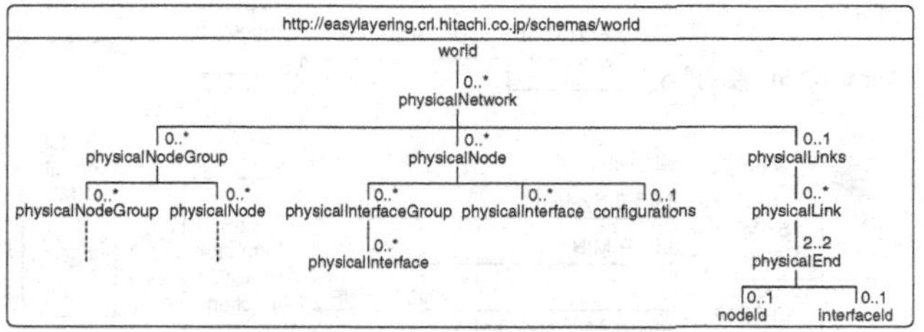

Fig. 4. XML tree of system-configuration XML

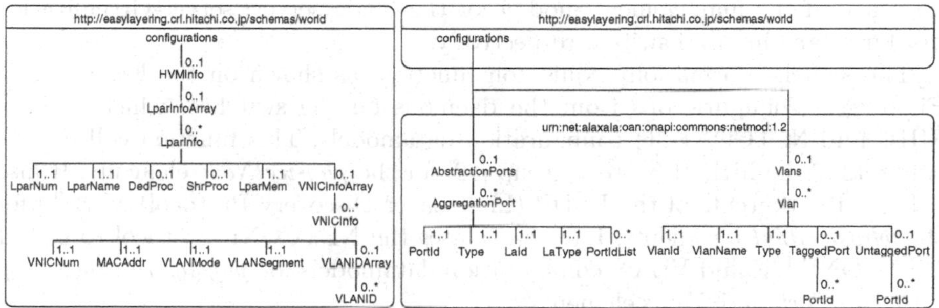

Fig. 5. XML elements for VM/VLAN configurations

The left side of Fig.5 shows the XML tree of a *configurations* element for a virtualized server. The *LparInfo* element in this XML tree has child nodes, corresponding to a name, a CPU core number, and an amount of memory of a VM. It also has a *VNICInfoArray* element that represents VNICs of the VM.

The right side of Fig.5 shows the XML tree of a *configurations* element for a switch. It has an *AbstractionPorts* element that represents LAG (link aggregation) [1] configurations and an *Vlans* element that represents VLAN configurations as the child nodes. These two elements have a set composed of *AggregationPort* elements and a set of *Vlan* elements as child nodes, respectively.

3.3 Configuration Acquisition Function

The server-information acquisition function, as shown on the upper side of Fig.6, gets configurations from the virtualized servers and generates the server information XML. To generate the server information XML, this function collects the system information including the list of server blades, virtual-machine configurations, and interface/LAG/VLAN configurations through the management

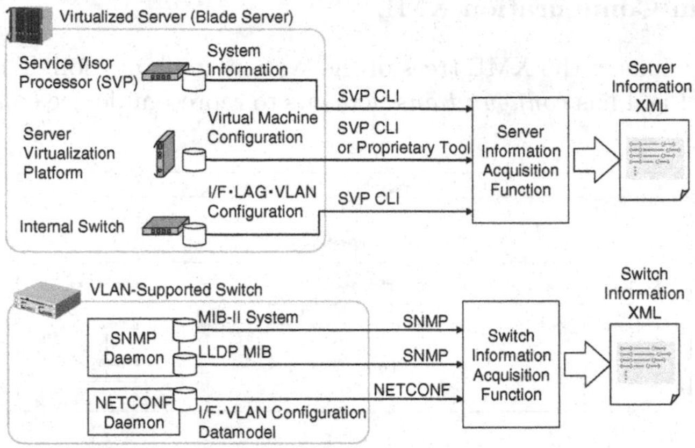

Fig. 6. Generating server/switch information XML

interface of the management module of the blade server, server-virtualization platform, and internal switch, respectively.

The switch-information acquisition function, as shown on the lower side of Fig.6, gets configurations from the daemons on the switches, which manage MIBs and NETCONF [6] configuration datamodels. This function collects the contents of the MIB-II System group [12] for the *physicalNode* elements. It also collects the contents of the LLDP (Link Layer Discovery Protocol) MIB [2] for the *physicalLinks* elements. Further, it uses the NETCONF protocol to collect NETCONF I/F and VLAN configuration datamodels for *physicalInterface*, *AggregationPort*, and *Vlans* elements.

The XML-file merge function gets the server-configuration XML and the switch-configuration XML, and it then aggregates them into a system-configuration XML. If there are multiple *physicalNetwork* elements with the same ID in those XMLs, this function aggregates those elements into a *physicalNetwork* element.

4 Evaluation

4.1 Evaluation Method

To evaluate the proposed function, we used the test network containing a server-virtualization supported blade server and four VLAN-supported switches. Five virtual machines and three VLANs were configured in this test network. In addition, a virtual-network-management-system prototype with the proposed function implemented by Perl and Java was set up. This prototype was run on a Windows Server 2003 PC, incorporating a Xeon 3GHz CPU and 2GB RAM.

We evaluated the performance of the proposed configuration-acquisition function by measuring the time the proposed function took to export a system-configuration XML file. Further, we evaluated the efficiency improvement for operators, by measuring the time they took to update configurations in the case when the operators used existing CLIs and the case when they used our prototype. The following steps are included in the measured time. First, the operator gets the VLAN configurations from devices. Second, he checks the configurations according to VLAN configuration data sheets. Finally, he updates the sheets if necessary.

4.2 Evaluation Result

The left side of Fig.7 shows the measurement results for the time taken to make the system-configuration XML with the prototype. The total time is 97.85 s, which is broken down in terms of each device as blade-server chassis, 38%, internal switch, 24%, layer-2/3 switch, 29%, and others, 9%.

And, the right side of Fig.7 shows the comparative measurement result for the time taken by the operator to update the configuration sheets. The conventional method took an average 1870 s and the proposed method took 1126 s; in other words, the proposed method reduced the time by 39.8% on average. Moreover, the proportions of the times for each task are not significantly different in the two cases (i.e., "by hand" and "by tool").

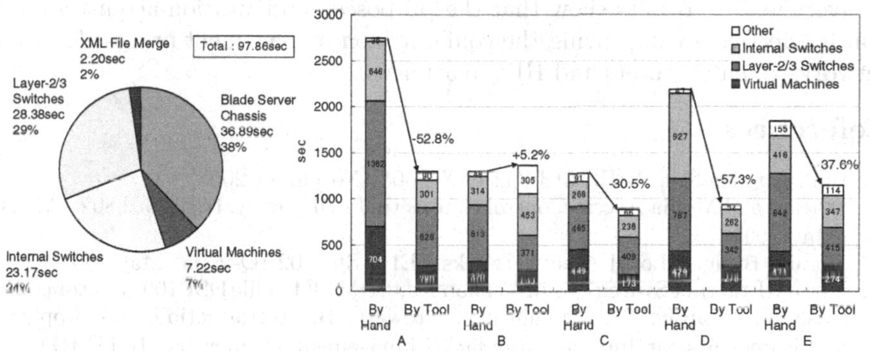

Fig. 7. Measurement result of evaluation

4.3 Discussion

The virtual-network-configuration acquisition function improved the efficiency of the configuration-update processes performed by operators without regard to device type. The reason for this improvement is considered to be as follows. Operators can get all information required to update the configuration sheets just by accessing the system-configuration XML.

Further, the proposed function would be effective in the case of dynamic changes of configurations, such as VM migrations. In such case, operators can easily acquire the latest configurations by using the proposed function at the notification about configuration changes from devices.

From a scalability point of view, the proposed function should be enhanced. The reason is that the number of queries to the devices increases in proportion to the number of managed devices in networks. On the other hand, a query to a device is independent from those to the other devices. Thus, parallelizing the queries is effective to suppress the time to collect configurations.

Further, the proposed function can be also applied to manage HPC platforms. Especially, it is useful in the case that HPC users use their own isolated platforms by means of server virtualization. However, to specify the user of a VLAN, we must develop the additional function that acquire user-information from an external authentication function and manage the user-VLAN mappings.

5 Conclusion

A configuration-acquisition function for virtual-network management systems was developed. This function collects configurations from virtualized servers and switches and integrates the configurations into the system-configuration XML.

The performance and effectiveness of the proposed function was evaluated by using a prototype of a virtual-network management system. In particular, it took 97.85 s to collect the configurations of five VMs and three VLANs . Furthermore, when operators used the prototype, the function reduced the time taken by operators to update the configuration documents for the test network by 39.8% on average. The results show that the proposed configuration-acquisition function is effective for improving the configuration-management process for virtual networks in data centers and HPC platforms.

References

1. Link Aggregation. IEEE Std 802.1AX-2008 (November 2008)
2. Station and Media Access Control Connectivity Discovery. IEEE Std 802.1AB-2005 (May 2005)
3. Virtual Bridged Local Area Networks. IEEE Std 802.1Q-2005 (May 2006)
4. Virtual Ethernet Switch Profile Version 1.0.0. DMTF Profile DSP1097 (October 2010)
5. Case, J., Mundy, R., Partain, D., Stewart, B.: Introduction and Applicability Statements for Internet Standard Management Framework. IETF RFC 3410 (December 2002)
6. Enns, R.: NETCONF Configuration Protocol. IETF RFC 4741 (December 2006)
7. Huang, W., Liu, J., Abali, B., Panda, D.K.: A Case for High Performance Computing with Virtual Machines. In: Proc. The 20th ACM International Conference on Supercomputing (ICS 2006), Queensland (June 2008)
8. Israel, R., Fang, Y., Cohen, P., Eichen, E.: Configuration Management of Large IP Telephony Networks. In: Proc. 2000 IEEE/IFIP Network Operations and Management Symposium, Honolulu, pp. 435–446 (April 2000)
9. Ito, M.: Japan Datacenter Services 2010-2013 Forecast and 2009 Review: Customer Perceptions and Needs. Market Analysis # JP2542801S (February 2010)
10. Kim, M.S., Leon-Garcia, A.: Autonomic Network Resource Management using Virtual Network Concept. In: Ata, S., Hong, C.S. (eds.) APNOMS 2007. LNCS, vol. 4773, pp. 254–264. Springer, Heidelberg (2007)
11. Kusano, K.: Japan Datacenter Network Infrastructure 2009-2012 Forecast. Market Analysis # JP209203S (July 2009)
12. McCloghrie, K., Rose, M.T.: Management Information Base for Network Management of TCP/IP-based internets: MIB-II. IETF RFC 1213 (March 1991)

Security and Performance Trade-off in PerfCloud*

Valentina Casola[1], Antonio Cuomo[2], Massimiliano Rak[3], and Umberto Villano[2]

[1] Dipartimento di Informatica e Sistemistica, Università Federico II di Napoli
casolav@unina.it
[2] RCOST and Dipartimento di Ingegneria, Università del Sannio
{antonio.cuomo,villano}@unisannio.it
[3] Dipartimento di Ingegneria dell'Informazione, Seconda Università di Napoli
massimiliano.rak@unina2.it

Abstract. Both cloud and GRID are computing paradigms that manage large distributed resources, and currently there is a lot of interest in their integration. An integrated architecture cloud-GRID requires fine-grained access control and identity federation among untrusted distributed domains in the cloud. This paper deals with the trade-off between security and performance in such architectures, comparing the overhead introduced by cloud services with different security levels. The quantitative results obtained in PerfCloud, an existing cloudgrid infrastructure, are presented and discussed.

1 Introduction

According to the definition by NIST, cloud computing is a model for enabling convenient, on-demand network access to a shared pool of configurable computing resources (e.g., networks, servers, storage, applications, services) that can be rapidly provisioned and released, with minimal management effort or service provider interaction [9]. On the other hand, GRID computing is basically a paradigm that aims at enabling access to high performance distributed resources in a simple and standard way. In GRIDs, users can compose complex stateful services in order to build up complex and computation-intensive tasks. GRID and clouds are at least similar, not to mention the use of many common underlying technologies. However, they are typically used for different purposes by different classes of users. In short, clouds are used by users that are prone to buy computing resources to get their results as soon as possible. On the other hand, GRID users wish to exploit the optimum set of resources that can solve their problem, overcoming the boundaries of a single enterprise. In fact, the two technologies complement gracefully each other, and currently their integration is actively investigated. The two principal integration approaches used are the

* The work described in this paper has been partly supported by MIUR-PRIN 2008 project "Cloud@Home: a New Enhanced Computing Paradigm"

M.R. Guarracino et al. (Eds.): Euro-Par 2010 Workshops, LNCS 6586, pp. 633–640, 2011.
© Springer-Verlag Berlin Heidelberg 2011

GRID-on-cloud (a cloud is exploited to build up and to manage a flexible GRID system [4]) and the *cloud-on-GRID* (the well-known and stable GRID infrastructure is exploited to build up a cloud environment).

In brief, adopting the *GRID-on-cloud* approach the GRID middleware is installed and configured on the top of a cloud system. The cloud "elasticity" makes it possible to add and to remove dynamically nodes to/from the resulting GRID infrastructure. The *cloud-on-GRID* approach is instead based on the development of typical cloud services (e.g., services to start up, to destroy, to manage virtual machines) as GRID services, offered by an existing GRID infrastructure [6,13]. Some of the most famous GRID environments are currently experimenting this solution with dedicated projects [13,10]. One of the tough tasks involved in cloud and GRID integration is to provide the integrated environment with a suitable security infrastructure. This is not trivial and might involve performance losses that could not be tolerable for all classes of users. The authors of this paper are involved in a project that aims to join the cloud-on-GRID and GRID-on-cloud approaches, by implementing a cloud on the top of a GRID, and integrating the cloud resources leased to users in the existing GRID. This solution, named *cloudgrid* [8], wishes to collect the advantages (possibly, not disadvantages) of the two computing paradigms. A previous paper [2] outlines the security requirements for a *cloudgrid* and proposes a possible solution, implemented in an existing prototype environment, PerfCloud [8]. This paper instead deals with the quantitative evaluation of the overheads introduced in the overall GRID infrastructure because of the cloud layer, pointing out the trade-off between the security level provided and the end-user GRID performance. It is worth noting that, even if the security/performance trade-off is a well known issue, very few quantitative studies are available on the topic. Besides exploring the cloud-GRID integration field, this paper is also intended to give a contribution for filling this gap. Almost surprisingly, it will be shown that the advanced authorization mechanism needed in the cloud layer turn out to have negligible impact on the GRID overall performance. The remainder of this paper is organized as follows. The next section illustrates the *cloudgrid* security requirements. In Section 3 the focus will be on the *PerfCloud* framework, showing in particular the architectural solutions used to meet security requirements. Section 4 presents a detailed analysis of the performance corresponding to each available security configuration. The paper closes with the conclusions and a discussion on our future work.

2 *Cloudgrid* Security Requirements

The integration of the GRID and cloud is of great interest, as it allows to re-use the effort spent in the last 20 years on GRID computing. In *PerfCloud*, an existing cloud-on-GRID infrastructure with provision for predictive performance evaluation [8], this problem is solved by integrating the virtual resources offered by the cloud into the underlying GRID. Given an existing computing GRID, users can gain access to virtualized resources (namely, to VCs, virtual clusters of machines) through a cloud interface, and these virtual resources are integrated in the existing GRID and can cooperate with its component systems. Fine-grain access control mechanisms are needed to grant different levels of privilege to users that can play a different role in accessing system resources (both physical and virtual). We have analyzed the different roles and corresponding security policies for the access to both administration and user cloud services, pointing out four different roles: the **System Administrator** and the **Grid User** to respectively manage and use the GRID platform and the physical resources; the **Cloud Administrator** and the **Cloud User** to respectively supervise the cloud environment and configure/use the assigned Virtual Clusters. It is interesting to point out that the a cloud administrator is able to create a new set of virtual clusters and assign them to cloud users, *but does not have administration rights over them, which are owned by the cloud users.* Even if offering to users full rights on the virtual cluster is one of the aims of clouds, this can have a side effect on the *cloudgrid* approach: in fact, a VC administrator has full right access to the VC but he can also manage the new physical GRID site. This represents a big security issue: an user of an hosted site could access physical resources if the cloud administrator does not enforce proper security policies or if it wants to abuse of his role on the physical resources. As a consequence, it is of fundamental importance that the *cloudgrid* approach provides a powerful role-based authorization mechanism.

Data integrity, confidentiality and privacy are not secondary requirements for the proposed architecture. Proper security mechanisms must be enforced not only at application level, but also in the other layers and components of the architecture (e.g., network, transport, service communication, internal application and databases). As we will discuss later, the adoption of secure protocols and encryption techniques has proven to be very useful in such distributed architectures. Furthermore, to fully enable the cloud approach, it is desirable to grant cooperation among users and virtual resources even when they are offered by potentially untrusted domains. So, a federated approach to security and, specifically, to Identity management is required [5].

3 The Security Infrastructure in *PerfCloud*

PerfCloud, our *cloudgrid* implementation, adopts Globus Toolkit 4 (GT4) as GRID middleware, and so we customized and enriched the default Globus configurations in order to meet the security requirements described in the previous section. In particular, GT4 uses the concept of Security Descriptors as standard method for configuring the security requirements and policies of clients and services [11]. GT4 authentication founds on PKI and the adoption of X.509 digital certificates with basic path authentication. The Security Descriptor (SD) makes it possible to specify the communication protocols and some mechanisms to improve security at message level (*Secure Message*), at session and transport level (*Secure Conversation* and *SecureTransport*); they are based on the implementation of WS-Security and WS-SecureConversation specifications [1].

As for the Authorization mechanisms, by default GT4 offers only simple mechanisms: (i) the basic *GRID mapfile* that statically assign to each GRID user an existing O.S. user with its group, (ii) *Embedded PDP*, in which it is possible to define a per-container, a per-service or per-resource mechanism handled by a Local Policy Decision Point (PDP).

However, GT4 also offers a set of APIs to integrate an external PDP, as XACML [12], to support more expressive authorization policies. In a *cloudgrid* archtecture, as the one implemented in *PerfCloud*, the default security solutions offered by Globus do not meet all the security requirements we have outlined above. The first limit is related to the adoption of a basic authentication path, which limits the access only to users authenticated internally to the Virtual Organization. We enriched this solution adopting an extended path validation that supports a federated approach, as described in [3]. Moreover, we extended the authorization mechanism in order to support XACML, and forced the security descriptor to adopt secure communication channels for all the cloud-related service and resources. The main drawback of this approach is an inevitable performance penalty, as complex authorization mechanisms or secure channels may heavily increase the platform overhead. The next section will evaluate quantitatively the actual impact of these choices.

4 Overhead Evaluation

The goal of the following analysis is to evaluate the overhead introduced by the multilayered *cloudgrid* architecture by performing measurements on *PerfCloud*. We have developed a synthetic PerfCloud *NULL* service, which just sends a reply when invoked. The response time measured in several working conditions (corresponding to the different security policies discussed in the previous section) will provide insight on the delay introduced by the *PerfCloud* middleware, unrelated to the service invoked and to the actual tasks to be performed on the target environment.

In order to understand how *PerfCloud* (and the *cloudgrid* approach) affects performance, we measured the response time of the above described target service on both physical and virtual clusters. The comparison between the figures obtained will make it possible to ascertain if the use of a GRID made up of both physical and virtual resources is a reasonable solution, or if the performance penalties incurred are too high.

4.1 Performance Evaluation Methodology

A complex system as the one described, in which different factors are involved in its performance, lends itself well to the *full factorial design* of experiments [7]. The selected factors and their N possible values are shown below:

- **Resource** (N=2), can be *Physical* or *Virtual*
- **Channel (transport)** (N=2), can be *HTTP* or *HTTPS*
- **Auth** (N=3), can be *None*, *Conversation* or *Message*
- **Authz** (N=2), can be *None*, *MapFile* or *XACML*

All the tests were performed in a dedicated environment, where the only source of load is a measurement client invoking the *NULL* service. This client repeats the test 50 times. Then we evaluated the mean, the standard deviation and the confidence interval. The session was repeated three times, and we chose the session with the lowest standard deviation, discarding the remainder.

According to the well-known methodology presented in [7], the next step of the analysis was the definition of a model taking in consideration the *main effects* (the contributions that come from a single factor). Then the *interaction effects* (the contributions that come from the mutual interaction of factors) were gradually introduced, until the evaluated error (meant as the difference between the measured value and the value predicted) could be considered negligible. In the next subsection, we will describe the construction of such model. It should be explicitly pointed out that this measurement technique does not allow to test system behavior under real workloads, as it corresponds to an *ideal* condition, where only the target service uses the target resource. However, this solution has the advantage to be easily reproducible, and so to perform all the tests under exactly the same conditions.

4.2 Experimental Results and Model Evaluation

Table 1 summarizes the performance results obtained for all the possible configurations. Each cell in the table reports the mean value and the confidence interval (in square parenthesis) of the response time, in milliseconds. In order to give an interpretation of the above presented results, we derived the following prediction model that corresponds to the DOE used [7]:

$y = \mu + R_i + C_j + Auth_k + AuthZ_h + Auth - C_{jk} + e_{ijkh}$

where i=(Physical,Virtual), j=(HTTP, HTTPS), k=(None, Conversation, Message), h=(None, MapFile, XACML), and μ is the global mean (i.e., the average

Table 1. Response times for the different configurations (ms)

		Physical Cluster		
AuthZ	Transport	None	Conversation	Message
None	HTTP	106 [102.61, 109.39]	370 [358.51, 381.49]	515 [497.33, 532.67]
	HTTPS	263 [256.50, 269.50]	853 [837.60, 868.40]	612 [590.02, 633.98]
MapFile	HTTP	107 [103.86, 110.14]	367 [356.49, 377.51]	508 [490.72, 525.28]
	HTTPS	262 [255.94, 268.06]	859 [843.31, 874.69]	617 [595.12, 638.88]
XACML	HTTP	108 [104.81, 111.19]	369 [358.87, 379.13]	521 [504.50, 537.50]
	HTTPS	266 [259.67, 272.33]	866 [850.20, 881.80]	627 [604.06, 649.94]
		Virtual Cluster		
AuthZ	Transport	None	Conversation	Message
None	HTTP	85 [81.86, 88.14]	328 [317.06, 338.94]	456 [438.67, 473.33]
	HTTPS	238 [231.96, 244.04]	797 [780.52, 813.48]	556 [535.59, 576.41]
MapFile	HTTP	86 [82.48, 89.52]	322 [311.42, 332.58]	453 [434.33, 471.67]
	HTTPS	239 [232.88, 245.12]	797 [780.35, 813.65]	556 [534.52, 577.48]
XACML	HTTP	86 [82.88, 89.12]	321 [310.09, 331.91]	452 [435.36, 468.64]
	HTTPS	245 [238.58, 251.42]	799 [782.67, 815.33]	563 [538.98, 587.02]

of all values). R, C, $Auth$ and $AuthZ$ (respectively Resource, Channel trasport protocol, Authentication security protocol and Authorization mechanism) are the independent factors that we decided to take into account in the model. They appear in the equation for y, according to the factor-level under evaluation. We will consider all the possible configurations described in the previous section with $R_{Physical}$ and $R_{Virtual}$, C_{HTTP} or C_{HTTPS}, and so on. These factors are all independent, and represent the *main effects* of the prediction model. $Auth - C$ is the contribution to the model that comes from the interaction between the Authentication security protocol and the Trasport protocol, and represents the way in which such coupling affects the mean. So, we will evaluate the different combinations $Auth - C_{None,HTTP}$, $Auth - C_{Conversation,HTTP}$ and so on. They are part of the so-called *interaction effects* of the prediction model. Finally, e is the error introduced by the model, and it depends on all factors taken in consideration. The other interactions (for example, $Auth - AuthZ$ or $Auth - R$) were computed, but not included in the model, because of their negligible impact. In fact, the model that includes only $Auth - C$ *explains for* the 99.85% of the measured values, as shown in Table 2. For brevity's sake, we present below just the results of the ANOVA analysis of the obtained model (Table 2). In this table we have reported for every effect the sum of the squares of all values (second column) and the variation of y as it is *explained* by the different effect. For example, in the considered model the main effect Channel *explains* the model for the 26.99% while the factor Authentication (Auth) *explains* the model for the 59.60%. In conclusion, the correctness of the prevision model is supported by the value of the error variation, which is under 1%. Further analysis, both visual and statistical, whose details are not shown here for brevity, shows that the residuals are uniformly distributed around zero, have homogeneous variance and that there is no polarization of the results.

Table 2. ANOVA table

Component	Sum of Squares	Variation (%)
Resource (R)	927,068.06	0.91%
Channel (C)	27,565,312.50	26.99%
Authentication (Auth)	60,868,636.11	59.60%
Authorization (AuthZ)	6,211.11	0.01%
Auth-C Interaction	12,606,925.00	12.34%
Errors	149,862.50	0.15%

4.3 Performance Considerations

The above model points out clearly the fundamental sources of overhead in a fully functional *cloudgrid* solution. The first result obtained, which was not completely unexpected, is the low impact of virtualization on overhead. In practice, there is no difference (in terms of security overhead) between a service hosted on a physical cluster and on a virtual one. In fact, the ratio of variation, explained by the factor R, is 0.91%. Moreover, looking at the results in Table 1, we can note that the invocation of a service on a virtual resource performs even better than the corresponding request on a physical one. This counterintuitive behavior is due to the fact that modern virtual engines introduce very small overhead (in our test, we used Xen 3, which declares less than 5% overhead). This can be compensated and sometimes overcome by the performance gain obtained by OS noise reduction. The virtual images, being targeted to a specific appliance, can exclude generic OS management services, which are instead needed in a general-purpose physical environment. It should noted, however, that we have implemented a service that does not stress much the system and the virtualization environment. For other kind of services, e.g., bandwidth-intensive ones, virtualization could become the bottleneck. A performance comparison between virtual and physical clusters is out of the scope of this paper.

Also the introduction of advanced authorization mechanisms as XACML, needed to deal with the different roles of the users, surprisingly, does not have a great effect on the overall system performance. The *AuthZ* factor simply does not affect the overhead, as shown by the ANOVA Table (less than 0.01% of variation explained). This can be explained by considering that even the basic GSI authorization mechanism needs to instantiate Java objects to take an authorization decision. As a result, the time required to invoke external authorization services is dwarfed by the time necessary to load the chain of GSI objects.

Unlike the previous factors, the Channel transport and the Authentication security protocol affect heavily system performance, both on virtual and physical resources. The model analysis shows that the introduced overhead depends on two factors: the adoption of security protocols at transport layer, i.e., the choice between HTTP and HTTPS, and the security protocols adopted at message layer, i.e., the cryptography applied to the XML-based SOAP message. Both factors have a great impact (with a variation on the model of about 30% and 60%, respectively). Also their interaction has a high impact (about 10%).

Considered that the measured overhead shows a minimum value of 85 ms and a maximum value of 866 ms (a value about 10 times higher), the parameters setup in the Security Descriptors should be performed with great care. From a security point of view, we can note that security at transport and security at message layer are independent of one another. They both aim at granting confidentiality and integrity of information, and they can reach the same result in different ways. The secure transport layer (HTTPS) has a lower impact on performance and, in terms of security, is considered equivalent to the message layer one. So the best solution is to disable completely the message layer security. When this is not possible, it should be avoided to enable both the security layers.

Some interesting considerations can also be done on the interaction of the two factors. Analyzing the result table (Table 1), it is possible to note that, enabling the transport layer, the performance of `Secure Conversation` (which offers a lower security level) becomes worse than the performance offered by the `Secure Message` approach. So, if for any reason both Transport and Message layer security must be enabled, the lowest overhead can be obtained by enabling the message level security protocol, which also offers the highest security level.

5 Conclusions and Future Work

In this paper we have considered the security issues linked to the use of a *cloudgrid* approach. We showed through extensive experimentation on our prototype *PerfCloud* that, in contrast with intuition, the *cloudgrid* approach does not introduce perceptible overhead, notwithstanding the presence of a virtualization layer and the need for complex authorization mechanisms. We have also proposed a trade-off analysis between performance and security.

Our plans for future research include the extension of the proposed analysis to the case of federated identities, which we outlined in another paper [3] as another necessary component in a complete security infrastructure for cloud and GRID integration.

References

1. Atkinson, B., et al.: Ws-security specification, web services security 1.0 (April 2002)
2. Casola, V., Lettiero, R., Rak, M., Villano, U.: Access control in cloud on grid: the perfcloud case study. To appear in the Proc. of SPCC 2010 (2010)
3. Casola, V., Rak, M., Villano, U.: Identity federation in cloud computing. In: Proc. of SPEDA 2010, Atlanta (August 2010)
4. Cherkasova, L., Gupta, D., Vahdat, A.: Optimizing grid site manager performance with virtual machines. In: Proc. of the 3rd USENIX Workshop on Real Large Distributed Systems (WORLDS 2006) (2006)
5. Cloud Security Alliance: Security guidance for critical areas of focus in cloud computing (2009)
6. Foster, I.T., Freeman, T., Keahey, K., Scheftner, D., Sotomayor, B., Zhang, X.: Virtual clusters for grid communities. In: CCGRID, pp. 513–520. IEEE Computer Society, Los Alamitos (2006)
7. Jain, R.: Art of Computer Systems Performance Analysis Techniques For Experimental Design Measurements Simulation And Modeling. Wiley Computer Publishing John Wiley & Sons, Chichester (May 1991)
8. Mancini, E.P., Rak, M., Villano, U.: Perfcloud: Grid services for performance-oriented development of cloud computing applications. In: Reddy, S. (ed.) WETICE, pp. 201–206. IEEE Computer Society, Los Alamitos (2009)
9. Mell, P., Grance, T.: The nist definition of cloud computing (2009)
10. Purdue University: Wispy project (2009), `http://www.rcac.purdue.edu/teragrid/resources/#wispy`
11. The Globus Security Team: Globus toolkit version 4, security: Authorization framework (2005), `http://www.globus.org/toolkit/docs/4.0/security/authzframe/`
12. The OASIS technical commitee: Xacml: extensible access control markup language (2005), `http://www.oasisopen.org/committees/xacml/repository/`
13. University of Chicago: Nimbus project (2009), `http://workspace.globus.org/clouds/nimbus.html`

A Distributed and Collaborative Dynamic Load Balancer for Virtual Machine

Jonathan Rouzaud-Cornabas

Laboratoire d'Informatique Fondamentale d'Orléans
Ensi de Bourges – Université d'Orléans
88 bd Lahitolle, 18020 Bourges cedex, France
jonathan.rouzaud-cornabas@univ-orleans.fr

Abstract. With the number of services using virtualization and clouds growing faster and faster, it is common to mutualize thousands of virtual machines within one distributed system. Consequently, the virtualized services, softwares, hardwares and infrastructures share the same physical resources, thus the performance of one depends of the resources usage of others. We propose a solution for VM load balancing (and rebalancing) based on the observation of the resources quota and the dynamic usage that leads to better balancing of resources. As it is not possible to have a single scheduler for the whole cloud and to avoid a single point of failure, our scheduler uses distributed and collaborative scheduling agents. We present scenarios simulating various cloud resources and VM usage experimented on our testbed P2P architecture.

1 Introduction

Nowadays, server farms are popular for running a large range of services from web hosting to e-commerce sites or enterprise systems. The common way to deal with those growing server farms is to mutualize services, softwares, hardwares and infrastructure using virtualization technologies. However, when multiple virtual machines share the same physical resources, the performance of each VM and its embedded application depends on the resources usage of other VM running on the physical host. So, the management of VM becomes critical. Currently, most of clouds (and grids) schedulers are solely based on quota negotiations and do not take into account real resources usage.

First, section 1.1 introduces the related works. After, we present our goals and confront them with the previous work in the section 1.2. Then, section 2 presents the architecture of our dynamic load balancer and explains how we efficiently place virtual machine to a host. Then, we come back on our implementation (section 3) and the experiments (section 4) that we have done through simulations to validate our algorithms and architecture.

1.1 Related Works

The scheduling of jobs on a grid is a NP-Complete problem. Moreover, the result of the scheduling process is not optimal too. It means that the schedulers are not

M.R. Guarracino et al. (Eds.): Euro-Par 2010 Workshops, LNCS 6586, pp. 641–648, 2011.
© Springer-Verlag Berlin Heidelberg 2011

searching for the optimal solution but a one that is good "enough" [1]. Dynamic scheduling algorithms are useful when it is not possible to predict the behavior of a task [2] and is the best algorithm to maximize the resource usage.

Work stealing has a better scalability and fault tolerance through the use of a decentralized approach [6] than work sharing (centralized). The work stealing method allows idle consumers to search among the other consumers to find additional work.

One kind of schedulers are P2P schedulers [3]. Within the peer-to-peer model, the cloud is seen as a set of nodes (i.e. peer) that makes available for each other a part (or the totality) of their resources. The main advantage of the P2P is that it does not contain a central coordination point and thus, avoid a single point of failure.

The live migration process allows a virtual machine to move from a host to another one without being stopped. From a virtualization point of view, a cloud is seen as a shared and distributed environment where concurrent users run VM on. Those VM have a heterogeneous behavior e.g. a website with peak traffic or a graphical interface. Accordingly, the resource usage can change at any given time, so taking into account the dynamic resources is essential. Some academic works proposed VM schedulers i.e. VM placement [7,5]. Automatic reallocation for virtual machine [9] i.e. VM migration, has been proposed too.

1.2 Motivations

There is some automatic solutions that allow sharing the load of multiple VM on the heterogeneous and distributed system but they mainly are dedicated to cluster or grid computing and not clouds. As VM behaviors can not be predicted due to those complex behaviors and non-deterministic events such as interactive input/output, dynamic approach is the best choice. In clouds, "black-box" monitoring is needed because the VM are heterogeneous and instrumenting them is too much time consuming. Moreover, with VM provided by users, instrumentations required to trust all the users within the cloud and that is impossible. Furthermore, clouds require the allocation and reallocation processes to be operating systems and applications agnostic. In addition, the placement must remain "good" enough for the maximum period of time to reduce the cost due to VM migration. Furthermore, dynamic load balancer on a cloud is a scalability challenge as one load balancer can not allocate VM for the whole cloud. But, distributed dynamic load balancer can achieve such goal.

To reach the goal of a decentralized virtual machine load balancer for clouds, we introduce our architecture enabling:

1. The monitoring of the VM and the hosts;
2. The placement of the VM on the best fitting host based on dynamic resources-centric algorithm;
3. The migration of VM if the load on a host is increasing, a special resource [1] is needed, a maintenance operation is taken place;

[1] For example, a VM with a GPU.

4. No single point of failure through the use of a distributed P2P architecture. The load balancer agents can cooperate together to share the load of the placement processes based on a work stealing algorithm;

Furthermore, in [4], the authors state that traditional distributed and dynamic load balancing methods have the following issues: they do not assume the heterogeneity of used hardware; processes, i.e. VM in our case, are assigned onto nodes based on nodes free resources only; many of them consider just the processor utilization as the only resource. Thus, our dynamic load balancing algorithm takes into account the heterogeneity of the hardware, takes into account free, static and quota resources for the processor and memory utilization.

2 Dynamic Load Balancer for Virtual Machine

2.1 Architecture

Within our architecture, each node provides a set of services as a hypervisor or a load balancer. Those services allow the placement and migration processes but also the collaboration between load balancers. Another service is a distributed hash table [8] that stores, distributes and replicates meta-data related to virtual machines (running state, location, etc) on each peer.

2.2 Monitoring Hosts

Using the static, free and used resources of a host and the running VM combined with the soft [2] and hard [3] resources quota, we are able to compute a score that is more relevant than a classical weight given to each host based on their static resources (and other static metrics).

In order to balance the load of the nodes of our architecture, a score is computed for each node. The computation of the score needs to be quick and does not require too much resources. But in the same time, the score needs to closely reflect the amount of resources used by each VM. To reach those goals, we introduced our score algorithm. It can be extended on-demand to take into account other resources than CPU and memory usage like network or hard drive bandwidth. It is divided in 2 parts. A **static score** that takes into account static resources e.g. the amount of CPU core on a node and the resources (soft and hard) quota reserved for a virtual machine. A **dynamic score** that is based on dynamic resources e.g. the amount of free memory.

The algorithm that computes score takes two arguments. A structure *host* containing the static resources of the node and a list of virtual machine *vmlist* that contains VM quota resources. For each virtual machine in the list, the RAM and CPU soft quota is added and multiplied by a static parameter α [4], then the result for each virtual machine is added into the variable $static\_vm\_soft$. The

[2] The amount of resources that is dedicated to the virtual machine.

[3] The maximum amount of resources that the VM can use.

[4] All the static parameters are set through experimentations (see section 4).

same thing is done with the hard quota into the variable *static_vm_hard* and the static parameter β. Secondary, the *static_host_score* is computed by dividing the processor speed $host(CPU)_{speed\_in\_Mhz}$ by a static parameter γ then it is multiplied by the number of core $host(CPU)_{number\_of\_core}$. The final static score *static_score* for the given *host* with the list of virtual machine *vmlist* is computed by summing the amount of memory to the result of last computation.

The the dynamic part of the score takes into account the free resources on the node and the resources used by the running VM. Our approach is based on a global scheduler on all cores of each host but our score can be extended to take into account the need of a dedicated core (or a part of it). For each CPU cores, it gets the amount of free CPU on it and sums them. Then it multiplies this result by the static variable (γ) and sums the result to the amount (in Kb) of RAM free. For each virtual machine, it retrieves the amount of CPU and memory used. Then it multiplies the amount of CPU used by all VM by a static value (β) and then sums it with the amount of RAM free. Finally, the dynamic score is computed by dividing the amount of free resources by the number of used resources by the VM.

The static part of the score is multiplied by a static value (κ) and then adds to the dynamic score that gives the score of a given node. Our approach permits a better placement and helps to limit the needs of migration by taking into account resources that can be potentially used by the VM (the soft and hard quota).

2.3 Virtual Machine Placement and Migration

The purpose of VM placement is to share the load of multiple VM on a cloud. When a new VM is added to the cloud, the placement algorithm looks for a node that fits the static resources requirements of the VM. We introduce an algorithm that takes into account the resources of each node to have a more efficient load balancing using the previously introduced score (see section 2.2) The algorithm can be divided into three parts:

1. the algorithm computes the global score of each node on the cloud (resources discovery).
2. based on the result of the global score, a node is elected (resources selecting).
3. after checking if the elected computer has enough resources i.e. the algorithm checks if the soft quota are respected on the host, the VM is started. If there is not enough resources, the algorithm is relaunched with an updated nodes list that excludes the previously elected node (placement).

The purpose of the migration algorithm is to automatically move a started VM from a node to another one to keep a "good enough" placement of the virtual machines on the distributed system. The objectives are: reduce the load on a host (i.e. its dynamic score), move a VM to a new host with more resources, move a VM to a new host with specialized resources (like a GPU) and move a VM to a new host before putting into maintenance the current one. The algorithm can be divided into two steps: electing a VM, if needed i.e. no VM given by the event and then, using the placement algorithm, to migrate the VM. In the first step, when no VM is given, a list of all VM running on the host is built and it is sorted from lower score to the highest one.

2.4 Decentralized Load Balancer for Virtual Machine

Our work stealing algorithm implementation is straightforward. First, each load balancer agent has two queue:

- a **local queue:** for the virtual machine to-place that the local load balancer agent is placing itself i.e. a list of task reserved for the local load balancer.
- a **shared queue:** for the virtual machine to-place that can be placed either by the local load balancer agent or by other ones through the use of work stealing.

To fit it in our decentralized peer-to-peer network, the second queue is available as a service for other load balancer agents. The local agent reserves a chunk of VM to-place for itself (by removing them from the shared queue and adding them to the local queue). When the local agent has placed all the virtual machine in the local queue, it preempts another buck. If there is no more task in the shared queue, it randomly chooses a victim load balancer agent and tries to take a buck from it. By having the two queue (local, shared), we have a better scalability with a limited latency due to lock. Moreover, we respect our goal of no point of failure by using a distributed algorithm.

3 Implementation

Architecture

Our P2P architecture is implemented using the Java based library JXTA because of its services of peer and service discovery and multi-cast communication. The major components of our architecture are the service components that implement one of the elementary tasks requested by the algorithms.

- **Score:** it computes the score of the node.
- **FreeResource:** it returns a set containing the amount of free resources.
- **LaunchVM:** it checks if a given VM can be started on the current node and starts it.
- **Migration:** it checks if a given VM can be migrated to the current node. If it is the case, the service migrates the VM.
- **LoadBalancer:** it receives to-place virtual machines. Then, it uses the placement algorithm to place each virtual machine on the cloud. Moreover, if in idle mode, it steals VM to-place from other load balancer.
- **Stealing:** it returns a buck of virtual machines that are not preempted by the local load balancer agent i.e. a buck that comes from the shared queue.

By using dynamic discovery service, our proposal can easily fit in a cloud where resources are added or removed. Some services like Score are also available through a multi-cast address allowing to send a request to all the agents at one time and without discovery process. It permits to have an efficient scaling score service because of the absence of concurrency in the placement and migration algorithms. Furthermore, the DHT allows to share the list of all the running VM.

4 Experimentation

To validate our approach based on a P2P network of agents and our algorithms, we have implemented our model on a custom cloud testbed.

4.1 Architecture Simulation

To simulate different nodes and virtual machines, we have chosen to implement three different resources scenarios for the nodes (see table 1) and two for the VM (see table 2).

Table 1. Host Configuration

	Nb of Core	Mhz	RAM in Gb
Host_1	2	3.2	4
Host_2	4	2.6	16
Host_3	8	2	32

Table 2. VM Configuration and Simulation Scenario

	CPU in Mhz	RAM in Gb
VM_1	300	0.512
VM_2	600	1.024

	Nb Host_1	Nb Host_2	Nb Host_3	Nb VM_1	Nb VM_2
#1. Cluster	10	0	0	10	10
#2. Heterogeneous cluster	5	3	3	40	20
#3. Larger Heterogeneous cluster	15	15	10	100	50
#4. Cloud	55	55	30	700	300

We have done four simulations as shown in the table 2.

The purpose was to test our architecture in different case of usage (homogeneous, heterogeneous) and to test its scalability (number of nodes, virtual machines, placement and migration choices, distributed load balancer). In our simulation, we uses the following static parameters for the score algorithm:

- $\alpha = 1$, $\beta = 1$: to give the same importance to the soft quota of processor or memory.
- $\gamma = 0.75$: because we want to give more weight to the virtual machine resources quota than the static resources on the node.
- $\delta = 1$: to give the same importance to the amount of free processor or free memory.

Moreover, we randomly increase or reduce CPU and memory usage of each VM every 30 seconds to simulate dynamic load.

4.2 Results

As shown on the figure 1 and 2, the amount of time taken by the startup process for a virtual machine without cooperative schedulers grows linearly with the number of nodes on the cloud. Indeed, with large size distributed systems, most of the interactions between agents can be parallelized. When a larger number of nodes (simulation #3 and #4) are part of the cloud, more interactions can be done in parallel on different agents and thus the overall throughput increases i.e. the number of VM placement in a given time grows.

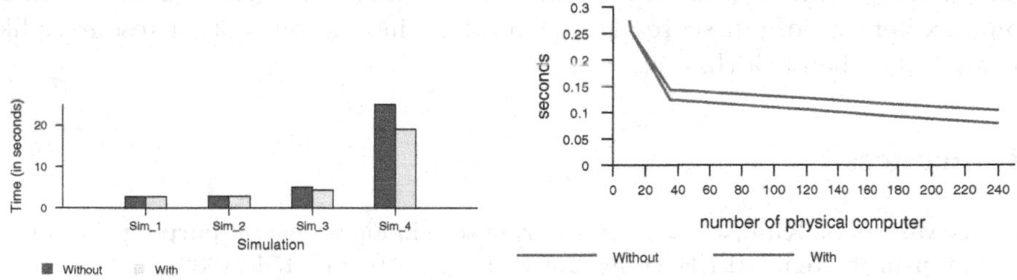

Fig. 1. Placement of a new Virtual Machine

Fig. 2. Placement of a new Virtual Machine

We compute the average time between the detection of an overloaded node and its solving. Each simulation was kept running for one day to evaluate if the placement of virtual machines was "good" enough. On the 1st simulation, no migration happens. During the second simulation, an average of five overloaded nodes has been detected. It took five seconds to detect the overload and solving it. During the third simulation, two migrations have been required and it took four seconds to solve it. On the last simulation, 15 migrations for the 1,000 virtual machines has been required and they took 19 seconds each. Consequently, we state that the placement of virtual machines on the distributed system is sufficiently "good" because the number of migrations is low.

With cooperative schedulers, both placement and migration processes are speed up as shown on the figures 1 and 2. In the two first simulation scenarios, it does not improve as there is overhead due to the placement process. But, it reduces the time for the placement of a VM from 5 to 4.34 seconds for the simulation #3 and from 25 to 19 for the simulation #4. It can be done because a vast majority of services can be parallelized.

5 Conclusion

Our paper presents a novel load balancer dedicated for VM on clouds. It is based on P2P architecture allowing a fully decentralized model. The load balancing decisions are based on dynamic-resources centric algorithm that computes a score.

This score is based on both static and dynamic resources usage of processor and memory but also uses the resources quota associated with each VM. Moreover, the load balancer agents can cooperate together through a distributed and decentralized facility. We have implemented our model using Java and JXTA. Then, we implement it within our cloud testbed to evaluate our model efficiency. As we show, the simulation results are encouraging. Indeed, we do not see any scalability bottleneck and the balancing of resources works great.

Futur works will tackle the over-migration issue when a VM is migrating constantly from a node to another. The fault tolerance of the stealing algorithm is still an open question for our work stealing algorithm. Another futur work will be to test our solution on a real cloud. Futhermore, we need to test more complex versions of our score algorithm taking into account other resources like network, I/O bandwidth, etc.

References

1. Casavant, T.L., Kuhl, J.G.: A taxonomy of scheduling in general-purpose distributed computing systems. IEEE Trans. Softw. Eng. 14(2), 141–154 (1988)
2. El-Rewini, H., Lewis, T.G., Ali, H.H.: Task scheduling in parallel and distributed systems, p. 290. Prentice-Hall, Inc., Upper Saddle River (1994)
3. Foster, I., Iamnitchi, A.: On death, taxes, and the convergence of peer-to-peer and grid computing. In: Kaashoek, M.F., Stoica, I. (eds.) IPTPS 2003. LNCS, vol. 2735, pp. 118–128. Springer, Heidelberg (2003)
4. Koutny, T., Safarik, J.: Load redistribution in heterogeneous systems. In: International Conference on Autonomic and Autonomous Systems, vol. 0, p. 24 (2007)
5. Krsul, I., Ganguly, A., Zhang, J., Fortes, J.A.B., Figueiredo, R.J.: Vmplants: Providing and managing virtual machine execution environments for grid computing. In: SC 2004: Proceedings of the 2004 ACM/IEEE Conference on Supercomputing, p. 7. IEEE Computer Society, Washington, DC, USA (2004)
6. Murata, Y., Takizawa, H., Inaba, T., Kobayashi, H.: A distributed and cooperative load balancing mechanism for large-scale p2p systems. In: SAINT-W 2006: Proceedings of the International Symposium on Applications on Internet Workshops, pp. 126–129. IEEE Computer Society, Washington, DC, USA (2006)
7. Song, Y., Wang, H., Li, Y., Feng, B., Sun, Y.: Multi-tiered on-demand resource scheduling for vm-based data center. In: IEEE International Symposium on Cluster Computing and the Grid, vol. 0, pp. 148–155 (2009)
8. Stoica, I., Morris, R., Liben-Nowell, D., Karger, D., Frans Kaashoek, M., Dabek, F., Balakrishnan, H.: Chord: A scalable peer-to-peer lookup service for internet applications. IEEE Transactions on Networking 11 (February 2003)
9. Wood, T., Shenoy, P., Venkataramani, A., Yousif, M.: Sandpiper: Black-box and gray-box resource management for virtual machines. Computer Networks 53(17), 2923–2938 (2009); Virtualized Data Centers

Towards GPGPU Assisted Computing in Virtualized Environments

Thilo Schmitt, Alexander Weggerle, Christian Himpel, and Peter Schulthess

Institute of Distributed Systems
Ulm University
James-Franck-Ring O-27/3210, 89069 Ulm, Germany
thilo.schmitt@uni-ulm.de
http://www-vs.informatik.uni-ulm.de/

Abstract. General Purpose Computation on Graphics Processing Units (GPGPU) makes it possible to use the massive computing power of modern graphics cards for generic high-performance computing. However, the new virtualization technologies will typically not support high-performance graphics cards and as a consequence GPGPU resources can not be used in typical virtualization setups. In this paper we present an approach to introduce accelerated 3D graphics support as well as GPGPU facilities into virtualized environments. We present our proof-of-concept "VirtGL" and discuss architectural considerations and a lean, straight-forward way of implementation. We then give an outlook on how this approach can easily be adopted for virtualizing GPGPU APIs like CUDA, Stream, OpenCL and alike.

Keywords: GPGPU, virtualization, virtualized 3D acceleration, High Performance Computing.

1 Introduction

Accelerated graphics access is a relatively new feature in the virtualization technology realm. Only a few virtualization solutions currently support full 3D-accelerated graphics. It is therefore difficult to do General Purpose Computation on Graphics Processing Units (GPGPU) in virtualized environments.

We suggest an approach for implementing fully accelerated 3D-graphics support. Our approach relays graphics commands through the virtualization layer to the readily available graphics card interface of the host system. As it avoids thick and multiple software layers the resulting implementation turns out to be fast, lean, robust and straight-forward.

"VirtGL" is a software package which brings accelerated 3D-graphics to virtualized guest operating systems. It reuses existing abstractions provided by the hosting operating system and lets them reappear in the guest environment. In other words: A "tunnel" between the guest's graphics interface abstraction and the pre-existing functionality in the host is created. With VirtGL we are able

M.R. Guarracino et al. (Eds.): Euro-Par 2010 Workshops, LNCS 6586, pp. 649–656, 2011.
© Springer-Verlag Berlin Heidelberg 2011

to provide high-end High Performance Computing facilities in virtualized environments. VirtGL integrates GPGPU techniques with virtualization technology, with low implementation costs as well as with minimal performance overhead.

2 Environment

In this section we give an overview of the environment, in which we have established VirtGL. We show the virtualization solution chosen (QEMU), the graphics card programming interface we use (OpenGL) and the operating system we targeted for a prototype driver on the virtualization guest side (Rainbow OS).

2.1 Virtualization

Several virtualization solutions are currently available for productive use. To add our new VirtGL device emulation to the virtualization software it needs to be available as source code. As one of the most important goals of our operating system project is a lean system, adding new complexity besides a new driver to our operating system was not an option. Thus, paravirtualization is not viable for our purposes. Accordingly, only the following virtualization solutions are considered to satisfy our requirements: VirtualBox Open Source Edition, Xen (version 3.0 or later), QEMU, Kernel Virtual Machine (KVM), Bochs.

The decision was made in favor of QEMU, because it is viable even without hardware virtualization. Device emulation modules in QEMU can easily be ported to KVM, Xen HVM and VirtualBox [9].

Our VirtGL device emulation uses memory mapped IO (MMIO) as the device's interface for the communication between the guest operating system and the host. QEMU devices can register such MMIO regions and corresponding handlers to be called on MMIO operations. Whenever the guest reads from or writes to a MMIO region, QEMU calls the according registered handlers. As a consequence the execution traps into QEMU. To determine the result of the access, the registered handler is called and the result is passed to the quest. So every read or write access to this region is immediately handled by the emulated device within QEMU.

2.2 Graphics Card Programming

The Open Graphics Library (OpenGL) [5] is a platform and programming language independent API. OpenGL is designed to offer a single and uniform interface to access various different graphics cards. To compensate for the different feature sets of the cards the API is capable to emulate in software missing features of the hardware. OpenGL programs use this API to view 2D- and 3D-data and images. The API does also support the use of shaders. Shaders are streaming processors, specially designed to execute a huge number of floating point operations, which are typically required to render a 3D scene. OpenGL shader language (GLSL) is used to program the shaders.

Shader programming can also be used for genereal purpose computation on graphics hardware (GPGPU). High-level abstractions were created to alleviate the programmer's job. With, for example, CUDA [8] and OpenCL [4] high-level languages, libraries and toolchains are made available to support the GPU programmer. These tools and interfaces are finally based on the above mentioned shader programming facilities like GLSL (as part of OpenGL).

2.3 Operating System

Rainbow OS is a transactional distributed memory (TDM) operating system for commodity 64-bit multicore architectures. The PCs constitute a cluster connected via Gigabit Ethernet [11]. Rainbow OS is almost completely implemented in a Java-like language. With our locally developed high-speed compiler SJC [1], Rainbow OS compiles into native x86 code, thereby avoiding the need for a Java Virtual Machine (JVM). Objects are accessed natively without interposed middleware layers or wrapper classes. So Rainbow OS offers to system programmers and application programmers the benefits of a strongly type-safe language coupled with fast runtime performance. Code and data structures of all applications as well as the kernel are accessible and shared by all nodes of the cluster (single system image) using a distributed memory abstraction. In order to guarantee a consistent memory perspective for both operating system components and application tasks Rainbow OS implements a unique transactional consistency mechanism [13].

3 VirtGL

3.1 Architecture

The initial and most important idea behind VirtGL was to develop a lean solution with low code complexity. Another important design goal was to develop the QEMU part without modifying the core of QEMU. We needed a module that was easily interchangeable between subsequent versions of QEMU and at a later time easily transferable to KVM.

VirtGL comprises two components: the *VirtGL device* and the *VirtGL driver*. The VirtGL device is a new emulated device, which is added as a module to the virtualization software. From the perspective of the guest system it is a hardware OpenGL interface. This is VirtGL's guest-system independent core. On the guest system's side a device driver for the VirtGL device is needed. That driver is guest-system specific by nature.

Important to note is, that the interface of the VirtGL device essentially is an OpenGL interface "in hardware" and the VirtGL driver making this interface accessible exposes itself as an OpenGL interface, too. The driver's interface can be directly used by the applications. Thus, particularly we *remove* the need for several layers of interfaces and wrappers in the guest system. Usually operating systems have a stack of interface levels with successively more abstract semantics:

- the graphics card exposes an intricate interface, which is vendor specific or even model specific,
- the device driver exposes an interface, which is typical for graphics, drivers and often is vendor specific,
- an abstraction interface that allows uniform access to all drivers,
- often several additional wrappers or filters,
- the actual graphics interface in standardized way (e.g. OpenGL) to be used by applications.

With VirtGL the situation is reduced to (cf. figure 1):

- the VirtGL driver exposes a standard graphics interface (e.g. OpenGL)
- the device driver in the guest OS exposes a standard graphics interface (e.g. OpenGL), which is at the same time the actual graphics interface to be used

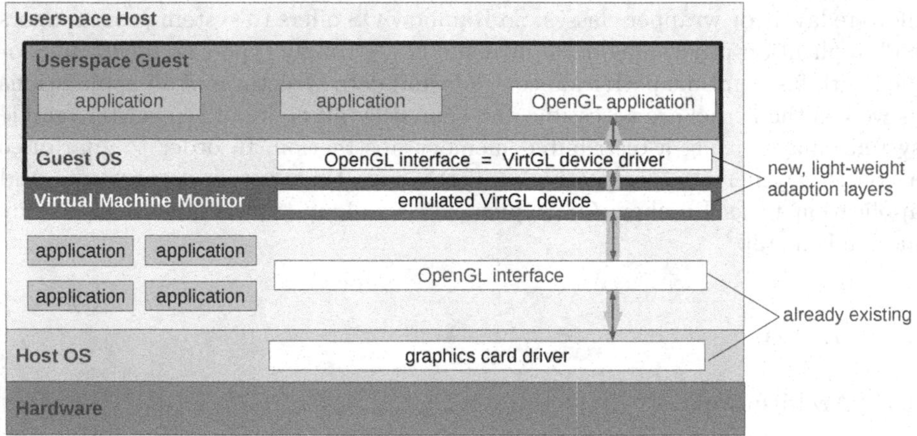

Fig. 1. VirtGL architecture

Not only the number of layers and interfaces is reduced. Also the mapping between the layers is much simpler. This is due to the fact that semantics do not change from one layer to the next; merely the way of identifying functions and passing parameters is different. Thus relaying a call from the software side to the hardware side is simple and efficiently implementable.

3.2 Implementation

Few changes were actually necessary in QEMU. From the point of view of QEMU this simply results in the addition of a simple PCI device. The changes essentially consist of: (1) the VirtGL emulation module: a C-file and its header file ("VirtGL core"); (2) a little patch that instructs QEMU to load the module just added; (3) adjusting the Makefile to link against certain libraries (OpenGL, window management).

The VirtGL core registers some callback routines during initialization time. These callback functions handle intercepted accesses to memory mapped I/O regions (see above). It is this piece of software that ultimately issues the OpenGL commands to the host system's OpenGL interface. The intercepted memory accesses tell the VirtGL core which OpenGL functions to call and which parameters to pass.

The guest system - in our case the locally developed Rainbow OS - merely provides a device driver for the VirtGL device. Because the VirtGL device is emulated as a traditional PCI device all the preexisting features in the operating system dealing with PCI device enumeration and configuration can be used. The VirtGL device is configured and commands are issued by reading and writing to MMIO regions. The device's PCI configuration space reports two MMIO regions which are required by the VirtGL device.

The first and most important region is the so called "command region", typically one page (4 KB) in size. All accesses are intercepted by QEMU and delegated to the VirtGL device emulation module. Such accesses result in a state change of the emulated VirtGL device. The second region is called the "direct data region". It has a configurable size, we currently chose to spend 2 MB. There is a corresponding memory block assigned and none of the accesses to this region are intercepted by QEMU. The direct data region is not really physical memory observable by the guest system. Rather it should be perceived as device memory embedded in the emulated PCI device (VirtGL graphics device) - very much like dedicated graphics RAM on real graphics cards.

Before an OpenGL command is issued, the parameters are written to the direct data region and then the command code assigned to the required OpenGL function is written to the command region and suitably intercepted. Thus, the device emulation will remain inactive as long as not all parameters are written. Writing the command code is intercepted to allow an immediate response. Because all parameters are known and the command code specifies the OpenGL function to be called, the command is immediately carried out.

3.3 Measurements

The performance of VirtGL was tested using the well-known GLXgears[1]. For a maximum of comparability the native GLXgears implementation was ported to Rainbow OS and QEMU.

In the virtualized QEMU environment of the guest system, the hardware timers and clocks might not provide correct values. However, during the measurements it is essential to have a reliable clock, so the code that determines the frames per second rate (FPS), was moved to the QEMU counterpart. Effectively, the time between two buffer swappings is measured to determine the FPS values. Due to the timing issues we are faced with in the virtualized guest system, the rotation of the gears was done in every frame with a constant angle[2].

[1] Part of the Mesa 3D Graphics Library 7.7

[2] The Mesa GLXgears implementation calculates dynamically a rotation angle, but this has no impact on the performance.

The test system was a Lenovo Thinkpad T410 with a Nvida NVS 3100M graphics card and an Intel Core i7 M620 CPU and 4 GB of RAM. The operating system was a recent Linux kernel (2.6.32.9) with the proprietary Nvidia graphics driver (190.53). The CPU frequency was set to 1.20 GHz in the first test and to 2.67 GHz in a second test run. The Linux host system was booted using the kernel parameter "`nosmp`" to suppress the influence of optimizations that could be achieved with more than one processor.

The tests ran for approximately one minute printing every 5 seconds the current FPS rate. Afterwards the frame rate was averaged over the measuring points. At the CPU frequency of 1.20 GHz we achieved a performance of approximately 93% (Rainbow 5280 FPS and native 5670). With an over 2 times higher CPU frequency (2.67 GHz) the performance of VirtGL was about 99% (Rainbow 5877 FPS and native 5903 FPS). The performance difference can be explained with the overhead of the virtualization. The higher the CPU frequency, the smaller the weighting of the overhead. The outcome shows that the CPU frequency has only a small impact and can be neglected.

4 Perspective

VirtGL currently supports only a tiny subset of OpenGL functions. We plan to extend the set of supported functions extensively in the future. Especially supporting more texture-related functions and integration of shader support is one of the most urgent needed extensions in VirtGL.

We also expect that relaying the shader functions would have only marginal negative effect on overall performance. The shader-related functions will typically only be used in the initialization part of the program and very rarely in the later program runtime. Texture operations might be used more frequently in GPGPU applications and the amount of data to be moved could be much more compared to typical 3D graphics applications. How this behavior impacts the overall performance remains unclear at the moment. Due to the fact, that VirtGL at the moment introduces one additional data copying step might be a downside. Preliminary measurements indicate that the impact is not as big as suspected at first. Thus, some refinements targeted on this issue might be needed and are currently in the evaluation phase.

As soon as all texture- and shader-related functions can be relayed from the guest to the host system, VirtGL will immediately be ready for the GPGPU use. A refined version of VirtGL would enable HPC applications in virtualized environments to use the GPGPU technology. Carrying the thought a bit further, VirtGL could enable GPGPU usage for HPC clouds: Infrastructure-as-a-Service providers could make GPGPU facilities available within their node instances, which are realized via virtualization.

5 Related Work

The research to provide accelerated 3D graphics to virtual machines is going on since several years. There are a number of different solutions. The most common solution is [7], which describes a way of reusing device drivers from the host in the virtual machine. This is a low-level approach which offers direct access to the host device driver. The authors made no attempt to use this approach to graphics cards. Due to the fact that the device driver has to be exclusively used by the virtual machine this approach is rather inappropriate for graphics cards, unless there are multiple graphics cards installed. This is also true for the approach of allowing a direct access to the graphics card itself from within the guest operating system.

There are a number of publications related to replacing the original library with a stub which forwards the OpenGL command stream. VirtualGL [12] is designed to provide accelerated 3D-graphics for remote display software like VNC. The data is sent over a network connection. This is a by far more indirect solution than the VirtGL approach; latencies can be expected to be dramatically higher and due to the interposed network connection overall performance should be considerably lower. A similar approach has WireGL [3], system for scalable interactive rendering on clusters. It focuses on distributing rendering resources and thus is not geared towards virtualization appliances.

In the past years several programs were published specializing in accelerated graphics for virtual machine guests. VMGL [6] uses the WireGL network protocol for communication between the guest and the host. Apart from displaying 3D data, the GPU can also be used for scientific calculations. Shi et al. [10] proposed a system to use the GPGPU libraries from inside an guest operating system. They use classical XML based remote procedure calls (RPC), which, due to its massive indirections and rather unfortunate data representation, imposes a considerable overhead compared to the custom-tailored VirtGL interface.

The system closest to VirtGL might be GViM [2], which makes the CUDA facilities of the host available inside the guest system. GViM uses queues of CUDA commands which are filled by the guest system's driver, eventually processed in the hypervisor and by then are ultimately issued to the host's CUDA interface. To achieve the functionality GViM introduces additional software layers. In contrast, our VirtGL package *removes* software layers and thus has a leaner design and a smaller footprint. Unlike GViM, VirtGL does not uncouple the processing of the commands from their issuing. VirtGL rather provides a direct interface to work with which entails immediate command execution/relaying.

None of the solutions found has the extremely lean and straight-forward characteristics of the VirtGL package. Most of the listed projects impose a considerable overhead, which VirtGL does not.

6 Conclusion

In this paper we presented an approach of re-using host system facilities in the guest environment. We used this approach to introduce accelerated 3D graphics support for virtualized environments. Our tests show that the approach is viable and that the solution has reasonable overall performance. We have found that our approach lends itself to a lean and simple software design, thus raising software quality. Compared to the implementation of a native graphics driver our development effort, the resulting code size and the program complexity is reduced by orders of magnitude. The approach also allows us to more easily keep up with fast evolving 3D-graphics technology.

VirtGL in its current state is not ready for production environments. At the moment it is rather a "proof of concept". Currently, a small subset of OpenGL functions is supported. Clearly we aim to support the complete OpenGL function set. One of the next steps would be to support modern shader functions and then to extend the approach with the OpenCL or CUDA interfaces. In the near future we will extend, improve and optimize VirtGL in several ways. In the more remote future VirtGL might facilitate GPGPU usage for HPC clouds.

References

1. Frenz, S.: Small Java Compiler, `http://www.fam-frenz.de/stefan/compiler.html`
2. Gupta, V., Gavrilovska, A., Schwan, K., Kharche, H., Tolia, N., Talwar, V., Ranganathan, P.: GViM: GPU-accelerated virtual machines. In: HPCVirt 2009: Proceedings of the 3rd ACM Workshop on System-level Virtualization for High Performance Computing, pp. 17–24. ACM, New York (2009)
3. Humphreys, G., Eldridge, M., Buck, I., Stoll, G., Everett, M., Hanrahan, P.: WireGL: a scalable graphics system for clusters. In: SIGGRAPH 2001: Proceedings of the 28th Annual Conference on Computer Graphics and Interactive Techniques. ACM, New York (2001)
4. Khronos Group: OpenCL, `http://www.khronos.org/opencl/`
5. Khronos Group: OpenGL, `http://www.opengl.org/`
6. Lagar-Cavilla, H.A., Tolia, N., Satyanarayanan, M., de Lara, E.: VMM-Independent Graphics Acceleration. In: Proceedings of the Third International ACM SIGPLAN/SIGOPS Conference on Virtual Execution Environments (VEE), San Diego, CA (2007)
7. LeVasseur, J., Uhlig, V., Stoess, J., Gotz, S.: Unmodified device driver reuse and improved system dependability via virtual machines. In: OSDI 2004: Proceedings of the 6th Conference on Symposium on Opearting Systems Design & Implementation. USENIX Association, Berkeley (2004)
8. NVIDIA: CUDA, `http://www.nvidia.com/object/cuda_home_new.html`
9. Richter, J.: Porting of the NE2000 Device Model. Großer beleg, TU Dresden, Germany (2009)
10. Shi, L., Chen, H., Sun, J.: vCUDA: GPU accelerated high performance computing in virtual machines. In: IPDPS 2009: Proceedings of the 2009 IEEE International Symposium on Parallel & Distributed Processing, pp. 1–11. IEEE Computer Society, Washington, DC, USA (2009)
11. Ulm University: Rainbow OS, `http://www.rainbow-os.net/`
12. VirtualGL, `http://www.virtualgl.org/`
13. Wende, M.: Communcation model of a distributed virtual memory. Ph.D. thesis, Ulm University (2003) (in German)

Providing Performance Guarantees to Virtual Machines Using Real-Time Scheduling*

Tommaso Cucinotta, Dhaval Giani, Dario Faggioli, and Fabio Checconi

Scuola Superiore Sant'Anna, Pisa, Italy

Abstract. In this paper we tackle the problem of providing Quality of Service guarantees to virtualized applications, focusing on computing and networking guarantees. We propose a mechanism for providing temporal isolation based on a CPU real time scheduling strategy. This allows not only to have control over the individual virtual machine throughput, but also on the activation latency and response-time by which virtualized software components react to external events. We show experimental results gathered on a real system validating the approach.

1 Introduction

When deploying virtualized distributed applications over a set of physical resources, by means of machine and network virtualization, one of the hot problems that is receiving an increasing attention [16, 14] is the one of how to provide a *stable performance* of *individual* virtualized applications. This problem is due to a multitude of factors: on the networking side, multiple data flows need to be streamed over a pool of shared physical network links; on the computing side, multiple Virtual Machines (VMs) need to be concurrently scheduled over a set of shared processors and cores; for storage, multiple data flows need to be concurrently supported during access to shared storage devices.

Sharing of physical resources constitutes a great opportunity for IaaS and PaaS providers. It allows for a better utilization of the underlying physical infrastructure. This is especially true with the increasing need [2] to deploy complex, distributed, interactive real-time applications over virtualized infrastructures (as common in the Cloud Computing world), a scenario implying a potential under-utilization of resources. An efficient utilization of resources in datacenters may also lead to the deployment of interactive applications on the same physical hosts occupied by HPC applications, which typically are CPU intensive and may rely on communication channels to pass data and synchronize themselves. In this case, it is crucial to provide CPU *and* I/O isolation between the two classes of workloads to avoid decreasing the customer satisfaction.

However, without an appropriate support for temporal isolation, concurrently running VMs may interfere each other in a way that it becomes impossible to guarantee a stable performance level to each one of them. This problem has been previously addressed in the case of compute-intensive VMs [6, 7], however it still remains a hot topic in the case of I/O-intensive and mixed workloads.

* The research leading to these results has received funding from the European Community's Seventh Framework Programme FP7 under grant agreements n. 214777 "IRMOS—Interactive Realtime Multimedia Applications on Service Oriented Infrastructures" and n. 248465 "S(o)OS – Service-oriented Operating Systems."

M.R. Guarracino et al. (Eds.): Euro-Par 2010 Workshops, LNCS 6586, pp. 657–664, 2011.
© Springer-Verlag Berlin Heidelberg 2011

2 Related Work

The interaction between CPU scheduling and I/O performance of virtualized environments was studied before, mainly in virtualization systems based on the Xen hypervisor [1]. The papers cited below all consider the Xen setup with device drivers in dedicated domains [10]. In [5], the authors proposed a monitoring infrastructure for Xen and estimated the CPU overhead induced by I/O virtualization using a set of HTTP-based benchmarks. In [3], the authors characterized the overheads of network virtualization in Xen using full system simulation; in this way, they were able to estimate the effects of the hardware architecture on the virtualization stack performance. To increase the control over I/O virtualization, various solutions were proposed; most of them used CPU scheduling to isolate the VMs from the performance perspective. In [11], the authors proposed to augment the Xen hypervisor with a set of mechanisms to account for and to control the CPU time spent on behalf of VMs doing I/O. In [17], the authors proposed an extension to the Xen credit-based scheduler improving its behavior in presence of multiple different applications with heavy I/O workloads, prioritizing the I/O bound ones. Also, in [13], the authors proposed to modify the Xen CPU scheduler and networking architecture to improve the performance of virtualized I/O on 10 Gbps Ethernet.

None of the approaches described above deal with service guarantees, most of them aim at improving fairness and/or throughput; we advocate the need for providing explicit guarantees in order to obtain predictable performance.

The existing solutions that support QoS, like for example Open vSwitch [18], or VMWare vNetwork [1], tend to be confined to the networking domain, and enforce QoS policing and shaping network traffic according to user-defined policies. A widely used virtual networking tool, VDE [9] uses the Linux bridging capabilities to achieve similar results. Our work differs from these latter approaches in that it tries to take into account isolation and CPU scheduling effects on I/O performance.

Finally, in our previous works [7, 8] we proposed to use CPU real-time scheduling for supporting proper timeliness guarantees to virtualized applications concurrently running on different VMs deployed on the same CPU. However, in these works the investigation was limited to CPU-bound workloads, while in this paper we consider also the effect of I/O-intensive workloads.

3 Proposed Approach

In this paper, we propose to provide stable computing and networking performance guarantees to VMs concurrently running on the same CPU(s) using an EDF-based soft real-time scheduling strategy for the CPU, which we developed in the context of the IRMOS project[2]. The proposed approach is particularly useful when mixing VMs with workloads that are heterogeneous with respect to the time granularity over which the temporal requirements of the hosted applications need to be fulfilled.

The IRMOS real-time scheduler [4] allows to reserve a "slice" of the processing capability of a system to a group of threads and/or processes (shortly, tasks). This is

[1] `http://www.vmware.com/products/vnetwork-distributed-switch`

[2] More information is available at: `http://www.irmosproject.eu`

done by specifying two scheduling parameters for each group: a budget Q and a period P, with the meaning that the tasks in the group are entitled to run on each of the CPUs (processor, or cores when present) available to the OS, for Q time units every period of P time units. This constitutes a scheduling guarantee and a limitation at the same time. Also, when a group is entitled to run on each CPU, the IRMOS scheduler employs a POSIX priority-based real-time scheduling strategy [12]. See [4] for further details.

With KVM, there is little control on how multiple VMs compete in accessing the available CPUs. In fact, the default Linux scheduling strategy (`SCHED_OTHER`) implements the Completely Fair Scheduler (CFS) policy, which tries to be as fair as possible across competing processes. Therefore, we used the scheduler described above to isolate the temporal behavior of concurrently running VMs, and at the same time provide them with their specifically required scheduling guarantees.

When dealing with compute-intensive VMs only, most of the time dedicated to a VM is spent by the host by running the corresponding KVM process. Therefore, providing proper CPU scheduling guarantees to the process, as achievable with our real-time IRMOS scheduler, allows for the achievement of a sufficient isolation degree between that VM and other VMs. The scheduling parameters for a VM can be set-up as follows. The scheduling period controls the activation latency of the VM and can be set equal to the minimum expected interarrival period of external requests triggering the VM services. The ratio budget over period controls how much computing capability of the host is reserved for the VM, thus the budget may be tuned by performing a preliminary benchmarking phase. Thanks to the hard reservation nature of our real-time scheduler, the performance obtained when the VM is running in isolation on the host, with given scheduling parameters, is only marginally affected by the workload imposed on the host by other VMs.

However, the situation becomes more complex when dealing with I/O-intensive workloads. In fact, in such case, the host may spend a significant part of the CPU time related to a VM outside the context of the KVM threads. The lowest level of the networking code executes in interrupt context, preempting the execution of VMs potentially unrelated to the I/O traffic that is being handled, thus "stealing" part of the budget reserved to the interrupted VMs, even under the use of our real-time scheduler. To deal with this problem, we suggest to overprovision the assigned budget, as compared to the minimum one detected when benchmarking the VM in isolation. Specifically, not only the budget should be increased of the amount necessary to deal with the interferences of multiple VMs at the cache level (this is unavoidable in modern systems), but also of a quantity that is strictly dependent on the overall networking traffic performed by the VMs hosted on the same system. Such aggregate figure is usually available to the infrastructure that handles the deployment of the VMs on the physical host.

Also, higher-level in-kernel networking code often executes in *softirq* context [15]. Furthermore, when using the PREEMPT-RT kernel [19], part of the low-level networking driver code runs in dedicated kernel threads, where it may be at risk of not getting a proper chance to run, compromising networking performance. In such case, we suggest to put all the threads relative to the same VM into the same reservation, comprising both KVM threads and kernel threads necessary for dealing with its (para-)virtualized networking. Our real-time scheduler allows for the provisioning of overall scheduling guarantees to the entire group of threads, even if not belonging to the same process. Fig. 1a depicts the overall architecture, showing how the temporal capsule extends also to the interrupt threads, which act as interconnecting channels between the kernel and the virtual machines. In the preliminary results reported below, we show how it is possible to achieve a proper degree of isolation in presence of I/O-intensive VMs, deferring to future work the adoption of more sophisticated techniques (see Section 5).

4 Experimental Results

For validating the proposed approach, in this section we report results gathered from an experimental set-up involving a real Linux system running KVM as hypervisor.

All the described experiments have been conducted by using two physical systems equipped with an Intel Quad Core Q6600 CPU running at 2.4 Ghz, 4 GB of RAM, and a Gigabit Ethernet card. One of the two systems played the role of *server*, and was running a Fedora 11 Linux distribution with a modified version of the kernel including our real-time scheduler. VMs were started with KVM in bridge mode and with 1 GB of guest memory. The networking was setup to use the `virtio` interface. The other system was used as *client*. On multi-core systems, the problem addressed in this paper appears when deploying VMs with an overall number of virtualized CPUs greater than the number of available physical CPUs. In order to keep a simple experimental set-up, the tests were run with only one core brought online, thus all the VMs running on it.

In what follows, resource-level experiments are shown first, demonstrating how the proposed technique improves isolation of I/O intensive traffic across concurrently running VMs, gathered running a synthetic network-benchmarking tool. Then, application-level results are shown, from an experiment involving a real Apache web server.

Resource-level isolation. In the following experiment, we investigate on the impact of different CPU share allocations over the networking throughput achievable by the VM. To this purpose, a VM was run alone on the server, with all of its threads attached to a unique real-time reservation for the VM, with a period of $100ms$ and different budgets varying from $10ms$ to $90ms$. We used `iperf` [3] to measure the network throughput

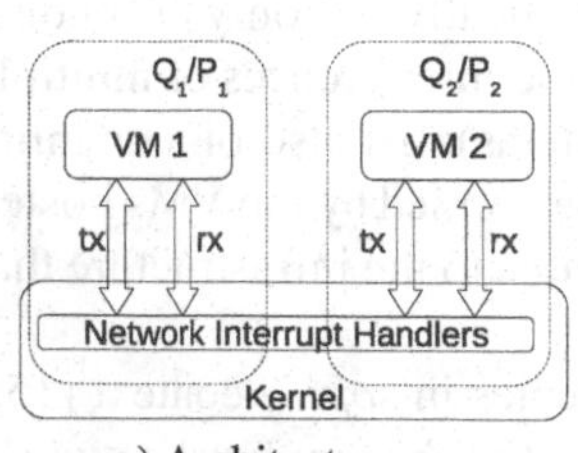

a) Architecture

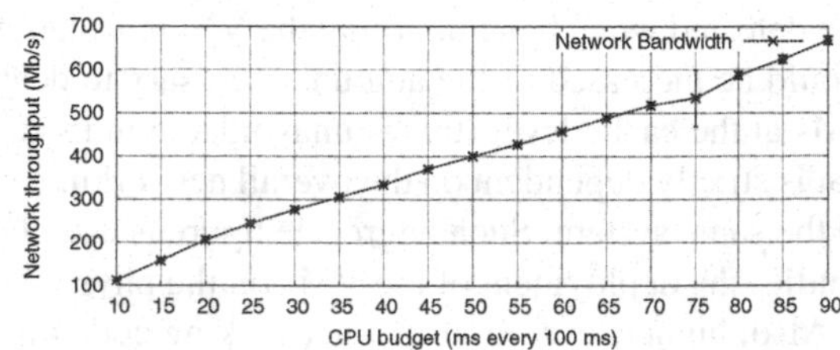

b) Network bandwidth with varying CPU reservation for a single VM

Fig. 1. System architecture and network bandwidth for a VM with various CPU reservations

[3] More information at: `http://sourceforge.net/projects/iperf/`.

between an `iperf` client running on the client machine, and an `iperf` server running inside the VM. The test was repeated 100 times for each budget value. As shown in Fig. 1b, there is a nearly linear relationship between the network throughput achieved by the VM and its CPU share. Each point corresponds to the average throughput over the 100 repetitions, and is flanked by a small vertical segment showing the standard deviation, which is barely noticeable except for a budget of $75ms$.

Now, in order to measure the degree of temporal isolation enforced by the real-time scheduler, we started two VMs on the same physical host and core, each one isolated in a different resource reservation. Each VM was running an `iperf` server. We launched two `iperf` clients on the client machine against the two VMs, and we measured the achieved throughput at varying scheduling parameters for both VMs.

The obtained results are shown in Fig. 2 and 3, from different perspectives. Fig. 2 shows (on the Y axis) the throughput obtained by a VM as a function of its own reservation share (on the X axis), at varying reservation share for the other VM (different curves). Ideally, if the temporal isolation were perfect, we should see perfectly superimposed curves. However, as expected, a performance drop is experienced by the VM under observation, quantified in a 20%–30% drop when the reservation share of the other VM is increased from 10% (similarly to the single-VM case in Fig. 1b) to 40%.

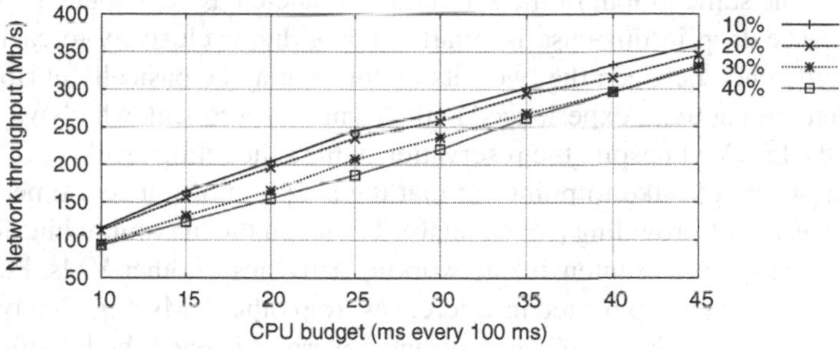

Fig. 2. Network throughput (Y axis) for a VM as a function of its own CPU share (X axis), at varying CPU shares for the other VM (different curves)

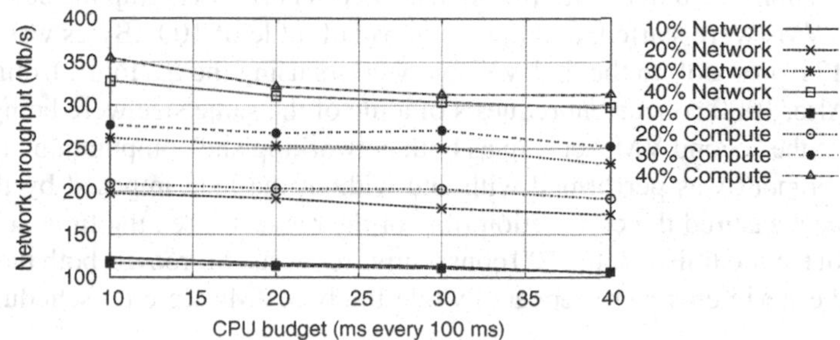

Fig. 3. Network throughput (Y axis) for a VM as a function of the CPU share of the other VM (X axis), at varying CPU shares for itself (different curves), in case of CPU- and I/O-intensive loads

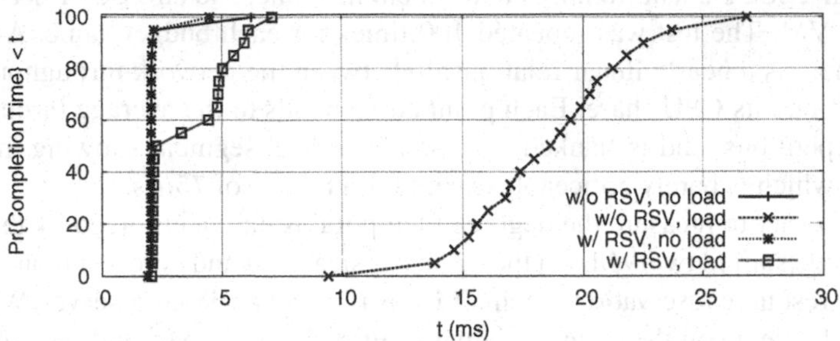

Fig. 4. CDF of the completion time of the requests to the first VM in various conditions

Fig. 3 shows the throughput (Y axis) obtained by the VM under observation as a function of the CPU share assigned to the other VM (X axis), and at varying CPU shares for itself (different curves labeled with "Network"). Again, if the isolation were perfect, we should see horizontal lines. Instead, we see again the performance drop that is achieved. Finally, we made a third experiment with a computation-intensive workload on the other VM (it was running Octave[4] inverting a 1000x1000 matrix). The results are shown on the same graph, in the set of curves labeled as "Compute". As expected, the performance drop in this case is smaller, being due exclusively to cache interference. The difference between the two sets of curves may be basically attributed to the increased interrupt activity experienced in the former experiment, which was "stealing" CPU from the first VM despite the reservation at the scheduling level.

However, we would like to point out that the adoption of our real-time scheduling strategy is capable of providing a controllable bound on the maximum interference that a VM may undergo due to intensive networking activities of other VMs. For example, in order to counteract the expected interferences from other VMs, Fig. 2 may be used in place of Fig. 1b for "looking-up" the (correctly overprovisioned) budget for sustaining a given VM throughput, depending on the expected networking load of other VMs.

Application-level results. To demonstrate the achievable level of isolation on a real-world application, a ramdisk with the Apache web server[5] was setup inside each VM[6].

The two VMs were started, and the download of a file of 100 kBytes was requested (via the HTTP protocol) to the first VM every $20ms$ using the `ab` tool[7], from the client machine. Also, 1000 concurrent requests of a file of the same size were being continuously sent to the second VM, serving as both networking and computation "load".

The experiment was performed with and without the load imposed by the second VM, and we measured the completion time of the requests, i.e., the time at which the download of the file finished, for 500 consecutive requests. Moreover, both the unloaded and loaded experiments were repeated while the two VMs were co-scheduled by the

[4] More information is available at: `http://www.octave.org`.

[5] More information is available at: `http://httpd.apache.org`

[6] By setting it up in a ramdisk, additional interference in the form of disk I/O was avoided.

[7] We modified ApacheBench (`ab`) to behave as described.

standard Linux kernel mechanisms, and with the first VM in a reservation with parameters $RSV(Q, P) = (4ms, 20ms)$. The Cumulative Distribution Function (CDF) of the completion time in all the four evaluated scenarios is shown in Fig. 4. The vertical line at 20 ms represents the time by which a request must complete, since another one should start (i.e., the deadline). It is easy to see how, in the unloaded case (curves labeled with "no load"), both with and without the reservation (curves labeled with "w/RSV" and "w/o RSV", respectively), the performance is good enough, since the completion time is almost constant at about $2.1ms$ among the various requests and it is always far from the deadline (with peaks of nearly $6.2ms$). However, in the loaded case, the original VM performance is completely subverted, and more than 30% of the requests for the first VM cannot complete within the $20ms$ deadline/period, with peaks of download-time of nearly $27ms$. When encapsulating the VM in a real-time reservation, instead, the download times returned to be well below the deadline, with a maximum of $7.1ms$.

5 Future Work and Conclusions

In this paper, the problem of provisioning QoS guarantees to VMs concurrently running on the same CPU was tackled. The focus was on VMs with I/O intensive workloads, where even if the guest OSes are for most of the time suspended for performing I/O, actually the host needs to execute the para-virtualized and native networking drivers necessary to deliver the packets, what is a major cause of interference between the VMs. Therefore, I/O-intensive and compute-intensive VMs may strongly interfere with each other, leading to a performance that is completely subverted as compared to the case in which they were running or benchmarked in isolation.

We showed that, by recurring to soft real-time scheduling strategies at the virtualization layer, it is possible to provide a good level of isolation between the concurrently running VMs. Furthermore, it is possible to achieve both a good throughput of the VMs and to keep the individual guarantees at the latency level, something that is not possible with the standard Linux scheduling strategies. However, the proposed solution is all but conclusive in this regard. In fact, as highlighted in the experimental section, still there is a degree of interference which is due to the resources that are implicitly shared among the VMs inside the host OS, namely network interface drivers and bridging logic that runs on the host OS. We plan to enhance the isolation with this regard by slightly reworking the networking driver infrastructure in Linux for such purpose, exploit some recent kernel features that allows for putting the networking code in a per-VM thread-/context. Also, we plan to experiment with the PREEMPT-RT branch of the kernel, in which part of the drivers logic is moved to dedicated kernel threads, thus it is possible to control when they execute with our real-time scheduler, and for which a variation of our real-time scheduler is already being ported.

Finally, we plan to investigate on the use of adaptation for fine-tuning the resource reservation parameters so as to better suit the needs of virtualized applications.

References

[1] Barham, P., et al.: Xen and the art of virtualization. In: SOSP 2003: Proc. Nineteenth ACM Symposium on Operating Systems Principles, New York, NY, USA (2003)

[2] Boniface, M., et al.: PaaS architecture for real-time quality of service management in clouds. In: International Conference on Internet and Web Applications and Services (2010)

[3] Chadha, V., et al.: I/O processing in a virtualized platform: a simulation-driven approach. In: VEE 2007: Proc. 3rd International Conference on Virtual Execution Environments, pp. 116–125. ACM, New York (2007)

[4] Checconi, F., et al.: Hierarchical multiprocessor CPU reservations for the linux kernel. In: Proc. OSPERT 2009, Dublin, Ireland (June 2009)

[5] Cherkasova, L., Gardner, R.: Measuring cpu overhead for I/O processing in the Xen virtual machine monitor. In: ATEC 2005: Proc. Annual Conference on USENIX Annual Technical Conference, Berkeley, CA, USA, p. 24 (2005)

[6] Cherkasova, L., Gupta, D., Vahdat, A.: Comparison of the three cpu schedulers in Xen. SIGMETRICS Perform. Eval. Rev. 35(2), 42–51 (2007)

[7] Cucinotta, T., Anastasi, G., Abeni, L.: Real-time virtual machines. In: Proceedings of the 29th IEEE Real-Time System Symposium (RTSS 2008) – WiP Session, Barcelona (December 2008)

[8] Cucinotta, T., Anastasi, G., Abeni, L.: Respecting temporal constraints in virtualised services. In: Proc. IEEE RTSOAA 2009, Seattle, Washington (July 2009)

[9] Davoli, R.: VDE: Virtual Distributed Ethernet. In: Proc. First International Conference on Testbeds and Research Infrastructures for the Development of Networks and Communities (TRIDENTCOM 2005), pp. 213–220 (2005)

[10] Fraser, K., Hand, S., Neugebauer, R., Pratt, I., Warfield, A., Warfield, A., Williamson, M., Williamson, M.: Reconstructing I/O (2004)

[11] Gupta, D., Cherkasova, L., Gardner, R., Vahdat, A.: Enforcing performance isolation across virtual machines in Xen. In: van Steen, M., Henning, M. (eds.) Middleware 2006. LNCS, vol. 4290, pp. 342–362. Springer, Heidelberg (2006)

[12] IEEE: Information Technology - Portable Operating System Interface - Part 1: System Application Program Interface Amendment: Additional Realtime Extensions (2004)

[13] Liao, G., et al.: Software techniques to improve virtualized i/o performance on multi-core systems. In: Proc. ACM/IEEE ANCS 2008, New York, NY, USA (2008)

[14] Lin, B., Sundararaj, A., Dinda, P.: Time-sharing parallel applications with performance isolation and control. In: Proc. 4th International Conference on Autonomic Computing (ICAC 2007), Jacksonville, FL, p. 28 (June 2007)

[15] Love, R.: Linux Kernel Development, 2nd edn. Novell Press (2005)

[16] Nathuji, R., Kansal, A., Ghaffarkhah, A.: Q-clouds: managing performance interference effects for qos-aware clouds. In: EuroSys 2010: Proc. 5th European Conference on Computer Systems, pp. 237–250. ACM, New York (2010)

[17] Ongaro, D., Cox, A.L., Rixner, S.: Scheduling i/o in virtual machine monitors. In: Proc. ACM SIGPLAN/SIGOPS VEE 2008. ACM, New York (2008)

[18] Pfaff, et al.: Extending networking into the virtualization layer. In: 8th ACM Workshop on Hot Topics in Networks (HotNets-VIII), New York City, NY (October 2009)

[19] Rostedt, S., Hart, D.V.: Internals of the rt patch. In: Proc. Ottawa Linux Symposium (OLS 2007), pp. 161–172 (June 2007)

Exploring I/O Virtualization Data Paths for MPI Applications in a Cluster of VMs: A Networking Perspective

Anastassios Nanos, Georgios Goumas, and Nectarios Koziris

Computing Systems Laboratory,
National Technical University of Athens,
{ananos,goumas,nkoziris}@cslab.ece.ntua.gr

Abstract. Nowadays, seeking optimized data paths that can increase I/O throughput in Virtualized environments is an intriguing task, especially in a high-performance computing context. This study endeavors to address this issue by evaluating methods for optimized network device access using scientific applications and micro-benchmarks.

We examine the network performance bottlenecks that appear in a Cluster of Xen VMs using both generic and intelligent network adapters. We study the network behavior of MPI applications. Our goal is to: (a) explore the implications of alternative data paths between applications and network hardware and (b) specify optimized solutions for scientific applications that put pressure on network devices. To monitor the network load and the applications' total throughput we build a custom testbed using different network configurations. We use the Xen bridge mechanism and I/O Virtualization techniques and examine the tradeoffs. Preliminary results show that a combination of these techniques is essential to overcome network virtualization overheads and achieve near-native performance.

1 Introduction

Today, with the advent of virtualization techniques, Cloud Computing infrastructures are becoming a great trend, providing flexibility, dedicated execution and isolation to a vast number of services. These infrastructures, built on clusters of multicores, offer huge processing power, ideal for mass deployment of compute-intensive applications. However, bridging the gap between I/O techniques in virtualized environments and application demands seems to be a major challenge. Numerous studies both in native [1,2] and virtualized environments [3,4,5] explore the implications of alternative data paths that increase the system's I/O throughput and help applications overcome significant bottlenecks in data retrieval from storage or network devices.

Typical HPC applications often utilize adaptive layers to overcome limitations that operating systems impose in order to ensure security, isolation and fairness in resource allocation and usage. These layers are usually communication libraries (e.g. MPI) or mechanisms to bypass the general purpose kernel-algorithms for (i) process scheduling (CPU affinity, process priority) and (ii)

M.R. Guarracino et al. (Eds.): Euro-Par 2010 Workshops, LNCS 6586, pp. 665–671, 2011.
© Springer-Verlag Berlin Heidelberg 2011

device access (user-level networking, direct I/O techniques such as zero-copy, page-cache bypass, etc.). Intelligent interconnects, suitable for HPC applications, provide adapters that offload protocol processing and achieve fast message exchange. To avoid the overhead associated with user-to-kernel–space communication, HPC interconnects often utilize a user-level networking approach. To use such a method in virtualized environments, several issues have to be taken into account.

Data retrieval from storage or network devices in virtualized environments is usually realized by software layers within the hypervisor, which allow VMs to interface with the hardware. A common implementation of such interfaces is a *split driver model*. These layers host a *backend* driver that communicates with the native driver and the device, while guest VM kernels host a *frontend* driver, exposing a generic device API to guest user– or kernel–space.

Similarly to operating systems, the hypervisor in virtualized environments multiplexes guest kernels which run on VMs and are not directly aware of the underlying hardware. Moreover, the application has to access specific resources on the network adapter's hardware. However, letting applications access I/O devices without regulation raises security issues.

Currently, only a subset of the aforementioned adaptive layers is implemented in virtualization platforms. For example, SR/MR-IOV [4] lets VMs exchange data with the network via a direct data path, bypassing the hypervisor and the privileged guest. Device access by multiple VMs is multiplexed in firmware running on the hardware itself. However, these features are only implemented for general purpose networking adapters (such as ethernet) and, as a result, cannot be used with High-performance interconnects such as Myrinet or InfiniBand.

Our work is focused on integrating HPC interconnect semantics into the VMM split driver model [5]. We aim to decouple data transfers from the virtualization layers and explore direct application-to-NIC data paths. In order to justify developing a framework to support standard features of HPC interconnects (user–level networking, zero–copy etc.) in VM environments, we need to examine the behavior of HPC applications in such environments [6]. In this work, we deploy network benchmarks and a real scientific application in a cluster of ParaVirtualized Xen [7] VMs and present some preliminary results.

The rest of this paper is organized as follows: Section 2 presents network performance measurements using common micro-benchmarks. In Section 3 we describe the evaluation of a real scientific application in a cluster of VMs. Section 4 discusses evaluation issues and related work. In Section 5, we conclude.

2 Network Performance in Xen VMs

In this section, we evaluate various network configurations using two popular network micro-benchmarks. Our testbed consists of two host machines, connected back-to-back. The host machines (H_0, H_1) are two dual quad-core Xeons@2.0GHz with two Neterion X3110 10GbE adapters, hosting 8 dual-core VMs ($n_1 \ldots n_8$) with 1.5GB of memory each. To determine the optimum data path of our testbed, we consider three configurations: `NATIVE`, the baseline of our testbed, running vanilla linux-kernel; `BRIDGED`, the default Xen setup, where all network traffic crosses the privileged guest (Dom0) either by copying or by *granting* the pages that hold the frames to the specified guest; `I/O Virtualization (IOV)`, our optimized setup. Specialized network adapters export PCI functions to the OS providing a direct VM-to-NIC data path.

We measure the bandwidth achieved by each VM separately on different hosts ($n_1 \rightarrow n_4$, $n_2 \rightarrow n_6$ and so on) and compare its sum to the aggregate bandwidth measured in the Native case ($H_0 \rightarrow H_1$).

Table 1. Bandwidth (MiB/sec) for netperf TCP_STREAM and iperf (1 proc)

	netperf					iperf				
	node1	node2	node3	node4	total	node1	node2	node3	node4	total
NATIVE					811.73					1238
BRIDGED	90.45	123.03	112.23	100.26	425.97	205.00	190.00	181.25	172.50	748.75
IOV	160.33	159.43	152.45	162.63	634.84	221.25	222.25	221.25	220.00	884.75

We used netperf to test the maximum achievable bandwidth that our testbed can sustain. Table 1 shows the bandwidth in MiB per second. The bandwidth achieved in the BRIDGED case is about 65% of the IOV case. On the other hand, IOV sustains 80% of the bandwidth achieved with the NATIVE case, but remains bound at only 50% of the theoretical maximum of the 10GbE link (1250MiB/sec).

3 Deploying an MPI Application in a Cluster of VMs

In order to project the results obtained by network benchmarks to a real scientific paradigm, we deploy an HPC application on top of our mini VM-cluster. Our application computes an advective process in a XxYxZ space for a time window T [8]. We choose a fixed grid size ($512x512x512$, $T = 512$), distributing X, Y or Z dimension across all 16 processes.

Our physical nodes (H_0 and H_1) provide 4 dual-core VMs each, resulting in an 8-node, 16-core cluster (n_1 to n_8). Each process communicates with its nearest neighbor, providing a linear communication pattern. We place processes across cores using three different placement patterns (Figure 1): *a. inter–node*, *b. intra–node*, *c. hybrid.* At first, we choose to place the processes ($P_1 \ldots P_{16}$) in a way that data cross the network in every MPI operation (inter-node). For example, P_2 communicates with P_1 and P_3: we place P_2 on n_5 in H_1 and $P_{1,3}$ on $n_{1,2}$ in H_0 respectively. In order to study how the process placement influences the application's behavior, we then choose the intra-node communication pattern: we place $P_1 \ldots P_8$ on $n_1 \ldots n_4$ in H_0 and $P_9 \ldots P_{16}$ on $n_5 \ldots n_8$ in H_1. Thus, network communication occurs only between n_4 and n_5 (intra–node).

Figure 2 presents the execution time of the advective equation application when using the inter–node and the intra–node cases. In the first bar we plot

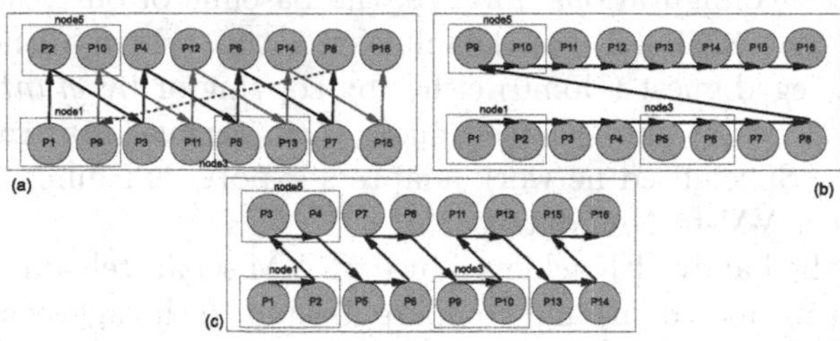

Fig. 1. Communication pattern according to process placement when using all 8 VMs

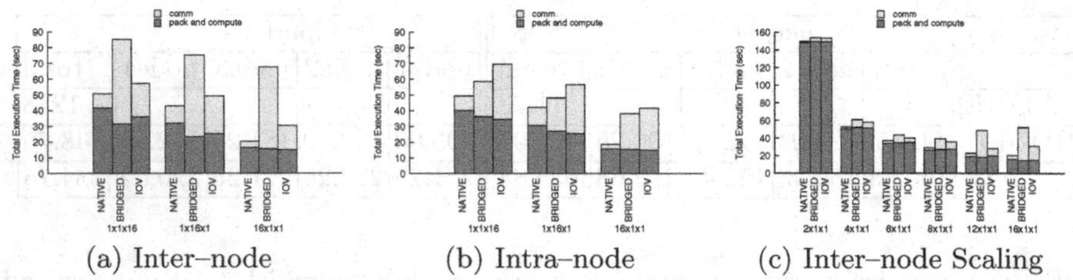

(a) Inter–node (b) Intra–node (c) Inter–node Scaling

Fig. 2. Advective equation execution time for the linear case ($1x1x16, 1x16x1, 16x1x1$)

the application's performance on a native linux kernel setup. In the second and third bar we plot the Xen case, with the BRIDGED and IOV configurations respectively.

This figure raises some interesting issues: (i) in the IOV case, the application execution time is almost half the time of the BRIDGED case for the inter-node communication pattern and its performance achieves 63% of the NATIVE case; (ii) there is significant performance degradation in the case of IOV in intra-node communication. In this case, the optimized configuration seems to be the BRIDGED case. An alternative, would be to provide a shared memory mechanism across VMs, as presented in [9]; (iii) the speed-up obtained using IOV techniques (Figure 2(a)) compared to the BRIDGED case is not proportional to the bandwidth measured with micro-benchmarks.

To gain further insight on the scalability of the advective application when adding cores, we deployed the application using 2 . . . 16 cores. To provide a baseline we deployed the application in a 4-node cluster of machines identical to $H_{0,1}$ (32 proc) using the inter-node placement pattern. Figure 3(a) presents the computation time and total execution time vs. the number of cores for the NATIVE and the BRIDGED case.

In general, it is important to note that the computation time is almost the same for all cases. Moreover, we observe that in the NATIVE case the communication part of the execution time becomes noticeable over 16 cores. This performance degradation appears in the Virtualized environment as well, and can be attributed to application characteristics. Since we are interested in the virtualization overheads on the communication part of the execution, we can study its behavior using 16 cores without loss of generality.

In the BRIDGED case, the application's performance starts to degrade when we add more than 8 cores. Since computation time remains the same in both cases, this degradation is due to the communication overhead associated with the Xen bridge mechanism. We also plot the total execution time of the IOV case (the computation time appears to be the same as in the NATIVE case). We observe a significant performance improvement with IOV due to optimizations in the network layers. Direct data paths allow messages to traverse the network, bypassing the hypervisor or the privileged guest. IOV's performance is nearly 80% of the NATIVE case.

Figure 2(c) presents the execution time breakdown for the $\{X\text{x}Y\text{x}Z\}$ = $\{2\ldots16\text{x}1\text{x}1\}$ process distribution using the inter–node communication pattern. In the BRIDGED case (2nd bar), the negative scaling factor as we add cores to the application is due to the communication part of the execution (light part); the computation part (dark part) remains constant. On the other hand, the IOV case follows the scaling pattern of the NATIVE case, with a constant overhead due to virtualized communication layers.

Based on Figure 1, we can also examine the application's behavior when customizing the number of communication (inter– or intra–node) messages. The total number of MPI operations per iteration between 16 processes is 15. Thus, according to the placement pattern (Figure 1): in case *a*, all MPI operations traverse the network, so the inter–node communication mechanism is the only means of data exchange (15/15 = 100%); in case *b*, only one MPI operation crosses the network, so the intra–node communication is dominant ($1/15 \approx 6\%$); in case *c*, there are 7 inter-node messages, leading in a hybrid model, which is the usual communication pattern in a native cluster of SMPs ($7/15 \approx 46\%$). We plot the speedup of the IOV case over the BRIDGED case vs. the percentage of inter–node messages when distributing dimension X, Y or Z across all 16 processes in Figure 3(b). We observe that when 50% of MPI operations traverse

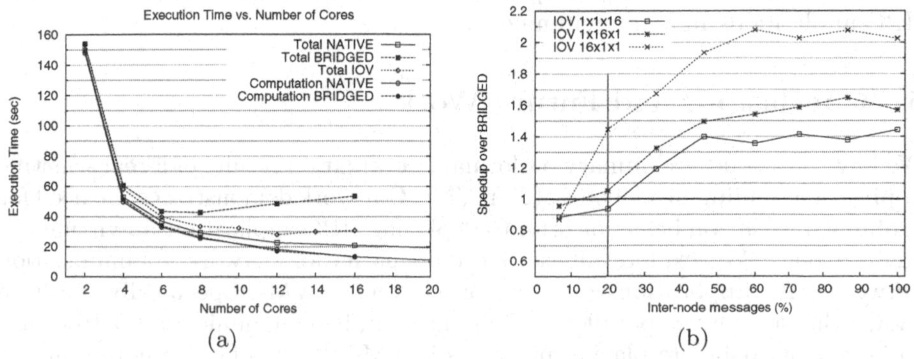

Fig. 3. Total Execution Time Breakdown for NATIVE, BRIDGED and IOV. Speedup.

the network, IOV outperforms the BRIDGED case by at least 40%. The only case where one should choose the BRIDGED case, is when network operations are lower than 20% of all MPI operations (for example Figure 1 case (b)).

4 Discussion and Related Work

In virtualized environments, the basic building blocks of the system (i.e. CPUs, memory and I/O devices) are multiplexed by the hypervisor in a secure, isolated and flexible manner. Different network configurations raise some interesting issues:

Xen Networking: Using I/O Virtualization techniques, our application outperforms the generic case. Nonetheless: (i) IOV requires specialized hardware, specific software support and its capabilities are often bound by hardware constraints; (ii) SR/MR-IOV is currently implemented for ethernet adapters, enforcing all communication libraries to stack their protocols above TCP/IP and ethernet.

HPC applications in clusters of VMs: As shown in Section 3, the computation part of the application's execution time in Xen is the same compared to the NATIVE case either in the BRIDGED or in the IOV mode; the overhead associated with the virtual environment is solely due to the communication part of the execution. Thus, by utilizing a direct optimized data path, the application achieves nearly 88% of the NATIVE case when all MPI operations traverse the network and 70% of the NATIVE case when only one process communicates over the network (Figure 1 for the communication pattern and Figure 2 for the total execution time, cases (a) and (b) respectively).

Several research papers [6,7], have analyzed Xen's performance. In [6] the authors investigate the overheads imposed by the Xen hypervisor using various linux kernel versions and they conclude that the perceived significant overheads are unwarranted. Huang et al. [9] design an inter-VM, intra-node communication library, implement it on top of a popular MPI library and evaluate its performance. They show that a VM-aware MPI library, in conjunction with VMM-bypass data paths [3] imposes very little overhead to the execution of HPC applications in VM environments.

5 Conclusions and Future Work

We have presented preliminary performance evaluation results of a real scientific application running in a cluster of Xen VMs. Our work demonstrates the need for profiling application behavior prior to deploying HPC applications in virtualized environments. We explore alternative data paths for network communication between HPC applications that run on clusters of VMs. Specifically, we have shown that for a given parallel HPC application, its communication pattern has to be examined before placing processes in VMs We should also note that the computation part of the application execution is not altered when migrating to a VM environment. These results show that HPC applications *can* be executed in

VM environments with very little overhead, provided that their communication pattern is examined and that all parallel processes are distributed in a way that data flow through the optimum ad-hoc data path (direct or indirect). We plan on evaluating message passing using shared memory techniques when processes co-exist in VM containers. Our agenda also consists of evaluating higher level frameworks for application parallelism based on MapReduce and its extensions in VM execution environments.

References

1. Geoffray, P.: OPIOM: Off-Processor I/O with Myrinet. Future Gener. Comput. Syst. 18(4) (2002)
2. Koukis, E., Nanos, A., Koziris, N.: GMBlock: Optimizing data movement in a block-level storage sharing system over myrinet. Cluster Computing
3. Liu, J., Huang, W., Abali, B., Panda, D.K.: High performance VMM-bypass I/O in virtual machines. In: ATEC 2006: Proc. of USENIX 2006 Annual Technical Conference. USENIX Association, Berkeley (2006)
4. PCI SIG: SR-IOV (2007), `http://www.pcisig.com/specifications/iov/single_root/`
5. Nanos, A., Koziris, N.: MyriXen: Message Passing in Xen Virtual Machines over Myrinet and Ethernet. In: 4th Workshop on Virtualization in High-Performance Cloud Computing, The Netherlands (2009)
6. Youseff, L., Wolski, R., Gorda, B., Krintz, C.: Evaluating the Performance Impact of Xen on MPI and Process Execution For HPC Systems. In: 1st Intern. Workshop on Virtualization Technology in Distributed Computing, VTDC 2006 (2006)
7. Barham, P., Dragovic, B., Fraser, K., Hand, S., Harris, T., Ho, A., Neugebauer, R., Pratt, I.A., Warfield, A.: Xen and the Art of Virtualization. In: SOSP 2003: Proc. of the 19th ACM Symposium on Operating Systems Principles. ACM, New York (2003)
8. Goumas, G., Drosinos, N., Koziris, N.: Communication-Aware Supernode Shape. IEEE Transactions on Parallel and Distributed Systems 20 (2009)
9. Huang, W., Koop, M.J., Gao, Q., Panda, D.K.: Virtual machine aware communication libraries for high performance computing. In: SC 2007: Proc. of the 2007 ACM/IEEE Conference on Supercomputing. ACM, New York (2007)

Building an Operator CDN the Virtual Way

Hareesh Puthalath, Karl-Åke. Persson, Bob Melander, Johan Kölhi, Victor Souza, Stefan Hellkvist, and Jan-Erik Mångs

Ericsson Research, Färögatan 6, Kista, Sweden
{hareesh.puthalath,karl-ake.persson,bob.melander,johan.kolhi, victor.souza,stefan.hellkvist,jan-erik.mangs}@ericsson.com

Abstract. Virtualization has opened an exciting and powerful way to experiment and evaluate complex distributed systems. In this paper we describe the experiences and lessons learned from building a distributed operator CDN consisting of 260+ virtual machine nodes in a six blade server unit. This provided us with a flexible platform to analyze a caching architecture we were developing. We also discuss the impact of virtual networking and virtual software routers on hardware resources.

1 Introduction

When faced with the task to design, implement and evaluate a complex distributed system with lots of advanced networking, and at your disposal are only very restricted manpower, a tight budget and hardware limited to a handful of servers in a rack, what can you do? That is one question this paper tries to answer and as will be shown a good part of the answer is centered on judicious use of virtualization.

The computer networks of operators, enterprises or other large organizations are today highly complex infrastructures.The introduction of Content Delivery Networks (CDNs) in operator networks [1] [2] is a good illustration of this evolution. A CDN is a system of strategically placed nodes in a network with copies of data requested by the end users of that network. The CDN logic redirects end user requests to CDN nodes with the appropriate copy satisfying some predefined optimization criteria. Common optimization criteria include higher bandwidth, lower latency and jitter from an end user perspective and lower traffic, higher availability, reduced traffic fluctuations in the operator network as well avoiding the bottleneck and higher transports costs at the origin server [8].

CDN development, experimentation and deployment encompass a wide range of issues spanning from understanding the pros and cons of different caching strategies, development of mechanisms and algorithms for content delivery, cache selection, request redirection and content migration, choosing placement and size of caches taking into account network topologies and traffic patterns. All of these aspects have impact on the performance of the system and the network it operates in.

Experimentation with systems like a CDN in operational networks is often not acceptable since bad configurations or unstable beta version functionality may jeopardize these business-critical infrastructures. Building a scaled down mirror infrastructure based on real hardware may be too costly or, for budget reasons, will be too small to

M.R. Guarracino et al. (Eds.): Euro-Par 2010 Workshops, LNCS 6586, pp. 673–680, 2011.
© Springer-Verlag Berlin Heidelberg 2011

be realistic and useful. Global testbeds like PlanetLab [7] and VINI [4] offer interesting alternatives in this regard. However, these testbeds are shared resources where utilization can vary greatly, the topology of available nodes may not suit the system to be evaluated or experimented with and testbed nodes may not be able to host the needed functionality. For these reasons simulators like OPNET, OMNET++ have thus far often been the only practical alternative. But this approach has inherent weaknesses such as that a model rather than the real system is evaluated and that good simulations models may be lacking for critical pieces of the system (e.g., "closed" vendor equipment).

Advances in hypervisors and virtual network appliances like Open vSwitch [3] have opened a promising middle way [6] [11] [5] [10] between pure hardware testbeds and simulators. The rest of the paper reports on our experiences when exploring this avenue, by having built a distributed network operator CDN with 260+ nodes in a purely virtual environment on six blade server unit. An exercise that pushed the limits of virtualization quite beyond what is typically the case in server consolidation.

2 An Operator Network with CDN Functionality

For the operator CDN study we created a network topology with distinct core and access networks, to resemble ISP networks of today.Figure 1 shows this system topology comprising the 260+ virtual nodes. It contains identical access networks that are interconnected via a core network of IP routers.In total there were 36 access networks and the core network consisted of 12 core routers. Being a distributed architecture,the CDN functionality was introduced to nodes placed in the access networks. They contained nodes for caching,cache control logic and emulating end users. There was also an infrastructure cluster containing DHCP,DNS and NFS servers.

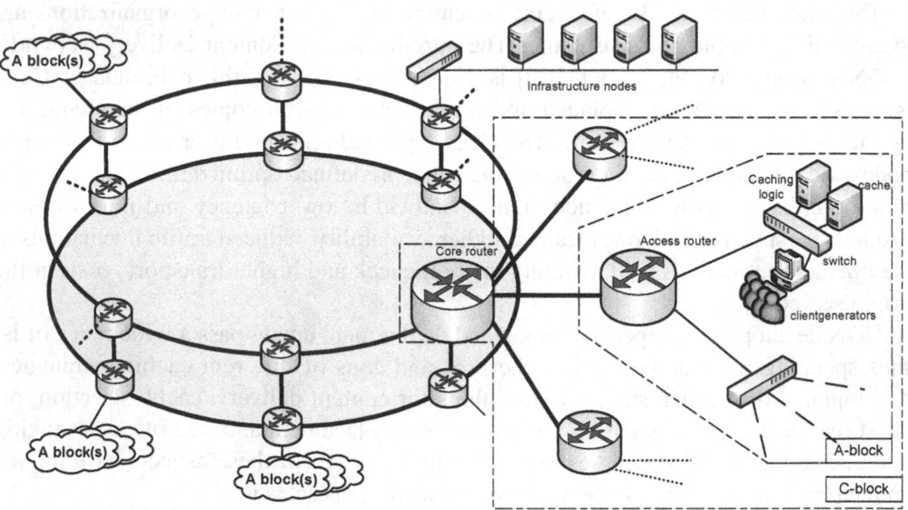

Fig. 1. Core and access networks with the A and C-block templates

3 Creating and Orchestrating a Virtual System

To manually create a virtual replica of complex systems like an operator deployed CDN comprising several hundreds of interconnected nodes is very impractical. The sheer number of nodes and the amount of configuration needed requires a way to automate such a process. We therefore resorted to an approach that lends itself to scripting, namely, identifying structurally recurring blocks in our system topology that can be replicated and customized.

3.1 Leveraging Structure for Automation: Network Lego Blocks

We utilized the structure present in our network to create what we call templates. It consists of a set of nodes (with associated VM images) and has a topology (utilizing one or more virtual switches). The template also has a control script which can instantiate and connect the virtual nodes and switches as per the defined topology. Thus the template acts as a kind of a basic Lego block for the virtual replica to be created.

We created two such templates, one for the access network (called A-block) and another aggregate one for the network core called C-block. A naming convention was used which enabled the template control scripts to interconnect nodes to create the right topology. Each node name embedded an identifier specifying which core, access and subnet block it belonged to.

3.2 Creation and Configuration of Nodes and Connectivity

The Lego blocks that can be created from the templates only provide generic VM nodes. They can in a way be viewed as the "stem cells" of the system. To become a CDN these nodes need to assume the appropriate functionality in the right location in the topology. We now describe how this process was automated.

Creation of virtual network and nodes. The first phase involves creation of the virtual nodes and network topology. We used two basic node types in the system. One was a virtual router node and the other was a generic node. The router node used the Vyatta open source distribution with all the routing packages. Configuration files were pushed out to the router nodes manually after topology creation. The generic node was a customized Linux image based on the Ubuntu 7.10 release. It was stripped of all unnecessary packages to reduce image size and memory consumption. It was also patched with appropriate run time environments necessary for the CDN modules and digital certificates for password-less ssh logins for remote management. The generic node later transforms into a specialized CDN node during the startup phase.

Automated IP configuration. The second phase is for nodes to establish network connectivity. Each CDN nodes when it configures its networking, requests an IP Address using DHCP (i.e., broadcasting on the locally connected LAN). Both the access and the core routers are setup to enable DHCP relay so that the requests reach the DHCP server in the infrastructure cluster. The DHCP server matches the node using its MAC address, and looks up its IP address assigned in its IP address plan. This IP address is sent back as a DHCP IP offer via the same relays. The offer also contains the default gateway, netmask and importantly the *host name*.

Node metamorphosis. Once the node has obtained network connectivity and has a hostname, it can begin the process to transform itself into a custom CDN node. It mounts an exported NFS volume as a local directory. The exported NFS volume contains various program binaries and other configuration information. Using its hostname as input, the node initiates a startup script which resolves which services and programs need to be launched for that node from the exported NFS volume. Once these programs are launched, the generic node is transformed into a specialized CDN node in the network, ready to accept test scenarios delivered over the virtual network.

4 Testbed and System Experimentation

The methods and procedures described in the previous section were used to instantiate the virtual CDN system on a hardware platform with virtualization support. It consisted of one single GEM (Generic Ericsson Magazine) unit; an Ericsson x86 prototype blade system. Each blade server employed an Intel Xeon Quad Core CPU running at 2.13GHz and had 24GB of RAM. The used GEM unit was equipped with six such blades and two gigabit Ethernet backplanes for internal chassis switching.

There was no storage in the blade servers or in the chassis. However, there were onboard flash disks on each blade server where VMware ESXi 3.5, bare metal, full virtualization hypervisors were installed. Virtual machines were instead stored on a separate iSCSI server (an HP Proliant DL180G5) running OpenFiler 2.2. VMware's Virtual Center management software and Perl API were used for the blade system and virtualization management.

4.1 Test Scenarios Control, Measurements and Visualization

Apart from having an automated process to create and instantiate the CDN system with its virtualized environment, a convenient way to experiment with such a large system is also desirable. To do this we developed experiment-conduction, measurement and visualization enablers and embedded them in the nodes of the system. This meant that once the system was started, no additional configurations steps were needed to perform experiments.

System test scenarios were controlled and distributed from a node in the infrastructure nodes group to all the client request generators. These scenarios consisted of user media consumption profiles mapped to areas. Areas consisted of one or more access networks. Scenarios and caching logic could be changed with the click of a button.

Measurement tools were developed for collecting information about the network. One measured transit traffic across the core routers in the system and another one, the total download traffic at the client locations. Each node periodically collected this information and sent it to a centralized measurement node for aggregation, analysis and display.

A generic visualization tool was created capable of displaying network topology and arbitrary information (like measurement data and statistics) coupled to nodes and links. In the CDN study this was used to visualize in real-time the status of the client request generators and the caches. It could show correlations between traffic and cache contents thus giving insights that could later be studied in detail offline. The ability to visually observe the system proved very useful to get an intuitive understanding of system behavior. It also enabled quicker verification of the created topology and experiment configuration.

5 Performance of Networking in Hypervisors

Understanding the performance and limitations of the underlying virtualization machinery is important to make a sound deployment (in terms of utilization and balance) of the VM nodes across the physical hardware cluster. For that reason a series of measurements using simple topologies were performed, in particular to understand achievable throughput and the requirements put by virtual networking (routers and switches) on the hardware. Those measurements were done using a single blade server.

5.1 Relation Between Virtual Networking and CPU Resources

The purpose of these measurements was to understand how the performance of concurrently communicating VMs impacts and are impacted by CPU load. Another purpose was to investigate how fairly the hypervisor schedules VMs and to benchmark the blade server capacity.

One to ten independent (i.e., not interconnected) links were carrying TCP traffic between one to ten pairs of virtual machines using the Netperf tool. A set of independent virtual machines with load generators were used to consume CPU cycles on the blade server but without generating any network traffic.

Each link pair consisted of two virtual nodes directly connected using a virtual switch. Both nodes used Ubuntu 8.04 with VMware tools installed and had no caps on their virtual CPUs. The separate load generators had similar Ubuntu installations but had no network connections. Each of these load generators was configured to create a constant CPU load of 350 MHz. This number was chosen to be able to increase the load in steps without consuming all CPU cycles at once.

All measurements were initiated by giving the following command to the client node of the links.

```
netperf -H 10.0.1.3 -l 60 -c -C -t TCP_STREAM
```

The measurement commands were sent from a separate control node (another Ubuntu VM) to the server nodes using multicast. This made sure all links measurements started simultaneously when more than one link was measured. The measurement was done starting with one link and increasing sequentially up to ten links. With each scenario, 0 to 20 load generators were added in steps of 5 giving a total of 40 measurements.

Fig. 2 (a) shows the result for 1-10 links when no load generators were used. Each individual link has its own color to show the TCP throughput distribution between the links. With one link, the figure reveals that the total throughput is about 1900 Mbps and with the two parallel and independent links it rises to about 3300 Mbps. The total throughput then drops to about 2200 Mbps when yet a third parallel and independent link is added. This observed behavior can be readily explained in terms of the underlying physical four cores CPU on the blade. The number of VMs in the one, two and three link scenarios is two, four and six, respectively.

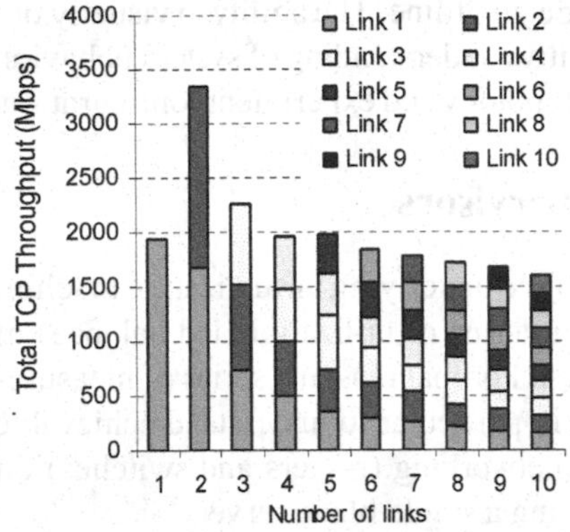

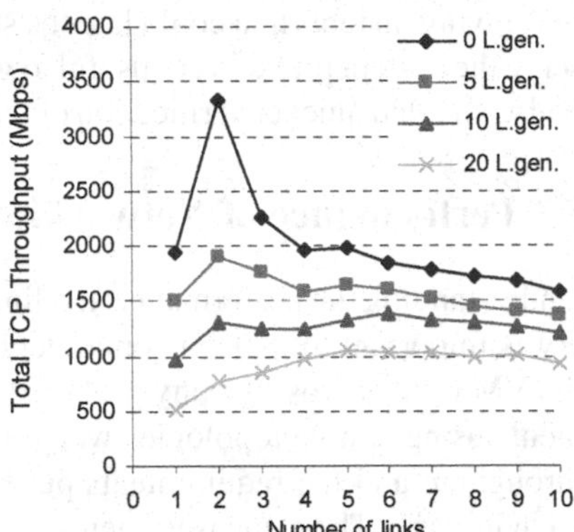

Fig. 2. (a) & (b) TCP throughput for varying numbers of independent server-client pairs

When instantiated, these VMs are mapped by the hypervisor onto the physical cores and in the one and two link cases, both the server and the sink nodes can be allocated their own core. With the used hardware, hypervisor and software configuration the single link pair server is able to achieve the throughput of 1900 Mbps. The two link pairs together do not quite achieve the double of that (3800 Mbps) even though all VMs can be mapped to separate cores, thus revealing a kind of "concurrency" related performance loss of 3800 - 3300 = 500 Mbps. With the addition of the third link, there are less physical cores (four) than VMs (six). This results in a more pronounced performance drop which can be explained by the increased scheduling of VMs across the cores. As more links, and thus more VMs, are added, the performance reduces further due to scheduling cost. There are thus two distinct modes with clearly differing behavior, one where VMs can be allocated their own core and one where multiplexing is needed.

The histogram in Figure 2(a) also shows that the scheduling of VMs performed by the hypervisor used has good fairness properties. All links have about the same amount of network traffic which gracefully degrades equally as the number of links is increased. This is very important since scheduling unbalances or in the worst case, starvation of VMs, will introduce bias in experiments and lead to misleading results.

Figure 2(b) shows the result for similar measurements but with a varying number of non-networked load generator VMs added to the system. For readability, only the total traffic for each measurement is shown. Again, there are two modes in the curves. The uppermost curve, corresponding to the case with zero load generators, is the same as the top of the bars in the Figure 2(a) histogram. As expected, with every increase in load from the load generators, a corresponding discrete drop in aggregate throughput follows. What can also be observed is that the throughput only drops slowly as the number of parallel links increases. With 40 virtual nodes running (20 non-networked load generators and 20 server and sink nodes) the aggregate throughput is slightly less than 1000 Mbps, some 500 Mbps lower than with no load generator case.

5.2 Performance of Virtual Routing

This measurement was done to investigate performance of virtual software routers. We used the Vyatta open source router (version 4.0). Maximum lossless throughput, latency, and host and guest CPU load was measured with two different setups. The first used a single Vyatta router. The second setup used five routers connected in series, $R1 \rightarrow R2 \rightarrow \ldots \rightarrow R5$. The interfaces of the router were connected to front panel connectors on the blade server via which an IXIA traffic generator was used to generate and measure UDP traffic of 1500 byte packet size. Figure 3 show the results from these measurements.

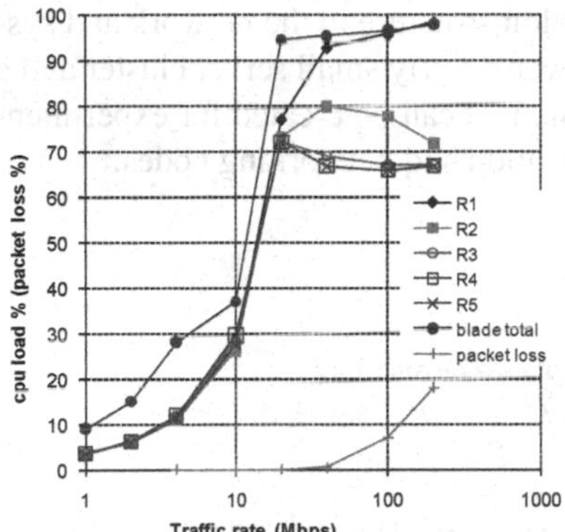

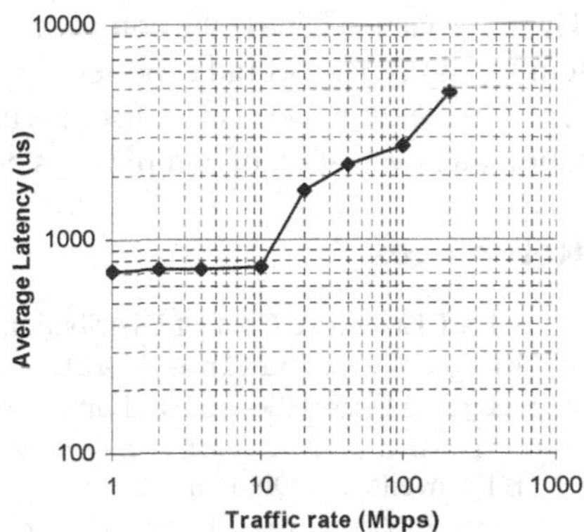

Fig. 3. (a) & (b) CPU load, packet loss and latency vs. injected traffic. 5 router path

In the single router case the achievable throughput was limited by a single core to slightly less than 200Mbps. Near that point delay and packet loss increase noticeably. For the case with multiple routers, until CPU saturation all routers show similar forwarding rates at each CPU usage. After CPU saturation, around 25 Mbps on each router, packet losses (measured at the egress port of the blade) starts happening. A likely explanation for the seemingly disproportionate spread in CPU load from this point onwards is that packet losses are concentrated to the routers near the ingress side. As a consequence, R5 will have less incoming packets that R4, which in turn will have less incoming packets than R3, etc.

6 Lessons Learnt and Conclusion

When starting the project it was assumed that available memory would be a major issue in creating a system with a very large number of virtual nodes. Instead the CPU consumption of the virtual routers limited the maximum number of nodes and the maximum throughput of the virtual network. Studies like [9] [11] performed using the Xen hypervisor show a similiar observation. There are efforts like [12] to improve inter-VM networking performance. Other studies [11] [5] have argued on the benefits of using a *container based virtualization* approach that exhibits a higher network performance though sacrificing transparency. We also observed that the bandwidth of a link would vary considerably depending on the momentarily available host CPU. But given enough CPU, the virtual links can attain high levels of performance but under heavy load the performance falls considerably, though in a fair manner.

By leveraging specific characteristics of the application, in our study the asymmetric distribution of load in a globally distributed CDN, large system topologies can be supported through reliance on statistical multiplexing. This enabled us to scale our network beyond available physical resources, while at the same time ensuring even and full utilization of our blades.

Generation and configuration of a system with 260+ virtual nodes proved to be a non-trivial task even though setting up each individual node is not that complicated. The approach to handle the complexity was to exploit structure in the network and system topology.The overall experience is that with even a fairly small server cluster and a state-of-the-art hypervisor, a useful virtual environment can be created for experimentation and evaluation of complex systems of application and networking nodes.

References

1. AT&T Enterprise Content Distribution,
`http://www.business.att.com/enterprise/Family/digital-media-solutions-enterprise/content-distribution-enterprise/`
2. BT Unveils Its CDN Plans,
`http://www.lightreading.com/document.asp?doc_id=174800`
3. Open vSwitch home page, `http://openvswitch.org/`
4. Bavier, A., Feamster, N., Huang, M., Peterson, L., Rexford, J.: In VINI veritas: realistic and controlled network experimentation. In: Proc. ACM SIGCOMM, pp. 3–14 (2006)
5. Bhatia, S., Motiwala, M., Muhlbauer, W., Mundada, Y., Valancius, V., Bavier, A., Feamster, N., Peterson, L., Rexford, J.: Trellis: a platform for building flexible, fast virtual networks on commodity hardware. In: CoNEXT 2008: Proceedings of the 2008 ACM CoNEXT Conference, pp. 1–6. ACM, New York (2008)
6. Chen, Y.F., Jana, R., Stern, D., Sun, H., Wei, B., Yang, M.: VP2P: A virtual machine-based P2P testbed for VoD delivery. In: 6th IEEE Consumer Communications and Networking Conference, CCNC 2009, January 10-13, pp. 1–5 (2009)
7. Culler, D., Roscoe, T., Peterson, L., Peterson, L., Anderson, T., Anderson, T.: A blueprint for introducing disruptive technology into the internet (2002)
8. Dilley, J., Maggs, B., Parikh, J., Prokop, H., Weihl, B.: Globally distributed content delivery. IEEE Internet Computing 6, 50–58 (2002)
9. Egi, N., Greenhalgh, A., Handley, M., Hoerdt, M., Mathy, L., Schooley, T.: Evaluating xen for router virtualization. In: Proceedings of 16th International Conference on Computer Communications and Networks, ICCCN 2007, August 13-16, pp. 1256–1261 (2007)
10. Gennaro, P.D., Bifulco, R., Canonico, R.: Link multiplexing in a Xen-based network emulation system. In: NGNM 2009 (2009)
11. Maier, S., Grau, A., Weinschrott, H., Rothermel, K.: Scalable network emulation: A comparison of virtual routing and virtual machines. In: 12th IEEE Symposium on Computers and Communications, ISCC 2007, July 1-4, pp. 395 –402 (2007)
12. Wang, J., Wright, K.-l., Gopalan, K.: Xenloop: a transparent high performance inter-vm network loopback. In: Proceedings of the 17th International Symposium on High Performance Distributed Computing (HPDC 2008), pp. 109–118 (2008)

A Survey Analysis of Memory Elasticity Techniques

Artur Baruchi and Edson Toshimi Midorikawa

Laboratory of Architecture and High Performance Computing
University of So Paulo
Av. Prof Luciano Gualberto. So Paulo. Brazil
{artur.baruchi,edson.midorikawa}@poli.usp.br

Abstract. Elasticity is an important feature in cloud computing environments. This feature allows a Virtual Machine to adapt resource allocation according to the nature of its workload. Until now, most memory elasticity implementations require human intervention. The implementation of memory elasticity is not very straightforward, due to old Operating System concepts; in general an Operating System assumes that all installed memory will be static and will not increase or decrease until the next shutdown. This paper compares two techniques for the implementation of memory elasticity, one based on the concept of Exponential Moving Average and the other based on Page Faults. To compare these modes of implementation, a method to measure allocation efficiency based on the space-time product was used. With an Exponential Moving Average, memory could be used more efficiently. When Page Faults were used as the main criteria to allocate or remove memory, the performance improved when compared to the Exponential Moving Average technique.

Keywords: Resource Management, Memory Management, Virtual Machines, Memory Elasticity.

1 Introduction

Resource elasticity is a new term that became popular with Cloud Computing. This term is a reference to the ability of resources to be removed or allocated according to current workload. The main advantage of this feature is more efficient use of resources. Elasticity can be implemented for any computational resource, like CPU cycles, I/O subsystems and memory. However, of the three, memory elasticity is more difficult to implement, due to old Operating System (OS) concepts.

To confront this problem, virtualization technology vendors have designed very innovative techniques, like Balloon Driver [16] and Memory Hashing [16] [4], to outline OS limitations. Moreover, implementation of virtualization in the x86 platform is not a simple affair; actually it requires considerable effort, for example, Paravirtualization [18], Binary Translation [3] and Virtualization at the processor level [15].

M.R. Guarracino et al. (Eds.): Euro-Par 2010 Workshops, LNCS 6586, pp. 681–688, 2011.
© Springer-Verlag Berlin Heidelberg 2011

The Virtualization concept is not new; it goes back to the 1970s [17], and it was briefly very popular with industries and research centers. However, during 1980s and 1990s more powerful computers and multitask OS became popular and Virtualization was practically consigned to little more than a footnote in the history books [14]. Now virtualization is being used as a means to making another old concept, known as The Computer as a Public Utility, feasible again [13].

This paper discusses the main issues in implementing memory elasticity and then presents two techniques to address these issues. The first is based on Page Faults, and the second is based on the Exponential Moving Average (EMA) concept. Both mechanisms have been implemented in Xen [5]. To compare the techniques, two benchmarks (one CPU bound and the other I/O bound) were used. Two analyses were carried out, one based on benchmark performance, and the other based on how accurately the memory was allocated and removed from Virtual Machines (VM).

This paper is organized as follows: in Section 2, we discuss the main issues concerning Memory Elasticity. In Section 3, the two techniques used to address the issues, as well as their implementation, are described. Methodology and Results are detailed in Section 4, and Section 5 contains our conclusions.

2 Memory Elasticity

Elasticity can be understood as the ability to adapt any given resource to a current workload, thus avoiding resource wastage. Basically, any resource can be elastic, but the effort to implement this feature can increase substantially, depending on the resource. This paper is focused on memory resources and compares two techniques to address this issue. When discussing resource elasticity, there are several issues that must be taken into account when designing an elasticity mechanism:

- To identify when a resource is scarce;
- To quantify the resource requirements of the system;
- To identify when and how much of a resource can be removed from the system without affecting its performance;

Addressing these problems is not very straightforward, and it is more complex when the resource being managed is memory. With memory we encounter difficulties with regards to old concepts of OS design. Since OS were designed [8], the premise has been that all available memory can be taken up by the OS and it will all be under the latters control. This has been effective up until now, but with the advent of virtualization and now cloud computing, these concepts must be revised.

Memory resources have become a bottleneck to improving virtualization techniques [12] and, contrary to CPU cycles, memory management implemented in OS cannot be ported to VMM. The VMM CPU scheduler is not that different from a CPU scheduler implemented in OS; there are obviously several peculiarities, but essentially it is the same concept.

Both techniques were developed by VMWare [16], and are now used in other VMMs [5] and even in the current Linux Kernel [4]. Balloon Driver is a mechanism that forces the OS algorithms to identify memory pages that can be swapped out (in other words, pages that the OS will probably not use) and used by VMM for something else.

3 Memory Elasticity Implementation

Both Memory Elasticity strategies were developed in Xen VMM. To fulfill the requirement of memory adaptation, the Balloon Driver mechanism present in Xen was used. According to this criterion, the prototype basically removes or adds the memory requested by the VM. The prototype was developed in C and all the communication between VM and Domain 0 (Dom0 a special VM in Xen with administration privileges) was carried out through a shared memory region called XenStore [6]. Finally, to adjust the memory allocation, a C library called Libvirt was used [2].

The prototypes were developed in a client/server scheme. The client side, running in VM has the objective of monitoring the VM and, according to the criterion, it calculates the amount of memory to request or to free up. Inside the Dom0, on the server side, the daemon receives the request from the client, checks whether it is possible to allocate the memory requested, and finally allocates or removes the amount of memory sent by the client.

3.1 Memory Elasticity Based on Page Faults

The first criterion used to design the prototype was the Page Fault rate. The premise is that if any given system has a high page fault rate, the current amount of memory will probably be insufficient to accommodate the workload imposed on the system. With this in mind, the client side of the prototype monitored the Major Page Fault Rate.

The daemon running inside the VM monitored the page fault rate from the last second. After three samples, it checked whether the page faults were increasing or decreasing. The three samples were used to avoid situations like cold starts [9] (when a new process starts, an increase in page faults is common, due to the allocation of pages to the new process).

After a memory requirement is detected, the amount of memory required is calculated as a function of the page fault rate of the previous one second. The amount of memory requested is the size of one page multiplied by the page fault rate of the second. This process was repeated until the page fault rate decreased.

The process of returning memory to the VMM is a little different. To remove some memory, the daemon needs to be sure that the VM is stable. One way to fulfill this requirement is to measure other aspects of the system, like CPU Usage and Load, IO wait and other items. The thresholds for these metrics are set by the administrator (for this paper, it was collected when the VM was idle). When the prototype detected a situation where the VM was able to return some memory, it was returned in slices of 5-10% of the current VM allocation. If the VM has the majority of the real memory allocated (more or equal to 51%), it is removed in slices of 10%; otherwise the slices amount to 5%.

3.2 Memory Elasticity Based on the Exponential Moving Average

The second criterion used to add or remove memory from a VM is based on the Exponential Moving Average (EMA) concept. The use of EMAs is very common in the financial market [11] to detect the price tendency of the share value of any given publically traded company. The main purpose of an EMA is to calculate the average of the last few samples and not the average of all samples. According to the amount of samples, the average can be more or less sensitive to changes (in a few samples, the EMA is more sensitive to peaks).

There are two kinds of Moving Average, the simplest form is just the arithmetic mean from the last few samples, whilst the second form, more complex, gives greater weight to the most recent values of the samples. This is called Exponential Moving Average, and it is the one used in this study.

The prototype monitored free memory every second. To identify the tendencies, two EMAs with different amounts of samples were used, one from the last 5 seconds and other from the last 25 seconds (these values were chosen empirically). To identify memory requirements, the crossing points (see Figure 1) of the EMA for the last 5 seconds (EMA5) and for the last 25 seconds (EMA25) were used, along with the direction of the cross. When EMA5 is increasing and crosses EMA25 (in an upwards direction), it constitutes an increasing tendency; otherwise there is a decreasing tendency of memory utilization and memory can be thus removed from the VM.

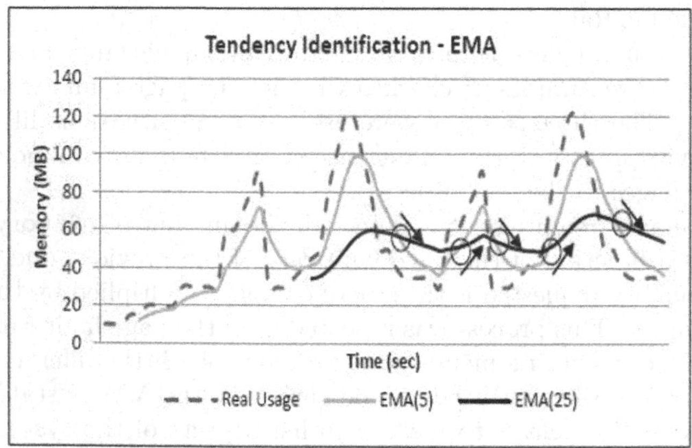

Fig. 1. Memory Tendency Identification, the arrows indicate the direction of crossing

4 Methodology and Results

To evaluate both strategies, two benchmarks were used. The first was the Linux Kernel compilation (CPU Bond) and the second was the DBench (IO Bond) [1]. Benchmarks were run 15 times on two Virtual Machines at the same time (to ensure that VMs were competing for memory), and the average and the student-t distribution were calculated with 95% confidence. Both VMs have the same hardware configuration (1 VCPU and 30GB of HD capacity). In order to compare the memory elasticity mechanism, two metrics were used:

- Benchmark Performance Evaluation (compilation time and throughput);
- Memory Allocation Efficiency (in MBxSec);

4.1 Performance Evaluation

The first method used to compare both strategies was the performance evaluation. It is important to verify the impact of the strategy on the environment. As can be seen in Figure 2, the performance of both strategies was statistically the same for the DBench, although the EMA strategy was a little bit better than the Page Fault strategy (higher values are more desirable).

When comparing the performance for Kernel Compilation (lower values are more desirable), the page fault strategy is more advantageous. The main reasons for this difference were the memory usage patterns of each benchmark. With

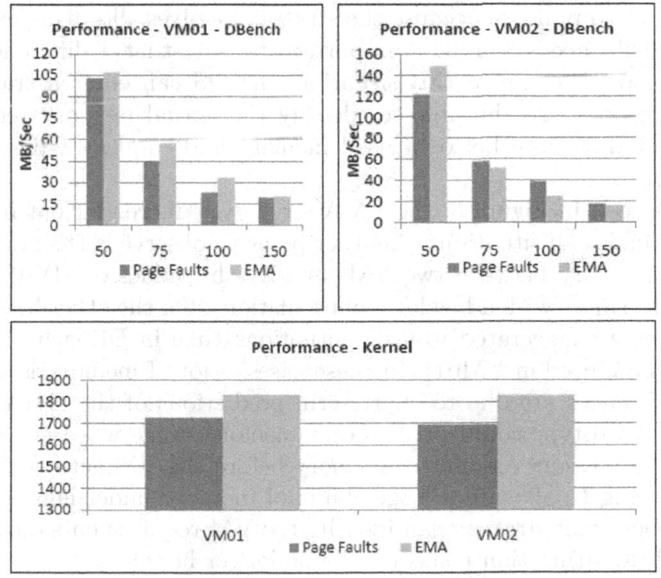

Fig. 2. Performance Comparison between strategies

Linux, the free memory was used as a buffer for IO operations and hence the DBench consumes all the available memory [10]. While the page fault strategy waits for page faults to occur in order to add some memory, the EMA strategy could detect an increase in the tendency of memory usage and add memory before it runs out.

For Kernel compilation, a limited amount of memory was used during execution, but it was possible to note a high page fault rate peak during a specific part of the compilation. This is the part of the compilation process that will differentiate a fast execution from a slow one. Due to a higher page fault rate in this part of the execution, the strategy based on page faults adds more memory and can decrease the page fault rate substantially. As a consequence, compilation time decreases as well.

4.2 Memory Allocation Efficiency

Memory Allocation Efficiency is based on the difference between the memory actually used and the memory available for use during the benchmark execution period. With this metric it is possible to evaluate the amount of memory being wasted and how effective the strategy is in detecting memory requirements.

This metric is known as Space-Time Product [7] and basically it is the difference between the area representing the amount of available memory and the area representing the used memory. The area of the graph can be calculated by the total amount of memory used and allocated by the prototype over the time spent by the benchmark for execution.

When the difference between available memory and used memory is near zero, efficiency tends to improve because the strategy involves allocating exactly what the VM actually needs. But it is important to note that a difference equal to zero is not good because in this situation, the OS can enter a trashing state or the strategy will not be able to identify the actual memory requirements. A satisfactory difference between used memory and total available memory is about 10% [19].

As can be seen in Figure 3, the EMA strategy is more efficient in allocating memory in almost all situations. Another point to observe is that the EMA can balance the memory between two VMs evenly (the values of MV01 and MV02 are almost the same, with a low level of oscillation). On the other hand, the page fault strategy is exaggerated in some situations (like in DBench running with 150 clients configured in VM01). In these cases, a lot of memory is wasted.

These differences are due to short term predictions of the EMA. With this strategy the prototype could predict that memory usage was increasing and it allocated the necessary amount of memory before the VM actually required it, thus not needing to allocate a large chunk of memory under emergency conditions. The page fault strategy can identify the VM requirements only when it is too late and the utilization peaks can be no longer handled.

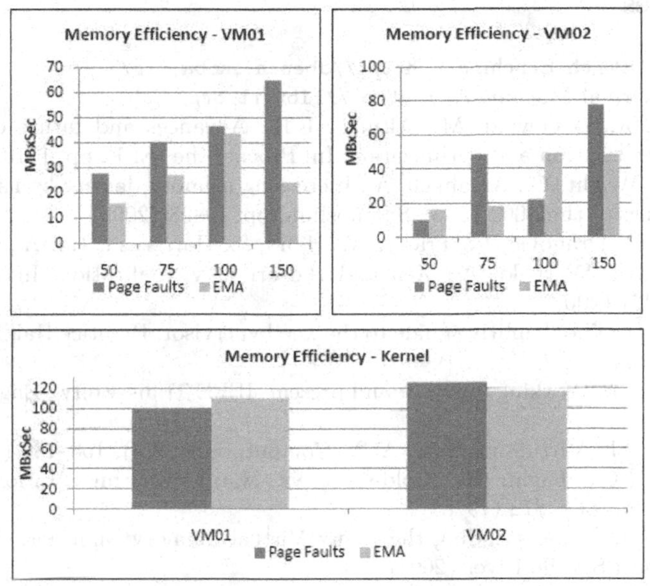

Fig. 3. Memory Allocation Efficiency of Benchmarks

5 Conclusions

This paper compared two strategies for designing memory elasticity in virtual environments. The first strategy is based on the Major Page Fault Rate and the second is based on the Exponential Moving Average concept. To compare both strategies, two benchmarks were used, one CPU intensive (Linux Kernel compilation) and other IO intensive (DBench that simulates a Samba Server). After the benchmarks were executed, the comparison was based on two metrics, firstly on performance and secondly on memory allocation efficiency, based on the Space-Time Product.

The Page Fault strategy exhibited better performance in the Linux Kernel compilation, due to its behavior regarding page fault peaks. For DBench, the page fault strategy is not as efficient, because of its difficulty in detecting the end of the peak. Memory wastage in the page fault strategy was very high when compared with the EMA strategy for both benchmarks.

The EMA strategy proved to be more efficient in identifying and managing memory for both benchmarks, and its performance was a little better than page faults for DBench and lower than the Kernel Compilation. The main difficulty, for both strategies, was the overhead imposed by Balloon Driver. Balloon Driver forces the OS to swap pages and the high-frequency activation and deactivation of this mechanism can cause higher overheads for the VM. The design of a more accurate mechanism for predicting memory usage and easing the Balloon Driver overhead will be evaluated in a future study.

References

1. Dbench. DBench Benchmark, http://dbench.samba.org/
2. Libvirt. Virtual Machine API, http://libvirt.org/
3. Ebcioglu, K., Gschwind, M., Altman, E.R.: Advances and future challenges in binary - translation and optimization. In: Proc. of the IEEE, pp. 1710–1722 (2001)
4. Eidus, I., Wright, C., Arcangeli, A.: Increasing memory density by using kvm. In: Proceedings of the 2009 Linux Symposium, pp. 19–28 (2009)
5. Barham, P., Dragovic, B., Fraser, K., Hand, S., Harris, T., Ho, A., Neugebauer, R., Pratt, I., Warfield, A.: Xen and the art of virtualization. In: SOSP 2003, pp. 164–177 (2003)
6. Chisnall, D.: The definitive guide to the xen hypervisor. Prentice Hall Press, Upper Saddle River (2007)
7. Denning, P.J.: Working sets past and present. IEEE Trans. Softw. Eng. 6(1), 64–84 (1980)
8. Denning, P.J.: Virtual memory. ACM Comput. Surv. 2(3), 153–189 (1970)
9. Easton, M.C., Fagin, R.: Cold-start vs. warm-start miss ratios. Commun. ACM 21(10), 866–872 (1978)
10. Gorman, M.: Understanding the Linux Virtual Memory Manager. Prentice Hall PTR, Upper Saddle River (2004)
11. James, F.E.: Monthly moving averages - an effective investment tool? Journal of Financial and Quantitative Analysis 3(03), 315–326 (1968)
12. Kamoun, F.: Virtualizing the datacenter without compromising server performance. Ubiquity (August 2009)
13. Parkhill, D.F.: The challenge of computer utility (1966)
14. Rosenblum, M., Garfinkel, T.: Virtual machine monitors: Current technology and future trends. Computer 38(5), 39–47 (2005)
15. Uhlig, R., et al.: Intel virtualization technology (2005)
16. Waldspurger, C.A.: Memory reource management in vmware esx server. In: Fifth Symposium on Operating Systems Design and Implementation, vol. 36, pp. 181–194 (2002)
17. Shaw, M., Gribble, S.D., Whitaker, A.: Survey of virtual machine research (1974)
18. Shaw, M., Gribble, S.D., Whitaker, A.: Denali: Lightweight virtual machines for distributed and networked applications (2001)
19. Zhao, W., Wang, Z., Luo, Y.: Dynamic memory balancing for virtual machines. SIGOPS Oper. Syst. Rev. 43(3), 37–47 (2009)

Vistas: Towards Behavioural Cloud Control

Alan Wood and Yining Zhao

University of York
{wood,hopezhao}@cs.york.ac.uk

Abstract. Vistas, a generalisation of the *object capability* concept, are presented which provide a scalable, distributed means for specifying and controlling the interaction rights that entities have in open distributed systems such as the Cloud. The operations for combining Vistas and examples of their use are discussed. Finally, a natural development of vistas to full *behavioural* control is outlined.

1 Introduction

The Cloud is perhaps the most genuinely 'open' computing model so far proposed. Active and passive entities — agents, services and resources — can appear within a cloud at any time and start interacting with existing entities. They may also create further entities and thus set up new interactions. All this occurs without any prior knowledge of their behaviours. It is important, therefore, to provide means for constraining this anarchic situation to conform to limited behavioural specifications in order for sensible computation to occur. Since the general Cloud model is decentralised and non-hierarchical, any appropriate behavioural constraint system must scale well over manifold entities and platforms, be dynamically adaptable, and be available to the entities and not merely part of the infrastructure.

The conventional way of limiting behaviour in computational environments is the *access control list* which prescribes, for each group of entities in the environment, some subset of a fixed collection of permissions. However, even in simple monolithic systems, this mechanism has many disadvantages; in open distributed environments the problems with ACLs mean that they become untenable.

The alternative to the ACL approach – *capabilities* — was first described over four decades ago [3] in the context of hardware-mediated protection mechanisms. Over time this concept has been applied to more software-oriented areas, such as operating systems [9], languages [8], and semantics [2]. The simplicity of implementation of the ACL technique, and its choice as the access control mechanism for the most popular operating systems, has meant that it has overshadowed the capability approach. However, with the advent of persistent and open distributed systems the specific advantages of the capability idea are becoming increasingly clear. A recent trend in the use of capabilities has been to apply them in a theoretical context, as an adjunct to type systems [4,5]. This view tends to relegate them to a formal 'trick' which can be applied in early stages and then erased: a kind of catalyst that facilitates the analysis and then disappears.

M.R. Guarracino et al. (Eds.): Euro-Par 2010 Workshops, LNCS 6586, pp. 689–696, 2011.
© Springer-Verlag Berlin Heidelberg 2011

There are, of course, advantages in this approach: if the information is erased before runtime, then there are no runtime resources required to support it. However, in spite of these positive aspects of the *static* view of capabilities, this paper takes the view that there is potential for significant gains in a dynamic approach — capabilities should be first-class, reified runtime objects which can thus be exploited in a variety of Cloud applications. These generalised capabilities are called *vistas*, which introduce a first level of behavioural specification. A richer level of behavioural control is provided by a further extension, *treaties*, which are outlined in §5.

2 Vistas: Constraining Rights

For the purposes of this paper, a simple generic *relational* view of objects will be taken [1,6]: objects consist of a number of *names* which entities can use in ways that are appropriate to the value referred to by the name. Then a *visibility* is defined to consist of an object reference and one of its names.

A *vista* is a collection of visibilities, which define the entitlements that a holder of the vista has to interact with the objects to which the vista applies. Thus, a vista makes visible to its holder a subset of its objects' names.

Vistas constitute a generalisation of conventional object-capabilities: a vista can encapsulate visibilities for *multiple* objects. How this affects the meaning of vista expressions will be clarified in later sections, but the semantics of vistas are identical to conventional object references when they contain visibilities for a unique object.

2.1 Vista Operations

Vistas represent the objects in the system: as far as the entities are concerned, the vistas *are* the objects, in the same way that object references in an OO system can be seen to *be* the objects. Consequently an expression of the form γ`.foo` is defined to be the selection of objects called `foo` that are made visible by the vista γ. This is directly analogous to an expression such as `o.foo` in an OO language which represents the object `foo` in `o`'s scope.

However, the main novelty of the vista model is that γ might contain *several* visibilities that make `foo` available, but on different objects. Consequently, any language that is using vistas must be able to handle *multiple* selections. Some implications of this are dealt with below (§2.1). The crucial point, though, is that a multiple selection does not prescribe what the result of *using* that selection is to be — it simply states that the members of that selection are *available* to be used.

Vista Constructors By analogy to the object-capability model, vistas are obtained by an entity in one of four ways [8]:

- *Initiality.* Some vistas will be available to an entity on its creation.
- *Parenthood.* If an entity creates an object, then it has the full vista for the new object. This vista will be the only way of referring to the new object.
- *Endowment.* When an entity creates an object, it may pass to the object any vistas that it holds. In an OO system this would correspond to passing the vistas as arguments to the object's constructor.
- *Introduction.* An entity can pass vistas to another by sending a message containing them, or by returning them as a result. In a non-distributed OO system this would correspond to calling a method on the other entity with the vista as an argument. Alternatively, this could be a 'physical' communication between distributed entities.

To these means of obtaining capabilities, the vista model adds:

- *Combination.* An entity can use various constructors on the vistas that it holds to produce new vistas. It is these operations that are the focus of this paper.

There are two fundamental principles in vista-enabled systems which are direct analogues of the basic requirements for capabilities:

Requirement 1. *Visibilities cannot be increased.*

Given the set of visibilities for an object implied by the vistas that an entity holds, it must not be possible for the entity to generate a vista that has *more* visibilities for that object. Consequently, any vista operations must conform, directly or indirectly, to this requirement.

The second principle is a consequence of Requirement 1:

Requirement 2. *Vistas cannot be forged.*

That is, there can be no way to create a valid vista other than by parenthood, or the constructors given below. Ensuring this is an implementational issue, that is essentially cryptological: a bit string representing a vista can neither be altered nor created by an entity to form a valid vista. Although it might be objected that how unforgeability is to be achieved is crucial to the viability of the vista concept, it is beyond the scope of this paper. The position taken here is that either unforgeability is solvable, or it isn't. If it were proved to be unsolvable, then the viability of vistas would be the least troublesome of consequences: the ramifications for *all* security would be much more severe. However, this property of vistas is important to bear in mind when considering their use.

The basic four vista operations are:

Sum	$\alpha + \beta$	is a vista representing *all* the visibilities of α and β.
Product	$\alpha \times \beta$	is a vista that represents ordered pairs of visibilities from α and β.
Difference	$\alpha - N$, $\alpha - \beta$	is a vista containing the visibilities of α *without* those, if any, referring to the names contained in the set N. Since a vista can be regarded as a set of visibilities, this operation is naturally overloaded to allow a vista as its second argument.
Intersection	$\alpha \wedge \beta$, $\alpha \wedge N$	is the vista containing visibilities, if any, that are common to α *and* β. This is extended to work with a set of names N as in the case of *difference.*

The safety of these constructors, in the sense of Requirement 1, is guaranteed since an entity can only form a combination if it already holds the vistas involved in the operation.

Interpretations. The definitions of the constructors are given purely in terms of their meanings as vistas. Since the intention is that vistas should be used in the generic open-system Cloud context, it is necessary to define them *independently* of any particular language or computational model. However, there are issues involved in the interpretation of vistas that impact on the properties of the virtual machines that Clouds support. For instance, both *difference* and *intersection* require that entities be able to discover, at run-time, the names associated with other entities in the system. The VMs will have to be the sources of this metadata. Since entities could be written in *any* language, the use of vista values within these languages will vary, but they must be consistent with their definitions given above. This section deals with some of these considerations.

Sum. It is *this* constructor that gives rise to vistas referring to multiple objects. Therefore languages must be able to interpret an expression α`.f` which results in a *set* of values.

The ability to handle multiple selections is common in most OO languages. Although the exact mechanism varies, several procedures can be applied to reduce the selections to at most one value. For instance at compile time most common OO languages use their class system to distinguish between multiple values of an expression such as `obj.doIt(3)`. Occasionally this can't be done statically and the final selection of the object to be applied is left until run-time. There is then the possibility that *no* value can be selected in which case a run-time exception might result.

However, many other mechanisms for dealing with multiple selections exist, and not all require reduction to a unique value. For instance, in a concurrent language it would be possible to handle *all* members of a multiple selection simultaneously. Alternatively, a *non-deterministic choice* of one of the visibilities could be made: such might be the case in a logic programming language.

In order to distinguish between these various ways of dealing with multiple selections languages can provide syntactic features. For instance, a simple language would only provide expressions of the form `vista.name` which expects to evaluate to a unique object, or raise an exception. A multi-cast language might provide a `..` operator, so that `vista..name(params)` would apply each of the values — vistas— of `name` to the `params`, and a concurrent language could provide a `||` operator that would cause `vista||name(params)` to be evaluated in parallel. These 'extra' selection operators could also do some further type-based filtering of the visibility set based on the supplied parameters. However, it should be noted that the `..` and `||` operators are *derived* versions of the basic `.` operator, and don't require a re-interpretation of the meaning of the vistas involved.

Difference. This is the fundamental visibility-reduction operation, and doesn't introduce any new linguistic issues, unlike *sum*, since the set of objects to which it applies isn't increased.

However, it gives rise to an interesting interpretation in terms of a generic OO view: since the effect of a difference expression is to reduce the visible members of an object's interface, it is, in effect, creating the interface for a new super-class of the original object, and 'inserting' this into the object's inheritance hierarchy.

Although this observation is of only marginal interest to the *user* of a vista-enabled language, it suggests two things: firstly, a way of *implementing* vistas in an OO language and, secondly, that the type-system for the VMs for Clouds need to provide facilities for *this* form of interface injection.[1]

Intersection. Intersecting with a set of names is a convenient way to specify a vista with *only* a particular set of visibilities: rather than having to subtract, and thus *know*, the visibilities that a vista *could* hold, it's easier to specify the ones that are required. In this form it is equivalent to a sum of selections.

Intersecting two vistas is a necessary operation since specifying the common visibilities would be difficult using a sum-of-selections expression as the names of the two vistas to be selected would need to accessed first.

Product. This constructor introduces an embryonic *behavioural* specification. Since it represents *ordered* pairs of visibilities, the 'language neutral' statement of its interpretation is that $\alpha \times \beta$ makes visible a name from α *followed by* a name from β. That is, an application of a visibility from a product vista involves evaluating *both* the elements of the pair. The intended semantics is that they are *both* evaluated unless the first fails in which case the second evaluation is abandoned.

Products, therefore, mandate that *both* elements be evaluated in the order specified. This implies that, as far as the evaluating entity is concerned, the two evaluations are atomic, in the sense that the entity cannot do anything until their evaluation has completed. However, there is no implication

[1] The term *interface injection* often refers to *adding* methods to an object — here we require their *removal*. The former usage is, in essence, dynamic sub-classing, whereas vistas require dynamic *super*-classing.

of atomicity in the evaluation of the pair itself — other events in the Cloud can (and probably *will*) occur 'in between' their execution. One consequence of this is that there is no way for the executing entity to process the result of the first evaluation of the product before the second is evaluated. This requires a different behavioural model, *treaties* (§5). However, even the limited restriction on behaviour that products provide gives useful control facilities as shown in the examples in §3.

In order to use product vistas, languages need to provide means for supplying *pairs* of arguments in applications of a product vista. This could be done by means of an API method or, more satisfactorily, syntax such as vista.<f,g>(<fs, gs>), which would select the <f,g> visibility from vista and then evaluate o_1.f(fs) followed by o_2.g(gs), where o_1, o_2 are the sets of objects whose f and g names are exposed.

3 Use-Case

There are many situations which benefit from the use of vistas— due to space limitations a single example will be given here which illustrates the main operations.

Security Proxy — Introducing Sum and Product Vistas. Alice will be going to University, so her parents set up a college tuition account for her. They wish there to be some control over how it is operated: they can deposit and withdraw funds and view the current balance; Alice is to be able to deposit and see the balance, but not withdraw. So they could request a *bank* object to create an *account* object — both are, of course, represented by vistas. They could then merely give Alice a restricted version of the *account* vista: $(\mathit{account} \wedge \{\texttt{deposit}, \texttt{balance}\})$.

On reflection, however, they want to add a layer of security to the account by requiring Alice to supply login details before using the account's balance facilities, while still allowing her unrestricted use of deposit. To do this they create a *guard* object which exposes a setlogin method. This method takes parameters which set a valid user's login details, and returns a vista for a function which takes details, checks them against the *guard*'s stored user details, returns if they are valid, or raises an exception if not. The vista that is sent to Alice is:

$$\mathit{alice} = (\mathit{guard}\texttt{.setlogin(aliceDetails)} \times \mathit{account}\texttt{.balance}) + \mathit{account}\texttt{.deposit}$$

allowing her to evaluate expressions such as $\mathit{alice}\texttt{.}\langle\texttt{aliceDetails}, \texttt{balance}\rangle$ and $\mathit{alice}\texttt{.deposit(5.96)}$ but both $\mathit{alice}\texttt{.}\langle\texttt{aliceDetails}, \texttt{withdraw(100)}\rangle$ and $\mathit{alice}\texttt{.withdraw(100)}$ would be illegal.

Now assume that Alice enrols at her chosen college. Her parents would be able to supply the college finance office with a vista:

$$\mathit{fees} = \mathit{guard}\texttt{.setlogin(uniDetails)} \times (\mathit{account} \wedge \{\texttt{withdraw}, \texttt{deposit}\})$$

which prevents them from seeing Alice's balance while being able to take the fees, and deposit Alice's earnings as a conference helper in the vacation.

Finally, Alice can send *her* account vista to friends and family so that they can `deposit` useful birthday presents. Since the `deposit` name is *not* protected by the *guard*, there would be no requirement for others to login in order to increase Alice's account.

4 Related Work

As mentioned in the Introduction, capabilities have been studied for the past 35 years, although there has been an increase in interest in their particular benefits relatively recently. This is probably due to the steady increase in the importance of distributed systems research, and internet-hosted systems in particular.

The work most closely related to that reported here has been in the general area of Coordination Languages and systems, particularly those deriving from the tuple-space model. Work by Iain Merrick using the idea of 'scopes' [7] showed the power of combination operations on capability-like objects, and derived in part from earlier work on the use of attributes in coordination.

The μKLAIM language and computational model has always had capabilities at its heart: the most recent work is very close to the proposals in this paper [4], in that the research uses 'pure' capabilities to supply control on process mobility and resource protection. The novel feature in that work is the amalgamation of static, compile-time, analysis of capabilities, with the necessity of dynamic run-time, capability processing. The former is possible since all processes are written in μKLAIM, and so are amenable to a consistent static analysis. However, the non-determinism inherent in both the tuple-space model, and the openness of the system mean that there are 'residual' capabilities that cannot be analysed away statically and thus must be processed by the middleware at run-time. Unlike vistas, their model does not see capabilities as first-class, expressible values, nor does their work address the problems of heterogeneous open systems such as clouds.

5 Future Work

Vistas provide a rich and subtle vocabulary of expressions to control interactions of entities in a Cloud, but in many situations they seem not to be powerful enough to express useful *behavioural* constraints. Take the bank account example in §3: it would be more natural to require Alice to login only once and then access the {`deposit`, `balance`} names arbitrarily often. However, this is not possible with vistas since there is no way of expressing the fact that she is in a 'logged in' state. WE are extending the vista concept to *treaties* which will allow a much wider range of behavioural control, due to the introduction of *state*.

There are many ways in which behaviours may be specified: the simplest, and the one that we are currently working with, is as a finite-state machine, or regular expression, where the state transitions are labelled by the names in the object's interface. A vista can be seen as a treaty having a single state with reflexive transitions labelled with the names in the vista's visibilities.

The concept of treaties gives significant advantages for behaviour control. For instance, due to their management of state, treaties are able to define actions with a fixed number of applications, and behaviours with 'end-states', and so garbage-collection can be *predictive*, which cannot be achieved using standard techniques in a heterogeneous, open, distributed Cloud. Treaties, due to the complexity of state-handling, give rise to significant challenges in implementation and distribution, but the potential benefits are great. Future work will be carried out to investigate the functionality and scalability of treaties.

References

1. Abadi, M., Cardelli, L.: A Theory of Objects. Springer, Heidelberg (1996)
2. Cardelli, L., Gordon, A.D.: Mobile Ambients. Theor. Comput. Sci. 240(1), 177–213 (2000)
3. Dennis, J.B., Van Horn, E.C.: Programming Semantics for Multiprogrammed Computations. Commun. ACM 9(3), 143–155 (1966)
4. Gorla, D., Pugliese, R.: Dynamic Management of Capabilities in a Network-aware Coordination Language. Journal of Logic and Algebraic Programming 78, 665–689 (2009)
5. Haller, P., Odersky, M.: Capabilities for External Uniqueness. Tech. rep., EPFL (2009)
6. Jacobs, B.: Objects and Classes, Co-Algebraically. In: Freitag, B., Jones, C., Lengauer, C., Schek, H.J. (eds.) Object Orientation with Parallelism and Persistence, pp. 83–103. Kluwer Academic, Dordrecht (1996)
7. Merrick, I.: Scope-Based Coordination for Open Systems. Ph.D. thesis, The University of York (2003)
8. Miller, M.S.: Robust Composition: Towards a Unified Approach to Access Control and Concurrency Control. Ph.D. thesis, Johns Hopkins University (2006)
9. Shapiro, J.S., Smith, J.M., Farber, D.J.: EROS: a Fast Capability System. In: Proc. 17th ACM Symposium on Operating Systems Principles, pp. 170–185. ACM, New York (1999)

Author Index